June 14–18, 2016
Antibes Juan-les-Pins, France

Association for
Computing Machinery

Advancing Computing as a Science & Profession

SIGMETRICS/ Performance 2016

Proceedings of the SIGMETRICS/Performance Joint International Conference on Measurement and Modeling of Computer Science

Sponsored by:

ACM SIGMETRICS

In Cooperation with:

IFIP

Association for
Computing Machinery

Advancing Computing as a Science & Profession

The Association for Computing Machinery
2 Penn Plaza, Suite 701
New York, New York 10121-0701

ISBN: 978-1-4503-4266-7 (Digital)

ISBN: 978-1-4503-4600-9 (Print)

Additional copies may be ordered prepaid from:

ACM Order Department
PO Box 30777
New York, NY 10087-0777, USA

Phone: 1-800-342-6626 (USA and Canada)
+1-212-626-0500 (Global)
Fax: +1-212-944-1318
E-mail: acmhelp@acm.org
Hours of Operation: 8:30 am – 4:30 pm ET

Printed in the USA

Foreword

A warm welcome to Antibes Juan-les-Pins and its new Palais des Congrès! We are honored to chair the organizing committee for the 2016 ACM SIGMETRICS / IFIP Performance joint conference and we hope you will enjoy its scientific program as well as the sunny Côte d'Azur.

The committee has prepared a superb program for the five days. Program Committee chairs Nidhi Hegde and Alexandre Proutière deserve our deepest thanks for leading the selection of 28 papers and 24 poster presentations (details on the selection process are in their message). Our sincere gratitude goes to many individuals for organizing the program of Tuesday and Saturday. In particular, Thrasyvoulos Spyropoulos has put together a 12-hour tutorial program with 6 speakers and Maria Carla Calzarossa has coordinated the 5 workshops hosted by the conference. The established MAMA, GreenMetrics and NetEcon events have renewed their trust in the co-location with SIGMETRICS. The workshop on Future Challenges in User-Centric Network, organized by the UCN@Sophia Laboratory of Excellence, will highlight the achievements of Sophia Antipolis researchers in the field of networking. We wish success and long life to the new workshop "Systems Analytics and Characterization". We are extremely grateful to our assistant Laurie Vermeersch and our merry students Alina, Arun, Dimitra, Dimitra, Hlib and Jithin who have taken care of local organization issues, to Nicolas Gast for his dedication and patience as Publicity Chair and webmaster, and to Patrick Loiseau for his efficient setting and management of the registration site.

It is a special pleasure to have the contributed papers of the main conference completed with two keynote speeches by Mor Harchol-Balter and Philippe Jacquet. The conference program also features invited lectures by the recipients of two of the 2016 ACM SIGMETRICS awards: John N. Tsitsiklis who was awarded the Achievement Award and Yi Lu for the Rising Star Research Award. The Test of Time Award will be presented to Bhuvan Urgaonkar, Giovanni Pacifici, Prashant Shenoy, Mike Spreitzer, and Asser Tantawi during the banquet, together with the best paper awards.

We have received generous financial contributions from Facebook, Huawei, IBM, Inria, Intel, Microsoft Research (UK), the Microsoft Research – Inria joint centre, NEC Laboratories, NetApp, Nokia, Orange, and the UCN@Sophia Laboratory of Excellence. Thanks to them, we could offer attractive registration fees. Most of these sponsors participate in the Industrial Research Fair during which many younger researchers will certainly find their next employer. We also thank the NSF, the Computer Performance Foundation, SIGMETRICS, and the RSD research group of CNRS for financing our student grants' program and our diligent Travel Grant Chair Bhuvan Urgaonkar for making it possible.

Organizers of previous editions have helped us during our turn as General Chairs. We thank Peter Harrison (General Chair of SIGMETRICS/Performance 2012) for providing essential information in the early stages of the organization. We are particularly indebted to Mor Harchol-Balter (General Chair of SIGMETRICS 2013) and Jim Xu (General co-chair of SIGMETRICS 2015) for sharing their files with us. Finally, we wish to acknowledge the efficiency of the ACM team, in particular Diana Brantuas, Irene Frawley, and April Mosqus.

Once again, we wish you a great stay in Antibes Juan-les-Pins. Enjoy the conference!

Sara Alouf and **Alain Jean-Marie,** *Inria, France*
SIGMETRICS/Performance 2016 General Chairs

Message from the Program Chairs

It is our pleasure to welcome you to ACM SIGMETRICS / IFIP Performance 2016, the 13th Joint International Conference on Measurement and Modeling of Computer Systems. This joint gathering occurs every three years, bringing together the flagship conferences of ACM SIGMETRICS and the IFIP Working Group 7.3 into a forum that attracts top quality papers in performance evaluation.

This year's program includes papers on topics that have been the foundation of our communities, including queueing, network resource allocation, and performance measurement. As we have seen over the last couple of years, some topics in particular have come to the forefront, such as graph theory and social networks, learning, energy optimization, memory systems, and network economics. We received 208 submissions, of which 28 were accepted into the program as full papers, a highly competitive acceptance rate of 13.5%. Additionally, 24 papers were accepted as poster presentations, and appear in abbreviated form in the proceedings.

The paper review process was as in previous years, starting with a first round where each paper was assigned to three reviewers. An online discussion period followed where some papers received up to two additional reviews. The Program Committee then met in person on Feb 13, 2016 at Columbia University in New York. After an entire day of intense deliberation, the committee selected 28 papers to be included as full papers in the program.

We deeply appreciate the enormous efforts by the program committee during the review, discussion, deliberation and decision process, and thank all 75 members wholeheartedly. After having witnessed the detailed and sincere discussions, we are confident that the program committee made up a great program. We also thank all authors for submissions of their best work. We are grateful for the support of the SIGMETRICS board. All conference organizers' efforts have been essential to bringing together this joint event. It is our pleasure to thank in particular the general chairs Sara Alouf and Alain Jean-Marie who have been extremely supportive, and our webmaster Nicolas Gast for his exceptional responsiveness to updates. We also greatly acknowledge the support of Laurent Charlin of the Toronto Paper Matching System that helped us in matching reviewers to submitted papers.

It has been our honor to serve as this year's program co-chairs. We look forward to an engaging and productive conference.

Nidhi Hegde
SIGMETRICS/Performance'16
Program Co-Chair
Bell Labs, France

Alexandre Proutière
SIGMETRICS/Performance'16
Program Co-Chair
KTH, Sweden

Table of Contents

SIGMETRICS / Performance 2016 Conference Organization ix

SIGMETRICS / Performance 2016 Sponsor & Supporters xii

Contributed Session 1: Queueing Theory

- **Delay, Memory, and Messaging Tradeoffs in Distributed Service Systems** 1
  David Gamarnik, John N. Tsitsiklis, Martin Zubeldia *(Massachusetts Institute of Technology)*
- **Optimal Heavy-Traffic Queue Length Scaling in an Incompletely Saturated Switch** 13
  Siva Theja Maguluri *(IBM T. J. Watson Research Center)*,
  Sai Kiran Burle, R. Srikant *(University of Illinois at Urbana-Champaign)*
- **A Necessary and Sufficient Condition for Throughput Scalability of Fork and Join Networks with Blocking** 25
  Yun Zeng *(The Ohio State University)*, Augustin Chaintreau *(Columbia University)*,
  Don Towsley *(University of Massachusetts)*, Cathy H. Xia *(The Ohio State University)*

Contributed Session 2: Graph Theory

- **Generalized Threshold-Based Epidemics in Random Graphs: The Power of Extreme Values** 37
  Michele Garetto *(University of Torino)*, Emilio Leonardi *(Politecnico di Torino)*,
  Giovanni-Luca Torrisi *(IAC-CNR)*
- **Reverse Ranking by Graph Structure: Model and Scalable Algorithms** 51
  Eliav Buchnik *(Tel Aviv University)*, Edith Cohen *(Google Research & Tel Aviv University)*
- **Improved Achievability and Converse Bounds for Erdös-Rényi Graph Matching** 63
  Daniel Cullina, Negar Kiyavash *(University of Illinois at Urbana-Champaign)*

Keynote Lecture

- **A Better Model for Task Assignment in Server Farms: How Replication can Help** 73
  Mor Harchol-Balter *(Carnegie Mellon University)*

Contributed Session 3: Data Centers and CDNs

- **Costly Circuits, Submodular Schedules and Approximate Carathéodory Theorems** 75
  Shaileshh Bojja Venkatakrishnan *(University of Illinois Urbana-Champaign)*,
  Mohammad Alizadeh *(Massachusetts Institute of Technology)*,
  Pramod Viswanath *(University of Illinois Urbana-Champaign)*
- **Reducing Latency Through Page-aware Management of Web Objects by Content Delivery Networks** 89
  Shankaranarayanan Puzhavakath Narayanan, Yun Seong Nam, Ashiwan Sivakumar *(Purdue University)*,
  Balakrishnan Chandrasekaran *(Duke University)*, Bruce Maggs *(Duke University & Akamai Technologies)*,
  Sanjay Rao *(Purdue University)*

Contributed Session 4: Caching

- **Optimizing TTL Caches under Heavy-Tailed Demands** 101
  Andrés Ferragut, Ismael Rodríguez, Fernando Paganini *(Universidad ORT Uruguay)*
- **Adaptive Caching Networks with Optimality Guarantees** 113
  Stratis Ioannidis, Edmund Yeh *(Northeastern University)*

Keynote Lecture

- **Breathing Mankind Thoughts** 125
  Philippe Jacquet *(Nokia Bell Labs)*

Contributed Session 5: Classification and Data Structure

- **Unsupervised Clustering Under Temporal Feature Volatility in Network Stack Fingerprinting** 127
  Zain Shamsi, Dmitri Loguinov *(Texas A&M University)*
- **Noisy Bloom Filters for Multi-Set Membership Testing** 139
  Haipeng Dai, Yuankun Zhong, Alex X. Liu, Wei Wang, Meng Li *(Nanjing University)*

Contributed Session 6: Graphs and Social Networks

- **Rumor Source Obfuscation on Irregular Trees** 153
  Giulia Fanti, Peter Kairouz, Sewoong Oh *(University of Illinois at Urbana-Champaign)*,
  Kannan Ramchandran *(University of California, Berkeley)*,
  Pramod Viswanath *(University of Illinois at Urbana-Champaign)*
- **Inference in OSNs via Lightweight Partial Crawls** 165
  Konstantin Avrachenkov *(INRIA)*, Bruno Ribeiro *(Purdue University)*, Jithin K. Sreedharan *(INRIA)*
- **Social Clicks: What and Who Gets Read on Twitter?** 179
  Maksym Gabielkov *(INRIA-MSR Joint Centre & Columbia University)*,
  Arthi Ramachandran, Augustin Chaintreau *(Columbia University)*, Arnaud Legout *(INRIA-MSR Joint Centre)*

Contributed Session 7: Learning and Optimization

- **Using Predictions in Online Optimization: Looking Forward with an Eye on the Past** 193
  Niangjun Chen, Joshua Comden, Zhenhua Liu, Anshul Gandhi *(Stony Brook University)*,
  Adam Wierman *(California Institute of Technology)*
- **Collaborative Filtering with Low Regret** 207
  Guy Bresler, Devavrat Shah, Luis Filipe Voloch *(Massachusetts Institute of Technology)*
- **Achieving Low-Delay and Fast-Convergence in Stochastic Network Optimization: A Nesterovian Approach** 221
  Jia Liu *(The Ohio State University)*

Contributed Session 8: Network Economics

- **On the Viability of a Cloud Virtual Service Provider** 235
  Liang Zheng, Carlee Joe-Wong, Christopher G. Brinton *(Princeton University)*,
  Chee Wei Tan *(City University of Hong Kong)*, Sangtae Ha *(University of Colorado)*,
  Mung Chiang *(Princeton University)*
- **The Value of Privacy: Strategic Data Subjects, Incentive Mechanisms and Fundamental Limits** 249
  Weina Wang, Lei Ying, Junshan Zhang *(Arizona State University)*

Contributed Session 9: Networking

- **Instability in Distributed Mobility Management: Revisiting Configuration Management in 3G/4G Mobile Networks** 261
  Yuanjie Li *(University of California, Los Angeles)*, Haotian Deng *(The Ohio State University)*,
  Jiayao Li *(University of California, Los Angeles)*, Chunyi Peng *(The Ohio State University)*,
  Songwu Lu *(University of California, Los Angeles)*
- **Transiently Secure Network Updates** 273
  Arne Ludwig *(Technische Universität Berlin)*, Szymon Dudycz *(University of Wroclaw)*,
  Matthias Rost *(Technische Universität Berlin)*, Stefan Schmid *(Aalborg University)*

Contributed Session 10: Theoretical Tools for Performance Analysis

- **On the Approximation Error of Mean-Field Models** 285
  Lei Ying *(Arizona State University)*
- **On the Duration and Intensity of Competitions in Nonlinear Pólya Urn Processes with Fitness** 299
  Bo Jiang *(University of Massachusetts, Amherst)*, Daniel R. Figueiredo *(Federal University of Rio de Janeiro)*, Bruno Ribeiro *(Purdue University)*, Don Towsley *(University of Massachusetts, Amherst)*
- **Asymptotics of Insensitive Load Balancing and Blocking Phases** 311
  Matthieu Jonckheere *(University of Buenos Aires and Conicet)*, Balakrishna J. Prabhu *(CNRS and Université de Toulouse)*

Contributed Session 11: Memory Systems

- **Understanding Latency Variation in Modern DRAM Chips: Experimental Characterization, Analysis, and Optimization** 323
  Kevin K. Chang *(Carnegie Mellon University)*, Abhijith Kashyap *(Carnegie Mellon University)*, Hasan Hassan *(Carnegie Mellon University & TOBB ETU)*, Saugata Ghose, Kevin Hsieh, Donghyuk Lee *(Carnegie Mellon University)*, Tianshi Li *(Peking University)*, Gennady Pekhimenko *(Carnegie Mellon University)*, Samira Khan *(University of Virginia)*, Onur Mutlu *(Carnegie Mellon University)*
- **Hash, Don't Cache (the Page Table)** 337
  Idan Yaniv, Dan Tsafrir *(Technion -- Israel Institute of Technology)*
- **Exploiting Core Criticality for Enhanced GPU Performance** 351
  Adwait Jog *(College of William and Mary)*, Onur Kayiran *(Advanced Micro Devices, Inc.)*, Ashutosh Pattnaik, Mahmut T. Kandemir *(The Pennsylvania State University)*, Onur Mutlu *(Carnegie Mellon University & ETH Zurich)*, Ravishankar Iyer *(Intel)*, Chita R. Das *(The Pennsylvania State University)*

Extended Abstracts

- **A Service System with Randomly Behaving On-demand Agents** 365
  Lam M. Nguyen, Alexander L. Stolyar *(Lehigh University)*
- **An Analysis of Load Imbalance in Scale-out Data Serving** 367
  Stanko Novakovic, Alexandros Daglis, Edouard Bugnion, Babak Falsafi *(Ecole Polytechnique Fédérale de Lausanne)*, Boris Grot *(University of Edinburgh)*
- **Analyzing the Power Consumption of the Mobile Page Load** 369
  Yi Cao, Javad Nejati, Pavan Maguluri, Aruna Balasubramanian, Anshul Gandhi *(Stony Brook University)*
- **Automated Test Location Selection For Cellular Network Upgrades** 371
  Mubashir Adnan Qureshi *(The University of Texas at Austin)*, Ajay Mahimkar *(AT&T)*, Lili Qiu *(The University of Texas at Austin)*, Zihui Ge, Sarat Puthenpura, Nabeel Mir, Sanjeev Ahuja *(AT&T)*
- **CAR: A Compression-Aware Refresh Approach to Improve Memory Performance and Energy Efficiency** 373
  Wenjie Liu *(Huazhong University of Science and Technology)*, Ping Huang, Kun Tang *(Virginia Commonwealth University)*, Ke Zhou *(Huazhong University of Science and Technology)*, Xubin He *(Virginia Commonwealth University)*
- **Contrasting Effects of Replication in Parallel Systems: From Overload to Underload and Back** 375
  Felix Poloczek *(University of Warwick / TU Berlin)*, Florin Ciucu *(University of Warwick)*
- **Explicit Back-off Rates for Achieving Target Throughputs in CSMA/CA Networks** 377
  Benny Van Houdt *(University of Antwerp)*
- **Freestyle Dancing: Randomized Algorithms for Dynamic Storage Load-Balancing** 381
  Liang Liu, Yating Wang, Lance Fortnow *(Georgia Institute of Technology)*, Jin Li *(Microsoft Research Technologies)*, Jun Xu *(Georgia Institute of Technology)*

- **Joint Data Purchasing and Data Placement in a Geo-Distributed Data Market** 383
  Xiaoqi Ren, Palma London, Juba Ziani, Adam Wierman *(California Institute of Technology)*
- **Majority Rule Based Opinion Dynamics with Biased and Stubborn Agents** 385
  Arpan Mukhopadhyay, Ravi R. Mazumdar *(University of Waterloo)*, Rahul Roy *(Indian Statistical Institute, Delhi)*
- **Mean Field Equilibria of Pricing Games in Internet Marketplaces** 387
  Vamseedhar Reddyvari Raja *(Texas A&M University)*, , Vinod Ramaswamy *(University of Colorado, Boulder)*,
  Srinivas Shakkottai *(Texas A&M University)*, Vijay Subramanian *(University of Michigan)*
- **Modeling SMR Drive Performance** 389
  Mansour Shafaei, Mohammad Hossein Hajkazemi, Peter Desnoyers *(Northeastern University)*,
  Abutalib Aghayev *(Carnegie Mellon University)*
- **Multipath Streaming: Fundamental Limits and Efficient Algorithms** 391
  Richard Combes *(Centrale-Supelec / L2S)*, Habib Sidi *(INRIA)*, Salah Elayoubi *(Orange Labs / SystemX)*
- **Network Calculus Analysis of a Feedback System with Random Service** 393
  Alireza Shekaramiz, Jorg Liebeherr, Almut Burchard *(University of Toronto)*
- **QoE Analysis of a Large-Scale Live Video Streaming Event** 395
  Adnan Ahmed, Zubair Shafiq *(The University of Iowa)*, Amir Khakpour *(Verizon Digital Media Services)*
- **Safe Randomized Load-Balanced Switching by Diffusing Extra Loads** 397
  Sen Yang *(Georgia Institute of Technology)*, Bill Lin *(University of California, San Diego)*,
  Jun Xu *(Georgia Institute of Technology)*
- **Searching For A Single Community in a Graph** 399
  Avik Ray, Sujay Sanghavi, Sanjay Shakkottai *(University of Texas at Austin)*
- **Shoot for the Moon and You Will Never Miss: Characterizing and Detecting Aimbots in Online Games** 401
  Daiping Liu *(University of Delaware)*, Xing Gao *(University of Delaware & College of William and Mary)*,
  Mingwei Zhang *(Intel Labs)*, Haining Wang *(University of Delaware)*
- **Spatial Multi-LRU Caching for Wireless Networks with Coverage Overlaps** 403
  Anastasios Giovanidis *(CNRS & Telecom ParisTech)*, Apostolos Avranas *(Telecom ParisTech & AUTh)*
- **SSD Failures in Datacenters: What, When and Why?** 407
  Iyswarya Narayanan *(The Pennsylvania State University)*,
  Di Wang, Myeongjae Jeon, Bikash Sharma, Laura Caulfield *(Microsoft Corporation)*,
  Anand Sivasubramaniam *(The Pennsylvania State University)*,
  Ben Cutler, Jie Liu, Badriddine Khessib, Kushagra Vaid *(Microsoft Corporation)*
- **The Power of d Choices for Redundancy** 409
  Kristen Gardner, Samuel Zbarsky, Mor Harchol-Balter, Alan Scheller-Wolf *(Carnegie Mellon University)*
- **Time-Based Bandwidth Allocation for Heterogeneous Storage** 411
  Hui Wang, Peter Varman *(Rice University)*
- **Towards Multi-Resource Fair Allocation with Placement Constraints** 415
  Wei Wang *(HKUST)*, Baochun Li, Ben Liang, Jun Li *(University of Toronto)*
- **Trading Discount for Reputation? – On the Design and Analysis of E-Commerce Discount Mechanisms** 417
  Hong Xie, Richard T. B. Ma *(National University of Singapore)*,
  John C. S. Lui *(The Chinese University of Hong Kong)*

Author Index 419

SIGMETRICS / Performance 2016 Conference Organization

General Chairs: Sara Alouf *(Inria, France)*
Alain Jean-Marie *(Inria, France)*

Program Chairs: Nidhi Hegde *(Bell Labs, France)*
Alexandre Proutière *(KTH, Sweden)*

Workshops Chair: Maria Carla Calzarossa *(University of Pavia, Italy)*

Tutorials Chair: Thrasyvoulos Spyropoulos *(Eurecom, France)*

Travel Grant Chair: Bhuvan Urgaonkar *(Pennsylvania State University, USA)*

Registration Chair: Patrick Loiseau *(Eurecom, France)*

Publicity Chair / Webmaster: Nicolas Gast *(Inria, France)*

Local Arrangements Chair: Laurie Vermeersch *(Inria, France)*

Local Arrangements Committee: Arun Kadavankandy *(Inria, France)*
Hlib Mykhailenko *(Inria, France)*
Dimitra Politaki *(Inria, France)*
Jithin Sreedharan *(Inria, France)*
Dimitra Tsigkari *(Inria, France)*
Alina Tuholukova *(Inria, France)*

Program Committee: Samuli Aalto *(Aalto University)*
Vaneet Aggarwal *(Purdue University)*
Animashree Anandkumar *(University of California Irvine)*
Matthew Andrews *(Bell Labs)*
Konstantin Avrachenkov *(Inria)*
Siddhartha Banerjee *(Cornell University)*
Randall Berry *(Northwestern University)*
Giuseppe Bianchi *(University of Roma Tor Vergata)*
Ricardo Bianchini *(Rutgers University, Microsoft)*
Thomas Bonald *(Telecom ParisTech)*
Sem Borst *(Bell Labs, Eindhoven University of Technology)*
Niklas Carlsson *(Linkoping University)*
Giuliano Casale *(Imperial College London)*
Ranveer Chandra *(Microsoft Research)*
Richard Combes *(Supelec)*
Mark Crovella *(Boston University)*
Moez Draief *(Huawei)*
Ken Duffy *(Hamilton Institute, National University of Ireland)*
Vijay Erramilli *(Guavus)*
Anja Feldmann *(TU Berlin)*

Program Committee (continued):

Anshul Gandhi *(Stony Brook University)*
Ayalvadi Ganesh *(University of Bristol)*
Nicolas Gast *(Inria)*
Bruno Gaujal *(Inria)*
Javad Ghaderi *(Columbia University)*
Leana Golubchik *(University of Southern California)*
Bruce Hajek *(University of Illinois at Urbana-Champaign)*
Longbo Huang *(Tsinghua University)*
Johan van Leeuwaarden *(Eindhoven University of Technology)*
Matthieu Jonckheere *(Universidad de Buenos Aires)*
Amin Karbasi *(Yale University)*
Richard La *(University of Maryland at College Park)*
Marc Lelarge *(Inria-ENS)*
Brian Levine *(University of Massachusetts Amherst)*
Alex Liu *(Michigan State University)*
Mingyan Liu *(University of Michigan)*
Zhenhua Liu *(Stony Brook University)*
Yi Lu *(University of Illinois at Urbana-Champaign)*
John C.S. Lui *(The Chinese University of Hong Kong)*
Peter Marbach *(University of Toronto)*
Laurent Massoulié *(Inria - Microsoft Research)*
Arif Merchant *(Google)*
Vishal Misra *(Columbia University)*
Erich Nahum *(IBM Research)*
Jayakrishnan Nair *(IIT Bombay)*
Thu Nguyen *(Rutgers University)*
Jason Nieh *(Columbia University)*
Sewoong Oh *(University of Illinois at Urbana-Champaign)*
Ana Radovanović *(Google)*
Bozidar Radunovic *(Microsoft Research)*
Gaurav Raina *(IIT Madras)*
Ori Rottenstreich *(Princeton University)*
Dan Rubenstein *(Columbia University)*
Srinivas Shakkottai *(Texas A&M University)*
Jinwoo Shin *(KAIST)*
Mark Squillante *(IBM Research)*
Christopher Stewart *(Ohio State University)*
Sasha Stolyar *(Lehigh University)*
Vijay Subramanian *(Northwestern University)*
Patrick Thiran *(EPFL)*
Bhuvan Urgaonkar *(Pennsylvania State University)*
Benny Van Houdt *(University of Antwerp)*
Rahul Vaze *(TIFR Bombay)*
Maaike Verloop *(IRIT-CNRS)*
Milan Vojnovic *(Microsoft Research)*
Anwar Walid *(Bell Labs)*

Program Committee (continued):

Neil Walton *(University of Amsterdam)*
Chuan Wu *(University of Hong Kong)*
Yung Yi *(KAIST)*
Haifeng Yu *(National University of Singapore)*
Se-Young Yun *(Microsoft Research)*
Li Zhang *(IBM Research)*
Zhi-Li Zhang *(University of Minnesota)*
Xia Zhou *(Dartmouth College)*
Gil Zussman *(Columbia University)*

SIGMETRICS / Performance 2016 Sponsor & Supporters

Sponsor: ACM SIGMETRICS
special interest group on performance evaluation

In cooperation with: ifip

Supporters:

Computer Performance Foundation

facebook

HUAWEI

IBM®

Inria informatics mathematics

intel

Microsoft Research

Microsoft Research - Inria JOINT CENTRE

NEC Laboratories America
Relentless passion for innovation

NetApp™

Supporters (continued):

Delay, Memory, and Messaging Tradeoffs in Distributed Service Systems

David Gamarnik
MIT, ORC
77 Massachusetts Ave.
Cambridge, MA 02139
gamarnik@mit.edu

John N. Tsitsiklis
MIT, LIDS
77 Massachusetts Ave.
Cambridge, MA 02139
jnt@mit.edu

Martin Zubeldia
MIT, LIDS
77 Massachusetts Ave.
Cambridge, MA 02139
zubeldia@mit.edu

ABSTRACT

We consider the following distributed service model: jobs with unit mean, exponentially distributed, and independent processing times arrive as a Poisson process of rate λN, with $0 < \lambda < 1$, and are immediately dispatched to one of several queues associated with N identical servers with unit processing rate. We assume that the dispatching decisions are made by a central dispatcher endowed with a finite memory, and with the ability to exchange messages with the servers.

We study the fundamental resource requirements (memory bits and message exchange rate), in order to drive the expected steady-state queueing delay of a typical job to zero, as N increases. We propose a certain policy and establish (using a fluid limit approach) that it drives the delay to zero when either (i) the message rate grows superlinearly with N, or (ii) the memory grows superlogarithmically with N. Moreover, we show that any policy that has a certain symmetry property, and for which neither condition (i) or (ii) holds, results in an expected queueing delay which is bounded away from zero.

Finally, using the fluid limit approach once more, we show that for any given $\alpha > 0$ (no matter how small), if the policy only uses a linear message rate αN, the resulting asymptotic (as $N \to \infty$) expected queueing delay is positive but upper bounded, uniformly over all $\lambda > 1$. This is a significant improvement over the popular "power-of-d-choices" policy, which has a limiting expected delay that grows as $\log(1/(1-\lambda))$ when $\lambda \uparrow 1$.

Categories and Subject Descriptors

G.3 [**Probability and Statistics**]: Queueing theory, Markov processes; C.2.1 [**Network Architecture and Design**]: Performance tradeoffs

Keywords

Distributed service, Dispatching policies, Performance tradeoffs.

SIGMETRICS '16, June 14 - 18, 2016, Antibes Juan-Les-Pins, France

ISBN 978-1-4503-4266-7/16/06...$15.00

DOI: http://dx.doi.org/10.1145/2896377.2901478

1. INTRODUCTION

This paper addresses the tradeoffs between various measures of performance (delay, message rate and memory) in the context of large scale queueing systems. More specifically, we consider the supermarket model [11], a service system that involves a stream of incoming jobs that are to be dispatched to the queue associated with one of multiple servers. This setting is the dynamic generalization of the classic balls and bins model [2], where N balls have to be sequentially placed into one of N bins.

There is a variety of ways that this system can be operated, which correspond to different system architectures and policies, with different delay performance. At one extreme, incoming jobs can be sent to a random queue. This policy has no informational requirements but incurs a substantial delay because it does not take advantage of resource pooling. At the other extreme, incoming jobs can be sent to a shortest queue, or to a server with the smallest workload. The latter policies have very good performance (small queueing delay), but rely on a substantial information exchange overhead.

Many intermediate policies have been explored in the literature, which achieve different performance levels while using varying degrees of resources such as messages and memory (e.g., the power-of-d-choices [11, 15] or the PULL algorithm [14]). Such policies have been individually analyzed, and the merits of each have been pointed out. However, a comparison is not always possible, because different policies often involve different types of decision making architectures. A more detailed discussion of the relevant literature and the various schemes therein is deferred to Section 4.

The performance-resources tradeoffs have been analyzed in the context of balls into bins models. In particular, the tradeoff between number of messages and maximum load was recently obtained by Lenzen and Wattenhofer [8]. Moreover, the tradeoff between the number of bits of memory available and the maximum load was studied in [1, 4]. To the best of our knowledge, the current study is the first to address these tradeoffs for a dynamic model.

1.1 Our contribution

Instead of focusing on yet another policy or decision making architecture, in this paper we step back and formulate a more fundamental problem. We consider a broad family of decision making architectures and policies, which includes most of those considered in the earlier literature, and work towards characterizing the attainable delay performance, for a given level of resources that are employed.

In more concrete terms, as far as delay is concerned, we

focus on the following qualitative criterion: does the average queueing delay go to zero, as the system size increases? Regarding resources, we allow the dispatcher to have some limited memory, where it can store information on the state of the queues. We also allow the exchange of messages, either from the dispatcher to the servers (queries), and from the servers to the dispatcher; these latter messages can be either responses to queries or spontaneous status updates.

The main question that we study is the following: What is the message rate (total over both directions) and/or memory size requirement that are necessary and sufficient in order to achieve vanishing delay, as the system size grows to infinity? We are able to provide a fairly complete answer to this question. Specifically,

a) If the message rate is proportional to the arrival rate **and** the memory size (in bits) is logarithmic in the number of servers, then *every* decision making architecture and policy, within a certain broad class of policies, results in a delay that does not vanish as the system size increases. The main constraints that we impose on the policies that we consider are: (i) there is no queueing at the dispatcher, and (ii) policies are symmetric, in a sense to be defined.

b) If either the message rate is superlinear in the arrival rate **or** the memory size is superlogarithmic in the number of servers, we provide a fairly simple and natural policy that results in a vanishing delay as the system size increases. Moreover, even if the message rate is proportional to the arrival rate and the memory is logarithmic in the number of servers, this same policy performs better than the alternatives considered earlier in the literature: among other properties, it has uniformly upper bounded queueing delay as $\lambda \uparrow 1$.

We analyze the proposed policy by considering a corresponding fluid limit. This results in expressions that provide a detailed characterization of the resulting queue lengths in the regime where delays do not vanish (case (b) above). Although we do not allow queueing at the dispatcher in our model, the negative result still holds even if we had a central queue with a finite buffer whose size is uniformly upper bounded independent of N. However, if the buffer size can grow with N, there exists a policy with a linear message rate and no memory that achieves vanishing queueing delay. Whether similar negative results can be established without our symmetry assumption is left as an open problem.

1.2 Outline of the paper

The rest of this paper is organized as follows. In Section 2 we introduce some notation. The model and the main results are presented in Section 3, where we also discuss the implications of the results and compare our policy to the so-called "power-of-d-choices" [11, 15]. In Section 4 we put our results in the context of some popular dispatching policies in the literature. In Sections 5, 6, and 7, we provide the proofs of the main results. Finally, in Section 8 we provide our conclusions and suggestions for future work.

2. NOTATION

We define the following sets:

$$\mathcal{S} \triangleq \left\{ s \in [0,1]^{\mathbb{Z}_+} : s_0 = 1;\ s_i \geq s_{i+1},\ \forall i \geq 0 \right\},$$

$$\mathcal{S}^1 \triangleq \left\{ s \in \mathcal{S} : \sum_{i=0}^{\infty} s_i < \infty \right\},$$

$$\mathcal{Q}_N \triangleq \left\{ x \in [0,1]^{\mathbb{Z}_+} : x_i = \frac{K_i}{N},\ \text{for some } K_i \in \mathbb{Z}_+,\ \forall i \right\}.$$

We define the weighted ℓ^2 norm $||\cdot||_w$ on $\mathbb{R}^{\mathbb{Z}_+}$ by

$$||x-y||_w^2 \triangleq \sum_{i=0}^{\infty} \frac{|x_i - y_i|^2}{2^i}.$$

We also define a partial order on $\mathbb{R}_+^{\mathbb{Z}_+}$ as follows:

$$x \geq y \Leftrightarrow x_i \geq y_i \quad \forall i \geq 0,$$
$$x > y \Leftrightarrow x \geq y,\ x \neq y, \text{ and } x_i > y_i, \text{ if } i \geq 1 \text{ and } y_i > 0.$$

For a given positive integer N, we define the set of server IDs $\mathcal{N} \triangleq \{1, \ldots, N\}$. We let Π_N be the set of probability distributions over $\mathcal{N}$, and let S_N denote the group of permutations over $\mathcal{N}$. We can also define the action of S_N over Π_N by letting, for every $\sigma \in S_N$ and $p \in \Pi_N$,

$$\sigma(p)(\sigma(i)) = p(i), \quad \forall i \in \mathcal{N}.$$

In words, the probability of $\sigma(i)$ under $\sigma(p)$ is the same as the probability of i under p. Finally, we denote by $\mathcal{P}(\mathcal{N})$ the power set of $\mathcal{N}$ and we further extend the action of S_N to $\Pi_{\mathcal{P}(\mathcal{N})}$ (the set of probability distributions over the power set $\mathcal{P}(\mathcal{N})$) so that, for any $\sigma \in S_N$ and $p \in \Pi_{\mathcal{P}(\mathcal{N})}$, and for all $r \in \mathcal{N}$,

$$\sigma(p)(\{\sigma(n_1), \ldots, \sigma(n_r)\}) = p(\{n_1, \ldots, n_r\}),$$

for all $\{n_1, \ldots, n_r\} \in \mathcal{P}(\mathcal{N})$. This means that the probability of selecting the subset of servers $\{\sigma(n_1), \ldots, \sigma(n_r)\}$ under $\sigma(p)$ is the same as the probability of selecting the subset $\{n_1, \ldots, n_r\}$ under p.

3. MODEL AND MAIN RESULTS

In this section we present our main results. In Section 3.1 we describe the model and our assumptions. In Section 3.2 we introduce and study three different variants of a certain pull-based dispatching policy. We study their fluid limits and state the validity of fluid approximations for the transient and the steady-state regimes. Then, in Section 3.3 we present a unified framework for a broad set of dispatching policies that includes most of the policies studied in previous literature, and present our negative result on the queueing delay for resource constrained policies.

3.1 Modeling assumptions

We consider a system consisting of N parallel servers, where each server has a processing rate equal to 1. Furthermore, each server is associated with an infinite capacity, FIFO queue. We use the convention that a job that is being served remains in the queue until its processing is completed. We assume that each server is work conserving: a server is idle if and only if the corresponding queue is empty. Jobs arrive to the system as a single Poisson process of rate λN (for some fixed $\lambda < 1$). Job sizes are i.i.d., independent from the arrival process, and exponentially distributed with mean 1. A central controller (dispatcher) is responsible for routing every incoming job to a suitable queue, immediately upon arrival. The dispatcher may have limited information on the state of the queues; it can only rely on a limited amount of local memory and on messages that provide partial information about the state of the system. These messages (which are assumed to be instantaneous) can be sent from the servers to the dispatcher at any time, or from the dispatcher to the server (in the form of queries) at the time of an arrival. Messages from the servers can only contain information about the state of their queue (number of remaining jobs and total remaining workload). Within this context, a system designer has the freedom to choose a messaging policy, the rules with which the memory is updated, and the dispatching policy. We are interested in the case where N is very large and where we have some constraints on the number of messages exchanged and on the memory size. The performance metric of interest is the expected delay in steady state of a typical job, i.e., the expected time between its arrival and the time at which it starts receiving service.

3.2 Our dispatching policy and its performance

In this section we introduce our policy, and study the properties of three of its variants.

3.2.1 Policy description

Let us fix N. We consider a policy whereby the dispatcher's memory is used to run a virtual queue that stores up to $C(N)$ server IDs (or tokens), so that the memory size is of order $C(N)\log_2(N)$ bits. Since there are only N distinct servers, we will assume throughout the rest of the paper that $C(N) \leq N$. While a server is idle, it sends messages to the dispatcher as a Poisson process of rate $\mu(N)$ to inform or remind the dispatcher of its idleness. Whenever the dispatcher receives a message, it adds the ID of the server that sent the message to the virtual queue of tokens that is kept in the memory, unless this ID is already stored or the virtual queue is full, in which case it discards the new message. When a new job arrives, if there is at least one server ID in the virtual queue, the job goes to the queue of a server chosen uniformly at random from the virtual queue and the corresponding token is deleted. If there are no tokens present, the job is sent to a queue chosen uniformly at random. This policy, called from now on the Resource Constrained Pull-Based (RCPB) policy or Pull-Based policy for short, is depicted in Figure 1.

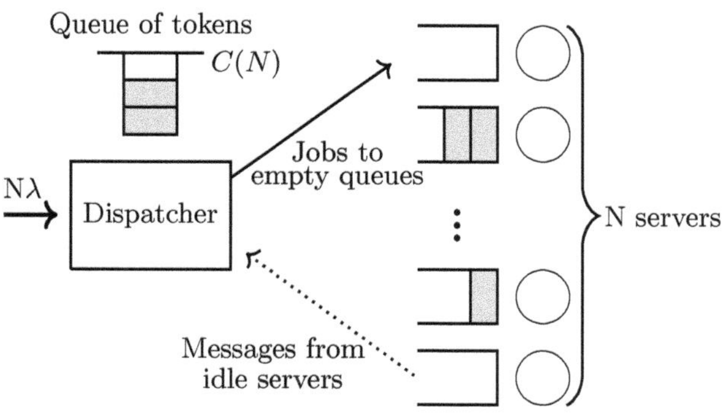

Figure 1: Resource Constrained Pull-Based policy. Jobs are sent to queues associated with idle servers, based on tokens in the virtual queue. If no tokens are present, a queue is chosen at random.

Note that under our policy, no messages are sent from the dispatcher to the servers, which is why it is called a "Pull-Based" policy [14]. We present a summary of our results for the three variants of our policy in Table 1, where we also introduce some mnemonic terms that we will use to refer to these variants. For our purposes, the most relevant subcase of the High Memory variant is when $\mu \geq \frac{\lambda}{1-\lambda}$, which achieves zero asymptotic delay with superlogarithmic memory and linear message rate.

Variant	Memory	Idle message rate	Delay
High Mem.	$C(N) \in \omega(1)$	$\mu(N) = \mu \geq \frac{\lambda}{1-\lambda}$	0
		$\mu(N) = \mu < \frac{\lambda}{1-\lambda}$	> 0
High Mess.	$C(N) = C \geq 1$	$\mu(N) \in \omega(1)$	0
Constr.	$C(N) = C \geq 1$	$\mu(N) = \mu > 0$	> 0

Table 1: The three variants (regimes) of our policy, and the resulting delays, in the limit as $N \to \infty$.

3.2.2 System state representation

For a fixed N, we can model the system as a continuous time Markov chain using as state the queue length vector, denoted by $\left(Q_i^N(t)\right)_{i=1}^N \in \mathbb{Z}_+^N$, together with the number of tokens, denoted by $M^N(t) \in \{0, 1, \ldots, C(N)\}$. Furthermore, as the system is symmetric with respect to the queues, we can replace the queue length vector by the more convenient representation $S^N(t) = \left(S_i^N(t)\right)_{i=0}^\infty$, where

$$S_i^N(t) \triangleq \frac{1}{N}\sum_{j=1}^N \mathbb{1}_{[i,+\infty)}\left(Q_j^N(t)\right), \quad i \in \mathbb{Z}_+,$$

is the fraction of queues with at least i jobs at time t.

3.2.3 Fluid model

We now introduce the fluid model of $S^N(t)$, associated with our policy.

Definition 1. (Fluid model) Given an initial condition $s^0 \in \mathcal{S}$, a function $s(t) : [0, \infty) \to \mathcal{S}$ is said to be a solution to the fluid model (or fluid solution) if

1. $s(0) = s^0$.
2. For all $t \geq 0$, $s_0(t) = 1$.
3. For almost all $t \in [0, \infty)$, and for every $i \geq 1$, $s_i(t)$ is differentiable and satisfies

$$\frac{ds_1(t)}{dt} = \lambda[1 - s_1(t)P_0(t)] - [s_1(t) - s_2(t)], \tag{1}$$

$$\frac{ds_i(t)}{dt} = \lambda[s_{i-1}(t) - s_i(t)]P_0(t) - [s_i(t) - s_{i+1}(t)], \tag{2}$$

for all $i \geq 2$, where $P_0(t)$ is given, for the three variants considered, by:

(i) High Memory: $P_0(t) = \left[1 - \frac{\mu[1-s_1(t)]}{\lambda}\right]^+$;

(ii) High Message: $P_0(t) = \left[1 - \frac{1-s_2(t)}{\lambda}\right]^+ \mathbb{1}_{\{s_1(t)=1\}}$;

(iii) Constrained: $P_0(t) = \left[\sum_{k=0}^{C}\left(\frac{\mu[1-s_1(t)]}{\lambda}\right)^k\right]^{-1}$.

Note that the fluid model does not include a variable associated with the number of tokens. This is because, as we will see, the virtual queue process $M^N(t)$ evolves on a much faster time scale than the processes of the queue lengths and does not have a deterministic limit. We thus have a process with two different time scales: on the one hand, the virtual queue evolves on a fast time scale (at least N times faster) and from its perspective the queue process $S^N(t)$ appears static; on the other hand, the queue process $S^N(t)$ evolves on a slower time scale; from its perspective, the virtual queue appears to be at equilibrium. This latter property is manifested in the drift of the fluid model: $P_0(t)$ is the probability that the virtual queue is empty when the rest of the system is fixed at the state $s(t)$ (and is given by a different expression for each variant).

We now provide some intuition for each of the drift terms in Equations (1) and (2).

(i) $\lambda[1 - P_0(t)]$: This term corresponds to arrivals to an empty queue while there are tokens in the virtual queue, taking into account that the virtual queue is nonempty with probability $1 - P_0(t)$, in the limit.

(ii) $\lambda[s_{i-1}(t) - s_i(t)]P_0(t)$: This term corresponds to arrivals to a queue with exactly $i-1$ jobs while there are no tokens in the virtual queue. This happens when the virtual queue is empty and when a queue with $i-1$ jobs is drawn uniformly at random, which happens with probability $P_0(t)[s_{i-1}(t) - s_i(t)]$.

(iii) $-[s_i(t) - s_{i+1}(t)]$: This term corresponds to departures from queues with exactly i jobs, which occur at a rate equal to the proportion $s_i(t) - s_{i+1}(t)$ of servers with exactly i jobs.

(iv) Finally, the expressions for $P_0(t)$ are obtained through an explicit calculation of the steady-state distribution of $M^N(t)$ when $S^N(t)$ is fixed at the value $s(t)$, while also letting $N \to \infty$.

3.2.4 Properties of the fluid solutions

The existence of fluid solutions is established by showing that the limit of every convergent subsequence of sample paths $(S^N(t))$ is a fluid solution. Moreover, the following theorem states their uniqueness for all initial conditions $s^0 \in \mathcal{S}$, and it also characterizes the (unique) equilibrium of the fluid model and its asymptotic stability for all initial conditions $s^0 \in \mathcal{S}^1 \subset \mathcal{S}$. The variants described below correspond to assumptions on memory and message rates described in the 2nd and 3rd columns of Table 1, respectively.

Theorem 1. (Uniqueness and stability of fluid solutions) *A fluid solution, as described in Definition 1, exists and is unique for any initial condition $s^0 \in \mathcal{S}$. Furthermore, within the set $\mathcal{S}^1$, the fluid model has a unique equilibrium s^*, given by $s_i^* = \lambda[\lambda P_0^*]^{i-1}$, for all $i \geq 1$, where P_0^* is given for the three variants considered by:*

(i) High Memory: $P_0^* = \left[1 - \frac{\mu(1-\lambda)}{\lambda}\right]^+$;

(ii) High Message: $P_0^* = 0$;

(iii) Constrained: $P_0^* = \left[\sum_{k=0}^{C} \left(\frac{\mu(1-\lambda)}{\lambda}\right)^k\right]^{-1}$.

This equilibrium is asymptotically stable, i.e.,

$$\lim_{t\to\infty} \|s(t) - s^*\|_w = 0,$$

for all initial conditions $s^0 \in \mathcal{S}^1$.

The proof for uniqueness and stability is given in Section 5. The proof of the existence is omitted due to space constraints.

3.2.5 Approximation theorems

The three results in this section justify the use of the fluid model as an approximation to the finite stochastic system. The first theorem states that the evolution of the process $S^N(t)$ is almost surely uniformly close, over any finite time horizon $[0, T]$, to the unique fluid solution $s(t)$.

Theorem 2. (Fluid limit) *Fix $T > 0$. If*

$$\lim_{N\to\infty} \left\|S^N(0) - s^0\right\|_w = 0, \qquad a.s.,$$

for some $s^0 \in \mathcal{S}$, then

$$\lim_{N\to\infty} \sup_{0\leq t\leq T} \left\|S^N(t) - s(t)\right\|_w = 0, \qquad a.s.,$$

where $s(t)$ is the fluid solution with initial condition s^0.

The proof of this theorem is omitted due to space constraints.

If we combine Theorems 2 and 1 we have that the finite system $S^N(t)$ can be approximated by the equilibrium of the fluid model s^* after some time, because

$$S^N(t) \xrightarrow{N\to\infty} s(t) \xrightarrow{t\to\infty} s^*,$$

almost surely. If we interchange the order of the limits over N and t, we obtain the limiting behavior of the invariant distributions π_s^N of the finite systems as N increases. In the next proposition and theorem, it is shown that the result is the same, i.e., that

$$S^N(t) \xrightarrow{t\to\infty} \pi_s^N \xrightarrow{N\to\infty} s^*,$$

in distribution, so that the interchange of limits is justified.

We start by showing that the stochastic process for any fixed N is positive recurrent.

Proposition 3. (Positive recurrence for finite N) *For any fixed N, the stochastic process $\left(S^N(t), M^N(t)\right)$ is positive recurrent and therefore has a unique invariant distribution π^N.*

Proof. In this case it is advantageous to work with the number of jobs in the queues $\left(Q_i^N(t)\right)_{i=1}^N$ instead of with $S^N(t)$. Then the positive recurrence follows by using the simple quadratic Lyapunov function

$$\Phi(Q, m) \triangleq \frac{1}{N} \sum_{i=1}^{N} Q_i^2. \tag{3}$$

□

We then show that the sequence of invariant measures converges in distribution to the Dirac measure concentrated on the equilibrium of the fluid model.

Theorem 4. (Interchange of limits) *For any N, let π^N be the unique invariant distribution of the stochastic process $\left(S^N(t), M^N(t)\right)$ and let $\pi_s^N(\cdot) = \sum_{m=0}^{C(N)} \pi^N(\cdot, m)$ be the marginal for S^N. Then,*

$$\lim_{N\to\infty} \pi_s^N = \delta_{s^*}, \quad \textit{in distribution.}$$

The proof is given in Section 6.

Putting everything together, we conclude that the fluid model is a very accurate approximation for the stochastic system when N is very large for the both transient regime (Theorems 2 and 1) and for the steady state regime (Theorem 4).

3.2.6 Delay

Having shown that we can approximate the stochastic system by its fluid model for large N, we can analyze the performance of the equilibrium of the fluid model and thus approximate the expected delay implied by our policy.

For the N-th system, we define the average delay (more precisely, the waiting time) of a job, in steady state, generically denoted by $\mathbb{E}\left[W^N\right]$, as the mean time that the job spends in queue until its service starts. Then by Little's law, we have that

$$\mathbb{E}\left[W^N\right] = \frac{1}{\lambda N}\mathbb{E}\left[\sum_{i=1}^{\infty} N S_i^N\right] - 1,$$

and taking limits as $N \to \infty$ we obtain the limiting queueing delay as

$$\mathbb{E}[W] \triangleq \lim_{N\to\infty} \mathbb{E}\left[W^N\right] = \frac{1}{\lambda}\left(\sum_{i=1}^{\infty} s_i^*\right) - 1,$$

where the interchange of the limit in N, and the expectation and the infinite sum can be justified by applying the Dominated Convergence Theorem using the geometric upper bound from Lemma 10.

High Memory and High Message variants.

For the High Memory variant with $\mu \geq \frac{\lambda}{1-\lambda}$, as well as for the High Message variant, the equilibrium is $s_1^* = \lambda$, and $s_i^* = 0$ for all $i \geq 2$, which yields the claimed zero queueing delay (cf. Table 1).

Constrained variant.

For the Constrained variant, even though we obtain a positive delay, our Pull-Based policy has some remarkable properties. First of all, as discussed above, the delay is

$$\mathbb{E}[W] = \frac{1}{\lambda}\sum_{i=1}^{\infty} s_i^* - 1 = \sum_{i=1}^{\infty} (\lambda P_0^*)^{i-1} - 1 = \frac{\lambda P_0^*}{1-\lambda P_0^*}. \quad (4)$$

Suppose that the message rate of each idle server is $\mu = \mu'\left(\frac{\lambda}{1-\lambda}\right)$ for some constant $\mu' > 0$. Since a server is idle (on average) a fraction $1-\lambda$ of the time, the resulting average message rate at each server is $\lambda\mu'$. We can rewrite the equilibrium probability as

$$P_0^* = \left[\sum_{k=0}^{C} (\mu')^k\right]^{-1}.$$

Substituting this in Equation (4) we can obtain an upper bound (uniform in $\lambda < 1$) for the delay in steady state

$$\mathbb{E}[W] \leq \left[\sum_{k=1}^{C} (\mu')^k\right]^{-1} \qquad \forall\, \lambda < 1. \qquad (5)$$

This implies that if $\mu' > 1$, the queueing delay decreases exponentially fast with the maximum number of tokens C. More importantly, for a fixed $\mu' > 0$ and C, the delay is in fact bounded as $\lambda \uparrow 1$. Finally, the delay is monotonically decreasing with μ' and C.

Phase transition of heavy traffic delay.

We have a phase transition between $\mu' = 0$ (which corresponds to a random uniform routing) and $\mu' > 0$. In the first case, we have the usual unbounded heavy traffic delay of the M/M/1 queue. However, when $\mu' > 0$ the delay is upper bounded uniformly in λ, as shown in Equation (5). This highlights the importance of sending messages while idle and the fact that an intelligent choice of the message budget is to set $\mu = \mu' \frac{\lambda}{1-\lambda}$. Note that this choice still results in a constant $(\lambda\mu')$ average message rate at each server, uniformly upper bounded by μ' for all N and all $\lambda < 1$. This is a key qualitative improvement over all other policies in the literature that have a non-vanishing delay; see the discussion below and in Section 4.

Comparison with the power-of-d-choices.

The expected steady-state delay for the power-of-d-choices policy was shown in [11, 15] to be

$$\mathbb{E}[W_{\text{Pod}}] = \sum_{i=1}^{\infty} \lambda^{\frac{d^i - d}{d-1}} - 1 \geq \lambda^d,$$

which means that the delay decreases at best exponentially with d, much like the delay decreases exponentially with C in our scheme. However, increasing d increases the number of messages sent, unlike our policy.

Furthermore, the delay in heavy traffic for the power-of-d-choices is shown in [11] to grow as $\log\left(\frac{1}{1-\lambda}\right)$ as $\lambda \uparrow 1$ for any fixed d. In contrast, the delay of our scheme has a constant upper bound, independent of λ.

In conclusion, our Pull-Based policy provides better expected delay (especially in heavy traffic) using fewer messages: the power-of-d-choices policy requires $2\lambda d N$ messages per unit of time, while our policy requires $\mu'\lambda N$ messages per unit of time and $C\log_2(N)$ bits of memory.

3.3 Delay lower bound for resource constrained policies

In this subsection we present a negative result that shows that resource constraints on the message rate and on the size of the memory result in asymptotically non-vanishing delays, for a broad class of symmetric policies.

3.3.1 *Unified framework for policies*

In order to provide a negative result for a class of policies, we need to be very precise on the family of policies considered, including details on the way that the memory is operated, and the precise meaning of "symmetry". We assume that in order to decide the destination of each arriving job, the dispatcher relies entirely on queries to a subset of servers regarding the state of their queues, and on a memory with C_N bits. The memory is updated only when either (i) the dispatcher receives a message from a server, or (ii) the dispatcher has just dispatched a job.

We define the set of memory states as $\mathcal{M} \triangleq \{1, \ldots, 2^{C_N}\}$. Furthermore, we define the set of possible states at a given queue as the set of nonnegative sequences $\mathcal{Q} \triangleq \mathbb{R}_+^{\mathbb{Z}_+}$, where a sequence specifies the remaining workload of each job in the queue, including the one that is being served. As long as a queue has a finite number of jobs, then the queue state is a sequence with a finite number of non-zero entries. We define next a broad class of memory-based dispatching policies.

Definition 2. (Memory-based dispatching policy) For a fixed N, a memory-based dispatching policy η^N has four components:

1. (Process of messages from servers) We have a bounded rate function $\mu^N : \mathcal{Q} \to \mathbb{R}_+$ which defines a set of modulated Poisson[1] counting processes
$$\left\{Y_n^N(t)\right\}_{n=1}^N.$$
The rate of $Y_n^N(\cdot)$ at each time t depends on the current queue state $Q_n^N(t)$ and equals $\mu^N(Q_n^N(t))$. Besides, the functions are uniformly upper bounded, i.e., $\mu^N(q) \leq \mu^N(0)$ for all $q \in \mathcal{Q}$.

2. (Memory update due to a new message from a server) Given a memory state $m \in \mathcal{M}$, whenever there is an arrival of a message from server $n \in \mathcal{N}$, containing the current queue state $q \in \mathcal{Q}$, the memory is updated according to a function
$$g_{pull}^N : \mathcal{M} \times \mathcal{N} \times \mathcal{Q} \to \mathcal{M}.$$

3. (Server sampling and dispatching rule) Given a memory state $m \in \mathcal{M}$, whenever a new job arrives to the system, the dispatcher sends queries to a subset of the servers, chosen according to the distribution specified by a function
$$\nu^N : \mathcal{M} \to \Pi_{\mathcal{P}(\mathcal{N})}.$$
Then, given the set of pairs $\{(n_1, q_{n_1}), \ldots, (n_r, q_{n_r})\}$ of sampled subset of servers and the state of the corresponding queues, the new arrival is dispatched according to a probability distribution specified by a function
$$f^N : \mathcal{M} \times \mathcal{B} \to \Pi_N,$$
where $\mathcal{B}$ is the subset of $\mathcal{P}(\mathcal{N} \times \mathcal{Q})$ where each element of $\mathcal{N}$ appears only once.

4. (Memory update due to a dispatched job) Immediately after a new job is dispatched to some queue, the memory is updated according to a function
$$g_d^N : \mathcal{M} \times \mathcal{B} \times \mathcal{N} \to \mathcal{M},$$
where the last argument of the function g_d^N is the identity of the server to which the job was dispatched.

[1]Although we will use Poisson processes for the analysis, our negative result can also be established even if the messages are more general renewal processes (e.g., with deterministic inter-arrival times).

Remark 1. Note that we only consider the memory used to store information between one arrival or message to the next. When counting the memory resources used by a policy, we do not take into account information that is used in zero time (e.g., the responses from the queries at the time of an arrival), or the memory required to evaluate the various functions that describe the policy. If that additional memory was accounted for, then the memory constraints would be more severe, and therefore our negative result would still hold.

The functions g_{pull}^N, ν^N, f^N, and g_d^N define a Markov process over the state space $\mathcal{Q}^N \times \mathcal{M}$, as follows. First of all, the states of the queues progress naturally through time as jobs get processed. Then, there are two sources of events: the exogenous arrivals and the messages that servers send to the dispatcher according to the processes $\{Y_n^N(\cdot)\}_{n=1}^N$. When a message from server n with queue state q arrives to the dispatcher, the memory is updated according to $g_{pull}^N(\cdot, n, q)$. When we have an arrival of a new job, there are three steps that occur sequentially but instantaneously: first, an element of the power set $\mathcal{P}(\mathcal{N})$ (i.e., a subset of $\mathcal{N}$) is selected according to ν^N and the current memory state; second, the job is sent to a queue according to the distribution obtained by f^N evaluated on the actual memory state, sampled subset of servers, and actual states of the queues associated with them; and third, the memory is updated once more according to g_d^N, taking into account the destination of the last job, as well as the IDs and the queue states of the sampled servers.

Remark 2. Here we are considering policies that send messages to the servers only at the time of an arrival and in one round of communication. This eliminates the possibility of having policies that sequentially poll the servers uniformly at random until they find an idle one. The reason behind this restriction is that, in practice, these queries involve some processing and travel time ϵ. Were we to consider a model with $\epsilon > 0$, the sequential polling policies would suffer greatly and would incur positive delay. In contrast our pull-based policy would only have to work with slightly delayed information, but the asymptotic vanishing result would still hold, as long as ϵ is small enough.

Remark 3. We could expand the set of policies by allowing the servers to also send messages whenever there is a service completion. This would result in some additional notation. However, the same negative result can be proved for this somewhat enlarged class of policies as well.

We now introduce a symmetry assumption on the policies.

Definition 3. (Symmetric policy) The memory-based dispatching policy η^N is symmetric if for every permutation of the servers $\sigma \in S_N$ (and associated permutations, also denoted by σ, over the sets $\mathcal{P}(\mathcal{N})$, Π_N, and $\Pi_{\mathcal{P}(\mathcal{N})}$), there exists some permutation σ_M of the memory states such that the following properties hold.

1. (Memory update due to new message from a server)
$$g_{pull}^N(\sigma_M(m), \sigma(n), q) = \sigma_M\left(g_{pull}^N(m, n, q)\right),$$
for all $(m, n, q) \in \mathcal{M} \times \mathcal{N} \times \mathcal{Q}$.

2. (Server sampling and dispatching rule)

$$\nu^N(\sigma_M(m)) = \sigma\left(\nu^N(m)\right),$$

for all $m \in \mathcal{M}$, and

$$f^N(\sigma_M(m),\{(\sigma(n_1),q_1),\ldots,(\sigma(n_r),q_r)\}) = \sigma\left(f^N(m,\{(n_1,q_1),\ldots,(n_r,q_r)\})\right),$$

for all $(m,\{(n_1,q_1),\ldots,(n_r,q_r)\}) \in \mathcal{M}\times\mathcal{B}$.

3. (Memory update due to a dispatched job)

$$g_d^N(\sigma_M(m),\{(\sigma(n_1),q_1),\ldots,(\sigma(n_r),q_r)\},\sigma(n)) = \sigma_M\left(g_d^N(m,\{(n_1,q_1),\ldots,(n_r,q_r)\},n)\right),$$

for all $(m,\{(n_1,q_1),\ldots,(n_r,q_r)\},n) \in \mathcal{M}\times\mathcal{B}\times\mathcal{N}$.

3.3.2 *Lower bound for queueing delay*

We are now ready to state the main result of this section.

Theorem 5. *Fix $C,\alpha > 0$. For any symmetric policy η^N with $C_N = C\log_2(N)$ bits of memory, with a time-average message rate bounded by αN almost surely, and with a unique steady state distribution, we have that the expected queueing delay is uniformly lower bounded, i.e.,*

$$\mathbb{E}\left[W^N\right] \geq b(C,\alpha) > 0,$$

where $\mathbb{E}\left[W^N\right]$ is the expected queueing delay in steady state, and $b(C,\alpha)$ is a constant that only depends on C and α.

A detailed proof is given in Section 7.

4. COMPARISON WITH OTHER POLICIES IN THE LITERATURE

In this section we put our results in perspective by reviewing various dispatching policies in the literature, focusing on their queueing delay and on the amount of resources they use.

4.1 Open-loop policies (without messages)

An optimal open-loop policy dispatches arriving jobs to the queues in a round robin fashion [13]. This policy does not require messages but needs $\log_2(N)$ bits of memory to store the ID of the next queue to receive a job. In the limit, each queue behaves similar to an D/M/1 queue, which still has a $\Omega\left(\frac{1}{1-\lambda}\right)$ delay (see [13]). This policy is not symmetric.

4.2 Policies based on queue lengths

4.2.1 *Join the shortest queue (SQ)*

If we only have access to the queue lengths, an optimal policy is to have each incoming job join a shortest queue. This policy is symmetric, achieves vanishing delay, and requires no memory, but uses $2\lambda N^2$ messages per unit of time (N queries and N responses for each arrival, with rate λN). Alternatively, joining a queue with the least remaining workload performs just as well.

4.2.2 *SQ(d) with memory (SQ(d,b))*

An improvement over the power-of-d-choices, proposed by Mitzenmacher et al. in [12], is obtained by using extra memory to store the b least loaded queues sampled at the time of the previous arrival. When a new job arrives, d queues are sampled uniformly at random and the job is sent to a least loaded queue among the d sampled and the b stored queues. This policy is symmetric, needs $2\lambda dN$ messages per unit of time and $\Omega(b\log_2(N))$ bits of memory, and has positive delay as expected. It compares unfavorably to our policy for the same reasons as for the power-of-d-choices.

4.2.3 *SQ(d) for divisible jobs*

More recently, Ying et al. [16] considered the case of having an arrival rate of $\frac{N\lambda}{m(N)}$ (with $m(N) \in \omega(1)$ and $m(N) \in o(N)$), where each job can be divided into $m(N)$ tasks with mean size 1. The dispatcher samples $dm(N)$ queues and does a water-filling of those queues with the $m(N)$ tasks. In this case, the number of messages sent per unit of time is $2\lambda dN$ and it needs no memory.

Even though this was not mentioned in [16], this policy can drive the queueing delay to 0 if $d \geq \frac{1}{1-\lambda}$. This policy does not fall into our framework because it works with divisible jobs. We could get a very similar policy by queueing $m(N)$ jobs in the dispatcher and dispatching them all at the same time, but this needs an unbounded buffer at the dispatcher.

4.3 Pull-based policies

In order to reduce the message rate, Badonnel and Burgess [3], Lu et al. [10], and then Stolyar [14] proposed that messages be sent from a server to the dispatcher whenever the server becomes idle, so that the dispatcher can keep track of the set of idle servers in real time. Then, an arriving job is to be sent to an empty queue (if there is one) or to a queue chosen uniformly at random if all queues are non-empty. This symmetric policy requires at most λN messages per unit of time and exactly N bits of memory (one bit for each server, indicating whether it is empty or not). Stolyar [14] has shown that when N goes to infinity, the expected delay vanishes.

These pull-based policies are very efficient and they were the inspiration for our own policy. In fact, the High Memory variant of our own policy can be viewed as a more memory-efficient version of Stolyar's PULL policy [14] where instead of requiring N bits of memory, we achieve the desired vanishing delay with any superlogarithmic memory size.

4.4 Memory, messages, and queueing delay

We now summarize the resource requirements (memory and message rate) and the asymptotic delay of the policies reviewed in this section that fall within our framework, together with our three variants.

Policy	Memory (bits)	Message rate	Delay
RRobin [13]	$\log_2(N)$	0	>0
JSQ	0	$2\lambda N^2$	0
JSQ(d) [11]	0	$2d\lambda N$	>0
JSQ(d,b) [12]	$\Omega(b\log_2(N))$	$2d\lambda N$	>0
Pull-based [14]	N	λN	0
High Memory	$\omega(\log_2(N))$	λN	0
High Message	$C\log_2(N)$	$\omega(N)$	0
Constrained	$C\log_2(N)$	$\mu'\lambda N$	>0

Note that there are several policies that achieve 0 queueing delay in the limit, but (as expected) all of them fall into one (or both) of two categories:

a) Those that need $\omega(N)$ messages. For example: JSQ and JLW require $\Theta(N^2)$ messages per unit of time.

b) Those that need $\omega(\log_2(N))$ bits of memory. For example, the PULL policy [14] requires N bits of memory.

This is consistent with our results: the only way to achieve vanishing delay is by having a superlogarithmic memory or a superlinear message rate. Alternatively, we could obtain a vanishing delay with a linear message rate and an unbounded central buffer [16].

5. PROPERTIES OF THE FLUID MODEL

We divide the proof of Theorem 1 into Lemmas 6 and 7, and Proposition 9 in which we establish uniqueness of solutions, uniqueness of an equilibrium, and asymptotic stability, respectively. The proof of existence is omitted due to space constraints.

5.1 Uniqueness of solutions

Lemma 6. *A fluid solution, as described in Definition 1, with initial condition $s^0 \in \mathcal{S}$, is unique.*

PROOF. The drift in the High Memory and Constrained variants is always Lipschitz-continuous, so the uniqueness of solutions is guaranteed by the Picard-Lindelöff theorem for infinite dimensional spaces [9]. On the other hand, the drift in the High Message variant is only continuous "almost everywhere" so we cannot guarantee the uniqueness of classical (differentiable) solutions. However, we can show the uniqueness of the possibly non-differential solutions of Definition 1. Uniqueness issues only appear when the trajectories hit the closure of the set where the drift is not Lipschitz-continuous, which in this case is the closure of

$$D = \{s \in \mathcal{S} : s_1 = 1 \text{ and } s_2 > 1 - \lambda\}.$$

The proof of the uniqueness for the High Message variant consists in concatenating up to three unique solutions, and has three steps:

1. If $s^0 \in \mathcal{S}\backslash\overline{D}$, then we have uniqueness up to the point in which the solution hits $\overline{D}$.

2. If $s^0 \in D$, we show that the solution stays in D until we have $s_2 = 1 - \lambda$, implying that it can only escape D through $\overline{D}\backslash D$. This is because $\dot{s}_1 > 0$ if $s_2 > 1 - \lambda$. Then, the uniqueness of the solution up to this point is guaranteed by the fact that the drift restricted to $\overline{D}$ is also Lipschitz-continuous.

3. Last, we show that once that it escapes D, it cannot go back in again, thus guaranteeing the uniqueness of the whole solution.

We omit the details due to space constraints. □

5.2 Existence and uniqueness of an equilibrium

Lemma 7. *The fluid model has the unique equilibrium $s^* \in \mathcal{S}^1$ defined in Theorem 1.*

PROOF. Suppose that $s^* \in \mathcal{S}^1$ is an equilibrium. Since $s^* \in \mathcal{S}^1$, we have $\sum_{i=1}^{\infty} s_i^* < \infty$ and we can sum the equilibrium conditions over all coordinates $j \geq i$ for all $i \geq 0$, and get the result. □

5.3 Asymptotic stability of the equilibrium

We will establish asymptotic stability by sandwiching a solution between two solutions that converge to s^*, similar to the argument in [15]. For this purpose, we first establish a monotonicity result.

Lemma 8. *Suppose that s^1 and s^2 are two fluid solutions with $s^1(0) \geq s^2(0)$. Then $s^1(t) \geq s^2(t)$, for all $t \geq 0$.*

The proof of this Lemma consists of checking the drift terms of the fluid model. It is straightforward and is omitted. Now we are ready to prove the convergence result.

Proposition 9. *The equilibrium s^* of the fluid model is asymptotically stable for all initial conditions $s^0 \in \mathcal{S}^1$, i.e.,*

$$\lim_{t\to\infty} \left\|s(t) - s^*\right\|_w = 0.$$

PROOF. Fix some $s^0 \in \mathcal{S}^1$. We define initial conditions $s^u(0)$ and $s^l(0)$ by letting

$$s_i^u(0) = \max\{s_i(0), s_i^*\},$$
$$s_i^l(0) = \min\{s_i(0), s_i^*\}.$$

We then have $s^u(0) \geq s^0 \geq s^l(0)$, $s^u(0) \geq s^* \geq s^l(0)$, and $s^u(0), s^l(0) \in \mathcal{S}^1$. Due to Lemma 8 we obtain that $s^u(t) \geq s(t) \geq s^l(t)$ and $s^u(t) \geq s^* \geq s^l(t)$, for all $t \geq 0$. Thus it suffices to prove that $\left\|s^u(t) - s^*\right\|_w$ and $\left\|s^l(t) - s^*\right\|_w$ converge to 0 as $t \to \infty$.

At this point it is convenient work with the representation $v^u(t)$, $v^l(t)$, and v^*, where $v_i \triangleq \sum_{j=i}^{\infty} s_j$. Then, the dynamics of $v^u(t)$ are of the form

$$\begin{aligned}
\frac{dv_1^u(t)}{dt} &= \lambda - s_i^u(t) = s_1^* - s_i^u(t) \\
\frac{dv_i^u(t)}{dt} &= \lambda s_{i-1}^u(t) P_0^u(t) - s_i^u(t) \qquad \forall\, i \geq 2 \\
&= \lambda[s_{i-1}^u(t) P_0^u(t) - s_{i-1}^* P_0^*] - [s_i^u(t) - s_i^*],
\end{aligned}$$

where in the last step we subtracted the equilibrium condition $0 = \lambda s_{i-1}^* P_0^* - s_i^*$ from the right-hand side.

Now we will prove the coordinate-wise convergence by induction on i. Note that, from the definition of v_i, we have $v_1^u(t) \geq v_i^u(t)$. Furthermore, we have $s_1^u(t) \geq s_1^*$, so that $\frac{dv_1(t)}{dt} \leq 0$. It follows that $v_1^u(0) \geq v_i^u(t) - v_i^u(0) \geq -v_i^u(0)$ uniformly in t. Then, for the base case, we have

$$0 \leq \int_0^{\infty} \left(s_1^u(\tau) - s_1^*\right) d\tau \leq v_1^u(0) < \infty,$$

which, together with the Lipschitz-continuity of s_1, implies $(s_1^u(\tau) - s_1^*) \to 0$ as $\tau \to \infty$. Now assume that we have $\int_0^{\infty} (s_k^u(\tau) - s_k^*)\, d\tau < \infty$ for all non-negative integers $k \leq i-1$. Then,

$$-v_i^u(0) \leq \int_0^{t} \left(\lambda\left[s_{i-1}^u(\tau) P_0^u(\tau) - s_{i-1}^* P_0^*\right] - \left[s_i^u(\tau) - s_i^*\right]\right) d\tau.$$

Adding and subtracting $\lambda s_{i-1}^* P_0^u(\tau)$ inside the integral, we can check that the former is less than or equal to

$$\int_0^t \left([s_{i-1}^u(\tau) - s_{i-1}^*] + [P_0^u(\tau) - P_0^*] - [s_i^u(\tau) - s_i^*]\right) d\tau, \quad (6)$$

where the first term is uniformly upper-bounded in t by the inductive hypothesis, and it can be checked that the second one is also uniformly upper bounded for all variants using the base case. This completes the induction. It is easily checked that this coordinate-wise convergence implies convergence in $\|\cdot\|_w$, which concludes the proof. □

Note that we proved asymptotic stability only for initial conditions $s^0 \in \mathcal{S}^1 \subset \mathcal{S}$, which correspond to the initial conditions with finite expected queue lengths.

6. INTERCHANGE OF LIMITS

We will prove Theorem 4 in this section, which shows that the sequence of the marginals of the invariant distributions $\{\pi_s^N\}_{N=1}^{\infty}$ converges in distribution to a measure concentrated on the unique equilibrium (in $\mathcal{S}^1$) of the fluid model. This, together with Proposition 3, guarantees that the properties derived from the equilibrium of the fluid model s^*, specifically for the queueing delay, are an accurate approximation for the steady state of the stochastic system for N large enough. First, we will find a uniform upper bound for $\mathbb{E}_{\pi^N}\left[V_1^N\right]$ in the following lemma.

Lemma 10. *Let π^N be the unique invariant distribution of our process, and let $V_1^N = \frac{1}{N}\sum_{i=1}^N Q_i^N$. We then have the uniform upper bounds*

$$\pi^N\left(Q_1^N \geq k\right) \leq \left(\frac{1}{2-\lambda}\right)^{\frac{k}{2}}, \quad \forall N, \quad \forall k,$$

and

$$\mathbb{E}_{\pi^N}\left[V_1^N\right] \leq 1 + \frac{2}{1-\lambda}, \qquad \forall N.$$

PROOF. Consider the linear Lyapunov function

$$\Psi(Q,m) = Q_1.$$

The bounded upward jumps allows us to use Theorem 2.3 from [7] to obtain that $\mathbb{E}_{\pi^N}[Q_1] < \infty$. Thus, all conditions in Theorem 1 in [5] are satisfied, yielding the upper bounds

$$\pi^N\left(Q_1^N \geq 1+2m\right) \leq \left(\frac{1}{2-\lambda}\right)^{m+1},$$

and

$$\mathbb{E}_{\pi^N}\left[Q_1^N\right] \leq 1 + \frac{2}{1-\lambda}.$$

The first part of the result is obtained by letting $m = (k-1)/2$ if k is odd or $m = k/2 - 1$ if k is even. Finally, using the definition of V_1^N and then symmetry, we have

$$\mathbb{E}\left[V_1^N\right] = \frac{1}{N}\sum_{i=1}^N \mathbb{E}[Q_i] = \mathbb{E}[Q_1],$$

which concludes the proof. □

Now we prove the interchange of limits.

PROOF OF THEOREM 4. Consider the set $\mathbb{Z}_+ \cup \{\infty\}$ endowed with the topology of Alexandroff's compactification, which is known to be metrizable. Moreover, the topology defined by the norm $\|\cdot\|_w$ on $[0,1]^{\mathbb{Z}_+}$ is equivalent to the product topology, which makes it compact. Then, $\mathcal{S}$ (cf. Section 2 for its definition) is also compact because it is a closed subset of $[0,1]^{\mathbb{Z}_+}$. As a result, we have that the product $\mathcal{S} \times (\mathbb{Z}_+ \cup \{\infty\})$ is a compact Polish space under the product topology. Then, $\{\pi^N\}_{N=1}^{\infty}$ is trivially tight and by Prohorov's theorem [6], it is also relatively compact in the weak topology, and any sequence has a weakly convergent subsequence.

Given a weakly convergent subsequence $\{\pi^{N_k}\}_{k=1}^{\infty}$ and its limit π, we can use Skorokhod's representation theorem to construct a probability space $(\Omega_0, \mathcal{A}_0, \mathbb{P}_0)$ and a sequence of random variables $\left(S^{N_k}(0), M^{N_k}(0)\right)$ distributed according to π^{N_k}, such that

$$\lim_{k\to\infty}\left\|S^{N_k}(0) - s(0)\right\|_w = 0 \qquad \mathbb{P}_0 - a.s. \qquad (7)$$

for some random variable $s(0) \sim \pi_s$, where π_s is the marginal of π. Furthermore, we use $\left(S^{N_k}(0), M^{N_k}(0)\right)$ as the initial conditions for a sequence of processes $\left\{\left(S^{N_k}(t), M^{N_k}(t)\right)\right\}_{k=1}^{\infty}$, which makes these processes stationary. Note that the initial conditions, distributed as π^{N_k}, do not necessarily converge to a deterministic initial condition (this is actually part of what we are trying to prove), so we cannot use Theorem 2 directly to find the limit of the sequence of processes $\left\{S^{N_k}(t)\right\}_{k=1}^{\infty}$. However, given any $\omega \in \Omega_0$ outside a zero P_0-measure set, we can restrict this sequence of stochastic processes to the probability space $(\Omega_\omega, \mathcal{A}_\omega, \mathbb{P}_\omega) =$

$$(\Omega_D \times \Omega_S \times \{\omega\}, \mathcal{A}_D \times \mathcal{A}_S \times \{\emptyset, \{\omega\}\}, \mathbb{P}_D \times \mathbb{P}_S \times \delta_\omega)$$

and apply Theorem 2 to this new space, to obtain

$$\lim_{k\to\infty}\sup_{0\leq t\leq T}\left\|S^{N_k}(t,\omega) - s(t,\omega)\right\|_w = 0, \quad \mathbb{P}_\omega - a.s.,$$

where $s(t,\omega)$ is the fluid solution with initial condition $s(0,\omega)$. Since this is true for all $\omega \in \Omega_0$ except for a set of zero P_0-measure, it follows that

$$\lim_{k\to\infty}\sup_{0\leq t\leq T}\left\|S^{N_k}(t) - s(t)\right\|_w = 0, \qquad \mathbb{P} - a.s.,$$

where $\mathbb{P} = \mathbb{P}_D \times \mathbb{P}_S \times \mathbb{P}_0$ and where $s(t)$ is another stochastic process whose randomness is only in the initial condition (its trajectory is the deterministic fluid solution for that specific initial condition).

The uniform bound on $\mathbb{E}_{\pi^N}[V_1^N]$ (Lemma 10) and the convergence of π^N to π imply that $\mathbb{E}_\pi[v_1] \leq 1 + 2/(1-\lambda)$ and therefore $v_1 < \infty$ a.s., or equivalently, $\pi_s\left(\mathcal{S}^1\right) = 1$. This means that every possible initial condition is in $\mathcal{S}^1$, almost surely (and not in $\mathcal{S}\backslash\mathcal{S}^1$). Now suppose that $\left\{S^{N_k}(0)\right\}_{k=1}^{\infty}$ does not converge $\mathbb{P}_0$-a.s. to s^* (i.e., that $\pi_s \neq \delta_{s^*}$). Then, the set of processes with initial conditions in $\mathcal{S}^1\backslash\{s^*\}$ has probability $\pi_s\left(\mathcal{S}^1\backslash\{s^*\}\right) > 0$ and for every such process $s(t,\omega)$ with initial condition $s(0,\omega)$ we have

$$\|s(0,\omega) - s^*\|_w > \|s(t,\omega) - s^*\|_w$$

for t large enough (this is due to the fact that these sample paths converge asymptotically to s^*, by Theorem 1). As a result,

$$\mathbb{E}_{\pi_s}\left[\|s(0) - s^*\|_w\right] > \mathbb{E}_{\pi_s}\left[\|s(t) - s^*\|_w\right]$$

for t large enough, which is a contradiction, because S^{N_k} is stationary and thus s also has to be stationary. Then, the limit of every convergent subsequence of the marginals $\{\pi_s^N\}_{N=1}^{\infty}$ has to be δ_{s^*}. □

7. PROOF OF THE NEGATIVE RESULT

We now prove our negative result for resource constrained policies. The proof proceeds through a sequence of lemmas. Due to space constraints, we will only prove it for the case in which the distribution for the sampling of servers, $\nu^N(m)$, is independent of m. The general case can be proven with a similar line of reasoning.

We first show that for any fixed time t, we can have any given finite number of arrivals before the next message or departure, with probability bounded away from zero, uniformly for all N.

Lemma 11. *Let η^N be a memory-based dispatching policy with message rate of at most αN for some $\alpha > 0$. If T_t^N is the (random) time of the first departure or message from a server after some fixed time $t > 0$, then for every $k \in \mathbb{Z}_+$ we have that $\mathbb{P}\left(k \text{ arrivals in } \left(t, T_t^N\right)\right) \geq P(\alpha, \lambda, k) > 0$, where $P(\alpha, \lambda, k)$ is a constant independent from N.*

PROOF. Because of the upper bound for the message rate of any server (cf. part 1 of Definition 2), we have that $\mu^N\left(Q_n^N(t)\right) \leq \mu^N(0)$ for all $t \geq 0$. In any interval $[0, t]$ we must have at most as many departures as arrivals to the system. Therefore, the time-average number of departures per unit of time is at most λN and thus we will have at least $(1-\lambda)N$ idle servers on the average. As a result, $\mu^N(0)$ has to be uniformly upper bounded by $\frac{\alpha}{1-\lambda}$ in order to have at most αN messages per unit of time, in average.

Starting at any time $t > 0$, we have k arrivals after an Erlang(k,λN) time. Moreover, we will have a departure no sooner than after an exponential time of rate N (which corresponds to the worst case in which all servers are busy), and we will have a message no sooner than after an exponential time of rate $N\frac{\alpha}{1-\lambda}$ (which corresponds to the worst case in which all servers are idle). Then, we get the uniform bound

$$\begin{aligned}
&\mathbb{P}\left(k \text{ arrivals in } \left(t, T_t^N\right)\right) \\
&\quad \geq \mathbb{P}\left(Erl(k, N\lambda) < exp\left(\frac{N\alpha}{1-\lambda} + N\right)\right) \\
&\quad \geq \mathbb{P}\left(Erl(k, \lambda) < exp\left(\frac{\alpha}{1-\lambda} + 1\right)\right),
\end{aligned}$$

which is a positive number, independent of N. □

We now state a simple lemma regarding the number of probability distributions over $\mathcal{N}$. It implies that unless many servers have the same probability, a distribution will have many distinct permutations.

Lemma 12. *If $p \in \Pi_N$ has at most u servers with the same probability of being selected, then*

$$\#\{\sigma(p) : \sigma \in S_N\} \geq \max\left\{\binom{N}{u}, \lceil N/u \rceil!\right\}.$$

The proof consists of a simple counting argument and is thus omitted.

The next step is to characterize the probability distributions on the set of servers induced by the dispatching rule function f^N when we take C_N to be logarithmic in N.

Lemma 13. *Consider a symmetric dispatching policy, with $C_N = C\log_2(N)$, and dispatching rule function f^N, and let r be a positive integer. Then for every $m \in \mathcal{M}$, for every subset $\{n_1, \ldots, n_r\} \in \mathcal{P}(\mathcal{N})$, and for every $(q_{n_1}, \ldots, q_{n_r}) \in \mathcal{Q}^r$, there exist at least $N-C-r$ servers with the same probability of being selected under $f^N(m, \{(n_1, q_1), \ldots, (n_r, q_r)\})$.*

PROOF. Fix $(q_1, \ldots, q_r) \in \mathcal{Q}^r$. First, note that there are $\binom{N}{r}$ different subsets $\{n_1, \ldots, n_r\}$, and N^C different memory states m. Then, with $(q_1, \ldots, q_r) \in \mathcal{Q}^r$ fixed, the argument of f^N can only take $\binom{N}{r}N^C$ different values, that lead to at most $\binom{N}{r}N^C$ different distributions. Let $p \in \Pi_N$ be one of those distributions, i.e., $p = f^N(m, \{(n_1, q_1), \ldots, (n_r, q_r)\})$ for some $m \in \mathcal{M}$ and $\{n_1, \ldots, n_r\} \in \mathcal{P}(\mathcal{N})$. Then, $\sigma(p) = f^N(\sigma_M(m), \{(\sigma(n_1), q_1), \ldots, (\sigma(n_r), q_r)\})$ is also a possible distribution due to the symmetry hypothesis. As a result,

$$\#\{\sigma(p) : \sigma \in S_N\} \leq \binom{N}{r}N^C, \tag{8}$$

which is the upper bound for the total number of different distributions implied by the limited number of different arguments for f^N.

On the other hand, if p has at most u servers with the same probability of being selected, Lemma 12 provides the lower bound

$$\#\{\sigma(p) : \sigma \in S_N\} \geq \max\left\{\binom{N}{u}, \lceil N/u \rceil!\right\},$$

which combined with Equation (8) yields

$$\max\left\{\binom{N}{u}, \lceil N/u \rceil!\right\} \leq \binom{N}{r}N^C. \tag{9}$$

Now, if $C + r < u < N - C - r$, then $\binom{N}{u} > \binom{N}{C+r+1} > \binom{N}{r}N^C$ for N large enough, which contradicts Equation (9). If $u \leq C + r$, then $\lceil N/u \rceil! \geq \lceil N/(C+r) \rceil! > \binom{N}{r}N^C$ for N large enough, which also contradicts Equation (9). Thus $u \geq N - C - r$. □

We are now ready to prove our main result.

PROOF OF THEOREM 5. Consider the system in steady state, fix some time $T > 0$ and let $\mathcal{C}^N(T)$ be the event that there are at least $C+1$ arrivals before the next message or departure. This event has probability bounded away from zero due to Lemma 11, and it is an event that depends only on the Poisson processes of arrivals, departures, and messages. We will show that, for N large enough, a policy will send at least one of those $C+1$ jobs to a non empty queue, with probability bounded away from zero.

Without loss of generality, we may assume that the expected delay is finite. This implies that there is no accumulation of jobs in the system, and that the expected number of busy servers is λN (because our system is in steady state). Then, by the Markov inequality, we have that the probability of $Q^N(T)$ having at least $N(\lambda - \epsilon)$ busy servers is greater than $\epsilon/(1-\lambda+\epsilon)$, for all $\epsilon \in (0, \lambda)$. Furthermore, since the message rate is at most αN, and since the number of sampled queues is independent from the arrivals (only depends on ν^N), it follows that the expected number of queues sampled at the time of an arrival is less than or equal to α/λ. Therefore, using the Markov inequality once more, we get that the probability of sampling less than β servers is lower bounded by $1-\alpha/(\lambda\beta)$, which is positive for $\beta > \alpha/\lambda$. Then, by the independence of the sampling, the probability that the number of sampled servers for each of the first $C+1$ arrivals after time T are fewer than β, is lower bounded by $(1-\alpha/(\lambda\beta))^{C+1}$. Moreover, due to the symmetry hypothesis, the sampling distribution ν^N is uniform over all subsets of the same size. This implies that we have a further subset of sample paths $\mathcal{C}'(T) \subset \mathcal{C}(T)$, with probability bounded away from zero uniformly in N, such that for the first $C+1$ arrivals after time T, all sampled servers are busy. From now on, we will focus on those sample paths.

Recall that a policy defines a continuous time Markov process, $\left(Q^N(t), M^N(t)\right)$, over the state space $\mathcal{Q}^N \times \mathcal{M}$. The evolution of this process between time T and the time of the $(C+1)$-st arrival, for all sample paths in $\mathcal{C}'(T)$, can be described in terms of some basic random variables, as follows.

Let t_k be the time of the k-th arrival after time T, let $\{U(k)\}_{k=1}^{C+1}$ be a collection of independent random subsets distributed as ν^N (the sampled servers at the time of each arrival), let $\{V(k)\}_{k=1}^{C+1}$ be a collection of i.i.d. random variables, uniform in $[0,1]$ (the seeds for the randomized selection of the destinations), and let $\{W(k)\}_{k=1}^{C+1}$ be a collection of i.i.d. exponential random variables with parameter 1 (the workloads of each incoming job). All the randomness in our system is modeled by these random variables, and the process $\left(Q^N(t), M^N(t)\right)$ between times T and t_{C+1} will be a deterministic function of them.

To begin with, the remaining workload of the jobs that are being processed, decreases at a rate of one unit of work per unit of time. Moreover, for all sample paths in $\mathcal{C}'(T)$, the memory process $M^N(t)$ is only updated at the time of an arrival. Consider the mapping $F_{f^N} : [0,1] \times \mathcal{M} \times \mathcal{B} \to \mathcal{N}$, such that $F_{f^N}(V(k), m, \{(n_1, q_1), \dots, (n_r, q_r)\})$ is distributed according to $f^N(m, \{(n_1, q_1), \dots, (n_r, q_r)\})$, and such that

$$\sigma\left(F_{f^N}(V(k), m, \{(n_1, q_1), \dots, (n_r, q_r)\})\right) = F_{f^N}(V(k), \sigma_M(m), \{(\sigma(n_1), q_1), \dots, (\sigma(n_r), q_r)\}), \quad (10)$$

for all $\sigma \in S_N$. Then, let

$$X(k) = F_{f^N}\left(V(k), M^N\left(t_k^-\right), \left\{\left(U(k), Q^N\left(t_k^-\right)\right)\right\}\right) \quad (11)$$

be the random destination of the new job. At the time of the k-th arrival, the following steps occur sequentially but in zero time.

1. A random subset of servers is chosen ($U(k)$).

2. Based on $U(k)$ and the state of their queues, a destination for the new job is chosen ($X(k)$) using the seed $V(k)$.

3. The memory is updated according to

$$M^N(t_k) = g_d^N\left(M^N(t_k^-), \left\{\left(U(k), Q^N(t_k^-)\right)\right\}, X(k)\right), \quad (12)$$

and a new job with workload $W(k)$ is added to queue $X(k)$ in Q^N.

Recall that for all sample paths in $\mathcal{C}'(T)$, the memory process is constant between arrivals, and thus its evolution after time T is completely determined by the previous update equation, for which we have $M^N(t_1^-) = M^N(T)$ and $M^N(t_k^-) = M^N(t_{k-1})$ for all $k \geq 2$.

For every sample path ω, let $E_k(\omega)$ be a least cardinality set such that $f^N\left(M^N(t_{k-1}, \omega), \left\{\left(U(k,\omega), Q^N(t_k^-, \omega)\right)\right\}\right)$ is uniform (or zero) in $E_k(\omega)^c$, and let $E^N(C+1)(\omega)$ be the union of those $E_k(\omega)$ for all $1 \leq k \leq C+1$. The sets $E_k(\omega)$ will have cardinality of at most $C+\beta$ by Lemma 13, for all $\omega \in \mathcal{C}'(T)$.

Using the construction of $\left(Q^N(t), M^N(t)\right)$ described above, we can define a mapping G, that takes as arguments

- the initial condition $\left(M^N(T,\omega), Q^N(T,\omega)\right)$,
- the arrival times $\{t_k(\omega)\}_{k=1}^{C+1}$, and the corresponding workloads $\{W(k,\omega)\}_{k=1}^{C+1}$,
- the subsets of sampled servers $\{U(k,\omega)\}_{k=1}^{C+1}$ and seeds $\{V(k,\omega)\}_{k=1}^{C+1}$,

and yields the set $E^N(C+1)(\omega)$.

Using the symmetry hypothesis in Equations (11) and (12), the symmetry of the map F_{f^N} from Equation (10), and proceeding recursively, it can be checked that the previous mapping G is "symmetric". In particular, for every permutation $\sigma \in S_N$ such that $\sigma(U(k,\omega)) = U(k,\omega)$, if $1 \leq k \leq C+1$, we have that $\sigma\left(E^N(C+1)(\omega)\right)$ is obtained when the argument of G is

- the initial condition $\left(\sigma_M\left(M^N(T,\omega)\right), Q^N(T,\omega)\right)$,
- the arrival times $\{t_k(\omega)\}_{k=1}^{C+1}$, and the corresponding workloads $\{W(k,\omega)\}_{k=1}^{C+1}$,
- the subsets of sampled servers $\{U(k,\omega)\}_{k=1}^{C+1}$ and seeds $\{V(k,\omega)\}_{k=1}^{C+1}$.

We omit the details of this claim due to space constraints. Note that, in order to obtain $\sigma\left(E^N(C+1)\right)$, we only need to change the initial memory state to $\sigma_M\left(M^N(T)\right)$. Then, due to the fact that we have only N^C memory states, we can only obtain at most N^C different sets $\sigma(E^N(C+1))$ by varying σ among those that have $\sigma(U(k,\omega)) = U(k,\omega)$, if $1 \leq k \leq C+1$, i.e., we have that

$$\#\left\{\sigma\left(E^N(C+1)\right) : \sigma \in A\right\} \leq N^C, \quad (13)$$

where

$$A = \{\sigma \in S_N : \sigma(U(k)) = U(k), \text{ if } 1 \leq k \leq C+1\}. \quad (14)$$

Recall that for all $\omega \in \mathcal{C}'(T)$, the number of sampled servers ($\#U(k,\omega)$) is at most β, so these permutations leave at most β servers fixed for each one of the $C+1$ arrivals, which translates into at most $(C+1)\beta$ servers fixed in total.

Now consider the collection of sample paths $\mathcal{C}_1'(T) \subset \mathcal{C}'(T)$ where at least one of the sets $E_k(\omega)$ is empty. For those sample paths, at least one of the jobs is dispatched according to a uniform distribution, and because we had at least $N(\lambda-\epsilon)$ non empty queues with probability bounded away from zero, at least one job is sent to a non empty queue with probability bounded away from zero (this last probability is conditioned on $\mathcal{C}_1'(T)$). If this event has overall probability bounded away from zero (without conditioning on $\mathcal{C}_1'(T)$), we are done. On the other hand, for all the sample paths in $\mathcal{C}'(T)\backslash\mathcal{C}_1'(T)$, none of the $E_k(\omega)$ are empty. In order to derive a contradiction, assume that the first $C+1$ jobs are sent to an empty queue for a collection of sample paths with "high probability" (in this context, "high probability" refers to probabilities converging to 1 as $N \to \infty$). This implies that the jobs are sent to servers in $E^N(C+1)$ with high probability. Otherwise, their destination would be distributed uniformly over E_k^c (which has cardinality of at least $N-\beta-C$ by Lemma 13), and they would go to a non empty queue with probability bounded way from zero, for the same reason as before. Then, each E_k must contain at least 1 idle server with high probability (and at most $C+\beta$ by Lemma 13), and thus $E^N(C+1)$ must contain between $C+1$ and $(C+\beta)(C+1)$ idle servers. This means that, if $a = \#E^N(C+1)$, then

$$\#\left\{\sigma\left(E^N(C+1)\right) : \sigma \in S_N\right\} = \binom{N}{a} \geq \binom{N}{C+1}.$$

If instead of using all permutations $\sigma \in S_N$, we take the subset A defined in Equation (14), then, if $b = \#\bigcup_{k=1}^{C+1} U(k)$ and $a' = \#\left(E^N(C+1)\backslash \bigcup_{k=1}^{C+1} U(k)\right)$, we have that

$$\#\{\sigma(E^N(C+1)) : \sigma \in A\} = \binom{N-b}{a'} \geq \binom{N-(C+1)\beta}{C+1},$$

because all sampled servers $U(k)$ (which are at most $(C+1)\beta$) are busy, and thus disjoint with the idle servers in $E^N(C+1)$ (which are at least $C+1$). However, we also had an upper bound for this quantity in Equation (13), which leads to a contradiction because $N^C < \binom{N-(C+1)\beta}{C+1}$ for N large enough. This concludes the proof. □

8. CONCLUSIONS AND FUTURE WORK

The main objective of this paper is to find necessary and sufficient conditions on the amount of resources (messages and memory) available to a central dispatcher, in order to achieve a vanishing queueing delay as the system size increases. This is done by defining a unified framework for a broad class of dispatching policies and by proving two separate results: First, we show that when we have a limited amount of memory and a modest budget of messages per unit of time, all dispatching policies result in queueing delay uniformly bounded away from zero. Second, we present two variants of a simple symmetric pull-based dispatching policy for which it is sufficient to have a little more memory or messages in order to have vanishing queueing delay. As an added bonus, we analyze a third variant of the same dispatching policy with positive queueing delay. We show that by wisely exploiting an arbitrarily small message rate (but still proportional to the arrival rate) we obtain a queueing delay which is finite and uniformly upper bounded even in heavy traffic, a significant qualitative improvement over the M/M/1 queueing delay obtained in the absence of messages.

There are several interesting directions for future research. In light of the symmetry assumption in Theorem 5, an immediate open question is whether the result still holds without this assumption. Our proof heavily relies on the symmetry assumption and is difficult to generalize. Second, we could relax the assumption of homogeneous servers, consider pools of servers with different service rates, and study the tradeoffs between resources and the stability region of a policy. In this setting we expect a result similar to our lower bound for queueing delay, stating that a symmetric resource constrained policy cannot be stable for every stabilizable system. Last but not least, it would be interesting to extend some or all of these results to the case of general job size distributions (e.g., heavy tailed) and/or different service disciplines such as processor sharing or LIFO, as these are prevalent in many applications.

9. REFERENCES

[1] N. Alon, E. Lubetzky, and O. Gurel-Gurevich. Choice-memory tradeoff in allocations. In *Proceedings of FOCS*, 2009.

[2] Y. Azar, A. Broder, A. Karlin, and E. Upfal. Balanced allocations. *SIAM Journal on Computing*, 29(1):180–200, 1999.

[3] R. Badonnel and M. Burgess. Dynamic pull-based load balancing for autonomic servers. In *Network Operations and Management Symposium*, 2008.

[4] I. Benjamini and Y. Makarychev. Balanced allocations: memory performance tradeoffs. *The Annals of Applied Probability*, 22(4):1642–1649, 2012.

[5] D. Bertsimas, D. Gamarnik, and J. Tsitsiklis. Performance of multiclass markovian queueing networks via piecewise linear lyapunov functions. *The Annals of Applied Probability*, 11(4):1384–1428, 2002.

[6] P. Billingsley. *Convergence of Probability Measures.* Wiley, second edition, 1999.

[7] B. Hajek. Hitting-time and occupation-time bounds implied by drift analysis with applications. *Advances in Applied Probability*, 14(3):502–525, 1982.

[8] C. Lenzen and R. Wattenhofer. Tight bounds for parallel randomized load balalcing. *Distributed Computing*, pages 1–16, 2014.

[9] S. Lobanov and O. Smolyanov. Ordinary differential equations in locally convex spaces. *Uspekhi Mat. Nauk*, 49:93–168, 1994.

[10] Y. Lu, Q. Xie, G. Kliot, A. Geller, J. Larus, and A. Greenberg. Join-Idle-Queue: A novel load balancing algorithm for dynamically scalable web services. *Performance Evaluation*, 68(11):1056–1071, Nov. 2011.

[11] M. Mitzenmacher. *The power of two choices in randomized load balancing.* PhD thesis, U.C. Berkeley, 1996.

[12] M. Mitzenmacher., B. Prabhakar., and D. Shah. Load balancing with memory. In *Proceedings of FOCS*, 2002.

[13] G. Stamoulis and J. Tsitsiklis. Optimal distributed policies for choosing among multiple servers. In *Proceedings of the CDC*, pages 815–820, 1991.

[14] A. Stolyar. Pull-based load distribution in large-scale heterogeneous service systems. *Queueing Systems*, 80(4):341–361, 2015.

[15] N. Vvedenskaya, R. Dobrushin, and F. Karpelevich. Queueing system with selection of the shortest of two queues: an asymptotic approach. *Problems of Information Transmission*, 32(1):15–27, 1996.

[16] L. Ying, R. Srikant, and X. Kang. The power of slightly more than one sample in randomized load balancing. In *Proceedings of INFOCOM*, 2015.

Optimal Heavy-Traffic Queue Length Scaling in an Incompletely Saturated Switch

Siva Theja Maguluri
Mathematical Sciences
IBM T. J. Watson Research Center
siva.theja@us.ibm.com

Sai Kiran Burle
Department of ECE and CSL
University of Illinois at Urbana-Champaign
burle2@illinois.edu

R. Srikant
Department of ECE and CSL
University of Illinois at Urbana-Champaign
rsrikant@illinois.edu

ABSTRACT

We consider an input queued switch operating under the MaxWeight scheduling algorithm. This system is interesting to study because it is a model for Internet routers and data center networks. Recently, it was shown that the MaxWeight algorithm has optimal heavy-traffic queue length scaling when all ports are uniformly saturated. Here we consider the case where a fraction of the ports are saturated and others are not (which we call the incompletely saturated case), and also the case where the rates at which the ports are saturated can be different. We use a recently developed drift technique to show that the heavy-traffic queue length under the MaxWeight scheduling algorithm has optimal scaling with respect to the switch size even in these cases.

Keywords

$n \times n$ Switch; Heavy Traffic Optimality; Drift Method; Performance Analysis

1. INTRODUCTION

The $n \times n$ switch is a model that has been widely used and studied to understand the behavior of Internet routers and data center switches. The importance of this model in the design of Internet routers is well known. In the mid to late 1990s when the Internet was exploding, it served as an important model to study and design scheduling algorithms for the switch fabric of Internet routers. The model is now used to understand the design of data centers used for cloud-computing services. Today's data centers consist of a massive number of servers organized in racks, which are interconnected through a data center network. An ideal data center network is a huge input queued switch with one port for each server. However, real switches are much smaller and they have to be interconnected appropriately, and routing and scheduling algorithms have to be designed, so that the overall network emulates an $n \times n$ switch. Designing such a network is a challenging and active area of research; see [1, 11] for example. Here, we do not explicitly consider a data center network, but only consider the $n \times n$ switch which is the underlying model (see [11] which argues why the model is appropriate even for a data center network) and study the behavior of the well-known MaxWeight algorithm [19] for this model.

As mentioned in [12], the $n \times n$ switch model also serves as a canonical theoretical example of a problem which exhibits the so-called multi-dimensional state-space collapse, which makes it difficult to study using traditional heavy-traffic theory. Recently, it has been shown in [8] that the heavy-traffic behavior of the mean queue length in an $n \times n$ switch operating under the MaxWeight scheduling algorithm can be precisely characterized using a non-trivial extension of a drift technique introduced in [5]. In particular, one of the key contributions of [8] is to extend the drift technique to cover the case of multi-dimensional state-space collapse. The result in [8] also resolved an open question on the scaling behavior of the heavy-traffic queue length in a switch operating under the MaxWeight algorithm. In particular, it showed that the total heavy-traffic-scaled queue length is $O(n)$ or the mean heavy-traffic-scaled delay experienced by a packet is $O(1)$. While there have been other results establishing $O(1)$ delay scaling, the significance of the result in [8] is that the result holds for the original MaxWeight algorithm introduced in [19], with no additional scheduling operations required.

The results in [8] were obtained under the assumption that every input and output port of the switch is saturated (i.e., close to capacity), and the arrival rates to each input port and each output port are close to capacity by the same amount. For the purposes of this paper, we call a switch where only some of ports are saturated an "incompletely saturated switch." The main purpose of this paper is to show that the MaxWeight algorithm has order-optimal scaling (in the number of ports of the switch) for the case of an incompletely saturated switch and for the case where each port has a different rate of saturation. The case of the incompletely saturated switch, in particular, is especially difficult and requires the use of a new test function whose drift is set to equal to zero in steady-state. The main reason for the difficulty here is that the geometry of the state-space collapse is different here than in the all-ports saturated case considered in [8]. The analysis in the case where each port has a different rate of saturation is similar to that of [8]; however, this is a theoretically important case since it corresponds to the situation where the drift vector is not the identity matrix in the diffusion limit [7]. In fact, the diffusion limit is no

SIGMETRICS '16, June 14 - 18, 2016, Antibes Juan-Les-Pins, France

ISBN 978-1-4503-4266-7/16/06...$15.00

DOI: http://dx.doi.org/10.1145/2896377.2901466

longer symmetric in the components of the limiting stochastic process (i.e., the diffusion limit is not symmetric across the ports), but here we show that the technique in [8] works even in this asymmetric situation to produce an exact formula for a certain linear combination of the queue lengths. This result can be further used to show optimal queue length scaling under some conditions on the saturation rates.

The rest of the paper is organized as follows. The model of an $n \times n$ switch and the MaxWeight algorithm are presented in Section 2. The case of an incompletely saturated switch is considered in Section 3. The case where different ports are saturated at different ports is presented in Section 4. For ease of exposition, here we assume that all ports are saturated since the proofs in the incompletely saturated case along with different rates of saturation at each port is cumbersome notationally. However, the reader should be able to see that the results carry over for this case as well. Concluding remarks are provided in the last section.

1.1 Related Work

The MaxWeight algorithm for general stochastic networks, of which the $n \times n$ switch is a special case, was presented in [19], where it was shown that the algorithm is throughput-optimal. The special case of the switch was considered in [9], where it was shown that the simpler algorithms such as MaxSize and Maximal matchings are not throughput-optimal. The case of non-stochastic arrivals was considered in [20], where in addition to the throughput-optimality of MaxWeight-type algorithms, a lower bound on the throughput loss of simpler algorithms such as Maximal matching was established.

Here we are interested in performance metrics beyond throughput optimality. In particular, we are interested in understanding whether the MaxWeight matching algorithm for switches achieves small queue lengths, at least under a heavy-traffic scaling regime. Using diffusion limits, the heavy-traffic optimality of the MaxWeight algorithm in a switch where only one port is saturated was established in [18], although the final step of interchanging the order of the heavy traffic scaling limit and letting time go to infinity was not undertaken there. Motivated by this result, [5] studied the switch directly in steady-state, established heavy-traffic optimality, and introduced a new drift method of studying stochastic networks in heavy-traffic. However, it should be emphasized that the results in [18, 5] apply only to the case of a single saturated port since they both rely on state of the system collapsing to a single dimension in the heavy-traffic limit. In a recent development, the case where all ports are uniformly saturated (thus, leading to the more difficult case of multi-dimensional state-space collapse) was studied in [8], where an exact expression for the heavy-traffic scaled queue length under the MaxWeight algorithm is derived. Additionally, this expression shows that the algorithm has heavy-traffic optimal scaling in the size of the switch, resolving an open conjecture stated in [12]. The results in [8] use and significantly extend the drift technique presented in [5].

State collapse in the case where multiple ports are saturated has been established in [2, 15, 16] and using the state-space collapse result in [15], a diffusion limit was established in [7]. However, properties of the diffusion limit (such as its steady-state distribution or mean queue lengths) were difficult to establish. The result in [8] can thus be interpreted as a derivation of the sum of the first moments of the limiting vector stochastic process, but obtained without going through the usual fluid/diffusion limit scaling arguments. An entirely different technique to study heavy-traffic optimality was presented in [14] where the authors approximate the scheduling decisions made by a switch which can change its schedule infinitely often to simulate a queueing network with product-form steady-state distribution as in [4]. The resulting algorithm is heavy-traffic optimal, but has a very high computational complexity. The optimal scaling of the queue length as a function of the switch size in the non-heavy-traffic limit appears to be still open. Alternatively, one can consider asymptotic regimes other than the heavy-traffic limit. The best known results in this regard are the ones in [10, 13], but these require algorithms that are more involved than the original MaxWeight algorithm.

2. SYSTEM MODEL AND BACKGROUND

In this section, we present the model of an input queued switch, the MaxWeight scheduling algorithm, and some lemmas that will later play a key role in the results.

Note on Notation: For ease of understanding, and to allow the reader to compare and contrast with the results in [8], here we use definitions and notation consistent with [8]. Since an $n \times n$ switch has n^2-dimensional queues, we often deal with the Euclidean space $\mathbb{R}^{n^2}$. However, we represent vectors in $\mathbb{R}^{n^2}$ as $n \times n$ matrices for convenience. Thus, $\mathbf{x}$ is a matrix with the $(i,j)^{\text{th}}$ component denoted by x_{ij}. Thus, for two vectors $\mathbf{x}$ and $\mathbf{y}$ in $\mathbb{R}^{n^2}$, their inner product $\langle \mathbf{x}, \mathbf{y} \rangle$ and Euclidean norm $\|\mathbf{x}\|$ are defined by

$$\langle \mathbf{x}, \mathbf{y} \rangle \triangleq \sum_{i=1}^{n}\sum_{j=1}^{n} x_{ij}y_{ij}, \quad \|\mathbf{x}\| \triangleq \sqrt{\langle \mathbf{x}, \mathbf{x} \rangle} = \sqrt{\sum_{i=1}^{n}\sum_{j=1}^{n} x_{ij}^2}.$$

For two vectors $\mathbf{x}$ and $\mathbf{y}$ in $\mathbb{R}^{n^2}$, $\mathbf{x} \leq \mathbf{y}$ means $x_{ij} \leq y_{ij}$ for every (i,j). We use $\mathbf{1}$ to denote the all ones vector. Let $\mathbf{e}^{(i)}$ denote the vector defined by $e_{ij}^{(i)} = 1$ for all j and $e_{i',j}^{(i)} = 0$ for all $i' \neq i$ and for all j. Thus, $\mathbf{e}^{(i)}$ is a matrix with i^{th} row being all ones and zeros every where else. Similarly, let $\widetilde{\mathbf{e}}^{(j)}$ denote the vector defined by $\widetilde{e}_{ij}^{(j)} = 1$ for all i and $\widetilde{e}_{i,j'}^{(j)} = 0$ for all $j' \neq j$ and for all i, i.e., it is a matrix with j^{th} column being all ones and zeros every where else. For a random process $\mathbf{q}(t)$ and a function $V(.)$, we will sometimes use $V(t)$ to denote $V(\mathbf{q}(t))$. We use $\text{Var}(.)$ to denote variance of a random variable.

2.1 The Switch Model and the MaxWeight Algorithm

For the purposes of queueing-theoretic analysis, an $n \times n$ switch can be treated as an $n \times n$ matrix of queues operating in a time-slotted discrete-time fashion. Let $a_{ij}(t)$ denote the number of packet arrivals to Queue (i,j), and we let $\mathbf{a} \in \mathbb{R}^{n^2}$ denote the vector $(a_{ij})_{ij}$. For every Queue (i,j), the arrival process $a_{ij}(t)$ is a stochastic process that is i.i.d. across time, with mean $\mathbb{E}[a_{ij}(t)] = \lambda_{ij}$ and variance $\text{Var}(a_{ij}(t)) = \sigma_{ij}^2$ for any time t. We assume that the arrival processes are independent across queues (the processes $a_{ij}(t)$ and $a_{i'j'}(t)$ are independent) and are also independent of the queue lengths or schedules chosen in the switch. We further assume that for all i,j,t, $a_{ij}(t) \leq a_{\max}$ for some $a_{\max} \geq 1$.The arrival rate vector is denoted by $\boldsymbol{\lambda} = (\lambda_{ij})_{ij}$ and the variance vector $(\sigma_{ij}^2)_{ij}$ is denoted by $(\boldsymbol{\sigma})^2$ or $\boldsymbol{\sigma}^2$. We will use $\boldsymbol{\sigma}$ to denote $(\sigma_{ij})_{ij}$. We denote the queue length of packets at input port i to be delivered at output port j at time t by $q_{ij}(t)$. Let $\mathbf{q} \in \mathbb{R}^{n^2}$ denote the vector of all queue lengths.

The key scheduling constraints are that (i) at most one packet can be removed from each queue in each time slot and (ii) at most one queue can be served in each row and each column in each time slot. These constraints arise from technological constrains in a real switch, where each row represents an input port and each column represents an output port; see [17] for example. The scheduling constraints can be captured in graph-theoretic language as follows. Let G denote a complete $n \times n$ bipartite graph with n^2 edges. Each node on the left side of the bipartite graph can be thought of as representing a row in the matrix of switches and each node on the right side represents a column. The schedule in each time slot is a matching on this graph G. Let s_{ij} be the amount of service provided to Queue (i, j) in a given time slot. Thus, $s_{ij} = 1$ if the link between input port i and output port j is matched or scheduled and $s_{ij} = 0$ otherwise and we denote $\mathbf{s} = (s_{ij})_{ij}$. Then, the set of feasible schedules, $\mathcal{S} \subset \mathbb{R}^{n^2}$ is the set of all vectors $\mathbf{s}$ which satisfy

$$\sum_{i=1}^{n} s_{ij} \leq 1, \sum_{j=1}^{n} s_{ij} \leq 1 \, \forall \, i, j \in \{1, 2, \ldots, n\}.$$

Let $\mathcal{S}^*$ denote the set of maximal feasible schedules. Then, it is easy to see that $\mathcal{S}^*$ is the set of all vectors $\mathbf{s}$ which satisfy

$$\sum_{i=1}^{n} s_{ij} = 1, \sum_{j=1}^{n} s_{ij} = 1 \, \forall \, i, j \in \{1, 2, \ldots, n\}.$$

A scheduling policy or algorithm picks a schedule $\mathbf{s}(t)$ in every time slot based on the current queue length vector, $\mathbf{q}(t)$. In each time slot, the order of events is as follows. Queue lengths at the beginning of time slot t are $\mathbf{q}(t)$. A schedule $\mathbf{s}(t)$ is then picked for that time slot based on the queue lengths. Then, arrivals for that time $\mathbf{a}(t)$ happen. Finally the packets are served and there is unused service if there are no packets in a scheduled queue. The queue lengths are then updated to give the queue lengths for the next time slot. The queue lengths therefore evolve as follows.

$$\begin{aligned} q_{ij}(t+1) &= [q_{ij}(t) + a_{ij}(t) - s_{ij}(t)]^+ \\ &= q_{ij}(t) + a_{ij}(t) - s_{ij}(t) + u_{ij}(t) \\ \mathbf{q}(t+1) &= \mathbf{q}(t) + \mathbf{a}(t) - \mathbf{s}(t) + \mathbf{u}(t), \end{aligned} \tag{1}$$

where $[x]^+ = \max(0, x)$ is the projection onto positive real axis, $u_{ij}(t)$ is the unused service on link (i, j). Unused service is 1 only when link (i, j) is scheduled, but has zero queue length; and it is 0 in all other cases. Thus, we have that when $u_{ij}(t) = 1$, we have $q_{ij}(t) = 0$, $a_{ij}(t) = 0$, $s_{ij}(t) = 1$ and $q_{ij}(t + 1) = 0$. Therefore, we have $u_{ij}(t)q_{ij}(t) = 0$, $u_{ij}(t)a_{ij}(t) = 0$ and $u_{ij}(t)q_{ij}(t + 1) = 0$. Also note that since $u_{ij}(t) \leq s_{ij}(t)$, we have that $\sum_{i=1}^{n} u_{ij} \in \{0, 1\}$ and $\sum_{j=1}^{n} u_{ij} \in \{0, 1\}$ for all i, j.

The MaxWeight Algorithm is a popular scheduling algorithm for switches. In every time slot t, each link (i, j) is given a weight equal to its queue length $q_{ij}(t)$ and the schedule with the maximum weight among the feasible schedules $\mathcal{S}$ is chosen at that time slot. In other words, using queue lengths as the weights, the permutation matrix with the maximum weight is picked in every time slot. This algorithm is presented in Algorithm 1.

Algorithm 1 MaxWeight Scheduling Algorithm for an input-queued switch

Consider the complete bipartite graph described earlier. Let the queue length $q_{ij}(t)$ be the weight of the edge between input port i and output port j. A maximum weight matching in this graph is chosen as the schedule in every time slot, i.e.,

$$\mathbf{s}(t) = \arg\max_{\mathbf{s} \in \mathcal{S}} \sum_{ij} q_{ij}(t) s_{ij} = \arg\max_{\mathbf{s} \in \mathcal{S}} \langle \mathbf{q}(t), \mathbf{s} \rangle \tag{2}$$

Ties are broken uniformly at random.

Note that there is always a maximum weight schedule that is maximal. If the MaxWeight schedule chosen at time t, $\mathbf{s}$ is not maximal, there exists a maximal schedule $\mathbf{s}^* \in \mathcal{S}^*$ such that $\mathbf{s} \leq \mathbf{s}^*$. For any link (i, j) such that $s_{ij} = 0$ and $s^*_{ij} = 1$, $q_{ij}(t) = 0$. If not, $\mathbf{s}$ would not have been a maximum weight schedule. Therefore, we can pretend that the actual schedule chosen is $\mathbf{s}^*$ and the links (i, j) that are in $\mathbf{s}^*$ but not in $\mathbf{s}$ have an unused service of 1. Note that this does not change the scheduling algorithm, but it is just a notational convenience. Therefore, without loss of generality, we assume that the schedule chosen in each time slot is a maximal schedule, i.e.,

$$\mathbf{s}(t) \in \mathcal{S}^* \text{ for all time } t. \tag{3}$$

Hence the MaxWeight schedule picks one of the $n!$ possible permutations from the set $\mathcal{S}^*$ in each time slot.

Under i.i.d. arrivals, the queue lengths process $\mathbf{q}(t)$ is a Markov chain. The switch is said to be stable under a scheduling policy if the sum of all the queue lengths is finite in an appropriate stochastic sense (see [17] for example). The capacity region of the switch is the set of arrival rates $\boldsymbol{\lambda}$ for which the switch is stable under some scheduling policy. A policy that stabilizes the switch under any arrival rate in the capacity region is said to be throughput optimal. It is well known [19, 9] that the capacity region $\mathcal{C}$ of the switch is convex hull of all feasible schedules,

$$\begin{aligned} \mathcal{C} =& \mathrm{Conv}(\mathcal{S}) \\ =& \left\{ \boldsymbol{\lambda} \in \mathbb{R}_+^{n^2} : \sum_{i=1}^{n} \lambda_{ij} \leq 1, \sum_{j=1}^{n} \lambda_{ij} \leq 1 \, \forall \, i, j \in \{1, \ldots, n\} \right\} \\ =& \left\{ \boldsymbol{\lambda} \in \mathbb{R}_+^{n^2} : \left\langle \boldsymbol{\lambda}, \mathbf{e}^{(i)} \right\rangle \leq 1, \left\langle \boldsymbol{\lambda}, \tilde{\mathbf{e}}^{(j)} \right\rangle \leq 1 \, \forall \, i, j \in \{1, \ldots, n\} \right\}. \end{aligned} \tag{4}$$

For any arrival rate vector $\boldsymbol{\lambda}$, $\rho \triangleq \max_{ij} \{ \sum_i \lambda_{ij}, \sum_j \lambda_{ij} \}$ is called the load. It is also known that the queue lengths process is positive recurrent under the MaxWeight algorithm whenever the arrival rate is in the capacity region $\mathcal{C}$ (equivalently, load $\rho < 1$) and therefore is throughput optimal.

For any arrival rate in the capacity region $\mathcal{C}$, due to positive recurrence of $\mathbf{q}(t)$, we have that a steady state distribution exists under MaxWeight policy. Let $\overline{\mathbf{q}}$ denote the steady state random vector. In this paper, we focus on the average queue length under the steady state distribution, i.e., $\mathbb{E}[\sum_{i,j} \overline{q}_{ij}]$, which can be shown to exist as in [8]. We consider a set of switch systems indexed by a parameter ϵ, with arrival rate $\boldsymbol{\lambda}^{\epsilon}$ so that the arrival rate approaches the vector $\boldsymbol{\nu}$ on the boundary of the capacity region $\mathcal{C}$ in the limit as $\epsilon \to 0$. This is called the heavy traffic limit. We are interested in the average queue length in heavy traffic limit, i.e., on $\lim_{\epsilon\to 0} \mathbb{E}[\sum_{i,j} \overline{q}_{ij}]$. In particular, in this paper, we will consider cases where the sum of the arrival rates at some rows and some columns approach 1, and they may approach 1 at different rates at each column and row.

2.2 Kingman bound for a discrete-time queue

To establish our results, we later show that the total queue length along each row and each column is lower bounded. For this purpose, we use a bound on the steady-state queue length in a simple discrete-time queue [5]. While the well-known Kingman bound is for continuous-time G/G/1 queues, due to the similarity in establishing the result, the bound for the discrete-time case is also called the Kingman bound in [5] and we use the same terminology here. We state the version of the result for the special case where a queue can serve only one packet per slot here since this is what is used in this paper. In this special case, instead of a bound, one has an exact expression for the mean queue length which we present below.

LEMMA 1. *Consider a single server operating in discrete time. In each time slot, packets arrive according to an i.i.d arrival process $\alpha(t)$ with mean λ and variance σ^2. Let q denote the queue length. Each packet needs exactly one time slot of service. The server operates according to any non-idling policy,* serving one packet in every time slot *whenever the queue is nonempty. Then, the queue is positive recurrent as long as $\lambda < 1$, and the steady state mean queue length is given by*

$$\mathbb{E}[q] = \frac{\sigma^2}{2(1-\lambda)} - \frac{\lambda}{2}.$$

We note that the first term on the right-hand side of the above equation is what is referred to as the Kingman bound in [5].

2.3 Moment bounds from Lyapunov drift conditions

In later sections in the paper, we establish state space collapse results by obtaining moment bounds on certain quantities related to the queue length vector based on drift of a Lyapunov function. A key ingredient in this approach is to obtain moment bounds from drift conditions. A lemma from [6] was used in [5] to obtain these bounds and a different result from [3] was used in [8] to obtain tighter bounds. Here we state [3, Theorem 1] in the form it was stated in [8].

LEMMA 2. *For an irreducible and aperiodic Markov chain $\{X(t)\}_{t\geq 0}$ over a countable state space $\mathcal{X}$, suppose $Z : \mathcal{X} \to \mathbb{R}_+$ is a nonnegative-valued Lyapunov function. We define the drift of Z at X as*

$$\Delta Z(X) \triangleq [Z(X(t+1)) - Z(X(t))]\, \mathcal{I}(X(t) = X),$$

where $\mathcal{I}(.)$ is the indicator function. Thus, $\Delta Z(X)$ is a random variable that measures the amount of change in the value of Z in one step, starting from state X. This drift is assumed to satisfy the following conditions:

C1 *There exists an $\eta > 0$, and a $\zeta < \infty$ such that for any $t = 1, 2, \ldots$ and for all $X \in \mathcal{X}$ with $Z(X) \geq \zeta$,*

$$\mathbb{E}[\Delta Z(X) | X(t) = X] \leq -\eta.$$

C2 *There exists a $D < \infty$ such that for all $X \in \mathcal{X}$,*

$$\mathbb{P}(|\Delta Z(X)| \leq D) = 1.$$

Further assume that the Markov chain $\{X(t)\}_t$ converges in distribution to a random variable $\overline{X}$. Then, for any $r = 1, 2, \ldots$,

$$\mathbb{E}[Z(\overline{X})^r] \leq (2\zeta)^r + (4D)^r \left(\frac{D+\eta}{\eta}\right)^r r!.$$

3. INCOMPLETELY SATURATED SWITCH

In this section, we consider the switch system when $n_1 \leq n$ input ports (rows) and $n_2 \leq n$ output ports (columns) are saturated. Without loss of generality, we assume that input ports (rows) $1, 2, ..., n_1$ and output ports (columns) $1, 2, ..., n_2$ are saturated. Thus, we consider a point $\boldsymbol{\nu}$ on the boundary of the capacity region that lies in Relint$(\mathcal{F}_{n_1 n_2})$, the relative interior of the face $\mathcal{F}_{n_1 n_2}$ defined by

$$\begin{aligned}
\mathcal{F}_{n_1 n_2} &= \Bigg\{ \boldsymbol{\lambda} \in \mathbb{R}_+^{n^2} : \sum_{j=1}^{n} \lambda_{ij} = 1 \,\forall\, i \in \{1, \ldots, n_1\}, \\
&\qquad \sum_{i=1}^{n} \lambda_{ij} = 1 \,\forall\, j \in \{1, \ldots, n_2\} \Bigg\} \\
&= \Big\{ \boldsymbol{\lambda} \in \mathbb{R}_+^{n^2} : \left\langle \boldsymbol{\lambda}, \mathbf{e}^{(i)} \right\rangle = 1 \,\forall\, i \in \{1, \ldots, n_1\}, \\
&\qquad \left\langle \boldsymbol{\lambda}, \widetilde{\mathbf{e}}^{(j)} \right\rangle = 1 \,\forall\, j \in \{1, \ldots, n_2\} \Big\}.
\end{aligned}$$

In other words, if we let $\delta_i = 1 - \sum_j \nu_{ij} = 1 - \left\langle \boldsymbol{\nu}, \mathbf{e}^{(i)} \right\rangle$ and $\widetilde{\delta}_j = 1 - \sum_i \nu_{ij} = \left\langle \boldsymbol{\nu}, \widetilde{\mathbf{e}}^{(j)} \right\rangle$, we have that $\delta_i = 0$ for $i = 1, ...n_1$, $\widetilde{\delta}_j = 0$ for $j = 1, ...n_2$ and $\delta_i > 0$ for $i > n_1$, $\widetilde{\delta}_j > 0$ for $j > n_2$.

We consider a sequence of systems indexed by ϵ. In this section, we consider an i.i.d arrival process $\mathbf{a}^{(\epsilon)}(t)$ with mean and variance given by

$$\begin{aligned}
\mathbb{E}[\mathbf{a}^{(\epsilon)}(t)] &= \boldsymbol{\lambda}^{(\epsilon)} = \boldsymbol{\nu}(1-\epsilon) \\
Var[\mathbf{a}^{(\epsilon)}(t)] &= \left(\boldsymbol{\sigma}^{(\epsilon)}\right)^2
\end{aligned}$$

such that as $\epsilon \to 0$, $\left(\boldsymbol{\sigma}^{(\epsilon)}\right)^2 \to \boldsymbol{\sigma}^2$. Define

$$\begin{aligned}
\gamma_i^{(\epsilon)} &\triangleq 1 - \sum_j \lambda_{ij}^{(\epsilon)} = 1 - (1-\delta_i)(1-\epsilon) \\
\widetilde{\gamma}_j^{(\epsilon)} &\triangleq 1 - \sum_i \lambda_{ij}^{(\epsilon)} = 1 - (1-\widetilde{\delta}_j)(1-\epsilon).
\end{aligned}$$

Note that $\gamma_i^{(\epsilon)} = \epsilon$ for $i \leq n_1$, and $\widetilde{\gamma}_j^{(\epsilon)} = \epsilon$ for $j \leq n_2$. For the unsaturated ports, $\lim_{\epsilon\downarrow 0} \gamma_i^{(\epsilon)} = \delta_i > 0$ for $i > n_1$, and $\lim_{\epsilon\downarrow 0} \widetilde{\gamma}_j^{(\epsilon)} = \widetilde{\delta}_j > 0$ for $j > n_2$.

3.1 Universal Lower Bound

We now present a lower bound on the steady state queue length that is satisfied by any scheduling algorithm.

PROPOSITION 1. *Consider a set of switch systems with the arrival processes $\mathbf{a}^{(\epsilon)}(t)$ described above, parameterized by $0 < \epsilon < 1$, such that the mean arrival rate vector is $\boldsymbol{\lambda}^{\epsilon} = \boldsymbol{\nu}(1-\epsilon)$ for some $\boldsymbol{\nu} \in$ Relint$(\mathcal{F}_{n_1 n_2})$, and the variance is $\left(\boldsymbol{\sigma}^{(\epsilon)}\right)^2$. The load is then $\rho = (1-\epsilon)$ and γ_i , $\widetilde{\gamma}_j$ are* *defined as above for $1 \le i,j \le n$. Fix a scheduling policy under which the switch system is stable for any $0 < \epsilon < 1$. Let $\mathbf{q}^{(\epsilon)}(t)$ denote the queue lengths process under this policy for each system. Suppose that this process converges in distribution to a steady state random vector $\overline{\mathbf{q}}^{(\epsilon)}$. Then, for each of these systems, the steady state mean queue length can be lower bounded as follows.*

$$\mathbb{E}\left[\sum_j \overline{q}_{ij}^{(\epsilon)}\right] \ge \frac{\sum_j \left(\sigma_{ij}^{(\epsilon)}\right)^2}{2\gamma_i} - \frac{1-\gamma_i}{2} \quad \textit{for all } 1 \le i \le n \quad (5)$$

$$\mathbb{E}\left[\sum_i \overline{q}_{ij}^{(\epsilon)}\right] \ge \frac{\sum_i \left(\sigma_{ij}^{(\epsilon)}\right)^2}{2\widetilde{\gamma}_j} - \frac{1-\widetilde{\gamma}_j}{2} \quad \textit{for all } 1 \le j \le n \quad (6)$$

Therefore, in the heavy-traffic limit as $\epsilon \downarrow 0$, if $\left(\boldsymbol{\sigma}^{(\epsilon)}\right)^2 \to \boldsymbol{\sigma}^2$, for the saturated ports, we have

$$\liminf_{\epsilon\downarrow 0} \epsilon\mathbb{E}\left[\sum_j \overline{q}_{ij}^{(\epsilon)}\right] \ge \frac{\sum_j \sigma_{ij}^2}{2} \quad \textit{for all } 1 \le i \le n_1$$

$$\liminf_{\epsilon\downarrow 0} \epsilon\mathbb{E}\left[\sum_i \overline{q}_{ij}^{(\epsilon)}\right] \ge \frac{\sum_i \sigma_{ij}^2}{2} \quad \textit{for all } 1 \le i \le n_2$$

and for the unsaturated ports, we have

$$\liminf_{\epsilon\downarrow 0} \epsilon\mathbb{E}\left[\sum_j \overline{q}_{ij}^{(\epsilon)}\right] \ge 0 \textit{ for all } i > n_1$$

$$\liminf_{\epsilon\downarrow 0} \epsilon\mathbb{E}\left[\sum_i \overline{q}_{ij}^{(\epsilon)}\right] \ge 0 \textit{ for all } i > n_2.$$

PROOF. The queue lengths at each port can be lower bounded by a single server queue as follows. Consider the total queue length at input port (row) i, $\sum_j q_{ij}^{(\epsilon)}(t)$. It can be lower bounded sample path wise by a coupled single server queue with arrival process $\sum_j a_{ij}^{(\epsilon)}(t)$ [8, Proposition 1]. The mean and variance of the arrival process for this single server queue are then $(1-\gamma_i)$ and $\left(\sigma_{ij}^{(\epsilon)}\right)^2$ respectively because of the independence of the arrival processes across the queues in the matrix. Then, using the Kingman bound for single server queue in Lemma 1, we get (5). Similarly lower bounding the total queue length for output port (column) j, $\sum_i q_{ij}^{(\epsilon)}(t)$ by a single server queue, we get (6). Taking the heavy traffic limits using the fact that $\gamma_i^{(\epsilon)} = \epsilon$, $\widetilde{\gamma}_j^{(\epsilon)} = \epsilon$ for saturated ports and $\lim_{\epsilon\downarrow 0} \gamma_i^{(\epsilon)} > 0$, $\lim_{\epsilon\downarrow 0} \widetilde{\gamma}_j^{(\epsilon)} > 0$ for unsaturated ports, give the heavy traffic limits. □

3.2 State Space Collapse

The heavy traffic rate vector $\boldsymbol{\nu}$ lies in the relative interior of the face $\mathcal{F}_{n_1 n_2}$ which is at the intersection of hyperplanes with the $n_1 + n_2$ normal vectors, $\{\mathbf{e}^{(i)}$ for $1 \le i \le n_1\} \cup \{\widetilde{\mathbf{e}}^{(j)}$ for $1 \le j \le n_2\}$. Call the cone spanned by these normal vector $\mathcal{K}_{n_1 n_2}$, i.e.,

$$\begin{aligned}\mathcal{K}_{n_1 n_2} = &\Big\{\mathbf{x} \in \mathbb{R}^{n^2} : \mathbf{x} = \sum_{i=1}^{n_1} w_i \mathbf{e}^{(i)} + \sum_{j=1}^{n_2} \widetilde{w}_j \widetilde{\mathbf{e}}^{(j)} \text{ where} \\ &\quad w_i \in \mathbb{R}_+ \text{ for } 1 \le i \le n_1, \widetilde{w}_j \in \mathbb{R}_+ \text{ for } 1 \le j \le n_2\Big\} \\ = &\Big\{\mathbf{x} \in \mathbb{R}^{n^2} : \mathbf{x} = \sum_{i=1}^{n} w_i \mathbf{e}^{(i)} + \sum_{j=1}^{n} \widetilde{w}_j \widetilde{\mathbf{e}}^{(j)} \text{ where} \\ &\quad w_i \in \mathbb{R}_+ \text{ for } 1 \le i \le n_1 \text{ and } w_i = 0 \text{ for } i > n_1, \\ &\quad \widetilde{w}_j \in \mathbb{R}_+ \text{ for } 1 \le j \le n_2 \text{ and } \widetilde{w}_j = 0 \text{ for } j > n_2\Big\}.\end{aligned}$$

The components of any vector $\mathbf{x}$ in the cone $\mathcal{K}_{n_1 n_2}$ can be written in the form, $x_{ij} = w_i + \widetilde{w}_j$ where $w_i \in \mathbb{R}_+$ for $1 \le i \le n_1$, $w_i = 0$ for $i > n_1$, $\widetilde{w}_j \in \mathbb{R}_+$ for $1 \le j \le n_2$, and $\widetilde{w}_j = 0$ for $j > n_1$.

Let $\mathbf{x}_{\|^{n_1 n_2}}$ denote the projection of $\mathbf{x}$ onto the cone $\mathcal{K}_{n_1 n_2}$, and let $\mathbf{x}_{\perp^{n_1 n_2}} \triangleq \mathbf{x} - \mathbf{x}_{\|^{n_1 n_2}}$ be the perpendicular component. For simplicity of notation, in this section, we use $\mathbf{x}_{\|}$ to mean $\mathbf{x}_{\|^{n_1 n_2}}$ and $\mathbf{x}_{\perp}$ to mean $\mathbf{x}_{\perp^{n_1 n_2}}$. We will show that under the MaxWeight Algorithm, all the moments of $\mathbf{q}_{\perp}$ are bounded in steady state independent of ϵ. Since the ℓ_1 norm of the queues length vector, $\|\mathbf{q}\|_1$ is $\Omega(1/\epsilon)$ as shown in the previous subsection, this establishes that the perpendicular component $\mathbf{q}_{\perp}$ is a negligible part of the queue lengths vector $\mathbf{q}$. Thus, we establish state space collapse.

For $\boldsymbol{\nu} \in \text{Relint}(\mathcal{F}_{n_1 n_2})$, the vector in the relative interior of the face $\mathcal{F}_{n_1 n_2}$, let $\nu_{min} \triangleq \min_{i,j} \nu_{ij}$. We assume that $\nu_{\min} > 0$. Then, $\nu'_{\min} > 0$ where

$$\nu'_{\min} \triangleq \min\left\{\nu_{min}, \min_{i>n_1}\left\{1 - \left\langle \boldsymbol{\nu}, \mathbf{e}^{(i)}\right\rangle\right\}, \min_{j>n_2}\left\{1 - \left\langle \boldsymbol{\nu}, \widetilde{\mathbf{e}}^{(j)}\right\rangle\right\}\right\}.$$

PROPOSITION 2. *Consider a set of switch systems under MaxWeight scheduling algorithm, with the arrival processes $\mathbf{a}^{(\epsilon)}(t)$, parameterized by $0 < \epsilon < 1$ and maximum possible arrivals in any queue $a_{\max}$. The mean arrival rate vector is $\boldsymbol{\lambda}^{\epsilon} = \boldsymbol{\nu}(1-\epsilon)$ for some $\boldsymbol{\nu} \in$ Relint($\mathcal{F}_{n_1 n_2}$) such that $\nu_{\min} \triangleq \min_{ij} \nu_{ij} > 0$. The load is then $\rho = (1-\epsilon)$. Let the variance $\left(\boldsymbol{\sigma}^{(\epsilon)}\right)^2$ of the arrival process be such that $\|\boldsymbol{\sigma}^{(\epsilon)}\|^2 \le \widetilde{\sigma}^2$ for some $\widetilde{\sigma}^2$ not dependent on ϵ. Let $\mathbf{q}^{(\epsilon)}(t)$ denote the queue lengths process of each system, which is positive recurrent. Therefore, the process $\mathbf{q}^{(\epsilon)}(t)$ converges to a steady state random vector in distribution, which we denote by $\overline{\mathbf{q}}^{(\epsilon)}$. Then, for each system with $0 < \epsilon \le \nu'_{\min}/2\|\boldsymbol{\nu}\|$, the steady state queue lengths vector satisfies*

$$\mathbb{E}\left[\|\overline{\mathbf{q}}_{\perp}^{(\epsilon)}\|^r\right] \le (M_r)^r \ \forall r \in \{1, 2, \ldots\},$$

where $\nu'_{\min}$ is defined as above and M_r is a function of $r, \widetilde{\sigma}, \boldsymbol{\nu}, a_{\max}, \nu'_{\min}$ but independent of ϵ.

PROOF. We omit the superscript $^{(\epsilon)}$ in this proof for simplicity of notation. For the Markov chain $\mathbf{q}$, consider the Lyapunov function $W_{\perp}(\mathbf{q}) \triangleq \|\mathbf{q}_{\perp}\|$. We will use Lemma 2 to obtain moment bounds from the drift of $W_{\perp}(.)$. Similar to [8, Proposition 2], under the MaxWeight scheduling algorithm, it can be shown that

$$\begin{aligned}&\mathbb{E}\left[\Delta W_{\perp}(\mathbf{q}) | \mathbf{q(t)} = \mathbf{q}\right] \\ &\le \frac{1}{2\|\mathbf{q}_{\perp}\|}\Big(\|\boldsymbol{\lambda}\|^2 + \|\boldsymbol{\sigma}\|^2 + n - 2\epsilon\left\langle \mathbf{q}_{\perp}, \boldsymbol{\nu}\right\rangle \\ &\quad + 2\mathbb{E}\left[\left\langle \mathbf{q}_{\|}, \mathbf{s}(t) - \boldsymbol{\nu}\right\rangle | \mathbf{q(t)} = \mathbf{q}\right] + 2\min_{\mathbf{r}\in\mathcal{C}}\left\langle \mathbf{q}, \boldsymbol{\nu} - \mathbf{r}\right\rangle\Big). \quad (7)\end{aligned}$$

Recall that since $\mathbf{s} \in \mathcal{S}^*$, $\left\langle \mathbf{e}^{(i)}, \mathbf{s}(t)\right\rangle = 1$ and $\left\langle \widetilde{\mathbf{e}}^{(j)}, \mathbf{s}(t)\right\rangle = 1$ for all i, j, t. Similarly, since $\boldsymbol{\nu} \in \mathcal{F}_{n_1 n_2}$, for $1 \le i \le n_1$ and $1 \le j \le n_2$, we have $\left\langle \mathbf{e}^{(i)}, \boldsymbol{\nu}\right\rangle = 1$ and $\left\langle \widetilde{\mathbf{e}}^{(j)}, \boldsymbol{\nu}\right\rangle = 1$. By the definition of the cone $\mathcal{K}_{n_1 n_2}$, the vector $\mathbf{q}_{\|}$ can be written as $\mathbf{q}_{\|} = \sum_{i=1}^{n_1} w_i \mathbf{e}^{(i)} + \sum_{j=1}^{n_2} \widetilde{w}_j \widetilde{\mathbf{e}}^{(j)}$. Putting all these together, we get $\langle \mathbf{q}_{\|}, \mathbf{s}(t) - \boldsymbol{\nu} \rangle = 0$. We now use the following claim to bound the last term in (7).

CLAIM 1. *For any* $\mathbf{q} \in \mathbb{R}^{n^2}$ *and* $\boldsymbol{\nu} \in Relint(\mathcal{F}_{n_1 n_2})$ *such that* $\nu_{\min} > 0$,

$$\boldsymbol{\nu} + \frac{\nu'_{\min}}{\|\mathbf{q}_\perp\|}\mathbf{q}_\perp \in \mathcal{C}.$$

PROOF. We will verify that $\boldsymbol{\nu} + \frac{\nu'_{\min}}{\|\mathbf{q}_\perp\|}\mathbf{q}_\perp$ satisfies all the conditions in the definition of $\mathcal{C}$ in (4) Note that $\frac{\mathbf{q}_\perp}{\|\mathbf{q}_\perp\|}$ is a unit vector along some direction. Since $\nu_{ij} > \nu'_{\min}$, clearly, $\boldsymbol{\nu} + \frac{\nu'_{\min}}{\|\mathbf{q}_\perp\|}\mathbf{q}_\perp \in \mathbb{R}_+^{n^2}$.

It is well known that for any $\mathbf{x} \in \mathcal{K}_{n_1 n_2}$, $\langle \mathbf{q}_\perp, \mathbf{x} \rangle \leq 0$. Since $\mathbf{e}^{(i)} \in \mathcal{K}_{n_1 n_2}$ for $1 \leq i \leq n_1$, we have $\left\langle \mathbf{q}_\perp, \mathbf{e}^{(i)} \right\rangle \leq 0$. Then, using the fact that $\boldsymbol{\nu} \in \mathcal{F}_{n_1 n_2}$, we have for $1 \leq i \leq n_1$,

$$\left\langle \boldsymbol{\nu} + \frac{\nu'_{\min}}{\|\mathbf{q}_\perp\|}\mathbf{q}_\perp, \mathbf{e}^{(i)} \right\rangle \leq 1$$

For $i > n_1$,

$$\left\langle \boldsymbol{\nu} + \frac{\nu'_{\min}}{\|\mathbf{q}_\perp\|}\mathbf{q}_\perp, \mathbf{e}^{(i)} \right\rangle = \left\langle \boldsymbol{\nu}, \mathbf{e}^{(i)} \right\rangle + \nu'_{\min}\left\langle \frac{\mathbf{q}_\perp}{\|\mathbf{q}_\perp\|}, \mathbf{e}^{(i)} \right\rangle$$
$$\overset{(a)}{\leq} \left\langle \boldsymbol{\nu}, \mathbf{e}^{(i)} \right\rangle + \nu'_{min} \qquad \leq \quad 1,$$

where (a) follows from Cauchy-Schwartz inequality and the-last inequality follows from the definition of $\nu'_{\min}$. It can similarly, be shown that $\left\langle \boldsymbol{\nu} + \frac{\nu_{\min}}{\|\mathbf{q}_\perp\|}\mathbf{q}_\perp, \tilde{\mathbf{e}}^{(j)} \right\rangle \leq 1$ for $1 \leq j \leq n_2$ as well as $j > n_2$, proving the claim. □

Using the claim, the last term in (7) can be bounded as

$$\begin{aligned} 2\min_{\mathbf{r}\in\mathcal{C}} \langle \mathbf{q}, \boldsymbol{\nu} - \mathbf{r} \rangle \leq & 2\left\langle \mathbf{q}, \boldsymbol{\nu} - \left(\boldsymbol{\nu} + \frac{\nu'_{\min}}{\|\mathbf{q}_\perp\|}\mathbf{q}_\perp\right)\right\rangle \\ = & -2\left\langle \mathbf{q}, \frac{\nu'_{\min}}{\|\mathbf{q}_\perp\|}\mathbf{q}_\perp \right\rangle \\ = & -2\nu'_{\min}\|\mathbf{q}_\perp\| \end{aligned}$$

Using this in (7) and bounding the $-2\epsilon \langle \mathbf{q}_\perp, \boldsymbol{\nu} \rangle$ term using Cauchy-Schwartz inequality, we get

$$\begin{aligned} &\mathbb{E}\left[\Delta W_\perp(\mathbf{q})|\, \mathbf{q}(\mathbf{t}) = \mathbf{q}\right] \\ \leq & \frac{\|\boldsymbol{\lambda}\|^2 + \|\boldsymbol{\sigma}\|^2 + n}{2\|\mathbf{q}_\perp\|} - \nu'_{\min} + \epsilon\|\boldsymbol{\nu}\| \\ \leq & \frac{\|\boldsymbol{\lambda}\|^2 + \|\boldsymbol{\sigma}\|^2 + n}{2\|\mathbf{q}_\perp\|} - \frac{\nu'_{\min}}{2} \text{ whenever } \epsilon \leq \frac{\nu'_{\min}}{2\|\boldsymbol{\nu}\|} \\ \leq & -\frac{\nu'_{\min}}{4} \text{ for all } \mathbf{q} \text{ such that } W_\perp(\mathbf{q}) \geq \frac{2(\|\boldsymbol{\lambda}\|^2 + \|\boldsymbol{\sigma}\|^2 + n)}{\nu'_{\min}}, \end{aligned}$$

Thus condition C.1 is valid with $\zeta = \frac{2(\|\boldsymbol{\lambda}\|^2 + \|\boldsymbol{\sigma}\|^2 + n)}{\nu'_{\min}}$ and $\eta = \frac{\nu'_{\min}}{4}$. Moreover ζ can be upper bounded by $\zeta \leq \frac{2(\|\boldsymbol{\nu}\|^2 + \|\boldsymbol{\sigma}\|^2 + n)}{\nu'_{\min}}$, an expression that doesn't contain ϵ. Condition C.2 can be verified using nonexpansivity of projection and the fact that maximum arrivals at every time are $a_{\max}$ [8]. Then from Lemma 2, we get the proposition. □

3.3 Upper Bound

In this subsection, we will use the state space collapse result from the previous section to show that under the MaxWeight algorithm, the steady state sum queue length have the same asymptotic scaling as in the universal lower bound in Section 3.1. We will obtain these results by setting the drift of a function to 0 in steady state. We use a novel function based on the geometry of the cone $\mathcal{K}_{n_1 n_2}$. For this purpose, define the following functions.

$$V_1(\mathbf{q}) \triangleq A\sum_{i=1}^{n_1}\left(\sum_{j=1}^{n} q_{ij}\right)^2$$
$$V_2(\mathbf{q}) \triangleq B\sum_{j=1}^{n_2}\left(\sum_{i=1}^{n} q_{ij}\right)^2$$
$$V_3(\mathbf{q}) \triangleq C\left(\sum_{i=1}^{n_1}\sum_{j=1}^{n} q_{ij} + \sum_{j=1}^{n_2}\sum_{i=1}^{n} q_{ij}\right)^2$$
$$V_4(\mathbf{q}) \triangleq V_1(\mathbf{q}) + V_2(\mathbf{q}) - V_3(\mathbf{q})$$

The terms A, B and C depend only on n_1, n_2, n and not on $\mathbf{q}$. We will pick them later to obtain the right upper bounds. For each of these functions, their drift is defined as

$$\Delta V(\mathbf{q}) \triangleq [V(\mathbf{q}(t+1)) - V(\mathbf{q}(t))]\,\mathcal{I}(\mathbf{q}(t) = \mathbf{q}).$$

We now state the main result in this section.

THEOREM 1. *Consider the set of switch systems operating under the MaxWeight algorithm, parameterized by* $0 < \epsilon < 1$ *as described in Proposition 2. Then, for each system with* $0 < \epsilon \leq \nu'_{\min}/2\|\boldsymbol{\nu}\|$, *the steady state queue lengths vector satisfies*

$$\begin{aligned} &2\epsilon(n - n_2)\mathbb{E}\left[\sum_{i=1}^{n_1}\sum_{j=1}^{n}\overline{q}_{ij}\right] + 2\epsilon(n - n_1)\mathbb{E}\left[\sum_{j=1}^{n_2}\sum_{i=1}^{n}\overline{q}_{ij}\right] \\ \leq & (n{+}n_1{-}1)\sum_{i=1}^{n_1}\sum_{j=1}^{n}\sigma_{ij}^2 + (n{+}n_2{-}1)\sum_{j=1}^{n_2}\sum_{i=1}^{n}\sigma_{ij}^2 + B_1(\epsilon, n), \end{aligned}$$

where $\lim_{\epsilon\to 0} B_1(\epsilon, n) = 0$. *Thus, in the heavy traffic limit as* $\epsilon \downarrow 0$, *we have*

$$\begin{aligned} &(n - n_2)\sum_{i=1}^{n_1}\sum_{j=1}^{n}\sigma_{ij}^2 + (n - n_1)\sum_{j=1}^{n_2}\sum_{i=1}^{n}\sigma_{ij}^2 \\ \leq & \lim_{\epsilon\to 0} 2\epsilon(n - n_2)\mathbb{E}\left[\sum_{i=1}^{n_1}\sum_{j=1}^{n}\overline{q}_{ij}\right] + 2\epsilon(n - n_1)\mathbb{E}\left[\sum_{j=1}^{n_2}\sum_{i=1}^{n}\overline{q}_{ij}\right] \\ \leq & (n + n_1 - 1)\sum_{i=1}^{n_1}\sum_{j=1}^{n}\sigma_{ij}^2 + (n + n_2 - 1)\sum_{j=1}^{n_2}\sum_{i=1}^{n}\sigma_{ij}^2. \end{aligned}$$

Moreover, for any $i > n_1$ *and* $j > n_2$,

$$\lim_{\epsilon\to 0}\epsilon\mathbb{E}\left[\overline{q}_{ij}\right] = 0.$$

We briefly discuss the result before presenting the proof of the theorem. In [8], the case when all the ports are saturated is considered and an exact expression for steady state sum queue length under MaxWeight algorithm was presented. In that case, i.e., when $n_1 = n$ and $n_2 = n$, this theorem does not give any queue length bounds. Thus, the result presented here does not subsume the result in [8]. To elaborate on Theorem 1, we now present the following special case of $n_1 = n_2 = n_{sat}$ which follows directly from the Theorem along with the universal lower bound in Proposition 2.

COROLLARY 1. *Suppose that $n_1 = n_2 = n_{sat}$ in the set of switch systems described in Theorem 1. Then, in the heavy traffic,*

$$\left(\sum_{i=1}^{n_1}\sum_{j=1}^{n}\sigma_{ij}^2+\sum_{j=1}^{n_2}\sum_{i=1}^{n}\sigma_{ij}^2\right)$$
$$\leq \lim_{\epsilon\to 0} 2\epsilon\mathbb{E}\left[\sum_{i=1}^{n_1}\sum_{j=1}^{n}\overline{q}_{ij}+\sum_{j=1}^{n_2}\sum_{i=1}^{n}\overline{q}_{ij}\right]$$
$$\leq \left(\frac{n+n_{sat}-1}{n-n_{sat}}\right)\left(\sum_{i=1}^{n_1}\sum_{j=1}^{n}\sigma_{ij}^2+\sum_{j=1}^{n_2}\sum_{i=1}^{n}\sigma_{ij}^2\right).$$

Moreover,

$$\max\left\{\sum_{i=1}^{n_1}\sum_{j=1}^{n}\sigma_{ij}^2,\sum_{j=1}^{n_2}\sum_{i=1}^{n}\sigma_{ij}^2\right\}\leq \lim_{\epsilon\to 0}2\epsilon\mathbb{E}\left[\sum_{i,j=1}^{n}\overline{q}_{ij}\right]$$
$$\leq\left(\frac{n+n_{sat}-1}{n-n_{sat}}\right)\left(\sum_{i=1}^{n_1}\sum_{j=1}^{n}\sigma_{ij}^2+\sum_{j=1}^{n_2}\sum_{i=1}^{n}\sigma_{ij}^2\right)$$

The second result follows from the universal lower bound in Proposition 2, the last part of the Theorem and $\sum_{i,j=1}^{n}\overline{q}_{ij}\leq \sum_{i=1}^{n_1}\sum_{j=1}^{n}\overline{q}_{ij}+\sum_{j=1}^{n_2}\sum_{i=1}^{n}\overline{q}_{ij}+\sum_{i>n_1,j>n_2}\overline{q}_{ij}$.

Remark: When n_{sat} is a constant or when n_{sat} is $o(n)$ or when n_{sat} is of the form $K_1 n$ for some constant $0<K_1<1$, we have optimal heavy traffic scaling under the MaxWeight algorithm. A similar conclusion can be obtained if n_1 and n_2 are different fractions of n.

We now present the proof of Theorem 1.

PROOF OF THEOREM 1. We consider the switch for a fixed $0<\epsilon\leq \nu'_{\min}/2\|\boldsymbol{\nu}\|$. For simplicity of notation, we again omit the superscript (ϵ) in this proof. Similar to the notation in [8], we use $\overline{\mathbf{q}}$ to denote the steady state queue length vector and $\overline{\mathbf{a}}$ to denote the steady state arrival vector which is identically distributed to the vector $\mathbf{a}(t)$ at any time t. We use $\mathbf{s}(\overline{\mathbf{q}})$ and $\mathbf{u}(\overline{\mathbf{q}})$ for the schedule and unused service to explicitly show their dependence on the queue lengths. If the queue length at time t is $\overline{\mathbf{q}}$, then the queue length at time $t+1$, $\overline{\mathbf{q}}+\overline{\mathbf{a}}-\mathbf{s}(\overline{\mathbf{q}})+\mathbf{u}(\overline{\mathbf{q}})$ is denoted by $\overline{\mathbf{q}}^+$. Since $\overline{\mathbf{q}}$ is the steady state queue length, it has the same distribution as $\overline{\mathbf{q}}^+$.

It can be easily shown using Lemma 2 that in steady state, $\mathbb{E}[V_1(\overline{\mathbf{q}})]$, $\mathbb{E}[V_2(\overline{\mathbf{q}})]$, $\mathbb{E}[V_3(\overline{\mathbf{q}})]$ and $\mathbb{E}[V_4(\overline{\mathbf{q}})]$ are all finite. See Lemma 5 in [8] for details. Since $\mathbb{E}[V_1(\overline{\mathbf{q}})]$ is finite in steady state, $\mathbb{E}[\overline{q}_{ij}]$ is also bounded for all i,j. Setting its drift to zero in steady state, we get

$$\mathbb{E}[u_{ij}(\overline{\mathbf{q}})]=\mathbb{E}[s_{ij}(\overline{\mathbf{q}})-\overline{a}_{ij}]\quad\forall i,j. \tag{8}$$

Setting the drift of V_4 to zero in steady state i.e. $\Delta V_4(\overline{\mathbf{q}})=0$, and expanding all the quadratic terms after using (1) for $\mathbf{q}(t+1)$, we get the following expression. Since it is very long, we break it into four parts, and write it as,

$$\mathcal{T}_1=\mathcal{T}_2+\mathcal{T}_3+\mathcal{T}_4,$$

where

$$\mathcal{T}_1 =2A\mathbb{E}\left[\sum_{i=1}^{n_1}\left(\sum_{j=1}^{n}\overline{q}_{ij}\right)\left(\sum_{j'=1}^{n}s_{ij'}(\overline{\mathbf{q}})-\overline{a}_{ij'}\right)\right]$$
$$+2B\mathbb{E}\left[\sum_{j=1}^{n_2}\left(\sum_{i=1}^{n}\overline{q}_{ij}\right)\left(\sum_{i'=1}^{n}s_{i'j}(\overline{\mathbf{q}})-\overline{a}_{i'j}\right)\right]$$
$$-2C\mathbb{E}\left[\left(\sum_{i=1}^{n_1}\sum_{j=1}^{n}\overline{q}_{ij}+\sum_{j=1}^{n_2}\sum_{i=1}^{n}\overline{q}_{ij}\right)\times\right.$$
$$\left.\left(\sum_{i'=1}^{n_1}\sum_{j'=1}^{n}(s_{i'j'}(\overline{\mathbf{q}})-\overline{a}_{i'j'})+\sum_{j'=1}^{n_2}\sum_{i'=1}^{n}(s_{i'j'}(\overline{\mathbf{q}})-\overline{a}_{i'j'})\right)\right]$$
$$\mathcal{T}_2 =A\mathbb{E}\left[\sum_{i=1}^{n_1}\left(\sum_{j=1}^{n}\overline{a}_{ij}-s_{ij}(\overline{\mathbf{q}})\right)^2\right]+B\mathbb{E}\left[\sum_{j=1}^{n_2}\left(\sum_{i=1}^{n}\overline{a}_{ij}-s_{ij}(\overline{\mathbf{q}})\right)^2\right]$$
$$-C\mathbb{E}\left[\left(\sum_{i=1}^{n_1}\sum_{j=1}^{n}\overline{a}_{ij}-s_{ij}(\overline{\mathbf{q}})+\sum_{j=1}^{n_2}\sum_{i=1}^{n}\overline{a}_{ij}-s_{ij}(\overline{\mathbf{q}})\right)^2\right]$$
$$\mathcal{T}_3 =-A\mathbb{E}\left[\sum_{i=1}^{n_1}\left(\sum_{j=1}^{n}u_{ij}(\overline{\mathbf{q}})\right)^2\right]-B\mathbb{E}\left[\sum_{j=1}^{n_2}\left(\sum_{i=1}^{n}u_{ij}(\overline{\mathbf{q}})\right)^2\right]$$
$$+C\mathbb{E}\left[\left(\sum_{i=1}^{n_1}\sum_{j=1}^{n}u_{ij}(\overline{\mathbf{q}})+\sum_{j=1}^{n_2}\sum_{i=1}^{n}u_{ij}(\overline{\mathbf{q}})\right)^2\right]$$
$$\mathcal{T}_4 =2A\mathbb{E}\left[\sum_{i=1}^{n_1}\left(\sum_{j=1}^{n}\overline{q}_{ij}^+\right)\left(\sum_{j'=1}^{n}u_{ij'}(\overline{\mathbf{q}})\right)\right]$$
$$+2B\mathbb{E}\left[\sum_{j=1}^{n_2}\left(\sum_{i=1}^{n}\overline{q}_{ij}^+\right)\left(\sum_{i'=1}^{n}u_{i'j}(\overline{\mathbf{q}})\right)\right]$$
$$-2C\mathbb{E}\left[\left(\sum_{i=1}^{n_1}\sum_{j=1}^{n}\overline{q}_{ij}^++\sum_{j=1}^{n_2}\sum_{i=1}^{n}\overline{q}_{ij}^+\right)\times\right.$$
$$\left.\left(\sum_{i'=1}^{n_1}\sum_{j'=1}^{n}u_{i'j'}(\overline{\mathbf{q}})+\sum_{j'=1}^{n_2}\sum_{i'=1}^{n}u_{i'j'}(\overline{\mathbf{q}})\right)\right]$$

We will simplify and bound each of these four terms to get a steady state queue length bound. Let us focus on the first term $\mathcal{T}_1$. Note that since $\mathbf{s}\in\mathcal{S}^*$, $\sum_{i=1}^{n}s_{ij}=1$ and $\sum_{j=1}^{n}s_{ij}=1$ for all i,j at all time. Using this, the expression $\mathbb{E}\left[\left(\sum_{j=1}^{n}\overline{q}_{ij}\right)\left(\sum_{j'=1}^{n}s_{ij'}(\overline{\mathbf{q}})-\overline{a}_{ij'}\right)\right]$ becomes $\mathbb{E}\left[\left(\sum_{j=1}^{n}\overline{q}_{ij}\right)\left(1-\sum_{j'=1}^{n}\overline{a}_{ij'}\right)\right]$. Arrival at any time is independent of the queue length at that time. Therefore, this expression reduces to $\mathbb{E}\left[\left(\sum_{j=1}^{n}\overline{q}_{ij}\right)\right]\left(1-\sum_{j'=1}^{n}\lambda_{ij'}\right)$. For $1\leq i\leq n_1$, $\left(1-\sum_{j'=1}^{n}\lambda_{ij'}\right)=\epsilon$ since $\boldsymbol{\lambda}=\boldsymbol{\nu}(1-\epsilon)$ and $\boldsymbol{\nu}\in\mathcal{F}_{n_1n_2}$. Using this and similarly bounding other parts of $\mathcal{T}_1$, we get

$$\mathcal{T}_1 =2A\epsilon\mathbb{E}\left[\sum_{i=1}^{n_1}\sum_{j=1}^{n}\overline{q}_{ij}\right]+2B\mathbb{E}\epsilon\left[\sum_{j=1}^{n_2}\sum_{i=1}^{n}\overline{q}_{ij}\right]$$
$$-2C(n_1+n_2)\epsilon\mathbb{E}\left[\left(\sum_{i=1}^{n_1}\sum_{j=1}^{n}\overline{q}_{ij}+\sum_{j=1}^{n_2}\sum_{i=1}^{n}\overline{q}_{ij}\right)\right]$$
$$=2\epsilon\left(A-C(n_1+n_2)\right)\mathbb{E}\left[\sum_{i=1}^{n_1}\sum_{j=1}^{n}\overline{q}_{ij}\right]$$
$$+2\epsilon\left(B-C(n_1+n_2)\right)\mathbb{E}\left[\sum_{j=1}^{n_2}\sum_{i=1}^{n}\overline{q}_{ij}\right]. \tag{9}$$

Now, we focus on the term $\mathcal{T}_2$. Again using the fact that

$\sum_{j=1}^{n} s_{ij} = 1$, the first term in $\mathcal{T}_2$ can be rewritten as

$$\sum_{i=1}^{n_1} \mathbb{E}\left[\left(\sum_{j=1}^{n}(\overline{a}_{ij} - s_{ij}(\overline{\mathbf{q}}))\right)^2\right] = \sum_{i=1}^{n_1} \mathbb{E}\left[(\sum_{j=1}^{n}\overline{a}_{ij} - 1)^2\right]$$
$$= \sum_{i=1}^{n_1} \mathbb{E}\left[(\sum_{j=1}^{n}\overline{a}_{ij} - (1-\epsilon) - \epsilon)^2\right]$$
$$\overset{(a)}{=} \sum_{i=1}^{n_1} Var\left(\sum_{j=1}^{n} a_{ij}\right) + \sum_{i=1}^{n_1}\epsilon^2$$
$$= n_1\epsilon^2 + \sum_{i=1}^{n_1}\sum_{j=1}^{n}\sigma_{ij}^2,$$

where (a) follows from $\mathbb{E}\left[(\sum_{j=1}^{n}\overline{a}_{ij})\right] = 1-\epsilon$ for $1 \le i \le n_1$. Similarly, the second term can be rewritten as

$$\sum_{j=1}^{n_2} \mathbb{E}\left[\left(\sum_{i=1}^{n}(\overline{a}_{ij} - s_{ij}(\overline{\mathbf{q}}))\right)^2\right] = n_2\epsilon^2 + \sum_{j=1}^{n_2}\sum_{i=1}^{n}\sigma_{ij}^2,$$

and the third term in $\mathcal{T}_2$ becomes

$$\mathbb{E}\left[\left(\sum_{i=1}^{n_1}\sum_{j=1}^{n}(\overline{a}_{ij} - s_{ij}(\overline{\mathbf{q}})) + \sum_{j=1}^{n_2}\sum_{i=1}^{n}(\overline{a}_{ij} - s_{ij}(\overline{\mathbf{q}}))\right)^2\right]$$
$$= \mathbb{E}\left[\left(\sum_{i=1}^{n_1}\sum_{j=1}^{n}\overline{a}_{ij} + \sum_{j=1}^{n_2}\sum_{i=1}^{n}\overline{a}_{ij} - n_1 - n_2\right)^2\right]$$
$$= \mathbb{E}\left[\left(\sum_{i=1}^{n_1}\sum_{j=1}^{n}\overline{a}_{ij} - n_1(1-\epsilon) + \sum_{j=1}^{n_2}\sum_{i=1}^{n}\overline{a}_{ij} - n_2(1-\epsilon) - n_1\epsilon - n_2\epsilon\right)^2\right]$$
$$\overset{(b)}{=} Var\left(\sum_{i=1}^{n_1}\sum_{j=1}^{n}\overline{a}_{ij} + \sum_{j=1}^{n_2}\sum_{i=1}^{n}\overline{a}_{ij}\right) + (n_1+n_2)^2\epsilon^2$$
$$= \sum_{i=1}^{n_1}\sum_{j=1}^{n}\sigma_{ij}^2 + \sum_{j=1}^{n_2}\sum_{i=1}^{n}\sigma_{ij}^2 + (n_1+n_2)^2\epsilon^2,$$

where in (b), the cross terms are 0 because of independence of the arrival processes across the queues. Putting it all together, the term $\mathcal{T}_2$ becomes

$$\mathcal{T}_2 = (A-C)\sum_{i=1}^{n_1}\sum_{j=1}^{n}\sigma_{ij}^2 + (B-C)\sum_{j=1}^{n_2}\sum_{i=1}^{n}\sigma_{ij}^2 + \epsilon^2\left(An_1 + Bn_2 - C(n_1+n_2)^2\right). \quad (10)$$

Now, we focus on the term $\mathcal{T}_3$. Recall that $u_{ij} \le s_{ij}$ and since $\mathbf{s} \in \mathcal{S}^*$, we have $\sum_{j=1}^{n} u_{ij}(\overline{\mathbf{q}}) \le 1$ and $\sum_{i=1}^{n} u_{ij}(\overline{\mathbf{q}}) \le 1$. Therefore the term $\mathcal{T}_3$ can be upper bounded by

$$\mathcal{T}_3 \le C\mathbb{E}\left[\left(\sum_{i=1}^{n_1}\sum_{j=1}^{n} u_{ij}(\overline{\mathbf{q}}) + \sum_{j=1}^{n_2}\sum_{i=1}^{n} u_{ij}(\overline{\mathbf{q}})\right)^2\right]$$
$$\le C(n_1+n_2)\mathbb{E}\left[\sum_{i=1}^{n_1}\sum_{j=1}^{n} u_{ij}(\overline{\mathbf{q}}) + \sum_{j=1}^{n_2}\sum_{i=1}^{n} u_{ij}(\overline{\mathbf{q}})\right]$$
$$\overset{(a)}{=} C(n_1+n_2)\mathbb{E}\left[\sum_{i=1}^{n_1}\sum_{j=1}^{n}(s_{ij}(\overline{\mathbf{q}}) - \overline{a}_{ij}) + \sum_{j=1}^{n_2}\sum_{i=1}^{n}(s_{ij}(\overline{\mathbf{q}}) - \overline{a}_{ij})\right]$$
$$= C(n_1+n_2)\mathbb{E}\left[\sum_{i=1}^{n_1}\epsilon + \sum_{j=1}^{n_2}\epsilon\right]$$
$$= C(n_1+n_2)^2\epsilon. \quad (11)$$

where (a) follows from (8).

We now focus on the last term $\mathcal{T}_4$ which is the most important of all the four terms. It can be rewritten as

$$\mathcal{T}_4 = \mathbb{E}\left[\sum_{i=1}^{n}\sum_{j=1}^{n} u_{ij}(\overline{\mathbf{q}})\left(f_{ij}(\overline{\mathbf{q}}^+)\right)\right]$$
$$= \mathbb{E}\left[\sum_{i=1}^{n}\sum_{j=1}^{n} u_{ij}(\overline{\mathbf{q}})\left(f_{ij}(\overline{\mathbf{q}}_{\|}^+) + f_{ij}(\overline{\mathbf{q}}_{\perp}^+)\right)\right], \quad (12)$$

where $f_{ij}(\overline{\mathbf{q}}^+)$ defined below in (13) is a linear function. Since the vector $\overline{\mathbf{q}}_{\|}^+$ lies in the cone $\mathcal{K}_{n_1 n_2}$, each of its components can be written as $bq_{ij'}^+ = w_i + \widetilde{w}_j$ where $w_i, \widetilde{w}_j \in \mathbb{R}_+$ for all i, j, $w_i = 0$ for $i > n_1$ and $\widetilde{w}_j = 0$ for $j > n_2$. Using this fact, $f_{ij}(\overline{\mathbf{q}}_{\|}^+)$ can be rewritten as in (14) below. We now pick $C = 1, A = (n+n_1), B = (n+n_2)$ to get (15).

$$f_{ij}(\overline{\mathbf{q}}^+) = \begin{cases} 2A\sum_{j'=1}^{n}\overline{q}_{ij'}^+ + 2B\sum_{i'=1}^{n}\overline{q}_{i'j}^+ - 4C\left[\sum_{i'=1}^{n_1}\sum_{j'=1}^{n}\overline{q}_{i'j'}^+ + \sum_{j'=1}^{n_2}\sum_{i'=1}^{n}\overline{q}_{i'j'}^+\right] & \text{if } i \le n_1 \text{ and } j \le n_2 \\ 2B\sum_{i'=1}^{n}\overline{q}_{i'j}^+ - 2C\left[\sum_{i'=1}^{n_1}\sum_{j'=1}^{n}\overline{q}_{i'j'}^+ + \sum_{j'=1}^{n_2}\sum_{i'=1}^{n}\overline{q}_{i'j'}^+\right] & \text{if } i > n_1 \text{ and } j \le n_2 \\ 2A\sum_{j'=1}^{n}\overline{q}_{ij'}^+ - 2C\left[\sum_{i'=1}^{n_1}\sum_{j'=1}^{n}\overline{q}_{i'j'}^+ + \sum_{j'=1}^{n_2}\sum_{i'=1}^{n}\overline{q}_{i'j'}^+\right] & \text{if } i \le n_1 \text{ and } j > n_2 \\ 0 & \text{if } i > n_1 \text{ and } j > n_2. \end{cases} \quad (13)$$

$$f_{ij}(\overline{\mathbf{q}}_{\|}^+) = \begin{cases} 2Anw_i + 2A\sum_{j'=1}^{n}\widetilde{w}_{j'} + 2Bn\widetilde{w}_j + 2B\sum_{i'=1}^{n} w_{i'} - 4C\left[(n+n_2)\sum_{i'=1}^{n} w_{i'} + (n+n_1)\sum_{j'=1}^{n}\widetilde{w}_{j'}\right] & \text{if } i \le n_1, j \le n_2 \\ 2Bn\widetilde{w}_j + 2B\sum_{i'=1}^{n} w_{i'} - 2C\left[(n+n_2)\sum_{i'=1}^{n} w_{i'} + (n+n_1)\sum_{j'=1}^{n}\widetilde{w}_{j'}\right] & \text{if } i > n_1, j \le n_2 \\ 2Anw_i + 2A\sum_{j'=1}^{n}\widetilde{w}_{j'} - 2C\left[(n+n_2)\sum_{i'=1}^{n} w_{i'} + (n+n_1)\sum_{j'=1}^{n}\widetilde{w}_{j'}\right] & \text{if } i \le n_1, j > n_2 \\ 0 & \text{if } i > n_1, j > n_2 \end{cases} \quad (14)$$

$$f_{ij}(\overline{\mathbf{q}}_{\|}^+) = \begin{cases} 2(n+n_1)nw_i + 2(n+n_2)n\widetilde{w}_j - 2\left[(n+n_2)\sum_{i'=1}^{n} w_{i'} + (n+n_1)\sum_{j'=1}^{n}\widetilde{w}_{j'}\right] & \text{if } i \le n_1, j \le n_2 \\ 2(n+n_2)n\widetilde{w}_j - 2\left[(n+n_1)\sum_{j'=1}^{n}\widetilde{w}_{j'}\right] & \text{if } i > n_1, j \le n_2 \\ 2(n+n_1)nw_i - 2\left[(n+n_2)\sum_{j'=1}^{n}\widetilde{w}_{j'}\right] & \text{if } i \le n_1, j > n_2 \\ 0 & \text{if } i > n_1, j > n_2 \end{cases} \quad (15)$$

Consider the $u_{ij}(\overline{\mathbf{q}})f_{ij}(\overline{\mathbf{q}}_{\|}^{+})$ part of $\mathcal{T}_4$. Since $u_{ij}(.)$ is non-negative, the negative parts in the expression $f_{ij}(\overline{\mathbf{q}}_{\|}^{+})$ in (15) can be upper bounded by 0. Then, using $n_1 \leq n$ and $n_2 \leq n$, we get

$$u_{ij}(\overline{\mathbf{q}})f_{ij}(\overline{\mathbf{q}}_{\|}^{+}) \leq \begin{cases} 4n^2 u_{ij}(\overline{\mathbf{q}})(w_i + \widetilde{w}_j) & \text{if } i \leq n_1, j \leq n_2 \\ 4n^2 u_{ij}(\overline{\mathbf{q}})\widetilde{w}_j & \text{if } i > n_1, j \leq n_2 \\ 4n^2 u_{ij}(\overline{\mathbf{q}})w_i & \text{if } i \leq n_1, j > n_2 \\ 0 & \text{if } i > n_1, j > n_2 \end{cases}.$$

Since $w_i = 0$ and $\widetilde{w}_j = 0$ for $i > n_1$ and $j > n_2$, this can compactly be written as

$$\begin{aligned} u_{ij}(\overline{\mathbf{q}})f_{ij}(\overline{\mathbf{q}}_{\|}^{+}) \leq & 4n^2 u_{ij}(\overline{\mathbf{q}})(w_i + \widetilde{w}_j) \quad \forall \quad i,j \\ =& 4n^2 u_{ij}(\overline{\mathbf{q}})(w_i + \widetilde{w}_j)\mathcal{I}(u_{ij}(\overline{\mathbf{q}}) > 1) \\ \stackrel{(a)}{=} & -4n^2 u_{ij}(\overline{\mathbf{q}})q_{\perp ij}^{+}\mathcal{I}(u_{ij}(\overline{\mathbf{q}}) > 1) \\ =& -4n^2 u_{ij}(\overline{\mathbf{q}})q_{\perp ij}^{+}. \end{aligned} \tag{16}$$

When $u_{ij}(\overline{\mathbf{q}}) > 0$, from the definition of unused service, we have that $\overline{q}_{ij}^{+} = 0 \Rightarrow q_{\| ij}^{+} + q_{\perp ij}^{+} = 0 \Rightarrow w_i + \widetilde{w}_j = -q_{\perp ij}^{+}$. This gives (a). In order to get an upper bound on $\mathcal{T}_4$, we now consider the expression We now consider the term $f_{ij}(\overline{\mathbf{q}}_{\perp}^{+})$. Since the cone $\mathcal{K}_{n_1 n_2}$ is defined by the vectors $\mathbf{e}^{(i)}$ and $\widetilde{\mathbf{e}}^{(j)}$ for $1 \leq i \leq n_1$, $1 \leq j \leq n_2$, from the property of projection onto convex cone, we have that $\left\langle \overline{\mathbf{q}}_{\perp}, \mathbf{e}^{(i)} \right\rangle \leq 0$ and $\left\langle \overline{\mathbf{q}}_{\perp}, \widetilde{\mathbf{e}}^{(j)} \right\rangle$ for $1 \leq i \leq n_1$, $1 \leq j \leq n_2$. Using this fact in (13) and denoting $\sum_{i=1}^{n_1} \left\langle \overline{\mathbf{q}}_{\perp}, \mathbf{e}^{(i)} \right\rangle + \sum_{j=1}^{n_2} \left\langle \overline{\mathbf{q}}_{\perp}, \widetilde{\mathbf{e}}^{(j)} \right\rangle$ by $\mathcal{A}$, we get

$$f_{ij}(\overline{\mathbf{q}}_{\perp}) = \begin{cases} -4\mathcal{A} & \text{if } i \leq n_1, j \leq n_2 \\ -2\mathcal{A} & \text{if } i > n_1, j \leq n_2 \\ -2\mathcal{A} & \text{if } i \leq n_1, j > n_2 \\ 0 & \text{if } i > n_1, j > n_2 \end{cases} \tag{17}$$

For any $\mathbf{x} \in \mathbb{R}^{n^2}$, let $\widehat{\mathbf{x}} \in \mathbb{R}^{n^2}$ denote the vector obtained by replacing the $(n - n_1)(n - n_2)$ components with $i > n_1$ and $j > n_2$ with zeros, i.e.,

$$\widehat{x}_{ij} = \begin{cases} x_{ij} & \text{if } i \leq n_1 \text{ or } j \leq n_2 \\ 0 & \text{if } i > n_1 \text{ and } j > n_2 \end{cases}$$

Then, noting that $\mathcal{A} \leq 0 \Rightarrow -4\mathcal{A} \geq -2\mathcal{A}$, from (17), we get

$$f_{ij}(\overline{\mathbf{q}}_{\perp}) \leq -4\mathcal{A}\hat{\mathbb{1}}$$

Since $f_{ij}(.) = 0$ for $i > n_1, j > n_2$, the term $\mathcal{T}_4$ in (12) can be written as

$$\begin{aligned} \mathcal{T}_4 =& \mathbb{E}\left[\left\langle \mathbf{u}(\overline{\mathbf{q}}), \mathbf{f}(\overline{\mathbf{q}}_{\|}^{+}) + \mathbf{f}(\overline{\mathbf{q}}_{\perp}^{+}) \right\rangle\right] \\ =& \mathbb{E}\left[\left\langle \widehat{\mathbf{u}}(\overline{\mathbf{q}}), \mathbf{f}(\overline{\mathbf{q}}_{\|}^{+}) \right\rangle + \mathbb{E}\left\langle \mathbf{u}(\overline{\mathbf{q}}), \mathbf{f}(\overline{\mathbf{q}}_{\perp}^{+}) \right\rangle\right] \\ =& \mathbb{E}\left[\left\langle \widehat{\mathbf{u}}(\overline{\mathbf{q}}), -4n^2\overline{\mathbf{q}}_{\perp} \right\rangle + \mathbb{E}\left\langle \mathbf{u}(\overline{\mathbf{q}}), -4\mathcal{A}\hat{\mathbb{1}} \right\rangle\right] \\ =& \mathbb{E}\left[\left\langle \widehat{\mathbf{u}}(\overline{\mathbf{q}}), -4n^2\overline{\mathbf{q}}_{\perp} - 4\mathcal{A}\hat{\mathbb{1}} \right\rangle\right] \\ \leq & \sqrt{\mathbb{E}\left[\|\widehat{\mathbf{u}}(\overline{\mathbf{q}})\|^2\right]\mathbb{E}\left[\|4n^2\overline{\mathbf{q}}_{\perp} + 4\mathcal{A}\hat{\mathbb{1}}\|^2\right]} \end{aligned} \tag{18}$$

Using the fact that $u_{ij} \in \{0, 1\}$ and (8), the first part here can be upper bounded as

$$\begin{aligned} \mathbb{E}\left[\|\widehat{\mathbf{u}}(\overline{\mathbf{q}})\|^2\right] =& \sum_{i=1}^{n_1} \mathbb{E}\left[\sum_{j=1}^{n} u_{ij}(\overline{\mathbf{q}})^2\right] + \sum_{j=1}^{n_2} \mathbb{E}\left[\sum_{i=1}^{n} u_{ij}(\overline{\mathbf{q}})^2\right] \\ =& \sum_{i=1}^{n_1} \mathbb{E}\left[\sum_{j=1}^{n} u_{ij}(\overline{\mathbf{q}})\right] + \sum_{j=1}^{n_2} \mathbb{E}\left[\sum_{i=1}^{n} u_{ij}(\overline{\mathbf{q}})\right] \\ =& \sum_{i=1}^{n_1} \mathbb{E}\left[\sum_{j=1}^{n} s_{ij}(\overline{\mathbf{q}}) - \overline{a}_{ij}\right] + \sum_{j=1}^{n_2} \mathbb{E}\left[\sum_{i=1}^{n} s_{ij}(\overline{\mathbf{q}}) - \overline{a}_{ij}\right] \\ =& (n_1 + n_2)\epsilon \end{aligned}$$

Using triangle inequality, we get that

$$\begin{aligned} \|4n^2\overline{\mathbf{q}}_{\perp} + 4\mathcal{A}\hat{\mathbb{1}}\| \leq & 4n^2\|\overline{\mathbf{q}}_{\perp}\| + 4|\mathcal{A}|\|\hat{\mathbb{1}}\| \\ \leq & 4n^2\|\overline{\mathbf{q}}_{\perp}\| + 4|\mathcal{A}|n \end{aligned}$$

where

$$\begin{aligned} |\mathcal{A}| \leq & \left(\sum_{i=1}^{n_1} \left|\left\langle \overline{\mathbf{q}}_{\perp}, \mathbf{e}^{(i)} \right\rangle\right| + \sum_{j=1}^{n_2} \left|\left\langle \overline{\mathbf{q}}_{\perp}, e^{(i)} \right\rangle\right|\right) \\ \leq & \|\overline{\mathbf{q}}_{\perp}\|(n_1 + n_2)\sqrt{n} \qquad \leq \|\overline{\mathbf{q}}_{\perp}\|n^{1.5}. \end{aligned}$$

Thus, $\mathcal{T}_4$ in (18) can be upper bounded as

$$\begin{aligned} \mathcal{T}_4 \leq & 4n^2(1 + \sqrt{n})\sqrt{\epsilon}\sqrt{\mathbb{E}\left[\|\overline{\mathbf{q}}_{\perp}\|^2\right]}\sqrt{(n_1 + n_2)} \\ \leq & 4n^2(1 + \sqrt{n})\sqrt{\epsilon}M_2\sqrt{(n_1 + n_2)} \end{aligned} \tag{19}$$

where the last inequality follows from state space collapse in Proposition 2. Using $A = n + n_1, B = n + n_2, C = 1$ in the bounds of $\mathcal{T}_1, \mathcal{T}_2, \mathcal{T}_3$, in (9),(10),(11) along with (19), we get

$$\begin{aligned} & 2\epsilon(n - n_2)\mathbb{E}\left[\sum_{i=1}^{n_1}\sum_{j=1}^{n} \overline{q}_{ij}\right] + 2\epsilon(n - n_1)\mathbb{E}\left[\sum_{j=1}^{n_2}\sum_{i=1}^{n} \overline{q}_{ij}\right] \\ \leq & (n + n_1 - 1)\sum_{i=1}^{n_1}\sum_{j=1}^{n} \sigma_{ij}^2 + (n + n_2 - 1)\sum_{j=1}^{n_2}\sum_{i=1}^{n} \sigma_{ij}^2 \\ & + \epsilon^2(nn_2 + nn_2 - 2n_1n_2) + \epsilon(n_1 + n_2)^2 \\ & + \sqrt{\epsilon}\sqrt{M_2(n_1 + n_2)2n^2(1 + 2n(n_1 + n_2))} \end{aligned}$$

This proves the first part of the theorem. The heavy traffic result follows from taking the limit as $\epsilon \downarrow 0$ and using the universal lower bound in Proposition 1. For any vector $\mathbf{x}$ and for $i > n_1$ and $j > n_2$, since $x_{\| ij} = 0$, $x_{ij} = x_{\perp ij}$ and so, $|x_{ij}| \leq \|\mathbf{x}_{\perp}\|$. Therefore, again using the state space collapse result, we have for $i > n_1$ and $j > n_2$,

$$\begin{aligned} \lim_{\epsilon \to 0} \epsilon\mathbb{E}\left[\overline{q}_{ij}\right] \leq & \lim_{\epsilon \to 0} \epsilon\mathbb{E}\left[\|\overline{\mathbf{q}}_{\perp}\|\right] \\ \leq & \lim_{\epsilon \to 0} \epsilon M_1 \qquad = \quad 0. \end{aligned}$$

□

The key step in such a proof based on drift of a quadratic function is to bound the cross terms between unused service and queue lengths as in the term $\mathcal{T}_4$. State space collapse plays an important role in obtaining a tight bound on this terms. In fact, in the proof here, we use state space collapse primarily to bound the term $\mathcal{T}_4$. We picked the function V_4 so that the fourth term $\mathcal{T}_4$ can be bounded by a $o(1/\epsilon)$ term as above using state space collapse. Typically, in heavy traffic proofs for various systems in the literature, [5, 8], the Lyapunov function is such that, when the queue length vector $\mathbf{q}$ is inside the region of state space collapse for that system (i.e., the cone $\mathcal{K}_{n_1 n_2}$ here), the term analogous to $\mathcal{T}_4$ is exactly 0. This fact, in addition to the state space collapse moment bounds on $\mathbf{q}_{\perp}$ when the queue lengths vector is not inside the region of collapse is used to obtain exact characterization of queue length in heavy traffic bounds. However, here, if the queue length vector $\mathbf{q}$ is inside the cone $\mathcal{K}_{n_1 n_2}$, we have that $\mathbf{q}_{\perp} = 0$ and so, the term $\mathcal{T}_4 \leq 0$ from (16). Since we only have $\mathcal{T}_4 \leq 0$ instead of $\mathcal{T}_4 = 0$, we obtain an upper bound and don't have an exact characterization. However, the upper bound we obtain is sufficient to show optimal queue length scaling under MaxWeight algorithm when at most a fraction of input and output ports are saturated.

4. DIFFERENT RATES OF SATURATION

In [8] as well as in the previous section, it is assumed that all the ports that are saturated, saturate at the same rate, i.e., the total arrival rate for each saturating port (row or column) is $1-\epsilon$. In this section, we consider the switch system when all ports are saturated, but at different rates. We consider the switch operating under the MaxWeight algorithm with an i.i.d arrival process as described in Section 2.1. The arrival rate is $\boldsymbol{\lambda}^\epsilon = \boldsymbol{\nu} - \epsilon \boldsymbol{k}$, where $\boldsymbol{k} \in \mathbb{R}_+^{n^2}$ and $\boldsymbol{\nu}$ is an arrival rate on the boundary of the capacity region $\mathcal{C}$ such that all the input and output ports are saturated and $\nu_{ij} > 0$ for all i,j. In other words, denoting the face $\mathcal{F}_{nn}$ by $\mathcal{F}^*$, we have that $\boldsymbol{\nu} \in \mathcal{F}^*$.

Define $\kappa_i(\boldsymbol{k}) = \sum_j k_{ij}$ and $\widetilde{\kappa}_j(\boldsymbol{k}) = \sum_i k_{ij}$. For simplicity of notation, we will suppress the dependence on $\boldsymbol{k}$. Note that $\sum_i \kappa_i = \sum_j \widetilde{\kappa}_j$. The load of each system is then $(1 - \epsilon \min_{i,j}\{\kappa_i, \widetilde{\kappa}_j\})$. Let $\kappa_{avg} \triangleq \sum_i \kappa_i/n = \sum_j \widetilde{\kappa}_j/n$, $\kappa_{\min} = \min_i \kappa_i$, $\widetilde{\kappa}_{\min} = \min_j \widetilde{\kappa}_j$ and similarly $\kappa_{\max}, \widetilde{\kappa}_{\max}$. Note that in [8], the setting when $\boldsymbol{k} = \boldsymbol{\nu}$, is studied, in which case $\kappa_i = 1$ and $\widetilde{\kappa_j} = 1$ for all i,j. In order to make sure that the heavy traffic parameter ϵ is comparable to this case, we assume without loss of generality that $\kappa_{avg} = 1$. In other words, we normalize the vector $\boldsymbol{k}$ by assuming that $\langle \boldsymbol{k}, \mathbf{1}\rangle = n$. Thus the total arrival rate to the switch is $n(1-\epsilon)$, which is same as in the uniform saturation case studied in [8]. Such a normalized $\boldsymbol{k}$ is called the saturation rate vector. We will study the switch in the heavy traffic limit as $\epsilon \downarrow 0$. As in Section 3, we will present a universal lower bound followed by state space collapse and an upper bound under the MaxWeight algorithm. More over, here we present an exact expression for a linear combination of queue lengths under the MaxWeight algorithm,

4.1 Universal Lower Bound

We first present a few universal lower bounds. We omit the proof, which is similar to the proof of Proposition 1 and follows from the Kingman bound in Lemma 1.

PROPOSITION 3. *Consider a set of switch systems with the arrival processes $\mathbf{a}^{(\epsilon)}(t)$ described in Section 2.1, parameterized by $0 < \epsilon < 1$, such that the mean arrival rate vector is $\boldsymbol{\lambda}^\epsilon = \boldsymbol{\nu} - \epsilon\boldsymbol{k}$ for some $\boldsymbol{\nu} \in \mathcal{F}^*$ and $\boldsymbol{k} \in \mathbb{R}_+^{n^2}$ is the normalized saturation rate vector so that $\langle \boldsymbol{k}, \mathbf{1}\rangle = n$. The variance of the arrival process is $\left(\boldsymbol{\sigma}^{(\epsilon)}\right)^2$. For each $0 < \epsilon < 1$, fix any scheduling policy under which the switch is stable and the queue lengths process $\mathbf{q}^{(\epsilon)}(t)$ converges in distribution to a steady state random vector $\overline{\mathbf{q}}^{(\epsilon)}$. Then, for each of these systems, the steady state queue lengths are lower bounded by*

$$\mathbb{E}\left[\sum_j \overline{q}_{ij}^{(\epsilon)}\right] \geq \frac{\sum_j \left(\sigma_{ij}^{(\epsilon)}\right)^2}{2\epsilon\kappa_i} - \frac{1-\kappa_i\epsilon}{2} \text{ for all } i$$

$$\mathbb{E}\left[\sum_i \overline{q}_{ij}^{(\epsilon)}\right] \geq \frac{\sum_i \left(\sigma_{ij}^{(\epsilon)}\right)^2}{2\epsilon\widetilde{\kappa}_j} - \frac{1-\widetilde{\kappa}_j\epsilon}{2} \text{ for all } j.$$

Consequently, we have that

$$\mathbb{E}\left[\sum_{ij} \overline{q}_{ij}^{(\epsilon)}\right] \geq \frac{1}{2\epsilon} \max\left\{\sum_{ij} \frac{\left(\sigma_{ij}^{(\epsilon)}\right)^2}{\kappa_i}, \sum_{ij} \frac{\left(\sigma_{ij}^{(\epsilon)}\right)^2}{\widetilde{\kappa}_j}\right\} - \frac{n(1-\epsilon)}{2} \text{ and}$$

$$\mathbb{E}\left[\sum_{ij} \overline{q}_{ij}^{(\epsilon)}(\kappa_i + \widetilde{\kappa}_j)\right] \geq \frac{\left\|\boldsymbol{\sigma}_{ij}^{(\epsilon)}\right\|^2}{\epsilon} - n + \frac{\epsilon}{2}\left(\sum_i \kappa_i^2 + \sum_j \widetilde{\kappa}_j\right)$$

Therefore, in the heavy-traffic limit as $\epsilon \downarrow 0$, if $\left(\boldsymbol{\sigma}^{(\epsilon)}\right)^2 \to \boldsymbol{\sigma}^2$, we have

$$\liminf_{\epsilon\downarrow 0} \epsilon\mathbb{E}\left[\sum_{ij} \overline{q}_{ij}^{(\epsilon)}\right] \geq \frac{1}{2} \max\left\{\sum_{ij} \frac{\left(\sigma_{ij}^{(\epsilon)}\right)^2}{\kappa_i}, \sum_{ij} \frac{\left(\sigma_{ij}^{(\epsilon)}\right)^2}{\widetilde{\kappa}_j}\right\} \text{ and}$$

$$\liminf_{\epsilon\downarrow 0} \epsilon\mathbb{E}\left[\sum_{ij} \overline{q}_{ij}^{(\epsilon)}(\kappa_i + \widetilde{\kappa}_j)\right] \geq \left\|\boldsymbol{\sigma}_{ij}^{(\epsilon)}\right\|^2.$$

4.2 State Space Collapse under MaxWeight policy

Since the heavy traffic rate vector $\boldsymbol{\nu}$ is on the face $\mathcal{F}^*$, the state space in the heavy traffic collapses to the cone $\mathcal{K}^*$ spanned by the $2n$ vectors $\{\mathbf{e}^{(i)}\forall i\} \cup \{\widetilde{\mathbf{e}}^{(j)}\forall j\}$. Using the notation defined in Section 3.2, this cone is denoted by $\mathcal{K}_{nn}$. We use $\mathcal{K}^*$ as a shorthand to this cone. The projection of a vector $\mathbf{x}$ onto this cone is $\mathbf{x}_{\|*}$ and the perpendicular component is $\mathbf{x}_{\perp *}$. In this use we use $\mathbf{x}_{\|}$ and $\mathbf{x}_{\perp}$ as shorthand for these to components respectively. We now state the state space collapse result. We again omit the proof because it is very similar to that of Proposition 2, but with the understanding that the symbols $\mathbf{q}_{\|}$ and $\mathbf{q}_{\perp}$ are now redefined.

PROPOSITION 4. *Consider a set of switch systems operating under the MaxWeight scheduling algorithm, with the arrival processes $\mathbf{a}^{(\epsilon)}(t)$ described in Section 2.1, parameterized by $0 < \epsilon < 1$, such that the mean arrival rate vector is $\boldsymbol{\lambda}^\epsilon = \boldsymbol{\nu} - \epsilon\boldsymbol{k}$ for some $\boldsymbol{\nu} \in \mathcal{F}^*$, $\nu_{\min} > 0$ and $\boldsymbol{k} \in \mathbb{R}_+^{n^2}$ is the normalized saturation rate vector so that $\langle \boldsymbol{k}, \mathbf{1}\rangle = n$. Let the variance $\left(\boldsymbol{\sigma}^{(\epsilon)}\right)^2$ of the arrival process be such that $\|\boldsymbol{\sigma}^{(\epsilon)}\|^2 \leq \widetilde{\sigma}^2$ for some $\widetilde{\sigma}^2$ not dependent on ϵ. Let $\mathbf{q}^{(\epsilon)}(t)$ denote the queue lengths process of each system, which is positive recurrent. Therefore, the process $\mathbf{q}^{(\epsilon)}(t)$ converges to a steady state random vector in distribution, which we denote by $\overline{\mathbf{q}}^{(\epsilon)}$. Then, for each system with $0 < \epsilon \leq \nu_{\min}/2\|\boldsymbol{k}\|$, the steady state queue lengths vector satisfies*

$$\mathbb{E}\left[\|\overline{\mathbf{q}}_{\perp}^{(\epsilon)}\|^r\right] \leq (M_r')^r \;\; \forall r \in \{1,2,\ldots\},$$

where M_r' is independent of ϵ.

4.3 Queue length bounds under the MaxWeight policy

We now state the main result obtaining an exact expression for a linear combination of heavy traffic scaled queue lengths.

THEOREM 2. *Consider the set of switch systems operating under the MaxWeight algorithm, parameterized by $0 <$*

$\epsilon < 1$ *as described in Proposition 2. Then, for each system with* $0 < \epsilon \leq \nu_{\min}/2\|\boldsymbol{k}\|$*, the steady state queue lengths vector satisfies*

$$\left(1-\frac{1}{2n}\right)\frac{\left\|\boldsymbol{\sigma}^{(\epsilon)}\right\|^2}{\epsilon}-B_2(\epsilon,n)$$
$$\leq \mathbb{E}\left[\sum_{ij}\overline{q}_{ij}^{(\epsilon)}(\kappa_i+\widetilde{\kappa}_j-1)\right] \leq \left(1-\frac{1}{2n}\right)\frac{\left\|\boldsymbol{\sigma}^{(\epsilon)}\right\|^2}{\epsilon}+B_3(\epsilon,n),$$

where $B_2(\epsilon,n)$ *and* $B_3(\epsilon,n)$ *are* $o(1/\epsilon)$*. Therefore, in the heavy traffic limit as* $\epsilon \downarrow 0$*, if* $\left(\boldsymbol{\sigma}^{(\epsilon)}\right)^2 \to \boldsymbol{\sigma}^2$*, we have*

$$\lim_{\epsilon\downarrow 0}\epsilon\mathbb{E}\left[\sum_{ij}\overline{q}_{ij}^{(\epsilon)}(\kappa_i+\widetilde{\kappa}_j-1)\right] = \left(1-\frac{1}{2n}\right)\|\boldsymbol{\sigma}\|^2.$$

PROOF. The proof is based on setting the drift of the following function to 0 in steady state.

$$V_5(\mathbf{q}) \triangleq \sum_i\left(\sum_j q_{ij}\right)^2+\sum_j\left(\sum_i q_{ij}\right)^2-\frac{1}{n}\left(\sum_{ij} q_{ij}\right)^2.$$

Since the proof is very similar to the proof of Theorem 1 in [8], we omit it here. The main difference how ever, is that here we have a bound on $\mathbb{E}\left[\sum_{ij}\overline{q}_{ij}^{(\epsilon)}(\kappa_i+\widetilde{\kappa}_j-1)\right]$ instead of the usual bound on $\mathbb{E}\left[\sum_{ij}\overline{q}_{ij}^{(\epsilon)}\right]$. We present a brief discussion her to illustrate this difference. By expanding all the terms after setting $\mathbb{E}[\Delta V_5(\overline{\mathbf{q}})]=0$, we get an expression of the form

$$\mathcal{T}_1' = \mathcal{T}_2'+\mathcal{T}_3'+\mathcal{T}_4',$$

where the terms $\mathcal{T}_1',\mathcal{T}_2',\mathcal{T}_3',\mathcal{T}_4'$ are analogous to $\mathcal{T}_1,\mathcal{T}_2,\mathcal{T}_3,\mathcal{T}_4$ in the proof of Theorem 1 (and identical to $\mathcal{T}_1,\mathcal{T}_2,\mathcal{T}_3,\mathcal{T}_4$ in the proof of Theorem 1 in [8]). Let us look at the term $\mathcal{T}_1'$.

$$\begin{aligned}
\mathcal{T}_1' =& 2\mathbb{E}\left[\sum_i\left(\sum_j\overline{q}_{ij}\right)\left(\sum_{j'}(s_{ij'}(\overline{\mathbf{q}})-\overline{a}_{ij'})\right)\right]\\
&+2\mathbb{E}\left[\sum_j\left(\sum_i\overline{q}_{ij}\right)\left(\sum_{i'}(s_{i'j}(\overline{\mathbf{q}})-\overline{a}_{i'j})\right)\right]\\
&-\frac{2}{n}\mathbb{E}\left[\left(\sum_{ij}\overline{q}_{ij}\right)\left(\sum_{i'j'}(s_{i'j'}(\overline{\mathbf{q}})-\overline{a}_{i'j'})\right)\right]\\
\overset{(a)}{=}&2\mathbb{E}\left[\sum_i\left(\sum_j\overline{q}_{ij}\right)\left(1-\sum_{j'}\lambda_{ij'}\right)\right]\\
&+2\mathbb{E}\left[\sum_j\left(\sum_i\overline{q}_{ij}\right)\left(1-\sum_{i'}\lambda_{i'j}\right)\right]\\
&-\frac{2}{n}\mathbb{E}\left[\left(\sum_{ij}\overline{q}_{ij}\right)\left(n-\sum_{i'j'}\lambda_{i'j'}\right)\right]\\
=&2\mathbb{E}\left[\sum_i\epsilon\kappa_i\left(\sum_j\overline{q}_{ij}\right)\right]+2\mathbb{E}\left[\sum_j\epsilon\widetilde{\kappa}_j\left(\sum_i\overline{q}_{ij}\right)\right]\\
&-\frac{2}{n}\mathbb{E}\left[\epsilon\left(\sum_{ij}\overline{q}_{ij}\right)\left(\sum_i\kappa_i\right)\right]\\
=&2\epsilon\mathbb{E}\left[\sum_{ij}\overline{q}_{ij}(\kappa_i+\widetilde{\kappa}_j-\kappa_{avg})\right],
\end{aligned}$$

where (a) follows from the fact that $\mathbf{s}\in\mathcal{S}^*$ and independence of the arrival process and the current queue length. Thus, we have

$$2\epsilon\mathbb{E}\left[\sum_{ij}\overline{q}_{ij}(\kappa_i+\widetilde{\kappa}_j-1)\right] = \mathcal{T}_2+\mathcal{T}_3+\mathcal{T}_4.$$

The theorem then follows from bounding the terms $\mathcal{T}_2',\mathcal{T}_3',\mathcal{T}_4'$ similar to Theorem 1. □

The following corollary shows that the above theorem implies optimal queue length scaling as a function of the switch size under certain conditions on the saturation rate vector $\boldsymbol{k}$. This considerably generalizes the result in [8].

COROLLARY 2. *Consider the set of switch systems operating under the MaxWeight algorithm described in Theorem 2. Suppose that the saturation rate vector* $\boldsymbol{k}$ *is such that* $\kappa_i(\boldsymbol{k})+\widetilde{\kappa}_j(\boldsymbol{k}) \geq 1$ *for all* i,j*, then the steady state queue lengths satisfy*

$$\frac{(1-\frac{1}{2n})}{\kappa_{\max}+\widetilde{\kappa}_{\max}-1}\frac{\left\|\boldsymbol{\sigma}^{(\epsilon)}\right\|^2}{\epsilon}-\frac{B_2(\epsilon,n)}{\kappa_{\max}+\widetilde{\kappa}_{\max}-1}$$
$$\leq \mathbb{E}\left[\sum_{ij}\overline{q}_{ij}^{(\epsilon)}\right] \leq \frac{(1-\frac{1}{2n})}{\kappa_{\min}+\widetilde{\kappa}_{\min}-1}\frac{\left\|\boldsymbol{\sigma}^{(\epsilon)}\right\|^2}{\epsilon}+\frac{B_3(\epsilon,n)}{\kappa_{\min}+\widetilde{\kappa}_{\min}-1}.$$

Therefore, in the heavy traffic limit as $\epsilon\downarrow 0$*, if* $\left(\boldsymbol{\sigma}^{(\epsilon)}\right)^2 \to \boldsymbol{\sigma}^2$*, we have*

$$\left(1-\frac{1}{2n}\right)\frac{\|\boldsymbol{\sigma}\|^2}{\kappa_{\max}+\widetilde{\kappa}_{\max}-1}$$
$$\leq \lim_{\epsilon\downarrow 0}\epsilon\mathbb{E}\left[\sum_{ij}\overline{q}_{ij}^{(\epsilon)}\right] \leq \left(1-\frac{1}{2n}\right)\frac{\|\boldsymbol{\sigma}\|^2}{\kappa_{\min}+\widetilde{\kappa}_{\min}-1}.$$

The corollary directly follows from the theorem. From Proposition 3, we have that under any scheduling policy,

$$\liminf_{\epsilon\downarrow 0}\epsilon\mathbb{E}\left[\sum_{ij}\overline{q}_{ij}^{(\epsilon)}\right] \geq \frac{\|\boldsymbol{\sigma}\|^2}{2}\max\left\{\frac{1}{\kappa_{\max}},\frac{1}{\widetilde{\kappa}_{\max}}\right\} \geq \frac{\|\boldsymbol{\sigma}\|^2}{2(\kappa_{\max}+\widetilde{\kappa}_{\max})}.$$

Thus, we have optimal heavy traffic scaling of sum queue length under the MaxWeight algorithm as long as the saturation rate is such that $(\kappa_{\min}+\widetilde{\kappa}_{\min}-1)$ is within a constant factor of $(\kappa_{\max}+\widetilde{\kappa}_{\max})$.

5. CONCLUSION

We consider the heavy-traffic queue length behavior in an input queued switch operating under the MaxWeight algorithm. It was recently shown in [8] that, in the heavy-traffic regime, the queue length scales optimally with the size of the switch when all the ports in the switch saturate at the same rate. In this paper, we considered two different cases. We first considered an incompletely saturated switch, where at most a fraction of the input ports as well at most a fraction of the output ports are saturated, and show optimal queue length scaling under the MaxWeight policy. We then consider a completely saturated switch, but when different ports saturate at different rates. We obtained an exact heavy traffic characterization of a linear combination of queue lengths and show that under some assumptions on the rates of saturation, MaxWeight algorithm achieves optimal scaling of sum queue lengths in heavy traffic.

The study of incompletely and nonuniformly saturated switches in this paper points out two additional open problems, in addition to the ones identified in [8].

- When a subset of ports are saturated, we obtain queue length bounds under the MaxWeight algorithm. While the bounds hold generally, in order to show optimal queue length scaling, we assume that at most a fraction of the ports are saturated. In addition to this, we have shown optimal queue length scaling when $(n-1)$ ports are saturated, a result not presented here due to space constraints. The more general case when $n-o(n)$ ports are saturated is still open.

- For the case when the rates of saturation are different, we obtain an exact expression for the heavy traffic limit of certain linear function of queue lengths under the MaxWeight algorithm. We have used this result to show optimal scaling of sum queue lengths in heavy traffic, under an assumption on the rates of saturation. Removing this assumption is another open problem.

6. ACKNOWLEDGEMENTS

We thank Prof. Alexander Stolyar and Prof. Michael Harrison for suggesting us the question about heavy traffic queue length behavior in a switch when different ports saturate at different rates. This research was supported by NSF Grants CNS-1161404 and ECCS-1202065.

References

[1] M. Alizadeh, S. Yang, M. Sharif, S. Katti, N. McKeown, B. Prabhakar, and S. Shenker. pFabric: Minimal near-optimal datacenter transport. In *Proceedings of the ACM SIGCOMM 2013 Conference on SIGCOMM*, SIGCOMM '13, pages 435–446, New York, NY, USA, 2013. ACM.

[2] M. Andrews, K. Jung, and A. Stolyar. Stability of the max-weight routing and scheduling protocol in dynamic networks and at critical loads. In *Proceedings of the Thirty-ninth Annual ACM Symposium on Theory of Computing*, STOC '07, pages 145–154, 2007.

[3] D. Bertsimas, D. Gamarnik, and J. N. Tsitsiklis. Performance of multiclass markovian queueing networks via piecewise linear Lyapunov functions. *Ann. Appl. Probab.*, 11(4):1384–1428, 11 2001.

[4] T. Bonald and A. Proutiere. Insensitivity in processor-sharing networks. *Performance Evaluation*, 49(1):193–209, 2002.

[5] A. Eryilmaz and R. Srikant. Asymptotically tight steady-state queue length bounds implied by drift conditions. *Queueing Systems*, 72(3-4):311–359, 2012.

[6] B. Hajek. Hitting-time and occupation-time bounds implied by drift analysis with applications. *Advances in Applied Probability*, pages 502–525, 1982.

[7] W. N. Kang and R. J. Williams. Diffusion approximation for an input-queued packet switch operating under a maximum weight algorithm. *Stochastic Systems*, 2012.

[8] S. T. Maguluri and R. Srikant. Heavy-traffic behavior of the maxweight algorithm in a switch with uniform traffic, 2015. arxiv preprint http://arxiv.org/abs/1503.05872.

[9] N. McKeown, V. Anantharam, and J. Walrand. Achieving 100% throughput in an input queued switch. In *Proceedings of IEEE INFOCOM*, pages 296–302, 1996.

[10] M. J. Neely, E. Modiano, and Y.-S. Cheng. Logarithmic delay for n× n packet switches under the crossbar constraint. *IEEE/ACM Transactions on Networking*, 15(3):657–668, 2007.

[11] J. Perry, A. Ousterhout, H. Balakrishnan, D. Shah, and H. Fugal. Fastpass: A centralized "zero-queue" datacenter network. In *Proceedings of the 2014 ACM Conference on SIGCOMM*, SIGCOMM '14, pages 307–318, New York, NY, USA, 2014. ACM.

[12] D. Shah, J. Tsitsiklis, and Y. Zhong. Optimal scaling of average queue sizes in an input-queued switch: an open problem. *Queueing Systems*, 68(3-4):375–384, 2011.

[13] D. Shah, J. N. Tsitsiklis, and Y. Zhong. On queue-size scaling for input-queued switches, 2015. arxiv preprint http://arxiv.org/abs/1405.4764.

[14] D. Shah, N. S. Walton, and Y. Zhong. Optimal queue-size scaling in switched networks. *Ann. Appl. Probab.*, 24(6):2207–2245, 12 2014.

[15] D. Shah and D. Wischik. Switched networks with maximum weight policies: Fluid approximation and multiplicative state space collapse. *The Annals of Applied Probability*, 22(1):70–127, 2012.

[16] R. Singh and A. Stolyar. Maxweight scheduling: Asymptotic behavior of unscaled queue-differentials in heavy traffic. *arXiv preprint arXiv:1502.03793*, 2015.

[17] R. Srikant and L. Ying. *Communication Networks: An Optimization, Control and Stochastic Networks Perspective.* Cambridge University Press, 2014.

[18] A. L. Stolyar. Maxweight scheduling in a generalized switch: State space collapse and workload minimization in heavy traffic. *Annals of Applied Probability*, pages 1–53, 2004.

[19] L. Tassiulas and A. Ephremides. Stability properties of constrained queueing systems and scheduling policies for maximum throughput in multihop radio networks. *IEEE Transactions on Automatic Control*, 37(12):1936–1948, 1992.

[20] T. Weller and B. Hajek. Scheduling nonuniform traffic in a packet-switching system with small propagation delay. *Networking, IEEE/ACM Transactions on*, 5(6):813–823, 1997.

A Necessary and Sufficient Condition for Throughput Scalability of Fork and Join Networks with Blocking

Yun Zeng
The Ohio State University
1971 Neil Ave
Columbus, OH
zeng.153@osu.edu

Augustin Chaintreau
Columbia University
1214 Amsterdam Ave
New York, NY
augustin@cs.columbia.edu

Don Towsley
University of Massachusetts
140 Governors Drive
Amherst, MA
towsley@cs.umass.edu

Cathy H. Xia
The Ohio State University
1971 Neil Ave
Columbus, OH
xia.52@osu.edu

ABSTRACT

Due to emerging applications such as cloud computing and big data analytics, modern information processing systems are growing increasingly large and complex. A critical issue concerns the throughput performance as the system grows in size. This paper models distributed information processing systems as fork and join queueing networks with blocking. We identify necessary and sufficient conditions for throughput scalability of such fork and join networks as they grow in size. Previous studies have either focused on special structured networks such as tandem or tree networks, or provided only necessary conditions for throughput scalability. In this paper, we show that such necessary conditions are not sufficient. We present a key topological concept called "minimum level" of the underlying graph, and develop lower and upper bounds for the throughput of arbitrary FJQN/Bs. The bounds depend on network degree, minimum level, deterministic cycle time, buffer sizes, and service time distributions, but not on network size. We show that level-boundedness and degree-boundedness are necessary and sufficient conditions to guarantee that the throughput of an FJQN/B is bounded away from zero as network size goes to infinity.

CCS Concepts

•**Networks** → **Network performance analysis;** *Topology analysis and generation;*

Keywords

Fork/join, queueing network, scalability, throughput, performance bound

SIGMETRICS '16, June 14 - 18, 2016, Antibes Juan-Les-Pins, France

ISBN 978-1-4503-4266-7/16/06...$15.00

DOI: http://dx.doi.org/10.1145/2896377.2901470

1. INTRODUCTION

Parallelism is widely implemented in modern computer and manufacturing systems to achieve high performance. In addition to applications to manufacturing systems such as assembly lines and supply chains, parallelism has become an indispensable method to analyze big data in distributed systems that would otherwise be inefficient or even infeasible. For instance, Google's MapReduce-based computing framework can sort one peta-byte data (10 trillion 100-byte records) in 33 minutes through a high degree of parallelism (on 8000 computers) [9]. Today, parallelism can be found in distributed stream processing [18], in query processing over distributed databases [12], and in many other distributed frameworks. Emerging applications such as cloud computing and big data analytics have driven these various systems to increase in size and scale. As the sizes of these systems continue to grow, it becomes increasingly important to understand how parallelism will influence throughput. Since experimentally constructing a large-scale parallel processing system and testing its performance may consume a tremendous amount of time and effort, theoretical guidance on the scaling behavior is of vital importance.

The above various parallel processing systems have been frequently modeled as Fork-Join Queueing Networks with Blocking (FJQN/Bs). A fork operation corresponds to a job being partitioned into multiple subtasks to be executed in parallel, whereas a join operation corresponds to the merging of outputs of subtasks to deliver a final product. Since the join operation requires the completion of a set of subtasks, it introduces a synchronization point. The outputs of subtasks that complete before synchronization are queued in buffers. Since typically all buffers are finite in capacity, operations can be blocked when one or more of the related buffers are filled. Different blocking mechanisms such as blocking before service, and blocking after service, have been introduced depending on the application [11]. FJQN/B models were introduced in the 80's motivated by manufacturing systems [1, 17]. Recent advances in cloud computing and distributed file systems have led to a renewed interest in these models.

The dynamics of an FJQN/B can be described using max-plus algebra [15]. However, exact analyses of such models have proven to be challenging due to the complexity introduced by synchronization and blocking. As recently surveyed in [21], a large body of published research focuses on performance bounds [5] or approximation techniques [22, 19] for various metrics (such as mean queue length, mean response time, etc). Notably, [20] provides a computational method that produces a tight upper bound for the throughput using probability mass fitting and critical path analysis. However, the method relies on discretization steps and critical path computation, which is impractical for large-scale networks. Other researchers study performance properties such as stability [3], duality and reversibility [10], and stochastic comparison results [4].

In this paper, we focus on the scaling properties of an FJQN/B as it grows in size. We say that a network is *throughput scalable* if its throughput is bounded from below by a positive constant independent of network size. In other words, throughput does not decrease to zero as the size of the network goes to infinity. Generally speaking, throughput can be limited by multiple factors, including network topology, processing speed, buffering/storage capacity, and the coordination of inputs and outputs between various processing nodes. These factors may be tolerable in a small network, but can accumulate and constrain the throughput of a large network. Here we focus on the impact of network topology and are concerned with the possible throughput degradation of an FJQN/B as it increases in size.

Research on the scaling properties of FJQN/Bs is limited but gaining increasing attention. Previous studies have mostly focused on specially structured networks. [16] shows that the throughput of a tandem queueing network with blocking is scalable. The author provides a positive lower bound on the system throughput independent of the network size and number of customers. [7] shows that the throughput of a tree-structured queueing network with blocking is scalable under the condition that the out-degree of the tree is upper bounded. [8] establishes a tight condition for the scalability of pattern grids where the precedence constraints of jobs are reproduced at every position of a lattice. All these studies provide *sufficient* conditions for various specially structured networks to be throughput scalable. The question remains how to guarantee the throughput scalability of a generally structured fork-join network with no regular topological features. In [23], the authors provide several *necessary* conditions for the throughput of a generally structured FJQN/B network to be scalable. Although these conditions are shown to be necessary, it is not clear whether they are sufficient to ensure throughput scalability. Such knowledge is essential in practice to construct scalability-guaranteed parallel processing systems with arbitrary and complex structures.

In this paper, we show that the necessary conditions in [23] are NOT sufficient. A counter example is given in Section 5.3. Instead, we present necessary and sufficient conditions on the throughput scalability of an FJQN/B. The network only needs to be directed, connected, and deadlock-free, with arbitrary topology and initial number of jobs in buffers. We analyze an infinite sequence of FJQN/Bs following which the individual FJQN/B can grow in size. We show that the throughput of every given network in the sequence is lower bounded by a strictly positive constant, and hence the sequence is throughput scalable, when the conditions are satisfied.

The main contributions of this paper include:

- We introduce a topological parameter for an FJQN/B, *minimum level*, which is determined by the optimal topological labelling on a circuit-free model variant of the FJQN/B. A topological labelling is a mapping of the nodes to integer values that are strictly increasing along the direction of arcs. The mapping that gives the minimum differences between the labels of neighboring nodes is called the optimal topological labelling, and the corresponding minimum difference is called the minimum level. The minimum level on the circuit-free variant is shown closely related to the cycle time on a deterministic non-blocking model variant of the FJQN/B.
- For any given FJQN/B with a finite number of nodes, we derive closed-form lower and upper bounds on the system throughput. The lower bound is achieved through an application of theory of last passage percolation and probability analysis; the upper bound is given by fork-join mechanism and the inverse of deterministic cycle time [2]. These bounds are functions of network degree, minimum level, deterministic cycle time, buffer sizes, and service time distributions. Critically, the bounds are independent of network size.
- We prove that, under mild service time assumptions, a sequence of FJQN/Bs is throughput scalable if and only if it is *level-bounded* and *degree-bounded*, i.e. the minimum level and the network degree of every network in the sequence is bounded from above.

The rest of this paper is organized as follows. Section 2 establishes the model and presents preliminaries on the network throughput. Section 3 introduces two variants of the network model with the concepts of minimum level and deterministic cycle time. Section 4 focuses on constructing upper and lower bounds for the throughput of any given FJQN/B. The necessary and sufficient conditions on throughput scalability is presented in Section 5. Section 6 concludes the research.

2. MODEL AND PRELIMINARIES

An FJQN/B is denoted as $N = (V, E, B)$, where V is a set of nodes, E is a set of directed arcs, and B is a set of buffer sizes on the arcs. Let (u, v) be the arc from node u to node v and let $B^{(u,v)}$ be the buffer size on arc (u, v). For any given FJQN/B, we assume $|V|$ is finite and the buffer sizes are positive and upper bounded. One example of an FJQN/B is given in Figure 1.

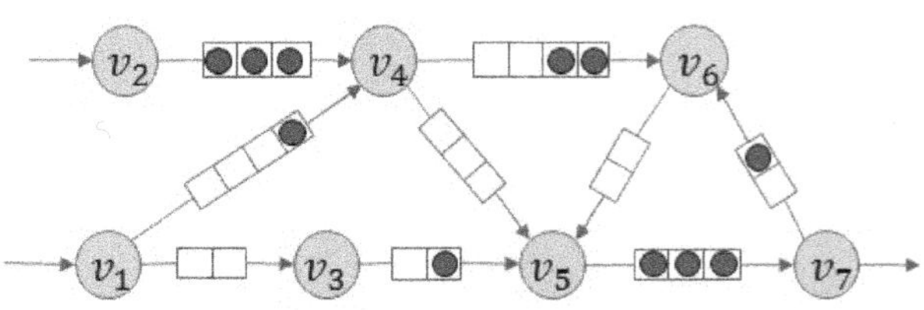

Figure 1: Example of FJQN/B. Blocked: v_2, v_5; **starved:** v_3, v_5

Each node $v \in V$ represents a server with a First Come First Serve (FCFS) scheduling policy. An FJQN/B has the following fork-join feature: each service consumes exactly one job from every upstream buffer and places exactly one job in every downstream buffer. In this paper, we assume that every server implement a blocking before service mechanism. An idle server starts processing only when there is at least one job in every upstream buffer and space in every downstream buffer for at least one job; otherwise, the server is blocked/starved (Figure 1) and does not work on any job. While being processed, jobs remain in the upstream buffers. As soon as processing is complete, one job is removed from each upstream buffer and one job is added to each downstream buffer.

Define the degree of a node v, denoted as $d(v)$, to be the total number of arcs connected to that node. We refer to the number of outgoing arcs from a node as the node's out-degree and to the number of incoming arcs as its in-degree. The network degree is defined as $D(N) = \max\{d(v)|v \in V\}$.

Nodes with no incoming arcs are *sources*. An infinite number of jobs are available at every source. Nodes with no outgoing arcs are *sinks*. Sinks are never blocked. We denote the set of all sources in the network as Q and the set of all sinks as Q'.

An FJQN/B is generally associated with an *initial marking* $M = \{M^{(u,v)}|(u,v) \in E\}$ and an *initial timing condition* $Y = \{Y_v|v \in V\}$, where $M^{(u,v)}$ is the number of jobs in the buffer on arc (u, v) at time 0 and Y_v is the time epoch at which server v is first available to provide service. Thus we extend the notation of an FJQN/B to $N = (V, E, B, M, Y)$.

Finally, a *circuit* is a sequence of arcs $(v_1, v_2), (v_2, v_3), \ldots,$ (v_{n-1}, v_n) such that $v_n = v_1$, $(v_i, v_{i+1}) \in E$, $\forall 1 \le i \le n-1$, and it contains no sub-circuit. A *cycle* is a sequence of arcs $(v_1, v_2), (v_2, v_3), \ldots, (v_{n-1}, v_n)$ such that $v_n = v_1$, either (v_i, v_{i+1}) or $(v_{i+1}, v_i) \in E$, $\forall 1 \le i \le n-1$, and it contains no sub-cycle. An FJQN/B with no circuit/cycle is called circuit-free/cycle-free. The system is said to be *deadlocked* if there exists a cycle such that every arc on the cycle along a certain orientation has zero initial marking while every arc along the opposite orientation has full initial marking. To make the problem non-trivial, we require the FJQN/B to be deadlock-free.

2.1 Service Times and Stochastic Order

Let $S_{m,v}$ be the m-th service time at server $v \in V$. We assume the service times are non-negative and integrable random variables defined on a common probability space $(\Omega, \mathcal{F}, P)$.

The service times on server $v \in V$ are given by a sequence $\{S_{m,v}\}_{m \ge 1}$. We assume the sequences are jointly stationary and ergodic. This assumption is essential to define throughput.

We denote the m-th service times on all nodes $v \in V$ as a service time vector

$$\boldsymbol{S}_m = (S_{m,1}, S_{m,2}, \ldots, S_{m,|V|}). \tag{1}$$

As m increases, we write the sequence of service time vectors in the following way:

$$\{\boldsymbol{S}\}_m := \{\boldsymbol{S}_1, \boldsymbol{S}_2, \ldots, \boldsymbol{S}_m, \ldots\}. \tag{2}$$

Throughout this paper, we rely on one or more of the following assumptions:

ASSUMPTION 1. *Service times among different servers are mutually independent. Service times on server v are independent and identically distributed (i.i.d.) with cumulative distribution function F_v.*

ASSUMPTION 2. *Service times are lower and upper bounded in the sense of stochastic ordering by non-negative and integrable random variables σ^- and σ^+, respectively. σ^- has positive mean. σ^+ has light-tailed distribution, i.e. $\exists\, t > 0$ such that $\mathbb{E}\left[e^{t\sigma^+}\right] < \infty$.*

ASSUMPTION 3. *The support of the distribution of σ^- is not bounded from above, i.e. $\sup\{x : F_{\sigma^-}(x) < 1\} = \infty$.*

The definition of stochastic order is given below.

Let $\boldsymbol{X}$ and $\boldsymbol{Y}$ be two integrable random vectors on $\mathbb{R}^n$.

DEFINITION 1. *$\boldsymbol{X}$ is smaller than $\boldsymbol{Y}$ in the sense of stochastic ordering, denoted $\boldsymbol{X} \le_{st} \boldsymbol{Y}$, iff*

$$E[f(\boldsymbol{X})] \le E[f(\boldsymbol{Y})], \tag{3}$$

for all nondecreasing functions $f : \mathbb{R}^n \to \mathbb{R}$ such that the expectations exist.

Let $\{\boldsymbol{S}\}_m := \{\boldsymbol{S}_1, \ldots, \boldsymbol{S}_m, \ldots\}$ and $\{\boldsymbol{S}'\}_m := \{\boldsymbol{S}'_1, \ldots, \boldsymbol{S}'_m, \ldots\}$ be two sequences of integrable random vectors on $\mathbb{R}^n$.

DEFINITION 2. *$\{\boldsymbol{S}\}_m$ is smaller than $\{\boldsymbol{S}'\}_m$ in the sense of stochastic ordering, denoted $\{\boldsymbol{S}\}_m \le_{st} \{\boldsymbol{S}'\}_m$, iff for all $m \ge 1$*

$$E[f(\{\boldsymbol{S}_1, \ldots, \boldsymbol{S}_m\})] \le E[f(\{\boldsymbol{S}'_1, \ldots, \boldsymbol{S}'_m\})], \tag{4}$$

for all nondecreasing functions $f : \mathbb{R}^{m \times n} \to \mathbb{R}$ such that the expectations exist.

2.2 Network Throughput

In this section, we define the throughput of an FJQN/B and summarize several throughput properties.

Denote by $T_{m,v}$ the m-th service completion time at node v. The throughput of node $v \in V$ is defined as

$$\theta_v = \mathbb{E}\left[\lim_{m \to \infty} \frac{m}{T_{m,v}}\right], \tag{5}$$

provided the limits exist. In words, the throughput of a node is the average number of service completions in a unit time in the long run.

The throughput of the network is determined by the lowest throughput among all nodes. Hence, the network throughput is defined as

$$\theta = \inf\left\{\mathbb{E}\left[\lim_{m \to \infty} \frac{m}{T_{m,v}}\right] \Big| v \in V\right\}, \tag{6}$$

provided the limits exist. We will use the notation $\theta(N)$ when we want to distinguish between different networks.

The following two lemmas have been established in [10].

LEMMA 1. *Consider an FJQN/B $N = (V, E, B, M, Y)$. The throughput at every node is identical and independent of the initial timing condition.*

$$\theta_v = \theta \perp Y, \ \forall v \in V. \tag{7}$$

For the rest of the paper, we always assume initial timing condition $Y_v = 0$, $\forall v \in V$ and denote an FJQN/B as $N = (V, E, B, M)$.

LEMMA 2. *Consider an FJQN/B $N = (V, E, B, M)$ and an arbitrary set of arcs $\Delta \subseteq E$. The Δ-dual of N is obtained by reversing the flow on arcs in Δ and setting the number of jobs to the number of available spaces initially present in the buffers of these arcs. If the Δ-dual and the original network share the same service times and initial timing condition, then they have the same throughput.*

The following comparison property has been derived in [11]. It addresses the monotonicity of the throughput with respect to buffer size.

LEMMA 3. *Consider an FJQN/B* $N = (V, E, B, M)$ *and an associated FJQN/B* $N' = (V, E, B', M)$ *such that* $B^{(u,v)} \leq B'^{(u,v)}$, $\forall (u, v) \in E$. *If they share the same service times, then we have* $\theta(N) \leq \theta(N')$.

The following comparison properties are consequences of Proposition 3.2 and Proposition 3.4 in [4] respectively. They present the monotonicity of the throughput with respect to the service times and the network inclusion.

LEMMA 4. *Consider an FJQN/B* $N = (V, E, B, M)$ *and two sequences of service time vectors* $\{\boldsymbol{S}(N)\}_m$ *and* $\{\boldsymbol{S}'(N)\}_m$. *If* $\{\boldsymbol{S}\}_m \leq_{st} \{\boldsymbol{S}'\}_m$, *then we have* $\theta(N; S) \geq \theta(N; S')$.

LEMMA 5. *Consider an FJQN/B* $N = (V, E, B, M)$ *and a sub-network* $\bar{N} = (\bar{V}, \bar{E}, \bar{B}, \bar{M})$ *with* $\bar{V} \subseteq V$, $\bar{E} \subseteq E$, $\bar{B}^{(u,v)} = B^{(u,v)}$, $\bar{M}^{(u,v)} = M^{(u,v)}$, $\forall (u, v) \in \bar{E}$. *If they share the same service times for shared nodes, then we have* $\theta(N) \leq \theta(\bar{N})$.

It is worth noting that the above lemmas do not depend on any of Assumptions 1 - 3. These lemmas will be used to construct throughput bounds in Section 4.

3. MODEL VARIANTS

In this section, we present two model variants of an FJQN/B: circuit-free network and no-blocking network. The two variants are used to derive lower and upper bounds for the network throughput respectively.

3.1 Circuit-free Network with Zero Initial Marking

Consider an FJQN/B $N = (V, E, B, M)$. We propose the following method to construct a circuit-free network with zero initial marking, denoted as N_a, without changing the network throughput:

1) For every arc $(u, v) \in E$, if $M^{(u,v)} \neq 0$ and $M^{(u,v)} \neq B^{(u,v)}$, then split the arc into two arcs and create an artificial node w in between. Set $B^{(u,w)} = B^{(u,v)} - M^{(u,v)}$, $M^{(u,w)} = 0$ and $B^{(w,v)} = M^{(w,v)} = M^{(u,v)}$. Set the service times on w equal to zero;
2) Reverse the direction of every arc whose buffer is initially full and change its initial marking to zero.

We then have the following lemma:

LEMMA 6. *Any FJQN/B* $N = (V, E, B, M)$ *is throughput equivalent to its circuit-free variant* N_a *with zero initial marking.*

Proof. The new network N_a has zero initial marking on every arc. Since the original FJQN/B is deadlock-free, every circuit in N will have at least one arc being split. Thus, N_a must be circuit-free. By Lemma 2 and zero service times on w, the throughput remains the same, i.e. $\theta(N_a) = \theta(N)$. □

3.1.1 Minimum Level

Here we propose an important topological concept for N_a: minimum level, which will be used to derive lower bounds on the throughput of N in Section 4.

Consider the underlying graph $G = (V, E)$ of the circuit-free network $N_a = (V, E, B)$. Let $l : V \to \mathbb{Z}$ denote a labelling of G. We are interested in topological labellings as defined below.

DEFINITION 3. *A labelling* $l : V \to \mathbb{Z}$ *is topological if*

$$\forall (i, j) \in E, l(j) - l(i) \geq 1. \tag{8}$$

The next lemma establishes the existence of a topological labelling on any directed circuit-free graph.

LEMMA 7. *For any given directed circuit-free graph, there exists a topological labelling.*

Proof. Since the network is circuit-free, we can label it according to the following procedure. Label all sources as zero. Then remove the sources and all arcs connected to them. Label all sources of the new network as one. Remove the sources and the connected arcs again. Repeat until all nodes are labelled.

It is worth noting that the above procedure is similar to Kahn's algorithm [13] for topological sorting. The difference with a topological labelling is that a topological sorting requires distinct labels for all nodes. □

Define the level of a directed circuit-free graph under a given topological labelling $l : V \to \mathbb{Z}$ as the maximum label difference between adjacent nodes in the graph, i.e.,

$$L_l(G) = \max\{l(j) - l(i) \mid i, j \in V,\ (i, j) \in E\}. \tag{9}$$

For the same graph, different topological labellings may result in different levels. Our interest is the optimal topological labelling l^* that minimizes the level, i.e.,

$$l_G^* = \underset{l:V \to \mathbb{Z}}{\operatorname{argmin}}\{L_l(G) \mid \forall (i, j) \in E, l(j) - l(i) \geq 1\}. \tag{10}$$

The minimum level of the graph is then given by the level under the optimal topological labelling, $L_{l_G^*}(G)$, which is unique to the graph. We will also refer to it as the minimum level of the circuit-free network N_a, i.e. $L^*(N_a) = L_{l_G^*}(G)$. Note that it is a topological feature that is generally unrelated to network size.

Figure 2 illustrates two different topological labellings for the same graph, with respective levels 5 and 2. It is not hard to verify that the minimum level of this graph is 2.

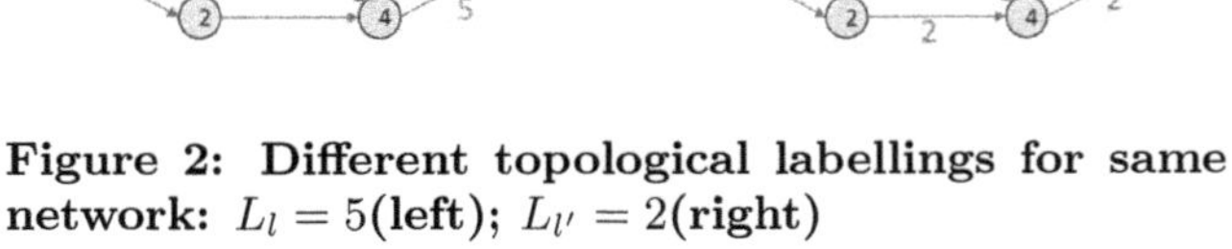

Figure 2: Different topological labellings for same network: $L_l = 5$**(left);** $L_{l'} = 2$**(right)**

3.1.2 Optimal Topological Labelling

In this section, we describe how to find the optimal topological labelling.

Given a directed circuit-free graph $G = (V, E)$, define variable x_k as the label of node $k \in V$. The problem of finding the optimal topological labelling method for graph G can be formulated as the following Integer Program:

$$\begin{array}{llcl}
\textbf{(IP)} & \min\ y & & \\
& \text{s.t. } x_k - x_j + y & \geq & 0,\ (k, j) \in E \\
& -x_k + x_j & \geq & 1,\ (k, j) \in E \\
& y, x_k & \in & \mathbb{Z},\ k \in V
\end{array}$$

Consider the following Linear Programming relaxation of (IP):

$$\begin{aligned}\textbf{(LP)}\quad & \min \quad y \\ \text{s.t. } x_k - x_j + y &\geq 0,\ (k,j) \in E \qquad (11)\\ -x_k + x_j &\geq 1,\ (k,j) \in E \qquad (12)\end{aligned}$$

where y and the x_k's become unrestricted.

The next lemma shows that the optimal solution to (IP) is easily obtained from the optimal solution of (LP). See Appendix A for the detailed proof.

LEMMA 8. *Let* $\mathbf{x}^* = (x_k^*, k \in V)$. *If* $(\mathbf{x}^*, y^*)$ *is the optimal solution to* **(LP)**, *then* $(\lceil \mathbf{x}^* \rceil, \lceil y^* \rceil)$ *must be the optimal solution to* **(IP)**. *Thus, the minimum level can be found in polynomial time by simply solving* **(LP)** *and rounding up the solution.*

Next, we discuss how the minimum level $L^*(N_a)$ relates to the cycles in the circuit-free network N_a.

Let $\boldsymbol{C}$ be the set of all cycles in N_a. Assume $\boldsymbol{C} \neq \varnothing$. Otherwise, N_a is a spanning tree and $L^*(N_a) = 1$.

Pick an arbitrary cycle $C^\alpha \in \boldsymbol{C}$. Define $C^{\alpha+}$ as the set of the arcs in cycle C^α with one orientation, and $C^{\alpha-}$ as the set of the arcs with the opposite orientation. Without loss of generality, we assume we always pick the + orientation such that $|C^{\alpha+}| \geq |C^{\alpha-}|$, where $|\cdot|$ denotes the cardinality measure. Since N_a is circuit-free, we have $|C^{\alpha+}|, |C^{\alpha-}| > 0$.

The next theorem establishes an important relationship between the minimum level and the cycles in N_a. A detailed proof is provided in Appendix B.

THEOREM 1. *The minimum level of* N_a *equals the ceiling of the maximum among all cycles in* N_a *of the ratio of* $|C^{\alpha+}|$ *to* $|C^{\alpha-}|$.

$$L^*(N_a) = \left\lceil \max\left\{ \frac{|C^{\alpha+}|}{|C^{\alpha-}|} \mid C^\alpha \in \boldsymbol{C} \right\} \right\rceil, \qquad (13)$$

where $\lceil \cdot \rceil$ *denotes the ceiling function.*

3.2 Deterministic Non-blocking Network

Under Assumptions 1, & 2, we can associate an FJQN/B $N = (V, E, B, M)$ with a deterministic non-blocking network, denoted as N_b, by the following steps:

1) For every arc $(u, v) \in E$, add an arc (v, u) so that $(u, v) - (v, u)$ forms a back-loop. Set $M^{(v,u)} = B^{(u,v)} - M^{(u,v)}$. Let (u, v) and (v, u) have infinite buffer sizes;
2) For every node $v \in V$, add a self-loop (v, v). Set $M^{(v,v)} = 1$. Let (v, v) have infinite buffer size;
3) For every node $v \in V$, replace the service time σ_v by its expected value $\mathbb{E}[\sigma_v]$.

And we have the following lemma:

LEMMA 9. *Any FJQN/B* $N = (V, E, B, M)$ *is throughput upper bounded by its deterministic non-blocking variant* N_b.

Proof. Assumption 1 guarantees the existence of the service time expectation. Assumption 2 guarantees that the expectation is finite. The service time on any node v in N_b is $\mathbb{E}[\sigma_v]$, which is a constant. N_b is non-blocking, as every arc in N_b has infinite buffer size. According to Corollary 8.24 in [2], N_b provides a throughput upper bound to N. □

3.2.1 *Deterministic Cycle Time*

Here we introduce an important parameter of N_b: the cycle time. We will use the cycle time of N_b to upper bound the throughput of N in Section 4.

The cycle time $c(N_b)$ is defined as the inverse of the throughput of N_b, namely $c(N_b) = 1/\theta(N_b)$.

To emphasize the deterministic nature of N_b, we refer to $c(N_b)$ as the deterministic cycle time.

Next, we discuss how to compute the deterministic cycle time. Let Ξ be the set of all circuits in N_b. For any circuit $\xi \in \Xi$, denote by $n_j(\xi)$ the total number of jobs on ξ and denote by $n_s(\xi)$ the number of nodes on ξ. According to Remark 8.21 in [2], the deterministic cycle time of N_b is given by the maximum among all circuits of the ratios of the total service time to the total number of jobs on ξ.

$$c(N_b) = \max_{\xi \in \Xi} \left\{ \frac{\sum_{v=1}^{n_s(\xi)} \mathbb{E}[\sigma_v]}{n_j(\xi)} \right\}. \qquad (14)$$

The deterministic cycle time is known to be computable in $O(n^3)$ by Karp's algorithm [14], where $n = |V|$.

3.3 Relationship Between Minimum Level and Deterministic Cycle Time

A given FJQN/B N has unique model variants N_a, N_b and unique minimum level $L^*(N_a)$, cycle time $c(N_b)$. Thus, we define the minimum level of an FJQN/B to be the minimum level of its associated circuit-free variant, i.e. $L^*(N) = L^*(N_a) = L^*$; we define the deterministic cycle time of an FJQN/B to be the deterministic cycle time of its associated deterministic non-blocking variant, i.e. $c(N) = c(N_b) = c$.

The relationship between the minimum level and the deterministic cycle time is given as follows.

THEOREM 2. *Consider a given FJQN/B* $N = (V, E, B, M)$. *Under Assumptions 1, & 2, the minimum level* L^* *and the deterministic cycle time* c *satisfy the following inequalities:*

$$\frac{(L^* - 1)\mathbb{E}[\sigma^-]}{\beta} \leq c \leq (1 + L^*)\mathbb{E}[\sigma^+], \qquad (15)$$

where β *is the upper bound to the buffer sizes of* N.

Proof. By (14) and Lemma 4,

$$\max_{\xi \in \Xi} \left\{ \frac{n_s(\xi)}{n_j(\xi)} \right\} \mathbb{E}[\sigma^-] \leq c \leq \max_{\xi \in \Xi} \left\{ \frac{n_s(\xi)}{n_j(\xi)} \right\} \mathbb{E}[\sigma^+]. \qquad (16)$$

There are three types of circuits in N_b: back-loops on arcs $(u, v) \in E$, self-loops on node $v \in V$, and loops along cycles in N. Notice that every cycle in N maps to a unique cycle C^α in N_a with some extra artificial nodes. Hence,

$$\frac{n_s(\xi)}{n_j(\xi)} = \begin{cases} 2/M^{(u,v)} & \text{,Back-loop} \\ 1 & \text{,Self-loop} \\ \frac{|C^{\alpha+}| + |C^{\alpha-}| - R_{C^\alpha}}{\sum_{(u,v) \in C^{\alpha*}} B^{(u,v)}} & \text{,Otherwise} \end{cases} \qquad (17)$$

where R_{C^α} is the number of artificial nodes on cycle C^α, and $C^{\alpha*}$ can be $C^{\alpha+}$ or $C^{\alpha-}$ depending on the orientation of ξ. In case $\boldsymbol{C} = \varnothing$, (15) is easily verified. In case $\boldsymbol{C} \neq \varnothing$, since every artificial node is the end of two arcs in opposite orientations, we have $0 \leq R_{C^\alpha} \leq |C^{\alpha-}|$ and hence

$$\frac{|C^{\alpha+}|}{\beta |C^{\alpha*}|} \leq \frac{n_s(\xi)}{n_j(\xi)} \leq \max\left\{ \frac{|C^{\alpha+}| + |C^{\alpha-}|}{|C^{\alpha*}|}, 2 \right\} \qquad (18)$$

Combining (16) and (18) yields

$$\max_{C^\alpha \in \boldsymbol{C}} \left\{ \frac{|C^{\alpha+}|}{\beta |C^{\alpha-}|} \right\} \mathbb{E}[\sigma^-] \leq c \leq \max_{C^\alpha \in \boldsymbol{C}} \left\{ \frac{|C^{\alpha+}| + |C^{\alpha-}|}{|C^{\alpha-}|} \right\} \mathbb{E}[\sigma^+] \tag{19}$$

By Theorem 1,

$$L^* - 1 < \max_{C^\alpha \in \boldsymbol{C}} \left\{ \frac{|C^{\alpha+}|}{|C^{\alpha-}|} \right\} \leq L^*. \tag{20}$$

Combining (19) and (20) completes the proof. □

4. THROUGHPUT BOUNDS

Throughput lower and upper bounds for a given FJQN/B are derived in this section as functions independent of network size. The upper bound depends on the network degree and the deterministic cycle time while the lower bound depends on the network degree and the minimum level.

THEOREM 3. *Consider a given FJQN/B $N = (V, E, B, M)$ with network degree D, minimum level L^*, deterministic cycle time c, and buffer size upper bound β. Under Assumptions 1 and 2,*

- *the network throughput has the following upper bound:*

$$\theta^u = \min \left\{ \frac{1}{\mathbb{E}[\max_{1 \leq i \leq \lceil D/2 \rceil} \sigma_i^-]}, \frac{1}{c} \right\}, \tag{21}$$

where $\{\sigma_i^-\}$ is a sequence of i.i.d. random variables with the same distribution as σ^-.

- *the network throughput has the following lower bound:*

$$\theta^l = \frac{t}{2(L^* + 1)\left(\ln(D+1) + \ln \mathbb{E}\left[e^{t\sigma^+}\right]\right)}, \tag{22}$$

where $t > 0$ is the parameter such that $\mathbb{E}\left[e^{t\sigma^+}\right] < \infty$.

4.0.1 Proof of Upper Bound

In this subsection, we prove the upper bound (21) of Theorem 3.

Consider an associated homogeneous FJQN/B N^+ where all service times are equal in distribution to σ^- in Assumption 2. By Lemma 4, $\theta(N^+) \geq \theta(N)$.

Suppose node v_0 determines the degree of the network, i.e. $d(v_0) = D$. Then v_0 has at least $\lceil D/2 \rceil$ upstream neighbors or at least $\lceil D/2 \rceil$ downstream neighbors. We assume v_0 has at least $\lceil D/2 \rceil$ downstream neighbors. The proof for the other case is similar.

Consider the subnetwork N_s^+ that only contains v_0 and the downstream neighbors $v_1, \ldots, v_{\lceil D/2 \rceil}$ and arcs in between. Because of the fork-join mechanism, v_0 will be blocked until all downstream buffers are empty. Hence, the average time it takes for each job to depart v_0 is at least $\mathbb{E}[\max_{1 \leq i \leq \lceil D/2 \rceil} \sigma_i^-]$, where σ_i^- is the random variable to the service time on node v_i in N_s^+. Thus, the throughput of N_s^+ is upper bounded as follows.

$$\theta(N_s^+) \leq \frac{1}{\mathbb{E}[\max_{1 \leq i \leq \lceil D/2 \rceil} \sigma_i^-]}. \tag{23}$$

By Lemma 5, the throughput of the original FJQN/B has the same upper bound. Hence,

$$\theta(N) \leq \theta(N^+) \leq \theta(N_s^+) \leq \frac{1}{\mathbb{E}[\max_{1 \leq i \leq \lceil D/2 \rceil} \sigma_i^-]}. \tag{24}$$

The other bound comes from Lemma 9 and the definition of the deterministic cycle time.

4.0.2 Proof of Lower Bound

In this subsection, we prove the lower bound (22) of Theorem 3.

Consider variant N_a and an associated homogeneous network N_a^- where all service times are equal in distribution to σ^+ in Assumption 2 and all buffer sizes are one. Since N_a and N_a^- share the same set of nodes and arcs, they have the same optimal topological labelling and the same minimum level $L^* = L^*(N_a) = L^*(N_a^-)$. By Lemmas 3, 4, and 6, $\theta(N_a^-) \leq \theta(N_a) = \theta(N)$.

Since $N_a^- = (V, E, B)$ is circuit-free, jobs never return to the same node after they pass through it. Because of the FCFS policy, the m-th service time at server v coincides with the service time of the m-th job that arrives to server v from every upstream buffer. Because of the fork-join feature and zero initial marking, the m-th job that arrives to server v will only join with or fork into the m-th job that arrives to any other server. We refer to this as job m. Then $S_{m,v}$ is the service time of job m at node v.

Denote by $T_{m,v}$ the m-th service completion time at node v, which is also the service completion time of job m at node v. According to the block before service mechanism, this completion time obeys the following recurrence equation:

$$\begin{aligned} T_{m,v} = S_{m,v} + \max \quad & \{T_{m,u} \big| (u,v) \in E\} \\ & \cup \{T_{m-1,v} \big| m > 1\} \\ & \cup \{T_{m-1,w} \big| (v,w) \in E, m > 1\} \end{aligned} \tag{25}$$

The initial condition is given by

$$T_{1,s} = S_{1,s}, \ s \in Q, \tag{26}$$

in which Q is the set of sources (nodes with no incoming arcs).

Recall that the throughput of an FJQN/B is related to the service completion time $T_{m,v}$ at an arbitrary node v. We will use the theory of *last passage percolation* to construct an upper bound on $T_{m,v}$, which leads to a lower bound on the network throughput.

The recurrence equation (25) corresponds to a last-passage percolation time (weight of a path with maximum weight) in a "time-expanded" graph. More precisely, we introduce a new graph $\mathcal{G} = (\mathcal{V}, \mathcal{E})$ which represents this collection of tasks and their preceding constraints as follows:

- $\mathcal{V} = \mathbb{Z}^+ \times V$ (27)
- $\mathcal{E} = \{(m,v) \to (m,u) \big| (u,v) \in E\} \cup \{(m,v) \to (m-1,v) \big| m > 1\} \cup \{(m,v) \to (m-1,w) \big| (v,w) \in E, m > 1\}$ (28)
- weight $S_{m,v}$ associated with each node (m,v) in $\mathcal{V}$.

Figure 3 illustrates an example of the time-expanded graph of a tandem queueing system with four nodes and buffer size 1 on every queue.

Denote by $\pi_{(m,v),(m',v')}$ a path from (m,v) to (m',v') in graph $\mathcal{G} = (\mathcal{V}, \mathcal{E})$, and denote by $W(\pi_{(m,v),(m',v')})$ the total weight of that path. We have the following lemma:

LEMMA 10. *$T_{(m,v)}$ is determined by the path with maximum weight from (m,v) to $(1,s)$ for all sources $s \in Q$,*

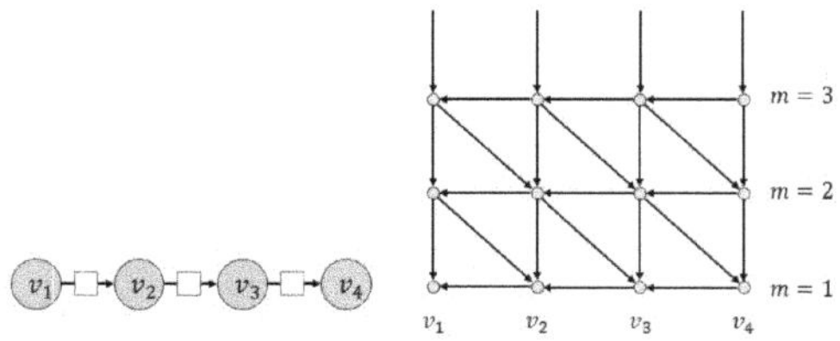

Figure 3: Example: tandem queueing system(left); time-expanded graph(right)

i.e.,

$$T_{m,v} = \max\{W(\pi) | \pi \textit{ from } (m,v) \textit{ to } (1,s),\ s \in Q\}. \quad (29)$$

Proof. The recurrence equation (25) implies that the service completion time takes the maximum at every step, which leads to the maximum weight among all paths to the sources. □

Now introduce the following function on N_a^- according to its optimal topological labelling $l^*_{N_a^-}$ and minimum level L^*:

$$\phi : (m,v) \to (L^* + 1) \cdot m + l^*_{N_a^-}(v). \quad (30)$$

By (28) and the definition of level, it follows that ϕ increases by at least one for every arc in $\mathcal{E}$.

$$\phi(m,v) - \phi(m',v') \geq 1,\ \forall (m,v) \to (m',v') \in \mathcal{E}. \quad (31)$$

Consider a path from (m,s) to $(1,s)$ for any source $s \in Q$. Since (m,s) and $(1,s)$ share the same label $l^*_N(s)$, we have

$$\phi(m,s) - \phi(1,s) = (L^* + 1) \cdot m. \quad (32)$$

Then by (31), this is an upper bound to the number of arcs on the path:

$$\left|\pi_{(m,s),(1,s)}\right| \leq (L^* + 1) \cdot m. \quad (33)$$

By Markov's inequality, we can bound the probability of the event that the weight of the path is larger than or equal to $xm/2$ in the following way:

$$\mathbb{P}\left[W(\pi_{(m,s),(1,s)}) \geq \tfrac{xm}{2}\right] \leq e^{-\frac{txm}{2}} \mathbb{E}\left[e^{tW(\pi_{(m,s),(1,s)})}\right]. \quad (34)$$

Since N_a^- is homogeneous, we have

$$\mathbb{E}\left[e^{tW(\pi_{(m,s),(1,s)})}\right] = \mathbb{E}\left[e^{t\sigma^+}\right]^{|\pi_{(m,s),(1,s)}|+1}. \quad (35)$$

Combining (34), (35), and (33) yields

$$\mathbb{P}\left[W(\pi_{(m,s),(1,s)}) \geq \tfrac{xm}{2}\right] \leq e^{-\frac{txm}{2}} \mathbb{E}\left[e^{t\sigma^+}\right]^{(c+1)\cdot m+1}. \quad (36)$$

On the other hand, by (28), the out-degree of every node (m,v) on $\mathcal{G}$ is at most $d(v)+1$. Since $d(v)$ is upper bounded by D, the out-degree of node on $\mathcal{G}_i$ is upper bounded by $D+1$. Together with (33), we obtain an upper bound on the number of paths between (m,s) and $(1,s)$ as follows.

$$\sum_{\pi \text{ from } (m,s) \text{ to } (1,s)} 1 \leq (D+1)^{(L^*+1)\cdot m}. \quad (37)$$

Define $\pi^*_{(m,s),(1,s)}$ to be the maximum weight path from (m,s) to $(1,s)$. To make the maximum weight larger than or equal to $xm/2$, the weight of at least one path must be larger than or equal to $xm/2$, i.e.

$$\{W(\pi^*_{(m,s),(1,s)}) \geq \tfrac{xm}{2}\} = \bigcup_{\pi \text{ from } (m,s) \text{ to } (1,s)} \{W(\pi) \geq \tfrac{xm}{2}\}. \quad (38)$$

Thus, for any $s \in Q$,

$$\begin{aligned} &\mathbb{P}\left[W(\pi^*_{(m,s),(1,s)})\} \geq \tfrac{xm}{2}\right] \\ \leq &\sum_{\pi \text{ from } (m,s) \text{ to } (1,s)} \mathbb{P}\left[W(\pi_{(m,s),(1,s)}) \geq \tfrac{xm}{2}\right] \\ \leq &e^{-\frac{txm}{2}} \mathbb{E}\left[e^{t\sigma^+}\right]^{(c+1)\cdot m+1} \cdot (D+1)^{(c+1)\cdot m} \\ = &\left(e^{-\frac{tx}{2}} \cdot (D+1)^{c+1} \cdot \mathbb{E}\left[e^{t\sigma^+}\right]^{c+1}\right)^m \mathbb{E}\left[e^{t\sigma^+}\right]. \end{aligned} \quad (39)$$

The first inequality comes from (38) and the second inequality comes from (37) and (36).

Now consider the relationship between $\pi^*_{(m,s),(1,s)}$ and $T_{m,s}$ given by (29). For any $m > 1$ and any $s_1 \in Q$, if T_{m,s_1} is determined by $\pi^*_{(m,s_1),(1,s_1)}$, then we have

$$\begin{aligned} \mathbb{P}\left[T_{m,s_1} \geq xm\right] &= \mathbb{P}\left[W(\pi^*_{(m,s_1),(1,s_1)}) \geq xm\right] \\ &\leq \mathbb{P}\left[W(\pi^*_{(m,s_1),(1,s_1)}) \geq \tfrac{xm}{2}\right]. \end{aligned} \quad (40)$$

If T_{m,s_1} is determined by $\pi^*_{(m,s_1),(1,s_2)}$ for any $s_2 \in Q$, $s_2 \neq s_1$, then we consider a third node $v \neq s_1, s_2$ in the original FJQN/B. For sufficiently large m, there must exist m' such that $1 < m' < m$ and $\pi_{(m,s_1),(m',v)}$, $\pi_{(m,s_2),(m',v)}$, $\pi_{(m',v),(1,s_1)}$, $\pi_{(m',v),(1,s_2)}$ all exist. Thus,

$$\begin{aligned} &W(\pi^*_{(m,s_1),(1,s_2)}) \\ \leq &W(\pi^*_{(m,s_1),(m',v)}) + W(\pi^*_{(m',v),(1,s_2)}) \\ \leq &W(\pi^*_{(m,s_1),(m',v)}) + W(\pi^*_{(m',v),(1,s_1)}) \\ &+ W(\pi^*_{(m',v),(1,s_2)}) + W(\pi^*_{(m,s_2),(m',v)}) \\ \leq &W(\pi^*_{(m,s_1),(1,s_1)}) + W(\pi^*_{(m,s_2),(1,s_2)}). \end{aligned} \quad (41)$$

Thus,

$$\begin{aligned} &\mathbb{P}\left[T_{m,s_1} \geq xm\right] \\ = &\mathbb{P}\left[W(\pi^*_{(m,s_1),(1,s_2)}) \geq xm\right] \\ \leq &\mathbb{P}\left[W(\pi^*_{(m,s_1),(1,s_1)}) + W(\pi^*_{(m,s_2),(1,s_2)}) \geq xm\right] \\ \leq &\mathbb{P}\left[W(\pi^*_{(m,s_1),(1,s_1)}) \geq \tfrac{xm}{2}\right] + \mathbb{P}\left[W(\pi^*_{(m,s_2),(1,s_2)}) \geq \tfrac{xm}{2}\right]. \end{aligned} \quad (42)$$

By (39), (40), (42), we have for any source $s \in Q$,

$$\mathbb{P}\left[T_{m,s} \geq xm\right] \leq 2\left(e^{-\frac{tx}{2}+(L^*+1)\left(\ln(D+1)+\ln \mathbb{E}\left[e^{t\sigma^+}\right]\right)}\right)^m \mathbb{E}\left[e^{t\sigma^+}\right]. \quad (43)$$

Since the distribution is light-tailed, we can find $t > 0$ such that $\mathbb{E}\left[e^{t\sigma^+}\right]$ is finite. Then the right-hand side in (43) converges to zero as $m \to \infty$ whenever

$$-\frac{tx}{2} + (L^* + 1)\left(\ln(D+1) + \ln \mathbb{E}\left[e^{t\sigma^+}\right]\right) \leq 0, \quad (44)$$

or equivalently

$$x \geq \frac{2}{t}(L^* + 1)\left(\ln(D+1) + \ln \mathbb{E}\left[e^{t\sigma^+}\right]\right). \quad (45)$$

And whenever (45) holds, we have

$$\mathbb{P}\left[\frac{T_{m,s}}{m} \geq x\right] \to 0 \text{ as } m \to \infty, \quad (46)$$

which implies

$$\mathbb{E}\left[\lim_{m\to\infty}\frac{T_{m,s}(N^-)}{m}\right] \le \frac{2}{t}(L^*+1)\left(\ln(D+1)+\ln\mathbb{E}\left[e^{t\sigma^+}\right]\right). \quad (47)$$

Thus

$$\begin{aligned}\theta_s(N^-) &= \mathbb{E}\left[\lim_{m\to\infty}\frac{m}{T_{m,s}(N^-)}\right] \\ &\ge \frac{t}{2(L^*+1)\left(\ln(D+1)+\ln\mathbb{E}\left[e^{t\sigma^+}\right]\right)}. \quad (48)\end{aligned}$$

Then according to Lemma 1, the throughput of the original FJQN/B is lower bounded as follows.

$$\theta(N) \ge \theta(N^-) = \theta_s(N^-) \ge \frac{t}{2(L^*+1)\left(\ln(D+1)+\ln\mathbb{E}\left[e^{t\sigma^+}\right]\right)}. \quad (49)$$

5. THROUGHPUT SCALABILITY

The throughput lower and upper bounds provided in Section 4 are independent of network size. In this section, we apply the bounds to an infinite sequence of FJQN/Bs and identify scalability conditions.

First, we introduce an infinite sequence of FJQN/Bs as follows:

$$\mathcal{N} = \{N_i\}_{i=1}^{\infty},\ N_i = (V_i, E_i, B_i, M_i). \quad (50)$$

Within the sequence, every network N_i has a finite number of nodes. We require the buffer sizes of all arcs of all networks in $\mathcal{N}$ to be upper bounded by $\beta < \infty$.

Define the throughput of the sequence $\mathcal{N}$ as

$$\Theta(\mathcal{N}) = \liminf \theta(N_i). \quad (51)$$

The throughput scalability of a sequence $\mathcal{N}$ is defined as follows.

Definition 4. *A sequence of FJQN/Bs $\mathcal{N}$ is throughput scalable if $\Theta(\mathcal{N}) > 0$.*

We next explore topological properties of a sequence of FJQN/Bs that are critical to ensure throughput scalability.

5.1 Degree-bounded & Level-bounded

Notice that in Theorem 3, the throughput bounds are independent of the network size. Thus, we can provide scalability conditions based on network degree and minimum level.

Definition 5. *A sequence of FJQN/Bs $\mathcal{N}$ is degree-bounded if there exists a constant $\Omega_d < \infty$ such that*

$$D(N_i) \le \Omega_d,\ \forall N_i \in \mathcal{N}. \quad (52)$$

For a given network $N_i \in \mathcal{N}$, the network degree is bounded from above by the number of nodes which is finite. Thus, $\mathcal{N}$ is NOT degree-bounded if

$$\limsup_{i\to\infty} D(N_i) = \infty. \quad (53)$$

Definition 6. *A sequence of FJQN/Bs $\mathcal{N}$ is level-bounded if there exists a constant $\Omega_l < \infty$ such that*

$$L^*(N_i) \le \Omega_l,\ \forall N_i \in \mathcal{N}. \quad (54)$$

For a given network $N_i \in \mathcal{N}$, the minimum level is bounded from above by the number of nodes in the associated circuit-free model variant which is finite. Thus, $\mathcal{N}$ is NOT level-bounded if

$$\limsup_{i\to\infty} L^*(N_i) = \infty. \quad (55)$$

We are now ready to answer the major question we proposed: how the throughput of an FJQN/B scales as the number of nodes goes to infinity.

5.2 Necessary and Sufficient Condition

We propose that level-bounded and degree-bounded are necessary and sufficient conditions for a sequence of FJQN/Bs to be throughput scalable.

Theorem 4. *Under Assumptions 1, 2, and 3, a sequence of FJQN/Bs is throughput scalable if and only if it is level-bounded and degree-bounded.*

Proof. *Part a: level-bounded and degree-bounded are sufficient conditions for throughput scalability.*

If the minimum level and the network degree are bounded by Ω_l and Ω_d respectively, then the lower bound in Theorem 3 gives $\forall i \in \mathbb{Z}^+$

$$\begin{aligned}\theta(N_i) &\ge \frac{t}{2(L^*(N_i)+1)\left(\ln(D(N_i)+1)+\ln\mathbb{E}\left[e^{t\sigma^+}\right]\right)} \\ &\ge \frac{t}{2(\Omega_l+1)\left(\ln(\Omega_d+1)+\ln\mathbb{E}\left[e^{t\sigma^+}\right]\right)} > 0, \quad (56)\end{aligned}$$

where $t > 0$ is the parameter such that $\mathbb{E}\left[e^{t\sigma^+}\right] < \infty$.

Thus,

$$\Theta(\mathcal{N}) = \liminf \theta(N_i) > 0. \quad (57)$$

Part b: level-bounded and degree-bounded are necessary conditions for throughput scalability.

The upper bound in Theorem 3 gives $\forall i \in \mathbb{Z}^+$

$$\theta(N_i) \le \min\left\{\frac{1}{\mathbb{E}[\max_{1\le j\le\lceil D(N_i)/2\rceil}\sigma_j^-]}, \frac{1}{c(N_i)}\right\}. \quad (58)$$

Let $Y_i = \max_{1\le j\le\lceil D(N_i)/2\rceil}\{\sigma_j^-\}$. We have

$$\mathbb{P}(Y_i \le x) = \mathbb{P}\left(\bigcap_{j=1}^{\lceil D(N_i)/2\rceil}\{\sigma_j^- \le x\}\right) = (F_{\sigma^-}(x))^{\lceil D(N_i)/2\rceil}. \quad (59)$$

Since $\sup\{x : F_{\sigma^-}(x) < 1\} = \infty$, we have $F_{\sigma^-}(x) < 1$, $\forall x < \infty$. If $\mathcal{N}$ is not degree-bounded, then by (53), $\forall x < \infty$,

$$\limsup_{i\to\infty}\mathbb{P}(Y_i \le x) = \limsup_{i\to\infty}(F_{\sigma^-}(x))^{\lceil D(N_i)/2\rceil} = 0. \quad (60)$$

Thus,

$$\limsup_{i\to\infty}\mathbb{E}[Y_i] = \infty. \quad (61)$$

Consequently,

$$\Theta(\mathcal{N}) = \liminf \theta(N_i) \le \liminf_{i\to\infty}\frac{1}{\mathbb{E}[Y_i]} = 0. \quad (62)$$

On the other hand, if $\mathcal{N}$ is not level-bounded, then by (55) and Theorem 2

$$\limsup_{i\to\infty} c(N_i) \ge \limsup_{i\to\infty}(L^*(N_i)-1)\mathbb{E}[\sigma^-]/\beta = \infty. \quad (63)$$

Thus,

$$\Theta(\mathcal{N}) = \liminf \theta(N_i) \leq \liminf_{i\to\infty} \frac{1}{c(N_i)} = 0. \quad (64)$$

□

This result has the following interpretation. Consider an FJQN/B and let it grow to infinitely large. We record the growing process and model it as a sequence of FJQN/Bs. If the minimum level and the network degree remain bounded as the FJQN/B grows in size, then the throughput is guaranteed to be lower bounded by a positive constant, i.e. it is scalable. If the minimum level or the network degree diverges to infinity as the FJQN/B grows, then the throughput decreases to zero, i.e. it is not scalable.

Alternatively, we can directly consider a large-scale FJQN/B. The network degree is relatively easy to determine. The minimum level is determined by solving the LP relaxation in Section 3.1.2. If the minimum level and the network degree are not large compared to the network size, then the network throughput will be significantly larger than zero. If the minimum level or the network degree is comparable to the size of the network, then the throughput of the network will be extremely small. Intuitively speaking, network degree is associated with a node with the largest number of connections while minimum level is associated with an arc on the most unbalanced cycle. These are places with the largest likelihood to get blocked; hence they become the throughput bottlenecks.

5.3 An Example: Level-bounded but Not C-balanced

In [23], several *necessary* conditions were provided for a generally structured FJQN/B network to be throughput scalable. In particular, under service time assumptions 1 - 3, to guarantee that the throughput of a sequence of FJQN/Bs is bounded away from zero, the networks must 1) have *bounded (in and out) degree* for all nodes and 2) be *c-balanced*, i.e there must exist a finite constant c, such that the path length ratio of any two (directed) paths in between any pair of fork and join nodes is bounded above by c.

The next example demonstrates that the above conditions are necessary but NOT sufficient. Consider an FJQN/B network N_L as shown in Figure 4. It has three fork nodes a, b, c, and three join nodes d, e, f. Suppose on every arc the buffer size is one and the initial marking is zero. There is one arc between b and e, and between c and d, but there are L arcs on $a \to b$, $a \to c$, $b \to d$, $c \to e$, $d \to f$, and $e \to f$.

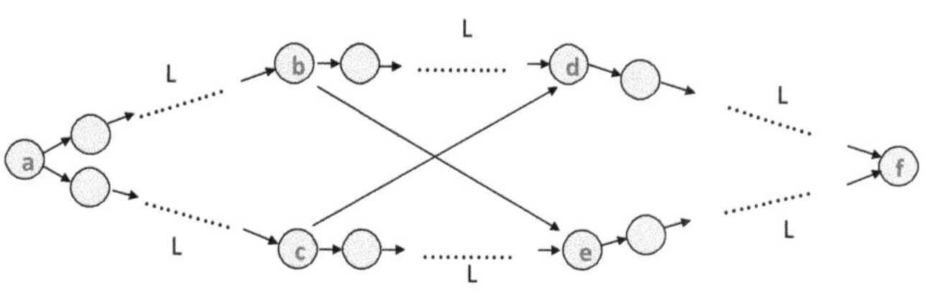

Figure 4: An example: c-balanced condition is necessary but not sufficient

It is easily checked that the necessary conditions 1) and 2) are satisfied. The maximum (in or out) degree is 2. In between any pair of fork and join nodes $(a, d), (a, e), (b, f), (c, f)$ or (a, f), the (directed) path length ratio is upper bounded by 2. Therefore, the network is 2-balanced.

However, consider the sequence $\mathcal{N} = \{N_L\}_{L=1}^{\infty}$. The throughput of the sequence is zero. To see this, consider the situation where all service times are replaced by $s := \mathbb{E}[\sigma^-]$. At time 0, all buffers are empty and the first job initiates service at node a. At time $t_1 = s$, the first job leaves a and forks into paths $a \to b$ and $a \to c$. At time $t_2 = s + Ls$, the first job departs b and c and forks into paths $b \to d$, $b \to e$, $c \to d$, $c \to e$. Since the job needs to go through all L nodes on $b \to d$ and $c \to e$, the join at d and e does not occur until $t_3 = t_2 + Ls$. During $[t_2, t_3)$, nodes b and c will be blocked because the buffers on $b \to e$ and $c \to d$ are occupied by the first job. Only until time t_3, can the second job initiate services at b and c. At time $t_4 = t_3 + s$, the second job leaves b and c and repeats blocking the third job for another Ls amount of time. It is not hard to see that exactly one job gets through this deterministic system for every $(L+1)s$ amount of time. Therefore,

$$\theta(N_L; \mathbb{E}[\sigma^-]) = \frac{1}{(L+1)s} \to 0 \text{ as } L \to \infty. \quad (65)$$

By Lemma 4 and Corollary 8.24 in [2], $\theta(N_L; \sigma) \leq \theta(N_L; \sigma^-) \leq \theta(N_L; \mathbb{E}[\sigma^-]) \to 0$ as $L \to \infty$, which indicates that $\Theta(\mathcal{N}) = \liminf \theta(N_L) = 0$.

Let's examine why this example is not throughput scalable from the aspect of level-boundedness. Consider the undirected cycle formed by paths $b \to d$, $b \to e$, $c \to d$, and $c \to e$, as shown in Figure 5.

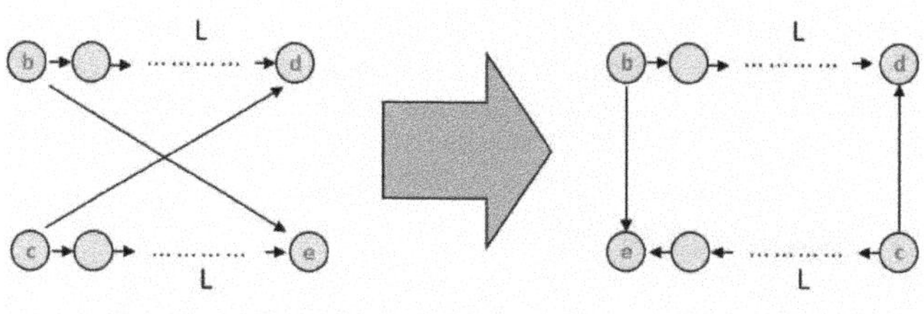

Figure 5: The counter example is not level-bounded

The opposite flow ratio of this cycle is $2L/2 = L$. And the opposite flow ratio of any other undirected cycle is less than 2. Based on Theorem 1,

$$\lim_{L\to\infty} L^*(N_L) = \lim_{L\to\infty} L = \infty, \quad (66)$$

which means $\mathcal{N}$ is not level-bounded. By Theorem 4, the sequence is not throughput scalable.

6. CONCLUSION

This paper investigates the throughput scalability of an arbitrary fork-join queueing network with blocking. Previous studies have either focused on special structured networks such as tandem or tree networks, or provided only necessary conditions for throughput scalability. In this paper, we show that such necessary conditions may not be sufficient. We introduce a key topological concept called "minimum level", and develop lower and upper bounds for the throughput of an FJQN/B. The bounds depend on network degree, minimum level, deterministic cycle time, buffer sizes, and the service time distributions, but not network size. As the size of the FJQN/B grows to infinity, we show that level-boundedness and degree-boundedness are the necessary and sufficient conditions to guarantee that the throughput will be bounded away from zero. The result can be applied to design throughput scalable parallel processing systems, to allocate the throughput bottleneck of a large-scale parallel processing system, and to describe the asymptotic behavior of the throughput as the system grows in size.

In this paper, we have focused on conditions on network topology to guarantee throughput scalability as an FJQN/B grows large in size. In practice, other factors, such as processing speed, buffering/storage capacity, etc., also play a role in throughput scalability. As future information processing network expands along with the technology advances, the processing and buffering capabilities may also grow. Future work could consider the situation where the buffer sizes also grow as the network grows in size. In addition, it is reasonable to have partial synchronization and partial production, as in real world the data transmission may fail but a processor cannot wait forever. A third direction is to extend our scalability analysis under light-tailed service time distributions to that under more general service time distributions, for instance, heavy-tailed distributions. Lastly, we have restricted our analyses to the FCFS service discipline. One future direction is to investigate the scalability conditions under other service disciplines such as processor sharing, priority rules, etc. Overall, the throughput scalability of fork-join queueing networks is a rich and valuable topic that deserves additional research.

7. ACKNOWLEDGMENTS

This work was supported in part by the US Department of Energy under Contract DE-AC02-06CH11357, by National Science Foundation grants ECCS-1232118, SES-1409214, and CNS-1254035.

8. REFERENCES

[1] M. H. Ammar and S. B. Gershwin. Equivalence relations in queueing models of fork/join networks with blocking. *Perf. Eval.*, 10(3):233–245, 1989.

[2] F. Baccelli, G. Cohen, G. J. Olsde, and J. P. Quadrat. *Synchronization and linearity: an algebra for discrete event systems.* John Wiley & Sons Ltd, 1992.

[3] F. Baccelli and Z. Liu. On the stability condition of a precedence-based queueing discipline. *Adv. Appl. Prob.*, 21:883–887, 1989.

[4] F. Baccelli and Z. Liu. Comparison properties of stochastic decision free petri nets. *IEEE Trans. on Automatic Control*, 37:1905–1920, 1992.

[5] S. Balsamo, L. Donatiello, and N. M. V. Dijk. Bound performance models of heterogeneous parallel processing systems. *IEEE Trans. Parallel Distrib. Syst.*, 9(10):1041–1056, 1998.

[6] M. S. Bazaraa, J. J. Jarvis, and H. D. Sherali. *Linear programming and network flows.* John Wiley & Sons, 2011.

[7] A. Chaintreau. *Processes of Interaction in Data Networks.* PhD thesis, INRIA-ENS, 2006.

[8] A. Chaintreau. Sharpness: a tight condition for scalability. *Structural Information and Communication Complexity*, pages 74–88, 2008.

[9] G. Czajkowski, M. Dvorsky, J. Zhao, and M. Conley. Sorting petabytes with mapreduce - the next episode. *http://googleresearch.blogspot.com/2011/09/sorting-petabytes-with-mapreduce-next.html*, 2011.

[10] Y. Dallery, Z. Liu, and D. Towsley. Equivalence, reversibility, symmetry and concavity properties in fork/join queueing networks with blocking. *Journal of the ACM*, 41:903–943, 1994.

[11] Y. Dallery, Z. Liu, and D. Towsley. Properties of fork/join queueing networks with blocking under various operating mechanisms. *IEEE Transactions on Robotics and Automation*, 13:503–518, 1997.

[12] S. Ghemawat, H. Gobioff, , and S.-T. Leung. The google file system. *ACM SIGOPS Op. Sys. Rev.*, 37(5):29–43, 2003.

[13] A. B. Kahn. Topological sorting of large networks. *Communications of the ACM*, 5(11):558–562, 1962.

[14] R. M. Karp. A characterization of the minimum cycle mean in a digraph. *Discrete mathematics*, 23(3):309–311, 1978.

[15] N. K. Krivulin. Max-plus algebra models of queueing networks. *arXiv preprint arXiv:1212.0578*, 2012.

[16] J. B. Martin. Large tandem queueing networks with blocking. *Queueing Systems*, 141(1-2):45–72, 2002.

[17] M. D. Mascolo, R. David, and Y. Dallery. Modeling and analysis of assembly systems with unreliable machines and finite buffers. *Inst. Elect. Eng. Trans.*, 23(4):315–330, 1991.

[18] L. Neumeyer, B. Robbins, A. Nair, and A. Kesari. S4: Distributed stream computing platform. In *Data Mining Workshops (ICDMW), 2010 IEEE International Conference on*, pages 170–177, 2011.

[19] Z. Qiu, J. F. Perez, and P. G. Harrison. Beyond the mean in fork-join queues: Efficient approximation for response-time tails. *Performance Evaluation*, 91:99–116, 2015.

[20] J. S. Tancrez, P. Chevalier, and P. Semal. *A tight bound on the throughput of queueing networks with blocking.* Springer Berlin Heidelberg, 2013.

[21] A. Thomasian. Analysis of fork/join and related queueing systems. *ACM CSUR*, 47:17, 2014.

[22] S. Varma and A. M. Makowski. Interpolation approximations for symmetric fork-join queues. *Perform. Eval.*, 20:245–265, 1994.

[23] C. H. Xia, Z. Liu, D. Towsley, and M. Lelarge. Scalability of fork/join queueing networks with blocking. In *Proc. of ACM Sigmetrics*, 2007.

APPENDIX

A. PROOF OF LEMMA 8

We show that if $(\mathbf{x}^*, y^*)$ is the optimal solution to **(LP)**, where $\mathbf{x}^* = (x_k^*, k \in V)$, then $(\lceil \mathbf{x}^* \rceil, \lceil y^* \rceil)$ must be the optimal solution to **(IP)**.

The optimal LP solution $(\mathbf{x}^*, y^*)$ must be feasible. By (11) and (12), we have

$$0 \le x_k^* - x_j^* + y^* \begin{cases} = \lceil x_k^* \rceil - \lceil x_j^* \rceil + \lceil y^* \rceil, \ x_j^* \in \mathbb{Z} \\ < \lceil x_k^* \rceil - \lceil x_j^* \rceil + 1 + \lceil y^* \rceil, \ x_j^* \notin \mathbb{Z} \end{cases} \quad (67)$$

$$1 \le x_j^* - x_k^* \begin{cases} = \lceil x_j^* \rceil - \lceil x_k^* \rceil, \ x_k^* \in \mathbb{Z} \\ < \lceil x_j^* \rceil - \lceil x_k^* \rceil + 1, \ x_k^* \notin \mathbb{Z} \end{cases} \quad (68)$$

Thus $\forall (k,j) \in E$,

$$\lceil x_k^* \rceil - \lceil x_j^* \rceil + \lceil y^* \rceil \geq 0 \quad (69)$$
$$-\lceil x_k^* \rceil + \lceil x_j^* \rceil \geq 1 \quad (70)$$

This means $(\lceil \mathbf{x}^* \rceil, \lceil y^* \rceil)$ is a feasible solution to the IP. Since the optimal solution value of the LP is the lower bound to the optimal solution value of IP, and $\lceil y^* \rceil$ is the smallest integer that is larger than or equal to y^*, we know that $(\lceil \mathbf{x}^* \rceil, \lceil y^* \rceil)$ is optimal to the IP. □

B. PROOF OF THEOREM 2

Consider the dual of **(LP)**. Let f_{kj} and g_{kj} be the dual variables to (11) and (12) respectively. Let $O_k = \{j \in V | (k,j) \in E\}$ and $I_k = \{j \in V | (j,k) \in E\}$ denote respectively the set of immediate downstream nodes and the set of immediate upstream nodes of node k. The dual can be written as follows:

$$\textbf{(D)} \quad \max \sum_{(k,j)\in E} g_{kj}$$

$$\text{s.t.} \sum_{j\in O_k} (f_{kj} - g_{kj}) - \sum_{j\in I_k} (f_{jk} - g_{jk}) = 0, \ k \in V \quad (71)$$

$$\sum_{(k,j)\in E} f_{kj} = 1 \quad (72)$$

$$f_{kj} \geq 0, \quad g_{kj} \geq 0, \ (k,j) \in E \quad (73)$$

Based on Lemma 7, we know that **(LP)** is guaranteed to have a feasible solution and the solution value has a lower bound of 1. Thus the optimal solution to **(LP)** exists and cannot go to negative infinity. By strong duality theorem, the optimal solutions to both the dual and the primal exist and they give equivalent optimal solution value.

In **(D)**, one can view the dual variable f_{kj} as one type of flow and g_{kj} as another type of flow both from k to j. Introduce the net flow on arc (k,j) as $h_{kj} = f_{kj} - g_{kj}$. Then (71) is the flow balance equation for the net flow with no supply or demand. One trivial solution is to have $f_{kj} = g_{kj}$ for all $(k,j) \in E$ (zero net flow on all arcs), which gives the objective value $\sum_{(k,j)\in E} g_{kj} = \sum_{(k,j)\in E} f_{kj} = 1$. We say a feasible solution is nontrivial if there exists at least one arc on which the net flow is not zero.

In Appendix C Lemma 11 we show that there is an one-to-one mapping between a non-trivial basic feasible solution of **(D)** and a cycle $C^\alpha \in \boldsymbol{C}$, and the non-trivial basic feasible solution must take the following form:

$$f_{kj} = \begin{cases} \frac{1}{|C^{\alpha-}|}, & \forall (k,j) \in C^{\alpha-} \\ 0, & \text{otherwise} \end{cases} \quad (74)$$

$$g_{kj} = \begin{cases} \frac{1}{|C^{\alpha-}|}, & \forall (k,j) \in C^{\alpha+} \\ 0, & \text{otherwise} \end{cases} \quad (75)$$

where $C^{\alpha-}, C^{\alpha+}$ are the sets of arcs in C^α in one direction and another.

Since every linear program has an optimal solution being basic, its corresponding cycle $C^\alpha \in \boldsymbol{C}$ must then generate the maximum objective value which equals to $|C^{\alpha+}|/|C^{\alpha-}|$ based on (75). That is, the optimal solution must correspond to the cycle such that

$$\sum_{(k,j)\in E} g_{kj}^* = \max\left\{ \frac{|C^{\alpha+}|}{|C^{\alpha-}|} \middle| C^\alpha \in \boldsymbol{C} \right\}, \quad (76)$$

and it will choose the direction of $|C^{\alpha-}|$ and $|C^{\alpha+}|$ such that $|C^{\alpha+}| \geq |C^{\alpha-}|$. According to the strong duality theorem, we have $y^* = \sum_{(k,j)\in E} g_{kj}^*$. Therefore, the optimal solution to **(IP)** must be $\lceil y^* \rceil$ based on Lemma 8. □

C. PROOF OF ONE-TO-ONE MAPPING

LEMMA 11. *Suppose $\boldsymbol{C} \neq \varnothing$. There is an one-to-one mapping between a cycle $C^\alpha \in \boldsymbol{C}$, and a non-trivial basic feasible solution to the dual* **(D)**. *That is, every non-trivial basic feasible solution of* **(D)** *corresponds to a cycle $C^\alpha \in \boldsymbol{C}$, and every cycle $C^\alpha \in \boldsymbol{C}$ corresponds to a non-trivial basic feasible solution to* **(D)** *which takes the following form:*

$$f_{kj} = \begin{cases} \frac{1}{|C^{\alpha-}|}, & \forall (k,j) \in C^{\alpha-} \\ 0, & \textit{otherwise} \end{cases} \quad (77)$$

$$g_{kj} = \begin{cases} \frac{1}{|C^{\alpha-}|}, & \forall (k,j) \in C^{\alpha+} \\ 0, & \textit{otherwise} \end{cases} \quad (78)$$

where $C^{\alpha-}, C^{\alpha+}$ are the sets of arcs in C^α in one direction and another.

Proof. *Part a: Mapping from a non-trivial basic feasible solution of (D) to a cycle.*

Let A be the coefficient matrix given by (71) and (72). In a basic feasible solution, the non-zero variables (including both f and g) must be associated with a basis of several *linearly independent columns* in A. In other words, if we take all non-zero variables from a basic feasible solution and look at their corresponding columns in A, then there does not exist a non-trivial linear combination on these columns to generate a column of all zeros.

Note that any non-trivial feasible solution to **(D)** must be formed by balanced non-zero net flow on cycle(s) because there is no starting or ending point [6, p.567-568]. Since the network is circuit-free, such a feasible solution to **(D)** can only be achieved by the following steps:

1) Pick a few cycles in $\boldsymbol{C}$. For every cycle, do 2) and 3);
2) Add $\delta > 0$ amount of net flow on all clockwise or counterclockwise arcs;
3) Add $-\delta$ amount of net flow on the rest arcs in that cycle;
4) For all (k,j) not in these cycles, set $f_{kj} = g_{kj}$.

Next, we show that, for any two cycles with non-zero net flow, no matter how the flow types are allocated on different arcs, the associated columns in A can generate a column of all zeros, thus being linearly dependent.

Consider an arbitrary cycle with non-zero net flow in $\boldsymbol{C}$ with n nodes, $n \leq |V|$. Denote the nodes as $k_1, k_2, \ldots, k_n$ and the arcs as $[k_1,k_2], [k_2,k_3], \ldots, [k_n,k_1]$, where $[k_i,k_j]$ can be (k_i,k_j) or (k_j,k_i) depending on the arc direction. Since non-zero net flow implies non-zero flow f or g, every arc in the cycle must have flow f or g, or both. The columns in A corresponding to either flow f or g on these arcs are shown in Matrix 1.

Matrix 1

	$A_{[k_1,k_2]}$	$A_{[k_2,k_3]}$	...	$A_{[k_n,k_1]}$
k_1	1/-1			-1/1
k_2	-1/1	1/-1		
...		-1/1	1/-1	
k_n			-1/1	1/-1
...				
$k_{\|V\|}$				
κ	1/0	1/0	1/0	1/0

Rows k_1 to $k_{|V|}$ correspond to constraint (71), and row κ corresponds to constraint (72). In first $|V|$ rows, the entries $1/-1$ are chosen according to the direction of the arcs and the flow types. For example, under column $A_{[k_1,k_2]}$, flow f from k_1 to k_2 (or flow g from k_2 to k_1) gives 1 to row k_1 and -1 to row k_2; flow f from k_2 to k_1 (or flow g from k_1 to k_2) gives -1 to row k_1 and 1 to row k_2. In every column, the two entries must be opposite in signs to represent the flow from one node to the other. In the last row κ, the entries 1/0 depend on the flow types. For example, if it is flow f on arc $[k_1, k_2]$, then the entry in column $A_{[k_1,k_2]}$ row κ is 1 or else it is 0.

Since the arcs form a cycle in the undirected sense, the columns in Matrix 1 without row κ are linearly dependent. In other words, by column operations, we can apply a non-trivial linear combination to the columns in Matrix 1 to get a column vector $(0, 0, \ldots, 0, a)^T$ in $(|V| + 1)$-dimension. If another cycle exists in the basis, then we can apply another non-trivial linear combination to the columns of the second cycle to get another column vector $(0, 0, \ldots, 0, b)^T$ in the same dimension. A third non-trivial linear combination can be applied to these two vectors to give a column of all zeros. Thus the columns are linearly dependent, which contradicts the requirement of a basic feasible solution. Hence, the basis will contain only one cycle, denoted as C^α.

Next we show that one arc can only have one type of flow in any non-trivial basic feasible solution. If an arc (k, j) has both flow f and g, then $A^f_{(k,j)} - A^g_{(k,j)}$ directly gives a column vector $(0, 0, \ldots, 0, 1)^T$ in $(|V| + 1)$-dimension. Since the solution is non-trivial, we must have non-zero net flow on a cycle whose corresponding columns as shown in Matrix 1 give another column vector $(0, 0, \ldots, 0, a)^T$ in $(|V| + 1)$-dimension. Again, a non-trivial linear combination can be applied to generate a column of all zeros, which makes the columns linearly dependent. Thus, a non-trivial basic feasible solution cannot have flow f and g together on one arc.

Overall, we know that a non-trivial basic feasible solution to **(D)** needs to satisfy the following requirements:
1) Non-zero net flow happens on exactly one cycle $C^\alpha \in \boldsymbol{C}$;
2) Flow $f = \delta > 0$ and flow $g = 0$ on all clockwise or counterclockwise arcs in C^α;
3) Flow $f = 0$ and flow $g = \delta > 0$ on the rest arcs in C^α;
4) For all (k, j) not in C^α, set $f_{kj} = g_{kj} = 0$.

Finally, (72) requires the summation of flow f to be 1. Therefore, we must have (74) and (75). This completes the mapping from a non-trivial basic feasible solution to a cycle.

Part b: Mapping from a cycle to a basic feasible solution of (D).

To show the mapping backward, consider an arbitrary cycle $C^\alpha \in \boldsymbol{C}$. Construct a solution according to (74) and (75). Clearly, it is non-trivial and feasible since $C^{\alpha-}, C^{\alpha+} > 0$ and all constraints (71) - (73) in **(D)** are satisfied. Based on the construct, on each arc in C^α, only one type of flow (either f or g but not both) exists.

To prove the solution is basic, we need to prove that the coefficient columns corresponding to the non-zero variables in the solution are linearly independent. Notice that the variables in the solution are zero except on the arcs of C^α. Thus we can use Matrix 1 which is the coefficient columns corresponding to the arcs on C^α. Apply row operations to Matrix 1 and get

Matrix 2

	(k_1, k_2)	(k_2, k_3)	...	(k_n, k_1)
k'_1				
k'_2	-1	1		
...	-1		1	
k'_n	-1			1
...				
$k'_{\|V\|}$				
κ'	n'			

Row k'_1 is obtained by adding rows $k_2, \ldots, k_n$ to row k_1. Row k'_n is obtained by adding rows $k_2, \ldots, k_{n-1}$ to row k_n and multiplying -1 if desired. Row k'_{n-1} is obtained by adding rows $k_2, \ldots, k_{n-2}$ to row k_{n-1} and multiplying -1 if desired. Similar to row $k'_{n-2}, \ldots, k'_3$. Row κ' is obtained by subtracting row k'_i $(i \geq 2)$ from row κ if the entry in row κ, column (k_i, k_{i+1}), is 1. The entries of row κ cannot be all 0, as the network is circuit-free and the cycle cannot be formed entirely by flow g. Thus, we have $n' > 0$.

Replace row k'_1 with row κ'. We get n rows that form a $n \times n$ triangular matrix. The determinant of it is the product of the diagonal entries, which is $n' > 0$. Thus, the rank of Matrix 2 (and Matrix 1) is n, which means the columns are linearly independent. Hence, the solution must be basic in this reduced n-dimension space. Since all the other variables are zero (no flow elsewhere), the solution must also be basic in the original $|V|$-dimension space.

Generalized Threshold-Based Epidemics in Random Graphs: the Power of Extreme Values

Michele Garetto
University of Torino
michele.garetto@unito.it

Emilio Leonardi
Politecnico di Torino
leonardi@polito.it

Giovanni-Luca Torrisi
IAC-CNR
torrisi@iac.rm.cnr.it

ABSTRACT

Bootstrap percolation is a well-known activation process in a graph, in which a node becomes active when it has at least r active neighbors. Such process, originally studied on regular structures, has been recently investigated also in the context of random graphs, where it can serve as a simple model for a wide variety of cascades, such as the spreading of ideas, trends, viral contents, etc. over large social networks. In particular, it has been shown that in $G(n,p)$ the final active set can exhibit a phase transition for a sub-linear number of seeds. In this paper, we propose a unique framework to study similar sub-linear phase transitions for a much broader class of graph models and epidemic processes. Specifically, we consider i) a generalized version of bootstrap percolation in $G(n,p)$ with random activation thresholds and random node-to-node influences; ii) different random graph models, including graphs with given degree sequence and graphs with community structure (block model). The common thread of our work is to show the surprising sensitivity of the critical seed set size to extreme values of distributions, which makes some systems dramatically vulnerable to large-scale outbreaks. We validate our results running simulation on both synthetic and real graphs.

1. INTRODUCTION AND RELATED WORK

Many fundamental phenomena occurring in various kinds of complex systems, ranging from technological networks (e.g., transportation, communication, energy), to biological networks (e.g., neural, ecological, biochemical) and social networks (in the real world or over the Internet) can be described by dynamical processes taking place over the underlying graph representing the system structure. Such processes modify over time the internal state of nodes and spread across the network following the edges of the graph.

One of the most widely studied example of such dynamical processes is the epidemic process, which starts from an initial set of infected nodes (usually referred to as seeds, chosen either deterministically or random) that can pass the infection to other (susceptible) nodes (under many possible models), possibly causing a major outbreak throughout the network.

SIGMETRICS '16, June 14–18, 2016, Antibes Juan-les-Pins, France.

DOI: http://dx.doi.org/10.1145/2896377.2901455

In our work we consider a generalized model for the spreading of an 'epidemic', in which nodes are characterized by an infection threshold r (either deterministic or random), and become infected when they collect from their neighbors an amount of influence larger than r. A special case of our model is the well known bootstrap percolation process, in which r is an integer ($r \geq 2$) and each edge exerts an influence equal to one: simply put, a node becomes infected when it has at least r infected neighbors.

Bootstrap percolation has a rich history, having been initially proposed in the area of statistical physics [1]. Due to its many physical applications (see [2] for a survey) it has been primarily studied over the years in the case of regular structures (lattices, grids, trees), most notably in a series of papers by Balogh and Bollobás (e.g., [3]). More recently, bootstrap percolation has been investigated also in the context of random graphs, which is the focus of this paper. In our work we are especially interested in epidemics occurring on very large, irregular structures such as those representing friendship relationships among people. This interest is motivated by the great popularity gained by online social platforms (e.g., Facebook, Twitter, Instagram, etc.), which, coupled with the increasing availability of always-on connectivity through mobile personal devices, has created an unprecedented opportunity for the rapid dissemination of various kinds of news, advertisements, viral videos, as well as a privileged environment for online discussion, creation and consolidation of beliefs, political opinions, memes and many other forms of collective reasoning. In this respect, bootstrap percolation provides a simple, primitive model that can be used to understand the diffusion of a generic 'idea' which requires a certain amount of 'reinforcement' from neighbors to be locally adopted.

Some results have already been obtained for particular random graph models. In particular, [4] first considered bootstrap percolation in the random regular graph $G(n,d)$, while [5] has extended the analysis to random graphs with given vertex degrees (configuration model). The above two papers assume that node degree is either fixed [4] or it has both finite expectation and finite second moment [5], implying that the cardinality of the seed set must scale linearly with n to observe a non-negligible growth of the epidemics. Both papers make use of the differential equation method to analyze the discrete Markov Chain associated with the epidemic process. The analysis in [5] also allows the threshold to vary among the nodes.

A very different technique has been recently proposed in [6] to study bootstrap percolation in Erdös–Rényi $G(n,p)$ graphs. This technique allows one to analyze also scenarios in which a sharp phase transition occurs with a number of seeds which is sublinear in n: below a critical seed set size, for which one can get a closed-form asymptotic expression, the infection essentially does not evolve, whereas above the critical size $n - o(n)$ nodes get infected with high probability[1]. In $G(n,p)$, this behavior is possible only when the average node degree itself grows with n (i.e., $p \gg 1/n$). The technique proposed in [6] has been applied by [7] to power-law random graphs generated by the Chung-Lu model (with power law exponent $2 < \beta < 3$), obtaining the interesting result that, under bounded average node degree, a sublinear seed set size is enough to reach a linear fraction of the nodes.

Also our work started from the approach proposed in [6], which provides a simple and elegant way to explore phase transitions taking place at sub-linear scale. To operate at this scale, we let, if needed, the average node degree grow with n, since this can be considered an acceptable assumption in many cases. Indeed, real social networks (and in particular online social networks), which evolve over time with the addition/removal of nodes/edges, often exhibit the so called densification phenomenon [8], meaning that the number of edges grows faster than the number of nodes (hence the average degree grows with time)[2].

The main thread of our work is to show the high 'vulnerability' (in terms of critical number of seeds) that arises in networks when we add inhomogeneities in any one of many possible ways (i.e., by adding variability in thresholds, edge weights, node degree, or network structure). Although this effect has already been observed in epidemic processes, the way in which inhomogeneities affect bootstrap percolation can be so dramatic that just extreme values of distributions (and not their particular shape) can determine the critical size of the seed set. We believe that this result, which apparently has not been recognized before, is of fundamental importance to better understand the dynamics of epidemics in complex systems.

2. NOTATION AND PRELIMINARIES

We start introducing some background material and notation taken from [6], which is necessary to follow the rest of the paper. As already mentioned, [6] provides a full picture of standard bootstrap percolation in Erdös–Rényi graphs $G(n,p)$. Nodes are characterized by a common integer threshold $r \geq 2$, and the process starts with an initial set $\mathcal{A}(0)$ of vertices (the seeds), of cardinality a, which are chosen uniformly at random among the nodes. We will use the same terminology adopted in [6], where infected nodes are called 'active', whereas non-infected nodes are said to be inactive. An inactive node becomes active as soon as at least r of its neighbors are active. Note that seeds are declared to be active irrespective of the state of their neighbors. Active nodes never revert to be inactive, so the set of active nodes grows monotonically.

The bootstrap percolation process naturally evolves through generations of vertices that become active. The first generation is composed of all those vertices which are activated by the seeds. The second generation of active nodes is composed by all the nodes which are activated by the joint effect of seeds and first generation nodes, etc. The process stops when either an empty generation is obtained or all nodes are active.

Now, it turns out that there is a useful reformulation of the problem that makes the process especially simple to analyze. This reformulation, which was originally proposed in [9], consists in changing the time scale, by introducing a virtual (discrete) time step $t \in \mathbb{N}$, such that a single active node is 'explored' at each time step (if the process has not yet stopped). By so doing, we forget about the generations, obtaining a more amenable process which is equivalent to the original one, in terms of the final size of the epidemic.

The above reformulation requires to introduce, besides the set $\mathcal{A}(t)$ of nodes which are active at time t, another set $\mathcal{Z}(t) \subseteq \mathcal{A}(t)$, referred to as *used* vertices, which is the subset of active vertices, of cardinality t, explored up to time t. More precisely, at time zero the set $\mathcal{A}(0)$ is initialized to the seed set, while the set of used vertices is initialized to the empty set: $\mathcal{Z}(0) = \emptyset$. Each node i is given a counter $M_i(t) \in \mathbb{N}$, initialized to 0 at time $t = 0$.

At time $t = 1$ we arbitrarily choose a node $z(1) \in \mathcal{A}(0)$ and we 'fire' its edges, incrementing by one the counter of all its neighbors. By so doing, we *use* node $z(1)$, adding it to the set of used nodes, so that $\mathcal{Z}(1) = \{z(1)\}$. We continue recursively: at each time t, we arbitrarily select an active node which has not been already used, i.e., $z(t) \in \mathcal{A}(t-1) \setminus \mathcal{Z}(t-1)$, and we distribute new 'marks' to its neighbors, which are not in $\mathcal{Z}(t-1)$, incrementing their counters. Node $z(t)$ is added to the set of used vertices: $\mathcal{Z}(t) = \mathcal{Z}(t-1) \cup \{z(t)\}$. We then check whether there are some inactive vertices, denoted by set $\Delta\mathcal{A}(t)$, that become active for effect of the marks distributed at time t (i.e., vertices whose counter reaches r at time t). Such newly activated vertices are added to the set of active vertices: $\mathcal{A}(t) = \mathcal{A}(t-1) + \Delta\mathcal{A}(t)$ (note that no vertices can be activated at time 1, being $r \geq 2$).

The process stops as soon as $\mathcal{Z}(t) = \mathcal{A}(t)$, i.e. when all active nodes have been used. Let $T = \min\{t : \mathcal{Z}(t) = \mathcal{A}(t)\}$. By construction, the final size A^* of the epidemic is exactly equal to T: $A^* := |\mathcal{A}(T)| = |\mathcal{Z}(T)| = T$.

The above reformulation of the problem is particularly useful because the counter associated to each inactive node can be expressed as:

$$M_i(t) = \sum_{s=1}^{t} I_i(s) \tag{1}$$

i.e., as the sum of t independent Bernoulli random variables $I_i(s)$ of average p, each associated with the existence/non existence of an edge in the underlying graph, between the node used at time s and node i. Indeed, it is perfectly sound to 'reveal' the edges going out of a node

[1]Throughout this paper we shall use the following (standard) asymptotic notation. Let $f, g : \mathbb{R} \to \mathbb{R}$ be two functions. We write: $f(x) = o(g(x))$ or $f(x) \ll g(x)$ and $g(x) = \omega(f(x))$ or $g(x) \gg f(x)$ if $\lim_{x\to\infty} \frac{f(x)}{g(x)} = 0$; $f(x) = O(g(x))$ if there exist $K > 0$, $x_0 \in \mathbb{R}$: $|f(x)| \leq K|g(x)|$, for any $x \geq x_0$; $f(x) \sim g(x)$ if $\lim_{x\to\infty} \frac{f(x)}{g(x)} = 1$. Unless otherwise specified, in this paper all limits are taken as $n \to \infty$.

[2]in practice, asymptotic results provide very good predictions of what happens in large (but finite) systems whenever the average degree is not too small, say significantly larger than r.

just when the node itself is used (principle of deferred decision). Moreover we can, for convenience, express the counters of all of the nodes at any time $t \geq 1$ just like (1), without affecting the analysis of the final size of the epidemics. Indeed, by so doing we introduce extra marks that are not assigned in the real process (where each edge is revealed at most one, in a single direction), specifically, when a used node is 'infected back' by a neighboring used node. However, this 'error' does not matter, since it has no impact on the percolation process. Note that counters $M_i(t)$ expressed in such a way are independent from node to node.

The dynamics of the epidemic process are determined by the behavior of the number $A(t)$ of 'usable' nodes (i.e., active nodes which have not been already used):

$$A(t) = |\mathcal{A}(t) \setminus \mathcal{Z}(t)| = a - t + S(t)$$

where a is the number of seeds, and $S(t)$ represents the number of vertices, which are not in the original seed set, that are active at time t. Note that the final size of the epidemics equals the first time T at which $A(T) = 0$. Moreover, by construction, the number of used vertices at time t equals t. Now, let $\pi(t) := \mathbb{P}(M_1(t) \geq r) = \mathbb{P}(\text{Bin}(t,p) \geq r)$ be the probability that an arbitrary node not belonging to the seed set is active at time t. There are $n-a$ such nodes, each active independently of others, hence $S(t)$ is equal in distribution to $\text{Bin}(n-a, \pi(t))$.

In essence, we need to characterize trajectories of process $A(t)$ which, besides a deterministic component $a-t$ (decreasing with time), includes a random variable $S(t)$ which is binomially distributed, with time-dependent parameter $\pi(t)$ (increasing with time):

$$A(t) = a - t + \text{Bin}(n-a, \mathbb{P}(\text{Bin}(t,p) \geq r)) \qquad (2)$$

In particular, whenever we can prove that, for a given t, $\mathbb{P}((\inf_{\tau \leq t} A(t)) < 0) \to 0$, then we can conclude that at least t vertices get infected w.h.p. Similarly, if, for a given t, $\mathbb{P}(A(t) < 0) \to 1$, we can conclude that the percolation terminates w.h.p. before t, thus the final number of infected vertices will be smaller than t. We now present a simplified form of the main theorem in [6], together with a high-level description of its proof.

THEOREM 2.1 (JANSON ET AL. [6]). *Consider bootstrap percolation in $G(n,p)$ with $r \geq 2$, and a number a of seeds selected uniformly at random among the n nodes. Let $p = p(n)$ be such that $p = \omega(1/n)$, $p = o(n^{-1/r})$. Define:*

$$t_c := \left(\frac{(r-1)!}{np^r}\right)^{1/(r-1)} \qquad (3)$$

$$a_c := \left(1 - \frac{1}{r}\right) t_c \qquad (4)$$

If $a/a_c \to \alpha < 1$ (subcritical case), then w.h.p. the final size is $A^* < 2a$. If $a/a_c \to \alpha \geq 1 + \delta$, for some $\delta > 0$ (supercritical case), then w.h.p. $A^* = n - o(n)$.

Note that, under the above assumptions on $p(n)$, the 'critical time' t_c is such that both $t_c = \omega(1)$ and $t_c = o(n)$, and the same holds for the critical number of seeds a_c, which differs from t_c just by the constant factor $(1-1/r)$, i.e., we get a phase transition for a sublinear number of seeds.

The methodology proposed in [6] to obtain the above result is based on the following idea: $A(t)$ is sufficiently concentrated around its mean that we can approximate it as $A(t) \approx \mathbb{E}(A(t)) = a - t + (n-a)\pi(t)$. Now, for a wide range of values of t (i.e., whenever $pt \to 0$, and in particular around t_c), $\pi(t)$ can be expressed as $\pi(t) = \frac{t^r p^r}{r!}(1 + O(pt + t^{-1}))$. Therefore function $\mathbb{E}(A(t))$ has a clear trend: it starts from a at $t = 0$ and first decreases up to a minimum value reached at $t \approx t_c$, after which it grows to a value of the order of n. Hence, time t_c acts as a sort of bottleneck: if $\mathbb{E}(A(t_c))$ is positive (negative), we are in the supercritical (subcritical) case. Finally, we can compute the asymptotic value of t_c by finding the minimum of function $f(t) = n\frac{t^r p^r}{r!} - t$.

The result then follows considering that, starting from a seeds, we get $\mathbb{E}(A(t_c)) = a - a_c + o(a_c)$, and that by changing a we deterministically move up or down the process $A(t)$. Hence, if we assume that a/a_c is asymptotically bounded away from 1 we obtain a sufficient 'guard factor' around the trajectory of the mean process to conclude that the real process is either supercritical or subcritical (see Fig. 1).

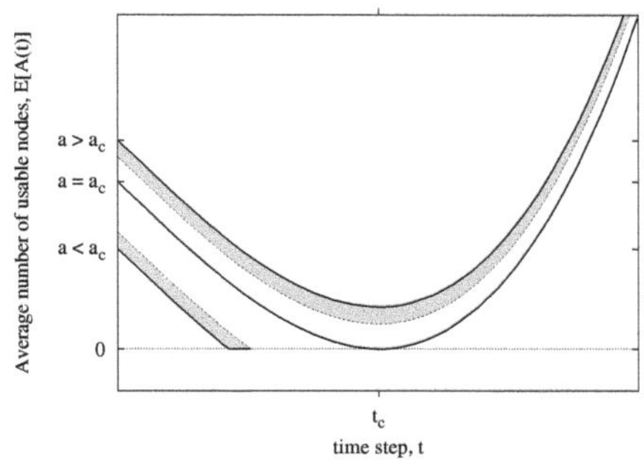

Figure 1: Example of (asymptotic) trajectories of the mean number of usable nodes, $\mathbb{E}(A(t))$, with $r = 3$. The plot also illustrates by shaded regions the concept of 'guard zone'.

We emphasize that in [6] authors use a martingale approach to show that $A(t)$ is sufficiently concentrated around its mean, which allows them to establish their results w.h.p.

As a final premise, it is better to clarify why we assume $r \geq 2$. The reason is that the case in which a node can be infected by just a single neighbor is degenerate, and leads to the trivial fact that a single seed is enough to infect the entire connected components it belongs to. Hence, one has to apply a totally different set of tools [10] to characterize the final size of the epidemic. This case, however, is not interesting to us, since the networks of many real systems are connected by construction, or they at least have a giant connected component. Hence, no phase transitions occur here in the number of seeds.

3. SUMMARY OF CONTRIBUTIONS

In this work we extend the approach of [6] along three 'orthogonal' directions that allow us to study more general threshold-based epidemic processes in inhomogeneous scenarios.

1. We consider a generalized version of bootstrap percolation in $G(n,p)$, in which thresholds of nodes are i.i.d. random variables $R_i > 0$, and infected nodes transmit a random amount of infection to their neighbors. Specifically, we assume that i.i.d.

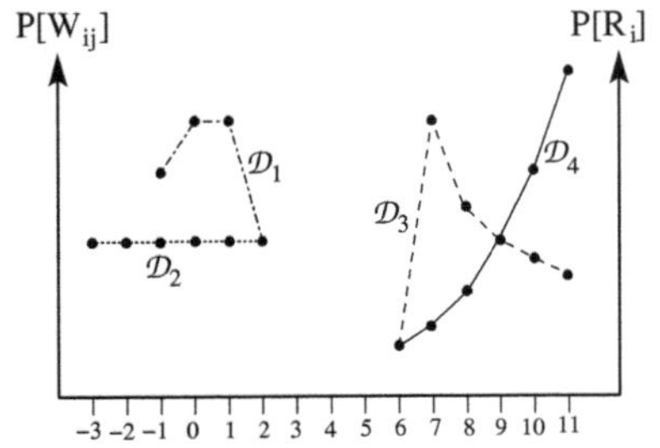

Figure 2: Examples of distributions of W_{ij} and R_i leading to the same (asymptotic) critical number of seeds a_c.

weights W_{ij} are assigned to the edges of the graph, representing the amount of infection transmitted through the edge. For this case, we obtain the asymptotic closed form expression of the critical number of seeds, and an exponential law for the probability that the process is supercritical or subcritical, strengthening the results in [6] (where results hold, instead, w.h.p.). The most significant outcome of our analysis is that the critical number of seeds typically does not depend on the entire distribution of R_i and W_{ij}, but just on values taken in proximity of the lower (for R_i) and upper (for W_{ij}) extreme of their support. For instance, in Figure 2 we show examples of two (discrete) distributions for W_{ij}, labelled $\mathcal{D}_1$ and $\mathcal{D}_2$, and two (discrete) distributions for R_i, labelled $\mathcal{D}_3$ and labelled $\mathcal{D}_4$. It turns out that any combination of them $(\mathcal{D}_a, \mathcal{D}_b)$, with $a \in \{1,2\}$ and $b \in \{3,4\}$ leads to the same asymptotic critical number of seeds a_c. Note that the various distributions have different means, and that one of them ($\mathcal{D}_2$) has even negative mean.

2. We extend the problem reformulation originally proposed in [9], where a single node is used at each time, to a similar reformulation in which a single edge is used at a time. This view is more convenient to apply the approach of [6] to other random graph models. In particular, we consider graphs with given degree sequence (configuration model), obtaining a closed-form expression of the asymptotic critical number of seeds. We then compute the scaling order of a_c for the particular (but most significant) case of power-law degree sequence, considering a wider range of parameters with respect to the one studied by [7]. Again, we observe the interesting phenomenon that in some cases the precise shape of the degree distribution (i.e., the power law exponent) does not matter, since a_c is determined by the largest degree.

3. We extend the analysis to the so-called block model, which provides a simple way to incorporate a community structure into a random graph model while preserving the analytical tractability of $G(n,p)$. We observe once more the interesting effect that the critical number of seeds might be determined by a single entry of the matrix of inter- (or intra-) community edge probabilities (i.e., the most vulnerable community).

Although we consider (for simplicity) the above three forms of inhomogeneity 'in isolation', it is not particularly difficult to combine them, if desired. Indeed, we show that all extensions above can be studied within a common framework. We emphasize that in this paper we generally assume that seeds are selected uniformly at random among the nodes, without knowledge of thresholds, weights, degrees, network structure. This differentiates our analysis from existing works addressing the so called influence maximization problem, i.e., finding the seed set that maximizes the final size of the epidemic (e.g., [11]). We observe that in the influence maximization framework many authors have already considered generalized models taking into account the impact of edge weights, node-specific thresholds, etc. (e.g., variants of the linear threshold model proposed in [12]). However, to the best of our knowledge, asymptotic properties of such generalized models are still not well understood. This paper makes a step forward in this direction analysing sublinear phase-transitions occurring when seeds are allocated uniformly at random in the network.

Interestingly, in all cases that we consider the epidemic is triggered among the most vulnerable nodes, and then it spreads out hitting less and less vulnerable components of the network. This fact can have dramatic consequences on the minimum number of seeds that can produce a network-wide outbreak.

In the following sections we present the above three contributions one at a time. Simulation experiments are presented along the way, to validate and better illustrate our analytical results.

4. GENERALIZED BOOTSTRAP PERCOLATION IN $G(n,p)$

4.1 System model

We start considering Erdös–Rényi random graphs $G(n,p)$, extending basic bootstrap percolation to the case in which node thresholds and/or node-to-node influences are i.i.d random variables. We denote by $R_i > 0$ the (real-valued) threshold associated to node i. We then assign a (real-valued) random weight W_{ij} to each edge of the graph, representing the influence that one node exerts on the other (see later). Node i becomes active when the sum of the weights on the edges connecting i to already active neighbors becomes greater than or equal to R_i.

Recall that each edge of the graph is 'used' by the process at most once. Hence our analysis encompasses both the 'symmetric' case in which the influence (possibly) given by i to j equals the influence (possibly) given by j to i, and the 'asymmetric' case in which weights along the two directions of an edge are different (i.i.d.) random variables. In both cases, we can consider a single random weight on each edge.

We do not pose particular restrictions to the distributions of R_i and W_{ij}, except for the following one, which avoids the degenerate case in which a node can get infected by a single edge (the case $r = 1$ in basic bootstrap percolation):

$$\operatorname{ess\,inf} R_i > \operatorname{ess\,sup} W_{ij} > 0. \tag{5}$$

Note that we can also allow W_{ij} to take negative values, which could represent, in the context of social networks, neighbors whose behavior steers us away from the adoption of an idea. This generalization produces, indeed, rather surprising results, as we will see. However, negative weights require to introduce some extra assumptions on the dynamics of the epidemic process, which are not needed when weights are always non-negative. Specifically, with negative weights we must assume that i) once a node becomes infected, it remains infected for ever; ii) some random delays are introduced in the infection process of a node and/or on the edges, to avoid that a node receives the combined effect of multiple (simultaneous) influences from active neighbors. We argue that assumption ii) is not particularly restrictive, since in many real systems influences received by a node take place atomically (e.g., a user reading ads, posts, twits, and the like). Assumption i) instead is crucial, because with negative weights counters no longer increase monotonically, and thus they can traverse the threshold many times in opposite directions. Assumption i) can be adopted, however, to study many interesting epidemic processes whose dynamics are triggered by nodes crossing the threshold for the first time[3].

The analysis of the general case can be carried out by exploiting the same problem reformulation described in Sec. 2, in which a single active node is used at each time step. Indeed, we can associate to inactive nodes a (real-valued) counter, initialized to 0 at time $t = 0$, which evolves according to:

$$M_i(t) = \sum_{s=1}^{t} I_i(s) W_{z(s),i} \tag{6}$$

where $I_i(s)$, $\forall s, \forall i$, is a Bernoulli r.v. with average p revealing the presence of edge $(z(s), i)$ and $W_{z(s),i}$ is the random weight associated to the same edge. Similarly to the basic case, the above expression of $M_i(t)$ can be extended to all nodes and all times, without affecting the results. By so doing, counters $M_i(t)$ are independent from node to node.

We then re-define $\pi(t)$, as the probability that an arbitrary node which is initially inactive (take node 1), has become active at any time $\tau \leq t$:

$$\pi(t) := \mathbb{P}\left(\sup_{\tau \leq t} M_1(\tau) \geq R_1\right)$$

With the above definition, the system behavior is still determined by trajectories of process (2). We have:

$$\begin{aligned}\pi(t) &= \mathbb{P}\left(\sup_{\tau \leq t} \sum_{s=1}^{\tau} I_1(s) W_{z(s),1} \geq R_1\right) \\ &\overset{(a)}{=} \sum_{\rho=0}^{t} \binom{t}{\rho} p^{\rho}(1-p)^{t-\rho} \cdot \mathbb{P}\left(\sup_{m \leq \rho} \sum_{s=1}^{m} W_{z(s),1} \geq R_1\right) \\ &= \sum_{\rho=0}^{t} \binom{t}{\rho} p^{\rho}(1-p)^{t-\rho} q_{\rho} \end{aligned} \tag{7}$$

where equation (a) is obtained by conditioning over the number ρ of variables $I_1(s) = 1$, and we have defined q_ρ:

$$q_\rho := \mathbb{P}\left(\sup_{m \leq \rho} \sum_{s=1}^{m} W_{z(s),1} \geq R_1\right) \tag{8}$$

which can be interpreted as the probability that a node, which has sequentially received the influence of ρ infected neighbors, has become active. Let $q_\infty := \lim_{\rho \to \infty} q_\rho$. Note that, as consequence of elementary properties of random walks, $q_\infty = 1$ when $\mathbb{E}[W_{ij}] \geq 0$ (recall also (5)). We introduce the following fundamental quantity:

$$\rho^* := \min\{\rho \geq 2 : \, q_\rho > 0\} \tag{9}$$

In words, ρ^* is the minimum number of infected neighbors that can potentially (with probability q_{ρ^*}) activate a node. Note that, as consequence of (5), it must be $\rho^* \geq 2$. For example, under the distributions shown in Fig. 2, we have $\rho^* = 3$, $q_{\rho^*} = \mathbb{P}(R_i = 6) \cdot \mathbb{P}(W_{ij} = 2)^3$.

4.2 Main results

We are now in the position to state our main results for the generalized bootstrap percolation model in $G(n,p)$. First, we define:

$$t_c := \left(\frac{(\rho^*-1)!}{np^{\rho^*} q_{\rho^*}}\right)^{\frac{1}{\rho^*-1}}; \qquad a_c := \left(1 - \frac{1}{\rho^*}\right) t_c$$

Moreover, we shall consider the function:

$$\begin{aligned} &H(x) := 1 - x + x \log x, \quad x > 0, \quad H(0) := 1, \\ &H(x) := +\infty, \quad x < 0 \end{aligned}$$

Theorem 4.1 (Super-critical case). *Under the assumptions: $1/(np) \to 0$, $p = o(n^{-1/\rho^*})$, $a/a_c \to \alpha$ for some $\alpha > 1$. Then,*

$$\forall\, \delta > 0, \quad \mathbb{P}\left(\left|\frac{A^*}{n} - q_\infty\right| > \delta\right) = O\left(\mathrm{e}^{-C_1(\rho^*,\alpha)a + o(a)}\right),$$

where $C_1(\rho^*, \alpha)$ is the constant:

$$C_1(\rho^*, \alpha) := \min_{x \in [\alpha\frac{\rho^*-1}{\rho^*}, \infty)} \frac{x^{\rho^*}}{\alpha(\rho^*-1)} H\left(\frac{x\rho^* - \alpha(\rho^*-1)}{x^{\rho^*}}\right).$$

For the sub-critical case, we define the function $h(x) := x - (\rho^*)^{-1} x^{\rho^*} - \alpha(1 - (\rho^*)^{-1})$, for $x \in [0,1]$, $\alpha \in (0,1)$, and we denote by $\varphi(\alpha)$ the only[4] solution of $h(x) = 0$, $x \in [0,1]$. Furthermore, having defined the interval $I := \left(0, (1-\alpha)(1-(\rho^*)^{-1})\right)$, it holds:

$$\forall \delta > 0, \exists \varepsilon_\delta \in I : [-\delta, \delta] \supseteq [h^{-1}(-\varepsilon_\delta) - \varphi(\alpha), h^{-1}(\varepsilon_\delta) - \varphi(\alpha)]$$

Theorem 4.2 (Sub-critical case). *Under the assumptions: $1/(np) \to 0$, $p = o(n^{-1/\rho^*})$ and $a/a_c \to \alpha$ for some $\alpha \in (0,1)$. Then, $\forall \delta > 0$,*

$$\mathbb{P}\left(\left|\frac{A^*}{a} - \frac{\rho^*}{\rho^*-1}\frac{\varphi(\alpha)}{\alpha}\right| > \delta\right) = O\left(\mathrm{e}^{-C_2(\rho^*,\alpha,\varepsilon_\delta)a + o(a)}\right),$$

where ε_δ and $\varphi(\alpha)$ are defined as above, and

$$C_2(\rho^*, \alpha, \varepsilon) := \frac{1}{\alpha(\rho^*-1)} H\left(1 + \varepsilon\rho^*\right).$$

Remark 4.3. *Note that the above results depend crucially on the extreme values of the distributions of R_i and W_{ij} through the expression of the percolation threshold a_c, which itself depends on ρ^*, defined in (9), and its associated probability q_{ρ^*}, see (8).*

[3]For example, on some online platforms, notifications that a user has watched a given viral video, bought a product, expressed interest for an event, etc., might be sent immediately (and once) to his friends, no matter if the user changes his mind later on.

[4]Function h is continuous and strictly increasing on $[0,1]$ with $h(0) = -\alpha(1-(\rho^*)^{-1}) < 0$ and $h(1) = (1-(\rho^*)^{-1})(1-\alpha) > 0$.

We shall provide here a sketch of the proof of Theorems 4.1 and 4.2. The complete proofs, including all mathematical details, can be found in [14].

At high level, we can show that almost complete percolation occurs under super-critical conditions, by:

i) analysing the trajectory of the mean of process (2), $\mathbb{E}[A(t)] = a - t + (n-a)\pi(t)$, finding conditions under which the above quantity is positive (with a sufficient guard factor) for any $t < (q_\infty - \delta)n$, for arbitrarily small $\delta > 0$.

ii) showing that the actual process $A(t)$ is sufficiently concentrated around its mean that we can conclude that $A(t) > 0$ w.h.p. for any $t < (q_\infty - \delta)n$.

For the sub-critical regime we can use similar arguments, showing that $\mathbb{E}[A(t)]$ becomes negative at early stages, and that $A(t)$ is sufficiently concentrated around its average that we can claim that the actual process stops at early stages w.h.p.

We start from the asymptotic approximation of $\pi(t)$:

$$\pi(t) = \frac{(pt)^{\rho^*}}{\rho^*!}(q_{\rho^*} + O(pt + t^{-1})). \quad (10)$$

which holds for any t such that $pt \to 0$. The above approximation allows us to write, for any $t \ll p^{-1}$:

$$\mathbb{E}[A(t)] = a - t + (n-a)\pi(t) = a - t + n\frac{(pt)^{\rho^*}}{\rho^*!}q_{\rho^*}(1 + o(1))$$

under the further assumption that $a = o(n)$. Thus, having defined for any $t \in \mathbb{R}_+$ function $f(t) = a - t + \frac{(pt)^{\rho^*}}{\rho^*!}q_{\rho^*}$, for n large enough we can determinate the sign of $\mathbb{E}[A(t)]$ for any $t \ll p^{-1}$ by analysing the behavior of $f(t)$. Elementary calculus reveals that $f(t)$ has a unique minimum at:

$$t_c = \left(\frac{(\rho^* - 1!)}{np^{\rho^*}q_{\rho^*}}\right)^{\frac{1}{\rho^*-1}}$$

with $f(t_c) = a - a_c$, $a_c = \left(1 - \frac{1}{\rho^*}\right)t_c$. Thus, we obtain an asymptotic closed-form expression for the critical number of seeds a_c (one can easily verify that, under the assumption $\frac{1}{n} \ll p \ll n^{\frac{1}{\rho^*}}$, it holds $t_c \to \infty$, $a_c \to \infty$, $pt_c \to 0$, $\frac{a_c}{n} \to 0$).

The difficult part of the proofs is to show that $A(t)$ is sufficiently concentrated around its expectation that we can establish exponential bounds (as $n \to \infty$) on the probability that the final size of the epidemics falls outside the intervals stated in Theorems 4.1 (super-critical case) and 4.2 (sub-critical case).

For the super-critical case, we adapt a methodology proposed in [6], which separately considers four time segments[5]: i) segment[6] $[a, Kt_c]$ (where K is a constant); ii) segment $[Kt_c, p^{-1}]$; iii) segment $[p^{-1}, cn]$ (where c is a constant); iv) segment $[cn, n(q_\infty - \delta)]$. Note that segment i) contains the most crucial, initial phase of the process.

The following lemma provides a fundamental property related to segment i), which provides the key to obtain the result in Theorem 4.1:

[5]The boundaries of all segments are to be meant as integers. However, to simplify the notation, we will omit $\lfloor\cdot\rfloor$ and $\lceil\cdot\rceil$ symbols.

[6]note that the process cannot stop at $t < a$.

LEMMA 4.4. *Under the assumptions of Theorem 4.1, let $K > \alpha(1 - (\rho^*)^{-1})$ be an arbitrarily fixed constant.*

$$\mathbb{P}\left(\inf_{t\in[a,Kt_c]}\{a - t + S(t)\} \le 0\right) = O\left(e^{-C_1(\rho^*,\alpha)a + o(a)}\right),$$

where $C_1(\rho^*, \alpha)$ is given in the statement of Theorem 4.1.

The detailed proof is reported in Appendix A. We outline here the three main ingredients to prove Lemma 4.4: i) we exploit standard concentration results for the binomial distribution, providing exponential bounds to $P(|S(t) - \mathbb{E}[S(t)]| > \epsilon t_c)$ at any t in the considered domain; ii) we employ the union bound to upper bound the probability $P(\sup_t |S(t) - \mathbb{E}[S(t)]| > \epsilon t_c)$ by $\sum_t P(|S(t) - \mathbb{E}[S(t)]| > \epsilon t_c)$; iii) we use the property $E[S(xt_c)] = x^{\rho^*}\frac{t_c}{\rho^*} + o(t_c)$.

We emphasize that in this paper we employ different techniques with respect to those used in [6], where authors rely on concentration results for $\sup_t |S(t) - \mathbb{E}[S(t)]|$ derived from Martingale theory (Doob's inequality). Instead, we combine deviation bounds specifically tailored to the binomial distribution (see Appendix A) with the union bound, obtaining a conceptually simpler approach which also permits us to obtain explicit exponential laws for probabilities related to the final size of the epidemics (i.e., a stronger result with respect to main Theorem 3.1 in [6], which holds just w.h.p.).

As immediate consequence of Lemma 4.4 we can say that the process does not stop before Kt_c with probability $1 - \zeta(n)$, being $\zeta(n) = O\left(e^{-C_1(\rho^*,\alpha)a + o(a)}\right)$.

Considering that $E[S(xt_c)] \sim x^{\rho^*}\frac{t_c}{\rho^*}$ quickly (super-linearly) increases after Kt_c (as long as approximation (10) holds), we can expect that the process is extremely unlikely to stop in segment $[Kt_c, p^{-1}]$, if it survives the first bottleneck segment. The proof of this fact is reported in Appendix A, where we also handle segment $[p^{-1}, cn]$.

Here we focus instead on the last temporal segment, where the value of q_∞ comes into play determining the final size of the epidemics. Indeed, we are going to show that $q_\infty n + o(n)$ are infected with probability $1 - \zeta(n)$. In general, we can assume that $q_\rho = q_\infty - v(\rho)$ with $v(\rho) \to 0$. Given an arbitrary $\hat{\rho}$ such that $\rho^* \le \hat{\rho} < cnp$, we make use of concentration inequality (24) to write:

$$\begin{aligned}
\pi(cn) &\ge \sum_{\rho=\hat{\rho}}^{cn}\binom{cn}{\rho}p^\rho(1-p)^{cn-\rho}q_\rho \\
&\ge \sum_{\rho=\hat{\rho}}^{cn}\binom{cn}{\rho}p^\rho(1-p)^{cn-\rho}(q_\infty - v(\hat{\rho})) \\
&= \mathbb{P}(\mathrm{Bin}(cn,p) \ge \hat{\rho})(q_\infty - v(\hat{\rho})) \\
&\ge (q_\infty - v(\hat{\rho}))(1 - e^{-cnpH(\hat{\rho}/(cnp))}) \\
&\ge q_\infty - (v(\hat{\rho}) + e^{-cnpH(\hat{\rho}/(cnp))}) \\
&\ge q_\infty - \frac{\epsilon}{2}
\end{aligned} \quad (11)$$

for any arbitrary $\epsilon > 0$ (and n large enough). We have:

$$\mathbb{P}\left(\inf_{t\in[cn,n(q_\infty-\epsilon)]} a - t + S(t) \le 0\right) \le \mathbb{P}(S(cn) + a \le n(q_\infty - \epsilon))$$
$$\le \mathbb{P}(\mathrm{Bin}(n, 1 - \pi(cn)) \ge n(1 - q_\infty + \epsilon))$$

Exploiting (25), the above probability goes to 0 faster than $\zeta(n)$ for any $\epsilon > 0$, proving that at least $n(q_\infty - \epsilon)$

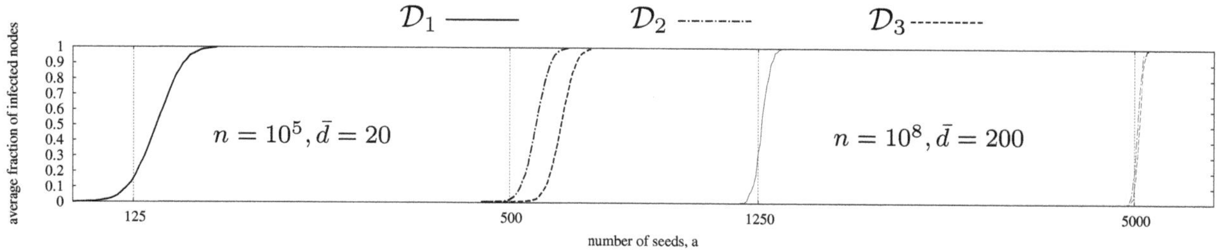

Figure 3: Phase transitions in $G(n,p)$ for different threshold distributions $\mathcal{D}_1$, $\mathcal{D}_2$, $\mathcal{D}_3$, averaging the results of 10,000 simulations. Analytical predictions are shown as vertical dotted lines.

nodes are infected. When $q_\infty < 1$, we can similarly show that no more than $n(q_\infty + \epsilon)$ nodes are infected. Indeed, considering that $\pi(n(q_\infty + \epsilon)) < q_\infty$, we can apply (24) to show that $\mathbb{P}(S(n(q_\infty + \epsilon) + a - n(q_\infty + \epsilon) < 0)$ goes to 1 faster than $\zeta(n)$, for any $\epsilon > 0$.

4.3 Validation

To validate our analysis, and understand how well asymptotic results can predict what happens in large (but finite) systems, we have run Monte-Carlo simulations of our generalized bootstrap percolation model. In each run we change both the identity of the seeds and the structure of the underlying $G(n,p)$ graph. We compute the average fraction of nodes that become infected, averaging the results of 10,000 runs.

We first look at the impact of random thresholds, while keeping equal weight $W_{ij} = 1$ on all edges. We consider three different distributions of R_i: i) constant threshold equal to 2 (denoted $\mathcal{D}_1$); ii) uniform threshold in the set $\{2,3,4,5\}$, (denoted $\mathcal{D}_2$); iii) two-valued threshold, with $\mathbb{P}(R_i = 2) = 1/4$ and $\mathbb{P}(R_i = 10) = 3/4$ (denoted $\mathcal{D}_3$); Note that all three distributions have $\rho^* = 2$, but their expected values are quite different. Moreover, $q_{\rho^*} = 1$ for $\mathcal{D}_1$, whereas $q_{\rho^*} = 1/4$ for both $\mathcal{D}_2$ and $\mathcal{D}_3$.

The asymptotic formula for the critical number of seeds gives in this scenario $a_c = n/(2\bar{d}^2 q_{\rho^*})$. We consider either a 'small' system, in which $n = 10^5$, $\bar{d} = 20$, or a 'large' system, in which $n = 10^8$, $\bar{d} = 200$. Results are shown in Fig. 3 using a log horizontal scale on which we have marked the values of a_c derived from the asymptotic formula. We use the same line style for each threshold distribution, and different line width to distinguish the small system (thick curves) from the large system (thin curves).

We make the following observations: i) the position of the phase transition (i.e., the critical number of seeds) is well estimated by the asymptotic formula; ii) despite having quite different shapes, distributions $\mathcal{D}_2$ and $\mathcal{D}_3$ lead asymptotically to the same critical number of seeds, as suggested by results obtained in the large system, where the corresponding curves are barely distinguishable (at $a_c = 5000$); iii) phase transitions become sharper for higher values of the critical number of seeds, confirming that the probability law by which the process is supercritical/subcritical depends strongly on a_c itself (as stated in Theorems 4.1 and 4.2).

We next move to a scenario in which the threshold is fixed, $R_i = 2$, and we vary the weights on the edges. We will consider, for simplicity, a simple case in which the influence exerted between two nodes can take just two values: +1, with probability z, and -1, with probability $1-z$. Note that the average influence, $\mathbb{E}[W_{ij}] = 2z-1$, can even be negative, if we select $z < 1/2$. In this scenario, we have $\rho^* = 2$, $q_{\rho^*} = z^2$, hence $a_c = n/(2(\bar{d}z)^2)$. We consider either a 'small' system, in which $n = 10^5$, $\bar{d} = 20$, or a 'large' system, in which $n = 10^7$, $\bar{d} = 200$, which produce the same value of a_c, for any z.

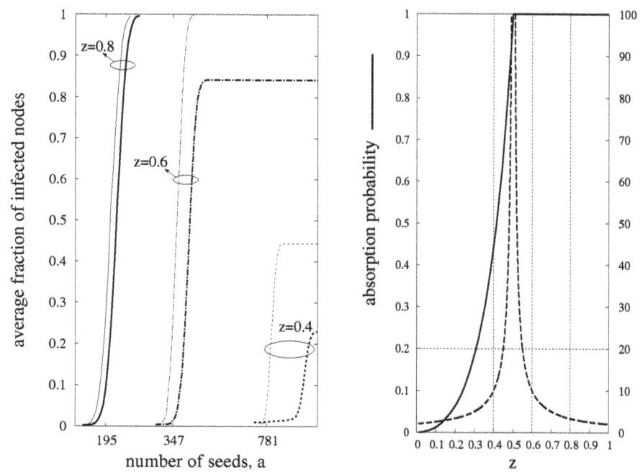

Figure 4: (left plot) Phase transitions in $G(n,p)$ for fixed threshold $R_i = 2$, and random weights ± 1, with $\mathbb{P}(W_{ij} = 1) = z$. (right plot) results for the corresponding simple random walk.

Results are shown in Fig. 4 (left plot), using a log horizontal scale on which we have marked the values of a_c derived from the asymptotic formula. We use the same line style for each value of z, and different line width to distinguish the small system (thick curves) from the large system (thin curves). We observe that in the small system the average fraction of infected nodes saturates to a value significantly smaller than one for $z = 0.6$, although we expect that, as $n \to \infty$, all nodes should get infected in this case (for which $q_\infty = 1$). In the large system, the discrepancy between simulation and asymptotic results disappears.

This phenomenon can be explained by considering that the counter of inactive nodes behaves as a simple random walk (i.e., with steps ± 1) with an absorbing barrier at $\rho^* = 2$. Recall [13] that for this simple random walk the absorption probability is 1 for $z \geq 1/2$, while it is equal to $(z/(1-z))^2$ for $z < 1/2$. Moreover, the mean time to absorption (conditioned to the event that the walk is absorbed) is $2/|1-2z|$ (see right plot in Fig. 4). On the other hand, the time horizon of this equivalent random walk is limited by the node degree, since a node cannot receive a number of contributions to its counter greater than the number of its neighbors. In the small system the average degree ($\bar{d} = 20$) is too small to approach the asymptotic prediction, whereas in the large system the average degree ($\bar{d} = 200$) is large enough (i.e., much larger than the mean time to absorption) to observe convergence of the final size to the asymptotic prediction obtained with q_∞. Interestingly, a finite fraction of nodes (asymptotically, around 0.44) gets infected with $z = 0.4$, a case in which the average node-to-node influence is negative!

5. RANDOM GRAPHS WITH ARBITRARY DEGREE DISTRIBUTION

Up to now we have considered the $G(n,p)$ random graph model, and we have followed the same problem reformulation adopted in [6], in which a single node is used at a time, revealing all its outgoing edges. This approach is especially suitable to $G(n,p)$, since marks $M_i(t)$ are i.i.d binomial random variables. We introduce now an alternative description of the percolation process, in which a single edge is used at a time. This approach is more convenient to analyze other random graph models, such as $G(n,M)$ (graphs with pre-established number of edges), $G(n,d)$ (where all nodes have the same degree), or the configuration model.

5.1 Edge-based reformulation for $G(n,M)$

We consider the (multi)-graph $\tilde{G}(n,M)$ in which, starting from a graph with no edges, M edges are sequentially added, each connecting two nodes selected (independently) uniformly at random. Note that by so doing we can generate parallel edges, as well as self loops. However, following the same approach as in Corollary 3 of [5], it is possible to show that sequences of events that occur w.h.p. over $\tilde{G}(n,M)$, occur w.h.p. also over $G(n,M)$, with $G(n,M)$ denoting the class of (simple)-graphs having M edges, with associated uniform probability law. Therefore our results apply to $G(n,M)$ as well.

To analyze bootstrap percolation in $\tilde{G}(n,M)$, we consider the following dynamical process: when a node becomes active, all edges connecting this node to other nodes which are still non active are denoted as 'usable', and added to a set $\mathcal{B}$ of usable edges. At a given time step t, one usable edge is selected uniformly at random from $\mathcal{B}(t-1)$, adding one mark to the endpoint that was inactive (when the edge became usable), provided that this endpoint is still inactive. The selected edge is then removed from $\mathcal{B}(t)$. Set $\mathcal{B}(0)$ is initialized with the edges connecting seeds to non-seeds. By construction, at most one node can become active at each time instant. Hence, denoting with $A(t)$ the number of active nodes at time t (initialized to a), we have $A(t) \leq a + t$.

Let $\pi(t)$ be the probability that a node, which is not a seed, has been activated at time $\tau \leq t$. While it is not easy to write an exact expression of $\pi(t)$, we can provide asymptotically tight bounds on $\pi(t)$, as follows:

$$1 - \sum_{j=0}^{r-1} \binom{t}{j} \left(\frac{1}{n}\right)^j \left(1 - \frac{1}{n}\right)^{t-j} \leq \pi(t) \leq$$
$$1 - \sum_{j=0}^{r-1} \binom{t}{j} \left(\frac{1}{n-a-t}\right)^j \left(1 - \frac{1}{n-a-t}\right)^{t-j}$$

This because we can reveal the endpoint of an active edge only when this edge is used, by choosing uniformly at random one of the nodes that were non active at the time instant τ' at which the considered edge became active. Hence, an inactive node i receives a mark at time τ with probability $\frac{1}{n-A(\tau')}$ (independently from other previously collected marks). Furthermore, by construction, we have $\frac{1}{n} \leq \frac{1}{n-A(\tau')} \leq \frac{1}{n-A(\tau)} \leq \frac{1}{n-a-\tau} \leq \frac{1}{n-a-t}$. At timescale $t = o(n)$, we can approximate $\pi(t)$ as:

$$\pi(t) = 1 - \sum_{j=0}^{r-1} \binom{t}{j} \left(\frac{1}{n}\right)^j \left(1 - \frac{1}{n}\right)^{t-j} + o(1) = \frac{1}{r!} \left(\frac{t}{n}\right)^r + o(1) \tag{12}$$

The dynamics of $\mathcal{B}(t)$ (whose size is denoted by $B(t)$) obey the following equation:

$$B(t) = B(0) + \Sigma(t) - t$$

where $\Sigma(t)$ represents the (cumulative) number of edges activated at $\tau \leq t$. The process stops at time $T = \min\{t : B(t) = 0\}$. Similarly to the $G(n,p)$ case, the number $S(t)$ of nodes that have become active by time t is the sum of $n - a$ identically distributed Bernoulli random variables with average $\pi(t)$. Indeed, $S(t) = \sum_{i \in \mathcal{V} \setminus \mathcal{A}(0)} \mathbb{1}_{M_i(t)=r}$.

Note that by construction marks are distributed only to inactive nodes, therefore a node i stops receiving marks as soon as $M_i(t) = r$. Differently from $G(n,p)$, however, variables $\mathbb{1}_{M_i(t)=r}$ are not independent, given that at most t marks have been distributed by time t (i.e., $\sum_i M_i(t) \leq t$). Note that we still have $\mathbb{E}[S(t)] = (n-a)\pi(t)$.

For what concerns the total number of edges activated by time t, $\Sigma(t)$, we can express it as the sum of random variables X_k associated with nodes in $\mathcal{A}(t)$, representing the numbers of edges activated along with node k (i.e. the number of edges connecting node k with inactive nodes):

$$\Sigma(t) = \sum_{k=1}^{A(t)} X_k.$$

We can evaluate X_k by dynamically unveiling, for every inactive edge, whether node k is one of its endpoints (but not both). It turns out $X_k = \text{Bin}\Big(M - \Sigma(\tau_k - 1) - B(0), \frac{2}{n-A(\tau_k-1)} - \frac{2}{(n-A(\tau_k-1))^2}\Big)$ where τ_k is the time instant at which the k-th node was activated. Indeed, $M - \Sigma(\tau_k - 1) - B(0)$ represents the number of edges still to be activated at time τ_k, while $\frac{2}{n-A(\tau_k-1)} - \frac{2}{(n-A(\tau_k-1))^2}$ is the probability that node k is an endpoint (but not both) of any such edges. Observe that variables X_k are not independent, as consequence of the fact that that sum of all edges in the graph is constrained to be M. However, X_k is conditionally independent from $X_{k'}$, with $k' < k$, given $\Sigma(\tau_k - 1)$ and $A(\tau_k - 1)$. Moreover, for any k we have:

$$\text{Bin}\Big(M - \Sigma(t) - B(0), \frac{2}{n} - \frac{2}{n^2}\Big) \leq_{st} X_k$$
$$\leq_{st} \text{Bin}\Big(M, \frac{2}{n-a-t} - \frac{2}{(n-a-t)^2}\Big). \tag{13}$$

In particular, the expectation of $\Sigma(t)$ satisfies:

$$\mathbb{E}\left[\frac{2(n-1)(M - \Sigma(t) - B(0))}{n^2} A(t)\right] \leq \mathbb{E}[\Sigma(t)] \leq \frac{2M\mathbb{E}[A(t)]}{n-a-t}.$$

Moreover, under the assumption $a \ll n$, since for $t \ll n$, $A(t) \leq a + t \ll n$ and $\Sigma(t) + B(0) = o(M)$, we have:

$$\mathbb{E}[\Sigma(t)] = \frac{2M}{n}\mathbb{E}[A(t)](1 + o(1)) = 2M\pi(t)(1 + o(1))$$

while $B(0) = \frac{2M}{n}a(1 + o(1)))$. Recalling (12), we have in conclusion:

$$\mathbb{E}[B(t)] = \left(\frac{2M}{n}a + \frac{2M}{r!}\left(\frac{t}{n}\right)^r - t\right)(1 + o(1))$$

Now, similarly to the case of $G(n,p)$, we can determine the critical number of seeds by: i) determining sufficient and necessary conditions under which $\mathbb{E}[B(t)] > \delta \frac{M}{n} a$ for some arbitrary $\delta > 0$ and any $t \ll n$; so doing we determine the critical number of seeds a_c. ii) Exploiting the fact that $B(t)$ is sufficiently concentrated around its mean for $t \le K\frac{M}{n}a_c$, where $K > 1$ is a properly defined constant. iii) Showing that for $K\frac{M}{n}a_c < t < M(1-\epsilon)$, $B(t)$ can be bounded from below away from 0.

For what concerns point i) we follow the same lines as for $G(n,p)$, defining function $g(t) = 2\frac{M}{n}a + \frac{2M}{r!}\frac{t^r}{n^r} - t$, and finding the minimum of $g(t)$, which is achieved at:

$$t_c = \left(\frac{(r-1)!n^r}{2M}\right)^{\frac{1}{r-1}} = \frac{2M}{n}\left(\frac{(r-1)!}{\frac{2M}{n}(\frac{2M}{n^2})^{r-1}}\right)^{\frac{1}{r-1}}$$

with $t_c = o(n)$ as long as $M \gg n$. Observe that $\frac{2M}{n}$ is the average node degree (replacing np in the expression of t_c obtained for $G(n,p)$) while $\frac{2M}{n^2}$ can be interpreted as the probability that two specific vertices are connected by at least an edge (replacing p for $G(n,p)$). Evaluating $g(t_c)$ and imposing $g(t_c) = 0$, we obtain the critical number of seeds:

$$a_c = \left(1 - \frac{1}{r}\right)\left(\frac{(r-1)!}{\frac{2M}{n}(\frac{2M}{n^2})^{r-1}}\right)^{\frac{1}{r-1}} \tag{14}$$

which is exactly the same as what we get in $G(n,p)$ through the substitution $\frac{2M}{n} \to np$ and $\frac{2M}{n^2} \to p$.

For what concerns ii) and iii) we can proceed in analogy with the case of $G(n,p)$, exploiting standard concentration results. In particular, we first focus on time instants $t \le K\frac{M}{n}a_c$ for suitable $K > 2$. We need to show that $B(t) > 0$ w.h.p. provided that $\mathbb{E}[B(t)] > \epsilon a_c$ for arbitrary $\epsilon > 0$ (i.e., $a > (1+\epsilon)a_c$). To this end observe that from (13), the fact that $\Sigma(K\frac{M}{n}a_c) = o(M)$ and $A(K\frac{M}{n}a_c) = o(n)$, and recalling the above mentioned property of conditional mutual independence of variables X_k, it descends that w.h.p., for any $t \le K\frac{M}{n}a_c$: $P(\Sigma(t) \le t - B(0)) \le P(\sum_1^{A(t)} \overline{X}_k \le t - B(0))$ with $\overline{X}_k$ mutually independent and $\overline{X}_k = \text{Bin}\Big(M(1-\epsilon), \frac{2}{n} - \frac{2}{n^2}\Big)$ for an arbitrarily small $\epsilon > 0$. At last observe that $P(\sum_1^{A(t)} \overline{X}_k \le t - B(0))$ can be easily bounded using inequalities (24) and (25).

For what concerns iii) we adopt arguments conceptually similar to the case of $G(n,p)$, exploiting the fact that $\mathbb{E}[B(t)]$ quickly (super-linearly) increases after $K\frac{M}{n}a_c$.

5.2 Configuration Model

The edge-based problem reformulation described in previous section can be easily extended to the configuration model $G(n,p(d))$, in which we specify a given degree sequence (possibly dependent on n) with associated empirical distribution function $p(d)$. For simplicity, we limit ourselves to describing the computation of the critical number number of seeds a_c. However, the approach can be made rigorous by following the same lines as for $G(n,M)$. As before, properties of multi-graphs $\tilde{G}(n,p(d))$ apply as well to simple-graphs $G(n,p(d))$.

Similarly to what we have done for $G(n,M)$, we focus on the evolution of the number of activable edges:

$$B(t) = B(0) + \Sigma(t) - t$$

and compute the critical time t_c by finding the minimum of $\mathbb{E}[B(t)]$.

The impact of node degree can be taken into account by evaluating the probability $\pi(t,d)$ that a node with degree d has been activated by time t. Moreover, we need to consider the amount of edges that a node contributes to $\mathcal{B}$ after being activated. There are in total $n\bar{d}$ 'end-of-edges' in the network, so the probability that a given end-of-edge is active at time t is $t/(n\bar{d})$. Hence, we can write:

$$\pi(t,d) = 1 - \sum_{j=0}^{r-1}\binom{d}{j}\left(\frac{t}{n\bar{d}}\right)^j\left(1 - \frac{t}{n\bar{d}}\right)^{d-j} + o(1), \tag{15}$$

Since $t/(n\bar{d})$ is small, we can approximate it as

$$\pi(t,d) = \frac{1}{r!}\left(\frac{dt}{n\bar{d}}\right)^r + o(1) \qquad (d \ge r)$$

Observe that since, by construction, a node gets activated thanks to exactly r active edges, it contributes $d - r$ new edges to $\mathcal{B}$. Then for $t \ll n$ since $A(t) \le t + a \ll n$ we can approximate the average value of $B(t)$ as:

$$\mathbb{E}[B(t)] \sim B(0) + n\sum_{d \ge r}\frac{1}{r!}\left(\frac{dt}{n\bar{d}}\right)^r (d-r)p(d) - t.$$

Now, if we define

$$d^* = \sum_{d \ge r}\left(\frac{d}{\bar{d}}\right)^r \frac{d-r}{\bar{d}} p(d) \tag{16}$$

we obtain $\mathbb{E}[B(t)] \sim B(0) + \frac{\bar{d}nt^r}{r!n^r}d^* - t$, from which we can derive the critical time t_c:

$$t_c = n\left(\frac{(r-1)!}{\bar{d}d^*}\right)^{\frac{1}{r-1}}$$

and the critical number of seeds:

$$a_c = \left(1 - \frac{1}{r}\right)n\left(\frac{(r-1)!}{\bar{d}^r d^*}\right)^{\frac{1}{r-1}} \tag{17}$$

One can easily check that the above formula is consistent with what we get in $G(n,p)$ or $G(n,M)$, for which $d^* \sim 1$. The above formula holds when seeds are selected uniformly at random. However, note that our analysis could be immediately extended to the important case in which seeds are chosen on the basis of the node degree. Indeed, what really matters is only the cardinality of the initial set of edges connecting seeds to non-seeds.

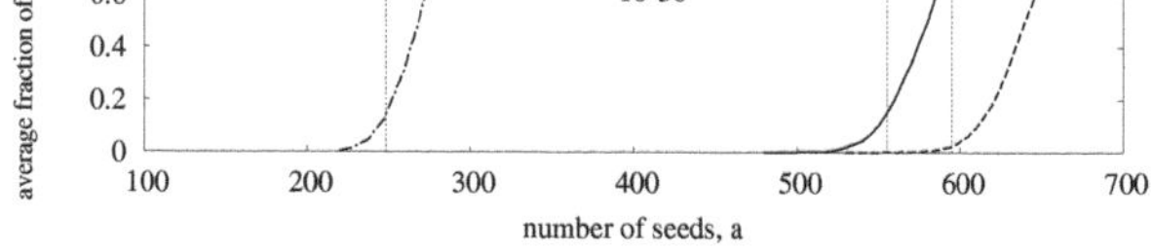

Figure 5: Phase transitions of basic bootstrap percolation with $r = 2$, in different random graph models with $n = 10^6$, $\bar{d} = 30$.

Figure 5 reports simulation results for three different random graph models having $n = 10^6$ nodes, and average node degree $\bar{d} = 30$. We consider basic bootstrap percolation with $r = 2$. We compare the $G(n,M)$ model, the regular $G(n,d)$ (in which nodes have constant degree), and a configuration model in which half of the nodes have degree 10 while the other half have degree 50 (curve labelled '10-50'). Analytical results obtained by (14) (for $G(n, M)$), and by (17) (for the other two graph models) are marked on the top margin. As expected, for fixed average degree, the critical number of seeds decreases for increasing variance of the degree distribution.

We experimented also with a real online social network, considering user-user friendship relations of Orkut, a former social networking site run by Google. In particular, we have used a crawled sub-graph of Orkut with $n = 3,072,441$ nodes [15], hereinafter referred to as Orkut graph, although it represents only a small percentage (11%) of the entire social network. The average node degree of this graph is $\bar{d} = 76.3$, and the maximum degree is $d_{\max} = 33,313$. An interesting question that arises here is the following: does a configuration model with the same number of nodes as the Orkut graph, and exactly the same degree sequence, produce also a similar value of a_c? If the answer is affirmative, it would tell us that the degree distribution alone, and not the entire network structure, could be used to predict (even analytically) the onset of large-scale outbreaks in this kind of systems (as suggested also by [16]). We partially answer this question by running simulations on both the original Orkut graph and the matched configuration model, as well as by analytically evaluating a_c using (17).

Besides basic bootstrap percolation, we explored also the interesting variation in which r is a deterministic function of the node degree. Indeed, note that (15) can be immediately generalized to $r = r(d)$, although in this case we do not get a closed-form expression for a_c, and the minimum of $\mathbb{E}[B(t)]$ has to be computed numerically (we omit the details of this computation).

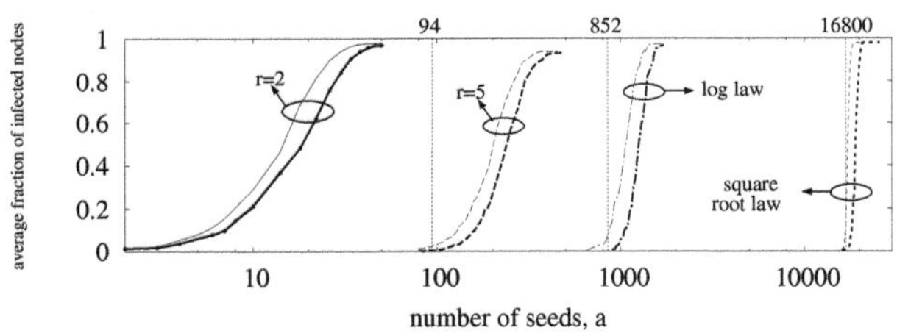

Figure 6: Phase transitions in the Orkut graph and the matched configuration model, for different threshold functions.

Results are shown in Fig. 6, where thick lines refers to the real Orkut graph, while thin lines refers to the matched configuration model. We use different line styles for i) basic bootstrap percolation with $r = 2$ or $r = 5$; ii) the logarithmic law $r(d) = \max\{2, \lceil \log_2(d) \rceil\}$; iii) the square root law $r(d) = \max\{2, \lceil \sqrt{d} \rceil\}$; Analytical predictions of a_c are shown as vertical dotted lines (except for $r = 2$, for which (17) provides a value of a_c even smaller than $r = 2$). We observe similar phase transitions in the Orkut graph and the associated configuration model, while the analysis captures quite well the point after which a major outbreak occurs.

5.3 Impact of power-law degree distribution

Large networks observed in a variety of different domains (social, technological, biological networks) are characterized by the scale-free property, which implies a power law degree distribution. Hence, it is interesting to understand the impact of power-law degree distributions on the critical seed set size. We will consider here power-law degree distributions of the form

$$p(d) = \frac{C}{d^\beta} \qquad \text{for } d_{\min} \le d \le d_{\max} \tag{18}$$

where β is the power-law exponent (typically larger than 2), and C is the normalization factor. We will further assume that $d_{\max} \to \infty$, while $d_{\min} = o(d_{\max})$. Note that by letting $d_{\min}$ scale up with n we can obtain an increasing average node degree (graph densification) in the most common case in which $\beta > 2$.

The reason why we introduce a maximum node degree $d_{\max}$ is instead more subtle, and has to do with the fact that $p(d)$ must be the limiting distribution function of a sequence of empirical distribution function (for each n) associated with the configuration model. Clearly, we cannot have in any case a degree larger than $n-1$, but it turns out that, for the common case of $\beta > 2$, nodes with very large degree are so rare that is preferable to avoid them at all, setting to zero $p(d)$ after a given $d_{\max} = n^\zeta$, with $\zeta < 1$. The maximum value of ζ, for $\beta > 1$, can be obtained by solving the inequality $\int_{n^\zeta}^{\infty} C x^{-\beta}\, dx > n^{-1}$. For example, when $\beta > 1$, $d_{\min} = \Theta(1)$, we have $\zeta \le 1/(\beta - 1)$. In practice, we never see nodes with extremely large degree[7], and it is actually customary in many random graph models to assume that the maximum degree is smaller than, say, $n^{1/2}$. In our model, we try to be more flexible by allowing a generic $d_{\max} = n^\zeta \ll n$, satisfying the above constraint (if $\beta > 1$).

In practice, one can starts with a desired distribution $p(d)$ of the form (18), having chosen $d_{\min}$ and $d_{\max}$ (depending on n), and construct a sequence $\{d_i\}_n$ of degrees for the configuration model by assigning to node i the degree $d_i = \inf\{d : 1 - F_n(d) < i/n\}$, where $F_n(d)$ is the cdf of $p(d)$. Under our assumptions we have, asymptotically,

$$C \sim \begin{cases} \frac{1-\beta}{d_{\max}^{1-\beta}} & \text{if } \beta < 1 \\ \frac{\beta-1}{d_{\min}^{\beta-1}} & \text{if } \beta > 1 \end{cases}$$

The following expression for the generic k-th moment of $p(d)$ will come in handy in the following:

$$\mathbb{E}[d^k] \sim \begin{cases} d_{\min}^k \frac{\beta-1}{\beta-k-1} & \text{if } \beta > k+1 \\ d_{\min}^{\beta-1} d_{\max}^{k+1-\beta} \frac{\beta-1}{k+1-\beta} & \text{if } 1 < \beta < k+1 \\ d_{\max}^k \frac{1-\beta}{k+1-\beta} & \text{if } \beta < 1 \end{cases} \tag{19}$$

Note that moments of order $k < \beta - 1$ depend only on $d_{\min}$ (e.g., the average node degree ($k = 1$), when $\beta > 2$). Instead, moments of order $k > \beta - 1$ may depend also (or exclusively) on $d_{\max}$.

Recall that our methodology to compute the critical seed set size requires that a_c is both $\omega(1)$ and $o(n)$. This regime implies that the average node degree $\bar{d}$ cannot be either too small nor too large. Recall that in the $G(n, p)$ model we need that $\bar{d} \gg 1$ and $\bar{d} \ll n^{\frac{r-1}{r}}$. Under a general degree distribution, it is not stricly necessary that $\bar{d} \gg 1$, since (look at formula (17)) we could just have $d^* \to \infty$, resulting into a number of seeds $o(n)$.

To better understand how the critical number of seeds depends on parameters of the power-law distribution, we

[7]In many real systems the tail of the degree distribution exhibits an exponential cut-off, and often the degree cannot exceed a maximum value imposed by physical or technological constraints.

evaluate its scaling order with n, assuming for simplicity that $d_{\min} = n^\gamma$, with $0 \le \gamma < \zeta$. When $\beta > 1$, we further assume $\zeta \le \frac{1}{\beta-1} - \gamma$ to avoid rare nodes having very large degree. We see from (16) that d^* depends essentially on the $(r+1)$-th moment of $p(d)$, i.e., $d^* = \Theta\left(\frac{\mathbb{E}[d^{r+1}]}{(\mathbb{E}[d])^{r+1}}\right)$ (assuming $\mathbb{E}[d] > r$). We can thus use the expressions in (19), and obtain that the scaling exponent of a_c is [8]

$$e(a_c) = \begin{cases} 1 - \frac{\gamma r}{r-1} & \text{if } \beta > r+2, \quad \gamma > 0 \\ 1 - \frac{\gamma(\beta-2)+\zeta(r+2-\beta)}{r-1} & \text{if } 2 < \beta < r+2, \quad \gamma \ge 0 \\ 1 - \frac{\zeta r}{r-1} & \text{if } \beta < 2, \quad \gamma \ge 0 \end{cases} \tag{20}$$

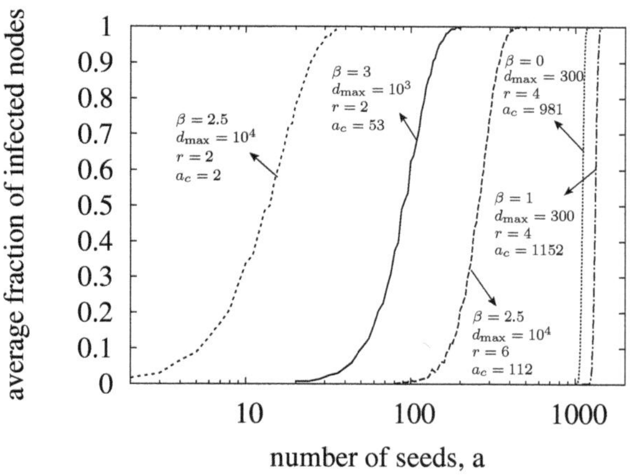

Figure 7: Phase transitions of basic bootstrap percolation in random graphs with $n = 10^6$ nodes and power-law degree.

We should mention that our results are only partially aligned with those obtained for Chung-Lu graphs[9] with power-law degree distribution in [7], where authors consider the case $2 < \beta < 3$, $\gamma = 0$. In particular, in [7] they suggest that, when $d_{\max} = \Theta(n^{1/(\beta-1)})$, a_c is of the order of $n^{\frac{\beta-2}{\beta-1}}$, independently of r. We emphasize that in [7] authors employ a totally different approach with respect to ours, partitioning the nodes into as sequence of bands, on the basis of node degree, the first of which associated to a fairly dense kernel of high-degree nodes. By directly applying the results of [6] to this kernel, they show that, once a fraction of nodes belonging to the kernel become active, the infection easily spreads recursively through the other bands.

Figure 7 reports simulation results under our power-law configuration model. The number of nodes is always $n = 10^6$, $d_{\min} = 10$, and we try different combinations of β, $d_{\max}$ and r. The values of a_c computed by (17) are also shown on the plot. We see that, with $\beta = 2.5$, $d_{\max} = n^{1/(\beta-1)} = 10^4$, very few seeds are needed with $r = 2$, and many more with $r = 6$. We also consider two cases with $\beta < 2$, $d_{\max} = 300$, $r = 4$, to show that, in accordance with (20), when $\beta < 2$, a_c depends essentially only on the extreme value of the node degree distribution (i.e., $d_{\max}$), and not on its shape. Indeed, the phase transitions obtained with $\beta = 0$ and $\beta = 1$ are not that far away, as predicted by our computed values of a_c, despite the fact that the average degree is quite different in the two cases (i.e., 84 ($\beta = 1$) vs 155 ($\beta = 0$)).

6. COMMUNITY BASED GRAPHS: THE BLOCK MODEL

Another important feature of many graphs representing real systems is the presence of a community structure (i.e., a non-negligible clustering coefficient). This feature is not captured by any of the random graph models considered so far. In this section, we extend the analysis of basic bootstrap percolation to the so called block model, which naturally extends the $G(n, p)$ model to incorporate a community structure. We will start from the simple case of just two communities, and then extend our results to $K < \infty$ communities.

6.1 The case of two communities

We consider a $G(n_1, n_2, p_1, p_2, q)$ block model comprising two communities of n_1 and n_2 nodes, respectively (with $n_1 + n_2 = n$). The sub-graph induced by nodes belonging to community i (with $i = 1, 2$) is an Erdös-Rényi's graph $G(n_i, p_i)$. Pairs of nodes belonging to different communities are independently connected with probability q. We assume $q < \min(p_1, p_2)$ and $q = \Omega(\max(\frac{1}{n_1}, \frac{1}{n_2}))$. We denote by $\mathcal{V}_i$ the set of nodes belonging to community i.

Bootstrap percolation in $G(n_1, n_2, p_1, p_2, q)$ can be reformulated in two different ways, which allow us to obtain different (complementary) results. We explain here our first approach. An alternative reformulation will be presented in Section 6.2.

In our first approach we assume that, at each discrete time step t, two active nodes (one in community 1 and one in community 2) are simultaneously used, whenever they are both available. If a community runs out of (active) usable nodes, while the other still has some available (active) usable nodes, a single node is used at a time. We denote by $\mathcal{A}_i(t)$ and $\mathcal{Z}_i(t)$, respectively, the set of active nodes and the set of used nodes in community i at time t. Let $A_i(t) = |\mathcal{A}_i(t) \setminus \mathcal{Z}_i(t)|$ be the cardinality of the set of active usable nodes in community i. Observe that it is entirely possible that, say, $A_1(t)$ hits zero at some point, but later on it increases again for effect of marks received by inactive nodes in $\mathcal{V}_1$ from nodes used in $\mathcal{V}_2$. This event makes an exact analysis of the system particularly difficult. Note that the process definitely dies at time T: $T := \min\{t \in \mathbb{N}^+ : \ A_1(t) = 0, A_2(t) = 0\}$.

We introduce a new quantity $T_i(t)$, representing the number of nodes that have been used in community i up to time t: $T_i(t) := |\mathcal{Z}_i(t)|$. From the above discussion, observe that $T_i(t)$ is not necessarily equal to t, for $t \le T$, in constrast to what happens in $G(n, p)$, where $|\mathcal{Z}_i(t)| = t$, $\forall t \le T$.

The number $S_1(t)$ of initially inactive nodes in $\mathcal{V}_1$ that are active at time t can then be expressed as:

$$S_1(t) = \text{Bin}(n - a_1, \widehat{\pi}_i(T_1(t), T_2(t))$$

where $\widehat{\pi}_1(t_1, t_2) = P(\text{Bin}(t_1, p_1) + \text{Bin}(t_2, q) \ge r)$. For $p_1 t_1 \ll 1$ we have:

$$\widehat{\pi}_1(t_1, t_2) \sim \sum_{\rho=0}^{r} \frac{(p_1 t_1)^\rho}{\rho!} \frac{(q t_2)^{r-\rho}}{(r-\rho)!}$$

(similar expressions can be written for $S_2(t)$ and $\widehat{\pi}_2(t_1, t_2)$ provided that $p_2 t_2 \ll 1$). Note that, whenever $t_1 =$

[8]The scaling exponent of a generic function $f(n)$ is defined as $e(f) := \lim_{n\to\infty} \frac{\log(f(n))}{\log(n)}$.

[9]Interestingly, our scaling exponent in (20), for $2 < \beta < 3$, $\gamma = 0$, perfectly matches quantity a_c^+ in [7] (Theorem 2.3).

$t_2 = t$, previous approximation simplifies to: $\widehat{\pi}_1(t,t) \sim \sum_{\rho=0}^{r} \frac{p_1^\rho q^{r-\rho}}{\rho!(r-\rho)!} t^r$. Moreover, if $q \ll p_1$, the latter further simplifies to $\widehat{\pi}_1(t,t) \sim \frac{(p_1)^r}{r!} t^r$, as in $G(n,p)$.

To characterize the system behavior, we stochastically upper and lower bound $S_i(t)$, for $i = 1,2$, by two virtual processes $\underline{S}_i(t)$ and $\overline{S}_i(t)$ obtained in the following shadow systems: a shadow reduced system, in which inter-community edges are removed, and thus each community evolves as in isolation. Note that process $\underline{S}_i(t)$ associated to the reduced system is equivalent to what we would get in a $G(n_i, p_i)$ model; a shadow augmented system (viewed by community i), in which we assume that a new node can *always* be used in the other community (if the other community has no usable nodes, an arbitrary inactive node in the other community is selected and used).

It immediately descends from their definitions that:

$$\begin{aligned} \underline{S}_1(t) &= \text{Bin}(n_1 - a_1, \widehat{\pi}_1(\underline{T}_1(t), 0)) \\ \overline{S}_1(t) &= \text{Bin}(n_1 - a_2, \widehat{\pi}_1(\overline{T}_1(t), t)) \end{aligned}$$

Furthermore, by induction over time, it can be immediately shown that: $\underline{S}_1(t) \leq_{st} S_1(t) \leq_{st} \overline{S}_1(t)$, where $\leq_{st}$ indicates the less or equal operator under usual stochastic ordering (also known as 'first order stochastic dominance'). Now, under the joint conditions $\mathcal{A}_1(\tau) \neq \mathcal{Z}_1(\tau)$ and $\mathcal{A}_2(\tau) \neq \mathcal{Z}_2(\tau)$ for any $\tau < t$, by construction $S_1(\tau) = \overline{S}_1(\tau)$ and $S_2(\tau) = \overline{S}_2(\tau)$ for any $\tau < t$, which allows us to conclude that also at time t: $S_1(t) = \overline{S}_1(t)$ and $S_2(t) = \overline{S}_2(t)$. Then, by induction over time:

$$\begin{aligned} &\{\mathcal{A}_1(\tau) \neq \mathcal{Z}_1(\tau), \mathcal{A}_2(\tau) \neq \mathcal{Z}_2(\tau), \forall \tau \leq t\} \\ &= \left\{ \inf_{\tau<t} \min(S_1(\tau) - \tau + a_1, S_2(\tau) - \tau + a_2) > 0 \right\} \\ &= \left\{ \inf_{\tau<t} \min(\overline{S}_1(\tau) - \tau + a_1, \overline{S}_2(\tau) - \tau + a_2) > 0 \right\}. \end{aligned}$$

In particular, whenever $\overline{S}_1(t)$ and $\overline{S}_2(t)$ both satisfy supercritical conditions, then necessarily $\mathcal{A}_i(t) \neq \mathcal{Z}_i(t)$ and $S_i(t) = \overline{S}_i(t)$, for any $t < \max(n_1, n_2) - o(\max(n_1, n_2))$. More formally, exploiting the results in 4.2, we get:

THEOREM 6.1. *Suppose $1/(n_i p_i) \to 0$, $p_i = o(n_i^{-1/r})$, $a_i / a_c^{(i)} \to \alpha_i$, for some $\alpha_i > 1$ with $i = \{1,2\}$, and:*

$$a_c^{(i)} = \left(1 - \frac{1}{r}\right) \left(\frac{(r-1)!}{n_i (\widehat{p}_i)^r}\right)^{(r-1)^{-1}}$$

where $\widehat{p}_i = \sqrt[r]{(r!) \cdot \sum_{\rho=0}^{r} \frac{p_i^\rho q^{r-\rho}}{\rho!(r-\rho)!}}$. Then, having defined $T = \inf_t \{\min_i (a_i - t + S_i(t)) < 0\}$ we have:

$$\forall \varepsilon > 0, P\left(1 - \frac{T}{\max_i(n_i)} > \varepsilon\right) = O\left(e^{-C_1(r, \min_i(\alpha_i))a + o(a)}\right)$$

where $C_1(r, \alpha)$ is the same function as in Theorem 4.1.

Theorem 6.1 provides sufficient (but not necessary) conditions for almost complete percolation of $G(n_1, n_2, p_1, p_2, q)$.

To complement previous result, suppose that $\underline{S}_1(t)$ satisfies supercritical conditions (while to avoid trivialities we assume $\overline{S}_2(t)$ to be sub-critical). In this case complete or almost complete percolation occurs in $\mathcal{V}_1$ as immediate consequence of Theorem 4.1 applied to community 1 in isolation, and the fact that $\underline{S}_1(t) \leq S_1(t)$. Then, under the assumption that $q \geq \Omega(\max(\frac{1}{n_1}, \frac{1}{n_2}))$, we obtain complete or almost complete percolation also in community 2, since any node in $\mathcal{V}_2$ would have finite probability of having at least r neighbors in $\mathcal{V}_1$[10].

It remains to analyze the case in which $\overline{S}_1(t)$ is supercritical (but $\underline{S}_1(t)$ is sub-critical), and $\overline{S}_2(t)$ is not supercritical (or viceversa). This case, which can occur only when q and p_1 are of the same order, is more involved and we leave it to future study.

6.2 Alternative approach for 2 communities

We now introduce a different approach to study the $G(n1, n2, p_1, p_2, q)$ block model, which allows us to understand how seeds should be optimally partitioned between the two communities in order to minimize their number and achieve almost complete percolation in the whole system. This time, we assume that at each time step t a single active node, selected uniformly at random among all usable active nodes in the system, is used.

To simplify the exposition, we will focus on a perfectly symmetric scenario in which $p_1 = p_2$ and $n_1 = n_2 = n/2$. However, the same approach can be easily extended to the general case $G(n_1, n_2, p_1, p_2, q)$.

Differently from our first reformulation, now we have, for any $t < T$:

$$T_1(t) + T_2(t) = t$$

where $T_i(t)$ denotes the (random) number of nodes used in community i up to time t.

Now, if we consider any two different sequences in which active nodes are selected, such that $T_1(t)$ in one sequence is larger than $T_1'(t)$ in the other sequence, we easily see that,

$$S_1(T_1(t), T_2(t)) \geq_{st} S_1(T_1'(t), T_2'(t)) \quad (21)$$

$$S_2(T_1(t), T_2(t)) \leq_{st} S_2(T_1'(t), T_2'(t)) \quad (22)$$

Furthermore, for $1 \ll t \ll p^{-1}$ we have:

$$\begin{aligned} &\mathbb{E}[S_1(T_1(t), T_2(t)) + S_2(T_1(t), T_2(t))] \sim \\ &\sum_{\rho=0}^{r} \frac{(pT_1(t))^\rho (qT_2(t))^{r-\rho}}{\rho!(r-\rho)!} + \sum_{\rho=0}^{r} \frac{(qT_1(t))^\rho (pT_2(t))^{r-\rho}}{\rho!(r-\rho)!} = \\ &f\left(\frac{T_1(t)}{t}\right) \quad (23) \end{aligned}$$

being $f(x) = \sum_\rho [\frac{(ptx)^\rho (qt(1-x))^{r-\rho}}{\rho!(r-\rho)!} + \frac{(qtx)^\rho (pt(1-x))^{r-\rho}}{\rho!(r-\rho)!}]$ a continuous function over $[0,1]$, indefinitely derivable in $(0,1)$ and satisfying the following properties: i) $f(x) = f(1-x)$; ii) $f(x)$ decreases for $x \in [0, 1/2)$ (and increases for $x \in (1/2, 1]$). Previous observations lead to:

THEOREM 6.2. *To minimize the number of seeds that are needed to achieve complete or almost complete percolation in the symmetric graph $G(n/2, n/2, p, p, q)$, with $q < p$ and $q = \Omega(\frac{1}{n})$, all seeds have to be placed within the same community.*

The proof is reported in the companion technical report [14]. At high level, the result descends from the fact that, for any given total number of seeds, extremal trajectories of $T_1(t)$ and $T_2(t)$ are obtained when all seeds are placed

[10] More in general, for $q \ll \frac{1}{n_2}$, we could study percolation in community 2 in isolation after: i) adding to a_2 the nodes in $\mathcal{V}_2$ that have at least r neighbors in $\mathcal{V}_1$; ii) reduce the threshold r for all inactive nodes in $\mathcal{V}_2$ to a stochastic threshold $R \leq r$ accounting for marks received from $\mathcal{V}_1$.

in the same community, as a consequence of (21), (22), and properties of (23).

Theorem 6.2 can be easily generalized to the asymmetric case (see [14]):

THEOREM 6.3. *To minimize the number of seeds that are needed to achieve complete or almost complete percolation in* $G(n_1, n_2, p_1, p_2, q)$ *with* $q = \Omega(\frac{1}{n})$*, all seeds have to be placed in the community having the maximum value of* $n_i(p_i)^r$.

6.3 Extension to the general block model

Results obtained for the case of two communities can be rather easily extended to a more general block model with $K < \infty$ heterogeneous communities, specified by a symmetric matrix P, whose element p_{jk} represents the probability that a node belonging to community j is connected to a node belonging to community k (with i.i.d. probabilities for all such pairs). Note that diagonal elements of P provide inter-community edge probabilities. In Appendix B, besides our system assumptions, we present two different upper bounds on the critical number of seeds. Interestingly, both bounds depends critically on extreme values of the model parameters, and in some cases a single community can determine the phase transition of the entire system.

7. CONCLUSIONS

We proposed a unique framework to study sub-linear phase transitions of threshold-based 'activation processes' in random graphs, adding inhomogeneities in the system along different (orthogonal) directions. We found that in several cases the critical seed set size depends critically just on extreme values of distributions, providing novel insights into the dynamics of epidemic processes in complex systems.

8. REFERENCES

[1] J. Chalupa, P.L. Leath, G.R. Reich, "Bootstrap percolation on a Bethe lattice," *J. Phys. C*, Vol. 12, L31–L35 (1979).

[2] J. Adler, U. Lev, "Bootstrap percolation: visualizations and applications," *Braz. J. Phys*, 33(3), (2003).

[3] J. Balogh, B. Bollobás, H. Duminil-Copin, R. Morris, "The sharp threshold for bootstrap percolation in all dimensions," *Trans. A. Math. Soc.*, 36, (2012).

[4] J. Balogh, B.G. Pittel, "Bootstrap percolation on the random regular graph," *Random Struct. Algor.*, 30(1–2), 257–286 (2007).

[5] H. Amini, "Bootstrap percolation and diffusion in random graphs with given vertex degrees," *Electron. J. Combin.* 17, R25 (2010).

[6] S. Janson, T. Luczak, T. Turova and T. Vallier. Bootstrap percolation on the random graph $G_{n,p}$. *Ann. Appl. Probab.*, 22(5):1989–2047, 2012.

[7] H. Amini and N. Fountoulakis, "Bootstrap percolation in power-law random graphs", *Journal of Statistical Physics*, 155:72–92, 2014.

[8] J. Leskovec, J. Kleinberg, and C. Faloutsos, "Graphs over time: Densification and shrinking diameters," *ACM Trans. on Knowledge Discovery from Data*, 1(1), 2007.

[9] G. Scalia-Tomba, "Asymptotic Final-Size Distribution for Some Chain-Binomial Processes", *Advances in Applied Probability*, 17(3), 477–495, 1985.

[10] A. Martin-Löf, "Symmetric Sampling Procedures, General Epidemic Processes and Their Threshold Limit Theorems", *Journal of Applied Probability* 23(2), 265–282, 1986.

[11] D. Kempe, J. Kleinberg, E. Tardos, "Maximizing the spread of influence in a social network," *in Proc. ACM SIGKDD*, 2003.

[12] D. Watts, "A simple model of global cascades in random networks," *In Proc. Natl. Acad. Sci*, pp. 5766–71, 2002.

[13] W. Feller, "An Introduction to Probability Theory and its Applications," Wiley, 1968.

[14] Companion technical report, available upon request.

[15] A. Mislove, M. Marcon, K.-P. Gummadi, P. Druschel, and B. Bhattacharjee, "Measurement and analysis of online social networks," *IMC '07.*

[16] P. Brach, A. Epasto, A. Panconesi, P. Sankowski, "Spreading rumours without the network," in Proc. ACM COSN, 2014.

[17] M. Penrose. *Random Geometric Graphs.* Oxford University Press, Oxford, 2004.

APPENDIX

A. THEOREM 4.1

First we introduce the following concentration inequalities for the binomial distribution $\text{Bin}(n,p)$, taken from [17]: Let $H(b) = 1 - b + b\log b$, for $b > 0$. Let $\mu = np$.

If $k \leq \mu$ then:

$$\mathbb{P}(\text{Bin}(n,p)) \leq k) \leq \exp\left(-\mu H\left(\frac{k}{\mu}\right)\right) \tag{24}$$

If $k > \mu$ then:

$$\mathbb{P}(\text{Bin}(n,p)) \geq k) \leq \exp\left(-\mu H\left(\frac{k}{\mu}\right)\right) \tag{25}$$

Proof of Lemma 4.4.

For any $\delta > 0$, We have $a = \alpha\, a_c + o(1) > (\alpha - \delta)a_c$, and so, by the definition of a_c, for any $t = a, \ldots, \lfloor Kt_c \rfloor$,

$$\{S(t) - t + a \leq 0\} \subseteq \{S(t) - t + (\alpha - \delta)(1 - (\rho^*)^{-1})t_c \leq 0\}$$
$$= \{S(t) \leq t - (\alpha - \delta)(1 - (\rho^*)^{-1})t_c\}$$

Hence:

$$\left\{\inf_{t[a,\lfloor Kt_c\rfloor]} S(t) - t + a \leq 0\right\} = \bigcup_{t\in[a,\lfloor Kt_c\rfloor]} \{S(t) - t + a \leq 0\}$$

$$\subseteq \bigcup_{t\in[a,\lfloor Kt_c\rfloor]} \{S(t) \leq t - (\alpha - \delta)(1 - (\rho^*)^{-1})t_c\}$$

Moreover, defining $x = t/t_c$, it can be be proved that:

$$E[S(xt_c)] = x^{\rho^*}\frac{t_c}{\rho^*} + o(t_c). \tag{26}$$

Using (26) and (24), we have for any $\delta > 0$,

$$P(S(t) \leq t - (\alpha - \delta)(1 - (\rho^*)^{-1})t_c) <$$
$$e^{-(1-\delta)x^{\rho^*}\frac{t_c}{\rho^*} H\left(\frac{xt_c - (\alpha-\delta)(1-(\rho^*)^{-1})t_c}{(1-\delta)x^{\rho^*}\frac{t_c}{\rho^*}}\right)}$$

Thus, by sub-additivity of probability:

$$P\left(\inf_{t[a,\lfloor Kt_c\rfloor]} S(t) - t + a \leq 0\right) \leq$$

$$\sum_{t\in[a,\lfloor Kt_c\rfloor]} e^{-(1-\delta)x^{\rho^*}\frac{t_c}{\rho^*} H\left(\frac{xt_c - (\alpha-\delta)(1-(\rho^*)^{-1})t_c}{(1-\delta)x^{\rho^*}\frac{t_c}{\rho^*}}\right)}$$

$$\leq \frac{K}{\alpha(1-(\rho^*)^{-1})(1+\delta)}$$
$$e^{-\inf_{x\in[a/t_c,K]}\left[\frac{(1-\delta)x^{\rho^*}a}{\alpha(1-(\rho^*)^{-1})\rho^*(1+\delta)} H\left(\frac{x-(\alpha-\delta)(1-(\rho^*)^{-1})}{(1-\delta)\frac{x^{\rho^*}}{\rho^*}}\right)\right]} \tag{27}$$

the assertion descends immediately taking the inf of (27) with respect to $\delta > 0$ and letting $K \to \infty$.

Segment $[Kt_c, p^{-1}]$. We basically follow [6], choosing $K = 8$ and defining a sequence of time instants $t_j = 8 \cdot 2^j t_c$ for $j = \{0, 1, 2 \cdots J\}$ with $J = \min\{j : pt_j \geq 1\}$. We first show that $\mathbb{E}[S(t_j)] > (1+\delta)t_{j+1}$ for every j and a properly specified $\delta > 0$. Then, applying again union bound and concentration inequality (24) we can prove that $P(S(t_j) \leq t_{j+1}$, for some $j)$ goes to zero faster than $\zeta(n)$. This implies $P(S(t) - t \leq 0$, for some $t \in [8t_c, \lceil p^{-1} \rceil])$ goes to 0 faster than $\zeta(n)$ under super-critical conditions. Indeed, given the monotonicity of $S(t)$, we have $\{a - t + S(t) < 0$ for some $t \in [t_j, t_{j+1}]\} \subseteq \{S(t_j) < t_{j+1}\}$. In conclusion, under super-critical conditions the process never stops before p^{-1} with probability $1 - \zeta(n)$.

Segment $[p^{-1}, cn]$. Beyond time p^{-1} we can no longer use (10). However, we can easily handle segment $[p^{-1}, cn]$ and already conclude that, in all cases, the process reaches at least a constant fraction of the nodes (if it survives the bottleneck). For this, we exploit the fact that $\pi(\lceil p^{-1} \rceil) \geq q_{\rho^*} P(\text{Bin}(p^{-1}, p) > R_i) > 2c$ for some constant $c > 0$. Using again union bound and concentration inequalities, we then show that the process never stops before cn with probability $1 - \zeta(n)$.

B. GENERAL BLOCK MODEL

Let $n_k(n)$ be the number of nodes in community k ($k = 1, \ldots, K$), with $n = \sum_k n_k$. We will assume that $n_k(n) \gg 1$, for any k. We focus on a community structure in which $p_{ik} < \min(p_{ii}, p_{kk})$ for any (i,k). Moreover, whenever $p_{ik} \neq 0$, we will assume that $p_{ik} = \Omega(\frac{1}{n_i}, \frac{1}{n_k})$. At last, but without loss of generality, we assume the graph to be connected at the community level; i.e. we assume P to be of maximal rank (equal to $K-1$). Indeed, if this in not true we can always partition the community-level graph into connected components and apply our results to each connected component.

We first generalize the result in Theorem 6.1:

THEOREM B.1. *Consider a block model with $K < \infty$ communities as defined before; suppose, for any k, that $1/(n p_{k,k}) \to 0$, $p_{k,k} = o(n^{-1/r})$, $a_k/a_c^{(k)} \to \alpha_k > 1$, with:*

$$\bar{a}_c^{(k)} = \left(1 - \frac{1}{r}\right)\left(\frac{(r-1)!}{n_k(\widehat{p}_{k,k})^r}\right)^{(r-1)^{-1}}$$

where:

$$\widehat{p}_{k,k} = \left((r!) \cdot \sum_{\substack{\rho_1 \cdots \rho_k \cdots \rho_K \\ with \sum \rho_j = r}} \frac{p_{k,k}^{\rho_k} \prod_{j \neq k} p_{jk}^{\rho_j}}{\rho_k! \prod_{j \neq k} \rho_j!} \right)^{\frac{1}{r}}$$

Let $T = \inf_t\{\min_k(a_k - t + S_k(t)) < 0\}$. We have:

$$\forall \varepsilon > 0, P\left(1 - \frac{T}{\max_k(n_k)} > \varepsilon\right) = O\left(\mathrm{e}^{-C_1(r, \min_k(r, \alpha_k))a + o(a)}\right)$$

where $C_1(r, \alpha)$ is the same function as in Theorem 4.1.

Theorem B.1 can be used to derive a simple upper bound to the minimum number of seeds that can produce super-critical conditions in all communities, in the case in which seeds are selected uniformly at random among all nodes. Indeed, Theorem B.1 coupled with standard concentration arguments lead to the result that a global number of seeds:

$$a = (1+\epsilon) n \max_k \frac{\bar{a}_c^{(k)}}{n_k} \tag{28}$$

for any $\epsilon > 0$, is enough to guarantee (almost) complete percolation of the entire graph.

More in general, given an arbitrary allocation of seeds among communities, Theorem B.1 can be used to check whether the considered seed allocation is able to trigger system-wide percolation. On this regard, note that Theorem B.1 can be applied to any community-level connected sub-graph of the entire system: if at least one sub-graph satisfies the conditions of Theorem B.1, we get (almost) complete percolation of the entire system, as consequence of the assumptions that: i) the graph is connected at community level; ii) for non null off diagonal elements of P, $p_{ik} = \Omega(\frac{1}{n_i}, \frac{1}{n_k})$. In particular, note that if we get (almost) complete percolation in just one community, the infection propagates to the entire system.

We can also ask ourselves which is the optimal seed allocation in the system, in the case in which we know the community membership of the nodes. A straightforward extension of Theorem 6.3 provides the answer to this question:

THEOREM B.2. *Consider a general block model graph with $K < \infty$ communities as defined before; assume that $1/(np_{k,k}) \to 0$, $p_{k,k} = o(n^{-1/r})$ for any k. In order to minimize the number of seeds that produce (almost) complete percolation of the entire graph, all seeds must be placed within a single community that maximizes quantity $n_k(p_k)^r$.*

As a consequence, it turns out that a number of seeds:

$$a = (1+\epsilon)\left(1 - \frac{1}{r}\right) \min_k \left(\frac{(r-1)!}{n_k(p_{k,k})^r}\right)^{(r-1)^{-1}} \tag{29}$$

for any $\epsilon > 0$, is enough to guarantee an almost complete percolation of the graph. Indeed, by placing these a nodes all within a single community that maximizes quantity $n_k(p_k)^r$, let this community be k_0, we have that process $\underline{S}_{k_0}(t)$, and thus process $S_{k_0}(t)$ is super-critical, which is enough to trigger system-wide percolation.

At last, we can exploit Theorem B.2 also to get a different upper bound to the critical number of seeds in the case in which seeds are selected uniformly at random among all nodes. Indeed, it turns out that $a\frac{n}{n_{k_0}}$ seeds, where a is the same as in (29), are enough, since w.h.p. at least $a(1-\varepsilon/2)$ seeds will fall within community k_0, producing super-critical conditions in community k_0 (and then in the entire system). In the case of very heterogeneous communities, this last bound might be tighter than (28).

Reverse Ranking by Graph Structure: Model and Scalable Algorithms

Eliav Buchnik*
School of Computer Science
Tel Aviv University, Israel
eliavbuh@gmail.com

Edith Cohen
Google Research, CA, USA
Tel Aviv University, Israel
edith@cohenwang.com

ABSTRACT

Distances in a network capture relations between nodes and are the basis of centrality, similarity, and influence measures. Often, however, the relevance of a node u to a node v is more precisely measured not by the magnitude of the distance, but by the number of nodes that are closer to v than u. That is, by the *rank* of u in an ordering of nodes by increasing distance from v.

We identify and address fundamental challenges in rank-based graph mining. We first consider single-source computation of reverse-ranks and design a "Dijkstra-like" algorithm which computes nodes in order of increasing approximate reverse rank while only traversing edges adjacent to returned nodes. We then define *reverse-rank influence*, which naturally extends reverse nearest neighbors influence [Korn and Muthukrishnan 2000] and builds on a well studied distance-based influence. We present near-linear algorithms for greedy approximate reverse-rank influence maximization. The design relies on our single-source algorithm. Our algorithms utilize near-linear preprocessing of the network to compute all-distance sketches. As a contribution of independent interest, we present a novel algorithm for computing these sketches, which have many other applications, on multi-core architectures.

We complement our algorithms by establishing the hardness of computing *exact* reverse-ranks for a single source and *exact* reverse-rank influence. This implies that when using near-linear algorithms, the small relative errors we obtain are the best we can currently hope for.

Finally, we conduct an experimental evaluation on graphs with tens of millions of edges, demonstrating both scalability and accuracy.

1. INTRODUCTION

Shortest-paths distances in a network are a classic measure of the relation between nodes and are the basis of similarity [29, 9], centrality [3, 33, 19, 4, 12, 31, 7, 10], and influence [21, 2, 15, 11] measures. Often, however, the relation of a node j to i is more correctly modeled not by the magnitude of the distance d_{ji} from j to i, but by i's position π_{ji} in an ordering of nodes according to increasing distance from j [14, 23, 37, 20]. A classic use of rank as an indicator of relevance in metric spaces is the k nearest neighbors (kNN) classifier, which classifies points based on the k closest labeled examples [14, 23]. In terms of popularity, kNN outweighs the respective distance-based classifiers, which instead use all examples within a certain distance.

*Part of the research was done during an internship at Google.

SIGMETRICS '16 June 14-18, 2016, Antibes Juan-Les-Pins, France

ACM ISBN 978-1-4503-4266-7/16/06.

DOI: http://dx.doi.org/10.1145/2896377.2901458

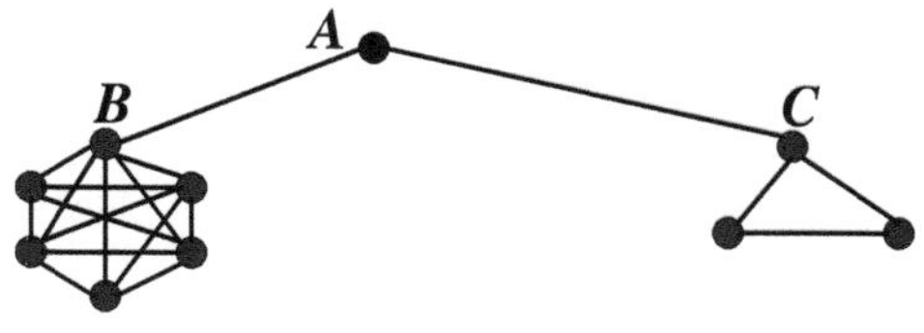

Figure 1: Example undirected social network (edge lengths are proportional to drawn lengths).

More formally, we view a node j as *ranking* other nodes according to their distance order from j. The *rank* π_{ji} is the position of i in increasing order from j. Accordingly, from the perspective of node j, we can refer to π_{ij} as a *reverse rank.*

An advantage of using rank is that it provides a different signal than distance by "factoring out" the effects of uneven density. This is illustrated in the toy social network in Figure 1: We expect node A to be more important to node C than it is to node B, even though, A is closer to B than to C ($d_{CA} > d_{BA}$). This is because B has a dense neighborhood of closer node than A, but C has only two nodes closer to it than A. In terms of ranks, we have $\pi_{CA} = 3$ and $\pi_{BA} = 6$ and thus $\pi_{CA} < \pi_{BA}$, which reflects this intuition.

The rank relation is asymmetric: In the example network in Figure 1, we have $\pi_{BA} = 6$, since there are 5 nodes closer to B than A, and $\pi_{AB} = 1$, since B is the closest node to A. Therefore, $\pi_{AB} \neq \pi_{BA}$ even though the distance is symmetric ($d_{AB} = d_{BA}$). The asymmetry $\pi_{BA} > \pi_{AB}$ reflects our intuition that the higher degree node (B) has more influence on its neighbor (A) than the reverse.

In particular, with tie breaking on distances, a node v has exactly one nearest neighbor, but can have 0 to many *reverse nearest neighbors*, which are nodes u which satisfy $\pi_{uv} = 1$. In our example, node A has no reverse nearest neighbors. The number of reverse nearest neighbors of a point v is a well studied notion of v's influence, proposed by Korn and Muthukrishnan [26], and considered in metric spaces and in graphs [27].

In the basic model all nodes both rank and get ranked. A natural extension [26] allows only a subset of the nodes to get ranked (*rankees*) and also permits nodes that provide ranks (*rankers*) to have different weights. In this model, π_{ij} relates a ranker i to rankee j. This distinction is useful when nodes have two or more types of entities, for example, users (rankers) and content (rankees). It also allows us to specify a special small set of certified rankees such that we can characterize properties of other nodes by this smaller set of ranks. Importance weights $\beta(i) \geq 0$ assigned to rankers can correspond to properties like purchase power or trust level. The ranks assigned by ranker i are then weighted by $\beta(i)$. This weighting is useful when we aggregate the scores of multiple rankers to obtain centrality/influence scores of rankees.

1.1 Contributions and Overview

Rank-based measures provide a natural alternative to distance-based ones, but algorithmically pose different challenges. We identify and motivate fundamental challenges and present scalable algorithmic tools which facilitating rank-based graph mining.

Reverse-rank Single-source computation

An important tool in working with distances is an efficient single-source computation. Dijkstra's algorithm from a source s computes the distances d_{si} for all nodes i in near-linear time. A powerful property of Dijkstra's algorithm is *sorted access*: Nodes are revealed in order of increasing distance from s. Thus, for any k, the k closest nodes to s are computed while traversing only edges adjacent to these k nodes. Therefore, if we are only interested in a prefix of the closest nodes, we can terminate the execution after they are computed, performing a fraction of the computation of a full execution. When we work with ranks, we would be instead interested in a prefix of the highest ranks. Such sorted access to rankings is also important for efficient aggregating rankings [16].

The *reverse-rank single-source problem* is, for a node $i \in U$, to compute the reverse ranks π_{ji} with respect to all nodes j. Moreover, we aim for an efficient algorithm that provides sorted-access: Listing nodes in increasing π_{ji} order with an algorithm that only traverses edges adjacent to listed nodes.

A naive solution for exact reverse-rank single source computation from i is to run Dijkstra's algorithm from each node j, until node i is processed. For the average node, this is equivalent to performing n runs of Dijkstra until revealing on average $n/2$ nodes. Note that even on sparse networks, this scales quadratically in the number of nodes, which is prohibitive even on mid-size networks. This is in sharp contrast to the shortest-path single-source computation which takes (near) linear time. Previous work [27] proposed ways to scalably identify the set of reverse nearest neighbors of nodes, but did not address higher reverse ranks. We are able here (Section 6) to provide an explanation, establishing that the naive solution is in a sense the best we can do for the exact problem: We leverage the theory of subcubic equivalence [36] and construct a reduction from graph radius computation to reverse-rank single source computation. The former is known to have subcubic equivalence to all-pairs shortest-paths computation (APSP) [1].

This hardness result, fortunately, applies to the *exact* problem. An important contribution we make here (see Section 4) is devising a novel, scalable, Dijkstra-like (sorted access), *approximate* reverse-rank single-source algorithm, which provides estimates $\hat{\pi}_{ij}$ with a small relative error. Since ranks are intrinsically slightly noisy measures of the actual relations, estimates with a small relative errors are often as good as the exact values.

An essential component of our design is a preprocessing step where we compute All-Distances Sketches (ADS) for all nodes [6, 13, 7]. The sketches provide us with a fast oracle which estimates $\hat{\pi}_{ij}$ from the distance d_{ji}. In Section 3 we review the sketches and estimators as applied in our context. We note that we can apply any ADS algorithm, and existing designs are suitable for sequential, shared-memory, and node-centric message-passing computations [6, 32, 13, 5, 7]. A stand-alone contribution we make here is engineering an ADS algorithm for multicore architectures which provides provable tunable tradeoff between overhead and concurrency. Our algorithm can be used for many other applications of the sketches which include estimating distances, closeness similarity, the distance distribution, and timed-influence [6, 32, 13, 5, 9, 15, 11, 7].

The estimation of single-source reverse ranks can be done by first running Dijkstra's algorithm to compute the single-source distances, and then apply the oracle we obtained in the preprocessing step to the computed distances. This method, however, will not provide us sorted access. Our sorted access algorithm, similarly to Dijkstra, also traverses a shortest-path tree rooted at the source, but critically, instead of doing so in distance order, which would violate rank-based sorted access, does so in order of increasing estimated reverse ranks. The correctness of our design relies on key insights on properties of reverse ranks.

Reverse-rank influence

Distance or reachability-based notions of centrality and influence of a set S of seed nodes are fundamental measures in network analysis. In the general form [11], distance-based influence is defined with respect to a non-increasing decay function $\alpha(x) \geq 0$ (smoothing kernel) and node weights $\beta(i) \geq 0$. The contribution of each node j to the influence of S is proportional to its weight $\beta(j)$ and decays with the distance of j from S, $d_{Sj} = \min_{i\in S} d_{ij}$:

$$\mathrm{Inf}^{(d)}(S) = \textstyle\sum_j \beta(j)\alpha(d_{Sj}) \,. \tag{1}$$

Well studied special cases include *Closeness centrality* [3, 33, 19, 4, 12, 31], where S contains a single node i, and the celebrated *reachability-based* influence model of [25], obtained when $\alpha(x) = 1$ for finite x and 0 otherwise. Distance-based influence with threshold function α ($\alpha(x) = 1$ for $x \leq T$ and $\alpha(x) = 0$ otherwise) was studied in [21, 2, 15] (With distance interpreted as elapsed time).

Here we define *reverse-rank influence*

$$\mathrm{Inf}^{(\pi^{-1})}(S) = \textstyle\sum_j \beta(j)\alpha(\pi_{jS}) \,, \tag{2}$$

where $\pi_{jS} = \min_{i\in S} \pi_{ji}$. The special case of $\mathrm{Inf}^{(\pi^{-1})}(v)$, the influence of a single node, with $\alpha(1) = 1$ and $\alpha(x) = 0$ otherwise is the number of reverse nearest neighbors of v, is the influence measure proposed in [26, 27]. Our more flexible definition (2) is able to account for the contribution of nodes with higher reverse-rank to the influence of our node. For example, by setting $\alpha(x) = 1/x$ we achieve the effect that a reverse rank of x contributes $1/x$ to the total influence of v; A node for which v is the 5th closest neighbor contributes to its influence 20% of what it would have contributed as a reverse nearest neighbor. With α being a T-threshold function, rankers u that rank v in their top T contribute $\beta(u)$ to v's influence.

Reverse-rank Influence Computation: We show (Section 6) that the computation of exact reverse-rank influence, even for a single node, and even when α is a threshold function, has subcubic equivalence to APSP. We therefore consider approximate influence $\widehat{\mathrm{Inf}}$ computed using approximate ranks $\hat{\pi}$. Clearly $\widehat{\mathrm{Inf}}(S)$ can be computed using $|S|$ single-source approximate reverse-rank computations (and using $\hat{\pi}_{jS} = \min_{i\in S} \hat{\pi}_{ji}$). Surprisingly, however, we show in Section 5, that even with large $|S|$, one single-source computation suffices.

Reverse-rank Influence Maximization: An important coverage problem which is extensively explored for reachability and distance-based influence, is *influence maximization (IM)* [25]: For a given $s \geq 1$, identify a set of s *seed* nodes with maximum influence. Intuitively, such a set provides the best "coverage" for its size with respect to the influence measure at hand. Here we consider IM with respect to our reverse-rank influence function $\mathrm{Inf}^{(\pi^{-1})}$. The reverse-rank IM problem with α being a threshold function with parameter T on our example user and movies data set is to find a set of s movies which maximizes the number of users for which there is at least one movie from S in their top T choices.

Similar to the distance-based influence function $\text{Inf}^{(d)}$, $\text{Inf}^{(\pi^{-1})}$ is monotone and submodular, and even for simple threshold α, when s is a parameter, the IM problem is NP hard. The most common and hugely successful algorithm for such coverage problems is the greedy algorithm [30], which iteratively builds a seed set by selecting in each step a node with maximum marginal contribution. For submodular and monotone functions, greedy has the property that each prefix of the sequence of size s has influence that is at least $1-(1-1/s)^s \geq 1-1/e$ of the influence of the optimal seed set of that size [30]. Exact greedy, however, does not scale well for very large graphs. For reverse-rank influence, an exact greedy sequence can be computed in cubic time in the number of nodes. When all nodes are both rankers and rankees, the graph is sparse, and we work with a threshold function α with parameter T, the computation reduces to $O(nT)$, by performing a single-source search from all nodes to find the T nearest neighbors and computing a greedy cover. But even this special case does not scale well for large graphs for larger values of T.

Approximate greedy and heuristics had been extensively studied for reachability-based [28, 22, 35, 10] and distance-based [15, 11] influence. In particular, the SKIM algorithm [10, 11] computes in near-linear time a full greedy permutation so that each prefix of size s has approximation ratio of $1-(1-1/s)^s - \epsilon$.

In Section 5 we present a near-linear algorithm for an approximate greedy sequence with respect to the *approximate* reverse-rank influence objective with threshold function: $\widehat{\text{Inf}}(S) = \{|z \in Z \mid \hat{\pi}_{zS} \leq T|\}$. We use the SKIM framework with our sorted-access approximate reverse-rank single-source computations as a critical component.

Experiments

Our experimental evaluation, detailed in Section 7 was focused on scalability and solution quality, using publicly available anonymized social graph data sets. Our ADS implementation runs on graphs with tens of millions of edges in tens of minutes on a single core, providing estimates with NRMSE (normalized mean square errors) of 6%-13%. Our multithreaded design achieved speedup factors of 3 to 4 on a machine with two CPUs and multiple cores.

With the preprocessing in place, our approximate reverse-rank single-source computations have similar running time to Dijkstra's algorithm (which computes single-source distances). In particular, a reverse-rank single-source computation was performed in less than 15 seconds on a single core on a graph with 4×10^6 nodes and 35×10^6 edges. For comparison, this should be contrasted with the running time of an exact reverse-rank single source computation, which would have taken an estimated 6000 hours on the same instance.

Using our implementation, we are able to visualize the reverse-rank distributions of some nodes in a large network, demonstrating how the distribution reveals information on the relative importance of a node in its locality. Prior to our work, it was not possible to scalably compute these distributions on large graphs.

Our approximate greedy IM implementation computes the full sequence on graphs with tens of millions of edges in minutes. We also observe that for small graphs or small values of T, where we could compute an exact greedy sequence, the solution quality of our approximate sequence was very close to the exact one.

2. PRELIMINARIES

We introduce some necessary notation. For a numeric function $r: X$ over a set X, the function $\text{k}_r^{\text{th}}(X)$ returns the kth smallest value in the range of r on X. If $|X| < k$, we define $\text{k}_r^{\text{th}}(X)$ as the supremum in the range of r. If r is not specified, we return the kth smallest value in X.

We work with networks modeled as directed or undirected graphs $G = (V, E)$ with nodes $V = [n] = \{1, \ldots, n\}$ and edges E with lengths $w(e) > 0$. We use $m = |E|$ for the number of edges. A subset or all nodes $U \subset V$ are specified as *rankee* nodes. We use the notation G^T for the *transpose graph*, which is the graph with edges reversed.

For nodes i, j, let d_{ij} be the shortest-paths distance from i to j. For $y \geq 0$, the *rankee y-neighborhood of i* is the set of rankee nodes within distance y from i. We denote the neighborhood by

$$N_i(y) = \{j \in U \mid d_{ij} \leq y\}$$

and its cardinality by $n_i(y) = |N_i(y)|$. The respective strict neighborhood is denoted by $\underline{N}_i(y) = \{j \in U \mid d_{ij} < y\}$ and its cardinality by $\underline{n}_i(y)$. For $i \in V$ and $j \in U$, π_{ij} denoted the *rank* of j with respect to i. When distances are unique, we have $\pi_{ij} = n_i(d_{ij})$, that is, equal to the number of rankee nodes that are at least as closer to i as j. When distances are not unique, we consider the range $(\underline{\pi}_{ij}, \overline{\pi}_{ij}]$, where

$$\begin{aligned} \underline{\pi}_{ij} &= \underline{n}_i(d_{ij}) , \\ \overline{\pi}_{ij} &= n_i(d_{ij}) . \end{aligned} \quad (3)$$

According to what we want to capture, we can define the rank π_{ij} as either, $\overline{\pi}_{ij}$, $\underline{\pi}_{ij}+1$, a uniform at random choice from the range, or as the midpoint of this range: $\pi_{ij} \equiv \frac{\underline{\pi}_{ij}+1+\overline{\pi}_{ij}}{2}$. Our algorithms and implementation can be adapted to support all these choices.

An important ingredient of our design is the computation of a data structure which allows us to efficiently estimate the number of rankees in a neighborhood. That is, for a query specified by a node i and $d \geq 0$, return $\hat{n}_i(d)$. The data structure can be viewed as a set of lists $L(i)$, one for each node $i \in V$. Each list $L(i)$ consists of pairs (d, y) where d is a distance value and $y = \hat{n}_i(d) > 0$ is an estimate on $n_i(d)$. The lists are sorted and increasing in both d and y. To estimate for $n_i(x)$ and $\underline{n}_i(x)$, from the list $L(i)$, we use

$$\hat{n}_i(d) = y \text{ such that } (x, y) = \arg \max_{(x,y)\in L(i)|x\leq d} x \quad (4)$$

$$\hat{\underline{n}}_i(d) = y \text{ such that } (x, y) = \arg \max_{(x,y)\in L(i)|x< d} x . \quad (5)$$

That is, we look at the pair $(x, y) \in L(i)$ such that $x \leq d$ (or $x < d$) is maximum and return y. From the relations (3), we can obtain estimates $\hat{\overline{\pi}}_{ij} = \hat{n}_i(d_{ij})$ and $\hat{\underline{\pi}}_{ij} = \hat{\underline{n}}_i(d_{ij})$ from $L(i)$ if we know d_{ij}.

The lists $L(i)$ are computed from All-Distances Sketches $\text{ADS}(i)$, which are the subject of the next section.

3. ALL-DISTANCES SKETCHES

We preprocess the graph to compute All-Distances Sketches (ADS) [6, 7] for the nodes in the graph. The sketches are defined with respect to a parameter k and a random permutation of rankee nodes. We find it convenient to work with $r(i) \in [0, 1]$ which is the permutation position of i divided by $|U|$. Alternatively, it is sometimes convenient to work instead with random hash based $r(i) \sim U[0, 1]$. The sketch $\text{ADS}(i)$ of a node $i \in V$ consists of a set of entries of the form (j, d_{ij}), consisting of a node $j \in U$ and the distance d_{ij}. We assume that $r(j)$ is either included in the entry or can be easily retrieved from j. The set of rankee nodes included in $\text{ADS}(i)$ is a random variable which depends on the assignment r:

$$j \in \text{ADS}(i) \iff r(j) \leq \text{k}_r^{\text{th}}\{h \in U \mid d_{ih} \leq d_{ij}\} . \quad (6)$$

This ADS definition (6) applies with unique and non-unique distances. A technical point is that for estimation with non-unique distances, we also maintain with $\text{ADS}(i)$, as auxiliary, entries (j, d_{ij}) that satisfy for some $z \in \text{ADS}(i)$ $r(j) = \text{k}_r^{\text{th}}\{h \in U \setminus \{z\} \mid d_{ih} \leq d_{iz}\}$ when these entries are not already included in $\text{ADS}(i)$ [8] (When distances are unique, all these entries are already in $\text{ADS}(i)$). With unique distances, the expected size of the sketches is exactly $\sum_{i=1}^{|U|} \min\{1, k/i\} \leq k \ln |U|$ with good concentration, but the sketch can be much smaller when distances are not unique, while providing the same statistical guarantees on estimate quality, which is why we separately treat non-unique distances rather than tie break.

Our implementation of ADS computation is based on PRUNED DIJKSTRA'S [6, 13, 7]. The pseudocode for the basic sequential version is provided as Algorithm 1 and uses $O(km \ln n)$ edge traversals. When applied with non-unique distances, the algorithm also includes the auxiliary entries.

Algorithm 1 ADS set for G via PRUNED DIJKSTRA'S

```
for rankee node u ∈ U by increasing r(u) do
    Run Dijkstra's algorithm from u on G^T
    foreach scanned node v do
        if d_vu > k^th{y | (x,y) ∈ ADS(v)} or
           |{x ∈ ADS(v) | d_vx ≤ d_vu}| > k then
            prune Dijkstra at v
        else
            ADS(v) ← ADS(v) ∪ {(r(u), d_vu)}
```

The term *scanned node* in the pseudocode refers to the event where the node $v \in V$ is popped from the Dijkstra priority queue. Each node can be scanned at most once in each (pruned) Dijkstra search. The scanned nodes are always a prefix of the nodes when sorted by increasing distance from u in G^T. When a node v is scanned, either u is inserted to $\text{ADS}(v)$ or the search is pruned at v. Therefore, the number of node scans is equal to the ADS size.

The algorithm builds the ADS of all nodes by considering one node $u \in U$ at a time and adding it as an entry in $\text{ADS}(v)$ for all relevant v. To do so efficiently, we maintain the entries in $\text{ADS}(v)$ as an array sorted by decreasing distances. The insertion condition then amounts to testing if $|\text{ADS}(v)| < k$ or if the entry (x, y) in the $|\text{ADS}(v)| - k$ position in the array (the kth smallest distance) has $y > d_{vu}$, or if it has $y = d_{vu}$ but either $|\text{ADS}(v)| = k$ or the entry (x, z) in the $|\text{ADS}(v)| - k - 1$ position has $z > d_{vu}$.

We refer to the kth smallest distance in $\text{ADS}(v)$ as the *threshold distance* and denote it by $\Delta(v)$. We also use the notation $*(v)$ for the bit indicating if the $k + 1$th smallest is equal to the kth smallest distance. The prune condition can then be written as

$$d_{vu} > \Delta(v) \textbf{ or } d_{vu} = \Delta(v) \textbf{ and } *(v) . \quad (7)$$

Observe that insertions can only affect the k last entries in the current ADS. Therefore, it suffices to keep only that "tail" part in active memory. When k is small we can keep it as an array and implement insertions by shifting. When k is larger we can use a data structure that supports efficient insertions.

3.1 Multithreading

PRUNED DIJKSTRA'S, as stated, sequentially performs possibly dependent searches from all rankee nodes. We propose here a design which allows us to control in a principled way the tradeoff between overhead and concurrency. We partition the $|U|$ pruned Dijkstra searches to batches, where each batch is a consecutive set of nodes when ordered by increasing r. All the searches in the same batch are made independent so that they can be executed concurrently. Each search computes a set of *proposed entries* to sketches $\text{ADS}(v)$, as contributions to a set $PE(v)$. A proposed entry is created when a node v is visited and the pruning condition (7) is not satisfied. The pruning, however, and hence the proposed entries, are computed with respect to the set of threshold distances and bits $(\Delta(v), *(v))$ for $v \in V$, as it was at the beginning of the batch. Pseudocode for an independent search thread is provided as Algorithm 2. Each such Dijkstra search may generate a proposed ADS entry for multiple nodes.

At the end of a batch, for each node v, the proposed entries $PE(v)$ from all the searches in the batch are merged with (the k-tail of) $\text{ADS}(v)$ (as it was in the beginning of the batch) to compute an updated $\text{ADS}(v)$ with respect to the end of the batch. The merge is performed by scanning the entries (u, d_{vu}) in $PE(v)$ in order of increasing r and applying the insertion procedure to $\text{ADS}(v)$ as used in Algorithm 1: If the pruning condition 7 does not hold, we insert u and update $\text{ADS}(v)$ (note that this updates $\Delta(v)$ and $*(v)$). Note that not all proposed entries are incorporated, since the insertion rule is not satisfied with respect to the updated $(\Delta(v), *(v))$ after processing previous $PE(v)$ entries.

Algorithm 2 A PRUNED DIJKSTRA thread (search from u)

```
Run Dijkstra's algorithm from u on G^T
foreach scanned node v do
    if d_vu > Δ(v) or d_vu = Δ(v) and *(v) then
        prune Dijkstra at v
    else
        PE(v) ← PE(v) ∪ {(u, d_vu)}
```

3.2 Concurrency/Overhead tradeoff analysis

The sequential algorithm has the property that all generated entries constitute final ADS entries. The multithreading algorithm computes proposed entries that may be eventually discarded. These discarded entries are the overhead of the multithreading algorithm.

More precisely, we define the overhead as the ratio of the expected number of discarded entries to the expected number of ADS entries per node. The overhead depends on how we partition the searches to batches. Placing each search in a separate batch would result in no overhead, but also no concurrency. Putting all searches in the same batch would have a very large overhead, as none of the searches would be pruned.

Note that the overhead of discarded entries corresponds to an overhead on edge traversals, which are the main cost of the algorithm. In particular, we can bound the total work performed by the multithreaded algorithm by multiplying the sequential bound of $km \ln |U|$ by $(1 + h)$, where h is a bound on the overhead.

We next propose batch partitions which allow us to bound the overhead. We first observe that the search is never pruned for the k nodes with lowest r values. Our first batch would contain these nodes, and we can perform those searches independently without overhead. At the end of this first batch, all generated proposed entries $PE(i)$ would be sorted by distance to form $\text{ADS}(i)$ with respect to those k nodes. As for subsequent batches, we propose exponentially increasing batch sizes and show the following:

LEMMA 3.1. *For a parameter $\mu > 0$, consider a partition to batches so that the jth batch ends at node in position $\lceil (1+\mu)^{j-1} k \rceil$ in the sorted order by increasing $r(v)$. Then the expected overhead is at most $h \leq \mu / \ln(1 + \mu) - 1$.*

PROOF. Consider processing a batch that starts at position $b_0 + 1$. The probability of a node in the batch to be included in $PE(i)$

is $\min\{1, \frac{k}{b_0+1}\}$. Note that to generate a proposed entry, the node needs to be with distance smaller than $\Delta(i)$, that is be among the k smallest distances among all the nodes processed up to the previous batch and itself. This probability is exactly that of being in one of the first k positions in a random permutation of b_0+1 nodes, which is $\min\{1, \frac{k}{b_0+1}\}$. Now we can consider the probability that a node in the batch is a final member of $\text{ADS}(i)$. If the node is in position b_0+j, the probability is $\min\{1, \frac{k}{b_0+j}\}$.

We now consider a batch that has nodes in permutation positions b_0+1 to b_t, such that $b_0 > k$. The ratio of good work to total work is

$$\frac{\sum_{j=1}^{b_t-b_0} 1/(b_0+j)}{(b_t-b_0)/(b_0+1)} = \frac{b_0+1}{b_t-b_0}\sum_{j=1}^{b_t-b_0}\frac{1}{b_0+j} \approx \frac{b_0+1}{b_t-b_0}\ln(\frac{b_t}{b_0+1})$$

Thus, if we choose $b_t = (1+\mu)b_0$ for some $\mu > 0$, we obtain the ratio $\ln(1+\mu)/\mu$. The overhead, by definition, is the inverse of this ratio minus 1. □

In particular, we can see that $\mu = 0.5$ results in overhead of 20% more edge traversals than the sequential algorithm. Using $\mu = 0.1$, has overhead of about 5%. The total number of batches is $O(\log_{1+\mu}(|U|/k)) \approx O(\frac{\log(|U|/k)}{\mu})$, which is logarithmic in the number of rankee nodes.

3.3 Cardinality estimation

We now discuss the computation of a list $L(i)$ from $\text{ADS}(i)$. Recall that $L(i)$ is a list of pairs the form $(d, \hat{n}_i(d))$. There is one pair for each unique distances d in $\text{ADS}(i)$, and we assume $L(i)$ is sorted by increasing d.

We review two estimators $\hat{n}_i(d)$: The bottom-k estimator and the HIP estimator. Both are unbiased, nonnegative, and have a small relative error, with good concentration which depend on the ADS parameter k. The HIP estimate is tighter: Estimates are at least as good as bottom-k, and with unique distances, has half the variance of the bottom-k estimator. The bottom-k estimator, however, is useful to us because it has some monotonicity property. We can compute the lists $L(i)$ using either estimator or both.

The bottom-k estimator: This inverse probability estimator [24] has coefficient of variation (CV) at most $1/\sqrt{k-2}$ [6, 7]. To estimate $n_i(x)$, we take the kth smallest r value among nodes in $N_i(x)$, which we denote by τ. If there are fewer than k nodes in $N_i(x)$, we return the number of entries as our estimate. Otherwise, we compute the probability p that an r-value is below τ. When $r(v) \sim U[0,1]$, $p = \tau$. We then use the estimate $\hat{n}_i(x) = (k-1)/p$.

The HIP estimator: This estimator has CV at most $1/\sqrt{k-2}$ and with unique distances is most $1/\sqrt{2k-2}$ [7] (see [8] for extension to non-unique distances). The estimates are obtained as follows: For each (non auxiliary) entry j in $\text{ADS}(i)$, we compute the threshold value

$$\tau_{ij} = \text{k}_r^{\text{th}}\{h \in \text{ADS}(i) \mid d_{ih} < d_{ij}\}\,. \tag{8}$$

We then compute p_{ij} as the probability of $r(j) < \tau_{ij}$. If there are fewer than k entries lower than d_{ij} then $p_{ij} = 1$. Otherwise, when $r(j) \sim U[0,1]$, we have $p_{ij} = \tau_{ij}$. We then take $a_{ij} = 1/p_{ij}$. Finally, the HIP estimate (summed over non-auxiliary entries) is

$$\hat{n}_i(x) = \sum_{j\in \text{ADS}(i) | d_{ij}\leq x} a_{ij}\,.$$

Computing the estimates The estimation list $L(i)$ for both the bottom-k and the HIP estimators can be computed by processing the entries of $\text{ADS}(i)$ in increasing distance order, maintaining the kth smallest values in the prefix processed so far and accordingly the kth smallest value τ, and computing the estimates $\hat{n}_i(d)$ when entries of distance d are processed.

An easy to verify property that is useful to us is that the neighborhood size estimates for each node are non-decreasing with distance from the node and therefore can only increase when the distance does:

LEMMA 3.2. *When $L(i)$ is computed using either bottom-k and HIP estimates, the estimates* (4) *and* (5) *satisfy*

$$d_1 \leq d_2 \implies \hat{n}_i(d_1) \leq \hat{n}_i(d_2)$$
$$d_1 \leq d_2 \implies \hat{\underline{n}}_i(d_1) \leq \hat{\underline{n}}_i(d_2)\,.$$

4. REVERSE-RANK SINGLE-SOURCE

As noted in the introduction, if we are interested in computing reverse-ranks from a source i to all nodes, we can compute the distances d_{ji} by applying Dijkstra's algorithm from i on G^T, and return estimated reverse-ranks from the distances using (4) and (5). The nodes, however, are processed in order of increasing distance, which does not necessarily corresponds to the order by increasing reverse ranks (recall the example in the introduction). Therefore, if we are only interested in correctly identifying nodes with highest reverse ranks and we apply this algorithm, we can not prune the computation and we will scan a much larger portion of the graph than needed.

In this section we present an approximate reverse-rank single-source algorithm that provides sorted-access: Computing nodes in order of increasing (approximate) reverse-rank. We start by establishing a basic monotonicity property of reverse-ranks that is essential for the correctness of our design.

4.1 SP monotonicity of reverse-ranks

We noted in the introduction that reverse-rank order does not necessarily correspond to distance order. For nodes on a shortest path, however, we can show that the reverse-ranks, and the respective bottom-k estimates, are monotone:

LEMMA 4.1. *Consider a shortest path $i_t, \ldots, i_0$ in G. Then $\overline{\pi}_{i_j i_0}$, $\underline{\pi}_{i_j i_0}$, and the bottom-$k$ estimates $\hat{\underline{\pi}}_{i_j i_0}$ and $\hat{\overline{\pi}}_{i_j i_0}$, are all non-decreasing with j.*

PROOF. Consider $j < h$, then $d_{i_j i_0} < d_{i_h i_0}$. The neighborhoods relations is $N_{i_j}(d_{i_j i_0}) \subseteq N_{i_h}(d_{i_h i_0})$. Therefore, $\overline{\pi}_{i_j i_0} \leq \overline{\pi}_{i_h i_0}$. Similarly, $\underline{N}_{i_j}(d_{i_j i_0}) \subseteq \underline{N}_{i_h}(d_{i_h i_0})$ and thus the cardinalities satisfy $\underline{\pi}_{i_j i_0} \leq \underline{\pi}_{i_h i_0}$.

In the case of bottom-k estimates, the claim follows again from containment of neighborhoods. Let τ_1 be the kth smallest r value in the contained set and let τ_2 be the kth smallest r value in the containing set. Then clearly, $\tau_1 \geq \tau_2$. Recall that the bottom-k cardinality estimate is $(k-1)/\tau$. We have $(k-1)/\tau_1 \leq (k-1)/\tau_2$. □

4.2 Algorithm and analysis

The pseudocode for our reverse-rank single source algorithms is presented as Algorithm 1. The algorithm has the same structure as Dijkstra's algorithm from source s in the transposed graph G^T. The algorithm maintains each unprocessed node j that is adjacent to an already processed node in a min priority queue. The entry contains $(j, \overline{d}_{js})$, where $\overline{d}_{js}$ is the upper bound on the distance from j to s. This upper bound serves as the priority in Dijkstra's algorithm and is the minimum over processed nodes h of $d_{hs} + w_{jh}$. Our reverse-rank single source algorithm uses instead a priority as follows. We first look at $\hat{n}_{\overline{d}_{js}}(j)$, which is an upper bound on the estimated reverse-rank, computed according to the best current upper bound $\overline{d}_{js}$ on the distance. From Lemma 3.2, $\hat{n}_{\overline{d}_{js}}(j) \geq \hat{n}_{d_{js}}(j)$. Therefore, when the upper bounds on the distances are tightened, the priority can only decrease. Now, two nodes in the priority queue can have the same estimate $\hat{n}_{\overline{d}_{js}}(j)$. In this case, we break ties according to the distance upper bounds $\overline{d}_{js}$, always preferring the node with lower $\overline{d}_{js}$. If both $\hat{n}_{\overline{d}_{js}}(j)$ and $\overline{d}_{js}$ are the same, the tie can be broken arbitrarily.

The next node h that is selected from the queue is the one with minimum priority according to lexicographic order on $(\hat{n}_{\overline{d}_{js}}(j), \overline{d}_{js})$. For this node h we set $d_{hs} \leftarrow \overline{d}_{hs}$ (a correctness proof that indeed $\overline{d}_{hs}$ is the distance is provided below). We then scan all in-coming edges (j, h). If j is not already in the priority queue, we insert it with $\overline{d}_{ji} = d_{hs} + w(j, h)$ and the respective priority. If j is already in the queue we compare $x \leftarrow d_{hs} + w(j, h)$ to the current $\overline{d}_{js}$. If $x < \overline{d}_{js}$, we update $\overline{d}_{js} \leftarrow x$ and update the priority to $\hat{n}_{\overline{d}_{js}}(j)$.

Note that the algorithm applies for both directed and undirected graphs. When applied to directed graphs, the algorithm returns reverse ranks only for nodes that can reach s. For completeness, we explain how to extends this, if needed, also for nodes v that can not reach s, that is, $d_{vs} = \infty$. We first need to precisely define the rank π_{vs} in this case. All rankee nodes that can not be reached from s can be viewed as having rank range $(|R_v|, |U|]$, where R_v is the set of rankee nodes reachable from v. Now note that we can estimate $|R_v|$ by the cardinality estimate associated with the maximum-distance entry in $L(v)$.

Algorithm 1: Approximate Reverse-rank Single-Source

```
Input: Source node s
Output: A sequence (v, d_sv, π̂_vs) in increasing π̂_vs
// Node object v:  v.dist, v.rDr are upper bounds
   on d_sv and π̂_vs.  Initialization v.Init(d, r):
   v.dist ← d; v.rDr ← r
Q ← ∅ // Initialize an empty min priority queue
Q of node objects prioritized by lex order of
(v.rDr, v.dist)
s.Init(1, 0)        // Initialize source node object
Q.add(s)                 // put source node in queue
while Q is not empty do
    v ← Q.extract_min()
    Output(v)                    // output and scan v
    foreach u | (u, v) ∈ E and u not scanned do
        d ← v.dist + w_vu
        if u ∉ Q then
            u.Init(n̂_u(d), d)
            Q.add(u)
        else
            if d < u.dist then
                Q.decrease_key(u, (n̂_u(d), d))  // Update
                priority of u in Q:  u.dist ← d;
                u.rDr ← n̂_u(d)
```

We now establish correctness, that is, when a node v is popped from the priority queue, its priority is its correct (approximate) reverse rank and distance. We also show that the algorithm traverses a shortest path tree (but not necessarily in increasing distance order).

THEOREM 4.1. *When Algorithm 1 is applied with exact cardinalities $n_i(d)$ or with bottom-k estimates $\hat{n}_i(d)$, it correctly computes reverse ranks (respectively, approximate reverse ranks) and distances. Moreover, the traversal forms a shortest-paths tree from s.*

PROOF. Let s be the source node. Consider a node i and its shortest path $s = x_0, \ldots, x_t = i$ from s. We show correctness by induction on the number of nodes t in the shortest path. Recall that the algorithm maintains a minimum heap sorted lexicographically by a priority that bound the (approximate) reverse rank and distance. We denote the distance upper bound by $\delta(s, i)$. Since it always corresponds to some actual path, $\delta(s, i) \geq d_{si}$. The reverse rank component of the priority is computed from $\delta(s, i)$ and therefore upper bound the reverse rank.

In each iteration we scan (traverse) the top of the heap. The base case where $t = 0$ is trivial: The source node s is inserted to the heap with priority equal to its reverse rank of 1 and distance of 0, and is then scanned. By the induction hypothesis, the priority is correct, that is $\delta(s, x_{t-1}) = d_{sx_{t-1}}$, for node x_{t-1} when it is scanned by the algorithm. At that point $\delta(s, x_t) \geq d_{sx_t} > d_{sx_{t-1}}$. Therefore from the monotonicity property (Lemma 4.1), the priority of x_t is lower than that of x_{t-1}, and therefore x_t was not yet scanned. When scanning x_{t-1}, the algorithm relaxes all outgoing edges including the edge (x_{t-1}, x_t). The relaxation procedure assigns $\delta(x_t, s)$ to the correct value and thus its heap priority is now its correct (approximate) reverse rank and distance. When it will be scanned, it will be with the correct priority. □

5. REVERSE-RANK INFLUENCE

In this section, we consider the computation and maximization of reverse-rank influence. Consider a graph with a set of rankee nodes $U \subset V$ and ranks π_{ji} defined for rankees $i \in U$ and $j \in V$. Let $\beta(j) \geq 0$ be the ranker weights of $j \in V$. For a set $S \subset U$ of seed nodes, the reverse-rank influence is $\text{Inf}(S) = \sum_{j \in Z} \beta(j)\alpha(\pi_{jS})$, where $Z \subset V$ is the set of ranker nodes (those with $\beta(z) > 0$). From Corollary 6.2, the exact computation of $\text{Inf}(S)$ has subcubic equivalence to APSP, even when restricted to threshold functions α and a single seed.

We therefore focus on scalably computing the approximate influence

$$\widehat{\text{Inf}}(S) = \sum_{j \in Z} \beta(j)\alpha(\hat{\pi}_{jS}) ,$$

where $\hat{\pi}_{jS} = \min_{i \in S} \hat{\pi}_{ji}$.

Note that to compute $\widehat{\text{Inf}}(S)$ it suffices to compute $\hat{\pi}_{jS}$ for all ranker nodes $j \in Z$. Moreover, when α is a threshold function for some $T \ll n$, or more generally, any function with $\alpha(x) = 0$ for all $x > T$, it suffices to compute $\hat{\pi}_{jS}$ only for nodes with $\hat{\pi}_{jS} \leq T$. A naive way to compute these values is to perform, from each seed $i \in S$, a single-source reverse ranks search from i, using Algorithm 1, and terminate the search when we scan a node with $\hat{\pi}_{ji} > T$. We can then combine the results of the different searches, computing the minimum $\hat{\pi}_{ji}$ of each node j that is scanned in at least one of the searches, to obtain the values $\hat{\pi}_{jS}$. This naive computation requires $|S||E| \log n$ operations (assuming the lists $L(j)$ are provided) when T is large. But even with smaller T, a node j can be scanned multiple times, once for each seed $i \in S$ with $\hat{\pi}_{ji} \leq T$. We now show how to remove the dependence on the number of seeds $|S|$.

THEOREM 5.1. *For a set of seeds S, we can compute the values $\hat{\pi}_{jS}$ for all $j \in V$ using $O(|S| + |E| \log n)$ operations. When $\alpha(x) = 0$ for $x \geq T$, $|E|$ is replaced by the number of incoming edges to nodes j that satisfy $\hat{\pi}_{jS} \leq T$. These bounds assume that the lists $L(j)$ are provided for $j \in V$.*

PROOF. We slightly modify Algorithm 1 by initializing the priority queue with entries with priorities $(i.\text{dist}, i.\text{rDr}) = (0, 1)$ for each node $i \in S$. The algorithm execution then proceeds as with a single source node. For correctness, we can show that nodes are scanned (popped from the queue) in increasing lex order of $(\hat{n}_j(d_{jS}), d_{jS})$, and at the point they are scanned we have $j.\text{dist} = d_{jS}$ and thus $j.\text{rDr} = \hat{n}_j(d_{jS})$.

To see that, note that d_{jS} suffices to obtain $\hat{\pi}_{jS}$. This is because, using Lemma 3.2, $\hat{n}_j(d_{jS}) \equiv \min_{i\in S} \hat{n}_j(d_{ji}) = \hat{n}_j(\min_{i\in S} d_{ji})$.

For correctness, we need to show that the monotonicity property (Lemma 4.1) to sets S: Consider a shortest path $i_t, \ldots, i_0$ from i_t to S (that is, i_0 is the closest S node to i_t). Note that this implies that i_0 is the closest S node to all i_j.

It follows from 4.1 that $\overline{\pi}_{i_j i_0}$, $\underline{\pi}_{i_j i_0}$, and the bottom-$k$ estimates $\hat{\underline{\pi}}_{i_j i_0}$ and $\hat{\overline{\pi}}_{i_j i_0}$ are non-decreasing with j. We observe that $\overline{\pi}_{i_j i_0} = \overline{\pi}_{i_j S}$ and similarly $\underline{\pi}_{i_j i_0} = \underline{\pi}_{i_j S}$ and this holds for the bottom-k estimates obtained using $d_{i_j S}$. Therefore, monotonicity holds also when i_0 is substituted with S. □

5.1 Influence Maximization

Here we consider uniform ranker weights $\beta(z) = 1$ and α that is a threshold function for some T. The influence of a set $S \subset U$ of rankee nodes is then the number of rankers that have at least one node from S among their top T rankees:

$$\text{Inf}(S) = |\{z \in Z \mid \pi_{zS} \leq T\}| . \qquad (9)$$

The goal of the IM problem is to find a set S of rankee nodes of a certain size which maximizes Inf(S). A common approach to such coverage problems is the greedy algorithm. Greedy repeatedly selects a rankee node which has maximum marginal influence. For each $s \geq 1$, the set S of the first s selected seeds is guaranteed to have influence that is at least $1 - (1 - 1/s)^s$ of the maximum possible by s seeds. Algorithm 2 is an exact greedy algorithm for our reverse-rank IM problem with influence function (9). The computation of the algorithm is dominated by Dijkstra computations from each ranker node that are stopped once T rankees are popped from the priority queue. Recall that when distance are not unique, we can work with multiple definition of the rank (see Section 2), but with all of them, we can determine the ranks once at most $T + 1$ rankees are popped. example, when we use $\overline{\pi}$, then if the $T + 1$ rankee has the same distance d as the T rankee, then all rankees of distance d are excluded (they have rank larger than T). Even when all nodes are rankees, and thus at most T nodes are popped in total in each Dijkstra run, the required computation is $\Omega(T|E|\log|V|)$, which does not scale well for large values of the threshold T.

5.2 Approximate Greedy IM

We next obtain a near-linear algorithm using two relaxations. First, the greedy selection, and thus the statistical guarantees we obtain, are with respect to the relaxed influence function (9) where $\hat{\pi}$ replaces π:

$$\widehat{Inf}(S) = |\{z \in Z \mid \hat{\pi}_{zS} \leq T\}| . \qquad (10)$$

Second, we do not compute an exact greedy sequence for $\widehat{Inf}(S)$ but instead use an approximate greedy algorithm: At each step, selects a node with marginal influence that is approximately (within a small relative error) the maximum.

Our design adapts the influence maximization algorithms SKIM and T-SKIM[10, 11] which are designed for reachability-based [25] and distance-based [21, 15, 11] influence with threshold functions. We quickly review SKIM, which remarkably, when all nodes are both rankers and rankees, computes a full approximate

Algorithm 2: Exact greedy reverse-rank IM

Input: Directed graph $G = (V, E)$, ranker nodes $Z \subset V$, rankee nodes $U \subset Z$, threshold T
Output: Exact greedy sequence seedlist

```
seedlist ←⊥ // Output list of (seed,marginal influence)
forall the rankee nodes u ∈ U do coverage[u] ← ∅
forall the ranker nodes z ∈ Z do
    coverers[z] ← ∅
    Run Dijkstra from z in G, until (we can determine that) π_zu > T
    foreach rankee u ∈ U with π_zu ≤ T do
        coverers[z] ← coverers[z] ∪ {u}
        coverage[u] ← coverage[u] ∪ {z}
while There are rankees u with |coverage[u]| > 0 do
    v ← arg max_{u∈U\S} |coverage[u]|
    Append (u, |coverage[u]|) to seedlist
    foreach z ∈ coverage[u] do
        foreach v ∈ coverers[z] do
            Remove z from coverage[v]
    Delete coverage[u]
return seedlist
```

greedy permutation in near linear time. To do so efficiently, SKIM samples nodes not covered by previously selected seeds, and maintains for each candidate seed node the number of sampled nodes it covers. Reachability-based SKIM performs a pruned reverse graph searches from the node to determine the nodes that cover it. The distance-based SKIM performs backward pruned Dijkstra searches. The node that first reaches some number K of samples has approximately maximum marginal influence and is selected as a seed. The *sample-size parameter* K determines a tradeoff between computation and accuracy. SKIM then updates the samples so that they are with respect to the updated marginal influences with the coverage of the new seed node removed. SKIM also updates the representation of the residual problem. The updates are performed using a respective forward (Dijkstra) search from the new seed to reveal all nodes that it covers. When a previously sampled node becomes covered, the samples of the nodes covering it are adjusted to reflect their reduced marginal coverage. Sampling is then resumed until another node reaches a sample size of K. We repeat the process of sampling, selecting a seed, and updating the residual problem until a desired number of seeds is selected, a desired coverage is achieved, or all nodes are covered.

Our Algorithm 3 , reverse-rank SKIM (RR-SKIM), follows the SKIM design, of iterating the selection of a new seed node (rankee) via sample building and updates. The reverse-rank problem, however, requires some critical adaptations.

When sample building, we repeatedly select random uncovered ranker nodes z. We then run Dijkstra's algorithm from z but stop the search when the approximate rank $\hat{\pi}_{zu}$ exceeds T. For each visited rankee node u, we increment the sample size sample_size[u] and also add u to a list inverted_sample[z] (the list of nodes where z is included in the sample). This process stops when the first rankee u reaches sample_size[u] $= K$. The node u then becomes the next seed node. We then apply our sorted-access reverse-rank single source computation from u, up to rank T, to determine the coverage of the new seed u. We mark all uncovered visited nodes as covered. For each newly covered ranker z, we scan inverted_sample[z] and decrement sample_size[v] for each $v \in$ inverted_sample[z]. We then delete inverted_sample[z]. For each covered ranker z, we maintain the (approximate) rank of the best seed best_seed[z]$.rank = \min_{v\in S} \hat{\pi}_{vz}$ and the corresponding minimum distance best_seed[z]$.dist = \min_{v\in S} d_{vz}$

(note that the node with minimum distance must have minimum estimated rank). The purpose of maintaining best_seed is to enable pruning of reverse searches. Pruning is critical for the near-linear computation bound of the algorithm (without it, we can construct examples were the bulk of covered nodes is revisited with each new seed, resulting in $\Omega(|\text{seedlist}|m)$ computation).

A search from the new seed u is always pruned at z when $\hat{\pi}_{uz} > T$, but is also pruned when

$$\hat{\pi}_{uz} > \text{best\_seed}[z].rank \text{ or } \quad (11)$$
$$\hat{\pi}_{uz} = \text{best\_seed}[z].rank \text{ and } d_{uz} \geq \text{best\_seed}[z].dist\ .$$

We now need to show that also with this pruning, the algorithm maintains the following invariant

LEMMA 5.1. *After the processing of a new seed node, all nodes z with $\min_{v\in S}\hat{\pi}_{vz} \leq T$ have best_seed$[z].rank = \min_{v\in S}\hat{\pi}_{zv}$ and best_seed$[z].dist = \min_{v\in S} d_{zv}$ and all other nodes have best_seed$[z].rank = +\infty$.*

PROOF. This property clearly holds when pruning only when $\hat{\pi}_{uz} > T$, since after inserting a new seed node u our reverse-rank search from u visits all nodes with $\hat{\pi}_{vz} \leq T$.

We establish the claim using induction on added seeds. The base of the induction is when S is empty and best_seed$[z].rank = +\infty$. Assume now that our invariant holds and let s_2 be a newly selected seed node. Let u_1 be a node on which we prune the search from s_2. From the condition (11) there exist a seed node s_1 such that $\hat{\pi}_{u_1,s_1} < \hat{\pi}_{u_1,s_2}$ or $\hat{\pi}_{u_1,s_1} = \hat{\pi}_{u_1,s_2}$ and $d_{u_1,s_1} \leq d_{u_1,s_2}$. From the definition of our estimators, $\hat{\pi}_{u_1,s_1} < \hat{\pi}_{u_1,s_2}$ implies $d_{u1,s_1} < d_{u_1,s_2}$. Combining, we obtain that $d_{u1,s_1} \leq d_{u_1,s_2}$.

Now assume to the contrary there is a node u_2 such that u_1 is on the shortest path from u_2 to s_2 and $\hat{\pi}_{u_2,s_2} < \hat{\pi}_{u_2,s_1}$ or $\hat{\pi}_{u_2,s_2} = \hat{\pi}_{u_2,s_1}$ and $d_{u_2,s_2} < d_{u_2,s_1}$. We show that this is not possible.

Using the above and triangle inequality we obtain $d_{u_2,s_1} \leq d_{u_2,u1} + d_{u_1,s_1} \leq d_{u_2,u_1} + d_{u_1,s_2} = d_{u_2,s_2}$. A property of our estimates is that for any three nodes $d_{u_2,s_1} \leq d_{u_2,s_2}$ implies $\hat{\pi}_{u_2,s_1} \leq \hat{\pi}_{u_2,s_2}$. □

The analysis of computation and approximation quality uses components from the analysis of T-SKIM[11]. An important critical component in the analysis is that we can "charge" edge traversals used for sample building to increases in sample sizes. When there are many non-rankee nodes, we can construct worst-case graph where non-rankees are repeatedly traversed without incrementing sample counts. In realistic models, however, and when all nodes are rankers or rankees, we would expect such popular ranker hub nodes to be covered quickly by the first few selected seeds. Another component of the analysis that carries over from T-SKIM is bounding the number of updates to best_seed$[z]$. The argument there critically relies on the sample based approximate greedy selection. The approximation quality of the algorithm can only be guaranteed probabilistically and with respect to approximate ranks $\hat{\pi}_{uz}$. To summarize, when we run the algorithm with $K = O(\epsilon^{-2}\log n)$, and prune sampling searches using the approximate ranks $\hat{\pi}$, we obtain the following.

THEOREM 5.2. *With very high probability, for all $s \geq 1$, the influence $\widehat{\text{Inf}}$ of the first s seed nodes is at least $1-(1-1/s)^s - \epsilon$ times the maximum possible $\widehat{\text{Inf}}$ with s seeds. When all nodes are both rankers and rankees, the algorithm uses $O(|E|\epsilon^{-1}\log^3 n + |E|\epsilon^{-2}\log n)$ operations.*

5.3 Approximability of the exact problem

Distance-based influence maximization is known to be at least as hard as max cover also in terms of inapproximability, by a seminal result of Feige [17]. Thus, we know that in a sense Greedy is the best scalable algorithm. What we can say about reverse-rank influence maximization with a threshold kernel T is that it is at least as hard as max cover, when each element can be a member of at most T sets. The problem is NP-hard for $T \geq 2$ (by reduction to max vertex cover), but Feige's inapproximability result does not apply. This leaves open the possibility that some polynomial-time algorithms have better approximation ratio than Greedy.

When $T = 1$, the influence function is simply the number of reverse nearest neighbors. In this case, the coverage sets of different nodes are disjoint and influence maximization is trivial: The greedy permutation which selects nodes in decreasing order according to number of reverse nearest neighbors is optimal.

When $T = 2$, each node can be covered by at most two other nodes, which is similar to max vertex cover, which is also NP hard, but has a polynomial approximation algorithms that achieves a slightly better approximation ratio than the greedy guarantee of $1-(1-1/s)^s$ [18]. The Linear Programming based algorithm, however, does not scale for large inputs and also does not seem to apply for our general case of $T > 2$.

6. HARDNESS OF EXACT REVERSE-RANK SINGLE SOURCE COMPUTATION

Exact single source reverse-rank computation from a node u will return π_{iu} for all nodes i. Clearly, it can be solved using an APSP computation. We show the following

THEOREM 6.1. *The reverse-rank single source problem has subcubic equivalence to APSP.*

We give a reduction from the *Graph Radius Problem*: The radius of a graph G, is defined as the minimum over nodes u of the maximum distance from v to another node

$$R = \min_{u\in V}\max_{v\in V} d_{uv}\ . \quad (12)$$

The graph radius problem on undirected graphs is known to have subcubic equivalence to APSP [1].

Given a graph $G = (V, E)$, and a length parameter x, we construct a new graph $G_x = (V', E')$ by adding a new node $V' = V \cup \{u\}$ and adding edges from u to all $v \in V$ with length x.

LEMMA 6.1. *Let G be a graph with radius R and consider $x > 0$. If $R > x$ then in G_x, for all nodes $v \in V$, $\pi_{vu} < |V|$. If $R < x$ then there must exist a node $z \in V$ such that $\pi_{zu} = |V|$ in G_x.*

PROOF. Suppose that $R > x$ then by definition of radius, for all nodes z, $\max_{v\in V} d_{zv} \geq R > x$. Therefore node u will not be the farthest from z and we have $\pi_{zu} < |V|$.

Suppose now that $R < x$. let $z \in V$ be such that $R = \max_{v\in V} d_{zv}$. Then for all $v \in V$, $d_{zu} = x > R \geq d_{zv}$ and thus $\pi_{zu} = |V|$. □

From the lemma, we can compute the graph radius R by performing a logarithmic number (in the representation of G) of exact reverse-rank single source computations on graphs the size of G. This concludes the proof of Theorem 6.1.

COROLLARY 6.2. *Exact computation of reverse-rank influence, even with a single seed node $|S| = 1$, uniform β, and a threshold function α, is sub-cubic equivalent to APSP.*

PROOF. We use the same construction and compute influence (centrality) of node u with α being a threshold function with $T = |V| - 1$. □

Algorithm 3: reverse-rank SKIM

Input: Directed graph $G = (V, E)$, ranker nodes $Z \subset V$, rankee nodes $U \subset V$, threshold T, parameter K
Output: Approximate greedy sequence seedlist

```
// Initialization
forall the nodes u ∈ V do best_seed[u].rank ← ∞
forall the rankee nodes v ∈ U do sample_size[v] ← 0
inverted_sample ←⊥ // Hash map of ranker nodes to sets of rankee nodes
coverage ← 0                    // Coverage of current seedlist
seedlist ←⊥                     // Output list
F ← random shuffle of the ranker nodes Z
while |coverage| < |Z| and (∃ unscanned u ∈ F or max_{u∈U} sample_size[u] > 0) do   // select seed
    x ←⊥                          // next seed node
    while ∃ unscanned u ∈ F do    // Build samples
        u ← next node in shuffled sequence F
        if best_seed[u].rank < ∞ then     // Node u is covered, skip it
            Continue
        // Find all rankees v with π̂_uv ≤ T
        Run a Dijkstra search from u in G, during which
        foreach scanned rankee node v ∈ U do
            if π̂_uv > T then terminate the search
            sample_size[v] ← sample_size[v] + 1
            inverted_sample[u] ← inverted_sample[u] ∪ {v}
            if sample_size[v] = K then
                x ← v                     // Next seed node
                abort sample building loop
    if x =⊥ then
        x ← arg max_{u∈U} sample_size[u]
        if sample_size[x] = 0 then abort main loop
    I_x ← 0                       // Estimated coverage of x
    // Compute I_x and update residual
    run pruned reverse-rank single-source search from x in transposed graph G^T, during which
    foreach scanned node v ∈ V with (π̂_vu, d_vu) do
        if π̂_vu > T or best_seed[v].rank < π̂_vu or
        best_seed[v].rank = π̂_vu and best_seed[v].dist ≤ d_vu
        then
            prune at v
        if best_seed[v] = ∞ and v ∈ Z then    // v is a newly covered ranker
            I_x ← I_x + 1 ; coverage ← coverage + 1
            forall the nodes w in inverted_sample[v] do
                sample_size[w] ← sample_size[w] − 1
            inverted_sample[v] ← ⊥              // Delete
        best_seed[v].rank ← π̂_vu
        best_seed[v].dist ← d_vu
    seedlist.append(x, I_x)
return seedlist
```

7. EXPERIMENTAL EVALUATION

We implemented and evaluated our algorithms for computing ADS, approximate reverse-rank single-source, and influence maximization. Our implementations are in C++ and were compiled using gcc (g++) with full optimization. Our testing machine runs Centos 6.5 and uses Dell PowerEdge R720 server with two Intel Xeon E5-2640 CPUs. Each with 12 cores (2.50GHz, 12×32kiB L1, 6×256kib L2, and 15MiB L3) and 264GiB of RAM. The disk capacity is 1T. We open sourced our implementation and it is available at https://github.com/eliavb/all_distance_sketch.

Table 1 shows the social graphs used for our evaluation, all taken from the SNAP project [34]. For each graph we list the number of nodes and edges and whether edges are directed. These data sets did not distinguish between edges, so we used uniform lengths of 1. Our implementations, however, are designed to work with general positive edge lengths.

7.1 Sequential ADS computation

Table 1 also lists, for each instance, performance figures (time and memory usage) of our optimized sequential implementation of *Pruned Dijkstras* (Algorithm 1). We list performance for ADS parameter values $k = 16, 64, 128$ (higher k implies larger sketch size and processing and higher estimation quality). The listed times are broken into *load time* – loading the graph into memory data structures, *ADS time* – computing the sketches, and *ests time* – process the ADS sketches to compute the distance to cardinality estimation lists $L(i)$. We can see that ADS computation was the dominant component. Overall, the preprocessing time is of the order of few hours, even on our largest data set. The table also lists the virtual memory usage of the different runs.

7.2 Multithreaded ADS algorithm

We next evaluate our implementation of the multithreaded ADS algorithm (Section 3.1). The evaluation was done by generating 1 to 14 concurrent threads. We used batch size parameter $\mu = 0.1$. The parameter $\mu = 0.1$ was selected since it had the best performance on a test of sweeping μ between 0.05 and 1 and considering 1–14 threads on the slashdot graph. We note that the amount of concurrency provided in the algorithmic design is much larger, but the architecture of our machine, mainly number of cores and shared caches, limited the benefit of using more threads. We show the results for executions with ADS parameter $k = 16$. The time to load the graph into memory and the total virtual memory used did not vary much for the same instance and different numbers of threads. Table 2 lists the load-time and virtual memory numbers for 7 threads. The table also shows the run time on a single thread. Note that it can be slightly larger than our optimized sequential implementation. Figure 2 shows the running times, as a fraction of the running time on a single-thread, as a function of the number of concurrent threads. We note that the number of threads listed is the concurrency generated by our program scheduler – the actual number of cores allocated by the OS was sometimes smaller and we had no control over it. We observe significant benefit of the multithreaded design, in particular for the larger graphs where we obtain up to a factor of 3 speedup, also with respect to the optimized sequential implementation. We note that most of the speedup is obtained using only $2 - 6$ threads.

Table 2: Multithreaded ADS computation

instance	load [Sec]	Memory [GiB]	1-thread [Sec]
Facebook	0.13	0.56	0.69
Slashdot	0.57	1.1	10.0
Twitter	23	2.2	120
YouTube	3.9	3.3	157
LiveJournal	36	11	1541

7.3 Reverse-rank single-source computation

Table 3 shows running times of our approximate reverse-rank single source computations, averaged over 1000 source nodes selected uniformly at random. The times listed are net per computation after loading the graph and pre-computed sketches $L(i)$ into

Table 1: **Test Instances and preprocessing time (single thread)**

instance (un/directed)	#nodes	#edges	load [Sec]	Preprocess ($k=16$) ADS [Sec]	Preprocess ($k=16$) mem [GB]	Preprocess ($k=16$) ests [Sec]	Preprocess ($k=64$) ADS [Sec]	Preprocess ($k=64$) mem [GB]	Preprocess ($k=64$) ests [Sec]	Preprocess ($k=128$) ADS [Sec]	Preprocess ($k=128$) mem [GB]	Preprocess ($k=128$) ests [Sec]
Facebook (u)	3,959	84,243	0.3	0.5	0.03	0.043	0.7	0.03	0.140	1.4	0.04	0.341
Slashdot (d)	77,360	905,468	0.5	5.7	0.1	0.276	23	0.22	1.91	42	0.4	5.35
Twitter (d)	456,626	14,855,842	22	88	0.9	2.00	338	1.4	13.5	523	2	39
YouTube (u)	1,134,890	2,987,624	3.3	116	1.4	6.69	404	3.3	41.6	770	5.3	118
LiveJournal (u)	3,997,962	34,681,189	32	1481	6.4	29.7	4,901	18	209	9,555	31.5	642

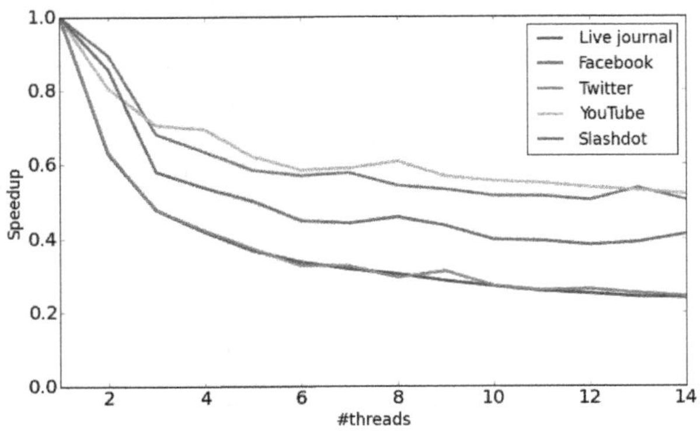

Figure 2: Multithreaded computation. Speedup (ratio of time to single-thread time) as a function of the number of threads.

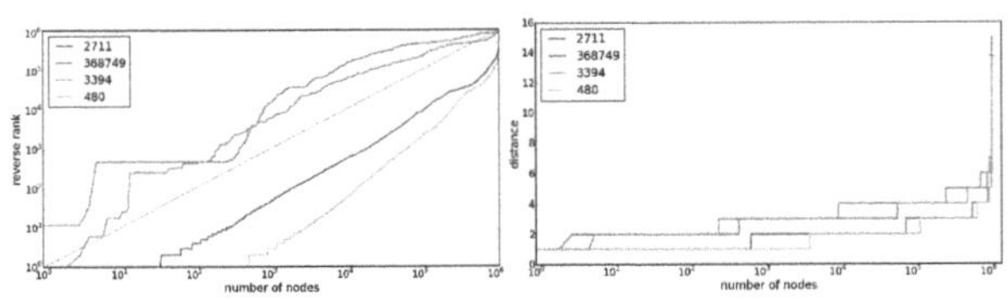

Figure 3: Cummulative distributions on YouTube graph. Left: Reverse-rank Right: Distance.

memory. We show running times for the different ADS parameter values $k = 16, 64, 128$. For reference, we also show running time for Dijkstra's algorithm (single-source distances) averaged over the same 1000 source nodes. We can observe that the running times of our reverse-rank single-source computation do not depend on the sketch parameter k and are similar to Dijkstra computations. The table also shows extrapolated running time for APSP computation. The extrapolation was obtained by multiplying the time for a single Dijkstra run by the number of nodes. This is listed for reference, since exact reverse-rank single-source computation is equivalent to an all-pairs computation.

The table also displays the average relative errors (ARE) for each sketch parameter. Since it was not possible to scalably compute the exact reverse-rank values even for a single source, we computed instead the estimation errors on the ranks using the Dijkstra runs: The errors were therefore averaged over all the ranks provided by 1000 different rankers instead of all the ranks "received" by 1000 different rankees. We can see that the ARE, as expected, decreases with the ADS parameter k and are within the theoretical bounds. Note that a fixed set of sketches was computed during preprocessing and used in all subsequent computations. Therefore the estimates on reverse-ranks of different source-destination pairs can be highly dependent.

7.4 Reverse-rank distributions

Our implementation allowed us, for the first time, to view the reverse rank distributions of nodes in a large network. Figure 3 (left) shows the cummulative reverse rank distributions $\overline{\pi}_{js}$ for 4 selected source nodes in the YouTube network. For each node s, we sort the (estimated) values $\overline{\pi}_{js}$ for all nodes j in increasing order. The cummulative distribution plot then shows the value y at each position x. The figure also includes a reference line where for any i there is a node with rank i. The reference line is in a sense corresponds to an "average" source node, which gives and receives the same influence.

We can get information on the relative importance of a node in its "locality," for varying locality ranges, from its reverse-rank distribution. Nodes that are important in their locality would have distributions that at least initially lie well below the reference line. This means that for some i, there are many more than i nodes that rank them below i. Node #2711 and #480 are example influential nodes that remain important across neighborhood scales. Node #368749 has low influence with distribution above the reference line across ranges. Node #3394 has low influence on most ranges except for its immediate neighborhood, where it has average influence, and on the longest scale, when looking at its 7×10^5 and above highest rankers (which is 35% of total nodes), which indicates that it lies closer to the "core" of the network. Note that we plot $\overline{\pi}$, meaning ties are broken "upwards," which biases towards being above the reference line.

Figure 3 (right) provides, for comparison, the cummulative distance distributions for the same nodes: For each number of hops y, we see the number x of nodes within y hops. The distance distribution captures the expansion rate, but does not quantify well the relative status of a node within its locality: A less influential member of a dense community would have higher expansion than an influential member of a sparser community. As a simplified example think of two nodes A and B with the same degree Δ such that all neighbors of A have degree $\ll \Delta$ and all neighbors of B have degree $\gg \Delta$. In this case we may view A as being influential in its neighborhood whereas B will not be. The reverse-rank distribution will correctly make this distinction whereas the distance-distribution will not.

7.5 Influence maximization

We next evaluate the performance of reverse-rank SKIM, in terms of both the quality of the coverage and the running time. The evaluation used the social graphs listed in Table 1, with uniform edge lengths and all nodes being both rankers and rankees. We used the $\pi \equiv \overline{\pi}$ (3) interpretation of rank. We study dependence on three parameters, T, k, and K: The threshold value T specifies the coverage rate. The ADS sketch parameter k determines the quality of $\hat{\overline{\pi}}$ as estimates of the true ranks π, and thus, the relation between $\widehat{\text{Inf}}$ (10), which we optimize for, and the true Inf. Finally, the sample size parameter K determines the quality of the coverage in terms

Table 3: Reverse-Rank Single Source computation, averaged over 1000 source nodes selected uniformly at random.

	reverse-rank single source						Dijkstra	APSP
	$k = 16$		$k = 64$		$k = 128$			
instance	[Sec]	ARE	[Sec]	ARE	[Sec]	ARE	[Sec]	$\approx$ [hours]
Facebook	0.006	0.11	0.006	0.072	0.006	0.067	0.002	0.002
Slashdot	0.071	0.34	0.077	0.12	0.074	0.076	0.06	1.3
Twitter	0.96	0.29	1.00	0.050	0.88	0.076	0.54	68
YouTube	1.44	0.24	1.51	0.041	1.34	0.023	0.98	309
LiveJournal	13	0.11	16	0.13	16	0.053	5.8	6440

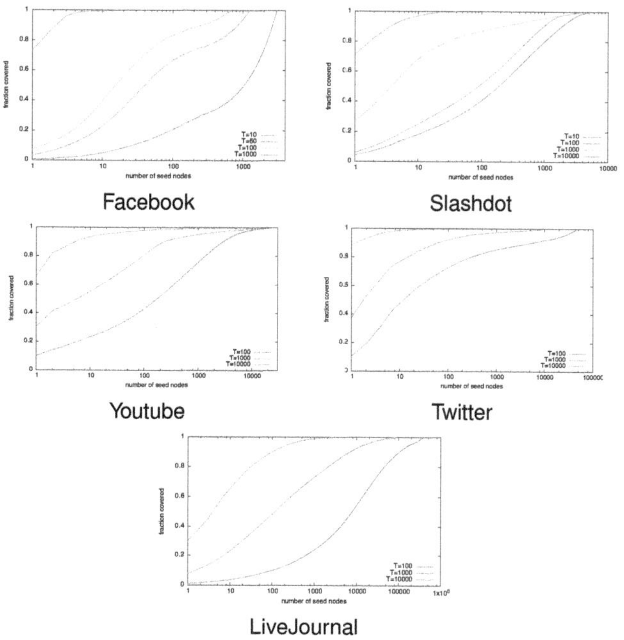

Figure 4: Fractional coverage $\widehat{\mathrm{Inf}(S)}/|V|$ as a function of seed set size $|S|$ for rR-SKIM, for varying T.

of the approximate influence $\widehat{\mathrm{Inf}}$ (10). Larger K mean that we are more likely to select seeds with marginal $\widehat{\mathrm{Inf}}$ influence that is closer to the maximum.

Recall that the computation of an exact greedy sequence, with respect to either $\widehat{\mathrm{Inf}}$ or Inf (Algorithm 2), is $\tilde{O}(T|E|)$, where the $\tilde{O}$ notation suppresses logarithmic factors. The computation of reverse-rank SKIM uses ADS computation of $\tilde{O}(k|E|)$ and additional computation with worst-case bound of $\tilde{O}(K|E|)$. Moreover, note that in actuality, the time is $\tilde{O}(K|E|\rho)$, where ρ is the ratio between the average and maximum (marginal) influence of a node, and with the typical skew we have $\rho \ll 1$. Therefore, the scalability advantage of SKIM to become more significant for larger T.

When evaluating the effect of the sample size K, we fixed the ADS parameter to be $k = 128$ for the four smaller graphs and $k = 64$ for the larger one and used several values of $T \leq 10^4$. We computed the exact greedy selection with respect to $\widehat{\mathrm{Inf}}$, which is obtained by selecting a node with maximum marginal $\widehat{\mathrm{Inf}}$ in each step. This was done on the four smaller graphs. On these graphs, sample size $K = 100$ was almost always within a fraction of a percent of the exact greedy coverage. The one exception was on Slashdot and $T = 10^4$ where the first seed had coverage that is 6% lower than the optimal one and the gap closed up for the first three seeds. With $K = 500$, the approximate greedy coverage almost exactly matched the exact greedy coverage. For LiveJournal, we only evaluated the coverage for sample size up to $K = 500$, but the performance with $K = 100$ already matched that. We note that these observed errors are much lower than the worst-case guarantees provided in our analysis. The explanation is the skew of the influence distribution is skewed, where the node of maximum marginal influence is well separated from the second maximum, and with very few nodes having influence that is more than a fraction of the maximum.

Our implementation allows us to examine the coverage to seed set size tradeoffs as a function of the threshold T. These tradeoffs provide structural insights on the networks and results are shown in Figure 4. Higher values of T as expected have higher coverage with fewer seeds. We can also see a highly skewed and asymmetric distribution of importance. For example, the LiveJournal graph with nearly four million nodes, there is a single node that 4×10^4 other nodes rank within their top $T = 100$. The first 11 nodes have 1.6×10^5 nodes ranking at least one of them in their top 100. For $T = 1000$, the top seed covers 3×10^5 nodes and the top 12 cover 7.5×10^5 (a quarter of all nodes).

Table 4 lists selected single thread running times for reverse-rank SKIM. Listed times do not include ADS computation (see Table 1), but this preprocessing time was only a fraction of the total. We note that the running time did not significantly depend on ADS size (the parameter k). The parameter k can impact running time only because it can generate longer neighborhood estimate lists $L(i)$. The size of these lists, even with very large k, is below the effective diameter of the graph, which was small in our data sets. The listed times in the table use $k = 128$ for the four smaller graphs and $k = 64$ for the largest one. They correspond to computing the full sequence (until all nodes are covered). Note that the running time can be significantly reduced if we stop when a desired coverage or number of seeds are reached. We can also observe that the running time grows linearly with the sample size K. An interesting observation is that for the largest graphs, the computation is faster for larger values of T – This is because SKIM works with the residual problem, and its size decreases more rapidly for higher values of T. This is in contrast to an exact greedy computation (Algorithm 2), where the running time increases rapidly with T. Selected running times, and the slowdown factor with respect to reverse-rank SKIM (including ADS computation), are provided in Table 5 (For technical reasons, we had to perform this comparison on a different machine). We can see that exact computation is feasible for small values of T, but the running time increases rapidly with T.

Finally, we evaluate the quality of our approximate greedy sequences which were optimized for $\widehat{\mathrm{Inf}}$, in terms of the exact influence objective Inf. To do so, we used a variation of Algorithm 2 to compute the exact influence of the sequence of seeds returned by reverse-rank SKIM. We observed that even for ADS parameter $k = 64$ and $k = 128$, the Inf coverage of the approximate greedy

Table 4: Reverse-rank SKIM running times [Sec]

Instance	$K = 100$			$K = 500$		
T:	10^2	10^3	10^4	10^2	10^3	10^4
Slashdot	10.22	16.35	-	17.37	32.81	-
Twitter	95.4	68.6	53.4	114	98	82
YouTube	151.3	138.6	228.9	289.3	256.6	346.9
LiveJournal	6533	3517	2040	8261	6123	4313

Table 5: Exact greedy running times and speedup factor of reverse-rank SKIM (including sketch computation)

Instance	T	[hours]	$\approx$ factor
YouTube	10^2	2.81	$\times 13$
YouTube	10^3	9.50	$\times 51$
YouTube	10^4	33.96	$\times 135$

sequence for $\widehat{\text{Inf}}$ generally almost matched, and never less than 8% of the exact greedy sequence for Inf.

8. CONCLUSION

Rank-based measures were used for decades as an alternative to distance-based measures. Here, we defined and motivated rank-based measures of centrality and influence, which we believe will become important tools in network mining and analysis. We then presented novel highly scalable algorithms for fundamental rank-based computations on graphs, including a Dijkstra-like approximate reverse rank single-source algorithm which facilitates reverse-rank influence computation and reverse-rank greedy influence maximization. We complement our work with hardness results that indicate that exact computation inherently scales poorly.

A contribution of broader interest is our novel multithreaded design for computing all-distance sketches (ADS) which provided the fastest implementation for computing these sketches on multi-core architectures. This design is relevant to many other applications of distance sketches.

Going forward, we plan to extend our reverse-rank IM computation to general decay functions and design a multithreaded implementation. We also hope to use our newly available tools to explore the relation between distance-based and rank-based influence.

Acknowledgements:. The authors would like to thank Shiri Chechik and Amos Fiat for discussions and pointers.

9. REFERENCES

[1] A. Abboud, F. Grandoni, and V. Vassilevska Williams. Subcubic equivalences between graph centrality problems, APSP and diameter. In *SODA*. ACM-SIAM, 2015.

[2] B. D. Abrahao, F. Chierichetti, R. Kleinberg, and A. Panconesi. Trace complexity of network inference. In *KDD*, 2013.

[3] A. Bavelas. A mathematical model for small group structures. *Human Organization*, 7:16–30, 1948.

[4] F. Bloch and M. O. Jackson. The formation of networks with transfers among players. *Journal of Economic Theory*, 133(1):83–110, 2007.

[5] P. Boldi, M. Rosa, and S. Vigna. HyperANF: Approximating the neighbourhood function of very large graphs on a budget. In *WWW*, 2011.

[6] E. Cohen. Size-estimation framework with applications to transitive closure and reachability. *J. Comput. System Sci.*, 55:441–453, 1997.

[7] E. Cohen. All-distances sketches, revisited: HIP estimators for massive graphs analysis. *TKDE*, 2015.

[8] E. Cohen. Multi-objective weighted sampling. In *HotWeb*. IEEE, 2015. full version: `http://arxiv.org/abs/1509.07445`.

[9] E. Cohen, D. Delling, F. Fuchs, A. Goldberg, M. Goldszmidt, and R. Werneck. Scalable similarity estimation in social networks: Closeness, node labels, and random edge lengths. In *COSN*. ACM, 2013.

[10] E. Cohen, D. Delling, T. Pajor, and R. F. Werneck. Sketch-based influence maximization and computation: Scaling up with guarantees. In *CIKM*. ACM, 2014.

[11] E. Cohen, D. Delling, T. Pajor, and R. F. Werneck. Timed influence: Computation and maximization. Technical Report cs.SI/1410.6976, arXiv, 2014.

[12] E. Cohen and H. Kaplan. Spatially-decaying aggregation over a network: Model and algorithms. *J. Comput. System Sci.*, 73:265–288, 2007. Full version of a SIGMOD 2004 paper.

[13] E. Cohen and H. Kaplan. Summarizing data using bottom-k sketches. In *ACM PODC*, 2007.

[14] T. M. Cover and P. E. Hart. Nearest neighbor pattern classification. *IEEE Transactions on Information Theory*, 13(1):21–27, 1967.

[15] N. Du, L. Song, M. Gomez-Rodriguez, and H. Zha. Scalable influence estimation in continuous-time diffusion networks. In *NIPS*. Curran Associates, Inc., 2013.

[16] R. Fagin, A. Lotem, and M. Naor. Optimal aggregation algorithms for middleware. *J. Comput. System Sci.*, 66, 2003.

[17] U. Feige. A threshold of $\ln n$ for approximating set cover. *J. Assoc. Comput. Mach.*, 45:634–652, 1998.

[18] U. Feige and M. Langberg. Approximation algorithms for maximization problems arising in graph partitioning. *J. Algorithms*, 41, 2001.

[19] L. C. Freeman. Centrality in social networks: Conceptual clarification. *Social Networks*, 1, 1979.

[20] J. Gao, H. V. Jagadish, B. C. Ooi, and S. Wang. Selective hashing: Closing the gap between radius search and k-nn search. In *ACM KDD*, 2015.

[21] M. Gomez-Rodriguez, D. Balduzzi, and B. Schölkopf. Uncovering the temporal dynamics of diffusion networks. In *ICML*, 2011.

[22] A. Goyal, W. Lu, and L.V.S. Lakshmanan. Celf++: Optimizing the greedy algorithm for influence maximization in social networks. In *WWW*. ACM, 2011.

[23] T. Hastie, R. Tibshirani, and J. Friedman. *The Elements of Statistical Learning*. Springer New York Inc., 2001.

[24] D. G. Horvitz and D. J. Thompson. A generalization of sampling without replacement from a finite universe. *Journal of the American Statistical Association*, 47(260):663–685, 1952.

[25] D. Kempe, J. M. Kleinberg, and É. Tardos. Maximizing the spread of influence through a social network. In *KDD*. ACM, 2003.

[26] F. Korn and S. Muthukrishnan. Influence sets based on reverse nearest neighbor queries. In *SIGMOD*, 2000.

[27] Yiu. M. L., D. Papadias, N. Mamoulis, and Y. Tao. Reverse nearest neighbors in large graphs. *IEEE TKDE*, 18, 2006.

[28] J. Leskovec, A. Krause, C. Guestrin, C. Faloutsos, J. VanBriesen, and Glance N. Cost-effective outbreak detection in networks. In *KDD*. ACM, 2007.

[29] D. Liben-Nowell and J. Kleinberg. The link prediction problem for social networks. In *CIKM*. ACM, 2003.

[30] G. Nemhauser, L. Wolsey, and M. Fisher. An analysis of the approximations of maximizing submodular set functions. *Mathematical Programming*, 14, 1978.

[31] T. Opsahl, F. Agneessens, and J. Skvoretz. Node centrality in weighted networks: Generalizing degree and shortest paths. *Social Networks*, 32, 2010. http://toreopsahl.com/2010/03/20/.

[32] C. R. Palmer, P. B. Gibbons, and C. Faloutsos. ANF: A fast and scalable tool for data mining in massive graphs. In *KDD*, 2002.

[33] G. Sabidussi. The centrality index of a graph. *Psychometrika*, 31(4):581–603, 1966.

[34] Stanford network analysis. `http://snap.stanford.edu`.

[35] Y. Tang, X. Xiao, and Y. Shi. Influence maximization: Near-optimal time complexity meets practical efficiency. In *SIGMOD*, 2014.

[36] V. Vassilevska Williams and R. Williams. Subcubic equivalences between path, matrix and triangle problems. In *FOCS*. IEEE, 2010.

[37] J. Weston, S. Bengio, and N. Usunier. WSABIE: scaling up to large vocabulary image annotation. In *IJCAI*, 2011.

Improved Achievability and Converse Bounds for Erdős-Rényi Graph Matching

Daniel Cullina
University of Illinois at Urbana-Champaign
1308 W Main St
Urbana, Illinois, 61801
cullina@illinois.edu

Negar Kiyavash
University of Illinois at Urbana-Champaign
1308 W Main St
Urbana, Illinois, 61801
kiyavash@illinois.edu

ABSTRACT

We consider the problem of perfectly recovering the vertex correspondence between two correlated Erdős-Rényi (ER) graphs. For a pair of correlated graphs on the same vertex set, the correspondence between the vertices can be obscured by randomly permuting the vertex labels of one of the graphs. In some cases, the structural information in the graphs allow this correspondence to be recovered. We investigate the information-theoretic threshold for exact recovery, i.e. the conditions under which the entire vertex correspondence can be correctly recovered given unbounded computational resources.

Pedarsani and Grossglauser provided an achievability result of this type. Their result establishes the scaling dependence of the threshold on the number of vertices. We improve on their achievability bound. We also provide a converse bound, establishing conditions under which exact recovery is impossible. Together, these establish the scaling dependence of the threshold on the level of correlation between the two graphs. The converse and achievability bounds differ by a factor of two for sparse, significantly correlated graphs.

1. INTRODUCTION

In this paper we consider the problem of graph deanonymization, or graph matching. In this problem, there are two correlated graphs on the same vertex set. Call these G_a and G_b. By correlated we mean that the presence or absence of a particular edge in G_a provides some information about the presence of that edge in G_b. The correspondence between the vertices can be obscured by randomly permuting the vertex labels of G_a. Given the permuted version of G_a and the unaltered G_b, what can be learned about the correspondence between their vertex sets?

We focus on one particular variant: the problem of perfectly recovering the vertex correspondence between two correlated Erdős-Rényi (ER) graphs. In some cases, the structural information in the graphs allow this correspondence to be recovered. We investigate the information-theoretic threshold for exact recovery, i.e. the conditions under which the entire vertex correspondence can be correctly recovered given unbounded computational resources.

This question was first addressed by Pedarsani and Grossglauser, who provided an information-theoretic sufficient condition [9]. Their result establishes the scaling dependence of the threshold on the number of vertices: in order for exact deanonymization to be feasible, n-vertex graphs G_a and G_b must have average degree at least $\Omega(\log n)$. Our main result is a new achievability bound that improves on the bound from [9]. We also provide a converse bound, establishing conditions under which exact recovery is impossible. Together, these establish the scaling dependence of the threshold on the level of correlation between the two graphs. Call G_a and G_b sparse if their average degree is sublinear. Call them significantly correlated if their intersection is larger than the intersection of similar independent graphs by a factor that grows to infinity. In this regime, our converse and achievability bounds differ by a constant factor of two.

One motivation for the study of graph deanonymization comes from networks associated with internet services. As these services have become ubiquitous, an enormous amount of data about the users of these services has been generated and collected. Much of this data is *structural*. It reflects interactions between multiple users: communications from one user to another, personal relationships, transactions, and many more examples. Other forms of data associated with single users still have informative network structure. Examples of this type of data include home towns, employers, educational institutions, hobbies and interests, and purchase history.

This data allows unprecedented opportunities for analysis, particularly when multiple data sources are combined. However, there are complex and difficult trade-offs between facilitating analysis and preserving privacy.

There are at least two fundamental reasons to attempt to learn vertex correspondences between networks. First, if multiple networks reflect a common underlying network of relationships, then one can obtain a better estimate of the underlying network by combining multiple sources to overcome the effects of noisy data and omissions. Second, if the data associated with one network is sensitive and the data associated with another network allows for the identification of users, then learning the vertex correspondence grants access to sensitive user information.

Responsible privacy management by data collectors requires an understanding of when sensitive information can

SIGMETRICS '16, June 14 - 18, 2016, Antibes Juan-Les-Pins, France

ISBN 978-1-4503-4266-7/16/06...$15.00

DOI: http://dx.doi.org/10.1145/2896377.2901460

and cannot be recovered from data. A large portion of the recent work on graph deanonymization has involved the evaluation of heuristic algorithms on datasets derived from real-world networks. These lines of work play a crucial role in advancing our understanding of the privacy of current systems. We attempt to complement these efforts by contributing to a foundational theory that will inform the design of future systems.

In addition to the practical motivations, this is an interesting and fundamental problem in the theory of random graphs. Throughout, we will discuss the connections to other questions regarding random graphs.

The remainder of the paper is organized as follows. In Section 2, we discuss some other work on information-theoretic limits of deanonymization. In Section 3, we introduce our notation and formalize the estimation problem and our model of correlated graphs. In Section 4, we state our main results. Section 5 contains the proof of our main achievability result and Section 6 contains the proof of our converse. In Section 7, we consider negatively correlated graphs and present achievability and converse bounds for their deanonymization. In Section 8, we suggest some directions for future work.

2. RELATED WORK

Pedarsani and Grossglauser [9] were the first to approach the problem of finding information-theoretic conditions for deanonymization. Since their work, a number of authors have considered extensions and variants of the deanonymization problem.

Ji et al. [5] investigated the feasibility of deanonymization under the configuration model of random graphs. The configuration model generates graphs with a specified degree sequence [2]. Real world networks differ from Erdős-Rényi graphs in several ways. One of the most obvious is that ER graphs have a binomial degree distribution (which becomes approximately Poisson for sparse ER graphs), which has a rapidly decaying upper tail. In contrast, the degree distributions of many real world networks have much heavier upper tails [1]. The configuration model allows for the replication of this feature.

Ji et al. [4] also investigated the effect of seed information on thresholds for deanonymization. A seed vertex pair consists of a vertex from G_a and the corresponding vertex from G_b. They found sufficient conditions for complete deanonymization using two information sources: first using only the edges between seed vertices and other vertices and second using all edges. In both cases, the dependence on the number of seeds was determined. This paper also found sufficient conditions for deanonymization of a fraction $1-\epsilon$ of the vertices.

Some practical deanonymization algorithms start by attempting to locate a few seeds. From these seeds, the graph matching is iteratively extended. Algorithms for the latter step can scale very efficiently. Narayanan and Shmatikov were the first to apply this method [8]. They evaluated their performance empirically on graphs derived from social networks.

More recently, there has been some work evaluating the performance of this type of algorithm on graph inputs from random models. Yartseva and Grossglauser examined a simple percolation algorithm for growing a graph matching [11]. They find a sharp threshold for the number of initial seeds required to ensure that final graph matching includes every vertex. The intersection of the graphs G_a and G_b plays an important role in the analysis of this algorithm. Kazemi et al. extended this work and investigated the performance of a more sophisticated percolation algorithm [6].

If the networks being deanonymized correspond to two distinct online services, it is unlikely that the user populations of the services are identical. Kazemi et al. investigate deanonymization of correlated graphs on overlapping but not identical vertex sets [7]. They determine that the information-theoretic penalty for imperfect overlap between the vertex sets of G_a and G_b is relatively mild. This regime is an important test of the robustness of deanonymization procedures.

3. MODEL

3.1 Notation

For a graph G, let $V(G)$ and $E(G)$ be the node and edge sets respectively. Let $[n]$ denote the set $\{1,\cdots,n\}$. All of the n-vertex graphs that we consider will have vertex set $[n]$. This is convenient for two reasons. First, it gives a concrete canonical way to encode the graph: take the adjacency matrix with rows and columns indexed by $[n]$. Second, there is a clear way to define the action of a permutation on the graph. We will always think of a permutation as a bijective function $[n] \to [n]$. The set of permutations of $[n]$ under the binary operation of function composition forms the group $S_{[n]}$.

We denote the collection of all two element subsets of $[n]$ by $\binom{[n]}{2}$. The edge set of a graph G is $E(G) \subseteq \binom{[n]}{2}$. Let $N = \binom{n}{2} = \left|\binom{[n]}{2}\right|$.

Represent a labeled graph on the vertex set $[n]$ by its edge indicator function $g : \binom{[n]}{2} \to [2]$. The group $S_{[n]}$ has an action on $\binom{[n]}{2}$. That is, there is a homomorphism l from $S_{[n]}$ to $S_{\binom{[n]}{2}}$. We can write the action of the permutation π on the graph G as the composition of functions $G \circ l(\pi)$, where $l(\pi)$ is the lifted version of π:

$$\begin{aligned} l(\pi) : \binom{[n]}{2} &\to \binom{[n]}{2} \\ \{i,j\} &\mapsto \{\pi(i), \pi(j)\}. \end{aligned}$$

Whenever there is only a single permutation under consideration, we will follow the convention $\sigma = l(\pi)$.

3.2 The Deanonymization Problem

We are considering the following problem. There are two correlated graphs on n vertices: G_a and G_b. By correlation we mean that for each vertex pair e, presence or absence of $e \in E(G_a)$, or equivalently the indicator variable $G_a(e)$, provides some information about $G_b(e)$. The true vertex labels of G_a are removed and replaced with meaningless labels. We model this by identifying the vertices of G_a with the set $[n]$ and applying a uniformly random permutation Π. This results in the graph $G_a \circ l(\Pi)$. The original vertex labels of G_b are preserved. We would like to know the conditions under which it is possible to discover the true correspondence between the vertices of G_a and the vertices of G_b. In other words, under what conditions can the random permutation Π be recovered exactly with high probability?

In this context, an achievability result demonstrates the existence of an algorithm or estimator that exactly recovers Π with high probability. We will refer to such an algorithm or estimator as a deanonymizer. A converse result is an upper bound on the probability of exact recovery that applies to any deanonymizer.

3.3 Correlated Erdős-Rényi Graphs

To fully specify this problem, we need to define a joint distribution over G_a and G_b. In this paper, we will focus on Erdős-Rényi (ER) graphs. We have already discussed some of the advantages and drawbacks of this model in Section 2.

We will generate correlated Erdős-Rényi graphs as follows. Let G_a and G_b be graphs on the vertex set $[n]$. We will think of (G_a, G_b) as a single function with codomain $\{0,1\}^2$ and abbreviate $(G_a(e), G_b(e))$ as $(G_a, G_b)(e)$ For each $e \in \binom{[n]}{2}$, the random variables $(G_a, G_b)(e)$ are i.i.d. and

$$(G_a, G_b)(e) = \begin{cases} (1,1) & \text{w.p. } p_{11} \\ (1,0) & \text{w.p. } p_{10} \\ (0,1) & \text{w.p. } p_{01} \\ (0,0) & \text{w.p. } p_{00}. \end{cases}$$

Call this distribution $ER(n, \mathbf{p})$, where $\mathbf{p} = (p_{11}, p_{10}, p_{01}, p_{00})$. Also define the marginal probabilities for G_a and G_b:

$$\begin{aligned} p_{1*} &= p_{11} + p_{10} \\ p_{0*} &= p_{01} + p_{00} \\ p_{*1} &= p_{11} + p_{01} \\ p_{*0} &= p_{10} + p_{00}. \end{aligned}$$

Note that $G_a \sim ER(n, p_{1*})$ and $G_b \sim ER(n, p_{*1})$.

Pedarsani and Grossglauser [9] introduced the following generative model for correlated Erdős-Rényi (ER) graphs. Essentially the same model was used in [4,5]. Let H be an ER graph on $[n]$ with edge probability r. Let G_a and G_b be independent random subgraphs of H such that each edge of H appears in G_a and in G_b with probabilities s_a and s_b respectively. We will refer to this as the *subsampling model.* The s_a and s_b parameters control the level of correlation between the graphs. This model is equivalent to $ER(n, \mathbf{p})$ with

$$\begin{aligned} p_{11} &= r s_a s_b \\ p_{10} &= r s_a (1 - s_b) \\ p_{01} &= r(1 - s_a) s_b \\ p_{00} &= 1 - r(s_a + s_b - s_a s_b). \end{aligned}$$

Solving for r from the above definitions, we obtain

$$r = \frac{p_{1*} p_{*1}}{p_{11}} = p_{11} + p_{10} + p_{01} + \frac{p_{10} p_{01}}{p_{11}}. \tag{1}$$

Observe that when G_a and G_b are independent, i.e. $p_{11} = p_{1*} p_{*1}$, we have $r = 1$. This reveals that the subsampling model is capable of representing any distribution over graph pairs in which $(G_a, G_b)(e)$ are i.i.d. and $p_{11} \geq p_{1*} p_{*1}$, i.e. the graphs have nonnegative correlation. The general $ER(n, \mathbf{p})$ can represent negatively correlated graphs as well. We will examine these in Section 7.

We will be concerned primarily with the *sparse* regime, defined by $p_{1*} \to 0$ and $p_{*1} \to 0$, or equivalently $p_{00} \to 1$. When we have the condition $\frac{p_{11} p_{00}}{p_{01} p_{10}} \to \infty$, we will say that the graphs are *significantly correlated.* From (1), we see that $r \to 0$ is equivalent to $p_{00} \to 1$ and $\frac{p_{11} p_{00}}{p_{01} p_{10}} \to \infty$.

In the subsampling model, it is possible to interpret H as representing some ground truth and G_a and G_b as incomplete observations of H. However, this understates the generality of this model. Let H be an $ER(n,r)$ graph and let A and B be the probability transition matrices of stochastic maps $[2] \to [2]$. Let $G_a(e)$ and $G_b(e)$ be noisy observations of $H(e)$ through the channels defined by A and B respectively, where all channels are independent. Then $(G_a, G_b) \sim ER(n, \mathbf{p})$, where

$$\begin{pmatrix} p_{0,0} & p_{0,1} \\ p_{1,0} & p_{1,1} \end{pmatrix} = A^T \begin{pmatrix} 1-r & 0 \\ 0 & r \end{pmatrix} B.$$

For some $e \in \binom{[n]}{2}$, consider the correlation ρ between $G_a(e)$ and $G_b(e)$. In the sparse, significantly correlated regime we have $p_{00} \to 1$, $\frac{p_{00} p_{11}}{p_{01} p_{10}} \to \infty$, and

$$\begin{aligned} \rho &= \frac{\mathbb{E}[G_a(e) G_b(e)] - \mathbb{E}[G_a(e)]\mathbb{E}[G_b(e)]}{\sqrt{(\mathbb{E}[G_a(e)^2] - \mathbb{E}[G_a(e)]^2)(\mathbb{E}[G_b(e)^2] - \mathbb{E}[G_b(e)]^2)}} \\ &= \frac{p_{11} p_{00} - p_{01} p_{10}}{\sqrt{p_{1*} p_{0*} p_{*1} p_{*0}}} \\ &= \frac{p_{11}}{\sqrt{p_{1*} p_{*1}}} (1 + o(1)) \\ &= \sqrt{s_a s_b} (1 + o(1)). \end{aligned}$$

Thus the intuition that in the symmetric case, $s = s_a = s_b$ measures the level of correlation between G_a and G_b is accurate.

Note that the condition $\frac{p_{00} p_{11}}{p_{01} p_{10}} \to \infty$ is much weaker than the condition $\rho = \Omega(1)$. For example, consider $p_{1*} = p_{*1} = n^{-\frac{1}{2}}$ and $p_{11} = n^{-1} \log n$. Then $\frac{p_{00} p_{11}}{p_{01} p_{10}} = \log(n)(1 + o(1))$ and $\rho = n^{-\frac{1}{2}} \log(n)(1 + o(1))$.

4. RESULTS

Our main achievability result applies for all regimes of $\mathbf{p}$.

THEOREM 1. *Let $(G_a, G_b) \sim ER(n, \mathbf{p})$, where $\mathbf{p}$ can depend on n. If*

$$\left(\sqrt{p_{11} p_{00}} - \sqrt{p_{01} p_{10}}\right)^2 \geq 2 \frac{\log n + \omega(1)}{n},$$

then there is a deanonymizer that succeeds with probability $1 - o(1)$.

Recall that in the sparse regime $p_{00} \to 1$ and in the significant correlation regime $\frac{p_{11} p_{00}}{p_{10} p_{01}} \to \infty$. Here, our achievability result takes a simpler form.

THEOREM 2. *Let $(G_a, G_b) \sim ER(n, \mathbf{p})$ where $p_{00} \to 1$ and $\frac{p_{11} p_{00}}{p_{10} p_{01}} \to \infty$. If $p_{11} \geq 2 \frac{\log n + \omega(1)}{n}$, then there is a deanonymizer that succeeds with probability $1 - o(1)$. If $p_{11} \leq \frac{\log n - \omega(1)}{n}$, then any deanonymizer succeeds with probability $o(1)$.*

PROOF OF THEOREM 2, ACHIEVABILITY PART. This follows from Theorem 1 and

$$\left(\sqrt{p_{11} p_{00}} - \sqrt{p_{01} p_{10}}\right)^2 = p_{11} p_{00} \left(1 - \sqrt{\frac{p_{10} p_{01}}{p_{11} p_{00}}}\right)^2 \to p_{11}.$$

□

The achievability half of Theorem 2 improves on a previous result by Pedarsani and Grossglauser [9]], which we restate here using our notation.

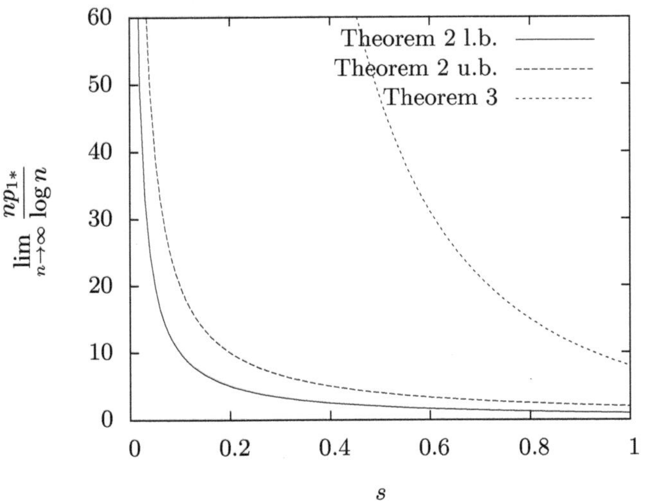

Figure 1: This plot depicts the trade-off between correlation ($s = s_a = s_b$) and density ($p_{1*} = p_{*1}$) in the feasibility of exact graph matching. Exact recovery of the permutation is possible above the threshold given by the Theorem 2 upper bound and impossible below the threshold given by the Theorem 2 lower bound. The upper bound of Pedarsani and Grossglauser [9], Theorem 3, is also plotted for comparison.

THEOREM 3 (PEDARSANI AND GROSSGLAUSER [9]). *Let $(G_a, G_b) \sim ER(n, \mathbf{p})$ where $p_{10} = p_{01}$, $p_{00} \to 1$, $\frac{p_{11}p_{00}}{p_{10}p_{01}} \to \infty$ and $\frac{p_{11}}{p_{1*}} = \omega(1/n)$. If $\frac{p_{11}^2}{p_{10}+p_{01}+p_{11}} \geq 8\frac{\log n + \omega(1)}{n}$, then there is a deanonymizer that succeeds with probability $1 - o(1)$.*

The bounds in Theorems 2 and 3 are plotted in Figure 4.

Theorem 3 applies to the symmetric case $p_{10} = p_{01}$ (and $s = s_a = s_b$). In this case we have reduced the achievability threshold by a factor of $\frac{4(p_{10}+p_{01}+p_{11})}{p_{11}} = \frac{4(2-s)}{s}$. This improvement becomes more significant as the graphs G_a and G_b become less correlated and s decreases. Additionally, the gap between the achievability and converse threshold has been reduced to a factor of 2 throughout this regime.

4.1 Perfect Correlation Limit

In the perfect correlation limit, i.e. $s = 1$, we have $G_a = G_b$. In this case, the size of the automorphism group of G_a determines whether it is possible to recover the permutation applied to G_a. This is because the composition of an automorphism with the true matching gives another matching with no errors. Whenever the automorphism group of G_a is nontrivial, it is impossible to exactly recover the permutation with high probability. We will return to this idea in Section 6 in the proof of the converse part of Theorem 2. Wright established that for $\frac{\log n + \omega(1)}{n} \leq p \leq 1 - \frac{\log n + \omega(1)}{n}$, the automorphism group of $G \sim ER(n, p)$ is trivial with probability $1 - o(1)$ and that elsewhere, it is nontrivial with probability $1 - o(1)$ [10]. In fact, he proved a somewhat stronger statement about the growth rate of the number of unlabeled graphs that implies this fact about automorphism groups.

Thus for $s = 1$, the converse part of Theorem 2 is tight and the achievability part is off by a factor of two. We conjecture that the converse is tight for all s.

Bollobás later provided a more combinatorial proof of this automorphism group threshold function [3]. The methods we use are closer to those of Bollobás.

4.2 MAP Estimation

The graph deanonymization problem is a statistical estimation problem. The Maximum a Posteriori (MAP) estimator minimizes the probability of error. The structure of the MAP estimator informs both our achievability and converse bounds. Hence if the MAP estimator does not recover the true permutation with high probability, then no other estimator can succeed. Note that because the permutations used to anonymize G_a are equiprobable, the MAP estimator is same as the Maximum Likelihood estimator.

For two graphs on $[n]$, G and H, let $G \cup H$ be the graph with edge set $E(G) \cup E(H)$ and let $G \cap H$ be the graph with edge set $E(G) \cap E(H)$. Define the size of the symmetric difference of the edge sets of G and H as

$$\begin{aligned}\Delta(G, H) &= |E(G \cup H)| - |E(G \cap H)| \\ &= \sum_{e \in \binom{[n]}{2}} |G(e) - H(e)|\end{aligned}$$

which is also the Hamming distance between the edge indicator vectors of G and H.

The MAP estimator for this problem can be derived as follows. In the following lemma we will be careful to distinguish graph-valued random variables from fixed graphs. Thus we name the former with upper-case letters and the latter with lower-case.

LEMMA 1. *Let $(G_a, G_b) \sim ER(n, \mathbf{p})$, let Π be a uniformly random permutation of $[n]$, and let $G_c = G_a \circ l(\Pi)$. Let $k = \frac{1}{2}\Delta(g_c \circ l(\pi)^{-1}, g_b)$. Then*

$$P[\Pi = \pi | (G_c, G_b) = (g_c, g_b)] \propto \left(\frac{p_{10}p_{01}}{p_{11}p_{00}}\right)^k.$$

PROOF. We compute the posterior probability as follows:

$$\begin{aligned}&P[\Pi = \pi | (G_c, G_b) = (g_c, g_b)] \\ &\overset{(a)}{=} \frac{P[(G_c, G_b) = (g_c, g_b) | \Pi = \pi] P[\Pi = \pi]}{P[(G_c, G_b) = (g_c, g_b)]} \\ &\overset{(b)}{\propto} P[(G_c, G_b) = (g_c, g_b) | \Pi = \pi] \\ &\overset{(c)}{=} P[(G_a, G_b) = (g_c \circ l(\pi)^{-1}, g_b) | \Pi = \pi] \\ &\overset{(d)}{=} P[(G_a, G_b) = (g_c \circ l(\pi)^{-1}, g_b)]\end{aligned}$$

where the constant of proportionality does not depend on π. Here we have applied Bayes rule in (a), the uniformity of Π in (b), the relationship between G_a, G_c and Π in (c), and the independence of (G_a, G_b) from Π (d).

Let $g_a = g_c \circ l(\pi)^{-1}$, $m_a = |E(g_a)| = |E(g_c)|$, and $m_b = |E(g_b)|$. Then

$$\begin{aligned}|\{e : (g_a, g_b)(e) = (1,1)\}| &= \frac{m_a + m_b}{2} - k \\ |\{e : (g_a, g_b)(e) = (1,0)\}| &= \frac{m_a - m_b}{2} + k \\ |\{e : (g_a, g_b)(e) = (0,1)\}| &= \frac{m_b - m_a}{2} + k \\ |\{e : (g_a, g_b)(e) = (0,0)\}| &= N - \frac{m_a + m_b}{2} - k.\end{aligned}$$

From the definition of the distribution of (G_a, G_b), we have

$$P[(G_a, G_b) = (g_a, g_b)]$$
$$= p_{11}^{\frac{m_a+m_b}{2}-k} p_{10}^{\frac{m_a-m_b}{2}+k} p_{01}^{\frac{m_b-m_a}{2}+k} p_{00}^{N-\frac{m_a+m_b}{2}-k}$$
$$\propto \left(\frac{p_{10}p_{01}}{p_{11}p_{00}}\right)^k$$

where we have kept the factors that depends on k and dropped the constant of proportionality that depends only on m_a and m_b. □

Thus the entries of posterior distribution, $P[\Pi = \pi | (G_c, G_b) = (g_c, g_b)]$, depend monotonically on $\Delta(g_a, g_b)$. If we fix any randomized estimation procedure, then the estimator $\hat{\Pi}$ is a random variable. It will be more convenient to work with the random permutation $\hat{\Pi} \circ \Pi^{-1}$ rather than $\hat{\Pi}$ directly. The estimator is correct when $\hat{\Pi} \circ \Pi^{-1} = I$, the identity permutation. In fact, it is easy to see that $\hat{\Pi} \circ \Pi^{-1}$ is independent of Π. For fixed g_a and g_b, any change in Π results in a corresponding change in $\hat{\Pi}$.

From here on, we do not need to consider the graph $G_a \circ l(\Pi)$. We can work directly with G_a and G_b and assume that $\pi = I$ is always the correct answer to the estimation.

The following quantity is central to both our converse and our achievability arguments (as well as the achievability proof of Pedarsani and Grossglauser [9]).

Definition 1. *Define $d(\pi, G_a, G_b)$ (abbreviated $d(\pi)$) to be $\Delta(G_a \circ \sigma, G_b) - \Delta(G_a, G_b)$, where $\sigma = l(\pi)$.*

This is the difference in matching quality between the permutation π and the identity permutation.

Lemma 2. *Let π be a permutation of $[n]$, let $\sigma = l(\pi)$, and let c_1 be the number of fixed points of σ. If $(G_a, G_b) \sim ER(n, \mathbf{p})$, then $\mathbb{E}[d(\pi)] = 2(N - c_1)(p_{00}p_{11} - p_{01}p_{10})$.*

Proof. Suppose $e \in \binom{[n]}{2}$ is not a fixed point of σ. Then

$$\begin{aligned}
&\mathbb{E}[|G_a(\sigma(e)) - G_b(e)| - |G_a(e) - G_b(e)|] \\
&= P[G_a(\sigma(e)) \neq G_b(e)] - P[G_a(e) \neq G_b(e)] \\
&= p_{*0}p_{1*} + p_{*1}p_{0*} - p_{01} - p_{10} \\
&= (p_{00} + p_{10})(p_{10} + p_{11}) + (p_{01} + p_{11})(p_{00} + p_{01}) \\
&\quad -(p_{01} + p_{10})(p_{00} + p_{01} + p_{10} + p_{11}) \\
&= 2p_{00}p_{11} - 2p_{01}p_{10}
\end{aligned}$$

and the value of $\mathbb{E}[d(\pi)]$ follows from linearity of expectation. □

Note that from Lemma 2 the expected value of $d(\pi)$ is influenced by the number of trivial cycles (i.e. fixed points) of σ. However, it does not depend on the distribution of lengths of the nontrivial cycles.

Remark 1. *Suppose that $\sigma = l(\pi)$ only contains cycles of length one and two. Thus the only cycles that contribute positively to $d(\pi, G, H)$ are those containing $e, e' \in \binom{[n]}{2}$ such that $(G, H)(e) = (1, 1)$ and $(G, H)(e') = (0, 0)$. The only cycles that contribute negatively to $d(\pi, G, H)$ are those containing $e, e' \in \binom{[n]}{2}$ such that $(G, H)(e) = (1, 0)$ and $(G, H)(e') = (0, 1)$.*

5. PROOF OF ACHIEVABILITY

Now we will prove the achievability half of Theorem 2. From Lemma 1, we know that the maximum a posteriori estimator is closely connected to the statistic $\Delta(G_a \circ \sigma, G_b)$. This measures the quality of the matching produced by the permutation π. We would like to show that with high probability, all non-identity permutations decrease the quality of the matching between G_a and G_b.

Here is the basic strategy. Throughout, we will analyze random graphs for some fixed permutation. First, in Lemma 3, we will relate the distribution of $\Delta(G_a \circ \sigma, G_b)$ to $\Delta(G_a \circ \sigma, G_a)$. In Section 5.1, we will precisely analyze the distribution of $\Delta(G_a \circ \sigma, G_a)$. This will allow us to obtain a tight bound on the probability that a particular permutation produces a better matching than the identity. In Section 5.2, we conclude the proof by applying the union bound over all permutations.

It will be convenient to name the following quantity from the statement of Theorem 1:

$$q = \left(\sqrt{p_{11}p_{00}} - \sqrt{p_{10}p_{01}}\right)^2.$$

Definition 2. *Let $R_\pi(z)$ be the generating function for the random variable $r = \frac{1}{2}\Delta(G_a, G_a \circ \sigma)$ where $G_a \sim ER(n, p_{1*})$:*

$$R_\pi(z) = \sum_r P[\Delta(G_a, G_a \circ \sigma) = 2r] z^r.$$

Lemma 3. *Let $(G_a, G_b) \sim ER(n, \mathbf{p})$, let π be a permutation of $[n]$, and let $2r = \Delta(G_a, G_a \circ \sigma)$. Conditioned on r, $d(\pi, G_a, G_b)$ has the generating function*

$$D_{r,G_b}(z) = \left(\frac{p_{00}z + p_{01}z^{-1}}{p_{0*}}\right)^r \left(\frac{p_{10}z^{-1} + p_{11}z}{p_{1*}}\right)^r.$$

Proof. Let $a(e) = |G_a(\sigma(e)) - G_b(e)| - |G_a(e) - G_b(e)|$. Then $d(\pi, G_a, G_b) = \sum_e a(e)$. Because $a(e)$ depends on G_b only at $G_b(e)$, the terms of the sum are conditionally independent. If $G_a(\sigma(e)) = G_a(e)$, then $|G_a(\sigma(e)) - G_b(e)| = |G_a(e) - G_b(e)|$ and the contribution of $a(e)$ to $d(\pi, G_a, G_b)$ is zero. If $G_a(\sigma(e)) \neq G_a(e)$, then $|G_a(\sigma(e)) - G_b(e)| \neq |G_a(e) - G_b(e)|$ and $a(e)$ is either 1 or -1.

Suppose that $G_a(e) = 0$ and $G_a(\sigma(e)) = 1$. Then

$$P[a(e) = 1 | G_a(e) = 0, G_a(\sigma(e)) = 1] = \frac{p_{00}}{p_{0*}}.$$

Suppose that $G_a(e) = 1$ and $G_a(\sigma(e)) = 0$. Then

$$P[a(e) = 1 | G_a(e) = 1, G_a(\sigma(e)) = 0] = \frac{p_{11}}{p_{1*}}.$$

Within each cycle of σ, the number of e such that $G_a(e) = 0$ and $G_a(\sigma(e)) = 1$ is equal to the number of e such that $G_a(e) = 1$ and $G_a(\sigma(e)) = 0$. Throughout all of σ, the number of e such that $G_a(e) = 0$ and $G_a(\sigma(e)) = 1$ is equal to $r = \frac{1}{2}\Delta(G_a, G_a \circ \sigma)$. Thus

$$D_{r,G_b}(z) = \left(\frac{p_{00}z + p_{01}z^{-1}}{p_{0*}}\right)^r \left(\frac{p_{10}z^{-1} + p_{11}z}{p_{1*}}\right)^r.$$

□

Now we will apply a standard technique to obtain tail probability bounds for large deviations from the mean.

Lemma 4. *Let $(G_a, G_b) \sim ER(n, \mathbf{p})$, let π be a permutation of $[n]$, and let $2r = \Delta(G_a, G_a \circ \sigma)$.*

If $\mathbb{E}[d(\pi)] \geq 0$*, then*

$$P[d(\pi) \leq 0] \leq R_\pi\left(1 - \frac{q}{p_{1*}p_{0*}}\right).$$

If $\mathbb{E}[d(\pi)] \leq 0$*, then*

$$P[d(\pi) \geq 0] \leq R_\pi\left(1 - \frac{q}{p_{1*}p_{0*}}\right).$$

PROOF. For all $0 < z \leq 1$

$$P[d(\pi) \leq 0|G_a] = \mathbb{E}[\mathbf{1}_{d(\pi)\leq 0}|G_a] \leq \mathbb{E}[z^{d(\pi)}|G_a] = D_{r,G_b}(z).$$

Starting from the expression of Lemma 3, we have

$$\begin{aligned} D_{r,G_b}(z) &= \left(\frac{p_{00}z + p_{01}z^{-1}}{p_{0*}}\right)^r \left(\frac{p_{10}z^{-1} + p_{11}z}{p_{1*}}\right)^r \\ &= \left(\frac{p_{01}p_{10}z^{-2} + p_{00}p_{10} + p_{01}p_{11} + p_{11}p_{00}z^2}{p_{0*}p_{1*}}\right)^r \\ &= \left(1 - \frac{p_{10}p_{01} + p_{11}p_{00} - p_{10}p_{01}z^{-2} - p_{11}p_{00}z^2}{p_{0*}p_{1*}}\right)^r. \end{aligned}$$

The value of z that minimizes $D_{r,G_b}(z)$ is

$$z^* = \left(\frac{p_{01}p_{10}}{p_{00}p_{11}}\right)^{1/4}.$$

From Lemma 2, $\mathbb{E}[d(\pi)] = 2(N - c_1)(p_{00}p_{11} - p_{01}p_{10})$, so $z^* \leq 1$ exactly when $\mathbb{E}[d(\pi)] \geq 0$. Substituting, we obtain

$$\begin{aligned} D_{r,G_b}(z^*) &= \left(1 - \frac{p_{10}p_{01} + p_{11}p_{00} - 2\sqrt{p_{00}p_{10}p_{01}p_{11}}}{p_{0*}p_{1*}}\right)^r \\ &= \left(1 - \frac{\left(\sqrt{p_{11}p_{00}} - \sqrt{p_{10}p_{01}}\right)^2}{p_{0*}p_{1*}}\right)^r \\ &= \left(1 - \frac{q}{p_{0*}p_{1*}}\right)^r \end{aligned}$$

Finally, the first claim follows from the definition of R_π:

$$\begin{aligned} P[d(\pi) \leq 0] &= \sum_r P[\Delta(G_a, G_a \circ \sigma) = 2r] P[d(\pi) \leq 0|G_a] \\ &\leq \sum_r P[\Delta(G_a, G_a \circ \sigma) = 2r] \left(1 - \frac{q}{p_{1*}p_{0*}}\right)^r \\ &= R_\pi\left(1 - \frac{q}{p_{1*}p_{0*}}\right). \end{aligned}$$

For all $1 \leq z < \infty$, $P[d(\pi) \geq 0|G_a] \leq D_{r,G_b}(z)$. The proof of the second claim matches the proof of the first claim with the appropriate inequalities flipped. □

5.1 Cycle combinatorics

A permutation $\sigma : \binom{[n]}{2} \to \binom{[n]}{2}$ decomposes into disjoint cycles. This partitions G_a into binary cyclic sequences. Let $a_{l,k,r}$ be the number of cyclic sequences of length l with k ones and r ones that followed by zeros. Define the corresponding generating function

$$a_l(x, y, z) = \sum_{k,r} a_{l,k,r} x^k y^{l-k} z^r.$$

Let c_l be the number of cycles of length l in σ. Then

$$R_\pi(z) = \prod_{l=1}^{n} a_l(p_{1*}, p_{0*}, z)^{c_l}$$

because R_π is the generating function for the random variable $\Delta(G_a \circ \sigma, G_a)$ and each one followed by a zero in a cycle of σ contributes to this quantity.

THEOREM 4. *Let* π *be a permutation of* $[n]$ *such that* $\sigma = l(\pi)$ *has* c_1 *fixed points. Then*

$$R_\pi\left(1 - \frac{q}{p_{1*}p_{0*}}\right) \leq (1 - 2q)^{\frac{N - c_1}{2}}.$$

The proof of Theorem 4 will use a few combinatorial lemmas. Let $b_{l,s}$ be the number of cyclic sequences of length l with s ones, none of which are consecutive.

LEMMA 5. *For all* $l, k, s \in \mathbb{N}$, $l \geq 1$,

$$\sum_r a_{l,k,r}\binom{r}{s} = b_{l,s}\binom{l - 2s}{k - s}.$$

PROOF. This identity is due the following bijection. The left side of the equation counts cyclic sequences with k ones, in which s of the ones that are followed by zeros have been marked. No two of these marked ones are consecutive. To produce one of the objects counted on the right side, create a new cyclic sequence by placing a one at each marked position and filling in the rest with zeros. There are $b_{l,s}$ such cycles. There are $l - 2s$ remaining unspecified positions in the first cycle. In these positions there must be $k - s$ ones and $l - k - s$ zeros. Record the symbols at these positions in a vector. There are $\binom{l-2s}{k-s}$ such vectors. □

LEMMA 6. *For* $l, s \in \mathbb{N}$, $l \geq 1$,

$$2^{l-2s} b_{l,s} = 2\sum_i \binom{l}{2i}\binom{i}{s}.$$

PROOF. For $s \geq 1$, both sides of the equation count the set of ternary cyclic sequences of length l with exactly s ones, such that in each interval separating a pair of ones there are an odd number of twos (which forces the interval to be nonempty). In such a sequence, the number of indices with either a one or a two is even. To obtain the expression on the right side, consider the subsequence induced by these symbols and let $2i$ be its length. In this subsequence, ones appear either only in even positions or only in odd positions, so there are $2\binom{i}{s}$ possible subsequences and $\binom{l}{2i}$ ways the subsequence can appear in the full sequences. To obtain the expression on the left side, consider the subsequence induced by the zeros and twos. There are $b_{l,s}$ ways this subsequence can appear in the full sequence. Regardless of the location of the ones, there are 2^{l-2s} possible induced sequences of zeros and twos: there are $l - s$ total symbols broken into s segments and there is a parity constraint on each segment.

For $s = 0$, both sides are equal to 2^l. □

LEMMA 7. *For all* $l \geq 1$*, the formal power series* $a_l(x, y, z)$ *satisfies*

$$a_l(x, y, z) = 2^{1-l}(x + y)^l \sum_i \binom{l}{2i}\left(1 + \frac{4xy(z - 1)}{(x + y)^2}\right)^i.$$

PROOF. Applying the binomial theorem to expand z^r, then Lemma 5, then the binomial theorem again, we obtain

$$\begin{aligned}
a_l(x,y,z) &= \sum_k \sum_r x^k y^{l-k} z^r a_{l,k,r} \\
&= \sum_k \sum_r x^k y^{l-k} a_{l,k,r} \sum_s \binom{r}{s} (z-1)^s \\
&= \sum_s \sum_k x^k y^{l-k} b_{l,s} \binom{l-2s}{k-s} (z-1)^s \\
&= \sum_s b_{l,s} x^s y^s (z-1)^s \sum_k x^{k-s} y^{l-k-s} \binom{l-2s}{k-s} \\
&= \sum_s b_{l,s} (xy(z-1))^s (x+y)^{l-2s} \\
&= (x+y)^l \sum_s b_{l,s} \left(\frac{xy(z-1)}{(x+y)^2}\right)^s.
\end{aligned}$$

Applying Lemma 6 followed by the binomial theorem, we obtain

$$\begin{aligned}
\sum_s b_{l,s} w^s &= \sum_s 2^{1-l+2s} \sum_i \binom{l}{2i} \binom{i}{s} w^s \\
&= 2^{1-l} \sum_i \binom{l}{2i} \sum_s \binom{i}{s} (4w)^s \\
&= 2^{1-l} \sum_i \binom{l}{2i} (1+4w)^i.
\end{aligned}$$

Combining these gives the lemma. □

PROOF OF THEOREM 4. Let $g = \sqrt{1-4q}$. Substituting p_{1*}, p_{0*}, and $1 - \frac{q}{p_{1*}p_{0*}}$ into the expression from Lemma 7, we obtain

$$\begin{aligned}
a_l\left(p_{1*}, p_{0*}, 1 - \frac{q}{p_{1*}p_{0*}}\right) &= 2^{1-l} \sum_i \binom{l}{2i} g^{2i} \\
&= 2^{-l} \sum_j \binom{l}{j} (1 + (-1)^j) g^j \\
&= \left(\frac{1+g}{2}\right)^l + \left(\frac{1-g}{2}\right)^l \\
&\le \left(\left(\frac{1+g}{2}\right)^2 + \left(\frac{1-g}{2}\right)^2\right)^{l/2} \\
&= \left(\frac{1+g^2}{2}\right)^{l/2} \\
&= (1-2q)^{l/2}.
\end{aligned}$$

Here we have used a standard p-norm inequality, which states that for a vector $\mathbf{x}$, $\|\mathbf{x}\|_l \le \|\mathbf{x}\|_2$ when $l \ge 2$.

We have shown

$$a_l\left(p_{1*}, p_{0*}, 1 - \frac{q}{p_{1*}p_{0*}}\right) \le (1-2q)^{l/2}$$

for $l \ge 2$. Because a cycle of length one cannot have a run boundary, $a_1(p_{1*}, p_{0*}, z) = 1$. Combining these with

$$R_\pi(z) = \prod_{l=1}^{n} a_l(p_{1*}, p_{0*}, z)^{c_l}$$

and $\sum_{l=1}^n l c_l = N$, we obtain the claim. □

5.2 Proof of Theorem 1

PROOF OF THEOREM 1. Let $S_{n,m}$ be the set of permutations of $[n]$ that move exactly m points and fix the other $n-m$. Then $|S_{n,m}| = \binom{n}{m} !m \le \frac{n!}{(n-m)!} \le n^m$, where $!m$ is the number of derangements of $[m]$, i.e. the permutations with no fixed points. If $\pi \in S_{n,m}$, then $e = \{i,j\}$ is a fixed point of σ if either i and j are both fixed points of π or i and j form a cycle of length 2 in π. Thus c_1, the number of fixed points of σ, satisfies $\binom{n-m}{2} \le c_1 \le \binom{n-m}{2} + \frac{m}{2}$. Thus

$$\begin{aligned}
N - c_1 &\ge \frac{n(n-1) - (n-m)(n-m-1) - m}{2} \\
&= \frac{m(2n-m-2)}{2}. \qquad (2)
\end{aligned}$$

The probability that there is some permutation that produces a better match than the identity permutation is

$$\begin{aligned}
P[\vee_{\pi \ne I} d(\pi) \le 0] &\le \sum_{\pi \ne I} P[d(\pi) \le 0] \\
&= \sum_{m=2}^{n} \sum_{\pi \in S_{n,m}} P[d(\pi) \le 0] \\
&\le \sum_{m=2}^{n} n^m \max_{\pi \in S_{n,m}} P[d(\pi) \le 0].
\end{aligned}$$

Here we applied the union bound, grouped permutations by the number of points that they move, and considered the worst case permutation in each group.

From Lemma 4 and Theorem 4,

$$P[d(\pi, G_a, G_b) \le 0] \le R_\pi(z^*) \le (1-2q)^{\frac{N-c_1}{2}},$$

where $q = \left(\sqrt{p_{11}p_{00}} - \sqrt{p_{10}p_{01}}\right)^2$. Substituting, we obtain

$$\begin{aligned}
&P[\vee_{\pi \ne I} d(\pi, G_a, G_b) \le 0] \\
&\le \sum_{m=2}^{n} n^m (1-2q)^{\frac{N-c_1}{2}} \\
&\overset{(a)}{\le} \sum_{m=2}^{n} n^m (1-2q)^{\frac{m(2n-m-2)}{4}} \\
&= \sum_{m=2}^{n} \left(n \exp\left(\frac{2n-m-2}{4} \log(1-2q)\right)\right)^m \\
&\overset{(b)}{\le} \sum_{m=2}^{n} \left(n \exp\left(\frac{-q(2n-m-2)}{2}\right)\right)^m \\
&\overset{(c)}{\le} \sum_{m=2}^{n} \left(n \exp\left(-\frac{q(n-2)}{2}\right)\right)^m.
\end{aligned}$$

Inequality (a) follows from (2), inequality (b) follows from $\log(1+x) \le x$, and inequality (c) follows from $m \le n$.

Let $x = n\exp(-q(n-2)/2)$. The condition $x = o(1)$ is equivalent to

$$q \ge 2\frac{\log(n\omega(1))}{n-2} = 2\frac{\log n + \omega(1)}{n},$$

which is exactly a hypothesis of the theorem. Thus for sufficiently large n, we have $x < 1$ and

$$P[\vee_{\pi \ne I} d(\pi, G_a, G_b) \le 0] \le \sum_{m=2}^{n} x^m < \frac{x^2}{1-x} = o(1).$$

Thus there is a deanonymizer that succeeds with probability $1 - o(1)$. □

6. PROOF OF CONVERSE

The converse statement depends on the following lemma.

LEMMA 8. *Let G_a and G_b be graphs on the vertex set $[n]$. For all $\pi \in Aut(G_a \cap G_b)$, $d(\pi, G_a, G_b) \le 0$.*

PROOF. Let $\sigma = l(\pi)$ and recall that

$$\Delta(G,H) = \sum_{e \in \binom{[n]}{2}} |G(e) - H(e)|$$
$$d(\pi, G_a, G_b) = \Delta(G_a \circ \sigma, G_b) - \Delta(G_a, G_b).$$

Let $e \in \binom{[n]}{2}$. Suppose that $(G_a, G_b)(e) = (1,1)$, so $(G_a \cap G_b)(e) = 1$. Because $\pi \in Aut(G_a \cap G_b)$, $(G_a \cap G_b)(\sigma(e)) = 1$. Then the contribution of e to both $\Delta(G_a, G_b)$ and $\Delta(G_a \circ \sigma, G_b)$ is zero.

Suppose $(G_a \cap G_b)(e) = 0$. The cycle of σ containing e is $C = \{\sigma^i(e) : i \in \mathbb{N}\}$. For all $e' \in C$, $(G_a \cap G_b)(e') = 0$ and $(G_a, G_b)(e')$ is $(0,0)$, $(0,1)$, or $(1,0)$. Thus the contribution of C to $\Delta(G_a, G_b)$ is equal to total number of edges in G_a and G_b in C. The contribution of C to $\Delta(G_a \circ \sigma, G_b)$ cannot be larger. □

It is well-known that Erdős-Rényi graphs with average degree less than $\log n$ have many automorphisms [3]. The following lemma is precise version of this fact that is suitable for our purposes.

LEMMA 9. *Let $G \sim ER(n,p)$. If $p \le \frac{\log n - c_n}{n}$ and $c_n \to \infty$, then there is some sequence $\epsilon_n \to 0$ such that $P[|Aut(G)| \le \epsilon_n^{-1}] \le \epsilon_n$.*

PROOF. Let X be the number of isolated vertices in G. A permutation that moves only isolated vertices is an automorphism of G, so $|Aut(G)| \ge X!$. We will use Chebyshev's inequality to bound the probability that there are few isolated vertices in G:

$$P[X \le \frac{1}{2}\mathbb{E}[X]] \le 4\frac{\mathbb{E}[X^2] - \mathbb{E}[X]^2}{\mathbb{E}[X]^2}.$$

The probability that a particular vertex is isolated is $(1-p)^{n-1}$. Thus $\mathbb{E}[X] = n(1-p)^{n-1}$. The probability that a particular pair of vertices are both isolated is $(1-p)^{2n-3}$. Thus $E\left[\binom{X}{2}\right] = \binom{n}{2}(1-p)^{2n-3}$. Then

$$\begin{aligned}
&\mathbb{E}[X^2]\mathbb{E}[X]^{-2} - 1 \\
&= \left(2E\left[\binom{X}{2}\right] + \mathbb{E}[X]\right)\mathbb{E}[X]^{-2} - 1 \\
&= \frac{(n^2-n)(1-p)^{2n-3}}{n^2(1-p)^{2n-2}} + E[X]^{-1} - 1 \\
&= (1-p)^{-1} - n^{-1}(1-p)^{-1} + E[X]^{-1} - 1 \\
&\le p + E[X]^{-1}.
\end{aligned}$$

Recall that $p \le \frac{\log n}{n}$, so $p \to 0$. Finally we compute the limiting behavior of the expected value of X:

$$\begin{aligned}
\mathbb{E}[X] &= n(1-p)^{n-1} \\
&= n\left(1 + \frac{p}{1-p}\right)^{-(n-1)} \\
&\ge n\left(\exp\left(\frac{p}{1-p}\right)\right)^{-n} \\
&= \exp\left(\log n - \frac{np}{1-p}\right) \\
&= \exp\left(\frac{c_n - p\log n}{1-p}\right).
\end{aligned}$$

Note that $p\log n \to 0$ and $c_n \to \infty$, so $\mathbb{E}[X] \to \infty$. Thus $P[X \le \frac{1}{2}\mathbb{E}[X]] \to 0$. □

PROOF OF THEOREM 2, CONVERSE PART. For all sufficiently large n, we have $\frac{p_{11}p_{00}}{p_{10}p_{01}} > 1$, so from Lemma 1, if $\Delta(G_a, G_b) \ge \Delta(G_a, G_b \circ \sigma)$, then the posterior probability of π is at least as large as the true permutation. From Lemma 8, there are at least $|Aut(G_a \cap G_b)|$ such permutations. Thus any estimator for Π succeeds with probability at most $1/|Aut(G_a \cap G_b)|$. The graph $G_a \cap G_b$ is distributed as $ER(n, p_{11})$. With high probability, the size of the automorphism group of an $ER(n, p_{11})$ graph goes to infinity with n. More precisely, if $p_{11} \le \frac{\log n - \omega(1)}{n}$, then from Lemma 9 there is some sequence $\epsilon_n \to 0$ such that

$$P\left[\frac{1}{|Aut(G_a \cap G_b)|} \ge \epsilon_n\right] \le \epsilon_n.$$

Any estimator succeeds with probability at most $2\epsilon_n$. □

7. NEGATIVE CORRELATION

In this section, we consider the problem of deanonymizing negatively correlated Erdős-Rényi graph. Such a pair of graphs have fewer edges in common that an independently generated pair. In the most extreme case the graphs avoid each other completely. Thus it is somewhat surprising that almost the same analysis yields an achievability result for both the positively and negatively correlated regimes.

In the sparse regime with significant negative correlation, we have $p_{00} \to 1$, $\frac{p_{00}p_{11}}{p_{01}p_{10}} \to 0$, and

$$\begin{aligned}
-\rho &= \frac{-p_{11}p_{00} + p_{01}p_{10}}{\sqrt{p_{1*}p_{0*}p_{*1}p_{*0}}} \\
&= \frac{p_{01}p_{10}}{\sqrt{p_{1*}p_{*1}}}(1 + o(1)) \\
&\le \sqrt{p_{1*}p_{*1}}(1 + o(1)) \\
&= o(1).
\end{aligned}$$

Thus it is impossible to achieve the same level of correlation as in the positive case. To counteract this, much higher edge densities are required to make deanonymization feasible.

The diameter of a graph is the maximum distance between a pair of vertices. As we have shown in Section 6, for positively correlated graph pairs, the threshold for perfect recovery of the permutation is closely related to the threshold for a single ER graph being connected, i.e. having a finite diameter. For negatively correlated pairs, the recovery threshold is related to the threshold for a single ER graph having a diameter of two.

The following lemma is analogous to Lemma 8. Let $G_a \backslash G_b$ be the graph with edge set $E(G_a) \setminus E(G_b)$.

LEMMA 10. *Let π be a permutation of $[n]$ that contains only cycles of length one and two. If $d(\pi, G_a \backslash G_b, G_b \backslash G_a) = 0$, then $d(\pi, G_a, G_b) \ge 0$.*

PROOF. The permutation $\sigma = l(\pi)$ also contains only cycles of length one and two. Recall Remark 1. Thus the only cycles that contribute positively to $d(\pi, G, H)$ are those containing $e, e' \in \binom{[n]}{2}$ such that $(G,H)(e) = (1,1)$ and $(G,H)(e') = (0,0)$. The only cycles that contribute negatively to $d(\pi, G, H)$ are those containing $e, e' \in \binom{[n]}{2}$ such that $(G,H)(e) = (1,0)$ and $(G,H)(e') = (0,1)$.

$(G_a \backslash G_b, G_b \backslash G_a)(e) = (0,0)$ for all e such that $(G_a, G_b)(e) = (1,1)$. Elsewhere $(G_a \setminus G_b, G_b \setminus G_a)(e) = (G_a, G_b)(e)$. In σ, there are no cycles that contribute positively to $d(\pi, G_a \setminus G_b, G_b \setminus G_a)$. Because $d(\pi, G_a \setminus G_b, G_b \setminus G_a) = 0$, there are also no cycles that contribute negatively. Thus there are also no cycles that contribute negatively to $d(\pi, G_a, G_b) \geq 0$. □

Let $N_a(u)$ be the neighborhood of vertex u in G_a.

LEMMA 11. *Let G_a and G_b be graphs on $[n]$ such that $E(G_a \cap G_b) = \varnothing$. Let $u, v \in [n]$ be distinct vertices. Let π be the permutation that exchanges u and v and fixes the rest of $[n]$. If $N_a(u) \cap N_b(v) = \varnothing$ and $N_a(v) \cap N_b(u) = \varnothing$, then $d(\pi, G_a, G_b) = 0$.*

PROOF. For all $i \in [n] \setminus \{u, v\}$, σ exchanges $\{u, i\}$ with $\{v, i\}$ and fixes all other vertex pairs. Then σ aligns two edges if there is some i such that either $G_a(\{u, i\}) = 1$ and $G_b(\{v, i\}) = 1$ or $G_a(\{v, i\}) = 1$ and $G_b(\{u, i\}) = 1$. Thus $d(\pi, G_a, G_b) = -|N_a(u) \cap N_b(v)| - |N_a(v) \cap N_b(u)| = 0$. □

LEMMA 12. *Let $(G_a, G_b) \sim ER(n, \mathbf{p})$ with $p_{11} = 0$. If $p_{01}p_{10} \leq \frac{\log n - \omega(1)}{n}$, then with probability $1 - o(1)$ there are $\omega(1)$ vertex pairs $u, v \in [n]$ such that $|N_a(u) \cap N_b(v)| = 0$ and $|N_a(v) \cap N_b(u)| = 0$.*

PROOF. Let $u, v \in [n]$ and let π be the permutation that exchanges u and v and fixes the rest of $[n]$. If $N_a(u) \cap N_b(v) = \varnothing$ and $N_a(v) \cap N_b(u) = \varnothing$, then $d(\pi, G_a, G_b) = 0$.

For each $i \in [n] \setminus \{u, v\}$,

$$P[G_a(\{u, i\}) = 1 \wedge G_b(\{v, i\}) = 1] = p_{1*}p_{*1} = p_{10}p_{01}.$$

Thus the probability that $|N_a(u) \cap N_b(v)| = 0$ and $|N_a(v) \cap N_b(u)| = 0$ is $(1 - 2p_{10}p_{01})^{n-2}$. Let X be the number of vertex pairs satisfying this property. Then $\mathbb{E}[X] = \binom{n}{2}(1 - 2p_{10}p_{01})^{n-2}$. Suppose that $p_{10}p_{01} \leq \frac{\log n - c_n}{n}$ where $c_n \to \infty$. A computation very similar to the one in Lemma 9 shows that

$$\mathbb{E}[X] \geq \frac{1 - o(1)}{2} \exp\left(2\frac{c_n - p_{10}p_{01}\log n}{1 - p_{10}p_{01}}\right)$$

Thus $\mathbb{E}[X] \to \infty$. Another computation similar to that of Lemma 9 shows that $\frac{\mathbb{E}[X^2] - \mathbb{E}[X]^2}{\mathbb{E}[X]^2} = o(1)$. Then Chebyshev's inequality implies that $P[X \leq \frac{1}{2}\mathbb{E}[X]] = o(1)$. □

THEOREM 5. *Let $(G_a, G_b) \sim ER(n, \mathbf{p})$ where $\frac{p_{11}p_{00}}{p_{10}p_{01}} \to 0$. If $p_{01}p_{10} \geq 2\frac{\log n + \omega(1)}{n}$, then there is a deanonymizer that succeeds with probability $1 - o(1)$. If $p_{01}p_{10} \leq \frac{\log n - \omega(1)}{n}$, then any deanonymizer succeeds with probability $o(1)$.*

PROOF. The conditions $p_{00} \to 1$ and $\frac{p_{11}p_{00}}{p_{10}p_{01}} \to 0$ imply $q \to p_{01}p_{10}$. Thus the first statement follows from Theorem 1.

For sufficiently large n, we have $\frac{p_{11}p_{00}}{p_{10}p_{01}} < 1$. From Lemma 1, if $\Delta(G_a, G_b) \leq \Delta(G_a, G_b \circ \sigma)$, then the posterior probability of π is at least as large as the true permutation. The statement of Lemma 10 identifies some permutation satisfying this condition. From Lemma 12, with probability $1 - o(1)$ there are $\omega(1)$ such permutations. Thus any deanonymizer succeeds with probability at most $o(1)$. □

8. CONCLUSION

We obtained new achievability and converse bounds for the problem of exact deanonymization of Erdős-Rényi graphs. For sparse, significantly correlated graphs, these bounds differ by a constant factor of two. Thus they establish the dependence of the threshold for deanonymization on the level of correlation between the graphs. We also investigated deanonymization of negatively correlated graphs. In sparse graphs, because it is impossible to achieve levels of negative correlation that match the possible levels of positive correlation, much higher edge density is required to facilitate deanonymization.

There are several directions that this work could be extended. For positive correlation, the perfect correlation limit suggests that the converse bound is tight and the achievability can be further improved. Thus the most obvious next step is to attempt to improve the achievability result to match the converse. In the analysis of the automorphism group of an Erdős-Rényi graph, different methods were required to handle the region just above the threshold. It may be possible to adapt these to the more general deanonymization problem.

Several follow-up works have applied the methods from the original paper of Pedarsani and Grossglauser [9]) to variations on the deanonymization problem. We discuss some of these in Section 2. It is likely that our results and methods can lead to improvements in the results obtained for these extensions.

In this paper, we have focused on exact recovery of the true graph matching. There are a number of natural relaxations of this condition. In many of the motivating problems related to data privacy, partial information leakage is still a serious issue. It remains to be seen which metrics for partial deanonymization are both relevant to practical privacy problems and tractable to analyze.

9. ACKNOWLEDGEMENTS

This work was in part supported by supported by MURI grant ARMY W911NF-15-1-0479 and NSF grant CCF 10-54937 - CAREER.

10. REFERENCES

[1] R. Albert and A.-L. Barabási. Statistical mechanics of complex networks. *Reviews of modern physics*, 74(1):47, 2002.

[2] B. Bollobás. A probabilistic proof of an asymptotic formula for the number of labelled regular graphs. *European Journal of Combinatorics*, 1(4):311–316, 1980.

[3] B. Bollobás. *Random graphs*. Springer, 1998.

[4] S. Ji, W. Li, N. Z. Gong, P. Mittal, and R. Beyah. On Your Social Network De-anonymizablity: Quantification and Large Scale Evaluation with Seed Knowledge. 2015.

[5] S. Ji, W. Li, M. Srivatsa, and R. Beyah. Structural Data De-anonymization: Quantification, Practice, and Implications. In *Proceedings of the 2014 ACM SIGSAC Conference on Computer and Communications Security*, pages 1040–1053. ACM, 2014.

[6] E. Kazemi, H. S Hamed, and M. Grossglauser. Growing a Graph Matching from a Handful of Seeds. In *Proceedings of the Vldb Endowment International Conference on Very Large Data Bases*, volume 8, 2015.

[7] E. Kazemi, L. Yartseva, and M. Grossglauser. When Can Two Unlabeled Networks Be Aligned Under Partial Overlap? In *Proceedings of the 53rd Annual*

Allerton Conference on Communication, Control, and Computing, 2015.

[8] A. Narayanan and V. Shmatikov. De-anonymizing social networks. In *Security and Privacy, 2009 30th IEEE Symposium on*, pages 173–187. IEEE, 2009.

[9] P. Pedarsani and M. Grossglauser. On the privacy of anonymized networks. In *Proceedings of the 17th ACM SIGKDD international conference on Knowledge discovery and data mining*, pages 1235–1243. ACM, 2011.

[10] E. M. Wright. Graphs on unlabelled nodes with a given number of edges. *Acta Mathematica*, 126(1):1–9, 1971.

[11] L. Yartseva and M. Grossglauser. On the performance of percolation graph matching. In *Proceedings of the first ACM conference on Online social networks*, pages 119–130. ACM, 2013.

A Better Model for Task Assignment in Server Farms: How Replication can Help

Mor Harchol-Balter
Carnegie Mellon University, Pittsburgh, PA, USA
harchol@cs.cmu.edu

ABSTRACT

An age-old problem in the design of server farms is the choice of the task assignment policy. This is the algorithm that determines how to assign incoming jobs to servers. Popular policies include Round-Robin assignment, Join-the-Shortest-Queue, Join-Queue-with-Least-Work, and so on.

While much research has studied assignment policies, little has taken into account server-side variability -- the fact that the server we choose might be temporarily and unpredictably slow. We show that when server-side variability dominates runtime, replication of jobs can be very beneficial. We introduce the Replication-d algorithm that replicates each arrival to d servers chosen at random, where the job is considered "done" as soon as the first replica completes. We provide an exact closed-form analysis of Replication-d.

We next introduce a much more general model, one which takes both the inherent job size distribution and the server-side variability into account. This is a departure from traditional queueing models which only allow for one "size" distribution. We propose and analyze a new task assignment policy, Replicate-Idle-Queue (RIQ), which is designed to perform well given these dual sources of variability.

CCS Concepts

- **Mathematics of computing →Queueing theory**
- **Mathematics of computing →Stochastic processes**
- *Mathematics of computing →Probabilistic algorithms*
- **Networks →Network performance evaluation**
- **Theory of computation → Online algorithms**
- *Theory of computation → Parallel algorithms*

Keywords Resource allocation; replication; power-of-d; queueing; load balancing

SIGMETRICS'16, June 14–18, 2016, Antibes Juan-Les-Pins, France.
ACM ISBN 978-1-4503-4266-7/16/06.
DOI: http://dx.doi.org/10.1145/2896377.2901900

Short Bio

Mor Harchol-Balter is a Professor of Computer Science at Carnegie Mellon. She received her Ph.D. from U.C. Berkeley in Computer Science, completed her postdoc at MIT, and joined CMU in 1999. From 2008-2011, she served as the Associate Department Head for Computer Science. Mor is a recipient of the McCandless Junior Chair, the NSF CAREER award, and several teaching awards, including the Herbert A. Simon Award.

Mor's work focuses on designing new resource allocation policies, including load balancing policies, power management policies, and scheduling policies, for distributed systems. She is known for both her new techniques in queueing-theoretic analysis and Markov chains, as well as her work in computer systems implementation. Mor has co-authored over 100 publications in top journals and conferences, including a textbook, *Performance Analysis and Design of Computer Systems*, published by Cambridge University Press, 2013.

Mor is heavily involved in the ACM SIGMETRICS / PERFORMANCE research community, where she has published over two dozen papers, and received multiple best paper awards, and where she served as Technical Program Chair in 2007 and as General Chair in 2013. She is best known for her enthusiastic talks and her many PhD students, most of whom are professors in top academic institutions.

Costly Circuits, Submodular Schedules and Approximate Carathéodory Theorems

Shaileshh Bojja Venkatakrishnan
University of Illinois
Urbana-Champaign
bjjvnkt2@illinois.edu

Mohammad Alizadeh
Massachusetts Institute of Technology
alizadeh@csail.mit.edu

Pramod Viswanath
University of Illinois
Urbana-Champaign
pramodv@illinois.edu

ABSTRACT

Hybrid switching – in which a high bandwidth circuit switch (optical or wireless) is used in conjunction with a low bandwidth packet switch – is a promising alternative to interconnect servers in today's large scale data centers. Circuit switches offer a very high link rate, but incur a non-trivial reconfiguration delay which makes their scheduling challenging. In this paper, we demonstrate a lightweight, simple and nearly-optimal scheduling algorithm that trades-off reconfiguration costs with the benefits of reconfiguration that match the traffic demands. Seen alternatively, the algorithm provides a fast and approximate solution towards a constructive version of Carathéodory's Theorem for the Birkhoff polytope. The algorithm also has strong connections to submodular optimization, achieves a performance at least half that of the optimal schedule and strictly outperforms state of the art in a variety of traffic demand settings. These ideas naturally generalize: we see that indirect routing leads to exponential connectivity; this is another phenomenon of the power of multi-hop routing, distinct from the well-known load balancing effects.

1. INTRODUCTION

Modern data centers are massively scaling up to support demanding applications such as large-scale web services, big data analytics, and cloud computing. The computation in these applications is distributed across tens of thousands of interconnected servers. As the number and speed of servers increases,[1] providing a fast, dynamic, and economic switching interconnect in data centers constitutes a topical networking challenge. Typically, data center networks use multi-rooted tree designs: the servers are arranged in racks and an Ethernet switch at the top of the rack (ToR) connects the rack of servers to one or more aggregation (or spine) layers. These designs use multiple paths between the ToRs to deliver uniform high bisection bandwidth, and consist of a large number of high speed electronic packet switches that provide fine-grained switching capabilities but at poor speed/cost ratios.

Recent work has proposed the use of high speed circuit switches based on optical [46, 16, 53] or wireless [27, 56, 25] links to interconnect the ToRs. These architectures enable a dynamic topology tuned to actual traffic patterns, and can provide a much higher aggregate capacity than a network of electronic switches at the same price point, consume significantly less power, and reduce cabling complexity. For instance, Farrington et al [15] report 2.8×, 6× and 4.7× lower cost, power, and cabling complexity respectively using optical circuit switching relative to a baseline network of electronic switches.

The drawback of circuit switches, however, is that their switching configuration time is much slower than electronic switches. Depending on the specific technology, reconfiguring the circuit switch can take a few milliseconds (e.g., for 3D MEMS optical circuit switches [46, 16, 53]) to tens of microseconds (e.g., for 2D MEMS wavelength-selective switches [40]). During this reconfiguration period, the circuit switch cannot carry any traffic. By contrast, electronic switches can make per-packet switching decisions at sub-microsecond timescales. This makes the circuit switch suitable for routing stable traffic or bursts of packets (e.g., hundreds to thousands of packets at a time), but not for sporadic traffic or latency sensitive packets. A natural approach is then to have a *hybrid* circuit/packet switch architecture: the circuit switch can handle traffic flows that have heavy intensity but also require sparse connections, while a lower capacity packet switch handles the complementary (low intensity, but densely connected) traffic flows [16].

With this hybrid architecture, the relatively low intensity traffic is taken care of by the packet switch — switch scheduling here can be done dynamically based on the traffic arrival and is a well studied topic [36, 28, 35]. On the other hand, scheduling the circuit switch, based on the heavy traffic demand matrix, is still a fundamental unresolved question. Consider an architecture where a centralized scheduler samples the traffic requirements at each of the ToR ports at regular intervals (W, of the order of 100μs–1ms), and looks to find the schedule of circuit switch configurations over the interval of W that is "matched" to the traffic requirements. The challenge is to balance the overhead of reconfiguring the circuits with the capability to be flexible and meet the traffic demand requirements.

The centralized scheduler must essentially decide a se-

[1] Servers with 10Gbps network interfaces are common today and 40/100Gbps servers are being deployed.

SIGMETRICS '16, June 14-18, 2016, Antibes Juan-Les-Pins, France

DOI: http://dx.doi.org/10.1145/2896377.2901479

quence of *matchings* between sending and receiving ToRs which the circuit switch then implements. For an optical circuit switch, for instance, the switch realizes the schedule by appropriately configuring its MEMS mirrors. As another example, in a broadcast-select optical ring architecture [9], the ToRs implement the controller's schedule by tuning in to the appropriate wavelength to receive traffic from their matching sender as dictated by the schedule.

Hence, we need a scheduling algorithm that decides the state (i.e., matching) of the circuit switch at each time and also a routing protocol to decide on an appropriate (direct or indirect) route packets can take to reach their destination ToR port. This is a challenging problem and entails making several choices on: (a) number of matchings, (b) choice of matchings (switch configuration), (c) durations of the matchings and (d) the routing protocol, in each interval W. Mathematically, this leads to a well defined optimization problem, albeit involving both combinatorial and real-valued variables. Even special cases of this problem [31] are NP hard to solve exactly.

Central to understanding this scheduling problem is finding a good sparse representation of the traffic matrix – a fundamental algorithmic question in Carathéodory's Theorem that has remained largely unanswered so far [38]. Recent papers have proposed heuristic algorithms to address this scheduling problem. In Solstice [34], the authors present a greedy perfect-matching based heuristic for a hybrid electrical-optical switch. Experimental evaluations show Solstice performing well over a simple baseline (where the schedules are provided by a truncated Birkhoff-von Neumann decomposition of the traffic matrix), although no theoretical guarantees are presented. Indirect routing in a distributed setting, but without considerations of configuration switching costs, is studied in another recent work [9].

1.1 Our Contributions

We first focus on routing policies where packets are sent from the source port to the destination port only via a direct link connecting the two ports, leading to *direct* or *single-hop* routing.

Approximate Carathéodory's Theorem: Our main result here is an approximately optimal, very simple and fast algorithm for computing the switch schedule in each interval. In turn this corresponds to a fast algorithm for computing a sparse approximate representation of a point on the Birkhoff polytope [10]. While Carathéodory's Theorem guarantees the *existence* of such a representation, an efficient *algorithm* to compute it has remained elusive so far. Our algorithm, which we christen Eclipse, has a performance that is at least half that of optimal for every instance of the traffic demands, and experimentally shows a strict and consistent improvement over the state-of-the-art [34]. A key technical contribution here is the identification of a submodularity structure [5] in the problem, which allows us to make connections between submodular function maximization and the circuit switch scheduling problem with reconfiguration delay.

Indirect Routing: Next, we consider routing polices where packets are allowed to reach their destination after (potentially) transiting through many intermediate ports, leading to *indirect* or *multi-hop* routing. This class of routing policies is motivated by our observation that if the number of matchings is limited, multi-hop routing can *exponentially* improve the *reachability* of nodes; a novel benefit of multi-hop routing distinct from the classical and well known load balancing effects [42, 49, 23]. We again identify submodularity in the problem, but the constraints for this submodular maximization problem are no longer linear and efficient solutions are challenging to find. However, for the important special case where the sequence of switch configurations have already been calculated (and the indirect routing policy has to be decided) we propose a simple and fast greedy algorithm that is near optimal universally for all traffic requirements. Detailed simulation results demonstrate strong improvements over direct routing, which are especially pronounced when the switch reconfiguration delays are relatively large.

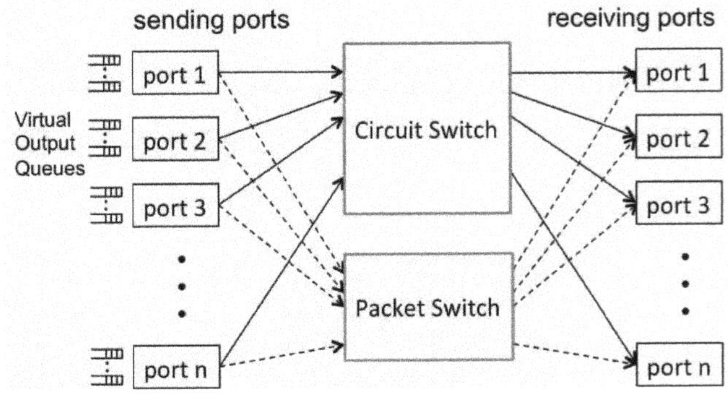

Figure 1: An illustration of our hybrid switch architechture.

The paper is organized as follows. In Section 2, the model, framework and the problem objective are formally stated along with a succinct summary of the state of the art. Section 3 focuses on direct routing and Section 4 on indirect routing. In Section 5, we present a detailed evaluation of the proposed algorithms on a variety of traffic inputs. Section 6 closes with a brief discussion. Technical aspects of the algorithm and its evaluation, including connections to submodularity and combinatorial optimization problems are deferred to the Appendix.

2. SYSTEM MODEL

In this section, we present our model for a hybrid circuit-packet switched network fabric, and formally define our scheduling problem. Our model closely follows [34].

2.1 Hybrid Switch Model

We consider an n-port network where each port is simultaneously connected to a circuit switch and a packet switch as shown in Figure 1. A set of nodes are attached to the ports and communicate over the network. The nodes could either be individual servers or top-of-rack switches.

We model the circuit switch as an $n \times n$ crossbar comprising of n input ports and n output ports. At any point in time, each input port can send packets to at most one output port and each output port can receive packets from at most one input port over the circuit switch. The circuit switch can be reconfigured to change the input-output connections. We assume that the packets at the input ports are organized in virtual-output-queues [41] (VOQ) which hold packets destined to different output ports.

In practice, the circuit switch is typically an optical switch-

[46, 16, 53].[2] These switches have a key limitation: changing the circuit configuration imposes a *reconfiguration delay* during which the switch cannot carry any traffic. The reconfiguration delay can range from few milliseconds to tens of microseconds depending on the technology [40, 33]. This makes the circuit switch suitable for routing stable traffic or bursts of packets (e.g., hundreds to thousands of packets at a time), but not for sporadic traffic or latency sensitive packets. Therefore, hybrid networks also use a (electrical) packet switch to carry traffic that cannot be handled by the circuit switch. The packet switch operates on a packet-by-packet basis, but has a much lower capacity than the circuit switch. For example, the circuit and packet switches might respectively run at 100Gbps and 10Gbps per port.

We divide time into slots, with each slot corresponding to a (full-sized) packet transmission time on the circuit switch. We consider a *scheduling window* of $W \in \mathbb{Z}$ time units. A central controller uses measurements of the aggregated traffic demand between different ports to determine a *schedule* for the circuit switch at the start of each scheduling window. The schedule comprises of a sequence of configurations and how long to use each configuration (Section 2.3). The controller communicates the schedule to the circuit switch, which then follows the schedule for the next scheduling window (W) without involving the controller. We assume that the delay for each reconfiguration is $\delta \in \mathbb{Z}$ time units.

2.2 Traffic Demand

Let $T \in \mathbb{Z}^{n \times n}$ denote the accumulated traffic at the start of a scheduling window. We assume T is a feasible traffic demand, i.e., T is such that $\sum_{j=1}^{n} T(i,j) \leq W$ and $\sum_{i=1}^{n} T(i,j) \leq W$ for all $i, j \in \{1, 2, \ldots, n\}$. The (i,j)th entry of T denotes the amount of traffic that is in the VOQ at node i destined for node j.

We assume that the controller knows T.[3] We also assume that non-zero entries in the traffic matrix T are bounded as $2\delta \leq T(i,j) \leq \epsilon W$ for all $i, j \in [n] : T(i,j) > 0$ and some parameter $0 < \epsilon < 1$. This is a mild condition because traffic between pairs of ports that is small relative to δ is better served by the packet switch anyway.

Previous measurement studies have shown that the inter-rack traffic in production data centers is sparse [34, 8, 3, 43]. Over short periods of time (e.g., 10s of milliseconds), most nodes communicate with only a small number of other nodes (e.g., few to low tens). Further, in many cases, a large fraction of the traffic is sent by a small fraction of "elephant" flows [3]. While our algorithms and analysis are general, it is important to note that such sparse traffic patterns are necessary for hybrid networks to perform well (especially with larger reconfiguration delay).

2.3 The Scheduling Problem

Given the traffic demand, T, our goal is to compute a schedule that maximizes the total amount of traffic sent over the circuit switch during the scheduling window W. This is desirable to minimize the load on the slower packet switch. In general, the scheduling problem involves two aspects:

1. Determining a schedule of circuit switch configurations: The algorithm must determine a sequence of circuit switch configurations: $(\alpha_1, P_1), (\alpha_2, P_2), \ldots, (\alpha_k, P_k)$. Here, $\alpha_i \in \mathbb{Z}$ denotes the duration of the ith switch configuration, and P_i is an $n \times n$ permutation matrix, where $P_i(s,t) = 1$ if input port s is connected to output port t in the ith configuration. For a valid schedule, we must have $\alpha_1 + \alpha_2 + \ldots + \alpha_k + k\delta \leq W$ since the total duration of the configurations cannot exceed the scheduling window W.
2. Deciding how to route traffic: The simplest approach is to use only direct routes over the circuit switch. In other words, each node only sends traffic to destinations to which it has a direct circuit during the scheduling window. Alternatively, we can allow nodes to use indirect routes, where some traffic is forwarded via (potentially multiple) intermediate nodes before being delivered to the destination. Here, the intermediate nodes buffer traffic in their VOQs for transmission over a circuit in a subsequent configuration.

In the next section, we begin by formally defining the problem in the simpler setting with direct routing and developing an algorithm for this case. Then, in Section 4, we consider the more general setting with indirect routing.
Remark 1. Prior work [34, 31] has considered the objective of *covering* the entire traffic demand in the least amount of time. For example, the ADJUST algorithm in [31] takes the traffic demand T as input and computes a schedule $(\alpha_1, P_1), \ldots, (\alpha_k, P_k)$ such that $\sum_{i=1}^{k} \alpha_i + k\delta$ is minimized while $\sum_{i=1}^{k} \alpha_i P_i \geq T$. Our formulation (and solution) is more general, since an algorithm which maximizes throughput over a given time period can also be used to find the shortest duration to cover the traffic demand (e.g., via binary search).
Remark 2. From a systems viewpoint, the traffic demand estimation can be done either by directly polling ToR switches or end-host NICs [33, 53], or indirectly through applications and flow information [16, 2]. For systems at scale, this represents a non-trivial task (and often taking 100s of μs [33]) necessitating the need for a window W to compute the schedule (vis-à-vis dynamic policies; see following Section 2.4).

2.4 Related Work

Before presenting the work in this paper, we briefly summarize related work on this topic. Scheduling in crossbar switches is a classical and well studied topic and traditionally it has been used to model the packet switch where the reconfiguration delay is very small. Hence the scheduling solutions proposed – ranging from centralized Birkhoff-von-Neumann decomposition scheduler [36] on one end to the decentralized load-balanced scheduler [11] on the other – did not account for reconfiguration delay.

With the proposals on hybrid circuit/packet switching systems [16, 53], simplified models that factor for the reconfiguration delay were considered. Early works often assumed the delay to be either zero [26] or infinity [48, 54]. The infinite delay setting corresponds to a problem where the number of matchings is minimized. However they still require $O(n)$ matchings. In a different context (satellite-switched time-division multiple access), works such as [22] also computed schedules that minimized the number of matchings. Moderate reconfiguration delays are considered in DOUBLE [48] and other algorithms such as [19, 31, 55] that explicitly take reconfiguration delay into account. The al-

[2]Designs based on point-to-point wireless links have also been proposed [27, 56]. Our abstract model is general.
[3]Our work is orthogonal to how the controller obtains the traffic demand estimate. For example, the nodes could simply report their backlogs before each scheduling window, or a more sophisticated prediction algorithm could be used.

gorithm ADJUST [31] minimizes the covering time but still requires around n configurations. All of these algorithms do not benefit from sparse demands and continue to require $O(n)$ configurations [34]. In a complementary approach, [12] considers conditions on the input traffic matrix under which efficient polynomial time algorithms to compute the optimal schedule exists. Yet other approaches have been to introduce speedup [35], or randomization in the algorithms [21], however they do not address the basic optimization problem underlying this scenario head-on. Such is the goal of this paper.

The above algorithms are "batch" policies [51] in which each computational call returns a schedule for an entire window of time. Another research direction is to consider "dynamic" policies where scheduling decisions are made time-slot by time-slot. A variant of the well known MaxWeight algorithm is presented in [52] and is shown to be throughput optimal. Fixed-Frame MaxWeight (FFMW) is a frame based policy proposed in [32] and has good delay performance. However it requires the arrival statistics to be known in advance. A hysteresis based algorithm that adapts many previously proposed algorithms for crossbar switch scheduling to the case with reconfiguration delay is presented in [51]. All these algorithms require perfect queue state information at every instant.

3. DIRECT ROUTING

The centralized scheduler samples the ToR ports and arrives at the traffic demand (matrix) T to be met in the upcoming slot. In this section, we develop an algorithm, named Eclipse, that takes the traffic demand, T, as input and computes a schedule of matchings (circuit configurations) and their durations to maximize throughput over the circuit switch; only direct routing of packets from source to destination ports are allowed here. Eclipse is fast, simple and nearly-optimal in every instance of the traffic matrix T. Towards a formal understanding of the notion of optimality, consider the following optimization problem:

$$\begin{aligned} \text{maximize} \quad & \left\| \min\left(\sum_{i=1}^{k} \alpha_i P_i, T \right) \right\|_1 \\ \text{s.t.} \quad & \alpha_1 + \alpha_2 + \ldots + \alpha_k + k\delta \le W \\ & k \in \mathbb{N}, P_i \in \mathcal{P}, \alpha_i \ge 0 \ \forall i \in \{1, 2, \ldots, k\}, \end{aligned} \qquad (1)$$

where $\mathbb{N} = \{1, 2, \ldots\}$ and $\mathcal{P}$ is the set of permutation matrices.

This optimization problem is NP-hard [31], and a recent work [34] in the literature has focused on heuristic solutions. Our proposed algorithm has some similarities to the prior work in [34] in that the matchings and their durations are computed successively in a *greedy* fashion. However, the algorithm is overall quite different in terms of both ideas and details; we uncover and exploit the underlying *submodularity* [44] structure inherent in the problem to design and analyze the algorithm in a principled way.

We also note that this problem can be viewed as finding permutation matrices $P_1, \ldots, P_k$ and weightings $\alpha_1, \ldots, \alpha_k$ such that their weighted sum is a good *approximation* of the traffic matrix T. Carathéodory's Theorem applied to the Birkhoff polytope guarantees the *existence* of such a dual representation; however till date we do not know of an efficient *algorithm* to compute this representation. A recent work [6] proposes a fast approximation algorithm but they implicitly assume availability of a dual representation to start with. We do not assume such an oracle, but are nevertheless able to provide an efficient algorithm to obtain an approximate Carathéodory expansion.

Algorithm 1: A general greedy algorithm template

Input : Traffic demand T, reconfiguration delay δ and scheduling window size W
Output: Sequence of matchings $P_1, \ldots, P_k$ and their corresponding durations $\alpha_1, \ldots, \alpha_k$:

```
sch ← {} ;                                    // schedule
k ← 0 ;
T_rem ← T ;                                   // traffic remaining
while Σ_{i=1}^{k} (α_i + δ) ≤ W do
    k ← k + 1;
    Decide on a duration α for the matching;
    M ← argmax_{M∈𝓜} ‖ min(αM, T_rem) ‖_1 ;
    sch ← sch ∪ {(α, M)} ;
    T_rem ← T_rem − min(αM, T_rem) ;
end
if Σ_{i=1}^{k} (α_i + δ) > W then
    sch ← sch \ {(α, M)};
end
k ← k − 1;
```

3.1 Intuition

Before a formal presentation and analysis of the algorithm, we begin with an intuitive and less-formal approach to how one might solve this optimization problem. Consider greedy algorithms with the template shown in Algorithm 1. The template starts with an empty schedule, and proceeds to add a new matching to the schedule in each iteration. This process continues until the total duration of the matchings exceeds the allotted time budget of W, at which point the algorithm terminates and outputs the schedule computed so far. In each iteration, the algorithm first picks the duration of the matching, α. It then selects the *maximum weight matching* in the traffic graph whose edge weights are thresholded by α (i.e., edge weights $> \alpha$ are clipped to α). The traffic graph is a bipartite graph between n input and n output vertices, with an edge of weight $T(i, j)$ between input node i and output node j. It remains to specify how to choose α in each iteration.

Consider an exercise where we vary the matching duration α from 0 to W and compute the maximum weight matching in the thresholded traffic graph for each α. For a typical traffic matrix, this results in a curve similar to the solid-blue line in Fig. 2. Notice that the value of the maximum weight matching is precisely equal to the sum-throughput that can be achieved in that round of the switch schedule. It is straightforward to see that the maximum weight matching curve has the following properties: (a) it is non-decreasing and (b) piecewise linear. These are explained as follows: when α is very small a lot of the edges in the traffic graph have a weight that is saturated at α. Hence it is likely to find a perfect matching with total weight of $n\alpha$. As such the slope of the curve when α is small is n. However, as α becomes large there are increasingly fewer edges whose weights are saturated at α and, correspondingly, the slope reduces. When α is so large that all of the edge weights

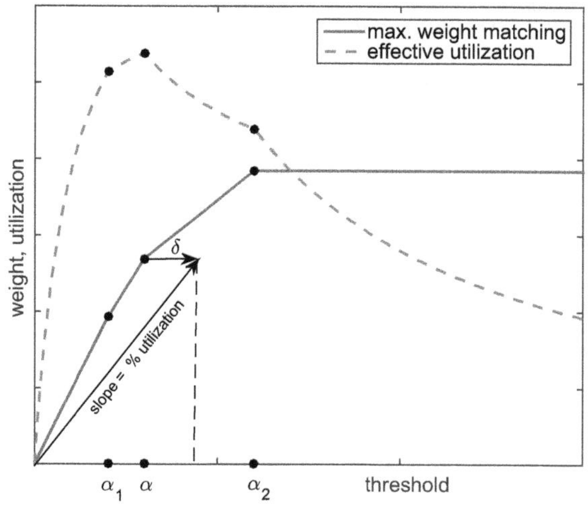

Figure 2: Throughput of max. weight matching as a function of threshold duration. The effective utilization curve of the matchings is also shown.

are strictly smaller than α, then the value of the maximum weight matching does not change even with any further increase in α and the curve ultimately flattens out.

Two operating points of interest, considering Fig. 2, are (a) the largest α where the slope of the curve is maximum ($= n$ in the typical case where every ingress/egress port has traffic) and (b) the smallest α where the value of the maximum weight matching is the largest. These points have been denoted by α_1 and α_2 in Fig. 2 respectively. Setting $\alpha = \alpha_1$ is interesting because it results in a matching where the links are all fully utilized. For example, the Solstice algorithm presented in [34] implicitly adopts this operating point. On the other hand, $\alpha = \alpha_2$ gives a matching that achieves the largest possible sum-throughput in that round.

However we note that both choices of α are less than ideal for the following reasons. Recall that after every round of switching we incur a delay of δ time units. As such if the value of α_1 is small (say comparable to δ) in each round, then the number of matchings, and hence the time wasted due to the reconfiguration delay, becomes large. As a concrete example, consider the transpose of the traffic matrix $T_1 = [A_1^t \mathbf{b}_1^t]$ where A_1 is a sparse $(n-1) \times n$ matrix and $\mathbf{b} = [2\delta, 2\delta, \ldots, 2\delta, 0, 0, \ldots, 0]$ comprises of some k entries of value 2δ and $n-k$ entries of value 0. In other words, we are considering an input where a node or a collection of nodes have a large number of small flows to a particular node or vice-versa. For such an instance it is clear that if we insist on matchings with 100% utilized links, then the maximum duration of the matching is 2δ (i.e., $\alpha_1 = 2\delta$). Thus, continuing the process described in Algorithm 1 results in a sequence of k matchings each of which is only 2δ time units long. Hence in the worst case (if $k > 1/(3\delta)$) about 1/3rd of the entire scheduling window is wasted just due to reconfiguration delay limiting the maximum possible throughput to $2n/3$. On the other hand, if we had ignored the entries in $\mathbf{b}$, then we could have scheduled just A_1 achieving a total throughput of $n - 2k\delta \approx n$ for large n. We point out that the phenomenon described above happens in a large family of instances, of which T_1 is a specific example. We also emphasize that such instances are pretty likely to occur in practice; for example, [43, Fig.5-b] shows traffic measurements in a Facebook data center where the interactions between Cache and Web servers lead to traffic matrices having this property.

Similarly for the operating point with $\alpha = \alpha_2$, consider the traffic matrix $T_2 = \begin{bmatrix} A_2 & \mathbf{0} \\ \mathbf{0} & B_2 \end{bmatrix}$ where A_2 is a sparse $(n-2) \times (n-2)$ matrix and $B_2 = \begin{bmatrix} 0 & 1 \\ 1 & 0 \end{bmatrix}$. This is a diametrically opposite situation from T_1 where a small collection of nodes interact only amongst themselves with no interaction outside. Such a situation occurs, for example, in multi-tenant cloud-computing data centers [45] where individual tenants run their jobs on small clusters of servers. In such a case, the value of the maximum weight matching can be maximum for a large α. For T_2 the maximum value occurs at $\alpha = 1 - \delta$ (i.e., $\alpha_2 = 1 - \delta$), resulting in a schedule with just one matching of duration $1 - \delta$ and potentially missing a lot of traffic for A_2. For example, if A_2 is uniformly k-sparse, we miss out roughly $(k-1)n/k$ units of traffic. On the other hand, by choosing the duration of the matching to be $1/k - \delta$ in each step we can achieve a sum throughput of $n - O(\delta) \approx n$.

In scenarios exemplified by T_2, setting $\alpha = 1$ is bad because the utilization of the resulting matching is poor, i.e., a vast majority of the matching links carry only a fraction of their capacity. This can be overcome by insisting that we choose only those matchings with utilization of at least 75% (say). However, in the case of T_1 we observe a poor performance in spite of all matchings having a utilization of 100%. The issue in this case is that the duration of the matchings are small compared to the reconfiguration delay. Hence to avoid this scenario we can insist on $\alpha \geq 20\delta$ (say) in Algorithm 1.

Our first main observation is that both of the above heuristics are captured if we consider the *effective utilization* of the matchings. We define effective utilization as the ratio $\text{mwm}(\alpha)/(\alpha + \delta)$ where $\text{mwm}(\alpha)$ denotes the value of the maximum weight matching at α. This ratio indicates the overall efficiency of a matching by including the reconfiguration delay into the duration. In Fig. 2 we plot the effective utilization of the matchings as the red-dotted curve. As can be seen there, the effective utilization at both α_1 and α_2 is suboptimal. We propose an algorithm that selects α to maximize effective utilization; a detailed description is deferred to Section 3.3.

The justification for selecting matchings according to the above is further reinforced by the *submodularity* structure of the problem (we discuss submodularity in Section 3.2). It turns out that for a certain class of submodular maximization problems with linear packing constraints, greedy algorithms take a form that precisely matches the intuitive thought process above [5]: the proposed intuitively correct algorithm is borne out naturally from submodular combinatorial optimization theory. We briefly recall relevant aspects of submodularity and associated optimization algorithms next.

3.2 Submodularity

A set function $f : 2^{[n]} \to \mathbb{R}$ is said to be *submodular* if it has the following property: for every $A, B \subseteq [n]$ we have $f(A \cup B) + f(A \cap B) \leq f(A) + f(B)$. Alternatively, submodular functions are also defined through the property of *decreasing marginal values*: for any S, T such that $T \subseteq S \subseteq [n]$ and $j \notin S$, we have

$$f(S \cup \{j\}) - f(S) \leq f(T \cup \{j\}) - f(T).$$

The difference $f(S \cup \{j\}) - f(S)$ is called the incremental marginal value of element j to set S and is denoted by $f_S(j)$. For our purpose we will only focus on submodular functions that are *monotone* and *normalized*, i.e., for any $S \subseteq T \subseteq [n]$ we have $f(S) \leq f(T)$ and further $f(\{\}) = 0$.

Many applications in computer science involve maximizing submodular functions with *linear packing constraints*. This refers to problems of the form:

$$\max f(S) \quad \text{s.t. } A\mathbf{x}_S \leq b \text{ and } S \subseteq [n],$$

where $A \in [0,1]^{m \times n}, b \in [1, \infty)^m$ and $\mathbf{x}_S$ denotes the characteristic vector of the set S. Each of the A_{ij}'s is a cost incurred for including element j in the solution. The b_i's represent a total budget constraint. A well-known example of a problem in the above form is the Knapsack problem (the objective function in this case is in fact modular).

With the above background, we formulate the optimization problem under direct routing as one of submodular function maximization. Recall that for any given input traffic matrix T, the schedule that is computed is described by a sequence of matchings and corresponding durations. Consider the set $\mathcal{M}$ of all perfect matchings in the complete bipartite graph $K_{n \times n}$ with n nodes in each partite. Then any round in the schedule is simply $(\alpha, P) \in \mathbb{Z} \times \mathcal{M}$. The key observation we make now is to view the schedules as a subset of $\mathbb{Z} \times \mathcal{M}$. Formally, define a *switch schedule* as any subset $\{(\alpha_1, M_1), \ldots, (\alpha_k, M_k)\}$ of $\mathbb{Z} \times \mathcal{M}$. The objective function in our case is the sum-throughput defined as

$$f(\{(\alpha_1, M_1), \ldots, (\alpha_k, M_k)\}) = \left\| \min \left(\sum_{i=1}^{k} \alpha_i M_i, T \right) \right\|_1, \quad (2)$$

where the minimum is taken entrywise and $\|\cdot\|_1$ refers to the entrywise L_1-norm of the matrix. We observe that the function f is submodular, deferring the proof to the Appendix.

THEOREM 1. *The function* $f : 2^{\mathbb{Z} \times \mathcal{M}} \to \mathbb{R}$ *defined by Equation* (2) *is a monotone, normalized submodular function.*

We have established that optical switch scheduling under the sum-throughput metric is a submodular maximization problem. With this, we are ready to present a greedy algorithm that achieves a sum-throughput of at least a constant factor of the optimal algorithm for *every* instance of the traffic matrix.

3.3 Algorithm

Algorithm 2 – Eclipse – captures our proposed solution under direct routing. Eclipse takes the traffic matrix T, the time window W and reconfiguration delay δ as inputs, and computes a sequence of matchings and durations as the output. The algorithm proceeds in rounds (the "while loop"), where in each round a new matching is added to the existing sequence of matchings. The sequence terminates whenever the sum of the matching durations exceeds the allocated time window W or whenever the traffic matrix T is fully covered.

Algorithm 2: Eclipse: greedy direct routing algorithm

Input : Traffic demand T, reconfiguration delay δ and scheduling window size W
Output: Sequence of matchings $P_1, \ldots, P_k$ and their corresponding durations $\alpha_1, \ldots, \alpha_k$:

```
sch ← {} ;                                  // schedule
k ← 0 ;
T_rem ← T ;                                 // traffic remaining
while Σ_{i=1}^k (α_i + δ) ≤ W do
    k ← k + 1;
    (α, M) ← argmax_{M∈𝓜, α∈ℝ+} ‖min(αM, T_rem)‖_1 / (α+δ) ;
    sch ← sch ∪ {(α, M)} ;
    T_rem ← T_rem − min(αM, T_rem) ;
end
if Σ_{i=1}^k (α_i + δ) > W then
    sch ← sch\{(α, M)};
end
k ← k − 1 ;
```

Consider any round t in the algorithm; let $(\alpha_1, M_1), \ldots, (\alpha_{t-1}, M_{t-1})$ denote the schedule computed so far in $t-1$ rounds (stored in variable `sch`) and let $T_{\text{rem}}(t)$ denote the amount of traffic yet to be routed. The matching that is selected in the t-th round is the one for which *utilization* – the percentage of the total matching capacity that is actually used – is maximum. Mathematically, we choose an (α, M) pair such that $\frac{\|\min(\alpha M, T_{\text{rem}})\|_1}{\alpha+\delta}$ is maximized. In [50], an extended version of this paper, we have given a proof that the maximum (for α) occurs on the support of T_{rem}. Hence this can be easily found by looking at the support of the (sparse) matrix T_{rem}. We also propose a simple binary-search procedure, discussed in Algorithm 3, that finds only a local maximum but performs extremely well in our evaluations (Section 5). This process of selecting a matching is repeated in each round until the sum-duration of the matchings exceeds the scheduling window W, when the last chosen matching is discarded and the remaining set of matchings are returned. Eclipse is simple and also fast, a fact the following calculation demonstrates.

Complexity: We begin with the complexity of Algorithm 3. Since i_{ub} is no more than the number of distinct entries of T, we have $i_{\text{ub}} \leq n^2$. In each iteration, the algorithm only considers entries of H that have indices between i_{lb} and i_{ub}. However, binary-search halves the effective size of H (i.e., those numbers in H with array indices $i_{\text{lb}}, i_{\text{lb}+1}, \ldots, i_{\text{ub}}$), and the number of iterations of the `while` loop is bounded by $\log n^2 = 2 \log n$. Within the `while` loop, computing the maximum weight matching can be done in $O(dn^{3/2} \log(W\epsilon))$ time (a basic fact of submodular optimization [14, 44]) where dn is the number of edges in bipartite graph formed by T (i.e., d is the average sparsity). Further $(1-\epsilon)$ approximate maximum weight matching can be computed in linear time, e.g. $O(dn\epsilon^{-1} \log \epsilon^{-1})$ [13], and efficient implementations in practice have been studied extensively in the literature [37, 39, 17]. Hence the overall time complexity is $O(dn^{3/2} \log n \log(W\epsilon))$. Now, in Algorithm 2 the number of iterations in the `while` loop is bounded by W/δ. As such the total complexity of the algorithm is $\tilde{O}(dn^{3/2} \frac{W}{\delta})$. An exact search over the support of T_{rem} in the maximization step results in a overall complexity of $\tilde{O}(d^2 n^{5/2} \frac{W}{\delta})$.

Algorithm 3: Finding the greedy maximum

Input : Traffic demand T, reconfiguration delay δ
Output: $(\alpha, M) \in \mathbb{Z} \times \mathcal{M}$ such that
$(\alpha, M) = \text{argmax}_{M \in \mathcal{M}, \alpha \in \mathbb{Z}} \frac{\|\min(\alpha M, T)\|_1}{(\alpha+\delta)}$

```
H ← distinct entries of T sorted in ascending order;
i_lb ← 1 and i_ub ← length(H);
while i_lb < i_ub do
    i ← (i_lb + i_ub)/2 ;
    T1 ← min{T, H(i)} ;  // thresholding T to H(i)
    T2 ← min{T, H(i + 1)} ;
    v1 ← (max. weight matching in T1)/(H(i) + δ) ;
    v2 ← (max. weight matching in T2)/(H(i + 1) + δ) ;
    if v1 < v2 then
        i_lb ← i;
    else if v1 > v2 then
        i_ub ← i;
    else
        return (H(i), max. weight matching in T1);
    end
end
```

Approximation Guarantee: Since the proposed direct routing algorithm is connected to submodular maximization with linear constraints, we can adapt standard combinatorial optimization techniques to show an approximation factor of $1 - 1/e$. Let OPT denote the sum-throughput of the optimal algorithm for given inputs T, δ and W. Let ALG2 denote the sum-throughput achieved by Eclipse. We then have the following.

THEOREM 2. *If the entries of T are bounded by $\epsilon W + \delta$ then Eclipse approximates the optimal algorithm to within a factor of $1 - 1/e^{(1-\epsilon)}$, i.e.,* $\texttt{ALG2} \geq (1 - 1/e^{(1-\epsilon)})\texttt{OPT}$.

The proof of the above Theorem is deferred to the Appendix. As a concluding remark, we note that the constant ϵ in the approximation factor comes from the requirement that $\alpha + \delta \leq \epsilon W$ hold. We observe that this mild technical condition, required to show that Eclipse is a constant factor approximation of the optimal algorithm, has an added implication. Informally, it ensures that no single matching occupies the bulk of the scheduling window.

4. INDIRECT ROUTING

In the previous section, we focused on direct routing where packets are forwarded to their destination ports only if a link *directly* connecting the source port to the destination port appeared in the schedule – this is essentially a "single-hop" protocol. In this section, we explore allowing packets to be forwarded to (potentially) multiple intermediate ports before arriving at its final destination. In terms of implementing this more involved protocol, we note that there is no extra overhead needed: the destination of any received packet is read first upon reception and since the queues are maintained on a per-destination basis at each ToR port, any received packet can be diverted to the appropriate queue. The key point of allowing indirect routing is the vastly increased range of ports that can be reached from a small number of matchings.

Consider Fig. 3 which illustrates a 6-port network and a sequence of 3 consecutive matchings in the schedule. With

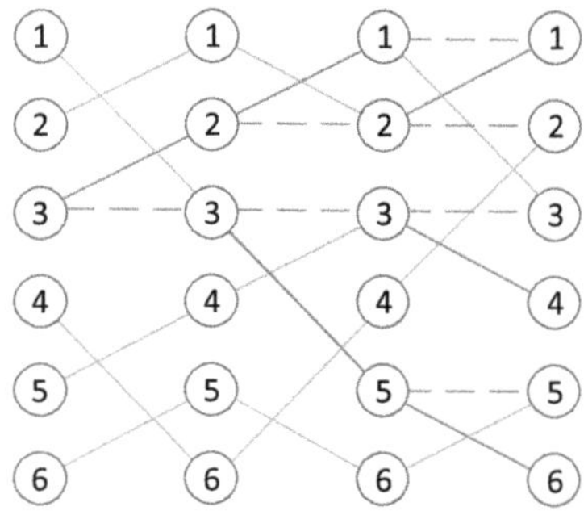

Figure 3: Reachability of nodes under multi-hop routing.

direct routing, port 3 can only forward packets to ports 2, 5 and 4 in rounds 1, 2 and 3 respectively, i.e., the set of egress ports *reachable* by port 3 is $\{2, 4, 5\}$. In the indirect routing framework of this section, port 3 can also forward packets to port 1. This can be achieved by first forwarding the packets to port 2 in the first round where the packets are queued. Then in the second round we let port 2 forward those packets to the destination port 1. Thus the *reachability* of the nodes is enhanced by allowing for indirect routing. Indirect routing can also be viewed as "multi-hop" routing.

Traditionally multi-hop routing has been used as a means of *load balancing*. This is known to be true in the context of networks such as the Internet where the benefits of "Valiant load-balancing" are legion [42, 49, 23]. The benefits of load balancing are also well known in the switching context – a classic example is the two-stage load-balancing algorithm in crossbar switches without reconfiguration delay [47]. The benefit of multi-hop routing in our context is *markedly different*: the reachability benefits of indirect routing are especially well suited to the setting where input ports are directly connected to only a few output ports due to the *small number* of matchings in the scheduling window. In fact, an elementary calculation shows that over a period of k matchings in the schedule, indirect routing can allow a node to forward packets to $O(2^k)$ other nodes, compared to only $O(k)$ nodes possible with direct routing. This is because of the recursion $f(k) = 2f(k-1) + 1$ where $f(k)$ denotes the number of nodes reachable by any node in k rounds. If a node (say, node 1) can reach $f(k-1)$ nodes in $k-1$ rounds, then in the k-th round (i) there is a new node directly connected to node 1 and (ii) each of the $f(k-1)$ nodes can be connected to a new node. Thus the number of nodes connected to node 1 in the k-th round becomes $f(k-1) + (f(k-1) + 1)$. Fig. 3 also illustrates this phenomenon where reachability from node 3 is shown. As a corollary we observe that $O(\log_2 n)$ rounds of matchings are sufficient to reach *all* other nodes in a n-port network.

As in the direct routing case, computing the optimal schedule remains a challenging problem. While it is clear that we can achieve a performance at least as good as with direct routing, the gain is different for each instance of the traffic matrix – precisely quantifying the gain in an instance-specific way appears to be challenging. Our main result is that the submodularity property of the objective function continues to hold, provided the variables are considered in an appropriate format. Further, if we restrict some of the variables (the matchings and their durations), then there is also a natural, simple and fast greedy algorithm to compute the switching schedules and routing policies that is approximately optimal for *each* instance of the traffic matrix. This algorithm serves as a heuristic solution to the more general problem of jointly finding the number of switchings, their durations, the switching schedules and routing policies. We present these results, following the same format as in the direct routing section, leaving numerical evaluations to a later section. We follow the model as discussed in Section 2.

4.1 Submodularity of objective function

We first adopt an alternative way of describing the switch schedule by specifying the multi-hop *path* taken by each packet. Such a formulation serves us well in the *causal* structure of the routed traffic patterns that naturally occur here.

For simplicity let us fix the number of rounds k in the schedule. Consider a fully connected k-round time-layered directed graph G consisting of $k+1$ partites, $V_0, V_1, \ldots, V_k$ (of n nodes each), with nodes in each partite i having directed edges to all the nodes in partite $i+1$. Let $\mathcal{P}$ denote the set of all paths in G that begin at a node in V_0 and end at a node in V_k. Any such $p \in \mathcal{P}$ describes a multi-hop route for a packet in the system. If we are able to choose a path for every packet in the traffic matrix T, subject to capacity constraints, then we have a valid sequence of switch configurations and routing policy for the schedule. Now, for a set of paths $(\beta_1, p_1), \ldots, (\beta_m, p_m)$, where β_i denotes the number of packets sharing the same path p_i, consider the sum-throughput given by a function $f : 2^{\mathbb{Z}\times\mathcal{P}} \to \mathbb{Z}$ defined as $f(\{(\beta_1, p_1), \ldots, (\beta_m, p_m)\}) \triangleq$

$$\sum_{i,j\in[n]} \min\left(\sum_{l=1}^{m} \beta_l \mathbf{1}_{\substack{p_l(0)=i,\\ p_l(k+1)=j}}, T_{ij}\right), \qquad (3)$$

where $p(0)$ and $p(k+1)$ denote the starting and ending nodes of path p and $\mathbf{1}_{\{.\}}$ is the indicator function. Then the main observation is that f is submodular.

THEOREM 3. *The function $f : 2^{\mathbb{Z}\times\mathcal{P}} \to \mathbb{Z}$ defined by Equation* (3) *is submodular.*

The proof is analogous to Theorem 1 and we omit it in the interests of space.[4] So far we have not imposed any restrictions on the set of paths that we choose for the schedule. This can be incorporated in the form of constraints to the problem, thus rephrasing the objective as a constrained submodular maximization problem.

Constraints: Since we are only choosing weighted paths, we can write constraints that ensure (i) the set of paths form a matching in each round and (ii) the total duration of the matchings is at most $W - k\delta$ [50]. However, the key challenge here is that the constraints are *nonlinear* – it is not clear whether an efficient (approximation) algorithm exists. The nonlinearities appear only in the sense of membership tests and a corresponding thresholding function – so it is possible that an efficient nearly-optimal greedy algorithm exists, but we leave this study for future work. We do note, however, that for the special case in which the configurations are fixed and we only have to decide on the indirect routing policies, the constraints take on a linear form – in this setting, we are able to construct fast and efficient greedy algorithms. This case represents a composition of direct routing (where switch schedules are computed) and indirect routing (where the multi-hop routing policies are described), and is discussed next.

Multi-Hop Routing Policies: Consider a fixed sequence $(\alpha_1, M_1), \ldots, (\alpha_k, M_k)$ of switch configurations and an input traffic demand matrix T. Let G denote the time-layered edge-capacitated graph obtained from the sequence of matchings, i.e., G consists of $k+1$ partites $V_0, \ldots, V_k$ with n nodes each, and M_i is the matching between partites V_{i-1} and V_i with edge capacity α_i on the matching edges. In addition to the matching edges, there are also edges, with unlimited edge capacities, connecting the j-th nodes of V_{i-1} and V_i for all $j \in [n], i \in [k]$. Let $R(e)$ denote the capacity of edge $e \in G$. In this setting, the capacity constraints on the end-to-end paths are the sole constraints in the optimization problem – we consider subsets $\{(\beta_1, p_1), \ldots, (\beta_m, p_m)\}$ that obey

$$\sum_{i=1}^{m} \beta_i \mathbf{1}_{\{e\in p_i\}} \le R(e) \quad \forall e \in G. \qquad (4)$$

Notice that the constraints above have a linear form, and there are a total of kn such constraints (one for each edge). Such a setting allows for a natural, simple, fast and nearly-optimal algorithm which we discuss below. Prior to that discussion, we remark that a naive approach to resolve the setting here is to formulate a *linear program* that maximizes the required objective. Indeed linear programming based approaches was the predominant technique used to solve this classical *multicommodity flow* problem [1, 24, 7]. However, despite many years of research in this direction the proposed algorithms were often too slow even for moderate sized instances [30]. Since then there has been a renewed effort in providing efficient *approximate* solutions to the multicommodity flow problem [20, 4]. The algorithm we propose is also a step in this direction, favoring efficiency over exactness of the solution. Note that in the path-formulation of the linear program there can be an exponential (in k) number of variables. Thus, in this form, there is no obvious efficient (exact) solution to this LP. On the other hand, the formulation we work with is able to handle this issue by appropriately *weighing the edges* and *picking the path* with the smallest weight; this latter step can be done efficiently – for example, using Dijkstra's algorithm.

4.2 Algorithm

We propose Eclipse++ (Algorithm 4) directly motivated from [5], which presents a fast and efficient multiplicative weights algorithm for submodular maximization under linear constraints. The structure of Algorithm 4 is similar in spirit to Eclipse (Algorithm 2) in the sense that (a) the algorithm proceeds in rounds, where one new path is added to the schedule in each round and (b) we select a path that offers the greatest utility per unit of cost incurred. However, unlike Algorithm 2 where there was only one linear constraint, we have multiple linear constraints now. This is addressed by assigning weights to the constraints and considering a *linear combination* of the costs as the true cost in each round. In the following, we describe the salient features of Eclipse++.

Recall the capacity constraints in Equation (4) for each edge $e \in G$; let w_e denote the weight assigned to the constraint involving edge e. We set $w_e = 1/R(e)$ for all e ini-

[4]The proof can be found in [50].

Algorithm 4: Eclipse++ : greedy indirect routing algorithm

Input : Traffic demand T, switch configurations with residue capacities $R_1, \ldots, R_k$, update factor λ
Output: Sequence of paths $p_1, \ldots, p_m$ and corresponding weights $\beta_1, \ldots, \beta_m$

```
sch ← {} ;                                   // schedule
T_rem ← T ;                           // traffic remaining
w_e ← 1/R(e) for all e ∈ E;
m ← 1;
while Σ_{e∈E} R(e)w_e ≤ λ and ||T_rem||_1 > 0 do
    (β_m, p_m) ← argmax_{p∈P, β∈Z} min(β, T_rem(p(0,p(k+1))) / Σ_{e∈E} β1_{e∈p} w_e ;
    sch ← sch ∪ {(β_m, p_m)} ;
    T_rem(p_m(0), p_m(k+1)) ← T_rem(p_m(0), p_m(k+1)) − β ;
    w_e ← w_e λ^{β_m 1_{e∈p}/R(e)}  ∀e ∈ G ;
    m ← m + 1;
end
if Σ_{i=1}^{m-1} β_i 1_{e∈p_i} ≤ R(e)  ∀e ∈ E then
    return sch
else
    return sch \ (β_{m-1}, p_{m-1})
end
```

tially, i.e., edges with a large capacity are assigned a small weight and vice-versa. We can now have another graph G_w (with same topology as G) whose edges are weighted by w_e. Now, for any path p the "effective cost" of the path per packet is simply the total cost of p in G_w. Thus for the path (β, p) carrying β packets, the effective cost is given by $\sum_{e\in E} \beta w_e \mathbf{1}_{e\in p}$. On the other hand, the benefit we get due to adding path (β, p) is given by $\min(\beta, T(p(0), p(k+1)))$ where $p(0)$ and $p(k+1)$ stand for the starting and terminating nodes along path p. Thus, the ratio $\frac{\min(\beta, T(p(0), p(k+1)))}{\sum_{e\in E} \beta w_e \mathbf{1}_{e\in p}}$ denotes the benefit of path p per unit cost incurred. In Algorithm 4 we select p such that the utility per unit cost is maximized.

Now, once we have selected a weighted path (β_1, p_1) in the first round, we update the weights w_e on the edges. This is done as $w_e \leftarrow w_e \lambda^{\beta_1/R(e)}$ for each edge $e \in p$, where λ is an input parameter. For the remaining edges the weights remain unchanged. Thus repeating the above iteratively until the `while` loop condition $\sum_{e\in E} R(e) w_e \le \lambda$ becomes invalid, we get a schedule that is the output of the algorithm. It can also be shown that if the schedule returned `sch` violates any of the constraints (Equation (4)) then it must have happened at the very last iteration and hence we return a schedule with the last added path removed from it. A detailed analysis and correctness of the algorithm proposed can be found in [50].

It only remains to show how the maximizer of

$$\frac{\min(\beta, T_{\text{rem}}(p(0, p(k+1))}{\sum_{e\in E} \beta \mathbf{1}_{\{e\in p\}} w_e} \tag{5}$$

is computed efficiently in each round (first line inside the `while` loop). Consider the set of shortest paths in G_w (smallest w_e-weighted path) from vertices in V_0 to vertices in V_k. Let p^* denote the shortest among them. Then by setting $\beta^* \leftarrow T_{\text{rem}}(p^*(0), p^*(k+1))$ we claim that Equation (5) is maximized. This is because,

$$\frac{\min(\beta, T_{\text{rem}}(p(0, p(k+1))}{\sum_{e\in E} \beta \mathbf{1}_{\{e\in p\}} w_e} \le \frac{\beta}{\sum_{e\in E} \beta \mathbf{1}_{\{e\in p\}} w_e} \le \frac{1}{\min \sum_{e\in E} \mathbf{1}_{\{e\in p\}} w_e}.$$

If $T_{\text{rem}}(p^*(0), p^*(k+1)) = 0$ we proceed to the second smallest shortest path and so on. This allows a very efficient implementation of the internal maximization step.

Approximation Guarantee: We show, as in the direct-routing scenario, that Eclipse++ has a constant factor approximation guarantee. Specifically, for a fixed instance of the traffic matrix, let `OPT` and `ALG4` denote the value of the objectives achieved by the optimal algorithm and Eclipse++ respectively. Let $\eta := \max_{i,j\in[n], e\in E} T(i,j)/R(e)$. Then one can show that $\texttt{ALG4} = \Omega(1/(nk)^{\eta})\texttt{OPT}$ for $\lambda = e^{1/\eta} nk$; the proof is analogous to the direct-routing case and follows [5, Theorem 1.1]. Further, if $\eta = O(\epsilon^2/\log(nk))$ for some fixed $\epsilon > 0$ then we get a approximation ratio of $(1-\epsilon)(1-1/e)$ by letting $\lambda = e^{\epsilon/(4\eta)}$ (using [5, Theorem 1.2]). An interesting regime where this occurs is when the traffic matrices are dense with small skew. For example, we get a constant factor approximation if the sparsity of the traffic matrix grows at least logarithmically fast. This is in stark contrast to direct routing, where sparse matrices generally perform better.

Complexity: The proposed algorithm is simple and fast. In this subsection, we explicitly enumerate the time complexity of the full algorithm and show that the complexity is at most cubic in n and nearly linear in k. Let W denote a bound on the total incoming or outgoing traffic for a node. In each iteration of the `while` loop at least one packet is sent. Therefore there are at most W iterations of the `while` loop. Now, in each iteration finding the shortest paths between nodes in V_0 to nodes in V_k takes $kn^2(\log k + \log n)$ operations using Dijkstra's algorithm [18]. Sorting the computed distances takes $kn^2(\log k + \log n)^2$ time and at most n^2 more operations to find a pair i, j such that $T_{\text{rem}}(i,j) > 0$. Finally the weights update step takes kn time. Therefore overall it takes $O(kn^2(\log k + \log n)^2)$ time per iteration. Hence the time complexity of the complete algorithm is $O(Wkn^3(\log k + \log n)^2)$.

5. EVALUATION

In this section, we complement our analytical results with numerical simulations to explore the effectiveness of our algorithms and compare them to state-of-the-art techniques in the literature. We empirically evaluate both the direct routing algorithm (Eclipse; Algorithm 2) and the indirect routing algorithm (Eclipse++; Algorithm 4).

Metric: We consider the total fraction of traffic delivered via the circuit switch (sum-throughput) over the duration of a fixed scheduling window as the performance metric throughout this section. Evaluating our algorithms under continuous traffic arrival models remains an important future direction.

Schemes compared: Our experiments compare Eclipse against two existing algorithms for direct routing:
Solstice [34]: This is the state-of-the-art hybrid circuit/packet scheduling algorithm for data centers. The key idea in Solstice is to choose matchings with 100% utilization. This is achieved by thresholding the demand matrix and selecting

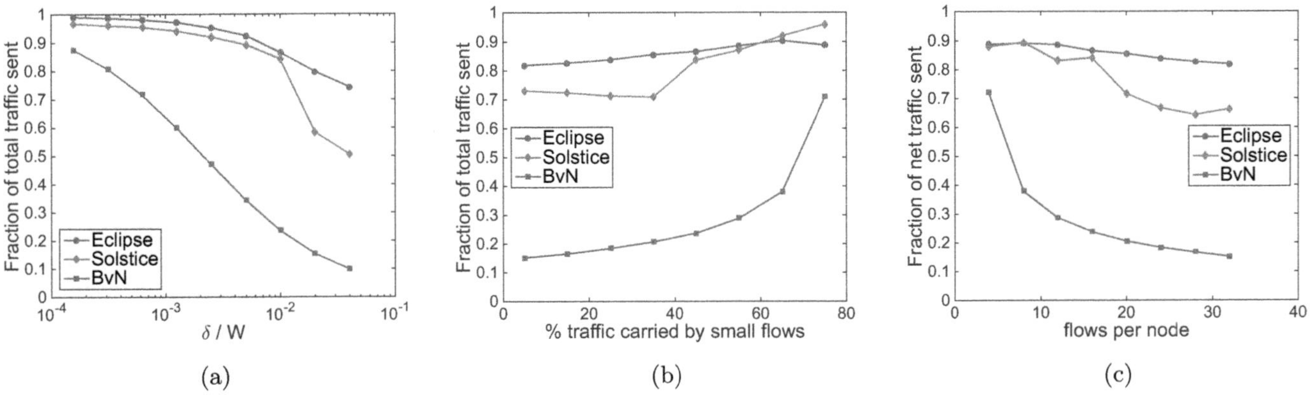

Figure 4: Performance comparison of Eclipse under single-block inputs.

a perfect matching in each round. The algorithm presented in [34] tries to minimize the total duration of the window such that the entire traffic demand is covered. In this paper, we have considered a more general setting where the scheduling window W is constrained. To compare against Solstice in this setting, we truncate its output once the total schedule duration exceeds W.

Truncated Birkhoff-von-Neumann (BvN) decomposition [10]: The second algorithm we compare against is the truncated BvN decomposition algorithm. BvN decomposition refers to expressing a doubly stochastic matrix as a convex combination of permutation matrices and this decomposition procedure has been extensively used in the context of packet switch scheduling [34, 29, 10]. However BvN decomposition is oblivious to reconfiguration delay and can produce a potentially large ($O(n^2)$) number of matchings. Indeed, in our simulations BvN performs poorly.

Indirect routing is relatively new and to the best of our knowledge our work is the first to consider use of indirect routing for centralized scheduling.[5] In our second set of simulations, we show that the benefits of indirect routing are in addition to the ones obtained from switch configurations scheduling. To this end, we compare Eclipse with Eclipse++ to quantify the additional throughput obtained by performing indirect routing (Algorithm 4) on a schedule that has been (pre)computed using Eclipse.

Traffic demands: We consider two classes of inputs: (a) single-block inputs and (b) multi-block inputs (explained in Section 5.1). Intuitively, single-block inputs are matrices which consist of one $n \times n$ 'block' that is sparse and skewed, and are similar to the traffic demands evaluated in the Solstice paper [34]. Multi-block inputs, on the other hand, denote traffic matrices that are composed of many sub-matrices each with disparate properties such as sparsity and skew.

Network size: The number of ports is fixed in the range of 50–200. We find that the relative performances stayed numerically stable over this range as well as for increased number of ports.

[5]Indirect routing in a distributed setting but without consideration of switch reconfiguration delay was studied in a recent work [9].

5.1 Direct Routing

While maintaining the sum-throughput as the performance metric, we vary the various parameters of the system model to gauge the performance in different situations.

Single-block Inputs

For a single-block input, our simulation setup consists of a network with 100 ports. The link rate of the circuit switch is normalized to 1, and the scheduling window length is also 1 ($W = 1$). We consider traffic inputs where the maximum traffic to or from any port is bounded by W. Further, we let the reconfiguration delay $\delta = W/100$. The traffic matrix is generated similar to [34] as follows. We assume 4 large flows and 12 small flows to each input or output port. The large flows are assumed to carry 70% of the link bandwidth, while the small flows deliver the remaining 30% of the traffic. To do this, we let each flow be represented by a random weighted permutation matrix, i.e., we have

$$T = \sum_{i=1}^{n_L} \frac{c_L}{n_L} P_i + \sum_{i'=1}^{n_S} \frac{c_S}{n_S} P_{i'} + N, \qquad (6)$$

where $n_L(n_S)$ denotes the number of large (small) flows and $c_L(c_S)$ denotes the total percentage of traffic carried by the large (small) flows. In this case, we have $n_L = 4, n_S = 12$ and $c_L = 0.7, c_S = 0.3$. Further, we have added a small amount of noise N — additive Gaussian noise with standard deviation equal to 0.3% of the link capacity — to the non-zero entries to introduce some perturbation. Each experiment below has been repeated 25 times.

Reconfiguration delay: In Fig. 4(a) we plot sum-throughput while varying the reconfiguration delay from $W/3200$ to $4W/100$. Eclipse achieves a throughput of at least 90% for $\delta \leq W/100$. We observe Eclipse to be consistently better than Solstice although the difference is not pronounced until $\delta > W/100$. The BvN decomposition algorithm has a large throughput when the reconfiguration delay is small. As δ increases, its performance gradually worsens.

Skew: We control the skew by varying the ratio of the amount of traffic carried by small and large flows in the input traffic demand matrix (c_L/c_S in Equation (6)). Fig. 4(b) captures the scenario where the percentage traffic carried by the small flows is varied from 5 to 75. We observe that Eclipse is very robust to skew variations and is able to con-

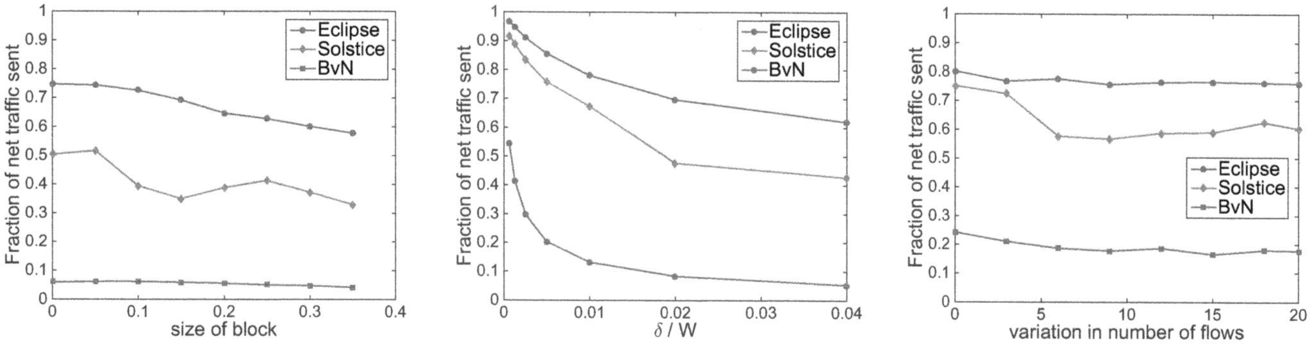

(a) (b) (c)

Figure 5: Performance comparison of Eclipse under multi-block inputs.

sistently maintain a throughput of about 85%. Solstice has a slightly better performance at low skew (when small-flows carry $\sim 75\%$ of traffic); but overall, is dominated by Eclipse.
Sparsity: Finally, we tested the algorithms' dependence on sparsity and plotted the results in Fig. 4(c). The total number of flows is varied from 4 to 32, while fixing the ratio of the number of large to small flows at 1:3. As the input matrix becomes less sparse, the performance of algorithms degrade as expected. However, for Eclipse, the reduction in the throughput is never more than 10% over the range of sparsity parameters considered. Solstice, on the other hand, is affected much more severely by decreased sparsity.

Multi-Block Inputs

Next, we consider a more complex traffic model for a 200 node network with block diagonal inputs of the form

$$T = \begin{bmatrix} B_1 & & \mathbf{0} \\ & \ddots & \\ \mathbf{0} & & B_m \end{bmatrix},$$

where each of the component blocks $B_1, B_2, \ldots, B_m$ can have its own sparsity (number of flows) and skew (fraction of traffic carried by large versus small flows) parameters. The different blocks model the traffic demands of different tenants in a shared data center network such as a public cloud data center. To begin with, we consider inputs with two blocks $T = \begin{bmatrix} B_1 & \mathbf{0} \\ \mathbf{0} & B_2 \end{bmatrix}$ where B_1 is a $n_1 \times n_1$ matrix with 4 large flows (carrying 70% of the traffic) and 12 small flows (carrying 30% of the traffic) and B_2 is a $(200-n_1)\times(200-n_1)$ matrix with uniform entries (up to sampling noise).
Size of block: Fig. 5(a) plots the throughput as the block size of B_2 is increased from 0 to 70. We observe a very pronounced difference in the performance of Eclipse and Solstice: Eclipse has roughly $1.5 - 2\times$ the performance of Solstice. These findings are in tune with the intuition discussed in Section 3.1 — the deteriorated performance of Solstice is due its insistence on perfect matchings in each round.
Reconfiguration delay: Fig. 5(b) plots throughput while varying the reconfiguration delay, for fixed size of B_2 to be 50×50. As expected, the throughput of Solstice and Eclipse both degrade as the reconfiguration delay δ increases. However, Eclipse throughput degrades at a much slower rate than Solstice. The gap between the two is particularly pronounced for $\delta/W \geq 0.02$, a numerical value that is well within range of practical system settings.
Varying numbers of flow: In the final experiment we consider block diagonal inputs with 8 blocks of size 25×25 each. Each block carries $10+\lfloor\sigma*(U-0.5))\rfloor$ equi-valued flows where $U \sim$ unif $(0,1)$ and σ is a parameter that controls the variation in the number of flows. When increasing σ from 0 to 20 we see from Fig.5(c) that Eclipse is more or less able to sustain its throughput at close to 80%; whereas Solstice is significantly affected by the variation.

5.2 Indirect Routing

In this section, we consider a 50 node network with traffic matrices having varying number of large and small flows as before. We compare the performance of the direct routing algorithm and the indirect routing algorithm that is run on the schedule computed by Eclipse. To understand the benefits of indirect routing, we focus on the regime where the reconfiguration delay δ/W is relatively large and the scheduling window W is relatively long compared to the traffic demand. This regime corresponds to realistic scenarios where the circuit switch is not fully utilized (Real data center networks often have low to moderate utilization; e.g, 10–50% [8]), but the reconfiguration delay is large. In this setting of relatively large δ/W, switch schedules are forced to have only a small number of matchings, and indirect routing is critical to support (non-sparse) demand matrices. The following experiments numerically demonstrate the added gains of indirect routing.
Sparsity: Fig. 6(a) considers a demand with 5 large flows and number of small flows varying from 7 to 49. The large and the small flows each carry 50% of the traffic. We let $\delta = 16W/100$ and consider a load of 20% (i.e., $W = 5$, and traffic load at each port is 1). We observe that the performance of the Eclipse++ is roughly 10% better than Eclipse.
Load: As the network load increases (Fig. 6(b)), we see that indirect routing becomes less effective. This is because at high load, the circuits do not have much spare capacity to support indirect traffic. However, at low to moderate levels of load, indirect routing provides a notable throughput gain over direct routing. For example, we see close to 20% improvement with Eclipse++ over Eclipse at 15% load.
Reconfiguration delay: Finally, we observe the effect of

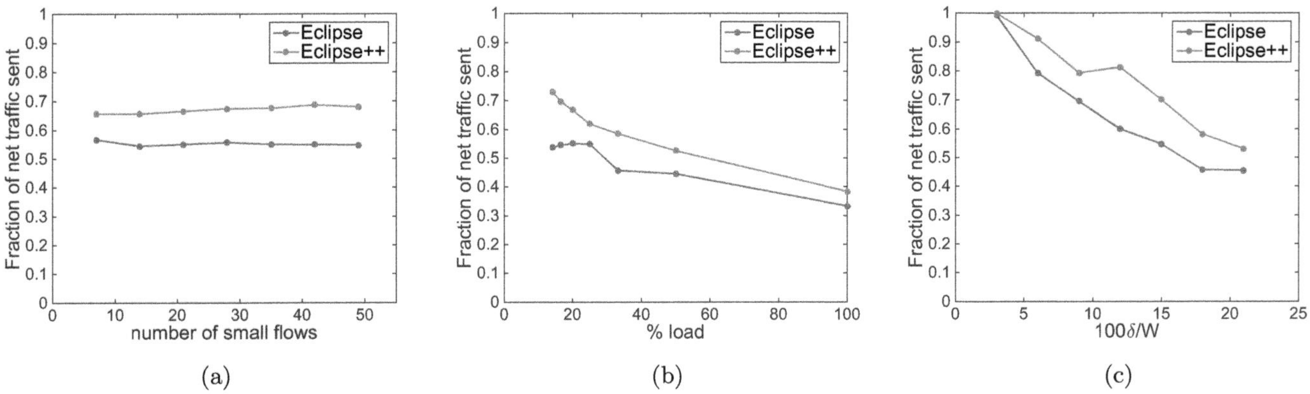

Figure 6: Performance of Eclipse++ and Eclipse. Here Eclipse++ uses the schedule computed by Eclipse.

δ/W on throughput by varying δ from $3W/100$ to $21W/100$. At smaller values of reconfiguration delay δ both Eclipse and Eclipse++ are able to achieve near 100% throughput. With increasing δ both algorithms degrade with Eclipse++ providing an additional gain of roughly 20% over Eclipse.

6. FINAL REMARKS

We have studied scheduling in hybrid switch architectures with reconfiguration delays in the circuit switch, by taking a fundamental and first-principles approach. The connections to submodular optimization theory allows us to design simple and fast scheduling algorithms and show that they are near optimal — these results hold in the direct routing scenario and indirect routing provided switch configurations are calculated separately. The problem of jointly deciding the switch configurations *and* indirect routing policies remains open. While submodular function optimization with nonlinear constraints is in general intractable, the specific constraints discussed in Section 4.1 perhaps have enough structure that they can be handled in a principled way; this is a direction for future work.

In between the scheduling windows of W time units, traffic builds up at the ToR ports. This dynamic traffic buildup is known locally to each of the ToR ports and perhaps this local knowledge can be used to pick appropriate indirect routing policies in a distributed, dynamic fashion. Such a study of indirect routing policies is initiated in a recent work [9], but this work omitted the switching reconfiguration delays. A joint study of distributed dynamic traffic scheduling in conjunction with a static schedule of switch configurations that account for reconfiguration delays is also an interesting direction of future research.

7. ACKNOWLEDGMENTS

The authors would like to thank Prof. Chandra Chekuri, Prof. George Porter and Prof. R. Srikant for the many helpful discussions. This work was partially supported by NSF grant CCF-1409106 and Army grant W911NF-14-1-0220.

8. REFERENCES

[1] R. Ahuja, T. Magnanti, and J. Orlin. *Network flows: theory, algorithms, and applications.* Prentice Hall, 1993.

[2] M. Al-Fares, S. Radhakrishnan, B. Raghavan, N. Huang, and A. Vahdat. Hedera: Dynamic flow scheduling for data center networks. In *NSDI*, volume 10, pages 19–19, 2010.

[3] M. Alizadeh, A. Greenberg, D. A. Maltz, J. Padhye, P. Patel, B. Prabhakar, S. Sengupta, and M. Sridharan. Data center tcp (dctcp). *SIGCOMM*, 2011.

[4] S. Arora, E. Hazan, and S. Kale. The multiplicative weights update method: a meta-algorithm and applications. *Theory of Computing*, 8(1):121–164, 2012.

[5] Y. Azar and I. Gamzu. Efficient submodular function maximization under linear packing constraints. In *Automata, Languages, and Programming*, pages 38–50. Springer, 2012.

[6] S. Barman. Approximating nash equilibria and dense bipartite subgraphs via an approximate version of caratheodory's theorem. In *Proceedings of the Forty-Seventh Annual ACM on Symposium on Theory of Computing*, pages 361–369. ACM, 2015.

[7] C. Barnhart and Y. Sheffi. A network-based primal-dual heuristic for the solution of multicommodity network flow problems. *Transportation Science*, 27(2):102–117, 1993.

[8] T. Benson, A. Akella, and D. A. Maltz. Network traffic characteristics of data centers in the wild. In *SIGCOMM*, 2010.

[9] Z. Cao, M. Kodialam, and T. Lakshman. Joint static and dynamic traffic scheduling in data center networks. In *INFOCOM*, 2014.

[10] C.-S. Chang, W.-J. Chen, and H.-Y. Huang. Birkhoff-von neumann input buffered crossbar switches. In *INFOCOM*, 2000.

[11] C.-S. Chang, D.-S. Lee, and Y.-S. Jou. Load balanced birkhoff-von neumann switches. In *High Performance Switching and Routing, 2001 IEEE Workshop on*, pages 276–280. IEEE, 2001.

[12] A. Dasylva and R. Srikant. Optimal wdm schedules for optical star networks. *IEEE/ACM Transactions on Networking (TON)*, 7(3):446–456, 1999.

[13] R. Duan and S. Pettie. Linear-time approximation for maximum weight matching. *J. ACM*, 61(1):1:1–1:23,

Jan. 2014.

[14] R. Duan and H.-H. Su. A scaling algorithm for maximum weight matching in bipartite graphs. In *SODA*, 2012.

[15] N. Farrington. *Optics in data center network architecture.* PhD thesis, Citeseer, 2012.

[16] N. Farrington, G. Porter, S. Radhakrishnan, H. H. Bazzaz, V. Subramanya, Y. Fainman, G. Papen, and A. Vahdat. Helios: a hybrid electrical/optical switch architecture for modular data centers. *SIGCOMM*, 2011.

[17] P. F. Felzenszwalb and R. Zabih. Dynamic programming and graph algorithms in computer vision. *Pattern Analysis and Machine Intelligence, IEEE Transactions on*, 33(4):721–740, 2011.

[18] M. L. Fredman and R. E. Tarjan. Fibonacci heaps and their uses in improved network optimization algorithms. *Journal of the ACM (JACM)*, 34(3):596–615, 1987.

[19] S. Fu, B. Wu, X. Jiang, A. Pattavina, L. Zhang, and S. Xu. Cost and delay tradeoff in three-stage switch architecture for data center networks. In *HPSR*, 2013.

[20] N. Garg and J. Koenemann. Faster and simpler algorithms for multicommodity flow and other fractional packing problems. *SIAM Journal on Computing*, 37(2):630–652, 2007.

[21] P. Giaccone, B. Prabhakar, and D. Shah. Randomized scheduling algorithms for high-aggregate bandwidth switches. *Selected Areas in Communications, IEEE Journal on*, 21(4):546–559, 2003.

[22] I. S. Gopal and C. K. Wong. Minimizing the number of switchings in an ss/tdma system. *Communications, IEEE Transactions on*, 33(6):497–501, 1985.

[23] A. Greenberg, P. Lahiri, D. A. Maltz, P. Patel, and S. Sengupta. Towards a next generation data center architecture: scalability and commoditization. In *Proceedings of the ACM workshop on Programmable routers for extensible services of tomorrow*, pages 57–62. ACM, 2008.

[24] M. Grötschel, L. Lovász, and A. Schrijver. *Geometric algorithms and combinatorial optimization.* Algorithms and combinatorics. Springer-Verlag, 1993.

[25] N. Hamedazimi, Z. Qazi, H. Gupta, V. Sekar, S. R. Das, J. P. Longtin, H. Shah, and A. Tanwer. Firefly: a reconfigurable wireless data center fabric using free-space optics. In *SIGCOMM*, 2014.

[26] T. Inukai. An efficient ss/tdma time slot assignment algorithm. *Communications, IEEE Transactions on*, 27(10):1449–1455, 1979.

[27] S. Kandula, J. Padhye, and P. Bahl. Flyways to de-congest data center networks. 2009.

[28] I. Keslassy, C.-S. Chang, N. McKeown, and D.-S. Lee. Optimal load-balancing. In *INFOCOM*, 2005.

[29] I. Keslassy, M. Kodialam, T. Lakshman, and D. Stiliadis. On guaranteed smooth scheduling for input-queued switches. In *INFOCOM*, 2003.

[30] T. Leighton, F. Makedon, S. Plotkin, C. Stein, É. Tardos, and S. Tragoudas. Fast approximation algorithms for multicommodity flow problems. *Journal of Computer and System Sciences*, 50(2):228–243, 1995.

[31] X. Li and M. Hamdi. On scheduling optical packet switches with reconfiguration delay. *Selected Areas in Communications, IEEE Journal on*, 21(7):1156–1164, 2003.

[32] Y. Li, S. Panwar, and H. J. Chao. Frame-based matching algorithms for optical switches. In *High Performance Switching and Routing, 2003, HPSR. Workshop on*, pages 97–102. IEEE, 2003.

[33] H. Liu, F. Lu, A. Forencich, R. Kapoor, M. Tewari, G. M. Voelker, G. Papen, A. C. Snoeren, and G. Porter. Circuit switching under the radar with reactor. In *NSDI*, 2014.

[34] H. Liu, M. K. Mukerjee, C. Li, N. Feltman, G. Papen, S. Savage, S. Seshan, G. M. Voelker, D. G. Andersen, M. Kaminsky, G. Porter, and A. C. Snoeren. Scheduling techniques for hybrid circuit/packet networks. In *ACM CoNEXT*, 2015.

[35] N. McKeown. The islip scheduling algorithm for input-queued switches. *Networking, IEEE/ACM Transactions on*, 7(2):188–201, 1999.

[36] N. McKeown, A. Mekkittikul, V. Anantharam, and J. Walrand. Achieving 100% throughput in an input-queued switch. *Communications, IEEE Transactions on*, 47(8):1260–1267, 1999.

[37] A. Mekkittikul and N. McKeown. A practical scheduling algorithm to achieve 100% throughput in input-queued switches. In *INFOCOM*, 1998.

[38] V. Mirrokni, R. P. Leme, A. Vladu, and S. C.-w. Wong. Tight bounds for approximate carathéodory and beyond. *arXiv preprint arXiv:1512.08602*, 2015.

[39] S. Pettie and P. Sanders. A simpler linear time 2/3- ε approximation for maximum weight matching. *Information Processing Letters*, 91(6):271–276, 2004.

[40] G. Porter, R. Strong, N. Farrington, A. Forencich, P. Chen-Sun, T. Rosing, Y. Fainman, G. Papen, and A. Vahdat. Integrating microsecond circuit switching into the data center. *SIGCOMM*, 2013.

[41] B. Prabhakar and N. McKeown. On the speedup required for combined input-and output-queued switching. *Automatica*, 35(12):1909–1920, 1999.

[42] M. O. Rabin. Efficient dispersal of information for security, load balancing, and fault tolerance. *Journal of the ACM (JACM)*, 36(2):335–348, 1989.

[43] A. Roy, H. Zeng, J. Bagga, G. Porter, and A. C. Snoeren. Inside the social network's (datacenter) network. In *SIGCOMM*, 2015.

[44] A. Schrijver. *Combinatorial Optimization - Polyhedra and Efficiency.* Springer, 2003.

[45] A. Shieh, S. Kandula, A. G. Greenberg, and C. Kim. Seawall: Performance isolation for cloud datacenter networks. In *HotCloud*, 2010.

[46] A. Singla, A. Singh, and Y. Chen. Osa: An optical switching architecture for data center networks with unprecedented flexibility. In *NSDI*, 2012.

[47] R. Srikant and L. Ying. *Communication Networks: An Optimization, Control and Stochastic Networks Perspective.* Cambridge University Press, New York, NY, USA, 2014.

[48] B. Towles and W. J. Dally. Guaranteed scheduling for switches with configuration overhead. *Networking, IEEE/ACM Transactions on*, 11(5):835–847, 2003.

[49] L. G. Valiant. A bridging model for parallel computation. *Communications of the ACM*, 33(8):103–111, 1990.
[50] S. B. Venkatakrishnan, M. Alizadeh, and P. Viswanath. Costly circuits, submodular schedules: Hybrid switch scheduling for data centers. *CoRR*, abs/1512.01271, 2015.
[51] C.-H. Wang and T. Javidi. Adaptive policies for scheduling with reconfiguration delay: An end-to-end solution for all-optical data centers. *arXiv preprint arXiv:1511.03417*, 2015.
[52] C.-H. Wang, T. Javidi, and G. Porter. End-to-end scheduling for all-optical data centers. In *Computer Communications (INFOCOM), 2015 IEEE Conference on*, pages 406–414. IEEE, 2015.
[53] G. Wang, D. G. Andersen, M. Kaminsky, K. Papagiannaki, T. Ng, M. Kozuch, and M. Ryan. c-through: Part-time optics in data centers. *SIGCOMM*, 2011.
[54] B. Wu and K. L. Yeung. Nxg05-6: Minimum delay scheduling in scalable hybrid electronic/optical packet switches. In *GLOBECOM*, 2006.
[55] B. Wu, K. L. Yeung, and X. Wang. Nxg06-4: Improving scheduling efficiency for high-speed routers with optical switch fabrics. In *GLOBECOM*, 2006.
[56] X. Zhou, Z. Zhang, Y. Zhu, Y. Li, S. Kumar, A. Vahdat, B. Y. Zhao, and H. Zheng. Mirror mirror on the ceiling: Flexible wireless links for data centers. *SIGCOMM*, 2012.

APPENDIX

A. DIRECT ROUTING - PROOFS

A.1 Proof of Theorem 1

PROOF. Clearly $f(\{\}) = 0$. Also for any $S \subseteq S' \in 2^{\mathbb{Z}\times\mathcal{M}}$ we have $\min\left\{\sum_{(\alpha,M)\in S}\alpha M, T\right\} \leq \min\left\{\sum_{(\alpha,M)\in S'}\alpha M, T\right\}$ implying $f(S) \leq f(S')$. Hence f is normalized and monotone. Next, for non-negative reals a, b, c the identity $\min(a+b,c) = \min(a,c) + \min(b, c - \min(a,c))$ holds. Therefore for $S \in 2^{\mathbb{Z}\times\mathcal{M}}$ and $(\alpha_0, M_0) \notin S$, we have $f(S \cup \{(\alpha_0, M_0)\}) =$

$$\Big\|\min\Big(\sum_{(\alpha,M)\in S}\alpha M + \alpha_0 M_0, T\Big)\Big\|_1 = \Big\|\min\Big(\sum_{(\alpha,M)\in S}\alpha M, T\Big) + \min\Big(\alpha_0 M_0, T - \min\Big(\sum_{(\alpha,M)\in S}\alpha M, T\Big)\Big)\Big\|_1 \Rightarrow$$

$$f_S((\alpha_0, M_0)) = \Big\|\min\Big(\alpha_0 M_0, T - \min\Big(\sum_{(\alpha,M)\in S}\alpha M, T\Big)\Big)\Big\|_1, \tag{7}$$

where $f_S((\alpha_0, M_0))$ denotes the incremental marginal value of adding (α_0, M_0) to the set S (see Section 3.2). Now, for $S \subseteq S' \in 2^{\mathbb{Z}\times\mathcal{M}}$ and $(\alpha_0, M_0) \notin S'$, since

$$T - \min\Big(\sum_{i\in S'}\alpha_i M_i, T\Big) \leq T - \min\Big(\sum_{i\in S}\alpha_i M_i, T\Big),$$

this together with Equation (7) implies

$$f_{S'}(\{(\alpha_0, M_0)\}) \leq f_S(\{(\alpha_0, M_0)\}).$$

Hence f is submodular. □

A.2 Proof of Theorem 2

PROOF. Recall the submodular sum-throughput function f defined in Equation (2). Let $\{(\alpha_1, M_1), \ldots, (\alpha_k, M_k)\}$ be the schedule returned by Algorithm 2. Let $S_i = \{(\alpha_1, M_1), \ldots, (\alpha_i, M_i)\}$ denote the schedule computed at the end of i iterations of the `while` loop and let S^* denote the optimal schedule. Now, since in the $i+1$-th iteration (α_{i+1}, M_{i+1}) maximizes $\frac{\|\min(\alpha M, T_{\text{rem}}(i+1))\|_1}{(\alpha+\delta)} = \frac{f_{S_i}(\{(\alpha,M)\})}{(\alpha+\delta)}$ we have for any $(\alpha, M) \notin S_i$,

$$\frac{f_{S_i}(\{(\alpha,M)\})}{(\alpha+\delta)} \leq \frac{f_{S_i}(\{(\alpha_{i+1},M_{i+1})\})}{(\alpha_{i+1}+\delta_{i+1})}$$
$$\Rightarrow f_{S_i}(\{(\alpha,M)\}) \leq \frac{(\alpha+\delta)}{(\alpha_{i+1}+\delta_{i+1})} f_{S_i}(\{(\alpha_{i+1},M_{i+1})\}). \tag{8}$$

Now consider $\texttt{OPT} - f(S_i)$ for some $i < k$. Since f is monotone we have

$$\begin{aligned}\texttt{OPT} - f(S_i) &= f(S^*) - f(S_i) \leq f(S_i \cup S^*) - f(S_i)\\ &\leq \sum_{(\alpha,M)\in J^*} f_{S_i}(\{(\alpha,M)\})\\ &\leq \sum_{(\alpha,M)\in J^*}\frac{(\alpha+\delta)}{(\alpha_{i+1}+\delta_{i+1})} f_{S_i}(\{(\alpha_{i+1},M_{i+1})\}) \qquad (9)\\ &\leq \frac{W}{(\alpha_{i+1}+\delta_{i+1})} f_{S_i}(\{(\alpha_{i+1},M_{i+1})\}), \qquad (10)\end{aligned}$$

where $J^* := S^* \backslash S_i$ denotes the set of matchings that are present in the optimal solution but not in S_i, Equation (9) follows from Equation (8), and Equation (10) follows because $\sum_{(\alpha,M)\in J^*}(\alpha+\delta) \leq \sum_{(\alpha,M)\in S^*}(\alpha+\delta) \leq W$. Next, observe that

$$\begin{aligned}f(S_{i+1}) &= f(S_i) + f_{S_i}(\{(\alpha_{i+1},M_{i+1})\})\\ \Rightarrow \texttt{OPT} - f(S_{i+1}) &= \texttt{OPT} - f(S_i) - f_{S_i}(\{(\alpha_{i+1},M_{i+1})\})\\ &\leq (\texttt{OPT} - f(S_i))\left(1 - \frac{(\alpha_{i+1}+\delta)}{W}\right) \qquad (11)\\ &\leq (\texttt{OPT} - f(S_0))\prod_{i'=1}^{i+1}\left(1 - \frac{(\alpha_{i'}+\delta)}{W}\right)\\ &\leq \texttt{OPT} \times e^{-\sum_{i'=1}^{i+1}(\alpha_{i'}+\delta)/W}, \qquad (12)\end{aligned}$$

where Equation (11) follows from Equation (10) and Equation (12) follows because of the identity $1 - x \leq e^{-x}$. Now, since after the k-th iteration the `while` loop terminates, this implies $\sum_{i'=1}^{k}(\alpha_{i'}+\delta) > W$. However, if the entries of the input traffic matrix T are bounded by $\epsilon W + \delta$, then no matching has a duration longer than ϵW. In particular $\alpha_k + \delta \leq \epsilon W \Rightarrow \sum_{i'=1}^{k-1}(\alpha_{i'}+\delta) \geq W(1-\epsilon)$. Thus, setting $i = k-2$ in Equation (12) we have

$$\texttt{OPT} - f(S_{k-1}) \leq \texttt{OPT} \times e^{-\sum_{i'=1}^{k-1}(\alpha_{i'}+\delta)/W} \leq \texttt{OPT} \times e^{-(1-\epsilon)}$$
$$\Rightarrow \texttt{OPT} - \texttt{ALG2} \leq \texttt{OPT} \times e^{-(1-\epsilon)}.$$

Hence we conclude $\texttt{ALG2} \geq \texttt{OPT}(1 - e^{-(1-\epsilon)})$. □

Reducing Latency Through Page-aware Management of Web Objects by Content Delivery Networks

Shankaranarayanan Puzhavakath Narayanan
Purdue University
spuzhava@purdue.edu

Yun Seong Nam
Purdue University
nam21@purdue.edu

Ashiwan Sivakumar
Purdue University
asivakum@purdue.edu

Balakrishnan Chandrasekaran
Duke University
balac@cs.duke.edu

Bruce Maggs
Duke University & Akamai Technologies
bmm@cs.duke.edu

Sanjay Rao
Purdue University
sanjay@purdue.edu

ABSTRACT

As popular web sites turn to content delivery networks (CDNs) for full-site delivery, there is an opportunity to improve the end-user experience by optimizing the delivery of entire web pages, rather than just individual objects. In particular, this paper explores page-structure-aware strategies for placing objects in CDN cache hierarchies. The key idea is that the objects in a web page that have the largest impact on page latency should be served out of the closest or fastest caches in the hierarchy. We present schemes for identifying these objects and develop mechanisms to ensure that they are served with higher priority by the CDN, while balancing traditional CDN concerns such as optimizing the delivery of popular objects and minimizing bandwidth costs. To establish a baseline for evaluating improvements in page latencies, we collect and analyze publicly visible HTTP headers that reveal the distribution of objects among the various levels of a major CDN's cache hierarchy. Through extensive experiments on 83 real-world web pages, we show that latency reductions of over *100 ms* can be obtained for 30% of the popular pages, with even larger reductions for the less popular pages. Using anonymized server logs provided by the CDN, we show the feasibility of reducing capacity and staleness misses of critical objects by 60% with minimal increase in overall miss rates, and bandwidth overheads of under 0.02%.

1 Introduction

Reducing the latency of web pages is critical for electronic commerce as it directly impacts user engagement and revenue [16,18,21]. Amazon, e.g., found that 100ms of latency costs 1% in sales [21], while Google Search found that a 400 millisecond delay resulted in a 0.59% reduction in searches per user [31].

SIGMETRICS '16, June 14-18, 2016, Antibes Juan-Les-Pins, France
© 2016 ACM. ISBN 978-1-4503-4266-7/16/06...$15.00
DOI: http://dx.doi.org/10.1145/2896377.2901472

The quest to reduce web-page latencies has triggered much effort in the networking community among both researchers and practitioners. On the one hand, we have seen the large-scale adoption of widely distributed Content Delivery Networks (CDNs), that involve placing caches at thousands of Internet vantage points, close to end users. On the other hand, we have seen the recent emergence of new protocols such as SPDY [19] that significantly influenced the HTTP 2.0 standard. Despite these efforts, web-page latencies remain significant, constituting 80-90% of overall application response time by some reports [20,31].

A key challenge in reducing the latencies of web-pages (the time to get an acceptable initial rendering of the page, formally defined in §3.1) is their complexity [10,22]. Web pages are comprised of tens to hundreds of static and dynamic objects such as images, style-sheets (CSS), and JavaScript (JS) files, which may be served from multiple domains. Web-page download process has complex dependencies [27,36], where some objects may have more impact on web-page latencies than others. The first objects fetched during a download (e.g., HTML, CSS, and JS) may need to be parsed or executed to decide which objects to fetch subsequently. Objects needed for an initial rendering of the page (e.g., to trigger a browser load event) may be more critical to the user experience than those that refine the initial rendering.

The need to accommodate the varying impact of individual objects on overall latencies has begun to receive attention from the community [12,19]. Specifically, SPDY allows servers to transmit objects out of order to reflect their priority in the page load process. While useful in single server settings, most web pages today are served from multiple domains, and make extensive use of CDNs. Simply enabling SPDY between clients and CDN servers addresses only part of the problem. It is also necessary to reduce the CDN retrieval time of critical objects, especially since CDNs are typically organized as a hierarchy of caches [14] with different capacities and latencies at each layer.

Our motivation arises in part from the results of a study we conducted in which we collected end-to-end measurements of clients downloading pages from a number of web sites. The data shows that (i) objects appearing on the same web page are often served from multiple layers of the CDN cache hierarchy; (ii) critical objects are not always served from the fastest caches; and (iii) delays in serving a small number of critical objects can disproportionately impact overall latency.

Motivated by these findings, we present a framework that allows CDNs to map objects more important for page latencies to faster cache layers. Our framework is enabled by the increasing shift of popular web-sites to CDNs for full-site delivery (e.g., for 89% of the pages in our study above, the main HTML document was served by the CDN). We consider a family of schemes for determining object priorities including a strategy based on content type, a strategy that prioritizes objects needed for an initial rendering of the page, and a scheme that explicitly takes the dependencies across objects of the page into account. We show how CDN cache placement and replacement algorithms may be redesigned to take object priorities into account, while still considering object popularity. We consider an approach where, to keep bandwidth overheads small, only objects most critical for latency are proactively refreshed to avoid staleness related misses. We present a family of schemes for proactive refreshing that differ in terms of which objects are refreshed.

We present an extensive evaluation study of our schemes using a combination of controlled experiments that emulate real web pages in hierarchical CDN settings, as well as trace data from a real CDN deployment. Our evaluations seek to understand the benefits of prioritization in CDN placement and refresh schemes, the relative benefits of different schemes for prioritization, and the sensitivity of our results to page popularity and composition.

Our evaluations with 83 real-world pages show that 30% of the most popular pages and 59% of the other pages show latency reduction larger than $100ms$, with some pages showing latency reductions as high as $500ms$. Both placement and proactive refreshing are important in achieving the benefits. For the vast majority of pages, considering content type in both placement and proactive refreshing provides most of the benefit. However, the additional benefits with other prioritization schemes can be significant in lower hit rate regimes, and when the penalty of going to the origin is higher. Finally, using trace driven simulations, we show the feasibility of the priority-based caching approach for reducing miss rates of page-critical objects in CDNs by 60% with minimal increase in overall miss rates. We also highlight the opportunity of minimizing stale misses for objects critical for latency by as much as 60% while incurring additional bandwidth costs of less than 0.02%.

2 Motivating measurement study

Web pages consist of tens to hundreds of objects of multiple content types (HTML, CSS, JS, images). A typical page load process involves significant dependencies across objects [27,36]. An initially downloaded HTML, CSS or JS (henceforth referred to as *HCJ*) object (which often embeds pointers to other objects) must be parsed (and executed) to identify further objects to download. Browser policies may dictate dependencies – e.g., execution of a JS must wait for a prior CSS to complete execution. Figure 1 shows an example dependency graph obtained using wprof [36]. Clearly, not all objects have the same impact on page latencies – e.g., $C1$ is much more important than $W1$. Further, content type need not necessarily reflect object importance – e.g., some *HCJ* objects may not be required for an initial rendering of a page most important for user experience, while Non-*HCJ* objects such as images may in fact be required. Moreover,

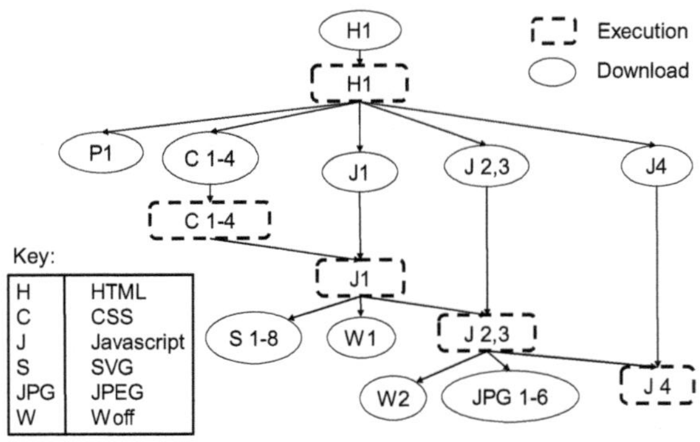

Figure 1: Dependency graph for a single load of www.apple.com. Each node shows download or execution of an object, and the directed arrow shows the dependency between them.

other objects may be dependent on Non-*HCJ* objects – e.g., a JS execution may wait on the arrival of a sprited image.

CDNs consist of a hierarchy of caches [14], typically consisting of clusters of servers deployed in multiple edge locations, and in parent locations. A user request that arrives at a server in an edge cluster (*First* server) could "hit" either at the memory or disk layer of that server. On a cache miss at the *First* server, requests could be directed to other servers in the CDN hierarchy (*Second* server), which could be a peer server in the same cluster or a server in a parent cluster. The latency of CDN served objects may vary widely depending on whether the object hits at the CDN and the layer that serves it.

To understand opportunities for reducing page latencies with CDNs by better mapping more important objects to faster CDN caches, we analyzed a prominent CDN that extensively provides edge caching (which we refer to as *CDN*). In the rest of this section, we discuss our measurement approach, and our findings.

2.1 Measurement methodology

We conduct end-to-end experiments by downloading real web pages from web clients and for each page measure the fraction of objects served from the different *CDN* layers. To determine the layer in the CDN hierarchy from which an object is served, we leverage HTTP pragma headers supported by CDNs for debugging purposes. Specifically, *CDN* supports the following pragma headers – *CDN*-x-cache-on, *CDN*-x-remote-cache-on and *CDN*-x-get-request-id. We set these pragma headers on all HTTP requests issued from the client. If the object is served by *CDN*, then the first contacted *CDN* server appends an X-Cache header in the HTTP response, and if a second *CDN* server is involved it appends an X-Cache-Remote header. The response also contains an X-*CDN*-Request-ID header with a dot-separated list of request IDs appended by each of the contacted *CDN* servers.

The X-Cache and X-Cache-Remote response headers contain values such as TCP MEM HIT, TCP HIT, TCP MISS, TCP REFRESH MISS, which respectively indicate a hit in the memory of that server, a disk hit, a server miss and a TTL expiry of a cached object with a new version fetched from the origin. We also count the number of request IDs in the X-*CDN*-Request-ID header to obtain the total number of *CDN* servers contacted. We use the values in these three headers to determine the layer from which the object was served. For instance, a TCP MEM HIT in the X-Cache header with one ID in the X-*CDN*-Request-ID header im-

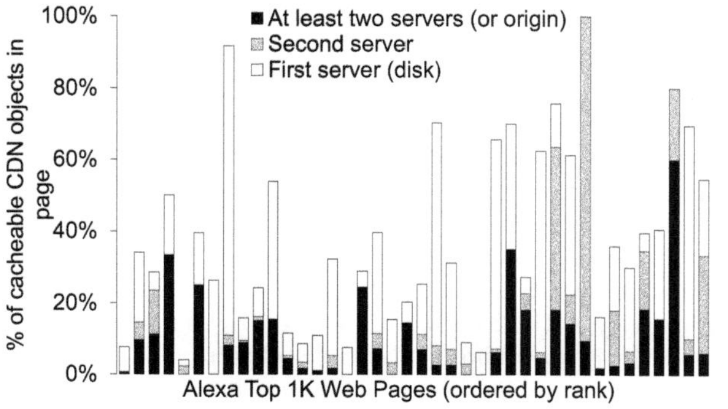

Figure 2: Breakdown of the different caching layers from which CDN-served objects of a web page are received. Fractions not shown hit at the memory layer of the first server

plies the object was served from the memory of the first *CDN* server. Like-wise a TCP MISS in the X-Cache header with a TCP MEM HIT in the X-Cache-Remote with two IDs implies the object was served from the second *CDN* server, while a MISS in both the headers means the object was fetched from origin. Note that, if we see a TCP MISS in both the headers with more than two IDs, due to limitations of the pragma headers, it is not possible to precisely tell if the object was served from the origin or another *CDN* server. But in our real runs we find these cases to be insignificant. For 90% of the pages fewer than 6 requests had more than two IDs in the X-*CDN*-Request-ID header.

We chose 100 Web pages for our measurement study across a wide range of popularity (Alexa US top sites [7]). Our measurement set has 40 pages in the Alexa rank top 1–1000 and 60 pages beyond rank 1000 which we refer to as *Top1K* and *Beyond1K* respectively in the rest of the paper. These pages were selected based on whether they had a good fraction of their objects served from *CDN*. Across all pages, at least 38% of the objects were served from *CDN* and for 25% of the pages more than 68% of the objects were served from *CDN*. Further, at least 92% of *CDN* served objects were cacheable for 90% of the pages. We also find that the main HTML for 89% of these pages were served from *CDN*.

Back-to-back downloads of the same page may artificially inflate the hit rates in subsequent runs owing to objects cached by the CDN from the earlier runs. To ensure our measurements themselves do not impact the hit rates, our entire set of measurements were spaced out across several weeks with consecutive downloads of the same page separated by 3 days – an analysis of the TTLs of objects in the pages indicated most objects would expire by this time.

2.2 Key findings

We now present key observations from our study.

• *Objects of a Web page may be served from different CDN caching layers incurring very different latencies:* Figure 2 presents the fraction of cacheable *CDN* objects served from each layer in the CDN hierarchy for a given run of the Alexa Top1K websites. Each stacked bar corresponds to a web page, and the segments in the bar show the breakdown – e.g., for the second most popular page (second stacked bar from the left), going from top to bottom, 19% of the cacheable *CDN* objects are served from the disk of the first server, 5% from the second server, 10% from at least 2 *CDN* servers (or origin) and the rest (66% – not shown) are served from the memory of the first server.

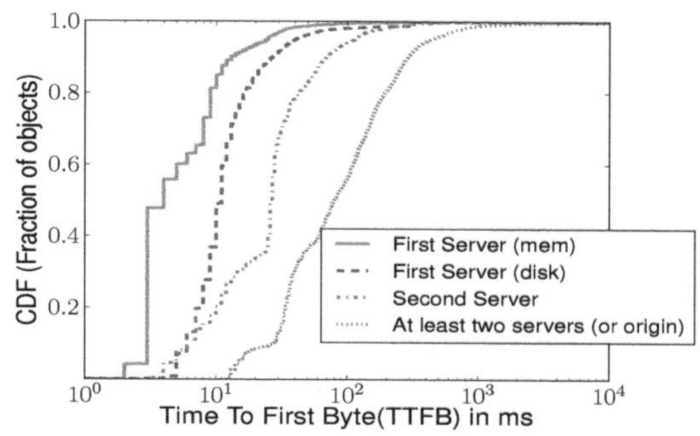

Figure 3: TTFB of objects served at different CDN layers

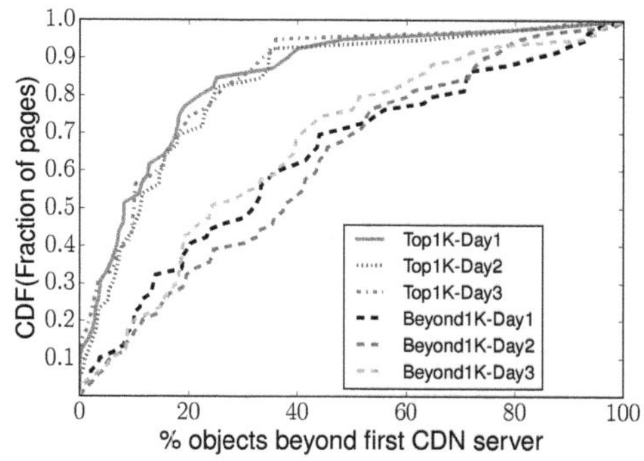

Figure 4: Fraction of cacheable CDN objects that are served from beyond the first CDN server across pages of two popularity classes for 3 different days

Figure 3 shows a distribution of the *Time To First Byte (TTFB)* of objects across all pages categorized by the layer from which it was served. The TTFB for an object is the time elapsed from when the request was sent from the client until the first byte of the response was received at the client, including the network time and retrieval time at the cache (or server). As expected, the TTFB observed across the different CDN layers vary substantially.

Figure 4 shows the fraction of cacheable CDN objects that are served from beyond the first contacted *CDN* server for the Top1K and Beyond1K classes for three different days. The figure shows that a significant fraction of objects are served from beyond the first *CDN* server even for the Top1K pages – e.g., the $50th(90th)$ %ile of objects served from beyond the first server were more than 11%(34%). Further, for the Beyond1K pages more objects are served from the farther layers in the CDN hierarchy – e.g., the $50th(90th)$ %ile of objects served from beyond the first server were more than 37%(74%). Moreover across multiple days, the hit rates remain similar for both the classes indicating the trends are consistent across many days and the hit rates are representative of the page popularity. We performed similar analysis across multiple days from different geographical locations and we find the trends to be similar. For instance, the median percentage of objects served from beyond the first server across the Top1K pages from another US location for three days were 15%, 12% and 10%, while for the Beyond1K pages they were 31%, 24% and 32%, with the 90%*ile* being higher than 38% and 71% across the days for the Top1K and Beyond1K respectively.

• *Critical objects are not always served from the fastest CDN layers:* Figure 5 shows a stacked bar graph with the number of objects served from each level in the dependency graph (as described earlier in this section) of *www.weather.com*. Each

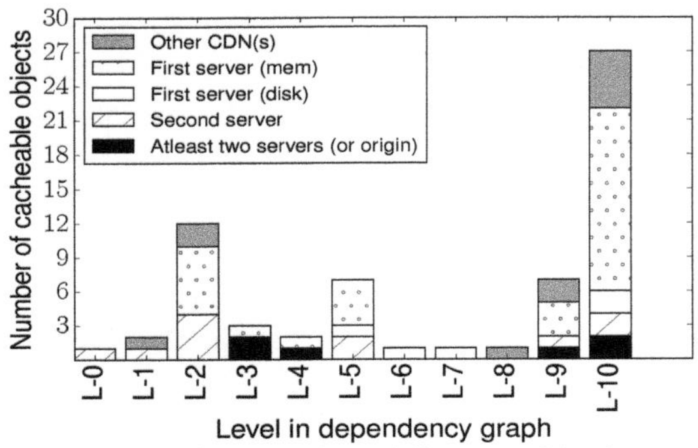

Figure 5: Number of objects from different caching layer at each level of the dependency graph for *www.weather.com*

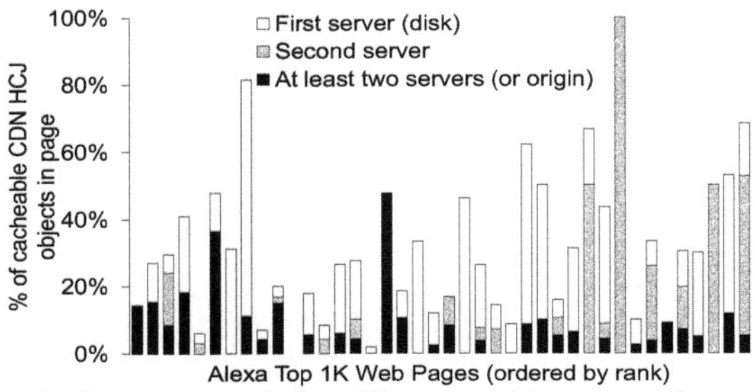

Figure 6: Breakdown of the different caching layers from which CDN-served *HCJ* objects (HTML, CSS, JS) are received.

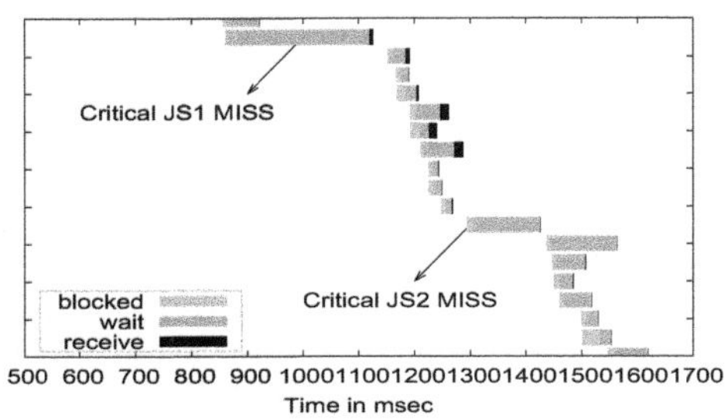

Figure 7: Serving delays in *HCJ* objects disproportionately impacts latency

bar corresponds to a level in the graph and the stacks in the bar show the number of objects served from the corresponding CDN layer. The figure shows that many critical objects (generally the internal nodes of the dependency graph) are served from beyond the first server indicating the potential to reduce page latencies by considering object priorities in CDN mechanisms.

Figure 6 shows a breakdown of the CDN layers from which the *HCJ* objects are served for the Alexa Top1K pages. While *HCJ* objects do not exactly correspond with objects important for a page load, we consider them here for simplicity. Note that a significant fraction of the *CDN* served cacheable objects are *HCJ* objects – e.g., 42% of *CDN* served cacheable objects are *HCJ* for 50% of the pages. The figure shows that in general across all pages a significant fraction of *HCJ* objects are served from different layers of the CDN hierarchy incurring vastly different latencies – e.g., for 50% of the Top1K pages more than 10% of the *CDN* served cacheable *HCJ* objects are served from higher layers with this fraction being greater than 48% for 10% of the pages.

• *Delays in serving a few critical objects can disproportionately impact page latency:* Figure 7 shows a section of the waterfall diagram which depicts how the objects arrive at a client during the download of an actual web page. The X-Axis is the time since the start of the download (only the relevant time segment is shown). Each bar corresponds to an object, and extends from when a request to that object was made, to when the object was fully downloaded at the client. Further, each bar shows the breakdown of the time spent waiting for a connection to the server (blocked), time spent waiting for the first byte of the response (wait) and time spent in receiving the object (receive). From the figure, we see that many objects were delayed because they depended on two JS objects, which got delayed (267*ms*, 135*ms* respectively with the time dominated by wait time). Further investigation showed both JS objects were cacheable and served from *CDN*, but were served beyond the first two servers in the hierarchy. Interestingly, many of the dependent objects hit in the CDN. Avoiding delays of these two JS objects would potentially reduce page load times by over 400*ms* (a 19% reduction).

• *Both true misses and stale misses contribute to objects being served from beyond the first* CDN *server:* We conducted a deeper analysis on the causes for the first *CDN* server misses. We found that even though true misses contribute greatly to the first server misses, we also find significant fractions of staleness related misses – e.g., the fraction of first server misses that were staleness related misses is more than 29% and 45% at the median and 75%*ile* respectively, with the rest being true misses.

3 Enabling page-awareness in CDNs

In §2, we have shown that there is opportunity to reducing web-page latency by mapping objects in a page most critical for latency to the fastest caches in the CDN hierarchy. In this section, we revisit CDN design to exploit this opportunity. In doing so, a number of issues must be tackled including (i) determining which objects to prioritize; (ii) reconciling the need to prioritize objects more critical for latency with the traditional CDN goals of placing more popular objects at the edge to save bandwidth, by appropriately tailoring cache placement and replacement policies; and (iii) avoiding staleness misses for important objects in addition to capacity misses. We discuss our schemes for each of these issues in the following sections.

3.1 Schemes for prioritization

We consider a range of schemes for assigning priorities to objects, which involve different trade-offs between the complexity of the priority-marking scheme, and the potential latency benefits as we discuss below:

• **Prioritizing objects based on content type: (*Type*)** Our first scheme is content-type based priority assignment, where objects are accorded priorities based on content type – specifically, HTML objects receive higher priority, followed by JS and CSS, and finally images and others. This, in fact, conforms to the best-practices for prioritization with the SPDY protocol, and is implemented by Chrome today [4].

• **Prioritizing objects needed for initial page rendering (*OLType*):** Content type may not accurately reflect the importance of an object to page latency. Objects needed for an initial acceptable rendering of a page are more critical to user experience than other objects. While images may be important for such an initial rendering, some *HCJ* objects may not be required. A commonly used indicator to identify such an initial version of the page is an Onload event triggered by the browser. The time to generate a browser Onload event, which we refer to as *Onload Time (OLT)*, is a commonly used metric to measure web page load performance [30]. This motivates our *OLType* strategy which prioritizes objects prior to the Onload event, and among such objects, prioritizes objects based on content type. More generically, this strategy could be refined to consider other indicators of an initial page load such as "above the fold" content, content related to most critical visual progress [2], or content with the highest utility to users [11].

• **Prioritization based on page dependency graph (*OLDep*):** While *Type* and *OLType* are fairly coarse-grained strategies, a more fine grained prioritization scheme is to consider the actual dependency graph associated with the page, and assign prioritizes based on the graph – e.g., in Figure 1, J1 would be accorded higher priority than J4. This motivates the *OLDep* algorithm. Like *OLType*, *OLDep* prioritizes objects needed to trigger the Onload event over other objects. However, among objects needed for the Onload event, it prioritizes objects based on their depth in the dependency graph, with *HCJ* objects preferred among those at the same depth. Likewise, objects after the Onload event are also prioritized based first on their depth in the dependency graph, and then their content-type.

3.2 Balancing popularity and priority in cache placement and replacement

CDNs have two potentially conflicting goals that they must consider in deciding whether to cache objects at a given edge location: (i) cost savings; and (ii) minimizing user latency. For cost savings, it is desirable to cache the most popular objects at the edge. However, for user latency savings, it is desirable to cache high priority objects at the edge. Since more popular objects might not be the highest priority and vice versa (e.g., page logos vs product related images), it is important to carefully reconcile these considerations.

A naive approach to tackling these issues is to use multiple LRU queues with one queue per priority level. When an eviction is required, incoming objects evict the least recently used objects in lower priority queues, before evicting the least recently used objects in the queue having the same priority as the incoming object. A key limitation of this approach is that objects with higher priority tend to remain in the cache even if they are no longer accessed, creating cache starvation for the popular, but low priority objects.

Instead, our approach is inspired by the notable Greedy-Dual-Size algorithm [13] which considers how to balance locality of access patterns with object size and the variable costs associated with fetching objects. We adapt this algorithm to balance object priority and popularity by assigning a utility to each object based on its priority (P_i), and implement our cache as a priority queue ordered by the utility of the objects. When an eviction is required, objects with the lowest utility value (which are located at the tail of the queue) are evicted first. To prevent high priority objects from residing permanently at the head of the queue, we gradually decrement the utility value of the objects in the queue that are no longer accessed. This may be achieved in a computationally efficient manner by maintaining a monotonically increasing global *clock* for the cache, which is added to the utility value of the object ($U(i)$) as follows:

$$U(i) = clock + 1 + (R-1) * \frac{P_{min} - P_i}{P_{min} - 1} \quad (1)$$

Here, P_{min} is the lowest assignable priority and is higher than P_{max}, the highest assignable priority. For simplicity, we fix $P_{max} = 1$ in our formulation and hence P_i varies between 1 and P_{min}. The parameter R is the ratio of the lowest and highest assignable priorities (P_{min}/P_{max}). A linear interpolation is used to assign the initial utility to objects with any priority. R is a knob that the CDN could tune to decide how much to favor hits to higher priority objects over lower priority objects, and we evaluate the impact of R with real traces in §6.1. The utility value of the object is updated using the above equation when the object is accessed from the cache. The monotonicity of the clock is maintained by incrementing the clock on an eviction to the utility value of the evicted object. Therefore, objects that are accessed more frequently will have a higher utility value than objects in the cache that do not see any further accesses. This ensures that high priority objects that are no longer accessed, eventually get evicted from the cache. Finally, note that an item is placed in the cache only if its utility exceeds the utility of the lowest utility object in the queue.

3.3 Priority based proactive refreshing

Staleness related misses could be avoided by proactively refreshing objects that are currently in the cache, but are about to expire in the near future, at the cost of some bandwidth related to unnecessary refreshes. Given the trade-off between reducing staleness misses and the bandwidth penalty, it is desirable to only proactively refresh those objects most important for page latency. We consider a family of strategies which primarily differ in terms of which objects are proactively refreshed:

• ***HCJ,*** which only proactively refreshes *HCJ* objects. The primary advantage of the scheme is the simplicity in identifying objects to refresh.

• ***BO,*** which only proactively refreshes all objects required for the page Onload event. While the strategy has the potential to better mirror objects most important for latency, it is more involved to identify these objects.

• ***HCJ BO,*** which only proactively refreshes *HCJ* objects needed for the page load event. This strategy has the potential to reduce the bandwidth overheads compared to *HCJ* while matching its latency benefits.

For all schemes, a refresh is triggered only when a request for the object is received and the following conditions are satisfied: (i) the object is unlikely to receive further accesses until it expires; and (ii) the estimated number of accesses in its lifetime is sufficiently high to warrant a proactive refresh. Specifically, we require that

$$A_i * e_i \leq T_{P_i} \quad (2)$$

$$A_i * l_i \geq K_{P_i} \quad (3)$$

Here, A_i, l_i, e_i, and P_i are respectively the average request rate, lifetime, time left to expiry and priority of the object. A_i is computed by tracking the number of accesses seen by the object since it entered the cache, and l_i and e_i are obtained from the cache-TTL or expiry-time of the object. T_{P_i} is ideally kept smaller (close to 1) to trigger just-in-time refreshes. Note that larger T_{P_i} and smaller K_{P_i} support more aggressive refreshing. We evaluate the impact of these parameters with real traces in §6.2. These thresholds may be set differently across priority classes to support more aggressive or conservative refreshing for each class.

4 Evaluation Methodology

Our evaluations have two primary goals. First, we seek to understand the potential latency benefits of our various

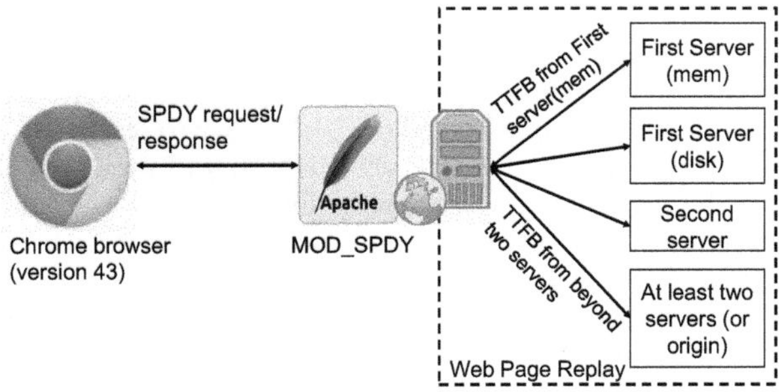

Figure 8: Experimental setup for evaluating latency benefits.

Placement schemes	Proactive refresh schemes
OBS	None
Type	*HCJ*
OLType	*BO*
OLDep	*HCJ BO*
	All

Table 1: Placement and refresh schemes studied in our evaluation.

schemes for priority-based placement and proactive refreshing, as well as their sensitivity to factors such as page popularity, CDN hit rates, page composition, and the relative latencies of various CDN cache layers. Second, we also seek to understand the impact of prioritization on CDN cache hit rates, and the bandwidth costs associated with the proactive refresh schemes.

We achieve the first goal by conducting a detailed emulation study of our schemes for the real-world pages analyzed in §2). Our emulations allow us to compare schemes in a fair manner while capturing the heterogeneity in latency (and object fetch times) across the CDN hierarchy, and realistic factors such as client execution times. We tackle the second goal by conducting a detailed analysis of traces from a real CDN. We present our experimental setup for latency comparisons in the rest of the section, latency benefits results in §5.1, and our trace-driven analysis in §6.

4.1 Methodology for latency comparisons

We use *Onload Time (OLT)* (defined in §3.1) to quantify the page load latency. We focus on OLT since it is objective, easy to determine, and widely used as a measure of page latency, while other indicators [2] are inherently more subjective. We do not consider the time to download the last byte for the page since many of the pages we evaluated tend to request objects indefinitely, and the time for an initial rendering is more important in practice.

We next discuss factors impacting our comparisons. A first factor is the CDN hit rates in terms of how many objects are served from each layer of the hierarchy. Of particular importance is the edge hit rate (*EHR,*) which we define as the fraction of objects served from the first CDN server (edge). A second factor is the composition of pages. Specifically, the fraction of *HCJ* and *BO* objects as well as the complexity of the dependency graph, can impact our comparisons. We compare our schemes with 83 real-world web pages analyzed in §2, which exhibit a wide range of diversity in terms of popularity and page composition. We highlight the characteristics of a page which impact the relative performance of schemes when appropriate. A third factor is the relative ratio of latency to the various layers of the CDN hierarchy, which we vary based on real measurements.

4.2 Schemes compared

Our schemes (Table 1) include:

Baseline for comparison (*OBS*): The *OBS* scheme corresponds to the placement observed when the page was loaded in the real-world measurements (§ 2). All objects served by *CDN* are fixed to the same layer from which it was served during the real page-load. All cacheable objects not served through *CDN* are split across the caching layers according to the hit-rates for cacheable objects observed in the real page-load.

Placement schemes: Our CDN placement schemes differ in their algorithms for assigning objects to the cache layers according to the fractions described above. We consider the *Type*, *OLType* and *OLDep* schemes are as described in § 3.1.

Proactive refresh strategies: This includes the *HCJ*, *BO* and *HCJ BO* schemes described in §3.3 which primarily differ in terms of which objects are proactively refreshed. We also consider the *None* and *All* strategies as baselines for comparison which indicate none or all of the objects are proactively refreshed.

To ensure fair comparisons with *OBS*, for all schemes, all non-cacheable objects were always pinned to the farthest layer (origin). All objects that observed a staleness miss with *OBS* were served from the same layer as they were with *OBS* if they were not proactively refreshed. For example, with no proactive refresh all objects that saw refresh misses in *OBS* were pinned, while with the *HCJ* strategy non-*HCJ* objects with refresh misses were pinned. All remaining objects were assigned to the CDN cache layers as per the placement strategy. In doing so, the total number of objects served from each CDN layer was ensured to be (i) the same as *OBS* in the absence of proactive refreshing; and (ii) the same as *OBS* augmented with that proactive refreshing strategy otherwise.

If only a subset of objects of a given priority class (e.g., a subset of *HCJ* objects with *Type*) can be accommodated at a given CDN layer to satisfy the constraints on the number of objects that could be served from each layer, our schemes pick objects from within the priority class randomly. To ensure a robust comparison, we generate 50 different placement configurations with each scheme. We load each web-page with each scheme for each of its 50 configurations, alternating across schemes. We clear the browser cache between runs to eliminate the impact of local browser caching. We usually summarize the performance of a scheme for a given page by presenting the median OLT across the 50 configurations, but we also report on higher percentiles.

Many of our schemes require knowledge of objects needed for Onload and their dependencies. Rather than detailed activity dependence graphs [36] that may vary across runs, we obtain more static object level dependencies [27, 37]. Through multiple controlled experiments that each delay an object in a page, we determine the objects needed for Onload based on whether the Onload event is delayed. Likewise, dependent objects may be determined based on delays observed in their download times. We determine object importance based on its depth in the dependency graph rather than consider critical paths which may vary across runs.

4.3 Experimental setup

Figure 8 presents our experimental setup. Web pages are hosted on a web server (corresponds to an edge server in a CDN cluster), where TTFBs to the different caching layers

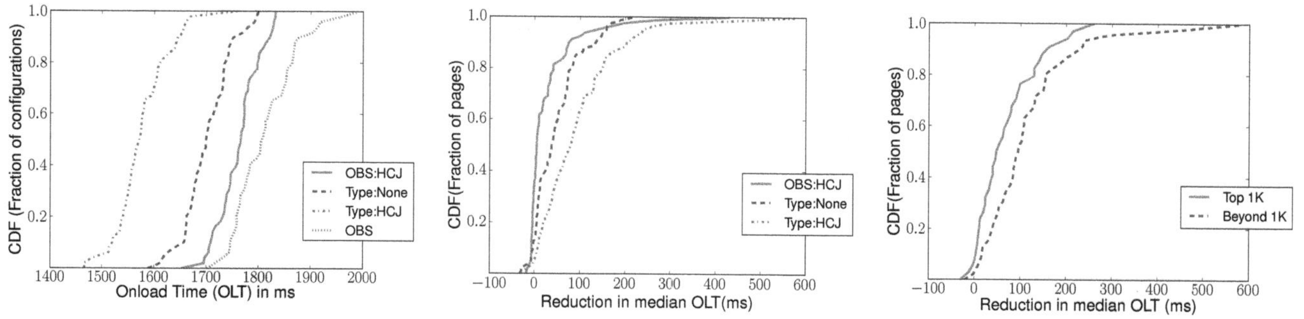

(a) OLT for *www.mercurynews.com* across schemes

(b) Median OLT reduction relative to *OBS* across all pages

(c) Median OLT reduction with *Type:HCJ* over *OBS* for Alexa Top1K and Beyond1K

Figure 9: Latency benefits of prioritized placement and proactive refresh strategies in isolation and combination.

are emulated and the page-load latency from an actual web browser is measured.

Web pages exhibit significant variability in the number of objects and aggregate download size for a given web page, even over short intervals of time. To ensure fair comparisons, we used an open source tool called web-page-replay [38]. Entire web pages including all constituent objects were first recorded through downloads from the actual web server(s). Then, the same recording was replayed for all schemes in later experiments. Some web pages still showed variability as they had JS that requested different URLs (e.g., using a random number or date) over different runs. We modified the web-page-replay code to replace such occurrences with constant values to ensure the same objects were requested for all schemes.

We focus our evaluations on settings where SPDY is enabled between the client and the edge server, in order to highlight that our benefits are complementary to SPDY. We also note that our schemes show similar benefits in the presence of traditional HTTP as well. We use apache mod_spdy server co-located with WPR, and Chrome browser (version 43.0) running SPDY (version 3.0) as the client in all our experiments. The client uses SPDY to forward object requests to the mod_spdy server, which in turn proxies the requests (and responses) to (and from) WPR. We modify the local DNS resolver configuration file in Linux to resolve all domains to localhost so that the requests are issued to the apache proxy during the replay experiments and no requests are served over the Internet. In all our experiments, the client uses the default priorities set by the SPDY implementation of Chrome when issuing requests to the server.

In order to minimize the impact of browser variability on page-load times, we disable all extensions, background and sync activities in the browser using Chrome command line flags [1]. We set the browser cache and user profile directories to RAMDisk [3] to minimize the impact of disk read/write variability on page-load times. We also clear the RAM disk across runs to ensure clean-slate page-loads where all objects are fetched from the emulated CDN layer.

5 Results

We begin by evaluating the potential benefits of our placement and proactive refresh schemes, focusing on content type prioritization (§5.1). We next compare all our placement strategies in the absence of proactive refresh (§5.2), and all our proactive refresh schemes in the absence of priority-based placements (§5.3), with a view to understanding the potential benefits of prioritizing objects based on factors other than content type. Finally, §5.4 evaluates the benefits when such richer prioritization is used as part of both placement and proactive refresh.

To emulate heterogeneous latencies associated with CDN cache hierarchies, by default, we use the median TTFB observed across all objects fetched from each layer in our measurement study (Figure 3), but we present a sensitivity study to our latency settings in §5.4.

We compare the performance of the schemes with 83 real-world web pages (out of the 100 pages analyzed in §2). The remaining 17 pages either did not consistently trigger an Onload, or had 100% of its objects being served from the edge server(mem), in which case all placement schemes are equivalent. In comparisons where both placement and proactive refresh strategies vary, we use names such as *Type:HCJ* (indicating placement using the *Type* strategy and proactive refreshing of *HCJ* objects). When schemes compared vary in only in their placement (or refresh) strategy, we abbreviate by only using names of the placement (or refresh) schemes.

5.1 Latency benefits of prioritization

In this section, we evaluate the potential benefits of prioritized placement and proactive refresh, in isolation and in combination. We focus on schemes that primarily distinguish objects based on their content type (*Type* and *HCJ*).

Figure 9(a) shows a CDF of the OLTs observed (across 50 placement configurations as described in §4) with *OBS*, *OBS:HCJ* indicating *OBS* placement with *HCJ* refresh strategy, *Type:None*, and *Type:HCJ* for a popular web-page *www.mercurynews.com* (Alexa Rank:1245). The breakdown of objects served from different layers in the real download (*OBS*) for this page was 54% at the edge server (34%mem, 20%disk), 26%remote, and 20%origin. The figure shows that both priority based placement and proactive refresh independently help reduce the OLT when compared to *OBS*. However, the combination of the two provides significantly higher benefits, reducing the OLT by more than 200ms.

Figure 9(b) shows the reduction in median OLT achieved by the three schemes relative to *OBS* for all pages. The figure shows that *Type:HCJ* provides significant reductions in OLT over *OBS*, despite the high EHRs for some of these pages. For instance, we see a median OLT reduction of more than 100ms for 40% of the pages and more than 200ms for 10% of the pages. Our results also show the importance of priority based placement only (*Type:None*), which reduces the median OLT by more than 50ms for 30% of the pages. Interestingly, we also find *OBS:HCJ* strategy providing sig-

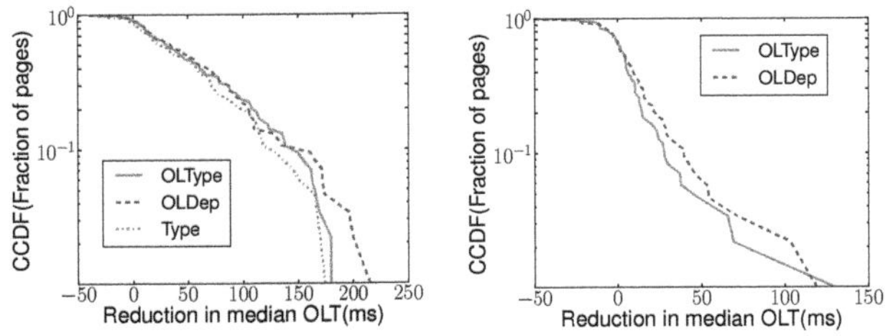

(a) Reduction relative to *OBS*. (b) Reduction relative to *Type*.

Figure 10: CCDF of median OLT reduction with *Type*, *OLType* and *OLDep* for all pages with Y-Axis in log-scale. Proactive refresh is disabled for all schemes.

nificant latency reductions when compared to *OBS* by avoiding refresh misses for some *HCJ* objects. For example, for 15% of the pages *OBS*:*HCJ* provides a latency reduction of more than 68ms. These correspond to pages where > 17% of all objects were *HCJ* and saw refresh misses. We also found similar trends for the reduction in 90*%ile* latency for all the schemes, though the benefits were marginally higher.

To understand the impact of prioritization for pages with different popularities, in Figure 9(c) we show the OLT reduction with *Type*:*HCJ* over *OBS* split by the Alexa Top1K and Beyond1K classes (§ 2). The figure shows that though the benefits are more pronounced for the Beyond1K pages, prioritization provides significant reduction in Median OLT even for the Top1K pages. For example, though *Type*:*HCJ* provides 93ms (225ms) reduction in median OLT for 50%(10%) of the Beyond1K pages, we see benefits of over 157ms for 10% of the Top1K pages also. Overall, our results clearly emphasize the importance of prioritization through better placement and proactive refresh strategies.

To ensure statistical significance, we conducted a Mann-Whitney-Wilcoxon (MWW) test [28] (a non-parametric test to compare two populations) to reject the null hypothesis that the OLT distributions observed with the two schemes being compared are identical. Typically, the MWW test confirms significance (at a significance level of 0.05) when our schemes provide latency reduction over 10 ms. However the null hypothesis cannot be rejected when our schemes show more marginal reductions, or marginal increases. These cases usually correspond to scenarios where prioritization schemes provide no benefit – e.g., 33% of the pages see no *HCJ* refresh misses at all, and hence the *OBS*:*HCJ* scheme provides no intrinsic benefits over *OBS* for these pages. Interestingly, the latency increase over *OBS* is significant for 1 page with *Type*:*HCJ*, and for 2 pages with *Type*:*None*. On further examination, we found that the increase could be attributed to limitations of *Type*-based prioritization. These pages had some important Non-*HCJ* objects required for the initial page rendering (Onload), which were not placed in the edge by *Type*, but interestingly were served from the edge in the *OBS* run. For such cases, more sophisticated prioritization schemes like *OLType* or *OLDep* could potentially provide benefits.

5.2 Comparing placement strategies

We next evaluate the benefits of *OLType* and *OLDep* which consider factors besides content type in placement decisions. Since our focus is on placement schemes, our comparisons are done without proactive refresh.

Figure 10(a) presents a CCDF of the median OLT reduction relative to *OBS* for all the placement schemes, and all the pages in our experiment set. While all schemes show significant reductions compared to *OBS*, *OLType* and *OLDep* provide only slightly higher benefits than *Type*. The benefits are marginal for most pages, however somewhat more significant at the tail. Note that the CCDF is shown with Y-Axis in log scale since the schemes show more prominent difference in the tail. Figure 10(b) shows the median OLT reduction of *OLType* and *OLDep* relative to *Type*. Across all pages, *OLDep* achieves a median OLT reduction higher than 35ms for 12% of the pages, while for 6% of the tail pages both schemes achieve median OLT reduction higher than 50ms relative to *Type*. Though we find higher benefits for the Beyond1K pages, we also see latency savings of more than 35ms for 14% of the Top1K pages as well, with as much as 71ms for the tail page. We have also verified the statistical significance of our results using the MWW test.

To better understand these results, and when different schemes are most helpful, we analyze the page composition into objects in 4 categories as follows – (i)*HCJ* and Non-*HCJ* objects; and (ii) required for Onload (*BO*) or not (*AO*). Figure 11(a) shows the composition of objects in these 4 categories for two example pages where *OLDep* and *OLType* show benefits over *Type*. In general, the benefits with these schemes depend both on the EHR, and the composition of the page, among other factors.

When do *OLType* and *OLDep* perform better than *Type*? Both *OLType* and *OLDep* prioritize objects before Onload. For *www.att.com*, the EHR is sufficiently high that all *BO* objects may be placed in the edge, hence both *OLType* and *OLDep* prioritize all *BO* objects to the edge. However, *Type* prioritizes *HCJ* objects (agnostic of whether they were required for Onload) over Non-*HCJ BO* objects, and is unable to accommodate all Non-*HCJ BO* objects at the edge. Indeed, Figure 11(b) confirms that for this page, *OLType* and *OLDep* perform better than *Type*. Note that the two schemes themselves perform comparably - this makes sense due to the high EHR both schemes are able to place all *BO* objects in the edge.

Interestingly, we observed many other pages where *Type* performs comparably to *OLType* and *OLDep* even though it is not able to place all Non-*HCJ BO* objects in the edge. On further analysis, we found that the Non-*HCJ* objects were leaves in the dependency graph for these pages – consequently, the performance with *Type* was relatively unaffected even though these objects were not placed in the edge. In contrast, for pages like *www.att.com* some of the Non-*HCJ* objects were internal nodes in the dependency graph, in the sense that a lot of object fetches were dependent on these objects (delaying the internal Non-*HCJ* objects delays a lot of other objects being fetched). For example, in *www.att.com* some of the Non-*HCJ* internal nodes were *sprited images* and the execution of JS code waits on these images. As a result, delaying these images delays all the objects to be fetched after executing the JS code. Thus careful placement of the internal Non-*HCJ* objects was particularly important to reduce the page latencies.

When does *OLDep* perform better than *OLType*? For *www.conduit.com*, 93% of the objects are required before Onload with more *HCJ BO* objects (60%) than can fit in the edge. While both *OLDep* and *OLType* prioritize *HCJ BO* objects, *OLDep* makes finer-grained distinctions, and prioritizes objects at the highest levels of the dependency graph, which are more critical for latency. Indeed, Figure 11(c) confirms that *OLDep* performs better than *OLType* for this

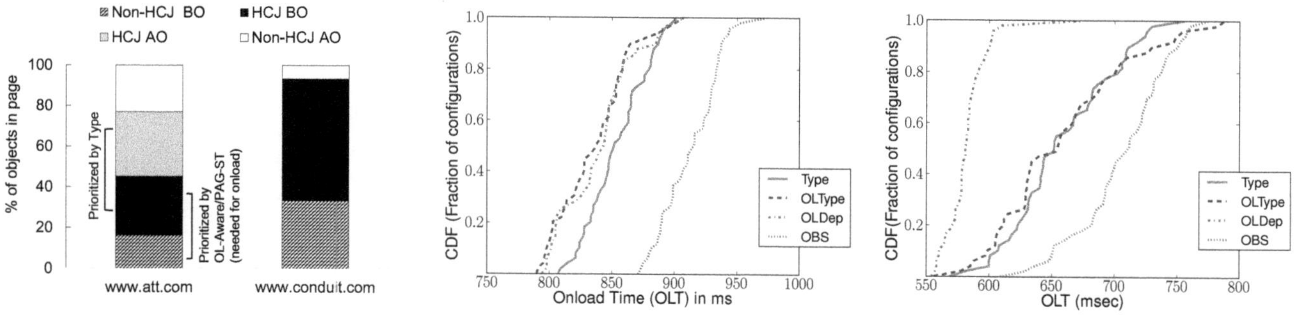

(a) Percentage of objects in each category (b) OLTs for *www.att.com* (EHR 84%) (c) OLTs for *www.conduit.com* (EHR 20%)

Figure 11: Impact of page composition on the relative performance of schemes

page. *OLType* and *Type* perform similar - this is because there are only a few *HCJ* AO objects and hence *OLType* and *Type* are choosing from relatively the same set of objects to place in the edge. More generally, *OLDep* also provides benefits over *OLType* for pages where all *HCJ BO* but not all *BO* objects fit in the edge, and some Non-*HCJ BO* objects are internal nodes in the dependency graph.

Finally, we found rare cases where *OLDep* performs worse than *Type*, when objects deeper in the dependency graph have more impact on the OLT than the objects closer to the root in the graph. For example, in *www.comcast.com*, a JS object (appearing as a leaf in the dependency graph) had a larger impact on the OLT owing to its higher execution times than other internal Non-*HCJ* objects, while *Type* placed all *HCJ* objects at the edge. While prioritizing objects occurring consistently on the critical path across runs (and clients) may help, determining such objects is not trivial, and we did not explore such a technique in depth given the small number of occurrences.

5.3 Comparing proactive refresh strategies

In this section, we fix the placement scheme as *OBS*, and compare the performance of various proactive refresh strategies described in §4. Since proactive refresh strategies differ only in their handling of refresh misses, we confine this study to only those pages(61 pages) that saw at least one stale access in the real page-load. Figure 12(a) shows that all strategies give significant latency reductions relative to *OBS*. For the vast majority of pages, the schemes perform similarly, though there are a small number of pages where *BO* and *All* perform better. Interestingly, we also find that the *HCJ BO* scheme performs similar to *HCJ* while incurring lesser bandwidth costs.

When does *BO* perform better than *HCJ*? We illustrate this using one of the pages *www.mercurynews.com*, where *BO* performs better than *HCJ*. Figure 12(b) shows the CDF of OLTs observed with each of the proactive refresh strategies. Clearly, all refresh schemes perform better than None, while *BO* performs even better than *HCJ* (and *HCJ BO*). We note that the page observed multiple refresh misses for Non-*HCJ BO* objects in the higher levels (L 9-14) of the dependency graph as shown in Figure 12(c). These objects have further dependent objects (in L15), and impacts the critical path of the page-load. Therefore, the *BO* scheme, which proactively refreshes all objects needed for Onload (including Non-*HCJ BO* objects), provides significant latency reductions.

Overall our results show that (i) *HCJ* suffices in most cases, though *BO* can provide further latency reduction for some pages; (ii) *BO* itself gives all the benefits of *ALL* with lower bandwidth costs; and (iii) *HCJ BO* provides comparable benefits to *HCJ* with lower bandwidth costs.

5.4 Sensitivity to origin TTFB

In this section, we achieve two goals. First, we evaluate the benefits achievable by considering factors other than content type in both placement and proactive refresh strategies together. Second, we study the sensitivity of the observed latency reductions with our schemes to heterogeneity in TTFBs for fetching objects. We focus on the TTFB to origin servers since they show the highest variability and have the highest impact on the page-load latency. Therefore, we conduct the sensitivity study by varying the TTFB to the highest layer retaining the same values for the other cache layers (used in §5). We compare *OLDep*:*BO* with *OBS* for three different ratios of *CDN* edge to origin server TTFBs viz. $1:4$, $1:8$ and $1:16$ (rounded-off) representing the $25th$, median and $75th$ percentiles respectively from the real downloads (see §2). Note that the ratio used in all our prior experiments (§5) is $1:8$.

Figure 13 shows the reduction in median OLT with *OLDep*:*BO* compared to *OBS* split by pages in Alexa Top1K and Beyond1K classes. Clearly, *OLDep*:*BO* which combines both placement and proactive refresh provides significant benefits – with $1:8$, the median latency reduction is $> 100ms$ for 30% of the Top 1K pages and $> 100ms$ for 59% of the Beyond 1K pages. As expected, the benefits with prioritization increases with larger origin TTFB. Interestingly, the benefits are higher for both the Top1K and Beyond1K pages when the origin TTFB is high (ratio $1:16$). For instance, the median OLT reduction for 50% of the Beyond1K pages is about $2X$ higher with $1:16$ than $1:8$, while for 50% of the Top1K pages we see almost $3X$ higher reduction with $1:16$ than $1:8$. Though not shown, the reduction in median OLT with *OLDep*:*BO* was as much as $> 1s$ for $1:16$ (and $586ms$ for $1:8$) at the tail.

We now study the relative benefits of *OLDep*:*BO* over *Type*:*HCJ*, with the various edge to origin ratios. Figure 14 shows a CCDF of the reduction in median and $90\%ile$ OLTs with *OLDep*:*BO* over *Type*:*HCJ* for all pages. The figure shows that the latency benefits of *OLDep*:*BO* over *Type*:*HCJ* increases with higher ratios. The trends hold for reductions in both the median and $90\%ile$ OLTs, with reductions in the median OLTs as high as $700ms$ for *www.mercurynews.com* which had many Non-*HCJ* refresh misses. Overall our results show that *OLDep*:*BO* gives higher benefits over *Type*:*HCJ* for pages at the tail, especially when the TTFB to origin is high.

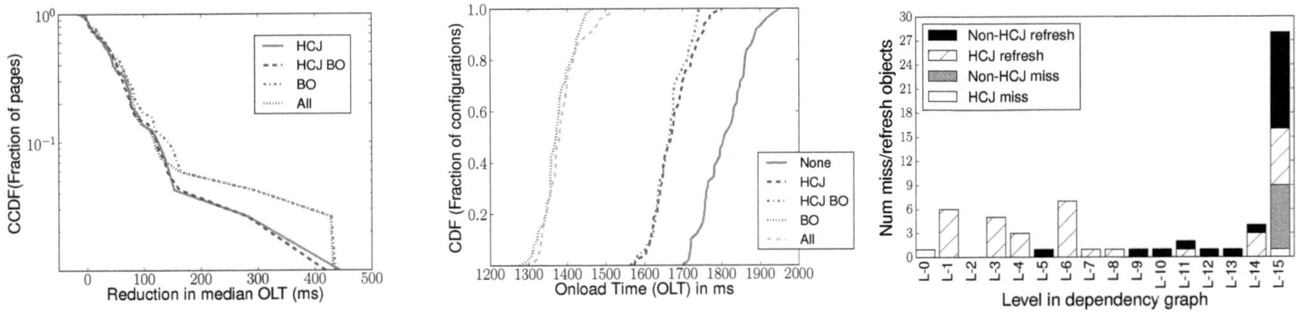

(a) CCDF of the median reduction in OLT relative to *OBS* with Y-Axis in log scale.

(b) OLTs for *www.mercurynews.com* with different refresh strategies.

(c) Composition of misses at each level of the dependency graph for *www.mercurynews.com*

Figure 12: Latency reduction with proactive refresh. All schemes use the *OBS* placement.

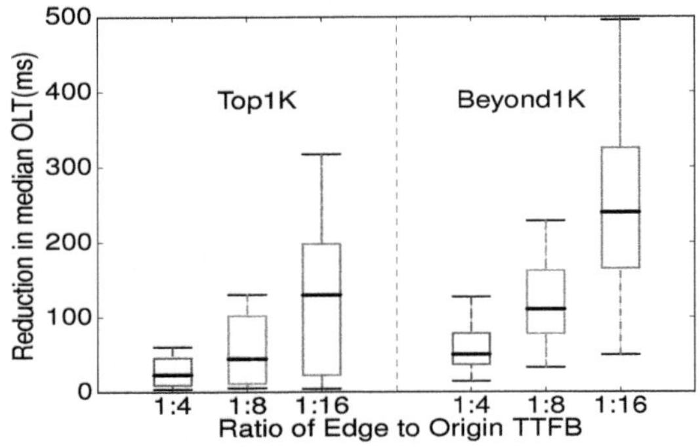

Figure 13: Median OLT reduction with *OLDep:BO* over *OBS* with three different edge to origin TTFB ratios split by Alexa Top1K and Beyond1K. The boxes show the 25th, 50th and 75th and the whiskers showing the 10th and 90th percentile pages.

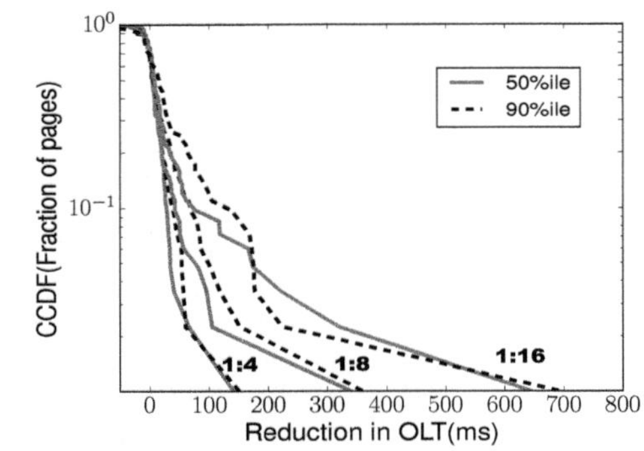

Figure 14: CCDF of the reduction in 50%*ile* and 90%*ile* OLTs for all pages with *OLDep:BO* over *Type:HCJ* for the three edge to origin TTFB ratios

6 Trace-driven evaluation

In this section, we conduct trace-driven simulations for evaluating the feasibility of priority-based caching and proactive refresh in CDNs. The request traces for this study were obtained from the edge cluster of a real CDN deployment, which serves a wide class of web traffic, and consists of 162 million requests for about 13.5 million distinct objects. The week long trace is non-sampled and consists of all client requests observed at each of the 18 servers in the edge cluster. For all simulations in this section, we set the cache capacity to those seen in the real deployment. Since the page structure (dependencies) and *Onload* information is not deducible from the trace, we use content-type based prioritization, and focus on miss-rate reduction (and bandwidth overhead) for all experiments in this section.

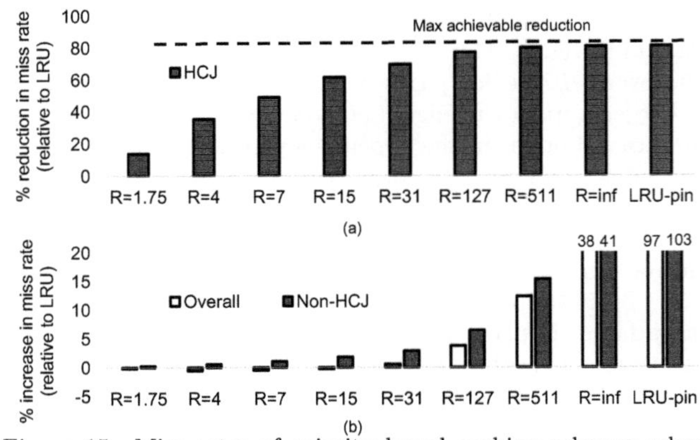

Figure 15: Miss rates of priority based caching schemes when compared to LRU(Size), and LRU-Pin.

6.1 Feasibility of priority based caching policy

We first show the feasibility of our approach in reducing the miss rate for the critical objects without significantly affecting the overall hit rates of the caches. We emulate the cache using our week-long trace for two caching algorithms - our priority-based caching described in §3.2, and (ii) LRU(size) - LRU with a size threshold, that is commonly employed by CDNs today. We evaluate our algorithm by varying the relative importance of the *HCJ* and Non-*HCJ* objects, which is captured by the parameter R, the ratio of the priority of *HCJ* objects to the priority of Non-*HCJ* objects. We also compare our algorithm with a variant of LRU which preferentially pins the *HCJ* objects to the cache and ensures that they are never evicted by a Non-*HCJ* object. However, *HCJ* objects may evict Non-*HCJ* objects and other *HCJ* objects similar to LRU. We use the same cache size and object-size threshold used by the LRU across all the schemes.

Figure 15(a) shows the reduction in miss rates for the *HCJ* objects for the different schemes relative to the miss rates observed with the LRU(size). The horizontal line at the top of the graph shows the maximum achievable reduction in miss rates, where the rest of the misses are compulsory misses in our trace. Figure 15(b) shows the corresponding increase in the overall miss rate as well as in the miss rate for Non-*HCJ* objects. From the figure, we see that as R increases, the reduction in miss rate for *HCJ* objects ramps up quickly for smaller R (flattens out at higher R), while the increase in miss rate for Non-*HCJ* objects increases gradually for smaller R and more rapidly for higher R. This shows the opportunity for the CDN to tune R, such that, it reduces

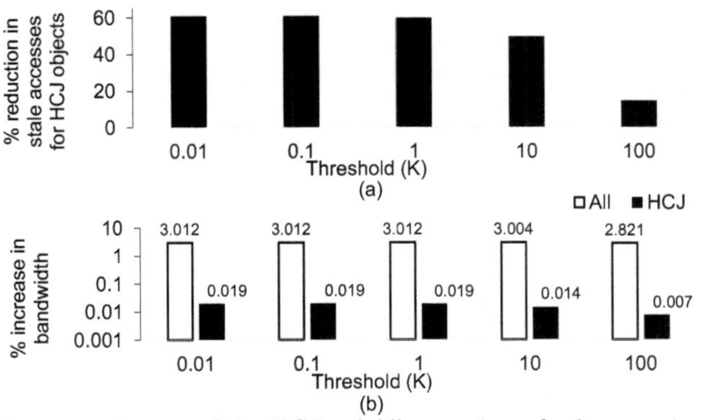

Figure 16: Impact of the *HCJ* and All proactive refresh strategies. Note that both schemes reduce stale accesses for HCJ objects by identical amounts.

the miss rate for *HCJ* objects without increasing the overall miss rate of the cache. In our trace, this occurs close to $R = 15$, which reduces the miss rate for *HCJ* objects by 61% without increasing the overall miss rate. We also see that while LRU-pin performs the best for *HCJ* objects, it drastically affects the overall miss rates. Our results show that our priority based caching scheme is able to significantly reduce the miss rates for *HCJ* objects, while incurring only a modest increase in the overall miss rate.

6.2 Bandwidth impact of proactive refresh schemes

We now show the benefits of prioritization in reducing the additional bandwidth costs associated with proactive refreshing. Since our traces do not have *Onload* information for objects, we focus our evaluation in this section on the *HCJ* and *All* proactive refresh schemes. We augment our priority-based caching algorithm with proactive refreshing as described in §3.3 and emulate the cache with our week long traces. In all our experiments, we set the threshold $T = 2$ (for just-in-time refreshes), but vary the parameter K for the *HCJ* objects to illustrate the bandwidth-cost and performance trade-off with conservative and aggressive proactive refreshing. Figure 16 compares the percentage reduction in stale accesses for *HCJ* objects, and the corresponding increase in bandwidth incurred with both the schemes. Note that the bandwidth costs estimated here are an upper bound since entire objects need not be fetched again if they are not modified at the origin, but that information is not available to us in the trace. The figure shows that both All and *HCJ* schemes reduce stale accesses for *HCJ* objects by 60%, while incurring an overall bandwidth increase of 3% and 0.02% respectively. Note that a smaller K (aggressive refreshing) results in fewer stale accesses, while a larger K (conservative refreshing) lowers the bandwidth costs of proactive refreshing. Overall, our results highlight the opportunity for priority-based proactive refresh in significantly reducing staleness for *HCJ* objects, while incurring only modest bandwidth penalties.

7 Related work

While SPDY [19] allows resource prioritization, it supports only priority based processing (and transmission) of objects from the server to a client [5]. Recent work [12] looks at re-prioritizing delivery of objects in a web page when they are pushed from a server to a mobile client. In contrast, our focus is on an orthogonal problem – enabling priority awareness within the CDN infrastructure. All our experiments including the *OBS* baseline are run with SPDY enabled, and our benefits are complementary to SPDY. Recent research has shown that SPDY is not always beneficial [17, 37]. Our proposals in this paper do not rely on SPDY - incorporating priority awareness in CDNs has benefits even with HTTP.

Our work builds on the rich literature on caching algorithms for web caches, proxy caches and CDNs (e.g., [6, 8, 9, 13, 24, 35, 39]). We adapt the well known Greedy-Dual-Size algorithm [13] which considers how to balance locality of access patterns with object size and the variable costs associated with fetching objects on a miss, given some network paths could be more expensive than others. Others have extended the algorithm to more explicitly bias it towards more popular objects [8, 24]). In contrast to all these works, our focus is on determining the importance of an object within a page for lowering page latency, and balancing object popularity and priority.

Prefetching to reduce web latencies has been extensively studied since the earliest days of the web (e.g., [29]). Many of the early works focused on client-side prefetching (e.g., [29]) in which clients initiate prefetching guided by predictions on which files are likely to be accessed soon (e.g., based on models that indicate which hyper-links a client is likely to click when on a given page [29]). Others [23, 25, 34, 40] have investigated prefetching in CDNs and proxy servers by using global access patterns to identify which objects should be proactively replicated to caches. While we leverage these techniques, we consider the more limited goal of avoiding refresh misses on objects already in the cache by proactively refreshing them. Further, we seek to proactively refresh objects that are more important for reducing page latencies, given refresh misses are a key component of overall miss rates for popular pages.

Researchers have explored how objects must be placed in a hierarchical caching system [15, 26, 32, 33] so that the average latencies are minimized given constraints on cache capacities [26] or bandwidth [33]. [32] propose mechanisms to improve end user response times by tracking the data location and minimizing the number of hops on hits and misses within the CDN hierarchy. In contrast, our focus is on placement of objects taking priority into account - specifically, objects that are not as popular may be placed lower in the hierarchy since they may be critical for page-load.

8 Conclusions

In this paper, we have made two contributions. First, we have shown that there is significant potential to reduce webpage latencies through page-structure-aware strategies for placing objects in CDN cache hierarchies. Second, we have presented several strategies to this end which differ in their degree of page-awareness, and conducted a detailed evaluation study of their benefits. Our evaluations with more than 80 real-world web pages show that for popular pages, more than 30% of pages see median OLT reductions higher than $100ms$, while for less popular pages, the median OLT reduction is more than $100ms$ for more than 59% of the pages, with some pages showing latency reductions as high as $500ms$. Both placement and proactive refreshing are important in achieving the benefits, though each can help in isolation. For the vast majority of pages, the *Type*:*HCJ* scheme provides most of the benefit. However, *OLDep*:*BO* can provide significant additional benefits for some pages, especially in lower hit rate regimes, when there are Non-

HCJ internal nodes in the dependency graph, and when the penalty of going to the origin is higher. Finally, using trace driven simulations, we show the feasibility of priority-based caching approach to reduce miss rates of page-critical objects in CDNs by 60% with minimal increase in overall miss rates. We also highlight the opportunity of minimizing staleness related misses for objects critical for latency by as much as 60% while incurring additional bandwidth costs of less than 0.02%.

9 Acknowledgements

We thank the anonymous reviewers for their constructive feedback and comments. We also thank Mangesh Kasbekar for his valuable inputs during discussions. This work was supported in part by the National Science Foundation (NSF) under Career Award No. 0953622, Award No. CCF-1535972, NSF Award Numbers 1162333, 1345284, and USAF Award FA8750-14-2-0150. Any opinions, findings and conclusions or recommendations expressed in this material are those of the authors and do not necessarily reflect the views of NSF or USAF.

10 References

[1] Chrome command-line switches. http://goo.gl/7t5nk5.
[2] Google Speed-index. https://goo.gl/TKMJTw.
[3] RAMDisk for faster browsing. http://goo.gl/qtbDTe.
[4] SPDY best practices. http://goo.gl/fPczq3.
[5] SPDY Protocol(draft3)-stream-priority. http://goo.gl/5PH7UH.
[6] M. Abrams et al. Caching proxies: Limitations and potentials. 1995.
[7] Alexa. Available at http://www.alexa.com/topsites.
[8] M. Arlitt et al. Performance evaluation of web proxy cache replacement policies. Technical report, 1998.
[9] J.-C. Bolot et al. Performance engineering of the world wide web: Application to dimensioning and cache design. *Computer Networks and ISDN Systems*, 1996.
[10] M. Butkiewicz et al. Understanding website complexity: measurements, metrics, and implications. In *Proc. of the ACM IMC*, 2011.
[11] M. Butkiewicz et al. Enabling the transition to the mobile web with websieve. In *Proc. of the ACM HotMobile*, 2013.
[12] M. Butkiewicz et al. Klotski: Reprioritizing web content to improve user experience on mobile devices. In *Proc. of the USENIX NSDI*, 2015.
[13] P. Cao et al. Cost-aware www proxy caching algorithms. In *Proc. of the USENIX USITS*, 1997.
[14] A. Chankhunthod et al. A hierarchical internet object cache. In *Proc. of the USENIX ATC*, 1996.
[15] H. Che et al. Hierarchical web caching systems: Modeling, design and experimental results. *IEEE Journal on Selected Areas in Communications*, 2002.
[16] J. Dean et al. The tail at scale. *Communications of the ACM*, 2013.
[17] J. Erman et al. Towards a SPDY'ier mobile web? In *Proc. of the ACM CoNEXT*, Dec 2013.
[18] B. Forrest. Bing and google agree: Slow pages lose users. http://goo.gl/BNjh3G, 2009.
[19] Google. SPDY: An experimental protocol for a faster web. http://goo.gl/vy63I4.
[20] J. Hamilton. The cost of latency. http://goo.gl/26j6S6, 2009.
[21] T. Hoff. Latency is everywhere and it costs you sales-how to crush it. http://goo.gl/T4vqjZ, 2009.
[22] S. Ihm et al. Towards understanding modern web traffic. In *Proc. of the ACM IMC*, 2011.
[23] Y. Jiang et al. Web prefetching: Costs, benefits and performance. In *Proc. of the 7th international WCW workshop. Boulder, Colorado*, 2002.
[24] S. Jin et al. Popularity-aware greedy dual-size web proxy caching algorithms. In *Proc. of the IEEE ICDCS*, 2000.
[25] R. Kokku et al. A non-interfering deployable web prefetching system. In *Proc. of the USENIX USITS*, 2002.
[26] M. R. Korupolu et al. Coordinated placement and replacement for large-scale distributed caches. *IEEE TKDE*, 2002.
[27] Z. Li et al. Webprophet: Automating performance prediction for web services. In *Proc. of the USENIX NSDI*, 2010.
[28] H. B. Mann et al. On a test of whether one of two random variables is stochastically larger than the other. *The annals of mathematical statistics*, 1947.
[29] V. N. Padmanabhan et al. Using predictive prefetching to improve world wide web latency. *ACM SIGCOMM CCR*, 1996.
[30] S. Souders. Onload event and post-onload requests. http://www.stevesouders.com/blog/2012/10/30/qa-nav-timing-and-post-onload-requests.
[31] S. Souders. Velocity and the bottom line. http://goo.gl/SaaVvv, 2009.
[32] R. Tewari et al. Design considerations for distributed caching on the internet. In *Proc. of the IEEE ICDCS*, 1999.
[33] A. Venkataramani et al. Bandwidth constrained placement in a wan. In *Proc. of the ACM Symposium on PODC*, 2001.
[34] A. Venkataramani et al. The potential costs and benefits of long-term prefetching for content distribution. *Computer Communications*, 2002.
[35] J. Wang. A survey of web caching schemes for the internet. *ACM SIGCOMM CCR*, 1999.
[36] X. S. Wang et al. Demystify page load performance with wprof. In *Proc. of the USENIX NSDI*, 2013.
[37] X. S. Wang et al. How Speedy is SPDY? In *Proc. of the USENIX NSDI*, April 2014.
[38] web-page replay. Record and play back web pages with simulated network conditions. https://www.code.google.com/p/web-page-replay/.
[39] R. P. Wooster et al. Proxy caching that estimates page load delays. *Computer Networks and ISDN Systems*, 1997.
[40] B. Wu et al. Objective-optimal algorithms for long-term web prefetching. *IEEE Transactions on Computers*, 2006.

Optimizing TTL Caches under Heavy-Tailed Demands

Andrés Ferragut
Universidad ORT Uruguay
ferragut@ort.edu.uy

Ismael Rodríguez
Universidad ORT Uruguay
rodriguez_i@ort.edu.uy

Fernando Paganini
Universidad ORT Uruguay
paganini@ort.edu.uy

ABSTRACT

In this paper we analyze the hit performance of cache systems that receive file requests with general arrival distributions and different popularities. We consider timer-based (TTL) policies, with differentiated timers over which we optimize. The optimal policy is shown to be related to the monotonicity of the hazard rate function of the inter-arrival distribution. In particular for decreasing hazard rates, timer policies outperform the static policy of caching the most popular contents. We provide explicit solutions for the optimal policy in the case of Pareto-distributed inter-request times and a Zipf distribution of file popularities, including a compact fluid characterization in the limit of a large number of files. We compare it through simulation with classical policies, such as least-recently-used and discuss its performance. Finally, we analyze extensions of the optimization framework to a line network of caches.

1. INTRODUCTION

Caching systems are widely deployed in computer networks to improve performance. By storing frequently requested content near end users, latency and access time are reduced and a lighter load is imposed on network resources. In recent years, with the exponential growth in available content in the Internet, caching has become an integral component of network architectures. Content Delivery Networks (CDNs) have become the standard approach used by content providers to serve large client populations. Current trends take this point further, using terms such as Content-Centric Networking (CCN) [21] or Information-Centric Networking (ICN) [1] to describe architectures designed to connect end users directly to content instead of a traditional server.

With the advent of these new technologies, there is a renewed interest in the performance analysis of caching systems, which has old roots in studies of CPU processing and memory paging [28]. Most models for cache performance analysis fall into two categories; the first are *replacement policies*, where a finite amount of memory is actively administered to maintain the most requested contents at hand. Within these, the Least-Frequently-Used (LFU) policy is known to be optimal under independent requests, albeit requiring a large state. A simpler algorithm is the Least-Recently-Used (LRU) policy [11,28], where upon arrival of a new request not presently stored, the object not requested for the longest time is evicted from the cache. Exact analysis of this policy has proven difficult, even with simple traffic models such as the *independent reference model (IRM)*, where successive requests are assumed independent and stationary. Further references on LRU models are given in Section 2.

Another class of cache management algorithms are *timer based* policies (Time-to-live, TTL). In this case the eviction of a file from the cache is performed after the expiration of some timer, which is independently set upon arrival of requests for each content. The main advantage of these policies is that eviction is decoupled amongst objects, thus simplifying analysis of the system. This simple policy also guarantees weak consistency, providing a bound on the storage of outdated content, which is the reason why it has been implemented in DNS systems and Web caching. The main disadvantage is that now memory usage can only be bounded on average. Another important point is that TTL caches with fixed timers can be used to approximate the behavior of the LRU system, as pointed out by Che et. al in [10]. This approximation procedure has been further developed in recent papers which we review in Section 2.

In this paper we study the *optimal* TTL policy for a cache, in the sense of maximizing the hit rate obtained, over the choice of timer parameters. Building upon the models in [5,16,29] and with very general hypotheses on the request arrival processes, we formulate the optimal timer policy as a nonlinear optimization program in Section 3. The key characteristic behind the structure of the optimal policy turns out to be the *hazard rate* function of the inter-request times. For the simple case where arrivals come from a Poisson process (constant hazard rate), it is well known that the optimal policy is to statically store the most popular files. A first contribution of this paper is to show that this holds as well for any interarrival distribution with *increasing* hazard rate. The most interesting case is, however, when hazard rates are *decreasing*; here the optimization problem can be transformed into a convex program, and the optimal policy characterized as choosing timer values that *equalize* the hazard rates of the stored contents. This implies in particular that the static policy (and hence, the LFU policy) is not always optimal. These results are described in Section 4.

SIGMETRICS '16, June 14-18, 2016, Antibes Juan-Les-Pins, France
© 2016 ACM. ISBN 978-1-4503-4266-7/16/06...$15.00
DOI: http://dx.doi.org/10.1145/2896377.2901459

The decreasing hazard rate case is important because it appears when inter-request distributions are heavy tailed, a typical model of bursty behavior. In Section 5 we develop this case in detail, assuming Pareto inter-arrival times, in combination with a Zipf power-law distribution for file popularities, also a commonly used model. The optimal policy is identified as a function of the tail parameters, where in particular no contents are permanently cached. A streamlined characterization of this optimal policy in the case of large number of files is obtained through a fluid limit, with explicit analytic expressions in terms of the model parameters. In particular, we show that the maximal hit rate achievable by TTL policies is strictly less than 1 for power-law popularities with tail parameter $\beta < 1$. For the case $\beta \geq 1$, we show that the maximal hit rate approaches 1 and that also the static policy is asymptotically optimal. We also analyze the memory usage of the TTL policy, showing through a law of large numbers that the cache operates close to its average capacity.

In Section 6 we evaluate the performance of the optimal TTL policies by simulation experiments. We validate our results and analyze the speed of convergence to the asymptotic limits. We also provide a practical variant of the TTL policy that enforces constant memory usage, with small deviations from the ideal case. Comparisons with static (LFU) policies as well as LRU replacement policies are carried out. The main observation is that both classical policies may be suboptimal, but each performs well in a certain regime which we can characterize through the hazard rate function of the request process.

In Section 7 we include some generalizations. In the first place we discuss how to generalize our optimization framework to consider timers which are themselves random, in particular exponentially distributed. We also investigate the situation of a line of caches, where contents displaced from one are moved upstream to the next. In the exponential and deterministic timer cases, we show how this situation can be analyzed through an appropriate Markov model, and results are given on how to optimize performance.

Conclusions are provided in Section 8. Some of the proofs can be found in the extended version of this paper [13].

2. BACKGROUND AND RELATED WORK

The performance analysis of caching algorithms goes back to the seminal works of [19, 28] on replacement algorithms. Despite the simplicity of replacement policies, analysis becomes complex even for a single cache: in [28], the author gives an explicit expression of the hit probability of the LRU policy, with exponential complexity. In [19], it is shown that under the IRM assumption, similar replacement policies such as first-in-first-out achieve the same hit probability. Since exact computation is intractable, [11] provides an approximate computational procedure, again under the IRM assumption. This method has been further extended recently by [30] to the case of networks of cache systems. In [18], another approach is given for list-based replacement policies.

Another line of work related to our results is the asymptotic characterization of cache performance. A first step in this direction is [14], which addresses the limit cost of the Move-to-Front rule in self-organizing lists. By exploiting the connection between MTF and the LRU policy, [23] provides an asymptotic expression for the hit probability under IRM assumptions and Zipf popularities with parameter $\beta > 1$. These results are extended in [25] to the case $\beta \leqslant 1$ and some LRU generalizations. Following a fundamentally different approach, the same limit result is obtained in [4] by using the Laplace transform of the asymptotic search cost. In our work, we follow a similar limit procedure to characterize the performance of the optimal TTL policies. Going beyond IRM, [22, 24, 26] show some insensitivity properties of LRU in the asymptotic regime, with dependent requests and $\beta > 1$, and also provide conditions for the capacity scaling for such insensitivity to hold. In this paper, we will show that in fact several policies achieve an optimal hit rate in this scenario, but for $\beta < 1$ temporal locality may have an impact.

By far, the most popular technique for analyzing cache performance of LRU under IRM is the so called "Che approximation", introduced in [10] in the context of Web caching. Here, a *characteristic time* is defined for the cache system which amounts to the average eviction time of the files. The authors of [17] provide additional evidence on why the approximation is good through a central limit argument. It turns out that this approximation amounts to choosing a uniform timer to approximate LRU behavior.

The analysis of policies based on timers goes back to [27] who gave expressions for the steady state hit probabilities, later extended in [3] to include update delay. More recently, [15, 16] laid the foundations for analyzing TTL policies under deterministic and random timers with general arrival processes. In [5] the analysis is extended to a family of TTL policies with the focus of approximating LRU performance in linear and tree networks, and a different policy is proposed in [6] with the aim of maximizing hit ratios by variance reduction. In [7] the Che approximation is analyzed in a more general setting and in [29], it is extended, using TTL cache tools, to renewal arrivals, showing good accuracy in the case of small caches and Zipf popularities. In particular, temporal locality in requests is observed to have an impact in cache performance. A reverse engineering approach based on utility maximization links TTL policies with list based ones, as recently shown in [12].

Building upon these models, the main contribution of our paper is to identify the structure of the optimal TTL based policy, give an exact analysis of the asymptotic behavior in the case of heavy tailed arrivals and show that it can outperform static and LRU policies in this setting.

3. SYSTEM MODEL

We now introduce our TTL cache model with the aim of determining the optimal TTL policy. We build on the models of [5, 16, 29] and introduce a unified notation for the system. The main assumption under TTL caches that simplifies analysis is that per content metrics can be dealt with separately. We first derive these metrics and then introduce our definition for the optimal policies.

The main tradeoff we want to analyze in these systems is between the hit probability, which is a property of the arriving requests and how they find the system upon arrival, and the memory occupation in steady state, which is a system property. Following [16], the correct mathematical setting to deal with the analysis of these metrics is the Palm formulation for stationary point process in the line [2], which enables to compute system-wide and job-related measures by conditioning upon arrivals. We follow this approach below to obtain the relevant metrics.

Consider a cache system that receives requests for files or content. Assume that requests for content n arrive into the system as a stationary point process [2] on $\mathbb{R}$ with intensity λ_n. Let $\{\tau_k^{(n)}\}_{k\in\mathbb{Z}}$ denote the arrival times, with the usual numbering convention $\tau_0^{(n)} \leqslant 0 < \tau_1^{(n)}$, and $X_k^{(n)} = \tau_{k+1}^{(n)} - \tau_k^{(n)}$ denote the interarrival times for content n. Define:

$$F_n(t) = P_0^{(n)}\left(X_k^{(n)} \leqslant t\right) \tag{1}$$

the interarrival time distribution in the Palm space of the arrival process, which is independent of k due to stationarity. We have:

$$E_0^{(n)}[X_k^{(n)}] = \int_0^\infty 1 - F_n(t)dt = \frac{1}{\lambda_n}.$$

The TTL policy is as follows: for every arrival k, a timer $T_n \in [0, \infty]$ is chosen; for most of this paper it will be assumed deterministic. Upon arrival of a request, the file is stored in the cache for a time T_n: if the next arrival occurs before T_n then the next request will be a *hit* and the timer is reset. If the interarrival time exceeds T_n the next request will be a *miss*, implying a performance penalty due to the need of retrieving the content from a remote repository.

From the above assumptions, the stationary hit probability is thus:

$$h_n := P_0^{(n)}\left(\tau_1^{(n)} \leqslant T_n\right) = P_0^{(n)}\left(X_0^{(n)} \leqslant T_n\right) = F_n(T_n). \tag{2}$$

From a system perspective, the main concern is cache occupation. Define by $Z_n(t) \in \{0, 1\}$ the stationary process indicating whether content n is stored at time t, i.e.:

$$Z_n(t) = \mathbf{1}_{\{\tau_{k(t)}^{(n)} + T_n > t\}},$$

where $\tau_{k(t)}^{(n)}$ is the last request before time t. The stationary occupation probability is given by $u_n := E[Z_n(t)]$. Due to stationarity, this probability can be computed at time 0 by using the Palm inversion formula [2]:

$$E[Z_n(0)] = \lambda_n E_0^{(n)}\left[\int_0^{\tau_1^{(n)}} Z_n(s)ds\right]$$

Noting that under the Palm space $\tau_0^{(n)} \equiv 0$, $Z_n(s) = \mathbf{1}_{\{T_n > s\}}$ for $s \in [0, \tau_1^{(n)}]$ and therefore:

$$\begin{aligned} u_n = E[Z_n(0)] &= \lambda_n E_0^{(n)}\left[\int_0^{\tau_1^{(n)}} \mathbf{1}_{\{T_n > s\}} ds\right] \\ &= \lambda_n E_0^{(n)}\left[\min\{X_0^{(n)}, T_n\}\right] \\ &= \lambda_n \int_0^{T_n} 1 - F_n(s)ds =: \hat{F}_n(T_n). \end{aligned} \tag{3}$$

Here $\hat{F}_n(t)$ is the well known *residual lifetime* distribution associated to F_n. Equation (3) simply states that the stationary probability u_n of storing the content is just the probability that the time elapsed since the last request is less than the timer T_n.

We are now ready to state the problem: consider a TTL cache system where requests come from independent arrival processes for each file. Let N be the total number of files, each having a popularity q_n stemming from a probability distribution, i.e. $\sum_{n=1}^N q_n = 1$. Without loss of generality, we shall assume that the files are labeled in decreasing order of popularity, i.e. q_n is a strictly decreasing sequence. We assume that the arriving requests for content n form a stationary and simple point process of intensity $\lambda_n = \lambda q_n > 0$. Here $0 < \lambda < \infty$ represents the total request rate into the system. Each content is assigned a timer value $T_n \in [0, \infty]$ possibly dependent on n.

From equation (2), the overall hit rate in the system is given by:

$$H(T_1, \ldots, T_n) := \sum_{n=1}^N \lambda_n F_n(T_n). \tag{4}$$

Suppose now the system should maintain a certain occupation level, due to memory constraints. One way to keep cache occupation at bay is to impose:

$$E\left[\sum_{n=1}^N Z_n(0)\right] \leqslant C,$$

where $C \leqslant N$ is the average memory allocated to the cache. Typically one should have $C \ll N$. Using eq. (3) the above constraint translates into:

$$\sum_n \hat{F}_n(T_n) \leqslant C \tag{5}$$

Therefore, the optimal TTL policy should solve the following optimization in the timer variables $T_1, \ldots, T_N$:

Problem 1 (TTL cache optimization).

$$\max \sum_{n=1}^N \lambda_n F_n(T_n),$$

$$s.t.: \sum_n \hat{F}_n(T_n) \leqslant C.$$

Problem 1 is a non-linear optimization with a non-linear constraint. Note also that typical timer policies that are feasible for Problem 1 include:

- The *static* policy that stores the C most popular contents, i.e. $T_n = \infty$ for $1 \leqslant n \leqslant C$ and $T_n = 0$ otherwise.
- The *homogeneous timer policy*, used in [10, 29] to approximate cache systems operating under the *Least Recently Used (LRU)* replacement algorithm, which amounts to choose $T_n \equiv T_C$ as the solution of:

$$\sum_{n=1}^N \hat{F}_n(T_C) = C \tag{6}$$

We want to characterize the optimal timer policy in terms of the interarrival distribution characteristics. To this end, it is useful to express Problem 1 in terms of the occupation probabilities by performing the change of variables:

$$u_n = \hat{F}_n(T_n) \Leftrightarrow T_n = \hat{F}_n^{-1}(u_n),$$

where $t = \hat{F}_n^{-1}(u) := \inf\{t : \hat{F}_n(t) \geqslant u\}$ is the generalized inverse function. With the change of variables Problem 1 becomes:

PROBLEM 2.

$$\max_{u_n \in [0,1]} \sum_{n=1}^{N} \lambda_n F_n(\hat{F}_n^{-1}(u_n)),$$
$$s.t.: \sum_{n=1}^{N} u_n \leqslant C.$$

Now we are dealing with a non-linear optimization with a linear constraint. We have the following:

LEMMA 1. *Let $F_n(t)$ have a density $f_n(t)$ in its support $[0, F_n^{-1}(1)]$ and define*

$$\eta_n(t) := \frac{f_n(t)}{1 - F_n(t)}, \quad t \in [0, F_n^{-1}(1)). \tag{7}$$

Then:

$$\frac{\partial}{\partial u_n} F_n(\hat{F}_n^{-1}(u_n)) = \frac{1}{\lambda_n} \eta_n \left(\hat{F}_n^{-1}(u_n)\right) = \frac{1}{\lambda_n} \eta_n(T_n). \tag{8}$$

PROOF. From eq. (3) we have that:

$$\frac{\partial}{\partial T_n} \hat{F}_n(T_n) = \lambda_n(1 - F_n(T_n)).$$

Applying the chain-rule and the inverse function theorem to the continuously differentiable function $\hat{F}_n$ we then have:

$$\frac{\partial}{\partial u_n} F_n(\hat{F}_n^{-1}(u_n)) = f_n(\hat{F}_n^{-1}(u_n)) \frac{\partial}{\partial u_n} \hat{F}_n^{-1}(u_n)$$
$$= \frac{f_n(\hat{F}_n^{-1}(u_n))}{\lambda_n(1 - F_n(\hat{F}_n^{-1}(u_n)))},$$

as stated. □

The function $\eta_n(t)$ is the well known *hazard rate* function associated to F_n and will play an important role in what follows.

4. OPTIMAL TIMER POLICY

We now discuss the structure of the optimal TTL policy under further assumptions on the hazard rate function. We begin with the simplest case where arrivals form a Poisson process.

4.1 Constant hazard-rate: the Poisson model

Assume requests for each file arrive according to a Poisson process of intensity $\lambda_n = \lambda q_n$. In this case $F_n(t) = \hat{F}_n(t) = 1 - e^{-\lambda q_n t}$, which is just a restatement of the memoryless property of the exponential distribution. Therefore, the hit and occupation probabilities coincide, $h_n = u_n$, as expected due to the PASTA property of Poisson arrivals. Problem 2 becomes:

$$\max_{u_n \in [0,1]} \sum_{n=1}^{N} \lambda_n u_n,$$
$$\text{s.t.: } \sum_{n=1}^{N} u_n \leqslant C.$$

Since this is a linear program, the solution should be attained at a vertex of the feasible region [8]. Since the weights $\lambda_n = \lambda q_n$ are strictly decreasing it is readily verified that the unique optimum is:

$$u_n^* = 1 \quad \text{for } 1 \leqslant n \leqslant C$$

and 0 otherwise. In the original timer variables, $T_n = \infty$ for the C most popular contents and 0 otherwise, i.e. the optimal policy is the static policy where the C most popular contents are stored. This result is well known in the context of the *independent reference model (IRM)* where the sequence of requests is *iid*. Under Poisson arrivals, the memoryless property ensures this is in fact the case, and thus we recover the static policy in the optimum.

The underlying fact here is that Problem 2 becomes linear because the hazard rate function of the exponential distribution is constant. We now analyze two cases where we deviate from this assumption, and hence of the IRM model.

4.2 The increasing hazard rate case

Assume now that the arrival processes are such that $\eta_n(t)$ is increasing in t within the support (IHR). In this case, once some time t has elapsed since a request it becomes increasingly likely to have a new request for the same file. This is associated with request processes that are in some sense more periodical than the Poisson process. A simple example is when $X_k^{(n)}$ follows an Erlang distribution with $m > 1$ stages, or the extreme case where $X_k^{(n)}$ approaches the deterministic distribution concentrated in $1/\lambda_n$.

Applying Lemma 1, if $\eta_n(t)$ is increasing, then:

$$\frac{\partial h_n(u_n)}{\partial u_n} = \frac{1}{\lambda_n} \eta_n \left(\hat{F}_n^{-1}(u_n)\right)$$

is increasing in u_n, since $\hat{F}_n^{-1}(u_n)$ is also increasing. Therefore, the objective function of Problem 2 is convex.

We are thus faced with *maximizing* a convex function over a convex domain. It is easy to see that also in this case there is a solution at an extremal point of the convex set: if u is not an extremal point, it can be written as a convex combination of two points in the set, and thus the function value should be less that the maximum value at the extremes.[1]

The extreme points of the set are again the static policies where $u_n = 1$ or 0. Since the support of the interarrival and lifetime distributions coincide, $F_n(F_n^{-1}(u_n)) = u_n$ whenever $u_n \in \{0, 1\}$. Therefore, the hit rate at the extreme policies are simply the sum of the arrival rates of the stored files, and again the optimal policy is to store the most popular contents statically. We have thus proved:

THEOREM 1. *Provided that the arrival distributions satisfy the increasing hazard rate (IHR) property, the optimal TTL caching policy defined by Problem 1 is to statically store the C most popular contents.*

In this case, the optimal hit rate is given by:

$$H^* = \sum_{n=1}^{C} \lambda_n. \tag{9}$$

4.3 The decreasing hazard rate case

We now turn our attention to the case where the hazard rates $\eta_n(t)$ are (strictly) decreasing in t (DHR). This assumption implies that after some time t has elapsed, requests are less and less likely to come. This type of interarrival distribution is associated with heavy tailed arrival processes (e.g. Pareto). This constitutes an important case

[1]The optimum is necessarily extremal if the function is strictly convex, which occurs for strictly increasing hazard rates.

in practice, since it can be used to model requests that come in "bursts" separated by a few very long interarrival times.

In this case, due to Lemma 1, the objective function in Problem 2 is strictly *concave* and we thus have a proper convex optimization problem. Let us write the Lagrangian of Problem 2:

$$\mathcal{L}(u,p) = \sum_n \lambda_n F_n\left(\hat{F}_n^{-1}(u_n)\right) - p\left(\sum_n u_n - C\right), \quad (10)$$

where $p \geqslant 0$ is the multiplier associated with the memory constraint. The saddle point conditions for the optimal u^* and the associated multiplier p^* are: $\sum_n u_n^* \leq C$, $p^* \geq 0$,

$$u_n^* = \operatorname*{argmax}_{u_n \in [0,1]} \mathcal{L}(u, p^*) \quad \forall n, \quad (11a)$$

$$p^*\left(\sum_n u_n^* - C\right) = 0. \quad (11b)$$

Applying Lemma 1, we have:

$$\frac{\partial \mathcal{L}}{\partial u_n} = \eta_n\left(\hat{F}_n^{-1}(u_n)\right) - p.$$

A first observation is that, if $C < N$, the multiplier p at the saddle point must be strictly positive, since otherwise $\mathcal{L}$ is increasing in $u_n \in [0,1]$ and therefore $u_n^* = 1 \ \forall n$, violating the constraint. Given this, we have three possibilities:

$$\begin{cases} \eta_n(0) \leqslant p^* & \Longrightarrow \quad u_n^* = 0, \\ \eta_n(0) > p^* \geqslant \eta_n(\infty) & \Longrightarrow \quad \eta_n\left(\hat{F}_n^{-1}(u_n^*)\right) = p^*, \\ \eta_n(\infty) > p^* & \Longrightarrow \quad u_n^* = 1. \end{cases} \quad (12)$$

Expressing these conditions in terms of the original TTL values, we have proved:

THEOREM 2. *Provided that the arrival distributions satisfy the decreasing hazard rate (DHR) property, the optimal TTL caching policy defined by Problem 1 is such that:*

$$\eta_n(T_n^*) \equiv \text{constant} \quad (13)$$

for every n such that $0 < T_n^* < \infty$.

REMARK 1. *The optimality condition* (13) *has the following economic interpretation: $\eta_n(T_n)$ is the marginal utility derived from increasing the timer to $T_n + dt$, since this is the probability that an arrival will occur immediately after T_n. For a given budget, then the optimal allocation is to equalize the marginal gains whenever possible.*

Despite this characterization, it is difficult to give an explicit expression for the timer values without choosing a suitable parametric family for the problem primitives F_n and q_n. We now deal with an important case that can be solved in detail.

5. HEAVY TAILED ARRIVALS AND POPULARITIES.

To obtain further results we now focus on a specific parametric form for the inter-arrival time distributions and file popularities. In both we will consider heavy-tailed distributions, reflecting the burstiness in time of demands for a specific content, and the natural fact that content files have widely disparate popularities. For simplicity we assume from now on that the total arrival rate of requests is $\lambda = 1$, which amounts to a choice of units.

A typical distribution for content popularities is the well known Zipf(β), defined by:

$$\lambda_n = \frac{1}{n^\beta S_N(\beta)}, \quad n = 1, \ldots, N; \quad (14)$$

where for the normalizing constant we are using the notation $S_N(\gamma) := \sum_{m=1}^N \frac{1}{m^\gamma}$.

Note that for $\gamma \in (-\infty, 1)$ when the series diverges we have the equivalent

$$S_N(\gamma) = \sum_{m=1}^N \frac{1}{m^\gamma} \sim \frac{N^{1-\gamma}}{1-\gamma} \quad \text{as } N \to \infty. \quad (15)$$

For the distribution F_n of inter-arrival times in requests for file n, we adopt a Pareto distribution with with parameter $\alpha > 1$, namely:

$$F_n(t) = 1 - \left(\frac{\theta_n}{\theta_n + t}\right)^\alpha.$$

Here θ_n is a scale-parameter, that must satisfy $\lambda_n = \frac{\alpha-1}{\theta_n}$ to be consistent with the mean arrival rate. It follows directly from the definition in (3) that $\hat{F}_n$ is also Pareto, given by:

$$\hat{F}_n(t) = 1 - \left(\frac{\theta_n}{\theta_n + t}\right)^{\alpha-1}.$$

Applying the change of variables of the preceding Section we obtain the convex problem:

$$\max_{u_n \in [0,1]} \sum_{n=1}^N \lambda_n \left[1 - (1-u_n)^{\frac{\alpha}{\alpha-1}}\right], \quad (16)$$

$$\text{s.t.:} \sum_{n=1}^N u_n \leqslant C. \quad (17)$$

We assume as before that $C < N$. Later on we will let the problem size N grow and choose a specific growth rate for $C(N)$.

The Lagrangian of our problem with respect to the capacity constraint is

$$\mathcal{L}(u,p) = \sum_{n=1}^N \left\{\lambda_n \left[1 - (1-u_n)^{\frac{\alpha}{\alpha-1}}\right] - pu_n\right\} + pC,$$

where $p \geqslant 0$. We have

$$\frac{\partial \mathcal{L}}{\partial u_n} = \lambda_n \frac{\alpha}{\alpha-1}(1-u_n)^{\frac{1}{\alpha-1}} - p.$$

As before, at the saddle point $p > 0$, otherwise $u_n = 1 \ \forall n$, which would violate the constraint. Given $p > 0$, we have two possibilities for the optimal u_n^*, corresponding to the two first cases in (12):

$$\begin{cases} \lambda_n \frac{\alpha}{\alpha-1} \leqslant p & \Rightarrow \ u_n^* = 0; \\ \lambda_n \frac{\alpha}{\alpha-1} > p & \Rightarrow \ u_n^* = 1 - \left(\frac{p(\alpha-1)}{\alpha\lambda_n}\right)^{\alpha-1}. \end{cases} \quad (18)$$

In this case, $u_n^* < 1$ always, so it is never optimal to store a file all the time.

Also, at least one file must be stored with positive probability, so the second case in (18) must hold for the largest λ_n, which occurs at $n = 1$; it will continue to hold until a maximum value

$$M := \max\left\{1 \leqslant n \leqslant N : \lambda_n = \frac{1}{n^\beta S_N(\beta)} > p\frac{(\alpha-1)}{\alpha}\right\}, \quad (19)$$

which corresponds to the number of files that are cached a nonzero amount of time in the optimal policy. The remaining files, if any, are never stored. Note that

$$C = \sum_{m=1}^{M} u_m^* < M, \tag{20}$$

so the number of stored files always exceeds capacity. In practice, if capacity is large the system will store all files a positive amount of time ($M = N$), but in a situation of more scarcity it is optimal to store only a number $M < N$ of objects.

5.1 Asymptotic behavior of the optimal policy

A more streamlined representation of the optimal storage policy can be obtained by taking the limit in the problem size, $N \to \infty$, where it is natural to also let the capacity grow, $C_N \to \infty$. A first observation that follows from (20) is that $M_N \to \infty$. This holds regardless of the growth rate of C_N.

From now on we will focus mainly on the case $C_N = cN$, $c < 1$, i.e. the cache size grows linearly with the number of files. We will characterize the asymptotic behavior of the optimal storage policy and the resulting cost. To analyze the growth rate of the resulting M_N we define

$$x_0 := \limsup_{N\to\infty} \frac{M_N}{N}. \tag{21}$$

Clearly from (20) we have $x_0 \in [c, 1]$. The following proposition provides an exact characterization. Its proof can be found in the extended version of this paper [13].

PROPOSITION 1. $x_0 = \min\{\frac{c}{c_{\alpha,\beta}}, 1\}$, *where*

$$c_{\alpha,\beta} := \frac{\beta(\alpha-1)}{1+\beta(\alpha-1)}. \tag{22}$$

Also the lim sup *in* (21) *is an actual limit.*

We thus characterize the optimal fraction of contents that get stored a positive amount of time in the system, in the asymptotic limit. There are two relevant cases, corresponding to those in the preceding example, characterized by the structural threshold $c_{\alpha,\beta} < 1$ defined in (22).

If $c < c_{\alpha,\beta}$, only a strict fraction $x_0 < 1$ of the objects will be cached. If $c > c_{\alpha,\beta}$, then $x_0 = 1$, furthermore in the proof we show that for large N we have $M_N = N$, i.e. it is optimal to cache all contents. In the border case we could have convergence to unit fraction from below, a case we will for simplicity not consider further.

5.1.1 Asymptotic file caching probabilities

Having characterized asymptotically how many objects are cached, we now turn to the fraction of time they must be stored. We begin by recalling the optimal solution policy (18), reproduced below with emphasis on the dependence with N:

$$u_n^{*,N} = \left[1 - \left(\frac{p_N S_N(\beta)(\alpha-1)}{\alpha} n^\beta\right)^{\alpha-1}\right] \mathbf{1}_{\{n \leqslant M_N\}}. \tag{23}$$

In order to characterize its asymptotic behavior in N, we will express this policy in terms of a continuous variable that represents the fraction n/N of the popularity rank. Specifically, define the function $u^{*,N}(x) = u^{*,N}_{\lfloor xN \rfloor}$, $x \in [0, 1]$.

The following theorem characterizes the limiting behavior of this function.

THEOREM 3. *If* $C_N = cN$ *for* $0 < c < 1$, *then as* $N \to \infty$, $u^{*,N}(x)$ *converges pointwise to*

$$u^*(x) = \left[1 - \kappa x^{(\alpha-1)\beta}\right]^+, \tag{24}$$

where $[w]^+ = \max\{w, 0\}$ *and the constant* κ *is such that the following constraint holds:*

$$\int_0^1 u^*(x)dx = c. \tag{25}$$

The proof is given in [13], by distinguishing the two cases present in the previous discussion. In particular it is shown that if $c < c_{\alpha,\beta}$ we have

$$u^*(x) = \left[1 - \left(\frac{x}{x_0}\right)^{\beta(\alpha-1)}\right] \mathbf{1}_{\{x<x_0\}}; \tag{26}$$

on the other hand if $c \geq c_{\alpha,\beta}$ the result spreads over $[0, 1]$:

$$u^*(x) = 1 - (1-c)(1+\beta(\alpha-1))x^{\beta(\alpha-1)}. \tag{27}$$

In Figure 1 below we show the asymptotic optimal policy functions for fixed values of $\alpha = 2$, $\beta = 0.8$ ($c_{\alpha,\beta} \approx 0.44$), and increasing values of the cache size parameter c. For comparison, we also plot the corresponding optimal policy calculated numerically for a catalog of $N = 1000$ files, showing that the approximation is indeed good.

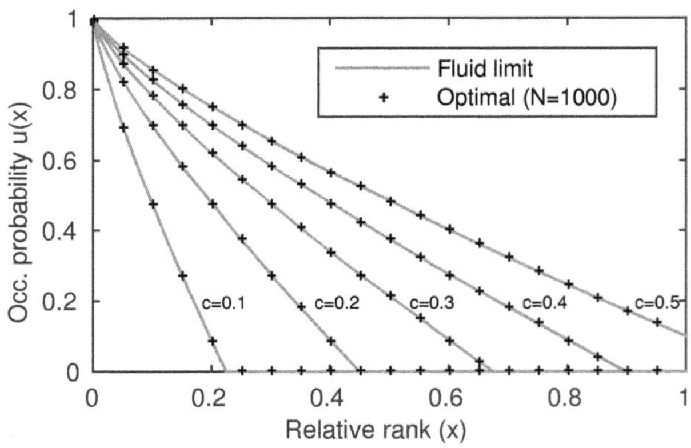

Figure 1: Asymptotic Optimal Policy

5.1.2 Asymptotic optimal cost

We are interested here in finding a limiting expression for large N for the optimal hit probability.

Here a new distinction appears in terms of popularity distribution. The most interesting case is when $\beta < 1$, i.e. the popularities are more heavy-tailed. In that case we will see that the optimal hit probability remains strictly below unity, and can be characterized asymptotically by integrating the optimal law described above. The proof of the following result can be found in [13].

THEOREM 4. *Suppose* $\beta < 1$, *and* $C_N = cN$ *for* $c < 1$. *Then as* $N \to \infty$, *the optimal hit probability converges to*

$$H^* = (1-\beta)\int_0^1 x^{-\beta}\left[1 - (1-u^*(x))^{\frac{\alpha}{\alpha-1}}\right]dx, \tag{28}$$

where $u^*(x)$ is the optimal policy from Theorem 3. In particular:

$$H^* = \begin{cases} \left(\frac{c}{c_{\alpha,\beta}}\right)^{1-\beta} \frac{\alpha\beta}{\alpha\beta+1-\beta}, & c < c_{\alpha,\beta} \\ 1-(1-\beta)(1-c)^{\frac{\alpha}{\alpha-1}}[1+\beta(\alpha-1)]^{\frac{1}{\alpha-1}}, & c \geqslant c_{\alpha,\beta} \end{cases} \quad (29)$$

Suppose we let $\beta \uparrow 1$ in the previous expressions. It is easily verified that we obtain $H^* \to 1$, indicating that the optimal policy becomes efficient when the popularity distribution has lighter tails. Indeed, we show below that this situation holds for $\beta \geqslant 1$, while maintaining the heavy tailed arrivals. Note that in this case the limiting H^* is no longer characterized by an integral of the continuum optimal policy, in particular the integral in (28) would become divergent.

PROPOSITION 2. *Consider a cache system as before with capacity $C_N = cN$, and $\lambda_n = \frac{1}{S_n(\beta)}\frac{1}{n^\beta}$ with $\beta \geqslant 1$. Then the optimal hit rate verifies $H^{*,N} \longrightarrow_N 1$ and moreover the static policy that stores only the C_N most popular contents is asymptotically optimal.*

PROOF. Since the static policy is feasible for Problem 2, we will have:

$$1 \geqslant H^{*,N} \geqslant \sum_{n=1}^{C_N} \lambda_n = \sum_{n=1}^{C_N} \frac{1}{S_N(\beta)}\frac{1}{n^\beta} = \frac{S_{C_N}(\beta)}{S_N(\beta)}.$$

If $\beta > 1$, then $S_N(\beta)$ has a finite limit $\zeta(\beta)$ as $N \to \infty$. Since C_N also goes to infinity we have:

$$\frac{S_{C_N}(\beta)}{S_N(\beta)} \xrightarrow[N]{} 1,$$

which proves this case.

When $\beta = 1$, $S_N(1)$ diverges but we have the well known equivalent $S_N(1) \sim \log(N)$ which upon substitution yields:

$$\lim_N \frac{S_{C_N}(1)}{S_N(1)} = \lim_N \frac{\log(c)+\log(N)}{\log(N)} \to_N 1.$$

□

REMARK 2. *Note that in the case $\beta > 1$, since the tail of the popularities decays fast enough, the same result holds provided $C_N \to \infty$, regardless of the speed of convergence. Therefore, as long as sufficient capacity is allocated in the cache, the hit rate can be made arbitrarily high.*

5.1.3 Some limiting cases

By considering some extreme cases, we can further compare the optimal policy with the static (LFU) case.

REMARK 3. *Suppose the tail parameter of the interarrival times $\alpha \to \infty$. In this case, it is easy to see that $c_{\alpha,\beta} \to 1$, $x_0 \to c$ and the optimal policy converges to $u(x) = \mathbf{1}_{\{x \leqslant x_0\}}$, which amounts to the static most popular policy. In fact, in this case, it is easy to show that the inter-request times converge, as $n \to \infty$ to exponential random variables with parameter λ_n, thus recovering the result of Poisson arrivals.*

REMARK 4. *Suppose that $\beta \to 0$, i.e. the popularities become more and more equal. In this case $c_{\alpha,\beta} \to 0$ and the optimal timer policy from (29) satisfies:*

$$H^* \xrightarrow[\beta\to 0]{} 1-(1-c)^{\frac{\alpha}{\alpha-1}}.$$

Note that $1-(1-c)^{\frac{\alpha}{\alpha-1}} > c$, which will be the hit rate of any static policy that stores a fraction c of the contents. Here the gain of TTL based policies is evident: under bursty arrivals, the timer policy is able to take advantage of the successive requests, enlarging the hit rate. The effect is greater as $\alpha \searrow 1$ (the heavier the tails of the interarrival times).

5.2 Capacity usage of the optimal policy

When using TTL policies, the memory constraint (5) imposes a limit of cache occupation only on average. One concern is that memory usage may overshoot the capacity constraint C by large amounts. We now show how to estimate memory usage and prove that in the asymptotic limit these overshoots are negligible.

Consider the total occupation process, given by $Z^N(t) := \sum_{n=1}^N Z_n(t)$. Under the optimal TTL policy, $E[Z(0)] = \sum_{n=1}^N u_n^{*,N} = C$ by construction. Moreover, since the occupation processes of every file are independent, we have:

$$\mathrm{Var}(Z^N(0)) = \sum_{n=1}^N \mathrm{Var}(Z_n(0)) = \sum_{n=1}^N u_n^{*,N}(1-u_n^{*,N}) \leqslant \frac{N}{4},$$

since each term comes from a Bernoulli random variable. By a direct application of Chebysev's inequality we have the following law of large numbers.

PROPOSITION 3. *Let the buffer size scale as $C_N = cN$ and let $N \to \infty$, then under the optimal TTL policy the occupation process verifies, for every $\delta > 0$:*

$$P\left(Z^N(t) > (1+\delta)C\right) \xrightarrow[N]{} 0.$$

Thus, the relative deviations from the average occupation are negligible in the limit.

By approximating the value of $\sum_{n=1}^N u_n^{*,N}(1-u_n^{*,N})$ by a Riemann integral as in the proof of Theorem 4, we can compute the asymptotic variability of the occupation process.

PROPOSITION 4. *Under the same scaling, the variance of the occupation process under the optimal TTL policy satisfies:*

$$\lim_N \frac{1}{N}\mathrm{Var}(Z^N(0)) = \int_0^1 u(x)(1-u(x))\,dx$$

where $u(x)$ is given by (26) for $c < c_{\alpha,\beta}$ or (27) for $c > c_{\alpha,\beta}$.

The above proposition shows that in fact the variance scales linearly with N. The constant can be readily calculated. For instance, a direct computation of the integral for the case $c < c_{\alpha,\beta}$ yields:

$$\frac{1}{N}\mathrm{Var}(Z^N(0)) \xrightarrow[N]{} \frac{c}{2\beta(\alpha-1)+1}.$$

Analogously, one can solve for $c > c_{\alpha,\beta}$.

6. NUMERICAL EXPERIMENTS

In this Section, we will analyze the performance of the optimal TTL policy in several scenarios, and compare with other policies such as the static policy that stores the most popular files, and the LRU replacement algorithm. We also provide a new approximation for finite N of the optimal hit rate, and provide a variation of the TTL policy that ensures constant memory usage, yet maintains high performance.

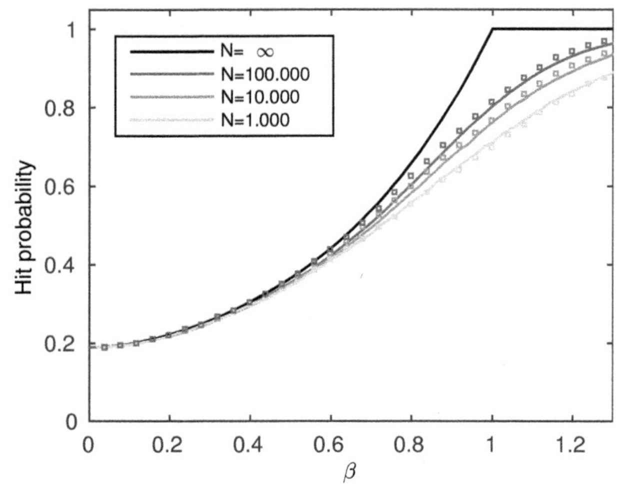

Figure 2: Hit probability as a function of β, asymptotic limit and simulations. $\alpha = 2$, $c = 0.1$.

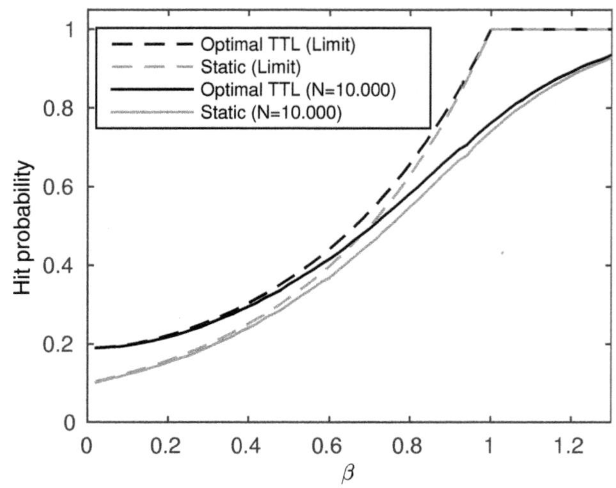

Figure 3: Optimal TTL policy and static policy performance as a function of β. $\alpha = 2$, $\beta = 0.1$.

To evaluate the algorithms, we implemented a discrete-event simulator on Java that emulates cache behavior under different policies (TTL, LRU, Static). The system is fed by general renewal arrival processes of intensity λ_n and total arrival rate $\lambda = 1$. Popularities are chosen as the Zipf(β) distribution as described before. Recall that a typical measured value for the popularity parameter is $\beta = 0.8$ [9].

To implement the optimal TTL policy described in Section 5 in the heavy-tailed case, we first solved the optimization Problem 2 in Matlab using the convex optimization library CVX [20]. Solving for the exact policy in large instances of this problem is computer intensive despite the convex structure. However, numerical trials show that, as long as the catalog size $N > 500$, the optimal occupation probabilities $u_n^{*,N}$ can be well approximated by the fluid limit function $u(x)$ from Theorem 3. Therefore, in our simulations, we simply derive the optimal occupation probabilities from the relative rank of the file and the fluid limit value, and set the timers accordingly. Note that this only requires knowledge of the tail parameters α, β of the distributions involved.

6.1 Convergence of the hit probability

We begin by analyzing the convergence to the limit H^* as the catalog size N grows. We simulated the system for different values of N with varying popularity parameter $\beta \in (0, 1.3)$. Inter-request times follow a Pareto distribution with $\alpha = 2$ and the storage capacity is fixed at $c = 0.1$ (i.e. 10% of the files stored on average). In Figure 2 we plot the simulation results as well as the limit given by equation (29) for $\beta < 1$. For $\beta \geqslant 1$ Proposition 2 shows that $H^* = 1$.

As N grows, the hit probability approaches the computed limit, although it does so slowly for critical values of β. This is not a limitation of approximating the optimal policy by the fluid limit $u(x)$, which indeed shows fast convergence; rather, the issue is the slow convergence of the Riemann sum to the integral in the proof of Theorem 4. Seeking a better estimate for finite N, we computed the difference between rectangular and trapezoidal approximations to the integral in question, and used a more precise approximation of $S_N(\beta)$. This yields the following correction for the hit rate with finite N:

$$H_N^* \approx \frac{(2N)^{1-\beta}}{(2N)^{(1-\beta)} - 1} H^* - \frac{(1+\beta).(2^{-\beta})}{(2N)^{(1-\beta)} - 1}. \tag{30}$$

These approximations are marked in Fig. 2 as boxes, showing that indeed the approximation captures the hit probability for finite N and can be used to predict system performance.

6.2 Comparison with the static policy

In the case of decreasing hazard-rates, it was shown that the optimal TTL policy outperforms the optimal static policy, which is also the limit of the least-frequently-used (LFU) policy in steady state. We now quantify this for the case analyzed in Section 5. Note that, under the same scaling $C_N = cN$, the asymptotic hit probability of the static policy can be computed for $\beta < 1$ as:

$$\lim_N \frac{1}{S_N(\beta)} \sum_{n=1}^{C_N} \frac{1}{n^\beta} = \lim_N \frac{S_{C_N}(\beta)}{S_N(\beta)} = \lim_N \frac{(cN)^{1-\beta}}{N^{1-\beta}} = c^{1-\beta}.$$

where we have used the equivalent in (15). For $\beta \geqslant 1$, Proposition 2 shows that the static policy also achieves maximal hit probability asymptotically.

In Figure 3 we plot the the asymptotic hit rates (dashed lines) as well as simulation results for the case of $\alpha = 2$, varying β. Here and in the remainder of the section we will use for simulations a catalog size $N = 10000$ and a cache size $C = 1000$, ($c = 0.1$). We remark that variations in c were explored as well, but they do not affect the qualitative conclusions which we draw in each case.

The main observation is that, when the arriving requests satisfy the decreasing hazard rate property, the static policy (and hence LFU) is no longer optimal. Indeed, because of its accommodation for traffic burstiness, the TTL policy performs better than the static policy across all ranges of β, with a stronger advantage in the case of more uniform popularities (lower values of β).

6.3 The effect of the hazard-rate on LRU

We now analyze the performance of the LRU policy, which is a popular policy within cache implementations due to its

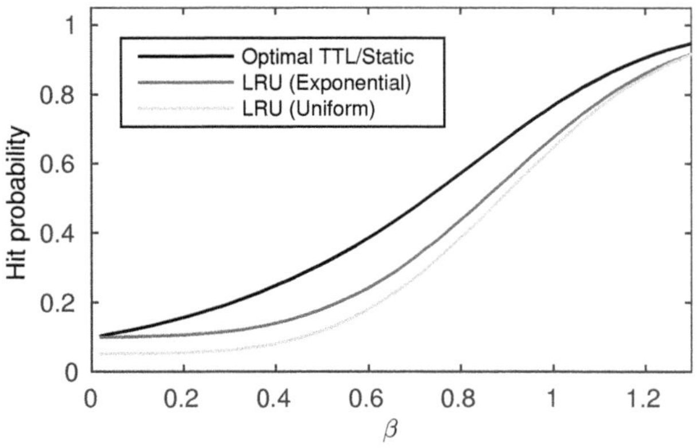

Figure 4: Optimal TTL policy vs. LRU in the Poisson and increasing hazard rate case. $c = 0.1$, $N = 10000$.

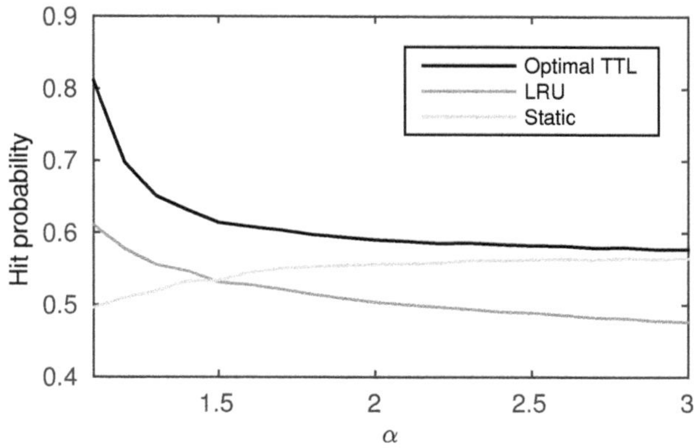

Figure 6: Hit rate of the optimal TTL, LRU and static policies for Pareto inter-request times with varying α. $\beta = 0.8$, $c = 0.1$, $N = 10000$.

simplicity, since it does not require previous knowledge of the request distribution and popularities. It turns out that our analysis based on hazard rates sheds some light on *when* LRU can provide near-optimal performance.

The main point is that LRU can be well approximated by an *homogeneous timer* policy: this is the key idea from Che et al. [10] and recently extended in [29] for general inter-request distributions. The eviction time T_C in LRU is approximately constant and homogeneous across files in a large system, and can be approximated by the solution of eq. (6) as discussed in Section 3. Therefore, in the situations when the optimal TTL policy assigns homogeneous timers, LRU performance should be near-optimal.

As a first example, we consider the constant (Poisson) together with the increasing hazard rate (IHR) case; in both the optimal TTL policy coincides with the static policy. For IHR we used inter-request times following a Uniform distribution in $[0, 2/\lambda_n]$.

Results are shown in Figure 4. In this case LRU is clearly suboptimal, and its deficiency becomes more severe in the IHR case. Note that in both cases, the optimal TTL solution is highly inhomogeneous due to the convexity of the objective function: some files are statically stored and the other ones never are (an extremal point). As in this case requests are more periodical in time, LRU is unable to quickly evict the less popular files once they get stored.

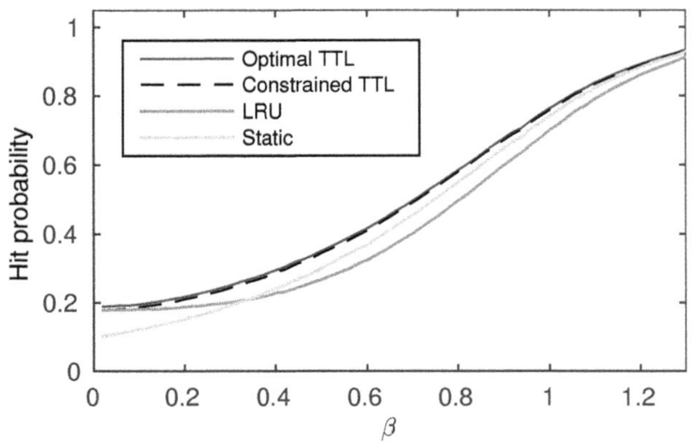

Figure 5: Optimal TTL policy, LRU and static policy for Pareto inter-request times with $\alpha = 2$, $c = 0.1$, $N = 10000$.

The situation is more interesting when inter-request times have the decreasing hazard rate property. In Figure 5 we plot the simulation results for Pareto ($\alpha = 2$) inter-arrival times, comparing the hit rates of LRU, the static policy, and the optimal TTL.

Note that in this case LRU may outperform the static policy. In fact, for lower values of β, LRU achieves near-optimal performance as compared to the TTL policy. An explanation for this lies in the fact that, in the DHR case, the optimal solution tends to equalize the hazard rates of the stored files: as $\beta \searrow 0$, popularities become similar and hazard rates become homogeneous. Therefore, the optimal timer policy has more homogeneous timers, and the LRU policy with its near fixed timer provides near optimal performance. This increase in the performance of LRU over the static policy was already observed in [29] for hyper-exponential distributions (which satisfy the DHR property) in some situations. Note also that in the limit case of Poisson arrivals, the LRU policy also approaches the optimal as $\beta \searrow 0$ in Figure 4.

One could wonder if the TTL's gains over LRU are based on the fact that capacity is imposed only on average, allowing the buffer occupation to go temporarily beyond C. To test this, we implemented also a variation of the optimal policy which we called *constrained TTL*. This is a similar to the Practical TTL policy described in [16] to maintain constant buffer occupation[2]: upon arrival of a request (with the buffer full), the object with the least time remaining in its timer is evicted immediately. If a timer expires, the object is not evicted until a request not present in the buffer arrives, and in that case the object with longest overdue timer is evicted. Thus, the constrained TTL policy maintains constant buffer occupation, and as shown in Figure 5 it achieves close-to-optimal performance.

As a final example, we analyze the performance of LRU against the optimal TTL and static policies with varying tail parameter α and fixed $\beta = 0.8$. As we can see in Fig. 6, as the burstiness of traffic increases ($\alpha \searrow 1$), LRU also outperforms the static policy, by storing temporarily less popular contents but which may be requested again soon,

[2]The main difference with [16] is that here timers are computed following the optimal TTL policy from Theorem 3.

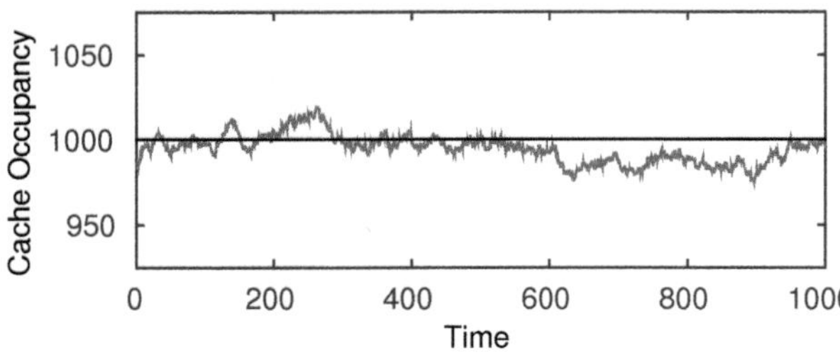

Figure 7: Capacity usage as a function of time for $N = 10000$ and $C = 1000$. Pareto arrivals with $\alpha = 2$ and $\beta = 0.8$.

due to the DHR property. As α grows, we approach the Poisson case as discussed in Section 5.1, and the static policy becomes optimal.

6.4 Capacity usage

Finally, we analyze the steady state memory usage of the optimal TTL policy. In Figure 7, we plot the number of stored objects under the optimal TTL policy as a function of time, for Pareto arrivals with $\alpha = 2$ and popularity parameter $\beta = 0.8$. The catalog and buffer size are the same as before. As expected from Proposition 3, the capacity usage has low overshoot from the average occupation. This also justifies why the Constrained TTL policy performs almost as well as the optimal. Using Proposition 4, one can estimate the occupation variance in this case as $Var(C(t)) \approx 40$, which is in accordance with the simulation.

7. GENERALIZATIONS

In this section we explore two generalizations of the optimal timer based policy characterized by Problem 1. We first analyze the case of exponentially distributed timers, first studied in detail in [16]. We show how to cast the optimal timer policy by writing an optimization problem by means of Laplace transforms. Then we proceed to analyze lines of cache networks, using both exponential and deterministic timers, and show also how to derive a timer based policy with desirable optimality properties.

7.1 Exponential timers

In Section 3 we assumed that timers associated to each file were deterministic. Random timers with general distribution are discussed in [16], in particular the case when $T_k^{(n)} \sim \exp(\mu_n)$. Under this policy, upon arrival of request k for content n, a random timer T_k^n is chosen independently for each arrival, and the file is evicted upon timer expiration as before. The authors of [16] derive the hit probability and occupation probability, which we reproduce here using our notation.

The hit probability for file n in steady state is simply:

$$P_0^{(n)}\left(X_0^{(n)} < T_0^{(n)}\right) = \int_0^\infty e^{-\mu_n x} dF_n(x) = F_n^*(\mu_n),$$

where $F_n^*(s)$ is the Laplace transform of the inter-request time X_0, i.e. $E_0^{(n)}\left[e^{-sX_0}\right]$.

By the same reasoning of Section 3, the occupation probability u_n can be computed as:

$$\begin{aligned} u_n = E[Z_n(0)] &= \lambda_n E_0^{(n)}\left[\min\{X_0^{(n)}, T_0^{(n)}\}\right] \\ &= \lambda_n \int_0^\infty e^{-\mu_n x}(1 - F_n(x))dx \\ &= \int_0^\infty e^{-\mu_n x} d\hat{F}_n(x) =: \hat{F}_n^*(\mu_n), \end{aligned} \tag{31}$$

where in the second equality we used the distribution function of the minimum of two independent random variables, and $\hat{F}_n^*(s)$ is the Laplace transform of the residual lifetime distribution $\hat{F}_n$.

Using these results, the optimal timer policy amounts to choosing the eviction frequencies $\{\mu_n\}$ according to:

PROBLEM 3 (OPTIMAL EXPONENTIAL TTL POLICY).

$$\max_{\mu_n \geqslant 0} \sum_{n=1}^N \lambda_n F_n^*(\mu_n)$$

$$s.t.: \sum_n \hat{F}_n^*(\mu_n) \leqslant C.$$

Problem 3 is different from Problem 1 with deterministic timers, but has a similar structure: instead of the inter-request distributions and their associated residual lifetimes, the corresponding Laplace transforms appear, evaluated at the eviction frequencies instead of the eviction times.

The Laplace transforms F_n^* and $\hat{F}_n^*$ are convex and decreasing functions over the positive real line. This means Problem 3 is seeking to *maximize* a convex function over a convex domain, not a convex optimization program. As argued before, the result should be at the extreme points of the convex set, but in this case this set can be the whole boundary $\sum_n \hat{F}_n^*(\mu_n) = C$.

As in Section 3, one can rewrite this problem in terms of the occupation probabilities, by performing the change of variables $u_n = (\hat{F}_n^*)^{-1}(\mu_n)$, obtaining the analogue of Problem 2:

PROBLEM 4.

$$\max_{u_n \in [0,1]} \sum_{n=1}^N \lambda_n F_n^*((\hat{F}_n^*)^{-1}(u_n)),$$

$$s.t.: \sum_n u_n \leqslant C.$$

In the case of Poisson arrivals, $F_n = \hat{F}_n$ and thus problem reduces to the linear program of Section 4.1, so the solution again degenerates to the static policy, as expected due to the PASTA property. Obtaining more general convexity conditions for general inter-request distributions under the same change of variables proves harder in this case, and will be pursued in future work.

7.2 Infinite line of TTL caches

We now extend our analysis of optimal TTL caching beyond the case of a single cache. Consider instead a line of TTL caches, with requests arriving at one end, and the following management policy: only one copy of each content is stored at some cache k in the line, with $k = 0$ representing the cache that receives external requests. When content n is requested, the object is moved to cache 0 and a timer is started. Upon timer expiration, it is evicted and moved to the next cache in line, where the process is repeated.

This "move to front" rule tends to keep popular objects in the first caches of the line, while less requested content drifts away and is stored further away from the users. Note again that one copy of the file is kept at any point in time.

We first analyze this policy in the case of Poisson arrivals with intensity λ_n and exponentially distributed timers of frequency μ_n. Since each file behaves independently, we begin by modeling the position of each file in the line. For simplicity, we will assume that the line is infinite, but the same analysis can be carried out for finite lines.

Let $L_n(t)$ denote the position of content n in the line over time. It is easy to see that, under the memoryless assumptions above, $L_n(t)$ is a continuous-time Markov chain with state space $k \in \{0, 1, 2, \dots\}$ and transition rates:

$$q_{k,k+1} = \mu_n, \quad q_{k,0} = \lambda_n.$$

This Markov chain is always stable, and by solving its global balance equations it can be shown that its invariant distribution is geometric:

$$\pi_n(k) = P(L_n = k) = \left(\frac{\lambda_n}{\lambda_n + \mu_n}\right)\left(\frac{\mu_n}{\lambda_n + \mu_n}\right)^k.$$

Therefore, the expected search cost of file n, measured by the number of hops needed to retrieve the content, is given in steady state by:

$$E[L_n] = \frac{\frac{\mu_n}{\lambda_n+\mu_n}}{1 - \frac{\mu_n}{\lambda_n+\mu_n}} = \frac{\mu_n}{\lambda_n}. \tag{32}$$

Assume now that caches have an average capacity C. The average occupation of cache k in the line is given by $\sum_n \pi_n(k)$. Since π_n is decreasing in k for each n, the most restrictive cache is the first in the line. Therefore, we can formulate an optimization problem to determine the eviction frequencies that minimize the average search cost:

PROBLEM 5.

$$\min_{\{\mu_n \geqslant 0\}} \sum_{n=1}^N \lambda_n E[L_n] = \sum_{n=1}^N \mu_n,$$

$$s.t.: \sum_{n=1}^N \pi_n(0) = \sum_{n=1}^N \frac{\lambda_n}{\lambda_n + \mu_n} \leqslant C.$$

The above is a convex optimization program that can be readily solved to yield the optimal eviction frequencies.

We now extend the above result to the case of deterministic timers. The key property is to show that the steady state distribution of $L_n(t)$ is again geometric, by using a method of stages. Namely, to model a deterministic timer distribution with value T_n, we divide the level k in S consecutive stages $k_1, \dots, k_S$, each with an exponential timer of parameter $S\mu_n$ and $\mu_n = T_n^{-1}$. With this change, the time in each stage follows an Erlang distribution of parameters S and $S\mu_n$. As the number of stages S grows large, this approximates the deterministic distribution concentrated at T_n, due to the law of large numbers.

This procedure yields a modified Markov chain $\tilde{L}_n(t)$, the state space is now $l \in \{0, 1, 2, \dots\}$ and the set $\{kS \leqslant l < (k+1)S\}$ corresponds to the event $\{L_n = k\}$, i.e. the object is cached in level k of the line. The transition rates for $\tilde{L}_n$ are given by:

$$\tilde{q}_{l,l+1} = S\mu_n, \quad \tilde{q}_{l,0} = \lambda_n,$$

and therefore by the same reasoning as before:

$$\tilde{\pi}_n(l) = P(\tilde{L}_n = l) = \left(\frac{\lambda_n}{\lambda_n + S\mu_n}\right)\left(\frac{S\mu_n}{\lambda_n + S\mu_n}\right)^l.$$

Accumulating this distribution over $\{kS \leqslant l < (k+1)S\}$, the stages of level k, yields again a geometric distribution:

$$\pi_n(k) = P(L_n(t) = k) = P\left(\tilde{L}_n \in \{kS, \dots, (k+1)S - 1\}\right)$$
$$= \left(\frac{\lambda_n}{\lambda_n + S\mu_n}\right)^S \left[\left(\frac{S\mu_n}{\lambda_n + S\mu_n}\right)^S\right]^k.$$

As the number of stages $S \to \infty$, we have the limit:

$$\left(\frac{S\mu_n}{\lambda_n + S\mu_n}\right)^S \xrightarrow[S\to\infty]{} e^{-\frac{\lambda_n}{\mu_n}} = e^{-\lambda_n T_n}.$$

We have thus proved:

PROPOSITION 5. *Let $L_n(t)$ denote the process tracking the level at which a file is stored in a line of TTL caches, where requests arrive as a Poisson process of intensity λ_n, and the file is evicted to the next cache in line after a deterministic time T_n. Then, L_n in steady state verifies:*

$$P(L_n(t) = k) = \left(1 - e^{-\lambda_n T_n}\right)\left(e^{-\lambda_n T_n}\right)^k, \tag{33}$$

and thus the average search cost is given by:

$$E[L_n] = \frac{e^{-\lambda_n T_n}}{1 - e^{-\lambda_n T_n}} = \frac{1}{e^{\lambda_n T_n} - 1}.$$

We can use this result to formulate the optimal TTL problem equivalent to Problem 5. However, while the search cost $E[L_n]$ for file n is convex in T_n, the occupation probability at cache $k = 0$ is given by $u_n = 1 - e^{-\lambda_n T_n}$, a concave function. Nevertheless, we can use the idea of Section 4, changing to variables u_n, posing the optimal TTL problem as:

PROBLEM 6.

$$\min_{\{u_n \in [0,1]\}} \sum_{n=1}^N \lambda_n E[L_n] = \sum_{n=1}^N \lambda_n \frac{1 - u_n}{u_n},$$

$$s.t.: \sum_{n=1}^N \pi_n(0) = \sum_{n=1}^N u_n \leqslant C.$$

By solving this convex optimization, the optimal timers are obtained from $T_n = -\frac{1}{\lambda_n}\log(1 - u_n^*)$.

REMARK 5. *Note that we could also have recast Problem 5 in terms of the occupation probabilities, and obtained the same convex program as Problem 6. This implies that the optimal performance is the same for exponential or deterministic timers. The reason behind it is that both yield a geometric distribution for the stage probabilities, so in essence we are optimizing over the parameter of this distribution, indirectly through the choice of timers or eviction frequencies.*

8. CONCLUSIONS

In this paper, we analyzed from a theoretical perspective the performance of caching systems operating under timer based eviction policies. Building upon previous results for the relevant performance metrics, we formulated an optimization problem that characterizes the optimal choice of timers that maximizes the hit probability. This enables us to understand the structural properties of the system. In particular, we proved that the convexity of this problem is tightly related to the monotonicity of the hazard rate of the inter-request times, and provided a detailed analysis of the case of heavy tailed inter-request distributions and popularities, which are relevant in practice. Through simulation and numerical evaluation, we also analyzed the performance of alternative cache management algorithms. We also pursued some generalizations to random timers and networks of caches which will be explored in future work.

9. ACKNOWLEDGMENTS

The authors would like to thank D. Sadoc-Menasche and R. Srikant for their inputs during useful discussions. The authors were partially supported by AFOSR US under grant FA_9550_15_1_0183.

10. REFERENCES

[1] B. Ahlgren, C. Dannewitz, C. Imbrenda, D. Kutscher, and B. Ohlman. A survey of information-centric networking. *IEEE Communications Magazine*, 50(7):26–36, 2012.

[2] F. Baccelli and P. Brémaud. *Elements of Queueing Theory*. Springer-Verlag, Berlin, 2013.

[3] O. Bahat and A. M. Makowski. Measuring consistency in TTL-based caches. *Performance Evaluation*, 62(1):439–455, 2005.

[4] J. Barrera and J. Fontbona. The limiting move-to-front search-cost in law of large numbers asymptotic regimes. *Annals of Applied Probability*, 20(2):722–752, 2010.

[5] D. S. Berger, P. Gland, S. Singla, and F. Ciucu. Exact analysis of TTL cache networks. *Performance Evaluation*, 79:2–23, 2014.

[6] D. S. Berger, S. Henningsen, F. Ciucu, and J. B. Schmitt. Maximizing cache hit ratios by variance reduction. *ACM SIGMETRICS Performance Evaluation Review*, 43(2):57–59, 2015.

[7] G. Bianchi, A. Detti, A. Caponi, and N. Blefari Melazzi. Check before storing: What is the performance price of content integrity verification in LRU caching? *ACM SIGCOMM Computer Communication Review*, 43(3):59–67, 2013.

[8] S. Boyd and L. Vandenberghe. *Convex optimization*. Cambridge university press, 2004.

[9] L. Breslau, P. Cao, L. Fan, G. Phillips, and S. Shenker. Web caching and zipf-like distributions: Evidence and implications. In *Proc. of IEEE/Infocom 1999*, pages 126–134.

[10] H. Che, Y. Tung, and Z. Wang. Hierarchical web caching systems: Modeling, design and experimental results. *IEEE Journal on Selected Areas in Communications*, 20(7):1305–1314, 2002.

[11] A. Dan and D. Towsley. An approximate analysis of the LRU and FIFO buffer replacement schemes. In *Proc. of ACM/SIGMETRICS 1990*, pages 143–152.

[12] M. Dehghan, L. Massoulie, D. Towsley, D. Menasche, and Y. C. Tay. A utility optimization approach to network cache design. In *Proc. of IEEE/Infocom 2016*, page to appear.

[13] A. Ferragut, I. Rodríguez, and F. Paganini. Optimizing TTL caches under heavy-tailed demands (extended version). Available at http://fi.ort.edu.uy/2243/17/publications.html.

[14] J. A. Fill. Limits and rates of convergence for the distribution of search cost under the move-to-front rule. *Theoretical Computer Science*, 164(1):185–206, 1996.

[15] N. C. Fofack, P. Nain, G. Neglia, and D. Towsley. Analysis of TTL-based cache networks. In *Proc. of Intl. Conf on Performance Evaluation Methodologies and Tools (VALUETOOLS)*, pages 1–10, 2012.

[16] N. C. Fofack, P. Nain, G. Neglia, and D. Towsley. Performance evaluation of hierarchical TTL-based cache networks. *Computer Networks*, 65:212–231, 2014.

[17] C. Fricker, P. Robert, and J. Roberts. A versatile and accurate approximation for LRU cache performance. In *Proc. of the 24th International Teletraffic Congress*, pages 57–64, 2012.

[18] N. Gast and B. V. Houdt. Transient and steady-state regime of a family of list-based cache replacement algorithms. In *Proc. of ACM/SIGMETRICS 2015*, pages 123–136.

[19] E. Gelenbe. A unified approach to the evaluation of a class of replacement algorithms. *IEEE Trans. on Computers*, 100(6):611–618, 1973.

[20] M. Grant and S. Boyd. CVX: Matlab software for disciplined convex programming, version 2.1. http://cvxr.com/cvx, Mar. 2014.

[21] V. Jacobson, D. K. Smetters, J. D. Thornton, M. F. Plass, N. H. Briggs, and R. L. Braynard. Networking named content. In *Proc. of the ACM/Conext*, pages 1–12, 2009.

[22] P. Jelenković and A. Radovanović. Asymptotic insensitivity of least-recently-used caching to statistical dependency. In *Proc. of IEEE/Infocom 2003*, pages 438–447.

[23] P. R. Jelenković. Asymptotic approximation of the move-to-front search cost distribution and least-recently used caching fault probabilities. *Annals of Applied Probability*, 9(2):430–464, 1999.

[24] P. R. Jelenković and A. Radovanović. Least-recently-used caching with dependent requests. *Theoretical computer science*, 326(1):293–327, 2004.

[25] P. R. Jelenković and A. Radovanović. The persistent-access-caching algorithm. *Random Structures & Algorithms*, 33(2):219–251, 2008.

[26] P. R. Jelenković, A. Radovanović, and M. S. Squillante. Critical sizing of LRU caches with dependent requests. *Journal of Applied Probability*, 43(4):1013–1027, 2006.

[27] J. Jung, A. W. Berger, and H. Balakrishnan. Modeling TTL-based internet caches. In *Proc. of IEEE/Infocom 2003*, pages 417–426.

[28] W. King. Analysis of paging algorithms. In *Proc. of IFIP Congress 1971*, pages 485–490.

[29] V. Martina, M. Garetto, and E. Leonardi. A unified approach to the performance analysis of caching systems. In *Proc. of IEEE/Infocom 2014*, pages 2040–2048.

[30] E. J. Rosensweig, J. Kurose, and D. Towsley. Approximate models for general cache networks. In *Proc. of IEEE/Infocom 2010*, pages 1–9.

Adaptive Caching Networks with Optimality Guarantees

Stratis Ioannidis and Edmund Yeh
E.C.E., Northeastern University
360 Huntington Ave, 409DA
Boston, MA, 02115
{ioannidis,eyeh}@ece.neu.edu

ABSTRACT

We study the problem of optimal content placement over a network of caches, a problem naturally arising in several networking applications, including ICNs, CDNs, and P2P systems. Given a demand of content request rates and paths followed, we wish to determine the content placement that maximizes the *expected caching gain*, i.e., the reduction of routing costs due to intermediate caching. The offline version of this problem is NP-hard and, in general, the demand and topology may be a priori unknown. Hence, a distributed, adaptive, constant approximation content placement algorithm is desired. We show that path replication, a simple algorithm frequently encountered in literature, can be arbitrarily suboptimal when combined with traditional eviction policies, like LRU, LFU, or FIFO. We propose a distributed, adaptive algorithm that performs stochastic gradient ascent on a concave relaxation of the expected caching gain, and constructs a probabilistic content placement within $1-1/e$ factor from the optimal, in expectation. Motivated by our analysis, we also propose a novel greedy eviction policy to be used with path replication, and show through numerical evaluations that both algorithms significantly outperform path replication with traditional eviction policies over a broad array of network topologies.

1. INTRODUCTION

We consider a *caching network*, i.e., a network of caches, each capable of storing a constant number of content items. Certain nodes in the network act as designated sources for content, and are guaranteed to always store specific items. Any node can generate a request for an item, which is forwarded over a fixed path toward a designated source. However, requests need not reach the end of this path: forwarding stops upon reaching a node that has cached the requested item. Whenever such a "cache hit" occurs, the item is sent over the reverse path towards the node that requested it.

Our goal is to *allocate items to caches optimally*, i.e., in a way that minimizes the aggregate routing costs due to content transfers across the network. This abstract problem naturally captures—and is directly motivated by—several important real-life networking applications. These include content and information-centric networks (CCNs/ICNs) [22, 32, 33], core and edge content delivery networks (CDNs) [7, 13], micro/femtocell networks [34], and peer-to-peer networks [12, 28], to name a few. For example, in hierarchical CDNs, requests for content can be served by intermediate caches placed at the network's edge, e.g., within the same administrative domain (e.g., AS or ISP) as the originator of the request; if, however, content is not cached locally, the request can be forwarded to a core server, that acts as a cache of last resort. Similarly, in CCNs, named data items are stored at designated sources, and requests for named content are forwarded to these sources. Intermediate routers can cache items carried by responses, and subsequently serve future requests. Both settings directly map to the abstract problem we study here.

In these and many other applications, it is natural to assume that the *demand*, determined by the frequencies of requests and the paths they follow, is dynamic and not a priori known. For this reason adaptive algorithms that (a) discover an optimal item placement without prior knowledge of this demand and (b) adapt to its changes are desired. Moreover, collecting information at a single centralized location may be impractical in large networks consisting of different administrative domains. Distributed algorithms, in which a node's caching decisions rely only on locally available information, allow the network to scale and are thus preferable.

Path replication [12] is a simple, elegant algorithm that attains both properties and is often encountered in the literature of the different applications mentioned above [10, 22, 25, 28, 33, 39]. Cast in the context of our problem, the algorithm roughly proceeds as follows: when an item traverses the reverse path towards a node that requested it, it is cached by *every intermediate node encountered.* When caches are full, evictions are typicaly implemented using traditional policies, like LRU, LFU, FIFO, etc.

This algorithm is intuitively appealing in its simplicity, and it is clearly both distributed and adaptive to demand. Unfortunately, the resulting allocations of items to caches come with no guarantees: we show in this paper that path replication combined with *any* of the above traditional eviction policies is arbitrarily suboptimal. To address this, our main goal is to design a *distributed, adaptive caching algorithm with provable performance guarantees.* To that end, we make the following contributions:

- We set the problem of optimal caching network design

SIGMETRICS '16, June 14–18, 2016, Antibes Juan-Les-Pins, France.

DOI: http://dx.doi.org/10.1145/2896377.2901467

on a formal foundation. We do so by rigorously defining the problem of finding an *allocation*, i.e., a mapping of items to network caches, that maximizes the *expected caching gain*, i.e., the routing cost reduction achieved due to caching at intermediate nodes. The deterministic, combinatorial version of the problem is NP-hard, though it is approximable within a $1 - 1/e$ factor [1, 34].

- We prove that the ubiquitous path replication algorithm, combined with LRU, LFU, or FIFO eviction policies, leads to allocations that are *arbitrarily suboptimal.* Our result extends to any *myopic* strategy, that ignores costs incurred upstream due to cache misses.
- We construct a distributed, adaptive algorithm that converges to a probabilistic allocation of items to caches that is within a $1 - 1/e$ factor from the optimal, *without* prior knowledge of the demand (i.e., items requested and routes followed) or the network's topology. The algorithm performs a projected gradient ascent over a concave objective approximating the expected caching gain.
- Motivated by this construction, we also propose a new eviction policy to be used with path replication: whenever an item is back-propagated over a path, the nodes on the path have the opportunity to store it and evict an existing content, according to a greedy policy we design.
- We conduct extensive simulations over a broad array of both synthetic and real-life topologies. We show that both algorithms significantly outperform path replication combined with traditional eviction policies. In all cases studied, the greedy heuristic performs exceptionally well, achieving at least 95% of the gain achievable by the projected gradient ascent algorithm, that comes with provable guarantees.

Our analysis requires overcoming several technical hurdles. To design our distributed algorithm, we show that it is always possible to construct a probabilistic allocation, mapping items to caches, that satisfies capacity constraints *exactly*, from a probabilistic allocation that satisfies capacity constraints only in *expectation.* This construction is simple and intuitive and can be performed in polynomial time. The concave relaxation we study is non-differentiable; this introduces additional technical difficulties when performing projected gradient ascent, which we address.

The remainder of this paper is structured as follows. We review related work in Section 2. We formally introduce our problem in Section 3, and discuss offline algorithms for it solution in Section 4. Our main results on distributed, adaptive algorithms in Section 5; we also prove an equivalence theorem on several variants of the expected caching gain maximization problem in Section 6. Finally, Section 7 contains our evaluations, and we conclude in Section 8.

2. RELATED WORK

Path replication is best known as the de facto caching mechanism in content-centric networking [22], but has a long history in networking literature. In their seminal paper, Cohen and Shenker [12] show that path replication, combined with constant rate of evictions leads to an allocation that is optimal, in equilibrium, when nodes are visited through uniform sampling. This is one of the few results on path replication's optimality—see also [19]; our work (c.f. Thm. 2) proves that, unfortunately, this result does not generalize to routing over arbitrary topologies. Many studies provide numerical evaluations of path replication combined with simple eviction policies, like LRU, LFU, etc., over different topologies (see, e.g., [25, 33, 39]). In the context of CDNs and ICNs, Rosensweig et al. [32] study conditions under which path replication with LRU, FIFO, and other variants, under fixed paths, lead to an ergodic chain. Che et al. [10] approximate the LRU policy hit probability through a TTL-based eviction scheme; this approach has been refined and extended in several recent works to model many traditional eviction policies [6, 15, 16, 29]; alternative analytical models are explored in [9, 18]. None of the above works however study optimality issues or guarantees.

Several papers have studied complexity and optimization issues in offline caching problems [2, 3, 5, 7, 14, 34]. With the exception of [34], these works model the network as a bipartite graph: nodes generating requests connect directly to caches, and demands are satisfied a single hop (if at all). Beyond content placement, Deghan et al. [13] jointly optimize caching and routing in this bipartite setting. In general, the *pipage rounding* technique of Ageev and Sviridenko [1] (see also [8, 36]) yields again a constant approximation algorithm in the bipartite setting, while approximation algorithms are also known for several variants of this problem [3, 5, 7, 14].

Among these papers on offline caching, the recent paper by Shanmugam et al. [34] is closest to the problem we tackle here; we rely and expand upon this work. Shanmugam et al. consider wireless nodes that download items from (micro/femtocel) base stations in their vicinity. Base stations are visited in a predefined order (e.g., in decreasing order of connection quality), with the wireless service acting as a "cache of last resort". This can be cast as an instance of our problem, with paths defined by the traversal sequence of base-stations, and the network graph defined as their union. The authors show that determining the optimal allocation is NP-hard, and that an $1 - 1/e$ approximation algorithm can be obtained through pipage rounding; we review these results, framed in the context of our problem, in Section 4.

All of the above complexity papers [1, 3, 5, 14], including [34], study *offline, centralized* versions of their respective caching problems. Instead, we focus on providing *adaptive, distributed* algorithms, that operate without any prior knowledge of the demand or topology. In doing so, we we produce distributed algorithms for (a) performing projected gradient ascent over the concave objective used in pipage rounding, and (b) rounding the objective across nodes; combined, these lead to our distributed, adaptive caching algorithm with provable guarantees (Thm. 4).

Adaptive replication schemes exist for asymptotically large, single-hop CDNs [20, 26, 27], but these works do not explicitly model a graph structure. The dynamics of the greedy path replication algorithm we propose in Section 5.3 resemble the greedy algorithm used to make caching decisions in [20], though our objective is different, and we cannot rely on a mean-field approximation in our argument. These dynamics are also similar (but not identical) to the dynamics of the "continuous-greedy" algorithm used for submodular maximization [36] and the Frank-Wolfe algorithm [11]; these can potentially serve as a basis for formally establishing its convergence, which we leave as future work.

The path replication eviction policy we propose also relates to greedy maximization techniques used in throughput-optimal backpressure algorithms—see, e.g., Stolyar [35] and, more recently, Yeh et al. [38], for an application to throughput-optimal caching in ICN networks. We minimize routing costs and ignore throughput issues, as we do not model congestion. Investigating how to combine these two research directions, capitalizing on commonalities between these greedy algorithms, is an interesting open problem.

3. MODEL

We consider a network of caches, each capable of storing at most a constant number of content items. Item requests are routed over given (i.e., fixed) routes, and are satisfied upon hitting the first cache that contains the requested item. Our goal is to determine an item allocation (or, equivalently, the contents of each cache), that minimizes the aggregate routing cost. We describe our model in detail below.

3.1 Cache Contents and Designated Sources

We represent a network as a directed graph $G(V, E)$. Content items (e.g., files, or file chunks) of equal size are to be distributed across network nodes. In particular, each node is associated with a cache, that can store a finite number of items. We denote by $\mathcal{C}$ the set of content items available, i.e., the *catalog*, and assume that G is symmetric, i.e., $(i, j) \in E$ if and only if $(j, i) \in E$.

We denote by $c_v \in \mathbb{N}$ the cache capacity at node $v \in V$: exactly c_v content items are stored in this node. For each node $v \in V$, we denote by

$$x_{vi} \in \{0,1\}, \qquad \text{for } v \in V, i \in \mathcal{C},$$

the variable indicating whether v stores content item i. We denote by $X = [x_{vi}]_{v\in V, i\in\mathcal{C}} \in \{0,1\}^{|V|\times|\mathcal{C}|}$ the matrix whose rows comprise the indicator variables of each node. We refer to X as the *global allocation strategy* or, simply, *allocation*. Note that the capacity constraints imply that

$$\textstyle\sum_{i\in\mathcal{C}} x_{vi} = c_v, \quad \text{for all } v \in V.$$

We associate each item i in the catalog $\mathcal{C}$ with a fixed set of *designated sources* $\mathcal{S}_i \subseteq V$, that always store i. That is:

$$x_{vi} = 1, \text{ for all } v \in \mathcal{S}_i.$$

Without loss of generality, we assume that the sets $\mathcal{S}_i$ are feasible, i.e., $\sum_{i:v\in\mathcal{S}_i} x_{vi} \leq c_v$, for all $v \in V$.

3.2 Content Requests and Routing Costs

The network serves content requests routed over the graph G. In short, a request is determined by (a) the item requested, and (b) the path that the request follows. Formally, a *path* p of length $|p| = K$ is a sequence

$$\{p_1, p_2, \dots, p_K\}$$

of nodes $p_k \in V$ such that edge (p_k, p_{k+1}) is in E, for every $k \in \{1, \dots, |p|-1\}$. Under this notation, a *request* r is a pair (i, p) where $i \in \mathcal{C}$ is the item requested, and p is the path traversed to serve this request. We say that a request (i, p) is *well-routed* if the following natural assumptions hold:

(a) The path p is simple, i.e., it contains no loops.
(b) The terminal node in the path is a designated source node for i, i.e., if $|p| = K$, $p_K \in S_i$.
(c) No other node in the path is a designated source node for i, i.e., if $|p| = K$, $p_k \notin S_i$, for $k = 1, \dots, K-1$.

We denote by $\mathcal{R}$ the set of all requests. Without loss of generality, we henceforth assume that all requests in $\mathcal{R}$ are well-routed. Moreover, requests for each element $\mathcal{R}$ arrive according to independent Poisson processes; we denote by $\lambda_{(i,p)} > 0$ the arrival rate of a request $(i, p) \in \mathcal{R}$.

An incoming request (i, p) is routed over the network G following path p, until it reaches a cache that stores i. At that point, a *response* message is generated, carrying the item requested. The response is propagated over p in the reverse direction, i.e., from the node where the "cache hit" occurred, back to the first node in p, from which the request originated. To capture costs (e.g., delay, money, etc.), we associate a *weight* $w_{ij} \geq 0$ with each edge $(i, j) \in E$, representing the cost of transferring an item across this edge. We assume that (a) costs are solely due to response messages that carry an item, while request forwarding costs are negligible, and (b) requests and downloads are instantaneous (or, occur at a smaller timescale compared to the request arrival process). We do not assume that $w_{ij} = w_{ji}$.

When a request $(i, p) \in \mathcal{R}$ is well-routed, the cost for serving it can be written concisely in terms of the allocation:

$$C_{(i,p)} = C_{(i,p)}(X) = \sum_{k=1}^{|p|-1} w_{p_{k+1}p_k} \prod_{k'=1}^{k} (1 - x_{p_{k'}i}). \tag{1}$$

Intuitively, this formula states that $C_{(i,p)}$ includes the cost of an edge (p_{k+1}, p_k) in the path p if *all* caches preceding this edge in p do not store i. If the request is well-routed, no edge (or cache) appears twice in (1). Moreover, the last cache in p stores the item, so the request is always served.

3.3 Maximizing the Caching Gain

As usual, we seek an allocation that minimizes the aggregate expected cost. In particular, let C_0 be the expected cost per request, when requests are served by the designated sources at the end of each path, i.e.,

$$C_0 = \textstyle\sum_{(i,p)\in\mathcal{R}} \lambda_{(i,p)} \sum_{k=1}^{|p|-1} w_{p_{k+1}p_k}.$$

Since requests are well-routed, C_0 is an upper bound on the expected routing cost. Our objective is to determine a feasible allocation X that maximizes the *caching gain*, i.e., the expected cost reduction attained due to caching at intermediate nodes, defined as:

$$\begin{aligned} F(X) &= C_0 - \textstyle\sum_{(i,p)\in\mathcal{R}} \lambda_{(i,p)} C_{(i,p)}(X) \\ &= \sum_{(i,p)\in\mathcal{R}} \lambda_{(i,p)} \sum_{k=1}^{|p|-1} w_{p_{k+1}p_k} \left(1 - \prod_{k'=1}^{k} (1 - x_{p_{k'}i})\right). \end{aligned} \tag{2}$$

In particular, we seek solutions to the following problem:

$$\begin{aligned} &\textsc{MaxCG} \\ &\text{Maximize:} \quad F(X) && \text{(3a)} \\ &\text{subj. to:} \quad X \in \mathcal{D}_1 && \text{(3b)} \end{aligned}$$

where $\mathcal{D}_1$ is the set of matrices $X \in \mathbb{R}^{|V|\times|\mathcal{C}|}$ satisfying the capacity, integrality, and source constraints, i.e.:

$$\begin{aligned} &\textstyle\sum_{i\in\mathcal{C}} x_{vi} = c_v, && \text{for all } v \in V, && \text{(4a)} \\ &x_{vi} \in \{0,1\}, && \text{for all } v \in V, i \in \mathcal{C}, \text{ and} && \text{(4b)} \\ &x_{vi} = 1, && \text{for all } v \in \mathcal{S}_i \text{ and all } i \in \mathcal{C}. && \text{(4c)} \end{aligned}$$

Problem MaxCG is NP-hard (see Shanmugam et al. [34] for a reduction from the 2-Disjoint Set Cover Problem). Our objective is to solve MaxCG using a *distributed*, *adaptive* algorithm, that produces an allocation within a constant

Table 1: Notation Summary

$G(V,E)$	Network graph, with nodes V and edges E
$\mathcal{C}$	Item catalog
c_v	Cache capacity at node $c \in V$
w_{uv}	Weight of edge $(u,v) \in E$
$\mathcal{R}$	Set of requests (i,p), with $i \in \mathcal{C}$ and p a path
$\lambda_{(i,p)}$	Rate of request $(i,p) \in \mathcal{R}$
x_{vi}	Variable indicating $v \in V$ stores $i \in \mathcal{C}$
y_{vi}	Marginal probability that $v \in V$ stores $i \in \mathcal{C}$
X	$\lvert V\rvert \times \lvert\mathcal{C}\rvert$ matrix of x_{vi}, for $v \in V$, $i \in \mathcal{C}$
Y	$\lvert V\rvert \times \lvert\mathcal{C}\rvert$ matrix of marginals y_{vi}, $v \in V$, $i \in \mathcal{C}$
$\mathcal{D}_1$	Set of feasible allocations $X \in \{0,1\}^{\lvert V\rvert\times\lvert\mathcal{C}\rvert}$
$\mathcal{D}_2$	Convex hull of $\mathcal{D}_1$
F	The expected caching gain (2) in $\mathcal{D}_1$, and its multi-linear relaxation (6) in $\mathcal{D}_2$
L	The concave approximation (10) of F

approximation of the optimal, *without* prior knowledge of the network topology, edge weights, or the demand.

4. PIPAGE ROUNDING

Before presenting our distributed, adaptive algorithm for solving MAXCG, we first discuss how to obtain a constant approximation solution in polynomial time in a *centralized*, *offline* fashion. To begin with, MAXCG is a submodular maximization problem under matroid constraints: hence, a solution within a 1/2 approximation from the optimal can be constructed by a greedy algorithm.[1] The solution we present below, due to Shanmugam et al. [34], improves upon this ratio using a technique called *pipage rounding* [1].

In short, the resulting approximation algorithm consists of two steps: (a) a *convex relaxation* step, that relaxes the integer program to a convex optimization problem, whose solution is within a constant approximation from the optimal, and (b) a *rounding* step, in which the (possibly) fractional solution is rounded to produce a solution to the original integer program. The convex relaxation plays an important role in our distributed, adaptive algorithm; as a result, we briefly overview pipage rounding as applied to MAXCG below, referring the interested reader to [1,34] for further details.

Convex Relaxation. To construct a convex relaxation of MAXCG, suppose that variables x_{vi}, $v \in V$, $i \in \mathcal{C}$, are independent Bernoulli random variables. Let ν be the corresponding joint probability distribution defined over matrices in $\{0,1\}^{|V|\times|\mathcal{C}|}$, and denote by $\mathbf{P}_\nu[\cdot]$, $\mathbb{E}_\nu[\cdot]$ the probability and expectation w.r.t. ν, respectively. Let y_{vi}, $v \in V$, $i \in \mathcal{C}$, be the (marginal) probability that v stores i, i.e.,

$$y_{vi} = \mathbf{P}_\nu[x_{vi} = 1] = \mathbb{E}_\nu[x_{vi}]. \tag{5}$$

Denote by $Y = [y_{vi}]_{v\in V, i\in\mathcal{C}} \in \mathbb{R}^{|V|\times|\mathcal{C}|}$ the matrix comprising the marginal probabilities (5). Then, for F given by (2):

$$\begin{aligned}\mathbb{E}_\nu[F(X)] &= \sum_{(i,p)\in\mathcal{R}} \lambda_{(i,p)} \sum_{k=1}^{|p|-1} w_{p_{k+1}p_k}\Big(1-\mathbb{E}_\nu\Big[\prod_{k'=1}^{k}(1-x_{p_{k'}i})\Big]\Big)\\ &= \sum_{(i,p)\in\mathcal{R}} \lambda_{(i,p)} \sum_{k=1}^{|p|-1} w_{p_{k+1}p_k}\Big(1-\prod_{k'=1}^{k}(1-\mathbb{E}_\nu[x_{p_{k'}i}])\Big)\\ &= F(Y). \end{aligned}\tag{6}$$

[1]Starting from items placed only at designated sources, this algorithm iteratively adds items to caches, selecting at each step a feasible assignment $x_{vi} = 1$ that leads to the largest increase in the caching gain.

Note that the second equality holds by independence, and the fact that path p is simple (no node appears twice). This extension of F to the domain $[0,1]^{|V|\times|\mathcal{C}|}$ is known as the *multi-linear relaxation* of F. Consider now the problem:

$$\text{Maximize:}\quad F(Y) \tag{7a}$$
$$\text{subject to:}\quad Y \in \mathcal{D}_2, \tag{7b}$$

where $\mathcal{D}_2$ is the set of matrices $Y = [y_{vi}]_{v\in V,i\in\mathcal{C}} \in \mathbb{R}^{|V|\times|\mathcal{C}|}$ satisfying the capacity and source constraints, with the integrality constraints relaxed, i.e.:

$$\textstyle\sum_{i\in\mathcal{C}} y_{vi} = c_v, \quad \text{for all } v \in V, \tag{8a}$$
$$y_{vi} \in [0,1], \quad \text{for all } v \in V, i \in \mathcal{C}, \text{ and} \tag{8b}$$
$$y_{vi} = 1, \quad \text{for all } v \in \mathcal{S}_i \text{ and all } i \in \mathcal{C}. \tag{8c}$$

Note that an allocation X sampled from a ν with marginals $Y \in \mathcal{D}_2$ only satisfies the capacity constraints *in expectation*; hence, X may not be in $\mathcal{D}_1$. Moreover, if X^* and Y^* are optimal solutions to (3) and (7), respectively, then

$$F(Y^*) \geq F(X^*), \tag{9}$$

as (7) maximizes the same function over a larger domain.

The multi-linear relaxation (7a) is not concave, so (7) is *not* a convex optimization problem. Nonetheless, (7) can be approximated as follows. Define $L : \mathcal{D}_2 \to \mathbb{R}$ as:

$$L(Y) = \sum_{(i,p)\in\mathcal{R}} \lambda_{(i,p)} \sum_{k=1}^{|p|-1} w_{p_{k+1}p_k} \min\{1, \sum_{k'=1}^{k} y_{p_{k'}i}\}. \tag{10}$$

Note that L is concave, and consider now the problem:

$$\text{Maximize:}\quad L(Y) \tag{11a}$$
$$\text{Subject to:}\quad Y \in \mathcal{D}_2. \tag{11b}$$

Then, the optimal value of (11) is guaranteed to be within a constant factor from the optimal value of (7)–and, by (9), from the optimal value of (3) as well. In particular:

THEOREM 1. *[1,34] Let Y^*, and Y^{**} be optimal solutions to* (7) *and* (11), *respectively. Then,*

$$F(Y^*) \geq F(Y^{**}) \geq (1-\frac{1}{e})F(Y^*). \tag{12}$$

A proof can be found in [21]. Problem (11) is convex; in fact, by introducing auxiliary variables, it can be converted to a linear program and, as such, the minimizer Y^{**} can be computed in strongly polynomial time [1].

Rounding. To produce a constant approximation solution to MAXCG, the solution Y^{**} of (11) is rounded. The rounding scheme is based on the following property of F: given a fractional solution $Y \in \mathcal{D}_2$, there is always a way to transfer mass between any two fractional variables y_{vi}, $y_{vi'}$ so that[2] (a) at least one of them becomes 0 or 1, (b) the resulting Y' under this transformation is feasible, i.e., $Y' \in \mathcal{D}_2$, and (c) the caching gain at Y' is at least as good as at Y, i.e., $F(Y') \geq F(Y)$.

This suggests the following iterative algorithm for producing an integral solution.

1. Start from Y^{**}, an optimal solution to the problem (11).

[2]Properties (a)-(c) are a direct consequence of the convexity of F when restricted to any two such variables, a property that Ageev and Sviridenko refer to as *ϵ-convexity* [1].

2. If the solution is fractional, find two variables y_{vi}, $y_{vi'}$ that are fractional: as capacities are integral, if a fractional variable exists, then there must be at least two.
3. Use the rounding described by properties (a)-(c) to transform (at least) one of these two variables to either 0 or 1, while increasing the caching gain F.
4. Repeat steps 2-3 until there are no fractional variables.

As each rounding step reduces the number of fractional variables by at least 1, the above algorithm concludes in at most $|V|\times|\mathcal{C}|$ steps, producing an integral solution $X' \in \mathcal{D}_1$. Since each rounding step can only increase F, X' satisfies:

$$F(X') \geq F(Y^{**}) \overset{(12)}{\geq} (1-\frac{1}{e})F(Y^*) \overset{(9)}{\geq} (1-\frac{1}{e})F(X^*),$$

i.e., is a $(1-\frac{1}{e})$-approximate solution to MAXCG.

5. DISTRIBUTED ADAPTIVE CACHING

5.1 Path Replication Suboptimality

Having discussed how to sove MAXCG offline, we turn our attention to distributed, adaptive algorithms. We begin with a negative result: the simple path replication algorithm described in the introduction, combined with LRU, LFU, or FIFO evictions, is arbitrarily suboptimal.

We prove this below using the simple star network illustrated in Figure 1, in which only one file can be cached at the central node. Intuitively, when serving requests from the bottom node, path replication with, e.g., LRU evictions, alternates between storing either of the two files. However, the optimal allocation is to permanently store file 2, (i.e., $x_{v2} = 1$): for large M, this allocation leads to a caching gain arbitrarily larger than the one under path replication and LRU. As $c_v = 1$, LFU and FIFO coincide with LRU, so the result extends to these policies as well.

Formally, assume that request traffic is generated only by node u: requests for items 1 and 2 are routed through paths $p_1 = \{u, v, s_1\}$ and $p_2 = \{u, v, s_2\}$, respectively. Let $\lambda_{(1,p_1)} = 1-\alpha$, $\lambda_{(2,p_2)} = \alpha$, for $\alpha \in (0, 1)$. As illustrated in Figure 1, the routing cost is 1 over both (s_1, v), (v, u) and $M \gg 1$ over (s_2, v). Then, the following holds:

THEOREM 2. *Let $X(t) \in \{0,1\}^2$ be the allocation of the network in Figure 1 at time t, under path replication with an LRU, LFU, or FIFO policy. Then, for $\alpha = \frac{1}{\sqrt{M}}$,*

$$\lim_{t\to\infty} \mathbb{E}[F(X(t))]/\max_{X\in\mathcal{D}_1} F(X) = O(1/\sqrt{M}).$$

PROOF. The worst case cost, when cache v is empty, is: $C_0 = \alpha\times(M+1)+(1-\alpha)\times 2 = \alpha M+2-\alpha$. Suppose that u permanently caches item 2. This results in an expected routing cost of $\alpha\times 1+(1-\alpha)\times 2 = 2-\alpha$. Hence, an optimal allocation X^* necessarily has a caching gain $F(X^*) > \alpha M + 2-\alpha-(2-\alpha) = \alpha M$. Consider now the path replication algorithm, in which either item is cached at v whenever it is back-propagated over the reverse path. As $c_v = 1$, the LRU, FIFO and LFU policies coincide, and yield exactly the same eviction decision. Moreover, as request arrivals are independent Poisson, the steady state probabilities that v stores item 1 or 2 are $1-\alpha$ and α, respectively. Hence, the expected routing cost in steady state is $\alpha^2 + \alpha(1-\alpha)\times(M+1)+(1-\alpha)\alpha\times 2+(1-\alpha)^2 = 1+\alpha M-\alpha^2 M+\alpha-\alpha^2)$, leading to a caching gain of $\alpha M+2-\alpha-(1+\alpha M-\alpha^2 M+\alpha-\alpha^2) = \alpha^2 M+1-2\alpha+\alpha^2$. Hence, the ratio of the expected caching gain under path replication with LRU, LFU, or FIFO evictions to $F(X^*)$ is at most $\alpha+\frac{(1-\alpha)^2}{\alpha M}$, and the theorem follows for $\alpha = 1/\sqrt{M}$. □

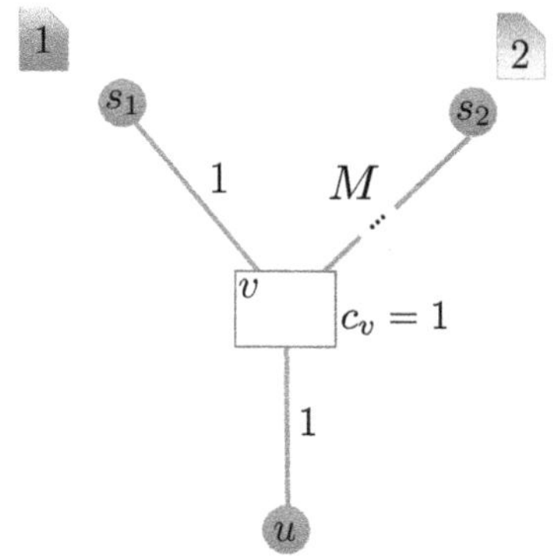

Figure 1: A simple caching network, with $\mathcal{C} = \{1, 2\}$, $S_1 = \{s_1\}$, $S_2 = \{s_2\}$. The cache at v has capacity $c_v = 1$, and the cost of the edge between v and s_2 is $M \gg 1$. Node u requests item 1 with rate $1-\alpha$, and item 2 with rate α. For $\alpha = \frac{1}{\sqrt{M}}$, path replication with LRU, LFU, or FIFO leads to an arbitrarily suboptimal caching allocation, in steady state.

Taking M to be arbitrarily large therefore makes this ratio arbitrarily small. Clearly, this argument applies to any eviction strategy that is *myopic*, *i.e.*, is insensitive to upstream costs. Accounting for the cost of an item's retrieval when caching seems necessary to provide any optimality guarantees; the algorithms we propose below indeed do so.

5.2 Projected Gradient Ascent

Given the negative result of Theorem 2, we now describe our distributed, adaptive algorithm for solving MAXCG. Intuitively, the algorithm performs a *projected gradient ascent* over function L, effectively solving the convex problem (11) in a distributed, adaptive fashion. The concavity of L ensures convergence (in contrast to minimizing F directly), while Theorem 1 ensures that the caching gain attained in steady state is within an $1-\frac{1}{e} \approx 0.62$ factor from the optimal. We describe the algorithm in detail below.

We deal with the following two challenges. First, in each step of gradient ascent, a node must estimate the contribution of its own caching allocation to the gradient of the (global) function L. The estimation should rely only on local information; additional care needs to be taken as L is not differentiable in the entire domain $\mathcal{D}_2$, so a *subgradient* needs to be estimated instead. Second, the final value of the convex relaxation (11), as well as intermediate solutions during gradient ascent, produce fractional values $Y \in \mathcal{D}_2$. To determine what to place in each cache, discrete allocations $X \in \mathcal{D}_1$ need to be determined from Y. Our algorithm *cannot* rely on pipage rounding to construct such cache allocations: each node must determine its cache contents in a distributed way, without explicitly computing F or L.

We address both challenges, by proving that (a) a *feasible* randomized rounding of any $Y \in \mathcal{D}_2$, and (b) the subgradient of L w.r.t. Y can both be computed in a distributed fashion, using only information locally available at each node.

Algorithm 1 Projected Gradient Ascent

```
Execute the following at each v ∈ V:
Pick arbitrary state y_v^(0) ∈ D_2^v.
for each period k ≥ 1 and each v ∈ V do
    Compute the sliding average ȳ_v^(k) through (16).
    Sample a x_v^(k) ∈ D_1^v from a μ_v that satisfies (17).
    Place items x_v^(k) in cache.
    Collect measurements
    At the end of the period, compute estimate z_v of
    ∂_{y_v} L(Y^(k)) through (18).
    Compute new state y_v^(k+1) through (15).
end for
```

5.2.1 *Algorithm Overview*

We begin by giving an overview of our distributed, adaptive algorithm. We partition time into periods of equal length $T > 0$, during which each node $v \in V$ collects measurements from messages routed through it. Each node keeps track of *its own marginals* $y_v \in [0,1]^{|\mathcal{C}|}$: intuitively, as in (5), each y_{vi} captures the probability that node $v \in V$ stores item $i \in \mathcal{C}$. We refer to y_v as the *state* at node v; these values, as well as the cache contents of a node, remain constant during a measurement period. When the period ends, each node (a) adapts its state vector y_v, and (b) reshuffles the contents of its cache, in a manner we describe below.

In short, at any point in time, the (global) allocation $X \in \mathcal{D}_1$ is sampled from a joint distribution μ that has a *product form*; for every v, there exist appropriate probability distributions μ_v, $v \in V$, such that:

$$\mu(X) = \prod_{v \in V} \mu_v(x_{v1}, \ldots, x_{v|\mathcal{C}|}). \tag{13}$$

Moreover, each marginal probability $\mathbf{P}_\mu[x_{vi} = 1]$ (i.e., the probability that node v stores i) is determined as a "smoothened" version of the current state variable y_{vi}.

State Adaptation. A node $v \in V$ uses local measurements collected from messages it receives during a period to produce a random vector $z_v \in \mathbb{R}_+^{|\mathcal{C}|}$ that is an unbiased estimator of a subgradient of L w.r.t. to y_v. That is, if $Y^{(k)} \in \mathbb{R}^{|V| \times |\mathcal{C}|}$ is the (global) matrix of marginals at the k-th measurement period, $z_{vi} = z_{vi}(Y^{(k)})$ is a random variable satisfying:

$$\mathbb{E}\left[z_v(Y^{(k)})\right] \in \partial_{y_v} L(Y^{(k)}) \tag{14}$$

where $\partial_{y_v} L(Y)$ is the set of subgradients of L w.r.t y_v. We specify how to produce such estimates in a distributed fashion below, in Section 5.2.2. Having these estimates, each node adapts its state as follows: at the conclusion of the k-th period, the new state is computed as

$$y_v^{(k+1)} \leftarrow \mathcal{P}_{\mathcal{D}_2^v}\left(y_v^{(k)} + \gamma_k \cdot z_v(Y^{(k)})\right), \tag{15}$$

where $\gamma_k > 0$ is a gain factor and $\mathcal{P}_{\mathcal{D}_2^v}$ is the projection to v's set of relaxed constraints:

$$\mathcal{D}_2^v = \{y_v \in [0,1]^{|\mathcal{C}|} : \sum_{i \in \mathcal{C}} y_{vi} = c_v, y_{vi} = 1, \text{for } i \text{ s.t } v \in \mathcal{S}_i\}.$$

State Smoothening. Upon performing the state adaptation (15), each node $v \in V$ computes the following "sliding average" of its current and past states:

$$\bar{y}_v^{(k)} = \sum_{\ell=\lfloor \frac{k}{2} \rfloor}^{k} \gamma_\ell y_v^{(\ell)} / \left[\sum_{\ell=\lfloor \frac{k}{2} \rfloor}^{k} \gamma_\ell\right]. \tag{16}$$

This "state smoothening" is necessary precisely because of the non-differentiability of L [30]. Note that $\bar{y}_v^{(k)} \in \mathcal{D}_2^v$, as a convex combination of points in $\mathcal{D}_2^v$.

Cache reshuffling. Finally, given $\bar{y}_v$, each node $v \in V$ reshuffles its contents, placing items in its cache *independently of all other nodes*: that is, node v selects a random allocation $x_v^{(k)} \in \{0,1\}^{|\mathcal{C}|}$ sampled independently of any other node in V, so that the joint distribution satisfies (13).

In particular, $x_v^{(k)}$ is sampled from a distribution μ_v that has the following two properties:

1. μ_v is a distribution over *feasible* allocations, satisfying v's capacity and source constraints, i.e., μ_v's support is:

$$\mathcal{D}_1^v = \{x_v \in \{0,1\}^{|\mathcal{C}|} : \sum_{j \in \mathcal{C}} x_{vj} = c_v, x_{vi} = 1, \text{for } i \text{ s.t } v \in \mathcal{S}_i\}.$$

2. μ_v is *consistent* with the marginals $\bar{y}_v^{(k)} \in \mathcal{D}_2^v$, i.e.,

$$\mathbb{E}_{\mu_v}[x_{vi}^{(k)}] = \bar{y}_{vi}^{(k)}, \text{ for } i \in \mathcal{C}. \tag{17}$$

It is not obvious that a μ_v that satisfies these properties exists. We show below, in Section 5.2.3, that such a μ_v exists, it has $O(|\mathcal{C}|)$ support, and can be computed in $O(c_v|\mathcal{C}|\log|\mathcal{C}|)$ time. As a result, having $\bar{y}_v$, each node v can sample a feasible allocation x_v from μ_v in $O(c_v|\mathcal{C}|\log|\mathcal{C}|)$ time.

The complete projected gradient ascent algorithm is summarized in Algorithm 1. A node may need to retrieve new items, not presently in its cache, to implement the sampled allocation $x_v^{(k)}$. This incurs additional routing costs but, if T is large, this traffic is small compared to regular response message traffic. Before we state its convergence properties, we present the two missing pieces, namely, the subradient estimation and randomized rounding we use.

5.2.2 *Distributed Sub-Gradient Estimation*

We now describe how to compute the estimates z_v of the subgradients $\partial_{y_v} L(Y)$ in a measurement period, dropping the superscript $\cdot^{(k)}$ for brevity. These estimates are computed in a distributed fashion at each node, using only information available from messages traversing the node. This computation requires additional "control" messages to be exchanged between nodes, beyond the usual request and response traffic.

The estimation proceeds as follows. Given a path p and a $v \in p$, denote by $k_p(v)$ is the position of v in p; i.e., $k_p(v)$ equals the $k \in \{1, \ldots, |p|\}$ such that $p_k = v$. Then:

1. Every time a node generates a new request (i, p), it also generates an additional control message to be propagated over p, in parallel to the request. This message is propagated until a node $u \in p$ s.t. $\sum_{\ell=1}^{k_p(u)} y_{p_\ell i} > 1$ is found, or the end of the path is reached. This can be detected by summing the state variables y_{vi} as the control message traverses nodes $v \in p$ up to u.
2. Upon reaching either such a node or the end of the path, the control message is sent down in the reverse direction. Every time it traverses an edge in this reverse direction, it adds the weight of this edge into a weight counter.
3. Every node on the reverse path "sniffs" the weight counter field of the control message. Hence, every node visited learns the sum of weights of all edges connecting it to visited nodes further upstream towards u; i.e., visited

node $v \in p$ learns the quantity:

$$t_{vi} = \sum_{k'=k_v(p)}^{|p|-1} w_{p_{k'+1}p_{k'}} \mathbb{1}_{\sum_{\ell=1}^{k'} y_{p_\ell i} \leq 1}.$$

4. Let $\mathcal{T}_{vi}$ be the set of quantities collected in this way at node v regarding item $i \in \mathcal{C}$ during a measurement period of duration T. At the end of the measurement period, each node $v \in V$ produces the following estimates:

$$z_{vi} = \frac{1}{T} \sum_{t \in \mathcal{T}_{vi}} t, \quad i \in \mathcal{C}. \tag{18}$$

Note that, in practice, this needs to be computed only for $i \in \mathcal{C}$ for which v has received a control message.

Note that the control messages in the above construction are "free" under our model, as they do not carry an item. Moreover, they can be piggy-backed on/merged with request/response messages, wherever the corresponding traversed subpaths of p overlap. It is easy to show that the above estimate is an unbiased estimator of the subgradient:

Lemma 1. *For $z_v = [z_{vi}]_{i \in \mathcal{C}} \in \mathbb{R}_+^{|\mathcal{C}|}$ the vector constructed through coordinates* (18)*,*

$$\mathbb{E}[z_v(Y)] \in \partial_{y_v} L(Y) \text{ and } \mathbb{E}[\|z_v\|_2^2] < W^2 |V|^2 |\mathcal{C}| (\Lambda^2 + \frac{\Lambda}{T}),$$

where $W = \max_{(i,j) \in E} w_{ij}$ *and* $\Lambda = \max_{v \in V, i \in \mathcal{C}} \sum_{(i,p) \in \mathcal{R}: v \in p} \lambda_{(i,p)}$.

Proof. First, let:

$$\overline{\partial_{y_{vi}}} L(Y) = \sum_{(i,p) \in \mathcal{R}: v \in p} \lambda_{(i,p)} \sum_{k'=k_p(v)}^{|p|-1} w_{p_{k'+1}p_{k'}} \mathbb{1}_{\sum_{\ell=1}^{k'} y_{p_\ell i} \leq 1} \tag{19a}$$

$$\underline{\partial_{y_{vi}}} L(Y) = \sum_{(i,p) \in \mathcal{R}: v \in p} \lambda_{(i,p)} \sum_{k'=k_p(v)}^{|p|-1} w_{p_{k'+1}p_{k'}} \mathbb{1}_{\sum_{\ell=1}^{k'} y_{p_\ell i} < 1} \tag{19b}$$

where $k_p(v)$ is the position of v in p, i.e., it is the $k \in \{1, \ldots, |p|\}$ such that $p_k = v$.

A vector $z \in \mathbb{R}^{|\mathcal{C}|}$ belongs to the subgradient set $\partial_{y_v} L(Y)$ if and only if $z_i \in [\underline{\partial_{y_{vi}}} L(Y), \overline{\partial_{y_{vi}}} L(Y)]$. If L is differentiable at Y w.r.t y_{vi}, the two limits coincide and are equal to $\frac{\partial L}{\partial y_{vi}}$. It immediately follows from the fact that requests are Poisson that $\mathbb{E}[z_{vi}(Y)] = \overline{\partial_{y_{vi}}} L(Y)$, so indeed $\mathbb{E}[z_v(Y)] \in \partial_{y_v} L(Y)$. To prove the bound on the second moment, note that $\mathbb{E}[z_{vi}^2] = \frac{1}{T^2} \mathbb{E}[(\sum_{t \in \mathcal{T}_{vi}} t)^2] \leq \frac{W^2 |V|^2}{T^2} \mathbb{E}\left[|\mathcal{T}_{vi}|^2\right]$ as $t \leq W|V|$. On the other hand, $|\mathcal{T}_{vi}|$ is Poisson distributed with expectation $\sum_{(i,p) \in \mathcal{R}: v \in p} \lambda_{(i,p)} T$, and the lemma follows. □

5.2.3 Distributed Randomized Rounding

We now turn our attention to the distributed, randomized rounding scheme executed each node $v \in V$. To produce a μ_v over $\mathcal{D}_1^v$ that satisfies (17), note that it suffices to consider μ_v such that $\mathbb{E}_{\mu_v}[x_v] = \bar{y}_v$, defined over the set:

$$\bar{\mathcal{D}}_1^v = \{x_v \in \{0,1\}^{|\mathcal{C}|} : \sum_{i \in \mathcal{C}} x_{vi} = c_v\}. \tag{20}$$

That is, subject to attaining correct marginals, one can ignore the source constraints: to see this, note that if $v \in S_i$, $\bar{y}_{vi} = 1$ for any $Y \in \mathcal{D}_2$. Hence, (17) ensures that v stores item i w.p. 1. We thus focus on constructing a distribution μ_v over $\bar{\mathcal{D}}_1^v$, under a given set of marginals $\bar{y}_v$. Note that a "naïve" construction in which x_{vi}, $v \in V$, $i \in \mathcal{C}$, are independent Bernoulli variables with parameters $\bar{y}_{vi}$ indeed satisfies

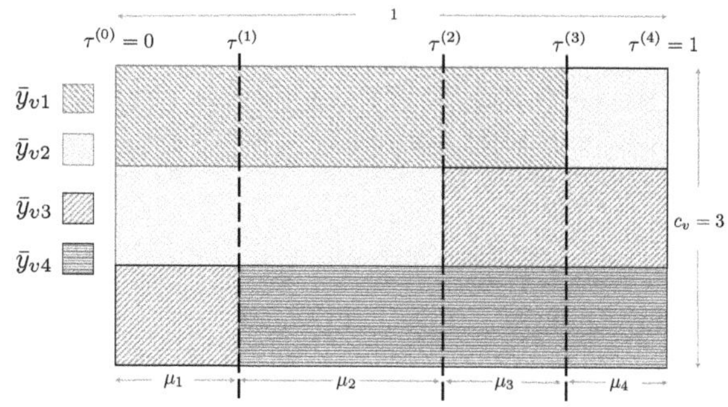

Figure 2: An allocation that satisfies $\mathbb{E}_\mu[x_{vi}] = \bar{y}_{vi}$, when $\sum_{i \in \mathcal{C}} \bar{y}_{vi} = c_v$. After placing the 4 rectangles in a 3×1 grid, assigning probabilities μ_1, μ_2, μ_3, μ_4 to each of the tuples $\{1,2,3\}$, $\{1,2,4\}$, $\{1,3,4\}$, $\{2,3,4\}$, respectively, yields the desired marginals.

(17), but *does not* yield vectors $x_v \in \bar{\mathcal{D}}_1^v$: indeed, such vectors only satisfy the capacity constraint in expectation, and may contain fewer or more items than c_v.

Before we formally present our algorithm we first give some intuition behind it, also illustrated in Figure 2. Let $c_v = 3$, $\mathcal{C} = \{1,2,3,4\}$, and consider a $\bar{y}_v \in \mathcal{D}_2^v$. To construct an allocation with the desired marginal distribution, consider a rectangle box of area $c_v \times 1$. For each $i \in \mathcal{C}$, place a rectangle of length $\bar{y}_{vi}$ and height 1 inside the box, starting from the top left corner. If a rectangle does not fit in a row, cut it, and place the remainder in the row immediately below, starting again from the left. As $\sum_{i=1}^{|\mathcal{C}|} \bar{y}_{vi} = c_v$, this space-filling method completely fills (i.e., tessellates) the $c_v \times 1$ box.

Consider now, for each row, all fractional values $\tau \in [0,1]$ at which two horizontal rectangles meet. We call these values the *cutting points*. Notice that there can be at most $|\mathcal{C}| - 1$ such points. Then, partition the $c_v \times 1$ box vertically, splitting it at these cutting points. This results in at most $|\mathcal{C}|$ vertical partitions (also rectangles), with c_v rows each. Note that each one of these vertical partitions correspond to tuples comprising c_v distinct items of $\mathcal{C}$. Each row of a vertical partition must contain some portion of a horizontal rectangle, as the latter tessellate the entire box. Moreover, no vertical partition can contain the same horizontal rectangle in two rows or more (i.e., a horizontal rectangle cannot "overlap" with itself), because $\bar{y}_{vi} \leq 1$, for all $\bar{y}_{vi} \in \mathcal{C}$. The desired probability distribution μ_v can then be constructed by setting (a) its support to be the c_v-tuples defined by each vertical partition, and (b) the probability of each c-tuple to be the length of the partition (i.e., the difference of the two consecutive τ cutting points that define it). The marginal probability of an item will then be exactly the length of its horizontal rectangle, i.e., $\bar{y}_{vi}$, as desired.

The above process is described formally in Algorithm 2. The following lemma establishes its correctness:

Lemma 2. *Alg. 2 produces a μ_v over $\bar{\mathcal{D}}_1^v$ s.t.* (17) *holds.*

A proof can be found in [21]. Note that, contrary to the "naïve" Bernoulli solution, the resulting variables x_{vi}, x_{vj}, where $i \neq j$, *may not be independent* (even though allocations are independent across caches). The algorithm's complexity is $O(c_v |\mathcal{C}| \log |\mathcal{C}|)$, as the sort in line 8 can be implemented in $O(c_v |\mathcal{C}| \log |\mathcal{C}|)$ time, while a match in 13 can be

Algorithm 2 PLACEMENT ALGORITHM

Input: capacity c_v, marginals $\bar{y}_v \in \mathbb{R}^{|\mathcal{C}|}$ s.t. $\bar{y}_v \geq \mathbf{0}$, $\sum_{i=1}^{|\mathcal{C}|} \bar{y}_{vi} = c_v$
Output: prob. distr. μ_v over $\{x \in \{0,1\}^{|\mathcal{C}|} : \sum_{i=1}^{|\mathcal{C}|} = c_v\}$ s.t. $\mathbb{E}_\mu[x_i] = \bar{y}_{vi}$, for all $i \in \mathcal{C}$.
$\texttt{sum} \leftarrow 0$
for all $i \in \mathcal{C}$ **do**
  $s_i \leftarrow \texttt{sum}$; $t_i \leftarrow \texttt{sum} + \bar{y}_{vi}$; $\tau_i \leftarrow t_i - \lfloor t_i \rfloor$
  $\texttt{sum} \leftarrow t_i$
end for
Sort all τ_i in increasing order, remove duplicates, and append 1 to the end of the sequence.
Let $0 = \tau^{(0)} < \tau^{(1)} < \ldots < \tau^{(K)} = 1$ be the resulting sequence.
for all $k \in \{0, \ldots, K-1\}$ **do**
  Create new vector $x \in \{0,1\}^{|\mathcal{C}|}$; set $x \leftarrow \mathbf{0}$.
  for all $\ell \in \{0, \ldots, c-1\}$ **do**
    Find $i \in \mathcal{C}$ such that $(\ell + \tau^{(k)}, \ell + \tau^{(k+1)}) \subset [s_i, t_i]$.
    Set $x_i \leftarrow 1$
  end for
  Set $\mu_v(x) = \tau^{(k+1)} - \tau^{(k)}$
end for
return μ_v

found in $O(\log |\mathcal{C}|)$ time if intervals are stored in a binary search tree. Moreover, the support of μ_v has size at most $|\mathcal{C}|$, so representing this distribution requires $O(c_v|\mathcal{C}|)$ space.

5.2.4 Convergence

We now establish the convergence of the smoothened marginals to a global maximizer of L:

THEOREM 3. *Let $\bar{Y}^{(k)} \in \mathcal{D}_2$ be the smoothened marginals at the k-th period of Algorithm 1. Then,*

$$\varepsilon_k \equiv \mathbb{E}[\max_{Y \in \mathcal{D}_2} L(Y) - L(\bar{Y}^{(k)})] \leq \frac{D^2 + M^2 \sum_{\ell=\lfloor k/2 \rfloor}^{k} \gamma_\ell^2}{\sum_{\ell=\lfloor k/2 \rfloor}^{k} \gamma_\ell},$$

where $D = \sqrt{2|V| \max_{v \in V} c_v}$, $M = W|V|\Lambda\sqrt{|V||\mathcal{C}|(1 + \frac{1}{\Lambda T})}$. *In particular, for* $\gamma_k = \frac{D}{M\sqrt{k}}$, *we have* $\varepsilon_k \leq O(1)\frac{MD}{\sqrt{k}}$, *where* $O(1)$ *is an absolute constant.*

PROOF. Under dynamics (15) and (16), from Theorem 14.1.1, page 215 of Nemirofski [30], we have that

$$\mathbb{E}[\max_{Y \in \mathcal{D}_2} L(Y) - L(\bar{Y}^{(k)})] \leq \frac{D^2 + M^2 \sum_{\ell=\lfloor k/2 \rfloor}^{k} \gamma_\ell^2}{\sum_{\ell=\lfloor k/2 \rfloor}^{k} \gamma_\ell}$$

where $D \equiv \max_{x,y \in \mathcal{D}_2} \|x - y\|_2 = \sqrt{\max_v 2|V|c_v}$ is the diameter of $\mathcal{D}_2$, and

$$M \equiv \sup_{Y \in \mathcal{D}_2} \sqrt{\sum_{v \in V} \mathbb{E}[\|z_v(Y)\|_2^2]} \leq W|V|\sqrt{|V||\mathcal{C}|(\Lambda^2 + \frac{\Lambda}{T})},$$

where the last equality follows from Lemma 1. □

The $O(1)\frac{MD}{\sqrt{k}}$ upper bound presumes knowledge of D and M when setting the gains γ_k, $k \geq 1$. Nonetheless, even when these are not apriori known, taking $\gamma_k = 1/\sqrt{k}$ suffices to ensure the algorithm converges with rate $1/\sqrt{k}$, up to (larger) constants, that depend on D and M. Moreover, the relationship between M and T captures the tradeoff induced by T: larger Ts give more accurate estimates of the subgradients, reducing the overall number of steps till convergence, but increase the length of each individual period.

Finally, Thms. 1 and 3 imply that the asymptotic expected caching gain under Algorithm 1 is within a constant factor from the optimal:

THEOREM 4. *Let $X^{(k)} \in \mathcal{D}_1$ be the allocation at the k-th period of Algorithm 1. Then, if $\gamma_k = \Theta(1/\sqrt{k})$,*

$$\lim_{k \to \infty} \mathbb{E}[F(X^{(k)})] \geq (1 - \frac{1}{e}) \max_{X \in \mathcal{D}_1} F(X).$$

PROOF. Given $\bar{Y}^{(k)}$, by Lemma 2, $X^{(k)}$ is sampled from a distribution μ over $\mathcal{D}_1$ that has product form (13). This product form implies that, conditioned on $\bar{Y}^{(k)}$, Eq. (6) holds; thus, $\mathbb{E}[F(X^{(k)}) \mid \bar{Y}^{(k)}] = F(\bar{Y}^{(k)})$, so $\lim_{k\to\infty} \mathbb{E}[F(X^{(k)})] = \lim_{k\to\infty} \mathbb{E}[F(\bar{Y}^{(k)})]$. From Thm. 3, $\lim_{k\to\infty} \mathbb{E}[L(\bar{Y}^{(k)})] = \max_{Y \in \mathcal{D}_2} L(Y)$. This implies that, for $\nu^{(k)}$ the distribution of $\bar{Y}^{(k)}$, and Ω the set of $Y \in \mathcal{D}_2$ that are maximizers of L, $\lim_{k\to\infty} \nu^{(k)}(\mathcal{D}_2 \setminus \Omega) = 0$. From Theorem 1, $F(Y) \geq (1 - 1/e) \max_{X \in \mathcal{D}_1} F(X)$ for any $Y \in \Omega$. The theorem therefore follows from the above observations, and the fact that F is bounded in $\mathcal{D}_2 \setminus \Omega$. □

We state these results under stationary demands but, in practice, we would prefer that caches adapt to demand fluctuations. To achieve this, one would fix γ to a constant positive value, ensuring that Algorithm 1 tracks demand changes. Though convergence to a minimizer is not guaranteed in this case, the algorithm is nonetheless guaranteed to reach states concentrated around an optimal allocation (see, e.g., Chapter 8 of Kushner & Yin [24]).

5.3 Greedy Path Replication

Algorithm 1 has certain drawbacks. First, to implement an allocation at the end of a measurement period, nodes may need to retrieve new items, which itself incurs additional traffic costs. Second, there is a timescale separation between how often requests arrive and when adaptations happen; an algorithm adapting at the request timescale may converge faster. Third, caches are synchronized, and avoiding such coordination is preferable. Finally, beyond request and response messages, the exchange of additional control messages are required to implement it.

In this section, we propose a greedy eviction policy, to be used with the path replication algorithm, that has none of the above drawbacks. This algorithm does not require any control traffic beyond the traffic generated by message exchanges. It is asynchronous, and its adaptations happen at the same timescale as requests. Each node makes caching decisions *only* when it receives a response message carrying an item: that is, a node decides whether to store an item exactly when it passes through, and requires no additional traffic to retrieve it. Finally, the eviction heuristic is very simple (though harder to analyze than Algorithm 1).

5.3.1 Algorithm Overview

In short, every $v \in V$ maintains an estimate z_v of $\partial_{x_v} L(X)$, i.e., a subgradient of L w.r.t. its allocation $x_v \in \{0,1\}^{|\mathcal{C}|}$. At any point in time, v stores all i s.t. $v \in S_i$; the remaining slots are occupied with items of *steepest gradient value*, namely, the items i that correspond to highest estimates z_{vi}. Crucially, a gradient estimate z_{vi} increases *only when a packet carrying i passes through v*. This ensures that an item entering the cache is always available. In more detail:

1. As in classic path replication, for each $(i,p) \in \mathcal{R}$, request messages are propagated until they reach a node u

Algorithm 3 GREEDY PATH REPLICATION

Execute the following at each $v \in V$:

Initialize $z_v = \mathbf{0}$.
while (true) **do**
  Wait for new response message.
  Upon receipt of new message, extract counter t_{vi} and i.
  Update z_v through (22).
  Sort z_{vj}, $j \in \mathcal{C}$, in decreasing order.
  if $x_{vi} = 0$ and i is in top c'_v items **then**
    Set $x_{vi} \leftarrow 1$; evict c'_v + 1-th item.
  end if
end while

caching the requested item $i \in \mathcal{C}$, i.e., for which $x_{ui} = 1$. Upon reaching such a node, a response message carrying the item is backpropagated over p.

2. The response message for a request (i, p) contains a weight counter that is initialized to zero by u. Whenever the response traverses an edge in the reverse path, the edge weight is added to the counter. The counter is "sniffed" by every node in p that receives the response. Hence, every node v in the path p that is visited by a response learns the quantity:

$$t_{vi} = \sum_{k'=k_v(p)}^{|p|-1} w_{p_{k'+1}p_{k'}} \mathbb{1}_{\sum_{\ell=1}^{k'} x_{p_\ell i} < 1}, \tag{21}$$

where, as before, $k_v(p)$ is the position of v in path p.

3. For each item i, each node v maintains again an estimate $z_v \in \mathbb{R}_+^{|\mathcal{C}|}$ of a subgradient in $\partial_{x_{vi}} L(X)$. This estimate is maintained through an *exponentially weighted moving average* (EWMA) of the quantities t_{vi} collected above. These are adapted each time v receives a response message. If v receives a response message for i at time t, then it adapts its estimates as follows: for all $j \in \mathcal{C}$,

$$z_{vj}(t) = z_{vj}(t') \cdot e^{-\beta(t-t')} + \beta \cdot t_{vi} \cdot \mathbb{1}_{i=j}, \tag{22}$$

where $\beta > 0$ is the EWMA gain, and $t' < t$ is the last time node v it received a response message prior to t. Thus, all estimates z_{vj} decay exponentially between responses, while only z_{vi}, corresponding to the requested item i, contains an additional increment βt_{vi}.

4. After receiving a response and adapting z_v, the node (a) sorts z_{vi}, $i \in C$, in a decreasing order, and (b) stores the top c'_v items, where $c'_v = c_v - |\{i : v \in S_i\}|$ is v's capacity excluding permanent items.

The above steps are summarized in Algorithm 3. Note that, upon the arrival of a response carrying item i, there are only two possible outcomes after the new z_v values are sorted: either (a) the cache contents remain unaltered, or (b) item i, which was previously not in the cache, is now placed in the cache, and another item is evicted. These are the only possibilities because, under (22), all items $j \neq i$ *preserve their relative order*: the only item whose relative position may change is i. As i is piggy-backed in the response, no additional traffic is needed to acquire it.

5.3.2 Formal Properties

Though simpler to describe and implement, Algorithm 3 is harder to analyze than Algorithm 1. Nonetheless, some intuition on its performance can be gained by looking into its fluid dynamics. In particular, let $X(t) = [x_{vi}(t)]_{v\in V, i\in\mathcal{C}}$ and $Z(t) = [z_{vi}(t)]_{v\in V, i\in\mathcal{C}}$ be the allocation and subgradient estimation matrices at time $t \geq 0$. Ignoring stochasticity, the "fluid" trajectories of these matrices are described by the following ODE:

$$X(t) \in \arg\max_{X\in\mathcal{D}_1} \langle X, Z(t)\rangle \tag{23a}$$

$$\frac{dZ(t)}{dt} = \beta\big(\underline{\partial L}(X(t)) - Z(t)\big) \tag{23b}$$

where $\langle A, B\rangle = \mathtt{trace}(AB^\top) = \sum_{v,i} A_{vi}B_{vi}$ is the inner product between two matrices, and $\underline{\partial L} \in \partial L$ is a subgradient of L at X.

PROOF. By the "baby Bernoulli" approximation of a Poisson process, and the fact that $e^x = 1 + x + o(x)$, for small $\delta > 0$ the EWMA adaptations have the form:

$$z_{vi}(t+\delta) = (1 - \beta\delta) z_{v_i}(t) + \beta\delta\phi_{vi} + o(\delta)$$

where $\mathbb{E}[\phi_{vi}] = \partial_{x_{vi}} L(X)$, and $\partial_{x_{vi}} L$ is given by (19b); note that the matrix $\underline{\partial L}$ is indeed a subgradient. The fluid dynamics (23) then follow by taking δ to go to zero, and replacing the ϕ_v's by their expectation. □

The dynamics (23) are similar (but not identical) to the "continuous greedy" algorithm for submodular maximization [36] and the Frank-Wolfe algorithm [11]. Eq. (23b) implies that $Z(t)$ indeed "tracks" a subgradient of L at X. On the other hand, the allocation selected by sorting—or, equivalently, by (23a)—identifies the most valuable items at each cache w.r.t. the present estimate of the subgradient. Hence, even if z_v is an inaccurate estimate of the subgradient at v, the algorithm treats it as correct and places the "most valuable" items in its cache. This is why we refer to this algorithm as "greedy". Note that (23a) also implies that

$$X(t) \in \arg\max_{Y\in\mathcal{D}_2} \langle Y, Z(t)\rangle.$$

This is because, subject to the capacity and source constraints, $\langle \cdot, Z\rangle$ is maximized by taking any set of top c'_v items, so an integral solution indeed always exists. The following lemma states that fixed points of the ODE (23), provided they exist, must be at maximizers of L.

LEMMA 3. *Let $X^* \in \mathcal{D}_2$ and $Z^* \in \mathbb{R}^{|V|\times|\mathcal{C}|}$ be such that $X^* \in \arg\max_{X\in\mathcal{D}_2} \langle X, Z^*\rangle$ and $Z^* \in \partial L(X^*)$. Then, $X^* \in \arg\max_{X\in\mathcal{D}_2} L(X)$.*

The lemma holds by the concavity of L, and is stated as Theorem 27.4 of Rockafellar [31], so we omit its proof. Though the conditions stated in the lemma are both necessary and sufficient in our case, the lemma does not imply that a *integral* solution (i.e., one in which $X^* \in \mathcal{D}_1$) need exist. In practice, the algorithm may converge to a chain-recurrent set of integral solutions. Though we do not study the optimality properties of this set formally, our numerical evaluations in Section 7 show that this greedy heuristic has excellent performance in practice, very close to the one attained by the maximizer of L.

6. OFFLINE PROBLEM EQUIVALENCE

Each iteration of the projected gradient ascent algorithm of Section 5 constructs probabilistic allocations that are (a) feasible, and (b) independent across nodes. This motivates us to study the following probabilistic relaxations of MAXCG, beyond the "independent Bernoulli" relaxation (7) we discussed in Section 4. First, consider the variant:

$$\text{Max.:} \quad \mathbb{E}_\mu[F(X)] = \textstyle\sum_{X\in\mathcal{D}_1} \mu(X)F(X) \tag{24a}$$

$$\text{subj. to:} \quad \mu \text{ is a pr. distr. over } \mathcal{D}_1 \text{ satisfying (13).} \tag{24b}$$

I.e., we seek random cache allocations sampled from a joint distribution μ having product form (13). In addition, consider the following (more general) variant of MAXCG:

$$\text{Maximize:} \quad \mathbb{E}_\mu[F(X)] = \textstyle\sum_{X\in\mathcal{D}_1} \mu(X)F(X) \tag{25a}$$

$$\text{subj. to:} \quad \mu \text{ is a pr. distr. over } \mathcal{D}_1. \tag{25b}$$

Our results and, in particular, Lemma 2, have the following surprising implication: all three relaxations (7), (24), and (25) *are in fact equivalent to* MAXCG.

THEOREM 5. *Let X^*, Y^*, μ^*, and μ^{**} be optimal solutions to* (3),(7), (24), *and* (25), *respectively. Then,*

$$F(X^*) = F(Y^*) = \mathbb{E}_{\mu^*}[F(X)] = \mathbb{E}_{\mu^{**}}[F(X)].$$

PROOF. We establish the following inequalities:

$$\mathbb{E}_{\mu^{**}}[F(X)] \le F(X^*) \le F(Y^*) \le \mathbb{E}_{\mu^*}[F(x)] \le \mathbb{E}_{\mu^{**}}[F(X)]$$

To see that $\mathbb{E}_{\mu^{**}}[F(X)] \le F(X^*)$, let $D = \texttt{supp}(\mu^{**}) \subseteq \mathcal{D}_1$ be the support of μ^{**}. Let $X' \in \arg\max_{X\in D} F(X)$ be an allocation maximizing F over D (as D is finite, this exists). Then, by construction, $\mathbb{E}_{\mu^{**}}[F(X)] \le F(X') \le F(X^*)$, as $X' \in \mathcal{D}_1$. $F(X^*) \le F(Y^*)$ by (9), as (7) is a relaxation of (3). To see that $F(Y^*) \le \mathbb{E}_{\mu^*}[F(X)]$, note that, by Lemma 2, since $Y^* \in \mathcal{D}_2$, there exists a measure μ' that has a product form and whose marginals are Y^*. Since μ' has a product form, it satisfies (6), and $F(Y^*) = \mathbb{E}_{\mu'}[F(X)] \le \mathbb{E}_{\mu^*}[F(X)]$. Finally, $\mathbb{E}_{\mu^*}[F(X)] \le \mathbb{E}_{\mu^{**}}[F(X)]$, as the former is the expected cost under a restricted class of distributions μ, namely, ones that have the product form (13). □

Theorem 5 is specific to MAXCG: e.g., Ineq. (9) can be strict in other problems solvable through the pipage rounding method. The theorem has some non-obvious, interesting implications. First, equivalence of (24) to (7) implies that satisfying capacity constraints in expectation, rather than exactly, *does not* improve the caching gain. Similarly, the equivalence of (24) to (25) implies that considering only distributions that describe *independent* caches does not restrict the caching gain attainable: independent caches are as powerful as fully randomized (or deterministic) caches. Finally, as MAXCG is NP-hard, so are all three other problems.

7. NUMERICAL EVALUATION

We simulate Algorithms 1 and 3 over synthetic and real networks, and compare their performance to path replication combined with **LRU**, **LFU**, **FIFO**, and random replacement (**RR**) caches. Across the board, greedy path replication performs exceptionally well, attaining at least 95% of the expected caching gain attained by Algorithm 1, while both significantly outperform traditional eviction policies.

Topologies. The networks we consider are summarized in Table 2. The first six graphs are deterministic. Graph **cycle** is a simple cyclic graph, and **lollipop** is a clique (i.e., complete graph), connected to a path graph of equal size. Graph **grid-2d** is a two-dimensional square grid, **balanced-tree** is a complete binary tree of depth 6, and **hypercube** is a 7-dimensional hypercube. Graph **expander** is a Margulies-Gabber-Galil expander [17]. The next 5 graphs are random, i.e., were sampled from a probability distribution. Graph **erdos-renyi** is an Erdős-Rényi graph with parameter $p = 0.1$, and **regular** is a 3-regular graph sampled uniformly at random (u.a.r.). The **watts-strogatz** graph is a graph generated according to the Watts-Strogatz model of a small-world network [37] comprising a cycle and 4 randomly selected edges, while **small-world** is the graph by Kleinberg [23], comprising a grid with additional long range edges. The preferential attachment model of Barabási and Albert [4], which yields powerlaw degrees, is used for **barabasi-albert**. Finally, the last 3 graphs represent the Deutche Telekom, Abilene, and GEANT backbone networks [33].

Graph	$\lvert V\rvert$	$\lvert E\rvert$	$\lvert\mathcal{C}\rvert$	$\lvert\mathcal{R}\rvert$	$\lvert Q\rvert$	c'_v	$F(Y^*)$
cycle	30	60	10	100	10	2	847.94
lollipop	30	240	10	100	10	2	735.78
grid-2d	100	360	300	1K	20	3	381.09
balanced-tree	127	252	300	1K	20	3	487.39
hypercube	128	896	300	1K	20	3	186.29
expander	100	716	300	1K	20	3	156.16
erdos-renyi	100	1042	300	1K	20	3	120.70
regular	100	300	300	1K	20	3	321.63
watts-strogatz	100	400	300	1K	20	3	322.49
small-world	100	491	300	1K	20	3	218.19
barabasi-albert	100	768	300	1K	20	3	113.52
geant	22	66	10	100	10	2	203.76
abilene	9	26	10	100	10	2	121.25
dtelekom	68	546	300	1K	20	3	94.79

Table 2: Graph Topologies and Experiment Parameters.

Experiment Setup. We evaluate the performance of different adaptive strategies over the graphs in Table 2. Given a graph $G(V, E)$, we generate a catalog $\mathcal{C}$, and assign a cache to each node in the graph. For every item $i \in \mathcal{C}$, we designate a node selected u.a.r. from V as a source for this item. We set the capacity c_v of every node v so that $c'_v = c_v - \lvert\{i : v \in S_i\}\rvert$ is constant among all nodes in V. We assign a weight to each edge in E selected u.a.r. from the interval $[1, 100]$. We then generate a set of requests $\mathcal{R}$ as follows. First, to ensure path overlaps, we select $\lvert Q\rvert$ nodes in V u.a.r., that are the only nodes that generate requests; let Q be the set of such query nodes. We generate a set of requests starting from a random node in Q, with the item requested selected from $\mathcal{C}$ according to a Zipf distribution with parameter 1.2. The request is then routed over the shortest path between the node in Q and the designated source for the requested item. We assign a rate $\lambda_{(i,p)} = 1$ to every request $(i, p) \in \mathcal{R}$.

The values of $\lvert\mathcal{C}\rvert$, $\lvert\mathcal{R}\rvert$ $\lvert Q\rvert$, and c_v for each experiment are given in Table 2. For each experiment, we also provide in the last column the quantity $F(Y^*)$, for $Y^* \in \arg\max_{Y\in\mathcal{D}_2} L(Y)$, i.e., the expected caching gain under a product form distribution that maximizes the relaxation L. By Thm. 1, this is within $1 - 1/e$ from the optimal expected caching gain.

Caching Algorithms and Measurements. We evaluate the performance of Algorithms 1 and 3, denoted by **PGA** (for Projected Gradient Ascent) and **GRD** (for Greedy), respectively. In the case of **PGA**, we tried different measurement periods $T = 1.0, 10.0, 20.0$, termed **PGA1**, **PGA10**, and **PGA20**, respectively. We implemented the algorithm both with state smoothening (16) and without (whereby allocations are sampled from marginals $Y^{(k)}$ directly). For brevity, we report

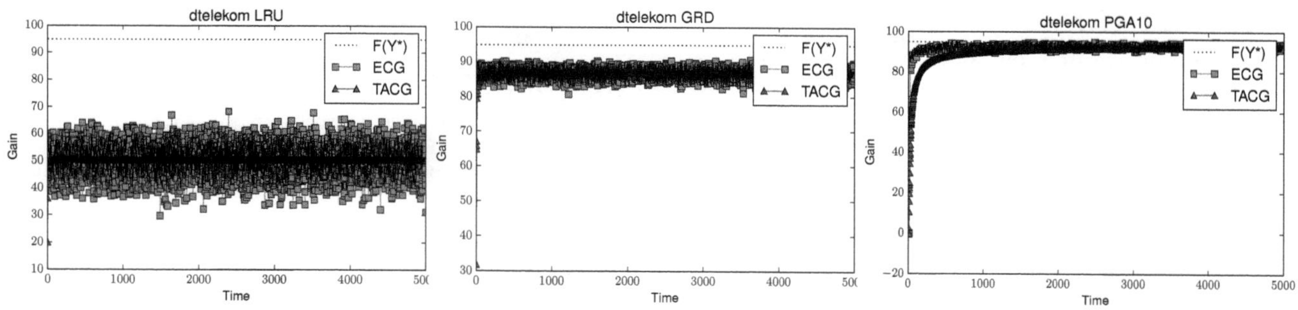

Figure 3: Trajectories of the expected caching gain ECG and the time average caching gain TACG under the LRU, GRD, and PGA algorithms, the latter with $T = 10$. The value $F(Y^*)$ for this experiment is shown in a dashed line.

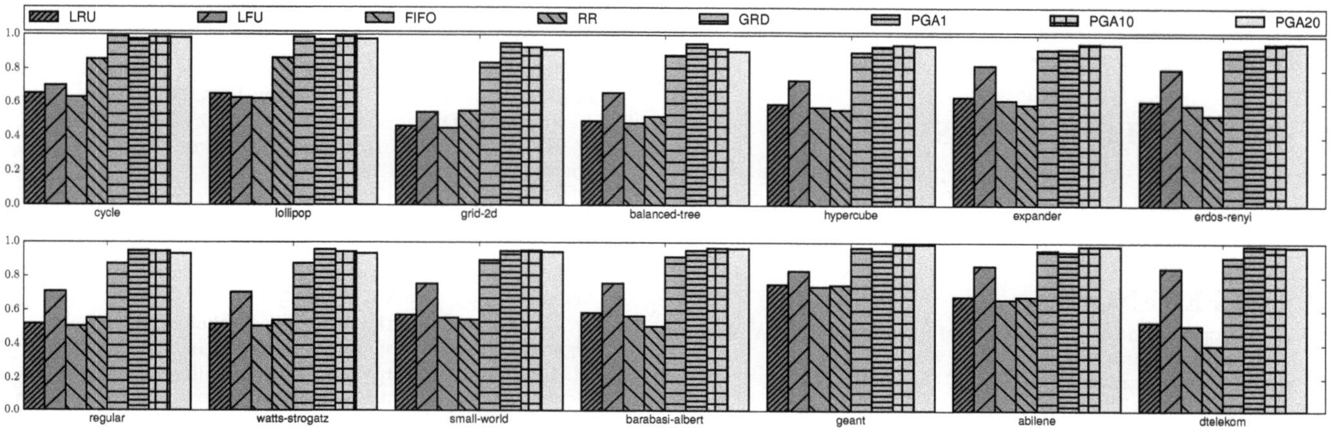

Figure 4: Ratio of expected caching gain ECG to $F(Y^*)$, as given in Table 2 under different networks and caching strategies. The greedy algorithm GRD performs almost as well as PGA in all cases. Both algorithms significantly outperform the remaining eviction policies.

only the non-smoothened versions, as time-average performance was nearly identical for both versions.

We also compare to path replication with LRU, LFU, FIFO, and RR eviction policies. In all cases, we simulate the network for 5000 time units. We collect measurements at epochs of a Poisson process with rate 1.0 (to leverage the PASTA property). In particular, at each measurement epoch, we extract the current allocation X, and compute the expected caching gain (ECG) as $F(X)$. In addition, we keep track of the actual cost of each request routed through the network, and compute the time average caching gain (TACG), measured as the difference of the cost of routing till the item source, minus the time average cost per request.

Results. Figure 3 shows the trajectories of the expected caching gain ECG and the time average caching gain TACG under the LRU, GRD, and PGA10 algorithms. All three algorithms converge relatively quickly to a steady state. PGA10 converges the slowest but it indeed reaches $F(Y^*)$, as expected. In addition, the greedy heuristic GRD performs exceptionally well, converging very quickly (faster than PGA) to a value close to $F(Y^*)$. In contrast, the allocations reached in steady state by LRU are highly suboptimal, close to 50% of $F(Y^*)$. Moreover, LRU exhibits high variability, spending considerable time in states with as low as 35% of $F(Y^*)$. We note that the relatively low variability of both GRD and PGA is a desirable feature in practice, as relatively stable caches are preferred by network administrators.

The above observations hold across network topologies and caching algorithms. In Figure 4, we plot the relative performance w.r.t ECG of all eight algorithms, normalized to $F(Y^*)$. We compute this as follows: to remove the effect of initial conditions, we focus on the interval $[1000, 5000]$, and average the ECG values in this interval.

We see that, in all cases, PGA attains $F(Y^*)$ for all three values of the measurement period T. Moreover, the simple heuristic GRD has excellent performance: across the board, it attains more than 95% of $F(Y^*)$, sometimes even outperforming PGA. Both algorithms consistently outperform all other eviction policies. We observe that RR and LFU perform quite well in several cases, and that "hard" instances for one appear to be "easy" for the other.

The differentiating instances, where performance is reversed, are the `cycle` and `lollipop` graphs: though small, these graphs contain long paths, in contrast to the remaining graphs that have a relatively low diameter. Intuitively, the long-path setting is precisely the scenario where local/myopic strategies like LRU, LFU, and FIFO make suboptimal decisions, while RR's randomization helps.

8. CONCLUSIONS

The main intuition from our analysis is that caching decisions *must account for upstream costs* to attain optimality guarantees. Establishing guarantees for Algorithm 3 remains an open question, of great interest especially in light of its performance in simulations. We believe that its relationship to the "continuous greedy" [36] and Frank-Wolfe [11] algorithms, as well as the algorithm in [20], can serve as a basis to characterizing its convergence. Determining the limit points of the fluid dynamics in (23) is key in this task.

Jointly optimizing caching *and* routing decisions is another open problem, even more pertinent in the presence of congestion, as in [38]. Ideally, one would reason about congestion within the context of MAXCG to produce joint routing and caching algorithms with delay *and* throughput optimality guarantees. Finally, Shanmugam et al. [34] show that caching fountain-coded content has interesting connections to the relaxation L; studying adaptive caching schemes in this setting also an important open question.

9. ACKNOWLEDGMENTS

E. Yeh gratefully acknowledges support from National Science Foundation grant CNS-1423250 and a Cisco Systems research grant.

10. REFERENCES

[1] A. A. Ageev and M. I. Sviridenko. Pipage rounding: A new method of constructing algorithms with proven performance guarantee. *Journal of Combinatorial Optimization*, 8(3):307–328, 2004.

[2] D. Applegate, A. Archer, V. Gopalakrishnan, S. Lee, and K. K. Ramakrishnan. Optimal content placement for a large-scale VoD system. In *CoNext*, 2010.

[3] I. Baev, R. Rajaraman, and C. Swamy. Approximation algorithms for data placement problems. *SIAM Journal on Computing*, 38(4):1411–1429, 2008.

[4] A.-L. Barabási and R. Albert. Emergence of scaling in random networks. *Science*, 286(5439):509–512, 1999.

[5] Y. Bartal, A. Fiat, and Y. Rabani. Competitive algorithms for distributed data management. *Journal of Computer and System Sciences*, 51(3):341–358, 1995.

[6] D. S. Berger, P. Gland, S. Singla, and F. Ciucu. Exact analysis of TTL cache networks. *IFIP Performance*, 2014.

[7] S. Borst, V. Gupta, and A. Walid. Distributed caching algorithms for content distribution networks. In *INFOCOM*, 2010.

[8] G. Calinescu, C. Chekuri, M. Pál, and J. Vondrák. Maximizing a submodular set function subject to a matroid constraint. In *Integer programming and combinatorial optimization*, pages 182–196. Springer, 2007.

[9] G. Carofiglio, M. Gallo, L. Muscariello, and D. Perino. Modeling data transfer in content-centric networking. In *Proceedings of the 23rd international teletraffic congress*, pages 111–118. International Teletraffic Congress, 2011.

[10] H. Che, Y. Tung, and Z. Wang. Hierarchical web caching systems: Modeling, design and experimental results. *Selected Areas in Communications*, 20(7):1305–1314, 2002.

[11] K. L. Clarkson. Coresets, sparse greedy approximation, and the frank-wolfe algorithm. *ACM Transactions on Algorithms*, 6(4):63, 2010.

[12] E. Cohen and S. Shenker. Replication strategies in unstructured peer-to-peer networks. In *SIGCOMM*, 2002.

[13] M. Dehghan, A. Seetharam, B. Jiang, T. He, T. Salonidis, J. Kurose, D. Towsley, and R. Sitaraman. On the complexity of optimal routing and content caching in heterogeneous networks. In *INFOCOM*, 2014.

[14] L. Fleischer, M. X. Goemans, V. S. Mirrokni, and M. Sviridenko. Tight approximation algorithms for maximum general assignment problems. In *SODA*, 2006.

[15] N. C. Fofack, P. Nain, G. Neglia, and D. Towsley. Analysis of TTL-based cache networks. In *VALUETOOLS*, 2012.

[16] C. Fricker, P. Robert, and J. Roberts. A versatile and accurate approximation for LRU cache performance. In *ITC*, 2012.

[17] O. Gabber and Z. Galil. Explicit constructions of linear-sized superconcentrators. *Journal of Computer and System Sciences*, 22(3):407–420, 1981.

[18] M. Gallo, B. Kauffmann, L. Muscariello, A. Simonian, and C. Tanguy. Performance evaluation of the random replacement policy for networks of caches. *Performance Evaluation*, 40(1):395–396, 2012.

[19] S. Ioannidis and P. Marbach. Absence of evidence as evidence of absence: A simple mechanism for scalable p2p search. In *INFOCOM*, 2009.

[20] S. Ioannidis, L. Massoulié, and A. Chaintreau. Distributed caching over heterogeneous mobile networks. In *SIGMETRICS*, 2010.

[21] S. Ioannidis and E. Yeh. Adaptive caching networks with optimality guarantees, 2016. arXiv:1604.03175.

[22] V. Jacobson, D. K. Smetters, J. D. Thornton, M. F. Plass, N. H. Briggs, and R. L. Braynard. Networking named content. In *CoNEXT*, 2009.

[23] J. Kleinberg. The small-world phenomenon: An algorithmic perspective. In *STOC*, 2000.

[24] H. J. Kushner and G. Yin. *Stochastic approximation and recursive algorithms and applications*, volume 35. Springer Science & Business Media, 2003.

[25] N. Laoutaris, S. Syntila, and I. Stavrakakis. Meta algorithms for hierarchical web caches. In *ICPCC*, 2004.

[26] M. Leconte, M. Lelarge, and L. Massoulié. Bipartite graph structures for efficient balancing of heterogeneous loads. In *SIGMETRICS*, 2012.

[27] M. Leconte, M. Lelarge, and L. Massoulie. Designing adaptive replication schemes in distributed content delivery networks. In *ITC*, 2015.

[28] Q. Lv, P. Cao, E. Cohen, K. Li, and S. Shenker. Search and replication in unstructured peer-to-peer networks. In *ICS*, 2002.

[29] V. Martina, M. Garetto, and E. Leonardi. A unified approach to the performance analysis of caching systems. In *INFOCOM*, 2014.

[30] A. Nemirovski. *Efficient methods in convex programming.* 2005.

[31] R. T. Rockafellar. *Convex analysis.* Princeton University Press, 1970.

[32] E. J. Rosensweig, D. S. Menasche, and J. Kurose. On the steady-state of cache networks. In *INFOCOM*, 2013.

[33] D. Rossi and G. Rossini. Caching performance of content centric networks under multi-path routing (and more). Technical report, Telecom ParisTech, 2011.

[34] K. Shanmugam, N. Golrezaei, A. G. Dimakis, A. F. Molisch, and G. Caire. Femtocaching: Wireless content delivery through distributed caching helpers. *Transactions on Information Theory*, 59(12):8402–8413, 2013.

[35] A. L. Stolyar. Maximizing queueing network utility subject to stability: Greedy primal-dual algorithm. *Queueing Systems*, 50(4):401–457, 2005.

[36] J. Vondrák. Optimal approximation for the submodular welfare problem in the value oracle model. In *STOC*, 2008.

[37] D. J. Watts and S. H. Strogatz. Collective dynamics of 'small-world' networks. *Nature*, 393(6684):440–442, 1998.

[38] E. Yeh, T. Ho, Y. Cui, M. Burd, R. Liu, and D. Leong. Vip: A framework for joint dynamic forwarding and caching in named data networks. In *ICN*, 2014.

[39] Y. Zhou, Z. Chen, and K. Li. Second-level buffer cache management. *Parallel and Distributed Systems*, 15(6):505–519, 2004.

Breathing Mankind Thoughts

Philippe Jacquet
Nokia Bell Labs, Nozay, France
Philippe.Jacquet@nokia.com

ABSTRACT

Mankind has never been connected as it is now and as it will be tomorrow. Nowadays thanks to the rise of social networks such as Tweeter and Facebook, we can follow in real time the thought of millions of people. In fact we can almost feel the thoughts of a whole humanity and maybe project ourselves in a position where we could predict the major trends in the collective behavior of this humanity.

However such an ambitious aim would require considerable resources in processing and networking which may be far from affordable. Indeed trends and topics are carried in a multiple of small texts written in various language and vocabularies like an hologram carries information in a dispersed way. Their capture and classification pose serious problems of data mining and analytics. Processes based on pure semantic analysis would require too much processing power and memory. We will present alternative methods based on string complexity also inspired on geolocalization in wireless networks which saves processing power by several order of magnitude. The ultimate goal is to detect when people are thinking about the very same topics before they become aware.

Beyond the problem of topic detection and classification one must also estimate the potential of an isolated topic to become a lasting trend. In other word one must probe the topic foundations, for example by challenging how trustworthy are its sources. Designing an efficient source finder algorithm is indissociable with building realistic models about topic propagation. If we suppose that topics propagate inside communities via the followers-followees links, the propagation is highly amplified by the unbalances in the graph topology. It is established that dominating and semi dominating nodes such as the CNN Tweeter site are the main accelerator of topic propagation. The difficulty is to find the actual source of a topic beyond those screening nodes and the search is prone to false positive and true negative effects. In fact we will show that finding a source of topic is similar to finding a common ancestor in a Darwin channel where spurious mutations complicate the task.

CCS Concepts

• Human-centered computing → Collaborative and social computing → Collaborative and social computing design and evaluation method → Social network analysis

SIGMETRICS'16, June 14–18, 2016, Antibes Juan-Les-Pins, France.
ACM ISBN 978-1-4503-4266-7/16/06.
DOI: http://dx.doi.org/10.1145/2896377.2901899

Keywords

Social networks; topic detection; string combinatorics; topic propagation

Short Bio

Philippe Jacquet graduated from Ecole Polytechnique, Paris, France in 1981, and from Ecole des Mines in 1984. He received his PhD degree from Paris Sud University in 1989. Since 1998, he has been a research director in Inria, a major public research lab in Computer Science in France. He has been a major contributor to the Internet OLSR protocol for mobile networks.
His research interests involve information theory, probability theory, quantum telecommunication, protocol design, performance evaluation and optimization, and the analysis of algorithms. Since 2012 he is with Nokia (formerly Alcatel-Lucent) Bell Labs as head of the department of mathematics of dynamic networks and information.

Unsupervised Clustering Under Temporal Feature Volatility in Network Stack Fingerprinting

Zain Shamsi and Dmitri Loguinov*
Department of Computer Science and Engineering
Texas A&M University, College Station, TX 77843 USA
{zain, dmitri}@cse.tamu.edu

ABSTRACT

Maintaining and updating signature databases is a tedious task that normally requires a large amount of user effort. The problem becomes harder when features can be distorted by observation noise, which we call *volatility*. To address this issue, we propose algorithms and models to automatically generate signatures in the presence of noise, with a focus on *stack fingerprinting*, which is a research area that aims to discover the operating system (OS) of remote hosts using TCP/IP packets. Armed with this framework, we construct a database with 420 network stacks, label the signatures, develop a robust classifier for this database, and fingerprint 66M visible webservers on the Internet.

Keywords

OS Fingerprinting; OS Classification; Internet Measurement

1. INTRODUCTION

With the immense growth of the Internet, classification of large networking datasets has become an important topic [1], [6], [9], [11], [14], [16], [19], [20], [26], [34], [35]. For classifiers to work, there must be a process that establishes signatures for known types of behavior and builds a database that contains all sufficiently different specimens found in the wild. To keep results up-to-date, new signatures must be periodically acquired and merged into the existing database. This is often a manual process that suffers from human error, poor repeatability, heuristic decisions, and database compositions incompatible across different classification methods.

To overcome these problems, we investigate algorithms and models for automated creation of clusters among the available samples, elimination of duplicates, and assignment of labels to the resulting signatures. We next explain the issues involved and our results.

*Supported by NSF grant CNS-1319984.

SIGMETRICS '16, June 14-18, 2016, Antibes Juan-Les-Pins, France
© 2016 ACM. ISBN 978-1-4503-4266-7/16/06...$15.00
DOI: http://dx.doi.org/10.1145/2896377.2901449

1.1 Motivation and Contributions

Performance of each classifier depends on not only its internal algorithms, but also database $\mathcal{D}$ and types of volatility experienced during measurement. This makes comparison between different approaches (e.g., Nmap [21], Snacktime [3], Hershel [25], p0f [33]) fairly complicated, especially if they utilize incompatible sets of features, databases, or assumptions on feature determinism. For example, consider method $\mathcal{M}_1$ with n signatures and $\mathcal{M}_2$ with $m \ll n$. It may appear that $\mathcal{M}_1$ is more powerful because its $\mathcal{D}$ is bigger; however, its classification accuracy may be lower due to the larger number of options to choose from and/or less reliable decision-making. Additionally, the specific model of distortion $\mathcal{X}$ (i.e., noise in certain features) applied during the experiment may have a dramatic impact on the result. In such cases, it is possible that $\mathcal{M}_1$ resorts to random guessing and makes inferior choices to those of $\mathcal{M}_2$.

To capture these aspects, our first contribution is to propose that each classification method be characterized by the number of signatures $d(1-\epsilon, \mathcal{X})$, which we call the *dimension*, between which it can differentiate with probability at least $1-\epsilon$ under a given $\mathcal{X}$. We also argue that database $\mathcal{D}$ should be customized to each pair $(\epsilon, \mathcal{X})$ to contain exactly $d(1-\epsilon, \mathcal{X})$-separable signatures. To determine the dimension and the corresponding $\mathcal{D}$, our second contribution is to propose an algorithm we call Plata[1], which disturbs each candidate signature in $\mathcal{D}$ using $\mathcal{X}$ and verifies that it can be matched to itself with probability at least $1-\epsilon$. Samples that fail to meet this criterion are eliminated and classification decisions among other signatures are redistributed in an iterative procedure that stops when all remaining candidates are $(1-\epsilon, \mathcal{X})$-separable. Assuming availability of labels for a subset of initial candidates, we explain how Plata automatically assigns them to the d generated clusters.

We apply these concepts to Hershel [25], which is a classifier that, unlike all previous tools in stack fingerprinting, allows random OS behavior and provides probabilities, rather than heuristic weights, for the match across any pair of samples. We focus on its temporal network features (i.e., delay jitter) since they are highly volatile and fairly well-understood, but difficult to separate using manual analysis. This leads to our third contribution that consists of building a Plata database using 9.7K webservers discovered in our campus network and passing all HTTP headers through simhash [16] to label the elements of $\mathcal{D}$. Using only delay features, we show that Hershel achieves 80%-separation under

[1]The city of La Plata in Argentina pioneered fingerprint databases in 1892.

500-ms random distortion on 117 signatures. Adding deterministic header values, this number jumps to $d(0.8, \mathcal{X}) = 398$, which is 3.4 times larger than the biggest database in prior work [25].

While Plata works well, its Monte Carlo simulations require a large amount of CPU time to compute the Hershel probabilities (i.e., over 24 hours using 16 cores). Therefore, our fourth contribution is to build a closed-form model for the matrix produced by Plata. This leads to an interesting discovery that Hershel's iid (independent and identically distributed) jitter assumption [25] is violated in practice, making the model disagree with simulations. We therefore create a novel classifier for temporal features that relies on one-way delay instead of jitter. We call the resulting method Hershel+ and show that it is not only more accurate, but also faster than Hershel after an appropriate expansion of integrals. It also admits a closed-form representation of the entire Plata matrix, which reduces the separation time to just 12 minutes and boosts our database dimension to 420 separable signatures. All of this forms our fifth contribution.

We finish the paper by scanning the Internet on port 80 and applying Hershel+ to the result. Among Internet-wide studies, this is the largest population to be fingerprinted (i.e., 66M IPs), using the most extensive database (i.e., 420 signatures), and the first such attempt with an automatically generated $\mathcal{D}$. Compared to the scan six years ago [25], we find that the number of Linux and embedded devices has almost doubled, while that of Windows has remained stable. We compare some of our results with those of Nmap and discover a major flaw in the operation of the latter that surfaces in scenarios with non-ideal network conditions (e.g., firewalls). More importantly, however, we conclude that stochastic network effects do not impede the use of temporal features, but they require a more careful database construction process. Our proposed framework of Plata and Hershel+ is a step in the direction of automated, repeatable, and streamlined classification of massive datasets.

2. BACKGROUND

2.1 Remote OS Classification

Stack fingerprinting is often used in market-share analysis [19], [20], Internet characterization [11], [14], research measurements [4], [8], [15], and security, where administrators aim to discover vulnerable devices and/or stealth intruders in the network [1], [17], [26]. We split the work across two main categories in Figure 1. In the first tier are classifiers that rely only on deterministic features, usually selected from the headers of various protocols (i.e., TCP, IP, UDP, ICMP). Among these, Nmap [21] is the most prominent tool with rules to identify over 4K network stacks. With hundreds of transmitted probes, several protocols that must pass remote firewalls, and complaints from network administrators during fingerprinting of their networks, Nmap is not generally considered suitable for Internet-scale use. Additional classifiers in this category include p0f [33], Xprobe [32], and several others [2], [18], [28]. They have a smaller presence and significantly fewer signatures, but most of their ideas have been ported to Nmap.

The second direction in Figure 1 handles random features, usually in the form of delays produced by the OS. One option is use the clock drift in the kernel, which can be derived from observing the timestamp option in streams of reply

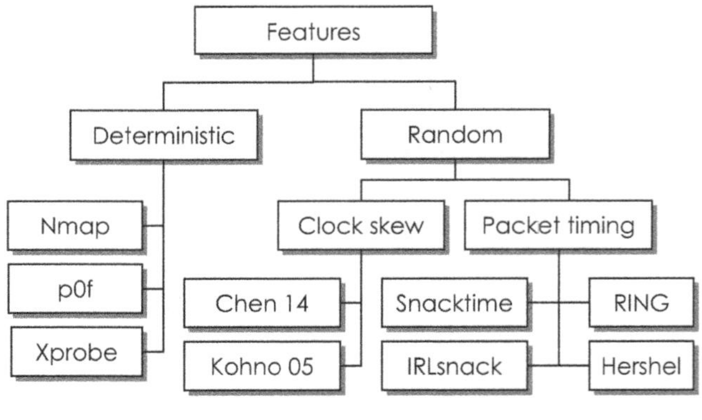

Figure 1: Taxonomy of previous work.

packets [13] or variation in timer frequency [6]. Another option is to monitor retransmission timeouts (RTOs) of SYN-ACKs for half-open connections, where the methods include Snacktime [3], RING [30], IRLsnack [14], and Hershel [25]. The last classifier uses a stochastic model that takes into account packet loss, delay jitter, and random header-field modifications by end-users, some of which we review below.

2.2 Database Creation

The majority of efforts in stack fingerprinting [2], [3], [6], [13], [18], [21], [25], [28], [30], [33] concentrate on introducing new features and designs to further distinguish between the OSes, thus improving the classification step; however, they universally rely on manual effort to construct databases. Since all of them rely only on deterministic features, database creation is fairly uncomplicated.

The closest related problem to ours is automatic discovery of features that can be used to differentiate one OS from another. For example, [5] proposes a set of rules built from sending out a large number of probes (i.e., 300K) to controlled hosts and randomly varying header fields to detect patterns that produce OS-specific responses. The authors show that this method can reliably differentiate between three stacks (i.e., Windows XP, Linux 2.6, and Solaris 9) in a LAN environment.

In [23], this idea is explored at a larger scale by increasing the number of network stacks and applying a wider range of machine-learning algorithms from the Weka tool [10]. However, their results from scaling this approach to more signatures are quite pessimistic – the authors conclude that over-fitting to non-deterministic header fields, training bias towards certain implementations, and lacking semantics lead to confusion for the learning algorithms.

3. OVERVIEW

We start by defining the type of decisions we are facing and the inherent challenges. While later sections use examples from stack fingerprinting, the same concepts are applicable to broader families of problems.

3.1 Terminology

Classifiers rely on vectors of distinctive features that identify each specimen, either uniquely or with some reasonably high probability. The former case arises when the features are *deterministic*, meaning all inspections of a given system produce the same result (e.g., the order of TCP options).

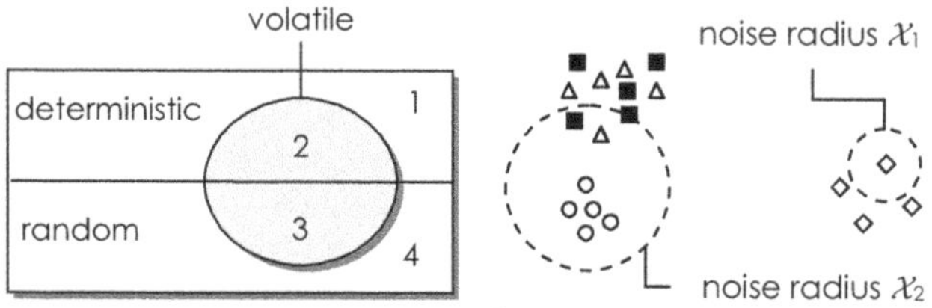

(a) types (b) separability

Figure 2: Classifier features.

The latter case occurs when the features are inherently *random* due to some non-deterministic processes running within the specimen (e.g., SYN-ACK retransmission delays). Features of either type may undergo additional modification due to influence of system owners or as byproduct of the measurement process, in which case we call them *volatile* (e.g., users tuning the TCP window size, queuing delays affecting packet spacing). All four types are illustrated in Figure 2(a).

Note that volatility and randomness are not the same – the former arises due to forces *external* to the object being classified, while the latter due to *internal*. This distinction is important when internal disturbances exhibit substantially larger variance than external, or produce patterns that cannot be accounted for in the volatility model alone. With this in mind, we call classifiers *simple* if they operate using only non-volatile deterministic features (i.e., type-1 in Figure 2(a)) and *complex* otherwise (i.e., types 2-4).

Consider an automaton that performs classification decisions for measurements x using some database $\mathcal{D}$. We call the matching process *membership* if it returns the probability that $x \in \mathcal{D}$, where determination of the most-likely match is not important. One example is intrusion detection that aims to decide whether payload x is malicious or benign against a database of known exploits. We call the process *identification* if the result must produce the one signature $y \in \mathcal{D}$ with the highest similarity to x. Stack fingerprinting falls into this category. In either case, the accuracy of the method is assessed by the percentage of correctly classified values under a particular model of volatility.

3.2 Challenges

We are now ready to describe the problem of creating $\mathcal{D}$. Assume a measurement of several, possibly duplicate, specimens. Membership classifiers are not overly concerned with high-precision duplicate elimination as these have no effect on accuracy, only on speed and memory consumption. Simple identification classifiers can construct $\mathcal{D}$ by retaining the observations with unique combinations of features, which makes the problem trivial. However, complex identification classifiers must instead ensure *separability* among the signatures, keeping only those that can be reliably distinguished from each other under various types of distortion $\mathcal{X}$. Inseparable specimens in $\mathcal{D}$ drop classification accuracy and increase overhead, while offering no tangible benefit.

To visualize this better, Figure 2(b) plots random features of four hypothetical systems – circles, squares, diamonds, and triangles – where each point is a random observation of the corresponding system. Assuming uniformly random noise centered at each sample, distortion $\mathcal{X}_1$ keeps circles and diamonds separable, but not necessarily triangles and squares. Dropping either of the last two leads to a separable 3-signature database. For larger radius of noise (e.g., $\mathcal{X}_2$ in the figure) the database may consist of only two separable signatures – diamonds and one of circles/squares/triangles.

Our goal in this paper is to study separation algorithms for volatile and/or random features, with application to inter-packet delays in wide-scale stack fingerprinting. This problem arises in single-packet techniques [3], [25], [30] whose classifier must heavily rely on temporal features. The general appeal of these methods includes low bandwidth consumption (i.e., no extra packets beyond those sent by the scanner), a reduced probability of tripping IDS, no requirement that the target respond on closed ports or multiple protocols, and good scalability in Internet-wide classification. However, unlike traditional tools [21] that rely on deterministic features, single-packet classifiers require prohibitively expensive manual effort to construct databases of non-trivial size. Since this problem has not been studied before, we address it below.

4. DATABASE CREATION USING PLATA

This section describes our technique for ensuring separability between observations with volatile/random features and building a database on top of such measurements.

4.1 Preliminaries

Traditional manual construction of $\mathcal{D}$ isolates each unique system and lets the classifier analyze it separately. In contrast, our framework assumes a one-step measurement process that remotely probes production systems $S_1, \ldots, S_n$ and builds the entire database without knowing which ones are duplicates of each other. We allow these specimens to exhibit feature randomness and aim to construct $\mathcal{D}$ that is $(1-\epsilon)$-separable under a known volatility model $\mathcal{X}$.

To capture random behavior, each specimen S_i must be observed several times to establish a distribution of its behavior. Let Δ_i be the corresponding random feature vector whose probability mass function (PMF)

$$p_i(\delta) := P(\Delta_i = \delta) \tag{1}$$

is built from observation. Note that $\delta = (\delta_1, \delta_2, \ldots)$ is a deterministic feature vector that consists of multiple scalar values. Using a pair of initial RTOs (SYN-ACK retransmission timeouts), Figure 3(a) shows the distribution of Δ_i for two Xerox printers in our dataset. Depending on the target jitter model $\mathcal{X}$, these two hosts may very well be $(1-\epsilon)$-separable; however, doing so manually for hundreds of thousands of points is close to impossible. To compound the issue, the majority of systems use random vectors with at least 3 dimensions and some with over 20.

Classifiers that deal with random features must provide a function $p(\delta|\delta', \mathcal{X})$ that produces a *similarity score* for each pair of deterministic vectors (δ, δ') under a given volatility model $\mathcal{X}$. This metric estimates the likelihood that δ' has been distorted to δ during remote measurement. Then, similarity between two observed systems (S_i, S_j) is given by the following expectation

$$p(\Delta_i|\Delta_j, \mathcal{X}) = \sum_{\delta} \sum_{\delta'} p(\delta|\delta', \mathcal{X}) p_i(\delta) p_j(\delta'). \tag{2}$$

For a given i, classifiers are typically concerned with finding j that produces the largest value in (2). However, we are facing a different problem that requires normalization. Let $\pi_i(\mathcal{X}) := \sum_{j=1}^{n} p(\Delta_i|\Delta_j, \mathcal{X})$ be the total similarity weight

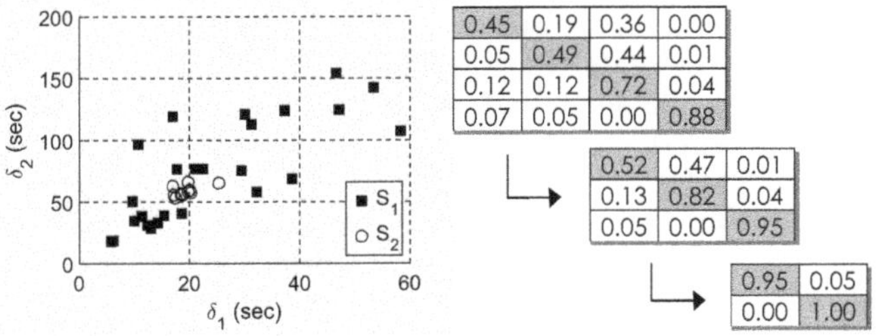

(a) random features (b) matrix reduction

Figure 3: Randomness of RTO features and elimination of duplicates in Plata.

of system S_i across all available options j. Depending on the classifier, π_i may not always be 1. To handle such cases, define

$$q(\Delta_i|\Delta_j, \mathcal{X}) = \frac{p(\Delta_i|\Delta_j, \mathcal{X})}{\pi_i(\mathcal{X})} \tag{3}$$

to be the probability that S_i gets classified as S_j. Now suppose systems $S_1, \dots, S_n$ are deployed in a production environment (e.g., wide-area Internet) and measured using remote probing. Therefore, instead of seeing Δ_i, the observer now samples $\Delta_i + \theta$, where random vector θ is driven by the same distortion model $\mathcal{X}$. We are thus interested in identifying the largest subset of $S_1, \dots, S_n$ in which each system can be matched back to itself with probability at least $1 - \epsilon$ under noise $\mathcal{X}$, i.e., $E[q(\Delta_i + \theta|\Delta_i, \mathcal{X})] \geq 1 - \epsilon$.

4.2 Matrix Construction

We next describe our database-construction framework, which we call Plata. It starts by building a confusion matrix $M = (M_{ij})$, where each cell $M_{ij} = E[q(\Delta_i + \theta|\Delta_j, \mathcal{X})]$ and the expectation is taken over θ. In general, classification decisions and vectors θ may be available only as output of some algorithm. For example, the former might be a C4.5 decision tree and the latter may require simulations of a specific queuing discipline. In such cases, the only solution is to run Monte-Carlo simulations that repeatedly distort Δ_i, classify the resulting observations, and average the result to obtain an approximation to M_{ij}.

To this end, suppose we generate r vectors $\theta_1, \dots, \theta_r$ by simulating $\mathcal{X}$. Using the PMF in (1), we obtain the same number of instances from random variable Δ_i, which we call $\delta_i^1, \dots, \delta_i^r$. Then, the approximate matrix is given by

$$\tilde{M}_{ij} = \frac{1}{r} \sum_{m=1}^{r} q(\delta_i^m + \theta_m|\Delta_j, \mathcal{X}). \tag{4}$$

Since this expands to

$$\tilde{M}_{ij} = \frac{1}{r} \sum_{m=1}^{r} \sum_{\delta'} q(\delta_i^m + \theta_m|\delta', \mathcal{X}) p_j(\delta'), \tag{5}$$

the overhead of constructing $\tilde{M}$ is determined by the product of r, matrix size n^2, the number of unique values δ', and complexity of computing $p(\delta|\delta', \mathcal{X})$, which typically is a linear function of the combined vector length $|\delta| + |\delta'|$.

4.3 Separation

Once complete, the diagonal of $\tilde{M}$ contains the probability of self-classification under $\mathcal{X}$. The next task is to iteratively eliminate specimens that disperse a significant fraction of classification decisions to non-diagonal cells until the target $(1 - \epsilon)$-separability is achieved, i.e., all $\tilde{M}_{ii} \geq 1 - \epsilon$. At each step, Plata removes row k with the smallest diagonal value and redistributes its probability weights to the remaining systems. The naive approach is to re-run Monte-Carlo simulations and build a new matrix with dimension $(n-1) \times (n-1)$; however, this is extremely expensive, especially when r is orders of magnitude larger than n.

The second option is to infer the new weights using a model and build a sequence of approximations that produce a final matrix similar to that in the naive method. Consider row i that needs to partition $\tilde{M}_{ik}$, i.e., the probability to classify i as k, among the other columns. If we assume that in the absence of system k, classification decisions follow the remaining probabilities in row i, the likelihood to classify $\delta_i^m + \theta_m$ as $j \neq k$ now becomes $\tilde{M}_{ij}/(1 - \tilde{M}_{ik})$. Multiplying this by the weight being removed and adding to the current $\tilde{M}_{ij}$, we get the following transformation that keeps row sums invariant

$$\tilde{M}_{ij} = \tilde{M}_{ij} + \frac{\tilde{M}_{ij}}{1 - \tilde{M}_{ik}} \tilde{M}_{ik}. \tag{6}$$

Note that if none of i's classifications went to system k, i.e., $\tilde{M}_{ik} = 0$, row i does not change. This process continues until all diagonal values are above $1 - \epsilon$. The remaining systems at that stage are added to the database and their number establishes the $(1 - \epsilon, \mathcal{X})$-dimension of the classifier. An example of this reduction process is shown in Figure 3(b), where the rows are sorted in ascending order of $\tilde{M}_{ii}$ for convenience of presentation. Setting $\epsilon = 0.2$, there are three rows that violate separability constraints. Since (S_1, S_2) are both similar to S_3, but none of them resembles S_4, intuition suggests the initial measurement may contain only two separable specimens. After removal of the first row, all diagonals receive a boost, but (S_2, S_3) are still inseparable. Another iteration produces the expected two vectors that match themselves with probability 0.95 or better.

Note that $1 - \epsilon$ can be used as a tuning parameter – larger values reduce the number of eventual vectors in the database, while smaller values preserve more, but at the risk of having more duplicates and poor classification accuracy. Although only $\tilde{M}_{ii}$ is compared against $1 - \epsilon$, the entire matrix needs to be recomputed after each iteration. This is necessary in order to properly distribute the weights of eliminated systems using (6). Thus, the complexity of each step is n^2, repeated $n - d$ times, where $d := |\mathcal{D}|$ is the size of the final database.

4.4 Labeling

Once database $\mathcal{D}$ is created, Plata needs to assign system-identifying labels to the available signatures. Assume a process that collects mappings from each S_i to the corresponding label l_i using some type of download (e.g., port-80 HTTP requests), oracle input, or other means, but possibly for a subset of the known specimens. Incomplete labeling may occur due to bandwidth constraints, obfuscation of certain systems by their administrators, and generic software names (e.g., apache) that fail to identify the underlying system. Since labels might be available for hosts that have been discarded during the matrix-separation step, we must again consider the entire set $S_1, \dots, S_n$. To this end, we classify each known specimen using $\mathcal{D}$ and produce a set of clus-

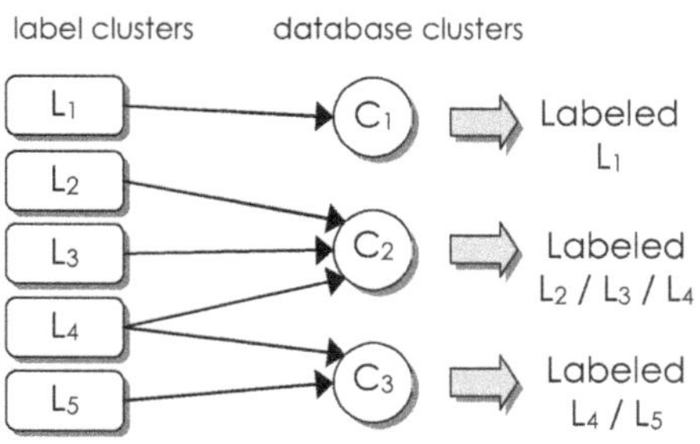

Figure 4: Applying labels to database clusters.

ters $C_1, \ldots, C_d$, where d is the $(1-\epsilon, \mathcal{X})$-dimension of the database/classifier obtained earlier by Plata.

To eliminate duplicate labels, a separate procedure clusters them into multiple categories $L_1, L_2, \ldots$ using some type of string-similarity matching. As shown in Figure 4, there is a directed edge between clusters L_k and C_j if there exists a system $S_i \in C_j$ such that its label $l_i \in L_k$. Note that this forms a bipartite graph in which L_k may point to multiple clusters C_j. Plata leaves the specifics of choosing the right label for each C_j to the application. One option is to combine the labels of all in-neighbors, as done in Figure 4. Another option is to assign weights to edges (e.g., equal to the number of corresponding S_i's) and enforce some minimum frequency before a label is considered valid. This can be further extended to allow for majority voting. For example, 100 hosts with label "Linux 2.4" and two with "Windows 7" mapping to C_j probably indicate the former is more appropriate than the latter.

5. OS FINGERPRINTING DATABASE

Plata is quite general and does not assume much beyond existence of similarity function p, algorithms to produce distortion θ, and ability to observe remote systems. We now apply this framework to one specific problem – OS stack fingerprinting under random/volatile features.

5.1 Classifier

As discussed earlier, the majority of stack fingerprinting tools treat all features as deterministic, in which case database construction is rather straightforward. The only exceptions are clock-skew methods [6], [13] and single-packet classifiers [3], [14], [25], [30]. The former direction has serious bandwidth overhead and suffers from inability to scale the database beyond a handful of hosts. The latter category, which is our focus, sends a single SYN packet to the target and observes a stream of SYN-ACKs, as illustrated in Figure 5. The vector of retransmission timeouts (RTOs) observed by the client forms the network features of the classifier. Combining unique RTO patterns with various fixed TCP/IP header fields, these algorithms can produce pretty robust OS identification.

The database for single-packet tools has evolved from 25 signatures in [3] to 98 in [14], eventually reaching 116 in [25], but the corresponding $(1-\epsilon, \mathcal{X})$-dimensions of the underlying classifiers remain unknown. So far, manual construction of $\mathcal{D}$ in these tools has relied on separation only across deterministic features (e.g., window size, TTL, RST bit) and never examined how to determine whether two hosts with the same fixed header values have sufficiently distinct

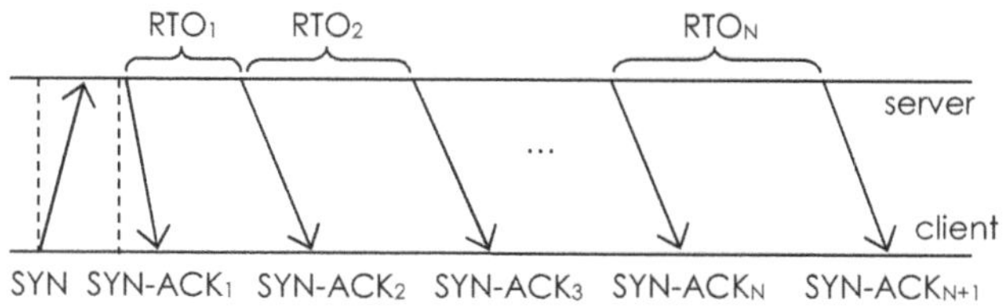

Figure 5: RTOs of half-open connections.

RTO vectors. To address this issue, we next apply Plata to temporal features of single-packet classifiers and build the first OS-fingerprinting database that is separable across random/volatile features.

5.2 Data Collection

We scan our campus network (three /16 blocks) on port 80 to obtain observations $\Delta_1, \ldots, \Delta_n$ from responsive hosts $S_1, \ldots, S_n$. Since each Δ_i may be random due to kernel-scheduling peculiarities, as in Figure 3(a), we persist in gathering $w = 50$ RTO vectors from each host, which is typically enough to capture whatever variation Δ_i may exhibit. Additionally, to exclude lossy vectors from being included in the database, the scanner continues until it receives w samples of the maximum length seen so far. Since packet loss in our network is low, quick convergence follows – the average number of SYN probes per responsive IP was 50.14.

As each S_i is a public server, care needs to be exercised to not overload the target with w back-to-back requests and cause unnecessary side-effects (e.g., rejected connections, CPU overload). However, as it turned out, even conservative 1-second inter-SYNs delays were too small. One such problem surfaced with certain printers, whose SYN-backlog queue [35] was smaller than w. When the queue was full, the printers terminated the oldest ongoing sequence of SYN-ACKs and started a new one. This caused the corresponding Δ_i to exhibit random truncation and presented difficulties in obtaining w loss-free observations. We eventually settled on delaying SYN probes by 240 seconds, i.e., double the TCP MSL (maximum segment life), which solved the problem.

The final caveat relates to OS kernel timing of RTOs. As speculated in [25], some hosts use a global timer that is independent of the SYN arrival time to generate SYN-ACKs for half-open connections. This causes the first RTO (and sometimes the remaining ones) to be randomized in some default range. In such cases, it is important to capture these effects in the database. We thus add random variable U to 240 seconds to avoid SYNs synchronization with any global clocks. Our U is uniform in $[0, 3]$ seconds, but other options are possible as well.

Along with the scan, a separate process opens a connection to each responsive host and attempts to download its root page over HTTP. This is known as *banner grabbing* – a general technique for discovering host type using some text-based protocol (e.g., telnet, finger, HTTP, FTP, and SMTP). This was used for OS fingerprinting in the 1990s, when Unix-based servers would readily volunteer their OS name and version. It has since fallen out of favor because these identification strings may be replaced by OS-oblivious names (e.g., Apache) or altogether removed, which makes the technique less reliable. However, banner grabbing works for our purpose since admins have no incentive to obfuscate

Grouping	RING	Snacktime	IRLsnack	Hershel
Deterministic only	28	209	209	344
Random only	23	52	50	117
Both	39	260	257	398

Table 1: Database dimensions.

OS names behind our campus firewall, and Plata only needs a subset of $S_1,\ldots,S_n$ to be labeled. This provides a fast, repeatable process that requires no manual intervention.

We receive SYN-ACKs from 9,879 IPs, assemble w loss-free RTO vectors from $n = 9{,}701$ hosts, and successfully complete a banner download from 9,594 of them.

5.3 Separating Features

Single-packet OS-fingerprinting tools use both deterministic and random features. For each S_i, we move the former into vector u_i and the latter into Δ_i. In general, Hershel treats u_i as volatile, which means it allows users to change TCP/IP header values without making the OS fundamentally different. However, there is no even remotely accurate model for distortion $\mathcal{X}$ applied by users to these features. We therefore limit our efforts to the better-understood network delay jitter and its volatility. If a realistic noise model $\mathcal{X}$ becomes available for u_i, Plata can be used to compact duplicate hosts even further.

The simplest way to achieve separation on the deterministic features is to combine u_i with the size of RTO vector Δ_i. Splitting the available hosts $S_1,\ldots,S_n$ into clusters based on the deterministic pair $(u_i, |\Delta_i|)$ produces the first row of Table 1, with 28 signatures for RING [30], 209 for Snacktime [3] and IRLsnack [14], and 344 for Hershel [25]. Note that hosts within each cluster have same-length RTO vectors and our next goal is to further subdivide them into smaller groups that are $(1-\epsilon,\mathcal{X})$-separable.

To decide on $\mathcal{X}$, assume the objective is to achieve sufficient accuracy during Internet-wide scanning, where each Δ_i is disturbed by random queueing delays along the path from the server back to the scanner. Due to constant SYN-ACK packet size, fixed transmission/propagation delays cancel out during RTO computation [25]. It is thus sufficient to use a FIFO-queue simulator that adds random delay jitter θ to each measurement, ensuring that no packets are reordered. As Hershel is fairly insensitive to the assumed model of jitter [25], we use exponentially distributed queueing delays with mean 500 ms, which results in θ being zero-mean Laplace. If better knowledge of network conditions is acquired, θ can be modified accordingly.

We generate r = 1K random noise vectors $\theta_1,\ldots,\theta_r$ and add them to each observation of Δ_i, resulting in wr = 50K disturbed samples per host S_i. We run Plata for each candidate classifier using their similarity function p and compute (5), in which $p_j(\delta') = 1/w$. This creates one matrix $\tilde{M}$ for each unique combination of deterministic features, which is fed to Plata's separation algorithm with $1-\epsilon = 0.8$. After all matrices are compacted, we combine the surviving specimens into the final database $\mathcal{D}$.

Going back to Table 1, the second row shows that RTO features alone allow single-packet tools to differentiate between 23−117 stacks under this combination $(\epsilon,\mathcal{X})$. Hershel more than doubles the dimension of its nearest competitor, which stems from its more sophisticated model for $p(\delta|\delta')$. Combining both deterministic and random features, Hershel ends up with 398 signatures, which is quite significant given the limited scope of the initial scan. Due to its higher accuracy and better separation ability, the rest of this paper stays with Hershel as the underlying classifier for Plata.

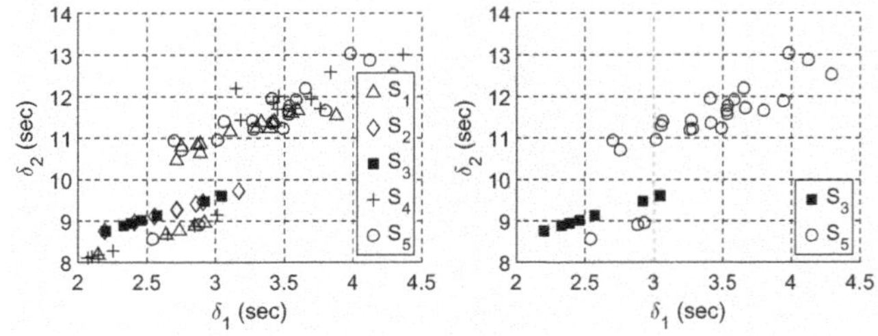

(a) candidate hosts (b) $(1-\epsilon)$-separable hosts

Figure 6: Plata example.

To demonstrate how matrix reduction works in practice, consider five actual Windows hosts in Figure 6(a) with $|\Delta_i| = 2$. While all of these OS kernels produce noisy RTOs, there are two distinct patterns. Figure 6(b) shows the result of Plata separation, which successfully extracts both patterns (Windows Server 2003 with two different service packs) out of the group and represents them using hosts (S_3, S_5).

5.4 Label Clustering

Note that Plata does not specify how to assign labels to clusters $\{L_j\}$. Besides ground-truth obtained from device owners, which may be infeasible for large decentralized networks, some of this information can be collected automatically. Our approach is to proceed along this route. Recall that HTTP headers contain the "Server:" string that sometimes identifies the version of the web server and uniquely ties it to a particular OS (e.g., Windows IIS). However, in other cases, the operating system can be inferred only from the HTML content of the page, as is the case with certain embedded devices (e.g., printers, cameras). We thus combine the "Server:" field with the entire HTML page and perform clustering using simhash [16], which is a well-known technique for detecting similar webpages. This creates 515 clusters $L_1, L_2,\ldots$, which we match to $d = 398$ Hershel signatures $C_1,\ldots,C_d$ using the procedure in Figure 4.

The final step is to perform manual verification of label sanity, determine which tags in the HTML to use (e.g., head, title), and convert low-level software versions to the corresponding OS name (e.g., IIS 7.5 to Windows Server 2008 R2). With enough coding effort to account for the various formats, most of this can be automated [29], but we found it easier to just show each page to a human and let them decide which of the found labels is appropriate. Plata does this by sequentially rendering one page from each L_k and recording the user's response. Even for $n \to \infty$, the number of unique clusters should remain reasonably small.

Results reveal that our label clustering works quite well – 326 out of 398 signatures (82%) receive a meaningful description. They are responsible for 98% of $n = 9{,}701$ measured hosts. Table 2 shows the top five most-popular signatures on our campus, where Plata successfully shrinks the most common Windows RTO pattern from 3,803 hosts down to 1. Heavy usage of Windows (43% of all servers) and Linux (12%) is no surprise, but we also find a large amount of HP LaserJet printers in fifth place. The $398 - 326 = 72$ unla-

Banner	Hosts	Deterministic features						Mean RTOs
		Win	TTL	DF	TCP options	MSS	RST	
Windows Vista / 7 / 8 / 2008 / 2012	3,803	8,192	128	1	MNWST	1,460	1, 0, 0, 1	3, 6, 12
Ubuntu / Debian / CentOS / Sci. Linux	822	5,792	64	1	MSTNW	1,460	0, 0 ,0, 0	4.3, 6, 12, 24.1, 48.2
Windows 2008 R2 / 2012	394	8,192	128	1	MNWST	1,460	0, 0, 0, 0	3, 6
Ubuntu / Redhat / CentOS / SUSE	366	14,480	64	1	MSTNW	1,460	0, 0, 0, 0	1.1, 2, 4, 8, 16
HP LaserJet Series	310	11,680	64	1	MNWNNT	1,460	0, 0, 0, 0	3, 6, 12

Table 2: Top 5 database signatures gathered from our campus scan (Win = window size, TTL = time to live, DF = do not fragment, MSS = max segment size, RST = reset packet features).

beled cases belong to network elements that either fail to provide a banner or supply one that contains no clue about the underlying OS. The latter case often happens with extremely rare devices for which we have only one banner to analyze. If Plata is exposed to additional data collection and user input (i.e., outside of our network), these gaps can be eliminated. The main benefit of our framework is that only a small fraction of n (i.e., 72/9701 = 0.7%) requires further attention.

Note that using automated banners for labeling does limit our ability to distinguish between OS versions. For example, the two Linux signatures in Table 2 are likely from different kernel versions. However, if the application requires more fine-granular labeling, additional effort – installing each OS in a test environment or contacting the owner – is needed in conjunction with Plata.

6. OPTIMIZING PLATA

While Plata works well, it bottlenecks on generating θ_m and recomputing $p(\delta_i^m + \theta_m|\delta', \mathcal{X})$ for each of the r random noise samples. This becomes especially noticeable in large groups, such as Windows with 3.8K hosts. Using 16 AMD Opteron cores @ 2.8 GHz and 64 GB of RAM, a parallelized C++ implementation requires over 24 hours to compute $\tilde{M}$. Although database creation is a one-time process, it is still desirable to have faster and more scalable algorithms that can tackle larger input. We address this next.

Analyzing (5), there are two obvious ways to reduce complexity – lowering r and making function $p(.)$ faster. However, for Hershel, we can attempt to do even better – replace Monte-Carlo simulations with a directly evaluated model that produces the expected probability that S_i gets classified as S_j under random noise θ. The rest of the section treats $\theta = (\theta_1, \theta_2, \dots)$ as a vector consisting of scalar random variables, with respect to which all expectations are taken. Since $M_{ij} := E[p(\Delta_i + \theta|\Delta_j, \mathcal{X})]$ can be written as

$$\sum_{\delta}\sum_{\delta'} E[p(\delta+\theta|\delta', \mathcal{X})]p_i(\delta)p_j(\delta'), \tag{7}$$

construction of M in Plata requires only knowing $E[p(\delta + \theta|\delta', \mathcal{X})]$ for two deterministic, same-length vectors δ, δ'.

6.1 Closed-Form Plata-Hershel Matrix

To understand the results that follow, we briefly review how Hershel deals with delay jitter. Assuming $f(x)$ is the distribution (density or PMF) of one-way jitter and $e_m = \delta_m - \delta'_m$ is the error term in the m-th RTO, the similarity between two deterministic vectors is [25]

$$p(\delta|\delta', \mathcal{X}) = \prod_{m=1}^{|\delta|} f(e_m). \tag{8}$$

Note that (8) treats error values $(e_1, e_2, \dots)$ as iid random observations. For the default model of $\mathcal{X}$, Hershel uses exponential one-way delay [25]. This produces Laplace jitter with density $f(x) = (\lambda/2)e^{-\lambda|x|}$, where parameter λ should conservatively reflect the amount of jitter anticipated in the network during actual measurement (i.e., $1/\lambda$ should upper-bound the real mean). With this in mind, our goal is to derive the following expectation

$$E[p(\delta+\theta|\delta', \mathcal{X})] = E\Big[\prod_{m=1}^{|\delta|} f(e_m+\theta_m)\Big], \tag{9}$$

where each θ_m is a random variable.

Given vectors δ and δ', we are interested in how similar Hershel considers them after the former undergoes random modification by the network. Suppose variables $(\theta_1, \theta_2, \dots)$ are iid Laplace with rate μ. Note that μ may not equal λ if separation is performed for purposes other than future scanning of the Internet. In that case, μ may be set to match the environment in which $S_1, \dots, S_n$ are probed (e.g., 5-ms average jitter for a campus network). Define $b_m = e^{-|e_m|}$ and consider the next result.

THEOREM 1. *For the Hershel classifier, the expected similarity between $\delta + \theta$ and δ' is*

$$E[p(\delta+\theta|\delta', \mathcal{X})] = \Big(\frac{\lambda\mu}{4}\Big)^{|\delta|} \prod_{m=1}^{|\delta|} \begin{cases} g_m & \lambda \neq \mu \\ h_m & \lambda = \mu \end{cases}, \tag{10}$$

where

$$g_m = \frac{2(\lambda b_m^{\mu} - \mu b_m^{\lambda})}{\lambda^2 - \mu^2}, \quad h_m = b_m^{\lambda}\Big(|e_m| + \frac{1}{\lambda}\Big). \tag{11}$$

The next logical step is to investigate whether matrix M built using (10) matches the Monte-Carlo version $\tilde{M}$. We consider a simple scenario with $|\delta| = 2$, $\delta = \delta'$, and $\lambda = \mu = 10$. This represents some diagonal cell M_{ii}, i.e., similarity score of S_i to itself, for a deterministic Δ_i. Setting $e_m = 0$ for all m, (10) produces 6.25, while Monte-Carlo simulations yield $\tilde{M}_{ii} = 6.7$. The error increases with RTO vector length and is more difficult to predict for off-diagonal values M_{ij}.

Further analysis uncovers that the source of this bias lies in Hershel's assumption on delay jitter. To illustrate this point, consider distorting a two-RTO vector δ using $\theta = (\theta_1, \theta_2)$. From the queuing model of [25], consecutive Laplace jitter values can be expressed using three iid exponential one-way delays X, Y, Z, i.e., $\theta_1 = Y - X$ and $\theta_2 = Z - Y$. While [25] is reasonable in arguing that X, Y, Z are independent due to the large gaps between SYN-ACKs, the same logic unfortunately does not apply to jitter because θ_1 and θ_2 share a common variable Y. For $e_m = 0$ and $|\delta| = 2$, the correct expectation of (9) is $E[f(\theta_1)f(\theta_2)]$. On the other hand, Theorem 1 uses Hershel to deduce the result

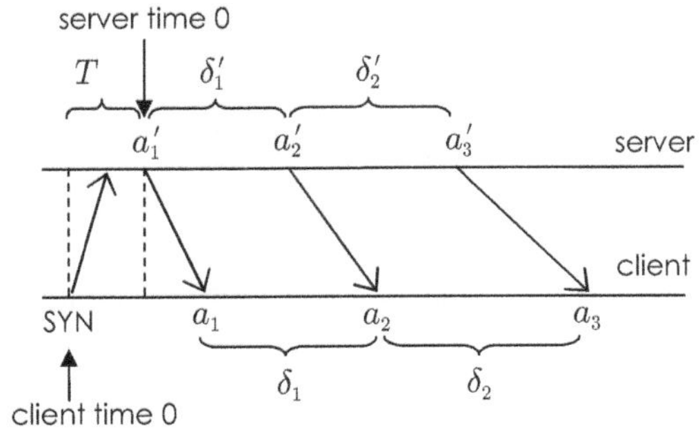

Figure 7: Features in Hershel (δ) and Hershel+ (a).

as $E[f(\theta_1)]E[f(\theta_2)] = \lambda^2/16$. We next expand the former term and show that it deviates from the latter for all λ.

THEOREM 2. *For $\mu = \lambda$ and $e_m = 0$, the expected Hershel similarity under dependent two-RTO jitter (θ_1, θ_2) is*

$$E[f(\theta_1)f(\theta_2)] = \frac{29\lambda^2}{432}. \tag{12}$$

Using $\lambda = 10$ in (12) produces 6.7 observed in simulations. While we succeeded in correctly modeling M_{ii} for two RTOs, doing the same for $i \neq j$ and longer vectors δ is very tedious.

6.2 Hershel+

We now show how the classification problem can be solved using only one-way delay (OWD). This requires a new model for $p(\delta|\delta', \mathcal{X})$ and additional constraints during creation of $\mathcal{D}$. For host S_i, define A_i to be a random vector of SYN-ACK transmission timestamps relative to the departure time of the first reply. Then, assuming that network delays are negligible, the distribution of elements inside A_i can be accurately obtained at the measurement client by subtracting the RTT of the first SYN-ACK from all observed values.

Now suppose that the scanner finds a remote host on the Internet and obtains a vector of SYN-ACK arrival instances as A, which are relative to the transmission time of the SYN. The main caveat here is that the forward SYN delay and server think time, which we collectively call T, are not just unknown in the public Internet, but also likely non-negligible. Consequently, the classifier must consider all options for T in its decision whether the observed A could have been produced by some known vector A_i. Delay randomness is handled similar to (7), which means that it is again sufficient to consider only deterministic pairs of delay vectors, i.e., by conditioning on $A = a = (a_1, a_2, \ldots)$ and $A_i = a' = (a_1', a_2', \ldots)$. This is illustrated in Figure 7. Supposing that Q_m is the m-th OWD from the server to the client, we have $a_m = T + a_m' + Q_m$.

With the new model, redefine the error as $e_m = a_m - a_m'$ and let $s = \min_m\{e_m\}$ be the largest possible value of T when a system equipped with a' is responsible for observation a. Then, the similarity function becomes

$$p(a|a', \mathcal{X}) = E\Big[\prod_{m=1}^{|a|} f_Q(e_m - T)\Big], \tag{13}$$

Distribution of OWD	Features used	Hershel	Hershel+
Pareto (mean = 0.5)	RTO only	22.1%	24.2%
Pareto (mean = 0.1)	RTO only	33.1%	33.3%
Uniform (mean = 0.5)	RTO only	21.7%	22.1%
Uniform (mean = 0.5)	All	99.9%	99.9%

Table 3: Accuracy on the Hershel database.

Distribution of T	Loss	Hershel	Hershel+
Exponential (mean = 0.1)	–	96.9%	97.6%
Pareto (mean = 0.1)	–	96.9%	97.4%
Pareto (mean = 0.1)	3.8%	95.2%	95.8%
Pareto (mean = 0.1)	10%	92.3%	92.9%

Table 4: Accuracy on the Plata database.

where $f_Q(x)$ is the density of OWD from model $\mathcal{X}$. Assuming $f_T(x)$ is the PDF of T, this leads to

$$p(a|a', \mathcal{X}) = \int_0^s \Big[\prod_{m=1}^{|a|} f_Q(e_m - x)\Big] f_T(x)dx. \tag{14}$$

We apply Hershel's exponential OWD with $f_Q(x) = \lambda e^{-\lambda x}$ and additionally represent T as a sum of two exponential variables (i.e., forward SYN delay and server think time), which leads to $f_T(x) = \nu^2 x e^{-\nu x}$, i.e., Erlang(2) distribution with some rate ν and mean $2/\nu$. The OWD classifier (14) is more complex than Hershel's as it requires numerical integration of a computationally expensive product of shifted density functions. Our next result shows that this can be avoided through additional derivations.

THEOREM 3. *The closed form for* (14) *is*

$$p(a|a', \mathcal{X}) = \mathbf{1}_{s\geq 0}\nu^2\lambda^{|a|}\psi \prod_{m=1}^{|a|} e^{-\lambda e_m}, \tag{15}$$

where $\mathbf{1}$ *is an indicator variable and*

$$\psi = \begin{cases} \frac{1-e^{-(\nu-\lambda|a|)s}(1+(\nu-\lambda|a|)s)}{(\nu-\lambda|a|)^2} & |a| \neq \frac{\nu}{\lambda} \\ \frac{s^2}{2} & |a| = \frac{\nu}{\lambda} \end{cases}. \tag{16}$$

Replacing Hershel's $p(\delta|\delta', \mathcal{X})$ with (15) and keeping the rest of the method unchanged gives rise to a technique we call Hershel+. Our next step is to verify that its accuracy is no worse than that of Hershel even when the assumed Erlang model for T, which uses $\nu = 4$ in all computation below, does not match the true distribution. To this end, we use the simulation setup from [25], where the only new parameter is T. In the first scenario, we keep T uniform in $[0, 1]$ seconds, maintain zero packet loss, and run both methods over Hershel's original database with 116 stacks. The result is shown in Table 3. As the new model only changes the RTO classifier, the most important comparison involves the first three rows of the table, which confirm superiority of Hershel+. In the second scenario, we fix the OWD to be uniform in $[0, 1]$ and use the larger Plata database. Table 4 shows that Hershel+ again edges out Hershel, despite its higher uncertainty related to T.

6.3 Closed-Form Plata-Hershel+ Matrix

Armed with the new classifier, we revisit the issue of obtaining a Plata matrix without Monte-Carlo simulations. To model $\mathcal{X}$, we disturb each A_i using a random OWD vector

$V = (V_1, V_2, \ldots)$, where all V_i are iid exponential with rate λ. We additionally apply noise to the forward SYN delay and server think time, which are collectively given by an Erlang(2) random variable W with rate ν. Note that we use λ and ν from Hershel+, although other options are possible.

Define matrix $H = (H_{ij})$ to consist of all pairwise Hershel+ similarities between the signatures in the database under distortion $V + W$. This requires computing

$$\zeta(a, a') := E[p(a + V + W|a', \mathcal{X})] \quad (17)$$

and setting $H_{ij} = E[\zeta(A_i, A_j)]$, where the second expectation is taken over random variables (A_i, A_j).

THEOREM 4. *Define* $v = (\lambda/2)^{|a|}\nu/4$. *Then,*

$$\zeta(a, a') = v \int_{-\infty}^{\infty} e^{-\lambda \sum_m |e_m + z|}(1 + \nu|z|)e^{-\nu|z|}dz. \quad (18)$$

Note that (18) can be computed by splitting the integral into $|a|+2$ regions such that $|z|$ and $|e_m+z|$ are conclusively resolved as being either positive or negative. Each of these smaller integrals expands in closed-form; however, due to the large number of terms involved and lacking structure, this result is difficult to represent symbolically. Algorithmically, however, this is simple to code using a bit-vector of size $|a|+1$ that keeps track of which of the terms $(z, e_1 + z, e_2 + z, \ldots)$ is positive. Moving from one interval to the next flips one bit from 0 to 1 and switches to the corresponding integral.

After verifying that (18) and its $|a| + 2$ sub-integrals produce correct results, we run Plata separation over H instead of $\tilde{M}$ and obtain 420 signatures, out of which 79 come out unlabeled. Recalling Table 1, notice that Hershel+ increases the dimension of its predecessor by 22 entries, indicating a more powerful classifier. Performance improvement is remarkable as well – the runtime reduces from over 24 hours to just 12 minutes. Added benefits include higher accuracy of Hershel+ decisions and alleviation of uncertainty if r is large enough to keep Monte-Carlo results convergent.

7. INTERNET SCAN

We now use Hershel+ to classify every visible webserver on the Internet against the previously constructed Plata database.

7.1 Classification Results

In July 2015, we sent 2.7B SYN probes on port 80 to every IP address advertised in BGP and obtained SYN-ACK responses from 66.4M hosts. This is almost double the 37M IPs used in the Hershel study [25]. The scan lasted 6 hours and operated at 125K packets per second.

Table 5 shows the Hershel+ output on the Internet data. We break down the result by OS category, showing the 5 most-popular signatures in each. Not surprisingly, Linux still dominates the webserver market. Although its top-5 signatures are separable at the feature level, limitations of our banner-based labeling do not allow identification of the specific version of these OSes. In second place, there is a large number of embedded devices, mostly routers and printers. This finding agrees with those in previous measurements at this scale [11], [25]. In third place, we combine hosts that map to a signature without a useful banner and those with a zero probability of matching to anything in $\mathcal{D}$. The former category is responsible for 94% of these cases, where 79 "mystery" signatures in $\mathcal{D}$ catch almost 12% of all Internet classification, despite being rare on our campus. Future work will attempt to uncover their OS.

Category	OS / Device	Hosts
Linux	Ubuntu / Redhat / CentOS	14,551,706
	Ubuntu / Redhat / SUSE	2,620,566
	Ubuntu / Debian / Redhat	2,381,733
	Ubuntu / CentOS / SUSE	1,831,519
	Ubuntu / Redhat / Sci. Linux	1,413,660
	Total in category	25,679,480
Embedded	3Com Routers	2,661,835
	Dell Laser / Xerox Printers	1,985,840
	Embedded Linux	1,869,053
	Cisco Embedded	1,699,418
	Citrix Netscaler	1,118,748
	Total in category	24,447,390
Unknown	No label in database	7,936,268
	Zero probability of match	474,585
	Total in category	8,410,853
Windows	Windows 7 / 8 / 2008 / 2012	2,186,229
	Windows XP / 2003	822,130
	Windows XP / 2000 / 2003	791,298
	Windows 2008 R2 / 2012	701,204
	Windows 2008 R2 / 2012	427,401
	Total in category	7,124,444
Other	FreeBSD	480,789
	FreeBSD	107,635
	Novell Netware	37,981
	Mac OSX Server	35,613
	Solaris 9 / Solaris 10	35,375
	Total in category	752,602

Table 5: OS classification of the Internet dataset.

Next, there is Windows in fourth place with 7M hosts. Unlike the previous categories, we can identify the specific type of Windows from its IIS version in the HTTP header. While it is by far the most popular desktop OS [19], its penetration of the webserver domain has been lagging behind Linux. This is in contrast to our campus scan, which was dominated by Windows. One explanation for Unix prevalence is migration of online services to enterprise clouds, which have traditionally favored Linux installations. Another is the possibility that Linux distributions more commonly enable a webserver in their default configurations or alias more IPs to the same physical server. And yet another is a higher percentage of Unix computers not being protected by a firewall (either corporate or host-level).

The table ends with 752K devices (1.1% of the total) in the "other" category that includes BSD, Mac, Novell, and Solaris. Compared to the previous large-scale fingerprinting effort [25] that used scans from July 2010, the table shows that Linux and embedded have doubled their numbers (i.e., from 13-14M to 25-26M), Windows remained pretty much unchanged (i.e., a slight drop from 7.5M to 7.1M), and the remaining group lost 68% of its membership (i.e., from 2.3M to 752K). In summary, 99.3% of all IPs are successfully classified and 87.3% have a label.

7.2 OS Popularity and Confidence

To better understand device deployment at different scales, we next examine the distribution of cluster size W for each of the 420 signatures in our database. Figure 8(a) shows the CCDF $P(W > x)$ using the initial campus scan. This plot is a close match to Pareto tail $(x/\beta)^{-\alpha}$, where $\alpha = 0.8$ and $\beta = 1$. Interestingly, the bottom 40% of the signatures map to a single host each. In contrast to the well-known stacks

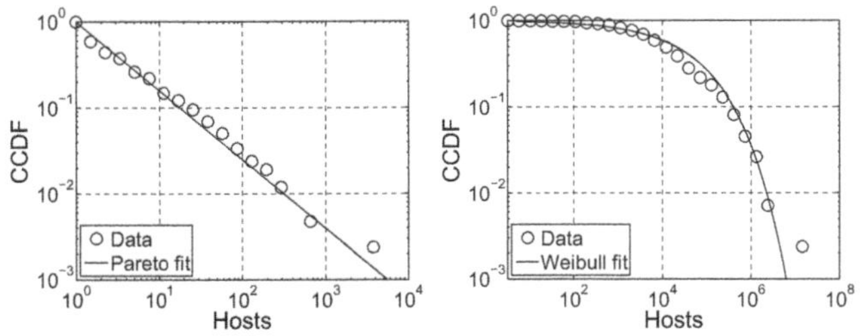

(a) campus (b) Internet

Figure 8: OS popularity distributions.

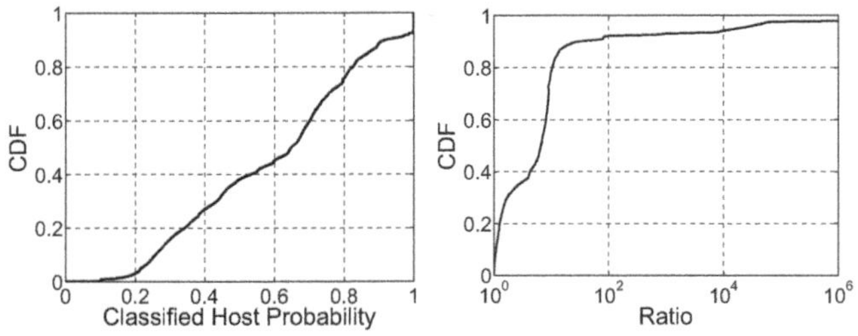

(a) CDF of top $p(a|A_j, \mathcal{X})$ (b) ratio top two $p(a|A_j, \mathcal{X})$

Figure 9: Hershel+ classification confidence.

in Table 2, these clusters enjoy more esoteric items such as security cameras, room-temperature controllers, UPS (uninterruptable power supplies), tape backup, humidity sensors, and even discontinued oscilloscopes. Figure 8(b) plots the same tail for the Internet scan, which is a good match to the Weibull distribution $\exp(-(x/\lambda)^k)$, where $k = 0.4$ and $\lambda = 45$K. Each of the top-14 signatures accounts for at least 1M hosts and the top-17 are responsible for 60% of IPs. The bottom 204 signatures match a combined 1% of the servers (i.e., 664K).

Another interesting issue is the amount of confidence with which Hershel+ selects the best OS during classification. Assuming a is a measurement from some IP, (14)-(15) can be used to obtain similarity score $p(a|A_j, \mathcal{X})$ for each OS j, the highest of which is selected as the match after normalization. Figure 9(a) plots the distribution of this probability across all 66.4M IPs. Observe that almost no classifications occur with less than 20% likelihood and over half the hosts fit some signature with probability at least 65%. The far end of the CDF shows 7% of the IPs with a 100% match, which are devices with truly unique combinations of features. In the same vein, to determine if the second-best match follows closely the top signature and how often the classifier might be "guessing," Figure 9(b) shows the CDF for the ratio of the two highest probabilities. In 17% of the cases, the second-best match is pretty close, i.e., within a factor of 1.2. Afterwards, the curve sharply rises and yields over 68% of IPs with a decisive winner (i.e., ratio 2:1 or better).

8. COMPARISON WITH NMAP

Since ground-truth for millions of Internet hosts is difficult to obtain, we next perform comparison against Nmap v6.49 [21]. During the scan, we randomly selected 1% of responsive hosts and invoked Nmap to fingerprint them as soon as the first SYN-ACK was received. Real-time execution was needed to minimize the possibility they left the network and other hosts appeared in their place (e.g., due to DHCP). We used Nmap's least-verbose mode to limit the traffic and complaints from target networks; however, this still resulted in 80 sent and 60 received packets per IP, as well as several notifications to campus network administrators about intrusive activity coming from our subnet. The complaints identified Nmap by name, which raises questions how often IDS tools not just detect, but drop its traffic.

Out of 664K IPs, Nmap was successful for only 481K (i.e., 72%). To rule out host departure, we verified that an overwhelming majority (99.8%) of the attempted IPs returned at least one reply to Nmap probes. The failed cases include responses unknown to the database and firewall obstruction of non-SYN packets. We uniformly subsampled these 481K IPs, excluded roughly 12% for which Hershel+ returned "unknown," and ended up with 603 cross-labeled samples for further manual analysis.

Category	Category match	String match	Total
Linux	301 (98.6%)	25 (8.1%)	305
Embedded	158 (75.5%)	34 (16.2%)	209
Windows	82 (95.3%)	82 (95.3%)	86
Other	3 (100%)	3 (100%)	3
Total	544 (90.2%)	144 (23.8%)	603

Table 6: Internet subsample classification.

8.1 Agreement

We first investigate how well Nmap and Hershel+ agree on the classification of the selected subset of hosts. Comparison with Nmap is far from straightforward since its stack names are human-created and rather fine-granular. The most detailed category in our Plata database is Windows, while the majority of other hosts are marked with just the name of the OS and/or device. Thus, it makes sense to separately consider whether Hershel+ matches the exact signature string of Nmap or just the category.

Table 6 shows the result of this process, where we group hosts based on Hershel+ classification. In the category match, we achieve over 98% agreement in Linux, 95% in Windows, and 100% in "other." With embedded systems, Nmap often claims the host is running Linux, whereas we have a specific (non-Linux) device name from the banner. Without tedious manual effort, it is difficult to know if Nmap has been exposed to these devices and whether it can reliably identify them. With that said, we still mark these cases as a mismatch, which drops the agreement rate to 75%.

As for OS strings, lower numbers were expected due to the difference in how the databases are labeled. The biggest drop occurs in Linux, where our $\mathcal{D}$ consists of just distribution names (e.g., Ubuntu, Redhat, SUSE), while Nmap provides both major and minor kernel versions (e.g., Linux 2.6.18-22). Nevertheless, there are 25 matching signatures for which both methods can identify only the Linux family. For embedded systems, Nmap produces a large variety of device names, many absent from our campus. Finally, the Windows group keeps the same 95% consensus rate since all 82 agreed-upon cases are exact string matches.

8.2 Disagreement

We now analyze the peculiar case of the four Windows hosts from Table 6 where Nmap and Hershel+ disagree. We

Vector	Win	TTL	DF	TCP options	MSS	RST	SYN-ACK arrival (sec)	Label
D_1	8,192	128	1	MNWST	1,464	1,0,0,1	0.00, 2.99, 9.00, 21.00	Windows 7 / 2008 R2
S_1	8,192	128	1	MNWST	1,464	1,0,0,1	0.22, 3.22, 9.22, 21.22	
S_2	8,192	64	1	MNWST	1,460	0,0,0,0	0.18, 3.17, 9.17	
D_2	16,384	128	0	MNWNNTNNS	1,380	0,0,0,0	0.00, 2.65, 9.21	Windows 2000 / 2003
S_3	16,384	128	0	MNWNNTNNS	1,460	0,0,0,0	0.21, 2.67, 9.22	
S_4	16,384	128	0	MNWNNTNNS	1,370	0,0,0,0	0.21, 3.07, 9.63	

Table 7: Hershel+ classification and features.

Vector	R_1	F_{11} = Win	F_{12} = TTL	F_{13} = DF	F_{14} = TCP options	F_{15} = MSS	$(R_2, \ldots, R_9)$	Label
D_1	1	$\emptyset$	$\emptyset$	$\emptyset$	$\emptyset$	$\emptyset$	0000 111 00	iPXE 1.0.0+
D_2	1	$\emptyset$	$\emptyset$	$\emptyset$	$\emptyset$	$\emptyset$	0000 111 01	Tomato 1.28
S_1	1	8,192	128	1	MNWST	1,464	0000 000 00	
D_3	1	$\emptyset$	64	1	MNNSNWNNT	1,460	1000 100 11	OpenBSD 4.3
S_2	1	8,192	64	1	MNWST	1,460	1000 100 11	
D_4	1	$\emptyset$	64	0	$\emptyset$	$\emptyset$	0000 111 01	D-Link DWL-624
S_3	1	16,384	128	0	MNWNNTNNS	1,460	0000 000 01	
S_4	1	16,384	128	0	MNWNNTNNS	1,370	0000 111 01	

Table 8: Nmap classification and features.

call these observations $S_1, \ldots, S_4$. Table 7 shows their features and the corresponding database signatures $D_1 - D_2$ for the Hershel+ classification. Notice that S_1 is an easy classification decision because the RTT is small (i.e., $\approx$ 220 ms) and D_1 matches all of its features. For S_2, Hershel+ prefers the same OS, overcoming a change in TTL/MSS and a loss of the RST packet at 21 sec. For the other two hosts, both matching to D_2, the only discrepancy is the MSS, which is a highly volatile field that depends on the MTU [25]. Judging from the OPT and RTO features, the accuracy of these decisions is not in doubt.

To explain the Nmap outcome for these IPs, we need to review its classification technique. Suppose vector $R = (R_1, \ldots, R_l)$ consists of indicator variables such that $R_i = 1$ iff probe i elicits a response from the network stack. We split R into several groups – a regular SYN to an open port (R_1), four TCP packets with extra flags (i.e., ECN, null, rainbow, ACK) to an open port ($R_2 - R_5$), three TCP packets to closed ports ($R_6 - R_8$), and UDP/ICMP probes ($R_9 - R_{10}$). For cases with $R_i = 1$, suppose F_{ij} records the j-th feature of that packet, where $F_{ij} = \emptyset$ indicates a missing optional header field. A combination of vector R and corresponding matrix F constitutes a signature $\Phi = (R, F)$.

Suppose a match in R_i carries weight w_i and that in feature F_{ij} some other weight w_{ij}. Then, Nmap computes similarity between an observation Φ and a signature $\Phi' = (R', F')$ from the database using the following

$$\frac{\sum_{i=1}^{l}(Y_i \mathbf{1}_{R_i=R'_i} w_i + R_i R'_i \sum_j Z_{ij} \mathbf{1}_{F_{ij}=F'_{ij}} w_{ij})}{\sum_{i=1}^{l}(Y_i w_i + R_i R'_i \sum_j Z_{ij} w_{ij})}, \quad (19)$$

where variable $Z_{ij} = 1$ iff field j in packet i is non-empty in both the observation and database (i.e., $F_{ij} \neq \emptyset, F'_{ij} \neq \emptyset$) and $Y_i = R_i$ for $i \in [6, 8]$ and 1 otherwise. The last rule ignores closed-port tests unless Φ contains a response to them. All signatures Φ' with at least 0.85 similarity are reported as likely matches.

This algorithm has no provisions for packet loss, which makes it increasingly unreliable as more probes are blocked. The issue is compounded by the usage of large weights $w_i \gg w_{ij}$, which ensure that a mismatch in a feature carries little impact compared to that in the receipt/non-receipt of a packet. As a result, presence of firewalls skews the score towards signatures Φ' that originally had fewer responses, regardless of their F_{ij}. Empty features cause $Z_{ij} = 0$ to remove the corresponding weight w_{ij} from consideration, gravitating the classifier towards results with more frequent occurrence of $\emptyset$. Finally, if the target does not respond to a given closed-port test, i.e., $Y_i = 0$, the denominator no longer contains the associated weight w_i. This allows Nmap to match $R_i = 0$ and $R'_i = 1$ with no penalty for $6 \leq i \leq 8$.

Armed with this insight, consider in Table 8 the Nmap features of $S_1 - S_4$, as well as their best matches – a network boot card, modem jail-break firmware, a decade-old OpenBSD 4.3, and an ancient D-link switch – where S_1 scores over 85% with both D_1 and D_2. From the table, notice that Nmap sampled the same SYN features as Hershel+, meaning they contacted similar network stacks. For inexplicable reasons, the database allows $\emptyset$ for mandatory values (e.g., Win, TTL, DF), where all four entries $D_1 - D_4$ contain at least one such case.

Based on Table 8, it is pretty clear that Nmap decisions are heavily influenced by the R vector and empty fields. Indeed, iPXE/Tomato have no features F_{ij} in common with S_1, OpenBSD 4.3 matches S_2 only in three fairly generic fields TTL/DF/MSS, and D-Link agrees with S_3/S_4 in just the DF bit. We thus find no evidence to suggest that Nmap signatures $D_1 - D_4$ are statistically probable, let alone better than the Hershel+ result in Table 7. In fact, D_3 and S_2 are conclusively different stacks judging from their ordering of non-NOP TCP options (i.e., MSWT vs MWST).

From a broader perspective, Table 9 shows the number of hosts for which Nmap decides that $D_1 - D_4$ exceed the 85% threshold. Remarkably, Tomato appears in 21% of the cases and OpenBSD in 13%. These results raise questions about Nmap's ability to provide meaningful classification, not just in the four cases we dissected, but generally in wide-area networks, where R is easily distorted by IDS, host-level packet filters, and network firewalls.

9. DISCUSSION AND CONCLUSION

Network stack fingerprinting has well-known pitfalls (e.g., scrubbers [7], [24], [22], [27], [31], traffic intercepts by middleboxes [12], load-balancers, RST injection by IDS), but nevertheless it is fascinating that a single SYN packet can

Signature	Subsample	Total
Tomato 1.28	132 (21.8%)	105,525 (21.9%)
OpenBSD 4.3	91 (15.0%)	64,050 (13.3%)
D-Link DWL-624	12 (1.9%)	6,454 (1.3%)
iPXE 1.0.0+	6 (0.9%)	5,723 (1.1%)

Table 9: Popularity of Nmap signatures.

elicit so much information about the target. With our algorithm for automated construction of databases and robust classification (i.e., Plata, Hershel+), single-packet tools may eventually become a legitimate competitor to Nmap for use over the public Internet. However, despite the recent developments in this field, there are still many open problems and avenues for improvement, which we discuss next.

One question is whether distortion $\mathcal{X}$ can include packet loss. This seems like a viable direction, which Plata can handle transparently in the Monte-Carlo version; however, deriving a Hershel+ matrix in closed-form requires additional research. Another avenue that is worth investigating is whether Hershel+ can increase accuracy by abandoning the single-packet assumption and sending multiple SYNs to each target IP. In these cases, it should be compared to other tools with retransmission, including their $(1-\epsilon, \mathcal{X})$-dimension under a common model of distortion. For Nmap, $\mathcal{X}$ may include blocking of ICMP/UDP packets to match the firewall assumptions of Hershel+, loss of SYN-ACKs, censorship of certain invalid flag combinations known to IDS, emulation of load-balancers, and presence of fingerprint scrubbers [24]. All of this requires a kernel-level driver that can intercept Nmap packets and reproduce the desired conditions, which is yet another direction for future work.

10. REFERENCES

[1] H. J. Abdelnur, R. State, and O. Festor, "Advanced Network Fingerprinting," in *Proc. RAID*, Sep. 2008, pp. 372–389.

[2] P. Auffret, "SinFP, Unification of Active and Passive Operating System Fingerprinting," *Journal in Computer Virology*, vol. 6, no. 3, pp. 197–205, Nov. 2010.

[3] T. Beardsley, "Snacktime: A Perl Solution for Remote OS Fingerprinting," Jun. 2003. [Online]. Available: http://www.planb-security.net/wp/snacktime.html.

[4] R. Beverly and A. Berger, "Server Siblings: Identifying Shared IPv4/IPv6 Infrastructure via Active Fingerprinting," in *Proc. PAM*, Mar. 2015, pp. 149–161.

[5] J. Caballero, S. Venkataraman, P. Poosankam, M. G. Kang, D. Song, and A. Blum, "FiG: Automatic Fingerprint Generation," in *Proc. NDSS*, Feb. 2007, pp. 27–42.

[6] Y.-C. Chen, Y. Liao, M. Baldi, S.-J. Lee, and L. Qiu, "OS Fingerprinting and Tethering Detection in Mobile Networks," in *Proc. ACM IMC*, 2014, pp. 173–180.

[7] A. Crenshaw, "OSfuscate," 2008. [Online]. Available: http://www.irongeek.com/i.php?page=security/code.

[8] R. Ensafi, D. Fifield, P. Winter, N. Feamster, N. Weaver, and V. Paxson, "Examining How the Great Firewall Discovers Hidden Circumvention Servers," in *Proc. ACM IMC*, Oct. 2015, pp. 445–458.

[9] J. Erman, M. Arlitt, and A. Mahanti, "Traffic Classification Using Clustering Algorithms," in *Proc. ACM SIGCOMM MineNet*, Sep. 2006, pp. 281–286.

[10] M. Hall, E. Frank, G. Holmes, B. Pfahringer, P. Reutemann, and I. H. Witten, "The WEKA data mining software: An update," *SIGKDD Explorations*, vol. 11, pp. 10–18, Jul. 2009.

[11] J. Heidemann, Y. Pradkin, R. Govindan, C. Papadopoulos, G. Bartlett, and J. Bannister, "Census and Survey of the Visible Internet," in *Proc. ACM IMC*, Oct. 2008, pp. 169–182.

[12] M. Honda, Y. Nishida, C. Raiciu, A. Greenhalgh, M. Handley, and H. Tokuda, "Is It Still Possible to Extend TCP?" in *Proc. ACM IMC*, Nov. 2011, pp. 181–194.

[13] T. Kohno, A. Broido, and K. C. Claffy, "Remote physical device fingerprinting," *IEEE Transactions on Dependable and Secure Computing*, vol. 2, no. 2, pp. 93–108, May 2005.

[14] D. Leonard and D. Loguinov, "Demystifying Service Discovery: Implementing an Internet-Wide Scanner," in *Proc. ACM IMC*, Nov. 2010, pp. 109–122.

[15] M. Luckie, R. Beverly, T. Wu, and M. Allman, "Resilience of Deployed TCP to Blind Attacks," in *Proc. ACM IMC*, Oct. 2015, pp. 13–26.

[16] G. S. Manku, A. Jain, and A. D. Sarma, "Detecting Near Duplicates for Web Crawling," in *Proc. WWW*, May 2007, pp. 141–149.

[17] C. McNab, *Network Security Assessment: Know Your Network*. O'Reilly Media, Inc., 2007.

[18] J. P. Medeiros, A. Brito, and P. M. Pires, "An Effective TCP/IP Fingerprinting Technique Based on Strange Attractors Classification," in *Proc. Data Privacy Management and Autonomous Spontaneus Security*, Sep. 2009, pp. 208–221.

[19] NetApplications, "Market Share Statistics for Internet Technologies." [Online]. Available: http://netmarketshare.com/.

[20] Netcraft Web Server Survey. [Online]. Available: http://news.netcraft.com/.

[21] Nmap. [Online]. Available: http://nmap.org/.

[22] G. Prigent, F. Vichot, and F. Harrouet, "IpMorph: fingerprinting spoofing unification," *Journal in Computer Virology*, vol. 6, no. 4, pp. 329–342, Nov. 2010.

[23] D. Richardson, S. Gribble, and T. Kohno, "The Limits of Automatic OS Fingerprint Generation," in *Proc. ACM AISec*, Oct 2010, pp. 24–34.

[24] G. Roualland and J.-M. Saffroy, "IP Personality." [Online]. Available: http://ippersonality.sourceforge.net/.

[25] Z. Shamsi, A. Nandwani, D. Leonard, and D. Loguinov, "Hershel: Single-Packet OS Fingerprinting," in *Proc. ACM SIGMETRICS*, Jun. 2014, pp. 195–206.

[26] B. Skaggs, B. Blackburn, G. Manes, and S. Shenoi, "Network Vulnerability Analysis," in *Proc. IEEE MWSCAS*, Aug. 2002, pp. 493–495.

[27] M. Smart, G. R. Malan, and F. Jahanian, "Defeating TCP/IP Stack Fingerprinting," in *Proc. USENIX Security*, Jun. 2000, pp. 229–240.

[28] G. Taleck, "SYNSCAN: Towards Complete TCP/IP Fingerprinting," *CanSecWest*, Apr. 2004.

[29] THC-RUT Fingerprint Database. [Online]. Available: https://www.thc.org/thc-rut/thcrut-os-fingerprints.

[30] F. Veysset, O. Courtay, O. Heen, and I. R. Team, "New Tool and Technique for Remote Operating System Fingerprinting," Apr. 2002. [Online]. Available: http://www.ouah.org/ring-full-paper.pdf.

[31] K. Wang, "Frustrating OS Fingerprinting with Morph," 2004. [Online]. Available: http://hackerpoetry.com/images/defcon-12/dc-12-presentations/Wang/dc-12-wang.pdf.

[32] F. V. Yarochkin, O. Arkin, M. Kydyraliev, S.-Y. Dai, Y. Huang, and S.-Y. Kuo, "Xprobe2++: Low Volume Remote Network Information Gathering Tool," in *Proc. IEEE/IFIP DSN*, Jun. 2009, pp. 205–210.

[33] M. Zalewski, "p0f v3: Passive Fingerprinter," 2012. [Online]. Available: http://lcamtuf.coredump.cx/p0f3.

[34] S. Zander, T. Nguyen, and G. Armitage, "Automated Traffic Classification and Application Identification Using Machine Learning," in *Proc. IEEE LCN*, Nov. 2005, pp. 250–257.

[35] X. Zhang, J. Knockel, and J. Crandall, "Original SYN: Finding Machines Hidden Behind Firewalls," in *Proc. IEEE INFOCOM*, Apr. 2015, pp. 720–728.

Noisy Bloom Filters for Multi-Set Membership Testing

Haipeng Dai Yuankun Zhong Alex X. Liu Wei Wang Meng Li
State Key Laboratory for Novel Software Technology, Nanjing University, Nanjing, Jiangsu, CHINA
{haipengdai,ww}@nju.edu.cn,alexliu@cse.msu.edu,{kun,121220046}@smail.nju.edu.cn

ABSTRACT

This paper is on designing a compact data structure for multi-set membership testing allowing fast set querying. Multi-set membership testing is a fundamental operation for computing systems and networking applications. Most existing schemes for multi-set membership testing are built upon Bloom filter, and fall short in either storage space cost or query speed. To address this issue, in this paper we propose Noisy Bloom Filter (NBF) and Error Corrected Noisy Bloom Filter (NBF-E) for multi-set membership testing. For theoretical analysis, we optimize their classification failure rate and false positive rate, and present criteria for selection between NBF and NBF-E. The key novelty of NBF and NBF-E is to store set ID information in a compact but noisy way that allows fast recording and querying, and use denoising method for querying. Especially, NBF-E incorporates asymmetric error-correcting coding technique into NBF to enhance the resilience of query results to noise by revealing and leveraging the asymmetric error nature of query results. To evaluate NBF and NBF-E in comparison with prior art, we conducted experiments using real-world network traces. The results show that NBF and NBF-E significantly advance the state-of-the-art on multi-set membership testing.

Keywords

Bloom filter, multi-set membership testing, noise, asymmetric error-correcting code, constant weight code

1. INTRODUCTION

1.1 Problem Statement and Motivation

This paper is on designing a compact data structure for multi-set membership testing allowing fast set querying. Given a set of sets $S = \{S_1, S_2, \ldots, S_\aleph\}$ where $S_i \cap S_j = \varnothing$ for any $1 \le i < j \le \aleph$, a multi-set membership testing algorithm builds an efficient data structure so that given an element e, the algorithm either finds $S_i \in S$ such that $e \in S_i$, or report that $e \notin S_1 \cup S_2 \ldots \cup S_\aleph$.

SIGMETRICS '16, June 14-18, 2016, Antibes Juan-Les-Pins, France

DOI: http://dx.doi.org/10.1145/2896377.2901451

Multi-set membership testing is a fundamental operation for computing systems and networking applications. For example, for frame forwarding in a layer-2 switch, multiple MAC addresses are mapped to a single port and fast querying for the associated port for a MAC address is crucial for frame forwarding [11, 25]. Here, MAC addresses correspond to elements and the associated port corresponds to the set. For Web traffic classification, URLs are classified into different groups on the fly for statistical purposes [11]. For approximate state machines, the simultaneous state of a large number of agents are tracked by a state machine [4]. For Web cache, each Web proxy maintains a compact summary of the cache directory of all other proxies and if a cache miss occurs it searches for the proxy wherein the request is a cache hit [8].

1.2 Limitations of Prior Art

Many existing solutions addressing multi-set membership testing are built upon Bloom filter [5, 6, 8, 9, 11, 13, 15, 23, 24]. Bloom filter is a compact data structure supporting membership query with no false negatives but with false positives, *i.e.*, it certainly answers yes if the query element belongs to the set and may mistakenly answer yes if not. Given a set of element S, Bloom filter first constructs a bit array with all bits initialized to 0. For inserting an element e to S, Bloom filter uses k independent hash functions with uniformly distributed outputs, say $h_1(\cdot), \ldots, h_k(\cdot)$, to map e to k bits in the array and set them to 1. For querying whether an element e belongs to S, Bloom filter returns true if all k mapped bits for e are 1.

Most of the Bloom filter based schemes regarding multi-set membership testing fall short in either storage space cost or query speed. On one hand, some prior art adopts a general framework that divides the whole storage space into multiple uniform cells and uses one or more cells to record set IDs of element [6, 9, 23]. This coarse granularity for storing set IDs leads to inefficient use of storage space. For the IBF scheme proposed in [6, 9], if two or more distinct set IDs are accidentally mapped to the same cell and mixed with each other, then no useful information can be extracted from this cell, which means the whole cell is wasted. kBF proposed in [23] improves IBF by allowing mixture from no more than 3 set IDs using a coding technique. However, kBF is still inefficient because it fails to decode any set IDs of elements mapped to the cell where more than 3 set IDs are mixed. On the other hand, other prior art mainly falls short in memory access overhead and query processing speed. Most of proposed schemes in these works assign multiple dedicated Bloom filters for recording in terms of set ID [5, 8], bit position in the binary expression of set IDs [15], and bit position in the encoding results of set IDs [11], or organizes multiple Bloom filters into a tree [24]. Consequently, the memory accesses of these schemes are generally several times higher than standard Bloom filters depending on the number of established Bloom filters, which results in much lower query processing speed. Still another scheme encodes set ID information of an element in its location by using offsets [13]. The offset is set to be proportional to the value of set ID. As both classification failure rate and memory access overhead grow proportionally to the maximum set ID value, this scheme is vulnerable to noise and has low query processing speed. One solution to alleviate this problem is to require that set IDs be no more than 64 [13], which largely limits its applications in reality.

1.3 Proposed Approach

In this paper, we propose a Noisy Bloom Filter (NBF) scheme as well as its enhanced version Error Corrected Noisy Bloom Filter (NBF-E) scheme for multi-set membership testing. Our NBF and NBF-E schemes simultaneously improve the storage space cost and query speed issues over prior art. NBF and NBF-E have two phases: construction phase and query phase. NBF encodes set IDs of input elements and records the results in a bit array in a noisy way to achieve compact storage in the construction phase, and denoises the recorded coding information to recover the set IDs in the query phase. Compared with NBF, NBF-E enhances the resilience to noise by using asymmetric error-correcting codes.

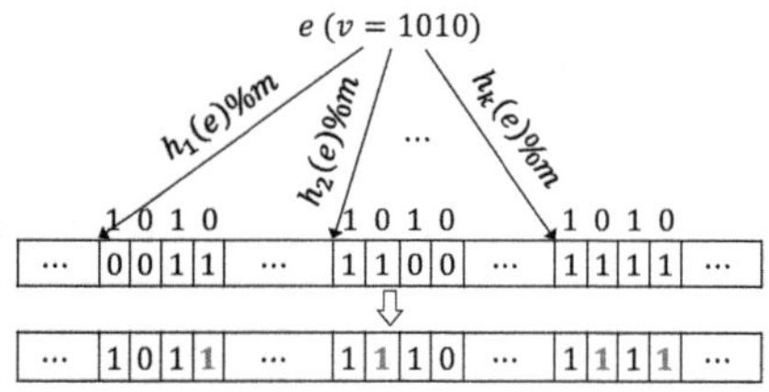

Figure 1: Construction phase of NBF/NBF-E

In the construction phase, given an element, NBF first maps it to k positions in its bit array using k hash functions. Then, NBF encodes the set ID of the element into a bit string with fixed length, and ORs the encoding result with the bitmaps starting from each of k hashed positions and lasting the same length of the encoding result. Figure 1 shows an example of the construction phase. An input element e is mapped to k positions in NBF using hash functions $h_1(e), h_2(e), \ldots h_k(e)$, its set ID is encoded as $v = 1010$, and is ORed with 4 consecutive bits starting from each of these k positions. The numbers marked in bold font and red color in the resulting NBF denote "noise" from the recorded information of other elements with respect to e.

In the query phase, NBF first computes the mapped positions for an input element e using the hash functions $h_1(e), h_2(e), \ldots h_k(e)$, and then fetches k related bitmaps starting from these k positions. To remove the potential noise from other elements, NBF performs AND operation across all bitmaps and yields the encoding result, which can be decoded to a set ID if it is valid. Figure 2 illustrates the querying procedure for the example stated in the construction phase. It can be seen that all noise is removed after the

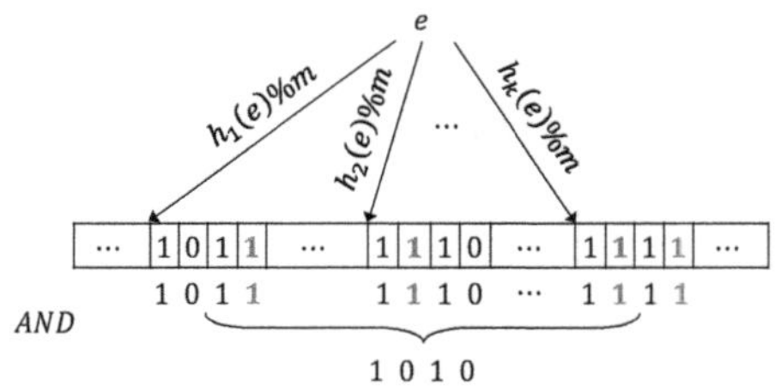

Figure 2: Query phase of NBF/NBF-E

AND operation and NBF finally obtains the correct encoding result 1010, and then decodes it to the original set ID. Besides, it is clear that when the number of total distinct sets equals 1, our NBF scheme is reduced to the standard Bloom filter as it encodes the set ID for all elements as 1 and writes it to or reads it from all k hashed bits.

Our proposed enhanced version NBF-E is built upon NBF, and it differs from NBF only in the encoding and decoding process. Particularly, NBF-E applies (binary) asymmetric error-correcting coding, or more specifically, (binary) Z channel coding, for encoding and decoding set IDs for elements. Asymmetric error-correcting coding is a type of forward error correction schemes which encode data by adding additional information such that introduced errors can be effectively detected and corrected, and it is particularly suitable for asymmetrical channels, or Z channel in our case. Z channel has $\{0, 1\}$ as input and output alphabets where the crossover $0 \to 1$ occurs with positive probability p whereas the crossover $1 \to 0$ never occurs. This precisely describes the error property of query results in our scenario, that is, only "0" bits prone to error but "1" bits do not. In our previous example as shown in Figure 2, noise only occurs to the "0" bits in the encoding result 1010 recorded in the Bloom filter and probably in the query result as we can image, but cannot occur to the "1" bits. By revealing this critical fact and using asymmetric error-correcting coding, we show theoretically that NBF-E achieves almost half of the false positive rate and twice faster decoding speed compared with schemes using traditional symmetric error-correcting coding.

Key intuition: The intuition behind storing element codes in bits, instead of in cells each of which consists of a fixed number of bits, is to save memory. Due to the abandon of delimits for storing data, encoding results for different element set IDs will overlap with each other. The intuition behind allowing this overlap is that NBF/NBF-E can effectively extract the original encoding results using AND operation to denoise mixed-in information from other elements in the query phase. The motivation behind storing encoding results in consecutive bits rather than in disjoint bits using multiple hash functions as [11, 15] do is to reduce memory access overhead. This guarantees each encoding result can be stored or fetched in one memory access. The motivation behind using asymmetric error-correcting coding technique in NBF-E is to enhance the resilience of recorded encoding results to noise by fully exploiting the asymmetric error nature of query results.

1.4 Key Technical Challenges

The first technical challenge is to minimize the classification failure and false positive for NBF scheme under a given memory constraint. To address this challenge, we first infer the expression of error rate for "0" bits in a set ID code, which is uniform and can be reasonably approximated as independent and identically distributed. Based on this, we further show that the number of error bits in the query results can be modeled with Binomial distributions. We then derive the expressions of classification failure rate and false positive rate. Furthermore, we optimize these two metrics in terms of number of hash functions and code size.

The second technical challenge is to best tradeoff the benefits brought by incorporating asymmetric error-correcting codes in NBF-E scheme and the aggravated noise arose from such codes. We first derive the expressions of classification failure rate and false positive rate for our NBF-E scheme. Among these two metrics, classification failure rate is much more complicated than its counterpart of NBF due to the asymmetric error-correcting ability of NBF-E, which hinders further optimization analysis. To address this challenge, we propose to analyze its upper bound, which is shown to be a relatively accurate estimate and is much easier to be analyzed than its exact value. Then, we obtain optimization results of classification failure rate and false positive rate in terms of number of hash functions and code size.

The third technical challenge is to provide guidance for choosing between NBF and NBF-E schemes. As NBF-E does not always outperform NBF due to its introduced noise, we need to answer the question of under which condition which scheme is more preferable than the other in terms of critical metrics, such as classification failure. This is a challenging task because of the fundamental difference, though seemingly small, between these two schemes. We address this challenge by employing appropriate relaxation techniques and using the lower bound, rather than exact value, of the number of asymmetric error-correcting codewords to make the comparison of classification failure rates for these two schemes feasible.

1.5 Advantages over Prior Art

Previous literature falls short in either storage space cost or query speed. To evaluate our NBF and NBF-E schemes in comparison with prior art, we conduct trace-driven experiments. Our results show that NBF/NBF-E significantly advances the state-of-the-art on multi-set membership testing. Suppose all schemes are under the same storage space constraint. In comparison with COMB, NBF-E has 13% higher correctness rate, 3.7 times smaller memory accesses and 3.3 times faster query processing speed. In comparison with Summary Cache, NBF/NBF-E has comparable correctness rate, 7.7 times lower memory accesses and about 6 times faster query processing speed. In comparison with kBF, NBF/NBF-E has 8.7 times higher correctness rate and about 6 times faster query processing speed. In comparison with IBF, NBF-E has hundreds of times higher correctness rate.

2. RELATED WORK

In this section, we briefly review related works regarding Bloom filters for multi-set membership testing.

2.1 Cell Based Approach

David *et al.* proposed Invertible Bloom Filter (IBF) which can be inverted to yield some or all of the inserted key IDs of elements [6,9]. An IBF consists of an array of cells each of which contains a counter, the XOR of all key IDs that hash into that cell, as well as the XOR of the hashes of all IDs that hash into the cell. In the query phase, the cells that record only a single element are first identified and recovered. Then, the set ID information of these elements is subtracted from IBF using XOR functions. Such identification and removal process will repeat until no further elements can be recognized. The major shortage of IBF is its memory inefficiency as it uses cells instead of bits. Xiong *et al.* proposed key-value Bloom Filter (kBF) that also stores values of elements in cells [23]. Each cell contains a counter and a possibly superimposed encoding result, and kBF can only infer original encodings from superimposed encoding results from at most three elements, which constrains its success rate of querying. Both of IBF and kBF are less memory efficient compared to our NBF scheme because NBF stores encoding results of set IDs in bits and allows the bit-level overlap.

2.2 Multiple Bloom Filter Based Approach

Fan *et al.* proposed a scalable web cache sharing scheme called Summary Cache, which in essence is a straightforward Bloom filter solution that allows multi-set membership testing [8]. It generates one Bloom filter for each set in the construction phase, and performs $k \times \aleph$ hashes for recording set IDs or querying which set the input element belongs to, where k is the number of hashes for each Bloom filter and $\aleph$ is the number of distinct sets. Chazelle *et al.* proposed Bloomier filter that consists of multiple suites of Bloom filters, or equivalently, a series of Bloom filters in Summary Cache [5]. Each suite for Bloomier filter contains $\aleph$ Bloom filters for $\aleph$ sets, and applies hash functions different from other suites to store and query set IDs. Especially, during the query phase, Bloomier filter searches all suites of Bloom filters one by one until it reaches a suite returning only one positive answer among $\aleph$ Bloom filters. The goal of Bloomier filter is to alleviate the false positive of the presented Bloom filter in Summary Cache. Lu *et al.* reported an improved solution based on Summary Cache which assumes each input set ID is L-bit long and generates one Bloom filter for each bit in set ID [15]. When performing Bloom filter construction or multi-set membership query, it uses $k \times L$ hash functions to record or determine the corresponding bit value in L-bit long set ID. As normally we have $L = O(\log \aleph)$, this solution is supposed to be much faster than Summary Cache scheme in [8]. Hao *et al.* proposed COMbinatorial Bloom filter (COMB) that encodes each set ID into an L-bit binary vector with θ 1*s* and $L-\theta$ 0*s* and then uses k hash functions for each of L bits in a single Bloom filter [11]. COMB needs to compute $k \times \theta$ hash functions for construction and query for each element. In comparison, our NBF scheme only needs to compute k hash functions. Yoon *et al.* proposed Bloom tree [24], which maintains a binary search tree with each node being a Bloom filter and the leaf nodes representing distinct values. To query a set ID for a given element is to determine a unique path from the root to a leaf node, and its query speed is t times that of standard Bloom filter where t is the depth of the Bloom tree. In summary, compared with the above schemes, NBF needs only k modulo operations and k memory accesses and is thus more time efficient. For example, NBF is 6 times faster than Summary Cache and 3.3 times faster than COMB in terms of query processing speed as demonstrated by our experimental results.

2.3 Offset Based Approach

Lee *et al.* proposed a new data structure called SVBF that encodes the set information in an offset to save s-

Table 1: Notations

Symbol	Meaning
m	Size of a Bloom filter in bits
B	Bit array of a Bloom filter
n	Number of stored elements
e	An element of a set
v	Set ID of element e
$\aleph$	Number of distinct set IDs of elements
$h_i(\cdot)$	The i-th hash function
k	Number of hash functions for a Bloom filter
f	Size of set ID code in bits
w	Constant Hamming weight of codes
d	Minimum Hamming distance of codes
t	Number of correcting error bits
p_e	Error rate for "0" bits of set ID code in query result
P_{cf}	Classification failure rate
P_{fp}	False positive rate

pace [13]. In particular, unlike standard Bloom filter that sets k hash values $h_i(e)\%m$ $(i = 1, \dots k)$ to 1 where % represents modular operation, SVBF sets the bit corresponding to $(h_i(e) + j)\%m$ $(i = 1, \dots k)$ to 1 where j $(0 < j \leq g)$ is the set ID, g is the maximum set ID, and m is the size of SVBF. In the query phase, SVBF first reads the next g consecutive bits from each base $h_i(e)\%m$ to get a bitmap B_i. Then, SVBF computes the bit-wise AND across all bitmaps to get the final bitmap B, and outputs the minimum offset where a bit is set to 1 as the set ID. The main limitation of SVBF is its bad scalability. On one hand, the classification failure of SVBF would increase rapidly as g increases because the probability that noisy bits from other elements appear between $h_i(e)\%m$ and $(h_i(e)+j)\%m$ increases nearly proportionally with j. On the other hand, as for each hash position in the query phase, SVBF needs to fetch all next g bits starting from this position, which may lead to memory accesses proportional to g when g becomes large. For these reasons, g is required to be no more than 64 to control classification failure and memory accesses in [13], which, however, constrains its applications. Compared with SVBF, NBF can scale to a much larger number of distinct set IDs (up to 1.83×10^{18}).

3. NOISY BLOOM FILTER (NBF)

In this section, we first describe the construction phase and query phase of our proposed Noisy Bloom Filter (NBF) scheme. Then, we give detailed theoretical analysis about the performance of NBF in terms of classification failure rate and false positive rate. In addition, we discuss parameter optimization to minimize classification failure rate as well as false positive rate. Table 1 summarizes notations used in this paper.

3.1 Construction Phase

In the construction phase, NBF first constructs a bit array B of size m with all bits initialized to 0. Suppose NBF needs to store n distinct elements $e_1, e_2, \dots, e_n$, each of which with an associated set ID v_i. Then, the recording process for an element e is to first map e into k different positions $h_1(e)\%m$, $h_2(e)\%m$, ..., $h_k(e)\%m$ using k distinct hash functions $h_1(.), h_2(.), \dots, h_k(.)$, where the symbol % represents modular operation.

Next, instead of recording the original set ID of e, NBF stores its corresponding constant weight code. Here constant weight code refers to a type of codes with constant Hamming weight. That is, the Hamming weight, namely the number of 1s in a code, for any codeword is a predefined constant w. We use $C(v)$ to denote the corresponding constant weight code for a set ID v. In practice, $C(v)$ can be computed by a well defined function, or obtained by querying a codebook that records all the mappings of set IDs and their corresponding codes. Furthermore, the number of codewords for constant weight code, *i.e.* $\binom{f}{w}$, should be sufficiently large to express all possible values for v, which is presumed to be bounded by $\aleph$. That is, NBF should carefully choose f and w such that $\binom{f}{w} \geq \aleph$. We will list the motivations for adopting constant weight code later in this subsection.

After that, NBF records the set ID of element e by ORing its constant weight code with the next f consecutive bits starting from each of the k hashed position. Specifically, NBF sets $B[(h_i(e)\%m + j)\%m] = B[(h_i(e)\%m + j)\%m] \mid C(v)[j]$ $(1 \leq i \leq k;\ 0 \leq j < f)$. As the length of the constant code f is typically set to be small to guarantee one memory access ($\lesssim 64$, which still allows expressing at most $\binom{64}{32} \approx 1.83 \times 10^{18}$ set IDs), all f relevant bits starting from each hashed position can be fetched or updated using one memory access operation. Note that modern architectures like X86 platform CPU can access data starting at any byte, *i.e.*, access data aligned on any boundary, not just on word boundaries [1, 17]. In addition, if $h_i(e)\%m + j > m$, NBF needs to wrap around and update an appropriate number of starting bits of B to make the total number of bits be f. This undoubtedly leads to one extra memory access.

The motivations for storing constant weight codes of input element set IDs rather than set IDs themselves or other non-constant weight codes are four-folds. First, constant weight codes are generally more space-efficient than directly storing set IDs. The cardinality of distinct values of input elements $\aleph$ could be far less than the largest set ID of input elements. As the length of codes should be designed to be uniform among elements and should accommodate the largest set ID of input elements, directly storing set IDs of elements could be a waste of space. For example, expressing elements with three distinct set IDs 1, 2 and $2^{32} - 1$ needs 32 bits, while constant weight codes 001, 010, 100 with three-bit length are sufficient to present all set IDs. Second, constant weight codes simply check the Hamming weight of the query result to verify its correctness, which is more efficient and explicit than other methods. Third, compared with other methods, constant weight codes can eliminate or alleviate the impact of distribution skewness of input element set IDs, guaranteeing the performance of NBF in general cases. The distribution of element set IDs is typically skewed and unpredictable, *e.g.*, traffic flows across large networks mostly follow Zipf or "Zipf-like" distribution which is highly skewed [19]. Using non-constant weight codes could introduce heavy noise to data stored in NBF if the codes of set IDs corresponding to large numbers of elements happen to have large Hamming weights, and therefore, it leads to high classification failure rate or high false positive rate. Fourth, constant weight codes can ensure fairness for set IDs in terms of query success rate, whereas other methods do not. As noise in NBF is approximately uniformly distributed, non-constant weight codes or set IDs with relatively less Hamming weight would suffer more from noise as they have more "0" bits (we will prove "0" bits are affected by noise while "1" bits are not), and are less likely to be successfully recovered.

3.2 Query Phase

To query an element e, NBF finds its associated set ID v by the following four steps. First, it computes k hash functions $h_1(e)\%m$, ..., $h_k(e)\%m$ to determine k positions from where the data records of e start. Second, for each $1 \leq i \leq k$, it reads the next consecutive f bits $B[(h_i(e)\%m + j)\%m]$ $(0 \leq j < f)$ and forms a bitmap B_i. Third, we conduct bitwise AND operation among all obtained k bitmaps, *i.e.*, $C(v) = B_1\&\ldots\&B_i\&\ldots\&B_k$ $(1 \leq i \leq k)$. Fourth, if the Hamming weight of the obtained code $C(v)$ is equal to w, then we report the corresponding v of $C(v)$, *i.e.* $C^{-1}(C(v))$, as the associated set ID of e. In the case that the Hamming weight is smaller than w, NBF reports that the element v doesn't exist in the Bloom filter and discards the query result.

There are two types of failures that can happen in the query phase of NBF: *classification failure* and *false positive.* In the case that the Hamming weight of $C(v)$ is larger than w, NBF cannot classify the query result into any predefined constant weight code, which we call it as *classification failure.* In the case that the element is not in the Bloom filter, but the Hamming weight of $C(v)$ is equal to w due to noises, NBF will falsely identify the element to a set with set ID v, which we call it as *false positive.*

3.3 Analysis

For theoretical analysis, we pay special attention to classification failure rate and false positive rate. In particular, we derive expected values of these parameters and discuss how to optimize them.

As the basis of further analysis, we begin with inferring the rate of a bit error in the query result, which is quantitatively evaluated by the equation in the following lemma.

LEMMA 1. *Given the NBF size m, number of stored elements n, code length f, code weight w and number of hash functions k, the error rate for "0" bits in a set ID code,* i.e. *the probability for any "0" bit in a set ID code changing to* 1 *in the query result, denoted by p_e is given by*

$$p_e = \left(1 - \left(1 - \frac{w}{m}\right)^{nk}\right)^k, \tag{1}$$

and the error rate for "1" bits is zero.

PROOF. Considering a "0" bit b in a recorded set ID code in B, the probability that another recorded set ID code with length f covers this bit is f/m, and the probability that the overlapped bit in this recorded set ID code taking value 1 is w/f, thus the probability that a "1" bit from another recorded set ID code overlaps with b is $f/m * w/f = w/m$. As there are $n \times k$ recorded set ID codes, the probability that b does NOT change its value is the probability that every overlapped bit takes value 0, *i.e.*, $(1 - w/m)^{nk}$. In contrast, the probability that b changes its value is $1 - (1 - \frac{w}{m})^{nk}$. Finally, a "0" bit in a set ID code changing to 1 in the query result after AND operation is conditioned on all k bits in k corresponding recorded set ID codes are "1", whose probability is $p_e = (1-(1-\frac{w}{m})^{nk})^k$. Next, it is easy to see the error rate for "1" bits is zero. This completes the proof. □

We continue to discuss the correlation between error rates of bits in a query result. For two bits b_p^i and b_q^i in a fetched bitmap B_i, their error rates are indeed statistically correlated because the "1" bits overlapped with b_p^i and b_q^i may come from the same set ID code and they are dependent of each other due to the constant weight constraint of set ID code. To see this, imagine a simple case that both b_p^i and b_q^i are covered by a set ID code $C(v)$ with code length f and Hamming weight w, then given that b_p^i is overlapped with a "1" bit in this code, the probability that b_q^i is also overlapped with a "1" bit in $C(v)$ is reduced from w/f to $(w-1)/(f-1)$, which means their error rates are correlated. However, for the corresponding two bits b_p^j and b_q^j at the same positions in another bitmap B_j that corresponds to the same element with B_i, their error rates should be almost independent of that of b_p^i and b_q^i. This is because any set ID code that covers b_p^j and b_q^j is unlikely to cover b_p^i and b_q^i due to the uniform distribution property of the outputs of the applied hash functions. Suppose the resulting bits in the query result is $b_p = b_p^1\&b_p^2\ldots\&b_p^k$ and $b_q = b_q^1\&b_q^2\ldots\&b_q^k$. As b_p equals 1 if and only if $b_p^i = 1$ for all $1 \leq i \leq k$ and the case is similar to b_q, it is clear that the correlation between error rates of any pair of bits b_p^i and b_q^i will be substantially weakened, which results in a weak correlation between b_p and b_q. For this reason, we approximately assume the error rates of bits conform to *independent and identical distribution (i.i.d.).* We will justify it by experimental results to several theorems below based on this assumption.

Next, we analyze the classification failure rate for query phase. Note that at the last step of query phase, classification failure occurs if the Hamming weight of the query result is larger than w, or equivalently, there is one or more "0" bits are corrupted. The theorem below formally gives the expression of classification failure rate.

THEOREM 1. *Given the NBF size m, number of stored elements n, code length f, code weight w and number of hash functions k, the classification failure rate P_{cf} for NBF is given by*

$$1 - (1 - p_e)^{f-w}, \tag{2}$$

where $p_e = (1 - (1 - \frac{w}{m})^{nk})^k$.

PROOF. Suppose there are exactly j $(1 \leq j \leq f - w)$ "0" bits are corrupted while the other $f - w - j$ "0" bits are not. Apparently, j conforms to Binomial distribution, *i.e.*, $j \sim$ *Binom*$(f - w, p_e)$ where $p_e = (1 - (1 - \frac{w}{m})^{nk})^k$ by following Lemma 1 and our *i.i.d.* assumption for error rates of bits in the query result. Thus the classification failure rate for j corrupted bits is given by $\binom{f-w}{j}p_e^j(1-p_e)^{f-w-j}$. By considering all possible cases of j $(1 \leq j \leq f - w)$, we have $P_{cf} = \sum_{j=1}^{f-w}\binom{f-w}{j}p_e^j(1-p_e)^{f-w-j}$, which is equivalent to Equation (2). This completes the proof. □

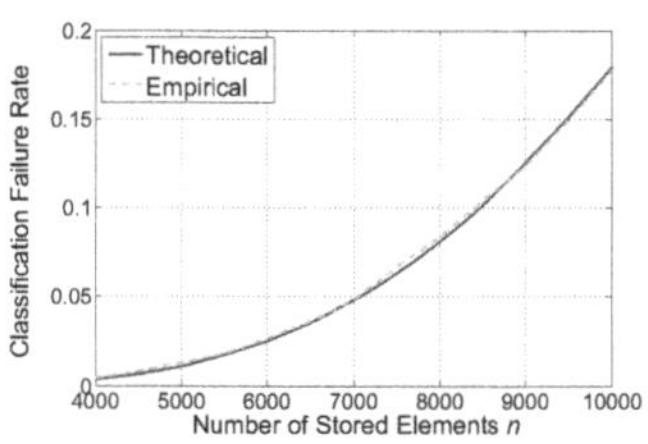

Figure 3: Comparison of Theoretical and Empirical Value of P_{cf}

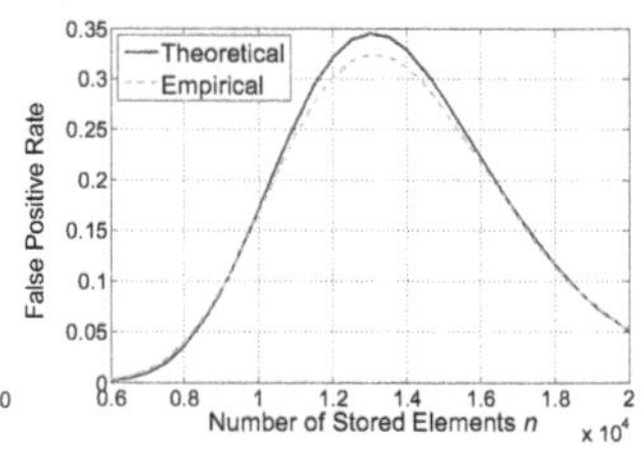

Figure 4: Comparison of Theoretical and Empirical Value of P_{fp}

As Figure 3 shows, the theoretical value of classification failure rate fits well with the empirical value when $m = 1.2 \times 10^5$, $f = 5$, $w = 2$, $k = 6$, and n increases from 4000 to 10000. The average approximation error is merely 5.3%.

In addition to classification failure rate, false positive rate is also a critical performance metric which refers to the probability with which an NBF mistakenly returns a positive answer for an absent element. The theorem below gives the formal expression of false positive rate.

THEOREM 2. *Given the NBF size m, number of stored elements n, code length f, code weight w and number of hash functions k, the false positive rate P_{fp} for NBF is given by*

$$\binom{f}{w} p_e^w (1 - p_e)^{f-w}, \tag{3}$$

where $p_e = (1 - (1 - \frac{w}{m})^{nk})^k$.

PROOF. A false positive happens if and only if there are exactly w bits corrupted which make the obtained result undistinguishable from valid results. By Theorem 1, each bit in the final result has probability p_e to take value 1 and probability $1 - p_e$ to take the opposite value. Therefore, the false positive rate is given by Equation (3). □

Figure 4 shows that the empirical value of false positive rate agrees well with the theoretical value when $m = 1.2 \times 10^5$, $f = 5$, $w = 2$, $k = 12$, and n grows from 6000 to 20000, and the average approximation error is only about 6.1%.

In what follows, we are dedicated to optimizing classification failure and false positive in terms of number of hash functions k.

THEOREM 3. *Given the fixed NBF size m, number of stored elements n, code length f, and code weight w, and the error rate for "0" bits in a set ID code p_e is sufficiently small, both of the classification failure rate P_{cf} and false positive rate P_{fp} for NBF can be minimized when*

$$k = \frac{m}{wn} \ln 2. \tag{4}$$

PROOF. For classification failure rate, by Equation (2), it is obvious that P_{cf} is minimized when p_e is minimized.

For false positive rate, taking the first-order partial derivative of $\ln P_{fp}$ with respect to p_e and following Equation (3) we have

$$\begin{aligned}\frac{\partial}{\partial p_e} \ln P_{fp} &= \frac{\partial}{\partial p_e} \ln \left[\binom{f}{w} p_e^w (1 - p_e)^{f-w}\right] \\ &= \frac{w}{p_e} - \frac{f - w}{1 - p_e}.\end{aligned} \tag{5}$$

By letting the above formula equal to zero, we obtain $p_e = \frac{w}{n}$. Furthermore, taking the second-order partial derivative of $\ln P_{fp}$ with respect to p_e and plugging in $p_e = \frac{w}{n}$ we have

$$\begin{aligned}\frac{\partial^2}{\partial^2 p_e} \ln P_{fp} &= -\frac{w}{p_e^2} - \frac{f - w}{(1 - p_e)^2} \\ &= -\frac{w}{(w/n)^2} - \frac{f - w}{(1 - w/n)^2} \\ &< 0.\end{aligned} \tag{6}$$

Thus, P_{fp} is maximized at point $p_e = \frac{w}{n}$. In contrast, in order to minimize P_{fp}, we need to minimize p_e or maximize p_e to make it being deviate from $\frac{w}{n}$ as much as possible. When p_e is sufficiently small such that $p_e < \frac{w}{n}$, minimizing p_e should be a reasonable choice to minimize P_{fp}.

Next, we study how to minimize p_e. In particular, we take the first-order partial derivative of $\ln p_e$ with respect to k and make an appropriate approximation

$$\begin{aligned}\frac{\partial}{\partial k} \ln p_e &= \frac{\partial}{\partial k} \ln(1 - (1 - \frac{w}{m})^{nk})^k \\ &\approx \frac{\partial}{\partial k} \ln(1 - e^{-\frac{wnk}{m}})^k \\ &= \ln(1 - e^{-\frac{wnk}{m}}) + \frac{wnk}{m} \frac{e^{-\frac{wnk}{m}}}{1 - e^{-\frac{wnk}{m}}}.\end{aligned} \tag{7}$$

It is easy to check the above derivative is equal to zero when $k = \frac{m}{wn} \ln 2$, and further this is a global minimum. To summarize, both of P_{cf} and P_{fp} are minimized when p_e is minimized at point $k = \frac{m}{wn} \ln 2$. This completes the proof. □

Discussion: We note that there is an interesting similarity between the optimal number of hash function for our proposed NBF and that for standard Bloom filter, which is given by $k' = \frac{m}{n} \ln 2$. As standard Bloom filter writes a single 1 to each of k hash bits whereas NBF writes w 1s, the total numbers of written 1s for both filters are the same, *i.e.*, $wnk = nk' = m \ln 2$. Therefore, on average each bit in both filters has the same probability 1/2 to be 1 or 0.

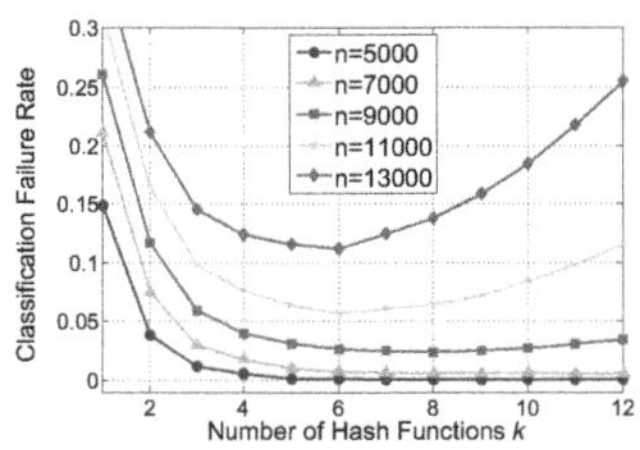

Figure 5: P_{cf} vs. k for NBF

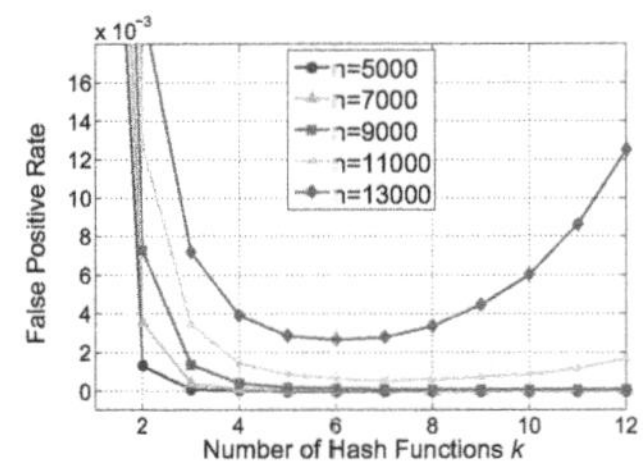

Figure 6: P_{fp} vs. k for NBF

Figures 5 and 6 show the classification failure rate P_{cf} and false positive rate P_{fp} when $m = 3 \times 10^5$, $f = 8$, $w = 3$, k increases from 1 to 12 and n increases from 5000 to 13000. Basically, all curves for P_{cf} and P_{fp} first drops until reaching a minimum, and then rises. For example, P_{cf} achieves the minimum points at $k = 14, 9, 8, 6, 6$, while P_{fp} attain its minimum at $k = 14, 10, 8, 7, 6$, when $n = 5000, 7000, 9000, 11000, 13000$ respectively. In comparison, the theoretical optimal k for $n = 5000, 7000, 9000, 11000, 13000$ are $k = 13.86, 9.90, 7.70, 6.30, 5.33$, respectively, which match well with the actual values. Note that the theoretical k is typically not an integer, while in practice k must be an integer. This corroborates with Theorem 3.

Next, we continue to optimize P_{cf} and P_{fp} in terms of f, and present theoretical findings in the theorem below.

THEOREM 4. *Both of the classification failure rate P_{cf} and the false positive rate P_{fp} for NBF decrease monotonically when the code size f decreases given that the number of hash functions k takes its optimal value, i.e., $k = \frac{m}{wn} \ln 2$, and the error rate for "0" bits in a set ID code p_e is sufficiently small.*

PROOF. For classification failure, plugging the expression of k in Equation (4) into Equation (2) we obtain $P_{cf} =$

$1-(1-(\frac{1}{2})^{\frac{m}{wn}\ln 2})^{f-w}$. As m, n and w are fixed, it is clear that P_{cf} decreases with an decreasing f.

For false positive, we plug the optimal value of k into Equation (3) and have

$$P_{fp} = \binom{f}{w}\left(\frac{1}{2}\right)^{\frac{m}{n}\ln 2}\left[1-\left(\frac{1}{2}\right)^{\frac{m}{wn}\ln 2}\right]^{f-w} \quad (8)$$

To search for the optimal value of f that minimizes P_{fp}, we take the first-order partial derivative of $\ln P_{fp}$ with respect to f

$$\begin{aligned}\frac{\partial}{\partial f}\ln P_{fp} &= \frac{\partial}{\partial f}\ln\left\{\binom{f}{w}\left(\frac{1}{2}\right)^{\frac{m}{n}\ln 2}\left[1-\left(\frac{1}{2}\right)^{\frac{m}{wn}\ln 2}\right]^{f-w}\right\} \\ &= \frac{\partial}{\partial f}\ln\frac{\prod_{i=0}^{w-1}(f-i)}{w!} - \ln\left[1-\left(\frac{1}{2}\right)^{\frac{m}{wn}\ln 2}\right] \\ &= \sum_{i=0}^{w-1}\frac{1}{f-i} - \ln\left[1-\left(\frac{1}{2}\right)^{\frac{m}{wn}\ln 2}\right] \quad (9)\end{aligned}$$

As $\frac{\partial^2}{\partial^2 f}\ln P_{fp} = -\sum_{i=0}^{w-1}\frac{1}{(f-i)^2} < 0$, f that makes the last formula equal to zero is a maximum. Furthermore, it is also a global maximum because $\sum_{i=0}^{w-1}\frac{1}{f-i}$ is a monotonically decreasing function with f and, therefore, there is at most one value letting the first-order partial derivative of $\ln P_{fp}$ equal to zero. Consider the case when $p_e = (\frac{1}{2})^{\frac{m}{wn}\ln 2}$ is sufficiently small and thereby the value of Formula (9) is always greater than zero, P_{fp} must decrease as f decreases. This completes the proof. □

Discussion: Despite of the result stated in Theorem 4, we should bear in mind that we can NOT arbitrarily cut down the value of f to minimize P_{cf} and P_{fp}, because we need an adequate number of codewords to accommodate all potential set IDs of input elements with cardinality $\aleph$. In other words, NBF should guarantee that $\binom{f}{w} \geq \aleph$. To this end, we can choose f and w that satisfy $w = f/2$ and thereby yield the minimum value of f under a given constraint $\binom{f}{w} \geq \aleph$. We will take this parameter setting in the later theoretical analysis in this paper.

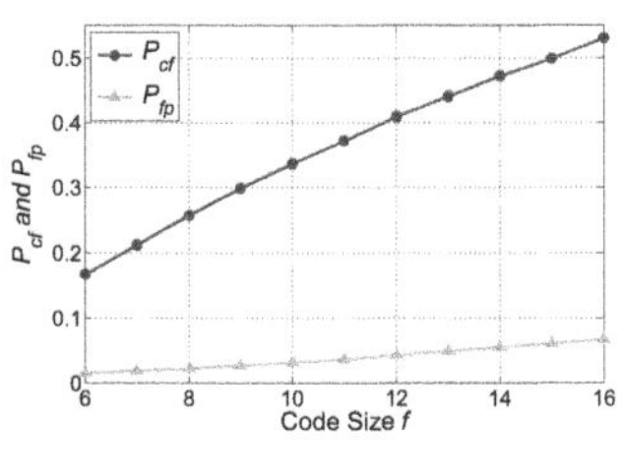

Figure 7: P_{cf} & P_{fp} vs. f for NBF

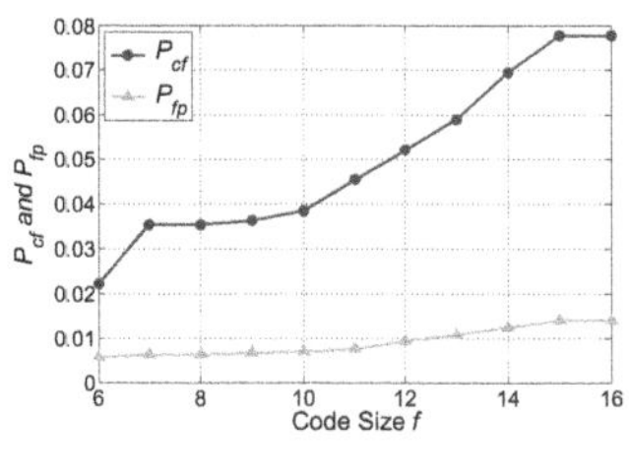

Figure 8: P_{cf} & P_{fp} vs. f for NBF-E

Figure 7 shows P_{cf} and P_{fp} when $m = 1.73\times 10^6$, $n = 10^5$, $w = 3$, $k = 4$, and f increases from 6 to 16. We can see that both P_{cf} and P_{fp} decease smoothly as f decreases. This observation well supports Theorem 4.

4. ERROR CORRECTED NOISY BLOOM FILTER (NBF-E)

In this section, we incorporate asymmetric error-correcting codes into our NBF framework, which is called NBF-E. Our goal is to further suppress the classification failure and/or false positive. First of all, we present the motivations of applying asymmetric error-correcting codes. Then, we elaborate on utilizing it in the construction phase and query phase for NBF-E. Next, we calculate the classification failure rate and false positive rate of NBF-E, and study their optimization.

4.1 Optimization Using Asymmetric Error-Correcting Code

Our motivation for employing Asymmetric Error-Correcting (AEC) codes is to leverage the asymmetric error property of NBF to bring down the classification failure rate and/or false positive rate of NBF. As revealed by Lemma 1, the error rates for "0" bits in query results being corrupted are uniform and are given by $p_e = (1-(1-w/m)^{nk})^k$, but, on the contrary, the probability for a "1" bit to be corrupted is zero. On one hand, the error rates for "0" bits resembles the bit error rate of common memory-less channel models in information theory and coding theory that assume errors occur randomly and with a certain probability. This inspires us to use traditional error-correcting codes to enhance the resilience of the query results to noise. On the other hand, the one-sided error property of query results, *i.e.*, the crossover $0 \to 1$ occurs with positive probability p_e whereas the crossover $1 \to 0$ never occurs as illustrated in Figure 9, is naturally the property of binary asymmetric channel, or to be specific, Z channel [12]. There has emerged a large body of literature studying on AEC codes for asymmetric channel in recent years such as [12,20,21,26,27]. These proposed AEC codes are commonly as good as or better than Symmetric Error-Correcting (SEC) codes in terms of error-correcting ability and decoding speed. The root reason is that their search space for correcting errors is much smaller due to the one-sided error pattern of Z channel.

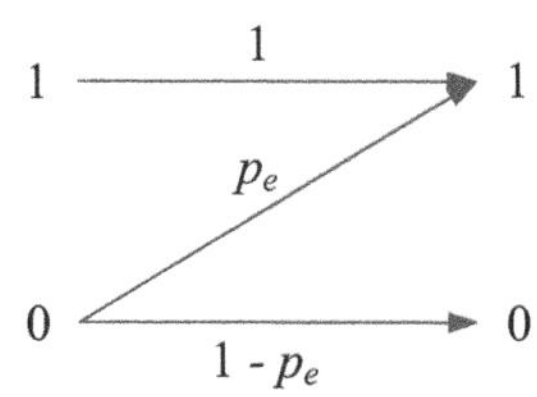

Figure 9: Binary Asymmetric Channel (Z Channel)

Notwithstanding, AEC codes have their weakness in slow encoding speed compared to SEC codes. For instance, the authors in [12] described a class of AEC codes such as Kim-Freiman codes, Constantin-Rao codes and Varshamov codes for which no simple algorithm is known. Surprisingly, our proposed constant weight codes capture the benefits of SEC codes in terms of fast encoding speed and the advantages of AEC codes in terms of strong error-correcting ability and fast decoding speed, while avoiding their major limitations. On one hand, we prove in Theorem 5 that AEC codes and SEC codes have exactly the same error-correcting ability for *present elements* that are already stored in the Bloom filter using constant weight codes, which means NBF-E can follow traditional encoding process as SEC codes do for constant weight codes. On the other hand, by the discussion for Theorems 8 and 9, the false positive rate for NBF-E using AEC codes is nearly half that of SEC codes in general cases, and, meanwhile, its expected decoding speed is twice higher than SEC codes.

We emphasize that our disclosure of inherent asymmetric error property of our proposed Bloom filters and proposition of adopting AEC codes would shed light to future researches including not only NBF-E extensions but also other Bloom filer based schemes. For example, suppose we have a priori knowledge regarding the distribution of set IDs, then we can use non-constant weight codes for the sake of better memory efficiency (*e.g.*, assign codes with light Hamming weights to frequent set IDs like Huffman Coding does). In this scenario, AEC codes should have stronger error-correcting ability than SEC codes even for present elements [12]. Besides, the decoding algorithm for AEC codes can be applied to the E-COMB scheme proposed in [11] to accelerate its decoding speed.

4.2 Construction Phase

Basically, the construction phase for NBF-E is the same as that for NBF except for the construction of constant weight codes.

Unlike NBF that merely needs to enumerate all codewords with length f and constant weight w, NBF-E additionally requires all codewords share the same Hamming distance d between each other. Under such an extra constraint, the maximum number of codewords, which is called $A(f,d,w)$, is generally impossible to be computed directly. There has emerged a large body of works to study effective enumerative methods of constant weight codes such as Steiner systems method [2] and geometric encoding method [22]. Among these methods, the method proposed in [18] yields essentially the optimal results and has complexity scale of $O(n(\log n)^c)$ where $c \geq 2$ is some fixed constant. As enumerative methods of constant weight code is out of the focus of this paper, we simply adopt the enumerative method proposed in [18] to generate codewords.

We first present some necessary definitions and theoretical results for Hamming distance and asymmetric distance, and then propose a critical theorem for asymmetric error-correcting codes in our case.

DEFINITION 1. *(Definition 2.6 in [12]) Given two codes* $x = (x_1, x_2, \dots, x_n)$, $y = (y_1, y_2, \dots, y_n) \in \{0,1\}^n$. *Let* $N(x,y) := \#\{i | x_i = 0 \text{ and } y_i = 1\}$.

(1) The Hamming distance is defined as:

$$d(x,y) := N(x,y) + N(y,x);$$

(2) The asymmetric distance is defined as:

$$\Delta(x,y) := \max\{N(x,y), N(y,x)\}.$$

THEOREM 5. *Symmetric error-correcting codes and asymmetric error-correcting codes have the same error-correcting ability for present elements when using constant weight codes.*

PROOF. By Lemma 2.1 in [12], we have $2\Delta(x,y) = d(x,y)$ for constant weight codes as all its codewords have the same weight. This also reveals the fact that the Hamming distance of constant weight codes $d(x,y)$ must be an even number. As a result, symmetric error-correcting codes for constant weight codes can correct up to $t_s = (d-2)/2 = (2\Delta(x,y) - 2)/2 = \Delta(x,y) - 1$ errors by Theorem 2.1.2 in [16], while asymmetric error-correcting codes can correct up to $t_a = \Delta(x,y) - 1$ errors by Theorem 2.1 in [12]. Then we have $t_s = t_a$, which means both of these two types of codes have the same error-correcting ability. □

Next, we present the Graham-Sloane lower bound, one of the most known lower bounds, for the maximum number of codewords $A(f,w,d)$ for binary constant weight codes.

THEOREM 6. *(Theorem 4 in [10]) Let q be the smallest prime power (prime power is a positive integer power of a single prime number) satisfying $q \geq f$, the minimum Hamming distance of codes d is an even number, then*

$$A(f,d,w) \geq \frac{1}{q^{d/2-1}} \binom{f}{w}. \tag{10}$$

As $A(f,w,d)$ is hard to be exactly determined, one reasonable choice is to alternatively use its lower bound by requiring that the lower bound should be no less than the cardinality of potential set IDs of input elements, *i.e.* $\frac{1}{q^{d/2-1}}\binom{f}{w} \geq \aleph$.

4.3 Query Phase

Compared to NBF, the only difference of the query phase for NBF-E is the decoding procedure using AEC codes.

Despite of the existence of efficient error-correcting algorithms for constant weight codes like [7], we use the following simple decoding algorithm and show the advantages of AEC codes over SEC codes in terms of decoding speed. For any obtained query result, normally we scan over the whole codebook to single out the codeword having the minimum Hamming distance with the query result as the corrected code, just as traditional SEC codes do. Here is the difference between SEC codes and AEC codes: for SEC codes, they are unaware of asymmetric error pattern and thus attempt to correct all obtained results even if the Hamming weight of the results is less than the code size f, which means these results are indeed invalid codes. For AEC codes, they will identify and ignore all such invalid codes by checking the Hamming weight of the results before scanning the codebook for decoding.

4.4 Analysis

In this section, we first derive the expressions of classification failure rate and false positive rate for NBF-E, and then study their optimization. After that, we study the necessary condition to use NBF-E rather than NBF for delivering insights to real applications.

We present the mathematical expressions of the classification failure rate and false positive rate for NBF-E in the following two theorems.

THEOREM 7. *Given the NBF-E size m, number of stored elements n, code length f, code weight w, number of hash functions k, and number of error-correcting bits t, the classification failure rate P_{cf} for NBF-E is given by*

$$\sum_{j=t+1}^{f-w} \binom{f-w}{j} p_e^j (1-p_e)^{f-w-j}, \tag{11}$$

where $p_e = (1-(1-\frac{w}{m})^{nk})^k$.

PROOF. As the proof is similar to that to Theorem 1, we omit it here to save space. □

THEOREM 8. *Given the NBF-E size m, number of stored elements n, code length f, code weight w and number of hash* *functions k, the false positive rate P_{fp} for NBF-E is given by*

$$\sum_{j=w}^{w+t} \binom{f}{j} p_e^j (1-p_e)^{f-j}, \tag{12}$$

where $p_e = (1-(1-\frac{w}{m})^{nk})^k$.

PROOF. For NBF-E, due to its error-correcting capability, we consider the even worse case in which NBF-E takes all codes with weight j that satisfies $w \le j \le w+t$ as valid codes with or without corruption, which leads to false positive. Consequently, the false positive rate for NBF-E can be obtained by summing up all probability for j ($w \le j \le w+t$) number of bits are corrupted, which is given by $\binom{f}{j} p_e^j (1-p_e)^{f-j}$. Then, the result follows. □

Discussion: Strictly speaking, Equation (12) is indeed an upper bound of false positive rate because in fact not all codes with j ($w \le j \le w+t$) number of bits are wrongly taken as valid set ID codes. For example, when $j = w$, only $A(f,d,w)$ out of $\binom{f}{w}$ codes are mistakenly regarded as valid as stated in Section 4.2. Nevertheless, we approximately take it as false positive rate for simplicity of analysis. Moreover, by similar analysis in the above proof, it is easy to see that the false positive for SEC codes is $P'_{fp} = \sum_{j=w-t}^{w+t} \binom{f}{j} p_e^j (1-p_e)^{f-j}$. Considering general cases where w is supposed to be around $n/2$, then we have $\binom{f}{w-t} p_e^{w-t} (1-p_e)^{f-w+t} > \binom{f}{w+t} p_e^{w+t} (1-p_e)^{f-w-t}$, which means P'_{fp} is nearly two times of P_{fp} for AEC codes.

Next, we analyze optimization of P_{cf} and P_{fp} of NBF-E in terms of the number of hash functions k. Before that, we present a critical lemma below to assist further analysis.

LEMMA 2. *(Theorem 1 in [3]) For Binomial distribution Binom(n, p), given that $p < \frac{k}{n}$, the upper bound of the lower tail of Binom(n, p), i.e. $F(k;n,p) = \sum_{j=k}^{n} \binom{n}{j} p^j (1-p)^{n-j}$, can be given by*

$$F(k;n,p) \le \exp\left\{-n\left[\frac{k}{n}\ln\frac{k/n}{p} + (1-\frac{k}{n})\ln\frac{1-k/n}{1-p}\right]\right\}. \tag{13}$$

Though Lemma 2 offers an upper bound, [3] shows that the gap between this bound and the exact value is quite small (only 3% for the numerical example in [3]). In this paper, we use this bound rather than the lower tail of Binomial distribution for the convenience of optimization analysis by assuming that they vary at nearly the same trend, which is a much weaker assumption than assuming they have the same value. We will justify its correctness in later simulations for theoretical results based on this assumption.

The following theorem presents the optimal value of the number of hash functions for NBF-E.

THEOREM 9. *Given the fixed NBF-E size m, number of stored elements n, code length f, and code weight w, and error rate for "0" bits in a set ID code p_e is sufficiently small, both of the classification failure rate P_{cf} and false positive rate P_{fp} for NBF-E can be minimized when*

$$k = \frac{m}{wn}\ln 2. \tag{14}$$

PROOF. We first consider the classification failure rate P_{cf}. According to Theorem 7 and Lemma 2, the upper bound for the classification failure rate is given by

$$\exp\left\{-\left[(t+1)\ln\frac{t+1}{(f-w)p_e} + ((f-w)-(t+1))\ln\frac{(f-w)-(t+1)}{(f-w)(1-p_e)}\right]\right\}. \tag{15}$$

where $p_e = (1-(1-\frac{w}{m})^{nk})^k$ is the error rate for "0" bits in a set ID code. To minimize the above formula is equivalent to maximize

$$(t+1)\ln\frac{t+1}{(f-w)p_e} + ((f-w)-(t+1))\ln\frac{(f-w)-(t+1)}{(f-w)(1-p_e)}. \tag{16}$$

We take the first-order partial derivative of the above formula with respect to p_e and then have

$$\frac{\partial}{\partial p_e}\left\{(t+1)\ln\frac{t+1}{(f-w)p_e} + ((f-w)-(t+1))\ln\frac{(f-w)-(t+1)}{(f-w)(1-p_e)}\right\} = -\frac{t+1}{p_e} + \frac{f-w-t-1}{1-p_e}, \tag{17}$$

and therefore its second-order partial derivative is

$$\frac{\partial}{\partial p_e}\left\{-\frac{t+1}{p_e} + \frac{f-w-t-1}{1-p_e}\right\} = \frac{t+1}{p_e^2} + \frac{f-w-t-1}{(1-p_e)^2} > 0, \tag{18}$$

which means Formula (16) achieves its minimum at point $p_e = \frac{t+1}{f-w}$. As p_e is sufficiently small and is less than $\frac{t+1}{f-w}$, we need to minimize p_e in order to maximize Formula (16), and finally minimize the classification failure rate.

We proceed to consider the false positive rate P_{fp}. Similar to the proof to Theorem 3, we can prove that $\binom{f}{j} p_e^j (1-p_e)^{f-j}$ when $w \le j \le w+t$ should decrease as p_e decreases under the condition that p_e is sufficiently small such that $p_e < \frac{j}{n}$. Thus, it is clear that $\sum_{j=w}^{w+t} \binom{f}{j} p_e^j (1-p_e)^{f-j}$ should decrease as p_e decreases given that $p_e < \frac{w}{n}$.

To sum up, both of P_{cf} and P_{fp} can be minimized when $p_e = (1-(1-\frac{w}{m})^{nk})^k$ is minimized, which can be achieved when $k = \frac{m}{wn}\ln 2$ indicated by the proof to Theorem 3. This completes the proof. □

Discussion: By Theorem 9, we can easily reach the conclusion that every bit in NBF-E takes the equal probability to be 1 or 0. Furthermore, w is generally set to be around $n/2$. Due to this symmetry, NBF-E should have roughly the same chance to process query results with Hamming weight varies from w to $w+t$ and query results with Hamming weight from $w-t$ to $w-1$. While AEC codes skip computing the latter kind of results that are indeed false positives, SEC codes compute both of them, which means the average decoding speed of SEC is twice slower than that of AEC codes.

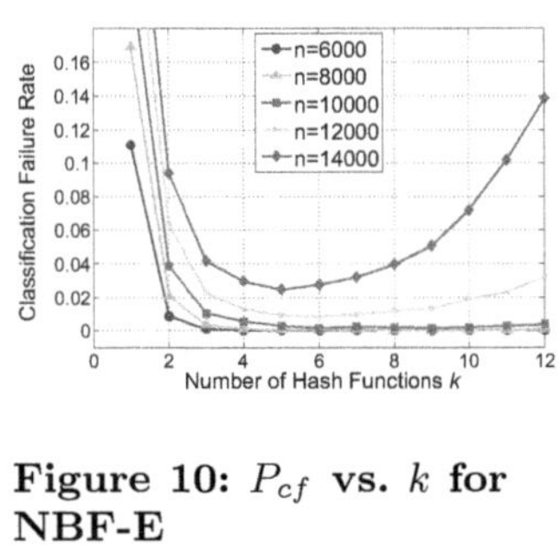

Figure 10: P_{cf} vs. k for NBF-E

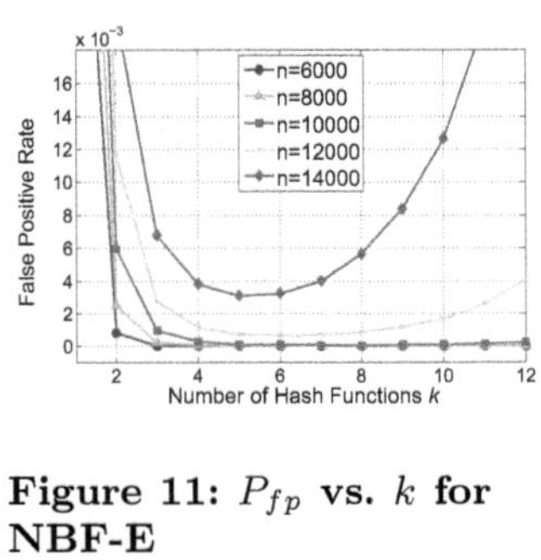

Figure 11: P_{fp} vs. k for NBF-E

Figures 10 and 11 show P_{cf} and P_{fp} when $m = 3 \times 10^5$, $f = 21$, $w = 3$, k increases from 1 to 12 and n increases from 6000 to 14000. The results well support Theorem 9. For instance, when $n = 6000, 8000, 10000, 12000, 14000$, P_{cf}

and P_{fp} achieve their minimum at $k = 11, 9, 6, 6, 5$ and at $k = 11, 8, 7, 6, 5$, respectively, while the theoretical optimal number of hash functions are $k = 11.55, 8.66, 6.93, 5.78, 4.95$, respectively.

THEOREM 10. *Both of the classification failure rate P_{cf} and the false positive rate P_{fp} for NBF-E decrease monotonically when the code size f decreases given that the number of hash functions k takes its optimal value, i.e., $k = \frac{m}{wn}\ln 2$, and the error rate for "0" bits in a set ID code p_e is sufficiently small.*

PROOF. We first consider the classification failure rate P_{cf}. Similar to the proof to Theorem 9, to minimize the upper bound of P_{cf}, we need to maximize

$$(t+1)\ln\frac{t+1}{(f-w)p_e} + ((f-w)-(t+1))\ln\frac{(f-w)-(t+1)}{(f-w)(1-p_e)}. \quad (19)$$

Taking the first-order partial derivative of the above formula with respect to f and considering the fact that $p_e = (1-(1-\frac{w}{m})^{nk})^k = (\frac{1}{2})^{\frac{m}{wn}}$ when $k = \frac{m}{wn}\ln 2$ has nothing to do with f, we obtain

$$\frac{\partial}{\partial f}\left\{(t+1)\ln\frac{t+1}{(f-w)p_e} + ((f-w)-(t+1))\ln\frac{(f-w)-(t+1)}{(f-w)(1-p_e)}\right\}$$
$$= \ln(1-\frac{t+1}{f-w}) - \ln(1-p_e), \quad (20)$$

and therefore its second-order partial derivative is

$$\frac{\partial}{\partial f}\left\{\ln(1-\frac{t+1}{f-w}) - \ln(1-p_e)\right\} = \frac{t+1}{f-w-t-1} > 0, \quad (21)$$

which means Formula (19) achieves its minimum at point $f = \frac{t+1}{p_e} + w$. As p_e is sufficiently small and therefore f is smaller than $\frac{t+1}{p_e} + w$, we need to minimize f in order to minimize P_{cf}.

Next we consider the false positive rate P_{fp}. Recall that we have proved in the proof to Theorem 4 that $\binom{f}{w}(\frac{1}{2})^{\frac{m}{n}\ln 2}[1-(\frac{1}{2})^{\frac{m}{wn}\ln 2}]^{f-w}$ decreases monotonically when f decreases given $k = \frac{m}{wn}\ln 2$. By similar analysis, we can prove $\binom{f}{j}(\frac{1}{2})^{\frac{mj}{wn}\ln 2}[1-(\frac{1}{2})^{\frac{m}{wn}\ln 2}]^{f-j}$ decreases monotonically as f decreases for $w \le j \le w+t$, and thereby $\sum_{j=w}^{w+t}\binom{f}{j}(\frac{1}{2})^{\frac{mj}{wn}\ln 2}[1-(\frac{1}{2})^{\frac{m}{wn}\ln 2}]^{f-j}$ decreases monotonically as f decreases as well. This completes the proof. □

Figure 8 illustrates P_{cf} and P_{fp} when $m = 1.73\times 10^6$, $n = 10^5$, $w = 3$, $k = 4$, and f increases from 6 to 16. It can be seen that both of P_{cf} and P_{fp} decease as f decreases, which confirms Theorem 10.

Apart from parameter optimization for NBF-E, another crucial and natural question is that under what condition is it better to use NBF-E rather than NBF or vice versa. We consider a constrained case and present our theoretical findings in the following theorem.

THEOREM 11. *Given the fixed Bloom filter size m, number of stored elements n, number of hash functions k, and code weight w, and the error rate for "0" bits in a set ID code p_e is sufficiently small, the necessary (but not sufficient) condition for choosing NBF-E rather than NBF in terms of classification failure rate P_{cf} is*

$$\left(1-\left(1-\frac{w}{m}\right)^{nk}\right)^k < \frac{2(f-w)}{(f^{\frac{w}{w-1}}-f)^2} \quad (22)$$

where f is the desirable code length for NBF, that is, the minimum integer satisfying $\binom{f}{w} \ge \aleph$ where $\aleph$ is the number of distinct set IDs of elements.

PROOF. Under the given parameter settings, NBF would choose a desirable code length f that is the minimum integer satisfying $\binom{f}{w} \ge \aleph$ where $\aleph$ is the cardinality of potential set IDs of input elements. For simplicity, we assume $\binom{f}{w} = \aleph$ for NBF. Essentially, if NBF-E is more preferable than NBF, it should be true that NBF-E with exact one error-correcting ability, namely $t = 1$, has less classification failure rate than the classification failure rate of NBF. Suppose the code length for such NBF-E is f', the above condition can be formally expressed as

$$\sum_{j=2}^{f'-w}\binom{f'-w}{j}p_e^j(1-p_e)^{f'-w-j} < 1-(1-p_e)^{f-w}, \quad (23)$$

or equivalently,

$$1-(1-p_e)^{f'-w} - (f'-w)p_e(1-p_e)^{f'-w-1} < 1-(1-p_e)^{f-w}, \quad (24)$$

where $p_e = (1-(1-\frac{w}{m})^{nk})^k$, following Theorem 1 and Theorem 7.

By rearranging Equation (24), we obtain

$$1+(f'-w-1)p_e > (1-p_e)^{-(f'-f-1)}. \quad (25)$$

According to the generalized Newton Binomial theorem [14], we have

$$(1-p_e)^{-(f'-f-1)}$$
$$= 1+(f'-f-1)p_e + \frac{1}{2}(f'-f)(f'-f-1)p_e^2 + O(p_e^3)$$
$$\approx 1+(f'-f-1)p_e + \frac{1}{2}(f'-f)(f'-f-1)p_e^2. \quad (26)$$

The last approximation holds since p_e is sufficiently small. Combing Inequality (25) and Equation (26) we have

$$p_e < \frac{2(f-w)}{(f'-f)(f'-f-1)} \approx \frac{2(f-w)}{(f'-f)^2}. \quad (27)$$

To simplify Inequality (27), we want to find an estimation of f'. By Theorem 6, f' is subject to $A(f', d, w) \ge \frac{1}{q^{d/2-1}}\binom{f'}{w}$ where q is the smallest prime power satisfying $q \ge f'$. As d should be at least $2t+2 = 4$ to ensure the error-correcting ability of NBF-E is at least 1 and q is approximately equal to f', this inequality can be also expressed as $A(f', d, w) \ge \frac{1}{f'}\binom{f'}{w}$. In practical design, we can set $\frac{1}{f'}\binom{f'}{w} = \aleph = \binom{f}{w}$ to guarantee the performance of NBF-E in the worst case. Then we have

$$f' = \frac{f'(f'-1)(f'-2)\dots(f'-w+1)}{f(f-1)(f-2)\dots(f-w+1)} > \left(\frac{f'}{f}\right)^w, \quad (28)$$

and therefore

$$f' < f^{\frac{w}{w-1}}. \quad (29)$$

Combining Inequalities (27) and (29) we have Inequality (22). Furthermore, as Inequality (22) is reached through a number of relaxations, it is indeed a necessary but not sufficient condition for selection. This completes the proof. □

Discussion: This result is consistent with our intuition that when the error rate for "0" bits $p_e = (1-(1-\frac{w}{m})^{nk})^k$ is quite small, the bit error rarely happens and most bits in the Bloom filter are 0, then applying NBF-E can effectively correct such error and reduce the classification failure rate, while not introducing much noise to data in NBF. In contrast, the situation will be reversed when p_e becomes large because the limited error correcting ability of AEC codes is of little use to severe noise while the additionally introduced noise by AEC codes will make the situation even worse. In addition, as Inequality (22) is a necessary but not sufficient condition, the right side of this inequality is essentially a *lower bound* of the threshold for selection between NBF and NBF-E, and can approximately serve as a threshold in practice. Finally, we note that Theorem 11 may not suit the general case where f, k and w can be arbitrarily set.

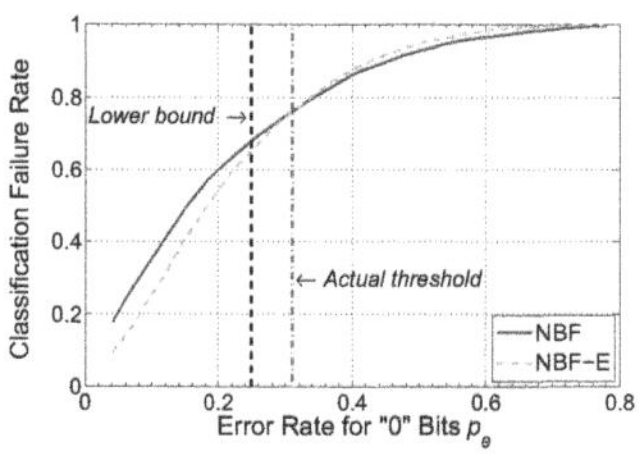

Figure 12: P_{cf} vs. f for NBF and NBF-E

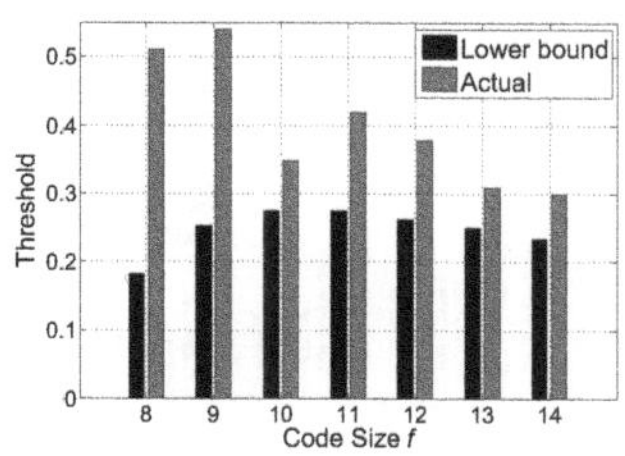

Figure 13: Lower Bound vs. Actual Value of Threshold for Selection

Figure 12 illustrates how P_{cf} changes when $m = 5 \times 10^4$, $f = 13$ for NBF and $f = 19$ for NBF-E, $w = 7$, $k = 3$, and P_e rises from about 0.04 to 0.78 for NBF and NBF-E. The results are shown in the solid blue curve and dotted green curve, respectively. We can observe P_{cf} for NBF-E is first superior, and then becomes inferior to that for NBF as P_e increases, which validates our discussion above. Furthermore, these two curves cross at point $P_e = 0.31$, as marked by the vertical red dot-dash line. This is the actual threshold value for selection between NBF and NBF-E. We also plot our theoretical lower bound of threshold $P_e = 0.25$ in the vertical black dash line in Figure 12. The lower bound of threshold $P_e = 0.25$ shown in the vertical black dash line in Figure 12 is unsurprisingly smaller than the actual threshold. The difference of P_{cf} for NBF and NBF-E at the lower bound of P_e is very small, which means using the lower bound for selection between NBF and NBF-E is reasonable.

Moreover, Figure 13 shows the lower bound and actual threshold values when $m = 5 \times 10^4$, $w = 7$, $k = 3$, and f varies from 8 to 14 as $\aleph$ increases. It can be seen that our lower bound for the threshold for selection precisely holds, and on average, the theoretical bound is equal to 58.2% of the actual threshold value.

5. EVALUATION

In this section, we conduct experiments to validate our NBF and NBF-E schemes and compare them to state-of-the-art solutions for multi-set membership testing.

5.1 Experimental Setup

We briefly describe the dataset we use in the experiments, and describe comparison algorithms as well as related parameter settings.

To evaluate the performance of NBF/NBF-E and other comparison algorithms, we deployed a traffic capturing system on a 10Gbps link of a backbone router to collect trace data. The traffic capturing system contains two sub-systems each of which is equipped with a 10G network card and uses netmap to capture packets. Especially, only 5-tuple flow IDs of packets consisting of source IP, source port, destination IP, destination port, and protocol type are recorded because of the high read/write overhead to capture the entire high-speed traffic. Each 5-tuple flow ID is stored as a 13-byte string, and used as an element in the experiments. The set ID of the set that the flow is belonged to is artificially generated. Overall, we collected up to 10 million flow IDs wherein 8 million flow IDs are distinct.

We use four algorithms, *i.e.*, COMB [11], Summary Cache (SC) [8], kBF [23], and IBF [9] for comparison purposes. To optimize query speed for COMB, SC, IBF and NBF/NBF-E, we use the following simple yet effective accelerating technique that is widely adopted in implementing standard Bloom filter or its variants: fetch k hashed bits (or bitmaps for NBF/NBF-E) one by one, and check if the value of current bit (or value of intermediate query result after performing AND operation for all obtained bitmaps for NBF/NBF-E) is 0; if yes, terminate immediately and return negative answer. Note that this technique can be refined specifically for NBF/NBF-E by checking whether the Hamming weight of the current result is smaller than a threshold (w for NBF/NBF-E) rather than checking whether it is 0. The reason we don't use it is to make a fair comparison between NBF/NBF-E and other schemes.

For computing platform, we used a standard off-the-shelf desktop computer equipped with an Intel(R) Core i7-3520 CPU @2.90GHz and 8GB RAM running Windows 10 to do our experiments. Throughout the experiments, we use the following parameter settings unless otherwise stated. The memory space allocated for any algorithm is $m = 2.16 \times 10^6$ bits, the number of stored elements $n = 10^5$, the number of hash functions is $k = 4$, the code length $f = 7$ for NBF, and $f = 15$ for NBF-E, the constant Hamming weight of codes in NBF or NBF-E is $w = 3$, and the number of distinct set IDs is $\aleph = 35$.

5.2 Correctness Rate

Our results show that our schemes, especially NBF-E, have nearly the best correction rates among all algorithms when changing k and $\aleph$, which is 8.7 times larger than kBF or IBF. The correctness rate here means the ratio of the number of correctly answered query elements to the total number of all query elements. As Figures 14 and 15 illustrate, NBF always has similar correctness rate with COMB, and NBF-E outperforms NBF or COMB by about 13%. Furthermore, it can be observed that SC has the best correctness rate. This is not surprising since SC allocates one standard Bloom filter to each set, and each Bloom filter absolutely returns a positive answer if the query element belongs to its associated set. The reason why SC cannot achieve 100% correctness rate at some points in Figures 14 and 15 is due to query failure, which means there are more than two Bloom filters corresponding to at least two sets return a positive answer because of false positive of standard Bloom filter, and therefore SC cannot determine which one the query element belongs to. Nevertheless, SC suffers from high memory access overhead and lower querying processing speed, and doesn't scale well with the number of distinct set IDs $\aleph$ as will be detailed later.

5.3 False Positive

Our results show that the false positive rate for

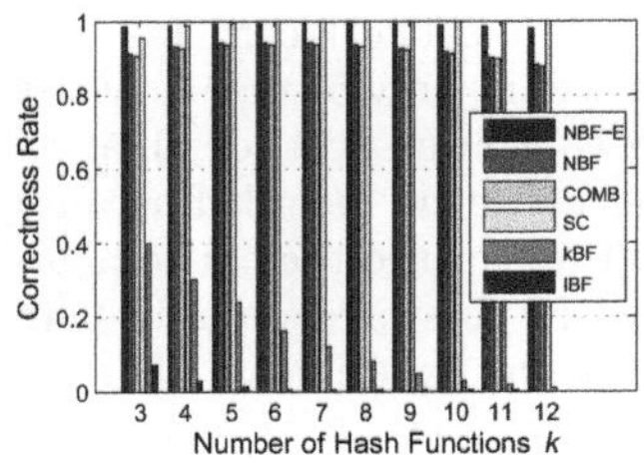

Figure 14: Correctness Rate vs. k

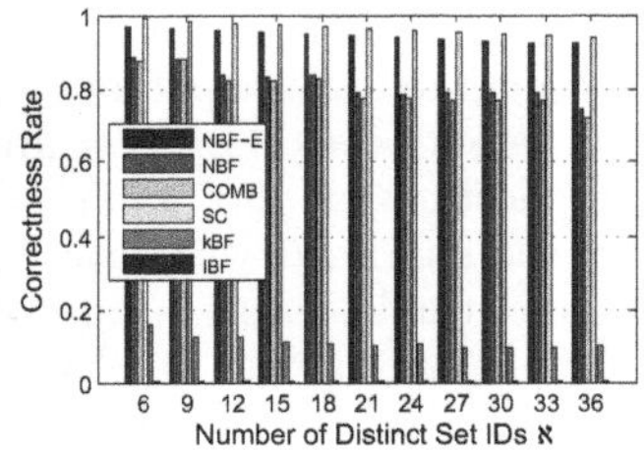

Figure 15: Correctness Rate vs. $\aleph$

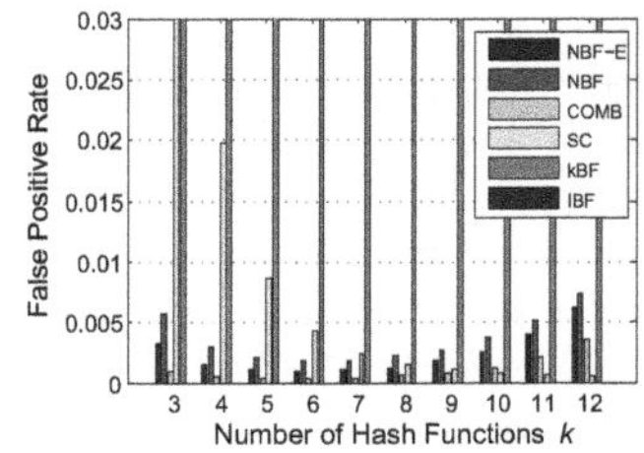

Figure 16: False Positive Rate vs. k

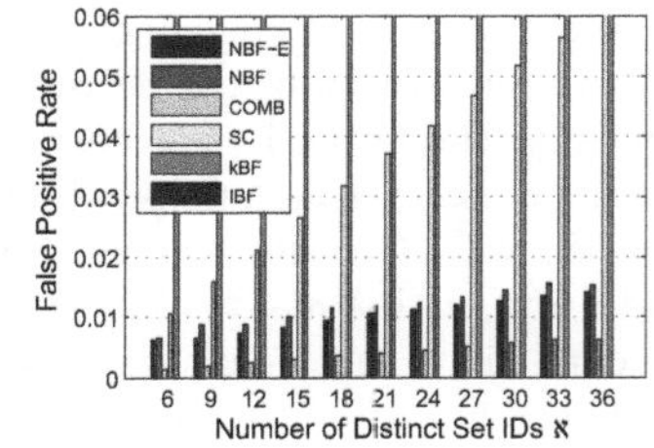

Figure 17: False Positive Rate vs. $\aleph$

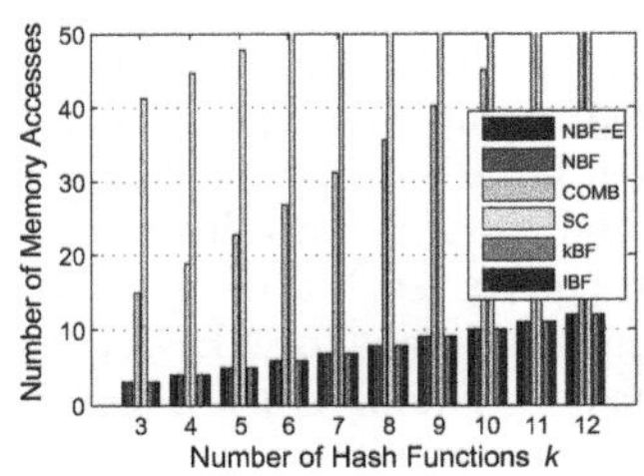

Figure 18: Memory Access vs. k when querying present elements

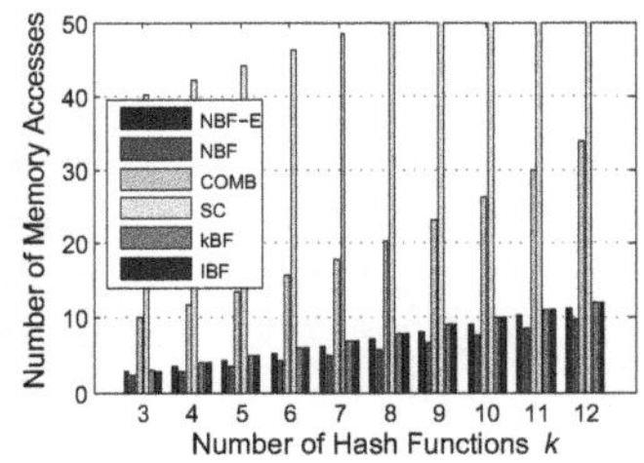

Figure 19: Memory Access vs. k when querying absent elements

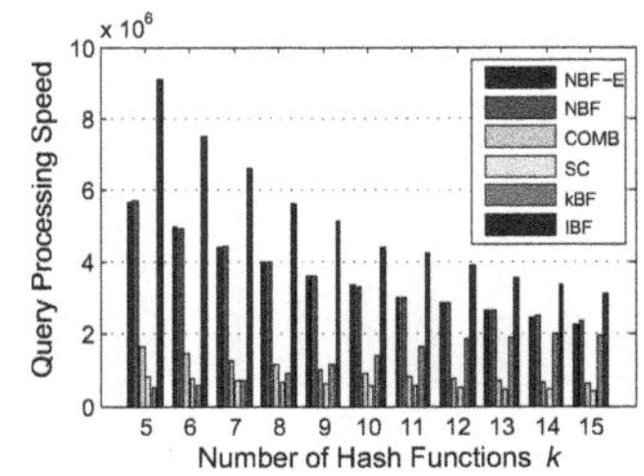

Figure 20: Querying Processing Speed vs. k when querying present elements

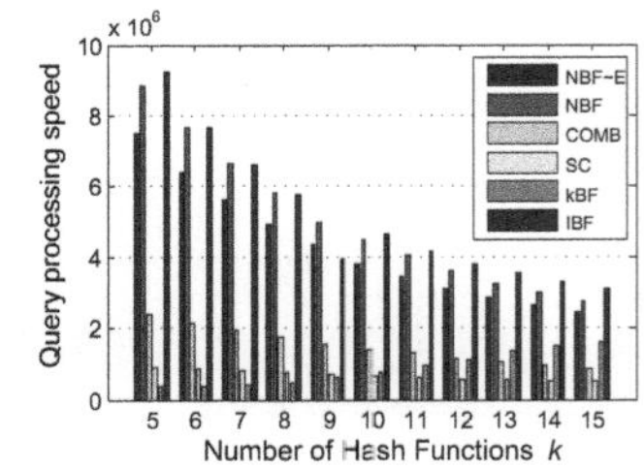

Figure 21: Querying Processing Speed vs. k when querying absent elements

NBF/NBF-E is about 6 *times less than kBF when changing* k *and* $\aleph$. From Figures 16 and 17, we observe that COMB generally exhibits better false positive rate than NBF/NBF-E as it uses k different hash functions to verify each bit in the query result while NBF/NBF-E uses k hash functions to verify all bits. However, this comes at the cost of much higher memory access overhead and query processing speed as will be described in Sections 5.4 and 5.5. The false positive rate for NBF/NBF-E is twice that of COMB and is smaller than 1%, which is practically acceptable. Moreover, the false positive rate for SC grows at a much faster speed than NBF/NBF-E and COMB as $\aleph$ increases. The reason is that the assigned memory for each standard Bloom filter in SC shrinks rapidly as $\aleph$ increases since the aggregate memory for all Bloom filters in SC in fixed, and, therefore, the false positive rate of each filter, as well as that of SC, rises dramatically. Note that the false positive rate for IBF is zero since it stores pairs of an element and its associated set ID, and returns the set ID only when the query element matches the associated element [9].

5.4 Memory Accesses

Our results show that NBF/NBF-E has a slightly smaller number of memory accesses compared to kBF and IBF, and uses only about 3.7 *and* 7.7 *times smaller memory accesses compared to COMB and SC respectively.* Figures 18 and 19 show the number of memory accesses for all six algorithms for present elements and absent elements respectively, when the number of hash functions k increases from 3 to 12. Here, present elements refer to those elements stored in the Bloom filters of these schemes while absent elements do not. It can be seen that all six algorithms have fewer memory accesses for false positives than that for present elements. This is because when using the accelerating technique described above, all these algorithms are capable to identify those false positives before carrying out all possible memory accesses, which are indispensable for present elements. We also observe that NBF has slightly fewer memory accesses than NBF-E for false positives. The reason is that NBF has higher opportunity to be terminated early than NBF-E because it has fewer "1" bits in its encoding result and the intermediate query result is more likely to become 0.

5.5 Query Processing Speed

Our results show that NBF (NBF-E) has about 3.2, 5.9 *and* 5.8 *times (*3.3, 6.4 *and* 6.5 *times) faster query processing speed compared to COMB, SC and kBF, when changing* k *and* $\aleph$. Figures 20 and 21 demonstrate the query processing speed, *i.e.* number of processed queries per second, for present elements and absent elements respectively, when the number of hash functions k rises from 5 to 15. We can see that all six algorithms have faster query processing speed for absent elements than that for present elements. The reason is the same as that of memory accesses, *i.e.*, the accelerating technique speeds up the querying process for absent elements. Moreover, due to the same reason why NBF outperforms NBF-E in terms of memory accesses, the query processing speed of NBF also exceeds that of NBF-E by nearly 16% for absent elements. As also shown in the two figures, IBF has the fastest query processing speed. This is because most cells in IBF in this scenario are mixed by two or more set IDs and cannot be decoded, IBF can quickly discover this fact by checking the count field in these cells and return "not found", which is much efficient than other algorithms.

6. CONCLUSION

The key contribution of this paper is to propose Noisy Bloom Filter (NBF) and Error Corrected Noisy Bloom Filter (NBF-E) for multi-set membership testing. The key advantages of NBF and NBF-E over the prior art are high space efficiency and high query processing speed. The key technical depth of this paper is in the analytical modeling of NBF and NBF-E, optimizing system parameters, finding the minimum classification failure rate and false positive rate, and criteria of selection between NBF and NBF-E. We validated our analytical models through simulations using real world network traces. Our experimental results show that NBF and NBF-E significantly advance state-of-the-art solution regarding multi-set membership testing with 3.7 times smaller memory accesses and 3.3 times faster query processing speed.

Acknowledgment

The work is partly supported by the National Natural Science Foundation of China under Grant Numbers 61502229, 61472184, 61373129, and 61321491, the Huawei Innovation Research Program (HIRP), and the Jiangsu High-level Innovation and Entrepreneurship (Shuangchuang) Program. Alex X. Liu is also affiliated with the Department of Computer Science and Engineering, Michigan State University, East Lansing, MI, USA.

7. REFERENCES

[1] https://software.intel.com/en-us/articles/data-alignment-when-migrating-to-64-bit-intel-architecture.

[2] E. Agrell, A. Vardy, and K. Zeger. Upper bounds for constant-weight codes. *IEEE Transactions on Information Theory*, 46(7):2373–2395, 2000.

[3] R. Arratia and L. Gordon. Tutorial on large deviations for the binomial distribution. *Bulletin of mathematical biology*, 51(1):125–131, 1989.

[4] F. Bonomi, M. Mitzenmacher, R. Panigrah, S. Singh, and G. Varghese. Beyond bloom filters: from approximate membership checks to approximate state machines. *ACM SIGCOMM Computer Communication Review*, 36(4):315–326, 2006.

[5] B. Chazelle, J. Kilian, R. Rubinfeld, and A. Tal. The bloomier filter: an efficient data structure for static support lookup tables. In *Proceedings of the fifteenth annual ACM-SIAM symposium on Discrete algorithms*, pages 30–39, 2004.

[6] D. Eppstein, M. T. Goodrich, F. Uyeda, and G. Varghese. What's the difference?: efficient set reconciliation without prior context. In *ACM SIGCOMM Computer Communication Review*, volume 41, pages 218–229. ACM, 2011.

[7] T. Etzion and A. Vardy. A new construction for constant weight codes. In *IEEE International Symposium on Information Theory and its Applications (ISITA)*, pages 338–342, 2014.

[8] L. Fan, P. Cao, J. Almeida, and A. Z. Broder. Summary cache: a scalable wide-area web cache sharing protocol. *IEEE/ACM Transactions on Networking*, 8(3):281–293, 2000.

[9] M. T. Goodrich and M. Mitzenmacher. Invertible bloom lookup tables. In *the 49th IEEE Annual Allerton Conference on Communication, Control, and Computing (Allerton)*, pages 792–799, 2011.

[10] R. L. Graham and N. Sloane. Lower bounds for constant weight codes. *IEEE Transactions on Information Theory*, 26(1):37–43, 1980.

[11] F. Hao, M. Kodialam, T. Lakshman, and H. Song. Fast dynamic multiple-set membership testing using combinatorial bloom filters. *IEEE/ACM Transactions on Networking*, 20(1):295–304, 2012.

[12] T. Kløve. *Error correcting codes for the asymmetric channel.* Technical Report. Department of Pure Mathematics, University of Bergen, 1981.

[13] M. Lee, N. Duffield, and R. R. Kompella. Maple: A scalable architecture for maintaining packet latency measurements. In *Proceedings of the ACM conference on Internet measurement conference*, pages 101–114, 2012.

[14] C.-s. Liu. The essence of the generalized newton binomial theorem. *Communications in Nonlinear Science and Numerical Simulation*, 15(10):2766–2768, 2010.

[15] Y. Lu, B. Prabhakar, and F. Bonomi. Bloom filters: Design innovations and novel applications. In *the 43rd Annual Allerton Conference*, 2005.

[16] I. P. Naydenova. Error detection and correction for symmetric and asymmetric channels. 2007.

[17] Y. Qiao, T. Li, and S. Chen. Fast bloom filters and their generalization. *IEEE Transactions on Parallel and Distributed Systems*, 25(1):93–103, 2014.

[18] B. Ryabko. Fast enumeration of combinatorial objects. In *Discrete Mathematics and Applications*, 1998.

[19] S. Sen and J. Wang. Analyzing peer-to-peer traffic across large networks. *IEEE/ACM Transactions on Networking*, 12(2):219–232, 2004.

[20] L. G. Tallini and B. Bose. Reed-muller codes, elementary symmetric functions and asymmetric error correction. In *IEEE International Symposium on Information Theory Proceedings (ISIT)*, pages 1051–1055. IEEE, 2011.

[21] L. G. Tallini and B. Bose. On L_1 metric asymmetric/unidirectional error control codes, constrained weight codes and σ-codes. In *IEEE International Symposium on Information Theory Proceedings (ISIT)*, pages 694–698, 2013.

[22] C. Tian, V. Vaishampayan, N. Sloane, et al. A coding algorithm for constant weight vectors: a geometric approach based on dissections. *IEEE Transactions on Information Theory*, 55(3):1051–1060, 2009.

[23] S. Xiong, Y. Yao, Q. Cao, and T. He. kBF: A Bloom Filter for key-value storage with an application on approximate state machines. In *Proceedings of the IEEE Conference on Computer Communications (INFOCOM)*, pages 1150–1158. 2014.

[24] M. K. Yoon, J. Son, and S.-H. Shin. Bloom tree: A search tree based on bloom filters for multiple-set membership testing. In *Proceedings of the IEEE Conference on Computer Communications (INFOCOM)*, pages 1429–1437. 2014.

[25] M. Yu, A. Fabrikant, and J. Rexford. Buffalo: Bloom filter forwarding architecture for large organizations. In *Proceedings of the 5th International Conference on Emerging Networking Experiments and Technologies*, pages 313–324. ACM, 2009.

[26] J. Zhang and F.-W. Fu. Constructions for binary codes correcting asymmetric errors from function fields. In *Theory and Applications of Models of Computation*, pages 284–294. Springer, 2012.

[27] H. Zhou, A. Jiang, and J. Bruck. Nonuniform codes for correcting asymmetric errors in data storage. *IEEE Transactions on Information Theory*, 59(5):2988–3002, 2013.

Rumor Source Obfuscation on Irregular Trees

Giulia Fanti
University of Illinois at Urbana-Champaign
fanti@illinois.edu

Peter Kairouz
University of Illinois at Urbana-Champaign
kairouz2@illinois.edu

Sewoong Oh
University of Illinois at Urbana-Champaign
swoh@illinois.edu

Kannan Ramchandran
University of California, Berkeley
kannanr@eecs.berkeley.edu

Pramod Viswanath
University of Illinois at Urbana-Champaign
pramodv@illinois.edu

ABSTRACT

Anonymous messaging applications have recently gained popularity as a means for sharing opinions without fear of judgment or repercussion. Messages in these applications propagate anonymously (without authorship metadata) over a network that is typically defined by social connections or physical proximity. However, recent advances in rumor source detection show that the source of such an anonymous message can be inferred by statistical inference attacks. Adaptive diffusion was recently proposed as a solution that achieves optimal source obfuscation over regular trees. However, in real social networks, node degrees differ from node to node, and adaptive diffusion can be significantly sub-optimal. This gap increases as the degrees become more irregular.

In order to quantify this gap, we model the underlying network as coming from standard branching processes with i.i.d. degree distributions. Building upon the analysis techniques from branching processes, we give an analytical characterization of the dependence between the probability of detection achieved by adaptive diffusion and the degree distribution. Further, this analysis provides a key insight: passing a rumor to a friend who has many friends makes the source more ambiguous. This leads to a new family of protocols that we call Preferential Attachment Adaptive Diffusion (PAAD). When messages are propagated according to PAAD, we give both the MAP estimator for finding the source and also an analysis of the probability of detection achieved by this adversary. The analytical results are not directly comparable, since the adversary's observed information has a different distribution under adaptive diffusion than under PAAD. Instead, we present results from numerical experiments that suggest that PAAD achieves a lower probability of detection, at the cost of increased communication for coordination.

Keywords

Anonymous Social Media; Rumor Spreading; Privacy

SIGMETRICS '16, June 14-18, 2016, Antibes Juan-Les-Pins, France

DOI: http://dx.doi.org/10.1145/2896377.2901471

1. INTRODUCTION

People have a right to share their thoughts without fear of political or economic repercussion. In cyberspace, freedom of expression often depends on a person's ability to remain anonymous to one's family, peers, or even government. Several anonymous messaging apps have emerged and evolved in recent years that allow users to post contents anonymously – first-generation apps like Whisper [1] and Yik Yak [2], second-generation ones like Secret [3](which is now out of business) and third generation ones like Blind [4]. These apps build upon an underlying connectivity network between their users, representing a social graph or a physical proximity graph, for instance. When a user posts a message, the message spreads to the user's neighbors, or 'friends', on the connectivity graph. If a friend approves the message by 'liking' it, the message propagates to the friend's friends, and so forth, spreading over the network.

The centralized architecture of existing anonymous messaging apps makes them vulnerable to deanonymization, since authorship information is stored on central servers. Third parties could access that information via hacking or government subpoena. A distributed architecture instead enables users to propagate messages directly to one another, circumventing centralized storage.

Perhaps surprisingly, even under distributed architectures, the source of a message can still be de-anonymized by global adversaries performing statistical inference. Recent work in rumor source detection shows that the spreading pattern itself reveals a great deal about the true message source [32, 30]. Existing platforms transmit messages to all neighbors immediately upon approval (e.g. when a user clicks 'like'). There is local randomness in each message's spread due to the time it takes for a user to see the message, and uncertainty regarding whether the user will like the message. This random process is typically modeled by the standard *random diffusion* process on graphs.

Rumor source detection algorithms, such as those proposed in [32, 30], exploit the inherent symmetry in how random diffusion propagates. In particular, it is shown in [32] that if an adversary, who knows the underlying contact network, observes which nodes received the message at a certain time, the source can be identified with probability bounded away from zero.

Under this vulnerability against statistical inference attacks, a natural question is, "how can a platform designer intervene with the spread of messages, in order to make rumor source inference difficult?" In other words, how can we add artificial delays on top of the natural human delays to obfuscate the source?

This question was asked in a recent work [14], which proposes a protocol called *adaptive diffusion.* This protocol protects the author's anonymity against the kinds of global adversaries typically assumed in rumor source detection literature. Adaptive diffusion breaks the symmetry of random diffusion by spreading messages faster in some directions on the underlying graph than others (detailed description in Section 2). It is shown in [14] that adaptive diffusion achieves perfect obfuscation when: *(a)* the underlying contact network is a regular tree, and *(b)* the adversary, who knows the underlying contact network, also observes the snapshot of who has seen the message at a certain point in time. A protocol is said to achieve perfect obfuscation, if it successfully hides among all nodes that have seen the message. Precisely, this happens if the probability of the true source being detected is $1/n$ when n nodes have received the message at the time of the attack.

Although adaptive diffusion achieves the best possible source obfuscation, the protocol design assumes a network that is regular and cycle-free. The assumption of cycle-free (i.e. tree-structured) network can be defended by observing that a message's spread on *any* connectivity graph will always be a tree embedded in the true connectivity graph; we assume here that that nodes cannot "be infected", or receive the message, more than once. Without loss of generality, a protocol designer can extract a spanning tree from a given social network, and use only those edges in the tree for spreading the messages. All the privacy guarantees we provide will naturally hold. Having more edges on top of this tree only makes it more difficult for the adversary to locate the source.

On the other hand, experimental results (Figures 6 and 7 and also in [14, Figure 8]) suggest that the performance of adaptive diffusion degrades significantly on certain classes of irregular trees.

In this paper, we ask the fundamental question of how the probability of detection depends on the topology of underlying network, when the network is an *irregular tree.* A precise characterization of the dependency will reveal why adaptive diffusion fails on irregular trees, and provide a guideline for designing novel spreading protocols that improve upon adaptive diffusion.

Model. We follow the setting introduced in [14] for modeling anonymous messaging. At time $t = 0$, a single user $v^* \in V$ starts to spread a message on a contact network $G = (V, E)$ where users and contacts are represented by nodes and edges, respectively. We assume a discrete-time system and model the delays due to user approval and intermittent network access via a deterministic delay of one time unit. Upon receiving the message, the messaging platform can choose to send the message to any of its neighbors the next time step, or add additional delay and wait. Therefore, if we do not intervene with how the messages are spread, then a message always propagates with a delay of one time unit per hop. If the contact network is an infinite d-regular tree, this process spreads to $(d-1)^T$ nodes at time T, but the source is trivially detected as the center of the snapshot. The validity of this model is discussed in Section 5.

Adaptive diffusion is introduced in [14] for hiding the source. The key idea is to add appropriate random delays in order to break the symmetry of the spread. This protocol is shown to achieve perfect obfuscation and is described in the next section.

After T time steps, let $V_T \subseteq V$, G_T, and $N_T \triangleq |V_T|$ denote the set of infected nodes, the subgraph of G containing only V_T, and the number of infected nodes, respectively. At a certain time T, an adversary observes the infected subgraph G_T (as well as the underlying connectivity graph G) and produces an estimate $\hat{v}$ of the source v^* of the message (with probability of detection $P_D = \mathbb{P}(\hat{v} = v^*)$).

There is a tradeoff between hiding the source and increased delay. Assuming a d-regular tree, adaptive diffusion spreads to $(d-1)^{T/2}$ nodes at time T, and it is shown to achieve perfect obfuscation in [14]. We say a protocol achieves a *perfect obfuscation* if the probability of source detection for the maximum likelihood estimator conditioned on n nodes being infected is upper bounded by

$$\mathbb{P}(\hat{v} = v^* | N_T = n) \quad = \quad \frac{1}{n} + o\Big(\frac{1}{n}\Big) . \qquad (1)$$

However, the detection probability can be significantly larger than $1/n$ when the degrees are not regular. To quantify this gap, we analyze the average probability of detection when the underlying contact network is generated from standard random irregular trees with i.i.d. degrees.

Contributions. We make the following contributions in this paper:

- We quantify the sub-optimality of adaptive diffusion, when the underlying contact network is a random irregular tree generated from i.i.d. degree distribution. We give an exact characterization of the detection probability, where the randomness is due to both the underlying network and also the protocol. In the process of the analyses, we prove a new concentration result for an extremal value on a Galton-Watson tree, which may be of independent interest.
- We give a general expression for the adversary's maximum a posteriori (MAP) detection rule for a broad class of protocols, that are generalizations of adaptive diffusion.
- We introduce a family of protocols that we call preferential attachment adaptive diffusion (PAAD). We characterize the probability of detection for this class of protocols. We present numerical experiments suggesting that PAAD achieves better obfuscation than adaptive diffusion.

Related Work. Most prior research on anonymous communication has focused on anonymous *point-to-point* communication, leading to the emergence of Tor [12], Freenet [8], Free Haven [11], and Tarzan [17]. In contrast, we study anonymous *broadcast* messaging. Anonymous broadcast communication has been studied extensively in the context of DC nets [7, 9, 36, 19, 20, 37]. Our work differs from this body of work by considering: (a) a different class of solutions, based on statistical spreading models rather than cryptographic encoding, and (b) a tree-structured network, rather than a fully-connected network.

Within the realm of statistical message spreading models, the problem of detecting the origin of an epidemic or the source of a rumor has been studied under the *diffusion* model. Recent advances in [34, 33, 38, 31, 16, 25, 39, 28, 29, 27, 15] show that it is possible to identify the source within a few hops with high probability. Drawing an analogy to epidemics, we refer to a person who has received the message as 'infected' and the act of passing the message as 'spreading the infection'. Just as infectious diseases often spread radially about patient zero geographically, under diffusion, the message spreads in a "ball" around the true source over the network. Thus, the author is very close to the center of that ball, making identification easy. Moreover, this is true independent of the size of that ball.

Recently, [26] modeled the rumor spreading and source identification problem as a "hide and seek" game. [26] studied optimal strategies for both the source and adversary under tree networks from a game theoretic perspective, and derived conditions under which a Nash equilibrium exists. In a different context, [5] studies privacy aware network formation games, where actions are adding/removing edges and the reward is measured by the utility of having friends subtracted by the loss in privacy.

Our problem formulation is closely related to the recent work of [14] where adaptive diffusion was presented, and its optimality under regular tree networks was shown. However, [14] does not study the performance of adaptive diffusion under irregular tree networks. In this work, we (a) prove that adaptive diffusion is sub-optimal under irregular trees, (b) characterize the sub-optimality gap, and (c) present a new class of statistical spreading protocols that improves over adaptive diffusion.

Outline. In Section 2, we describe adaptive diffusion protocol introduced in [14]. We then present our theoretical analysis of adaptive diffusion over irregular random trees in Section 3. Section 4 describes our proposed preferential-attachment adaptive diffusion algorithm, and demonstrates through simulation that it outperforms regular adaptive diffusion on irregular random trees. We discuss some implications of this work and open questions in Section 5. We give the proofs of the main results in Section 6 and in the extended version of this paper [13].

2. ADAPTIVE DIFFUSION

For completeness, adaptive diffusion is described in full detail in the appendix (see Protocol 1). Adaptive diffusion as introduced in [14] refers to a family of protocols parametrized by d_O, where d_O indicates the degree of the regular tree network for which the protocol is customized. Since we consider irregular trees in this paper, it is not obvious how to choose the parameter d_O; we set $d_O = \infty$ throughout this paper for two reasons: first, this choice is universal, independent of the topology of the underlying graph. Second, it has been suggested via numerical experiments that this choice of d_O achieves a performance close to the optimal choice (e.g. Figure 5 in [14]). The downside of this choice is that some nodes in an (infinite tree) network will never receive the message. Henceforth, we refer to adaptive diffusion with the choice of $d_O = \infty$ as simply 'adaptive diffusion'. However, it should be noted that in practice, it is preferable to choose a finite d_O to ensure that the messages spread in all directions eventually, as we discuss in Section 5.

As illustrated in Figure 1, adaptive diffusion ensures that at every even time step the infected subtree is a balanced tree with the true source v^* at one of the leaves. At even time T, the infected balanced tree has radius $T/2$ and the center of this sub-tree is called the *virtual source*, denoted by v_T. Notice that two time steps are needed to spread the infection from one balanced tree of radius $T/2$ rooted at v_T to another balanced tree of radius $T/2 + 1$ rooted at the next virtual source v_{T+2}. The odd time steps are intermediate steps, necessary to make such transitions. Since the propagation of the messages is fully described by the dynamics of the virtual sources, adaptive diffusion only needs to provide a (randomized) rule for choosing the virtual source's location at each (even) time.

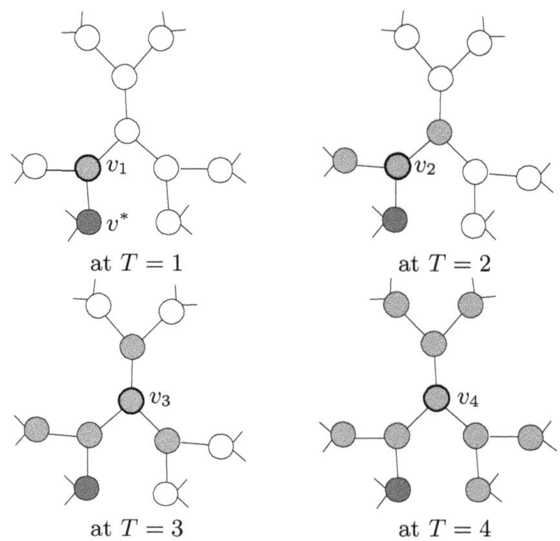

Figure 1: A sample path of adaptive diffusion.

At time $t = 0$, the source v^* chooses a neighbor to be the next virtual source uniformly at random, and infects it. Let v_1 denote this new virtual source as shown in Figure 1. The next time step is spent spreading the infection one more hop to appropriate neighbors, in order to maintain the balanced tree of depth one rooted at the new virtual source, which remains $v_2 = v_1$. Our choice of $d_O = \infty$ implies that the virtual source never stays the same over consecutive even time steps, so v_{T+2} is always adjacent to v_T. In other words, in subsequent even time steps, a new virtual source is chosen from one of the current virtual source's neighbor uniformly at random, excluding previous virtual sources. The odd time steps are spent maintaining the balanced infection structure.

3. ANALYSIS OF ADAPTIVE DIFFUSION

At a certain time T, the adversary attacks and observes the set of infected nodes thus far. Given the snapshot at time T, the underlying network, and the knowledge of what protocol is used, the attacker performs statistical inference to detect the source using maximum a posteriori (MAP) estimator. It is proved in [14] that adaptive diffusion achieves (near) perfect obfuscation for *regular* trees. The key idea is that, by construction, all leaves in the infection are equally likely to have been the source, and there are as many leaf nodes in the boundary as in the interior of the infection.

On *irregular* trees, adaptive diffusion is known to be sub-optimal, and the gap depends on the underlying topology of the irregular tree. In order to quantify this gap and characterize the dependence on the underlying tree, we analyze adaptive diffusion on the following model of a random tree and provide rigorous analysis for the average case performance, where the randomness is due to both the underlying contact network as well as the protocol.

We assume adaptive diffusion spreads over a random irregular tree according to a branching process with i.i.d. degrees according to some distribution D. Specifically, at time $t = 0$, the source v^* draws a degree d_{v^*} from D, and generates d_{v^*} child nodes. The source picks one of these neighbors uniformly at random to be the new virtual source. The infection spreads as per adaptive diffusion, and each infected node draws its degree from D generating $D-1$ new (uninfected) children nodes.

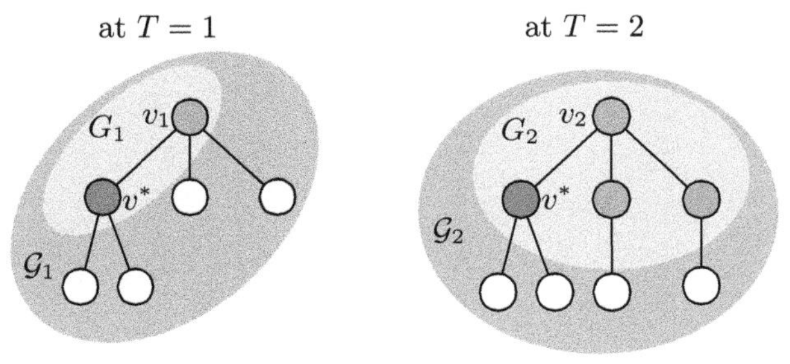

Figure 2: Example of the branching process modeling adaptive diffusion on irregular trees.

We denote the sub-tree of infected nodes as G_T and the branching tree generated at time T as $\mathcal{G}_T$. The structure of the contact network outside of $\mathcal{G}_T$ is independent of G_T conditioned on the uninfected neighbors $\partial\mathcal{G}_T$, where $\partial\mathcal{G}_T$ denotes the leaves of the tree $\mathcal{G}_T$. To ensure that the graph grows indefinitely, we assume that the minimum degree of a node is at least two.

3.1 Probability of Detection Given a Snapshot

The adversary observes this random process at time T, i.e. $\mathcal{G}_T$, knowing that the interior G_T are the infected nodes, and estimates one of the leaf nodes of G_T as an estimate of the true source which started the random process. The following theorem analyzes the probability of detecting the true source for any estimate $\hat{v}$, given a snapshot $\mathcal{G}_T$.

THEOREM 3.1. *Under the above described random process of adaptive diffusion, an adversary observes the snapshot $\mathcal{G}_T$ at an even time $T > 0$ and estimates $\hat{v} \in \partial G_T$. For any estimator $\hat{v}$, the conditional probability of detection is*

$$\mathbb{P}(\hat{v} = v^*|\mathcal{G}_T) = \frac{1}{d_{v_T}} \prod_{\substack{w\in\phi(\hat{v},v_T)\\ \setminus\{v_T,\hat{v}\}}} \frac{1}{(d_w-1)}, \qquad (2)$$

where v_T is the center of $\mathcal{G}_T$, $\phi(\hat{v}, v_T)$ is the (unique) path from $\hat{v}$ to v_T, G_T is the interior of $\mathcal{G}_T$ which is the infected sub-tree, and ∂G_T is the set of leaves of G_T.

A proof is provided in the extended version [13]. Intuitively, Equation (2) is the probability that the virtual source starting from $\hat{v}$ ends up at v_T (up to some constant factor for normalization). This gives a simple rule for the adversary to achieve the best detection probability by computing the MAP estimate:

$$\hat{v}^{(T)}_{\text{MAP}} \in \arg\max_{\hat{v}} \mathbb{P}(\hat{v}^{(T)} = v^*|\mathcal{G}_T) . \qquad (3)$$

COROLLARY 3.2. *Under the hypotheses of Theorem 3.1, the MAP estimator in (3) can be computed as*

$$\hat{v}^{(T)}_{\text{MAP}} = \arg\min_{v\in\partial G_T} \prod_{\substack{w\in\phi(v,v_T)\\ \setminus\{v_T,v\}}} (d_w-1), \qquad (4)$$

achieving a conditional probability of detection

$$\mathbb{P}(\hat{v}^{(T)}_{\text{MAP}} = v^*|\mathcal{G}_T) = \max_{v\in\partial G_T} \frac{1}{d_{v_T} \prod_{\substack{w\in\phi(v,v_T)\\ \setminus\{v_T,v\}}} (d_w-1)} . \qquad (5)$$

When applied to regular trees, this recovers known results of [14], which confirms that adaptive diffusion provides strong anonymity guarantees under d-regular trees. But more importantly, Corollary 3.2 characterizes how the anonymity guarantee depends on the general topology of the snapshot. We illustrate this in two extreme examples: a regular tree and an extreme example in Figure 3.

For a d-regular tree, where all nodes have the same degree, the size of infection at even time T is the number of nodes in a d-regular tree of depth $T/2$:

$$N_T = \frac{d(d-1)^{T/2}}{d-2} + \frac{2}{d-2} . \qquad (6)$$

To achieve a perfect obfuscation, we want the probability of detection to decay as $1/N_T$. We can apply Corollary 3.2 to this d-regular tree and show the probability of detection is $((d-1)/d)(d-1)^{-T/2})$, which recovers one of the known results in [14, Proposition 2.2]. This confirms that adaptive diffusion achieves near-perfect obfuscation, up to a small factor of $(d-1)/(d-2)$.

On the other hand, when there exists a path to a leaf node consisting of low-degree nodes, adaptive diffusion can be sub-optimal, and the gap to optimality can be made arbitrarily large. Figure 3 illustrates such an example. This is a tree where all nodes have the same degree $d = 5$, except for those nodes along the path from the center v_T to a leaf node v, including v_T and excluding v. The center v_T has degree two and the nodes in the path have degree three. Hence, the shaded triangles indicate d-regular subtrees of appropriate heights. The size of this infection is $N_T = ((d-1)^{T/2+1}/(d-2)^2)(1+o(1))$. Ideally, one might hope to achieve a probability of detection that scales as $1/(d-1)^{T/2}$. However, Corollary 3.2 shows that the adaptive diffusion achieves probability of detection $1/2^{T/2}$, with the leaf node v achieving this maximum in Equation (5). Hence, there is a multiplicative gap of $((d-1)/2)^{T/2}$. By increasing d, the gap can be made arbitrarily large. On the other hand, such an extreme topology is rare under the i.i.d tree model.

We want to emphasize that the results in [14] only use elementary proof techniques and only work for regular trees. In comparison, we develop new proof techniques for the combinatorial problem of counting the number of instances that can start from a leaf v and generate a snapshot $\mathcal{G}_T$.

3.2 Concentration of Probability of Detection

Depending on the topology, adaptive diffusion can be significantly sub-optimal. A natural question is "what is the

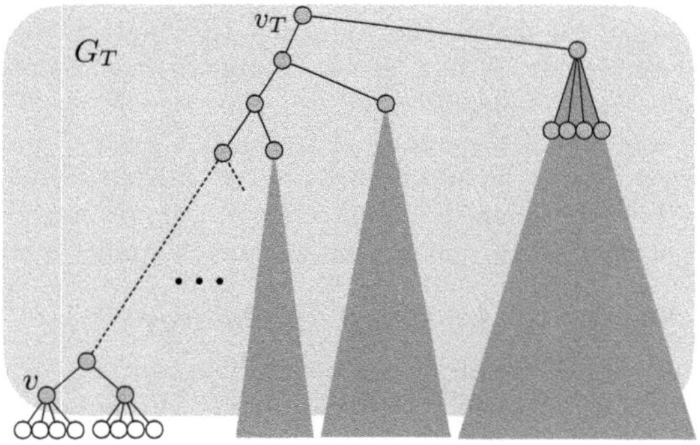

Figure 3: An example of a snapshot emphasizing the sub-optimality of the adaptive diffusion.

typical topology of a graph resulting from the random tree model?" Under the model introduced in the beginning of Section 3, we give a concrete answer. Perhaps surprisingly, this typical topology can be characterized by solving a simple convex optimization.

We are interested in the following extremal value

$$\Lambda_{G_T} \equiv d_{v_T} \min_{v \in \partial G_T} \prod_{\substack{w \in \phi(v, v_T) \\ \setminus \{v_T, v\}}} (d_w - 1) , \quad (7)$$

which captures the topology of the snapshot. We want to characterize the typical value of this function over random tree G_T resulting from the adaptive diffusion process.

Observe that the distribution of the balanced tree G_T follows a simple branching process known as Galton-Watson process. This is because G_T resulting from adaptive diffusion has the same distribution, independent of the location of the source v^*. We consider a given degree distribution D. We use D to denote both a random variable and its distribution—the distinction should be clear from context. The random variable D has support $\boldsymbol{f} = (f_1, \ldots, f_\eta)$ associated with probability $\boldsymbol{p} = (p_1, \ldots, p_\eta)$ such that the degree of node v is i.i.d. with

$$d_v = \begin{cases} f_1 & \text{with probability } p_1 , \\ \vdots & \vdots \\ f_\eta & \text{with probability } p_\eta , \end{cases} \quad (8)$$

where $2 < f_1 < f_2 < \cdots < f_\eta$ are integers and the positive p_i's sum to one. We also assume D's support set has at least two elements, i.e., $\eta \geq 2$.

Note that the adaptive diffusion always passes the virtual source token to a uniformly-chosen neighbor. It is straightforward to show that adaptive diffusion starting from a leaf node v^* has the same distribution over graphs as the following branching process, denoted $\overline{G}_T$: at time $T = 0$ a root node, which we denote as the virtual source v_T, creates D offspring. At each subsequent even time step, each leaf node in G_T creates new offspring independently according to $D - 1$ (where we subtract one because each leaf is already connected to its parent). This process is repeated until time step T, which generates a random tree G_T. More precisely, the two branching processes are equal in distribution: $\overline{G}_T \overset{D}{=} G_T$. This can be seen by observing that conditioned on the path of nodes $\phi(v^*, v_T)$, the branching processes are identical. Since the node degrees in this path are drawn independently, the path is equally distributed whether it starts from the virtual source v_T or the leaf node v^*.

The following theorem provides a concentration inequality on the extremal quantity Λ_{G_T}, which in turn determines the probability of detection as provided by Corollary 3.2:

$$\mathbb{P}(\hat{v}_{\text{MAP}}^{(T)} = v^* | G_T) = \frac{1}{\Lambda_{G_T}} . \quad (9)$$

THEOREM 3.3. *For an even $T > 0$, suppose a random tree G_T is generated from the root v_T according to the Galton-Watson process with i.i.d. degree distribution D, where $\boldsymbol{f}$ and $\boldsymbol{p}$ are defined as in (8), then the following results hold:*

(a) *If $p_1(f_1 - 1) > 1$, for any positive $\delta > 0$, there exists positive constants $C_{D,\delta}$ and $C'_{D,\delta}$ that depend only on the degree distribution and the choice of δ such that*

$$\mathbb{P}\left(\left| \frac{\log(\Lambda_{G_T})}{T/2} - \log(f_1 - 1) \right| > \delta \right) \leq e^{-C_{D,\delta} T} , \quad (10)$$

for an even time $T \geq C'_{D,\delta}$.

(b) *If $p_1(f_1 - 1) < 1$, define the mean number of children:*

$$\mu_D \equiv \sum_{i=1}^{\eta} p_i (f_i - 1) ,$$

and the set

$$\mathcal{R}_D = \{ \boldsymbol{r} \in S_\eta \mid \log(\mu_D) \geq D_{\text{KL}}(\boldsymbol{r} \| \boldsymbol{\beta}) \} , \quad (11)$$

where S_η denotes the η-dimensional probability simplex, $D_{\text{KL}}(\cdot\|\cdot)$ denotes Kullback-Leibler divergence, and $\boldsymbol{\beta}$ is a length-η probability vector in which $\beta_i = p_i(f_i - 1)/\mu_D$. Further, define $\boldsymbol{r}^*$ as follows:

$$\boldsymbol{r}^* = \operatorname*{arg\,min}_{\boldsymbol{r} \in \mathcal{R}_D} \langle \boldsymbol{r} , \log(\boldsymbol{f} - 1) \rangle , \quad (12)$$

where $\langle \boldsymbol{r}, \log(\boldsymbol{f} - 1) \rangle = \sum_{i=1}^{\eta} r_i \log(f_i - 1)$. Then for any $\delta > 0$, there exists positive constants $C_{D,\delta}$ and $C'_{D,\delta}$ that only depend on the degree distribution D and the choice of $\delta > 0$ such that

$$\mathbb{P}\left(\left| \frac{\log(\Lambda_{G_T})}{T/2} - \langle \boldsymbol{r}^*, \log(\boldsymbol{f} - 1) \rangle \right| > \delta \right) \leq e^{-C_{D',\delta} T} \quad (13)$$

for an even time $T \geq C'_{D,\delta}$.

The results in parts (a) and (b) can be merged, in the sense that the solution of (12) is $\boldsymbol{r}^* = [1, 0, \ldots, 0]$ when $p_1(f_1 - 1) > 1$. A proof of this theorem is provided in Section 6. Putting it together with (9), it follows that the probability of detection concentrates around

$$-\frac{2}{T} \log \left(\mathbb{P}(\hat{v}_{\text{MAP}}^{(T)} = v^*) \right) \simeq \langle \boldsymbol{r}^* , \log(\boldsymbol{f} - 1) \rangle ,$$

in case (b) and around $\log(f_1 - 1)$ in case (a). Here $\simeq$ indicates concentration for large enough T. We want to emphasize that $\boldsymbol{r}^*$ can be computed using off-the-shelf optimization tools, since the program in (12) is a convex program of dimension η. This follows from the fact that the objective is linear in $\boldsymbol{r}$ and the feasible region is convex since KL divergence is convex in $\boldsymbol{r}$.

For example, if D is 3 w.p. 0.7 or 4 w.p. 0.3, then this falls under case (a). The theorem predicts the probability of detection to decay as $(3 - 1)^{-T/2}$. On the other hand, if

$$D = \begin{cases} 2 & \text{with probability } 0.3 \\ 3 & \text{with probability } 0.7 \end{cases} ,$$

then this falls under case (b) with $\mu_D = 1.7$, $\beta_1 = 0.3/1.7$, and $\beta_2 = 1.4/1.7$. In this case, the exponent is a solution of the following optimization for $\boldsymbol{r} = [r, 1-r]$:

$$\begin{aligned} \underset{r\in\mathbb{R}}{\text{minimize}} \quad & r\log 1 + (1-r)\log 2 \\ \text{subject to} \quad & r\log\frac{1.7r}{0.3} + (1-r)\log\frac{1.7(1-r)}{1.4} \le \log(1.7) \\ & r \in [0,1] \end{aligned}$$

It follows that the optimal solution is $\boldsymbol{r}^* \simeq [0.64,\ 0.36]$ and the probability of detection decays as $2^{-0.36(T/2)}$. Figure 4 confirms this prediction with simulations for these examples.

Theorem 3.3 provides a simple convex program that computes the probability of detection for any degree distribution. For random trees, this quantifies the gap between what adaptive diffusion can guarantee and the perfect obfuscation one desires. We define the rescaled log-multiplicative gap as

$$\Delta_D \equiv \frac{2}{T}\log\frac{\mathbb{P}(v_{\rm MAP}^{(T)} = v^*)}{1/\mathbb{E}[|\partial G_T|]},$$

where $|\partial G_T|$ is the total number of candidates in a snapshot. It is not difficult to show that $\mathbb{E}[|\partial G_T|] = \mu_D^{T/2}$, and it follows that $\Delta_D \simeq \log\mu_D - \langle \boldsymbol{r}^*, \log(\boldsymbol{f}-1)\rangle$. For example, $\Delta_D = 0$ for regular trees, and $\Delta_D = \log_2 2.3 - \log_2 2 = 0.20$ for the first example under case (a) and $\Delta_D = \log_2 1.7 - 0.36 = 0.41$ for the second example under case (b).

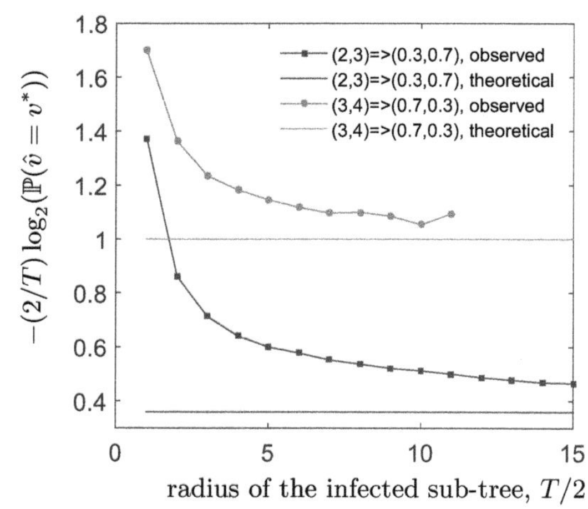

Figure 4: Simulated detection probability converges to the theoretical prediction.

3.3 Simulation Results

In Figure 4, we simulate adaptive diffusion and use the MAP estimator in Equation (4) to detect the source. Data points represent the probability of detection, averaged over 10,000 trials, where the randomness is both in the protocol and the underlying random tree. The horizontal axis denotes successive even time steps of adaptive diffusion—or equivalently, the radius of the infected sub-tree. The notation $(3,4) \Rightarrow (0.5, 0.5)$ in the legend indicates that each node in the tree has degree 3 or 4, each with probability 0.5. In this case, we have $p_1(f_1-1) > 1$, corresponding to case (a) in Theorem 3.3; our analysis predicts that the exponent is $\log_2(f_1-1) = 1$. This is indicated by a solid red line in Figure 4. For the other distribution with support $\boldsymbol{f} = (2,3)$ with probabilities $\boldsymbol{p} = (0.3, 0.7)$, we have $p_1(f_1-1) < 1$. This is case (b) in the theorem, and the analysis predicts that the exponent is 0.36 as we computed in the previous section. This is indicated by a solid blue line.

We observe that the empirical exponent $-\log(\mathbb{P}(\hat{v} = v^*))/(T/2)$ converges to the theoretical prediction, albeit slowly. The size of this experiment was limited by computational considerations, since the graph size grows exponentially in time.

3.4 Sketch of the Proof of Theorem 3.3

We provide a sketch of a proof of Theorem 3.3, first for case (a). We suppose $\eta = 2$ to simplify the notation and highlight the key insights. The random snapshot G_T is distributed according to T steps of Galton-Watson process starting from the root node v_T, with degree distribution D. Note that v_T is the center of G_T and not the source of the message. We want to prove that, with high probability, there exists a path from the root v_T to a leaf v which (mostly) consists of nodes with degree f_1, such that

$$\min_v \prod_{w\in\phi(v_T,v)\setminus\{v_T,v\}} (d_w - 1) \simeq (f_1-1)^{T/2-1},$$

where $\simeq$ indicates that we allow for vanishing fraction of nodes to deviate from the minimum degree f_1.

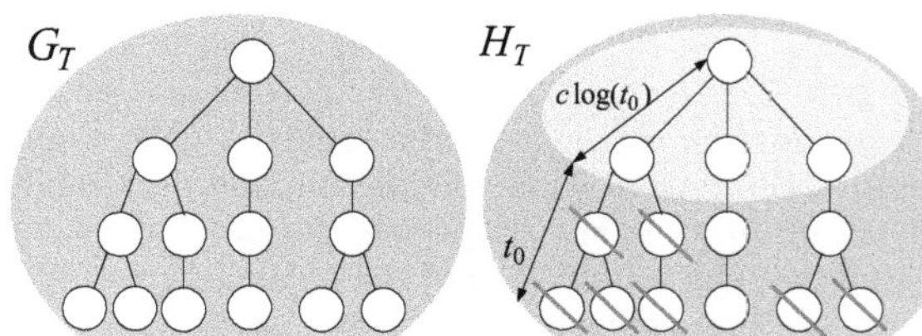

Figure 5: Pruning of a snapshot. We prune all descendants of nodes with degree 3 that are more than $c\log(t_0)$ hops from the root, where $t_0 + c\log t_0 = T/2$.

The main idea is to consider the sub-tree of G_T where we remove all nodes with degree f_2 and also all its descendants. First, if this pruned tree reaches the boundary at $T/2$, which is referred to as surviving until $T/2$ time steps, then we know that in the original G_T there exists a path from the root to a leaf consisting only of nodes with degree f_1. Furthermore, The pruned tree is also a Galton-Watson process, but with a different degree distribution:

$$\tilde{D} = \begin{cases} 1 & \text{with probability } p_2 \\ f_1 & \text{with probability } p_1 \end{cases}.$$

Under the assumption of case (a) that $(f_1-1)p_1 > 1$, we know from standard analysis of branching processes [22] that this pruned process survives for $T/2$ time steps with a strictly positive probability for any T. By delaying the pruning until an appropriately chosen $O(\log T)$ time steps, we can make this survival probability as large as we want.

In case (b), the same argument proves that the pruned process will not survive, and there will not be a path of minimum degree nodes reaching the boundary. We need to relax the pruning, and allow r_2 proportion of the nodes in a path to have degree f_2 for some $r_2 \in [0,1]$. We search over all possible choices of $\boldsymbol{r} = [1-r_2,\ r_2]$ such that the process barely survives while minimizing Λ_{G_T}:

$$\begin{aligned} \underset{r_2\in[0,1]}{\text{minimize}} \quad & (f_1-1)^{(1-r_2)T/2}(f_2-1)^{(r_2)T/2} \\ \text{subject to} \quad & \mathbb{P}(\text{survival}) > 0 \end{aligned}$$

Note that we have the same objective as in (12), up to a logarithm and scaling. The challenge in analyzing the constraint is that the pruned process is now dynamic, in the sense that we do not fix the number of f_2 nodes allowed in any path (as we did in case (a), allowing zero f_2 nodes), but rather let this allowed number grow proportionally to the tree depth. To analyze this dynamically-pruned process, we define a multi-type branching process, where the type of a node encodes the quantity we are interested in, namely the product of degrees in the path from the root. We analyze all possible pruning in this multi-type branching process, and show that it survives if and only if the conditions in (11) is satisfied. The complete proof is provided in Section 6.

4. PREFERENTIAL ATTACHMENT

Our analysis reveals that adaptive diffusion can be significantly sub-optimal, when the underlying graph degrees are highly irregular. To bridge this gap, we introduce a family of protocols we call *Preferential Attachment Adaptive Diffusion (PAAD)*. We analyze the performance of PAAD and provide numerical simulations showing that PAAD improves over adaptive diffusion when degrees are irregular.

The reason for this gap is that in typical random trees, there are nodes that are significantly more likely to be the source, compared to other typical candidate nodes. To achieve near-perfect obfuscation, we want all candidate nodes to have similar posterior probabilities of being the source. To balance the posterior probabilities of leaf nodes, we suggest passing the virtual source with higher probability to high-degree nodes. We propose a family of protocols based on this idea, and make this intuition precise in Theorem 4.1.

PAAD is based on adaptive diffusion, but we modify how virtual sources are chosen. We parametrize this family of protocols by a non-negative integer g. When a new virtual source is to be chosen, instead of choosing uniformly among its neighbors (except for the previous virtual source), the new virtual source is selected with probability weighted by the size of its g-hop neighborhood. Let $\mathcal{N}_g(v)$ denote the set of g-hop neighbors of node v, and let $\mathcal{N}_g(v,w)$ denote the same set, removing any nodes z for which $w \in \phi(z,v)$, where $\phi(z,v)$ denotes the path between z and v. Then for instance, if $g=1$, then each time the virtual source is passed from v_T to v_{T+2}, it is passed to a neighbor $w \in \mathcal{N}_1(v_T, v_{T-2})$ with probability proportional to $d_w - 1$:

$$\mathbb{P}(v_{T+2}=w) = \frac{d_w - 1}{\sum_{w'\in\mathcal{N}_1(v_T,v_{T-2})}(d_{w'}-1)} .$$

For general g, the probability is proportional to the size of the candidate w's g-hop local neighborhood, excluding those in the direction of the current virtual source v_T. Each virtual source v_T chooses the next virtual source as follows: for any node $w \in \mathcal{N}_1(v_T, v_{T-2})$,

$$P(v_{T+2}=w) = \frac{|\mathcal{N}_g(w,v_T)|}{\sum_{w'\in\mathcal{N}_1(v_T,v_{T-2})}|\mathcal{N}_g(w',v_T)|} .$$

PAAD encourages the virtual source to traverse high-degree nodes. This balances the posterior probabilities, by strengthening the probability of leaf nodes whose path contain high-degree nodes, while weakening those with low-degree nodes.

This intuition is made precise in the following theorem, which analyzes the probability of detection for a given snapshot. Define the probability that the sequence of decisions on choosing the virtual sources results in the path from a source v to the current virtual source v_T as $Q(\mathcal{G}_T, v) \equiv \prod_{t=1}^{T/2}\mathbb{P}(v_{2t}=w_t)$, where $\phi(v,v_T) = (w_0 = v, w_1, w_2, \ldots, w_{T/2-1}, w_{T/2} = v_T)$. The specific probability depends on the choice of g and the topology of the underlying tree. Note that the progression of the virtual source now depends on g-hop neighborhood, and we therefore define $\mathcal{G}_T$ to include the current infected subgraph G_T and its $(g+1)$-hop neighborhood.

THEOREM 4.1. *Suppose a node v^* starts to spread a message at time $t=0$ according to PAAD, where the underlying irregular tree is generated according to the random branching process described in the beginning of Section 3. At a certain even time $T \geq 0$, an adversary observes the snapshot of the infected subtree $\mathcal{G}_T$ and computes a MAP estimate of the source v^*. Then, the following results hold:*

(a) *The MAP estimator is*

$$\hat{v}_{\text{MAP}} = \arg\max_{v\in\partial G_T} d_v\, Q(\mathcal{G}_T, v) \tag{14}$$

where ∂G_T denotes the leaves of G_T.

(b) *The conditional probability of detection achieved by the MAP estimator is*

$$\mathbb{P}(\hat{v}_{\text{MAP}} = v^*|\mathcal{G}_T) = \frac{\max_{v\in\partial G_T} d_v\, Q(\mathcal{G}_T,v)}{\sum_{w\in\partial G_T} d_w\, Q(\mathcal{G}_T,w)} \tag{15}$$

The proof relies on the techniques developed for Theorem 3.1, and is omitted due to space limitation. The example from Figure 3 illustrates the power of PAAD. For this class of snapshots, it is straightforward to show that under adaptive diffusion, $P_D^{AD} = 2^{-T/2}$, whereas under 1-hop PAAD,

$$P_D^{PAAD} \leq \frac{2}{(d-1)^{T/2-1}-1} .$$

Notice from these expressions that P_D^{PAAD} scales as $(d-1)^{-T/2}$, which achieves perfect obfuscation, whereas regular adaptive diffusion scales as $2^{-T/2}$.

This shows that there exist snapshots where PAAD significantly improves over adaptive diffusion. However, such examples are rare under the random tree model, and there are also examples of snapshots where adaptive diffusion can achieve a better obfuscation than PAAD. To complete the analysis, we would like to show the analog of Theorem 3.3 for PAAD. However, the observed snapshot is no longer generated by a standard Galton-Watson branching process, due to the preferential attachment. The analysis techniques developed for Theorem 3.3 do not generalize, and new techniques seem to be needed for a technical analysis. This is outside the scope of this manuscript, but we show simulations suggesting that PAAD improves over adaptive diffusion.

4.1 Simulation Results

PAAD requires each virtual source to know some information about its local neighborhood on the contact network; in exchange, we observe empirically that it hides the source better than traditional adaptive diffusion. Figure 6 shows the probability of detection over graphs with a degree distribution of support $\boldsymbol{f} = (2,5)$ with probability $\boldsymbol{p} = (0.5, 0.5)$. The results are averaged over 10,000 realizations of the random graph and the spreading sequence. This plot shows empirically that preferential attachment adaptive diffusion exhibits better hiding properties than regular adaptive diffusion, and that the benefit of preferential attachment increases with the size of the neighborhood considered for preferential attachment (e.g., one-hop vs. two-hop). Notice that our lower bound on probability of detection is $1/|\partial G_T|$ rather than $1/N_T$, as in [14]; this is because we constrain the source to always be at one of the leaves of the graph, so $1/|\partial G_T|$ lower bounds the probability of detection.

Figure 7 computes the ratio of the observed probability of detection to a lower bound on the probability of detection (i.e., $1/|\partial G_T|$), for both adaptive diffusion (AD) and one-hop PAAD. Empirically, we observe that the advantage of PAAD is greater when the degree distribution is more imbalanced (i.e., when $f_{\max} - f_{\min}$ is large).

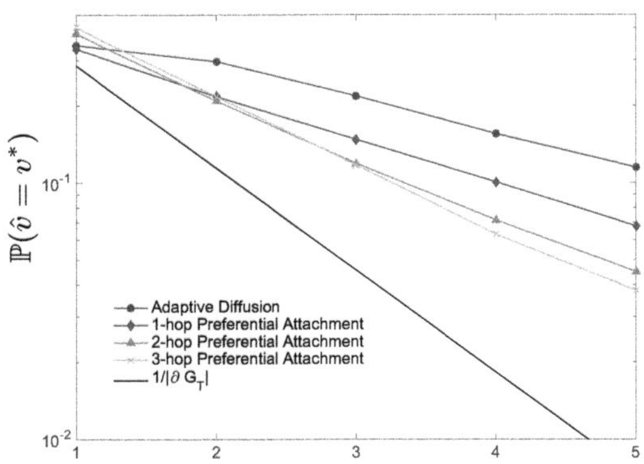

Figure 6: Probability of detection of regular adaptive diffusion compared to 1-, 2-, and 3-hop preferential attachment adaptive diffusion (PAAD).

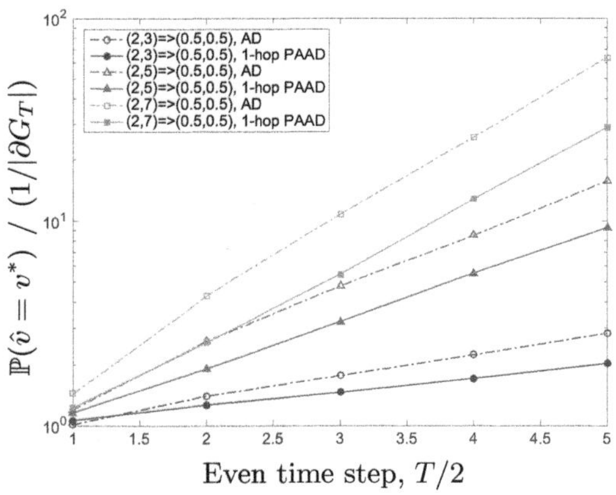

Figure 7: Ratio of observed probability of detection to lower-bound probability of detection, for a range of degree distributions. PAAD has better anonymity properties than regular adaptive diffusion over random, irregular trees.

5. DISCUSSION

We characterize how the probability of detection depends on the degree distribution of the underlying random tree, when messages spread as per adaptive diffusion. This suggests a novel family of protocols, we call preferential attachment adaptive diffusion. We analytically calculate the conditional probability of detection of this family of protocols; numerical results suggest improvements over adaptive diffusion. Ideally, we would like to prove an upper bound on the average probability of detection under adaptive diffusion: $\mathbb{P}(\hat{v}^{(T)}_{\text{MAP}} = v^*) = \sum_{\mathcal{G}_T} \mathbb{P}(\mathcal{G}_T)\,\mathbb{P}(\hat{v}^{(T)}_{\text{MAP}} = v^*|\mathcal{G}_T)$, averaged over all instances of the graphs. We conjecture this has the similar scaling as the concentration result in Theorem 3.3. The challenge is in proving a sharper concentration of Λ_{G_T}.

Proving a result analogous to Theorem 3.3 for PAAD is an interesting research direction, with technical challenges due to the fact that snapshot G_T is no longer a Galton-Watson tree. Although the distribution of the snapshot can be modeled by a multi-type branching process, it is an interesting open question how to analyze the typical value of $Q(\mathcal{G}_T, v)$. Similarly, it would be interesting to analyze adaptive diffusion and PAAD when the source is not constrained to be a leaf. This is more practical, in the sense that a natural message spreading should spread to all directions eventually. We believe the techniques developed in this paper can be generalized to handle this more general adaptive diffusion.

A related question is how to give plausible deniability to users that "approve" sensitive messages. Initial investigations exist [18], but technical and algorithmic questions remain, such as fundamental tradeoffs between privacy, spreading rate, and the utility lost, measured by the increased amount of spam in the network.

It has been recently shown that it is difficult to locate multiple sources [35]. It might be possible to spread the messages faster than adaptive diffusion and still achieve perfect obfuscation by creating multiple pseudo-sources. This approach sacrifices some social relevance, since the message spreads from remote nodes that may dislike the message.

Finally, recent work explores how to identify the first node in a randomly growing network [6, 21, 23, 24]. Unlike diffusion, the network itself is growing according to some mechanism, e.g., preferential attachment. [6], explores fundamental limits on the size of a candidate set to ensure that the true *source* or root of the random network is in the candidate set with high probability. A natural question is how to grow such a network to hide the identity of the root.

6. PROOF OF THEOREM 3.3

To facilitate the analysis, we consider an alternative random process that generates unlabeled graphs G'_T according to the same distribution as G_T (i.e., the infected, unlabeled subgraph embedded in $U(G_D^{(T)})$ from the proof of Theorem 3.1). For a given degree distribution D and a stopping time T, the new process is defined as a Galton-Watson process in which the set of offsprings at the first time step is drawn from D and the offsprings at subsequent time steps are drawn from $D-1$. At time $t=0$, a given root node v_T draws its degree d_{v_T} from D, and generates d_{v_T} child nodes. The resulting tree now has depth 1. In each subsequent time step, the process traverses each leaf v of the tree, draws its degree from D, and generates $d_v - 1$ children. The random process continues until the tree has depth $T/2$, since under adaptive diffusion, the infected subgraph at even time T has depth $T/2$. Because the probability of detection in Equation (5) does not depend on the degrees of the leaves of G_T, the random process stops at depth $T/2$ rather than $T/2+1$. We call the output of this random process G'_T. The distribution of G'_T is identical to the distribution as the previous random process imposed on G_T, which follows from the proof of Theorem 3.1. We therefore use G_T to denote the resulting output in the remainder of this proof.

Distribution D is a multinomial distribution with support $\boldsymbol{f} = (f_1, \ldots, f_\eta)$ and probabilities $\boldsymbol{p} = (p_1, \ldots, p_\eta)$. Without loss of generality, we assume $2 \le f_1 < \ldots < f_\eta$. Let μ_D denote the mean number of *children* generated by D:

$$\mu_D = \sum_{i=1}^{\eta} p_i(f_i - 1).$$

There are two separate classes of distributions, which we deal with as separate cases.

Case 1: When $p_1(f_1 - 1) > 1$, we claim that with high probability, there exists a leaf node v in ∂G_T such that on the unique path from the root v_T to this leaf v, all nodes in this path have the minimum degree f_1, except for a vanishing fraction. To prove this claim, consider a different graph H_T derived from G_T by pruning large degree nodes:

1. For a fixed, positive c, find t_0 such that $T/2 = t_0 + c\log(t_0)$.

2. Initialize H_T to be identical to G_T.

3. For each node $v \in H_T$, if the hop distance $\delta_H(v, v_T) \le c\log(t_0)$, do not modify that node.

4. For each node $v \in H_T$, if the hop distance $\delta_H(v, v_T) > c\log(t_0)$ and $d_v > f_1$, prune out all the children of v, as well as all their descendants (Figure 5).

We claim that this pruned process survives with high probability. The branching process that generates H_T is equivalent to a Galton-Watson process that uses distribution $D-1$ for the first $c\log(t_0)$ generations, and a different degree distribution $D'-1$ for the remaining generations; D' has support $\boldsymbol{f}' = (f_1, 1)$, probability mass $\boldsymbol{p}' = (p_1, 1-p_1)$, and mean number of children $\mu_{D'} = p_1(f_1 - 1)$.

Note that $f_1 \ge 3$ by the assumption that $p_1(f_1 - 1) > 1$. Hence, the inner branching process up to $c\log t_0$ has probability of extinction equal to 0. This means that at a hop distance of t_0 from v_T, there are at least $(f_1-1)^{c\log(t_0)}$ nodes. Each of these nodes can be thought of as the source of an independent Galton-Watson branching process with degree distribution $D' - 1$. By the properties of Galton-Watson branching processes ([22], Thm. 6.1), since $\mu_{D'} > 1$ by assumption, each independent branching process' asymptotic probability of extinction is the unique solution of $g_{D'}(s) = s$, for $s \in [0, 1)$, where $g_{D'}(s) = p_1\, s^{f_1-1} + (1-p_1)$ denotes the probability generating function of the distribution D'. Call this solution $\theta_{D'}$. The probability of any individual Galton-Watson process going extinct in the first generation is exactly $1 - p_1$. It is straightforward to show that $g_{D'}(s)$ is convex, and $g_{D'}(1-p_1) > 1 - p_1$, which implies that the probability of extinction is nondecreasing over successive generations and upper bounded by $\theta_{D'}$. Then for the branching process that generates H_T, the overall probability of extinction (for a given time T) is at most $\theta_{D'}^{(f_1-1)^{c\log t_0}}$. Increasing the constant c therefore decreases the probability of extinction. If there exists at least one leaf at depth T (i.e., extinction did not occur), then there exists at least one path in H_T of length $t_0 - c\log t_0$ in which every node (except possibly the final one) has the minimum degree f_1. This gives

$$\frac{\log(\Lambda_{H_T})}{T/2} \le \frac{t_0\log(f_1-1) + c\log(t_0)\log(f_\eta - 1)}{t_0 + c\log(t_0)} \quad (16)$$

$$\le \log(f_1 - 1) + \frac{c\log t_0}{t_0}\log\frac{f_\eta - 1}{f_1 - 1}, \quad (17)$$

with probability at least $1 - \theta_{D'}^{(f_1-1)^{c\log t_0}} = 1 - \theta_{D'}^{t_0^{c\log(f_1-1)}} = 1 - e^{-C_{D'}t_0}$, where $C_{D'} = \log(\theta_{D'})$ and the upper bound in (16) comes from assuming all the interior nodes have maximum degree f_η. Since H_T is a subgraph of a valid snapshot G_T, there exists a path in G_T from the virtual source v_T to a leaf of the tree where the hop distance of the path is exactly $T/2$, and at least t_0 nodes have the minimum degree f_1. Since the second term in (17) is $o(t_0)$, the claim follows. The lower bound $\log(\Lambda_{H_T})/(T/2) \ge \log(f_1 - 1)$ holds by definition. Therefore, for any $\delta > 0$, by setting T (and consequently, t_0) large enough, we can make the second term in (17) arbitrarily small. Thus, for $T \ge C'_{D,\delta}$, where $C'_{D,\delta}$ is a constant that depends only on the degree distribution and δ, the result holds.

Case 2: Consider the case when $p_1(f_1 - 1) < 1$. By the properties of Galton-Watson branching processes ([22], Thm. 6.1), the previous pruned random process that generated graphs H_T goes extinct with probability approaching 1. This implies that with high probability there is no path from the root to a leaf consisting only of min-degree nodes.

Instead, we introduce a Galton-Watson process with multiple types, derived from the original process. Our approach is to assign a numeric *type* to each node in G_T according to the number of non-minimum-degree nodes in the unique path between that node and the virtual source. If a node's path to v_T contains too many nodes of high degree, then we prune the node's descendants. The challenge is to choose the smallest pruning threshold that still ensures the pruned tree will survive with high probability. This threshold allows us to precisely characterize Λ_{G_T} for most of the instances.

To simplify the discussion, we start by considering a special case in which D allows nodes to take only two values of degrees, i.e., $\eta = 2$. We extend the results for $\eta = 2$ to larger, finite values of η in the extended version [13]. With a slight abuse of notation, consider a new random process H_T derived from G_T by pruning large degree nodes in the following way:

1. For a fixed, positive c, find t_0 s.t. $T/2 = t_0 + c\log(t_0)$.

2. Initialize H_T to be identical to G_T.

3. For each node $v \in H_T$, if the hop distance $\delta_H(v, v_T) \le c\log(t_0)$, do not modify that node, and assign it type 0.

4. For each node $v \in H_T$, if the hop distance $\delta_H(v, v_T) > c\log(t_0)$, assign v a type ξ_v, which is the number of nodes in $\phi(w, v) \setminus \{v\}$ that have the maximum possible degree f_2, where w is the closest node in H_T to v such that $\delta_H(w, v_T) \le c\log(t_0)$ (Figure 8).

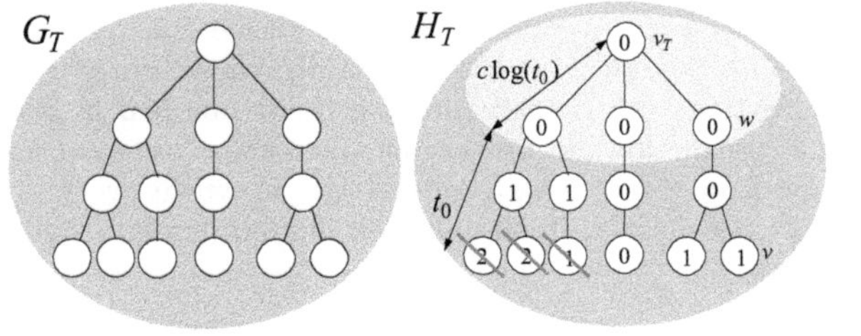

Figure 8: Pruning of a snapshot using multiple types. In this example, the distribution D allows nodes to have degree 2 or 3. We take $t_0 = 2$ and $r = 0.5$, so all descendants of nodes with type $rt_0 = 1$ are pruned.

5. Given a threshold $r \in (0,1)$, if a node v has type $\xi_v \geq rt_0$, prune out all the descendants of v. For example, in Figure 8, if $t_0 = 2$ and the threshold is $r = 0.5$, we would prune out all descendants of nodes with $\xi_v \geq 1$.

We show that for an appropriately-chosen threshold r, this pruned tree survives with high probability. By choosing the smallest possible r, we ensure that Λ_{H_T} consists (in all but a vanishing fraction of nodes) of a fraction r nodes with maximum degree, and $(1-r)$ of minimum degree. This allows us to derive the bounds on $\log(\Lambda_{H_T})/(T/2)$ stated in the claim, which hold with high probability.

Let $k \equiv rt_0$. The process that generates H_T is equivalent to a different random branching process that generates nodes in the following manner: set the root's type $\xi_{v_T} = 0$. At time $t = 0$, the root v_T draws a number of children according to distribution D, and generates d_{v_T} children, all type 0. Each leaf generates type 0 children according to child degree distribution $D-1$ until $c\log(t_0)$ generations have passed. At that point, each leaf v in this branching process (which necessarily has type 0) reproduces as follows: if its type $\xi_v > k$, then v does not reproduce. Otherwise, it either generates $(f_1 - 1)$ children with probability p_1, each with state ξ_v, or $(f_2 - 1)$ children with probability p_2, each with state $\xi_v{+}1$. This continues for t_0 generations. Mimicking the notation from Case 1, we use D' to denote the distribution that gives rise to this modified, multi-type random process (in the final t_0 generations); this is a slight abuse of notation since the branching dynamics are multi-type, not defined by realizations of i.i.d. degree random variables.

Lemma 6.1. *Consider a Galton-Watson branching process with child degree distribution $D-1$, where each node has at least one child with probability 1, and $\mu_{D-1} > 1$. Then the number of leaves in generation t, $Z^{(t)}$, satisfies $Z^{(t)} \geq e^{C_\ell t}$ with probability at least $1 - e^{C'_\ell t}$, where both C_ℓ and C'_ℓ are constants that depend on the degree distribution.*

We omit the proof due to space limitations. The first $c\log(t_0)$ generations ensure that with high probability, we have at least $e^{C_\ell \log t_0}$ independent multi-type Galton-Watson processes originating from the leaves of the inner subgraph; this follows from Lemma 6.1. Here we have encapsulated the constant c from the first $c\log(t_0)$ generations in the constant C_ℓ. For example, in Figure 8, there are 3 independent Galton-Watson processes starting at the leaves of the inner subgraph. We wish to choose r such that the expected number of new leaves generated by *each* of these processes, at *each* time step, is large enough to ensure that extinction occurs with probability less than one. For brevity, let $\alpha \equiv p_1(f_1 - 1)$ and let $\beta \equiv p_2(f_2 - 1)$. Let $x^{(t)}$ denote the $(k+1)$-dimensional vector of the expected number of leaves generated with each type from 0 to k in generation t. This vector evolves according to the following $(k+1) \times (k+1)$ transition matrix M:

$$x^{(t+1)} = x^{(t)} \underbrace{\begin{bmatrix} \alpha & \beta & & \\ & \ddots & \ddots & \\ & & \ddots \;\; \alpha & \beta \\ & & & 0 \end{bmatrix}}_{M}.$$

The last row of M is 0 because a node with type k does not reproduce. Since the root of each process always has type 0, we have $x^{(0)} = \boldsymbol{e}_1$, where $\boldsymbol{e}_1$ is the indicator vector with a 1 at index 1 and zeros elsewhere. Let $Z^{(t)}$ denote the expected number of new leaves created in generation t. This gives

$$\mathbb{E}[Z^{(t)}] = \boldsymbol{e}_1 M^t \mathbb{1}^{\intercal}_{(k+1)}, \tag{18}$$

where $^\intercal$ denotes a transpose, and $\mathbb{1}_{(k+1)}$ is the $(k+1)$ all-ones vector. When $t < k$, this is a simple binomial expansion of $(\alpha+\beta)^t$. For $t \geq k$, this is a truncated expansion up to k:

$$\mathbb{E}[Z^{(t)}] = \sum_{i=0}^{k} \binom{t}{i} \alpha^{t-i} \beta^i. \tag{19}$$

We seek a necessary and sufficient condition on r for non-extinction, such that $(1/t)\log(\mathbb{E}[Z^{(t)}]) > 0$. Consider a binomial random variable W with parameter $\beta/(\alpha+\beta) = \beta/\mu_D$ and t trials. Equation (19) implies that for large t,

$$\begin{aligned} \mathbb{E}[Z^{(t)}] &= (\alpha+\beta)^t \, \mathbb{P}(W \leq k). & (20) \\ &= \mu_D^t \exp\Big\{ -t\, D_{\mathrm{KL}}\Big(r \,\|\, \frac{\beta}{\mu_D}\Big) + o(t) \Big\}, & (21) \end{aligned}$$

by Sanov's theorem [10]. Here $D_{\mathrm{KL}}(r\|\beta/\mu_D)$ denotes the Kullback-Leibler divergence between the two Bernoulli distributions defined by r and β/μ_D, such that $D_{\mathrm{KL}}(r\|\beta/\mu_D) = (1-r)\log((1-r)/(\alpha/\mu_D)) + r\log(r/(\beta/\mu_D))$. We wish to identify the smallest r for which $(1/t)\log(\mathbb{E}[Z^{(t)}])$ is bounded away from zero. Such an r is a sufficient (and necessary) condition for the multi-type Galton-Watson process to have a probability of extinction less than 1. To achieve this, we define the following set of r such that Eq. (21) is strictly positive, for some $\epsilon > 0$:

$$\mathcal{R}_{\alpha,\beta}(\epsilon) = \big\{ r \mid \log(\mu_D) \geq D_{\mathrm{KL}}(r\|\beta/\mu_D) + \epsilon \big\}, \tag{22}$$

Suppose we now choose a threshold $r \in \mathcal{R}_{\alpha,\beta}(\epsilon)$. This is the regime where the modified Galton-Watson process with threshold r has a chance for survival. In other words, the probability of extinction $\theta_{D'}$ is strictly less than one. Precisely, $\theta_{D'}$ is the unique solution to $s = g_{D'}(s)$, where $g_{D'}(s)$ denotes the probability generating function of the described multi-type Galton-Watson process. Using the same argument as in Case 1, we can construct a process where the probability of extinction is asymptotically zero. Precisely, we modify the pruning process such that we do not prune any leaves in the first $c\log(t_0)$ generations. This ensures that with high probability, there are at least $e^{C_\ell \log(t_0)}$ independent multi-type Galton-Watson processes evolving concurrently after time $c\log(t_0)$, each with probability of extinction $\theta_{D'}$. Hence with probability at least $1 - e^{-2C_{D'}t_0}$ (for an appropriate choice of a constant $C_{D'}$ that only depends on the degree distribution D' and the choice of r), the overall process does not go extinct.

Our goal is to find the choice of r with minimum product of degrees $\log(\Lambda_{G_T})/(T/2)$ that survives. We define r_1 as: $r_1 \equiv \arg\min_{r\in\mathcal{R}_{\alpha,\beta}(\epsilon)} (1-r)\log(1-f_1) + r\log(1-f_2)$. Since $\mathcal{R}_{\alpha,\beta}(\epsilon)$ is just an interval and we are minimizing a linear function with a positive slope, the optimal solution is $r_1 = \inf_{r\in\mathcal{R}_{\alpha,\beta}(\epsilon)} r$. This is a choice that survives with high probability and has the minimum product of degrees. Precisely, with probability at least $1 - e^{-C_{D'}T}$, where $C_{D'}$ depends on D' and ϵ, we have that $\frac{\log(\Lambda_{G_T})}{T/2} \leq \langle[1-r_1, r_1], \log(f - 1)\rangle + \frac{c\log(t_0)}{t_0}\log(f_2 - 1)$, where we define the standard inner product $\langle[1-r_1, r_1], \log(\boldsymbol{f} - 1)\rangle \triangleq (1-r_1)\log(f_1-1) + r_1\log(f_2-1)$. It follows that

$$\frac{\log(\Lambda_{G_T})}{T/2} - \langle[1-r^*, r^*], \log(\boldsymbol{f}-1)\rangle \leq (r_1 - r^*)\log\left(\frac{f_2-1}{f_1-1}\right) + \frac{c\log(t_0)}{t_0}\log(f_2-1) \quad (23)$$

By setting ϵ small enough and t_0 large enough, we can make this arbitrarily small. For any $\delta > 0$, there exists a positive $\epsilon > 0$ such that the first term is bounded by $\delta/2$. Further, recall that $T/2 = c\log(t_0) + t_0$. For any choice of ϵ, there exists a $t_{D',\epsilon}$ such that for all $T \geq t_{D',\epsilon}$ the vanishing term in Eq. (21) is smaller than ϵ. For any given $\delta > 0$, there exists a positive $t_{D',\delta}$ such that $T \geq t_{D',\delta}$ implies that the second term is upper bounded by $\delta/2$. Putting everything together (and setting ϵ small enough for target δ), we get

$$\mathbb{P}\Big(\frac{\log(\Lambda_{G_T})}{T/2} \geq \langle[1-r^*, r^*], \log(\boldsymbol{f}-1)\rangle + \delta\Big) \leq e^{-C_{D',\delta}T} \quad (24)$$

for all $T \geq C'_{D',\delta}$, where $C_{D',\delta}$ and $C'_{D',\delta}$ are positive constants that only depend on the degree distribution D' and the choice of $\delta > 0$.

For the lower bound, we define the following set of r such that Eq. (21) is strictly negative:

$$\overline{\mathcal{R}}_{\alpha,\beta}(\epsilon) = \{r \mid \log(\mu_D) \leq D_{\text{KL}}(r\|\beta/\mu_D) - \epsilon\}. \quad (25)$$

Choosing $r \in \overline{\mathcal{R}}_{\alpha,\beta}(\epsilon)$ causes extinction with probability approaching 1. Explicitly, $\mathbb{P}(Z^{(t)} \neq 0)$ is the probability of non-extinction at time t, and $\mathbb{P}(Z^{(t)} \neq 0) \leq \mathbb{E}[Z^{(t)}]$. By Equation (21), we have $\mathbb{E}[Z^{(t)}] \leq e^{t(\log(\mu_D) - D_{\text{KL}}(r\|\beta/\mu_D) + o(t))}$ where $\log(\mu_D) - D_{\text{KL}}(r\|\beta/\mu_D) \leq -\epsilon$. The probability of extinction is at least $1 - \mathbb{E}[Z^{(t)}] \geq 1 - e^{-t(\epsilon + o(t))}$. So defining $r_2 \equiv \arg\max_{r\in\overline{\mathcal{R}}_{\alpha,\beta}(\epsilon)} (1-r)\log(1-f_1) + r\log(1-f_2)$, we have $\frac{\log(\Lambda_{G_T})}{T/2} \geq \langle[1-r_2, r_2], \log(\boldsymbol{f}-1)\rangle + \frac{c\log(t_0)}{t_0}\log(f_1-1)$, with probability at least $1 - e^{-C_{D',2}T}$ where $C_{D',2}$ is again a constant that depends on D' and ϵ. It again follows that

$$\frac{\log(\Lambda_{G_T})}{T/2} - \langle[1-r^*, r^*], \log(\boldsymbol{f}-1)\rangle \geq (r_2 - r^*)\log\left(\frac{f_2-1}{f_1-1}\right) + \frac{c\log(t_0)}{t_0}\log(f_1-1)\ , \quad (26)$$

where $r_2 - r^*$ is strictly negative. Again, for any given $\delta > 0$, there exists a positive $\epsilon > 0$ such that the first term is lower bounded by $-\delta/2$, and for any choice of ϵ, there exists a $t_{D',\epsilon}$ such that for all $T \geq t_{D',\epsilon}$ the vanishing term in Eq. (21) is smaller than ϵ. Note that this ϵ might be different from the one used to show the upper bound. We ultimately choose the smaller of the two ϵ values. For any given $\delta > 0$, there exists a positive $t_{D',\delta}$ such that $T \geq t_{D',\delta}$ implies that the second term is lower bounded by $-\delta/2$. Putting everything together (and setting ϵ small enough for the target δ), we get that

$$\mathbb{P}\Big(\frac{\log(\Lambda_{G_T})}{T/2} \leq \langle[1-r^*, r^*], \log(\boldsymbol{f}-1)\rangle - \delta\Big) \leq e^{-C_{D',\delta}T}$$

for all $T \geq C'_{D',\delta}$, where $C_{D',\delta}$ and $C'_{D',\delta}$ are positive constants that only depend on the degree distribution D' and the choice of $\delta > 0$. This gives the desired result.

The general case for $\eta > 2$ (i.e., when the distribution has support greater than two) appears in the extended version [13].

Acknowledgement

We would like to thank the anonymous reviewers for their helpful comments. This work has been supported by NSF CISE awards CCF-1422278 and CCF-1553452, and SaTC award CNS-1527754.

7. REFERENCES

[1] Whisper, 2012. http://whisper.sh.

[2] Yik yak, 2013. http://www.yikyakapp.com/.

[3] Secret, 2014. https://www.secret.ly.

[4] Team blind, 2015. http://us.teamblind.com/.

[5] D. Acemoglu, A. Makhdoumi, A. Malekian, and A. E. Ozdaglar. Privacy-constrained network formation. MIT Department of Economics Working Paper, 2015.

[6] S. Bubeck, L. Devroye, and G. Lugosi. Finding adam in random growing trees. *arXiv preprint arXiv:1411.3317*, 2014.

[7] D. Chaum. The dining cryptographers problem: Unconditional sender and recipient untraceability. *Journal of cryptology*, 1(1), 1988.

[8] I. Clarke, O. Sandberg, B. Wiley, and T.W. Hong. Freenet: A distributed anonymous information storage and retrieval system. In *Designing Privacy Enhancing Technologies*, 2001.

[9] H. Corrigan-Gibbs and B. Ford. Dissent: accountable anonymous group messaging. In *CCS*. ACM, 2010.

[10] T. M. Cover and J. A. Thomas. *Elements of information theory*. John Wiley & Sons, 2012.

[11] R. Dingledine, M.J. Freedman, and D. Molnar. The free haven project: Distributed anonymous storage service. In *Designing Privacy Enhancing Technologies*, 2001.

[12] R. Dingledine, N. Mathewson, and P. Syverson. Tor: The second-generation onion router. Technical report, DTIC Document, 2004.

[13] G. Fanti, P. Kairouz, S. Oh, K. Ramchandran, and P. Viswanath. Hiding the rumor source. *arXiv preprint arXiv:1509.02849*, 2015.

[14] G. Fanti, P. Kairouz, S. Oh, and P. Viswanath. Spy vs. spy: Rumor source obfuscation. In *SIGMETRICS Perform. Eval. Rev.*, volume 43, pages 271–284, 2015.

[15] S. Feizi, K. Duffy, M. Kellis, and M. Medard. Network infusion to infer information sources in networks. 2014.

[16] V. Fioriti and M. Chinnici. Predicting the sources of an outbreak with a spectral technique. *arXiv:1211.2333*, 2012.

[17] M.J. Freedman and R. Morris. Tarzan: A peer-to-peer anonymizing network layer. In *Proc. CCS*. ACM, 2002.

[18] G. Giakkoupis, R. Guerraoui, A. Jégou, A. Kermarrec, and N. Mittal. Privacy-conscious information diffusion in social networks. pages 480–496, 2015.

[19] S. Goel, M. Robson, M. Polte, and E. Sirer. Herbivore: A scalable and efficient protocol for anonymous communication. Technical report, 2003.

[20] P. Golle and A. Juels. Dining cryptographers revisited. In *Advances in Cryptology-Eurocrypt 2004*, 2004.

[21] E. Gwynne and S. Bubeck. Asymptotic behavior of the eden model with positively homogeneous edge weights. *arXiv preprint arXiv:1508.05140*, 2015.

[22] T. E. Harris. *The theory of branching processes.* Courier Corporation, 2002.

[23] V. Jog and P. Loh. Persistence of centrality in random growing trees. *arXiv preprint arXiv:1511.01975*, 2015.

[24] V. Jog and P. Loh. Analysis of centrality in sublinear preferential attachment trees via the cmj branching process. *arXiv preprint arXiv:1601.06448*, 2016.

[25] W. Luo, W. Tay, and M. Leng. How to identify an infection source with limited observations. 2013.

[26] W. Luo, W. P. Tay, and M. Leng. Rumor spreading and source identification: A hide and seek game. *arXiv preprint arXiv:1504.04796*, 2015.

[27] E. A. Meirom, C. Milling, C. Caramanis, S. Mannor, A. Orda, and S. Shakkottai. Localized epidemic detection in networks with overwhelming noise. 2014.

[28] C. Milling, C. Caramanis, S. Mannor, and S. Shakkottai. Network forensics: Random infection vs spreading epidemic. In *SIGMETRICS*. ACM, 2012.

[29] C. Milling, C. Caramanis, S. Mannor, and S. Shakkottai. Detecting epidemics using highly noisy data. In *MobiHoc*, pages 177–186, 2013.

[30] P. C. Pinto, P. Thiran, and M. Vetterli. Locating the source of diffusion in large-scale networks. *Physical review letters*, 109(6):068702, 2012.

[31] B. A. Prakash, J. Vreeken, and C. Faloutsos. Spotting culprits in epidemics: How many and which ones? In *ICDM*, volume 12, pages 11–20, 2012.

[32] D. Shah and T. Zaman. Detecting sources of computer viruses in networks: theory and experiment. In *ACM SIGMETRICS Performance Evaluation Review*, volume 38, pages 203–214. ACM, 2010.

[33] D. Shah and T. Zaman. Finding rumor sources on random graphs. *arXiv preprint arXiv:1110.6230*, 2011.

[34] D. Shah and T. Zaman. Rumors in a network: Who's the culprit? *Information Theory, IEEE Transactions on*, 57:5163–5181, Aug 2011.

[35] S. Spencer and R. Srikant. On the impossibility of localizing multiple rumor sources in a line graph. *ACM SIGMETRICS Performance Evaluation Review*, 43(2):66–68, 2015.

[36] J. van den Hooff, D. Lazar, M. Zaharia, and N. Zeldovich. Vuvuzela: Scalable private messaging resistant to traffic analysis. In *SOSP*. ACM, 2015.

[37] L. von Ahn, A. Bortz, and N.J. Hopper. K-anonymous message transmission. In *CCS*. ACM, 2003.

[38] Z. Wang, W. Dong, W. Zhang, and C.W. Tan. Rumor source detection with multiple observations: Fundamental limits and algorithms. In *ACM SIGMETRICS*, 2014.

[39] K. Zhu and L. Ying. A robust information source estimator with sparse observations. *arXiv:1309.4846*, 2013.

APPENDIX

Protocol 1 Adaptive Diffusion [14]

Input: contact network $G = (V, E)$, source v^*, time T, degree d
Output: set of infected nodes V_T

$V_0 \leftarrow \{v^*\}$, $h \leftarrow 0$, $v_0 \leftarrow v^*$
v^* selects one of its neighbors u at random
$V_1 \leftarrow V_0 \cup \{u\}$, $h \leftarrow 1$, $v_1 \leftarrow u$
let $\mathcal{N}(u)$ represent u's neighbors
$V_2 \leftarrow V_1 \cup \mathcal{N}(u) \setminus \{v^*\}$, $v_2 \leftarrow v_1$
$t \leftarrow 3$
for $t \leq T$ **do**
    v_{t-1} randomly selects $u \in \mathcal{N}(v_{t-1}) \setminus \{v_{t-2}\}$
    $h \leftarrow h + 1$
    $v_t \leftarrow u$
    for all $v \in \mathcal{N}(v_t) \setminus \{v_{t-1}\}$ **do**
        Infection Message(G,v_t,v,V_t)
        if $t + 1 > T$ **then**
            break
        Infection Message(G,v_t,v,V_t)
    $t \leftarrow t + 2$
procedure Infection Message(G,u,v,V_t)
    if $v \in V_t$ **then**
        for all $w \in \mathcal{N}(v) \setminus \{u\}$ **do**
            Infection Message(G,v,w,G_t)
    else
        $V_t \leftarrow V_{t-2} \cup \{v\}$

Inference in OSNs via Lightweight Partial Crawls

Konstantin Avrachenkov
INRIA
Sophia Antipolis,France
k.avrachenkov@inria.fr

Bruno Ribeiro
Dept. of Computer Science
Purdue University
West Lafayette, IN, USA
ribeiro@cs.purdue.edu

Jithin K. Sreedharan
INRIA
Sophia Antipolis,France
jithin.sreedharan@inria.fr

ABSTRACT

Are Online Social Network (OSN) A users more likely to form friendships with those with similar attributes? Do users at an OSN B score content more favorably than OSN C users? Such questions frequently arise in the context of Social Network Analysis (SNA) but often crawling an OSN network via its Application Programming Interface (API) is the only way to gather data from a third party. To date, these partial API crawls are the majority of public datasets and the synonym of lack of statistical guarantees in incomplete-data comparisons, severely limiting SNA research progress. Using regenerative properties of the random walks, we propose estimation techniques based on short crawls that have proven statistical guarantees. Moreover, our short crawls can be implemented in massively distributed algorithms. We also provide an adaptive crawler that makes our method parameter-free, significantly improving our statistical guarantees. We then derive the Bayesian approximation of the posterior of the estimates, and in addition, obtain an estimator for the expected value of node and edge statistics in an equivalent configuration model or Chung-Lu random graph model of the given network (where nodes are connected randomly) and use it as a basis for testing null hypotheses. The theoretical results are supported with simulations on a variety of real-world networks.

Keywords

Bayesian inference, Graph sampling, Random walk on graphs, Social network analysis

1. INTRODUCTION

What is the fraction of male-female connections against that of female-female connections in a given Online Social Network (OSN)? Is the OSN assortative or disassortative? Edge, triangle, and node statistics of OSNs find applications in computational social science (see e.g. [30]), epidemiology [31], and computer science [5, 15]. Computing these statistics is a key capability in large-scale social network analysis and machine learning applications. But because data collection in the wild is often limited to partial OSN crawls through Application Programming Interface (API) requests, observational studies of OSNs – for research purposes or market analysis – depend in great part on our ability to compute network statistics with incomplete data. Case in point, most datasets available to researchers in widely popular public repositories are partial OSN crawls[1]. Unfortunately, these incomplete datasets have unknown biases and no statistical guarantees regarding the accuracy of their statistics. To date, the best methods for crawling networks ([4, 14, 32]) show good real-world performance but only provide statistical guarantees asymptotically (i.e., when the entire OSN network is collected).

This work addresses the fundamental problem of obtaining unbiased and reliable node, edge, and triangle statistics of OSNs via partial crawling. *To the best of our knowledge our method is the first to provide a practical solution to the problem of computing OSN statistics with strong theoretical guarantees from a partial network crawl.* More specifically, we (a) provide a provable finite-sample unbiased estimate of network statistics (and their spectral-gap derived variance) and (b) provide the approximate posterior of our estimates that performs remarkably well in all tested real-world scenarios.

More precisely, let $G = (V, E)$ be an undirected labeled network – not necessarily connected – where V is the set of vertices and $E \subseteq V \times V$ is the set of edges. Unlike the usual definition of E where each edge is only present once, to simplify our notation we consider that if $(u, v) \in E$ then $(v, u) \in E$. Both edges and nodes can have labels. Network G is unknown to us except for $n > 0$ *arbitrary* initial seed nodes in $I_n \subseteq V$. Nodes in I_n must span all the different connected components of G. From the seed nodes we crawl the network starting from I_n and obtain a set of crawled edges $\mathcal{D}_m(I_n)$, where $m > 0$ is a parameter that regulates the number of website API requests. With the crawled edges $\mathcal{D}_m(I_n)$ we seek an unbiased estimate of

$$\mu(G) = \sum_{(u,v) \in E} g(u, v)\,, \tag{1}$$

for any function $g(u, v)$ over the node pair (u, v). Note that functions of the form eq. (1) are general enough to compute

[1]Public repositories such as SNAP [26] and KONECT [24] contain a majority of partial website crawls, not complete datasets or uniform samples.

SIGMETRICS'16, June 14-18, 2016, Antibes Juan-Les-Pins, France
© 2016 ACM. ISBN 978-1-4503-4266-7/16/06...$15.00
DOI: http://dx.doi.org/10.1145/2896377.2901477

node statistics

$$\mu_{\text{node}}(G) = \sum_{(u,v)\in E} h(v)/d_v ,$$

where d_u is the degree of node $u \in V$, $h(v)$ is any function of the node v, and statistics of triangles such as the local clustering coefficient of G first provided by [32]

$$\mu_{\triangle}(G) = \frac{1}{|V|} \sum_{(u,v)\in E} \Big\{ \frac{\mathbf{1}(d_v > 2)}{d_v}$$

$$\frac{\sum_{a\in N_v} \sum_{b\in N_v, b\neq a} \mathbf{1}((v,a) \in E \cap (v,b) \in E \cap (a,b) \in E)}{\binom{d_v}{2}} \Big\},$$

where the expression inside the sum is zero when $d_v < 2$ and N_v are the neighbors of $v \in V$ in G. Our task is to find estimates of general functions of the form $\mu(G)$ in eq. (1).

Contributions

In our work we provide a partial crawling strategy using short dynamically adjustable random walk tours starting at a "virtual" super-node without invoking the notion of lumpability [21]. A random walk tour is a random walk sample path that starts and ends at the same node on the graph. We use these tours to compute a frequentist unbiased estimator of $\mu(G)$ (including its variance) regardless of the number of nodes, $n > 0$, in the seed set and regardless of the value of $m > 0$, unlike previous asymptotically unbiased methods [4, 14, 25, 32, 33]. We also provide a Bayesian approximation of the posterior of $\mu(G)$ given the observed tours $P[\mu(G)|\mathcal{D}_m(I_n)]$, which is shown to be consistent. In our experiments we note that the posterior is remarkably accurate using a variety of networks large and small. Furthermore, when the network is formed by randomly wiring connections while preserving degrees and attributes of the nodes in the observed network, we devise an estimation technique for the expected true value with partial knowledge of the original graph.

Related Work

The works of Massoulié et al. [28] and Cooper et al. [10] are the ones closest to ours. Massoulié et al. [28] estimates the size of a network based on the return times of random walk tours. Cooper et al. [10] estimates number of triangles, network size, and subgraph counts from weighted random walk tours using results of Aldous and Fill [1, Chapter 2 and 3]. The previous works on finite-sample inference of network statistics from incomplete network crawls [16, 22, 23, 18, 19, 27, 34] need to fit the partial observed data to a probabilistic graph model such as ERGMs (exponential family of random graphs models). Our work advances the state-of-the-art in estimating network statistics from partial crawls because: (a) we estimate statistics of arbitrary edge functions without assumptions about the graph model or the underlying graph; (b) we do not need to bias the random walk with weights as in Cooper et al.; this is particularly useful when estimating multiple statistics reusing the same observations; (c) we derive upper and lower bounds on the variance of estimator, which both show the connection with the spectral gap; and, finally, (d) we compute a posterior over our estimates to give practitioners a way to access the confidence in the estimates without relying on unobtainable quantities like the spectral gap and without assuming a probabilistic graph model.

The remainder of the paper is organized as follows. In Section 2 we introduce key concepts and defines the notation used throughout this manuscript. Section 3 presents the algorithms to build the super-node and proves the equivalence between them. The frequentist estimators and their properties are explained in Section 4. Section 5 contains the main result of the posterior distribution in Bayesian framework. Section 6 consists of experimental results over real-world networks. Finally, in Section 7 we present our conclusions.

2. SUPER-NODE RATIONALE

In this section we present definitions and concepts using throughout the reminder of the paper. Then we substantiate an intuitive reasoning that our random walk tours are shorter than the "regular random walk tours" because the "node" that they start from is an amalgamation of a multitude of nodes in the graph.

Preliminaries

Let $G = (V, E)$ be an unknown undirected graph with N number of nodes and $M = |E|/2$, number of edges. Our goal is to find an unbiased estimate of $\mu(G)$ in eq. (1) and its posterior by crawling a small fraction of G. We are given a set of $n > 0$ initial *arbitrary* nodes denoted $I_n \subset V$. If G has disconnected components I_n must span all the different connected components of G.

Unless stated otherwise our network crawler is a classical random walk (RW) over the following augmented multigraph $G' = (V', E')$ with N' nodes and M' edges. A multigraph is a graph that can have multiple edges between two nodes. In $G'(I_n)$ we aggregate all nodes of I_n into a single node, denoted hereafter S_n, the *super-node*. Thus, $V'(I_n) = \{V \backslash I_n\} \cup \{S_n\}$. The edges of $G'(I_n)$ are $E'(I_n) = E\backslash\{E \cap \{I_n \times V\}\} \cup \{(S_n, v) : \forall(u,v) \in E$, s.t. $u \in I_n$ and $v \in V\backslash I_n\}$, i.e., $E'(I_n)$ contains all the edges in E including the edges from the nodes in I_n to other nodes, and I_n is merged into the super-node S_n. Note that $G'(I_n)$ is necessarily connected as I_n spans all the connected components of G. For compactness of notation we sometimes refer to $G'(I_n)$ as G' when I_n is clear from the context. *We also use S_n and I_n interchangeably to denote both the super-node at $G'(I_n)$ and each individual nodes of I_n at G.*

A random walk on $G'(I_n)$ has transition probability from node u to an adjacent node v, $p_{uv} := \alpha_{u,v}/d_u$, where d_u is the degree of u and $\alpha_{u,v}$ is the number of edges between $u \in V'$ and $v \in V'$. Let $\mathbf{P} = \{p_{uv}\}$. We note that the theory presented in the paper can be extended to more sophisticated random walks as well. Let π_i be the stationary distribution at node i in the random walk on $G'(I_n)$.

A random walk *tour* is defined as the sequence of nodes $X_1^{(k)}, \ldots, X_{\xi_k}^{(k)}$ visited by the random walk during successive k-th and $k+1$-st visits to the super-node S_n. Here $\{\xi_k\}_{k\geq 1}$ denote the successive return times to S_n. Tours have a key property: from the renewal theorem tours are independent since the returning times act as renewal epochs. Moreover, let $Y_1, Y_2, \ldots, Y_n$ be a random walk on $G'(I_n)$ in steady state.

Note that the random walk on $G'(I_n)$ is equivalent to a random walk on G where all the nodes in I_n are treated as *one single node.* Figure 1 shows an example of the formation of $G'(I_n)$.

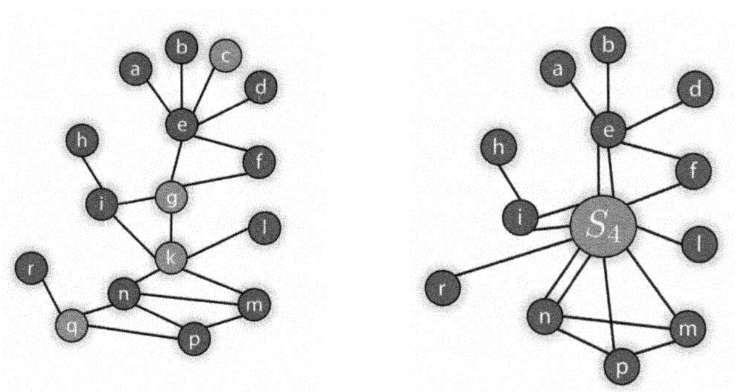

(a) The original graph G with $I_4 = \{c, g, j, q\}$.

(b) The modified graph $G'(I_n)$ with super-node S_4.

Figure 1: Graph modification with the super-node

Why a Super-node

The introduction of super-node is primary motivated by the following closely-related reasons:

- *Tackling disconnected or low-conductance graphs:* When the graph is not well connected or has many connected components, forming a super-node with representatives from each of the components make the modified graph connected and suitable for applying random walk theory. Even when the graph is connected, it might not be well-knit, i.e., it has low conductance. Since the conductance is closely related to mixing time of Markov chains, such graph will prolong the mixing of random walks. But with proper choice of super-node, we can reduce the mixing time and, as we show, improve the estimation accuracy.

  If we consider self loops from S_n to itself while forming the modified graph G', i.e. all the connections between I_n ($E \cap \{I_n \times I_n\}$), then G' becomes a contracted graph [9]. Then [9, Lemma 1.15] says that if S_n is formed from $n = 2$ vertices, the spectral gaps of the two graphs $\delta_{G'}$ and δ_G are related as follows: $\delta_{G'} \geq \delta_G$. The spectral gap $\delta_{G'} = 1 - \lambda_2$, where λ_2 is the second largest eigenvalue of $\mathbf{P}$, and δ_G can be defined accordingly on the random walk on the original graph. The above argument with spectral gaps can be extended to $n > 2$ by induction and hence $\delta_{G'} \geq \delta_G$ follows. The improvement in the spectral gap proves that the modified graph will become well-knit (low conductance). Note that G' in our case does not involve self loops around S_n, but this is for the ease of computation as the function values over the self loops are known (from the knowledge of I_n and further API queries with them), and hence allowing self loops will only slower down the estimation of $\mu(G)$ outside the super-node.

- *No lumpability for random walks:* The theory of lumpability [21, Section 6.3] provides ways to exactly partition a Markov chain. Unfortunately, lumping states in a classical random walk will not give an accurate representation of the random walk Markov chain and, thus, we consider a super-node S_n where all the nodes inside the super-node are merged into one node rather than partitioning the states. The edges from S_n are the collection of all the edges from the nodes inside the super-node which are connected to nodes outside super-node, and Markov chain property still holds on this formation. The graph modification with S_n is illustrated with an example in Figure 1.

- *Faster estimate with shorter tours:* The expected value of the k-th tour length $\mathbb{E}[\xi_k] = 1/\pi_{S_n}$ is inversely proportional to the degree of the super-node d_{S_n}. Hence, by forming a massive-degree super-node we can significantly shorten the average tour length. This property is of great practical importance as it reduces the number of API queries required per tour.

3. STATIC AND DYNAMIC SUPER-NODES

In what follows we describe the algorithms to build super-nodes. The static super-node technique selects the nodes I_n before starting the experiment, while the dynamic super-node recruits the nodes on the fly.

3.1 Static Super-node Algorithm

The static super-node is selected by n nodes from G without replacement to form I_n. If the graph is disconnected, I_n must contain at least one node of each component of interest. To construct I_n we can crawl each component of the graph G. For instance, one can make I_n be the n largest degree nodes seen in a set of random walks with a total of $k > n$ steps (as in Avrachenkov et al. [3]). Because random walks are biased towards large-degree nodes the resulting super-node S_n tends to have large degrees.

Once I_n is chosen we form the virtual graph $G'(I_n)$ and start m random walk tours from the virtual super-node S_n. We stop each tour when the walk comes back to S_n. One practical issue in building I_n is knowing how many nodes we need to recruit to keep the random walk tours short. To ameliorate the situation in what follows we consider a dynamic algorithm to select the super-node.

3.2 Dynamic Super-node Algorithm

In a dynamic super-node, nodes are added into the super-node *on-demand* using a different random walk called the super-node recruiting walk. The super-node S_j starts with $j \geq 1$ nodes. S_j must span nodes in all graph components. The algorithm is as follows:

1. Run a super-node recruiting walk independent of all previous tours starting from S_n, $n \geq j$. Once a node of interest i, or set of nodes, are reached, stop the super-node recruiting walk.

2. Add a newly recruited node i to the super-node S_n, $n \geq j$, $S_{n+1} = S_n \cup \{i\}$. If node i appears in any of the previous tours, break these tour into multiple tours where i either ends or starts a new tour.

3. Generate a random number k_{redo} from the negative binomial distribution with number of successes as the number of previous tours (not counting the broken tours) and probability of success $d_{S_n}/d_{S_{n+1}}$, where $d_{S_{n+1}}$ is the degree of the new super-node that includes i and d_{S_n} is the degree of the super-node without i.

4. Perform $k_{\text{redo}} - k_{\text{broken}} > 0$ tours, where k_{broken} is the number of broken tours that start with node i and have length greater than two. These tours start at node i in

$G'(S_i)$ with a first step into nodes in $N(i)\backslash S_{i+1}$, where $N(i)$ are the neighbors of i in $G'(S_i)$. The tour ends at either S_n or i. Note that in $G'(S_{i+1})$ these tours start at S_{i+1} and end at S_{i+1} with length greater than two. If $k_{\text{redo}} - k_{\text{broken}} < 0$ then randomly remove tours starting at i until only k_{redo} tours remain.

5. Redo steps 2–4 until all recruited nodes are added to the super-node.

6. We can now proceed normally with new super-node tours (or recruit more nodes if necessary by redoing steps 1–4).

The step 4 calculates the number of tours that might have happened in the past when the new node i was part of S_n. This retrospective event can be recreated by sampling from a negative binomial distribution with appropriate parameters.

3.3 Equivalence Between Dynamic and Static Super-node Sample Paths

In what follows we show that the tours of a dynamic super-node S_n^{dyn} and the tours of the same super-node as a static super-node have the same probability distribution.

Theorem 1. *Let $\mathcal{D}_m^{(dyn)}$ denote the set of m tours according to the super-node dynamic algorithm over $n \geq 1$ steps, resulting in super-node S_n and $\mathcal{D}_m^{(st)}$ denote the set of m tours according to the static super-node algorithm using super-node S_n. The dynamic super-node sample paths and the static super-node sample paths are equivalent in distribution, that is, $P[\mathcal{D}_m^{(dyn)}(S_n) = Q] = P[\mathcal{D}_m^{(st)}(S_n) = Q]$, $n \geq 1, \forall S_n \subset V, \forall Q$, where $m > 1$ is the number of tours.*

PROOF. We prove by induction. Let $\sigma(\omega, S, \mathcal{E})$ be a deterministic function that is given an infinite random vector ω, where $\omega(1), \omega(2), \ldots \sim \text{Uniform}(0,1)$ are i.i.d. random variables, and a vector of starting nodes S and terminal nodes $\mathcal{E}$ as inputs and outputs a sample path of a random walk on the original graph G that starts at a node $u \in S$ with probability proportional to d_u and ends when it reaches any node in $\mathcal{E}$.

In what follows I_i denotes a set of i nodes as well as a vector of i nodes, $i \geq 1$. We add an arbitrary node outside I_i, $v \in V\backslash I_i$, into the first position $I_{i+1} = (v, I_i)$ and consider the deterministic sample path function:

$$\sigma^{(\text{dyn})}(\omega, I_i, v) = \begin{cases} (v, \sigma') & \text{, if } \omega(1) \leq d_v/\text{vol}(I_{i+1}) \\ \sigma(\omega', I_i, I_{i+1}) & \text{, otherwise,} \end{cases}$$

where $\text{vol}(S) = \sum_{t \in S} d_t$, $\sigma' = \sigma((\omega(2), \ldots), \{v\}, I_{i+1})$, $\omega' = ((\omega(1) - p_v)/(1 - p_v), \omega(2), \ldots)$, with $p_v = d_v/\text{vol}(I_{i+1})$. Note that by construction

$$\mathcal{D}_m^{(\text{st})}(I_i) = \{\sigma(\omega_k, I_i, I_i) : k = 1, \ldots, m, |\sigma(\omega_k, I_i, I_i)| > 2\}$$

and if we aggregate the nodes I_i into a single super-node S_i these are independent sample paths of a random walk on the super-node graph $G'(I_i)$ starting from super-node S_i. Similarly, if the choice of nodes in I_i are independent of the random vectors $\{\omega_k\}_{k=1}^m$ then

$$\mathcal{D}_m^{(\text{dyn})}(I_i) = \{r : r := \sigma^{\text{dyn}}(\omega_k, I_{i-1}, u), k = 1, \ldots, m, |r| > 2\},$$

where $u \in I_i \backslash I_{i-1}$, and $\mathcal{D}_m^{(\text{dyn})}(I_i)$ are the sample paths of the random walk described by the dynamic super-node algorithm with node addition sequence I_i.

Our proof is by induction on i. For $S_1 = \{v\}$, $v \in V$ it is clear that $\sigma^{\text{dyn}}(\omega, \emptyset, v) = \sigma(\omega, I_1, I_1)$, $\forall \omega$. By induction assume that $\sigma^{\text{dyn}}(\omega, I_{i-1}, u) = \sigma(\omega, I_i, I_i)$, $\forall \omega$, $i \geq 2$ and $u \in I_i \backslash I_{i-1}$. By construction the only possible difference between the sample paths of σ and σ^{dyn} is how they select the sample paths starting with u, the first node in the vector I_i. But by our induction assumption these two deterministic functions are equivalent and u is selected with probability $d_u/\text{vol}(I_i)$. Thus, using the same deterministic rule σ selects v, the first element of vector I_{i+1}, with probability $d_v/\text{vol}(I_{i+1})$ making $\sigma^{\text{dyn}}(\omega, I_i, v) = \sigma(\omega, I_{i+1}, I_{i+1})$ and yielding

$$P[\mathcal{D}_m^{(\text{dyn})}(I_n) = Q] = P[\mathcal{D}_m^{(\text{st})}(I_n) = Q], \quad \forall n, I_n, Q.$$

To finish the proof note that for $v \in I_{i+1} \backslash I_i$, the the deterministic rule σ guarantees that we are selecting tours starting from v with probability $d_v/\text{vol}(I_{i+1})$. This rule is equivalent to the dynamic super-node algorithm that starts k_{redo} tours from v once v is added to the super-node, where k_{redo} is a negative binomial random variable with success probability $\text{vol}(I_i)/\text{vol}(I_{i+1})$. The success probability in the algorithm is $d_{I_i}/d_{I_{i+1}}$ because by definition the algorithm, like our definition of $\mathcal{D}_m^{(\text{dyn})}(I_{i+1})$, disregards tours of size two which only contain nodes in I_{i+1}. □

4. FREQUENTIST APPROACH

In what follows we present our main results for the estimators.

4.1 Estimator of $\mu(G)$

Theorem 2 proposes an unbiased estimator of $\mu(G)$ in equation (1) via random walk tours. Later in Section 5 we present the approximate posterior distribution of this unbiased estimator.

To compute an estimate of $\mu(G)$ using super-node tours we define a function f and a set H over the modified graph $G'(I_n)$ as follows.

(a) If $\forall (u, v) \in E$, s.t. $u \in I_n$, $v \in V \backslash I_n$ the function $g(u, v)$ can be obtained with little overhead (using extra API queries to find all the neighbors of $u \in I_n$ and further querying them to find the function $g(u, v)$), then we define f as

$$f(u, v) = \begin{cases} g(u, v) & \text{, if } u \neq S_n, v \neq S_n \\ 0 & \text{, if } u \text{ or } v = S_n \text{ .} \end{cases} \tag{2}$$

Define $H = \{(u, v) : (u, v) \in E \text{ s.t. } u \in I_n \textbf{ or } v \in I_n\}$.

(b) Otherwise we define f as

$$f(u, v) = \begin{cases} g(u, v) & \text{if } u \neq S_n, v \neq S_n \\ \frac{1}{k_{xS}} \sum_{w \in I_n} g(u, w) & \text{if } u \text{ or } v = S_n, \end{cases} \tag{3}$$

where $x = u$ if $u \neq S_n$, $x = v$ if $v \neq S_n$ and k_{yS} is the number of neighbors of node $y \in V \backslash I_n$ that are in I_n. Define $H = \{(u, v) : (u, v) \in E \text{ s.t. } u, v \in I_n\}$.

Let $\mu(G')$ be contribution from G' to the true value $\mu(G)$ and $\mu(G') = \sum_{(u,v) \in E'} f(u, v)$.

Theorem 2. *Let G be an unknown undirected graph where $n > 0$ initial* arbitrary *set of nodes is known $I_n \subseteq V$ which span all the different connected components of G. Consider a random walk on the augmented multigraph G' described in Section 2 starting at super-node S_n. Let $(X_t^{(k)})_{t=1}^{\xi_k}$ be the k-th random walk tour until the walk first returns to S_n and let $\mathcal{D}_m(S_n)$ denote the collection of all nodes in $m \geq 1$ such tours, $\mathcal{D}_m(S_n) = \left((X_t^{(k)})_{t=1}^{\xi_k}\right)_{k=1}^{m}$. Then,*

$$\hat{\mu}(\mathcal{D}_m(S_n)) = \overbrace{\frac{d_{S_n}}{2m}\sum_{k=1}^{m}\sum_{t=2}^{\xi_k} f(X_{t-1}^{(k)}, X_t^{(k)})}^{\text{Estimate from crawls}} + \overbrace{\sum_{(u,v)\in H} g(u,v)}^{\text{Given knowledge from nodes in } I_n}, \tag{4}$$

is an unbiased estimate of $\mu(G)$, i.e., $\mathbb{E}[\hat{\mu}(\mathcal{D}_m(S_n))] = \mu(G)$. Moreover the estimator is strongly consistent, i.e., $\hat{\mu}(\mathcal{D}_m(S_n)) \to \mu(G)$ a.s. for $m \to \infty$.

The proof of Theorem 2 is in Appendix A. Theorem 2 provides an unbiased estimate of network statistics from random walk tours. The length of tour k is short if it starts at a massive super-node as the expected tour length is inversely proportional to the degree of the super-node, $\mathbb{E}[\xi_k] \propto 1/d_{S_n}$. This provides a practical way to compute unbiased estimates of node, edge, and triangle statistics using $\hat{\mu}(\mathcal{D}_m(S_n))$ (eq. (4)) while observing only a small fraction of the original graph. Because random walk tours can have arbitrary lengths, we show in Lemma 2, Section 4.4, that there are upper and lower bounds on the variance of $\hat{\mu}(\mathcal{D}_m(S_n))$. For a bounded function f, the upper bounds are shown to be always finite.

4.2 Confidence interval of the estimator

In what follows we give confidence intervals for the estimator presented in Theorem 2. Let

$$\bar{f}_m = m^{-1}\sum_{k=1}^{m}\left(\frac{d_{S_n}}{2}\sum_{t=2}^{\xi_k} f(X_{t-1}^{(k)}, X_t^{(k)})\right),$$

$$\hat{\sigma}_m^2 = m^{-1}\sum_{k=1}^{m}\left(\frac{d_{S_n}}{2}\sum_{t=2}^{\xi_k} f(X_{t-1}^{(k)}, X_t^{(k)}) - \bar{f}_m\right)^2.$$

If $\Phi(x)$ is the CDF of the standard Gaussian distribution, then for a known constant $c > 0$ [6]:

$$\sup_x \left| P\left\{\sqrt{m}\left(\frac{\bar{f}_m - \mu(G')}{\hat{\sigma}_m}\right) < x\right\} - \Phi(x)\right| \leq \frac{c\beta}{\sigma^3\sqrt{m}}, \tag{5}$$

where

$$\beta = \mathbb{E}\left[\left|\frac{d_{S_n}}{2}\sum_{t=2}^{\xi_k} f(X_{t-1}^{(k)}, X_t^{(k)}) - \mu(G')\right|^3\right],$$

$$\sigma^2 = \operatorname{Var}\left[\sum_{t=2}^{\xi_k} f(X_{t-1}^{(k)}, X_t^{(k)})\right].$$

Moreover, $\sigma^2 < \infty$ for a bounded function f as we will prove in Lemma 2(i) in Section 4.4 and $\beta < \infty$ through the C_r inequality [17, Chapter 3, Theorem 2.2].

Therefore, with $\epsilon > 0$ and large m (number of tours) within the confidence interval $[\hat{\mu}(\mathcal{D}_m(S_n)) - \epsilon, \hat{\mu}(\mathcal{D}_m(S_n)) + \epsilon]$ yields

$$P\left(|\mu(G) - \hat{\mu}(\mathcal{D}_m(S_n))| \leq \epsilon\right) \approx 1 - 2\Phi\left(\frac{\epsilon\sqrt{m}}{\hat{\sigma}_m}\right).$$

with the rate of convergence given by equation (5).

4.3 Estimation and hypothesis testing in random graph models

Here we study $\mu(G)$ when the connections in graph G are made randomly while keeping the node attributes and node degrees the same as the observed graph. Two types of random graph generation are considered here: configuration model and Chung-Lu model. These models can be regarded as null hypotheses in graph hypothesis testing problem. First we estimate the expected value $\mathbb{E}[\mu(G)]$ in these random graph models. Then we seek, *with how much certainty* the value $\mu(G)$ of the observed graph could possibly belong to a random network with the same node attributes and degrees as that of the observed graph, all this with partial knowledge of the original graph.

4.3.1 Estimators for Configuration model and Chung-Lu random graphs

Configuration model is an important class of random graph model. For a given degree sequence over the nodes, the configuration model creates random edge connections by uniformly selecting pairs of half edges. We assume that the number of nodes N and number of edges M are known (The estimation of N and M can be done explicitly, for instance using the techniques in [28] and [10]). The probability that the nodes u and v are connected in the configuration model is $d_u d_v/(2M-1)$ if $u \neq v$ and the probability of a self-edge from node u to itself is $\binom{d_u}{2}/(2M-1)$.

Another important model, Chung-Lu random graph [8] is a generalized version of Erdős-Renyi graphs and is closely related to configuration model. Chung-Lu model takes the positive weights $w_1, \ldots, w_N$ corresponding to nodes $1, \ldots, N$ as input and generates a graph with average degrees as these weights. The edges are created between any two vertices u and v independently of all others with probability $w_u w_v / \sum_{k=1}^{N} w_k$, when $u \neq v$, and for the self loops at node u, with a probability $\binom{w_u}{2}/\sum_{k=1}^{n} w_k$.

In the case of Chung-Lu random graphs, from [2], it is known that the weights $w_1, \ldots, w_N$ in fact becomes the actual degrees $d_1, \ldots, d_N$ asymptotically and the following concentration bound exists: for $c > 0$,

$$\mathbb{P}\left(\max_{1\leq i\leq N}\left|\frac{d_i}{w_i} - 1\right| \geq \beta\right) \leq \frac{2}{N^{c/4} - 1}, \text{ if } \beta \geq \frac{c\log N}{w_{\min}} = o(1).$$

Thus we take the sequence $\{w_k\}$ as $\{d_k\}$ of the observed graph. One main advantage in using Chung-Lu model compared to configuration model is that the edges are independent to each other.

For brevity we will use G_{obs} for the observed graph, G_{conf} for an instance of the configuration model with the same degree sequence $\{d_k\}$ as that of G and $G_{\text{C-L}}$ for the Chung-Lu graph sample with weights as $\{d_k\}$. Note that $\mu(G_{\text{conf}})$ and $\mu(G_{\text{C-L}})$ are random variables. Thus we look for $\mathbb{E}[\mu(G_{\text{conf}})]$ and $\mathbb{E}[\mu(G_{\text{C-L}})]$, where the expectation is with respect to the probability distribution of the configuration model and Chung-Lu model respectively. The values of $\mathbb{E}[\mu(G_{\text{C-L}})]$ and $\mathbb{E}[\mu(G_{\text{conf}})]$ are nearly the same, but for higher moments the values are different since configuration model introduces correlation between edges.

Now the expected value in the Chung-Lu model is

$$\mathbb{E}[\mu(G_{\text{C-L}})] = \sum_{\substack{(u,v)\in E\cup E^c \\ u\neq v}} g(u,v)\,\frac{d_u d_v}{2M} + \sum_{\substack{(u,v)\in E\cup E^c \\ u=v}} g(u,v)\,\frac{\binom{d_u}{2}}{2M}. \quad (6)$$

In order to calculate $\mathbb{E}[\mu(G_{\text{C-L}})]$, we need to know the missing edge set E^c. The set E^c is revealed once the entire graph is crawled, which is not possible in the context of this paper. The idea is to estimate $\mathbb{E}[\mu(G_{\text{C-L}})]$ from the tours of a random walk. Since the classical random walk which we have used so far, could sample only from E, we resort to a new random walk that could make samples from E^c as well.

We use random walk with uniform restarts (RWuR) [4] in which if the crawler is at a node i, with a probability $d_i/(d_i+\alpha)$ the crawler chooses one of the neighbors uniformly (RW strategy) and with a probability $\alpha/(d_i+\alpha)$, the crawler chooses the next node by uniformly sampling all the nodes. The parameter $\alpha > 0$ controls the rate of uniform sampling (which has higher cost in many OSNs).

Define a new function f' whose value depends on the crawling strategy as follows: let u, v be the nodes chosen by the crawling technique (RWuR or RW) in order,

$$f'(u,v) = \begin{cases} g(u,v)\frac{d_u d_v}{2M-1} & \text{if } u,v \neq S_n \\ \sum_{w\in I_n} g(u,w)\frac{d_u d_w}{2M-1} & \text{if } u\neq S_n, v = S_n \\ & (u,v) \text{ selected} \\ & \text{by unif. sampling} \\ \frac{1}{k_{uS}}\sum_{w\in I_n} g(u,w)\frac{d_u d_w}{2M-1} & \text{if } u\neq S_n, v = S_n \\ & (u,v) \text{ selected by RW} \end{cases} \quad (7)$$

where k_{uS} is defined in (3). In the new graph G' there will be k_{uS} multiple edges between u and S_n and k_{uS} is introduced in the last term is to take into account this. In case of classical random walk, the second criteria does not exist.

We denote $W'_k = \sum_{t=2}^{\xi_k} f'(X^{(k)}_{t-1}, X^{(k)}_t)$ when RWuR is employed as the random walk technique for crawling the graph and $W''_k = \sum_{t=2}^{\xi_k} f'(X^{(k)}_{t-1}, X^{(k)}_t)$, when the classical random walk is used for crawling. Let

$$R = \frac{1}{2}\sum_{\substack{(u,v)\in I_n\times I_n \\ u\neq v}} g(u,v)\frac{d_u d_v}{(2M-1)} + \frac{1}{2}\sum_{\substack{(u,v)\in I_n\times I_n \\ u=v}} g(u,v)\frac{\binom{d_u}{2}}{(2M-1)}.$$

The value R can be calculated a priori from the knowledge of I_n. In the lemma below we propose an estimator for $\mathbb{E}[\mu(G_{\text{C-L}})]$ and proves that it is unbiased.

Lemma 1. *The estimator*

$$\hat{\mu}_C(\mathcal{D}_m(S_n)) = \frac{1}{m}\sum_{k=1}^{m}\left[\frac{N'(d_{S_n}+\alpha)}{2\alpha}W'_k - \frac{N' d_{S_n}}{2\alpha}W''_k + R\right],$$

is an unbiased estimator of $\mathbb{E}[\mu(G_{\text{C-L}})]$ *of the Chung-Lu model.*

PROOF. See Appendix A □

4.3.2 A hypothesis testing problem for the Chung-Lu model

The Chung-Lu model or configuration model can be regarded as a null hypothesis model and comparing $\mu(G_{\text{obs}})$ to $\mathbb{E}[\mu(G_{\text{C-L}})]$ or $\mathbb{E}[\mu(G_{\text{conf}})]$ answers many questions like whether the connections are formed based on degrees alone with no other influence or whether the edges are formed purely at random?

Let $G_{\text{C-L}}(V_{\text{C-L}}, E_{\text{C-L}})$ be a sample of the Chung-Lu model with weights $\{d_k\}$. Like the estimator of $\mathbb{E}[\mu(G_{\text{C-L}})]$, the estimator of $\text{Var}(G_{\text{C-L}})$, $\widehat{\text{Var}}_{\text{C-L}}(\mathcal{D}_m(S_n))$ can be constructed as follows: modify $g(u,v)\frac{d_u d_v}{2M}$ to $g^2(u,v)\frac{d_u d_v}{2M}(1-\frac{d_u d_v}{2M})$ in the function f' in (7).

By invoking Lindeberg central limit theorem [17, Chapter 7, Section 2], for independent non-identically distributed Bernoulli random variables[2], we get

$$\sum_{(u,v)\in E_{\text{C-L}}} f(u,v) \sim \text{Normal}\left(\mathbb{E}[\mu(G_{\text{C-L}})], \text{Var}(G_{\text{C-L}})\right).$$

Hence a natural check is whether $\mu(G_{\text{obs}})$ is a sample from the above distribution. Since we have only one sample $\mu(G_{\text{obs}})$, a simple test is to check whether

$$|\hat{\mu}(\mathcal{D}(S_n)) - \hat{\mu}_C(\mathcal{D}(S_n))| \leq a\sqrt{\widehat{\text{Var}}_{\text{C-L}}(\mathcal{D}_m(S_n))},$$

holds for any $a = 1,2,3$ and for a large value of m . This condition is satisfied by a Gaussian sample with probabilities 0.6827, 0.9545, or 0.9973 respectively. On the other hand, the lower a is, the more certain that the sample belongs to this particular Gaussian distribution.

4.4 Impact of spectral gap on variance

In this section we derive results on higher moments of the estimator $\hat{\mu}(\mathcal{D}(S_n))$. Lemma 2, which follows, introduces upper and lower bounds on the variance of the i.i.d. the tour sum $\sum_{t=2}^{\xi_k} f(X^{(k)}_{t-1}, X^{(k)}_t)$, and also shows that all the moments exist. Moreover, the results in the lemma establish a connection between the estimator variance and the spectral gap.

Let $\mathbf{S} = \mathbf{D}^{1/2}\mathbf{P}\mathbf{D}^{-1/2}$, where $\mathbf{P} = \{p_{uv}\}$ is the random walk transition probability matrix as defined in Section 2 and $\mathbf{D} = \text{diag}(d_1, d_2, \ldots, d_{|V'|})$ is a diagonal matrix with the node degrees of G'. The eigenvalues $\{\lambda_i\}$ of $\mathbf{P}$ and $\mathbf{S}$ are same and $1 = \lambda_1 > \lambda_2 \geq \ldots \geq \lambda_{|V'|} \geq -1$. Let jth eigenvector of $\mathbf{S}$ be $(w_{ji}), 1 \leq i \leq |V|$. Let δ be the spectral gap, $\delta := 1-\lambda_2$. Let the left and right eigenvectors of $\mathbf{P}$ be v_j and u_j respectively. $d_{tot} := \sum_{v\in V'} d_v$. Define $\langle r, s\rangle_{\hat{\pi}} = \sum_{(u,v)\in E'} \hat{\pi}_{uv} r(u,v)s(u,v)$, with $\hat{\pi}_{uv} = \pi_u p_{uv}$, and matrix $\mathbf{P}^*$ with (j,i)th element as $p^*_{ji} = p_{ji} f(j,i)$. Also let $\hat{f}$ be the vector with $\hat{f}(j) = \sum_{i\in V'} p^*_{ji}$.

Lemma 2. *The following holds*

(i). Assuming the function f is bounded, $\max_{(i,j)\in E'} f(i,j) \leq B < \infty$, $B > 0$ and for tour $k \geq 1$,

$$\text{Var}\left[\sum_{t=2}^{\xi_k} f(X^{(k)}_{t-1}, X^{(k)}_t)\right]$$

[2]The necessary condition to hold this central limit theorem, the Lindeberg condition is satisfied by the sequence of independent Bernoulli random variables with different success probabilities $\{p_k\}$, if $0 < p_k < 1$. This is always true in our case when we assume $d_k > 0$ for all k.

$$\leq \frac{1}{d_{S_n}^2}\left(2d_{tot}^2 B^2 \sum_{i\geq 2}\frac{w_{S_n i}^2}{(1-\lambda_i)} - 4\mu^2(G_{S_n})\right)$$
$$- \frac{1}{d_{S_n}} B^2 d_{tot} + B^2$$
$$< B^2\left(\frac{2d_{tot}^2}{d_{S_n}^2 \delta} + 1\right).$$

Moreover,

$$\mathbb{E}\left[\left(\sum_{t=2}^{\xi_k} f(X_{t-1}^{(k)}, X_t^{(k)})\right)^l\right] < \infty \quad \forall l \geq 0.$$

(ii).

$$\mathrm{Var}\left[\sum_{t=2}^{\xi_k} f(X_{t-1}^{(k)}, X_t^{(k)}))\right]$$
$$\geq 2\frac{d_{tot}}{d_{S_n}}\sum_{i=2}^{r}\frac{\lambda_i}{1-\lambda_i}\langle f, v_i\rangle_{\hat{\pi}}(u_i^\intercal \hat{f}) + \frac{1}{d_{S_n}}\sum_{(u,v)\in E'} f(u,v)^2$$
$$+ \frac{1}{d_{tot} d_{S_n}}\left\{\sum_{(u,v)\in E'} f(u,v)^2\right\}^2$$
$$+ \frac{1}{d_{tot} d_{S_n}}\sum_{u\in V'} d_u\left\{\sum_{u\sim v} f(u,v)\right\}^2$$
$$- \frac{4}{d_{S_n}^2}\left\{\sum_{(u,v)\in E'} f(u,v)\right\}^2$$
$$- \frac{8}{d_{tot}}\left\{\sum_{(u,v)\in E'} f(u,v)\right\}^2 \sum_{i\geq 2}\frac{w_{S_n i}^2}{(1-\lambda_i)}$$
$$- \frac{4}{d_{tot} d_{S_n}}\left\{\sum_{(u,v)\in E'} f(u,v)\right\}^2. \quad (8)$$

PROOF. See Appendix B. □

5. BAYESIAN APPROACH

In this section we consider Bayesian formulation of our problem and derive the posterior of $\mu(G)$ given the tours and provide a consistent maximum a posteriori estimator (MAP).

Approximate posterior

For the same scenario of Theorem 2 for $m \geq 2$ tours let

$$\hat{F}_h = \frac{d_{S_n}}{2\lfloor\sqrt{m}\rfloor}\sum_{k=((h-1)\lfloor\sqrt{m}\rfloor+1)}^{h\lfloor\sqrt{m}\rfloor}\sum_{t=2}^{\xi_h} f(X_{t-1}^{(k)}, X_t^{(k)}) + \sum_{(u,v)\in H} g(u,v),$$

which is similar to equation (4) but first sums a range of $\lfloor\sqrt{m}\rfloor$ tours rather than all m tours. Let σ_F^2 be the variance of $\hat{F}_h$. Assuming priors

$$\mu(G)|\sigma_F^2 \sim \mathrm{Normal}(\mu_0, \sigma_F^2/m_0)$$
$$\sigma_F^2 \sim \text{Inverse-gamma}(\nu_0/2, \nu_0\sigma_0^2/2),$$

then for large values of m, the marginal posterior density of $\mu(G)$ can be approximated by a *non-standardized t - distribution*

$$\phi(x|\nu, \widetilde{\mu}, \widetilde{\sigma}) = \frac{\Gamma\left(\frac{\nu+1}{2}\right)}{\Gamma\left(\frac{\nu}{2}\right)\widetilde{\sigma}\sqrt{\pi\nu}}\left(1 + \frac{(x-\widetilde{\mu})^2}{\widetilde{\sigma}^2\nu}\right)^{-\frac{\nu+1}{2}}, \quad (9)$$

with degrees of freedom parameter

$$\nu = \nu_0 + \lfloor\sqrt{m}\rfloor,$$

location parameter

$$\widetilde{\mu} = \frac{m_0\mu_0 + \lfloor\sqrt{m}\rfloor\hat{\mu}(\mathcal{D}_m(S_n))}{m_0 + \lfloor\sqrt{m}\rfloor},$$

and scale parameter

$$\widetilde{\sigma}^2 = \frac{\nu_0\sigma_0^2 + \sum_{k=1}^{\lfloor\sqrt{m}\rfloor}(\hat{F}_k - \hat{\mu}(\mathcal{D}_m(S_n)))^2 + \frac{m_0\lfloor\sqrt{m}\rfloor(\hat{\mu}(\mathcal{D}_m(S_n))-\mu_0)^2}{m_0+\lfloor\sqrt{m}\rfloor}}{(\nu_0 + \lfloor\sqrt{m}\rfloor)(m_0 + \lfloor\sqrt{m}\rfloor)}.$$

The derivation is detailed in Section 5.1 later.

Remark 1. Note that the approximation (9) is Bayesian and Theorem 2 is its frequentist counterpart. In fact, the motivation of our Bayesian approach comes from the frequentist estimator. From the approximate posterior in (9), the Bayesian MAP estimator is

$$\hat{\mu}_{\mathrm{MAP}} = \arg\max_x \phi(x|v, \widetilde{\mu}, \widetilde{\sigma}) = \widetilde{\mu}.$$

Thus for large values of m, the Bayesian estimator $\hat{\mu}_{\mathrm{MAP}}$ is essentially the frequentist estimator $\hat{\mu}(\mathcal{D}_m(S_n))$, which is unbiased, and hence the MAP estimator is consistent.

The above remark shows that the approximate posterior in (9) provides a way to access the confidence in the estimate $\hat{\mu}(\mathcal{D}_m(S_n))$. The Normal prior for the average gives the largest variance given a given mean. The inverse-gamma is a non-informative conjugate prior if the variance of the estimator is not too small [13], which is generally the case in our application. Other choices of prior, such as uniform, are also possible yielding different posteriors without closed-form solutions [13].

Remark 2. Another asymptotic result in Bayesian analysis, the classic Bernstein-von Mosses Theorem [36, Chapter 10] is not useful in our scenario. The Bernstein-von Mosses Theorem states that irrespective of the prior distribution, when μ is the random parameter of likelihood, then posterior distribution of $\sqrt{m}(\mu - \hat{\mu}_m^{\mathrm{MLE}})$ converges to Normal$(0, I(\mu_0)^{-1})$, where $\hat{\mu}_m^{\mathrm{MLE}}$ is the maximum likelihood estimator (MLE) and $I(\mu_0)$ is the Fisher information at the true value μ_0. But note that in cases like ours, where the distribution of $W_k = \sum_{t=2}^{\xi_k} f(X_{t-1}^{(k)}, X_t^{(k)})$ is unknown, $k \geq 1$, the Fisher information is also unknown. In contrast, our approximate posterior of $\mu(G)$ uses only the available information and does not need to guess the distribution of W_k.

5.1 Derivation of approximate posterior

In this section we derive the approximation (9) of the posterior. The approximation relies first on showing that $\hat{\mu}(\mathcal{D}_m(S_n))$ has finite second moment. By Lemma 2 the variance of $\sum_{t=2}^{\xi_k} f(X_{t-1}^{(k)}, X_t^{(k)})$, $k \geq 1$, is also finite.

We are now ready to give the approximation in equation (9). Let $m' = \lfloor\sqrt{m}\rfloor$,

$$\hat{F}_h = \frac{d_{S_n}}{2m'}\sum_{k=((h-1)m'+1)}^{hm'}\sum_{t=2}^{\xi_h} f(X_{t-1}^{(k)}, X_t^{(k)}) + \sum_{(u,v)\in H} g(u,v).$$

and $\{\hat{F}_h\}_{h=1}^{m'}$ and because the tours are i.i.d. the marginal posterior density of μ is

$$P[\mu|\{\hat{F}_h\}_{h=1}^{m'}] = \int_0^\infty P[\mu|\sigma_F^2, \{\hat{F}_h\}_{h=1}^{m'}]P[\sigma_F^2|\{\hat{F}_h\}_{h=1}^{m'}]d\sigma_F^2 .$$

For now assume that $\{\hat{F}_h\}_{h=1}^{m'}$ are i.i.d. normally distributed random variables, and let

$$\hat{\sigma}_{m'} = \sum_{h=1}^{m'} (\hat{F}_h - \hat{\mu}(\mathcal{D}_m(S_n)))^2,$$

then [20, Proposition C.4]

$$\mu|\sigma_F^2, \{\hat{F}_h\}_{h=1}^{m'} \sim \text{Normal}\left(\frac{m_0\mu_0 + \sum_{h=1}^{m'} \hat{F}_h}{m_0 + m'}, \frac{\sigma_F^2}{m_0 + m'}\right),$$

$$\sigma_F^2|\{\hat{F}_h\}_{h=1}^{m'} \sim \text{Inverse-Gamma}\Bigg(\frac{\nu_0 + m'}{2}, \frac{\nu_0\sigma_0^2 + \hat{\sigma}_{m'} + \frac{m_0 m'}{m_0+m'}(\mu_0 - \hat{\mu}(\mathcal{D}_m(S_n)))^2}{2}\Bigg),$$

are the posteriors of parameters μ and σ_F^2, respectively. The non-standardized t-distribution can be seen as a mixture of normal distributions with equal mean and random variance inverse-gamma distributed [20, Proposition C.6]. Thus, if $\{\hat{F}_h\}_{h=1}^{m'}$ are i.i.d. normally distributed then the posterior of $\mu(G)$ given $\mathcal{D}_{m'}(S_n)$ is a non-standardized t-distributed with parameters

$$\tilde{\mu} = \frac{m_0\mu_0 + \sum_{h=1}^{m'} \hat{F}_h}{m0 + m'},$$

$$\tilde{\sigma}^2 = \frac{\nu_0\sigma_0^2 + \sum_{k=1}^{m'} (\hat{F}_k - \hat{\mu}(\mathcal{D}_m(S_n)))^2 + \frac{m_0 m'(\hat{\mu}(\mathcal{D}_m(S_n)) - \mu_0)^2}{m_0+m'}}{(\nu_0 + m')(m_0 + m')}, \qquad \nu = \nu_0 + m'$$

where $\tilde{\mu}, \tilde{\sigma}^2$ and ν are location, scale and degree of freedom parameters of the student-t distribution. Left to show is that $\{\hat{F}_h\}_{h=1}^{m'}$ converge *in distribution* to i.i.d. normal random variables as $m \to \infty$. As the spectral gap of $G'(I_n)$ is greater than zero, $|\lambda_1 - \lambda_2| > 0$, Lemma 2 shows that for $W_k = \sum_{t=2}^{\xi_k} f(X_{t-1}^{(k)}, X_t^{(k)})$, $\sigma_W^2 = \text{Var}(W_k) < \infty, \forall k$. From the renewal theorem we know that $\{W_k\}_{k=1}^{m}$ are i.i.d. random variables and thus any subset of these variables is also i.i.d.. By construction $\hat{F}_1, \ldots, \hat{F}_{m'}$ are also i.i.d. with mean $\mu(G)$ and finite variance. Applying the Lindeberg-Lévy central limit theorem [11, Section 17.4] yields

$$\sqrt{m'}(\hat{F}_h - \mu(G)) \xrightarrow{d} \text{Normal}(0, \sigma_W^2), \quad \forall h .$$

Thus, for large values of m (recall that $m' = \lfloor\sqrt{m}\rfloor$), $\{\hat{F}_h\}_{h=1}^{m'}$ are approximately i.i.d. normally distributed

$$\hat{F}_h \sim \text{Normal}(\mu(G), \sigma_W^2/m') , \quad \forall h .$$

This completes the derivation of the approximation (9). In what follows we present our results over real-world networks.

6. EXPERIMENTS ON REAL-WORLD NETWORKS

In this section we demonstrate the effectiveness of the theory developed above with the experiments on real data sets of various social networks. We have chosen to work with the datasets where the value $\mu(G)$ is available. This way it is possible to check the correctness of the results obtained via experiments. We assume the contribution from super-node to the true value is known a priori and hence we look for $\mu(G')$ in the experiments. In the case that the edges of the super-node are unknown, the estimation problem is easier and can be taken care separately. One option is to start multiple random walks in the graph and form connected subgraphs. Later, in order to estimate the bias created by this subgraph, do some random walk tours from the largest degree node in each of these sub graph and use the idea in Theorem 3.

In the figures we display both the approximate posterior generated from $\hat{F}_h$ with one only run of the experiment and empirical posterior created from multiple runs. For the approximate posterior, we have used the following parameters $m_0 =, \nu_0 = 0, \mu_0 = 0.1, \sigma_0 = 1$ (see (9)). The green line in the plots shows the actual value $\mu(G')$.

We have used the dynamic super-node algorithm explained in Section 3.2. From the experiments, it is observed that the static super-node and dynamic super-node produces similar results which is in corroboration with Theorem 1. In the following experiments, we opt a simple strategy to decide when to run super-node recruiting walk: run the super-node recruiting walk when the number of original tours reaches multiples of a fixed integer and it stops when a node of degree exceeding a specific threshold is reached.

6.1 Friendster

First we study a network of moderate size, a connected subgraph of Friendster network with 64,600 nodes and 1,246, 479 edges (data publicly available at the SNAP repository [26]). Friendster is an online social networking website where nodes are individuals and edges indicate friendship. Here, we consider two types of functions:

$$1.\ f_1 = d_{X_t}.d_{X_{t+1}} \qquad 2.\ f_2 = \begin{cases} 1 \text{ if } d_{X_t} + d_{X_{t+1}} > 50 \\ 0 \text{ otherwise} \end{cases}$$

These functions reflect assortative nature of the network. The final super-node size is 10,000. Figures 2 and 3 display the results for functions f_1 and f_2, respectively. A good match between the approximate and empirical posteriors can be observed from the figures. Moreover the true value $\mu(G')$ is also fitting well with the plots. The percentage of graph crawled is 7.43% in terms of edges and is 24.44% in case of static super-node with uniform sampling.

6.2 Dogster network

The aim of this example is to check whether there is any affinity for making connections between the owners of same breed dogs [12]. The network data is based on the social networking website Dogster. Each user (node) indicates the dog breed; the friendships between dogs' owners form the edges. Number of nodes is 415,431 and number of edges is 8,265,511.

In Figure 4, two cases are plotted. Function f_1 counts the number of connections with different breeds as pals and

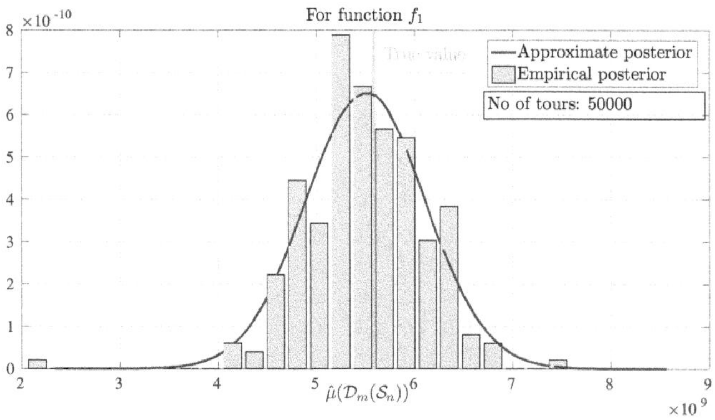

Figure 2: Friendster subgraph, function f_1

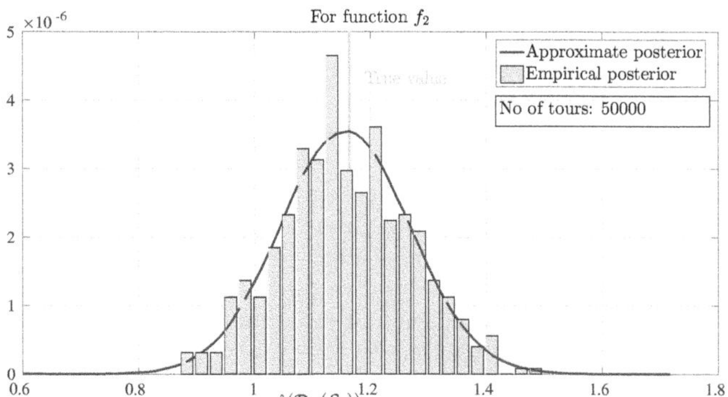

Figure 3: Friendster subgraph, function f_2

function f_2 counts connections between same breeds. The final super-node size is 10,000. The percentage of the graph crawled in terms of edges is 2.72% and in terms of nodes is 14.86%. While using the static super-node technique with uniform sampling, the graph crawled is 5.02% 2.72% (in terms of edges) and 37.17% (in terms of nodes) with the same super-node size. These values can be reduced much further if we allow a bit less precision in the match between approximate distribution and histogram.

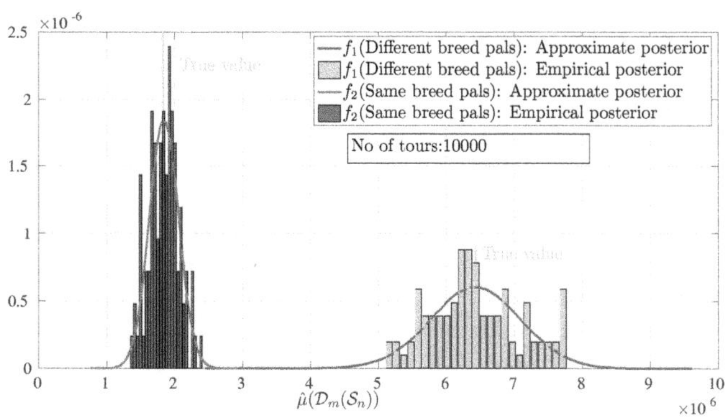

Figure 4: Dog pals network

In order to better understand the correlation in forming edges, we now consider the *configuration model*. We use the estimator $\hat{\mu}_C(\mathcal{D}(S_n))$ proposed in Section 4.3.1 (note that the estimator is same for Chung-Lu model and configuration model). It is important to recollect that this estimator does not require the knowledge of the complete network (in fact the Figures 5 and 6 are based on estimates from RWuR crawls which covered 8.9% of the graph). This is shown in blue line in Figure 5 and red line in Figure 6, and the true value is the net expected value given by (6). Moreover we run our original estimator $\hat{\mu}(\mathcal{D}(S_n))$ and calculated the approximate posterior on one random instance of the configuration model with same degree sequence of the original graph. Figure 5 compare function f_2 for the configuration model and original graph. The figure shows that in the correlated case (original graph), the affinity to form connection between same breed owners is around 7.5 times more than that in the uncorrelated case. Figure 6 shows similar figure in case of f_1.

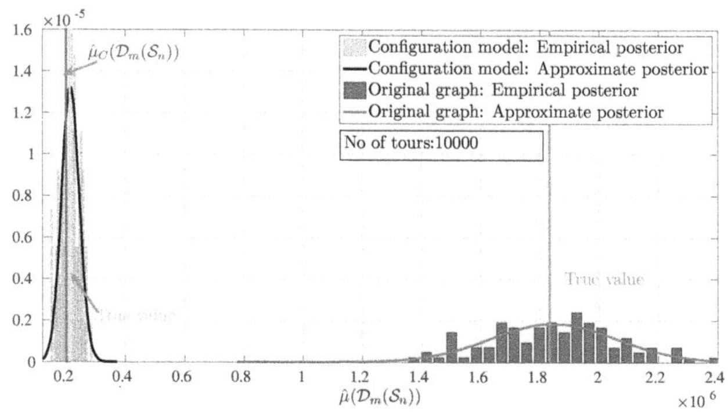

Figure 5: Dog pals network: Comparison between configuration model and original graph for f_2, number of connection between same breeds

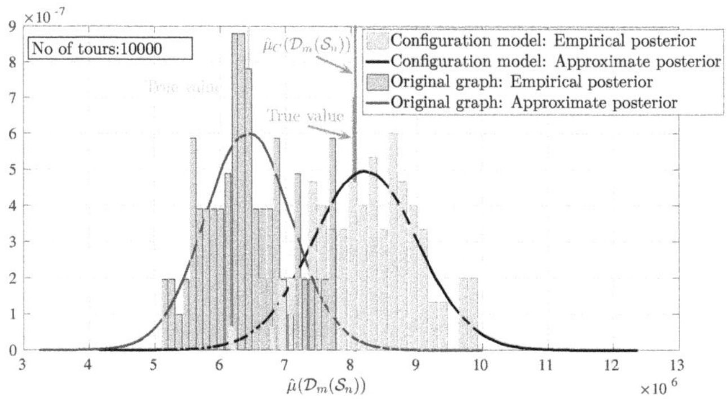

Figure 6: Dog pals network: Comparison between configuration model and original graph for f_1, number of connection between different breeds

6.3 ADD Health data

Though our main result in the approximation (9) holds when the number of tours is large, in this section we check with a small dataset. We consider ADD network project[3], a friendship network among high school students in US. The graph has 1545 nodes and 4003 edges.

We take two types of functions. Figure 7 shows the affinity in same gender or different gender friendships and Figure 8 displays the inclination towards same race or different race

[3]http://www.cpc.unc.edu/projects/addhealth

in friendships. The random walk tours covered around 10% of the graph. We find that the theory works reasonably well for this network data, for instance, the true values in both the cases in Figure 7 are nearly the same, and this is evident from the approximate posterior calculated from only one run. We have not added the empirical posterior in the figures since for such small sample sizes, the empirical distribution does not lead to a meaningful histogram.

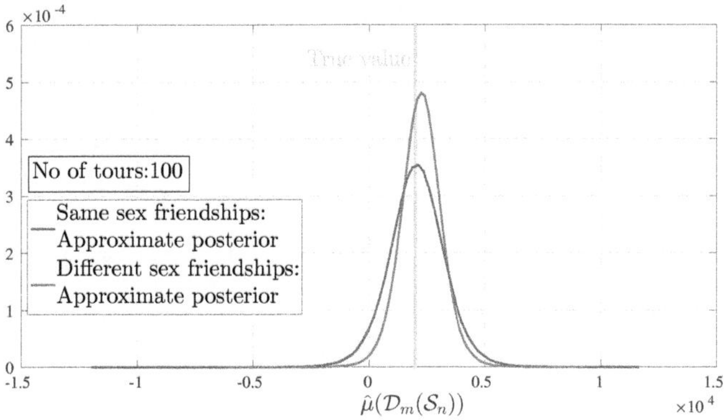

Figure 7: ADD network: effect of gender in relationships

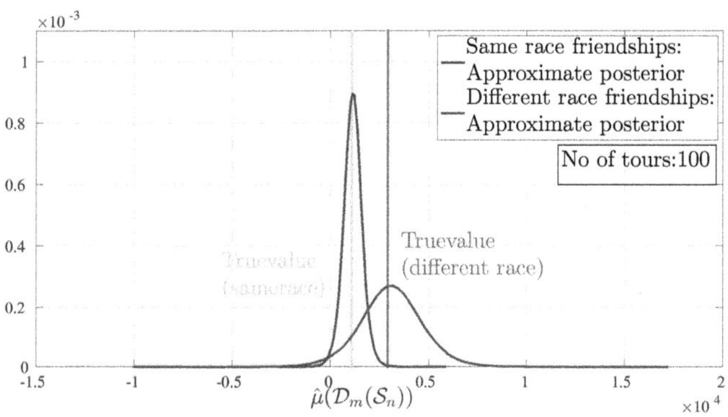

Figure 8: ADD network: effect of race in friendships

6.4 Check for Chung-Lu random graph model in Dogester

We use the same dataset and functions as in Section 6.2. Consider the function f_1, which is one when the owners of different breed dogs form connection, zero otherwise. For the Chung-Lu model, $\hat{\mu}_C(\mathcal{D}(S_n))$, the estimator of $\mathbb{E}[\mu(G_{\text{C-L}})]$ is 8.066×10^6 and $\widehat{\text{Var}}_C(\mathcal{D}(S_n))$, the estimator of $\text{Var}_C[\mu(G_{\text{C-L}})]$ is 6.3938×10^{11}. For the original graph, the estimated value $\mu(\mathcal{D}(S_n)) = 6.432\times 10^6$. Now

$$|\hat{\mu}_C(\mathcal{D}(S_n)) - \mu(\mathcal{D}(S_n))| \le a\sqrt{\widehat{\text{Var}}_C(\mathcal{D}(S_n))},$$

is satisfied for $a = 3$, but not for $a = 1, 2$. This implies there is a slight probability (0.0428) that $\mu(G)$ belongs to the values from different configurations of Chung-Lu model.

For function f_2, which is one when the owners of same breed dogs form connection, zero otherwise, $\hat{\mu}_C(\mathcal{D}(S_n)) = 1.995\times 10^5$, $\widehat{\text{Var}}_C(\mathcal{D}(S_n)) = 2.9919\times 10^4$ and for the original graph $\mu(\mathcal{D}(S_n)) = 1.831\times 10^6$. We find that

$$|\hat{\mu}_C(\mathcal{D}(S_n)) - \mu(\mathcal{D}(S_n))| \nleq a\sqrt{\widehat{\text{Var}}_C(\mathcal{D}(S_n))} \text{ for } a = 1, 2, 3.$$

Hence the probability that $\mu(G)$ belongs to the values generated by the random network made from Chung-Lu model is less than 0.0027, which is negligible. These two inferences can also be observed in Figures 6 and 5.

7. CONCLUSIONS

In this work we have introduced a method that by crawling a fraction of a large network can produce, to the best of our knowledge, the first non-asymptotic unbiased estimates of network node and edge characteristics. Our method is based on random walk tours and a dynamic super-node algorithm. We derive variance lower and upper bounds of this estimator and show its connection to the spectral gap of a random walk on the graph. One of our contributions is introducing an approximate Bayesian posterior of the network metric of interest using crawled data (random walk tours). We also derived a technique to study how a network looks "random" to a metric by estimating the same metric if the network was drawn from a Chung-Lu network or a configuration model with the same node labels and node degrees, all using random walk crawls without ever knowing the full original network. Our simulations over real-world networks show great accuracy of our estimators and approximations. In particular, the simulations clearly show that the derived posterior distribution fits very well with the data even when as few as 2.7% of the edges and less than 15% of the nodes in the network are observed by the crawl.

8. ACKNOWLEDGMENTS

This work was supported in part by NSF grant CNS-1065133 and ARL Cooperative Agreement W911NF-09-2-0053 and ADR "Network Science" of the Alcatel-Lucent Inria joint Lab. Research was partially conducted within the context of the THANES Associate Team, jointly supported by INRIA (France) and FAPERJ (Brazil). The authors would like to thank Arun Kadavankandy for the useful discussions.

9. REFERENCES

[1] D. Aldous and J. A. Fill. Reversible markov chains and random walks on graphs, 2002. Unfinished monograph, recompiled 2014, available at http://www.stat.berkeley.edu/~aldous/RWG/book.html.

[2] K. Avrachenkov, A. Kadavankandy, L. O. Prokhorenkova, and A. Raigorodskii. Pagerank in undirected random graphs. In *WAW*, 2015.

[3] K. Avrachenkov, N. Litvak, M. Sokol, and D. Towsley. Quick detection of nodes with large degrees. *Internet Mathematics*, 10(1-2):1–19, 2014.

[4] K. Avrachenkov, B. Ribeiro, and D. Towsley. Improving random walk estimation accuracy with uniform restarts. In *Algorithms and Models for the Web-Graph*, pages 98–109. Springer, 2010.

[5] F. Benevenuto, T. Rodrigues, M. Cha, and V. Almeida. Characterizing user behavior in online social networks. In *ACM SIGCOMM IMC*, pages 49–62. ACM, 2009.

[6] V. Bentkus and F. Gotze. The berry-esseen bound for student's statistic. *The Annals of Probability*, pages 491–503, 1996.

[7] P. Brémaud. *Markov chains: Gibbs fields, Monte Carlo simulation, and queue.* Springer, 2013.

[8] F. Chung and L. Lu. The average distances in random graphs with given expected degrees. *Proceedings of the National Academy of Sciences*, 99(25):15879–15882, 2002.

[9] F. R. Chung. *Spectral graph theory*, volume 92. American Mathematical Society, 1997.

[10] C. Cooper, T. Radzik, and Y. Siantos. Fast low-cost estimation of network properties using random walks. In *Algorithms and Models for the Web Graph*, pages 130–143. Springer, 2013.

[11] H. Cramér. *Mathematical methods of statistics*. Princeton university press, 1999.

[12] Dogster and C. friendships network dataset KONECT. http://konect.uni-koblenz.de/networks/petster-carnivore, May 2015.

[13] A. Gelman et al. Prior distributions for variance parameters in hierarchical models (comment on article by browne and draper). *Bayesian analysis*, 1(3):515–534, 2006.

[14] M. Gjoka, M. Kurant, C. T. Butts, and A. Markopoulou. Practical recommendations on crawling online social networks. *IEEE Journal on Selected Areas in Communications*, 29(9):1872–1892, 2011.

[15] M. Gjoka, M. Kurant, and A. Markopoulou. 2.5 k-graphs: from sampling to generation. In *IEEE INFOCOM*, pages 1968–1976, 2013.

[16] S. Goel and M. J. Salganik. Respondent-driven sampling as Markov chain Monte Carlo. *Statistics in medicine*, 28(17):2202–2229, 2009.

[17] A. Gut. *Probability: A Graduate Course*. Springer Science & Business Media, 2013.

[18] M. S. Handcock and K. J. Gile. Modeling social networks from sampled data. *The Annals of Applied Statistics*, 4(1):5–25, mar 2010.

[19] D. D. Heckathorn. Respondent-driven sampling: A new approach to the study of hidden populations. *Social Problems*, 44(2):174–199, 05 1997.

[20] S. Jackman. *Bayesian analysis for the social sciences*. John Wiley & Sons, 2009.

[21] J. G. Kemeny and J. L. Snell. *Finite Markov Chains*. Springer, 1983.

[22] J. H. Koskinen, G. L. Robins, and P. E. Pattison. Analysing exponential random graph (p-star) models with missing data using Bayesian data augmentation. *Statistical Methodology*, 7(3):366–384, may 2010.

[23] J. H. Koskinen, G. L. Robins, P. Wang, and P. E. Pattison. Bayesian analysis for partially observed network data, missing ties, attributes and actors. *Social Networks*, 35(4):514–527, oct 2013.

[24] J. Kunegis. Konect: the Koblenz network collection. In *WWW*, pages 1343–1350, 2013.

[25] C.-H. Lee, X. Xu, and D. Y. Eun. Beyond random walk and metropolis-hastings samplers: why you should not backtrack for unbiased graph sampling. In *ACM SIGMETRICS Performance Evaluation Review*, volume 40, pages 319–330, 2012.

[26] J. Leskovec and A. Krevl. SNAP Datasets: Stanford large network dataset collection. http://snap.stanford.edu/data, June 2014.

[27] J. G. Ligo, G. K. Atia, and V. V. Veeravalli. A controlled sensing approach to graph classification. *IEEE Transactions on Signal Processing*, 62(24):6468–6480, 2014.

[28] L. Massoulié, E. Le Merrer, A.-M. Kermarrec, and A. Ganesh. Peer counting and sampling in overlay networks: random walk methods. In *ACM PODS*, pages 123–132, 2006.

[29] S. P. Meyn and R. L. Tweedie. *Markov chains and stochastic stability*. Springer Science & Business Media, 2012.

[30] R. Ottoni, J. P. Pesce, D. B. Las Casas, G. Franciscani Jr, W. Meira Jr, P. Kumaraguru, and V. Almeida. Ladies first: Analyzing gender roles and behaviors in pinterest. In *ICWSM*, 2013.

[31] R. Pastor-Satorras and A. Vespignani. Epidemic spreading in scale-free networks. *Physical review letters*, 86(14):3200, 2001.

[32] B. Ribeiro and D. Towsley. Estimating and sampling graphs with multidimensional random walks. In *ACM SIGCOMM IMC 2010*, Nov 2010.

[33] B. Ribeiro, P. Wang, F. Murai, and D. Towsley. Sampling directed graphs with random walks. In *IEEE INFOCOM*, pages 1692–1700, 2012.

[34] S. K. Thompson. Targeted random walk designs. *Survey Methodology*, 32(1):11, 2006.

[35] H. C. Tijms. *A first course in stochastic models*. John Wiley and Sons, 2003.

[36] A. W. Van der Vaart. *Asymptotic statistics*. Cambridge university press, 2000.

APPENDIX

A. PROOF OF THEOREM 2

First, in Lemma 3 we show that the estimate of $\mu(G')$ from each tour is unbiased.

Lemma 3. *Let $X_1^{(k)}, \ldots, X_{\xi_k}^{(k)}$ be the nodes traversed by the k-th random walk tour on G', $k \geq 1$ starting at super-node S_n. Then the following holds, $\forall k$,*

$$\mathbb{E}\Big[\sum_{t=2}^{\xi_k} f(X_{t-1}^{(k)}, X_t^{(k)})\Big] = \frac{2}{d_{S_n}} \mu(G'). \qquad (10)$$

Proof. The random walk starts from the super-node S_n, thus

$$\mathbb{E}\Big[\sum_{t=2}^{\xi_k} f(X_{t-1}^{(k)}, X_t^{(k)})\Big] = \sum_{(u,v)\in E'} \mathbb{E}\Big[\Big(\text{No. of times Markov chain crosses } (u,v) \text{ in the tour}\Big) f(u,v)\Big]. \qquad (11)$$

Consider a renewal reward process with inter-renewal time distributed as $\xi_k, k \geq 1$ and reward as the number of times Markov chain crosses (u, v). From renewal reward theorem,

$$\{\text{Asymptotic frequency of transitions from } u \text{ to } v\} = \mathbb{E}[\xi_k]^{-1} \mathbb{E}\Big[\Big(\text{No. of times Markov chain crosses } (u,v) \text{ in the tour}\Big) f(u,v)\Big].$$

The left-hand side is essentially $2\pi_u p_{uv}$. Now (11) becomes

$$\mathbb{E}\Big[\sum_{t=2}^{\xi_k} f(X_{t-1}^{(k)}, X_t^{(k)})\Big] = \sum_{(u,v)\in E'} f(u,v)\, 2\pi_u\, p_{uv}\, \mathbb{E}[\xi_k]$$
$$= \frac{2}{d_{S_n}} \sum_{(u,v)\in E'} f(u,v),$$

which concludes our proof. □

In what follows we prove Theorem 2 using Lemma 3.

PROOF THEOREM 2. By Lemma 3 the estimator $W_k = \sum_{t=2}^{\xi_k - 1} f(X_{t-1}^{(k)}, X_t^{(k)})$ is an unbiased estimate of $(2/d_{S_n})\mu(G')$. By the linearity of expectation the average estimator $\bar{W}(m) = m^{-1}\sum_{k=1}^{m} W_k$ is also unbiased.

We now consider two cases depending on f is defined as (2) or (3). When f is as in (2), it is trivial. For the function described in (3), $\mathbb{E}[W_k]$ can be rewritten as,

$$\frac{2}{d_{S_n}}\mathbb{E}[W_k] = \sum_{\substack{(u,v)\in E'\\ u\neq S_n, v\neq S_n}} g(u,v) + \sum_{\substack{(u,v)\in E'\\ u\neq S_n, v=S_n}} \frac{1}{k_{uS}} \sum_{w\in I_n} g(u,w).$$

Note that in the graph G' there are k_{uS} multiple edges between u and S_n, when u and S_n are connected, and each contributes $\sum_{w\in I_n} g(u,w)$ to the net expectation. Moreover the multiplying factor of two in the left-hand side of the above expression takes into account edges in both the directions since the random walk is reversible and graph is undirected. Hence

$$\frac{2}{d_{S_n}}\mathbb{E}[W_k] = \sum_{\substack{(u,v)\in E\\ u\notin I_n, v\notin I_n}} g(u,v) + \sum_{\substack{(u,v)\in E\\ u\notin I_n, v\in I_n}} g(u,v).$$

Finally for the estimator

$$\hat{\mu}(\mathcal{D}_m(S_n)) = \frac{d_{S_n}}{2m}\bar{W}(m) + \sum_{\substack{(u,v)\in E\\ \text{s.t. } u,v\in I_n}} f(u,v).$$

has average

$$\mathbb{E}[\hat{\mu}(\mathcal{D}_m(S_n))] = \sum_{\substack{(u,v)\in E\\ \text{s.t. } u\notin I_n \text{ or } v\notin I_n}} g(u,v) + \sum_{\substack{(u,v)\in E\\ \text{s.t. } u,v\in I_n}} g(u,v) = \mu(G).$$

Furthermore, by strong law of large numbers with $\mathbb{E}[W_k] < \infty$, $\hat{\mu}(\mathcal{D}_m(S_n)) \to \mu(G)$ a.s. as $m \to \infty$. This completes our proof. □

sectionProof of Lemma 1

PROOF. For RWuR, stationary distribution of node u, $\hat{\pi}_u = \frac{d_i+\alpha}{2M'+N'\alpha}$ and transition probability from node u to v, $\hat{p}_{uv} = \frac{\alpha/N'+1}{d_u+\alpha}$ if u and v are connected, $\frac{\alpha/N'}{d_u+\alpha}$ otherwise [4].

Let $f''(u,v) = g(u,v)\frac{d_u d_w}{2m-1}$ and f' as defined in (7). Let $V'' = V - I_n$. We have

$$V\times V = \{V''\cup I_n\}\times\{V''\cup I_n\}$$
$$= \{V''\times V''\}\cup\{V''\times I_n\}\cup\{I_n\times V''\}\cup\{I_n\times I_n\}.$$

Now the value in the set $\{V''\times I_n\}$ can be expresses in terms of $V'\times V'$ as,

$$\sum_{(u,v)\in V''\times I_n} f''(u,v) = \sum_{u\in V''}\sum_{w\in I_n} f''(u,w)$$
$$= \sum_{\substack{u\neq S_n, v=S_n\\ (u,v)\in V'\times V'}} \sum_{w\in I_n} f''(u,w).$$

$$\mathbb{E}[W_k']$$
$$= \sum_{(u,v)\in E'} f'(u,v)2\hat{\pi}_u\hat{p}_{uv}\mathbb{E}[\xi_k] + \sum_{(u,v)\in(E')^c} f'(u,v)2\hat{\pi}_u\hat{p}_{uv}\mathbb{E}[\xi_k]$$
$$= \frac{2\alpha/N'}{d_{S_n}+\alpha}\sum_{(u,v)\in E'\cup(E')^c} f'(u,v) + \frac{2}{d_{S_n}+\alpha}\sum_{(u,v)\in E'} f'(u,v)$$
$$= 2\sum_{\substack{(u,v)\in E'\\ u\neq S_n, v\neq S_n}} f''(u,v)\frac{\alpha/N'+1}{d_{S_n}+\alpha} + 2\sum_{\substack{(u,v)\in E'\\ u\neq S_n, v=S_n}} \frac{\alpha/N'+k_{uS}}{d_{S_n}+\alpha}\sum_{w\in I_n} f''(u,w)$$
$$+ 2\sum_{\substack{(u,v)\in (E')^c\\ u\neq S_n, v\neq S_n}} \frac{\alpha/N'}{d_{S_n}+\alpha} f''(u,v) + 2\sum_{\substack{(u,v)\in (E')^c\\ u\neq S_n, v=S_n}} \frac{\alpha/N'}{d_{S_n}+\alpha}\sum_{w\in I_n} f''(u,w)$$
$$= \frac{\alpha/N'}{d_{S_n}+\alpha}\Bigg[\sum_{(u,v)\in V''\times V''} f''(u,v) + \sum_{(u,v)\in V''\times I_n} f''(u,v)\Bigg]$$
$$+ \frac{1}{d_{S_n}+\alpha}\Bigg[\sum_{\substack{(u,v)\in E'\\ u\neq S_n, v=S_n}} k_{uS}\Bigg(\frac{1}{k_{uS}}\sum_{w\in I_n} f''(u,w)\Bigg)\Bigg].$$

A multiplying factor 2 will be added to the first term in the above expression since RWuR is reversible and the graph under consideration is undirected. The last term can be removed by using classical random walk tours $\{W_k''\}$ with appropriate bias. The unbiasedness of the estimator then follows from the linearity of expectation. □

B. PROOF OF LEMMA 2

(i). The variance of the estimator at tour $k \geq 1$ starting from node S_n is

$$\mathrm{Var}_{S_n}\Bigg[\sum_{t=2}^{\xi_k} f(X_{t-1}^{(k)}, X_t^{(k)}))\Bigg]$$
$$\leq B^2\mathbb{E}[(\xi_k-1)^2] - \Bigg(\mathbb{E}\Bigg[\sum_{t=2}^{\xi_k} f(X_{t-1}^{(k)}, X_t^{(k)}))\Bigg]\Bigg)^2. \quad (12)$$

It is known from [1, Chapter 2 and 3] that

$$\mathbb{E}[\xi_k^2] = \frac{2\sum_{i\geq 2} w_{S_n i}^2(1-\lambda_i)^{-1}+1}{\pi_{S_n}^2}.$$

Using Theorem 3 eq. (12) can be written as

$$\mathrm{Var}\Bigg[\sum_{t=2}^{\xi_k} f(X_{t-1}^{(k)}, X_t^{(k)}))\Bigg]$$
$$\leq \frac{1}{d_{S_n}^2}\Bigg(2d_{\text{tot}}^2 B^2(\sum_{i\geq 2} w_{S_n m}^2(1-\lambda_i)^{-1}) - 4\mu^2(G')\Bigg)$$
$$-\frac{1}{d_{S_n}}B^2 d_{\text{tot}} + B^2.$$

The latter can be upper-bounded by $B^2(2d_{\text{tot}}^2/(d_i^2\delta)+1)$.

For the second part, we have

$$\mathbb{E}\left[\left(\sum_{t=2}^{\xi_k} f(X_{t-1}^{(k)}, X_t^{(k)})\right)^l\right] \leq B^l \mathbb{E}[(\xi_k - 1)^l)]$$
$$\leq C(\mathbb{E}[(\xi_k)^l] + 1),$$

for a constant $C > 0$ using C_r inequality [17, Chapter 3, Theorem 2.2]. From [29], it is known that there exists an $a > 0$, such that $\mathbb{E}[\exp(a\,\xi_k)] < \infty$, and this implies that $\mathbb{E}[(\xi_k)^l] < \infty$ for all $l \geq 0$. This proves the theorem.

(ii). We denote $\mathbb{E}_\pi f$ for $\mathbb{E}_\pi[f(Y_1, Y_2)]$ and Normal(a, b) indicates Gaussian distribution with mean a and variance b. With the trivial extension of the central limit theorem of Markov chains [29] of node functions to edge functions, we have for the ergodic estimator $\bar{f}_n = n^{-1}\sum_{t=2}^n f(Y_{t-1}, Y_t)$,

$$\sqrt{n}(\bar{f}_n - \mathbb{E}_\pi f) \xrightarrow{d} \text{Normal}(0, \sigma_a^2), \tag{13}$$

where

$$\sigma_a^2 = \text{Var}(f(Y_1, Y_2)) + 2\sum_{l=2}^{n-1} \frac{(n-1)-l}{n} \text{Cov}(f(Y_0, Y_1), f(Y_{l-1}, Y_l)) < \infty.$$

We derive σ_a^2 in Lemma 4. Note that σ_a^2 is also the asymptotic variance of the ergodic estimator of edge functions.

Consider a renewal reward process at its k-th renewal, $k \geq 1$, with inter-renewal time ξ_k and reward as $W_k = \sum_{t=2}^{\xi_k} f(X_{t-1}^{(k)}, X_t^{(k)})$. Let $\bar{W}(n)$ be the average cumulative reward gained up to m-th renewal, i.e., $\bar{W}(m) = m^{-1}\sum_{k=1}^m W_k$. From the central limit theorem for the renewal reward process [35, Theorem 2.2.5], with $l_n = \text{argmax}_k \sum_{j=1}^k \mathbf{1}(\xi_j \leq n)$, after n total number of steps yields

$$\sqrt{n}(\bar{W}(l_n) - \mathbb{E}_\pi f) \xrightarrow{d} \text{Normal}(0, \sigma_b^2), \tag{14}$$

with $\sigma_b^2 = \dfrac{\nu^2}{\mathbb{E}[\xi_k]}$ and

$$\begin{aligned}\nu^2 &= \mathbb{E}[(W_k - \xi_k \mathbb{E}_\pi f)^2] = \mathbb{E}_i\left[\left(W_k - \xi_k \frac{\mathbb{E}[W_k]}{\mathbb{E}[\xi_k]}\right)^2\right] \\ &= \text{Var}_{S_n}(W_k) + (\mathbb{E}[W_k])^2 + \left(\frac{\mathbb{E}[W_k]}{\mathbb{E}[\xi_k]}\right)^2 \mathbb{E}[(\xi_k)^2] \\ &\quad -2\frac{\mathbb{E}[W_k]}{\mathbb{E}[\xi_k]}\mathbb{E}[W_k \xi_k].\end{aligned}$$

In fact it can be shown that (see [29, Proof of Theorem 17.2.2])

$$|\sqrt{n}(\bar{f}_n - \mathbb{E}_\pi f) - \sqrt{n}(\bar{W}(l_n) - \mathbb{E}_\pi f)| \to 0 \quad \text{a.s.}.$$

Therefore $\sigma_a^2 = \sigma_b^2$. Combining this result with Lemma 4 shown below we get (8). □

Lemma 4.

$$\begin{aligned}&\lim_{n\to\infty} \frac{1}{n}\text{Var}_\pi\left(\sum_{k=2}^n f(Y_{k-1}, Y_k)\right) \\ &= 2\sum_{i=2}^r \frac{\lambda_i}{1-\lambda_i}\langle f, v_i\rangle_{\hat{\pi}}\,(u_i^\intercal \hat{f}) + \frac{1}{d_{tot}}\sum_{(i,j)\in E} f(i,j)^2 \\ &\quad + \frac{1}{d_{tot}^2}(\sum_{(i.j)\in E} f(i,j)^2)^2 + \frac{1}{d_{tot}^2}\sum_{i\in V} d_i\Big(\sum_{i\sim j} f(i,j)\Big)^2\end{aligned}$$

Proof. We extend the arguments in the proof of [7, Theorem 6.5] to the edge functions. We have,

$$\begin{aligned}&\lim_{n\to\infty}\frac{1}{n}\text{Var}_\pi\left(\sum_{k=2}^n f(Y_{k-1}, Y_k)\right) \\ &= \frac{1}{n}\Big(\sum_{k=2}^n \text{Var}_\pi(f(Y_{k-1}, Y_k)) \\ &\quad + 2\sum_{\substack{k,j=2\\k<j}} \text{Cov}_\pi(f(Y_{k-1}, Y_k), f(Y_{j-1}, Y_j))\Big) \\ &= \text{Var}_\pi(f(Y_{k-1}, Y_k)) \\ &\quad + 2\sum_{l=2}^{n-1}\frac{(n-1)-l}{n}\text{Cov}_\pi(f(Y_0, Y_1), f(Y_{l-1}, Y_l)).\end{aligned} \tag{15}$$

Now the first term in (15) is

$$\text{Var}_\pi(f(Y_{k-1}, Y_k)) = \langle f, f\rangle_{\hat{\pi}} - \langle f, \Pi\hat{f}\rangle_{\hat{\pi}}, \tag{16}$$

where $\Pi = \mathbf{1}\pi^\intercal$.

For the second term in (15),

$$\begin{aligned}&\text{Cov}_\pi(f(Y_0, Y_1), f(Y_{l-1}, Y_l)) \\ &\quad = \mathbb{E}_\pi(f(Y_0, Y_1), f(Y_{l-1}, Y_l)) - (\mathbb{E}_\pi[f(Y_0, Y_1)])^2.\end{aligned}$$

$$\begin{aligned}&\mathbb{E}_\pi(f(Y_0, Y_1), f(Y_{l-1}, Y_l)) \\ &= \sum_i\sum_j\sum_k\sum_m \pi_i\, p_{ij}\, p_{jk}^{(l-2)}\, p_{km} f(i,j) f(k,m) \\ &= \langle f, P^{(l-2)}\hat{f}\rangle_{\hat{\pi}}.\end{aligned} \tag{17}$$

Therefore,

$$\text{Cov}_\pi(f(Y_0, Y_1), f(Y_{l-1}, Y_l)) = \langle f, (\mathbf{P}^{(l-2)} - \Pi)\hat{f}\rangle_{\hat{\pi}}.$$

Taking limits, we get

$$\begin{aligned}&\lim_{n\to\infty}\sum_{l=2}^{n-1}\frac{n-l-1}{n}(\mathbf{P}^{(l-2)} - \Pi) \\ &\overset{(a)}{=} \lim_{n\to\infty}\sum_{k=1}^{n-1}\frac{n-k}{n}(\mathbf{P}^k - \Pi) + (\mathbf{I} - \Pi) - \lim_{n\to\infty}\frac{3}{n}\sum_{k=1}^{n-3}(\mathbf{P}^k - \Pi) \\ &= (\mathbf{Z} - \mathbf{I}) + (\mathbf{I} - \Pi) = \mathbf{Z} - \Pi,\end{aligned} \tag{18}$$

where the first term in (a) follows from the proof of [7, Theorem 6.5] and since $\lim_{n\to\infty}(\mathbf{P}^n - \Pi) = 0$, the last term is zero using Cesaro's lemma [7, Theorem 1.5 of Appendix].

We have,

$$\mathbf{Z} = \mathbf{I} + \sum_{i=2}^r \frac{\lambda_i}{1-\lambda_i} v_i u_i^\intercal,$$

Thus

$$\begin{aligned}&\lim_{n\to\infty}\frac{1}{n}\text{Var}_\pi\left(\sum_{k=2}^n f(Y_{k-1}, Y_k)\right) \\ &= \langle f, f\rangle_{\hat{\pi}} - \langle f, \Pi\hat{f}\rangle_{\hat{\pi}} + 2\langle f, \left(\mathbf{I} + \sum_{i=2}^r \frac{\lambda_i}{1-\lambda_i} v_i u_i^\intercal - \Pi\right)\hat{f}\rangle_{\hat{\pi}} \\ &= \frac{1}{d_{tot}}\sum_{(i,j)\in E} f(i,j)^2 + \frac{1}{d_{tot}^2}(\sum_{(i.j)\in E} f(i,j)^2)^2 \\ &\quad + \frac{1}{d_{tot}^2}\sum_{i\in V} d_i\Big(\sum_{i\sim j} f(i,j)\Big)^2 + 2\sum_{i=2}^r \frac{\lambda_i}{1-\lambda_i}\langle f, v_i\rangle_{\hat{\pi}}\,(u_i^\intercal \hat{f})\end{aligned}$$

□

Social Clicks: What and Who Gets Read on Twitter?

Maksym Gabielkov
INRIA-MSR Joint Centre,
Columbia University
maksym.gabielkov@inria.fr

Arthi Ramachandran
Columbia University
arthir@cs.columbia.edu

Augustin Chaintreau
Columbia University
augustin@cs.columbia.edu

Arnaud Legout
INRIA-MSR Joint Centre
arnaud.legout@inria.fr

ABSTRACT

Online news domains increasingly rely on social media to drive traffic to their websites. Yet we know surprisingly little about how a social media conversation mentioning an online article actually generates clicks. Sharing behaviors, in contrast, have been fully or partially available and scrutinized over the years. While this has led to multiple assumptions on the diffusion of information, each assumption was designed or validated while ignoring actual clicks.

We present a large scale, unbiased study of *social clicks*—that is also the first data of its kind—gathering a month of web visits to online resources that are located in 5 leading news domains and that are mentioned in the third largest social media by web referral (Twitter). Our dataset amounts to 2.8 million shares, together responsible for 75 billion potential views on this social media, and 9.6 million actual clicks to 59,088 unique resources. We design a reproducible methodology and carefully correct its biases. As we prove, properties of clicks impact multiple aspects of information diffusion, all previously unknown. (i) Secondary resources, that are not promoted through headlines and are responsible for the long tail of content popularity, generate more clicks both in absolute and relative terms. (ii) Social media attention is actually long-lived, in contrast with temporal evolution estimated from shares or receptions. (iii) The actual influence of an intermediary or a resource is poorly predicted by their share count, but we show how that prediction can be made more precise.

1. INTRODUCTION

In spite of being almost a decade old, social media continue to grow and are dramatically changing the way we access Web resources. Indeed, it was estimated for the first time in 2014 that the most common way to reach a Web site is from URLs cited in social media[1]. Social media account for 30% of the overall visits to Web sites, which is higher than visits due to organic search results from search engines. However, the context and dynamics of social media referral remain surprisingly unexplored.

[1]http://j.mp/1qHkuzi

SIGMETRICS '16, June 14 - 18, 2016, Antibes Juan-Les-Pins, France

ACM ISBN 978-1-4503-4266-7/16/06. . . $15.00
DOI: http://dx.doi.org/10.1145/2896377.2901462

Related works on the click prediction of results of search engines [21] do not apply to social media referral because they are very different in nature. To be exposed to a URL on a search engine, a user needs to make an explicit request, and the answer will be tailored to the user profile using behavioral analysis, text processing, or personalization algorithms. On the contrary, on social media, a user just needs to create a social relationship with other users, then he will automatically receive contents produced by these users. At a first approximation, a web search service provides pull based information filtered by algorithms and social media provide a push based information filtered by humans. In fact, our results confirm that the temporal dynamics of clicks in this case is very different.

For a long time, studying clicks on social media was hindered by unavailability of data, but this paper proves that today, this can be overcome[2]. However, no sensitive individual information is disclosed in the data we present. Using multiple data collection techniques, we are able to jointly study Twitter conversations *and clicks* for URLs from five reputable news domains during a month of summer 2015. Note that we do not have complete data on clicks, but we carefully analyze this selection bias and found that we collected around 6% of all URLs, and observed 33% of all clicks. We chose to study news domains for multiple reasons described below.

First, news are a primary topic of conversation on social media[3], as expected due to their real time nature. In particular, Twitter is ranked third behind Facebook and Pinterest in total volume of web referral traffic, and often appears second after Facebook when web users discuss their exposure to news[1]. Knowing which social media generates traffic to news site is important to understand how users are exposed to news.

Second, diffusion of news are generally considered highly influential. Political opinion is shaped by various editorial messages, but also by intermediaries that succeed in gener-

[2]Like any social media studies, we rely on open APIs and search functions that can be rendered obsolete after policy changes, but all the collection we present for this paper follow the terms of use as of today, and the data will remain persistently available. http://j.mp/soTweet

[3]For instance, more than one in two American adult reports using social media as the top source of political news, which is more than traditional network such as CNN [22].

ating interest in such messages. This is also true for any kind of public opinion on subjects ranging from a natural disaster to the next movie blockbusters. Knowing who relays information and who generates traffic to news site is important to identify true influencers.

Last, news exhibit multiple forms of diffusion that can vary from a traditional top-down promotion through headlines to a word-of-mouth effect of content originally shared by ordinary users. Knowing how news are relayed on social media is important to understand the mechanisms behind influence.

This paper offers the first study of social web referral at a large scale. We now present the following contributions.

- We validate a practical and unbiased method to study web referral from social media at scale. It leverages URL shorteners, their associated APIs, in addition to multiple social media search APIs. We identify four sources of biases and run specific validation experiments to prove that one can carefully minimize or correct their impact to obtain a representative joint sample of shares/receptions/clicks for all URLs in various online domains. As an example, a selection bias leads to collecting only 6.41% of the URLs, but we validate experimentally that this bias can be entirely corrected. (Section 2)
- We show the limitations of previous studies that ignored click conversion. First, we analyze the long-tail content popularity primarily caused by the large number of URLs mentioned that are not going through official headline promotions and show their effect to be grossly underestimated: those typically receive a minority of the receptions[4], indeed almost all of them are shared only a handful of times, and we even show a large fraction of them generate no clicks at all, sometimes even after thousands of receptions. In spite of this, they generate a *majority* of the clicks, highlighting an efficient curation process. In fact, we found evidence that the number of shares, ubiquitously displayed today on media's web presence to indicate popularity, appears an inaccurate measure of actual readership. (Section 3)
- We show that that clicks dynamics reveal the attention of social media to be long-lived, a significant fraction of clicks by social media referrals are produced over the following days of a share. This stands in sharp contrast with social media *sharing behavior*, previously shown to be almost entirely concentrated within the first hours, as we confirm with new results. An extended analysis of the tail reveals that popular content tend to attract many clicks for a long period of time, this effect has no equivalent in users' sharing behavior. (Section 4)
- Finally we leverage the above facts to build the first analysis of URL or user influence based on clicks and Clicks-Per-Follower. We first validate our estimation, show it reveals a simple classification of information intermediaries, and propose a refined influence score motivated by statistical analysis. URLs and users influence can be leveraged to predict a significant fraction of future social media referral, with multiple applications to the performance of online web services. (Section 5)

[4]See Section 2.1 for definition.

2. MEASURING SOCIAL MEDIA CLICKS

Our first contribution is a new method leveraging features of social media shorteners to study for the first time in a joint manner how URLs get promoted on a social media and how users decide to click on those. This method is scalable using no privileged accounts, and can in principle apply to different web domains and social media than those we consider here. After presenting how to reproduce it, we analyze multiples biases, run validation experiment, and propose correction measures. As a motivation for this section, we focus on estimating the distribution of Click-Per-Follower (CPF), which is the probability that a link shared on a social media generates a click from one of the followers receiving that share.

Background on datasets involving clicks.

As a general rule, datasets involving clicks of users are highly sensitive and rarely described let alone shared in a public manner, for two reasons.

First, they raise ethical issues as the behavior of individual users online (*e.g.*, what they read) can cause them real harm. Users share a lot of content online, sometimes with dramatic consequence as this spreads, but they also have an expectation of privacy when it comes to what they read. This important condition makes it perilous to study clicks by collecting individual behaviors at scale. We carefully analyze the potential privacy threat of our data collection method and show that it merely comes from minutiae of social web referral that can be accounted for and removed at no expense.

Second, clicks on various URLs have important commercial value to a news media, a company, or a brand: if a movie orchestrates a social media campaign, the producing company, the marketing company, and the social media itself might not necessarily like to disclose its success in gathering attention, especially when it turns out to be underwhelming. These issues have hindered the availability of any such information beyond very large seasonal aggregates. Moreover due to the inherent incentives in disclosing this information (social media buzz, or the lack thereof), one may be tempted to take any of those claims with a grain of salt. In fact, *prior to our paper, no result can be found to broadly estimate the Click-Per-Follower of a link shared on social media.*

2.1 Obtaining raw data & terminology

For our study, we consider five domains of news media chosen among the most popular on Twitter: 3 news media channels BBC, CNN, and Fox News, one newspaper, The New York Times, and one strictly-online source, The Huffington Post. Our goal is to understand how URLs from these news media appear and evolve inside Twitter, as well as how those URLs are clicked, hence bringing web traffic revenue to each of those medias.

To build our dataset, we crawled two sources: Twitter to get the information on the number of shares and receptions (defined below), and `bit.ly` to get the number of clicks on the shortened URLs. At the beginning of our study, we monitored all URLs referencing one of the five news media using the Twitter 1% sample, and we found that 80% of the URLs of these five domains shared on Twitter are shortened with `bit.ly`, using a professional domain name such as `bbc.in` or `fxn.ws`. In the following, we only focus on the URLs shortened by `bit.ly`.

Twitter Crawl. We use two methods to get tweets from the Twitter API. The first method is to connect to the Streaming API[5] to receive tweets in real time. One may specify to access a 1% sample of tweets. This is the way we discover URLs for this study[6].

The second method to get tweets, and *the one we use after a URL is discovered*, is to use the search API[7]. This is an important step to gather all tweets associated with a given URL, providing a holistic view of its popularity, as opposed to only tweets appearing in the 1% sample. However, this API call has some limitations: (i) we cannot search for tweets older than 7 days (related to the time the API is called), (ii) the search API is rate-limited at 30 requests per minute for an application-only authentication and 10 requests per minute for a user authentication. This method proved sufficient to obtain during a month a comprehensive view of the sharing of each URL we preliminary discovered.

bit.ly Crawl. The `bit.ly` API provides the hourly statistics for the number of clicks on any of its URLs, including professional domains. The number of API calls are rate-limited, but the rate limit is not disclosed[8]. During our crawl, we found that we cannot exceed 200 requests per hour. Moreover, as the `bit.ly` API gives the number of clicks originating from each web referrer, we can distinguish between clicks made from `twitter.com`, `t.co`, and others, which allows us to remove the effect of traffic coming from other sources.

In the rest of this article, we will use the following terms to describe a given URL or online article.

Shares. Number of times a URL has been published in tweets. An original tweet containing the URL or a retweet of this tweet are both considered as a new share.

Receptions. Number of Twitter users who are potentially exposed to a tweet (*i.e.*, who follow an account that shared the URLs). Note that those may not have necessarily seen or read the tweet in the end. As an example, if a tweet is published by a single user with N followers, the number of receptions for this tweet is N. This metric is related but different from the number of "impressions" (number of people who actually saw the tweets in their feed). Impressions are typically impossible to crawl without being the originator of the tweet (see a study by Wang*et al.* [26] comparing those two metrics).

Clicks. Number of times a URL has been clicked by a visitor originating from `twitter.com` or `t.co`.

[5]https://dev.twitter.com/streaming/overview

[6]One can also specify to the Streaming API a filter to receive tweets containing particular keywords (up to 400 keywords) or sent by particular people (up to 5000 userIDs) or from particular locations. For the volume of tweets that we gathered, this method can be overwhelmed by rate limit, leading to real time information loss, especially during peak hours, that are hard to recover from.

[7]https://dev.twitter.com/rest/reference/get/search/tweets

[8]http://dev.bitly.com/rate_limiting.html

Click-Per-follower (CPF). For a given URL, the CPF is formally defined as the ratio of the clicks to the receptions for this URL. For example, if absolutely all followers of accounts sharing a URL go visit the article, the CPF is equal to 1.

Limitations.

The rest of this section will demonstrate the merit of our method, but let us first list a serie of limitations. (i) *It only monitors searchable public shares in social media.* Facebook, an important source of traffic online, does not offer the same search API[9]. Everything we present in this article can only be representative of public shares made on Twitter. (ii) *It only deals with web resource exchanged using `bit.ly` or one of its professional accounts.* This enables to study leading news domain which are primarily using this tool to direct traffic to them. Our observations are also subject to the particular choice of domains (5 news channel, in English, primarily from North America). (iii) *It is subject to rate limits.* `bit.ly` API caps the number of request to an undisclosed amounts and Twitter implements a 1 week window on any information requested. This could be harmful to study even larger domains (*e.g.*, all links in `bit.ly`) as this is impractical, but as we will see it was not a limitation for those cases considered in this study. (iv) *It measures attention on social media only through clicks.* While in practice merely viewing a tweet can already convey some information, we consider that no interest was shown by the user unless they are actively visiting the article mentioned.

2.2 Ensuring users' privacy

Since we only collect information on URLs shared, viewed, and visited, we do not *a priori* collect individual data that are particularly sensitive in nature. Note also, that all those data are publicly available today. However, the scale of our data might *a posteriori* contains sufficient information to derive those individual behaviors from our aggregates. As an extreme example, if a user is the *only* user on that social media receiving an article, and that this article is clicked, that information could be used to infer that this user most likely read that webpage.

We found a few instance of cases like the above, but in practice those particular cases can be addressed. First, before we analyze the raw data we apply a preprocessing *merging* step in which all URLs shorteners that lead to the same developed URLs were merged together (ignoring information contained after the symbols "?" and "#" which may be used in URL to inform personalization). This also helps our analysis further as it allows to consider the importance of a given article independently of the multiplication of URLs by which it is shortened. After considering the data after this processing step, we found that case of clicked URLs with less than 10 receptions never occurred. Moreover, we found only a handful of URLs with less than 50 receptions, showing that in all cases we considered, all but a extremely small number of users are guaranteed to be k-anonymous with $k = 50$. Equivalently, it means that their behavior is indistinguishable from at least 49 other individuals. In practice, for most users, the value of k will be much larger. Finally,

[9]Although, very recently as of October 2015 Facebook provides search over public posts http://www.wired.com/2015/10/facebook-search-privacy/.

we observe that no explicit information connect clicks from multiple URLs together. Clicks are measured at a hourly rate, it is therefore particularly difficult to use this data to infer that the same user has clicked on multiple URLs and use it for reidentification.

Finally, we computed the probability for a discovered URLs to receive at least one click as a function of its number of receptions, and found that observed URLs with less than 500 receptions are a minority (3.96%), and *among those* 9.80% actually receive clicks. This shows that, while our study dealing with links from popular sources online raised little privacy issue, one could in practice extend this method for more sensitive domains simply by ignoring clicks from those URLs if a larger value of k-anonymity is required (such as $k = 500$) to protect users.

Removing clicks from all URLs with less than k receptions would in practice affect the results very marginally.

2.3 Selection bias and a validated correction

The most important source of bias in our experiment comes from the URL discovery process. As we rely on a 1% sample of tweets from Twitter, there are necessarily URLs that we miss, and those we obtain are affected by a *selection bias*. First, Twitter does not always document how this sample is computed, although it is arguably random. (Our experiments confirmed that it a uniform random sample.) Second, the 1% sample yields a uniform sample of tweets, but not the URLs contained in these tweets. We are much more likely to observe a URLs shared 100 times than one shared only in a few tweets. We cannot recover the data about the missed URLs, but we can correct it by giving more weight to unpopular URLs in our dataset when we compute statistics. We note that this selection bias was present in multiple studies before ours, but given our focus on estimating the shape of online news, it is particularly damaging.

To understand and cope with this bias, we conduct a validation experiment in which we collected all tweets for one of the news sources (*i.e.*, `nytimes.com`) using the Twitter search API. Note that `bit.ly` rate limits would not allow us to conduct a joint analysis of audience for such volumes of URLs. This collection was used to compare our sample, and validate a correction metric.

Figure 1 compares distributions of the number of shares among URLs in our sample and in the validation experiment for the same time period. We see that 1% sample underestimates unpopular URLs that are shared less often. However, this bias can be systematically corrected by reweighting each URL in the 1% sample using the coefficient $\frac{1}{1-(1-\alpha)^s}$, where $\alpha = 0.01$ is the probability of a tweet to get into the sample and s is the number of shares that we observed for that URL from the search API. We then obtain a partial but representative view of the URLs that are found online, which also indirectly validates that Twitter 1% sampling indeed resembles a random choice. All the results in this paper take into account this correction.

Finally, we need to account for one particular effect of our data: URLs shorteners were first discovered separately, and crawled each for a complete view of their shares, but shorteners are subsequently merged (as explained in Section 2.2) into articles leading to the same developed URL. It is not clear which convention applies to best assign weight among merged URLs that have been partially observed, so we relied on simple case analysis to decide on the best choice. Our analysis showed that not to overwhelm the correction in favor of either a small or a large article, the best is to sum all shares of shorteners leading to the same article before applying the re-weighting exactly as done above.

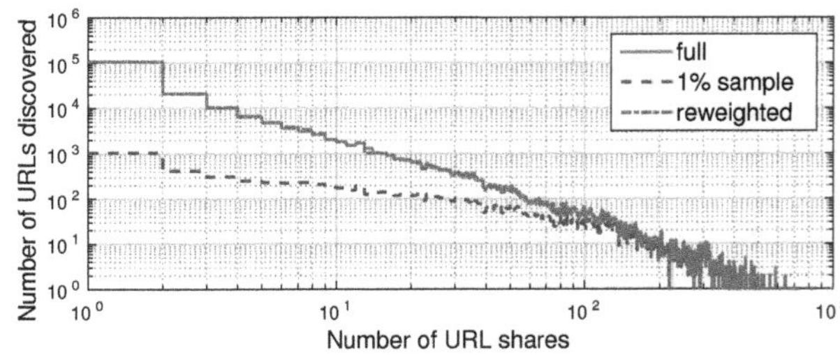

Figure 1: **1% sample bias and correction.** *The bias due to the 1% sample is significant, but can be fully corrected using reweighting.*

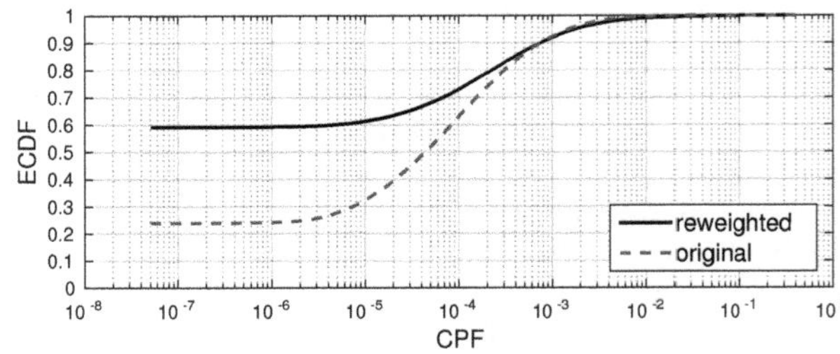

Figure 2: **CPF distribution with and without selection bias.** *The number of URLs with low CPF is significantly underestimated if the bias due to the 1% sample is not corrected.*

Social media CPF and the effect of selection bias.

To illustrate the effect of the selection bias, Figure 2 presents the two empirical distributions of CPF obtained from the Twitter crawl by dividing for each article its sum of clicks by its number of receptions (all measured after 24 h), and after re-weighting each value according to the above correction.

We highlight multiple observations: First, CPF overall is low (as one could expect) given that what counts in our data as a *reception* does not guarantee that the user even has seen the tweet, for instance if she only accesses Twitter occasionally this tweet might have been hidden by more recent information. In fact, we estimate that a *majority* (59%) of the URLs mentioned on Twitter are not clicked at all. Note that this would not appear in the data without reweighting, where only 22% of URLs are in that case, which illustrates how the selection bias present in the Twitter 1% sample could be misleading. Finally, for most of the URLs that do generate clicks, the CPF appear to lie within the $[10^{-5}; 10^{-3}]$ range. It is interesting to observe that removing the selection bias also slightly reinforce the distribution for high values of CPF. This is due to a minority of niche URLs shared only to a limited audience but that happens to generate in comparison a larger number of clicks. This effect will be analyzed further in the next section.

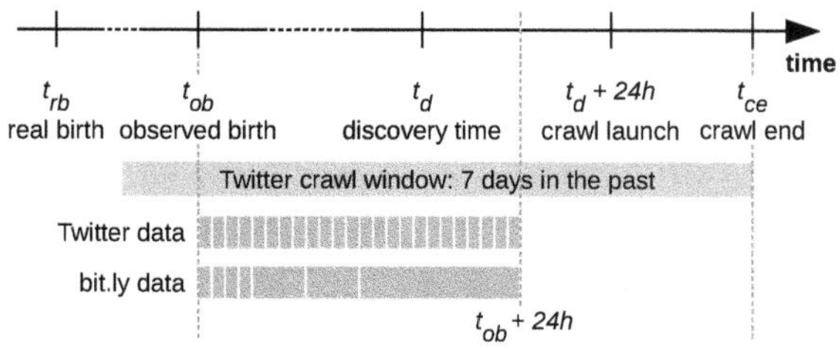

Figure 3: **Time conventions and definitions for URL life description.**

2.4 Other forms of biases

Limited time window.

On Figure 3, we present the time conventions and definitions we are using to describe the lifespan of a URL. We monitored the 1% tweet sample, and each time t_d we found a tweet containing a new URL (shortened by `bit.ly`) from one of the five news media we consider, we schedule a crawl of this URL at time t_d + 24h, the crawl ends at time t_{ce}. The rational to delay by 24 hours the crawl is to make sure that each URL we crawl has a minimum history of 24 hours. The crawl of each URL consists of the three following steps.

1. We query the Twitter search API for all tweets containing this URL. We define the time t_{ob} of observed birth of the URL as the timestamp of the earliest tweet found containing this URL.

2. We query the `bit.ly` API to get the number of clicks on the URL. Due to the low limit on the number of queries to the `bit.ly` API, we make 7 calls asking for the number of clicks in the 1st, 2nd, 3rd, 4th, 5th through 8th, 9th through 12th, and 13th through 24th hours after t_{ob}.

3. After this collection was completed, we crawled `bit.ly` a second time to obtain information on clicks completed after a day (up to 2 weeks).

Note that this technique inherently leverages a partial view on both side of the temporal axis. On the one hand, some old information could have been ignored, due to the limited time window of our search. In fact, we cannot be sure that no tweet mentioned that URL a week before. On the other hand, we empirically measured that for a majority of URLs $t_d - t_{ob} \leq 1$ hour which means that the oldest observation of that URLs in the week was immediately before our discovery. Moreover, for an overwhelming majority of the URLs (97.6%) $t_d - t_{ob} \leq 5$ days. This implies that for all of those our earliest tweets were preceded by at least two days where this URLs was never mentioned (see Figure 3). Given the nature of news content, we deduce that earlier tweets are non-existent (we conclude that t_{rb} is equal to t_{ob}), or even if they are missed, not creating any more clicks at the time of our observations. Finally, we note that recent information occurring after our observation time is missing, especially as we cannot retroactively collect tweets after 24 h. While this could in theory be continuously done in a sliding window experiment, we observe that an overwhelming majority of tweets mentioning a URLs occurred immediately after our discovery (within a few hours). We also note that the effect of those tweets would not affect the clicks seen before 24 h.

The effect of multiple receptions.

An online article may be shown multiple times, sometimes using the same shorteners, to the same user. This comes from multiple reasons. Two different accounts that a user follows may share the same link, or a given Twitter account may share multiple times the same URL, which is not so uncommon. This necessarily affects how one should count receptions of a given URLs, and how to estimate its CPF although it's not clear whether receiving the same article multiple times impacts its chance to be seen. Note finally, that even if we know the list of Twitter users who shared a URL, we cannot accurately compute how many saw the URLs at least once without gathering the list of followers of those who share, in order to remove duplicates, *i.e.*, overlaps between sets of followers. Because of the low rate limit of the Twitter API, it would take us approximately 25 years with a single account to crawl the followers of users who shared the URLs in our dataset. However, we can compute an upper bound of the number of receptions as a sum of the number of followers. This is an upperbound because we don't consider the overlap between the followers, that is any share from a different user counts as a new reception. Note that this already removes multiplicity due to several receptions coming from the same account.

To assess the bias introduced by this estimation, we consider a dataset that represents the full Twitter graph as of July 2012 [8]. This graph provides not only the number of followers, but also the full list of followers for each account, at a time where the API permitted such crawl. Therefore, this graph allows to compute both an estimate and the ground truth of the number of receptions. We computed our estimated reception and the ground truth reception for each URLs on the 2012 dataset. We note that some users that exist today might not have been present in the 2012 dataset. Therefore, we extracted from our current dataset all Twitter users that published one of the monitored URLs and found that 85% of these users are present in the 2012 dataset, which is large enough for our purpose.

Figure 4 shows the difference between our estimation of the number of receptions and the real number of receptions based on the 2012 dataset. We observe that for an overwhelming majority (more than 97% of URLs) the two values are of the same order (within a factor 2). We also observe that for 75% of them, the difference is less than 20%.

This implies that the CPF values we obtain are conservative (they may occasionally underestimate the actual probability by about 20-50%) but within a small factor of values computed using other conventions (*i.e.*, for instance, if multiple receptions to the same user are counted only once). For the sake of validating this claim, and measuring how overlaps affect CPF estimation, we ran a "mock" experiment where we draw the distribution among URLs of the CPF assuming that the audience is identical to the followers found in the 2012 dataset. We compare the CPF when multiple receptions are counted (as done in the rest of this paper), and when duplicate receptions to the same user are removed. Note that since 2012 the number of followers have evolved (typically increased) as Twitter expanded, hence receptions are actually underestimated. The absolute values we ob-

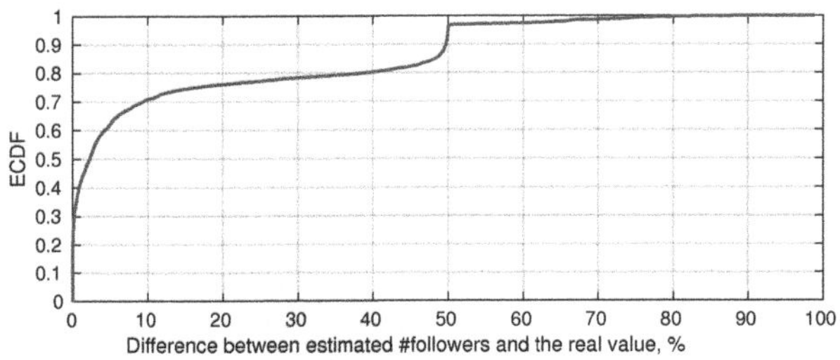

Figure 4: **Bias of the estimation of the number of receptions.** The figure present the ECDF of the relative difference of the real number of receptions and our estimate. The lists of followers are taken from the 2012 Twitter dataset [8]. *For 75% of the receptions, the estimation error is less than 20%, which is good enough for this study.*

serve are hence not accurate (typically ten times larger). However, we found that the CPF for multiple conventions always are within a factor two of each other. It confirms that the minority of URLs where overlaps affect receptions are URLs shared to a small audience that typically do not impact the distribution.

3. LONG TAIL & SOCIAL MEDIA

For news producers and consumers, social media create new opportunities by multiplying articles available and exposed, and enabling personalization. However, with no analysis of consuming behaviors that is, clicks, which we show vastly differ from sharing behaviors, it remains uncertain how the users of social media today take advantage of such features.

3.1 Background

Social media such as Twitter allow news consumption to expand beyond the constraints of a fixed number of headlines and printed articles. Today's landscape of news is *in theory* only limited by the expanding interests of the online audience. Previous studies show that almost all online users exhibit an uncommon taste at least in a part of their online consumption [9], while others point to possible bottlenecks in information discovery that limits the content accessed [5]. To fully leverage opportunities open by social media, works propose typically to leverage either a distributed social curation process (*e.g.*, [32, 11, 27, 20]) or some underlying interest clusters to feed a recommender system (*e.g.*, [30, 19]). However, with no evidence on the actual news consumed by users, it is hard to validate whether todays' information has benefited from those opportunities. For instance, online media like those in our study continue to select a few set of headlines articles to be promoted via their official Twitter account, followed by tens of millions of users or more, effectively reproducing traditional curation under a new format. Those are usually leading to large cascades of information. What remains to measure is *how much* web traffic comes from such promoted content, and how much from different type of content reaching users organically through the distributed process of online news sharing. To answer these questions, we rely on a detailed study of the properties of the long tail and the effect of promotion on content accessed.

Long tail of online news: What to expect?.
Pareto's principle, or the law of diminishing return, states that a majority of the traffic (say, for instance 80%) should primarily comes from a restricted, possibly very small, fraction of the URLs. Those are typically referred to as the *blockbusters*. This prediction is however complemented with the fact that most web traffic exhibits a long tail effect. The later focuses on the set of URLs that are requested infrequently, also referred to as *niche*. It predicts that, when it comes to generating traffic, whereas the contribution of each niche URLs is small, they are in such great numbers that they collectively contribute a significant fraction of the overall visits. Those properties are not contradictory and usually coexist, but a particular one might prevail. When it is the case, it pays off for a content producer who has limited resource and wishes to maximize its audience to focus either on promoting the most popular content, or, on the contrary, on maintaining a broad catalog of available information catering to multiple needs.

And what questions remains to answer?.
Beyond the above qualitative trends, we wish here to answer a set of precise questions by leveraging the consumption of online news. What level of sharing defines a blockbuster URL that generates an important volume of clicks, or a niche one; for instance, should we consider a moderate success a URL that is shared 20 times or clicked 5 times? Does it mean that niche URLs have overall a negligible effect in bringing audience to an online site? Since the headlines selected by media to feature in their official Twitter feed benefit from a large exposure early on, could it be that they account for almost all blockbuster URLs? More generally, what fraction of traffic is governed by blockbuster and niche clicks? Moreover, do any of those property vary significantly among different online news sources, or is it the format of the social media itself (here, Twitter) that governs users behaviors, in the end, determining how content gets accessed?

3.2 Traditional vs. social media curation

To answer the above questions, we first introduce a few definitions:

Primary URL. A primary URL is a URL contained in a tweet sent by an official account of the 5 news media we picked for this study. Such URLs are spread through the traditional curation process because they are selected by new media to appear in the headlines.

Secondary URL. All URLs that are not primary are secondary URLs. Although they refer to official and authenticated content from the same domain, none benefited from the broad exposure that the official Twitter of this source offers. Such URLs are spread trough the social media curation process.

We see from the sharing activities (tweet and retweet) that primary URLs accounts for 60.47%, hence a majority, of the receptions in the network. This comes from the fact that, although primary URLs only account for 17.43% of the shares overall, non-primary URLs are typically shared to less followers.

If we assume that clicks are linearly dependent on the receptions then we will wrongly conclude that clicks are predominantly coming from primary or promoted content. In

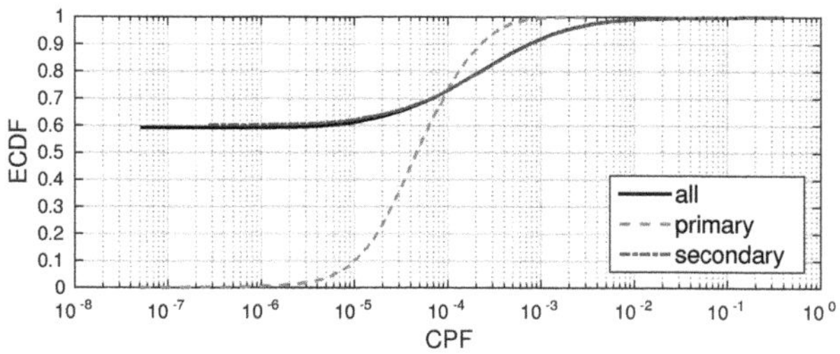

Figure 5: **The empirical CDF of the CPF for primary and secondary URLs.** Primary URLs account for 2% of all URLs after selection bias is removed, are always receiving clicks, whereas secondary URLs account for 98% URLs, and 60% of them are never clicked.

fact, one could go even further and expect primarily URLs to generate an ever larger fraction of the clicks. Those URLs, after all, are the headlines that are carefully selected to appeal to most, they also contain important breaking news, and are disseminated through a famous trusted channel (a verified Twitter account with a strong brand name). It is however, the opposite that holds. As our new data permits to observe for the first time, *secondary URLs, who receive a minority of receptions, generate a significant majority of the clicks (60.66% of them).* Note that our methodology plays a key role in proving this result, as without correcting the sampling bias, this trend is less pronounced (non-primary URLs are estimated in the raw data to receive 52.01% of the clicks).

We present in Figure 5 the CPF distribution observed among primary and secondary URLs separately. This allows to compare for the first time the effective performance of traditional curation (primary URLs) with the one performed through a social media (secondary URLs). Primary URLs account for less than 2% of the URLs overall and all of them are clicked at least once. Secondary URLs, in contrast, very often fail to generate any interest (60% of them are never clicked), and are typically received by a smaller audience. However, secondary URLs that are getting clicked outperform primary URLs in terms of CPF.

This major finding has several consequences. First, it suggests that social media like Twitter already play an important role, both to personalize the news exposed to generate more clicks, and also to broaden the audience of a particular online domain by considering a much larger set of articles. Consequently, serving traffic for less promoted or even non-promoted URLs is critical for online media, it even creates a majority of the visits and hence advertising revenue. Simple curating strategies focusing on headlines and traditional curation would leave important opportunities unfulfilled (more on that immediately below). In addition, naive heuristics on how clicks are generated in social media are too simplistic, and we need new models to understand how clicks occur. Beyond carefully removing selection bias due to sampling, there is a need to design CPFs model which accounts for various types of sharing dynamics.

Variation across news domain.

One could formulate a simple hypothesis in which the channel, or in this case the social network, that is used to share information governs how its users decide to share and click URLs, somewhat independently of the sources. But we found that the numbers reported above for the overall data vary significantly between online news media (as shown in Table 1 where they are sorted from the most to the least popular), proving that multiple audiences use Twitter differently.

Most of the qualitative observations remain: a majority of URLs (50-70%) are not clicked, and primarily URLs always generate overall more receptions than they generate clicks. But, we also observe striking differences. First, domains that are less popular online (in terms of mentions and clicks) shown on the right in Table 1 typically rely more on traditional headline promotion to receive clicks: `nyti.ms` and `fxn.ws` stand as the two extreme examples with 60% and 90% of their clicks coming from headlines, whereas the Huffington Post and the BBC which receive more clicks, present opposite profiles. These numbers suggest that most famous domains like those receive the same absolute order of clicks from primary URLs (roughly between 0.5 and 1.2 million), but that some differ in successfully fostering broader interest to their content beyond those. Although those domain cater to different demographics and audience, Twitter users represent a relatively young crowd and this may be interpreted as an argument that editorial strategy based on a breadth of topics covered might be effective as far as generating clicks from this population is concerned.

3.3 Blockbusters and the share button

Our results show that information sharing on social media plays a critical role for online news; it complements curation offered traditionally through headlines. These two forms of information selection appear strikingly similar: in traditional curation 2% of articles are chosen and produce a disproportionate fraction (near 39%) of the clicks; the sharing process of a social media also results in a minority of secondary URLs (those clicked at least 90 times, about 7% of them) receiving almost 50% of the click traffic. Together, those blockbuster URLs capture about 90% of the traffic. Each typically benefits from a very large amount of receptions (from Figure 6, we estimate that 90% of the clicks come from URLs with at least 150,000 receptions). More details on each metric distribution and how those URLs generate clicks can be seen in Figure 6.

Before our study, most analysis of blockbusters content made the following assumptions: since the primary ways to promote a URL is to share or retweets this article to your followers, one could identify blockbusters using the number of times a URL was shared. This motivates today's ubiquitous use of the "share number" shown next to an online article with various button in Twitter, Facebook, and other social media. One could even envision that, since a fraction of the users clicking an article on a social media decide to retweet it, the share number is a somewhat reduced estimate of the actual readership of an article. However, our joint analysis of shares and clicks reveal limitations of the share number.

First, 59% of the shared URLs are never clicked or, as we call them, *silent.* Note that we merged URLs pointing to the same article, so out of 10 articles mentioned on Twitter, 6 typically on niche topics are never clicked[10].

Because silent URLs are so common, they actually account for a significant fraction (15%) of the whole shares we collected, more than one out of seven. An interesting

[10]They could, however, be accessed in other ways: inside the domain's website, via a search engine etc.

	bbc.in	huff.to	cnn.it	nyti.ms	fxn.ws
# URLs	13.14k	12.38k	6.39k	5.60k	1.82k
# clicks (million)	3.05	2.29	2.01	1.53	0.79
% primary shares	7.24%	10.34%	22.94%	31.86%	41.06%
% primary receptions	31.16%	61.78%	75.37%	78.97%	84.76%
% primary clicks	15.01%	30.81%	61.29%	60.31%	89.79%
% unclicked URLs	51.19%	59.85%	70.16%	64.94%	62.54%
Clicks from all URLs shared <100 times	51.10%	75.70%	33.67%	22.59%	34.89%
Clicks from secondary URLs shared <100 times	46.11%	55.28%	24.73%	14.83%	6.62%
Threshold share to get 90% clicks	8	6	22	34	90
Threshold receptions to get 90% clicks	215k	110k	400k	560k	10,000k
Threshold clicks to get 90% clicks	70	62	180	170	2,000

Table 1: **Variation of metrics across different newssource.**

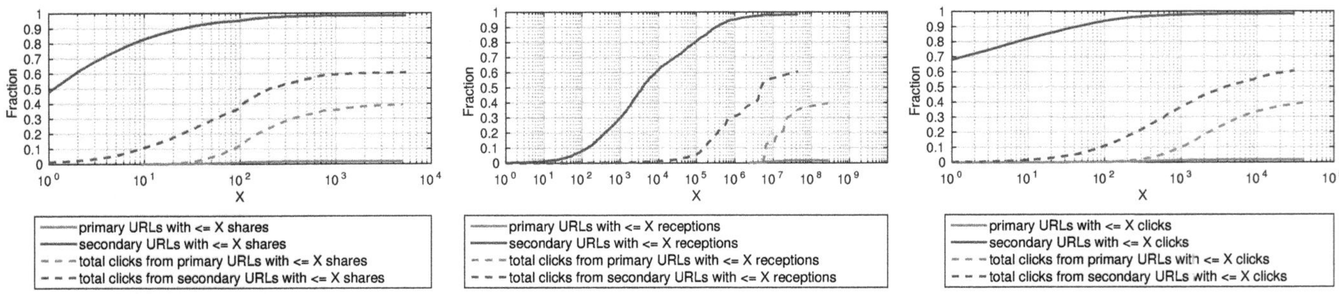

(a) Shares. (b) Receptions. (c) Clicks.

Figure 6: **Fraction of Primary/Secondary URLs (divided by all URLs) with less than X shares, receptions and clicks, shown along with the cumulative fraction of all clicks that those URLs generate (dashed lines).**

paradox is that there seems to be vastly more niche content that users are willing to mention in Twitter than the content that they are actually willing to click on. We later observe another form of a similar paradox.

Second, when it comes to popular content, sharing activity is not trivially correlated with clicks. For instance, URLs receiving 90 shares or more (primary or secondary) comprises the top 6% most shared, so about the same number of URLs as the blockbusters, but they generate way less clicks (only 45%). Conversely we find that blockbuster URLs are shared much less. Figure 6 shows that 90% of the clicks are distributed among all URLs shared 9 times and more.

The 90% click threshold of any metric (clicks, shares, receptions) is the value X of this metric such that the subset of URLs with metric *above* X receives 90% of the clicks. We present values of the 90% click threshold for different domains in Table 1. We observe that the threshold for share is always significantly smaller than other metrics, which means that any URLs shared even just a few times (such as 6 or 8) may be one generating clicks significantly.

The values of 90% click thresholds, when compared across domains, reveals another trend: most popular domains (shown on the left) differ not because their most successful URLs receive more clicks, but because clicks gets generated even for URLs shared a few times only. For instance, in `fxn.ws`, URLs with less than 90 mentions are simply not contributing much to the click traffic; they could entirely disappear and only 10% of the clicks to that domain would be lost. In contrast, for `bbc.in` and `huff.to` the bulk of clicks are generated even among URLs shared about 6-8 times. Similarly, for Fox News 90% of clicks belong to URLs generating at least 10 million receptions on Twitter, this goes down by a factor 50x to 100x when it comes to more popular domains receiving 3 or 4 times more clicks overall. In other words, although massive promotion remains an effective medium to get your content known, the large popularity of the most successful domains is truly due to a long-tail effect of niche URLs.

In summary, the pattern of clicks created from social media clearly favors a blockbuster model: infrequent niche URLs—whatever numerous they are—are generally seen by few users overall and hence have little to no effect on clicks, while successful URLs are seen by a large number (at least 100,000) of the users. But those blockbusters are not easy to identify: massive promotion of articles through official Twitter accounts certainly work, but it appeals less to users as far as clicks are concerned, and in the end, most of the web visits come from other URLs. All evidence suggest that for a domain to expand and grow, the role of other URLs, sometimes shared not frequently, is critical. We note also that relying on the number of shares to characterize the success of an article, as commonly done today for readers of online news, is imprecise (more on that in Section 5).

4. SOCIAL MEDIA ATTENTION SPAN

We now analyze how our data on social media attention reveals different temporal dynamics than those previously observed and analyzed in related literature. Indeed, prior to our work, most of the temporal analysis of social media relied on sharing behavior, and concluded that their users have a *short attention span*, as most of the activity related to an item occurs within a small time of its first appearance. We now present contrasting evidence when clicks are taken into account.

4.1 Background

Studying the temporal evolution of diffusion on social media can be a powerful tool, either to interpret the attention received online as the result of an exogenous or endogenous process [6], to locate the original source of a rumor [24], or to infer *a posteriori* the edges on which the diffusion spreads from the timing of events seen [10]. More generally, examining the temporal evolution of a diffusion process allows to confirm or invalidate simple model of information propagation based on epidemic or cascading dynamics. One of the most important limitation so far is that prior studies focus only on the evolution of the collective volume of attention (*e.g.*, hourly volumes of clicks [25], views [6, 5]), hence capturing the *implicit* activity of the audience, while ignoring the process by which the information has been propagated. Alternatively, other studies focus on *explicit* information propagation only (*e.g.*, tweets [31], URLs shorteners, diggs [28]) ignoring which part of those content exposure leads to actual clicks and content being read. Here for the first time we combine explicit shares of news with the implicit web visits that they generate.

Temporal patterns of online consumption was gathered using videos popularity on YouTube [6, 5] and concluded to some evolution over days and weeks. However, this study considered clicks originating from any sources, including YouTube own recommendation systems, search engine and other mentions online. One hint of the short attention span of social media was obtained through URLs shorteners[11]. Using generic `bit.ly` links of large popularity, this study concludes that URLs exchanged using `bit.ly` on Twitter today typically fades after a very short amount of time (within half an hour). Here we can study jointly for the first time the two processes of social media sharing and consumption. Prior work [1] dealt with very different content (*i.e.*, videos on YouTube), only measured overall popularity generated from all sources, and only studied temporal patterns as a user feature to determine their earliness. Since the two processes are necessarily related, the most important unanswered question we address is whether the temporal property of one process allows to draw conclusion on the properties of the others, and how considering them jointly shed a new light on the diffusion of information in the network.

4.2 Contrast of shares and clicks dynamics

For a given URL and type of events (*e.g.*, clicks), we define this URL half-life as the time elapsed between its birth and half of the event that we collected in the entire data (*e.g.*, the time at which it received half of all the clicks we measured). Intuitively, this denotes a maturity age at which we can expect interest for this URL to start fading away. Prior report[1] predicted that the click half-life for generic `bit.ly` links using Twitter is within two hours. Here we study in addition half-life based on other events such as shares and receptions, and we consider a different domain of URLs (online news). We found, for instance that for a majority of URLs, the half-life for any metric is below one hour (for 52% of the URLs when counting clicks, 63% for shares, and 76% for receptions). This offers no surprise; we already proved that most URLs gather a very small attention overall, it is therefore expected that this process is also ephemeral.

But this metric misrepresents the dynamic of online traffic as it hides the fact that most traffic comes from unusual URLs, those that are more likely to gather a large audience over time. We found for instance that only 30% of the overall clicks gathered in the first day are made during the first hour. This fraction drops to 20% if it is computed for clicks gathered over the first two weeks; overall the number of clicks made in the second week (11.12%) is only twice smaller than in the first hour. Share and receptions dynamics are, on the contrary, much more short lived. While we have no data beyond 24 hours for those metrics due to Twitter limitations, we observe that 53% of shares and 82% of all receptions on the first day occur during the first hour, with 91% and 97% of those created during the first half of the day. By the time that we reach the limit of our observation window, it appears that the shares and receptions are close to zero. In fact, the joint correlation between half-life defined on shares and clicks (not shown here, due to lack of space) revealed that those gathering most of the attention are heavily skewed towards longer clicks lifetime. Note that we are reporting results aggregated for all domains but each of them follow the same trend with minor variations.

4.3 Dynamics & long tail

To understand the effect of temporal dynamics on the distribution of online attention, we draw in Figure 7 for shares, receptions and clicks the evolution with time. Each plot presents, using a dashed line, the distribution of events observed after an hour. In solid line we present how the distribution increases cumulatively as time passes, whereas the dashed-dotted line shows the diminishing rate of hourly events observed at a later point. Most strikingly, we observe that shares and especially receptions dropped by order of magnitude at the end of 24 h. Accordingly, the cumulative distribution of receptions seen at 24 h is only marginally different from the one observed in the first hour. Clicks, and to some extent shares, present a different evolution. Clicks drop more slowly, but more importantly it does not drop uniformly. The more popular a tweet or a URL the more likely it will be shared or clicked after a big period of time.

We highlight a few consequences of those results. Social media have often been described as entirely governed by fast successive series of flash crowds. Although that applies to shares and receptions, it misrepresents the dynamics of clicks which, on the contrary, appear to follow some long term dynamics. This opens opportunities for accurate traffic prediction that we analyze next. In addition, our dynamics motivate to further investigate the origins and properties of the reinforcing effect of time on popularity, as our results suggest that gathering clicks for news on social media rewards URLs that are able to maintain a sustained attention.

5. CLICK-PRODUCING INFLUENCE

In this section, we propose a new definition of influence based on the ability to generate clicks, and we show how it differs from previous metrics measuring mere receptions. We then show how influence and properties of sharing on social media can be leveraged for accurate clicks prediction.

[11] http://bitly.is/1IoOqkU

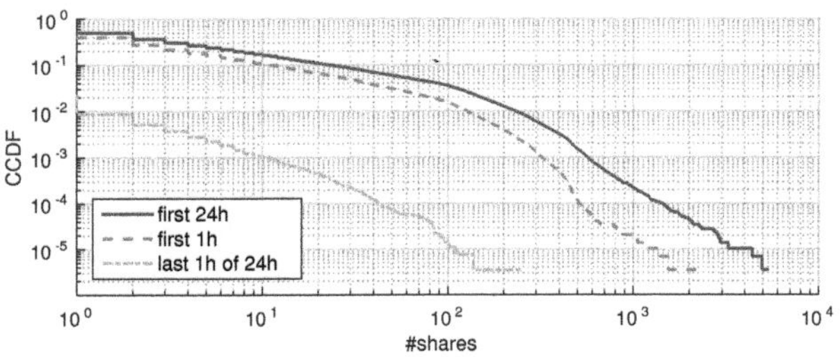

(a) Shares.

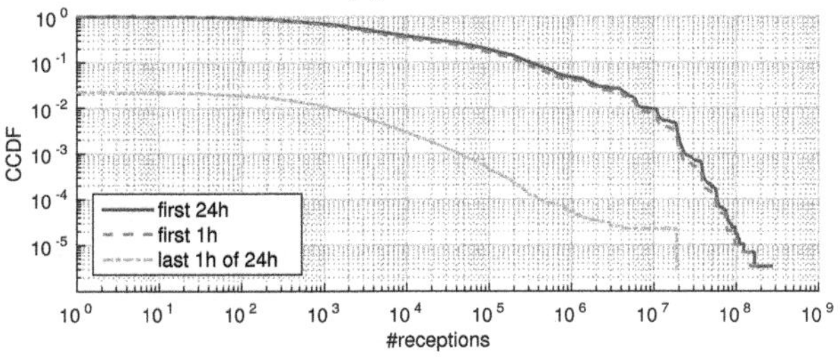

(b) Receptions.

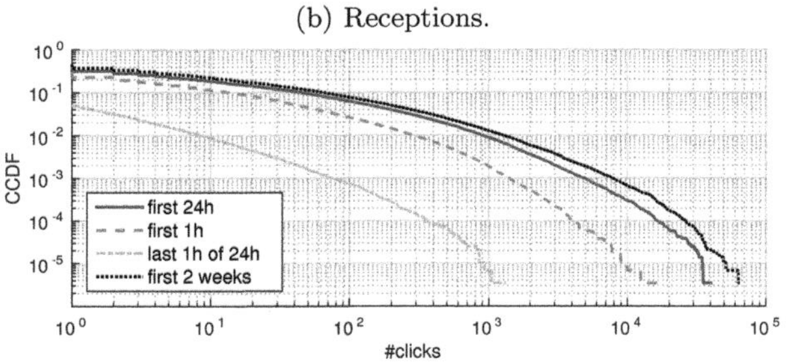

(c) Clicks.

Figure 7: **Evolution of the empirical CCDF with time for three metrics.**

5.1 Background

Information diffusion naturally shapes collective opinion and consensus [12, 7, 18], hence the role of social media in redistributing influence online has been under scrutiny ever since blogs and email chains [2, 17]. Information on traditional mass media follows a unidirectional channel in which pre-established institutions concentrate all decisions. Although the emergence of opinion leaders digesting news content to reach the public at large was pre-established long time ago [12], social media presents an extreme case. They challenge the above vision with a distributed form of influence: social media allow *in theory* any content item to be tomorrow's *headline* and any user to become an *influencer*. This could be either by gathering direct followers, or by seeing her content spreading faster through a set of intermediary node.

Prior works demonstrated that news content exposure benefits from a set of information intermediaries [29, 20], proposed multiple metrics to quantify influence on social media like Twitter [4, 3], proposed models to predict its long term effect [14, 16], and designed algorithms to leverage inherent influence to maximize the success of targeted promotion campaign [13, 23] or prevent it [15]. So far, those influence metrics, models, and algorithms have been validated assuming that observing a large number of receptions is a reliable predictor of actual success, hence reducing influence to the ability to generate receptions. We turn to a new definition in which influence is measured by actual clicks, which are more directly related to revenue through online advertising, and also denote a stronger interaction with content.

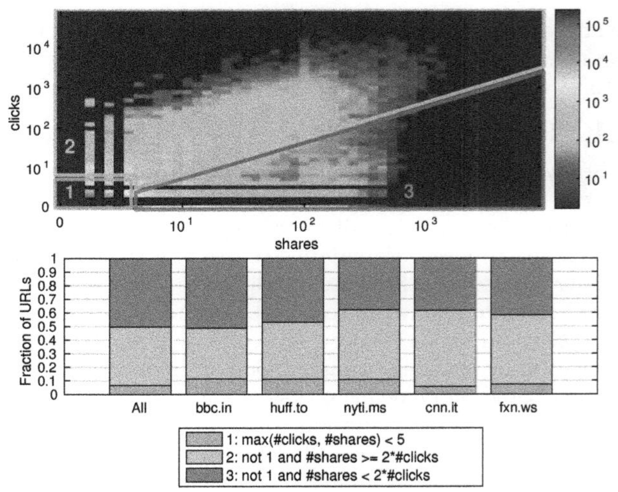

Figure 8: **Joint distribution of shares and clicks, and volume of shares created by different subset of URLs.**

5.2 A new metric and its validation

A natural way to measure the influence (or the lack thereof) for a URL is to measure its ability to generate clicks. We propose to measure a URL's influence by its CPF. To illustrate how it differs from previous metrics, in Figure 8 we present the joint distribution of shares (used today to define influence online) and clicks among URLs in our data using a color-coded heatmap. We observe that the two metrics loosely correlate but also present important differences. URLs can be divided into three subsets: the bottom left corner comprising URLs who have gathered neither shares nor clicks (cluster 1 in green), and two cluster of URLs separated by a straight line (cluster 2 in cyan and cluster 3 in red). Immediately below the figure we present how much share events are created by each cluster. Not shown here is the same distribution for clicks, which confirms that those are entirely produced by URLs in the cluster 2 shown in cyan. This produces another evidence that relying on shares, which classify all those URLs as influential, can be strikingly misleading. While about 40% to 50% of the shares belong to URLs in the cluster 3 in red, those are collectively generating a negligible amount of clicks (1%).

Ideally, we would like to create a similar metric to quantify the influence of a user. Unfortunately, it is not straightforward. One can define the *participatory influence* of a user as the median CPF of URLs that she decides to share. However, this metric is indirect since clicks generated by these URLs are aggregated with many others. In fact, even if this metric is very high, we cannot be sure that the user was responsible for the clicks we observe on those URLs. To understand the bias that this introduces we compare the CPF of the URLs that users were the only ones to send with the CPF of the other URLs they sent. There are 1,358 users in our dataset that are the only ones tweeting at least one of their URL shorteners (note that for validation we did

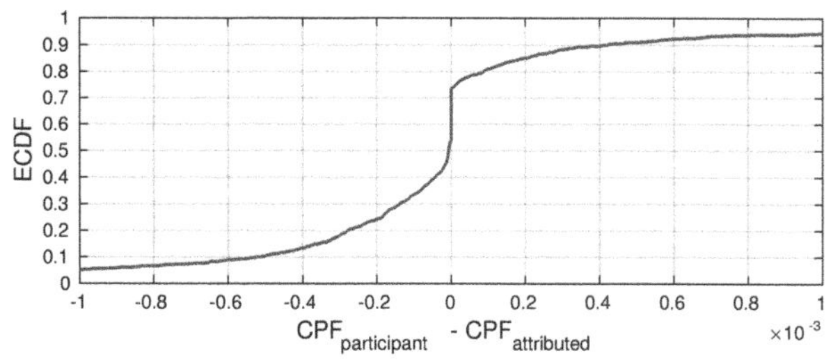

Figure 9: **Bias of the estimation of CPF.**

not merge the URL shorteners). For each user, using those URLs whose transmission on Twitter can be attributed to them, we can compare the CPF of attributed URLs, and ones they participated in sharing without being the only ones. Figure 9 presents the relative CPF difference between these two metric computation. We see that for 90% of users with attributed clicks the difference between the participating CPF and attributed CPF is below 4×10^{-4}. We also see that the difference is more frequently negative. Overall using the participating CPF is a conservative estimate of their true influence.

However, one limitation of the above metric is that a very large fraction of users share a small number of URLs. If that or those few URLs happen to have a large CPF, we assign a large influence although we gather small evidence for it. We therefore propose a refined metric based on the same principles as a statistical confidence test. For each user sharing k URLs, we compute a CPF threshold based on the top 95% percentile of the overall CPF distribution, and we count how many (l) of those URLs among k have a CPF above the threshold. Since choosing a URL at random typically succeeds with probability $p = 0.05$, we can calculate the probability that a user obtain at least l such URLs purely due to chance:

$$\sum_{n=l}^{k} \binom{k}{n} p^n (1-p)^{k-n} = 1 - \sum_{n=0}^{l-1} \binom{k}{n} p^n (1-p)^{k-n} .$$

When this metric is very small, we conclude that the user must be influential. In fact, we are guaranteed that those URLs are chosen among the most influential in a way that is statistically better than a random choice. It also naturally assigns low influence to users for which we have little evidence, as the probability in this case cannot be very small. After computing this metric and manually looking at the results, we found that it clearly distinguish between users, with a minority of successful information intermediaries receiving the highest value of influence.

5.3 Influence and click prediction

So far, our results highlight a promising open problem: as most clicks are generated by social media in the long term, based on early sharing activity, it should be possible to predict, from all the current URLs available on a domain, the click patterns until the end of the day. Moreover, equipped with influence at the user level, we ought to leverage context beyond simple count of events for URLs to make that prediction more precise.

To focus in this article on the most relevant outcomes, we omit the details of the machine learning methodology and validation that we use to compute this prediction. They are however, presented in Appendix A for references. We now present a summary of our main findings:

- One can leverage early information on a URL influence in order to predict its future clicks. For instance, a simple linear regression is shown, based on the number of clicks received by each URL during its first hour, to correctly predict its clicks at the end of the day, with a Pearson R^2 correlation between the real and predicted values being 0.83.
- We found that this result was robust across different classifications methods (such as SVMs) but it varies with information used. Being able to observe clicks at 4 h, for instance, increased the correlation coefficient of the prediction to 0.87, while information on share after 4 h leads to lower correlations of the prediction of 0.65.
- Including various features for the first 5 users sharing the URLs (in terms of followers, or the new influence score) is not sufficient to obtain prediction of the same quality. However, this information can be used in complement to the 1 h of shares to reach the same precision as with clicks only.

6. CONCLUSION

As we have demonstrated, multiple aspects of the analysis of social media are transformed by the dynamics of clicks. We provide the first publicly available dataset[12] to jointly analyze sharing and reading behavior online. We examined the multiple ways in which this information affects previous hypotheses and inform future research. Our analysis of social clicks showed the ability of social media to cater to the myriad taste of a large audience. Our research also highlights future area that require immediate attention. Chiefly among those, predictive models that leverage temporal property and user influence to predict clicks have been shown to be particularly promising. We hope that our methodology, the data collection effort that we provide, and those new observations will help foster a better understanding of how to best address future users' information needs.

7. ACKNOWLEDGMENTS

This material is based upon work supported by the National Science Foundation under grant no. CNS-1254035.

8. REFERENCES

[1] A. Abisheva, V. R. K. Garimella, D. Garcia, and I. Weber. Who watches (and shares) what on YouTube? And when?: Using Twitter to understand YouTube viewership. In *Proc. of ACM WSDM'14*. New York, NY, USA, Feb. 2014.

[2] L. A. Adamic and N. Glance. The political blogosphere and the 2004 U.S. election: divided they blog. In *Proc. of ACM SIGKDD LinkKDD'05*. Chicago, IL, USA, Aug. 2005.

[3] E. Bakshy, J. M. Hofman, W. A. Mason, and D. J. Watts. Everyone's an influencer: quantifying influence on Twitter. In *Proc. of ACM WSDM'11*. Hong Kong, PRC, Feb. 2011.

[12] http://j.mp/soTweet

[4] M. Cha, H. Haddadi, F. Benevenuto, and K. Gummadi. Measuring user influence in Twitter: The million follower fallacy. In *Proc. of AAAI ICWSM'10*, Washington, DC, USA, May 2010.

[5] M. Cha, H. Kwak, P. Rodriguez, Y.-Y. Ahn, and S. Moon. Analyzing the video popularity characteristics of large-scale user generated content systems. *IEEE/ACM TON*, 17(5):1357–1370, 2009.

[6] R. Crane and D. Sornette. Robust dynamic classes revealed by measuring the response function of a social system. In *PNAS*, 105(41):15649–15653, Oct. 2008.

[7] M. H. Degroot. Reaching a consensus. *Journal of the American Statistical Association*, 69(345):118–121, Mar. 1974.

[8] M. Gabielkov, A. Rao, and A. Legout. Studying social networks at scale: macroscopic anatomy of the Twitter social graph. In *Proc. of ACM SIGMETRICS'14*, Austin, TX, USA, Jun. 2014.

[9] S. Goel, A. Broder, E. Gabrilovich, and B. Pang. Anatomy of the long tail: ordinary people with extraordinary tastes. In *Proc. of ACM WSDM'10*, New York, NY, USA, Feb. 2010.

[10] M. Gomez-Rodriguez, J. Leskovec, and A. Krause. Inferring networks of diffusion and influence. *ACM TKDD*, 5(4), Feb. 2012.

[11] N. Hegde, L. Massoulié, and L. Viennot. Self-organizing flows in social networks. In *Proc. of SIROCCO'13*, pages 116–128, Ischia, Italy, Jul. 2013.

[12] E. Katz. The two-step flow of communication: An up-to-date report on an hypothesis. *Public Opinion Quarterly*, 21(1):61, 1957.

[13] D. Kempe, J. M. Kleinberg, and É. Tardos. Maximizing the spread of influence through a social network. In *Proc. of ACM SIGKDD KDD'03*, Washington, DC, USA, Aug. 2003.

[14] J. M. Kleinberg. Cascading behavior in networks: Algorithmic and economic issues. *Algorithmic game theory*, Cambridge University Press, 2007.

[15] M. Lelarge. Efficient control of epidemics over random networks. In *Proc. of ACM SIGMETRICS'09*, Seattle, WA, USA, June 2009.

[16] M. Lelarge. Diffusion and cascading behavior in random networks. *Games and Economic Behavior*, 75(2):752–775, Jul. 2012.

[17] D. Liben-Nowell and J. M. Kleinberg. Tracing information flow on a global scale using Internet chain-letter data. In *PNAS*, 105(12):4633, 2008.

[18] C. G. Lord, L. Ross, and M. R. Lepper. Biased assimilation and attitude polarization: The effects of prior theories on subsequently considered evidence. *Journal of Personality and Social Psychology*, 37(11):2098, Nov. 1979.

[19] L. Massoulié, M. I. Ohannessian, and A. Proutiere. Greedy-Bayes for targeted news dissemination. In *Proc. of ACM SIGMETRICS'15*. Portland, OR, USA, Jun. 2015.

[20] A. May, A. Chaintreau, N. Korula, and S. Lattanzi. Filter & Follow: How social media foster content curation. In *Proc. of ACM SIGMETRICS'14*, Austin, TX, USA, Jun. 2014.

[21] H. B. McMahan, G. Holt, D. Sculley, M. Young, and D. Ebner. Ad click prediction: a view from the trenches. In *Proc. of ACM SIGKDD KDD'13*, Chicago, IL, USA, Aug. 2013.

[22] A. Mitchell, J. Gottfried, J. Kiley, and K. E. Matsa. Political polarization & media habits. Technical report, Pew Research Center, Oct. 2014, http://pewrsr.ch/1vZ9MnM.

[23] J. Ok, Y. Jin, J. Shin, and Y. Yi. On maximizing diffusion speed in social networks. In *Proc. of ACM SIGMETRICS'14*, Austin, TX, USA, Jun. 2014.

[24] P. Pinto, P. Thiran, and M. Vetterli. Locating the source of diffusion in large-scale networks. *Physical review letters*, 109(6):068702, Aug. 2012.

[25] G. Szabo and B. A. Huberman. Predicting the popularity of online content. *Communications of the ACM*, 53(8), Aug. 2010.

[26] L. Wang, A. Ramachandran and A. Chaintreau. Measuring click and share dynamics on social media: a reproducible and validated approach. In. *Proc. of AAAI ICWSM NECO'16*, Cologne, Germany, May 2016.

[27] F. M. F. Wong, Z. Liu, and M. Chiang. On the efficiency of social recommender networks. In. *Proc. of IEEE INFOCOM'15*, Hong Kong, PRC, Apr. 2015.

[28] F. Wu and B. A. Huberman. Novelty and collective attention. In *PNAS*, 104(45):17599–17601, Nov. 2007.

[29] S. Wu, J. M. Hofman, W. A. Mason, and D. J. Watts. Who says what to whom on Twitter. In *Proc. of WWW'11*. Hyderabad, India, Mar. 2011.

[30] J. Xu, R. Wu, K. Zhu, B. Hajek, R. Srikant, and L. Ying. Jointly clustering rows and columns of binary matrices. In *Proc. of ACM SIGMETRICS'14*, Austin, TX, USA, Jun. 2014.

[31] J. Yang and J. Leskovec. Patterns of temporal variation in online media. In *Proc. of ACM WSDM'11*. Hong Kong, PRC, Feb. 2011.

[32] R. B. Zadeh, A. Goel, K. Munagala, and A. Sharma. On the precision of social and information networks. In *Proc. of ACM COSN'13*. Boston, MA, USA, Oct. 2013.

APPENDIX

A. CLICK PREDICTION METHOD

As we design influence score from CPF and long term dynamics, we expect that it can be useful to predict clicks on URLs. In this section, we evaluate the efficiency of those metrics to predict the clicks for a URL. We consider two types of features: those related to the timing of shares (*e.g.*, number of shares in the first hour or number of receptions in the first 4 hours) and those based on the users who initially shared the URL (*e.g.*, number of followers of the user). Table 2 lists the different features that were used. For the user features, we only consider the first five users to share the URL, and we use the influence score as defined in Section 5.2. We choose to predict the number of clicks for a URL instead of the CPF to better account for the very different characteristics of URLs independently of the receptions.

Sharing-Based Features	Time scales	User-Based Features
• shares	• 1 h	• # primary URLs
• clicks	• 4 h	• # followers
• receptions	• 24 h	• verified account?
		• score (median)
		• score (95th percentile)
		• score (median) + score (95th percentile)

Table 2: **Features used for the click prediction.**

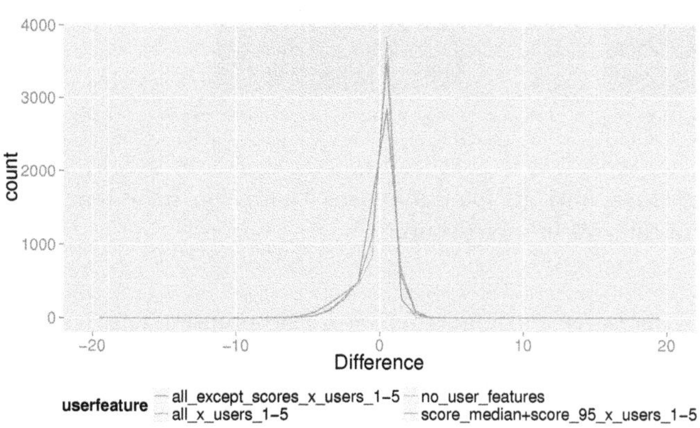

Figure 10: **Distribution of predicted clicks vs. actual clicks.**

We predict clicks on the following scale: 0 clicks, $(0, 10]$ clicks, $(10, 100]$ clicks, $(100, 1000]$ clicks, $(1000, 5000]$ clicks, and $(5000, +\infty)$ clicks. We use the standard *python* implementation in *scikit-learn* to apply the linear regression to estimate the logarithm of the number of clicks with all the features in logarithmic scale. We concentrate on a single domain (`nyti.ms`) to avoid noise from different domains, and we randomly split the data into a training set and a test set of equal size.

To evaluate the quality of our prediction, we use a standard measure of quality (confusion matrix) as well as computing the difference between the predicted number of clicks and the true number of clicks. In a confusion matrix, each row corresponds to the real value, each column corresponds to the predicted value and the corresponding elements are the number of samples in those classes. The better the classification, the more samples lie along the diagonal. Samples close to the diagonal were misclassified but not as egregiously as those further away. Confusion matrices help us understand the classifier performance by *class*. However, we are interested in how close our predicted clicks are to the real clicks, captured by the latter measure. We define the fraction of underestimated clicks for a URL to be $\frac{\text{true \# clicks}-\text{predicted \# clicks}}{\text{true \# clicks}}$ when *predicted # clicks* < *true # clicks*. Similarly, we define the fraction of overestimated clicks for a URL to be $\frac{\text{predicted \# clicks}-\text{true \# clicks}}{\text{true \# clicks}}$ when *predicted # clicks* > *true # clicks*.

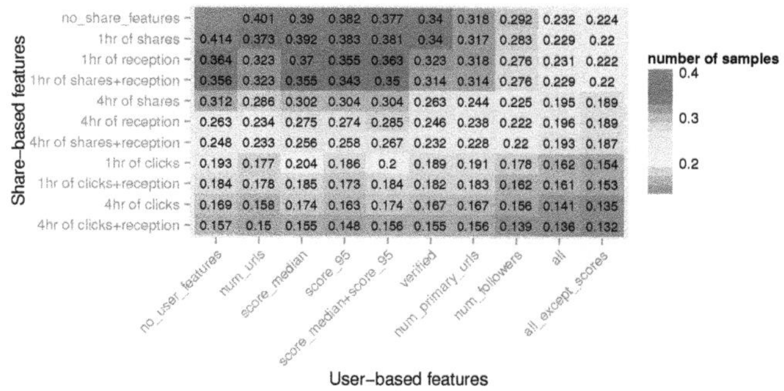

Figure 11: **Fraction of clicks that was missed or underestimated in classification.**

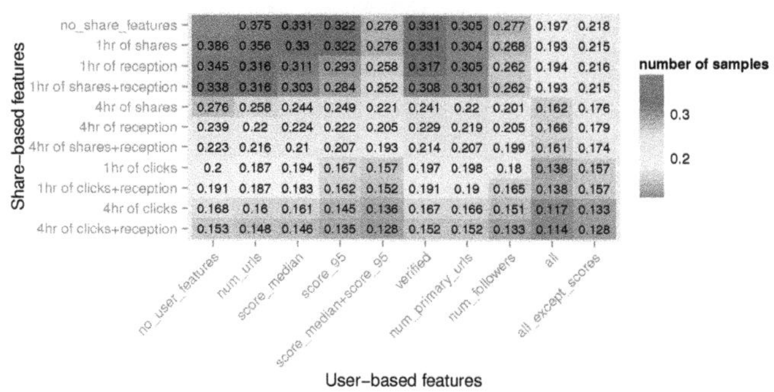

Figure 12: **Fraction of clicks that were overestimated in classification.**

Figure 10 shows the distribution of the difference in estimated clicks from the real ones. Here, we fix the user-based features to be the the information about 1 h of clicks and we evaluate the impact of user-based features. We see that the vast majority of URLs have no clicks and are successfully predicted to have none. The histogram is quite tightly clustered indicating that most of our estimates are quite close to the real value. Each color in the figure indicates the prediction quality with the use of additional user features for the classifier.

To better understand the contributions of sharing and user features, we look at the fraction of underestimated clicks and overestimated clicks for various combinations of sharing and user features. Figure 11 and Figure 12 compare the results across all sharing and user features, the color indicates the quality of the classification. In both cases, lower values indicate a better classification, *i.e.*, there are fewer clicks that

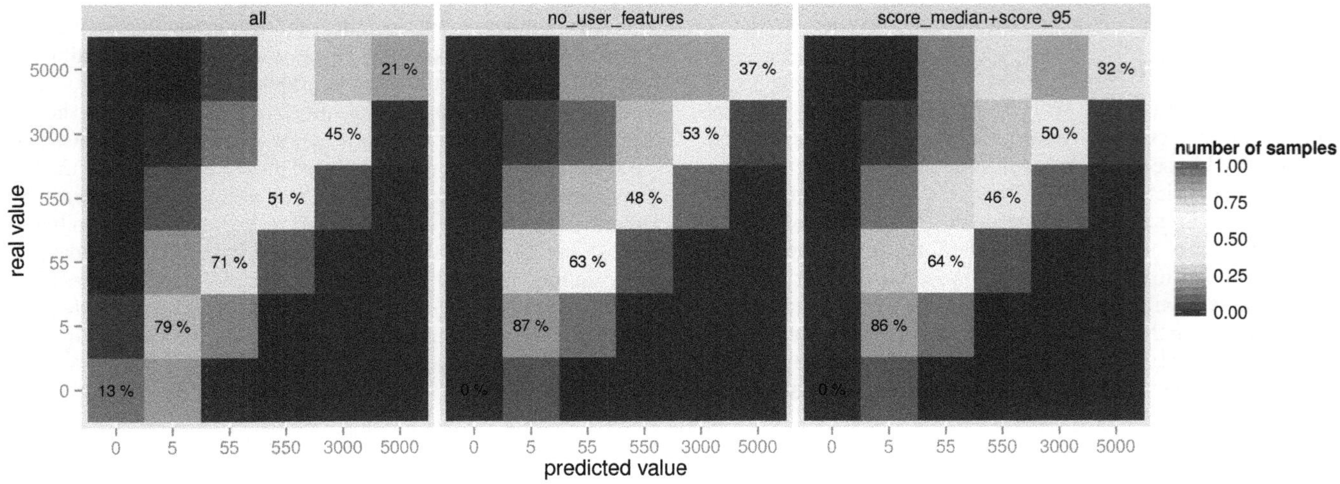

Figure 13: **Confusion matrices with 1 h of clicks and all user features (left), no user features (middle), and user scores(right).** The values are the number of samples in each group.

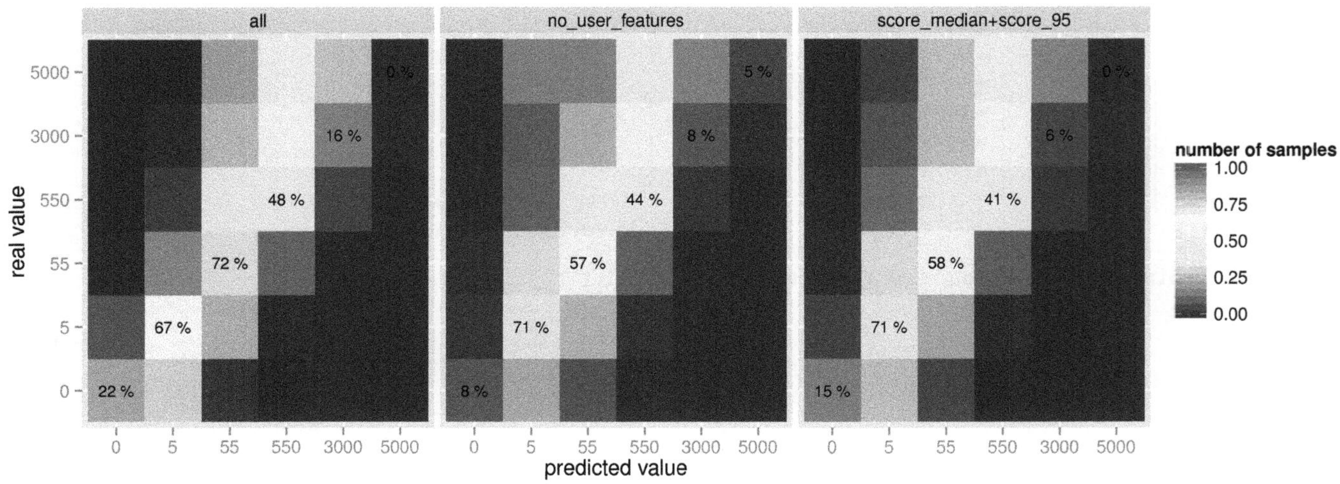

Figure 14: **Confusion matrices with 4 h of shares and receptions and all user features (left), no user features (middle), and user scores(right).** The values are the number of samples in each group.

are missed or overestimated. In the figures, the redder the value, the better the quality of the classification with those features. Unsurprisingly, the initial number of clicks for a URL proves to be a good feature. Knowing the number of clicks in the first hour is much more important than knowing the number of shares or receptions in the first hour, or even for the first 4 hours. Taken independently, user features do not provide good click estimates. However, they prove to be useful when used in conjunction with sharing features. For example, the fraction of underestimated clicks reduces marginally when considering the additional features of median and 95th percentile scores with the sharing feature of 4 h of shares (from 31.2% of clicks missed to 30.4% of clicks missed).

Figure 13 and Figure 14 show the confusion matrices for 1 h of clicks and 4 h of shares + 4 h of receptions, respectively. In general, we see that the user features provide definite improvement in prediction quality. Combination of all user features provides a significant improvement in prediction quality. The number of followers of the first five users who shared the URL gives the greatest improvement in the number of underestimated clicks, and the user influence scores prove to be useful in controlling the overestimation of clicks.

Using Predictions in Online Optimization: Looking Forward with an Eye on the Past*

Niangjun Chen†, Joshua Comden‡, Zhenhua Liu‡, Anshul Gandhi‡, Adam Wierman†
†California Institute of Technology, Pasadena, CA, E-mail: {ncchen,adamw} @caltech.edu
‡Stony Brook University, NY, E-mail:{joshua.comden, zhenhua.liu, anshul.gandhi}@stonybrook.edu

ABSTRACT

We consider online convex optimization (OCO) problems with switching costs and noisy predictions. While the design of online algorithms for OCO problems has received considerable attention, the design of algorithms in the context of noisy predictions is largely open. To this point, two promising algorithms have been proposed: Receding Horizon Control (RHC) and Averaging Fixed Horizon Control (AFHC). The comparison of these policies is largely open. AFHC has been shown to provide better worst-case performance, while RHC outperforms AFHC in many realistic settings. In this paper, we introduce a new class of policies, Committed Horizon Control (CHC), that generalizes both RHC and AFHC. We provide average-case analysis and concentration results for CHC policies, yielding the first analysis of RHC for OCO problems with noisy predictions. Further, we provide explicit results characterizing the optimal CHC policy as a function of properties of the prediction noise, e.g., variance and correlation structure. Our results provide a characterization of when AFHC outperforms RHC and vice versa, as well as when other CHC policies outperform both RHC and AFHC.

1. INTRODUCTION

In an online convex optimization (OCO) problem, an algorithm interacts with an environment in a sequence of rounds. In round t the algorithm chooses an action x_t from a convex decision/action space F, the environment reveals a convex cost function h_t, and the algorithm pays cost $h_t(x_t)$. The goal of the algorithm is to minimize cost over a horizon T.

OCO has a rich history, with applications in wide-ranging areas of computer science and beyond [54, 27, 21, 50, 33, 34, 35, 36, 37]. In recent years, OCO has seen considerable interest from applications in the networking and distributed systems communities. In particular, OCO has enabled novel designs for dynamic capacity planning, load shifting and demand response for data centers [29, 34, 35, 36, 40], geographical load balancing of internet-scale systems [33, 47], electrical vehicle charging [15, 29], video streaming [41, 25], and thermal management of systems-on-chip [51, 52, 7].

Applications of OCO in the networking and distributed systems communities typically differ in two significant ways from the classical OCO literature: (i) actions incur *switching costs* and (ii) *noisy predictions* about the future are available.

Switching costs capture the cost that is incurred by systems when moving from one state to another. This is modeled by adding an extra term to the cost paid by the algorithm in each round, i.e., the cost becomes $h_t(x_t) + \beta \parallel x_t - x_{t-1} \parallel$, where $\parallel \cdot \parallel$ is a norm (often the one-norm), and $\beta \in \mathbb{R}^+$. This additional term models, e.g., the cost of turning servers on/off in dynamic capacity planning [29, 34, 35, 36, 40, 17] or the cost of changing a quality level in the case of video streaming [24, 25]. The addition of switching costs makes the algorithmic problem harder as it forces current actions to depend on beliefs about future cost functions.

Predictions are of great importance in networking and distributed systems. Despite the considerable noise that is often inherent in forecasts, predictions can be extremely useful. For example, predictions of future demand are critical in the case of dynamic capacity planning in data centers to ensure sufficient capacity [16, 30, 19, 29, 34, 35, 36, 40, 17]. Unfortunately, designing online algorithms that exploit noisy predictions is an open, challenging topic.

In this paper, we focus on *OCO problems that have both switching costs and noisy predictions.* While there is a significant literature on OCO problems with switching costs [13, 4, 20, 5, 33, 34, 6], there is much less work studying the impact of predictions [33, 13, 34]. Further, the analytic work that does focus on predictions typically assumes perfect lookahead, the lone exception being Chen et al. [13].

Two promising algorithms. Perhaps the most natural starting point for studying algorithms for OCO problems with switching costs and noisy predictions is the class of Model Predictive Control (MPC) algorithms. MPC is a prominent and widely-studied class of algorithms in the control theory community [8, 48, 31, 12, 18, 38], and much of the work studying predictions in OCO problems has focused on MPC and its variants, e.g., [33, 15, 14].

From these works, two promising algorithms have emerged: Receding Horizon Control (RHC) and Averaging Fixed Horizon Control (AFHC). (See Section 3 for formal definitions of these two algorithms.) Both algorithms use a prediction horizon/window of size w, but make decisions in very different ways. RHC considers, at each point in time, the predictions available in the current horizon, determines the trajectory of w actions that minimize the cost within that horizon, and then commits *only* the first action in that trajectory. By contrast, AFHC works by averaging the actions of multiple Fixed Horizon Control (FHC) algorithms, each of which work similarly to RHC but commit to *all* w actions in a given prediction horizon.

*This work is partially supported by the NSF through CNS-1464388, CNS-1464151, CNS-1319820, NETS-1518941 and an A*STAR NSS (PhD) scholarship.

SIGMETRICS '16, June 14–18, 2016, Antibes Juan-Les-Pins, France.

DOI: http://dx.doi.org/10.1145/2896377.2901464

Receding Horizon Control (RHC) has a long history in the control theory literature [8, 48, 31, 12, 18, 38], but was first studied analytically in the context of OCO in [33]. In [33], RHC was proven to have a competitive ratio (the ratio of the cost incurred by RHC to the cost incurred by the offline optimal algorithm) of $1+O(1/w)$ in the one-dimensional setting, where w is the size of the prediction window. However, the competitive ratio of RHC is $1+\Omega(1)$ in the general case, and thus does *not* decrease to one as the prediction window grows in the worst case; this is despite the fact that predictions are assumed to have no noise (the perfect lookahead model). To this point there is no analytic work characterizing the performance of RHC with noisy predictions.

The poor worst-case performance of RHC motivated the proposal of Averaging Fixed Horizon Control (AFHC) [33], which provides an interesting contrast. While RHC is entirely "forward looking", AFHC keeps an "eye on the past" by respecting the actions of FHC algorithms in previous timesteps and thus avoids switching costs incurred by moving too quickly between actions. As a result, AFHC achieves a competitive ratio of $1 + O(1/w)$ in both single and multi-dimensional action spaces, under the assumption of perfect lookahead, [33]. Further, strong guarantees on the performance of AFHC have been established in the case of noisy predictions [13].

Surprisingly, while the competitive ratio of AFHC is smaller than that of RHC, RHC provides *better* performance than AFHC in many practical cases. Further, RHC is seemingly more resistant to prediction noise in many settings (see Figure 1 for an example), though no analytic results are known for this case. Thus, at this point, two promising algorithms have been proposed, but it is unclear in what settings each should be used and it is unclear if there are other algorithms that dominate these two proposals.

Contributions of this paper. The goal of this paper is to provide new insights into the design of algorithms for OCO problems with noisy predictions. In particular, our results highlight the importance of *commitment* in online algorithms, and the significant performance gains that can be achieved by tuning the *commitment level* of an algorithm as a function of structural properties of the prediction noise such as variance and correlation structure.

In terms of commitment, receding horizon control (RHC) and averaging fixed horizon control (AFHC) represent two extreme algorithm designs – RHC commits to only one action at a time whereas AFHC averages over algorithms that commit to actions spanning the whole prediction horizon. While the non-committal nature of RHC enables quick response to improved predictions, it makes RHC *susceptible to switching costs.* On the other hand, the cautious nature of AFHC averts switching costs but makes it entirely *dependent on the accuracy of predictions.*

Motivated by these deficiencies in existing algorithm design, we introduce a new class of policies, **Committed Horizon Control** (CHC), that allows for arbitrary levels of commitment and thus subsumes RHC and AFHC. We present both average-case analysis (Theorems 1 and 6) and concentration results (Theorems 7) for CHC policies. In doing so, we provide the *first analysis* of RHC with noisy predictions.

Our results demonstrate that intermediate levels of commitment can provide significant reductions in cost, to the tune of more than 50% (e.g., Figure 4(a), Figure 5(a) and Figure 6(a)). Further, our results also reveal the impact of correlation structure and variance of prediction noise on the optimal level of commitment, and provide simple guidelines on how to choose between RHC and AFHC.

These results are enabled by a key step in our proof that transforms the control strategy employed by the offline optimal algorithm, OPT to the strategy of CHC via a trajectory of intermediate strategies. We exploit the structure of our algorithm at each intermediate step to bound the difference in costs; the sum of these costs over the entire transformation then gives us a bound on the difference in costs between OPT and CHC .

To summarize, this paper makes the following contributions to the literature on OCO with noisy predictions:

- We provide the first analysis of RHC for OCO problems with noisy predictions.
- We characterize when RHC/AFHC is better as a function of the correlation structure and variance of prediction noise.
- We introduce and analyze a new class of Committed Horizon Control (CHC) policies that generalizes AFHC and RHC.
- We highlight how the commitment level of a policy should be tuned depending on structural properties of prediction noise. By optimizing the level of commitment, CHC policies can achieve performance improvements of more than 50% over AFHC and RHC.

2. PROBLEM FORMULATION

We consider online convex optimization (OCO) problems with switching costs and noisy predictions. We first introduce OCO with switching costs (Section 2.1) and then describe the model of prediction noise (Section 2.2). Finally, we discuss the performance metric we consider in this paper – the competitive difference – and how it relates to common measures such as regret and competitive ratio (Section 2.3).

2.1 OCO with switching costs

An OCO problem with switching costs considers a convex, compact decision/action space $F \subset \mathbb{R}^n$ and a sequence of cost functions $\{h_1, h_2, \ldots\}$, where each $h_t : F \to \mathbb{R}^+$ is convex, and F is a compact set.

At time t, the following sequence occurs: (i) the online algorithm first chooses an action, which is a vector $x_t \in F \subset \mathbb{R}^n$, (ii) the environment chooses a cost function h_t from a set $\mathcal{C}$, and (iii) the algorithm pays a stage cost $h_t(x_t)$ and a switching cost $\beta \|x_t - x_{t-1}\|$, where $\beta \in \mathbb{R}^+$, and $\|\cdot\|$ can be any norm in $\mathbb{R}^n$, and F is bounded in terms of this norm, i.e., $\|x - y\| \leq D$ for all $x, y \in F$.

Motivated by path planning and image labeling problems [45, 13, 42], we consider a variation of the above that uses a *parameterized* cost function $h_t(x_t) = h(x_t, y_t)$, where the parameter $y_t \in \mathbb{R}^m$ is the focus of prediction. This yields a total cost over T rounds of

$$\min_{x_t \in F} \sum_{t=1}^{T} h(x_t, y_t) + \beta \|x_t - x_{t-1}\|, \tag{1}$$

Note that prior work [13] considers only the case where a least-square penalty is paid each round, i.e., an online LASSO formulation with $h(x_t, y_t) = \frac{1}{2}\|y_t - Kx_t\|_2^2$. In this paper, we consider more general h. We impose that $h(x_t, y_t)$ is separately convex in both x_t and y_t along with the following smoothness criteria.

DEFINITION 1. *A function h is α-Hölder continuous in the second argument for $\alpha \in \mathbb{R}^+$, i.e., for all $x \in F$, there exists $G \in \mathbb{R}^+$, such that*

$$|h(x, y_1) - h(x, y_2)| \leq G \|y_1 - y_2\|_2^{\alpha}, \forall y_1, y_2.$$

G and α control the sensitivity of the cost function to a disturbance in y.

For this paper, we focus on $\alpha \leq 1$, since the only α-Hölder continuous function with $\alpha > 1$ is the constant function [2].

When $\alpha = 1$, h is *G-Lipschitz* in the second argument; if h is differentiable in the second argument, this is equivalent to $\|\partial_y h(x,y)\|_2 \leq G, \quad \forall x, y$.

2.2 Modeling prediction noise

Predictions about the future play a crucial role in almost all online decision problems. However, while significant effort has gone into designing predictors, e.g., [53, 43, 44, 26], much less work has gone into *integrating* predictions efficiently into algorithms. This is, in part, due to a lack of tractable, practical models for prediction noise. As a result, most papers that study online decision making problems, such as OCO, use numerical simulations to evaluate the impact of prediction noise, e.g., [1, 3, 36, 40].

The papers that do consider analytic models often use either i.i.d. prediction noise or worst-case bounds on prediction errors for tractability. An exception is the recent work [13, 15] which introduces a model for prediction noise that captures three important features of real predictors: (i) it allows for correlations in prediction errors (both short range and long range); (ii) the quality of predictions decreases the further in the future we try to look ahead; and (iii) predictions about the future are refined as time passes. Further, [13] shows that it is tractable in the context of OCO. Thus, we adopt the model from [13] for this paper.

Specifically, throughout this paper we model prediction error via the following equation:

$$y_t - y_{t|\tau} = \sum_{s=\tau+1}^{t} f(t-s)e(s), \qquad (2)$$

where $y_{t|\tau}$ is the prediction of y_t made at time $\tau < t$. This model characterizes prediction error as white noise being passed through a causal filter. In particular, the prediction error is a weighted linear combination of per-step noise terms $e(s)$ with weights $f(t-s)$, where f is a deterministic impulse response function. The noise terms $e(s)$ are assumed to be uncorrelated with mean zero and positive definite covariance R_e; let $\sigma^2 = \mathrm{tr}(R_e)$. Further, the impulse response function f is assumed to satisfy $f(0) = I$ and $f(t) = 0$ for $t < 0$.

Note that i.i.d. prediction noise can be recovered by imposing that $f(0) = I$ and $f(t) = 0$ for all $t \neq 0$. Further, the model can represent prediction errors that arise from classical filters such as Wiener filters and Kalman filters (see [13]). In both cases the impulse response function decays as $f(s) \sim \eta^s$ for some $\eta < 1$.

These examples highlight that the form of the impulse response function captures the degree of short-term/long-term correlation in prediction errors. The form of the correlation structure plays a key role in the performance results we prove, and its impact can be captured through the following definition. For any $k > 0$, let $\|f_k\|^2$ be the two norm square of prediction error covariance over k steps of prediction, i.e.,

$$\|f_k\|^2 = \mathrm{tr}(\mathbb{E}[\delta y_k \delta y_k^T]) = \mathrm{tr}(R_e \sum_{s=0}^{k} f(s)^T f(s)), \qquad (3)$$

where $\delta y_k^T = y_{t+k} - y_{t+k|t} = \sum_{s=t+1}^{t+k} f(t+k-s)e(s)$. Derivation of (3) can be found in Appendix B.1 Equation (19).

2.3 The competitive difference

For any algorithm ALG that comes up with feasible actions $x_{ALG,t} \in F, \forall t$, the cost of the algorithm over the horizon can be written as

$$\mathrm{cost}(ALG) = \sum_{t=1}^{T} h(x_{ALG,t}, y_t) + \beta \|x_{ALG,t} - x_{ALG,t-1}\| \quad (4)$$

We compare the performance of our online algorithm against the optimal offline algorithm OPT, which makes the optimal decision with full knowledge of the trajectory of y_t.

$$\mathrm{cost}(OPT) = \min_{x_t \in F} \sum_{t=1}^{T} h(x_t, y_t) + \beta \|x_t - x_{t-1}\| \qquad (5)$$

The results in this paper bound the *competitive difference* of algorithms for OCO with switching costs and prediction noise. Informally, the competitive difference is the additive gap between the cost of the online algorithm and the cost of the offline optimal.

To define the competitive difference formally in our setting we need to first consider how to specify the instance. To do this, let us first return to the specification of the prediction model in (2) and expand the summation all the way to time zero. This expansion highlights that the process y_t can be viewed as a random deviation around the predictions made at time zero, $y_{t|0} := \hat{y}_t$, which are specified externally to the model:

$$y_t = \hat{y}_t + \sum_{s=1}^{t} f(t-s)e(s). \qquad (6)$$

Thus, an instance can be specified either via the process y_t or via the initial predictions $\hat{y}_t$, and then the random noise from the model determines the other. The latter is preferable for analysis, and thus we state our definition of competitive difference (and our theorems) using this specification.

DEFINITION 2. *We say an online algorithm ALG has (expected)* ***competitive difference*** *at most $\rho(T)$ if:*

$$\sup_{\hat{y}} \mathbb{E}_e [\mathrm{cost}(ALG) - \mathrm{cost}(OPT)] \leq \rho(T). \qquad (7)$$

Note that the expectation in the definition above is with respect to the prediction noise, $(e(t))_{t=1}^{T}$, and so both terms $\mathrm{cost}(ALG)$ and $\mathrm{cost}(OPT)$ are random. Unlike ALG, the offline optimal algorithm OPT knows each exact realization of e before making the decision.

Importantly, though we specify our results in terms of the competitive difference, it is straightforward to convert them into results about the competitive ratio and regret, which are more commonly studied in the OCO literature. Recall that the **competitive ratio** bounds the ratio of the algorithm's cost to that of OPT, and the **regret** bounds the difference between the algorithm's cost and the offline *static* optimal.

Converting a result on the competitive difference into a result on the competitive ratio requires lower bounding the offline optimal cost, and such a bound can be found in Theorem 6 of [33]. Similarly, converting a result on the competitive difference into a result on the regret requires lower bounding the offline static optimal cost, and such a bound can be found in Theorem 2 of [13].

3. ALGORITHM DESIGN

There is a large literature studying algorithms for online convex optimization (OCO), both with the goal of designing algorithms with small regret and algorithms with small competitive ratio.

These algorithms use a wide variety of techniques. For example, there are numerous algorithms that maintain sublinear regret, e.g., *online gradient descent* (OGD) based algorithms [54, 21] and *Online Newton Step and Follow the Approximate Leader* algorithms [21]. (Note that the classical setting does not consider switching costs; however, [4] shows that similar regret bounds can be obtained when switching costs are considered.) By contrast, there only exist algorithms that achieve constant competitive ratio in limited settings, e.g., [34] shows that, when F is a one-dimensional normed space, there exists a deterministic online algorithm that is 3-competitive. This is because, in general, obtaining a constant competitive ratio is impossible in the worst-case: [10] has shown that any deterministic algorithm must be $\Omega(n)$-competitive given metric decision space of size n and [9] has shown that any randomized algorithm must be $\Omega(\sqrt{\log n / \log\log n})$-competitive.

However, all of the algorithms and results described above are in the worst-case setting and do not consider algorithms that have noisy predictions available. Given noisy predictions, the most natural family of algorithms to consider come from the family of Model Predictive Control (MPC) algorithms, which is a powerful, prominent class of algorithms from the control community. In fact, the only analytic results for OCO problems with predictions to this point have come from algorithms inspired by MPC, e.g., [8, 48, 31, 12]. (Note that there is a large literature on such algorithms in control theory, e.g., [18, 38] and the references therein, but the analysis needed for OCO is different than from the stability analysis provided by the control literature.)

To this point, two promising candidate algorithms have emerged in the context of OCO: Receding Horizon Control (RHC) [32] and Averaging Fixed Horizon Control (AFHC) [33]. We discuss these two algorithms in Section 3.1 below and then introduce our novel class of Committed Horizon Control (CHC) algorithms, which includes both RHC and AFHC as special cases, in Section 3.2. The class of CHC algorithms is the focus of this paper.

3.1 Two promising algorithms

At this point the two most promising algorithms for integrating noisy predictions into solutions to OCO problems are RHC and AFHC.

Receding Horizon Control (RHC): RHC operates by determining, at each timestep t, the optimal actions over the window $(t+1, t+w)$, given the starting state x_t and a prediction window (horizon) of length w.

To state this more formally, let $y_{\cdot|\tau}$ denote the vector $(y_{\tau+1|\tau}, \ldots, y_{\tau+w|\tau})$, the prediction of y in a w timestep prediction window at time τ. Define $X^{\tau+1}(x_\tau, y_{\cdot|\tau})$ as the vector in F^w indexed by $t \in \{\tau+1, \ldots, \tau+w\}$, which is the solution to

$$\min_{x_{\tau+1},\ldots,x_{\tau+w}} \sum_{t=\tau+1}^{\tau+w} h(x_t, y_{t|\tau}) + \sum_{t=\tau+1}^{\tau+w} \beta \left\| x_t - x_{t-1} \right\|, \quad (8)$$

$$\text{subject to} \quad x_t \in F.$$

Algorithm 1 (Receding Horizon Control). *For all $t \leq 0$, set $x_{RHC,t} = 0$. Then, at each timestep $\tau \geq 0$, set*

$$x_{RHC,\tau+1} = X_{\tau+1}^{\tau+1}(x_{RHC,\tau}, y_{\cdot|\tau}) \quad (9)$$

RHC has a long history in the control theory literature, e.g., [8, 18, 38, 12]. However, there are few results known in the OCO literature, and most such results are negative. In particular, the competitive ratio of RHC with perfect lookahead window w is $1+O(1/w)$ in the one-dimensional setting. The performance is not so good in the general case. In particular, outside of the one-dimensional case the competitive ration of RHC is $1 + \Omega(1)$, i.e., the competitive ratio does not decrease to 1 as the prediction window w increases in the worst case [34].

Averaging Fixed Horizon Control (AFHC): AFHC provides an interesting contrast to RHC. RHC ignores all history – the decisions and predictions that led it to be in the current state – while AFHC constantly looks both backwards and forwards. Specifically, AFHC averages the choices made by Fixed Horizon Control (FHC) algorithms. In particular, AFHC with prediction window size w averages the actions of w FHC algorithms, each with different predictions available to it. At time t, a FHC algorithm determines the optimal actions $x_{t+1}, \ldots, x_{t+w}$ given a prediction window (horizon) of length w as done in RHC. But, then FHC implements all actions in the trajectory $x_{t+1}, \ldots, x_{t+w}$ instead of just the first action x_t. Fixed Horizon Control algorithms are individually more naive than RHC, but by averaging them AFHC can provide improved worst-case performance compared to RHC. To define the algorithm formally, let

$$\Omega_k = \{i : i \equiv k \mod w\} \cap [-w+1, T] \text{ for } k = 0, \ldots, w-1.$$

Algorithm 2 (Fixed Horizon Control, version k). *$FHC^{(k)}(w)$, is defined in the following manner. For all $t \leq 0$, set $x_{FHC,t}^{(k)} = 0$. At timeslot $\tau \in \Omega_k$ (i.e., before $y_{\tau+1}$ is revealed), for all $t \in \{\tau+1, \ldots, \tau+w\}$, use (8) to set*

$$x_{FHC,t}^{(k)} = X_t^{\tau+1}\left(x_{FHC,\tau}^{(k)}, y_{\cdot|\tau}\right). \quad (10)$$

Note that, for $k \geq 1$, the algorithm starts from $\tau = k - w$ rather than $\tau = k$ in order to calculate $x_{FHC,t}^{(k)}$ for $t < k$.

While individual FHC can have poor performance, surprisingly, by averaging different versions of FHC we can obtain an algorithm with good performance guarantee. Specifically, $AFHC$ is defined as follows.

Algorithm 3 (Averaging Fixed Horizon Control). *For all k, at each timeslot $\tau \in \Omega_k$, use $FHC^{(k)}$ to determine $x_{FHC,\tau+1}^{(k)}, \ldots, x_{FHC,\tau+w}^{(k)}$, and for $t = 1, \ldots, T$, set*

$$x_{AFHC,t} = \frac{1}{w} \sum_{k=0}^{w-1} x_{FHC,t}^{(k)}. \quad (11)$$

In contrast to RHC, AFHC has a competitive ratio of $1 + O(1/w)$ regardless of the dimension of the action space in the perfect lookahead model [33][1]. This improvement of AFHC over RHC is illustrated in Figure 1(a), which shows for a specific setting with perfect lookahead, AFHC approaches the offline optimal with increasing prediction window size while RHC is relatively constant. (The setting used for the figure uses a simple model of a data center with a multi-dimensional action space, and is described in Appendix A.)

Comparing RHC and AFHC: Despite the fact that the worst-case performance of AFHC is dramatically better than RHC, RHC provides better performance than AFHC in realistic settings when prediction can be inaccurate in the lookahead window. For example, Figure 1(b) highlights that RHC can outperform AFHC by an arbitrary amount if the predictions are noisy. Specifically, if we make predictions accurate for a small window γ and then inaccurate for the remaining $(w - \gamma)$ steps of the lookahead window, AFHC is affected by the inaccurate predictions whereas RHC only acts on the correct ones. The tradeoff between the worst-case bounds and average-case performance across AFHC and RHC is also evident in the results shown in Figure 3 of [33].

The contrast between Figure 1(a) and 1(b) highlights that, at this point, it is unclear when one should use AFHC/RHC. In particular, AFHC is more robust but RHC may be better in many specific settings. Further, the bounds we have described so far say nothing about the impact of noise on the performance (and comparison) of these algorithms.

[1] Note that this result assumes that there exists $e_0 > 0$, s.t. $h(x, y) \geq e_0 \cdot x, \forall x, y$, and the switching cost is $\beta \cdot (x_t - x_{t-1})^+$ where $(x)^+ = \max(x, 0)$.

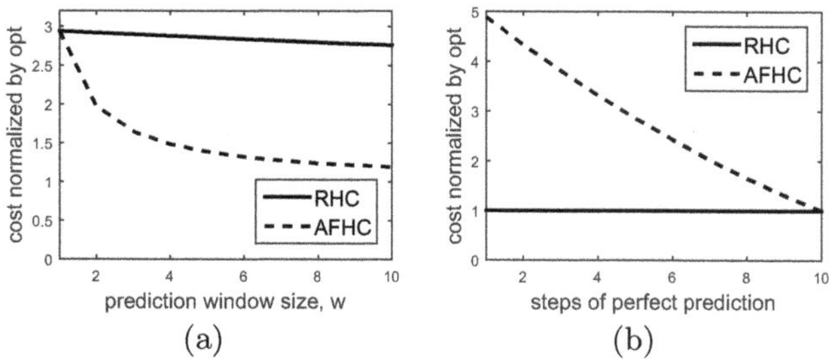

Figure 1: Total cost of RHC and AFHC, normalized by the cost of the offline optimal, versus: (a) prediction window size, (b) number of steps of perfect prediction with $w = 10$. Note (a) and (b) were produced under different cost settings, see Appendix A.

3.2 A general class of algorithms

The contrast between the performance of receding horizon control (RHC) and averaging fixed horizon control (AFHC) in worst-case and practical settings is a consequence of the fact that RHC is entirely "forward looking" while AFHC keeps an "eye on the past". However, both algorithms are extreme cases in that RHC does not consider any information that led it to its current state, while AFHC looks back at w FHC algorithms – every set of predictions that led to the current state.

One way to view this difference between RHC and AFHC is in terms of *commitment.* In particular, AFHC has FHC algorithms that commit to the w decisions at each timestep and then the final choice of the algorithm balances these commitments by averaging across them. In contrast, RHC commits only one step at a time.

Building on this observation, we introduce the class of Committed Horizon Control (CHC) algorithms. The idea behind the class is to allow commitment of a fixed number, say v, of steps. The minimal level of commitment, $v = 1$, corresponds to RHC and the maximal level of commitment, $v = w$, corresponds to AFHC. Thus, the class of CHC algorithms allows variation between these extremes.

Formally, to define the class of CHC algorithms we start by generalizing the class of FHC algorithms to allow limited commitment. An FHC algorithm with commitment level v uses a prediction window of size w but then executes (commits to) only the first $v \in [1, w]$ actions which can be visualized by Figure 2. To define this formally, let

$$\Psi_k = \{i : i \equiv k \mod v\} \cap [-v+1, T] \text{ for } k = 0, \dots, v-1.$$

Fixed horizon control with lookahead window w and commitment level v, $FHC^{(k)}(v, w)$, is defined in the following manner. For notational convenience, we write $x^{(k)} \equiv x^{(k)}_{FHC(v,w)}$.

ALGORITHM 4 (FHC WITH LIMITED COMMITMENT). *For all $t \leq 0$, set $x^{(k)}_{FHC,t} = 0$. At timeslot $\tau \in \Psi_k$ (i.e., before $y_{\tau+1}$ is revealed), for all $t \in \{\tau+1, \dots, \tau+v\}$, use* (8) *to set*

$$x^{(k)}_t = X^{\tau+1}_t \left(x^{(k)}_\tau, y_{\cdot|\tau}\right). \tag{12}$$

Note that, for $k \geq 1$, the algorithm starts from $\tau = k - v$ rather than $\tau = k$ in order to calculate $x^{(k)}_t$. We can see that FHC with limited commitment is very similar to FHC as both use (8) to plan w timesteps ahead, but here only the first v steps are committed to action.

CHC(v, w), the CHC algorithm with prediction window w and commitment level v, averages over v FHC algorithms

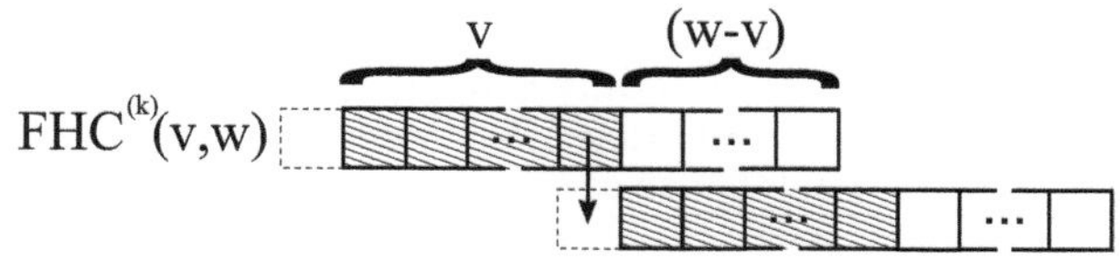

Figure 2: Fixed Horizon Control with commitment level v: optimizes once every v timesteps for the next w timesteps and commits to use the first v of them.

with prediction window w and commitment level v. Figure 3 provides an overview of CHC. For conciseness in the rest of the paper, we will use $x^{(k)}_t$ to denote the action decided by FHC$^{(k)}(v, w)$ at time t.

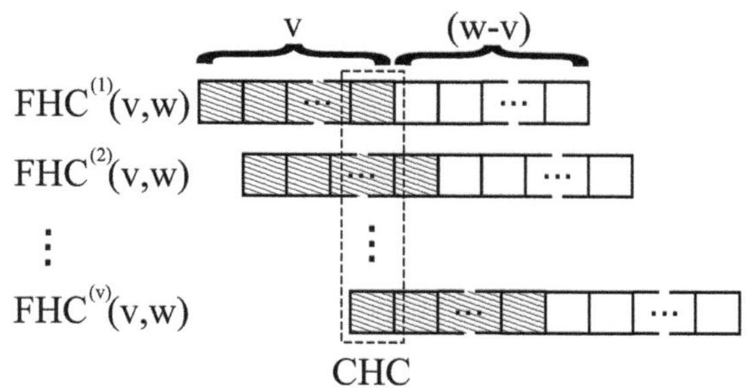

Figure 3: Committed Horizon Control: at each timestep, it averages over all v actions defined by the v FHC algorithms with limited commitment.

ALGORITHM 5 (COMMITTED HORIZON CONTROL). *At each timeslot $\tau \in \Psi_k$, use $FHC^{(k)}(v, w)$ to determine $x^{(k)}_{\tau+1}, \dots, x^{(k)}_{\tau+v}$, and at timeslot $t \in 1, \dots, T$, $CHC(v, w)$ sets*

$$x_{CHC,t} = \frac{1}{v} \sum_{k=0}^{v-1} x^{(k)}_t \tag{13}$$

RHC and AFHC are the extreme levels of commitment in CHC policies and, as we see in the analysis that follows, it is often beneficial to use intermediate levels of commitment depending on the structure of prediction noise.

4. AVERAGE-CASE ANALYSIS

We now present the main technical results of this paper, which analyze the performance of committed horizon control (CHC) algorithms and address several open challenges relating to the analysis of receding horizon control (RHC) and averaging fixed horizon control (AFHC). In this section we characterize the average case performance of CHC as a function of the commitment level v of the policy and properties of the prediction noise, i.e., the variance of prediction noise $e(s)$ and the form of the correlation structure, $f(s)$. Concentration bounds are discussed in Section 5. All proofs are presented in Appendix B.

Our main result establishes *bounds on the competitive difference of CHC under noisy predictions.* Since CHC generalizes RHC and AFHC, our result also provides the *first* analysis of RHC with noisy predictions and further enables a comparison between RHC and AFHC based on the properties of the prediction noise.

Prior to this paper, only AFHC has been analyzed in the case of OCO with noisy predictions [13]. Further, the analysis of AFHC in [13] depends delicately on the structure of the algorithm and thus cannot be generalized to other policies, such as RHC. Our results here are made possible by a *novel* analytic technique that transforms the control strategy employed by OPT, one commitment length at a time, to the control strategy employed by $FHC^{(k)}(v, w)$. At each intermediate step, we exploit the optimality of $FHC^{(k)}(v, w)$ within the commitment length to bound the difference in costs; the sum of these costs over the entire transformation gives a bound on the difference in costs between OPT and $FHC^{(k)}(v, w)$. We then exploit Jensen's inequality to extend this bound on competitive difference to CHC.

Theorem 1 below presents our main result characterizing the performance of CHC algorithms under noisy predictions for functions that are α-Hölder continuous in the second argument; in particular, $\alpha = 1$ corresponds to the class of function that is Lipschitz continuous in the second argument.

THEOREM 1. *Assuming that the prediction error follows (2), then for h that is α-Hölder continuous in the second argument, we have*

$$\mathbb{E}\text{cost}(CHC) \leq \mathbb{E}\text{cost}(OPT) + \frac{2T\beta D}{v} + \frac{2GT}{v}\sum_{k=0}^{v-1}\|f_k\|^{\alpha}. \quad (14)$$

Note that, while Theorem 1 is stated in terms of the competitive difference, it can easily be converted into results about the competitive ratio and regret as explained in Section 2.

There are two terms in the bound on the competitive difference of CHC: (i) The first term $\frac{2T\beta D}{v}$ can be interpreted as the price of switching costs due to limited commitment; this term decreases as the commitment level v increases. (ii) The second term $\frac{2GT}{v}\sum_{k=0}^{v-1}\|f_k\|^{\alpha}$ represents the impact of prediction noise on the competitive difference and can be characterized by $\|f_k\|$ (defined in (3)), which is impacted by both the variance of $e(s)$ and the structural form of the prediction noise correlation, $f(s)$.

Theorem 1 allows us to immediately analyze the performance of RHC and AFHC as they are special cases of CHC. We present our results comparing the performance of RHC and AFHC by analyzing how the optimal level of commitment, v, depends on properties of the prediction noise.

In order to make concrete comparisons, it is useful to consider specific forms of prediction noise. Here, we consider four cases: (i) i.i.d. prediction noise, (ii) prediction noise with long range correlation, (iii) prediction noise with short range correlation, and (iv) prediction noise with exponentially decaying correlation. All four cases can be directly translated to assumptions on the correlation structure, $f(\cdot)$. Recall that many common predictors, e.g., Wiener and Kalman filters, yield f that is exponentially decaying.

i.i.d. prediction noise. The assumption of i.i.d. prediction noise is idealistic since it only happens when the forecast for y_t is optimal based on the information prior to time t for all $t = 1, \ldots, T$ [23]. However, analysis of the i.i.d. noise is instructive and provides a baseline for comparison with more realistic models. In this case, Theorem 1 can be specialized as follows. Recall that $\mathbb{E}[e(s)e(s)^T] = R_e$, and $\text{tr}(R_e) = \sigma^2$.

COROLLARY 2. *Consider i.i.d. prediction error, i.e.,*

$$f(s) = \begin{cases} I, & s = 0 \\ 0, & \textit{otherwise.} \end{cases}$$

If h satisfies is α-Hölder continuous in the second argument, then the expected competitive difference of CHC is upper bounded by

$$\mathbb{E}\text{cost}(CHC) \leq \mathbb{E}\text{cost}(OPT) + \frac{2T\beta D}{v} + 2GT\sigma^{\alpha},$$

which is minimized when $v^* = w$.

This can be proved by simply applying the form of $f(s)$ to (14). Corollary 2 highlights that, in the i.i.d. case, the level of commitment that minimizes the competitive difference always coincides with the lookahead window w, independent of all other parameters. This is intuitive since, when prediction noise is i.i.d., increasing commitment level does not increase the cost due to prediction errors. Combined with the fact that increasing the commitment level decreases the costs incurred by switching, we can conclude that $AFHC$ *is optimal* in the i.i.d. setting.

Long range correlation. In contrast to i.i.d. prediction noise, another extreme case is when prediction noise has strong correlation over a long period of time. This is pessimistic and happens when past prediction noise has far-reaching effects on the prediction errors in the future, i.e., the current prediction error is sensitive to errors in the distant past. In this case, prediction only offers limited value since prediction errors accumulate. For long range correlation, we can apply Theorem 1 as follows.

COROLLARY 3. *Consider prediction errors with long range correlation such that*

$$\|f(s)\|_F = \begin{cases} c, & s \leq L \\ 0, & s > L, \end{cases}$$

where $L > w$. If h is α-Hölder continuous in the second argument, the expected competitive difference of CHC is upper bounded by

$$\mathbb{E}\text{cost}(CHC) - \mathbb{E}\text{cost}(OPT) \leq \frac{2T\beta D(\alpha+2) - 4GTc^{\alpha}\sigma^{\alpha}}{\alpha+2}v^{-1} + \frac{2^{3+\frac{\alpha}{2}}GTc^{\alpha}\sigma^{\alpha}}{\alpha+2}v^{\alpha/2}.$$

If $\frac{\beta D}{Gc^{\alpha}\sigma^{\alpha}} > \alpha(2w)^{1+\frac{\alpha}{2}} + 2$, then $v^* = w$; if $\frac{\beta D}{Gc^{\alpha}\sigma^{\alpha}} < \frac{2}{\alpha+2}$, then $v^* = 1$, otherwise v^* is in between 1 and w.

Corollary 3 highlights that, in the case of long range correlation, the level of commitment that minimizes the competitive difference depends on the variance σ^2, the switching cost β, the smoothness G, α, and diameter of the action space D.

The term $\frac{\beta D}{Gc^{\alpha}\sigma^{\alpha}}$ can be interpreted as a measure of the relative importance of the switching cost and the prediction loss. If $\frac{\beta D}{Gc^{\alpha}\sigma^{\alpha}} = \frac{2}{\alpha+2} \in O(1)$, i.e., the one step loss due to prediction error is on the order of the switching cost, then $v^* = 1$ and RHC optimizes the performance bound; if $\frac{\beta D}{Gc^{\alpha}\sigma^{\alpha}} = \alpha(2w)^{1+\frac{\alpha}{2}} + 2 \in \Omega(w)$, then $v^* = w$ and $AFHC$ optimizes the performance bound. Otherwise, $v^* \in (1, w)$.

We illustrate these results in Figure 4(a) which plots the competitive difference as a function of the commitment level for various parameter values. The case for the dashed line satisfies $\frac{\beta D}{Gc^{\alpha}\sigma^{\alpha}} > \alpha(2w)^{1+\frac{\alpha}{2}} + 2$ and shows competitive difference decreases with increasing levels of commitment. Here, the window size is 100, and thus AFHC minimizes the competitive difference, validating Corollary 3. The dot-dashed line satisfies $\frac{\beta D}{Gc^{\alpha}\sigma^{\alpha}} < \frac{2}{\alpha+2}$ and shows the increase in competitive difference with commitment, highlighting that RHC is optimal. The solid line does not satisfy either of these conditions and depicts the minimization of competitive difference at intermediate levels of commitment (marked with a circle). Figure 4(b) illustrates the relationship between α and the optimal commitment level v^* (marked with a circle that corresponds to the same v^* as in Figure 4(a)). As α increases, the prediction loss increases, and thus the optimal commitment level decreases to allow for updated predictions.

Short range correlation. Long range correlation is clearly pessimistic as it assumes that the prediction noise is always

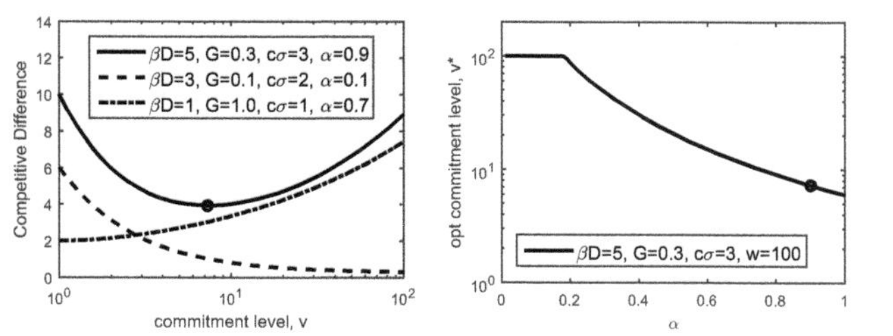

(a) (b)

Figure 4: Illustration of Corollary 3, for long range dependencies. (a) shows the time averaged expected competitive difference as a function of the commitment level, and (b) shows the optimal commitment level as a function of α.

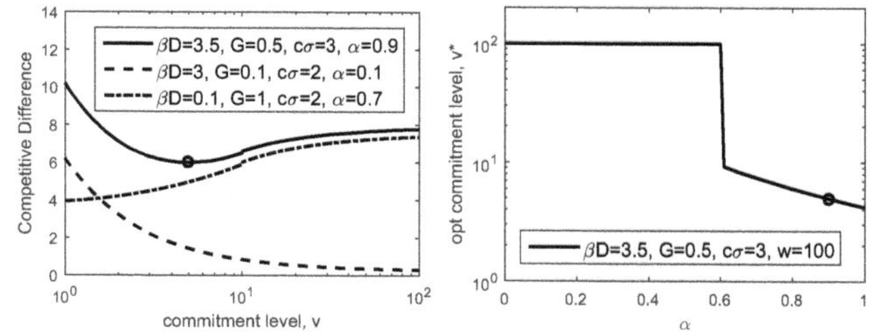

(a) (b)

Figure 5: Illustration of Corollary 4, for short range correlations. (a) shows the time averaged expected competitive difference as a function of the commitment level, and (b) shows the optimal commitment level as a function of α.

correlated within the lookahead window. Here, we study another case where prediction noise can be correlated, but only within a small interval that is less than the lookahead window w. This is representative of scenarios where only limited past prediction noises affect the current prediction. For such short range correlation, Theorem 1 gives us:

COROLLARY 4. *Consider prediction errors with short range correlation such that*

$$\|f(s)\|_F = \begin{cases} c, & s \leq L \\ 0, & s > L, \end{cases}$$

where $L \leq w$. If h is α-Hölder continuous in the second argument, the expected competitive difference of CHC is upper bounded by:

if $v > L$

$$\mathbb{E}\text{cost}(CHC) - \mathbb{E}\text{cost}(OPT) \leq \frac{2T\beta D}{v} + 2GT(c\sigma)^{\alpha}(L+1)^{\alpha/2} - \frac{2GT}{v}\frac{(c\sigma)^{\alpha}}{\alpha+2}((L+1)^{\alpha/2}(\alpha L - 2) + 1);$$

if $v \leq L$

$$\mathbb{E}\text{cost}(CHC) - \mathbb{E}\text{cost}(OPT) \leq \frac{2T\beta D}{v} + \frac{4GTc^{\alpha}\sigma^{\alpha}}{v(\alpha+2)}((v+1)^{(\alpha+2)/2} - 1).$$

If $\frac{\beta D}{Gc^{\alpha}\sigma^{\alpha}} > H(L)$, where $H(L) = \frac{1}{\alpha+2}((L+1)^{\alpha/2}(\alpha L - 2) + 1)$, then $v^* = w$; if $\frac{\beta D}{Gc^{\alpha}\sigma^{\alpha}} < \min(H(L), \frac{2}{\alpha+2})$, then $v^* = 1$, otherwise v^* is in between 1 and w.

Corollary 4 shows that the structure of the bound on the competitive difference itself depends on the relative values of v and L. In terms of the optimal commitment level, Corollary 4 shows that, similar to Corollary 3, the term $\frac{\beta D}{Gc^{\alpha}\sigma^{\alpha}}$ comes into play; however, unlike Corollary 3 (where $L > w$), the optimal commitment level now also depends on the length of the interval, L, within which prediction errors are correlated. Note that $H(L)$ is increasing in L. If $\frac{\beta D}{Gc^{\alpha}\sigma^{\alpha}} > H(L)$, i.e., the prediction loss and L are small compared to the switching cost, then $v^* = w$ and thus *AFHC* optimizes the performance bound. On the other hand, if the prediction loss and L are large compared to the switching cost, then $v^* = 1$, and thus *RHC* optimizes the bound; otherwise, v^* lies is between 1 and w, and thus intermediate levels of commitment under *CHC* perform better than *AFHC* and *RHC*.

Note that when prediction noise is i.i.d., we have $L = 0$ and $H(L) < 0$; hence we have $\frac{\beta D}{Gc^{\alpha}\sigma^{\alpha}} > H(L)$ and thus $v^* = w$, which corresponds to the conclusion of Corollary 2.

We illustrate these results in Figure 5(a), which plots the competitive difference as a function of the commitment for various parameter values. The dashed line satisfies $\frac{\beta D}{Gc^{\alpha}\sigma^{\alpha}} > H(L)$ and shows the drop in competitive difference with increasing levels of commitment. The competitive difference is lowest when the commitment level is 100, which is also the window size, thus validating the optimality of AFHC as per Corollary 4. The dot-dashed line satisfies $\frac{\beta D}{Gc\sigma} < \min(H(L), \frac{2}{\alpha+2})$ and shows the increase in competitive difference with commitment, highlighting that RHC is optimal. The solid line does not satisfy either of these conditions and depicts the minimization of competitive difference at intermediate levels of commitment. Figure 5(b) illustrates the relationship between α and the optimal commitment level v^*. As α increases, loss due to prediction noise increases; as a result, v^* decreases.

Exponentially decaying correlation. Exponentially decaying correlation is perhaps the most commonly observed model in practice and is representative of predictions made via Wiener [49] or Kalman [28] filters. For clarity of illustration we consider the case of $\alpha = 1$ here. In this case, Theorem 1 results in the following corollary.

COROLLARY 5. *Consider prediction errors with exponentially decaying correlation, i.e., there exists $a < 1$, such that*

$$\|f(s)\|_F = \begin{cases} ca^s, & s \geq 0 \\ 0, & s < 0. \end{cases}$$

If h is 1-Hölder continuous, then the expected competitive difference of CHC is upper bounded by

$$\mathbb{E}\text{cost}(CHC) - \mathbb{E}\text{cost}(OPT) \leq \frac{2T\beta D}{v} + \frac{2GTc\sigma}{1-a^2} - \frac{a^2(1-a^{2v})GTc\sigma}{v(1-a^2)^2}.$$

When $\frac{\beta D}{Gc\sigma} \geq \frac{a^2}{2(1-a^2)}$ the commitment that minimizes the performance bound is $v^* = w$, i.e., AFHC minimizes the performance bound. When $\frac{\beta D}{Gc\sigma} < \frac{a^2}{2(1+a)}$, $v^* = 1$, i.e., RHC minimizes the performance bound.

Corollary 5 shows that when the prediction noise σ and the correlation decay a are small, the loss due to switching costs is dominant, and thus commitment is valuable; on the other hand, when σ and a are large, then the loss due to inaccurate

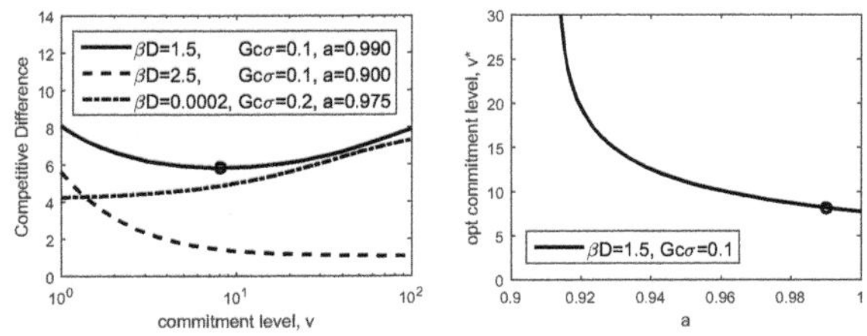

(a) (b)

Figure 6: Illustration of Corollary 5, for exponentially decaying correlations. (a) shows the time averaged expected competitive difference as a function of the commitment level, and (b) shows the optimal commitment level as a function of the decay parameter, *a*.

predictions is dominant, and thus a smaller commitment is preferable to exploit more updated predictions.

We illustrate these results in Figure 6(a), which plots the competitive difference as a function of the commitment for various parameter values. The dashed line satisfies $\frac{\beta D}{Gc\sigma} > \frac{a^2}{2(1-a^2)}$ and shows the drop in competitive difference with increasing levels of commitment. The competitive difference is lowest when the commitment level is 100, which is also the window size, thus validating the optimality of AFHC as per Corollary 5. The dot-dashed line satisfies $\frac{\beta D}{Gc\sigma} > \frac{a^2}{2(1+a)}$ and shows the increase in competitive difference with commitment, highlighting that RHC is optimal. The solid line does not satisfy either of these conditions and depicts the minimization of competitive difference at intermediate levels of commitment. Figure 6(b) illustrates the relationship between a and the optimal commitment level v^*. As a increases, correlation decays more slowly, thus the loss due to prediction noise becomes dominant; as a result, v^* decreases.

Strong convexity. All of our results to this point depend on the diameter of the action space D. While this is common in OCO problems, e.g., [54, 27], it is not desirable.

Our last result in this section highlights that it is possible to eliminate the dependence on D by making a stronger structural assumption on h – strong convexity. In particular, we say that $h(\cdot)$ is m−strongly convex in the first argument w.r.t. the norm of the switching cost $\|\cdot\|$ if $\forall x_1, x_2, y$,

$$h(x_1, y) - h(x_2, y) \geq \langle \partial_x h(x_2, y) \cdot (x_1 - x_2) \rangle + \frac{m}{2} \|x_1 - x_2\|^2.$$

Strong convexity is used in the online learning literature to obtain performance bounds that are independent of the diameter of action space, see, e.g., [22, 46]. Under the assumption of strong convexity, we obtain the following.

THEOREM 6. *If h is m-strongly convex in the first argument with respect to $\|\cdot\|$ and α-Hölder continuous in the second argument, we have*

$$\mathbb{E}\text{cost}(CHC) - \mathbb{E}\text{cost}(OPT) \leq \frac{2\beta^2 T}{mv} + 2GT\sum_{k=0}^{v-1} \|f_k\|^\alpha.$$

Theorem 6 is useful when the diameter of the feasible set D is large or unbounded; when D is small, we can apply Theorem 1 instead. As above, it is straightforward to apply the techniques in Corollaries 2 – 5 to compute v^* for strongly convex h under different types of prediction noise[2].

[2]We only need to change βD with β^2/m in the bounds of the corollaries to draw parallel conclusions.

5. CONCENTRATION BOUNDS

Our results to this point have focused on the performance of CHC algorithms *in expectation.* In this section, we establish bounds on the *distribution* of costs under CHC algorithms. In particular, we prove that, under a mild additional assumption, the likelihood of cost exceeding the average case bounds proven in Section 4 decays exponentially.

For simplicity of presentation, we state and prove the concentration result for CHC when the online parameter y is one-dimensional. In this case, $R_e = \sigma^2$, and the correlation function $f : \mathbb{N} \to R$ is a scalar valued function. The results can be generalized to the multi-dimensional setting at the expense of considerable notational complexity in the proofs.

Additionally, for simplicity of presentation we assume (for this section only) that $\{e(t)\}_{t=1}^T$ are uniformly bounded, i.e., $\exists \epsilon > 0$, s.t. $\forall t$, $|e(t)| < \epsilon$. Note that, with additional effort, the boundedness assumption can be relaxed to $e(t)$ being subgaussian, i.e., $\mathbb{E}[\exp(e(t)^2/\epsilon^2)] \leq 2$, for some $\epsilon > 0$.[3]

Given $\{\hat{y}_t\}_{t=1}^T$, the competitive difference of CHC is a random variable that is a function of the prediction error $e(t)$. To state our concentration results formally, let $V_1 T$ be the upper bound of the expected competitive difference of CHC in (14), i.e., $V_1 T = \frac{2T\beta D}{v} + \frac{2GT}{v}\sum_{k=1}^{v} \|f_k\|^\alpha$.

THEOREM 7. *Assuming that the prediction error follows (2), and h is α-Hölder continuous in the second argument, we have*

$$\mathbb{P}(\text{cost}(CHC) - \text{cost}(OPT) > V_1 T + u)$$
$$\leq \exp\left(\frac{-u^2\alpha^2}{2^{1+2\alpha}G^2\varepsilon^2 T F(v)}\right),$$

for any $u > 0$, where $F(v) = \left(\frac{1}{v}\sum_{k=0}^{v-1}(v-k)^\alpha |f(k)|^\alpha\right)^2$.

This result shows that the competitive difference has a sub-Gaussian tail, which decays much faster than the normal large deviation bounds obtained by bounding moments, i.e., Markov Inequality, the rate of decay is dependent on the sensitivity of h to disturbance in the second argument (G, α), the size of variation (ε), and the correlation structure $(F(v))$. This is illustrated in Figure 7, where we show the distribution of the competitive difference of CHC under different prediction noise correlation assumptions. We can see that, for prediction noise that decays fast (i.i.d. and exponentially decaying noise with small a) in Figure 7(a), the distribution is tightly concentrated around the mean, whereas for prediction noise that are fully correlated (short range correlation and long range correlation) in Figure 7(b), the distribution is more spread out.

If we consider the time-averaged competitive difference, or the *regret* against the offline optimal, we can equivalently state Theorem 7 as follows.

COROLLARY 8. *Assuming that the prediction error follows (2), and h is α-Hölder continuous, then probability that the competitive difference of CHC exceeds V_1 can be bounded by*

$$\mathbb{P}\left(\frac{1}{T}[\text{cost}(CHC) - \text{cost}(OPT)] > V_1 + u\right)$$
$$\leq \exp\left(\frac{-u^2}{2^{1+2\alpha}G^2\varepsilon^{2\alpha}F(v)/T}\right),$$

where $F(v) = \left(\frac{1}{v}\sum_{k=0}^{v-1}(v-k)|f(k)|^\alpha\right)^2$. Assuming $f(s) \leq C$ for $s = 0, \ldots, v$, then $\lim_{T\to\infty} F(v)/T = 0$ if either $v \in O(1)$, or $f(s) \leq c\eta^s$ for some $\eta < 1$.

[3]This involves more computation and worse constants in the concentration bounds. Interested readers are referred to Theorem 12 and the following remark of [11] for a way to generalize the concentration bound.

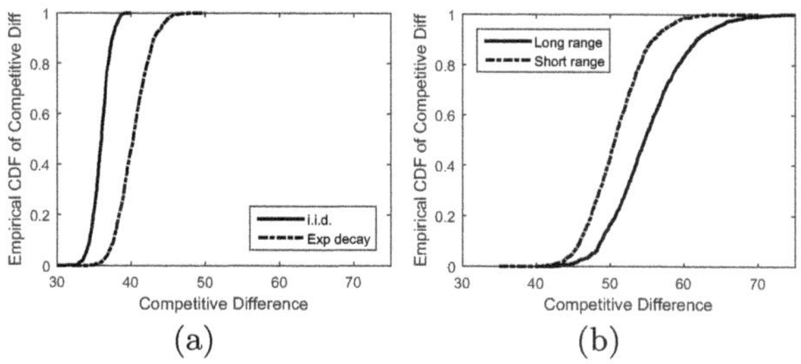

Figure 7: The cumulative distribution function of average-case bounds under different correlation structures: (a) i.i.d prediction noise; exponentially decaying, $a = 2/3$; (b) long range; short range, $L = 4$. Competitive differences simulated with random realization of standard normal $e(t)$ 1000 times under the following parameter values: $T = 100, v = 10, \beta D = 1, G = 0.1, \alpha = 1, c = 1$.

Corollary 8 shows that, when either the commitment level v is constant, or the correlation $f(s)$ is exponentially decaying, the parameter of concentration $F(v)/T$ for the regret of CHC tends to 0. The full proof is given in Appendix B.6. To prove this result on the concentration of the competitive difference, we make heavy use of the fact that h is α-Hölder continuous in the second argument, which implies that the competitive difference is α-Hölder continuous in e. This allows application of the method of bounded difference, i.e., we bound the difference of $V(e)$ where one component of e is replaced by an identically-distributed copy. More specifically, we use the following lemma, the one-sided version of one due to McDiarmid:

LEMMA 9 ([39], LEMMA 1.2). *Let $X = (X_1, \ldots, X_n)$ be independent random variables and Y be the random variable $f(X_1, \ldots, X_n)$, where function f satisfies $|f(x) - f(x'_k)| \leq c_k$ whenever x and x'_k differ in the kth coordinate. Then for any $t > 0$, $\mathbb{P}(Y - \mathbb{E}Y > t) \leq \exp\left(\frac{-2t^2}{\sum_{k=1}^n c_k^2}\right)$.*

6. CONCLUDING REMARKS

Online convex optimization (OCO) problems with switching costs and noisy predictions are widely applicable in networking and distributed systems. Prior efforts in this area have resulted in two promising algorithms – Receding Horizon Control (RHC) and Averaging Fixed Horizon Control (AFHC). Unfortunately, it is not obvious when each algorithm should be used. Further, thus far, only AFHC has been analyzed in the presence of noisy predictions, despite the fact that RHC is seemingly more resistant to prediction noise in many settings.

In this paper, we provide the first analysis of RHC with noisy predictions. This novel analysis is made possible by the introduction of our new class of online algorithms, Committed Horizon Control (CHC), that allows for arbitrary levels of commitment, thus generalizing RHC and AFHC. Our analysis of CHC provides explicit results characterizing the optimal commitment level as a function of the variance and correlation structure of the prediction noise. In doing so, we characterize when RHC/AFHC is better depending on the properties of the prediction noise, thus addressing an important open challenge in OCO.

Our focus in this paper has been on the theoretical analysis of CHC and its implications for RHC and AFHC. The superiority of CHC suggests that it is a promising approach for integrating predictions into the design of systems, especially those that operate in uncertain environments. Going forward, it will be important to evaluate the performance of CHC algorithms in settings where RHC and AFHC have been employed, such as dynamic capacity provisioning, geographical load balancing, and video streaming.

7. REFERENCES

[1] M. A. Adnan, R. Sugihara, and R. K. Gupta. Energy efficient geographical load balancing via dynamic deferral of workload. In *IEEE Int. Conf. Cloud Computing (CLOUD)*, pages 188–195, 2012.

[2] Hölder condition. https://en.wikipedia.org/wiki/Holder_condition.

[3] G. Ananthanarayanan, A. Ghodsi, S. Shenker, and I. Stoica. Effective straggler mitigation: Attack of the clones. In *Proc. NSDI*, volume 13, pages 185–198, 2013.

[4] L. Andrew, S. Barman, K. Ligett, M. Lin, A. Meyerson, A. Roytman, and A. Wierman. A tale of two metrics: Simultaneous bounds on competitiveness and regret. In *Conf. on Learning Theory (COLT)*, pages 741–763, 2013.

[5] M. Asawa and D. Teneketzis. Multi-armed bandits with switching penalties. *IEEE Transactions on Automatic Control*, 41(3):328–348, 1996.

[6] N. Bansal, A. Gupta, R. Krishnaswamy, K. Pruhs, K. Schewior, and C. Stein. A 2-competitive algorithm for online convex optimization with switching costs. In *LIPIcs-Leibniz International Proceedings in Informatics*, volume 40. Schloss Dagstuhl-Leibniz-Zentrum fuer Informatik, 2015.

[7] A. Bartolini, M. Cacciari, A. Tilli, and L. Benini. A distributed and self-calibrating model-predictive controller for energy and thermal management of high-performance multicores. In *Design, Automation & Test in Europe Conference & Exhibition (DATE), 2011*, pages 1–6. IEEE, 2011.

[8] A. Bemporad and M. Morari. Robust model predictive control: A survey. In *Robustness in identification and control*, pages 207–226. Springer, 1999.

[9] A. Blum, H. Karloff, Y. Rabani, and M. Saks. A decomposition theorem and bounds for randomized server problems. In *Proc. Symp. Found. Comp. Sci. (FOCS)*, pages 197–207, Oct 1992.

[10] A. Borodin, N. Linial, and M. E. Saks. An optimal on-line algorithm for metrical task system. *J. ACM*, 39(4):745–763, 1992.

[11] S. Boucheron, G. Lugosi, and O. Bousquet. Concentration inequalities. In *Advanced Lectures on Machine Learning*, pages 208–240. Springer, 2004.

[12] E. F. Camacho and C. B. Alba. *Model predictive control.* Springer, 2013.

[13] N. Chen, A. Agarwal, A. Wierman, S. Barman, and L. L. H. Andrew. Online convex optimization using predictions. In *Proc. ACM SIGMETRICS*, pages 191–204. ACM, 2015.

[14] N. Chen, L. Gan, S. H. Low, and A. Wierman. Distributional analysis for model predictive deferrable load control. In *Decision and Control (CDC), 2014 IEEE 53rd Annual Conference on*, pages 6433–6438. IEEE, 2014.

[15] L. Gan, A. Wierman, U. Topcu, N. Chen, and S. H. Low. Real-time deferrable load control: Handling the uncertainties of renewable generation. *SIGMETRICS Perform. Eval. Rev.*, 41(3):77–79, Jan. 2014.

[16] A. Gandhi, Y. Chen, D. Gmach, M. Arlitt, and M. Marwah. Minimizing Data Center SLA Violations and Power Consumption via Hybrid Resource Provisioning. In *Proceedings of the 2011 International Green Computing Conference*, pages 49–56, Orlando, FL, USA, 2011.

[17] A. Gandhi, M. Harchol-Balter, and I. Adan. Server farms with setup costs. *Performance Evaluation*, 67:1123–1138, 2010.

[18] C. E. Garcia, D. M. Prett, and M. Morari. Model predictive control: theory and practice—a survey. *Automatica*, 25(3):335–348, 1989.

[19] D. Gmach, J. Rolia, L. Cherkasova, and A. Kemper. Workload analysis and demand prediction of enterprise data center applications. In *Proc. IEEE Int. Symp. Workload Characterization*, IISWC '07, pages 171–180. IEEE Computer Society, 2007.

[20] S. Guha and K. Munagala. Multi-armed Bandits with Metric Switching Costs. In *Automata, Languages and Programming*, volume 5556 of *Lecture Notes in Computer Science*, pages 496–507. Springer Berlin Heidelberg, 2009.
[21] E. Hazan, A. Agarwal, and S. Kale. Logarithmic regret algorithms for online convex optimization. *Machine Learning*, 69(2-3):169–192, 2007.
[22] E. Hazan, A. Agarwal, and S. Kale. Logarithmic regret algorithms for online convex optimization. *Machine Learning*, 69(2-3):169–192, 2007.
[23] Innovation process. https://en.wikipedia.org/wiki/Innovation_(signal_processing).
[24] V. Joseph and G. de Veciana. Variability aware network utility maximization. *arXiv preprint arXiv:1111.3728*, 2011.
[25] V. Joseph and G. de Veciana. Jointly optimizing multi-user rate adaptation for video transport over wireless systems: Mean-fairness-variability tradeoffs. In *Proc. IEEE INFOCOM*, pages 567–575, 2012.
[26] T. Kailath, A. H. Sayed, and B. Hassibi. *Linear estimation*. Prentice-Hall, Inc., 2000.
[27] A. Kalai and S. Vempala. Efficient algorithms for online decision problems. *Journal of Computer and System Sciences*, 71(3):291–307, 2005.
[28] R. E. Kalman. A new approach to linear filtering and prediction problems. *J. Fluids Engineering*, 82(1):35–45, 1960.
[29] S.-J. Kim and G. B. Giannakis. Real-time electricity pricing for demand response using online convex optimization. In *IEEE Innovative Smart Grid Tech. Conf.*, pages 1–5, 2014.
[30] A. Krioukov, P. Mohan, S. Alspaugh, L. Keys, D. Culler, and R. Katz. NapSAC: Design and implementation of a power-proportional web cluster. In *Proceedings of the 1st ACM SIGCOMM Workshop on Green Networking*, Green Networking '10, pages 15–22, New Delhi, India, 2010.
[31] D. Kusic, J. O. Kephart, J. E. Hanson, N. Kandasamy, and G. Jiang. Power and performance management of virtualized computing environments via lookahead control. *Cluster computing*, 12(1):1–15, 2009.
[32] W. Kwon and A. Pearson. A modified quadratic cost problem and feedback stabilization of a linear system. *IEEE Transactions on Automatic Control*, 22(5):838–842, 1977.
[33] M. Lin, Z. Liu, A. Wierman, and L. L. Andrew. Online algorithms for geographical load balancing. In *Int. Green Computing Conference (IGCC)*, pages 1–10. IEEE, 2012.
[34] M. Lin, A. Wierman, L. Andrew, and E. Thereska. Dynamic right-sizing for power-proportional data centers. *IEEE/ACM Trans. Networking*, 21(5):1378–1391, Oct 2013.
[35] Z. Liu, I. Liu, S. Low, and A. Wierman. Pricing data center demand response. In *Proc. ACM Sigmetrics*, 2014.
[36] Z. Liu, A. Wierman, Y. Chen, B. Razon, and N. Chen. Data center demand response: Avoiding the coincident peak via workload shifting and local generation. *Performance Evaluation*, 70(10):770–791, 2013.
[37] L. Lu, J. Tu, C.-K. Chau, M. Chen, and X. Lin. Online energy generation scheduling for microgrids with intermittent energy sources and co-generation. In *Proc. ACM SIGMETRICS*, pages 53–66. ACM, 2013.
[38] D. Q. Mayne, J. B. Rawlings, C. V. Rao, and P. O. Scokaert. Constrained model predictive control: Stability and optimality. *Automatica*, 36(6):789–814, 2000.
[39] C. McDiarmid. On the method of bounded differences. *Surveys in combinatorics*, 141(1):148–188, 1989.
[40] B. Narayanaswamy, V. K. Garg, and T. Jayram. Online optimization for the smart (micro) grid. In *Proc. ACM Int. Conf. on Future Energy Systems*, page 19, 2012.
[41] D. Niu, H. Xu, B. Li, and S. Zhao. Quality-assured cloud bandwidth auto-scaling for video-on-demand applications. In *Proc. IEEE INFOCOM*, pages 460–468, March 2012.
[42] C. Rhemann, A. Hosni, M. Bleyer, C. Rother, and M. Gelautz. Fast Cost-volume Filtering for Visual Correspondence and Beyond. In *Proceedings of the 2011 IEEE Conference on Computer Vision and Pattern Recognition*, CVPR '11, pages 3017–3024, 2011.
[43] A. P. Sage and J. L. Melsa. Estimation theory with applications to communications and control. Technical report, DTIC Document, 1971.
[44] S. Sastry and M. Bodson. *Adaptive control: stability, convergence and robustness*. Courier Dover Publications, 2011.
[45] J. Schulman, Y. Duan, J. Ho, A. Lee, I. Awwal, H. Bradlow, J. Pan, S. Patil, K. Goldberg, and P. Abbeel. Motion planning with sequential convex optimization and convex collision checking. *The International Journal of Robotics Research*, 33(9):1251–1270, 2014.
[46] S. Shalev-Shwartz. Online learning and online convex optimization. *Foundations and Trends in Machine Learning*, 4(2):107–194, 2011.
[47] H. Wang, J. Huang, X. Lin, and H. Mohsenian-Rad. Exploring smart grid and data center interactions for electric power load balancing. *ACM SIGMETRICS Performance Evaluation Review*, 41(3):89–94, 2014.
[48] X. Wang and M. Chen. Cluster-level feedback power control for performance optimization. In *High Performance Computer Architecture*, pages 101–110. IEEE, 2008.
[49] N. Wiener. *Extrapolation, interpolation, and smoothing of stationary time series*, volume 2. MIT press, Cambridge, MA, 1949.
[50] L. Xiao. Dual averaging methods for regularized stochastic learning and online optimization. *J. Machine Learning Research*, 9999:2543–2596, 2010.
[51] F. Zanini, D. Atienza, L. Benini, and G. De Micheli. Multicore thermal management with model predictive control. In *Proc. IEEE. European Conf. Circuit Theory and Design (ECCTD)*, pages 711–714, 2009.
[52] F. Zanini, D. Atienza, G. De Micheli, and S. P. Boyd. Online convex optimization-based algorithm for thermal management of MPSoCs. In *Proc. ACM Great Lakes Symp. VLSI*, pages 203–208, 2010.
[53] X. Y. Zhou and D. Li. Continuous-time mean-variance portfolio selection: A stochastic LQ framework. *Applied Mathematics & Optimization*, 42(1):19–33, 2000.
[54] M. Zinkevich. Online convex programming and generalized infinitesimal gradient ascent. In *Proc. Int. Conf. Machine Learning (ICML)*, pages 928–936. AAAI Press, 2003.

APPENDIX

A. EXPERIMENTAL SETUP FOR FIG. 1

Setting for Figure 1(a): This example corresponds to a simple model of a data center. There are $(w+1)$ types of jobs and $(w+2)$ types of servers available to process these jobs. Each server has a different linear cost $\{a(t), b, c : 0 < a(t) < b < c\}$ (low, medium, high respectively) depending on the job type. The low cost is a monotonically increasing function of time that asymptotically approaches the constant medium cost (i.e. $a(t) = \alpha + (b-\alpha)\frac{t-1}{t}$, where $0 < \alpha < b$). The switching cost β only applies when a server is turned on (shut down costs can be included in the turning on cost) and has a magnitude greater than the difference between the medium and low costs (i.e. $\beta > b - \alpha$). The high cost is constant but greater than the difference between the medium and low costs multiplied by the prediction window size plus the switching cost. (i.e. $c > (b-\alpha)w+\beta$). One special server (server 0) can process all jobs with medium cost. Label all other servers 1 through $(w+1)$ and all job types 1 through $(w+1)$. Let server $s \in \{1, ..., w+1\}$ be able to process job type s with low cost, job type $s-1$ with high cost, and all other job types with medium cost.

We assume perfect prediction within the prediction window, w. The trace that forms Figure 1(a), is one in which the whole work load is only with one job type at each timestep starting with job type 1 and sequentially cycles through all job types every $(w+1)$ timesteps.

This forces RHC to switch every timestep and FHC to switch every w timesteps to avoid a future high cost but take advantage of a low cost at the current timestep.

The offline optimal puts all of the workload on server 0 that processes all jobs with medium cost and so never incurs a switching cost after the first timestep.

RHC and AFHC try to take advantage of the low cost but the trace tricks them with a high cost one timestep beyond the prediction window. Switching to server 0 is always slightly too expensive by $(b-\alpha)\frac{1}{t}$ within the prediction window. The values used in Figure 1(a) are as follows: cycling workload of size 1 for 100 timesteps, $\alpha = 0.9$, $b = 1$, $\beta = 2$, $c = 0.1(w+1)+3$.

Setting for Figure 1(b): Similar to Figure 1(a), the setting in which this example was constructed corresponds to a simple model of a data center. The key difference is that predictions are noisy. There are $(w+1)$ types of jobs and $(w+1)$ types of servers available to process these jobs. Each server has a different linear cost $\{a, c : 0 < a < c\}$ (low, high respectively) depending on the job type. The switching cost β only applies when a server is turned on (shut down costs can be included in the turning on cost) and has a magnitude less than the difference between the high and low cost (i.e. $\beta < c - a$). Label all servers 1 through $(w+1)$ and all job types 1 through $(w+1)$. Let server $s \in \{1, ..., w+1\}$ be able to process job type s with low cost, and all other job types with high cost.

We assume perfect prediction within only the first γ timesteps of the prediction window, w. The trace that forms Figure 1(b), is one in which the whole work load is only with one job type at each timestep starting with job type 1 and sequentially cycles through all job types every $(w+1)$ timesteps. Error in the last $w-\gamma$ timesteps of the prediction window is produced by making those predictions be equal to the prediction of the last perfect prediction (i.e. the γ-th timestep within the prediction window).

RHC equals the offline optimal solution in this setting which is to switch the whole workload at every timestep to the server with the unique low cost. AFHC on the other hand puts $(w-\gamma)/w$ of the workload on servers with high cost and only γ/w of the workload on the server with the unique low cost. The values used in Figure 1(b) are as follows: cycling workload of size 1 for 30 timesteps, $a = 1$, $c = 6$, $\beta = 0.1$.

B. PROOF OF ANALYTIC RESULTS

We first introduce some additional notation used in the proofs. For brevity, for any vector x we write $x_{i..j} = (x_i, \ldots, x_j)$ for any $i \le j$. Let x^* denote the offline optimal solution to (5), and let the cost of an online algorithm during time period $[t_1, t_2]$ with boundary conditions x_S, x_E and with online data $y_{t_1..t_2}$ be

$$g_{t1,t2}(x; x_S; x_E; y) = \sum_{t=t_1}^{t_2} h(x_t, y_t) + \beta \|x_S, x_{t_1}\| + \sum_{t=t_1+1}^{t_2} \beta \|x_{t-1}, x_t\| + \beta \|x_{t_2}, x_E\|.$$

If x_E is omitted, then by convention $x_E = x_{t_2}$ (and thus $\beta \|x_{t_2} - x_E\| = 0$). If x_S is omitted, then by convention $x_S = x_{t_1 - 1}$. Note that $g_{t_1,t_2}(x)$ depends only on x_i for $t_1 - 1 \le i \le t_2$.

B.1 Proof of Theorem 1

To characterize the suboptimality of CHC in the stochastic case, we first analyze the competitive difference of fixed horizon control with commitment level v, $FHC^k(v)$. Without loss of generality, assume that $k = 0$. Subsequently we omit k and v in FHC for simplicity. Construct a sequence of T-tuples $(\xi^1, \xi^2, \ldots, \xi^{M_1})$, where $M_1 = \#\{t \in [1,T] \mid t \mod v = 1\} \le \lceil T/v \rceil$, such that $\xi^1 = x^*$ is the offline optimal solution, and $\xi_t^\tau = x_{FHC,t}$ for all $t < \tau v + 1$ hence, $\xi^{M_1} = x_{FHC}$. At stage τ, to calculate $\xi^{\tau+1}$, apply FHC to get $(\tilde{x}_{\tau v+1}, \ldots, \tilde{x}_{\tau v+w}) = X^\tau(\xi^\tau_{\tau v}, y_{\cdot|\tau v})$, and replace $\xi^\tau_{\tau v+1:(\tau+1)v}$ with $\tilde{x}_{\tau v+1:(\tau+1)v}$ to get $\xi^{\tau+1}$, i.e.,

$$\xi^{\tau+1} = (\xi_1^\tau, \ldots, \xi_{\tau v}^\tau, \tilde{x}_{\tau v+1}, \ldots, \tilde{x}_{(\tau+1)v}, \xi^\tau_{(\tau+1)v+1}, \ldots, \xi_T^\tau).$$

By examining the terms in ξ^τ and $\xi^{\tau+1}$, we have

$$\begin{aligned} & g_{1,T}(\xi^{\tau+1}; y) - g_{1,T}(\xi^\tau; y) \\ = & -\beta \left\|x^*_{(\tau+1)v+1} - x^*_{(\tau+1)v}\right\| + \beta \left\|x^*_{(\tau+1)v+1} - \tilde{x}_{(\tau+1)v}\right\| \\ & - \beta \left\|x^*_{\tau v+1} - \xi^\tau_{\tau v}\right\| + \beta \left\|\tilde{x}_{\tau v+1} - \xi^\tau_{\tau v}\right\| \\ & - \sum_{t=\tau v+1}^{(\tau+1)v} \left(h(x_t^*, y_t) + \beta \left\|x_t^* - x_{t-1}^*\right\|\right) \\ & + \sum_{t=\tau v+1}^{(\tau+1)v} \left(h(\tilde{x}_t, y_t) + \beta \left\|\tilde{x}_t - \tilde{x}_{t-1}\right\|\right) \end{aligned} \quad (15)$$

By construction of $(\tilde{x}_{\tau v+1}, \ldots, \tilde{x}_{(\tau+1)v})$, it is the optimal solution for $g_{\tau v+1,(\tau+1)v}(x; \xi^\tau_{\tau v}; \tilde{x}_{(\tau+1)v+1}; y_{\cdot|\tau})$, hence

$$\begin{aligned} & \sum_{t=\tau v+1}^{(\tau+1)v} \left(h(\tilde{x}_t, y_{t|\tau v}) + \beta \left\|\tilde{x}_t - \tilde{x}_{t-1}\right\|\right) \\ & + \beta \left\|\tilde{x}_{\tau v+1} - \xi^\tau_{\tau v}\right\| + \beta \left\|\tilde{x}_{(\tau+1)v+1} - \tilde{x}_{(\tau+1)v}\right\| \\ \le & \sum_{t=\tau v+1}^{(\tau+1)v} \left(h(x_t^*, y_{t|\tau v}) + \beta \left\|x_t^* - x_{t-1}^*\right\|\right) \\ & + \beta \left\|x^*_{\tau v+1} - \xi^\tau_{\tau v}\right\| + \beta \left\|\tilde{x}_{(\tau+1)v+1} - x^*_{(\tau+1)v}\right\|, \end{aligned}$$

Substituting the above inequality into (15) and by triangle inequality, we have

$$\begin{aligned} & g_{1,T}(\xi^{\tau+1}; y) - g_{1,T}(\xi^\tau; y) \\ \le & 2\beta \left\|x^*_{(\tau+1)v+1} - \tilde{x}_{(\tau+1)v+1}\right\| + \sum_{t=\tau v+1}^{(\tau+1)v} \left|h(x_t^*, y_{t|\tau v}) - h(x_t^*, y_t)\right| \\ & + \sum_{t=\tau v+1}^{(\tau+1)v} \left|h(\tilde{x}_t, y_t) - h(\tilde{x}_t, y_{t|\tau v})\right| \\ \le & 2\beta D + 2G \sum_{t=\tau v+1}^{(\tau+1)v} \left\|y_t - y_{t|\tau v}\right\|_2^\alpha, \end{aligned} \quad (16)$$

Summing these inequalities from $\tau = 0$ to $\tau = M_1$ and noting that $\xi^{M_1} = x_{FHC^1(v)}$ and $\xi^1 = x^*$, we have

$$\begin{aligned} \mathrm{cost}(FHC^1(v)) \le & \mathrm{cost}(OPT) + 2M_1\beta D + 2G \sum_{\tau=0}^{M_1} \sum_{t=\tau v+1}^{(\tau+1)v} \left\|y_t - y_{t|\tau v}\right\|_2^\alpha \\ = & \mathrm{cost}(OPT) + 2M_1\beta D + 2G \sum_{t=1}^{T} \left\|y_t - y_{t|t-\phi^1(t)}\right\|_2^\alpha. \end{aligned} \quad (17)$$

where $\phi^k(t) = \arg\min_{u \in \Psi_k, u \le t} |t - u|$. For $k = 1$, $\phi^1(t) = u$ whenever $u = \tau v$ and $t \in [u, u+v-1]$ for some τ. We only have M_1 terms of the switching cost $\left\|x^*_{(\tau+1)v+1} - \tilde{x}_{(\tau+1)v+1}\right\|$ since $(M_1+1)v + 1 > T$. By the same argument, we have

$$\mathrm{cost}(FHC^k(v)) \le \mathrm{cost}(OPT) + 2M_k\beta D + 2G \sum_{t=1}^{T} \left\|y_t - y_{t|\phi^k(t)}\right\|_2^\alpha$$

Recall that $x_{CHC,t} = \frac{1}{v}\sum_{k=1}^{v} x_{FHC,t}^{(k,v)}$, by convexity of the cost function and Jensen's inequality, we have

$$\begin{aligned}
&\text{cost}(CHC) \le \frac{1}{v}\sum_{k=0}^{v-1}\text{cost}(FHC^k(v)) \\
\le&\text{cost}(OPT) + \frac{2\sum_{k=0}^{v-1}M_k\beta D}{v} + \frac{2G}{v}\sum_{t=1}^{T}\sum_{k=0}^{v-1}\left\|y_t - y_{t|t-\phi^k(t)}\right\|_2^\alpha \\
\le&\text{cost}(OPT) + \frac{2T\beta D}{v} + \frac{2G}{v}\sum_{t=1}^{T}\sum_{k=0}^{v-1}\left\|y_t - y_{t|t-\phi^k(t)}\right\|_2^\alpha \\
\le&\text{cost}(OPT) + \frac{2T\beta D}{v} + \frac{2G}{v}\sum_{t=1}^{T}\sum_{k=0}^{v-1}\left\|y_t - y_{t|t-(k+1)}\right\|_2^\alpha. \quad (18)
\end{aligned}$$

where the third inequality is because $\sum_{k=0}^{v-1}M_k = T$ since by definition M_k is the number of elements in $[1,T]$ that is congruent to k modulus v; and the fourth inequality is because for all t, $t-\phi^k(t)$ always range from 1 to v when k goes from 0 to $v-1$.

Finally, we show that $\mathbb{E}\left\|y_\tau - y_{\tau|\tau-(k+1)}\right\|_2^\alpha \le \|f_k\|^\alpha$ to finish the proof. Note that for $\alpha = 2$, by (2), we have

$$\begin{aligned}
&\mathbb{E}\left\|y_\tau - y_{\tau|\tau-(k+1)}\right\|_2^2 = \mathbb{E}\left\|\sum_{s=\tau-k}^{\tau} f(\tau-s)e(s)\right\|_2^2 \\
=&\mathbb{E}\text{tr}\left(\sum_{s_1,s_2=0}^{k} e(\tau-s_1)^T f(s_1)^T f(s_2) e(\tau-s_2)\right) \\
=&\text{tr}\left(\sum_{s_1,s_2=0}^{k} f(s_1)^T f(s_2)\mathbb{E}e(\tau-s_2)e(\tau-s_1)^T\right) \\
=&\text{tr}\left(R_e\sum_{s=0}^{k} f(s)^T f(s)\right) = \|f_k\|^2, \quad (19)
\end{aligned}$$

where the second equality is due to cyclic invariance of trace and linearity of expectation, and third equality is due to the fact that $e(s)$ are uncorrelated. When $\alpha \le 2$, $F(x) = x^{\alpha/2}$ is a concave function, hence by Jensen's inequality,

$$\begin{aligned}
&\mathbb{E}\left\|y_\tau - y_{\tau|\tau-(k+1)}\right\|_2^\alpha = \mathbb{E}F(\left\|y_\tau - y_{\tau|\tau-(k+1)}\right\|_2^2) \\
\le&F(\mathbb{E}\left\|y_\tau - y_{\tau|\tau-(k+1)}\right\|_2^2) = \|f_k\|^\alpha.
\end{aligned}$$

B.2 Proof of Corollary 3

Taking expectation over the prediction error and assuming long range correlation, we have for all $k \le v \le w$

$$\begin{aligned}
\|f_k\|^2 &= \sum_{s=0}^{k}\text{tr}(R_e f(s)^T f(s)) = \sum_{s=0}^{k}\langle R_e^{1/2}, f(s)\rangle^2 \\
&\le \sum_{s=0}^{k}(\left\|R_e^{1/2}\right\|_F \|f(s)\|_F)^2 = (k+1)c^2\sigma^2,
\end{aligned}$$

where the inequality is due to Cauchy-Schwarz and $\|f_k\| = \sqrt{k+1}c\sigma$. To compute competitive difference of CHC, note that

$$\begin{aligned}
&\sum_{k=0}^{v-1}\|f_k\|^\alpha = \sum_{k=0}^{v-1}(\sqrt{k+1}c\sigma)^\alpha \le c^\alpha\sigma^\alpha\int_1^{v+1}k^{\alpha/2}dk \\
=&\frac{2c^\alpha\sigma^\alpha}{\alpha+2}((v+1)^{\frac{\alpha+2}{2}}-1). \quad (20)
\end{aligned}$$

Thus, by Theorem 1,

$$\begin{aligned}
&\mathbb{E}\text{cost}(CHC) - \mathbb{E}\text{cost}(OPT) \le \frac{2T\beta D}{v} + \frac{2GT}{v}\sum_{k=0}^{v-1}(\sqrt{k+1}c\sigma)^\alpha \\
\le&\frac{2T\beta D}{v} + \frac{4GTc^\alpha\sigma^\alpha}{v(\alpha+2)}((v+1)^{1+\alpha/2}-1) \\
=&\frac{2T\beta D(\alpha+2) - 4GTc^\alpha\sigma^\alpha}{\alpha+2}v^{-1} + \frac{4GTc^\alpha\sigma^\alpha}{\alpha+2}v^{\alpha/2}\left(\frac{v+1}{v}\right)^{1+\alpha/2} \\
\le&\frac{2T\beta D(\alpha+2) - 4GTc^\alpha\sigma^\alpha}{\alpha+2}v^{-1} + \frac{2^{3+\frac{\alpha}{2}}GTc^\alpha\sigma^\alpha}{\alpha+2}v^{\alpha/2},
\end{aligned}$$

where the last inequality is because $(v+1)/v \le 2$ for $v \ge 1$. If $\beta D(\alpha+2) \le 2Gc^\alpha\sigma^\alpha$, which implies $\frac{\beta D}{Gc^\alpha\sigma^\alpha} \le \frac{2}{\alpha+2}$, then the right hand side is an increasing function of v, hence the commitment level that minimizes the performance guarantee is $v^* = 1$.

On the other hand, if $\beta D(\alpha+2) > 2Gc^\alpha\sigma^\alpha$, then let $A = \frac{\beta D(\alpha+2)-2Gc^\alpha\sigma^\alpha}{\alpha+2}$, $B = \frac{2^{2+\alpha/2}Gc^\alpha\sigma^\alpha}{\alpha+2}$, then the right hand side is $F(v) = 2T(Av^{-1} + Bv^{\alpha/2})$, by examining the gradient $F'(v) = 2T(-Av^{-2} + \frac{\alpha}{2}Bv^{-(1-\alpha/2)})$, since $F'(v) > 0$ iff $v^2F'(v) > 0$ and $v^2F'(v)$ is an increasing function in v, we can see that when $v < (\frac{2A}{\alpha B})^{2/(\alpha+2)}$, $F(v)' < 0$ and $F(v)$ is a decreasing function, when $v > (\frac{2A}{\alpha B})^{2/(\alpha+2)}$, $F(v)' > 0$ and $F(v)$ is an increasing function, hence when $v = (\frac{2A}{\alpha B})^{2/(\alpha+2)}$, $F(v)' = 0$ is the global minimum point of $F(v)$.

Therefore, when $(\frac{2A}{\alpha B})^{2/(\alpha+2)} \ge w$, we have $v^* = w$, this happens when $\frac{\beta D}{Gc^\alpha\sigma^\alpha} > \alpha(2w)^{1+\frac{\alpha}{2}} + 2$. When $\frac{\beta D}{Gc^\alpha\sigma^\alpha} \in \left(\frac{2}{\alpha+2}, \alpha(2w)^{1+\frac{\alpha}{2}} + 2\right)$, v^* is between 1 to w, in this case, $v^* = \left(\frac{\beta D(\alpha+2)-2Gc^\alpha\sigma^\alpha}{2^{2+\alpha/2}\alpha Gc^\alpha\sigma^\alpha}\right)^{2/(\alpha+2)}$.

B.3 Proof of Corollary 4

Taking expectation over the prediction error, when $k < L$, similar to the proof of Corollary 3, $\|f_k\|^2 \le (k+1)c^2\sigma^2$. When $k \ge L$, $\|f_k\|^2 \le (L+1)c^2\sigma^2$. Hence if $v > L$, we have

$$\begin{aligned}
&\sum_{k=0}^{v-1}\|f_k\|^\alpha = \sum_{k=0}^{L-1}\|f_k\|^\alpha + \sum_{k=L}^{v-1}\|f_k\|^\alpha \\
\le&\frac{2(c\sigma)^\alpha}{\alpha+2}((L+1)^{\frac{\alpha+2}{2}}-1) + (v-L)(c\sigma)^\alpha(L+1)^{\alpha/2} \\
=&v(c\sigma)^\alpha(L+1)^{\alpha/2} \\
&+\frac{(c\sigma)^\alpha}{\alpha+2}\left((L+1)^{\alpha/2}(2(L+1)-(\alpha+2)L)-1\right) \\
=&v(c\sigma)^\alpha(L+1)^{\alpha/2} \\
&-\frac{(c\sigma)^\alpha}{\alpha+2}\left((L+1)^{\alpha/2}(\alpha L-2)+1\right),
\end{aligned}$$

where the first inequality if by (20). Hence, by Theorem 1,

$$\begin{aligned}
&\mathbb{E}\text{cost}(CHC) - \mathbb{E}\text{cost}(OPT) \le \frac{2T\beta D}{v} + \frac{2GT}{v}\sum_{k=0}^{v-1}\|f_k\|^\alpha \\
\le&\frac{2T\beta D}{v} + 2GT(c\sigma)^\alpha(L+1)^{\alpha/2} \\
&-\frac{2GT}{v}\frac{(c\sigma)^\alpha}{\alpha+2}((L+1)^{\alpha/2}(\alpha L-2)+1)
\end{aligned}$$

The right hand side can be written as $2T(\frac{A-B}{v}+C)$, where $A = \beta D, B = G(c\sigma)^\alpha H(L), C = G(c\sigma)^\alpha(L+1)^{\alpha/2}$ and

$H(L)=\frac{1}{\alpha+2}\left((L+1)^{\frac{\alpha}{2}}(\alpha L-2)+1\right)$. When $A>B$, then the right hand side is a decreasing function in v, hence $v^*=w$; this happens when $\frac{\beta D}{Gc^\alpha\sigma^\alpha}>H(L)$. When $A<B$, then the right hand side is an increasing function in v, hence we want v^* to be small, i.e., $v\le L$, this happens when $\frac{\beta D}{Gc^\alpha\sigma^\alpha}<H(L)$. When $v\le L$, $\sum_{k=0}^{v-1}\|f_k\|^\alpha\le\frac{2(c\sigma)^\alpha}{\alpha+2}((v+1)^{1+\frac{\alpha}{2}}-1)$, hence

$$\mathbb{E}\text{cost}(CHC)-\mathbb{E}\text{cost}(OPT)\le\frac{2T\beta D}{v}+\frac{2GT}{v}\sum_{k=0}^{v-1}\|f_k\|^\alpha$$
$$\le\frac{2T\beta D(\alpha+2)-4GTc^\alpha\sigma^\alpha}{v(\alpha+2)}+\frac{4GT(c\sigma)^\alpha}{v(\alpha+2)}((v+1)^{1+\alpha/2})$$

If $\frac{\beta D}{Gc^\alpha\sigma^\alpha}\le\frac{2}{\alpha+2}$, then the right hand side is an increasing function in v, hence $v^*=1$.

B.4 Proof of Corollary 5

Taking expectation over the prediction error, assuming that there exists $a<1$, such that for all s, $\|f(s)\|_F\le ca^s$, we have

$$\|f_k\|^2=\sum_{s=0}^{k}\text{tr}(R_e f(s)^T f(s))=\sum_{s=0}^{k}\langle R_e^{1/2},f(s)\rangle^2$$
$$\le\sum_{s=0}^{k}(\left\|R_e^{1/2}\right\|_F\|f(s)\|_F)^2=\sum_{s=0}^{k}c^2\sigma^2a^{2s}=c^2\sigma^2\frac{1-a^{2k}}{1-a^2},$$

where the inequality is due to Cauchy-Schwarz, hence for h that is G-Lipschitz in the second argument, we have $\|f_k\|\le\frac{c\sigma(1-a^{2(k+1)}/2)}{1-a^2}$, where the inequality is because $\sqrt{1-a^2}\ge(1-a^2)$, and $1-a^{2(k+1)}\le1-a^{2(k+1)}+a^{4(k+1)}/4=(1-a^{2(k+1)}/2)^2$, hence,

$$\mathbb{E}\text{cost}(CHC)-\mathbb{E}\text{cost}(OPT)$$
$$\le\frac{2T\beta D}{v}+\frac{2GT}{v}\sum_{k=0}^{v-1}\frac{c\sigma(1-a^{2(k+1)}/2)}{1-a^2}$$
$$\le\frac{2T\beta D}{v}+\frac{2GTc\sigma}{1-a^2}-\frac{GTc\sigma}{v(1-a^2)}\sum_{k=1}^{v}a^{2k}$$
$$\le\frac{2T\beta D}{v}+\frac{2GTc\sigma}{1-a^2}-\frac{GTc\sigma}{v(1-a^2)}\frac{a^2(1-a^{2v})}{1-a^2}.$$

Let $A=2T\beta D$, $B=\frac{a^2GTc\sigma}{1-a^2}$ and $C=\frac{2GTc\sigma}{1-a^2}$, then

$$\mathbb{E}\text{cost}(CHC)-\mathbb{E}\text{cost}(OPT)\le\frac{A}{v}-\frac{B(1-a^{2v})}{v}+C$$
$$=\frac{(A-B)+Ba^{2v}}{v}+C.$$

Hence when $A\ge B$, $(A-B)+Ba^{2v}>0$, and the RHS is a decreasing function in v, hence $v^*=w$, and this happens when $2T\beta D\ge\frac{a^2GTc\sigma}{1-a^2}$ which implies $\frac{\beta D}{Gc\sigma}\ge\frac{a^2}{2(1-a^2)}$.

On the other hand, if $A<B-Ba$, then $(A-B)+Ba^{2v}\le A-B+Ba<0$, and the right hand side is an increasing function in v, hence $v^*=1$, and this happens when $2T\beta D<\frac{a^2GTc\sigma}{1-a^2}(1-a)$, which implies $\frac{2\beta D}{Gc\sigma}\le\frac{a^2}{2(1+a)}$.

B.5 Proof of Theorem 6

The proof follows in the same fashion as that of Theorem 1. Recall that we have

$$g_{1,T}(\xi^{\tau+1};y)-g_{1,T}(\xi^\tau;y)$$
$$\le2\beta\left\|x^*_{(\tau+1)v+1}-\tilde{x}_{(\tau+1)v+1}\right\|+\sum_{t=\tau v+1}^{(\tau+1)v}|h(x^*_t,y_{t|\tau v})-h(x^*_t,y_t)|$$
$$+\sum_{t=\tau v+1}^{(\tau+1)v}|h(\tilde{x}_t,y_t)-h(\tilde{x}_t,y_{t|\tau v})|$$
$$\le2\beta\left\|x^*_{(\tau+1)v+1}-\tilde{x}_{(\tau+1)v+1}\right\|+2G\sum_{t=\tau v+1}^{(\tau+1)v}\left\|y_t-y_{t|\tau v}\right\|_2^\alpha,\tag{21}$$

Since h is m-strongly convex, $g_{\tau v+1,(\tau+1)v}$ is also m-strongly convex, hence

$$g_{\tau v+1,(\tau+1)v}(\tilde{x}_{\tau v+1:(\tau+1)v};\xi^\tau_{\tau v};\tilde{x}_{(\tau+1)v+1};y_{\cdot|\tau v})$$
$$\le g_{\tau v+1,(\tau+1)v}(x^*_{\tau v+1:(\tau+1)v+1};\xi^\tau_{\tau v};\tilde{x}_{(\tau+1)v+1};y_{\cdot|\tau v})$$
$$-\partial g_{\tau v+1,(\tau+1)v}(\tilde{x}_{\tau v+1:(\tau+1)v})\cdot(x^*_{\tau v:(\tau+1)v}-\tilde{x}_{\tau v:(\tau+1)v})$$
$$-\frac{m}{2}\sum_{t=\tau v+1}^{(\tau+1)v}\|x^*_t-\tilde{x}_t\|^2$$

By the optimality of $\tilde{x}_{\tau v+1:(\tau+1)v}$ minimizes the cost function $g_{\tau v+1,(\tau+1)v}(x;\xi^\tau_{\tau v};\tilde{x}_{(\tau+1)v+1};y_{\cdot|\tau v})$, we have the first order condition

$$\partial g_{\tau v+1,(\tau+1)v}(\tilde{x}_{\tau v+1:(\tau+1)v})\cdot(x^*_{\tau v+1:(\tau+1)v}-\tilde{x}_{\tau v+1:(\tau+1)v})\ge0,$$

hence

$$\sum_{t=\tau v+1}^{(\tau+1)v}(h(\tilde{x}_t,y_{t|\tau v})+\beta\|\tilde{x}_t-\tilde{x}_{t-1}\|)$$
$$+\beta\|\tilde{x}_{\tau v+1}-\xi^\tau_{\tau v}\|+\beta\left\|\tilde{x}_{(\tau+1)v+1}-\tilde{x}_{(\tau+1)v}\right\|$$
$$\le\sum_{t=\tau v+1}^{(\tau+1)v}\left(h(x^*_t,y_{t|\tau v})+\beta\|x^*_t-x^*_{t-1}\|-\frac{m}{2}\|\tilde{x}_t-x^*_t\|^2\right)$$
$$+\beta\|x^*_{\tau v+1}-\xi^\tau_{\tau v}\|+\beta\left\|\tilde{x}_{(\tau+1)v+1}-x^*_{(\tau+1)v}\right\|,$$

Substituting the above inequality into (21) and summing over τ, we have

$$\text{cost}(FHC^1(v))-\text{cost}(OPT)=\sum_{\tau=0}^{M}g_{1,T}(\xi^{\tau+1};y)-g_{1,T}(\xi^\tau;y)$$
$$\le2\beta\sum_{\tau=0}^{M-1}\left\|x^*_{(\tau+1)v+1}-\tilde{x}_{(\tau+1)v+1}\right\|-\sum_{\tau=0}^{M}\sum_{t=\tau v+1}^{(\tau+1)v}\frac{m}{2}\|\tilde{x}_t-x^*_t\|^2$$
$$+2G\sum_{\tau=0}^{M}\sum_{t=\tau v+1}^{(\tau+1)v}\left\|y_t-y_{t|\tau v}\right\|_2^\alpha$$
$$\le\sum_{\tau=1}^{M}\left(2\beta\|x^*_{\tau v+1}-\tilde{x}_{\tau v+1}\|-\frac{m}{2}\|x^*_{\tau v+1}-\tilde{x}_{\tau v+1}\|^2\right)$$
$$+2G\sum_{\tau=0}^{M}\sum_{t=\tau v+1}^{(\tau+1)v}\left\|y_t-y_{t|\tau v}\right\|_2^\alpha$$
$$\overset{(a)}{\le}\frac{2\beta^2M}{m}+2G\sum_{t=1}^{T}\left\|y_t-y_{t|t-\phi^1(t)}\right\|^\alpha.$$

where (a) is because for any t,

$$2\beta \|x_t^* - \tilde{x}_t\| - \frac{m}{2}\|x_t^* - \tilde{x}_t\|^2$$
$$= -\frac{m}{2}(\|x_t^* - \tilde{x}_t\| - \frac{2\beta}{m})^2 + \frac{2\beta^2}{m} \leq \frac{2\beta^2}{m}.$$

Summing over k from 0 to $v-1$ as in (18) and taking expectation on both sides as in (19) finishes the proof.

B.6 Proof of Theorem 7

By the proof of Theorem 1 and assuming one dimensional setting, we have

$$\text{cost}(CHC) - \text{cost}(OPT) \leq \frac{2\beta TD}{v} + \frac{2G}{v}\sum_{\tau=1}^{T}\sum_{k=0}^{v-1}|y_\tau - y_{\tau|\tau-k}|^\alpha$$
$$= \frac{2\beta TD}{v} + \frac{2G}{v}\sum_{\tau=1}^{T}\sum_{k=1}^{v}\left|\sum_{s=\tau-k+1}^{\tau} f(\tau-s)e(s)\right|^\alpha \quad (22)$$

which is a function of the randomness of prediction noise $e = (e(1), \ldots, e(T))$, let

$$l(e) := \frac{2\beta TD}{v} + \frac{2G}{v}\sum_{\tau=1}^{T}\sum_{k=1}^{v}\left|\sum_{s=\tau-k+1}^{\tau} f(\tau-s)e(s)\right|^\alpha$$

be the upper bound of the competitive difference of CHC in terms of the random variables $e(1), \ldots, e(T)$. For every i, let $e(i)'$ be an independent and identical copy of $e(i)$, and let $e_i' = (e(1), \ldots, e(i-1), e(i)', e(i+1), \ldots, e(T))$ be the vector that differ from e by the replacing the ith coordinate with an identical copy of $e(i)$, then let δ_{is} be the kronecker delta, we have

$$|l(e) - l(e_i')| \leq \frac{2G}{v}\sum_{\tau=1}^{T}\sum_{k=1}^{v}\left|\sum_{s=\tau-k+1}^{\tau} \delta_{is} f(\tau-s)e(s)\right|^\alpha$$
$$- \frac{2G}{v}\sum_{\tau=1}^{T}\sum_{k=1}^{v}\left|\sum_{s=\tau-k+1}^{\tau} \delta_{is} f(\tau-s)e_i'(s)\right|^\alpha$$
$$\leq \frac{2G}{v}\sum_{\tau=1}^{T}\sum_{k=1}^{v}\left|\sum_{s=\tau-k+1}^{\tau} \delta_{is} f(\tau-s)(e(s) - e_i'(s))\right|^\alpha$$

where the last inequality is due to the fact that $F(x) = x^\alpha$ is a α-Hölder continuous with constant 1, hence $\forall x, y, |x^\alpha - y^\alpha| \leq |x-y|^\alpha$. Therefore,

$$|l(e) - l(e_i')| \leq \frac{2G}{v}\sum_{\tau=1}^{T}\sum_{k=1}^{v}\left|\sum_{s=\tau-k+1}^{\tau} \delta_{is} f(\tau-s)(e(s) - e_i'(s))\right|^\alpha$$
$$\overset{(a)}{\leq} \frac{2G}{v}\sum_{k=1}^{v}\sum_{\tau=1}^{T}\sum_{s=\tau-k+1}^{\tau} \delta_{is}|f(\tau-s)|^\alpha|e(s) - e_i'(s)|^\alpha$$
$$\overset{(b)}{=} \frac{2G}{v}|e(i) - e_i'(i)|^\alpha\sum_{k=1}^{v}\sum_{s=0}^{k-1}|f(s)|^\alpha$$
$$\leq \frac{2^{1+\alpha}G\varepsilon^\alpha}{v}\sum_{s=0}^{v-1}(v-s)|f(s)|^\alpha \quad (23)$$

where (a) is because for all $\alpha \leq 1$, $(\sum_{i=1}^{k}|a_i|)^\alpha \leq \sum_{i=1}^{k}|a_i|^\alpha$, to prove this, note that we only need to show that

$$\forall x, y \geq 0, (x+y)^\alpha \leq x^\alpha + y^\alpha \quad (24)$$

and iterate this inequality k times. To prove the above, note that when $x = 0$ or $y = 0$ or $\alpha = 1$, the inequality is trivially true. Otherwise, wlog assume $x \geq y$, and let $t = y/x \leq 1$. (24) is equivalent to $(1+t)^\alpha \leq 1 + t^\alpha$, this is true by examining the function $F(t) = 1 + t^\alpha - (1+t)^\alpha$, note that $F(0) = 0$, and for $\alpha < 1$, $F(t)' = \alpha(t^{\alpha-1} - (1+t)^{\alpha-1}) > 0$, since a^x hence $F(t) \geq 0$ for all t, which proves (a).

(b) is because let $s' = \tau - s$, then

$$\sum_{k=1}^{v}\sum_{\tau=1}^{T}\sum_{s=\tau-k+1}^{\tau} \delta_{is}|f(\tau-s)|^\alpha|e(s) - e_i'(s)|^\alpha$$
$$= \sum_{k=1}^{v}\sum_{\tau=1}^{T}\sum_{s'=0}^{k-1} \delta_{i(\tau-s')}|f(s')|^\alpha|e(\tau-s') - e_i'(\tau-s')|^\alpha$$
$$= \sum_{k=1}^{v}\sum_{s'=0}^{k-1}|f(s')|^\alpha\left(\sum_{\tau=1}^{T}\delta_{i(\tau-s')}|e(\tau-s') - e_i'(\tau-s')|^\alpha\right)$$
$$= |e(i) - e_i'(i)|^\alpha\sum_{k=1}^{v}\sum_{s'=0}^{k-1}|f(s')|^\alpha$$

Let $c_i = 2^{1+\alpha}G\varepsilon^\alpha\sum_{k=0}^{v-1}\frac{(v-k)|f(k)|^\alpha}{v}$, then by (23), $|l(e) - l(e_i')|^2 \leq c_i^2$, by Lemma 9, we have

$$\mathbb{P}(\text{cost}(CHC) - \text{cost}(OPT) \geq V_1 T + u)$$
$$\leq \exp\left(\frac{-2u^2}{\sum_{i=1}^{T}c_i^2}\right) = \exp\left(\frac{-u^2}{2^{1+2\alpha}G^2\varepsilon^{2\alpha}TF(v)}\right)$$

where $F(v) = \left(\frac{1}{v}\sum_{k=0}^{v-1}(v-k)|f(k)|^\alpha\right)^2$.

B.7 Proof of Corollary 8

By Theorem 7,

$$\mathbb{P}\left(\frac{1}{T}[\text{cost}(CHC) - \text{cost}(OPT)] > V_1 + u\right)$$
$$= \mathbb{P}(\text{cost}(CHC) - \text{cost}(OPT) > V_1 T + uT)$$
$$\leq \exp\left(\frac{-2u^2}{\sum_{i=1}^{T}c_i^2}\right) = \exp\left(\frac{-u^2}{2^{1+2\alpha}G^2\varepsilon^{2\alpha}F(v)/T}\right).$$

If $v \in O(1)$, then $F(v)$ is bounded since $f(s)$ is bounded, hence $F(v)/T \to 0$ as $T \to \infty$.

Otherwise, if $f(s) \leq c\eta^s$ for $\eta < 1$, denote $a = \eta^\alpha$, then

$$\sum_{k=0}^{v-1}(v-k)|f(k)|^\alpha \leq c^\alpha\left(v\sum_{k=0}^{v-1}a^k - a\sum_{k=0}^{v-1}\frac{d}{da}(a^k)\right)$$
$$= c^\alpha\left(v\frac{1-a^v}{1-a} - a\frac{d}{da}\left(\frac{1-a^v}{1-a}\right)\right) = c^\alpha\frac{v - a(v+1) + a^{v+1}}{(1-a)^2}$$

then

$$F(v) = \left(\frac{1}{v}\sum_{k=0}^{v-1}(v-k)|f(k)|^\alpha\right)^2 \leq \left(\frac{c^\alpha(v - \eta^\alpha(v+1) + \eta^{\alpha(v+1)})}{(1-a)^2 v}\right)^2$$
$$\leq \left(\frac{c^\alpha}{(1-\eta^\alpha)^2} + \frac{c^\alpha\eta^\alpha}{(1-\eta^\alpha)^2 v}\right)^2 \in O(1).$$

Hence in this case $F(v)/T \to 0$ as $T \to \infty$.

Collaborative Filtering with Low Regret *

Guy Bresler
IDSS/LIDS/EECS, MIT
32 Vassar Street
Cambridge, Massachusetts
guy@mit.edu

Devavrat Shah
IDSS/LIDS/EECS, MIT
32 Vassar Street
Cambridge, Massachusetts
devavrat@mit.edu

Luis F Voloch
LIDS/EECS, MIT
32 Vassar Street
Cambridge, Massachusetts
voloch@mit.edu

ABSTRACT

There is much empirical evidence that item-item collaborative filtering works well in practice. Motivated to understand this, we provide a framework to design and analyze various recommendation algorithms. The setup amounts to online binary matrix completion, where at each time a random user requests a recommendation and the algorithm chooses an entry to reveal in the user's row. The goal is to minimize regret, or equivalently to maximize the number of +1 entries revealed at any time. We analyze an item-item collaborative filtering algorithm that can achieve fundamentally better performance compared to user-user collaborative filtering. The algorithm achieves good "cold-start" performance (appropriately defined) by quickly making good recommendations to new users about whom there is little information.

1. INTRODUCTION

1.1 Background

Whenever a business contains a large collection of items for sale, it is of interest to help customers find the items that are of most interest to them. Before the creation and widespread adoption of the Internet, this was done by trained store salesmen, who can recommend items based on experience and the customers' revealed preferences.

After the creation of the Internet, this "recommendation system" has been largely taken off the hands of trained salesmen and is now largely handled by automated, statistically driven policies. For many companies, the efficacy of their recommendation systems stands at the core of their business. Amazon and Netflix are prominent examples.

A natural and clever first idea in designing an automated recommendation system is to use content specific data. In this spirit, one may use words in the title and book's cover, or a user's age and geographic location as inputs to recommendation heuristics. This type of recommendation system, based on content-specific data, is called content filtering.

In contrast to content filtering, a technique called collaborative filtering (CF) provides recommendation in a content-agnostic way. CF works by exploiting patterns in general purchase or usage data. For instance, if 90% of users agree on two items (that is, 90% of users either like both items or dislike both items), a CF algorithm may recommend the second item after a user has expressed positive feedback for the first item.

The term collaborative filtering was coined in [16], and this technique is used in virtually all recommendation systems. There are two main paradigms in neighborhood-based collaborative filtering: the user-user paradigm and the item-item paradigm. To recommend to a user in the user-user paradigm, one first looks for similar users, and then recommends items liked by those similar users. In the item-item paradigm, in contrast, items similar to those liked by the user are found and subsequently recommended. Much empirical evidence exists that the item-item paradigm performs well in many cases [26, 23], and in this paper, motivated to understand the reasons behind this, we introduce a mathematical model and formally analyze the performance of a simple, intuitive algorithm that follows the item-item paradigm. The algorithm, called ITEM-ITEM-CF, is described in Section 3.

1.2 Organization

The rest of this paper is organized as follows. For the remainder of Section 1 we formally introduce the model, give an informal overview of the main results, and discuss related works. In Section 2 we describe the assumptions we make, motivated by theoretical lower bounds and empirical observations. In Section 3 we describe our algorithm and in Section 4 we prove the correctness of its main set of routines. In Section 5 we put all the pieces together and give our main results pertaining to the performance of ITEM-ITEM-CF. In Section 6 we further discuss our results and future work.

1.3 Model

We consider a system with N users and collection of items $\mathcal{I}$. For each item $i \in \mathcal{I}$, user u has binary preference $L_{u,i}$ equal to +1 (like) or −1 (dislike). Recommendation systems typically operate in an *online*[1] setting, meaning that when a user logs into a virtual store (such as Amazon), a recommendation must be made immediately. At each dis-

*This work was supported in parts by NSF CMMI-1462158, CNS-1523546 and ARO MURI Award W911NF-11-1-0036.

SIGMETRICS '16, June 14-18, 2016, Antibes Juan-Les-Pins, France
© 2016 ACM. ISBN 978-1-4503-4266-7/16/06...$15.00
DOI: http://dx.doi.org/10.1145/2896377.2901469

[1]Online refers to decisions being made sequentially and with limited information.

crete time step $t = 1, 2, 3, \ldots$ a uniformly random user $U_t \in \{1, .., N\}$ requests a recommendation. The recommendation algorithm selects an item I_t to recommend from the set of available items $\mathcal{I}$, after which U_t gives feedback L_{U_t, I_t}. The recommendation must depend only on previous feedback: I_t is required to be measurable with respect to the sigma-field generated by the history (U_1, I_1, L_{U_1, I_1}), ...,$(U_{t-1}, I_{t-1}, L_{U_{t-1}, I_{t-1}})$.

We impose the constraint that the recommendation algorithm may only recommend each item to a given user at most once. This captures the situation where users do not want to watch a movie or read a book more than once and focuses attention on the ability to recommend new items.

For each recommendation, the algorithm may therefore either recommend an item that has been previously recommended to *other* users (in which case it has some information about the item) or recommend a new item from $\mathcal{I}$.

We are interested in the situation where there are many items, and will assume that $\mathcal{I}$ is infinite. For a given item i, the corresponding ith column $L_{\cdot,i} \in \{-1, +1\}^N$ containing each user's preference is called the *type* of item i. It is convenient to represent the population of items by a probability measure μ over $\{-1, +1\}^N$. When the algorithm selects an item that has not yet been recommended, the item's type is drawn from this distribution in an i.i.d. manner. Recommending a new item corresponds to adding a column to the rating matrix, with binary preferences jointly distributed according to μ.

1.4 Performance measure and main results

As is standard in the online decision-making literature, algorithm performance is measured by regret relative to an all-knowing algorithm that makes no bad recommendations. The regret at time T is therefore

$$\mathcal{R}(T) \triangleq \frac{1}{N} \sum_{t=1}^{T \cdot N} \frac{1}{2} (1 - L_{U_t, I_t}) .$$

Recall that at time t user $U_t \in \{1, \ldots, N\}$ desires a recommendation, I_t is the recommended item, and $L_{u,i}$ is equal to $+1$ (resp. -1) if u likes (resp. dislikes) item i. The regret $\mathcal{R}(T)$ is the number of bad recommendations per user after having made an average of T recommendations per user. Dependence on the algorithm is implicit through I_t.

We now describe two high-level objectives in designing a recommendation system and the corresponding guarantees obtained for our proposed algorithm ITEM-ITEM-CF, which is described in Sections 3 and 3.1. The results are stated in more detail in Section 5.

1.4.1 Cold-start time

With no prior information, the algorithm should give reliable recommendations as quickly as possible. The *cold-start time* $T_{\text{cold-start}}$ of a recommendation algorithm is defined as

$$\min \left\{ T + \Gamma : T, \Gamma \geq 0, \mathbb{E}\left[\mathcal{R}(T + \Delta) - \mathcal{R}(T)\right] \leq 0.1\Delta, \forall \Delta > \Gamma \right\}. \tag{1}$$

This is the first time after which the slope of the expected regret is bounded by 0.1: after $T_{\text{cold-start}}$ the algorithm makes a bad recommendation to a randomly chosen user with probability at most 0.1.[2]

[2]The choice 0.1 is arbitrary. We will assume that users like only a small fraction of the items, so the cold-start time is the minimum time after which the algorithm can recommend significantly better than random.

Our results: As described in Section 2, we assume that each user likes at least $\nu > 0$ fraction of the items. In Theorem 5.1 we show that algorithm ITEM-ITEM-CF achieves $T_{\text{cold-start}} = \widetilde{\mathcal{O}}(\frac{1}{\nu})$ for $N \geq N_0$.[3] Note that one must typically randomly sample $\Omega(\frac{1}{\nu})$ items to find a *single* liked item, and our results show that this amount of time-investment suffices in order to give consistently good recommendations. Further, in Section 6.2 we show that user-user collaborative filtering cannot achieve such cold-start performance, and give intuition for why that is the case.

1.4.2 Improving accuracy

The algorithm should give increasingly more reliable recommendations as it gains information about the users and items. This is captured by having *sublinear expected regret* $\mathbb{E}\left[\mathcal{R}(T)\right] = o(T)$.

Our results: Proposition 2.1 shows that without assumptions on the item space, it is impossible for any online algorithm to achieve sublinear regret for any positive length of time. In this paper we assume that the item space has doubling dimension (a measure of complexity of the space, defined and motivated later) bounded by d. In Theorem 5.2 we show that after time $T_{\text{cold-start}}$ (until which we incur linear regret), algorithm ITEM-ITEM-CF achieves sublinear expected regret $\widetilde{\mathcal{O}}(T^{\frac{d+1}{d+2}})$ up until a certain time $T_{\max}$. After $T_{\max}$ the expected regret again grows linearly (but with much smaller slope), and this behavior is shown in Theorem 5.3 to be unavoidable. As will be made explicit, performance improves with increasing number of users: $T_{\max}$ (and hence the length of the sublinear time-period) increases with N and the eventual linear slope decreases with N, both of which illustrate the so-called collaborative gain.

We would like to note that the mathematical formulation of cold-start time is new, to the best of our knowledge. The strong guarantee we obtain on cold-start time (independent of doubling dimension d) is distinct from and does not follow as an implication of the sub-linear regret result (which *does* depend on d).

1.5 Related Works

In this section we discuss connections to related work. We begin by describing some relevant literature in multi-armed bandits, which deals with explore-exploit trade-offs similar to the ones faced by a recommendation algorithm. We then, for completeness, describe matrix factorization methods of recommendation systems, which is another popular model of recommendation system. We conclude by discussing other relevant works.

1.5.1 Multi-armed Bandits

In the multi-armed bandit problem, at each time t the player must choose an arm $i \in \mathcal{X}$ (hence multi-armed) to pull in a slot machine (bandit). Upon pulling arm i, the player receives a random reward distributed according to an i.i.d. random variable with mean r_i.

The goal of the player is to minimize the expected regret,

[3]Here and throughout, $r = \widetilde{\mathcal{O}}(x)$ means $r \leq Cx \log^c x$ for some numerical constants c and C.

which in this context is defined as

$$\bar{\mathcal{R}}(T) = \mathbb{E}\left[\sum_{t=1}^{T} r^* - r_{I_t}\right]. \quad (2)$$

Here I_t is the random variable denoting the arm pulled at time t and $r^* \triangleq \sup_{i \in \mathcal{X}} r_i$ is the supremum of expected reward of all arms. The means $\{r_i\}$ are unknown to the player, so the decision about which arm to pull depends on estimates of the means. Hence, the expected regret is the difference in expected reward compared with an oracle algorithm that always pulls the arm with the highest expected reward.

The survey by [6] thoroughly covers many other variants of multi-armed bandits, and points to [33] as the earliest work in bandits. The multi-armed bandit work that is most relevant to us, however, is when $\mathcal{X}$ is a very large set. In this case we can interpret arms as items, and pulling an arm as recommending an item to a user. When $\mathcal{X}$ is very large (possibly uncountably infinite), however, some structure on $\mathcal{X}$ must be assumed in order for any algorithm to achieve nontrivial regret.

The papers [22, 7] use notions of dimensionality similar to the one in this paper in order to control the structure of the space of arms $\mathcal{X}$: [22] assumes that the arm space is endowed with a metric, and [7] assumes that the arms have a dissimilarity function (which is not necessarily a metric). The expected rewards are then related to this geometry of the arms. In the former work, the difference in expected rewards is Lipschitz[4] in the distance, and in the latter work the dissimilarity function constrains the slope of the reward around its maxima. In contrast, *what is Lipschitz about our setting?* For us, the difference in reward is Lipschitz when averaged over all users. That is

$$\mathbb{E}_u\left[|L_{u,i} - L_{u,j}|\right] \leq 2 \cdot \gamma_{i,j}, \quad (3)$$

where γ_{ij} is a distance between items that will be defined in Section 2.

The expected regret upper bound of the algorithms in [22, 7] is $\widetilde{\mathcal{O}}(T^{\frac{d'+1}{d'+2}})$, where d' is a weaker notion (than the one we use) of the covering number of $\mathcal{X}$, and is closely related to the doubling dimension (which we define later) in the case of a metric. The regret bound in Theorem 5.2 for the sublinear regime is of the same form, but two important aspects of our model require a different algorithm and more intricate arguments: (*i*) in our case, no repeat recommendations (i.e. pulling the same arm) can be made to the same user, and (*ii*) we do not have an oracle for distances between users and items, and instead we must estimate distances by making carefully chosen exploratory recommendations.

Aside from these differences, the nature of the collaborative filtering problem leads to additional novelty relative to existing work on multi-armed bandits. First, we formalize the cold-start problem and prove strong guarantees in this regard. Second, all of our bounds are in terms of system parameters. This allows, for example, to see the role of the number of users N as an important resource allowing for collaboration.

[4]That is, $|\mathbb{E}[r_i] - \mathbb{E}[r_j]| \leq C \cdot d(i,j)$, where d is the distance between arms, and C is a constant.

1.5.2 *Matrix Factorization*

Besides neighborhood-based methods of collaborative filtering, matrix factorization is another branch of collaborative filtering that is widely used in practice. The winning team in the Netflix Challenge, for instance, used an algorithm based on matrix factorization, and due to its importance we will briefly cover some aspects of it here[5].

Using the language of recommendations, the set-up for matrix factorization is that we have a (possibly incomplete) $n \times m$ matrix L of ratings (where rows represent users and columns represent rows) that we would like to factor as $L = AW$, where A is $n \times r$ and W is $r \times m$, and r is as small as possible. When L is complete, the singular value decomposition is known to provide the factorization.When L is incomplete, however, a popular approach in practice (cf. [24]) is to find the decomposition by solving the regularized optimization problem

$$\arg\min_{A,W} \sum_{(u,i)\text{ observed}} \left(L_{u,i} - A_u^T W_i\right) + \lambda\left(||A_u||^2 + ||W_i||^2\right) \quad (4)$$

via, for instance, stochastic gradient descent (cf. [37]). This, in effect, is looking for a sparse low-rank factorization of L.

In many contexts, including that of recommendations, it also makes sense to want a nonnegative factorization. Intuitively, this enforces that we interpret each item as being composed of different attributes to various extents (rather than as a difference of attributes). [25] provided theoretical guarantees for fixed r, and [34] then showed that this problem is NP-hard with r as a variable. The first provable guarantee under nontrivial conditions came only later in [2]. They give an algorithm that runs in time that is polynomial in the m, n, and the inner rank, granted that L satisfies the so-called separability condition introduced by [14][6].

In Section 2.4 we compare low-rank structure with low doubling dimension. Specifically, we argue that there are simple scenarios where the rank of a matrix is high, but its doubling dimension is small.

1.5.3 *Other Related Works*

The papers [19] and [10] on online learning and matrix completion are also relevant. In their case, however, the matrix entries to be predicted are not chosen by the algorithm and hence there is no explore-exploit trade-off. The paper [21] considers collaborative filtering under a mixture model in the *offline* setting, and they make separation assumptions between the item types (called genres in their paper). The work [11] considers a setting similar to ours (but with finite number of user and item types) and proves certain guarantees on a moving horizon approximation rather than the cumulative anytime regret. The paper [4] proves asymptotic consistency guarantees on estimating the ratings of unrecommended items. The recent paper [27] considers a different model in which repeat recommendations are also not allowed, but they make recommendations by exploiting existing information about users' interests.

It is possible that using the similarities between users, and not just between items as we do, is also useful. This

[5]As noted in [24], matrix factorization techniques have some advantages over neighborhood-based methods, such as the ease of combining it with content-specific data and of including implicit feedback.

[6][30] surveys of all these and more results.

has been studied theoretically in the user-user collaborative filtering framework in [5], via bandits in a wide variety of settings (for instance [1, 32, 9]), with focus on benefits to the cold-start problem [15, 8], and in practice (cf. [12, 3]). In this paper, in order to capture the power of purely item-item collaborative filtering, we intentionally avoid using any user-user similarities.

A latent source model of user types is used by [5] to give performance guarantees for user-user collaborative filtering. The assumptions on users and items are closely related since K items types induce at most 2^K user types and vice versa (the K item types liked by a user fully identify the user's preferences, and there are at most 2^K such choices). Since we study algorithms that cluster similar items together, in this paper we assume a latent structure of items. We note that unlike the standard mixture model with minimum separation between mixture components (as assumed in [5]), our setup does not have any such gap condition. In contrast, we allow an effectively arbitrary model, and we prove performance guarantees based on a notion of dimensionality of the item space.

2. STRUCTURE IN DATA

The main intuition behind all variants of collaborative filtering is that users and items can typically be clustered in a meaningful way even ignoring context specific data. Items, for example, can often be grouped into a few different types that tend to be liked by the same users (see fig. 1). It is with this intuition and empirical observation in mind that the two main paradigms in neighborhood-based collaborative filtering, user-user and item-item, operate.

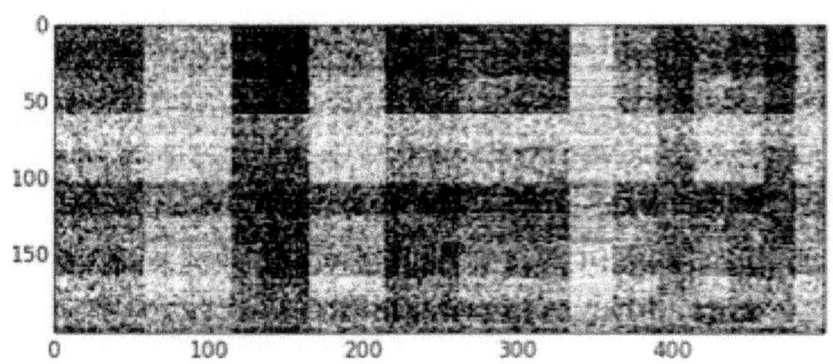

Figure 1: Observed clustering of users and items (from [5]). This is the densest subset of users (rows) and items (columns), where the darker spots indicate likes and the lighter spots indicate dislikes. One can see that the items and users can be grouped in relatively few types, where items of the same type tend to be liked by users of the same type.

In this section we will develop the appropriate notions to capture structure in data. First, in Section 2.1 we show that without structural assumptions, the expected regret of any online algorithm grows linearly with time. In Section 2.2, we then develop our intuition for the structure present in data and define a distance between item types. In Section 2.3 we then define the precise structural assumption that we will make: that the item space has finite doubling dimension. Finally, in Section 2.4 we give an example of how to relate the concepts of doubling dimension and low rank.

2.1 Need for Structure

As discussed, a good recommendation algorithm suggests items to users that are liked, but have not been recommended to them before. In order to motivate the need for assumptions on the item space, we begin by stating the intuitive result that in the worst case when μ has little structure, no online algorithm can do better than recommending random items.

PROPOSITION 2.1 (LOWER BOUND). *Under the uniform distribution μ over $\{-1,+1\}^N$, for all $T \geq 1$, the expected regret satisfies*

$$\mathcal{R}(T) \geq T/2$$

for any online recommendation algorithm. Conversely, the algorithm that recommends a random item at each time step achieves $\mathcal{R}(T) = T/2$.

Proposition 2.1 states that no online algorithm can have sublinear regret for any period of time unless some structural assumptions are made. Hence, to have any *collaborative gain* we need to capture the fact that items tend to come in clusters of similar items. We make two assumptions.

(**A1**) The distribution μ over the item space has doubling dimension at most d for a given $d \geq 0$.

(**A2**) Each user likes a random item drawn from μ with probability between ν and 2ν, and each item is liked by a fraction between ν and 2ν of the users, for a given $\nu \in (0, 1/4)$.

Assumption **A1** captures structure in the item space through the notion of doubling dimension, defined and motivated in Section 2.3. Assumption **A2** is made to avoid the extreme situations where almost no items are liked (in which case recommendation is impossible) or most items are liked (in which case the regret benchmark becomes meaningless).

2.2 Item Types

To more formally describe item types and the conditions on μ, let us first define a distance between the item types. We endow the N-dimensional Hamming cube $\{-1,+1\}^N$ with the normalized Hamming metric: for any two item types $x, y \in \{-1,+1\}^N$, define their distance

$$\gamma_{x,y} \equiv \gamma(x,y) \triangleq \frac{1}{N}\sum_{k=1}^{N}\frac{1}{2}|x_k - y_k|.$$

We see that $\gamma_{x,y}$ is the fraction of users that disagree on item types x and y. Since each item has a unique type, we write γ_{ij} for items i and j to denote the distance between their types.

One can plausibly go about capturing the empirical observation that items tend to belong to clusters that are liked by similar set of users by assuming that there are K different item types, i.e., the measure μ assigns positive mass to only K vectors in $\{-1,+1\}^N$. [5] assumes similar structure, but over users rather than items. In addition, they assume that the types are well-separated (that is, $\gamma_{x,y}$ is lower bounded for each two different types x and y with positive mass). This allows for clustering perfectly with high probability, which in turn leads to a small regret.

However, enforcing that the types are well-separated is counter-intuitive and not necessary for the following reason. If two types x and y are extremely close to each other, that should only make the problem easier: In our setting, two similar item types have (by definition) the same 'like' or 'dislike' from most users, so for the purpose of recommendation the distinction between type of x and y is insignificant.

It turns out that we can exploit this intuition when the item space has sufficient structure, as captured by a certain notion of dimensionality.

2.3 Doubling Dimension

In order to capture this intuition that our mixture assumption should (*i*) give significant mass around item types and (*ii*) not have separation assumptions, we define a notion of doubling dimension of μ, and then further discuss its advantages. Let $\mathcal{B}(x, r) = \{y \in \{-1, +1\}^N : \gamma_{x,y} \le r\}$ be the ball of radius r around x with respect to metric γ[7].

DEFINITION 2.1. *(Doubling Dimension) A distribution μ on $\{-1, +1\}^N$ is said to have dimension d if d is the least number such that for each $x \in \{-1, +1\}^N$ with $\mu(x) > 0$ we have*

$$\sup_{r>0} \frac{\mu(\mathcal{B}(x, 2r))}{\mu(\mathcal{B}(x, r))} \le 2^d. \tag{5}$$

Further, a measure that has finite doubling dimension is called a doubling measure.

The above definition is a natural adaptation to probability measures on metric spaces of the well-known notion of doubling dimension for metric spaces (cf. [20, 18, 13]). As noted in, for instance [13], this is equivalent to enforcing that $\mu(B_\gamma(x, \alpha r)) \le \alpha^d \cdot \mu(B_\gamma(x, r))$ for any $r > 0$ and any $x \in \{-1, +1\}^N$ with $\mu(x) > 0$. For Euclidean spaces, the doubling dimension coincides with the ambient dimension, which reinforces the intuition that metric spaces of low doubling dimension have properties of low dimensional Euclidean spaces.

Despite its simplicity, measures of low doubling dimension capture the observed clustering phenomena. Proposition 2.2 below, which follows directly from the definition, shows that a small doubling dimension ensures that the balls around any item type must have a significant mass.

PROPOSITION 2.2. *Let μ be an item space for N users with doubling dimension d. Then for any item type $x \in \{-1, 1\}^N$ with $\mu(x) > 0$ we have*

$$\mu(\mathcal{B}(x, r)) \ge r^d.$$

Doubling measures also induce many other nice properties on the item space. To that end, let us first define an ε-net for an item space.

DEFINITION 2.1 (ε-NET). *For any $\varepsilon > 0$, a collection of items $\mathcal{C}$ is called an ε-net of the item space represented by distribution μ on $\{-1, +1\}^N$ if (a) for any pair $i, j \in \mathcal{C}$, we have $\gamma_{ij} > \varepsilon/2$, and (b) for any item ℓ with $\mu(\ell) > 0$, there exists $i \in \mathcal{C}$ so that $\gamma_{i\ell} \le \varepsilon$.*

Proposition 2.3 below shows that an ε-net of items can only have few items close to any given item.

PROPOSITION 2.3. *Let μ be an item space for N users with doubling dimension d and let $\mathcal{C}$ be an ε-net for μ. For j an arbitrary item, let $c_j \in \mathcal{C}$ be such that $\gamma_{j,c_j} < \varepsilon$, and let $m_{c_j} \triangleq \mu(\mathcal{B}(c_j, \varepsilon))$. Then, for each $r \in [\varepsilon/2, 1/2]$, there are at most $m_{c_j} \left(\frac{4}{\varepsilon}\right)^d \left(\frac{4r+5\varepsilon}{4\varepsilon}\right)^d$ items in $\mathcal{C}$ within radius r of j.*

[7]We omit the dependence of the ball on γ throughout.

To further illustrate and gain intuition for doubling dimension, let us consider a simple item space with K clusters.

EXAMPLE 2.1. *Consider an item space μ over N users that assigns probability at least $w > 0$ to K distinct item types with separation at least $\sigma > 0$. Then, since $\mu(\mathcal{B}(x, \alpha)) \le 1$, and $\mu(\mathcal{B}(x, \alpha/2)) \ge w$, we have that*

$$d = \log_2 \left(\max_{x:\mu(x)>0} \sup_r \frac{\mu(\mathcal{B}(x, r))}{\mu(\mathcal{B}(x, r/2))} \right) \le \log_2 \left(\frac{1}{w} \right).$$

Similarly, if we only know that there are at most K equally likely item types we can bound the doubling dimension as

$$d = \log_2 \left(\max_{x:\mu(x)>0} \sup_r \frac{\mu(\mathcal{B}(x, r))}{\mu(\mathcal{B}(x, r/2))} \right) \le \log_2 K. \tag{6}$$

With the example above in mind, we would like to emphasize that doubling dimension assumptions are strictly more general than the style of assumptions made in [5] (finite K with separation assumptions) because (a) doubling measures require no separation assumptions (that is, two item types x and y that are arbitrarily close to each other can have positive mass) and (b) the number of types of positive mass is not bounded by a finite K anymore, but instead can grow with the number of users.

Finally, note that doubling dimension is not only a proof technique: it can be estimated from data and tends to be small in practice. To illustrate this point, we calculated the doubling dimension on the Jester Jokes Dataset[8] and for the MovieLens 1M Dataset[9]. For the MovieLens dataset we considered only movies that have been rated by at least 750 users (to ensure some density).

In both datasets we calculated the empirical doubling dimension d_i (that is, the smallest d_i such that $\mu(\mathcal{B}(i, 2r)) \le 2^{d_i} \mu(\mathcal{B}(i, r))$ for each r) around each item i. Under a simple noise assumption, figs. 2 and 3 show that all the d_i tend to be small. The appendix B describes the precise experiments.

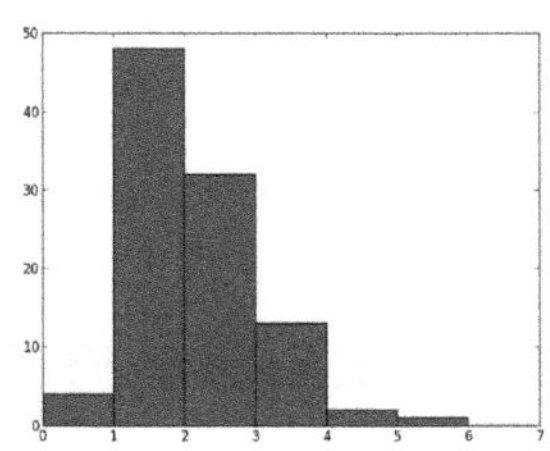

Figure 2: Jester Doubling Dimensions

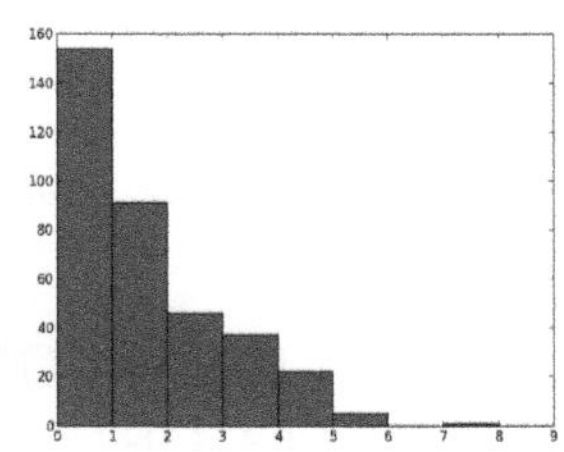

Figure 3: MovieLens Doubling Dimensions

2.4 Low Rank and Doubling Dimension

As mentioned in Section 1.5, a common assumption behind matrix factorization methods is that the matrix has low rank. In this section we would like to draw a connection between rank properties of the rating matrix L and the doubling dimension of the item space *induced* by L. In particular, we will show that low doubling dimension can be a weaker requirement than low rank of L. To that end, we

[8][17], and data available on http://goldberg.berkeley.edu/jester-data/

[9][31], and data available on http://grouplens.org/datasets/movielens/

will first define what we mean by the item space induced by a rating matrix.

DEFINITION 2.2. *(Item Space Induced by Rating Matrix) Let L be an $N \times M$ binary rating matrix. Then the item space μ induced by L is*

$$\mu(x) = \frac{1}{M}\sum_{j=1}^{M} \mathbf{1}_{L_j = x}, \text{ for each } x \in \{-1,+1\}^N,$$

where L_j is the jth column of L.

That is, the item space induced by a rating matrix assigns mass to item types according to the empirical frequency of the item type in L.

The example below shows that there are rating matrices of high binary rank, but whose corresponding doubling dimension is constant (at most 2). Consider the $N \times N$ matrix L_N whose j^{th} column's first j entries are $+1$ and the remaining -1. That is, each of its columns differ from its adjacent columns in exactly one entry. For instance, for $N = 4$ we have

$$L_4 = \begin{pmatrix} +1 & +1 & +1 & +1 \\ -1 & +1 & +1 & +1 \\ -1 & -1 & +1 & +1 \\ -1 & -1 & -1 & +1 \end{pmatrix}.$$

The matrix L_N clearly has rank N. However, the doubling dimension of its induced item space is at most 2. We can see this because for each x and $r \in \{0, ..., N-1\}$

$$\frac{1+r}{N} \le \mu\left(\mathcal{B}\left(x, \frac{r}{N}\right)\right) \le \frac{1+2r}{N},$$

which we can use in turn to conclude that

$$d \le \max_x \max_r \log_2\left(\frac{\mu\left(\mathcal{B}\left(x, \frac{2r}{N}\right)\right)}{\mu\left(\mathcal{B}\left(x, \frac{r}{N}\right)\right)}\right) \le \log_2\left(\frac{\frac{1+4r}{N}}{\frac{1+r}{N}}\right) \le 2.$$

Hence, the doubling dimension of the induced item space can be substantially smaller than the rank of the rating matrix. Since the rank is a way of counting the number of item types, this reinforces the fact that *the number of types is not particularly important, but the geometric structure between them is.*

3. ITEM-ITEM COLLABORATIVE FILTERING ALGORITHM

In this section we describe our algorithm, ITEM-ITEM-CF. The algorithm carries out a certain procedure over increasingly longer epochs (blocks of time), where the epoch index is denoted by $\tau \ge 1$. In each epoch the algorithm carefully balances *Explore* and *Exploit* steps.

In the Explore steps of epoch τ, a partition $\{P_k^{(\tau+1)}\}$ of a set of items is created for use in the subsequent epoch. Each epoch has a target precision ε_τ (specified below) such that if two items i and j are in the same block $P_k^{(\tau+1)}$, then usually $\gamma_{ij} \le \varepsilon_{\tau+1}$.

In the Exploit steps of epoch τ, the partition $\{P_k^{(\tau)}\}$ created in the previous epoch is used for recommendation. Exploit recommendations to a user u are made as follows: u samples a random item i from a random block $P_k^{(\tau)}$, and if u likes i ($L_{u,i} = +1$) then the rest of $P_k^{(\tau)}$ is recommended to u in subsequent Exploit steps. After all items in $P_k^{(\tau)}$ have been recommended to u, the user repeats the process by sampling random items in random blocks until liking some item j in $P_{k'}^{(\tau)}$, upon which the rest of $P_{k'}^{(\tau)}$ is recommended.

In the first epoch there is no possibility of exploiting a partition created in a previous epoch, so the algorithm begins with a purely exploratory "cold-start" period. The pseudocode of the algorithm is as follows.

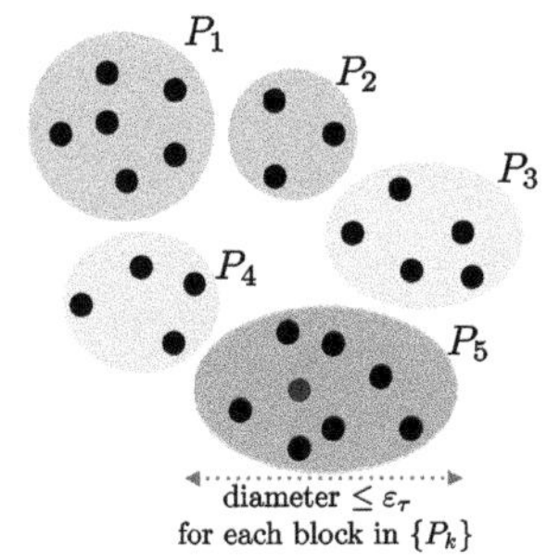

Figure 4: Partition resulting from exploration in the previous epoch

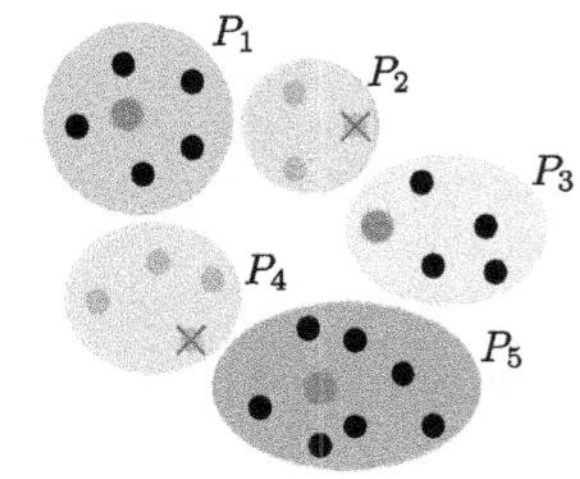

Figure 5: During exploitation, items in P_k are recommended only when from a block when a user likes an item in the block

ITEM-ITEM-CF(N)

1 **Algorithm parameters:**

$\varepsilon_N = \left(\frac{2^{5d+18}}{\nu} \cdot 630(2d+11)(d+2)^4 \frac{1}{N}\right)^{\frac{1}{d+5}}$, $C = \frac{\nu}{148}\frac{1}{20}$

$\varepsilon_\tau = \max\left(\frac{1}{2^\tau}, \varepsilon_N\right) \cdot C$, for $\tau \ge 1$ (target accuracy for epoch)

$M_\tau = \frac{2^{\max(3.5d,8)}}{\nu}\frac{(3d+1)}{\varepsilon_\tau^{d+2}}\ln(\frac{2}{\varepsilon_\tau})$, for $\tau \ge 1$ (items per epoch)

$D_\tau = \frac{\nu}{2} M_\tau$, for $\tau \ge 1$ (duration of epoch)

2 **Cold-Start:**

$\{P_k^{(1)}\}$ = MAKE-PARTITION($M_1, \varepsilon_1, \varepsilon_1$)

3 **Subsequent epochs:**

for $\tau \ge 1$
  do for $t = 1$ to $N \cdot D_\tau$
    do U_t = random user
      w.p. $1 - \varepsilon_\tau$: *exploit* $\{P_k^{(\tau)}\}$ to recommend an item to U_t
      w.p. ε_τ: U_t *explores* to help construct partition $\{P_k^{(\tau+1)}\}$ (see Section 3.1)

3.1 Explore: making a partition

Recall that during epoch τ the goal of the explore recommendations is to create a partition $\{P_k^{(\tau+1)}\}$ of items such that whenever $i, j \in P_k^{(\tau+1)}$ then $\gamma_{ij} \le \varepsilon_{\tau+1}$. We later prove that this can be done by executing the routine MAKE-PARTITION($M_{\tau+1}, \varepsilon_{\tau+1}, \varepsilon_{\tau+1}$) described below, which at any point makes recommendations to a randomly chosen user. Hence, given the random user making the recommendation, ITEM-ITEM-CF provides explore recommendations in whatever order MAKE-PARTITION would have recommended (had it been run sequentially)[10].

[10]For instance, suppose that time t is the first in some epoch τ. We might have that times $t+5$ and $t+30$ are the first two explore recommendations of the epoch, then for those two recommendations the algorithm makes whatever the first

MAKE-PARTITION first finds a *net* $\mathcal{C}$ for the item space (using the subroutine GET-NET described later). To each item in the net there is associated a block in a partition. M randomly sampled items are assigned to the blocks as follows: for each sampled item j, an item $i \in \mathcal{C}$ is found that is similar to j, and j is assigned to the partition block P_i (if there is more than one item i similar to j, the algorithm chooses among the relevant blocks at random). Finally, the algorithm breaks up large blocks into blocks of size on the order of $1/\varepsilon$. This guarantees that there will be many blocks in the partition, which turns out to be important in Theorem 5.1 showing brief cold-start time [11].

MAKE-PARTITION(M, ε, δ)

$\mathcal{C} =$ GET-NET$(\varepsilon/2, \delta/2)$
$\mathcal{M} = M$ randomly drawn items from item space
for each $i \in \mathcal{C}$, let $P_i = \varnothing$
for each $j \in \mathcal{M}$, let $S_j = \{i \in \mathcal{C} \mid$ SIMILAR$(i, j, 0.6\varepsilon, \frac{\delta}{4M|\mathcal{C}|})\}$
if $|S_j| > 0$ **then** $P_i = P_i \cup \{j\}$, for i chosen u.a.r. from S_j
for each i, **if** $|P_i| > 1/\varepsilon$, **then** partition P_i into blocks of size $\geq \frac{1}{2\varepsilon}$ and $\leq 1/\varepsilon$
return $\{P_i\}$

The subroutine SIMILAR is used in MAKE-PARTITION; it determines whether most users have the same preference (like or dislike) for two given items i and j.This is accomplished by sampling many random users and counting the number of disagreements on the two items.

SIMILAR$(i, j, \varepsilon, \delta)$

$q_{\varepsilon,\delta} = \lceil 630 \frac{d+1}{\varepsilon} \ln\left(\frac{1}{\delta}\right) \rceil$
for $n = 1$ **to** $q_{\varepsilon,\delta}$
  do sample a uniformly random user u
    let $X_u = \mathbf{1}_{L_{u,i} \neq L_{u,j}}$
if $\frac{1}{q_{\varepsilon,\delta}} \sum_{\text{sampled } u} X_u \geq 0.9\varepsilon$ **then**
    return FALSE
return TRUE

The subroutine GET-NET below is a natural greedy procedure for constructing an ε-net. Given parameters ε and δ, it finds a set of items $\mathcal{C}$ that is an ε-net for μ with probability at least $1 - \delta$ (proven in the appendix). It does so by keeping a set of items $\mathcal{C}$ and whenever it samples an item i that currently has no similar item in $\mathcal{C}$, it adds i to $\mathcal{C}$.

GET-NET(ε, δ)

$\mathcal{C} = \varnothing$, COUNT $= 0$, MAX-SIZE $= (4/\varepsilon)^d$
MAX-WAIT $= (\frac{5}{\varepsilon})^d \ln\left(\frac{2 \cdot \text{MAX-SIZE}}{\delta}\right)$, $\delta' = \frac{\delta}{4 \cdot \text{MAX-WAIT} \cdot \text{MAX-SIZE}^2}$
while COUNT $\leq$ MAX-WAIT and $|\mathcal{C}| <$ MAX-SIZE
  do draw item i from μ
    if SIMILAR$(i, j, \varepsilon, \delta')$ for any $j \in \mathcal{C}$ **then**
      COUNT $=$ COUNT $+ 1$
    else $\mathcal{C} = \mathcal{C} \cup i$, COUNT $= 0$
return $\mathcal{C}$

two recommendations would have been in MAKE-PARTITION. If the execution of MAKE-PARTITION has finished, the algorithm resorts to an exploit recommendation instead.

[11]It is crucial that blocks in the partition are not too small because we would like the reward for exploration to be large when a user finds a likable item. Although the algorithm does not explicitly ensure that blocks are not too small (as it did in ensuring the blocks are not too large) it comes as a byproduct of a property proven in Proposition 2.3: there are not many items in the net close to any given item.

4. CORRECTNESS OF EXPLORE

This section establishes correctness of the explore procedure as well as some of its properties that will be utilized for establishing the main result of the paper. Concretely, we will prove that with high probability the procedure MAKE-PARTITION produces a partition of similar items during each epoch. To that end, in Section 4.1, we prove that SIMILAR succeeds in deciding whether two items are close to each other. In Section 4.2 we prove that the procedure GET-NET succeeds in finding a set of items that is an ε-net for μ. We then put all the pieces together and prove that MAKE-PARTITION, the routine at which the explore recommendations are aimed at completing, succeeds in creating a partition of similar items. Finally, in Section 4.3 we prove that with high probability during any given epoch there will be enough explore recommendations.

4.1 Guarantees for SIMILAR

The procedure SIMILAR is used throughout GET-NET and MAKE-PARTITION, and it is aimed at testing whether two items are approximately ε-close to each other. Lemma 4.1 below shows that given two items i and j, SIMILAR indeed succeeds in determining that the items are similar when $\gamma_{i,j} \leq 0.8\varepsilon$, and that the items are not similar when $\gamma_{i,j} \geq \varepsilon$.

LEMMA 4.1. *Let i and j be arbitrary items, $\delta, \varepsilon \in (0,1)$, and $S_{i,j}$ be the event that* SIMILAR$(i, j, \varepsilon, \delta)$ *returns* TRUE. *Then we have that*

(i) if $\gamma_{i,j} \leq 0.8\varepsilon$, then $\mathbb{P}(S_{ij}) \geq 1 - \delta$, and

(ii) if $\gamma_{ij} \in [k\varepsilon, (k+1)\varepsilon)$ where $k \in \{1, \ldots, \lfloor \frac{1}{\varepsilon} \rfloor\}$, then $\mathbb{P}(S_{ij}) \leq \frac{\delta}{4} \left(\frac{1}{4k}\right)^d \frac{1}{k^2}$.

The lemma above bounds the probability of false positive and missed detection for deciding whether or not two items are similar. Further, the lemma states that the probability of a false-positive decreases quickly as the items get further apart. Lemma 4.2 below shows that, when one of the items is drawn from μ, SIMILAR still works and that the false positive rate is small, despite the possibility that it may be much more likely to draw an item that is far from i. Lemma 4.2 uses the doubling dimension of μ for the first time, and in this context the doubling dimension guarantees that SIMILAR (which is a random projection) preserves relative distances.

LEMMA 4.2. *Let i be an arbitrary item, let J be a randomly drawn item from an item space μ of doubling dimension d, and let S_{iJ} be the event that* SIMILAR$(i, J, \varepsilon, \delta)$ *returns* TRUE. *Then we have $\mathbb{P}(\gamma_{iJ} \geq \varepsilon \mid S_{iJ}) \leq \delta$.*

PROOF. By Bayes' rule we get

$$\mathbb{P}(\gamma_{i,J} \geq \varepsilon \mid S_{iJ}) = \frac{\mathbb{P}(\gamma_{i,J} \geq \varepsilon, S_{iJ})}{\mathbb{P}(\gamma_{i,J} \geq \varepsilon, S_{iJ}) + \mathbb{P}(\gamma_{i,J} < \varepsilon, S_{iJ})}, \tag{7}$$

where the probability is with the respect to the random choice of J and the random users in SIMILAR. Now if

$$\delta \mathbb{P}(S_{iJ}, \gamma_{iJ} < \varepsilon) \geq (1 - \delta) \mathbb{P}(S_{iJ}, \gamma_{iJ} \geq \varepsilon) \tag{$\star$}$$

holds, we get

$$\mathbb{P}(\gamma_{i,J} \geq \varepsilon \mid S_{iJ}) = \frac{1}{1 + \frac{\mathbb{P}(\gamma_{i,J} < \varepsilon, S_{iJ})}{\mathbb{P}(\gamma_{i,J} \geq \varepsilon, S_{iJ})}} \leq \frac{1}{1 + \frac{1-\delta}{\delta}} = \delta. \tag{8}$$

Hence, it suffices to show ($\star$). Recall that $\mathcal{B}(i,r)$ is the ball of radius r centered at i. Note that

$$\mathbb{P}(\gamma_{iJ} < \varepsilon, S_{iJ}) \geq \mathbb{P}(S_{iJ} \mid \gamma_{iJ} \leq \varepsilon/2)\, \mu(\mathcal{B}(i,\varepsilon/2)),$$

and

$$\begin{aligned}\mathbb{P}(\gamma_{iJ} \geq \varepsilon, S_{iJ}) &= \sum_{k=0}^{\lceil \log_2(\frac{1}{\varepsilon}) \rceil} \mathbb{P}\left(S_{iJ} \mid \gamma_{iJ} \in [2^k\varepsilon, 2^{k+1}\varepsilon)\right) \\ &\quad \times \mu\left(\mathcal{B}\left(i, 2^{k+1}\varepsilon\right) \setminus \mathcal{B}\left(i, 2^k\varepsilon\right)\right) \\ &\leq \sum_{k=0}^{\lceil \log_2(\frac{1}{\varepsilon}) \rceil} \mathbb{P}\left(S_{iJ} \mid \gamma_{iJ} \in [2^k\varepsilon, 2^{k+1}\varepsilon)\right) \mu\left(\mathcal{B}\left(i, 2^{k+1}\varepsilon\right)\right).\end{aligned}$$

Let us first lower bound $\mathbb{P}(S_{iJ} \mid \gamma_{ij} \leq \varepsilon/2)\, \mu(\mathcal{B}(i,\varepsilon/2))$. Letting $p \triangleq \mu(\mathcal{B}(i,\varepsilon/2))$, Lemma 4.1 gives

$$\mathbb{P}(S_{iJ} \mid \gamma_{iJ} \leq \varepsilon/2)\, \mu(\mathcal{B}(i,\varepsilon/2)) \geq (1-\delta)\, p. \tag{9}$$

We will now upper bound $\mathbb{P}(S_{iJ}, \gamma_{iJ} \geq \varepsilon)$. Using the doubling dimension of the item space, which implies that $\mu(\mathcal{B}_\gamma(i, 2^{k+1}\varepsilon)) \leq (2^{k+2})^d p$, we have that

$$\begin{aligned}\mathbb{P}(\gamma_{iJ} \geq \varepsilon, S_{iJ}) &\leq \sum_{k=0}^{\lceil \log_2(\frac{1}{\varepsilon}) \rceil} \mathbb{P}\left(S_{iJ} \mid \gamma_{iJ} \in [2^k\varepsilon, 2^{k+1}\varepsilon)\right) \mu\left(\mathcal{B}_\gamma\left(i, 2^{k+1}\varepsilon\right)\right) \\ &\leq \sum_{k=0}^{\lceil \log_2(\frac{1}{\varepsilon}) \rceil} \mathbb{P}\left(S_{iJ} \mid \gamma_{iJ} \in [2^k\varepsilon, 2^{k+1}\varepsilon)\right) \left(2^{k+2}\right)^d p.\end{aligned}$$

We now use the second half of Lemma 4.1, and arrive at

$$\mathbb{P}(\gamma_{iJ} \geq \varepsilon, S_{iJ}) \leq \sum_{k=0}^{\lceil \log_2(\frac{1}{\varepsilon}) \rceil} \left(\frac{\delta}{4}\left(\frac{1}{4 \cdot 2^k}\right)^d \frac{1}{2^{2k}}\right)\left(2^{k+2}\right)^d p, \tag{10}$$

which in turn is at most $p\frac{\delta}{4}\sum_{k=0}^{\infty}\frac{1}{2^{2k}} \leq p\frac{\delta}{2}$. We can now check that the sufficient condition from eq. ($\star$) is satisfied:

$$\begin{aligned}\delta\mathbb{P}(S_{iJ}, \gamma_{iJ} < \varepsilon) \geq \delta p(1-\delta) &\geq \frac{\delta}{2}p(1-\delta) \\ &\geq (1-\delta)\,\mathbb{P}(S_{iJ}, \gamma_{iJ} \geq \varepsilon),\end{aligned}$$

which completes the proof. □

4.2 Making the Partition

In the previous section we proved that the procedure SIMILAR works well in deciding whether two items are similar to each other at some desired precision. In this section, we will prove that with SIMILAR as a building block we can partition items into blocks of similar items.

We will begin with a lemma showing that the subroutine GET-NET, used in the beginning of MAKE-PARTITION, succeeds at producing an ε-net of items with high probability. The proof is omitted due to space constraints.

LEMMA 4.3. *With probability at least $1-\delta$ the routine* GET-NET(M,ε,δ) *returns an ε-net for μ that contains at most $\left(\frac{4}{\varepsilon}\right)^d$ items.*

It is now only left to prove that the main tool used during exploration, MAKE-PARTITION, indeed produces a partition of similar items. This is done in Lemma 4.4 below. The additional properties stated in the Lemma regarding size of the blocks will be crucial later in ensuring good cold-start performance.

LEMMA 4.4. *Let $\varepsilon, \delta \in (0,1)$, and let M be at least $12 \cdot \left(\frac{12}{\varepsilon}\right)^{d+1} \ln\left(\frac{2}{\delta}\left(\frac{8}{\varepsilon}\right)^d\right)$. Then with probability at least $1-\delta$ the subroutine* MAKE-PARTITION(M,ε,δ) *returns a partition $\{P_k\}$ of a subset of M randomly drawn items such that*

(*i*) *For each block P_k and $i,j \in P_k$ we have $\gamma_{i,j} \leq 1.2 \cdot \varepsilon$,*

(*ii*) *Each block P_k contains at least $\frac{1}{2\varepsilon}$ items,*

(*iii*) *Each block P_k contains at most $1/\varepsilon$ items,*

(*iv*) *There are at most $2M\varepsilon$ blocks.*

PROOF. We will show that properties (*i*) and (*ii*) hold with probability at least $1-\delta$, and note that (*iii*) follows directly from the algorithm and that (*iv*) follows from (*ii*).

Let C be the event that the set $\mathcal{C}$ returned by GET-NET is not an $\frac{\varepsilon}{2}$-net for μ, and let $\mathcal{M}$ be the set of M items sampled. Let $E_{i,j}$ be the event $\{S_{i,j}, \gamma_{ij} > 0.6\varepsilon\} \cup \{S_{i,j}^c, \gamma_{ij} < 0.5\varepsilon\}$, where S_{ij} is the event that SIMILAR$(i,j,0.6\varepsilon,\delta/(4M|\mathcal{C}|))$ returns TRUE. Intuitively, event $E_{i,j}$ occurs when SIMILAR is incorrect. Furthermore, let $E = \bigcup_{c \in \mathcal{C}} \bigcup_{j \in \mathcal{M}} E_{c,j}$.

Let F be the event that for some block P_k there exists $i,j \in P_k$ such that $\gamma_{ij} > 1.2\varepsilon$, and let B be the event that all blocks in the partition have size at least $\frac{1}{2\varepsilon}$. Hence, $B^c = \bigcup_k B_k^c$, where B_k^c is the even that P_k has size less than $\frac{1}{2\varepsilon}$.

Since event F guarantees condition (*i*) and event B guarantees condition (*ii*) it suffices to show that

$$\mathbb{P}(F^c \cup B^c) \leq \delta.$$

We will do so by conditioning on C^c and E^c where after a couple of union bounds we arrive at

$$\mathbb{P}(F^c \cup B^c) \leq \mathbb{P}(F^c \mid C^c, E^c) + \mathbb{P}(B^c \mid C^c, E^c) + \mathbb{P}(C) + \mathbb{P}(E).$$

Now showing (*i*) $\mathbb{P}(B^c \mid C^c, E^c) \leq \delta/2$, (*ii*) $\mathbb{P}(F^c \mid C^c, E^c) = 0$, (*iii*) $\mathbb{P}(E) \leq \delta/4$, and (*iv*) $\mathbb{P}(C) \leq \delta/4$ (of which we omit the proof) completes the argument. □

4.3 Sufficient Exploration

Any given recommendation in epoch τ is used for exploration with probability ε_τ. In the lemma below, we show that during each epoch there are enough Explore recommendations for the procedure MAKE-PARTITION to terminate.

LEMMA 4.5. *With probability at least $1-\varepsilon_{\tau+1}$, during the τth epoch the algorithm has enough explore recommendations for* MAKE-PARTITION$(M_{\tau+1}, \varepsilon_{\tau+1}, \varepsilon_{\tau+1})$ *to terminate.*

5. REGRET ANALYSIS

In this section we prove the main results of the paper. In Section 5.1 we prove the Quick Recommendations Lemma, which is the main lemma that will that will be used in Theorems 5.1 and 5.2, which are proved in Section 5.2.

5.1 Quick Recommendations Lemma

In Section 3 we described the algorithm, which starts recommending items to a user as soon as it knows one item that the user likes. Below we show that indeed shortly after the beginning of the epoch the slope of the regret is small.

LEMMA 5.1 (QUICK RECOMMENDATIONS LEMMA). *For* $\tau \geq 1$ *let* $\mathcal{R}^{(\tau)}(T) = \frac{1}{N}\sum_{t=T_\tau}^{T_\tau+TN} \frac{1}{2}(1 - L_{U_t,I_t})$ *denote the number of bad recommendations made to users during the first* TN *recommendations of epoch* τ. *Then we have*

$$\mathbb{E}\left[\mathcal{R}^{(\tau)}(T)\right] \leq \frac{148\varepsilon_\tau}{\nu}T \tag{11}$$

whenever $T \in [T_{\min,\tau}, D_\tau]$ *and where* $T_{\min,\tau} \triangleq \frac{12}{\varepsilon_\tau}\ln(\frac{1}{\varepsilon_\tau})$. *For* $T < T_{\min,\tau}$, *we trivially have* $\mathbb{E}\left[\mathcal{R}^{(\tau)}(T)\right] \leq T$.

PROOF. Let $\mathcal{R}'^{(\tau)}(T)$ denote the number of bad recommendations made to users during the first TN *exploit* recommendations of epoch τ. Then, since the expected number of explore recommendations by time TN of epoch τ is $\varepsilon_\tau TN$, we get that

$$\mathbb{E}\left[\mathcal{R}^{(\tau)}(T)\right] \leq \varepsilon_\tau T + \mathbb{E}\left[\mathcal{R}'^{(\tau)}(T)\right].$$

Furthermore, as described in the algorithm, during epoch $\tau - 1$ the algorithm spends a small fraction of the recommendations (in the explore part) to create a partition $\{P_k\}$ (which we call $\{P_k^{(\tau)}\}$ in the pseudocode) of M_τ random items to be exploited during epoch τ. Let $\mathcal{E}_\tau$ be the event that the partition $\{P_k^{(\tau)}\}$ to be used during epoch τ satisfies the conditions specified in Lemma 4.4 (with $M = M_\tau$ $\varepsilon = \varepsilon_\tau$, $\delta = \varepsilon_\tau$). Then we get

$$\mathbb{E}\left[\mathcal{R}^{(\tau)}(T)\right] \leq \varepsilon_\tau T + \mathbb{E}\left[\mathcal{R}'^{(\tau)}(T)\right] \leq 2\varepsilon_\tau T + \mathbb{E}\left[\mathcal{R}'^{(\tau)}(T) \mid \mathcal{E}_\tau\right],$$

where the last inequality is due to Lemma 4.4, which guarantees that $\mathbb{P}(\mathcal{E}_\tau) \leq \varepsilon_\tau$.

For the rest of the proof, we will show that $\mathbb{E}\left[\mathcal{R}'^{(\tau)}(T)\right]$ is at most $\frac{45}{\nu}\varepsilon_\tau T$. We will do so by first rewriting this in terms of the number of bad exploit recommendations to each user

$$\mathbb{E}\left[\mathcal{R}'^{(\tau)} \mid \mathcal{E}_\tau\right] \leq \frac{1}{N}\mathbb{E}\left[\sum_u \mathcal{R}_u'^{(\tau)}(T) \mid \mathcal{E}_\tau\right],$$

where $\mathcal{R}_u'^{(\tau)}(T)$ is the number of bad recommendations made to user u during the first TN exploit recommendations of epoch τ. We will now bound the latter term by conditioning on a nice property of users (denoted by $g_{u,T}$), and showing that this property holds for most users. Let $g_{u,T}$ be the event that user u has tried at most $16\frac{T}{D_\tau}P^{(\tau)}$ blocks during the first TN recommendations of epoch τ (we omit τ in the notation of $g_{u,T}$ since it is clear from the context here). Here we use notation $P^{(\tau)} = |\{P_k^{(\tau)}\}|$ to denote the total number of blocks in the partition for epoch τ. Then we get that $\frac{1}{N}\mathbb{E}\left[\sum_u \mathcal{R}_u'^{(\tau)}(T) \mid \mathcal{E}_\tau\right]$ is at most

$$\frac{1}{N}\sum_u \mathbb{E}\left[\mathcal{R}_u'^{(\tau)}(T) \mid \mathcal{E}_\tau, g_{u,T}\right] + T\frac{1}{N}\sum_u \mathbb{P}\left(g_{u,T}^c \mid \mathcal{E}_\tau\right).$$

We dedicate Lemma 5.3 to showing that $\frac{1}{N}\sum_u \mathbb{P}\left(g_{u,T}^c \mid \mathcal{E}_\tau\right) \leq \frac{42}{\nu}\varepsilon_\tau$. Hence, it suffices to show that for each $T > T_{\min,\tau}$ we have

$$\frac{1}{N}\sum_u \mathbb{E}\left[\mathcal{R}_u'^{(\tau)}(T) \mid \mathcal{E}_\tau, g_{u,T}\right] \leq \frac{104}{\nu}\varepsilon_\tau T, \tag{$\bigstar$}$$

which we prove now. We will first rewrite the regret by summing over the number of bad recommendations due to each of the blocks as

$$\sum_u \mathbb{E}\left[\mathcal{R}_u'^{(\tau)}(T) \mid \mathcal{E}_\tau, g_{u,T}\right] = \sum_u \mathbb{E}\left[\sum_k W_{u,k,T} \mid \mathcal{E}_\tau, g_{u,T}\right],$$

where $W_{u,k,T}$ is the random variable denoting the number of bad exploit recommendations to user u from block P_k among the first TN exploit recommendations of epoch τ. We can further rewrite to get that

$$\frac{1}{N}\sum_u \mathbb{E}\left[\sum_k W_{u,k,T} \mid \mathcal{E}_\tau, g_{u,T}\right] \tag{12}$$
$$\leq \frac{1}{N}\sum_u\sum_k \mathbb{E}\left[W_{u,k,T} \mid \mathcal{E}_\tau, g_{u,T}, s_{u,k,T}\right]\mathbb{P}\left(s_{u,k,T} \mid \mathcal{E}_\tau, g_{u,T}\right),$$

where $s_{u,k,T}$ denotes the event that by time T user u has sampled an item from block P_k. Here we used the fact that $W_{u,k,T}$ is identically equal to zero on $s_{u,k,T}^c$ because the user hasn't sampled an item from the block, so the expectation $\mathbb{E}\left[W_{u,k,T} \mid \mathcal{E}_\tau, g_{u,T}, s_{u,k,T}^c\right]$ is also zero.

Now note that by conditioning on $g_{u,T}$, we know that user u has sampled at most $16\frac{T}{D_\tau}P^{(\tau)}$ blocks. Now given $g_{u,T}$ as well as $\mathcal{E}_\tau$, the indices of the sampled blocks are not revealed. Let K be a random variable that selects one of the indices of the blocks uniformly at random. Then, it follows that with respect to randomness in K,

$$\mathbb{P}\left(s_{u,K,T} \mid \mathcal{E}_\tau, g_{u,T}\right) \leq \frac{16\frac{T}{D_\tau}P^{(\tau)}}{P^{(\tau)}} = 16 \cdot \frac{T}{D_\tau}.$$

We can re-write (12) in this notation and apply the above discussed bound to obtain

$$\begin{aligned}
&\frac{1}{N}\sum_u \mathbb{E}\left[\sum_k W_{u,k,T} \mid \mathcal{E}_\tau, g_{u,T}\right] \\
&\leq \frac{P^{(\tau)}}{N}\sum_u \mathbb{E}\left[W_{u,K,T} \mid \mathcal{E}_\tau, g_{u,T}, s_{u,K,T}\right]\mathbb{P}\left(s_{u,K,T} \mid \mathcal{E}_\tau, g_{u,T}\right) \\
&\leq \frac{P^{(\tau)}}{N}\sum_u \mathbb{E}\left[W_{u,K,T} \mid \mathcal{E}_\tau, g_{u,T}, s_{u,K,T}\right]\frac{16T}{D_\tau} \\
&= \frac{16T}{ND_\tau}\sum_u\sum_k \mathbb{E}\left[W_{u,k,T} \mid \mathcal{E}_\tau, g_{u,T}, s_{u,k,T}\right].
\end{aligned}$$

The last quantity above can be bounded as

$$\underbrace{\leq}_{Lemma\ 5.2} \frac{16T}{ND_\tau}\left(\sum_k (1 + 1.2\varepsilon_\tau |P_k^{(\tau)}|)N\right)$$
$$\underbrace{\leq}_{Lemma\ 4.4} 52\varepsilon_\tau T\frac{M_\tau}{D_\tau} \overset{D_\tau = \frac{\nu}{2}M_\tau}{\widehat{=}} \frac{104}{\nu}\varepsilon_\tau T.$$

The first inequality follows from Lemma 5.2 by realizing that each block, $P_k^{(\tau)}$ corresponds to a collection of items such that for any $i, j \in P_k^{(\tau)}$, we have $\gamma_{ij} < 1.2\varepsilon_\tau$. The second inequality can be justified as: from Lemma 4.4, $1/2\varepsilon_\tau \leq |P_k^{(\tau)}| \leq 1/\varepsilon_\tau$ and hence

$$\sum_k (1 + 1.2\varepsilon_\tau |P_k^{(\tau)}|) \leq \sum_k (3.2\varepsilon_\tau |P_k^{(\tau)}|) \leq 3.2\varepsilon_\tau \sum_k |P_k^{(\tau)}|,$$

which is $3.2\varepsilon_\tau M_\tau$. This, along with some arithmetic, completes the proof of eq. ($\bigstar$) and hence the lemma. □

The lemma below was used in the proof of Lemma 5.1. Informally, it says that our recommendation policy, which recommends the whole block to a user after the user likes an item in the block, succeeds in finding most likable items to recommend and in not recommending many bad items.

LEMMA 5.2 (PARTITION LEMMA). *Let P_k be a set of items such that for each $i, j \in P_k$ we have $\gamma_{ij} < \varepsilon$, and consider the usual recommendation policy that* ITEM-ITEM-CF *uses during its "exploit" steps (where when user u samples a random item $i \in_R P_k$, only if u likes i will u be recommended the remaining items). Let $s_{u,k}$ be the event that user u has sampled an item from P_k, let $W_{u,k}$ (W for wrong) denote the number of wrong recommendations made to u from P_k, and let $A_{u,k}$ (A for absent) denote the number of items in P_k that u likes that are not recommended to u. Then we have*

$$\sum_u \mathbb{E}\left[A_{u,k} + W_{u,k} \mid s_{u,k}\right] \leq (1 + \varepsilon|P_k|)N.$$

PROOF. For each block P_k and user u, let $\ell_{u,k} = |\{i \in P_k \mid L_{u,i} = +1\}|$ denote the number of items in P_k that u likes. Note that $\mathbb{E}\left[A_{u,k} \mid s_{u,k}\right] = \ell_{u,k} \cdot \frac{(|P_k| - \ell_{u,k})}{|P_k|}$ and $\mathbb{E}\left[W_{u,k} \mid s_{u,k}\right] = (|P_k| - \ell_{u,k}) \cdot \frac{\ell_{u,k}}{|P_k|} + 1 \cdot \frac{(|P_k| - \ell_{u,k})}{|P_k|}$. This is because with probability $\ell_{u,k}/|P_k|$ user u will sample an item from P_k that u likes and will then be recommended $(|P_k| - \ell_{u,k})$ bad items, and with probability $(|P_k| - \ell_{u,k})/|P_k|$ the first (and thus only) item from P_k recommended to u is bad. Likewise, with probability $(|P_k| - \ell_{u,k})/|P_k|$ the user will sample an item that the user dislikes, and then fail to be recommended $\ell_{u,k}$ items that the user likes. Hence we have that $\mathbb{E}\left[\sum_u A_{u,k} + W_{u,k} \mid s_{u,k}\right]$ is equal to

$$\underbrace{\sum_u \frac{(|P_k| - \ell_{u,k})}{|P_k|}}_{\leq N} + 2\sum_u \frac{\ell_{u,k}(|P_k| - \ell_{u,k})}{|P_k|}.$$

Now,

$$2\sum_u \frac{\ell_{u,k}(|P_k| - \ell_{u,k})}{|P_k|} \overset{\text{by definition}}{=} \frac{2}{|P_k|}\sum_u \sum_{i,j \in P_k} \mathbf{1}_{L_{u,i} \neq L_{u,j}}$$

$$= \frac{2}{|P_k|}\sum_{i,j \in P_k} \underbrace{\sum_u \mathbf{1}_{L_{u,i} \neq L_{u,j}}}_{=\gamma_{ij} \cdot N} \underbrace{\leq}_{\gamma_{ij} < \varepsilon} \frac{2}{|P_k|}\sum_{i,j \in P_k} \varepsilon N$$

$$\leq \frac{2}{|P_k|}\binom{|P_k|}{2}\varepsilon N \leq \varepsilon|P_k|N. \tag{13}$$

Putting it all together we get $\mathbb{E}\left[\sum_u A_{u,k} + W_{u,k} \mid s_{u,k}\right]$ is equal to

$$\underbrace{\sum_u \frac{(|P_k| - \ell_{u,k})}{|P_k|}}_{\leq N} + 2\underbrace{\sum_u \frac{\ell_{u,k}(|P_k| - \ell_{u,k})}{|P_k|}}_{\varepsilon|P_k|N} \leq (\varepsilon|P_k| + 1)N. \quad \square$$

The lemma below was also needed in the proof of Lemma 5.1.

LEMMA 5.3 (AUXILIARY CLAIM). *Consider an arbitrary epoch τ, and let $g_{u,T}$ be the event that by the $(TN)^{th}$ exploit recommendation of epoch τ user u has tried at most $16\frac{T}{D_\tau}|\{P_k^{(\tau)}\}|$ blocks from the partition $\{P_k^{(\tau)}\}$ constructed during the* MAKE-PARTITION$(M_\tau, \varepsilon_\tau, \varepsilon_\tau)$ *of the previous epoch, and let $\mathcal{E}_\tau$ be the event that $\{P_k^{(\tau)}\}$ satisfies the conditions specified in Lemma 4.4. Then*

$$\frac{1}{N}\sum_u \mathbb{P}\left(g_{u,T}^c \mid \mathcal{E}_\tau\right) \leq \frac{42}{\nu}\varepsilon_\tau$$

holds for any $T \in \left(\frac{12}{\varepsilon_\tau}\ln(1/\varepsilon_\tau), D_\tau\right]$.

PROOF. Let us make a few definitions. Let $N_{u,T}$ be the event that by the TN^{th} exploit recommendation user u has been recommended at most $1.1T$ items, *and* that u likes at least $0.9\nu M_\tau$ among the items in $\{P_k^{(\tau)}\}$. Also, let $H_{u,T}$ be the event that by the TN^{th} exploit recommendation there are still at least $\frac{\nu}{5}M_\tau$ items liked by u in blocks that haven't been sampled by u. Then we get $\mathbb{P}\left(g_{u,T}^c \mid \mathcal{E}_\tau\right)$ is at most

$$\mathbb{P}\left(g_{u,T}^c \mid H_{u,T}, N_{u,T}, \mathcal{E}_\tau\right) + \mathbb{P}\left(H_{u,T}^c \mid N_{u,T}, \mathcal{E}_\tau\right) + \mathbb{P}\left(N_{u,T}^c \mid \mathcal{E}_\tau\right).$$

By showing that for $T \in \left(\frac{12}{\varepsilon_\tau}\ln(1/\varepsilon_\tau), D_\tau\right]$ the following points (of which we omit the proofs) hold the lemma follows:
(A) $\mathbb{P}\left(g_{u,T}^c \mid H_{u,T}, N_{u,T}, \mathcal{E}_\tau\right) \leq \varepsilon_\tau$,
(B) $\frac{1}{N}\sum_u \mathbb{P}\left(H_{u,T}^c \mid N_{u,T}, \mathcal{E}_\tau\right) \leq \frac{40}{\nu}\varepsilon_\tau$,
(C) $\mathbb{P}\left(N_{u,T}^c \mid \mathcal{E}_\tau\right) \leq \varepsilon_\tau$. $\square$

5.2 Main Results

In Section 3 we described how ITEM-ITEM-CF starts recommending items to a user as soon as it finds one item that the user likes. This leads to a short cold-start time. We are now ready to bound the cold-start time of ITEM-ITEM-CF (the proof is presented in the Appendix).

THEOREM 5.1 (COLD-START PERFORMANCE). *Suppose assumptions* **A1** *and* **A2** *are satisfied. Then the algorithm* ITEM-ITEM-CF *has cold-start time $T_{\text{cold-start}} = \frac{f(\nu,d)}{N} + \widetilde{O}(1/\nu)$.*

It follows that the algorithm ITEM-ITEM-CF has cold-start time $\widetilde{O}(1/\nu)$ for N sufficiently large. This differs from the results of [5] for the user-user paradigm, where the cold-start time increases with user space complexity and the effect is not counteracted with more users present. (Section 6.2 contains a more in-depth discussion.)

The next result shows that after the cold-start period and until a time $T_{\max}$, the expected regret is sublinear.

THEOREM 5.2 (UPPER BOUND ON REGRET). *Suppose assumptions* **A1** *and* **A2** *are satisfied. Then the algorithm* ITEM-ITEM-CF *achieves expected regret for $T_{\min} < T \leq T_{\max}$ given by*

$$\mathbb{E}\left[\mathcal{R}(T)\right] \leq T_{\min} + \alpha(\nu, d) \cdot (T - T_{\min})^{\frac{d+1}{d+2}} \log_2(T - T_{\min}),$$

and for $T \geq T_{\max}$

$$\mathbb{E}\left[\mathcal{R}(T)\right] \leq \beta + \varepsilon_N\left(T - T_{\max}\right).$$

Here $T_{\min} = \widetilde{O}\left(\frac{1}{\nu}\right) + \frac{f(d,\nu)}{N}$, $T_{\max} = g(\nu, d)N^{\frac{d+2}{d+5}}$, $\varepsilon_{N,d,\nu} = h(d,\nu)\left(\frac{1}{N}\right)^{\frac{1}{d+5}}$, and
$\beta = T_{\min} + \alpha(\nu, d) \cdot (T_{\max} - T_{\min})^{\frac{d+1}{d+2}} \log_2(T_{\max} - T_{\min})$.

The reader is directed to the proof (presented in the Appendix) for the exact constants. Also note that $T_{\max}$ increases with N and the asymptotic slope ε_N decreases as a function with N, both of which illustrate the so-called collaboration gain. Note that the regret bound in Theorem 5.2

has an asymptotic linear regime. The next result (whose proof is in the Appendix) shows that with a finite number of users such linear regret is unavoidable.

THEOREM 5.3 (LINEAR REGRET IS UNAVOIDABLE). *Let μ be an item space satisfying assumptions* **A1** *and* **A2**. *Then any online algorithm must have expected asymptotic regret* $\mathbb{E}[\mathcal{R}(T)] \geq C(\nu, N) \cdot T$, *where* $C(\nu, N) = (1 - 2\nu)/N$.

6. CONCLUSION

In this section we further discuss our results and give suggestions for future work in the subject.

6.1 Discussion

In this paper we provided a formal expected regret analysis of ITEM-ITEM-CF, a simple recommendation algorithm following the item-item paradigm in collaborative filtering. We first proved that unless some structural assumption is made, no online recommendation algorithm can have sublinear expected for any period of time.

We then motivated using the doubling dimension d of the item space as a measure of structure in the data, and showed that the algorithm achieves expected regret $\tilde{\mathcal{O}}\left(T^{\frac{d+1}{d+2}}\right)$ for a period of time that increases with the number of users. Furthermore, we proved that the asymptotic linear regime following the sublinear regime is unavoidable.

6.2 Comparison with user-user CF

In this section we will contrast the cold-start performance of user-user collaborative filtering to that of our item-item algorithm. In particular, we give a heuristic argument showing that the cold-start time for user-user algorithms grows with the complexity of the user space. This is in contrast to our Theorem 5.1, where for any doubling dimension of the item space, if there are sufficiently many users then the cold-start time is independent of system complexity.

We consider a simple scenario with K user clusters. First, let $\tilde{\gamma}_{uv}$ denote the probability that users u and v agree on an item randomly drawn from the item space. We have K equally sized clusters of users, such that $\tilde{\gamma}_{uv} = 0$ for users u, v in the same cluster, and $\tilde{\gamma}_{uv} \in (0.1\nu, 0.2\nu)$ for users u, v in different clusters.

Consider now a given user u. A user-user algorithm seeks to find another user v who is similar to u, so that the items liked by v can be recommended to u. In order to recommend with at most (say) 0.1 probability of error, the similar user v should have distance $\tilde{\gamma}_{uv}$ at most 0.1ν. The extra factor ν is present because inference can only effectively be made from the ν fraction of liked items.

Concretely, we sample a random user v, and attempt to decide if it is from the same cluster as u. Suppose u and v have rated q items in common. The problem then reduces to a classical hypothesis test: after observing q items in common from two users, determine whether or not they are from the same cluster. The goal is to understand what is the minimal value of q needed so that the above procedure works with at least probability $1/2$.

We consider the maximum a posteriori rule for deciding that v is from u's cluster. If u and v disagree on any single item, then they cannot be from the same cluster. Conversely, if u and v agree on all q sampled items, the MAP rule declares v to be from u's cluster only if

$$\frac{K-1}{K}(1-0.2\nu)^q \leq \frac{1}{K}.$$

This means that if q is too small, we will never declare v to be from u's cluster and therefore will be unable to make recommendations.

Rearranging gives $q \geq \Omega(\log(K)/\nu)$. Hence, an algorithm based on user similarity needs at least $T = \Omega(\log(K)/\nu)$ steps simply to determine if two users are similar to each other, a prerequisite to making good recommendations. In contrast, we have shown that ITEM-ITEM-CF achieves cold start time $\tilde{\mathcal{O}}(1/\nu)$, which in particular does not increase with the complexity of the item space.

This contrast between cold-start times highlights the *asymmetry between item-item and user-user* collaborative filtering. The intuition is that it is much faster to compare two items than two users: it takes a long time to make many recommendations to two particular users, but comparing two items can be done in *parallel* by sampling different users.

6.3 Two roles of Doubling Dimension

In Section 2.1 we make the assumption that μ has small doubling dimension. This is crucial in the proofs for two distinct reasons. First, it guarantees that the *ε-net grows slowly* as ε-decreases (polynomially in $1/\varepsilon$). This is important in Lemma 4.4 for ensuring that the blocks of ε similar items are large enough and the reward for exploration pays off (as when the algorithm finds an item liked by the user, it can now recommend the many other items in the block). It is in this "slowly-growing ε-net" sense that doubling dimension/covering numbers are used, for instance, as [22, 7]. Second, the doubling dimension ensures that SIMILAR, which is a random projection, works with high probability (as proved in Lemma 4.2) in preserving relative distances. It is in this *random projection preserves relative distances* sense that it is used, for instance, in [13].

6.4 Future Works

This paper analyzes a collaborative filtering algorithm based on item similarity, and proves guarantees on its regret. Our algorithm exploits structure only in the item space. It would be desirable to have a matching lower bound, in the spirit of the lower bound for multi-armed bandits in metric spaces shown in [22] and [7]. Furthermore, many practitioners use a hybrid of user-user and item-item paradigms [36] and [35], and formally analyzing such algorithms is an open problem.

Finally, the main challenge of the cold-start problem is that initially we do not have any information about item-item similarities. In practice, however, some similarity can be inferred via content specific information. For instance, two books with similar words in the title can have a prior for having a higher similarity than books with no similar words in the title. In practice such hybrid content/collaborative filtering algorithms have had good performance [29]. Formally analyzing such hybrid algorithms has not been done and can shed light onto how to best combine content information with the collaborative filtering information.

7. REFERENCES

[1] N. Alon, N. Cesa-Bianchi, C. Gentile, S. Mannor, Y. Mansour, and O. Shamir. Nonstochastic multi-armed bandits with graph-structured feedback. *arXiv Technical Report arXiv:1409.8428*, 2014.

[2] S. Arora, R. Ge, R. Kannan, and A. Moitra. Computing a nonnegative matrix factorization–provably. In *STOC*, 2012.

[3] A. Bellogin and J. Parapar. Using graph partitioning techniques for neighbour selection in user-based collaborative filtering. In *RecSys*, 2012.

[4] G. Biau, B. Cadre, and L. Rouviere. Statistical analysis of k-nearest neighbor collaborative recommendation. *The Annals of Statistics*, 38(3):1568–1592, 2010.

[5] G. Bresler, G. Chen, and D. Shah. A latent source model for online collaborative filtering. In *NIPS*, 2014.

[6] S. Bubeck and N. Cesa-Bianchi. Regret analysis of stochastic and nonstochastic multi-armed bandit problems. *arXiv preprint arXiv:1204.5721*, 2012.

[7] S. Bubeck, R. Munos, G. Stoltz, and C. Szepesvari. X-armed bandits. *JMLR*, 2011.

[8] S. Caron and S. Bhagat. Mixing bandits: A recipe for improved cold-start recommendations in a social network. In *Workshop on Social Network Mining and Analysis*, 2013.

[9] N. Cesa-Bianchi, C. Gentile, and G. Zappella. A gang of bandits. In *NIPS*, 2013.

[10] N. Cesa-Bianchi and O. Shamir. Efficient transductive online learning via randomized rounding. In *Empirical Inference*, pages 177–194. Springer, 2013.

[11] O. Dabeer. Adaptive collaborating filtering: The low noise regime. In *ISIT*, 2013.

[12] A. S. Das, M. Datar, A. Garg, and S. Rajaram. Google news personalization: scalable online collaborative filtering. In *WWW*, 2007.

[13] S. Dasgupta and K. Sinha. Randomized partition trees for nearest neighbor search. *Algorithmica*, 2014.

[14] D. Donoho and V. Stodden. When does non-negative matrix factorization give a correct decomposition into parts? In *NIPS*, 2003.

[15] C. Gentile, S. Li, and G. Zappella. Online clustering of bandits. *ICML*, 2014.

[16] D. Goldberg, D. Nichols, B. M. Oki, and D. Terry. Using collaborative filtering to weave an information tapestry. *Commun. ACM*, 1992.

[17] K. Goldberg, T. Roeder, D. Gupta, and C. Perkins. Eigentaste: A constant time collaborative filtering algorithm. *Information Retrieval*, 2001.

[18] S. Har-Peled and M. Mendel. Fast construction of nets in low-dimensional metrics and their applications. *SIAM Journal on Computing*, 35(5):1148–1184, 2006.

[19] E. Hazan, S. Kale, and S. Shalev-Shwartz. Near-optimal algorithms for online matrix prediction. *COLT*, 2012.

[20] J. Heinonen. *Lectures on analysis on metric spaces.* Springer, 2001.

[21] J. Kleinberg and M. Sandler. Using mixture models for collaborative filtering. In *STOC*, 2004.

[22] R. Kleinberg, A. Slivkins, and E. Upfal. Bandits and experts in metric spaces. *arXiv preprint arXiv:1312.1277*, 2013.

[23] Y. Koren and R. Bell. Advances in collaborative filtering. In *Recommender Systems Handbook*, pages 145–186. Springer US, 2011.

[24] Y. Koren, R. Bell, and C. Volinsky. Matrix factorization techniques for recommender systems. *IEEE*, 2009.

[25] D. D. Lee and H. S. Seung. Algorithms for non-negative matrix factorization. In *NIPS*, 2001.

[26] G. Linden, B. Smith, and J. York. Amazon.com recommendations: Item-to-item collaborative filtering. *IEEE Internet Computing*, 7(1):76–80, 2003.

[27] L. Massoulie, M. Ohannessian, and A. Proutiere. Greedy-bayes approach for targeted news dissemination. *Sigmetrics*, 2015.

[28] C. McDiarmid. Concentration. In *Probabilistic methods for algorithmic discrete mathematics.* Springer, 1998.

[29] P. Melville, R. J. Mooney, and R. Nagarajan. Content-boosted collaborative filtering for improved recommendations. In *AAAI/IAAI*, 2002.

[30] A. Moitra. Algorithmic aspects of machine learning. *Online Manuscript*, 2014.

[31] J. Riedl and J. Konstan. Movielens dataset, 1998.

[32] A. Slivkins. Contextual bandits with similarity information. *The Journal of Machine Learning Research*, 2014.

[33] W. R. Thompson. On the likelihood that one unknown probability exceeds another in view of the evidence of two samples. *Biometrika*, pages 285–294, 1933.

[34] S. A. Vavasis. On the complexity of nonnegative matrix factorization. *SIAM Journal on Optimization*, 2009.

[35] K. Verstrepen and B. Goethals. Unifying nearest neighbors collaborative filtering. In *Recsys*, 2014.

[36] J. Wang, A. De Vries, and M. Reinders. Unifying user-based and item-based collaborative filtering approaches by similarity fusion. In *ACM SIGIR*, 2006.

[37] T. Zhang. Solving large scale linear prediction problems using stochastic gradient descent algorithms. In *ICML*, 2004.

APPENDIX

A. PROOFS

A.1 Proof of Theorem 5.1

First recall the usual definitions: $D_\tau = \frac{\nu}{2}M_\tau$, $T_\tau = T_{MP} + \sum_{\tau'<\tau} D_{\tau'}$, and $T_{MP} = f(\nu, d)/N$, where $f(\nu, d)$ is the number of recommendations required for the initial MAKE-PARTITION call (as stated in Lemma 4.4), and $T_{min,\tau} = \frac{12}{\varepsilon_\tau}\ln\left(\frac{1}{\varepsilon_\tau}\right)$ (as stated in Lemma 5.1). We will show the bound in the definition of cold-start time with $T = T_{MP}$ and $\Gamma = T_{min,1} = \widetilde{\mathcal{O}}(1/\nu)$, which implies $T_{\text{cold-start}} = T_{MP} + T_{min,1}$.

We shall establish the following two properties:

(*i*) For any $\Delta > 0$, $\mathbb{E}\left[\mathcal{R}(T_{\text{MP}} + T_{\text{min},1} + \Delta) - \mathcal{R}(T_{\text{MP}})\right] \le 0.1(T_{\text{min},1} + \Delta)$, for $T_{\text{MP}} + T_{min,1} + \Delta \le T_2$. This condition says that the desired property holds for times involving the first epoch.

(*ii*) $\mathbb{E}\left[\mathcal{R}(T_\tau + \Delta) - \mathcal{R}(T_\tau)\right] \le 0.05(\Delta + D_{\tau-1})$, for $\Delta \le D_\tau$ and any $\tau \ge 2$.

Before we show how the above two properties imply the desired result, we note that (*i*) follows directly from Lemma 5.1, and (*ii*) will be proved at the end.

Now let us complete the proof using (i) and (ii). Consider a time of the form $T_{\text{cold-start}} + \Delta = T_{MP} + T_{min,1} + \Delta$, for any $\Delta > 0$. Let $\tau^* \ge 1$ be the epoch to which $T_{MP} + T_{min,1} + \Delta$ belongs, i.e.

$$T_{\tau^*} < T_{MP} + T_{min,1} + \Delta \le T_{\tau^*+1}.$$

Define $t = T_{MP} + T_{min,1} + \Delta - T_{\tau^*} > 0$. We separately deal with $\tau^* = 1$ and $\tau^* > 1$. If $\tau^* = 1$, (i) implies the desired result. For $\tau^* > 1$, we use (ii) as follows:

$$\begin{aligned}
&\mathbb{E}\left[\mathcal{R}\left(T_{\text{MP}} + T_{\text{min},1} + \Delta\right) - \mathcal{R}\left(T_{\text{MP}}\right)\right] \underbrace{\le}_{t = T_{\text{cs}} + \Delta - T_{\tau^*}} \\
&\underbrace{\mathbb{E}\left[\mathcal{R}\left(T_2\right) - \mathcal{R}\left(T_{\text{MP}}\right)\right]}_{\le 0.1 \cdot D_1 \text{ by } (i)} \\
&+ \mathbf{1}_{\tau^* \ge 3}\left(\sum_{\tau=2}^{\tau^*-1} \underbrace{\mathbb{E}\left[\mathcal{R}\left(T_\tau\right) - \mathcal{R}\left(T_{\tau-1}\right)\right]}_{\le 0.05(D_\tau + D_{\tau-1}) \text{ by } (ii)}\right) \\
&+ \overbrace{\mathbb{E}\left[\mathcal{R}\left(T_{\tau^*} + t\right) - \mathcal{R}\left(T_{\tau^*}\right)\right]}^{\le 0.05(t + D_{\tau-1}) \text{ by } (ii)} \\
&\le 0.05\left(t + 2\sum_{\tau=1}^{\tau^*-1} D_\tau\right) \\
&\le 0.1 \cdot (\Delta + T_{\text{min},1}).
\end{aligned}$$

This establishes the desired result that $T_{\text{cold-start}} = T_{MP} + T_{min,1} = f(\nu, d)/N + \widetilde{\mathcal{O}}(1/\nu)$.

Proof of (ii): Now we show the remaining property (ii). Lemma 5.1 tells us that for $\Delta \in (T_{min,\tau}, D_\tau)$ we have that $\mathbb{E}\left[\mathcal{R}\left(T_\tau + \Delta\right) - \mathcal{R}\left(T_\tau\right)\right] \le \frac{148}{\nu}\varepsilon_\tau \Delta$, i.e.

$$\mathbb{E}\left[\mathcal{R}\left(T_\tau + T_{min,\tau}\right) - \mathcal{R}\left(T_\tau\right)\right] \le \frac{148}{\nu}\varepsilon_\tau T_{min,\tau}.$$

Thus, for $\Delta < D_\tau$, we have that

$$\mathbb{E}\left[\mathcal{R}\left(T_\tau + \Delta\right) - \mathcal{R}\left(T_\tau\right)\right] \le \frac{148}{\nu}\varepsilon_\tau T_{min,\tau} + \underbrace{\frac{148}{\nu}\varepsilon_\tau}_{\le 0.05 \text{ for } \tau \ge 2}\Delta \quad . \tag{14}$$

In above we used the fact that for $\Delta < T_{min,1}$, $\mathcal{R}\left(T_\tau + \Delta\right) \le \mathcal{R}\left(T_\tau + T_{min,1}\right)$. Using the fact that $T_{min,\tau} \triangleq \frac{12}{\varepsilon_\tau}\ln\left(\frac{1}{\varepsilon_\tau}\right) \le 0.05\left(\frac{300}{\varepsilon_\tau}\ln\left(\frac{1}{\varepsilon_\tau}\right)\right) = 0.05 D_{\tau-1}$, we conclude

$$\mathbb{E}\left[\mathcal{R}\left(T_\tau + \Delta\right) - \mathcal{R}\left(T_\tau\right)\right] \le 0.05\left(\Delta + D_{\tau-1}\right). \quad \square$$

A.2 Proof of Theorem 5.2

Recall that ITEM-ITEM-CF starts by running the routine MAKE-PARTITION$(M_1, \varepsilon_1, \varepsilon_1)$. This consumes at most

$$MP(1) \triangleq \left(\frac{8}{\varepsilon_1}\right)^{d+1} 4 \cdot 630\left(d+1\right)^3 M_1 \ln^2\left(\frac{8}{\varepsilon_1}\right)\ln\left(M_1\right) \tag{15}$$

recommendations (by Lemma 4.4), and hence finishes in at most $T_{MP} \triangleq MP(1)/N$ time steps. For this initial exploratory period $T \le T_{MP}$ we will bound the regret with the trivial bound $\mathcal{R}(T) \le T$.

Let us now deal with the regime between T_{min} and T_{max}. Recall that the target ε_τ used in the τth epoch is decreasing as $\frac{C}{2^\tau}$, until it plateaus at ε_N when $\frac{C}{2^\tau} \le \varepsilon_N$, where $C = \frac{\nu}{148 \cdot 20}$. Hence $\tau^* \triangleq \lceil \log_2 \frac{C}{\varepsilon_N} \rceil$ is the first epoch in which ε_N is used. For a function g defined later, we will show that

$$T_{MP(1)} + \sum_{\tau'=1}^{\tau^*-1} D_\tau \ge g(\nu, d) N^{\frac{d}{d+5}} \triangleq T_{max}. \tag{16}$$

Now since $\varepsilon_N = \left(\frac{2^{5d+18}}{\nu} \cdot 630(2d+11)(d+2)^4 \frac{1}{N}\right)^{\frac{1}{d+5}}$, we get that

$$\tau^* \ge \frac{1}{d+5}\log_2\left(\left(\frac{\nu}{148 \cdot 20}\right)^{d+5} \frac{\nu}{630(2d+11)(d+2)^4} \frac{1}{2^{5d+18}} \cdot N\right). \tag{17}$$

Also,

$$T_{MP(1)} + \sum_{\tau=1}^{\tau^*-1} D_\tau \ge \sum_{\tau=1}^{\tau^*-1} D_\tau = \sum_{\tau=1}^{\tau^*-1} \frac{\nu}{2} M_\tau, \tag{18}$$

where we used the fact that $D_\tau = \frac{\nu}{2}M_\tau$. Recall $M_\tau \triangleq C_M \frac{1}{\varepsilon_\tau^{d+2}}\ln\left(\frac{2}{\varepsilon_\tau}\right)$, where $C_M = \frac{2^{\max(3.5d, 8)}}{\nu}(3d+1)$, and for $\tau \le \tau^*$ we have $\varepsilon_\tau = C/2^\tau$, where $C = \nu/(148 \cdot 20)$. Then we get

$$\begin{aligned}
T_{MP(1)} + \sum_{\tau=1}^{\tau^*-1} D_\tau &\ge \frac{\nu C_M}{2C^{d+2}} \sum_{\tau=1}^{\tau^*-1} 2^{\tau(d+2)} \ge \frac{\nu C_M}{4C^{d+2}} 2^{\tau^*(d+2)} \\
&\ge \underbrace{\frac{\nu C_M}{4C^{d+2}}\left(\frac{\nu}{630(2d+11)(d+2)^4} \frac{1}{2^{5d+18}}\right)^{\frac{d+2}{d+5}}}_{g(\nu, d)} \cdot N^{\frac{d+2}{d+5}} \triangleq T_{max},
\end{aligned} \tag{19}$$

as wished. Hence, between T_{min} and T_{max} the target ε_τ for the epochs is indeed halving for each subsequent epoch. Let $\tau(T)$ be the epoch of time T. Then, by Lemma 5.1, for $T \in [T_{min}, T_{max}]$, where $T_{min} = T_{MP} + T_{min,1}$, the expected regret satisfies $\mathcal{R}(T) - T_{MP} \le \frac{148}{\nu}\sum_{\tau=1}^{\tau(T)} \varepsilon_\tau D_\tau$, which we can further bound as

$$\begin{aligned}
\mathcal{R}(T) - T_{MP} &\le \frac{C_M}{2}\log_2\left(\frac{2^{\tau(T)}}{2C}\right)\sum_{\tau=1}^{\tau(T)} 2^{\tau(d+1)} \\
&\le \frac{C_M}{2}\log_2\left(\frac{2^{\tau(T)}}{2C}\right) 2^{(\tau(T)+1)(d+1)}.
\end{aligned} \tag{20}$$

Now, since for $T > T_{min}$ epoch

$$\tau(T) \leq 1 + \frac{1}{d+2}\log_2\left(\frac{T-T_{MP}}{C_M}\frac{1}{\log(2/C)}\right),$$

we get that

$$\mathcal{R}(T) \leq T_{MP} + \tag{21}$$

$$\frac{C_M}{2}\log_2\left(\frac{T-T_{MP}}{C_M C(d+2)}\frac{1}{\log(2/C)}\right)2^{2(d+1)}2^{(\tau(T)+1)(d+1)} \tag{22}$$

$$\leq T_{MP} + \underbrace{\frac{C_M}{2}\log_2\left(\frac{1}{CC_M(d+2)}\frac{1}{\log(2/C)}\right)2^{4(d+1)}}_{\triangleq C'} \tag{23}$$

$$\cdot \log_2(T-T_{MP})\, 2^{\frac{d+1}{d+2}\log_2\left(\frac{T-T_{MP}}{C_M}\frac{1}{\log(2/C)}\right)} \tag{24}$$

$$\leq T_{MP} + \underbrace{C'\left(\frac{1}{C_M}\frac{1}{\log(2/C)}\right)^{\frac{d+1}{d+2}}}_{\triangleq \alpha(\nu,d)}(T-T_{MP})^{\frac{d+1}{d+2}}\log_2(T-T_{MP}),$$

as we wished, which completes the proof of the sublinear regret regime.

The case $T > T_{max}$ now follows. Recall that by Lemma 5.1 we get $\mathcal{R}(T) \leq T_{MP} + \frac{148}{\nu}\sum_{\tau=1}^{\tau(T)}\varepsilon_\tau D_\tau$,which we can in turn split between before T_{max} and after T_{max} as

$$\mathcal{R}(T) \leq T_{MP} + \frac{148}{\nu}\sum_{\tau=1}^{\tau^*-1}\varepsilon_\tau D_\tau + \frac{148}{\nu}\sum_{\tau=\tau^*}^{\tau(T)}\varepsilon_\tau D_\tau \tag{25}$$

$$\leq \underbrace{T_{MP} + \alpha(\nu,d)T_{max}^{\frac{d+1}{d+2}}\log_2(T_{max})}_{\triangleq \beta} + \varepsilon_N(T-T_{max}), \tag{26}$$

as claimed, and where the last inequality is due to the sublinear regime proved above. $\square$

A.3 Proof of Theorem 5.3

Let $\{i_1, ..., i_{k_T}\}$ be the set of distinct items that have been recommended up to time TN. Then we have

$$\mathbb{E}[\mathcal{R}(T)] = \frac{1}{N}\mathbb{E}\left[\sum_{t=1}^{TN}\frac{1}{2}(1-L_{U_t,I_t})\right]$$

$$= \frac{1}{N}\mathbb{E}\left[\sum_{k=1}^{k_T}\sum_{t=1}^{TN}\frac{1}{2}\mathbf{1}_{I_t=i_k}(1-L_{U_t,i_k})\right]$$

$$\geq \frac{1}{N}\mathbb{E}\left[\sum_{k=1}^{k_T}\frac{1}{2}(1-L_{U_{T_k},i_k})\right],$$

where T_k is the first time in which the item i_k is recommended to any user. Now note that for each k by (A_2) we have that $\mathbb{E}\left[\frac{1}{2}(1-L_{U_{T_k},i_k})\right] \geq 1-2\nu$, since when we have no prior information about i_k the best we can do is to recommend it to the user that likes the largest fraction of items. Hence we get

$$\mathbb{E}[\mathcal{R}(T)] \geq \frac{1-2\nu}{N}k_t. \tag{27}$$

Since each item can be recommended to each user at most once, we see that by the TN^{th} recommendation at least T different items must have been recommended (that is, $k_t \geq T$). We can then conclude that

$$\mathbb{E}[\mathcal{R}(T)] \geq \underbrace{\frac{1-2\nu}{N}}_{C(\nu,d)}, \tag{28}$$

as we wished. $\square$

A.4 Chernoff Bound

We state a standard version of the Chernoff Bound [28]:

THEOREM A.1 (CHERNOFF BOUND). *Let $X_1, \cdots, X_n$ be independent random variables that take value in $[0,1]$. Let $X = \sum_{i=1}^n X_i$, and let $\bar{X} = \sum_{i=1}^n \mathbb{E}X_i$. Then, for any $\varepsilon \geq 0$,*

$$\mathbb{P}\left(X \geq (1+\varepsilon)\bar{X}\right) \leq \exp\left(-\frac{\varepsilon^2}{2+\varepsilon}\bar{X}\right), \text{ and}$$

$$\mathbb{P}\left(X \leq (1-\varepsilon)\bar{X}\right) \leq \exp\left(-\frac{\varepsilon^2}{2}\bar{X}\right).$$

B. EMPIRICAL DOUBLING DIMENSION EXPERIMENTS

The jester dataset contains ratings of one hundred jokes by over seventy thousand users. The dataset is fairly dense (as the average number of ratings per user is over fifty), which makes it a great dataset for calculating the doubling dimension. For the MovieLens 1M Dataset we consider the only movies that have been rated by at least 750 users (to ensure some density).

The Jester ratings are in $[-10, 10]$, with an average of 2, so we make ratings greater than 2 a $R_{u,i} = +1$, and ratings at most 2 a $R_{u,i} = -1$. For the MovieLens 1M Dataset we make ratings $1, 2, 3$ into -1, and $4, 5$ into $+1$. We then estimate the doubling dimension as follows:

- For each pair of items (i, j), we calculate $\hat{d}_{i,j,\Delta}$ as fraction of users that agree on them, where the Δ subscript is put to denote our assumption that each entry has a noise probability of Δ (that is, $\mathbb{P}(R_{u,i} \neq L_{u,i}) = \Delta$), where R is the empirical ratings matrix and L is the true, noiseless, ratings matrix.
- Assuming that each entry has a noise probability of $\Delta = 0.20$, we estimate the true distance $d_{i,j}$ as the solution to $\hat{d}_{i,j,\Delta} = (1-d_{ij})(2\Delta(1-\Delta)) + d_{i,j}(\Delta^2 + (1-\Delta)^2)$.
- For each item i and r in $\{0, \frac{1}{N}, ..., \frac{N-1}{N}, 1\}$, let $N_{i,r}$ be the number of items such that $d_{i,j} \leq r$.
- For each item i let d_i be the least such that $N_{i,2r}/N_{i,r} \leq 2^{d_i}$ for each r in $\{0, \frac{1}{N}, ..., \frac{1}{2}\}$.
- Figs 2 and 3 show the histogram of the $\{d_i\}$.

Achieving Low-Delay and Fast-Convergence in Stochastic Network Optimization: A Nesterovian Approach*

Jia Liu
Dept. of Electrical and Computer Engineering
The Ohio State University, Columbus, OH 43210, USA
liu@ece.osu.edu

ABSTRACT

Due to the rapid growth of mobile data demands, there have been significant interests in stochastic resource control and optimization for wireless networks. Although significant advances have been made in stochastic network optimization theory, to date, most of the existing approaches are plagued by either slow convergence or unsatisfactory delay performances. To address these challenges, in this paper, we develop a new stochastic network optimization framework inspired by the Nesterov accelerated gradient method. We show that our proposed Nesterovian approach offers utility-optimality, fast-convergence, and significant delay reduction in stochastic network optimization. Our contributions in this paper are three-fold: i) we propose a Nesterovian joint congestion control and routing/scheduling framework for both single-hop and multi-hop wireless networks; ii) we establish the utility optimality and queueing stability of the proposed Nesterovian method, and analytically characterize its delay reduction and convergence speed; and iii) we show that the proposed Nesterovian approach offers a three-way performance control between utility-optimality, delay, and convergence.

CCS Concepts

•Networks → Network resources allocation; Network control algorithms; Network performance modeling;

1. INTRODUCTION

Fueled by the massive amounts of mobile data and the rapid integration of new devices, recent years have witnessed an active research on stochastic resource control and optimization for wireless networks (see, e.g., [1–5], and [6] for a survey). The large body of work in this area has given rise to a beautiful queue-length-based control algorithmic framework (QCA), based on which congestion control, scheduling, and routing algorithms are naturally coupled by queueing states. Such algorithms do not need statistical knowledge of either the arrivals or the channel fading distributions. Rather, they only require instantaneous queue-lengths and channel state information (CSI) to make control decisions. Further, these algorithms can be interpreted by the Lagrangian dual decomposition framework plus the subgradient method in convex optimization [1,2], where queue-lengths can be viewed as Lagrangian dual variables and the queue-length evolutions play the role of subgradient updates.

However, the QCA approaches suffer from several notable limitations. First, for the existing QCA approaches, it is well-known that an $O(1/K)$ utility-optimality gap is achieved at the expense of an $O(K)$ penalty in steady-state queue-length, where $K > 0$ is a system parameter. Hence, a small utility-optimality gap implies a large K and results in large queueing delay. To alleviate this queueing delay problem, there have been significant recent efforts (e.g., [4,7–9], etc.) on improving the utility-optimality and delay trade-off scaling law (see Section 2 for more in-depth discussions). Second, due to the subgradient nature of the queue-length-based weight adjustment, the QCA framework is oblivious to the curvature of the objective function [1–4]. The resultant "zigzagging" phenomenon [10] entails unsatisfactory convergence speed. To overcome this limitation, several second-order congestion control and routing/scheduling algorithms have recently been proposed to enhance the convergence speed (see, e.g., [11,12]). However, due to the high complexity in Hessian inverse computation, these second-order designs require large information exchange overhead and may not work well for large-scale networks. The limitations of these existing works motivate us to pursue a new *Nesterovian* approach in this paper.

More specifically, in this work, our goal is to develop a low-complexity weight adjustment scheme based on the much simpler first-order Nesterov's accelerated gradient descent (AGD) method [13,14] to reduce the queueing delay and increase the convergence speed of the QCA approaches, while without affecting their utility-optimality performance and without increasing their algorithmic complexity. Our fundamental rationale behind this approach is that the AGD method, first appeared in Nesterov's seminal work [13], is known for being an order-optimal first-order optimization method in terms of convergence rate [14]. Our key idea is to separate the weights and queue-lengths in the QCA framework, which then allows us to develop a weight updating scheme based on a Nesterovian scheme to accelerate the algorithm's convergence speed in the dual domain. Surpris-

*The work of Jia Liu has been supported in part by NSF grants CNS-1527078 and CNS-1446582.

SIGMETRICS '16, June 14-18, 2016, Antibes Juan-Les-Pins, France.
© 2016 ACM. ISBN 978-1-4503-4266-7/16/06...$15.00
DOI: http://dx.doi.org/10.1145/2896377.2901474

ingly, it turns out that the theoretical findings of adopting a Nesterovian approach in network optimization are far *richer* than just convergence acceleration.

However, due to a number of technical challenges, developing a Nesterovian solution for stochastic network optimization is highly non-trivial. First, since the original Nesterov's AGD method was developed for unconstrained deterministic convex optimization, it is unclear how to modify the algorithm for wireless network utility maximization, which is not only constrained but also a stochastic optimization problem with a far more complex structure. Second, unlike the clear relationship between Lagrangian dual variables and queue-lengths in the QCA approaches, the relationship between the Nesterov's AGD method and the network states (e.g., queue-lengths, channel states, etc.) is unknown, which will cause difficulty in the trade-off analysis between delay and network utility. Third, due to the memory of past iterations' values, the structure of a Nesterovian approach is quite different from that of the QCA approaches. Hence, many existing analytical techniques used in QCA for utility optimality and delay tradeoff are not applicable.

The main contribution of this paper is that we develop a Nesterovian wireless network utility optimization framework that addresses the aforementioned technical challenges. This framework entails a series of new theoretical results on delay reduction and convergence speed, while maintaining utility-optimality. The main results and technical contributions of this paper are as follows:

- Motivated by the Nesterov's AGD idea, we propose a new weight adjustment scheme for joint congestion control and routing/scheduling in wireless networks. Our work not only establishes a connection between Nesterov's AGD method and the queue-length and channel state information to allow simple implementation in practice, it also extends the classical Nesterov's AGD method from unconstrained determinstic optimization to constrained stochastic network optimization.
- We establish the utility optimality and the queuing stability of the proposed Nesterovian approach. More precisely, under our Nesterovian congestion control and scheduling scheme with a β-parameterized memory term ($\beta \in [0, 1)$ is a system parameter), we show that a utility-optimality gap $O(1/K)$ can be achieved with an $O((1-\beta)K)+O((1+\beta)\sqrt{K})$ cost in queueing-delay, where K is the same parameter as used in the traditional QCA framework. Moreover, in the asymptotic regime of K with β being chosen as $\beta = 1 - O(1/\sqrt{K})$, our Nesterovian approach achieves an $[O(1/K), O(\sqrt{K})]$ utility-delay trade-off, which is a much stronger result compared to the $[O(1/K), O(K)]$ trade-off scaling obtained by the QCA approaches.
- We investigate the choices of system parameters β and K, and their impacts on convergence. More specifically, we characterize the linear convergence rate factor of our Nesterovian approach and further show that it achieves superior convergence performance even compared with some state-of-the-art momentum-based schemes (e.g., [15]) in certain cases. Further, integrating with the results in the previous bullet, our Nesterovian approach offers a three-way performance control between utility, delay, and convergence speed. We offer insights on how to implement the proposed Nesterovian approach in a *distributed* fashion for multi-hop networks. We show that the distributed Nesterovian method only requires one-hop local message exchange, which is identical to the QCA schemes and hence does *not* incur any additional information exchange overhead in practical implementations.

The remainder of this paper is organized as follows. In Section 2, we review related works. Section 3 introduces the network model and problem formulation. Section 4 presents our Nesterovian approach and the performance analysis of the proposed algorithm. In Section 5, we extend the proposed algorithm to multi-hop networks. Section 6 presents numerical results and Section 7 concludes this paper.

Notation: In this paper, we use boldface to denote matrices/vectors. We let $\mathbf{A}^\top$ be the transpose of $\mathbf{A}$. We let $\mathbf{I}_N$ and $\mathbf{O}_N$ denote the $N \times N$ identity and all-zero matrices, respectively. We let $\mathbf{1}_N$ and $\mathbf{0}_N$ denote the N-dimensional all-one and all-zero vectors, respectively. We will often omit "N" for brevity if the dimension is clear from the context. We use $\|\cdot\|$ and $\|\cdot\|_1$ to denote L^2- and L^1-norms, respectively. $\mathbf{A} \succeq 0$ (or $\mathbf{A} \preceq 0$) means that $\mathbf{A}$ is positive (resp., negative) semidefinite. $\mathbf{A} \succeq \mathbf{B}$ means $\mathbf{A} - \mathbf{B} \succeq 0$.

2. RELATED WORK

In this section, we first provide a synopsis of the state-of-the-art on delay reduction in the QCA literature that is most related to our work. Then, we provide a brief overview of the Nesterov's AGD method and its applications.

Delay Reduction for QCA: As mentioned in Section 1, there have been significant efforts on reducing the delay of the QCA approaches. For example, in [4, 16–19], virtual queues are used to reduce delay, where the virtual queue-lengths evolve based on service rates that are a fraction of the actual service rates. The key finding in these earlier efforts is that a slight sacrifice of throughput can lead to notable improvements in delay. More recent research on delay-reduction can be found in [7–9]. In [8], a virtual backlog mechanism with place-holder bits instead of real data was proposed. It was shown that, by accepting some non-zero packet dropping probability, this approach achieves an $[O(1/K), O(\log^2(K))]$ utility-delay trade-off. An exponential Lyapunov virtual backlog method combined with a threshold-based packeting-dropping scheme was proposed in [7] to achieve an even stronger $O(\log(K))$ delay. Although enjoying a log-type delay scaling, a common limitation of [7, 8] is that choosing the size of place-holder bits in [8] and the threshold value in [7] require *non-causal* global arrival and channel statistics (cf. [7, Eq. (17)], [8, Eq. (45)]), which is usually hard to obtain. If the parameters are not set appropriately, these schemes may result in non-negligible packet dropping probability. To address this problem, a per-iteration learning step was proposed in [9] to learn the optimal size of place-holder bits. However, the per-iteration learning component significantly increases the complexity. We note that, in some sense, all these delay reduction schemes can be viewed as sacrificing throughput-optimality (reflected in reduced service rates or packet dropping) for delay reduction, which is undesirable in practice. In contrast, *without sacrificing any throughput-optimality and without requiring any non-causal statistical knowledge*, our Nesterovian approach achieves an $O(\sqrt{K})$ delay scaling. We also note that although attempts to get rid of the back-pressure nature of the QCA framework have also been proposed in the literature (see, e.g., [20, 21]), convergence performance was not addressed in these works.

The Nesterov's AGD Method: A Primer: For this paper to be self-contained, here we provide an overview of the Nesterov's AGD method. Historically, the AGD method was proposed by Nesterov in 1983 for unconstrained convex optimization [13]. Specifically, consider a general unconstrained optimization problem $\min_{\mathbf{x}\in\mathbb{R}^n} f(\mathbf{x})$, where $f(\cdot)$ is twice continuously differentiable and convex. Let $\mathbf{H}(\mathbf{x})$ denote the Hessian matrix evaluated at $\mathbf{x}$. We assume that there exist two constants $0 \le \phi \le \Phi$ such that $\phi\mathbf{I} \preceq \mathbf{H}(\mathbf{x}) \preceq \Phi\mathbf{I}$, $\forall \mathbf{x}$ (thus Φ is a Lipschitz constant of the gradient of $f(\cdot)$). Then, the Nesterov's AGD method operates as follows [14, Chap. 2.2]:

- Choose an initial point $\mathbf{x}[0]$. Define an auxiliary variable $\mathbf{y}$ and let $\mathbf{y}[0] = \mathbf{x}[0]$. Choose $\alpha_0 \in (0,1)$. Let $\kappa = \Phi/\phi$ be the condition number of $f(\cdot)$.
- In iteration $t \ge 0$: a) Compute $f'(\mathbf{x}[k])$ and let:

$$\mathbf{y}[t+1] = \mathbf{x}[t] - (1/\Phi)f'(\mathbf{x}[t]). \tag{1}$$

b) Compute $\alpha[t+1] \in (0,1)$ by solving the quadratic equation $\alpha^2[t+1] + [\alpha^2[t] - (1/\kappa)]\alpha[t+1] - \alpha^2[t] = 0$. Let:

$$\beta[t] = \frac{\alpha[t](1-\alpha[t+1])}{(\alpha^2[t] + \alpha[t+1])}, \text{ and} \tag{2}$$

$$\mathbf{x}[t+1] = \mathbf{y}[t+1] + \beta[t](\mathbf{y}[t+1] - \mathbf{y}[t]). \tag{3}$$

It can be shown that the Nesterov's AGD method achieves: i) order-optimal $O(1/t^2)$ convergence rate for weakly convex problems ($\phi = 0$); and ii) an $O(1/\sqrt{\kappa})$ linear convergence factor for strongly convex problems (see [14] for details). In each iteration, the Nesterov's AGD method first performs a basic gradient descent step to move from $\mathbf{x}[t]$ to $\mathbf{y}[t+1]$ (cf. (1)), and then "slides" a little bit further (controlled by $\alpha[t]$ and $\beta[t]$) from $\mathbf{y}[t+1]$ in the direction with respect to $\mathbf{y}[t]$ (cf. (3)). Unfortunately, the intuition behind the Nesterov updates in (1) and (3) is difficult to grasp. Over the years, researchers have made numerous attempts to explain why the acceleration works, rather than settling on the mysterious (yet beautiful) algebraic manipulations in the original proof. Recent efforts in this area include, e.g., viewing AGD as a linear coupling of gradient descent and mirror descent [22], interpretation through discretization of certain second-order ordinary differential equation (ODE) in physics [23], and a geometric explanation inspired by the ellipsoid method [24]. Although interpreting the Nesterov's AGD method is beyond the scope of this paper, we hope that our Nesterovian network optimization approach could also provide some insights from a networking angle.

We note that the Nesterov's AGD method exploits past memory (cf. (3)), which is similar to another family of first-order methods termed "multi-step methods" (or called "heavy ball") that also leverage memory for convergence acceleration [25–28]. However, the key difference is that the Nesterov's method exploits both past iterates and gradients, while the multi-step methods only use past iterates. Also, the Nesterov's method is convergence-rate order-optimal for general convex problems, while multi-step methods only work for strongly convex problems ($\phi > 0$). We also note that, since its inception, the Nesterov's method has found applications in signal processing (e.g., [29] and references therein). However, to our knowledge, the Nesterov's AGD idea remains unexplored in network system optimization.

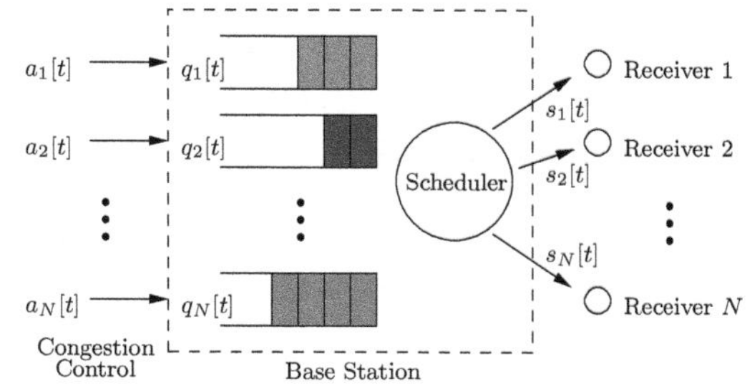

Figure 1: An illustration of the single-hop cellular downlink.

3. NETWORK MODEL AND PROBLEM FORMULATION

From this section to Section 4, we focus on a single-hop model with N links, which could model a cellular downlink/uplink channel with N users, or a set of communicating pairs in an ad hoc network. We will discuss in Section 5 how to extend the results to multi-hop networks.

Network model: In the single-hop case, we use a cellular downlink system as shown in Figure 1 to facilitate discussions. We assume a time-slotted system with time being indexed by $t = 0, 1, 2, \ldots$. Suppose that the channel fading is characterized by a total of M states and denoted by vectors $\boldsymbol{\pi}_1, \ldots, \boldsymbol{\pi}_M$, where each $\boldsymbol{\pi}_m \in \mathbb{R}^N$, $m = 1, \ldots, M$, corresponds to the N links' channel states under state m. Let $\mathcal{C}_{\boldsymbol{\pi}_m}$ denote the achievable rate region for $\boldsymbol{\pi}_m$, which is defined as $\mathcal{C}_{\boldsymbol{\pi}_m} \triangleq Conv\{x_1^{(m)}, \ldots, x_N^{(m)}\}$, where $Conv\{\cdot\}$ represents convex hull and $x_n^{(m)}$ denotes a feasible rate of link n that can be scheduled under channel state m. We assume that, for each link n and channel state m, $x_n^{(m)} \le s^{\max} < \infty$. We use a vector $\mathbf{x}^{(m)} = [x_1^{(m)}, \ldots, x_N^{(m)}]^\top \in \mathbb{R}^N$ to denote the feasible rates of all receivers under channel state m. We assume that the channel states are independent and identically distributed across time-slots[1]. Let $\boldsymbol{\pi}[t]$ denote the channel state vector in time-slot t and let $p_m \triangleq \Pr\{\boldsymbol{\pi}[t] = \boldsymbol{\pi}_m\}$ be the stationary distribution of the channel state being in state m. We let $\bar{\mathcal{C}}$ denote the mean achievable rate region, which can be computed as:

$$\bar{\mathcal{C}} \triangleq \left\{ \mathbf{x} \,\middle|\, \mathbf{x} = \sum_{m=1}^{M} p_m \mathbf{x}^{(m)}, \ \forall \mathbf{x}^{(m)} \in \mathcal{C}_{\boldsymbol{\pi}_m} \right\}. \tag{4}$$

We note that, in this paper, neither the channel state statistics nor $\bar{\mathcal{C}}$ is assumed to be known at the base station.

Queue-stability: As shown in Figure 1, each link n is associated with a queue. We denote the queue-length in time-slot t as $q_n[t]$. In every time-slot t, the controller observes the current channel state $\boldsymbol{\pi}[t]$ and then chooses a service rate vector $\mathbf{s}[t] \triangleq [s_1[t], \ldots, s_N[t]]^\top \in \mathcal{C}_{\boldsymbol{\pi}[t]}$ and a congestion control rate vector $\mathbf{a}[t] \triangleq [a_1[t], \ldots, a_N[t]]^\top \in \mathbb{R}_+^N$. Clearly, the queue-length process $\{q_n[t]\}$ evolves as:

$$q_n[t+1] = \{q_n[t] - s_n[t] + a_n[t]\}^+, \quad \forall n, \tag{5}$$

where $\{\cdot\}^+ \triangleq \max\{0, \cdot\}$. We let $\mathbf{q}[t] \triangleq [q_1[t], \ldots, q_N[t]]^\top$ denote the queue-length vector in time-slot t. Same as in [2, 3], in this paper, we say that a network is *stable* if the

[1]Following the same arguments as in [8, 30], our results can be generalized to Markovian channel state processes.

steady-state total queue-length is finite, i.e.,

$$\limsup_{t\to\infty} \mathbb{E}\left\{\|\mathbf{q}[t]\|_1\right\} < \infty. \quad (6)$$

Problem formulation: Let $\bar{a}_n \triangleq \lim_{T\to\infty} \frac{1}{T}\sum_{t=0}^{T-1} a_n[t]$ denote the average arrival rate of link n under congestion control. Each receiver n is associated with a utility function $U_n(\bar{a}_n)$, which represents the utility gained by receiver n when its data is injected at rate $\bar{a}_n$. We assume that $U_n(\cdot)$, $\forall n$, is concave, monotonically increasing, and twice continuously differentiable, and strongly concave, i.e., there exist constants $0 < \phi \le \Phi < \infty$ such that

$$\phi \le -U_n''(a_n) \le \Phi, \quad \forall a_n \in [0, a^{\max}], \quad (7)$$

where $a^{\max}$ is an arrival rate upper bound for burst control. As an example, the function $\log(\epsilon + a_n)$ with some constant $\epsilon > 0$ satisfies (7). Our goal is to maximize $\sum_{n=1}^{N} U_n(\bar{a}_n)$, subject to achievable rate region $\mathcal{C}_{\boldsymbol{\pi}[t]}$ in each time-slot and the queue-stability constraint. Putting together the models presented above, we have the following joint congestion control and scheduling (CCS) optimization problem:

$$\textbf{CCS:} \text{ Maximize } \sum_{n=1}^{N} U_n(\bar{a}_n)$$

$$\text{subject to Queue-length stability constraint in (6),}$$
$$s_n[t] \in \mathcal{C}_{\boldsymbol{\pi}[t]},\ a_n[t] \in [0, a^{\max}]\ \forall n, t.$$

4. A NESTEROVIAN APPROACH FOR STOCHASTIC NETWORK OPTIMIZATION

In this section, we first introduce the Nesterovian algorithm in Section 4.1. In Section 4.2, we will present the main theoretical results. Then, in Section 4.3, we will discuss the key insights and intuition of the theoretical results. Section 4.4 provides the proofs for the main theorems.

4.1 The Nesterovian Algorithm

Our proposed Nesterovian joint congestion control and scheduling algorithm is described in Algorithm 1:

Algorithm 1: A Nesterovian Approach for Joint Congestion Control and Scheduling.

Initialization:

1. Choose parameters $K > 0$ and $\beta \in [0, 1)$. Set $t = 0$.
2. Let queue-states $q_n[0] = 0$ and $\Delta q_n[-1] = 0$, $\forall n$.
3. Associate each link n with a non-negative weight w_n and set the initial weights $w_n[0] = w_n[-1] = 0$, $\forall n$.

Main Loop:

4. *MaxWeight Scheduler:* In time-slot $t \ge 0$, observe the current weight vector $\mathbf{w}[t] \triangleq [w_1[t], \ldots, w_N[t]]^\top$ and the current channel state $\boldsymbol{\pi}[t]$. Then, the scheduler chooses a service rate vector $\mathbf{s}[t]$ as follows:

$$\mathbf{s}[t] = \arg\max_{\mathbf{x}\in\mathcal{C}_{\boldsymbol{\pi}[t]}} (\mathbf{w}[t])^\top \mathbf{x}. \quad (8)$$

5. *Congestion Controller:* For each link n, given its current weight $w_n[t]$, the data injection rate $a_n[t]$ is an integer-valued random variable that satisfies:

$$\mathbb{E}\{a_n[t]|w_n[t]\} = \min\left\{U_n'^{-1}\left(\frac{w_n[t]}{K}\right), a^{\max}\right\}, \quad (9)$$

$$\mathbb{E}\{a_n^2[t]|w_n[t]\} \le A < \infty, \quad \forall w_n[t], \quad (10)$$

where $U_n'^{-1}(\cdot)$ represents the inverse function of the first-order derivative of $U_n(\cdot)$. In (9), $a^{\max}$ is a positive constant satisfying $a^{\max} > 2s^{\max}$. In (10), the second moment bound A will be used in establishing subsequent theoretical results.

6. *Queue-Length and Nesterovian Weight Updates:* Update the queue-lengths following (5). Let $\Delta q_n[t] \triangleq q_n[t+1] - q_n[t]$, $\forall n$, be the resultant queue-length changes. Next, for all links, update the weights in the following (projected) **Nesterovian** manner:

$$w_n[t+1] = \{w_n[t] + \Delta q_n[t] + \beta[(w_n[t] + \Delta q_n[t]) - (w_n[t-1] + \Delta q_n[t-1])]\}^+,\ \forall n. \quad (11)$$

Let $t = t + 1$. Go to Step 4 and repeat the scheduling and congestion control processes.

Some important remarks on Algorithm 1 are in order:

1) Relation to QCA: We can see that the congestion control and scheduling components in Algorithm 1 are similar to those in the QCA schemes (see, e.g., [2,3,30]). However, in both scheduling and congestion control components, the weights in (8) and (9) are *not* based on current queue-lengths (or a direct function of current queue-lengths). We will see later that this *separation* of weights and queue-lengths leads to significant delay reductions. Note also that when $\beta = 0$, our Nesterovian algorithm reduces to the traditional QCA approach. Hence, the QCA approach can be viewed as a special case of our Nesterovian algorithm.

2) Nesterovian weight update: The weight update idea in (11) is motivated by the Nesterov updates in (1) and (3). To see this, one only needs to do the following: i) Let $\beta[t] \equiv \beta$, $\forall t$; ii) Let $\mathbf{x}[t] = \mathbf{w}[t]$ and $f'(\mathbf{x}[t]) = \Delta\mathbf{q}[t]$ in (1) (ignoring the scaling factor $1/\Phi$); and lastly iii) Substitute (1) into (3) and apply the non-negative projection. We note that changing $\beta[t]$ to a constant step-size β not only simplifies the computation to allow easy implementations in practice, it also leads to an elegant three-way performance control relationship between utility-optimality, delay, and convergence speed, which will be presented later.

3) First-order memory: One can see that the weight update in (11) integrates a β-parameterized first-order memory of the weights $w_n[t-1]$ and queue-length changes $\Delta q_n[t-1]$ from the previous time-slot. By contrast, the weight updates in traditional QCA approaches are of zero-order memory in the sense that queue-lengths only inherit the absolute weight values from the current time-slot. As will be seen shortly, this algorithmic structural difference necessitates new proof techniques in establishing our theoretical results.

4) Zero-valued initial states: We note that, in Algorithm 1, the zero-valued initial states of the w_n- and q_n-variables are necessary for the delay reduction and queue-length scaling results to be established in Theorem 1. If the initial queueing buffers are non-empty, these zero-valued initial states can still be met by turning off the injection rates $a_n[t]$ and let the scheduler drain all the existing packets. As long as the number of existing packets is finite, this evacuation period must also be finite. Hence, this finite period of injection rate shutdown will not affect the utility-optimality of the average injection rates over an infinite time horizon.

4.2 Main Theoretical Results

Our first main result is on the queue-length reduction performance of the proposed Nesterovian algorithm:

THEOREM 1 (QUEUE-LENGTH REDUCTION). *Given $\beta \in [0,1)$, the scaling of the steady-state total queue-length:*

$$\limsup_{t\to\infty} \mathbb{E}\{\|\mathbf{q}[t]\|_1\} = O((1-\beta)K) + O((1+\beta)\sqrt{K}). \quad (12)$$

Further, if $\beta \uparrow 1$ at a speed faster than $\beta = 1 - O(1/\sqrt{K})$, then Eq. (12) implies that $\limsup_{t\to\infty} \mathbb{E}\{\|\mathbf{q}[t]\|_1\} = O(\sqrt{K})$.

Several important remarks on Theorem 1 are in order: i) If β is fixed and $K \to \infty$, the second term on the right-hand-side of (12) is dominated by the first term. Hence, $\limsup_{t\to\infty} \mathbb{E}\{\|\mathbf{q}[t]\|_1\} \approx O((1-\beta)K)$. Note that in the traditional K-parameterized QCA algorithm (see, e.g., [3,4]), the total queue-length grows as $O(K)$. Hence, Theorem 1 shows that the steady-state total queue-length under a β-parameterized Nesterovian scheme is approximately $(1-\beta)$–fraction of that of the traditional QCA approaches.

ii) Rather than fixing β, if we allow β to vary in relation to K, then Theorem 1 implies that if β approaches 1 fast enough as $K\to\infty$, the total queue-length scales as $O(\sqrt{K})$. This significantly outperforms the $O(K)$ delay of the QCA algorithms, yet *without sacrificing any throughput and without requiring non-causal global statistics as in [7, 8].*

iii) Incorporating the weight and queue-length changes from the previous time-slot in (11) can be loosely viewed as a way to memorize the queue states' and weights' evolution in history. Remarkably, Theorem 1 shows that simply learning from "immediate past" makes a big difference in steady-state queue-length reduction.

Next, we let $U(\mathbf{a}) = \sum_{n=1}^{N} U_n(a_n)$ denote the utility sum of Problem CCS and let $\mathbf{a}^*$ be the optimal solution. Also, we let $a_n^\infty \triangleq \mathbb{E}\{\min\{U_n'^{-1}(w_n^\infty/K), a^{\max}\}\}$, $\forall n$, be the mean steady-state congestion control rates achieved by our algorithm (the existence of steady-state will be proved later in Section 4.4). Further, we let $\mathbf{a}^\infty \triangleq [a_1^\infty, \ldots, a_N^\infty]^\top$. Then, the second key result in this paper can be stated as follows:

THEOREM 2 (UTILITY-OPTIMALITY). *The mean of the stationary rate vector $\mathbf{a}^\infty$ under Algorithm 1 tsatisfies $\|\mathbf{a}^\infty - \mathbf{a}^*\| = O(1/\sqrt{K})$. Meanwhile, the acheived utility objective value can be bounded as $U(\mathbf{a}^*) - U(\mathbf{a}^\infty) = O(1/K)$. These imply that $\mathbf{a}^\infty \to \mathbf{a}^*$ asymptotically as K increases.*

Theorem 2 says that our Nesterovian approach is utility-optimal and the optimality is *independent* of β. In other words, the new addition of the β-parameterized memory term in (11) does *not* affect the utility-optimality of the traditional QCA methods, which exactly achieves our goal.

The third main result in this work is on the convergence speed performance. In this paper, the convergence speed metric is defined in terms of the number of time-slots required by the sequence $\{\mathbb{E}\{\mathbf{a}[t]|\mathbf{w}[t]\}\}$ to reach the $O(1/\sqrt{K})$-neighborhood of $\mathbf{a}^*$ as stated in Theorem 2.

THEOREM 3 (CONVERGENCE RATE). *Let $K \in (\Phi, \infty)$ and $\beta \in [0,1)$. Let $\mathbf{H}^* \in \mathbb{R}^{N\times N}$ denote the Hessian matrix of the objective function of Problem CCS evaluated at $\mathbf{a}^*$. Then, $\{\mathbb{E}\{\mathbf{a}[t]|\mathbf{w}[t]\}\}$ converges linearly[2] with a factor $R_{(K,\beta)}$ satisfying:*

$$R_{(K,\beta)} \le \frac{1}{2}\max_{\lambda_i^*,\forall i}\left\{\left|(1+\beta)\Big(1-\frac{\lambda_i^*}{K}\Big) \pm \sqrt{(1+\beta)^2\Big(1-\frac{\lambda_i^*}{K}\Big)^2 - 4\beta\Big(1-\frac{\lambda_i^*}{K}\Big)}\right|\right\} < 1, \quad (13)$$

where λ_i^*, $i = 1, \ldots, N$, denote the eigenvalues of $\mathbf{H}^*$. Further, minimizing $R_{(K,\beta)}$ over K and β yields the smallest convergence factor bound: $R^* = (\sqrt{\Phi} - \sqrt{\phi})/\sqrt{\Phi}$, which is achieved by letting $K \to \Phi$ and $\beta^* = (\sqrt{\Phi}-\sqrt{\phi})/(\sqrt{\Phi}+\sqrt{\phi})$.

Theorem 3 implies that K and β can be optimized to achieve $R^* = (\sqrt{\kappa}-1)/\sqrt{\kappa}$, where $\kappa \triangleq \Phi/\phi$ is the condition number of the Hessian $\mathbf{H}$. Note that R^* is always *smaller* than that of the QCA approaches, where $R_{\text{QCA}} = (\kappa - 1)/(\kappa + 1)$ (cf. e.g., [2]). This implies that our Nesterovian approach converges faster than QCA, particularly when κ is large (i.e., when the problem is ill-conditioned).

Further, based on Theorem 3 and by comparing the convergence factor bounds, it can be shown that when $\beta > \sqrt{1-\phi/K}$, the Nesterovian approach converges faster than our previous heavy-ball approach in [15]. This shows that the proposed Nesterovian approach further improves the convergence speed of the heavy-ball approach in cases where β is chosen close to 1 (implying low-delay).

The proofs of Theorems 1–3 can be found in Section 4.4. In what follows, we will further discuss some insights of the theoretical results.

4.3 Discussions

1) Intuition behind delay reduction: From the connection between the QCA approaches and the Lagrangian dual decomposition (see, e.g., [2–4,31]), the QCA algorithms can be interpreted as using queue-lengths as the dual variables to solve Problem CCS. One drawback of this approach is that a large amount of packets need to be kept in each queue *only* to maintain the "right amount of pressure," which we denote as $w_n^*(K)$, $\forall n$ here. As will be seen in Section 4.4, $w_n^*(K)$ scales as $O(K)$ as K increases to approach optimal network utility. However, this "queue-lengths as dual" approach is *not* necessary since the $w_n^*(K)$ is merely a mathematical construct and needs not be associated with queue-lengths. In theory, one has the freedom to choose any quantity to play the role of the dual variables.

Indeed, there are several existing works based on the above intuition to reduce delay. To our knowledge, the idea that is most related to ours is [8], where the authors proposed to use $\mathcal{W}_n \in [0, w_n^*(K))$ amount of "place-holder bits" in each queueing buffer n and use the weight $w_n[t] = q_n[t] + \mathcal{W}_n$ to conduct scheduling, and the weights evolve as:

$$w_n[t+1] = [w_n[t] + \Delta q_n[t]]^+ = [q_n[t] + \Delta q_n[t] + \mathcal{W}_n]^+, \forall n. \quad (14)$$

However, as mentioned in Section 2, determining an appropriate value for each $\mathcal{W}_n$ is a non-trivial task since doing so requires non-causal global knowledge $w_n^*(K)$, $\forall n$, which is unavailable at the initial state. Now, consider the Nesterovian weight update in (11), which is re-stated below:

$$w_n[t+1] = \{w_n[t] + \Delta q_n[t] + \beta[(w_n[t] + \Delta q_n[t]) - (w_n[t-1] + \Delta q_n[t-1])]\}^+, \ \forall n. \quad (15)$$

[2]We say that $\{x_k\}_{k=1}^{\infty}$ converges linearly to x^* if there exists a factor $R \in (0,1)$ such that $\|x_{k+1} - x^*\| \le R\|x_k - x^*\|$, $\forall k$.

Table 1: Three-way performance control.

	Type I	Type II	Type III
Utility Optimality Gap	Small	Small	Large
Queueing Delay	Low	High	Low
Convergence Speed	Slow	Fast	Fast
K	Large	Large	Optimized for convergence
β	Close to 1	Optimized for convergence	Close to 1

Comparing (14) and (15), we can see that the memory term $\beta[(w_n[t]+\Delta q_n[t])-(w_n[t-1]+\Delta q_n[t-1])]$ plays a similar role as the place-holder bits $\mathcal{W}_n$ in the sense that it effectively reduces the size of required $\Delta q_n[t]$ to maintain the pressure level. Moreover, the use of memory term has the following advantages: i) Unlike the artificial notion of place-holder bits whose initial value is difficult to set, the memory term only requires two time-slots of weight and queue-length update history, which not only have a real physical meaning but also render easy implementations; ii) The memory term can also be viewed as a simple way to implicitly learn and adapt to the unknown $\mathbf{w}_n^*(K)$, thus eliminating the need for an explicit per-iteration learning step as in [9]; and (iii) Unlike the possibility of using an overly aggressive $\mathcal{W}_n$-value that results in packet dropping, our Nesterovian weight update scheme evolves gracefully and does *not* incur packet dropping and thus retaining full throughput-optimality.

2) Thee-way performance trade-offs: Collectively, Theorems 1–3 imply a three-way control between utility-optimality, delay, and convergence. By appropriately choosing K and β, one can simultaneously improve *two* out of the three performance metrics by trading-off the third. We summarize the three-way performance control in Table 1.

As shown in Table 1, Control Type I corresponds to achieving utility-optimality and low-delay at the cost of slower convergence, by setting K large and β close to 1. To see this, we note from Theorem 2 that a large K implies small utility-optimality gap $O(1/K)$. Also, by setting β close to 1, Theorem 1 indicates that a big $(1-\beta)$–fraction delay reduction. However, as $K\to\infty$ and $\beta\to 1$, it can be verified from Theorem 3 that $\lim_{\beta\to 1,K\to\infty} R_{(K,\beta)}\to 1$, which implies an increasingly slower convergence. Likewise, Control Type II corresponds to achieving utility-optimality and fast-convergence at the cost of less delay reduction, by setting K large and optimizing β for convergence. To see this, from Theorem 2, we have that a large K implies a small $O(1/K)$ utility-optimality gap. Also, by Theorem 3, β can be optimized under a given K to minimize $R_{(K,\beta)}$ to increase the convergence. However, the obtained β may or may not be close to 1. Thus, the delay performance gain may not be dramatic. Control Type III can be verified similarly as Trade-off Type II, so we omit the details for brevity.

4.4 Proofs of the Main Theorems

In this subsection, we provide the proofs for the main theorems stated in Section 4.2.

Proof of Theorem 1. Since the proof of Theorem 1 is lengthy, we structure the proof of into several key steps.

Step 1): A K-Parameterized Deterministic Problem: Consider a deterministic problem where the channel state process is not random but fixed at its mean level, i.e., $C_{\boldsymbol{\pi}[t]}=\bar{\mathcal{C}}$, $\forall t$. The congestion control and scheduling variables are not time-varying and denoted as a_n and s_n, $\forall n$. The K-parameterized deterministic problem can be written as:

$$\textbf{K-DCCS:}\ \text{Maximize}\quad K\sum\nolimits_{n=1}^{N} U_n(a_n)$$

$$\text{subject to}\quad a_n-s_n\le 0,\ \forall n,\ s_n\in\bar{\mathcal{C}},\ a_n\in[0,a^{\max}],\ \forall n.$$

We associate dual variables $w_n\ge 0$, $\forall n$ with the constraints $a_n-s_n\le 0$, $\forall n$ to obtain the Lagrangian as follows:

$$\Theta_K(\mathbf{w})\triangleq\max_{\mathbf{a},\mathbf{s}}\left\{K\sum_{n=1}^{N}U_n(a_n)+\sum_{n=1}^{N}w_n(s_n-a_n)\right\},\quad(16)$$

where the vector $\mathbf{w}\triangleq[w_1,\dots,w_N]^\top\in\mathbb{R}_+^N$ contains all dual variables. Then, the Lagrangian dual problem of Problem K-DCCS can be written as:

$$\textbf{D-K-DCCS:}\ \text{Minimize}\quad \Theta_K(\mathbf{w})$$

$$\text{subject to }\mathbf{w}\in\mathbb{R}_+^N.$$

It can be verified that Problem K-DCCS is convex and satisfies the Slater condition [10]. Hence, the optimal objective value of Problem K-LD-CCS is the same as that of Problem D-K-DCCS, i.e., strong duality holds. Let $\mathbf{w}^*(K)$ be the optimal dual solution to Problem D-K-DCCS. Due to the strict convexity of Problem K-LD-CCS, $\mathbf{w}^*(K)$ is unique. Further, we have the following result of $\mathbf{w}^*(K)$:

Lemma 1 (Linear scaling of $\mathbf{w}^*(K)$). *For a given K, $\mathbf{w}^*(K)=K\mathbf{w}^*(1)$, or equivalently, $\mathbf{w}^*(K)=O(K)$.*

Proof. Dividing K on both sides of (16), we have

$$\frac{1}{K}\Theta_K(\mathbf{w})=\max_{\mathbf{a},\mathbf{s}}\left\{\sum_{n=1}^{N}U_n(a_n)+\sum_{n=1}^{N}\widehat{w}_n(s_n-a_n)\right\},\quad(17)$$

where $\widehat{w}_n=w_w/K$. Note that the right hand side (RHS) of (17) is precisely $\Theta_1(\mathbf{w})$, for which the maximizer is $\widehat{\mathbf{w}}=\mathbf{w}^*(1)$. Hence, we have $\Theta_K(\mathbf{w})$ is maximized at $K\mathbf{w}^*(1)$. □

Step 2): A Special-Structured Block Matrix: Now, we define a β-parameterized block matrix $\boldsymbol{\Gamma}(\beta)$ as follows:

$$\boldsymbol{\Gamma}(\beta)\triangleq\begin{bmatrix}(1+\beta)\mathbf{I}_N & -\beta\mathbf{I}_N\\ \mathbf{I}_N & \mathbf{0}_N\end{bmatrix}\in\mathbb{R}^{2N\times 2N},\quad(18)$$

where $0<\beta<1$. Next, we prove a lemma about the eigenvalues of $\boldsymbol{\Gamma}(\beta)$ that will be useful in proving Theorem 1.

Lemma 2 (Eigen-spectrum of $\boldsymbol{\Gamma}(\beta)$). *$\boldsymbol{\Gamma}(\beta)$ only has two distinct eigenvalues β and 1, and both eigenvalues are of algebraic multiplicity N. Hence, $\boldsymbol{\Gamma}(\beta)$ is a non-expansive linear transformation in $\mathbb{R}^{2N}$.*

Proof. Let λ denote an eigenvalue of $\boldsymbol{\Gamma}(\beta)$ and consider the characteristic equation $\det(\boldsymbol{\Gamma}(\beta)-\lambda\mathbf{I}_{2N})=0$, which can be written in block-wise fashion as:

$$\det\begin{bmatrix}(1+\beta-\lambda)\mathbf{I}_N & -\beta\mathbf{I}_N\\ \mathbf{I}_N & -\lambda\mathbf{I}_N\end{bmatrix}=0.\quad(19)$$

We claim that $\lambda\neq 1+\beta$ and thus the block $(1+\beta-\lambda)\mathbf{I}_N$ in (19) is invertible. To verify this, suppose on the contrary that $\lambda=1+\beta$ and (19) holds. In this case, we have:

$$\det\begin{bmatrix}\mathbf{0}_N & -\beta\mathbf{I}_N\\ \mathbf{I}_N & -(1+\beta)\mathbf{I}_N\end{bmatrix}=\det(\beta\mathbf{I}_N)=-\beta^N\neq 0,$$

contradicting to the assumption that (19) holds. Given that the block $(1+\beta-\lambda)\mathbf{I}_N$ is invertible, it follows from the Schur complements determinantal formulae [32] that

$$
\begin{aligned}
(19) =& \det\left[(1+\beta-\lambda)\mathbf{I}_N\right]\times \\
& \det\left[(-\lambda\mathbf{I}_N)-\mathbf{I}_N((1+\beta-\lambda)\mathbf{I}_N)^{-1}(-\beta\mathbf{I}_N)\right] \\
=&(1+\beta-\lambda)^N\det\left[\left(-\lambda+\frac{\beta}{1+\beta-\lambda}\right)\mathbf{I}_N\right] \\
=&[\lambda^2-(1+\beta)\lambda+\beta]^N=(\lambda-1)^N(\lambda-\beta)^N=0. \quad (20)
\end{aligned}
$$

Hence, the result stated in the lemma follows. □

The spectral result in Lemma 2 implies that $\mathbf{\Gamma}(\beta)$ is a *non-expansive* linear operator. This result will play a key role in our subsequent analysis of the proposed Nesterov's method.

Step 3): Mean Weight Deviation: Our next key step toward proving Theorem 1 is to establish the following mean deviation result of the weights:

THEOREM 4 (MEAN WEIGHT DEVIATION BOUND). *For a given K, there exists a constant C that depends on Φ, $s^{\max}$, and $a^{\max}$, such that $\mathbb{E}\{\|\mathbf{w}^{\infty}-\mathbf{w}^*(K)\|\}\leq C\sqrt{K}$, where $\mathbf{w}^{\infty}$ denotes the weights $\mathbf{w}[t]$ in steady-state.*

PROOF. We start by rewriting the Nesterovian weight update in (11) in the following equivalent vector form:

$$
\begin{aligned}
\mathbf{w}[t+1] =& \mathbf{w}[t]+\Delta\mathbf{q}[t]+\beta[(\mathbf{w}[t]+\Delta\mathbf{q}[t]) \\
& -(\mathbf{w}[t-1]+\Delta\mathbf{q}[t-1])]+\mathbf{u}[t], \quad (21)
\end{aligned}
$$

where $\mathbf{u}[t]$ is the projection term representing unused services: $\mathbf{u}[t]\triangleq\{\beta(\mathbf{w}[t-1]+\Delta\mathbf{q}[t-1])-(1+\beta)(\mathbf{w}[t]+\Delta\mathbf{q}[t])\}^+$. Note that the memory term in (21) depends on two consecutive time-slots of memory (i.e., $\mathbf{w}[t]$, $\mathbf{w}[t-1]$, $\Delta\mathbf{q}[t]$, and $\Delta\mathbf{q}[t-1]$), which is challenging in subsequent analysis. To overcome this challenge, we define a $2N$-dimensional vector $\mathbf{z}[t]$ as follows (we simplify the notation of $\mathbf{w}^*(K)$ to $\mathbf{w}^*$):

$$
\mathbf{z}[t]\triangleq\begin{bmatrix}\mathbf{w}[t]-\mathbf{w}^*\\ \mathbf{w}[t-1]-\mathbf{w}^*\end{bmatrix}. \quad (22)
$$

Then, it can be readily verified that (21) can be rewritten in terms of $\mathbf{z}[t]$ as follows:

$$
\mathbf{z}[t+1]=\mathbf{\Gamma}(\beta)\mathbf{z}[t]+\mathbf{\Gamma}'(\beta)\begin{bmatrix}\Delta\mathbf{q}[t]\\ \Delta\mathbf{q}[t-1]\end{bmatrix}+\begin{bmatrix}\mathbf{u}[t]\\ \mathbf{0}_N\end{bmatrix}, \quad (23)
$$

where $\mathbf{\Gamma}'(\beta)\triangleq\begin{bmatrix}(1+\beta)\mathbf{I} & -\beta\mathbf{I}\\ \mathbf{0} & \mathbf{0}\end{bmatrix}$. We define a quadratic Lyapunov function $V(\mathbf{z}[t])\triangleq\frac{1}{2}\|\mathbf{z}[t]\|^2$ and consider its conditional expectation of one-slot drift:

$$
\mathbb{E}\{\Delta V(\mathbf{z}[t])|\mathbf{z}[t]\}\triangleq\frac{1}{2}\mathbb{E}\{\|\mathbf{z}[t+1]\|^2-\|\mathbf{z}[t]\|^2|\mathbf{z}[t]\}. \quad (24)
$$

Let $1_{\mathcal{A}}(\mathbf{x})$ be the indicator function that takes value 1 if $\mathbf{x}\in\mathcal{A}$ and 0 otherwise. After some algebraic derivations and upper-bounding (see Appendix A for details), we have:

PROPOSITION 1. *Let $B\triangleq N[A+(s^{\max})^2]$. There exist constants $\delta,\eta>0$ such that*

$$
\begin{aligned}
\mathbb{E}\{\Delta V(\mathbf{z}[t])|\mathbf{z}[t]=\mathbf{z}\}\leq& -\frac{\delta}{\sqrt{K}}\big(\|\mathbf{w}[t]-\mathbf{w}^*\|1_{\mathcal{B}^c}(\mathbf{w}[t])+ \\
& \|\mathbf{w}[t-1]-\mathbf{w}^*\|1_{\mathcal{B}^c}(\mathbf{w}[t-1])\big)+\eta\big(1_{\mathcal{B}}(\mathbf{w}[t])+1_{\mathcal{B}}(\mathbf{w}[t-1])\big),
\end{aligned}
$$

where $\mathcal{B}\triangleq\{\mathbf{w}:\|\mathbf{w}-\mathbf{w}^*\|\leq\sqrt{(1/2)B\Phi K}\}$, and $\mathcal{B}^c$ denotes the complement of $\mathcal{B}$.

Note that $\{\mathbf{z}[t]\}$ is a continuous Markov chain in $\mathbb{R}^{2N}$ and Proposition 1 ensures the Foster-Lyapunov criterion for positive Harris-recurrence. Thus, a steady-state exists [33]. Now, we consider the T-step conditional mean Lyapunov drift. For notational simplicity, we define the following sets:

$$
\begin{aligned}
\Omega_1&\triangleq\{\mathbf{z}\in\mathbb{R}^{2N}:\|\mathbf{w}[t]-\mathbf{w}^*\|\in\mathcal{B},\|\mathbf{w}[t-1]-\mathbf{w}^*\|\in\mathcal{B}\},\\
\Omega_2&\triangleq\{\mathbf{z}\in\mathbb{R}^{2N}:\|\mathbf{w}[t]-\mathbf{w}^*\|\in\mathcal{B},\|\mathbf{w}[t-1]-\mathbf{w}^*\|\notin\mathcal{B}\},\\
\Omega_3&\triangleq\{\mathbf{z}\in\mathbb{R}^{2N}:\|\mathbf{w}[t]-\mathbf{w}^*\|\notin\mathcal{B},\|\mathbf{w}[t-1]-\mathbf{w}^*\|\in\mathcal{B}\},\\
\Omega_4&\triangleq\{\mathbf{z}\in\mathbb{R}^{2N}:\|\mathbf{w}[t]-\mathbf{w}^*\|\notin\mathcal{B},\|\mathbf{w}[t-1]-\mathbf{w}^*\|\notin\mathcal{B}\}.
\end{aligned}
$$

By telescoping (24) from $t=0$ to $T-1$, we have that

$$
\begin{aligned}
\mathbb{E}\{V(\mathbf{z}[T])|\mathbf{z}[0]\}-V(\mathbf{z}[0])&\overset{(a)}{=}\sum_{t=0}^{T-1}\mathbb{E}\{\Delta V(\mathbf{z}[t])|\mathbf{z}[0]\}\\
&=\sum_{t=0}^{T-1}\int_{\mathbb{R}^{2N}}p_{\mathbf{z}[t]|\mathbf{z}[0]}(\mathbf{z})\mathbb{E}\{\Delta V(\mathbf{z}[t])|\mathbf{z}[t]=\mathbf{z}\}d\mathbf{z}\\
&=\sum_{i=1}^{4}\sum_{t=0}^{T-1}\int_{\Omega_i}p_{\mathbf{z}[t]|\mathbf{z}[0]}(\mathbf{z})\mathbb{E}\{\Delta V(\mathbf{z}[t])|\mathbf{z}[t]=\mathbf{z}\}d\mathbf{z}, \quad (25)
\end{aligned}
$$

where (a) follows from the fact that $\mathbf{z}[t]$ is a continuous state Markov chain in $\mathbb{R}^{2N}$. It then follows from Proposition 1 and the definitions of Ω_i, $i=1,\ldots,4$, that each term in (25) can be respectively upper-bounded as:

$$
\sum_{t=0}^{T-1}\int_{\Omega_1}\mathbb{E}\{\Delta V(\mathbf{z}[t])|\mathbf{z}[t]=\mathbf{z}\}d\mathbf{z}\leq 2\eta\int_{\Omega_1}\sum_{t=0}^{T-1}p_{\mathbf{z}[t]|\mathbf{z}[0]}(\mathbf{z})d\mathbf{z}. \quad (26)
$$

$$
\begin{aligned}
\sum_{t=0}^{T-1}\int_{\Omega_2}\mathbb{E}\{\Delta V(\mathbf{z}[t])|\mathbf{z}[t]=\mathbf{z}\}d\mathbf{z}\leq&\ \eta\int_{\Omega_2}\sum_{t=0}^{T-1}p_{\mathbf{z}[t]|\mathbf{z}[0]}(\mathbf{z})d\mathbf{z}\\
&-\frac{\delta}{\sqrt{K}}\int_{\Omega_2}\sum_{t=0}^{T-1}p_{\mathbf{z}[t]|\mathbf{z}[0]}(\mathbf{z})\|\mathbf{w}[t-1]-\mathbf{w}^*\|d\mathbf{z}. \quad (27)
\end{aligned}
$$

$$
\begin{aligned}
\sum_{t=0}^{T-1}\int_{\Omega_3}\mathbb{E}\{\Delta V(\mathbf{z}[t])|\mathbf{z}[t]=\mathbf{z}\}d\mathbf{z}\leq&\ \eta\int_{\Omega_3}\sum_{t=0}^{T-1}p_{\mathbf{z}[t]|\mathbf{z}[0]}(\mathbf{z})d\mathbf{z}\\
&-\frac{\delta}{\sqrt{K}}\int_{\Omega_3}\sum_{t=0}^{T-1}p_{\mathbf{z}[t]|\mathbf{z}[0]}(\mathbf{z})\|\mathbf{w}[t]-\mathbf{w}^*\|d\mathbf{z}. \quad (28)
\end{aligned}
$$

$$
\begin{aligned}
\sum_{t=0}^{T-1}\int_{\Omega_4}\mathbb{E}\{\Delta V(\mathbf{z}[t])|\mathbf{z}[t]=\mathbf{z}\}d\mathbf{z}\leq&-\frac{\delta}{\sqrt{K}}\int_{\Omega_4}\sum_{t=0}^{T-1}\big(\\
&\|\mathbf{w}[t]-\mathbf{w}^*\|+\|\mathbf{w}[t-1]-\mathbf{w}^*\|\big)p_{\mathbf{z}[t]|\mathbf{z}[0]}(\mathbf{z})d\mathbf{z}. \quad (29)
\end{aligned}
$$

Adding (26) to (29), we have that

$$
\begin{aligned}
\mathbb{E}\{V(\mathbf{z}[T])|\mathbf{z}[0]\}-V(\mathbf{z}[0])\leq&\ \eta\int_{\cup_{i=1}^{3}\Omega_i}\sum_{t=0}^{T-1}p_{\mathbf{z}[t]|\mathbf{z}[0]}(\mathbf{z})d\mathbf{z}\\
&-\frac{\delta}{\sqrt{K}}\Big[\int_{\Omega_2}\sum_{t=0}^{T-1}\|\mathbf{w}[t-1]-\mathbf{w}^*\|p_{\mathbf{z}[t]|\mathbf{z}[0]}(\mathbf{z})d\mathbf{z}+\\
&\int_{\Omega_3}\sum_{t=0}^{T-1}\|\mathbf{w}[t]-\mathbf{w}^*\|p_{\mathbf{z}[t]|\mathbf{z}[0]}(\mathbf{z})d\mathbf{z}+\int_{\Omega_4}\sum_{t=0}^{T-1}\big(\|\mathbf{w}[t]\\
&-\mathbf{w}^*\|+\|\mathbf{w}[t-1]-\mathbf{w}^*\|\big)p_{\mathbf{z}[t]|\mathbf{z}[0]}(\mathbf{z})d\mathbf{z}\Big]. \quad (30)
\end{aligned}
$$

Note that for any $\mathbf{z}\in\mathbb{R}^{2N}$, $\lim_{T\to\infty}\frac{1}{T}\sum_{t=0}^{T-1}p_{\mathbf{z}[t]|\mathbf{z}[0]}=p_{\mathbf{z}}^{\infty}$ for all $\mathbf{z}[0]$, where $p_{\mathbf{z}}^{\infty}$ denotes the stationary distribution of the continuous state Markov chain $\mathbf{z}[t]$. Moving $V(\mathbf{z}[0])$ to the right hand side (RHS) of (30), dividing both sides of (30) by T, and letting $T\to\infty$ yields:

$$0 \leq -\frac{\delta}{\sqrt{K}}\Bigg[\int_{\Omega_2 \cup \Omega_3} \|\mathbf{w}^\infty - \mathbf{w}^*\| p_{\mathbf{z}}^\infty d\mathbf{z} +$$
$$\int_{\Omega_4} 2\|\mathbf{w}^\infty - \mathbf{w}^*\| p_{\mathbf{z}}^\infty d\mathbf{z}\Bigg] + \eta \int_{\cup_{i=1}^3 \Omega_i} p_{\mathbf{z}}^\infty d\mathbf{z}. \quad (31)$$

Rearranging terms and adding $\frac{\delta}{\sqrt{K}} \int_{\Omega_2 \cup \Omega_3} \|\mathbf{w}^\infty - \mathbf{w}^*\| p_{\mathbf{z}}^\infty d\mathbf{z} + \frac{\delta}{\sqrt{K}} \int_{\Omega_1} 2\|\mathbf{w}^\infty - \mathbf{w}^*\| p_{\mathbf{z}}^\infty d\mathbf{z}$ to both sides of (31) yields:

$$\frac{\delta}{\sqrt{K}} \int_{\mathbb{R}^{2N}} 2\|\mathbf{w}^\infty - \mathbf{w}^*\| p_{\mathbf{z}}^\infty d\mathbf{z} \leq \eta \int_{\cup_{i=1}^3 \Omega_i} p_{\mathbf{z}}^\infty d\mathbf{z} +$$
$$\frac{\delta}{\sqrt{K}}\Bigg[\int_{\Omega_2 \cup \Omega_3} \|\mathbf{w}^\infty - \mathbf{w}^*\| p_{\mathbf{z}}^\infty d\mathbf{z} + \int_{\Omega_1} 2\|\mathbf{w}^\infty - \mathbf{w}^*\| p_{\mathbf{z}}^\infty d\mathbf{z}\Bigg]$$
$$\overset{(a)}{\leq} \eta \int_{\cup_{i=1}^3 \Omega_i} p_{\mathbf{z}}^\infty d\mathbf{z} + 4\delta\sqrt{(1/2)B\Phi} \leq \eta + \delta\sqrt{8B\Phi}, \quad (32)$$

where (a) follows from the definitions of Ω and $\mathcal{B}$. Note that the left-hand-side (LHS) of (32) is exactly $\frac{2\delta}{\sqrt{K}} \mathbb{E}\{\|\mathbf{w}^\infty - \mathbf{w}^*\|\}$. Multiplying both sides of (32) by $\frac{\sqrt{K}}{2\delta}$ yields:

$$\mathbb{E}\{\|\mathbf{w}^\infty - \mathbf{w}^*\|\} \leq \Big(\frac{\eta}{2\delta} + \sqrt{2B\Phi}\Big)\sqrt{K} = O(\sqrt{K}). \quad (33)$$

This completes the proof of Theorem 4. □

Step 4): Final Step to Prove Theorem 1: Recall that the Nesterovian update can be written as:

$$\mathbf{w}[t+1] = \mathbf{w}[t] + \Delta\mathbf{q}[t] + \beta[(\mathbf{w}[t] + \Delta\mathbf{q}[t])$$
$$- (\mathbf{w}[t-1] + \Delta\mathbf{q}[t-1])] + \mathbf{u}[t],$$

Rearranging terms and noting that $\mathbf{u}[t] \geq \mathbf{0}$, we have

$$\Delta\mathbf{q}[t] \leq \big(\mathbf{w}[t+1] - \mathbf{w}[t]\big) - \beta\big(\mathbf{w}[t] - \mathbf{w}[t-1]\big)$$
$$- \beta(\Delta q[t] - \Delta q[t-1]). \quad (34)$$

Telescoping the inequality in (34) from $t = 0$ to $T-1$ yields:

$$\sum_{t=0}^{T-1} \Delta\mathbf{q}[t] \leq \big(\mathbf{w}[T] - \mathbf{w}[0]\big) - \beta\big(\mathbf{w}[T-1] - \mathbf{w}[-1]\big)$$
$$= -\beta(\Delta q[T-1] - \Delta q[-1]) = \mathbf{w}[T] - \beta\mathbf{w}[T-1] - \beta\Delta\mathbf{q}[T-1],$$

where the last equality holds because, by assumption, $\mathbf{w}[0] = \mathbf{w}[-1] = \mathbf{q}[-1] = \mathbf{0}$. Also, since $\mathbf{q}[0] = \mathbf{0}$, we have

$$\|\mathbf{q}[T]\|_1 = \|\mathbf{q}[0] + \sum_{t=0}^{T-1} \Delta\mathbf{q}[t]\|_1$$
$$\leq \|\mathbf{w}[T] - \beta\mathbf{w}[T-1] - \beta\Delta\mathbf{q}[T-1]\|_1.$$

Taking expectation on both sides, letting $T \to \infty$, and noting that in steady-state $\mathbb{E}\{\Delta\mathbf{q}[\infty]\} = \mathbf{0}$, we have:

$$\limsup_{T\to\infty} \mathbb{E}\{\|\mathbf{q}[T]\|_1\} \leq \mathbb{E}\{\mathbf{w}^\infty - \beta\mathbf{w}^\infty\} \overset{(a)}{\leq} \mathbf{w}^* + O(\sqrt{K}) -$$
$$\beta(\mathbf{w}^* - O(\sqrt{K})) = (1-\beta)\mathbf{w}^* + (1+\beta)O(\sqrt{K}), \quad (35)$$

where (a) follows from Theorem 4 and $\|\cdot\|_1 \leq \sqrt{N}\|\cdot\|$ (simplifying $\mathbf{w}^*(K)$ to $\mathbf{w}^*$). This proves the first part of Theorem 1. Moreover, in the asymptotic regime where $1 - \beta = O(\frac{1}{\sqrt{K}})$, it follows from (35) that

$$\limsup_{T\to\infty} \mathbb{E}\{\|\mathbf{q}[t]\|_1\} = O(\sqrt{K}). \quad (36)$$

This completes the proof of Theorem 1.

Proof of Theorem 2. We first prove the optimality gap for the stationary rates $a_n^\infty \triangleq \mathbb{E}\{\min\{U_n^{'-1}(w_n^\infty/K), a^{\max}\}\}$. Note that $\mathbb{E}\{a_n[t]|w_n[t]\} = \min\{U_n^{'-1}(w_n[t]/K), a^{\max}\}$ and $a_n^* = U_n^{'-1}(w_n^*/K)$, $\forall n$. Thus, we have

$$\|\mathbf{a}^\infty - \mathbf{a}^*\|^2 = \sum_{n=1}^N \Bigg[\mathbb{E}\Big\{\min\Big\{U_n^{'-1}\Big(\frac{w_n^\infty}{K}\Big), M\Big\}\Big\} - U_n^{'-1}\Big(\frac{w_n^*}{K}\Big)\Bigg]^2$$
$$\overset{(a)}{\leq} \sum_{n=1}^N \mathbb{E}\Bigg\{\Bigg[\min\Big\{U_n^{'-1}\Big(\frac{w_n^\infty}{K}\Big), M\Big\} - U_n^{'-1}\Big(\frac{w_n^*}{K}\Big)\Bigg]^2\Bigg\}$$
$$\overset{(b)}{\leq} \sum_{n=1}^N \mathbb{E}\Bigg\{\Bigg[U_n^{'-1}\Big(\frac{w_n^\infty}{K}\Big) - U_n^{'-1}\Big(\frac{w_n^*}{K}\Big)\Bigg]^2\Bigg\}$$
$$\overset{(c)}{=} \sum_{n=1}^N \mathbb{E}\Bigg\{\Bigg[\Big[U_n^{'-1}\Big(\frac{\tilde{w}_n}{K}\Big)\Big]'\Big(\frac{w_n^\infty}{K} - \frac{w_n^*}{K}\Big)\Bigg]^2\Bigg\}$$
$$\overset{(d)}{=} \sum_{n=1}^N \mathbb{E}\Bigg\{\Bigg[\Big[\frac{1}{U_n''(\frac{\tilde{w}_n}{K})}\Big]^2\Big(\frac{w_n^\infty}{K} - \frac{w_n^*}{K}\Big)\Bigg]^2\Bigg\}$$
$$\overset{(e)}{\leq} \sum_{n=1}^N \mathbb{E}\Big\{\frac{1}{\phi^2}(w_n^\infty - w_n^*)^2 \frac{1}{K^2}\Big\} \overset{(f)}{=} \frac{1}{\phi^2 K^2}\mathbb{E}\Big\{\sum_{n=1}^N (w_n^\infty - w_n^*)^2\Big\}$$
$$= \frac{1}{\phi^2 K^2}\mathbb{E}\{\|\mathbf{w}^\infty - \mathbf{w}^*\|^2\}, \quad (37)$$

where (a) follows from the convexity of quadratic function and Jensen's inequality; (b) follows from the non-expansion property of the $\min\{\cdot\}$ function; (c) follows by using mean value theorem for some $\tilde{w}_n \in [\min\{w_n^\infty, w_n^*\}, \max\{w_n^\infty, w_n^*\}]$; (d) follows from inverse function lemma; (e) follows from the strong convexity assumption in (7); and (f) follows from exchanging the order or summation and expectation.

Consider the term $\mathbb{E}\{\|\mathbf{w}^\infty - \mathbf{w}^*\|^2\}$ in (37). From the proof of Proposition 1, we have (cf. Eq. (62) in Appendix A) the following one-slot mean Lyapunov drift bound:

$$\mathbb{E}\{\Delta V(\mathbf{z}[t])|\mathbf{z}[t]\} \leq -\frac{1}{\Phi K}(\|\mathbf{w}[t] - \mathbf{w}^*\|^2 +$$
$$\|\mathbf{w}[t-1] - \mathbf{w}^*\|^2) + B. \quad (38)$$

Following the same argument in the proof of Theorem 4, we telescope the inequality in (38) from $t = 0$ to $T-1$ to obtain:

$$\mathbb{E}\{V(\mathbf{z}[T])|\mathbf{z}[0]\} - V(\mathbf{z}[0]) = \sum_{t=0}^{T-1} \mathbb{E}\{V(\mathbf{z}[t+1]) - V(\mathbf{z}[t])|\mathbf{z}[0]\}$$
$$= \sum_{t=0}^{T-1} \int_{\mathbb{R}^{2N}} p_{\mathbf{z}[t]|\mathbf{z}[0]}(\mathbf{z})\mathbb{E}\{V(\mathbf{z}[t+1]) - V(\mathbf{z}[t])|\mathbf{z}[t] = \mathbf{z}\}d\mathbf{z}$$
$$= \sum_{t=0}^{T-1} \int_{\mathbb{R}^{2N}} p_{\mathbf{z}[t]|\mathbf{z}[0]}(\mathbf{z})\mathbb{E}\{\Delta V(\mathbf{z}[t])|\mathbf{z}[t]\}d\mathbf{z} \leq -\frac{1}{\Phi K}\sum_{t=0}^{T-1}$$
$$\int_{\mathbb{R}^{2N}} p_{\mathbf{z}[t]|\mathbf{z}[0]}(\mathbf{z})(\|\mathbf{w}[t] - \mathbf{w}^*\|^2 + \|\mathbf{w}[t-1] - \mathbf{w}^*\|^2)d\mathbf{z} + TB. \quad (39)$$

Dividing both sides by $\frac{2T}{\Phi K}$, rearranging terms, and letting $T \to \infty$, we have

$$\limsup_{T\to\infty} \frac{1}{T}\sum_{t=0}^{T-1} \int_{\mathbb{R}^{2N}} p_{\mathbf{z}[t]|\mathbf{z}[0]}(\mathbf{z}) \|\mathbf{w} - \mathbf{w}^*\|^2 d\mathbf{z} \leq \frac{1}{2}B\Phi K. \quad (40)$$

Note that the LHS of (40) is precisely $\mathbb{E}\{\|\mathbf{w}^\infty - \mathbf{w}^*\|^2\}$. Hence, it follows that

$$\|\mathbf{a}^\infty - \mathbf{a}^*\|^2 \le \frac{1}{\phi^2 K^2}\mathbb{E}\{\|\mathbf{w}^\infty - \mathbf{w}^*\|^2\} \le \frac{B\Phi}{2\phi^2}\frac{1}{K}. \quad (41)$$

Taking square root on both sides of (41) yields:

$$\|\mathbf{a}^\infty - \mathbf{a}^*\| \le \frac{\sqrt{B\Phi}}{\phi}\frac{1}{\sqrt{K}} = O\Big(\frac{1}{\sqrt{K}}\Big),$$

i.e., the result in the first half of Theorem 2.

Next, we prove the optimality gap result for the objective value, i.e., $U(\mathbf{a}^\infty_{(K)}) \ge U(\mathbf{a}^*) - O(1/K)$. To this end, similar to the proof of Theorem 4, we define an augmented vector and its quadratic Lyapunov function as follows:

$$\mathbf{y}[t] \triangleq \begin{bmatrix} \mathbf{w}[t] \\ \mathbf{w}[t-1] \end{bmatrix} \quad \text{and} \quad \tilde{V}(\mathbf{y}[t]) = \frac{1}{2}\|\mathbf{y}[t]\|^2.$$

Following the same steps in the proof of Theorem 4, one can verify that

$$\mathbf{y}[t+1] = \mathbf{\Gamma}(\beta)\mathbf{y}[t] + \mathbf{\Gamma}'(\beta)\begin{bmatrix} \Delta\mathbf{q}[t] \\ \Delta\mathbf{q}[t-1] \end{bmatrix} + \begin{bmatrix} \mathbf{u}[t] \\ \mathbf{0}_N \end{bmatrix}.$$

where $\mathbf{\Gamma}(\beta)$ and $\mathbf{\Gamma}'(\beta)$ are the same as defined earlier. Then, following the same steps as in the proof of Proposition 1, we can show that the conditional expectation of the one-slot Lyapunov drift can be bounded as follows:

$$\mathbb{E}\{\Delta\tilde{V}(\mathbf{y}[t])|\mathbf{y}[t]\} \le -(\mathbf{y}[t])^\top\mathbb{E}\{\tilde{\mathbf{a}}[t] - \tilde{\mathbf{s}}[t]|\mathbf{y}[t]\} + B. \quad (42)$$

Note that (42) is in the same form as in [3, Eq. (24)]. Then, following the same arguments in [3], we have that $U(\mathbf{a}^\infty_{(K)}) \ge U(\mathbf{a}^*) - O(1/K)$. This completes the proof. □

Proof of Theorem 3. We first show the ranges of K and β that suffice for convergence. Due to the one-to-one mapping between $\mathbb{E}\{\mathbf{a}[t]|\mathbf{w}[t]\}$ and $\mathbf{w}[t]$, the convergence of $\mathbb{E}\{\mathbf{a}[t]|\mathbf{w}[t]\}$ can be equivalently analyzed by examining the convergence of $\mathbf{w}[t]$. Using the fact that $\Delta\mathbf{q}[t] = \frac{1}{K}\mathbf{H}^*(\mathbf{w}[t] - \mathbf{w}^*) + o(\|\mathbf{w}[t] - \mathbf{w}^*\|)$, where $\mathbf{H}^*$ denotes the Hessian matrix of $\Theta_K(\mathbf{w})$ evaluated at $\mathbf{w}^*$, we can rewrite (11) in a local neighborhood of $\mathbf{w}^*$ as:

$$\mathbf{z}[t+1] \le \begin{bmatrix} (1+\beta)(\mathbf{I}_N - \frac{1}{K}\mathbf{H}^*) & -\beta(\mathbf{I}_N - \frac{1}{K}\mathbf{H}^*) \\ \mathbf{I}_N & \mathbf{O}_N \end{bmatrix}\mathbf{z}[t].$$

where $\mathbf{z}[t]$ is defined the same as in the proof of Theorem 1. For convenience, we let $\widehat{\mathbf{\Gamma}}$ denote the coefficient matrix and consider the eigenvalue equation:

$$\begin{bmatrix} (1+\beta)(\mathbf{I}_N - \frac{1}{K}\mathbf{H}^*) & -\beta(\mathbf{I}_N - \frac{1}{K}\mathbf{H}^*) \\ \mathbf{I}_N & \mathbf{O}_N \end{bmatrix}\begin{bmatrix} \mathbf{v}_1 \\ \mathbf{v}_2 \end{bmatrix} = \lambda_{\widehat{\mathbf{\Gamma}}}\begin{bmatrix} \mathbf{v}_1 \\ \mathbf{v}_2 \end{bmatrix}.$$

Noting from the second row that $\mathbf{v}_1 = \lambda_{\widehat{\mathbf{\Gamma}}}\mathbf{v}_2$, we have that

$$\Big[\lambda^2_{\widehat{\mathbf{\Gamma}}}\mathbf{I} - \lambda_{\widehat{\mathbf{\Gamma}}}(1+\beta)\Big(\mathbf{I} - \frac{1}{K}\mathbf{H}^*\Big) + \beta\Big(\mathbf{I} - \frac{1}{K}\mathbf{H}^*\Big)\Big]\mathbf{v}_2 = \mathbf{0}.$$

Let λ_i^*, $i = 1, \ldots, N$, denote the eigenvalues of $\mathbf{H}^*$. Through eigenvalue decomposition, it can be verified that $\lambda_{\widehat{\mathbf{\Gamma}}}$ satisfies the following quadratic equations:

$$\lambda^2_{\widehat{\mathbf{\Gamma}},i} - (1+\beta)\Big(1 - \frac{\lambda_i^*}{K}\Big)\lambda_{\widehat{\mathbf{\Gamma}},i} + \beta\Big(1 - \frac{\lambda_i^*}{K}\Big) = 0, \quad \forall i. \quad (43)$$

It then follows from (43) that

$$R_{(K,\beta)} \le \max_i \lambda_{\widehat{\mathbf{\Gamma}},i} = \frac{1}{2}\max_{\lambda_i^*,\forall i}\Big\{\Big|(1+\beta)\Big(1 - \frac{\lambda_i^*}{K}\Big) \pm \sqrt{\Delta_i}\Big|\Big\}, (44)$$

where $\Delta_i \triangleq (1+\beta)^2(1-\frac{\lambda_i^*}{K})^2 - 4\beta(1-\frac{\lambda_i^*}{K})$. Next, we consider (44) for the following two cases, where we let $\alpha_i \triangleq 1 - \lambda_i^*/K$ for notational convenience:

- $\Delta_i \ge 0$: Then, $|\lambda_{\widehat{\mathbf{\Gamma}},i}| < 1$ is equivalent to $(1+\beta)^2\alpha_i^2 - 4\beta\alpha_i \ge 0$ and $-2 < (1+\beta)\alpha_i \pm \sqrt{\Delta_i} < 2$, which, after simplifications, yields $K \ge [(1+\beta)/(1-\beta)]^2\lambda_i^*$, $\forall i$
- $\Delta_i < 0$: Then, $|\lambda_{\widehat{\mathbf{\Gamma}},i}| < 1$ is equivalent to $(1+\beta)^2\alpha_i^2 - 4\beta\alpha_i < 0$ and $0 \le \frac{1}{4}[(1+\beta)^2\alpha_i^2 - \Delta_i] < 1$, which, after simplifications, yields: $\lambda_i^* < K < [(1+\beta)/(1-\beta)]^2\lambda_i^*$, $\forall i$.

Combining both cases and noting that they should hold for all λ_i^*, we can conclude that $K > \Phi$. This completes the proof of the first half of the theorem.

To prove the second half of the theorem, we minimize the upper bound in (44), i.e.,

$$\underset{K\in(\Phi,\infty),\beta\in[0,1)}{\text{Minimize}} \Big\{\frac{1}{2}\max_{\lambda_i^*,\forall i}\Big\{\Big|(1+\beta)\Big(1 - \frac{\lambda_i^*}{K}\Big) \pm \sqrt{\Delta_i}\Big|\Big\}\Big\}. (45)$$

First, we claim that the upper bound in (44) is monotonically decreasing with respect to the λ_i^*-variables. To see this, we again consider two cases.

- $\Delta_i \ge 0$: In this case, $\alpha \in [4\beta/(1+\beta)^2, 1)$. In this interval, Δ_i monotonically increases as λ_i decreases. Hence, the upper bound in (44) is monotonically decreasing.
- $\Delta_i < 0$: From (44), we have $\lambda_{\widehat{\mathbf{\Gamma}},i} = 2\sqrt{\beta(1 - \lambda_i^*/K)}$, which is monotonically increasing as λ_i^* decreases.

Combining both cases, we have that (45) can be written as:

$$\min_{\beta\in[0,1)}\Big\{\min_{K\in(\Phi,\infty)}\Big\{\Big|(1+\beta)\Big(1 - \phi/K\Big) \pm \sqrt{(1+\beta)^2(1-\phi/K)^2 - 4\beta(1-\phi/K)}\Big|\Big\}\Big\}. \quad (46)$$

For notational simplicity, we let $\psi(K,\beta) \triangleq |(1+\beta)(1 - \phi/K) \pm \sqrt{(1+\beta)^2(1-\phi/K)^2 - 4\beta(1-\phi/K)}|$. Then, based on the positivity of the discriminant in (46), the search domain in the optimization problem in (46) can be divided into three subdomains:

- $\beta \in [0, (\sqrt{\kappa}-1)/(\sqrt{\kappa}+1))$, $K \in (\Phi, \infty)$,
- $\beta \in [(\sqrt{\kappa}-1)/(\sqrt{\kappa}+1), 1)$, $K \in (\Phi, ((1+\beta)/(1-\beta))^2\phi)$,
- $\beta \in [(\sqrt{\kappa}-1)/(\sqrt{\kappa}+1), 1)$, $K \in [((1+\beta)/(1-\beta))^2\phi, \infty)$,

where $\kappa \triangleq \Phi/\phi$ is the condition number. It can be readily verified that (46) is minimized to $(\sqrt{\kappa}-1)/\sqrt{\kappa}$ by $K^* = \Phi$ and $\beta^* = (\sqrt{\kappa}-1)/(\sqrt{\kappa}+1)$. This completes the proof of the second half of the theorem. □

5. EXTENSION TO MULTI-HOP NETWORKS

In this section, we will generalize our Nesterovian algorithmic framework to multi-hop networks. In the multi-hop setting, the utility optimization problem becomes the joint congestion control and routing optimization as in [1–3]. We first state the network model and problem formulation.

Network Model and Problem Formulation: *1) Network model:* Consider a time-slotted communication network system as in the single-hop case. We represent the communication network by a directed graph $\mathcal{G} = \{\mathcal{N}, \mathcal{L}\}$, where $\mathcal{N}$ and $\mathcal{L}$ are the sets of nodes and links, with $|\mathcal{N}| = N$ and $|\mathcal{L}| = L$, respectively. We assume that $\mathcal{G}$ is connected.

There are F end-to-end flows in the network, indexed by $f = 1, \ldots, F$. Each flow f has a source node and a destination node, represented by $\mathrm{Src}(f), \mathrm{Dst}(f) \in \mathcal{N}$, respectively. To avoid triviality, we assume that $\mathrm{Src}(f) \neq \mathrm{Dst}(f)$ for all f. The data of flow f travel from $\mathrm{Src}(f)$ to $\mathrm{Dst}(f)$ through the network, possibly via multi-hop and multi-path routing.

2) Congestion control: As in [2, 3], we assume that the source node $\mathrm{Src}(f)$ has a continuously-backlogged transport layer reservoir that contains session f's data. In each time-slot t, a transport layer congestion controller determines the amount of data $a_f[t]$ to be released from this reservoir into a network layer source queue, where the data awaits to be routed to node $\mathrm{Dst}(f)$ through the network. In other words, $\{a_f[t]\}$ acts as the arrival process to the source queue. For burst control, we let $a_f[t] \leq a_f^{\max}, \forall t$. We let $\bar{a}_f \geq 0$ denote the time-average rate at which data of session f is injected at $\mathrm{Src}(f)$ under congestion control, i.e., $\bar{a}_f = \lim_{T\to\infty} \frac{1}{T}\sum_{t=0}^{T-1} a_f[t]$. Each session is associated with a utility function $U_f(\bar{a}_f)$, which represents the utility gained by session f when data is injected at rate $\bar{a}_f$. We assume that $U_f(\cdot)$ is strictly concave, monotonically increasing, and twice continuously differentiable.

3) Routing: We let $x_l^{(f)}[t] \geq 0$ denote the rate offered to route session f's data in time-slot t at link l. We let $\bar{x}_l^{(f)} \triangleq \lim_{T\to\infty} \frac{1}{T}\sum_{t=0}^{T-1} x_l^{(f)}[t]$ represent the time-average routing rate of session f at link l. The time-varying model of the channel states at each link remains the same as in the single-hop case. As in [2, 31, 34], we define the *network capacity region* as the largest set of congestion control rates such that there exists a routing policy for which the time-average routing rates satisfy the following constraints:

$$\sum_{l\in\mathcal{O}(n)} \bar{x}_l^{(f)} \geq \sum_{l\in\mathcal{I}(n)} \bar{x}_l^{(f)} + \bar{a}_f 1_f(n), \ \forall f, \forall n \neq \mathrm{Dst}(f), \quad (47)$$

where $\mathcal{O}(n)$ and $\mathcal{I}(n)$ represent the sets of outgoing and incoming links at node n, respectively; $1_f(n)$ is an indicator function that takes the value 1 if $n = \mathrm{Src}(f)$ and 0 otherwise.

4) Queue-stability: We assume that each node has a separate queue for each flow f. Let $q_n^{(f)}[t] \geq 0$ represent the queue-length of flow f at node n at time t. Since data leave the network upon reaching destinations, we have $q_{\mathrm{Dst}(f)}^{(f)}[t] = 0, \forall t$. Then, $q_n^{(f)}[t]$, $n \neq \mathrm{Dst}(f)$ evolves as:

$$q_n^{(f)}[t+1] = \Big(q_n^{(f)}[t] - \sum_{l\in\mathcal{O}(n)} x_l^{(f)}[t]\Big)^+ + \sum_{l\in\mathcal{I}(n)} \widehat{x}_l^{(f)}[t] + a_f[t]1_f(n), \quad (48)$$

where $(\cdot)^+ \triangleq \max\{0, \cdot\}$ and $\widehat{x}_l^{(f)}[t]$ is the *actual* routing rate. Note that $\widehat{x}_l^{(f)}[t] \leq x_l^{(f)}[t]$ since $\mathrm{Tx}(l)$ may have less than $x_{l,[t]}^{(f)}$ amount of data to transmit. Let $\mathbf{q}[t] \triangleq [q_n^{(f)}[t], \forall f, \forall n \neq \mathrm{Dst}(f)]^T$ group all queue lengths at time t. Similar to the single-hop case, under a congestion control and routing scheme, we say that the network is stable if the norm of steady-state queue-lengths is finite, i.e., $\limsup_{t\to\infty} \mathbb{E}\{\|\mathbf{q}[t]\|_1\} < \infty$.

5) Problem formulation: In the multi-hop case, our goal is again to develop an optimal joint congestion control and routing scheme to maximize the total utility $\sum_{f=1}^{F} U_f(\bar{a}_f)$, subject to the network capacity region and stability constraints. Putting together the models presented above yields the following joint congestion control and routing (CCR) optimization problem:

$$\textbf{CCR: } \mathrm{Max} \ \sum_{f=1}^{F} U_f(\bar{a}_f)$$

$$\text{s.t. Routing constr. in (47); Stability of all queues,}$$
$$x_l^{(f)}[t] \in \mathcal{C}_{\boldsymbol{\pi}[t]}, \ \forall l, t, f, \quad a_f[t] \geq 0, \ \forall f, t.$$

5.1 A Nesterovian Joint Congestion and Routing Optimization Algorithm

Similar to the the QCA schemes in the multi-hop case, in our multi-hop Nesterovian algorithm, the weights are replaced by *weight differentials* for dynamic routing. Let $\mathcal{E}(l)$ denote the two end nodes of link l. The Nesterovian congestion control and routing algorithm is stated as follows:

Algorithm 2: A Nesterovian Approach for Joint Congestion Control and Routing.

Initialization:

1. Choose parameters $K > 0$ and $\beta \in [0, 1)$. Set $t = 0$.
2. Let queue-states: $q_n^{(f)}[0], \Delta q_n^{(f)}[-1] = 0, \forall n, f$.
3. Associate each link l with a weight $w_n^{(f)} \geq 0$ and set the initial weights $w_n^{(f)}[0] = w_n^{(f)}[-1] = 0, \forall n, f$.

Main Loop:

4. *Weight Differentials:* In time-slot $t \geq 1$, we let $\Delta w_l^{(f)}[t] = \max\{w_n^{(f)}[t] - w_{\mathcal{E}(l)\setminus n}^{(f)}[t], 0\}$ denote the *weight differential of each flow* f, $\forall n, l \in \mathcal{O}(n)$. Let $\Delta w_l^*[t] = \max_f \Delta w_l^{(f)}[t]$ and let $f_l^*[t] = \arg\max_f \Delta w_l^{(f)}[t]$ (breaking ties arbitrarily). Let $\Delta\mathbf{w}^*[t] \triangleq [w_1^*[t], \ldots, w_L^*[t]]^\top$ be the maximum weight differentials vector over all links.
5. *Routing and MaxWeight Scheduling:* Given $\Delta\mathbf{w}^*[t]$ and channel state $\boldsymbol{\pi}[t]$, the scheduler chooses a service rate vector $\mathbf{x}[t] \in \mathbb{R}^L$ to transmit flow $f_l^*[t]$ at each link l:
$$\mathbf{x}[t] = \arg\max_{\mathbf{x}\in\mathcal{C}_{\boldsymbol{\pi}[t]}} (\Delta\mathbf{w}^*[t])^\top \mathbf{x}. \quad (49)$$
6. *Congestion Controller:* For each flow f and in each time-slot t, let w be the value of $w_{\mathrm{Src}(f)}[t]$ that the source node $\mathrm{Src}(f)$ observes. Then, $\mathrm{Src}(f)$ sets $a_f[t]$ to be an integer-valued random variable that satisfies:
$$\mathbb{E}\{a_f[t]|w\} = \min\Big\{U_f^{'-1}\Big(\frac{w}{K}\Big), a^{\max}\Big\}, \quad (50)$$
$$\mathbb{E}\{a_n^2[t]|w\} \leq A < \infty, \quad (51)$$
where $U_f^{'-1}(\cdot)$ represents the inverse function of first-order derivative of $U_f(\cdot)$. In (50) and (51), $a^{\max}$ and A are positive constants with $a^{\max} > 2s^{\max}$.
7. *Queue-Length and Nesterovian Weight Updates:* Update queue-lengths following (48). Let $\Delta q_n^{(f)}[t] \triangleq q_n^{(f)}[t+1] - q_n^{(f)}[t]$, $\forall n$, be the queue-length change of flow f at node n following the update in (48). Next, update the weights in the following (projected) **Nesterovian** manner:
$$w_n^{(f)}[t+1] = \{w_n^{(f)}[t] + \Delta q_n[t] + \beta[(w_n^{(f)}[t] + \Delta q_n^{(f)}[t]) - (w_n^{(f)}[t-1] + \Delta q_n^{(f)}[t-1])]\}^+, \ \forall n, f. \quad (52)$$

Let $t = t+1$. Go to Step 4 and repeat the whole dynamic routing, scheduling and congestion control processes.

Distributed Implementation: We note that, as in the QCA algorithms, the congestion control and dynamic routing components in the multi-hop version of the Nesterovian

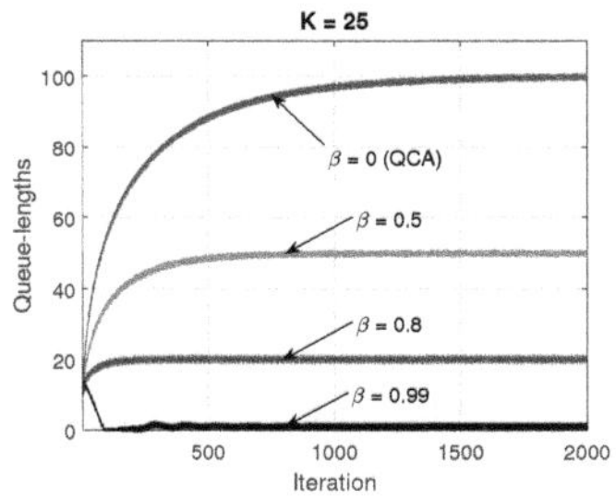

Figure 2: The impact of β on queueing delay.

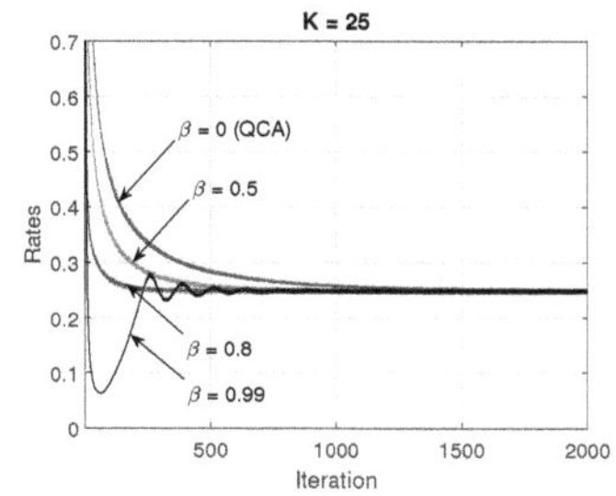

Figure 3: The impact of β on convergence speed.

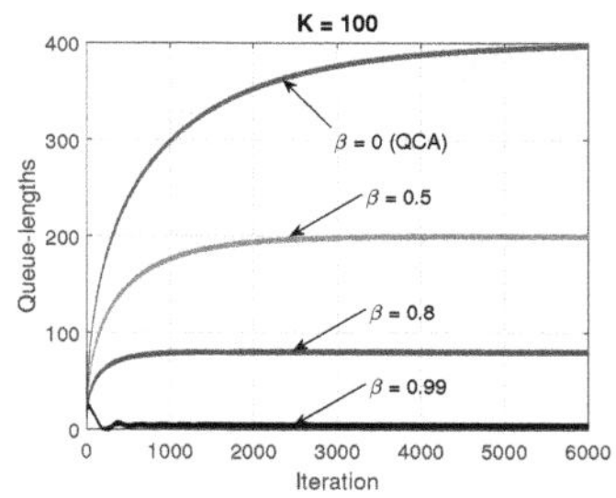

Figure 4: The impact of K on queueing delay.

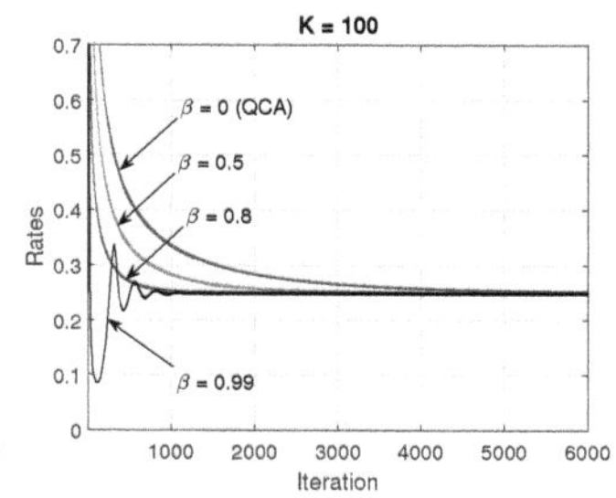

Figure 5: The impact of K on convergence speed.

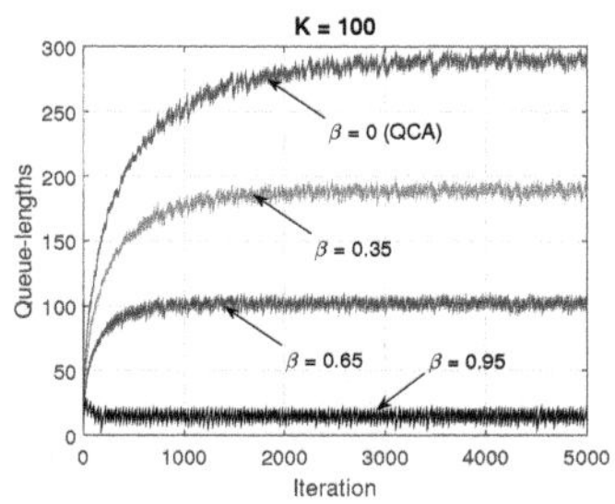

Figure 6: The impact of β on queueing delay for a 15-user cellular downlink with fading ($K = 100$).

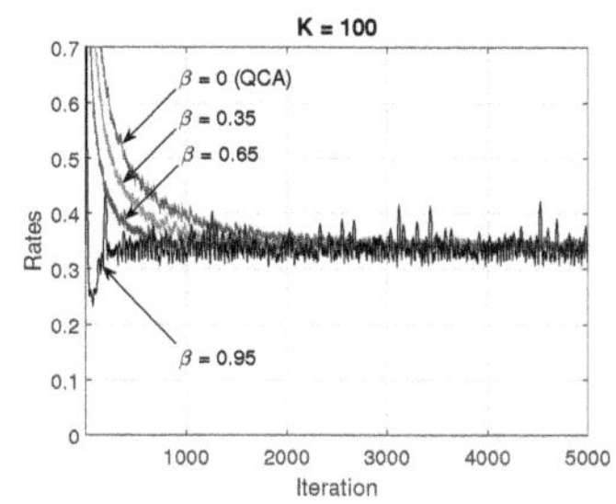

Figure 7: The impact of β on convergence for a 15-user cellular downlink with fading ($K = 100$).

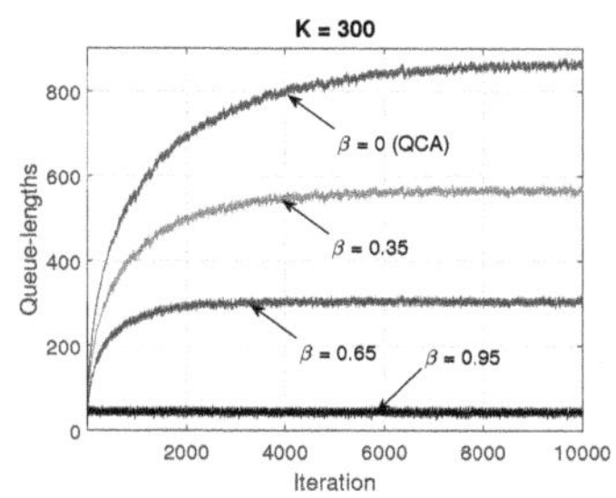

Figure 8: The impact of β on queueing delay for a 15-user cellular downlink with fading ($K = 300$).

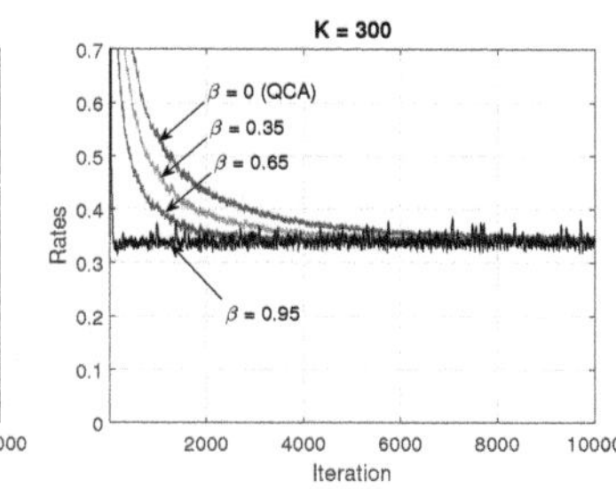

Figure 9: The impact of β on convergence for a 15-user cellular downlink with fading ($K = 300$).

algorithm only require weight information either locally or from one-hop neighbors. Also, the Nesterovian weight updates in (52) only require two time-slots of local history. Thus, the congestion control and dynamic routing naturally lend themselves to *distributed* implementation in exactly the *same* fashion as that in the QCA algorithms. In other words, compared to QCA algorithms, our multi-hop Nesterovian algorithm does *not* incur any additional complexity in terms of messaging passing between nodes.

On the other hand, also same as in the QCA algorithms, we can see that the scheduling problem in (49) require global weight information from all links and could be challenging for developing distributed solutions (depending on the structure of $\mathcal{C}_{\pi[t]}$). In many cases, it can be shown that the scheduling problem in (49) is NP-hard and even developing centralized solutions is difficult. Fortunately, due to the same messaging passing requirement, many distributed algorithms (e.g., [35, 36]) developed for the QCA framework can be applied in the scheduling component in our Nesterovian algorithm. One example is to adopt our weight adjustment scheme to Q-CSMA [36] by setting the attempt probability of each link in the form of $e^{w[t]}/(e^{w[t]}+1)$ (cf. [36, Eq. (10)]). Then, under the time-scale separation assumption, one can follow the same line of arguments in [36] to establish the throughput optimality with fewer iterations to update weights in the outer time-scale.

Performance Analysis: The delay reduction at source nodes, convergence rates, and utility-optimality results in Theorems 1–3 in the single-hop case can be generalized to the multi-hop cases. Also, their proofs follow the same steps and arguments but with more complicated notation. Due to space limitation, we omit these results and their proofs in this paper for brevity.

6. NUMERICAL RESULTS

In this section, we conduct some numerical studies to verify the theoretical results presented in Section 4. To better visualize the insights of our theoretical results and not being blurred by random noises, we first use a 4-link non-fading cellular network as an example. We assume that each link has unit capacity and only one link can be activated in each time-slot. We use $\log(0.001 + a)$ as the utility function for each link, i.e., the well-known proportional fairness metric [6]. Due to the symmetry of the setting, the optimal congestion control rates are $\bar{a}_1^* = \bar{a}_2^* = \bar{a}_3^* = \bar{a}_4^* = \frac{1}{4}$. To see the impact of β on delay and convergence, we let $K = 25$ and increase β from 0 to 0.99 ($\beta = 0$ corresponds to QCA). Due to the symmetry of the setting, we only plot the results of link 1. As shown in Figure 2, as β increases, the average queue-lengths are 100.1, 50.1, 20.2, and 1.1, respectively, which confirm the $(1-\beta)$-fraction reduction result in Theorem 1. We see from Figure 3 that, for all choices of β, the congestion control rates with different β's all converge to the same optimal solution, confirming Theorem 2 that utility-optimality is not affected byβ. However, varying β significantly affects the convergence speed: As β increases from 0 to 0.99, the convergence speed initially increases and then decreases. Particularly, we see from Figure 2 and Fig. 3 that, by letting $\beta = 0.99$, we achieve both utility-optimality and low-delay at the expense of slower convergence, hence confirming the three-way performance trade-off. Next, we increase K from 25 to 100 and conduct another set of experiments on the same network. The results are shown in Figure 4 and Figure 5, respectively. With a larger K, the congestion control rates again converge to the same optimal solution with a smaller variance, but at the cost of larger delay and slower convergence, again confirming Theorems 1–3.

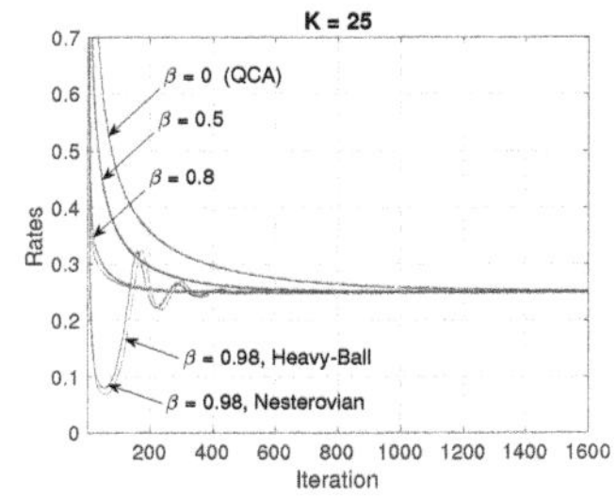

Figure 10: Convergence behaviors of the Nesterovian and Heavy-Ball approaches (Non-fading).

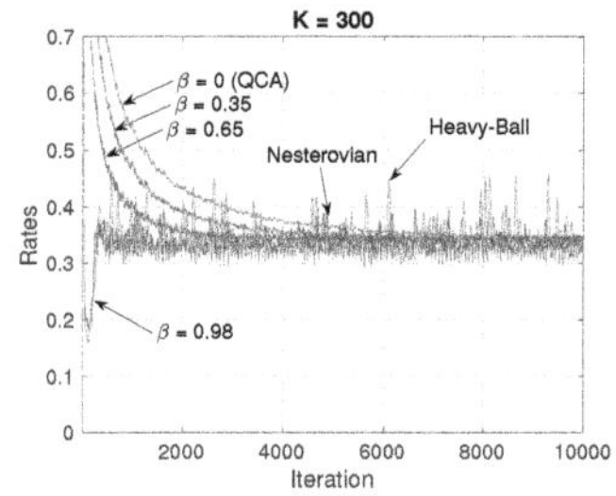

Figure 11: Convergence behaviors of the Nesterovian and Heavy-Ball approaches (Fading).

Now, we test our Nesterovian algorithm in a larger 15-user cellular downlink system with quasi-static block fading (channel states vary from one slot to the next but remain constant in each slot). Again, we assume that only one user can be activated in each time-slot. First, we let $K = 100$ and set *beta* to 0 (i.e., QCA), 0.35, 0.65, 0.95, respectively. For fewer random noise, we only plot the congestion control rate and queue-length of user 1 in Figure 6 and Figure 7, respectively. In Figure 6, as β grows, the queue-length again decreases monotonically and follows the $(1-\beta)$-fraction reduction in Theorem 1. In Figure 7, the congestion control rates under different β's all converge to the same optimal solution, which is approximately $\frac{5}{15} = \frac{1}{3}$. Next, we increases K to 300 and conduct another set of experiments. The results are illustrated in Figure 8 and Figure 9, respectively. We can see that, with a larger K, the congestion control rates again converge to the same optimal solution with a smaller variance, but at the cost of larger delay and longer convergence time, again confirming Theorems 1 and 2.

Finally, we compare the convergence behaviors of our Nesterovian algorithm to another state-of-the-art momentum-based algorithm termed "Heavy-Ball" [15]. The results for non-fading and fading cases are illustrated in Figures 10 and 11, respectively. From Figures 10 and 11, we can see that the convergence processes are similar when β is small. However, as shown in Figure 10, the convergence speed of our Nesterovian approach outperforms that of the Heavy-Ball approach when β is large (meaning aggressive delay reduction), which confirms our theoretical conclusion in Section 4.2. Further, from Figure 11, we can see that when β is large (0.98), the variance of the data rates under Nesterovian approach is much smaller than that of the Heavy-Ball approach.

7. CONCLUSION

In this paper, we have developed a Nesterovian algorithmic framework for stochastic network optimization, which offers not only utility-optimality and queue-stability, but also dramatic delay reduction and fast convergence. We established the utility-optimality of the proposed Nesterovian algorithmic framework and characterized the delay reduction and convergence speed performances; Also, we offered design rules for systems parameters, as well as insights on a three-way control between utility-optimality, delay, and convergence. Collectively, these results shed lights on a new cross-layer network optimization theory that based on the Nesterov's AGD method. Nesterovian cross-layer network optimization is an exciting and yet under-explored area. In our future research, we will further explore how to incorporate other Nesterovian variants into stochastic network control and optimization and investigate tight queue-length upper bounds rather than Big-O characterizations.

8. REFERENCES

[1] X. Lin and N. B. Shroff, "The impact of imperfect scheduling on cross-layer congestion control in wireless networks," *IEEE/ACM Trans. Netw.*, vol. 14, no. 2, pp. 302–315, Apr. 2006.

[2] A. Eryilmaz and R. Srikant, "Joint congestion control, routing, and MAC for stability and fairness in wireless networks," *IEEE J. Sel. Areas Commun.*, vol. 24, no. 8, pp. 1514–1524, Aug. 2006.

[3] M. J. Neely, E. Modiano, and C.-P. Li, "Faireness and optimal stochastic control for heterogeneous networks," *IEEE/ACM Trans. Netw.*, vol. 16, no. 2, pp. 396–409, Apr. 2008.

[4] A. Eryilmaz and R. Srikant, "Fair resource allocation in wireless networks using queue-length-based scheduling and congestion control," *IEEE/ACM Trans. Netw.*, vol. 15, no. 6, pp. 1333–1344, Dec. 2007.

[5] A. L. Stolyar, "Maximizing queueing network utility subject to stability: Greedy primal-dual algorithm," *Queueing Systems*, vol. 50, no. 4, pp. 401–457, 2005.

[6] X. Lin, N. B. Shroff, and R. Srikant, "A tutorial on cross-layer optimization in wireless networks," *IEEE J. Sel. Areas Commun.*, vol. 24, no. 8, pp. 1452–1463, Aug. 2006.

[7] M. J. Neely, "Super-fast delay tradeoffs for utility optimal fair scheduling in wireless networks," *IEEE J. Sel. Areas Commun.*, vol. 24, no. 8, pp. 1489–1501, Aug. 2006.

[8] L. Huang and M. J. Neely, "Delay reduction via lagrange multipliers in stochastic network optimization," *IEEE Trans. Autom. Control*, vol. 56, no. 4, pp. 842–857, Apr. 2011.

[9] L. Huang, X. Liu, and X. Hao, "The power of online learning in stochastic network optimization," in *Proc. ACM Sigmetrics*, Austin, TX, Jun.16-20, 2014, pp. 153–165.

[10] M. S. Bazaraa, H. D. Sherali, and C. M. Shetty, *Nonlinear Programming: Theory and Algorithms*, 3rd ed. New York, NY: John Wiley & Sons Inc., 2006.

[11] J. Liu, C. H. Xia, N. B. Shroff, and H. D. Sherali, "Distributed cross-layer optimization in wireless networks: A second-order approach," in *Proc. IEEE INFOCOM*, Turin, Italy, Apr. 14-19, 2013.

[12] J. Liu, N. B. Shroff, C. H. Xia, and H. D. Sherali, "Joint congestion control and routing optimization: An efficient second-order distributed approach," *IEEE/ACM Trans. Netw.*, 2015, accepted, to appear.

[13] Y. Nesterov, "A method of solving a convex programming problem with convergence rate $O(1/k^2)$," *Soviet Math. Doklady*, vol. 27, no. 2, pp. 372 – 376, 1983.

[14] ——, *Introductory Lectures on Convex Programming.* Boston/Dordrecht/London: Kluwer Academic Publishers, 2004.

[15] J. Liu, A. Eryilmaz, N. B. Shroff, and E. S. Bentley, "Heavy-ball: A new approach to tame delay and

convergence in wireless network optimization," in *Proc. IEEE INFOCOM*, 2016.

[16] R. J. Gibbens and F. P. Kelly, "Resource pricing and the evolution of congestion control," *Automatica*, vol. 35, pp. 1969–1985, 1999.

[17] S. Kunniyur and R. Srikant, "Analysis and design of an adaptive virtual queue algorithm for active queue management," in *Proc. ACM SIGCOMM*, San Diego, CA, Aug. 2001, pp. 123–134.

[18] A. Laksmikantha, C. Beck, and R. Srikant, "Robustness of real and virtual queue-based active queue management schemes," *IEEE/ACM Trans. Netw.*, vol. 13, no. 1, pp. 81–93, Feb. 2005.

[19] E. Athanasopoulou, L. Bui, T. Ji, R. Srikant, and A. Stolyar, "Back-pressure-based packet-by-packet adaptive routing in communication networks," *IEEE/ACM Trans. Netw.*, vol. 21, no. 1, pp. 244–257, Feb. 2013.

[20] N. Walton, "Concave switching in single and multihop networks," in *Proc. ACM Sigmetrics*, Austin, TX, Jun. 11-14, 2014, pp. 139 – 151.

[21] M. Bramson, B. D'Auria, and N. Walton, "Proportional switching in FIFO networks." [Online]. Available: http://arxiv.org/abs/1412.4390

[22] Z. A. Zhu and L. Orecchia, "Linear coupling: An ultimate unification of gradient and mirror descent," MIT CSAIL, Tech. Rep., January 2015. [Online]. Available: http://arxiv.org/pdf/1407.1537v4.pdf

[23] W. Su, S. Boyd, and E. J. Candes, "A differential equation for modeling Nesterov's accelerated gradient method: Theory and insights," *Journal of Machine Learning Research*, 2015, accepted, to appear. [Online]. Available: http://arxiv.org/abs/1503.01243

[24] S. Bubeck, Y. T. Lee, and M. Singh, "A geometric alternative to Nesterov's accelerated gradient descent," June 2015. [Online]. Available: http://arxiv.org/abs/1506.08187

[25] B. T. Polyak, "Some methods of speeding up the convergence of iteration methods," *USSR Computational Mathematics and Mathematical Physics*, vol. 4, no. 5, pp. 1–17, 1964.

[26] ——, *Introduction to Optimization.* New York, NY: Optimization Software, Inc., May 1987.

[27] E. Ghadimi, I. Shames, and M. Johansson, "Multi-step gradient methods for networked optimization," *IEEE Trans. Signal Process.*, vol. 61, no. 21, pp. 5417–5429, Nov. 2013.

[28] P. Ochs, T. Brox, and T. Pock, "iPiasco: Inertial proximal algorithm for strongly convex optimization," *Journal of Mathematical Imaging and Vision (JMIV)*, 2015.

[29] D. Jakovetic, J. M. F. Xavier, and J. M. F. Moura, "Convergence rates of distributed nesterov-like gradient methods on random networks," *IEEE Trans. Signal Process.*, vol. 62, no. 4, pp. 868 – 882, Feb. 2014.

[30] A. Eryilmaz, R. Srikant, and J. R. Perkins, "Stable scheduling policies for fading wireless channels," *IEEE/ACM Trans. Netw.*, vol. 13, no. 2, pp. 411–424, Apr. 2005.

[31] X. Lin and N. B. Shroff, "Joint rate control and scheduling in multihop wireless networks," in *Proc. IEEE CDC*, Atlantis, Paradise Island, Bahamas, Dec. 2006, pp. 1484–1489.

[32] R. A. Horn and C. R. Johnson, *Matrix Analysis.* New York, NY: Cambridge University Press, 1990.

[33] S. P. Meyn and R. L. Tweedie, *Markov Chains and Stochastic Stability*, 2nd ed. Cambridge, UK: Cambridge University Press, 2009.

[34] M. J. Neely, E. Modiano, and C. E. Rohrs, "Power allocation and routing in multibeam satellites with time-varying channels," *IEEE/ACM Trans. Netw.*, vol. 11, no. 2, pp. 138–152, Feb. 2003.

[35] L. Jiang and J. Walrand, "A distributed CSMA algorithm for throughput and utility maximization in wireless networks," *IEEE/ACM Trans. Netw.*, vol. 18, no. 3, pp. 960–972, Jun. 2010.

[36] J. Ni, B. Tan, and R. Srikant, "Q-CSMA: Queue-length-based CSMA/CA algorithms for achieving maximum throughput and low delay in wireless networks," *IEEE/ACM Trans. Netw.*, vol. 20, no. 3, pp. 825–836, Jun. 2012.

APPENDIX

A. PROOF OF PROPOSITION 1

As stated in Section 4.4, in $\mathbb{R}^{2N}$, the Nesterovian update in (11) can be rewritten as:

$$\mathbf{z}[t+1] = \mathbf{\Gamma}(\beta)\mathbf{z}[t] + \mathbf{\Gamma}'(\beta)\begin{bmatrix} \Delta\mathbf{q}[t] \\ \Delta\mathbf{q}[t-1] \end{bmatrix} + \begin{bmatrix} \mathbf{u}[t] \\ \mathbf{0}_N \end{bmatrix}. \quad (53)$$

For convenience, we define $\Delta\tilde{\mathbf{q}}[t] \triangleq \left[\Delta\mathbf{q}^\top[t]+\mathbf{u}[t],\ \Delta\mathbf{q}^\top[t-1]\right]^\top$. Then, the right-hand-side of (53) can be written as:

$$\mathbf{z}[t+1] = \mathbf{\Gamma}(\beta)\mathbf{z}[t] + \mathbf{\Gamma}'(\beta)\Delta\tilde{\mathbf{q}}[t]. \quad (54)$$

Also, based on the queueing evolution in (5), we can further explicitly express $\Delta\tilde{\mathbf{q}}[t]$ as follows:

$$\Delta\tilde{\mathbf{q}}[t] = \begin{bmatrix} \mathbf{a}[t] - \mathbf{s}[t] + \mathbf{u}'[t] + \mathbf{u}[t] \\ \mathbf{a}[t-1] - \mathbf{s}[t-1] + \mathbf{u}'[t-1] \end{bmatrix}, \quad (55)$$

where $\mathbf{a}[t] \triangleq [a_1[t], \ldots, a_N[t]]^\top$, $\mathbf{s}[t] \triangleq [s_1[t], \ldots, s_N[t]]^\top$, $\forall t$, and $\mathbf{u}'[t] \triangleq [u'_1[t], \ldots, u'_N[t]]^\top$, $\forall t$, represents the projection term in (5), meaning the unused services in each time-slot.

Also, it can be readily verified that $\mathbf{\Gamma}'(\beta)$ has only two distinct eigenvalues 0 and $(1+\beta)$. Hence, the largest eigenvalues of $\mathbf{\Gamma}'(\beta)$ is bounded by 2 since $\beta \in [0,1)$. Due to the non-expansive properties of the projection terms $\mathbf{u}'[t]$ and $\mathbf{u}[t]$, we further have that

$$\|\Delta\tilde{\mathbf{q}}[t]\| \leq \|\tilde{\mathbf{a}}[t] - \tilde{\mathbf{s}}[t]\|, \quad (56)$$

where $\tilde{\mathbf{a}}[t] \triangleq \left[\mathbf{a}^\top[t],\ \mathbf{a}^\top[t-1]\right]^\top$ and $\tilde{\mathbf{s}}[t] \triangleq \left[\mathbf{s}^\top[t],\ \mathbf{s}^\top[t-1]\right]^\top$.

Now, consider the conditional expectation of the one-slot Lyapunov drift in (24), for which we have:

$$\mathbb{E}\{\Delta V(\mathbf{z}[t])|\mathbf{z}[t]\} = \frac{1}{2}\mathbb{E}\{\|\mathbf{z}[t+1]\|^2 - \|\mathbf{z}[t]\|^2|\mathbf{z}[t]\}$$
$$= \frac{1}{2}\mathbb{E}\{(\mathbf{z}[t+1] - \mathbf{z}[t])^\top(\mathbf{z}[t+1] + \mathbf{z}[t])|\mathbf{z}[t]\}$$
$$\overset{(a)}{=} \frac{1}{2}\mathbb{E}\{[(\mathbf{\Gamma}(\beta) - \mathbf{I})\mathbf{z}[t] + \mathbf{\Gamma}'(\beta)\Delta\tilde{\mathbf{q}}[t]]^\top[(\mathbf{\Gamma}(\beta) + \mathbf{I})\mathbf{z}[t]$$
$$+ \mathbf{\Gamma}'(\beta)\Delta\tilde{\mathbf{q}}[t]]|\mathbf{z}[t]\}$$

$$= \frac{1}{2}\mathbb{E}\{\mathbf{z}^\top[t](\|\mathbf{\Gamma}(\beta)\|^2 - \mathbf{I})\mathbf{z}[t] + \mathbf{z}^\top[t](2\mathbf{\Gamma}(\beta)\mathbf{\Gamma}'(\beta))\Delta\tilde{\mathbf{q}}[t] + \|\mathbf{\Gamma}'(\beta)\Delta\tilde{\mathbf{q}}[t]\|^2|\mathbf{z}[t]\}$$

$$\overset{(b)}{\leq} \frac{1}{2}\mathbb{E}\{4\mathbf{z}^\top[t]\Delta\tilde{\mathbf{q}}[t] + 4\|\Delta\tilde{\mathbf{q}}[t]\|^2|\mathbf{z}[t]\}$$

$$\overset{(c)}{\leq} \mathbb{E}\left\{2\|\tilde{\mathbf{a}}[t] - \tilde{\mathbf{s}}[t]\|^2 + 2\langle(\tilde{\mathbf{a}}[t] - \tilde{\mathbf{s}})[t], \mathbf{z}[t]\rangle \Big| \mathbf{z}[t]\right\}$$

$$= 2\mathbf{z}^\top[t]\mathbb{E}\{\tilde{\mathbf{a}}[t]-\tilde{\mathbf{s}}[t]|\mathbf{z}[t]\}+2\mathbb{E}\left\{\|\tilde{\mathbf{a}}[t]\|^2+\|\tilde{\mathbf{s}}[t]\|^2|\mathbf{z}[t]\right\}, \quad (57)$$

where (a) follows from (54), (b) follows the spectral property of $\mathbf{\Gamma}(\beta)$ in Lemma 2 (i.e., the eigenvalues of $\mathbf{\Gamma}(\beta)$ are less or equal to 1), and and (c) from the non-expansive property of the projection terms. Further, from the second moment constraint of congestion control in (10) in our Nesterovian algorithm, we have $\mathbb{E}\{\|\tilde{\mathbf{a}}[t]\|^2| \ \mathbf{z}[t]\} \leq 2AN$. From the assumption that $s_n[t] \leq s^{\max}$, we can conclude that $\mathbb{E}\{\|\tilde{\mathbf{s}}[t]\|^2|\mathbf{z}[t]\} \leq 2N(s^{\max})^2$. Hence, by defining $B \triangleq 2N[A + (s^{\max})^2]$ (Notice here that B is independent of K), we have:

$$\mathbb{E}\{\Delta V(\mathbf{z}[t])|\mathbf{z}[t]\} \leq 2\mathbf{z}^\top[t]\mathbb{E}\{\tilde{\mathbf{a}}[t] - \tilde{\mathbf{s}}[t]|\mathbf{z}[t]\} + B \overset{(a)}{=} 2\mathbf{z}^\top[t] \times \left(\mathbb{E}\{\tilde{\mathbf{a}}[t]|\mathbf{z}[t]\}-\tilde{\mathbf{s}}^*\right)+\mathbb{E}\{2\mathbf{z}^\top[t](\tilde{\mathbf{s}}^*-\tilde{\mathbf{s}}[t])|\mathbf{z}[t]\}+B, \quad (58)$$

where $\tilde{\mathbf{s}}^* \triangleq [(\mathbf{s}^*)^\top, (\mathbf{s}^*)^\top]^\top$ and $(\mathbf{s}^*, \mathbf{w}^*)$ is a pair of optimal primal and dual solutions to Problem D-CCS. In (58), (a) follows from adding and subtracting $\tilde{\mathbf{s}}^*$ as well as the fact that $\tilde{\mathbf{a}}[t]$ is independent of the channel state and determined solely by $\mathbf{w}[t]$. Consider the term $\mathbf{z}^\top[t](\tilde{\mathbf{s}}^* - \tilde{\mathbf{s}}[t])$ in (58). From the design of the scheduler in (8), we have the pair of relationships holding true:

$$(\mathbf{w}^*)^\top\mathbf{s}^* \geq (\mathbf{w}^*)^\top\mathbf{s}[t], \quad (\mathbf{w}[t])^\top\mathbf{s}[t] \geq (\mathbf{w}[t])^\top\mathbf{s}^*.$$

Adding these two inequalities and rearranging terms yields: $(\mathbf{w}[t] - \mathbf{w}^*)^\top(\mathbf{s}^* - \mathbf{s}[t]) \leq 0$. It then follows that

$$\mathbf{z}^\top[t](\tilde{\mathbf{s}}^* - \tilde{\mathbf{s}}[t]) = [(\mathbf{w}[t] - \mathbf{w}^*)^\top, (\mathbf{w}[t-1] - \mathbf{w}^*)^\top]\times \left\{\begin{bmatrix} \mathbf{s}^* \\ \mathbf{s}^* \end{bmatrix} - \begin{bmatrix} \mathbf{s}[t] \\ \mathbf{s}[t-1] \end{bmatrix}\right\} = \sum_{\tau=t-1}^{t} (\mathbf{w}[\tau]-\mathbf{w}^*)^\top(\mathbf{s}^*-\mathbf{s}[\tau]) \leq 0$$

Hence, we can further rewrite (58) as:

$$\mathbb{E}\{\Delta V(\mathbf{z}[t])|\mathbf{z}[t]\} \leq 2\mathbf{z}^\top[t](\mathbb{E}\{\tilde{\mathbf{a}}[t]|\mathbf{z}[t]\} - \tilde{\mathbf{s}}^*) + B = \sum_{\tau=t-1}^{t}\sum_{n=1}^{N} 2(w_n[\tau] - w_n^*)\left[U_n^{'-1}\left(\frac{w_n[\tau]}{K}\right) - U_n^{'-1}\left(\frac{w_n^*}{K}\right)\right] + B. (59)$$

Since $U_n(\cdot)$ is concave and increasing, $\forall n$, we have

$$(w_n[\tau] - w_n^*)^\top\left[U_n^{'-1}\left(\frac{w_n[\tau]}{K}\right) - U_n^{'-1}\left(\frac{w_n^*}{K}\right)\right] \leq 0.$$

Thus, by using Cauchy-Schwatz inequality, we can equivalently rewrite (59) as:

$$\mathbb{E}\{\Delta V(\mathbf{z}[t])|\mathbf{z}[t]\} \leq -\sum_{\tau=t-1}^{t}\sum_{n=1}^{N} 2\,|w_n[\tau] - w_n^*| \times \left|U_n^{'-1}\left(\frac{w_n[\tau]}{K}\right) - U_n^{'-1}\left(\frac{w_n^*}{K}\right)\right| + B. \quad (60)$$

By the strong convexity of $-U_n(\cdot)$ (cf. Eq. (7)) and the Lipschitz continuity of $U_n'(\cdot)$, we have

$$\phi\,|a_{n,1} - a_{n,2}| \leq |U_n'(a_{n,1}) - U_n'(a_{n,2})| \leq \Phi\,|a_{n,1} - a_{n,2}|.$$

Therefore, by the inverse function lemma, we have

$$\frac{1}{\Phi}\left|\frac{w_n[t]}{K} - \frac{w_n^*}{K}\right| \leq \left|U_n^{'-1}\left(\frac{w_n[t]}{K}\right) - U_n^{'-1}\left(\frac{w_n^*}{K}\right)\right| \leq \frac{1}{\phi}\left|\frac{w_n[t]}{K} - \frac{w_n^*}{K}\right|. \quad (61)$$

Hence, we can further upper-bound (60) as:

$$\mathbb{E}\{\Delta V(\mathbf{z}[t])|\mathbf{z}[t]\} \leq -\frac{2}{\Phi K}\sum_{\tau=t-1}^{t}\sum_{n=1}^{N}(w_n[\tau] - w_n^*)^2 + B = -\frac{2}{\Phi K}\sum_{\tau=t-1}^{t}\|\mathbf{w}[\tau] - \mathbf{w}^*\|^2 + B. \quad (62)$$

Now, suppose that $\|\mathbf{w}[\tau] - \mathbf{w}^*\| \geq c\sqrt{K}$, $\tau = t-1, t$, where c will be specified shortly. Then, we have

$$\frac{1}{\|\mathbf{w}[\tau] - \mathbf{w}^*\|} \leq \frac{1}{c\sqrt{K}}, \quad \tau = t-1, t.$$

From (62), we that

$$\mathbb{E}\{\Delta V(\mathbf{z}[t])|\mathbf{z}[t]\} \leq -\frac{2}{\Phi\sqrt{K}}\sum_{\tau=t-1}^{t}\left[\|\mathbf{w}[\tau]-\mathbf{w}^*\|\frac{\|\mathbf{w}[\tau]-\mathbf{w}^*\|}{\sqrt{K}} + \frac{B}{2}\right]$$

$$= -\frac{2}{\Phi\sqrt{K}}\sum_{\tau=t-1}^{t}\|\mathbf{w}[\tau]-\mathbf{w}^*\|\left[\frac{\|\mathbf{w}[\tau]-\mathbf{w}^*\|}{\sqrt{K}} + \frac{B\Phi\sqrt{K}}{2\|\mathbf{w}[\tau]-\mathbf{w}^*\|}\right]$$

$$\leq -\frac{2}{\Phi\sqrt{K}}\sum_{\tau=t-1}^{t}\|\mathbf{w}[\tau] - \mathbf{w}^*\|\left(c - \frac{B\Phi}{2c}\right). \quad (63)$$

Therefore, by choosing $c > \sqrt{(1/2)BL}$, we have

$$\mathbb{E}\{\Delta V(\mathbf{z}[t])|\mathbf{z}[t]\} \leq -\frac{2\hat{\delta}}{\Phi\sqrt{K}}\sum_{\tau=t-1}^{t}\|\mathbf{w}[\tau] - \mathbf{w}^*\| \quad (64)$$

for some $\hat{\delta} = c - \frac{BL}{2c} > 0$. Plugging in $c > \sqrt{(1/2)B\Phi}$ to define a ball $\mathcal{B} \triangleq \{\mathbf{w} : \|\mathbf{w} - \mathbf{w}^*\| \leq \sqrt{(1/2)B\Phi K}\}$, we have

$$\mathbb{E}\{\Delta V(\mathbf{z}[t])|\mathbf{z}[t]\} \leq -\frac{\delta}{\sqrt{K}}\left[\|\mathbf{w}[t] - \mathbf{w}^*\| + \|\mathbf{w}[t-1] - \mathbf{w}^*\|\right], \text{ if } \mathbf{w}[t] \in \mathcal{B}^c. \quad (65)$$

where $\delta \triangleq \frac{2\hat{\delta}}{\Phi}$. On the other hand, when $\|\mathbf{w}[\tau] - \mathbf{w}^*\| \leq \sqrt{(1/2)B\Phi K}$, $\tau = t-1, t$, it trivially holds that

$$-\frac{\delta}{\sqrt{K}}\|\mathbf{w}[t] - \mathbf{w}^*\| \leq \eta, \quad \tau = t-1, t, \quad (66)$$

for some $\eta > 0$. Combining (65) and (66) yields the result stated in Proposition 1. This completes the proof.

On the Viability of a Cloud Virtual Service Provider

Liang Zheng* Carlee Joe-Wong* Christopher G. Brinton*
Chee Wei Tan† Sangtae Ha§ Mung Chiang*
*Princeton University †City University of Hong Kong §University of Colorado
{liangz, cjoe, cbrinton, chiangm}@princeton.edu cheewtan@cityu.edu.hk sangtae.ha@colorado.edu

ABSTRACT

Cloud service providers (CSPs) often face highly dynamic user demands for their resources, which can make it difficult for them to maintain consistent quality-of-service. Some CSPs try to stabilize user demands by offering sustained-use discounts to jobs that consume more instance-hours per month. These discounts present an opportunity for users to pool their usage together into a single "job." In this paper, we examine the viability of a middleman, the cloud virtual service provider (CVSP), that rents cloud resources from a CSP and then resells them to users. We show that the CVSP's business model is only viable if the average job runtimes and thresholds for sustained-use discounts are sufficiently small; otherwise, the CVSP cannot simultaneously maintain low job waiting times while qualifying for a sustained-use discount. We quantify these viability conditions by modeling the CVSP's job scheduling and then use this model to derive users' utility-maximizing demands and the CVSP's profit-maximizing price, as well as the optimal number of instances that the CVSP should rent from the CSP. We verify our results on a one-month trace from Google's production compute cluster, through which we first validate our assumptions on the job arrival and runtime distributions, and then show that the CVSP is viable under these workload traces. Indeed, the CVSP can earn a positive profit without significantly impacting the CSP's revenue, indicating that the CSP and CVSP can coexist in the cloud market.

1. INTRODUCTION

Cloud computing is forecasted to grow to a market size of $112 billion in 2018 [11], in large part due to its Infrastructure-as-a-Service (IaaS) offerings. IaaS attracts customers from individuals and organizations of all sizes, who can benefit from pay-as-you-go pricing that allows users to rent computing resources by the hour, eliminating setup and maintenance costs. Yet as more cloud service providers (CSPs) offer these services, the IaaS market has become increasingly competitive, with CSPs competing to offer ever-lower prices to users [1, 8, 30]. Compounding this difficulty, the number and variety of tasks that users submit to the cloud create a highly dynamic environment with many jobs that require different amounts of resources arriving and departing at different times. CSPs do take advantage of this job heterogeneity to optimize their capacity provisioning, but their pay-as-you-go pricing means that they cannot completely prevent localized instances of high demand and high user waiting times [21, 26, 27, 38]. Thus, many providers are turning to different pricing plans to match their IaaS prices to real-time user demands.

SIGMETRICS '16, June 14-18, 2016, Antibes Juan-Les-Pins, France

DOI: http://dx.doi.org/10.1145/2896377.2901452

1.1 Existing Cloud Pricing

IaaS resources are generally virtualized in units of instances. Each instance consists of a remote virtual machine (VM) with specified amounts of CPU, memory, storage, and other attributes. Users submit jobs by requesting the use of their desired types of instances. Each job consists of one or multiple parallel or dependent tasks, with each task run on a single instance and charged collectively with other tasks in the job. Users pay for the execution of their jobs per instance per hour. Most CSPs offer three types of instance pricing: usage-based, auction-based, and volume-discount pricing, as summarized in Table 1.

Usage-based pricing, also known as pay-as-you-go, is the simplest pricing scheme, charging users at a fixed unit (per-instance, per-hour) price [30, 40]. Auction-based pricing, such as Amazon's Elastic Compute Cloud (EC2) spot pricing [4] and Google's preemptible VMs [15], introduces more freedom to respond to real-time market demand: users bid for instances and the CSP sets dynamic thresholds for successful bids. While several works have shown that user cost can be reduced by such bidding, jobs run under this scheme may be interrupted prior to completion [22, 24, 39].

Volume-discount pricing offers another way for CSPs to stabilize user demand, without auction pricing's potential for interruptions. Under this scheme, users are charged a lower unit price if their usage exceeds a given threshold, *e.g.*, 25% of a one-month billing cycle for Google Cloud Platform [14]. Amazon EC2 allows users to rent reserved instances for 1 or 3 years at a reduced rate [3]. In our work, we follow Google's terminology and use *sustained-use discount* to refer to the discount afforded to longer-lasting jobs. We focus on this type of pricing in the paper.

1.2 The Cloud Virtual Service Provider

Sustained-use discounts appear to only benefit users with longer-lasting jobs. However, if users with shorter jobs could

Table 1: Different types of cloud pricing.

Scheme	Job Runtime	Unit Price	Typical Job Types
Usage-based	Short-term	Highest	Scientific computing, backend batch processing
Auction-based	Interruptible; no guaranteed deadline	Lowest	Word counting, multimedia processing
Volume-discount	Long-term	Discounted	Real-time web service, remote monitoring

pool their jobs together, they could jointly create a *virtualized* longer "job" to take advantage of the sustained-use discount.[1] This creates an opening for cloud virtual service providers (CVSPs) to rent long-term instances from CSPs offering these discounts. The CVSP can then attract users with shorter jobs by selling them this rented capacity at a small markup: users still pay lower per-instance, per-hour prices than they would by buying directly from the CSP, and the CVSP can also make a profit. Figure 1 illustrates this pooling scheme: individual users consume relatively little resources, but when pooled together they take up most of the VM time. In the remainder of the paper, we use CSP to denote the cloud service provider from which the CVSP rents instances to resell to users.

This type of user pooling to resell resources has been practiced in a variety of other contexts, *e.g.*, mobile virtual network operators (MVNOs) in the U.S. often offer cheaper mobile data plans to their users than the four major network operators [23]. Many cloud storage companies, like Dropbox, sell a version of virtualized cloud resources in which they store user data on rented VMs and add services like file sharing on top of the storage resources [12]. No work has yet studied virtual cloud services in which VMs are only resold to users without significant additional services.

While their business model seems generally reasonable, more careful consideration reveals some uncertainty as to whether CVSPs can viably support their users' demands. In particular, CVSPs need to balance offering lower prices to users with providing acceptable quality-of-service (QoS) to them. On the one hand, if the CVSPs do not attract enough users to their platform, they will not achieve the high usage volumes necessary to receive the CSP's sustained-use discounts, and must charge users higher prices. On the other hand, attracting too many users could cause congestion, forcing users to wait long amounts of time before their jobs complete. Indeed, in a worst-case scenario, users' waiting times may grow to infinity as congestion builds up at the CVSP. Users may then decide to move their jobs to the CSP, even if it is more expensive. It is therefore unclear *whether virtual CSPs can viably exist in the IaaS market.* We establish conditions for CVSPs' viability in this paper.

1.3 Research Challenges and Contributions

The viability of a CVSP's business model depends on users' demands for its services: while the CVSP must attract enough users to qualify for the sustained-use discounts, it must also keep their demands low enough to provide acceptable QoS in order to compete with the CSP. We take QoS to be determined by users' waiting times in this paper

[1]If a CVSP attracts too many users, the CSP may refuse to rent VMs to the CVSP to avoid cannibalizing its business. Full consideration of the CSP's actions is beyond the scope of this paper, but we show numerically that the CVSP does not completely take over the CSP's business, allowing both to exist in the market (Section 5).

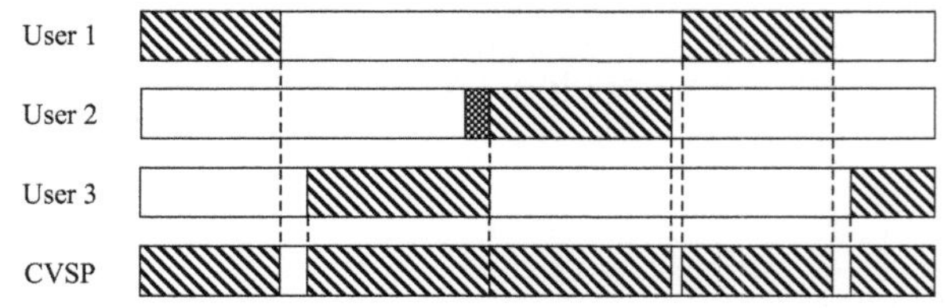

Figure 1: A simple one-instance example of a CVSP that pools usage from three users, reselling them VMs from CSPs. Shaded regions indicate when jobs are running for each user, while the grid-shaded region indicates that user 2 has to wait until user 3 finishes. Blank regions indicate idle time.

and define a CVSP's *viability* as its ability to qualify for sustained-use discounts while providing finite waiting times for some fixed, nonzero level of user demand.

In reality, users' demands are not fixed; they are influenced by the CVSP's decisions. CVSPs that charge users very low prices, for instance, will attract many users to their platform. However, these high demand levels may force users to wait long amounts of time for their jobs to run. Even if the CVSP is viable at a given demand level, if users' waiting times are finite but long, then they may not submit their future jobs to the CVSP. Yet this effect also depends on the number of VMs rented by the CVSP: if the CVSP has rented enough VMs, then user jobs could be run simultaneously, possibly compensating for the congestion induced by lower CVSP prices. Complicating matters is the sustained-use discount offered by the CSP that may increase with the CVSP's usage time on an instance, further increasing the CVSP's profit at high user demands. Thus, it is unclear *what prices the CVSP should charge its users* or *how many VM instances it should rent from the CSP.*

In order to model these CVSP decisions, we first develop a model for users' received QoS, given their demand levels, and use it to assess the CVSP's viability. We then evaluate users' strategically optimal demands and the CVSP's corresponding optimal economic strategy. We finally verify our results with evaluations on a one-month dataset of cloud workload traces. After a brief review of related work in Section 2, this paper establishes the following:

CVSPs' operational viability (Section 3): To determine the CVSP's viability, we first evaluate users' received QoS, given their demand levels. As such, we develop a model to characterize the system under Poisson-distributed user arrivals [29, 36, 37] and Pareto-distributed job running times [10, 25]. We then find the expected user waiting time and conditions under which it remains bounded. On relating these conditions to the expected system idle time, we show that the CVSP faces a tradeoff between lowering the user waiting time and lowering the system idle time to qualify for sustained-use discounts. We find that if users' average job runtimes are sufficiently small, then the CVSP can ensure finite waiting times and qualify for the discounts simultaneously: though shorter jobs consume fewer resources, sufficiently many short jobs will both consume enough resources to qualify for sustained-use discounts and allow for shorter user waiting times. However, if the threshold for the sustained-use discounts is too high, then the CVSP is not viable for any job runtimes: users' waiting times will grow to infinity at usage levels compatible with these discounts.

The optimal CVSP strategy (Section 4): We use our system characterization to formulate the CVSP's optimal (profit-maximizing) strategy, *i.e.*, its optimal prices and number of VMs. We first introduce a model of user demand, in which we suppose that users choose the frequency of job submissions and the number of jobs that they submit to the CVSP depending on the CVSP's QoS and price provided to users. We therefore observe a dependence among different users' actions: each user's demand affects the average waiting time in the system, which in turn affects other users' optimal demands. We find the equilibrium job arrival rate given this dependence, and then use the viability conditions derived in Section 3 to find the CVSP's profit-maximizing price and number of VMs to rent.

Experiments on a real-world data trace (Section 5): We finally simulate our model on a real-world user trace that contains the scheduling events of more than 600,000 jobs and 25 million tasks over one month. We first verify that users' job arrival rates follow a Poisson distribution and that the job runtimes follow a Pareto distribution. We then simulate the market dynamics, using these to verify that by choosing the right price to charge users and number of VMs to rent from the CSP, the CVSP can (i) obtain a sustained-use discount while maintaining a tolerable waiting time for users; and (ii) make a positive profit. Moreover, we show that the CVSP's market share is limited, giving the CSP more incentive to allow the CVSP to exist: the CVSP rents only a portion of the CSP's total capacity, stabilizing demand for this portion of the CSP's capacity and leaving the rest for the CSP to market directly to users.

2. RELATED WORK

Cloud and datacenter workloads have been extensively studied. User requests are often modeled as Poisson processes for analytic convenience [2,35], though a number of early studies showed that the workload interarrival times experienced by traditional datacenters were not exponentially distributed [17]. However, as datacenter services become more popular and users become more experienced in scaling and managing their workloads, these traffic dynamics are changing. Recent measurements on different traces have suggested that job arrivals are in fact Poisson distributed [29,36,37], consistent with our own findings in this work. Furthermore, other works have used the Pareto distribution to model job service times [10,25], as we do here, while still others have characterized cloud workloads without leveraging user behavior [21,31].

Other works have considered cloud resource provisioning and dynamic scheduling from a purely operational perspective [2,5,6,16,26,38]. Power usage is a particularly important concern for CSPs, *e.g.,* the authors of [26,38] used the heterogeneity of VM resources and workloads to minimize power consumption and scheduling delay, while [5,6] considered the tradeoffs between power consumption and scheduling. Furthermore, authors in [13] derived equilibrium algorithms for cloud resource scheduling. While the CVSP does need to schedule user jobs on its rented instances, it does not need to provision resources or consider energy costs, leaving these to the CSP.

Table 2: Key terms and symbols.

Symbol	Definition
L	Number of users who subscribe to the CVSP.
M	Number of instances that the CVSP rents from the CSP.
N	Expected number of tasks within one job.
λ_l	Poisson distribution parameter for the lth user's arrival rate.
Λ	Poisson distribution parameter for the system arrival rate, where $\Lambda = \sum_{l=1}^{L} \lambda_l$.
$\tilde{\Lambda}$	Instance arrival rate, where $\tilde{\Lambda} = N\Lambda/M$.
t	Time duration of two adjacent job arrivals.
$\tau, \underline{\tau}$	Job runtime and the minimum runtime.
α	Pareto distribution parameter for job runtime.
φ	Expected waiting time.
T	A month's time.
θ	The expected idle-to-runtime ratio of an instance's usage
ϵ	Fraction of an instance's usage of the total time in a billing cycle.
p	Unit price that users pay the CVSP.
π	Full unit price without sustained usage that the CSPs charge.
ω	Fraction of full price that the CVSP pays.

Some works have treated cloud pricing as a game between CSPs and the users to reach an equilibrium [7,9,33]. As an alternative, others have used auctions for distributed cloud resource allocation [18,32,39]. Given that user demands are crucial to datacenter efficiency, the authors in [19] designed a prediction-based pricing scheme for demand response in data centers. We instead propose using the CVSP as a middleman to mitigate uncertainty in user demand, thus reducing user cost and increasing operational efficiency for CSPs.

3. CVSP VIABILITY

In this section, we consider the CVSP's ability to balance user QoS with qualifying for sustained-use discounts. To do so, we analyze a simple job scheduler for the CVSP that allows us to find users' expected job waiting times and the expected system idle time. We suppose that users' jobs are all run on the same type of VM instances and that they have equal priorities: each job request is fulfilled as soon as enough CVSP instances are available.[2] We first formalize the user arrival distribution (Section 3.1), and then derive the job waiting time and the system idle time, using these to establish CVSP viability in Section 3.2.

3.1 System Model

We consider a system of L users, each of whom is expected

[2]While the scheduler does not consider all nuances of user jobs, *e.g.,* dependencies between job tasks, we expect that its qualitative results will hold in practice, and we numerically validate our assumptions in Section 5.

to submit jobs consisting of N tasks at a time.[3] Each task is required to run on a separate instance, *i.e.*, they cannot simultaneously share resources on the same instance. We suppose that the CVSP has rented M ($M \geq N$) instances to allocate to its users. Without loss of generality, we assume that the lth user's job arrival rate follows a Poisson distribution with mean λ_l, $l = 1, 2, \ldots, L$ [29,36,37]. Thus, the arrival rate from the point of view of the system (our focus in this section) is denoted by $\Lambda = \sum_{l=1}^{L} \lambda_l$, and the time t between two job arrivals is exponentially distributed. As a heavy-tailed distribution is often used to model job runtimes [10,25], we assume that the time τ for which each job will run in the system follows a Pareto distribution with parameter $\alpha > 1$ and a minimum runtime $\underline{\tau}$.[4] We suppose that each task within a given job must run for the same amount of time, which has the expected value $\frac{\alpha\underline{\tau}}{\alpha-1}$. All times in this paper are assumed to be given in hours. We summarize our notation in Table 2.

We assume that users request resources from the CVSP independently over a continuous time interval. After receiving a job request of N tasks from a user, the CVSP randomly allocates the tasks to N instances. Since we do not distinguish between different instances, each instance has the same probability of being available at any given time, and thus of being assigned a task. The probability that an instance will be chosen for a given job request is then $1 - \binom{M-1}{N} / \binom{M}{N} = \frac{N}{M}$, where $\binom{M}{N}$ is the binomial coefficient representing the number of combinations of selecting N items from a set of M items. Now, it can be established that the task arrival rate for each instance also has a Poisson distribution:

LEMMA 1. *If (i) job arrivals follow a Poisson distribution with parameter Λ, (ii) each submitted job requires N tasks, and (iii) the CVSP can run the jobs on M instances, then the task arrival rate for each of the instances follows a Poisson distribution with parameter $\frac{N}{M}\Lambda$.*

PROOF. Suppose that for a given instance, t is the time interval between the starting times of two adjacent requests. We can derive the probability density function of t:

$$f(t) = \sum_{j=1}^{\infty} \left(\frac{N}{M}\right)\left(1 - \frac{N}{M}\right)^{j-1} \frac{\Lambda^j t^{j-1} e^{-\Lambda t}}{(j-1)!}$$
$$= \frac{N}{M}\Lambda e^{-\Lambda t} \sum_{j=1}^{\infty} \frac{\left((1-\frac{N}{M})t\right)^{j-1}}{(j-1)!} = \frac{N}{M}\Lambda e^{-\frac{N}{M}\Lambda t}.$$

To understand the above derivations, we note that $\frac{\Lambda^j t^{j-1} e^{-\Lambda t}}{(j-1)!}$ is the probability of the jth Poisson arrival in time t according to the Erlang distribution, $\left(1 - \frac{N}{M}\right)^{j-1}$ is the probability that the first $j-1$ users' jobs are all assigned to the other instances, and one of the jth user's jobs is assigned to this instance with probability $\frac{N}{M}$. Since $f(t) = \frac{N}{M}\Lambda e^{-\frac{N}{M}\Lambda t}$ is the probability density function of an exponential distribution with parameter $\frac{N}{M}\Lambda$, the job arrival rate for this instance follows the Poisson distribution with parameter $\frac{N}{M}\Lambda$. □

Henceforth, we refer to Λ and $\frac{N}{M}\Lambda$ as the *system arrival rate* and the *instance arrival rate*, respectively. For ease of notation, $\tilde{\Lambda} = \frac{N}{M}\Lambda$ will denote the instance arrival rate.

[3]Our results remain the same if N instead represents the expected number of tasks per job; we assume in this section that each job has N tasks for simplicity.

[4]On Google's Cloud Platform, all jobs run for a minimum of 10 minutes, or $\underline{\tau} = 1/6$ of an hour.

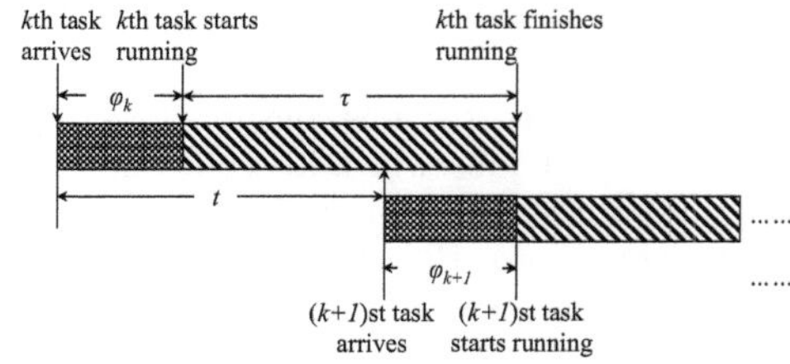

(a) Waiting time.

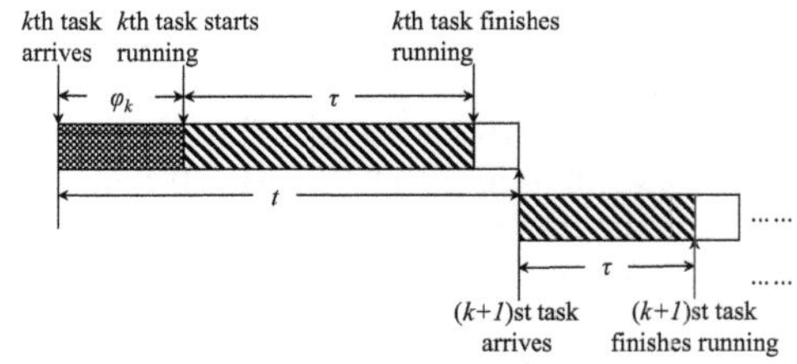

(b) Idle time.

Figure 2: Waiting time and idle time between two consecutive task arrivals. A new task must wait if it arrives before all previous tasks have finished running. On the other hand, there will be idle time for the system if the next task has not arrived by the time the previous task has finished running.

Although the result in Lemma 1 is not qualitatively surprising, it allows us to quantify the expected time between two task arrivals at an instance as $\tilde{\Lambda}^{-1} = \frac{M}{N\Lambda}$. Thus, if the next task is expected to arrive before the current task finishes running, *i.e.*, $\tilde{\Lambda}^{-1} < \frac{\alpha\underline{\tau}}{\alpha-1}$ (recall $\frac{\alpha\underline{\tau}}{\alpha-1}$ is the expected task runtime), we would expect to observe larger waiting times that could diverge to infinity. Conversely, if the expected task runtime is shorter than the expected time between adjacent task arrivals, *i.e.*, $\tilde{\Lambda}^{-1} \geq \frac{\alpha\underline{\tau}}{\alpha-1}$, the system may experience idle time between jobs. We formalize this intuition in the next section.

3.2 Balancing QoS with System Idle Time

We now evaluate the CVSP's viability using the above system model by first finding the conditions for finite job waiting times and then the conditions under which the CVSP's system idle time is low enough to qualify for sustained-use discounts.

3.2.1 User Waiting Time

We assume that each instance runs its assigned tasks in a first-come-first-served manner: a new arrival to an instance will only begin to run as soon as all of the tasks that arrived before it have completed. We let φ_k denote the waiting time of the kth arrival, as illustrated in Figure 2: the kth task first waits for time φ_k and then spends time τ to run. Two possibilities can then happen to the $(k+1)$st task: either it arrives before the kth task has finished (Figure 2(a); $t < \varphi_k + \tau$) and has to wait for time $\varphi_{k+1} = \varphi_k + \tau - t$ before it is launched, or it arrives after the kth task finishes (Figure 2(b); $t \geq \varphi_k + \tau$) and does not wait ($\varphi_{k+1} = 0$).

Taking these two possibilities into consideration, the expected waiting time of the next task arrival can be written

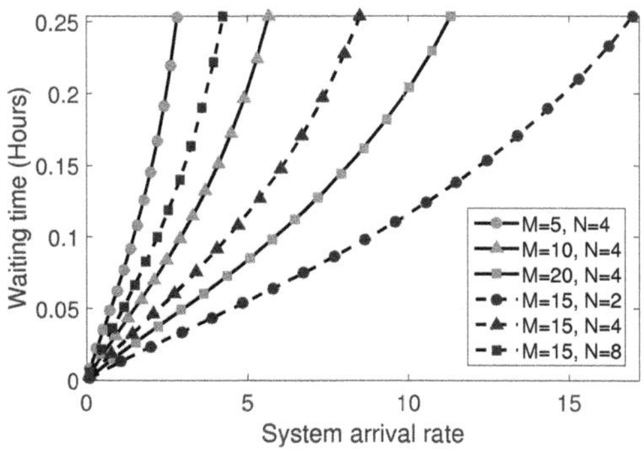

Figure 3: An illustration that the expected waiting time increases with the system arrival rate Λ.

in terms of the waiting time of the previous task: $\varphi_{k+1} = \int_{\underline{\tau}}^{\infty}\left(\int_0^{\varphi_k+\tau}(\varphi_k+\tau-t)\tilde{\Lambda}e^{-\tilde{\Lambda}t}\mathrm{d}t\right)\frac{\alpha\underline{\tau}^\alpha}{\tau^{\alpha+1}}\mathrm{d}\tau$, where we have abused on notation and use φ_{k+1} to refer to the expected waiting time of the $(k+1)$st task instead of the actual waiting time. This expression can be further simplified to

$$\varphi_{k+1} = \varphi_k - \frac{1}{\tilde{\Lambda}} + \frac{\alpha}{\alpha-1}\underline{\tau} + \frac{\alpha}{\tilde{\Lambda}}\left(\tilde{\Lambda}\underline{\tau}\right)^\alpha e^{-\tilde{\Lambda}\varphi_k}\Gamma\left(-\alpha, \tilde{\Lambda}\underline{\tau}\right), \quad (1)$$

where $\Gamma(s,z) \equiv \int_z^\infty x^{s-1}e^{-x}\mathrm{d}x$ is the upper incomplete gamma function.

Note that (1) is a fixed-point function for the expected task waiting times, and, in particular, is a recursion $\varphi_{k+1} = g(\varphi_k)$ for the implied function g. If the CVSP does not rent enough instances, *i.e.*, if M is too small, it is possible that φ_{k+1} will diverge to infinity. In such cases, the CVSP would not be viable, since users would eventually have to wait forever. To ensure finite waiting times, we derive a lower bound on M for which the waiting time converges to a fixed point:

PROPOSITION 1. *If the number of instances rented by the CVSP satisfies*

$$M \geq \left\lceil \frac{\alpha N}{\alpha - 1}\Lambda\underline{\tau}\right\rceil, \quad (2)$$

then asymptotically as $k \to \infty$, all of the tasks have a finite expected waiting time

$$\varphi = \frac{1}{\tilde{\Lambda}}\log\left(\frac{\alpha\left(\tilde{\Lambda}\underline{\tau}\right)^\alpha\Gamma\left(-\alpha, \tilde{\Lambda}\underline{\tau}\right)}{1-\frac{\alpha\underline{\tau}}{\alpha-1}\tilde{\Lambda}}\right), \quad (3)$$

where log *denotes the natural logarithm.*

PROOF. We show that the fixed-point iteration (1) converges if and only if (2) holds. For ease of notation, we first rewrite (1) by replacing $a = \frac{1}{\tilde{\Lambda}} - \frac{\alpha}{\alpha-1}\underline{\tau}$ and $b = \frac{\alpha}{\tilde{\Lambda}}\left(\tilde{\Lambda}\underline{\tau}\right)^\alpha\Gamma\Big(-\alpha, \tilde{\Lambda}\underline{\tau}\Big)$ and obtain:

$$g(\varphi_k) = \varphi_k - a + be^{-\tilde{\Lambda}\varphi_k}.$$

To show that (2) is a necessary condition, we note that (2) is equivalent to $a \geq 0$. If $a < 0$, then since $b > 0$, we have $g(\varphi_k) \geq \varphi_k - a = \varphi_0 - ka \to \infty$ as $k \to \infty$, so the iteration cannot converge.

To show that (2) is a sufficient condition, we use Banach's fixed-point theorem. We first show that $g(\varphi_k)$ maps $[0, R]$ to itself for some $R > 0$, and then that $g'(\varphi_k) \in (-1, 1)$ for all φ, *i.e.*, that g is a contraction mapping on $[0, R]$. Since $\varphi_0 = 0$, i.e., the first waiting time is 0 (since there are no preceding tasks), this is sufficient to show convergence.

We first show that if $\varphi_k \in [0, R]$, then $g(\varphi_k) \geq 0$. Since $g(\varphi_k)$ is convex with respect to φ_k, by letting its first-order derivative $g'(\varphi_k) = 1 - b\tilde{\Lambda}e^{-\tilde{\Lambda}\varphi_k} = 0$, we have

$$\begin{aligned}\min_{\varphi_k}\varphi_{k+1} &= g_{\min}(\varphi_k) = g\Big(\frac{1}{\tilde{\Lambda}}(\log b + \log\tilde{\Lambda})\Big) \\ &= \frac{1}{\tilde{\Lambda}}(\log b + \log\tilde{\Lambda}) - a + \frac{1}{\tilde{\Lambda}} \\ &= \frac{1}{\tilde{\Lambda}}(\log b + \log\tilde{\Lambda}) + \frac{\alpha}{\alpha-1}\underline{\tau} \geq 0.\end{aligned}$$

We now verify that for some $R > 0$, if $\varphi_k \in [0, R]$, then $g(\varphi_k) \leq R$. Since g is a convex function, we have $g(\varphi_k) \leq \max\left\{R - a + be^{-\tilde{\Lambda}R}, b - a\right\}$. Thus, we require that $R \geq \max\left\{R - a + be^{-\tilde{\Lambda}R}, b - a\right\}$, *i.e.*, that $R \geq b - a$ and that

$$a \geq be^{-\tilde{\Lambda}R} \iff \log\left(\frac{a}{b}\right) \geq -\tilde{\Lambda}R,$$

so that $R \geq \frac{-\log(a/b)}{\tilde{\Lambda}}$. For $R \geq \max\left\{b - a, \frac{-\log(a/b)}{\tilde{\Lambda}}\right\}$, g maps $[0, R]$ to itself.

We now show that $|g'(\varphi_k)| < 1$. Since $b > 0$ and $\tilde{\Lambda} > 0$, we see that $g'(\varphi_k) = 1 - b\tilde{\Lambda}e^{-\tilde{\Lambda}\varphi_k} < 1$ for $\varphi_k \geq 0$. To show that $g'(\varphi_k) > -1$, we note that $\min g'(\varphi_k) = g'(\min\varphi_k)$ due to the monotonic increase of $g'(\varphi_k)$. We thus deduce that

$$1 - b\tilde{\Lambda}e^{-\tilde{\Lambda}(\min\varphi_k)} > -1 \iff \frac{-\alpha}{\alpha-1}\frac{N}{M}\Lambda\underline{\tau} < \log 2,$$

which always holds since $\alpha > 1$. Thus, the recursion (1) converges to an equilibrium. Furthermore, by setting $\varphi_k = \varphi_{k+1}$ in (1), the result in (3) can be obtained. □

Note that a finite task waiting time φ necessarily implies a finite waiting time for the job as a whole. As a remark, we observe that the condition in (2) is equivalent to $\tilde{\Lambda}^{-1} \geq \alpha\underline{\tau}/(\alpha-1)$, *i.e.*, the expected time between task arrivals should be larger than the expected runtime, and this necessarily means that the denominator in (3) is positive.

Intuitively, to ensure a finite waiting time, the next task should on average arrive after the previous task has finished running. Proposition 1 implies that finite waiting times are more likely to occur when jobs have a shorter runtime (α is larger) and arrive less often (Λ is smaller). These conditions imply that jobs require fewer resources, allowing the CVSP to rent fewer VMs while still maintaining an upper bound on users' expected waiting times. We can mathematically verify this intuition in the following corollary:

COROLLARY 1. *The waiting time φ, as defined in (3), increases with the instance arrival rate $\tilde{\Lambda}$.*

PROOF. Although Corollary 1 is intuitively true, its proof is not straightforward. To show the monotonic increase of $\varphi(\tilde{\Lambda})$, we prove that, for any $z \geq 1$, $\varphi(\frac{1}{z}\tilde{\Lambda})$ decreases with z. Similar to the proof of Proposition 1, we further rewrite $\varphi(z)$ by replacing $a(z) = \frac{z}{\tilde{\Lambda}} - \frac{\alpha\underline{\tau}}{\alpha-1}$ and $b(z) = \frac{\alpha z}{\tilde{\Lambda}}(\frac{1}{z}\tilde{\Lambda}\underline{\tau})^\alpha\Gamma(-\alpha, \frac{1}{z}\tilde{\Lambda}\underline{\tau})$ and obtain $\varphi(z) = \frac{1}{\tilde{\Lambda}}\log\left(b(z)a(z)^{-1}\right)^z$. Due to the monotonic increase of the logarithm function, $\varphi(z)$ monotonically decreases if $g(z) = \left(b(z)a(z)^{-1}\right)^z$ monotonically decreases.

By taking the first-order derivative of $g(z)$ with respect to z, we have

$$\frac{\partial g(z)}{\partial z} = \left(\log\frac{b(z)}{a(z)}\right)\left(\frac{b(z)}{a(z)}\right)^{z} a(z)^2\left(\frac{\partial b(z)}{\partial z}a(z) - b(z)\frac{\partial a(z)}{\partial z}\right),$$

where $\frac{\partial b(z)}{\partial z}a(z) \leq b(z)\frac{\partial a(z)}{\partial z}$ is equivalent to

$$\underline{\tau}\left(z - \frac{\alpha}{\alpha-1}\tilde{\Lambda}\underline{\tau}\right)\underline{\tau}^{-\alpha-1}e^{-\frac{1}{z}\tilde{\Lambda}\underline{\tau}} \leq \alpha(z - \tilde{\Lambda}\underline{\tau})\int_{\underline{\tau}}^{\infty}\tau^{-\alpha-1}e^{-\frac{1}{z}\tilde{\Lambda}\tau}d\tau.$$

By leveraging the condition in (2), $\frac{\alpha}{\alpha-1}\frac{1}{z}\tilde{\Lambda}\underline{\tau} \leq \log 2$ leads to $\underline{\tau}\left(z - \frac{\alpha}{\alpha-1}\tilde{\Lambda}\underline{\tau}\right) \leq \alpha(z - \tilde{\Lambda}\underline{\tau})$. Combing with the fact that $\underline{\tau}^{-\alpha-1}e^{-\frac{1}{z}\tilde{\Lambda}\underline{\tau}} \leq \int_{\underline{\tau}}^{\infty}\tau^{-\alpha-1}e^{-\frac{1}{z}\tilde{\Lambda}\tau}d\tau$, we find that $\frac{\partial b(z)}{\partial z}a(z) \leq b(z)\frac{\partial a(z)}{\partial z}$ always holds. □

To illustrate Corollary 1, Figure 3 shows the joint effects of the number of instances M that the CVSP rents and the expected number of instances N that each user will request on the waiting time φ. As expected, the waiting time decreases with the number of rented instances (as shown by the solid curves with grey markers). Also, the instance arrival rate $\tilde{\Lambda} \equiv N\Lambda/M$ decreases as the number of instances M increases. However, the waiting time increases with N, as does $\tilde{\Lambda}$ (as shown by the dashed curves with blue markers). As Λ approaches the upper bound in (2), we see that the waiting time increases rapidly, eventually approaching infinity as predicted by Proposition 1.

3.2.2 System Idle Time and CVSP Viability

The second requirement for the CVSP's viability is to ensure that its expected idle time falls below the threshold required to qualify for a sustained-use discount. Intuitively, less idle time occurs when users submit jobs more frequently and fewer instances have been rented by the CVSP, *i.e.*, the opposite conditions as required for a finite waiting time in Proposition 1. We now find conditions under which both objectives can hold.

We define the *idle-to-runtime ratio* of the system to be the expected ratio of each instance's idle time to the time for which jobs run on the instance. To derive this ratio, we take an integral over the range $\tau \leq t$, and arrive at the following proposition:

PROPOSITION 2. *The expected idle-to-runtime ratio is*

$$\theta = \alpha\left(\tilde{\Lambda}\underline{\tau}\right)^{\alpha}\Gamma\left(-\alpha-1, \tilde{\Lambda}\underline{\tau}\right). \quad (4)$$

PROOF. When $\tau \leq t$, the idle time is $t - \tau$ after a job finishes running and before the next job arrives. So the idle-to-runtime ratio for the system is given by $\frac{t-\tau}{\tau}$. Since τ and t follow the Pareto and exponential distributions respectively, the expected idle-to-runtime ratio is integrated over $\tau \leq t$ and $\tau \geq \underline{\tau}$. The proof is readily obtained by evaluating

$$\int_{\underline{\tau}}^{\infty}\left(\int_{\underline{\tau}}^{t}\frac{1}{\tau}(t-\tau)\frac{\alpha\underline{\tau}^{\alpha}}{\tau^{\alpha+1}}d\tau\right)\tilde{\Lambda}e^{-\tilde{\Lambda}t}dt$$
$$= \int_{\underline{\tau}}^{\infty}\left(\frac{1}{\alpha+1}\underline{\tau}^{\alpha}t^{-\alpha} + \frac{\alpha}{\alpha+1}\underline{\tau}^{-1}t - 1\right)\tilde{\Lambda}e^{-\tilde{\Lambda}t}dt$$
$$= \frac{\alpha}{\alpha+1}\left(\tilde{\Lambda}\underline{\tau}\right)^{-1}e^{-\tilde{\Lambda}\underline{\tau}} - \frac{\alpha}{\alpha+1}\left(\tilde{\Lambda}\underline{\tau}\right)^{\alpha}\Gamma\left(-\alpha, \tilde{\Lambda}\underline{\tau}\right).$$

Using integration by parts, *i.e.*, $\Gamma(-\alpha, \tilde{\Lambda}\underline{\tau}) = (-\alpha-1)\Gamma(-\alpha-1, \tilde{\Lambda}\underline{\tau}) + (\tilde{\Lambda}\underline{\tau})^{-\alpha-1}e^{-\tilde{\Lambda}\underline{\tau}}$, the above integral can be further reduced to $\alpha(\tilde{\Lambda}\underline{\tau})^{\alpha}\Gamma(-\alpha-1, \tilde{\Lambda}\underline{\tau})$. □

The CVSP qualifies for a sustained-use discount if the idle-to-runtime ratio is sufficiently low. Suppose that the CSP offers sustained-use discounts once the overall usage of each CVSP's instance exceeds a fraction $\epsilon \in (0, 1]$ of the total time in an instance billing cycle. Equivalently, the CVSP must satisfy $\frac{1}{\theta+1} \geq \epsilon$, where $\frac{1}{\theta+1}$ is the fraction of time used to run tasks when the instance is either idle or running a task. This condition holds for higher instance arrival rates (larger $\tilde{\Lambda}$):

COROLLARY 2. *The idle-to-runtime ratio θ given in (4) decreases as the instance arrival rate $\tilde{\Lambda}$ increases. Furthermore, the CVSP qualifies for a sustained-use discount if the number of instances that it rents satisfies*

$$M \leq \left\lfloor\left(\frac{1}{\alpha}+1\right)\left(\frac{1}{\epsilon}-1\right)N\Lambda\underline{\tau}\right\rfloor. \quad (5)$$

PROOF. By taking the first-order derivative of θ with respect to $\tilde{\Lambda}$, we have

$$\frac{\partial\theta}{\partial\tilde{\Lambda}} = \alpha\underline{\tau}(\tilde{\Lambda}\underline{\tau})^{\alpha-1}(\alpha\Gamma(-\alpha-1, \tilde{\Lambda}\underline{\tau}) - (\tilde{\Lambda}\underline{\tau})^{-\alpha-1}e^{-\tilde{\Lambda}\underline{\tau}})$$
$$\overset{(a)}{=} -\frac{\alpha\underline{\tau}}{\alpha+1}(\tilde{\Lambda}\underline{\tau})^{\alpha-1}\left(\frac{e^{-\tilde{\Lambda}\underline{\tau}}}{(\tilde{\Lambda}\underline{\tau})^{\alpha+1}} + \alpha\Gamma(-\alpha, \tilde{\Lambda}\underline{\tau})\right)$$
$$\leq 0,$$

where (a) is due to $\Gamma(-\alpha, \tilde{\Lambda}\underline{\tau}) = (-\alpha-1)\Gamma(-\alpha-1, \tilde{\Lambda}\underline{\tau}) + (\tilde{\Lambda}\underline{\tau})^{-\alpha-1}e^{-\tilde{\Lambda}\underline{\tau}}$. Since θ decreases with $\tilde{\Lambda}$, we then need to prove $\theta \leq \frac{1}{\epsilon} - 1$ at $\tilde{\Lambda} = 0$. By substituting $\lim_{\tilde{\Lambda}\to 0}\Gamma(-\alpha-1, \tilde{\Lambda}\underline{\tau}) = \frac{1}{\alpha+1}(\tilde{\Lambda}\underline{\tau})^{-\alpha-1}$ and combining with $\theta \leq \frac{1}{\epsilon} - 1$, we have $\theta \leq \frac{\alpha}{\alpha+1}\left(\frac{N}{M}\Lambda\underline{\tau}\right)^{-1} \leq \frac{1}{\epsilon} - 1$, which leads to (5). □

We thus find that the CVSP is viable if the conditions in Proposition 1 and Corollary 2 are simultaneously satisfied:

$$\left\lceil\frac{\alpha N}{\alpha-1}\Lambda\underline{\tau}\right\rceil \leq M \leq \left\lfloor\left(\frac{1}{\alpha}+1\right)\left(\frac{1}{\epsilon}-1\right)N\Lambda\underline{\tau}\right\rfloor, \quad (6)$$

so that users experience finite waiting times and the CVSP qualifies for a sustained-use discount. Indeed, we find that (6) has a solution when $\frac{\alpha}{\alpha-1} \leq \frac{(\alpha+1)(1-\epsilon)}{\alpha\epsilon}$, leading to

COROLLARY 3. *There exists an instance arrival rate $\tilde{\Lambda}$ for which (6) is satisfied,* i.e., *the CVSP is viable, if*

$$\alpha \geq \sqrt{\frac{1-\epsilon}{1-2\epsilon}}, \quad (7)$$

which has a positive solution α only if $\epsilon < \frac{1}{2}$.

Since the expected runtime decreases as α increases, we conclude that jobs with shorter runtimes are more suitable for the CVSP. Intuitively, if the majority of users' job runtimes are sufficiently small, then even if many jobs are submitted to the system, each job will not have to wait for very long. Thus, the CVSP can maintain low waiting times and low idle-to-runtime ratios, thus qualifying for a sustained-use discount, by attracting smaller jobs. Indeed, these smaller jobs are exactly those that ought to be attracted to the CVSP; jobs with longer runtimes naturally qualify for a

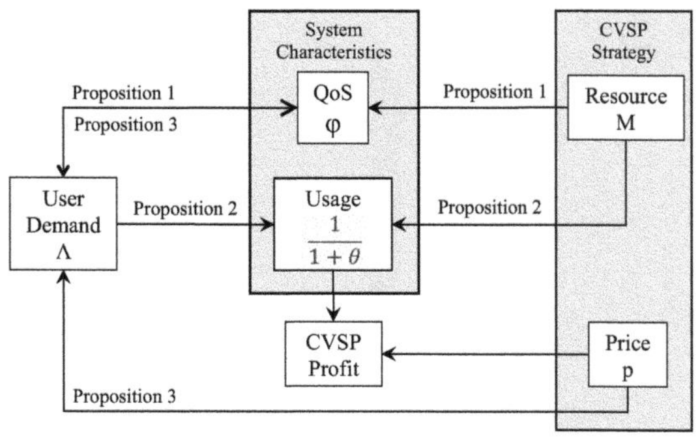

Figure 4: Tradeoffs between different parameters, showing their economic and behavioral impacts.

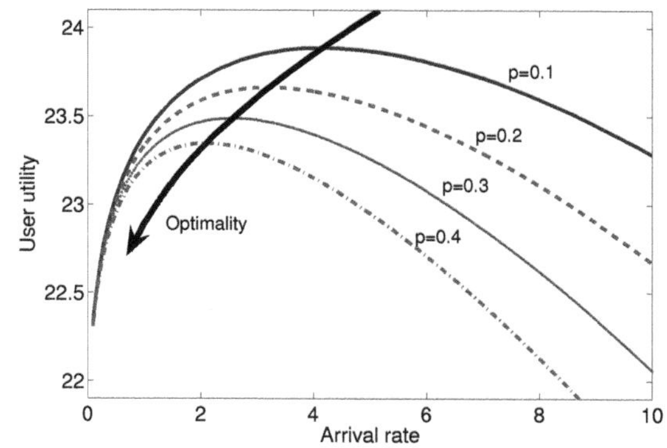

Figure 5: Example of the utility-maximizing demand Λ decreasing with price p for a single user.

sustained-use discount at the CSP and need not make use of the CVSP.

However, if the sustained-use threshold ϵ is too large, shorter average runtimes are not enough to ensure finite job waiting times. As ϵ grows, the CVSP must attract more and more jobs to lower the system idle time; after a certain point, jobs will need to wait for too many preceding jobs to finish, and the waiting time will grow to infinity despite the short job runtimes. While we do not expect the threshold of $\epsilon = 0.5$ in Corollary 3 to hold exactly, this result indicates that even relatively generous thresholds, like $\epsilon = 75\%$ utilization, may not allow for CVSP viability.

4. THE OPTIMAL CVSP STRATEGY

By leveraging the characteristics of the CVSP workload derived in Section 3, we can now derive the users' and the CVSP's optimal strategies. Both must trade off between possibly conflicting objectives: users would like both low waiting times and low instance prices, while the CVSP desires as little idle time as possible in order to qualify for a larger sustained-use discount. The user and CVSP decisions can be broken down as follows:

- *User demand (job arrival rates)*: Users' demands are dictated by their job arrival rates λ_l, $l = 1, ..., L$, which determine the frequency of job submission. Intuitively, users' demands increase as their waiting times φ decrease and the CVSP's price p drops. We assume that users adjust their demands to maximize their expected utilities, which are a function of these factors.
- *Waiting time (user QoS)*: Though each user's demand λ_l is expected to decrease as the waiting time φ increases, φ increases with the system arrival rate Λ (Corollary 1), which paradoxically corresponds to a higher demand λ_l from user l. Moreover, each user's demand depends on the other users' demands via the waiting time φ. Given this dependence, we find an equilibrium system arrival rate at which all of the users can simultaneously maximize their utilities. Since φ also depends on M, the number of instances rented by the CVSP, this equilibrium demand indirectly depends on M.
- *CVSP profit (idle-to-runtime ratio)*: We suppose that the CVSP's objective is to maximize its profit, which depends on the idle-to-runtime ratio θ: a lower θ (less idle time) leads to the CVSP obtaining a higher sustained-use discount from the CSP. The CVSP can influence θ through two decision variables: the price p that it charges users, which in turn influences users' demands Λ, and the number of instances M that it rents from the CSPs. Intuitively, a smaller M can lead to a lower θ, but may also lead to a longer waiting time and thus lower user demand. Therefore, different values of M and p can lead to lower or higher profit.

Figure 4 visualizes the above discussion (Proposition 3 is given in Section 4.1).

In the rest of this section, we first derive a relationship between the user demand, the CVSP price, and the expected waiting time (Section 4.1). We then formulate the CVSP's profit maximization problem (Section 4.2), which the CVSP solves to determine the optimal M and p.

4.1 User Demands

We first derive users' optimal demands by considering their utilities. We define an overall utilization rate for each user as the ratio of his or her expected job runtime to the expected waiting time, multiplied by the user's job arrival rate and the number of tasks per job, *i.e.*, $r_l = \lambda_l \frac{\alpha \underline{\tau} N}{(\alpha-1)\varphi}$. User utility generally increases with this rate, but with diminishing returns (*i.e.*, only increasing modestly when the runtime is already much larger than the waiting time). As such, we model this using the standard concave utility function $\log(1 + r_l)$ [20,39], with the lth user's utility given by:

$$U(\lambda_l \,|\, p) = \gamma_l \log\left(1 + \lambda_l \frac{\alpha \underline{\tau} N}{(\alpha - 1)\varphi}\right) - p\lambda_l \frac{\alpha \underline{\tau} N}{\alpha - 1}. \quad (8)$$

Here, $p\lambda_l \frac{\alpha \underline{\tau} N}{\alpha - 1}$ is the expected amount that user l pays to the CVSP given its expected job runtime $\frac{\alpha \underline{\tau}}{(\alpha-1)}$, and $\gamma_l > 0$ is a normalization constant that encodes the user's relative utilities from its waiting time and payment to the CVSP.

Note that the waiting time φ depends on *all* users' job arrival rates. Thus, due to λ_l's contribution to the waiting time, the utility in (8) for user l may not be concave in user l's demand λ_l. However, we see in Figure 5 that user l's utility does first increase and then decrease in λ_l. For instance, given a price $p = \$0.1$, the user's maximum utility occurs at $\lambda_l = 4.2$, corresponding to a waiting time of 0.046 hours. Higher arrival rates decrease user utility due to (i) higher costs and (ii) longer expected waiting times. User utility can therefore be maximized by setting $\partial U(\lambda_l \,|\, p)/\partial \lambda_l = 0$.

We now derive the system's job arrival rate $\Lambda = \sum_{l=1}^{L} \lambda_l$ assuming that all users maximize their own utilities, *i.e.*, $\partial U(\lambda_l \,|\, p)/\partial \lambda_l = 0$ for all $l = 1, \ldots, L$. We find that each user's utility-maximizing arrival rate satisfies $\gamma_l \varphi - p\varphi^2 = \lambda_l(\gamma_l \frac{\partial \varphi}{\partial \Lambda} + p\frac{\alpha \mathcal{T}}{\alpha - 1} N\varphi)$, leading to the following equilibrium system arrival rate:

PROPOSITION 3. *If all users choose the job arrival rates that maximize their utilities, then the system arrival rate satisfies*

$$\Lambda = \sum_{l=1}^{L} \frac{\gamma_l \varphi - p\varphi^2}{\gamma_l \frac{\partial \varphi}{\partial \Lambda} + p\frac{\alpha \mathcal{T}}{\alpha - 1} N\varphi}. \tag{9}$$

We thus find that Λ decreases for higher prices: if the CVSP charges users a higher price p, they are less willing to endure larger job waiting times, leading to a lower demand. We illustrate in Figure 5 that the utility-maximizing Λ decreases with p, as shown in the bolded black arrow curve.

4.2 Profit Maximization

We now characterize the CVSP's sustained-use discount in terms of the idle-to-runtime ratio θ. Letting π denote the CSP's full unit price without discounts, we expect the discount to increase as θ decreases, *i.e.*, the unit price should be cheaper when the CVSP has less idle time. Letting $1 - \omega$ denote the discount, *i.e.*, ω is the fraction of the full price that the user must pay, we define ω as a linear function of the idle-to-runtime ratio θ:

$$\omega(\theta) = \delta_1 \theta + \delta_2, \tag{10}$$

where $\delta_1 > 0$ and $\delta_2 > 0$ are two small fractions, satisfying $\omega(\theta) \in (0, 1]$ for any $\theta \leq \frac{1-\epsilon}{\epsilon}$. This threshold corresponds to $\epsilon \leq \frac{1}{1+\theta}$, *i.e.*, the fraction of time during which some tasks are running should be larger than ϵ. In Appendix A, we give a real-world example of (10) for Google Cloud Platform.

The CVSP's objective in choosing how many instances to rent and how much to charge is to maximize its own profit. The monthly payment to CSPs and the revenue received from users are $\omega(\theta)\pi\frac{T}{\theta+1}$ and $p\frac{T}{\theta+1}$ respectively, where T represents a month's time, and $\frac{T}{1+\theta}$ corresponds to the expected amount of time that a job is running on each instance. The CVSP thus solves the following optimization problem to maximize its profit:

$$\text{maximize} \quad M\Big(p - \omega(\theta)\pi\Big)\frac{T}{\theta + 1} \tag{11a}$$

$$\text{subject to} \quad \omega(\theta)\pi \leq p \leq \pi \tag{11b}$$

$$\omega(\theta) = \delta_1 \theta + \delta_2 \tag{11c}$$

$$\left\lceil \frac{\alpha N}{\alpha - 1} \Lambda \mathcal{T} \right\rceil \leq M \leq \left\lfloor \frac{\alpha + 1}{\alpha} \frac{1 - \epsilon}{\epsilon} N \Lambda \mathcal{T} \right\rfloor \tag{11d}$$

$$\text{variable:} \quad M \in \mathbb{Z}^+, p \in \mathbb{R}^+, \tag{11e}$$

where (11b) ensures that the price is lower than the full price and higher than the price with sustained-use discount, so that users are motivated to use the CVSP in the first place and the CVSP can have positive profit. The left-hand side of (11d) ensures a finite waiting time as in Proposition 1, and the right-hand side ensures a usage larger than ϵ as stated in Corollary 2. The waiting time φ, idle-to-runtime ratio θ, and equilibrium system demand Λ used in (11) are respectively given in (3), (4), and (9).

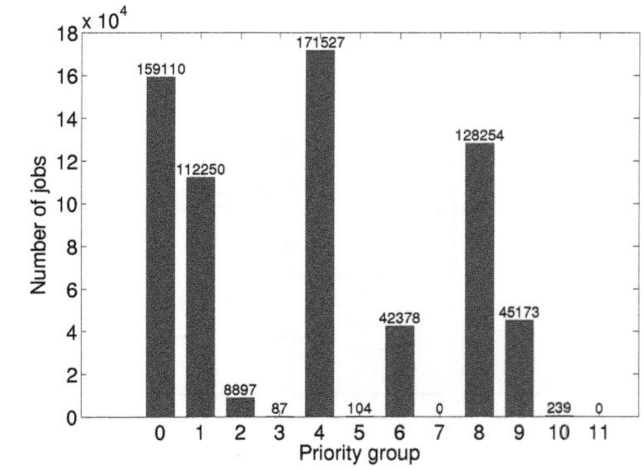

Figure 6: Numbers of jobs in different priority groups for our dataset.

If a joint solution to (3), (4), and (9) can be found subject to the constraints (11b–11d), then the profit maximization (11) has a solution. We expect that such a solution does exist, since these three equations can be reduced to one nonlinear equation in p and M. Although (11) is a discontinuous, mixed integer, nonlinear programming problem, it can be numerically solved by exhaustively considering all possible values of M and doing a line search for the optimal p.[5] In the next section, we analyze how the CVSP profits from different combinations of M and p. This not only provides insights into the interactions between the CVSP's strategy and user behavior, but also demonstrates that there is a feasible set for (11), *i.e.*, that the CVSP can make money in the IaaS market.

5. DATA-DRIVEN EVALUATION

To verify our models and results, we employ a trace from Google's production compute cluster, spanning 672,003 jobs over roughly a month-long period in May 2011 [34]. We begin in Section 5.1 by analyzing the job arrival and runtime distributions, showing that they match our assumptions within a tolerable margin of error. Then, in Section 5.2, we use simulations to validate the system characterization and profit maximization derived in Sections 3 and 4, respectively. Overall, we illustrate that all three parties – CSPs, CVSP, and users – can benefit from an optimal cloud resource reselling mechanism.

5.1 Model Validation

Data trace. The user trace contains timestamp records of machine events, job events, and task events; as the resource utilization of different jobs was studied in [26,38], we do not consider these parameters in our analysis. When a job is submitted, the user can specify its priority as one of 12 integer groups from 0 to 11. In general, a higher numbered group will be used for a more urgent job, while lower-prioritized jobs may be, *e.g.*, remote monitoring products or backend batch processing. Since jobs' priorities will affect their waiting times and runtimes, *e.g.*, due to higher-priority

[5]Since the value of M is at most 1000 for all practical purpose, (11) can be solved in a reasonable amount of time.

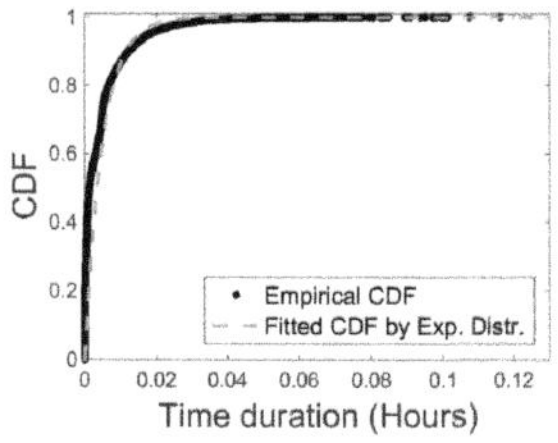

(a) Priority group 0 ($\Lambda = 200$, p-value $= 0.0015$).

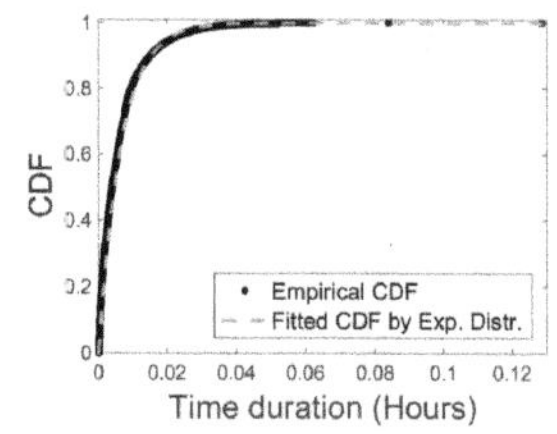

(b) Priority group 1 ($\Lambda = 150$, p-value $= 0.1998$).

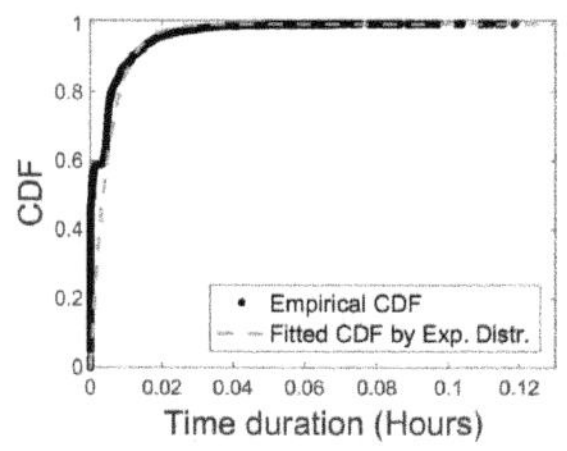

(c) Priority group 4 ($\Lambda = 195$, p-value $= 0.001$).

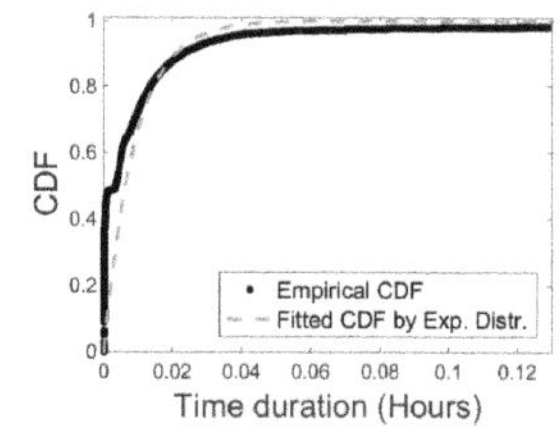

(d) Priority group 6 ($\Lambda = 110$, p-value $= 0.001$).

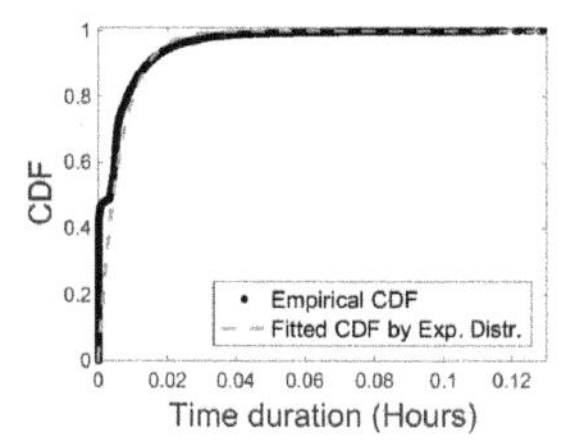

(e) Priority group 8 ($\Lambda = 160$, p-value $= 0.001$).

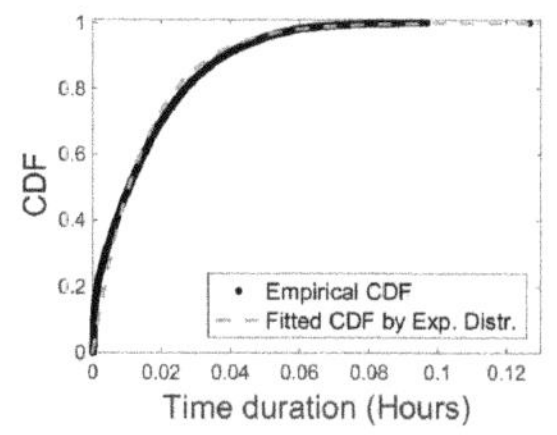

(f) Priority group 9 ($\Lambda = 66$, p-value $= 0.0625$).

Figure 7: Comparison between the empirical and fitted exponential CDFs of the duration between job submissions for different priority groups. The curves qualitatively match in each case, and the priority groups 0, 1 and 9 have non-rejected p-values.

jobs being allocated more resources faster, we consider the priority groups separately.

Figure 6 shows the number of jobs in each priority group.[6] For brevity, we show only the results for the most used groups in the body of the paper. Overall, we find that the job arrival and runtime distributions are comparable to the Poisson and Pareto distributions assumed in Section 3.

Poisson-distributed arrival rates. We validate our assumption of Poisson arrivals by examining the distributions of job interarrival times for the priority groups with substantial sample sizes, as shown in Figure 7. In all of the plots, the black dotted line gives the empirical cumulative density function (CDF), and the blue dashed line represents the best-fit CDF from an exponential distribution. Visually, the curves are qualitatively similar in each case. To investigate these fits statistically, we use the Lilliefors test on the null hypothesis that the waiting times come from an exponential distribution, at the significance level of 0.1% (*i.e.,* if the test returns a p-value ≤ 0.001, it rejects the hypothesis of an exponential distribution). The resulting p-values are given in the captions; the Lilliefors test does not reject the

[6]We exclude jobs submitted before the beginning of the trace as we do not know their runtimes or arrival times.

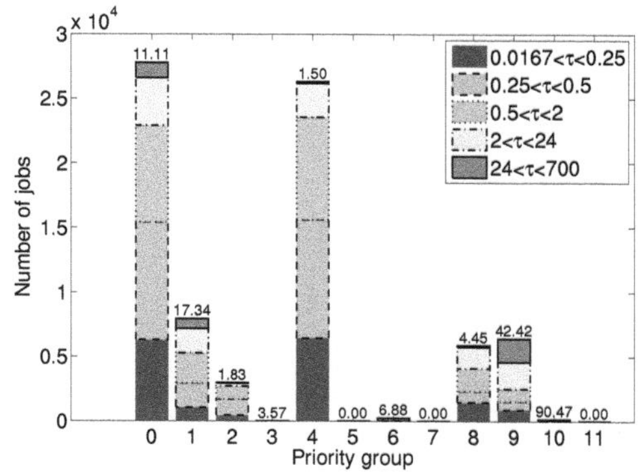

Figure 8: Distribution of the job runtime in each priority group. The number on each bar indicates the average runtime in the priority group.

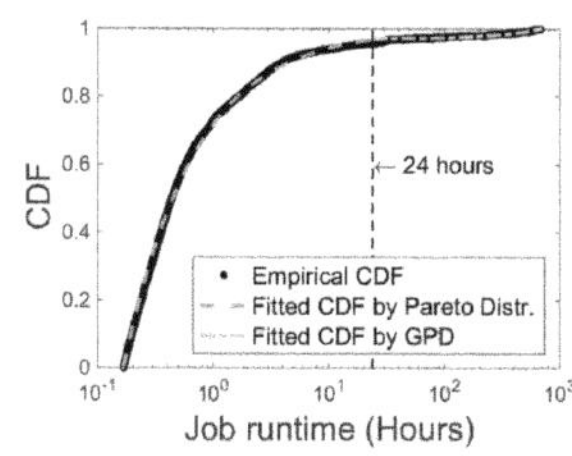

(a) Priority group 0 ($\alpha = 0.71$, $\xi = 2.14$, $\sigma = 21187.83$, $\mu = 27.98$).

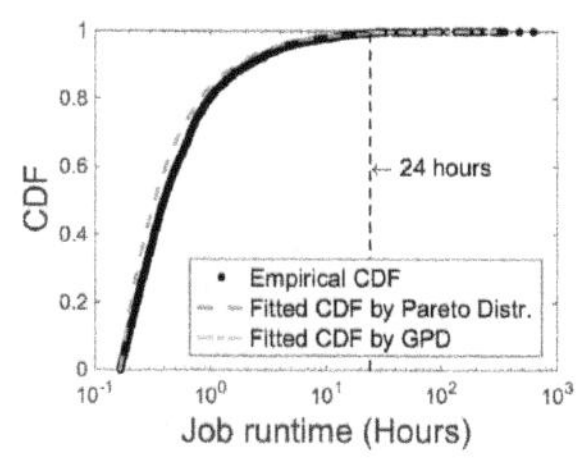

(b) Priority group 4 ($\alpha = 1.01$, $\xi = 524.18$, $\sigma = 5037.03$, $\mu = 0.96$).

Figure 9: Comparison of the empirical and piecewise-fitted CDFs of the job runtime distributions. Qualitatively, the CDFs appear to be very similar for both groups. The R-squared fit statistics are $R^2 = 0.997, 0.872$ for the Pareto and Generalized Pareto (GPD) fits respectively for priority group 0; $R^2 = 0.9913, 0.9319$ for the Pareto and GPD fits respectively for priority group 4.

hypothesis for the jobs in priority groups 0, 1, and 9, though it does for the jobs in priority groups 4, 6, and 8. The CDFs for priority groups 4, 6, and 8 in Figure 7(c), 7(d), and 7(e) have a small kink around a 20-second interarrival time, suggesting that Google may impose a small minimum delay on jobs whose tasks are not scheduled simultaneously. The kink is likely the reason that the p-value for this group does not reject the null hypothesis.

Pareto-distributed job runtimes. Figure 8 depicts the number of jobs with various runtimes in each priority group, identified by the stacked color bars.[7] We notice that the longest running jobs, *i.e.,* those running for more than one day, as shown in the red bars with solid outlines, are mostly in either the highest or lowest priority groups. Jobs with lower priority may be long-running computational jobs, which are not latency-sensitive, while higher priority jobs may be real-time, long-term applications that cannot tolerate interruptions.

As with the arrival rates, we choose to examine only the

[7]The total number of jobs in Figure 8 is less than that shown Figure 6 because we additionally exclude the jobs that were unable to finish within the trace period; we cannot determine the total runtimes of those jobs.

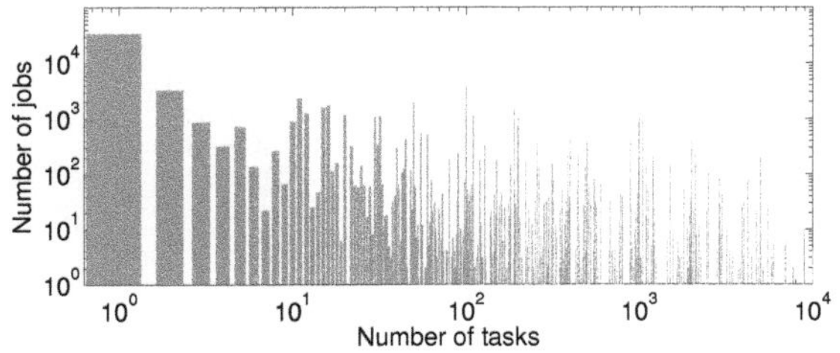

(a) Usage $\frac{1}{\theta+1} < 0.25$ (average $N = 192$).

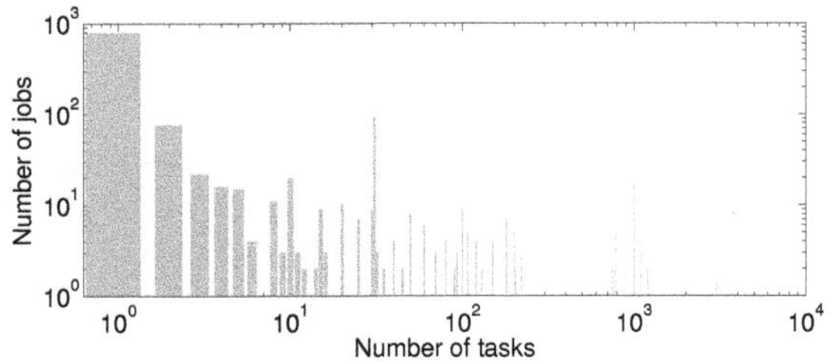

(b) Usage $\frac{1}{\theta+1} \geq 0.25$ (average $N = 67$).

Figure 10: Number of jobs comprising different numbers of tasks in different ranges of job runtimes. Those with shorter runtimes (10(a)) have more tasks than those with longer runtimes (10(b)).

runtimes of priority groups 0 and 4, which have the most jobs in Figure 8. In each plot of Figure 9, the empirical CDF, denoted by the dotted black lines, evinces a power-law distribution at the beginning with a more complex tail. To incorporate the dual nature of the distribution in fitting the CDF, we use the following piecewise probability density function that makes the first segment a Pareto distribution and the tail a generalized Pareto distribution (similar to the process used for job stragglers in [28]):

$$f(\tau) = \begin{cases} \dfrac{\alpha \underline{\tau}^{\alpha}}{\tau^{\alpha+1}}, & \text{if } \underline{\tau} \leq \tau \leq \hat{\tau}, \\ \dfrac{1}{\sigma}\left(1 + \xi \dfrac{\tau - \mu}{\sigma}\right)^{-\left(\frac{1}{\xi}+1\right)}, & \text{if } \tau \geq \hat{\tau}, \end{cases}$$

where the CDF is $F(\tau) = 1 - (\underline{\tau}/\tau)^{\alpha}$ for $\underline{\tau} \leq \tau \leq \hat{\tau}$ and $F(\tau) = 1 - (\underline{\tau}/\hat{\tau})^{\alpha} + \left(1 + \xi\frac{\hat{\tau}-\mu}{\sigma}\right)^{-\frac{1}{\xi}} - \left(1 + \xi\frac{\tau-\mu}{\sigma}\right)^{-\frac{1}{\xi}}$ for $\tau \geq \hat{\tau}$. Setting the domain boundary at $\hat{\tau} = 24$ hours, we fit the parameter α for the Pareto distribution (the dashed blue curves in Figure 8) and the parameters σ, ξ, and μ for the generalized Pareto distribution (the dash-dot green lines). We observe that the fitted CDF fits the empirical data well visually, and quantitatively, all of the R-squared fit statistics are above $R^2 = 0.87$. Although α in Figure 9(a) is less than 1, implying an infinite expected runtime in theory, it is close to 1; since all runtimes are in practice finite, we assign a value to α that is slightly larger than 1 to simulate the job runtimes in Section 5.2.

Expected number of tasks. Another important property of the jobs is the number of tasks; as in Section 3, N can affect the instance arrival rate (cf. Lemma 1), and henceforth the expected waiting time (cf. Proposition 1) and the idle-to-runtime ratio (cf. Proposition 2). Moreover, jobs that require more tasks than the CVSP's number of rented instances M will not be able to run on the CVSP. The average number of tasks for all jobs recorded in the trace is 190, though a large majority of jobs comprise fewer than 100 tasks.

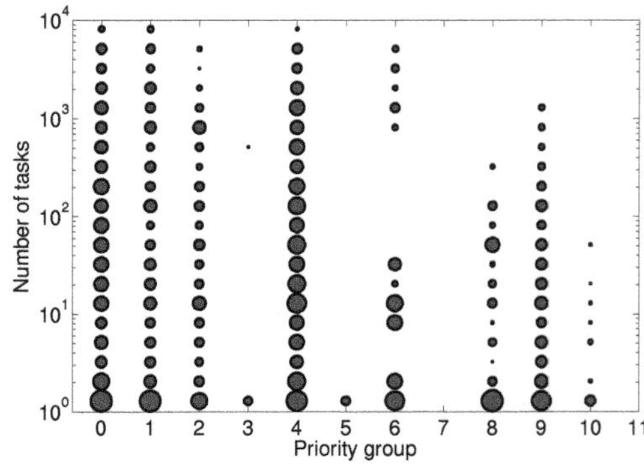

Figure 11: The number of jobs in the priority groups that have comprise numbers of tasks in given ranges. A larger circle implies that more jobs in that priority group have that number of tasks, with the size of dots in logarithmic scale. Most jobs have fewer than 100 tasks.

In Figure 10, we show the histograms for the number of tasks per job, over jobs of all priorities. Since Google offers sustained-use discounts when the job usage exceeds one quarter of a month (cf. Appendix A), we consider jobs above and below this usage threshold separately. As expected, jobs with shorter runtimes (in Figure 10(a)) have more tasks than the jobs with longer runtimes (in Figure 10(b)): jobs that can be divided into more tasks are more likely to have lower per-task runtimes. Thus, some jobs with short runtimes may wish to use the CVSP in order to receive a sustained-use discount, but will not be eligible to do so if the CVSP does not have enough instances. We show in the next section that it is optimal for the CVSP to rent only a limited number of instances, forcing these jobs to use services from the CSP instead and allowing both the CVSP and CSP to coexist in the IaaS market.

Figure 11 shows the numbers of tasks for jobs in each of the priority groups. We observe that, as we would expect from Figure 10, most jobs have fewer than 100 tasks. There is little visual consistency between the numbers of tasks for jobs with different priorities, but priority groups 0 and 4 clearly have the most jobs of all the priority groups, as is consistent with Figure 8. Interestingly, both of these priority groups appear to have somewhat more jobs that require a large number of tasks. We conjecture that priority groups with more jobs are more likely to include relatively rare jobs that have large numbers of tasks.

5.2 Trace-based Simulations

We use jobs from the trace that belong to priority group 0 to simulate the behavior of the CSPs, CVSP, and users. We first consider the CSP's revenue from these jobs with sustained-use discounts, before the CVSP enters the market. We then consider the CVSP's revenue and user utility after the CVSP enters the market. This trace was taken before Google introduced sustained-use discounts, so we cannot fully measure the effect of the sustained-use discounts in practice, but the job workload data still allow us to approximate its anticipated effects.

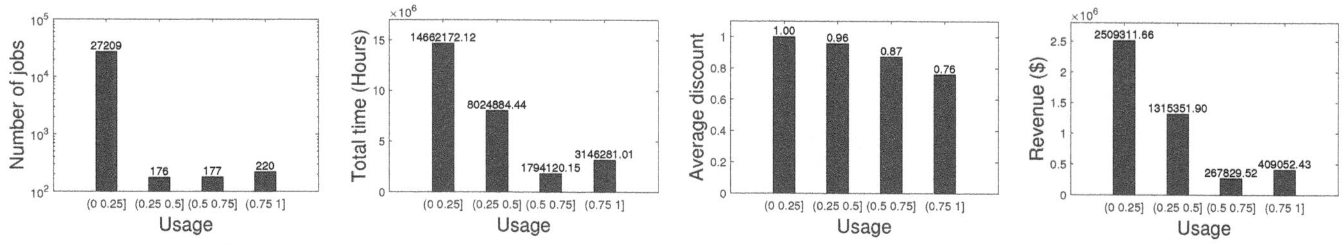

(a) Number of jobs. (b) Total time. (c) Average fraction paid. (d) Revenue.

Figure 12: The number of jobs, the total time for which users need to pay, the average fraction paid after the sustained-use discount, and the revenue for the CSP before the CVSP enters the market. All quantities are broken out for jobs whose usage is in a different range of runtimes.

5.2.1 CSP Revenue without the CVSP

We take the full price offered by the CSP to be $p =$ \$0.17, which is in between the current prices that Google charges for different instance types [14]. Assuming that the users of the CSP acted so as to maximize their utilities, we can then use the workload trace to reverse-engineer the users' utility parameters. From (8), we write $U(\lambda_l \,|\, p) = \gamma \log\left(1 + \lambda_l \frac{\alpha\mathcal{T}N}{(\alpha-1)\varphi}\right) - p\lambda_l \frac{\alpha\mathcal{T}}{\alpha-1}N$, assuming that all users have the same γ parameter for simplicity. As in Proposition 3, we can solve for the system arrival rate as

$$\Lambda = \frac{L(\gamma - p\varphi)}{p\frac{\alpha\mathcal{T}}{\alpha-1}N}. \tag{12}$$

We take the system arrival rate to be $\Lambda = 200$, as discovered in Figure 7(a). We also find from the workload trace that the expected number of tasks per job is $N = 138$, with $L = 306$ unique users submitting jobs. Furthermore, the jobs experience an average delay of $\varphi = 6.85 \times 10^{-3}$ hours between the time when they are submitted and the time they begin to run. We can then use (12) to find that $\gamma = 9$.

Given these user utilities, we now calculate the CSP's revenue under the sustained-use discounts, assuming no change in user demand (*i.e.,* the CVSP has not yet entered the market). We suppose that the CSP follows the pricing discounts specified in Appendix A. In Figure 12(a), we count the number of jobs that fall into each runtime range of the piecewise discount function, *e.g.,* jobs falling into the $(0, 0.25]$ range run for less than one-quarter of the month discovered in the dataset. We can then obtain the total instance hours consumed by the jobs in each range by calculating $\sum_{i=\in\{\text{All jobs}\}} N_i\tau_i$, as shown in Figure 12(b). Though there are about the same numbers of jobs in the ranges $(0.25, 0.5]$, $(0.5, 0.75]$, and $(0.75, 1]$, those in the range $(0.25, 0.5]$ have a much larger number of instance hours, suggesting that these jobs have a larger average number of tasks. In Figure 12(c), we show the average sustained-use discount for all jobs in different usage ranges, and we finally obtain the revenue of the CSP from jobs in each range in Figure 12(d). Jobs in the range $(0, 0.25]$ each run for less than a quarter of the month, so we expect them to have relatively low per-job revenue. However, there are enough jobs in this range for them to dominate the CSP's total revenue.

This result raises the question of whether the CSP would allow the CVSP to exist in the market: given that the CSP makes most of its revenue from shorter jobs, it might be reluctant to allow these jobs migrate to the CVSP. However, the CVSP will not be able to handle all of these jobs: it can only admit jobs whose number of tasks N does not exceed M, the number of instances rented by the CVSP. Thus, by limiting the CVSP's number of instances, the CSP can limit its revenue loss. Indeed, the CVSP itself has an incentive to keep its number of instances limited, since a larger value of M will increase the idle time on each instance, decreasing the sustained-use discount that the CVSP receives (cf. the bounds in (6)). We show in the next section that it is optimal for the CVSP to rent only a few hundred instances. Losing this limited number of jobs can in fact increase the CSP's profit, reducing its per-job account tracking and billing costs, as verified later in Figure 14. The CVSP's lower unit price might even attract more user job submissions than the CSP could attract on its own, increasing the CSP revenue overall due to higher user demand.

5.2.2 CVSP Profit and Impact on CSP Revenue

We now show that the CVSP makes a positive profit. We assume that users will offload jobs to the CVSP as long as (i) the price offered by the CVSP is cheaper than what the users can obtain from their CSPs and (ii) the CVSP has enough instances to accommodate the job's tasks. Thus, the number of jobs that the CSPs will lose depends on the CVSP's price p and the number of instances M. While in reality user demand may increase due to the CVSP's lower prices, we consider a conservative scenario in which jobs merely defect from the CSP, so the overall demand does not increase. Indeed, we show in the next section that user utilities do not change significantly when the price changes: users' utilities are much more sensitive to the waiting time and number of instances M than they are to the price.

Table 3 summarizes the number of users L who have at least one job that defects to the CVSP as well as their average number of tasks per job N and the resulting system arrival rate of the CVSP Λ. We see that Λ increases as the number of rented instances M increases and as the price p decreases: more instances allows the CVSP to support jobs with more tasks, and a lower price means more jobs can lower their costs by defecting to the CVSP. As we would expect, the average number of tasks per job N also increases with the number of rented instances, but it decreases as the price p decreases. As p decreases, jobs with longer runtimes can lower their costs by defecting to the CVSP, as the lower price p at the CVSP becomes even lower than their sustained-use discounts from the CSP. These jobs are likely to have fewer tasks (cf. Figure 10).

In Figure 13, we plot the idle-to-runtime ratio and CVSP profit as the CVSP's decision points M and p are varied.

Table 3: **Variation of user behavior with price incentive p and rented instances M.**

M	$p = 0.160$			$p = 0.145$			$p = 0.130$		
	L	N	Λ	L	N	Λ	L	N	Λ
100	257	1.0550	40.77	260	1.0547	41.36	261	1.0545	41.65
200	260	1.0737	41.28	264	1.0733	41.87	265	1.0731	42.16
300	260	1.0983	41.79	264	1.0981	42.39	265	1.0979	42.69
400	261	1.1048	41.83	265	1.1045	42.44	266	1.1043	42.74
500	266	1.1382	42.07	270	1.1377	42.68	271	1.1376	42.98

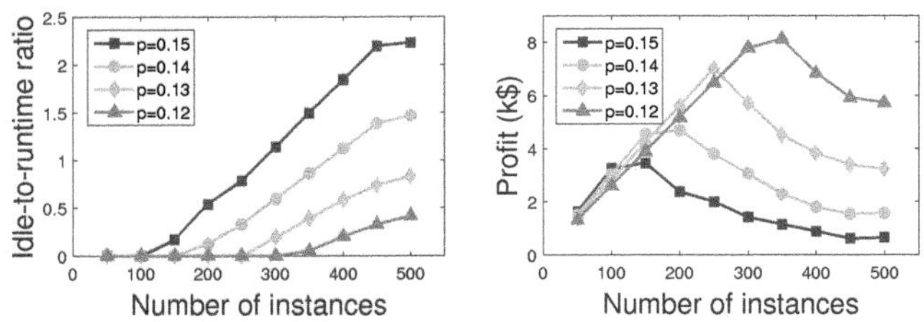

(a) Idle-to-runtime ratio. (b) CVSP Profit.

Figure 13: Idle-to-runtime ratio and profit as the CSVP varies its price p and the number of rented instances M. As p and M increase, the idle-to-runtime ratio increases monotonically. The profit is non-monotonic, necessitating a numerical search for the optimal p and M that solve (11).

The minimum price, p = \$0.12, represents the maximum sustained-use discount offered by the CSP; the CVSP will not offer a price lower than \$0.12 as in that case its revenue would be negative. We observe in Figure 13(a) that the system has less idle time with a smaller number of instances and a lower price: as the price p decreases, Λ increases, yielding fewer available resources and less idle time. In all cases, the idle-to-runtime ratio θ is ≤ 3, indicating that $\frac{1}{1+\theta} \geq 0.25$ and the CVSP can qualify for a sustained-use discount, earning a positive profit.

We confirm this reasoning in Figure 13(b). The CVSP's profit, however, is not monotonic: Figure 13(b) shows that if relatively few instances are available ($M < 300$), then a higher price p can yield higher CVSP profit as in (11). For a small number of instances, the CVSP cannot support as many jobs without increasing users' expected waiting time, making a lower demand (as driven by higher price) desirable. However, even though less idle time can increase the CVSP's sustained-use discount from the CSP, the lower arrival rate caused by the fewer available resources can drive the profit down. Numerically, we find that the CVSP's maximum profit is roughly \$8,000, for $M = 350$ and p = \$0.12. Thus, the CVSP limits itself to only a few hundred instances; we show in the next section that this represents only a limited number of user jobs, indicating that the CSP loses relatively little revenue. The CSP thus has little incentive to drive the CVSP out of the market.

Figure 14 compares the CSP revenue before and after the CVSP enters the market, for selected values of p and M. Though the CSP loses some revenue, it retains more than 85% of its original revenue, as represented by the dashed black line. The CSP could easily compensate for this small revenue loss. For instance, offloading shorter jobs to the

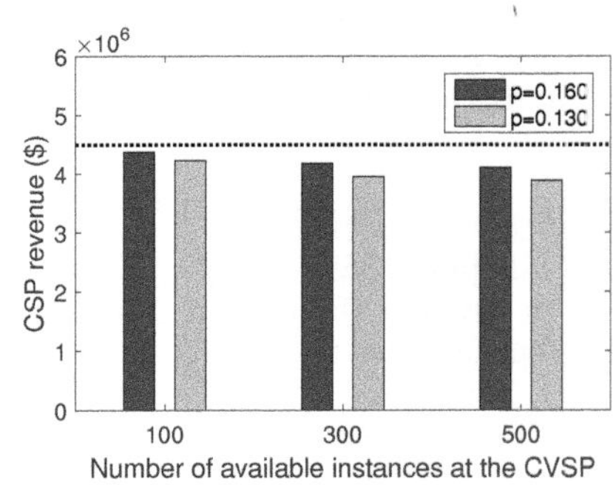

Figure 14: CSP revenue after jobs defect to the CVSP. The dashed line represents its revenue before the CVSP enters the market.

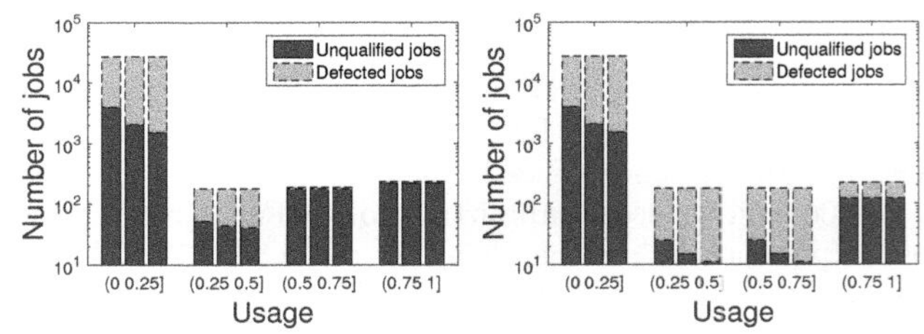

(a) $p = 0.160$. (b) $p = 0.130$.

Figure 15: Jobs defecting to the CVSP for different usage ranges, price p, and number of rented instances M. The left, center, and right bars in each group corresponds to $M = 100, 300, 500$ respectively. A larger M and lower p lead to more jobs defecting.

CVSP reduces the CSP's cost of tracking those user accounts and billing users for those jobs. The CSP may also benefit from an increase in user demand at the CVSP, due to users taking advantage of lower CVSP prices and submitting more jobs than they would otherwise have submitted to the CSP.

5.2.3 *User Utility at the CVSP*

We now analyze users' utilities at the CVSP after the CVSP enters the market. As in Table 3, we again assume that users will offload jobs to the CVSP as long as the price offered is cheaper than what the users can obtain from their CSPs and the CVSP has enough instances to accommodate the job's tasks.

Figure 15 shows the number of jobs that defect from the CSP to the CVSP for different prices p and numbers of instances M. We observe that only a limited number of jobs defect to the CSP. When the price is relatively high, at p = \$0.16, longer-running jobs do not defect to the CVSP,

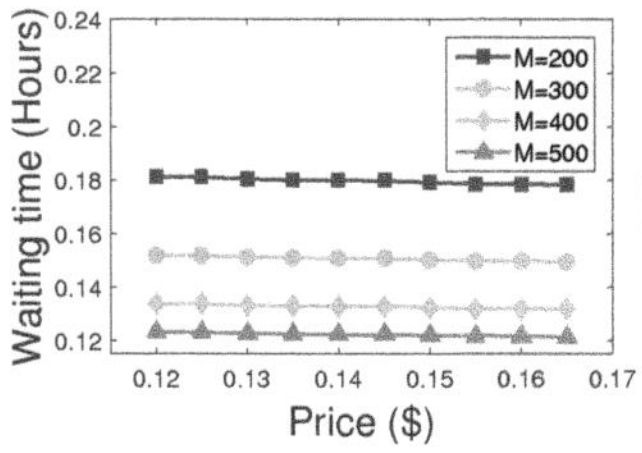

(a) Waiting time.

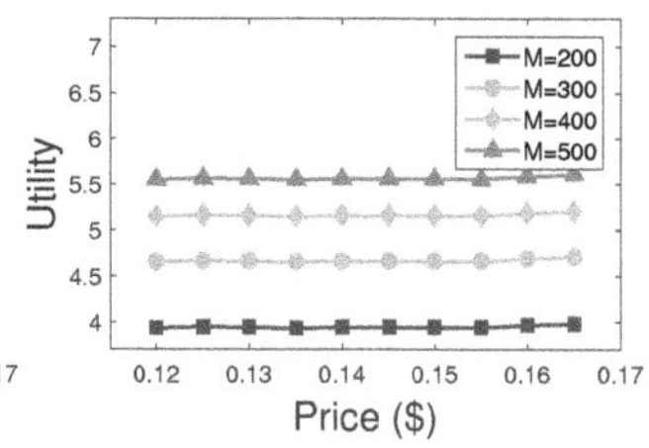

(b) Utility.

Figure 16: User waiting time φ and utility U for different prices p and rented instances M. Both are relatively flat with respect to price, but φ decreases and U increases with the number of instances M.

as they can qualify for the sustained use discounts on their own. Even some jobs with shorter running times, *i.e.,* usage in the range $(0, 0.25]$, do not defect, as they have more tasks than the CVSP has instances. More jobs defect when the price is cheaper and when the CVSP rents more instances, since under these conditions more jobs can save money at the CVSP and are eligible (*i.e.,* have few enough tasks) to run at the CVSP, respectively.

Figure 16 shows the average waiting time and utility for users at the CVSP, given the defected jobs as calculated in Figure 15. We observe that neither the waiting time nor utility changes very much with price. This result suggests that user utility, and thus user demand, is largely determined by the waiting time. This finding is consistent with the relatively large weight $\gamma = 9$ that we derived from (12) for the waiting time component of user utility. Figure 16(a) also illustrates that more rented instances M intuitively yield a shorter waiting time (Corollary 1). Consequently, user utility increases with the number of rented instances, as shown in Figure 16(b).

6. CONCLUSION

CVSPs can take advantage of sustained-use IaaS discounts to reduce cloud computing costs for users with short-term jobs, without a significant decrease in CSP revenue. In this work, we give conditions under which the CVSP's business model is viable: we show that sustained-use discount thresholds that are too large, as well as job runtimes that are too long, result in job waiting times growing to infinity at the CVSP. We use our characterization of the CVSP's job scheduling to find users' optimal demands at the CVSP in order to maximize a utility function of the job waiting times, the CVSP price, and the user demand. This determines the CVSP's optimal profit-maximizing price, as well as the optimal number of instances that it should rent from the CSP. We verify our job workload assumptions with a month-long Google datacenter trace and show that it is optimal for the CVSP to rent only a limited number of instances from the CSP. Thus, we obtain a win-win situation: the CVSP can earn a positive profit, and users can save money, without significantly impacting the CSP revenue.

As a first investigation into the viability of CVSPs, our work does not incorporate all practical features of the IaaS market. In particular, we do not explicitly model the CSP's optimal behavior, *i.e.,* the sustained-use discounts it should offer so as to maximize its own profit. Since multiple CSPs may offer different sustained-use discounts in order to attract jobs from their competitors, this results in the variety in formulating CVSP strategy depending on the deal with each CSP. We expect that including this CSP competition can lead to a more in-depth understanding of the CVSP's role in the IaaS market. We also plan to investigate the robustness of our findings to our assumptions of Poisson job arrivals and Pareto runtime distributions.

Acknowledgments

The work in this paper was in part supported by the NSF Waterman Award Grant CNS-1347234, and the Research Grants Council of Hong Kong under Projects No. RGC 11207615.

APPENDIX

A. SUSTAINED-USE DISCOUNTS

Users can get a better deal from their CSPs for long-term commitments. Google Cloud Platform offers no discount for the first quarter of usage, and then 20%, 40%, and 60% off for the second, third and fourth quarter of the monthly usage respectively [14]. For instance, at the third quarter of the usage, the discount is calculated as $\big(0.25 \times 1 + 0.25 \times 0.8 + (\frac{1}{\theta+1} - 0.5) \times 0.6\big)/\frac{1}{\theta+1}$ for $0.5 < \frac{1}{\theta+1} \leq 0.75$. Thus, we have the following sustained-use discount expression to model the Google Cloud Platform:

$$\omega(\theta) = \begin{cases} 1, & \theta \geq 3 \\ 0.05\theta + 0.85, & 1 \leq \theta < 3 \\ 0.15\theta + 0.75, & \frac{1}{3} \leq \theta < 1 \\ 0.3\theta + 0.7, & 0 \leq \theta < \frac{1}{3}. \end{cases}$$

which is consistent with the formulation in (10). However, in this case, the sustained-use discount is piecewise linear.

2. REFERENCES

[1] O. Agmon Ben-Yehuda, M. Ben-Yehuda, A. Schuster, and D. Tsafrir. The rise of RaaS: the resource-as-a-service cloud. *Communications of the ACM*, 57(7):76–84, 2014.

[2] M. Al-Fares, S. Radhakrishnan, B. Raghavan, N. Huang, and A. Vahdat. Hedera: Dynamic flow scheduling for data center networks. In *Proc. of NSDI*, 2010.

[3] Amazon EC2. Reserved Instances, 2015. https://aws.amazon.com/ec2/purchasing-options/reserved-instances/.

[4] Amazon EC2. Spot Instances, 2015. http://aws.amazon.com/ec2/spot/.

[5] M. Andrews, S. Antonakopoulos, and L. Zhang. Energy-aware scheduling algorithms for network stability. In *Proc. of IEEE INFOCOM*, 2011.

[6] M. Andrews and L. Zhang. Scheduling algorithms for optimizing the tradeoffs between delay, queue size and energy. In *Proc. of IEEE CISS*, 2012.

[7] D. Ardagna, B. Panicucci, and M. Passacantando. A game theoretic formulation of the service provisioning problem in cloud systems. In *Proc. of WWW*, 2011.

[8] M. Armbrust, A. Fox, R. Griffith, A. D. Joseph, R. Katz, A. Konwinski, G. Lee, D. Patterson, A. Rabkin, I. Stoica, and M. Zaharia. A view of cloud

computing. *Communications of the ACM*, 53(4):50–58, 2010.

[9] X.-R. Cao, H.-X. Shen, R. Milito, and P. Wirth. Internet pricing with a game theoretical approach: concepts and examples. *IEEE/ACM Trans. on Networking*, 10(2):208–216, 2002.

[10] J. Chen, C. Wang, B. B. Zhou, L. Sun, Y. C. Lee, and A. Y. Zomaya. Tradeoffs between profit and customer satisfaction for service provisioning in the cloud. In *Proc. of ACM HPDC*, pages 229–238, 2011.

[11] L. Columbus. Roundup of cloud computing forecasts and market estimates Q3 update, 2015.

[12] B. Darrow. AWS in fight of its life as customers like Dropbox ponder hybrid clouds and Google pricing. 2014. https://gigaom.com/2014/07/25/aws-in-fight-of-its-life-as-customers-like-dropbox-ponder-hybrid-clouds-and-google-pricing/.

[13] N. Devanur, J. Garg, R. Mehta, V. V. Vazirani, and S. Yazdanbod. A market for scheduling, with applications to cloud computing. *arXiv preprint arXiv:1511.08748*, 2015.

[14] Google Cloud Platform. Compute Engine Pricing. *https://cloud.google.com/compute/*, 2015.

[15] Google Cloud Platform. Preemptible Virtual Machines. *https://cloud.google.com/preemptible-vms/*, 2015.

[16] A. Greenberg, J. R. Hamilton, N. Jain, S. Kandula, C. Kim, P. Lahiri, D. A. Maltz, P. Patel, and S. Sengupta. VL2: a scalable and flexible data center network. In *ACM SIGCOMM computer communication review*, volume 39, pages 51–62, 2009.

[17] S. Kandula, S. Sengupta, A. Greenberg, P. Patel, and R. Chaiken. The nature of data center traffic: measurements & analysis. In *Proc. of ACM IMC*, 2009.

[18] E. Kutanoglu and S. D. Wu. On combinatorial auction and lagrangean relaxation for distributed resource scheduling. *IIE transactions*, 31(9):813–826, 1999.

[19] Z. Liu, I. Liu, S. Low, and A. Wierman. Pricing data center demand response. In *Proc. of ACM SIGMETRICS*, 2014.

[20] R. Mahindra, H. Viswanathan, K. Sundaresan, M. Y. Arslan, and S. Rangarajan. A practical traffic management system for integrated LTE-WiFi networks. In *Proc. of ACM MobiCom*, 2014.

[21] A. K. Mishra, J. L. Hellerstein, W. Cirne, and C. R. Das. Towards characterizing cloud backend workloads: insights from Google compute clusters. *ACM SIGMETRICS Performance Evaluation Review*, 37(4):34–41, 2010.

[22] C. Ng, D. C. Parkes, and M. Seltzer. Virtual worlds: Fast and strategyproof auctions for dynamic resource allocation. In *Proc. of ACM EC*, 2003.

[23] I. Paul. 10 alternative carriers that can save you serious cash on your smartphone bill. PC World, 2015. http://www.pcworld.com/article/2878298/10-alternative-carriers-that-can-save-you-serious-cash-on-your-smartphone-bill.html.

[24] D. Poola, K. Ramamohanarao, and R. Buyya. Fault-tolerant workflow scheduling using spot instances on clouds. *Procedia Computer Science*, 29:523–533, 2014.

[25] C. M. Ramsay. Exact waiting time and queue size distributions for equilibrium M/G/1 queues with Pareto service. *Queueing Systems*, 57(4):147–155, 2007.

[26] C. Reiss, A. Tumanov, G. R. Ganger, R. H. Katz, and M. A. Kozuch. Heterogeneity and dynamicity of clouds at scale: Google trace analysis. In *Proc. of ACM SoCC*, 2012.

[27] S. Ren, Y. He, and F. Xu. Provably-efficient job scheduling for energy and fairness in geographically distributed data centers. In *Proc. of IEEE ICDCS*, 2012.

[28] X. Ren, G. Ananthanarayanan, A. Wierman, and M. Yu. Hopper: Decentralized speculation-aware cluster scheduling at scale. 2015.

[29] G. Sakellari and G. Loukas. A survey of mathematical models, simulation approaches and testbeds used for research in cloud computing. *Simulation Modelling Practice and Theory*, 39:92–103, 2013.

[30] S. Sen, C. Joe-Wong, S. Ha, and M. Chiang. A survey of smart data pricing: Past proposals, current plans, and future trends. *ACM Computing Surveys (CSUR)*, 46(2):15, 2013.

[31] B. Sharma, V. Chudnovsky, J. L. Hellerstein, R. Rifaat, and C. R. Das. Modeling and synthesizing task placement constraints in Google compute clusters. In *Proc. of ACM SoCC*, 2011.

[32] K. Song, Y. Yao, and L. Golubchik. Exploring the profit-reliability trade-off in Amazon's spot instance market: A better pricing mechanism. In *Proc. of IEEE/ACM IWQoS*, 2013.

[33] P. Upadhyaya, M. Balazinska, and D. Suciu. How to price shared optimizations in the cloud. *Proc. of the VLDB Endowment*, 2012.

[34] J. Wilkes and C. Reiss. ClusterData-2011-2. *https://github.com/google/cluster-data*, 2015.

[35] C. Wilson, H. Ballani, T. Karagiannis, and A. Rowtron. Better never than late: Meeting deadlines in datacenter networks. In *ACM SIGCOMM Computer Communication Review*, 2011.

[36] Y. Yao, L. Huang, A. Sharma, L. Golubchik, and M. Neely. Data centers power reduction: A two time scale approach for delay tolerant workloads. In *Proc. of IEEE INFOCOM*, 2012.

[37] M. Zaharia, D. Borthakur, J. Sen Sarma, K. Elmeleegy, S. Shenker, and I. Stoica. Delay scheduling: A simple technique for achieving locality and fairness in cluster scheduling. In *Proc. of EuroSys*, 2010.

[38] Q. Zhang, M. F. Zhani, R. Boutaba, and J. L. Hellerstein. Dynamic heterogeneity-aware resource provisioning in the cloud. *IEEE Trans. on Cloud Computing*, 2(1):14–28, 2014.

[39] L. Zheng, C. Joe-Wong, C. W. Tan, M. Chiang, and X. Wang. How to bid the cloud. In *Proc. of ACM SIGCOMM*, 2015.

[40] Y. Zhou and D. Wentzlaff. The sharing architecture: sub-core configurability for IaaS clouds. In *Proc. of ACM ASPLOS*, pages 559–574, 2014.

The Value of Privacy: Strategic Data Subjects, Incentive Mechanisms and Fundamental Limits

Weina Wang
School of Electrical, Computer and Energy Engineering
Arizona State University
Tempe, AZ 85287
weina.wang@asu.edu

Lei Ying
School of Electrical, Computer and Energy Engineering
Arizona State University
Tempe, AZ 85287
lei.ying.2@asu.edu

Junshan Zhang
School of Electrical, Computer and Energy Engineering
Arizona State University
Tempe, AZ 85287
junshan.zhang@asu.edu

ABSTRACT

We study the value of data privacy in a game-theoretic model of trading private data, where a data collector purchases private data from strategic data subjects (individuals) through an incentive mechanism. The private data of each individual represents her knowledge about an underlying state, which is the information that the data collector desires to learn. Different from most of the existing work on privacy-aware surveys, our model does not assume the data collector to be trustworthy. Then, an individual takes full control of its own data privacy and reports only a privacy-preserving version of her data.

In this paper, the value of ϵ units of privacy is measured by the minimum payment of all nonnegative payment mechanisms, under which an individual's best response at a Nash equilibrium is to report the data with a privacy level of ϵ. The higher ϵ is, the less private the reported data is. We derive lower and upper bounds on the value of privacy which are asymptotically tight as the number of data subjects becomes large. Specifically, the lower bound assures that it is impossible to use less amount of payment to buy ϵ units of privacy, and the upper bound is given by an achievable payment mechanism that we designed. Based on these fundamental limits, we further derive lower and upper bounds on the minimum total payment for the data collector to achieve a given learning accuracy target, and show that the total payment of the designed mechanism is at most one individual's payment away from the minimum.

1. INTRODUCTION

From the monetary coupons offered for revealing opinions of a product to the large-scale trade of personal information by data brokers such as Acxiom [20], the commoditization of private data has been trending up when big data analytics is playing a more and more critical role in advertising, scientific research, etc. However, in the wake of a number of recent scandals, such as the Netflix data breach and the Veterans Affairs data theft, data privacy is emerging as one of the most serious concerns of big data analytics. This raises a fundamental question "whether big-data and privacy can go hand-by-hand or giving up our privacy is inevitable in the big-data era." One common practice of collecting private data is called informed consent. With information on "who is collecting the data, what data is collected, and how the data will be used," data subjects decide upon whether to report data or not. The data collector is supposed to use the data only in the manner disclosed to data subjects. This practice, however, has two fundamental issues: (i) data subjects have no control of data privacy after transferring private data to the data collector; and (ii) the data collector has to take full responsibility of protecting users' private data, which not only costs significant investment on infrastructure and maintenance, but also may lead to reputation damage if data breach occurs. In some applications, such as collecting certain browsing history records to enhance the phishing and malware protection of web browsers [10, 11], the data collectors prefer to avoid holding individuals' raw data for subpoena concerns.

Taking a forward-looking view, we envisage a market model for private data analytics such that private data is treated as a commodity and traded in the market. In particular, the data collector will use an incentive mechanism to pay (or reward) individuals for reporting informative data, and individuals control their own data privacy by reporting noisy data with the appropriate level of privacy protection (or level of noise added) being strategically chosen to maximize their payoffs. A distinctive merit of this privacy protection approach is that data subjects take full control of their own privacy and the data collector gets informative data but does not need to bear the responsibility of protecting data privacy. This differentiates our approach from the existing work [15, 12, 22, 26, 13, 24, 14], where the data collector is assumed to be a trustworthy entity who is willing to and has the capability to protect users' privacy.

One significant challenge of the proposed paradigm is that the data collector has no direct control (perhaps no information either) over the quality of reported data. To tackle this challenge, we cast the problem into a game-theoretic setting, which allows us to quantify two fundamental tradeoffs: the tradeoff between cost and accuracy from the data collector's perspective, and the tradeoff between reward and privacy from an individual's perspective (the value of privacy for a data subject). In return, with the reward (incentive) as the bridge, it establishes the tradeoff of data privacy concerned

SIGMETRICS '16, June 14–18, 2016, Antibes Juan-Les-Pins, France.

ISBN 978-1-4503-4266-7/16/06...$15.00

DOI: http://dx.doi.org/10.1145/2896377.2901461

by an individual versus data quality concerned by the data collector.

Specifically, we consider a game-theoretic model of collecting private data in hypothesis testing, where the data collector is interested in learning information from a population of N individuals. An illustration of our model is shown in Figure 1. The information is represented by a binary random variable W, which is called the *state*. Each individual i possesses a binary *signal* S_i, which is her private data, representing her knowledge about the state W. Conditional on the state W, the signals are independently generated such that the probability for each signal S_i to be the same as W is θ, where $0.5 < \theta < 1$. To protect her privacy, an individual reports only a privacy-preserving version of her signal, denoted by X_i, or chooses to not participate after considering both the payment from the data collector and the loss of privacy. The data collector needs to decide the amount of payment and the payment mechanism to get informative reports, i.e., not completely random data. Intuitively, the higher the payment is, the more informative the reported data should be. We will answer the following fundamental questions in this paper: *What is the minimum payment needed from the data collector to obtain reported data with a privacy level ϵ? Which payment mechanism can be used to collect private data with minimum cost?* This setting without accounting for data privacy has garnered much attention in the literature (see, e.g., [23, 1, 21]), including the application of estimating the underlying value of a new technology by eliciting opinions from individuals.

Intuitively, the data collector can purchase more informative data (so higher privacy) by offering higher payment. However, the strategic behavior of the privacy-aware individuals makes this more complicated. Due to privacy concerns, an individual's action/strategy is the conditional distributions of the reported data given the realizations of the signal. But the actions of the individuals are not observable to the data collector. Instead, what the data collector receives is the reported data, generated randomly according to the individuals' strategies, so the payments can only be designed based on the reported data. This differs our problem from the conventional mechanism design.

Furthermore, the privacy-aware individuals weigh the privacy loss against the payment to choose the best quantity of privacy to trade. To make an individual willing to trade ϵ level of privacy, the data collector needs to make sure doing this benefits the individual most. We reiterate that the data collector has access only to the reported data instead of the individuals' actions. Note that only compensating the privacy cost incurred is not sufficient. The payment mechanism needs to ensure that ϵ is the best privacy level such that when an individual uses a less-private strategy, the decrease in her payment is faster than the decrease in her privacy cost, and similarly, when an individual uses a more-private strategy, the increase in her payment is slower than the increase in her privacy cost. In other words, with a game-theoretic approach, we consider an individual's best response in a Nash equilibrium, and the value of data privacy is measured by the minimum payment that makes this equilibrium strategy have a privacy level of ϵ, which represents the monetary value of data privacy in a market for private data.

Summary of Main Results

It is assumed that individuals use the celebrated notion of differential privacy [8, 7] to evaluate their data privacy. When an individual i uses an ϵ-differentially private randomization strategy to generate X_i, the privacy loss incurred is ϵ, and the individual's cost of privacy loss is a function of ϵ, whose form is assumed to be publicly known. The value of ϵ units of privacy, denoted by $V(\epsilon)$, is measured by the minimum payment of all nonnegative payment mechanisms under which an individual's best response in a Nash equilibrium is to report the data with privacy level ϵ, where nonnegativity ensures that individuals would not be *charged* for reporting data. We are interested in the range that $\epsilon > 0$, simply because when $\epsilon = 0$, the reported data is independent of the private data and thus would be of no use for data analysis. Our contributions are summarized as follows:

1. We establish a lower bound on $V(\epsilon)$. First we characterize the strategies of individuals at a Nash equilibrium to prove that from a payment perspective, it suffices to focus on nonnegative payment mechanisms at which the best response of an individual in a Nash equilibrium is a symmetric randomized response with a privacy level of ϵ. This strategy generates the reported data by flipping the signal with probability $\frac{1}{e^{\epsilon}+1}$: for convenience, this is called the ϵ-strategy. Next we prove that the expected payments resulting from any Nash equilibrium of any payment mechanism can be "replicated" by a genie-aided payment mechanism, where the payments are determined with the aid of a genie who knows the underlying state W. This makes the analysis of the Nash equilibria more tractable by decoupling the individuals in the payments. The lower bound is then given by necessary conditions for ϵ to be the best privacy level in the genie-aided mechanism. We remark that although the genie-aided mechanism that achieves the lower bound is not implementable, it can be well-approximated, when the number of individuals is large, by the feasible payment mechanism that we design to establish the upper bound.

2. We observe that the equilibrium strategies exhibit some interesting characteristics: the strategy of an individual in a Nash equilibrium is either a symmetric randomized response, which treats the realizations of the private signal symmetrically, or a non-informative strategy, where the reported data is independent of the signal. This characterization holds regardless of the prior distribution of the state, and it also holds for more general probability models of the signals. This characterization advances our understanding of the behavior of privacy-aware individuals. It is worth pointing out that finding an equilibrium strategy of a privacy-aware individual under some payment mechanism involves non-convex optimization.

3. We prove an upper bound on $V(\epsilon)$ by designing a payment mechanism $\boldsymbol{R}^{(N,\epsilon)}$, in which the strategy profile consisting of ϵ-strategies constitutes a Nash equilibrium. The expected payment to each individual at this equilibrium gives an upper bound on $V(\epsilon)$. This upper bound converges to the lower bound exponentially fast as the number of individuals N becomes large, which indicates that the lower and upper bounds are asymptotically tight.

4. The above fundamental bounds on the value of privacy can be further used to study the *payment–accuracy prob-*

lem, where the data collector aims to minimize the total payment while achieving an accuracy target in learning the state W. Given an accuracy target τ, which can be regarded as the maximum allowable error, let $F(\tau)$ denote the minimum total payment for achieving τ. We obtain lower and upper bounds on $F(\tau)$ based on the lower and upper bounds on the value of privacy. The upper bound is given by the designed mechanism $\boldsymbol{R}^{(N,\epsilon)}$ with properly chosen parameters, which shows that the total payment of the designed mechanism is at most one individual's payment away from the minimum.

2. RELATED WORK

Most existing work on privacy-aware surveys [15, 12, 22, 26, 13, 24, 14] assumes that there is a trusted data curator or data collector. The private data is either already kept by the data collector, or is elicited using mechanisms that are designed with the aim of truthfulness. What the data collector purchases is the "right" of using individuals' data in an announced way. Our work differs from the existing work by considering a data collector who is not trusted by individuals. In this scenario, the data collector directly purchases the private data, in which privacy is embedded.

In the seminal work by Ghosh and Roth [15], individuals' data is already known to the data collector, and individuals bid their costs of privacy loss caused by data usage, where each individual's privacy cost is modeled as a linear function of ϵ if her data is used in an ϵ-differentially private manner. The goal of the mechanism design is to elicit truthful bids of individuals' cost functions, i.e., the coefficients. Subsequent work [12, 22, 26, 24] explores various models for individuals' valuation of privacy, especially the correlation between the coefficients and the private bits.

This line of work has been extended to the scenario that the data is not available yet and needs to be reported by the individuals to the data collector, but the data collector is still trusted [13, 33, 3, 14]. Notably, Ghosh, Ligett and Roth [14] study the model in which the collected data is non-verifiable. The goal of the mechanism design there is to incentivize truthful data reporting (without adding any noise) from individuals. For more work on the interplay between differential privacy and mechanism design, Pai and Roth [25] give a comprehensive survey.

The local model of differential privacy, which is a generalization of randomized response [32] and is formalized in [19], has been studied in the literature [8, 7, 16, 6, 9, 18, 29, 30, 2, 27]. The hypothesis testing formulation in our paper is similar to a setting in [18], where the authors find an optimal mechanism that maximizes the statistical discrimination of the hypotheses subject to local differential privacy constraint. In practice, Google's Chrome web browser has implemented the RAPPOR mechanism [10, 11] to collect users' data, which guarantees that only limited privacy will be leaked by using randomized response in a novel manner. However, users may still not be willing to report data in the desired way due to the lack of an incentive mechanism.

3. SYSTEM MODEL

We consider a single-bit learning problem with privacy-aware individuals as shown in Figure 1. Recall that the data collector is interested in learning the state W, which is a binary random variable. For example, the state W can describe the underlying value of some new technology. Let P_W denote the prior PMF of W. We assume that $P_W(1) > 0$ and $P_W(0) > 0$.

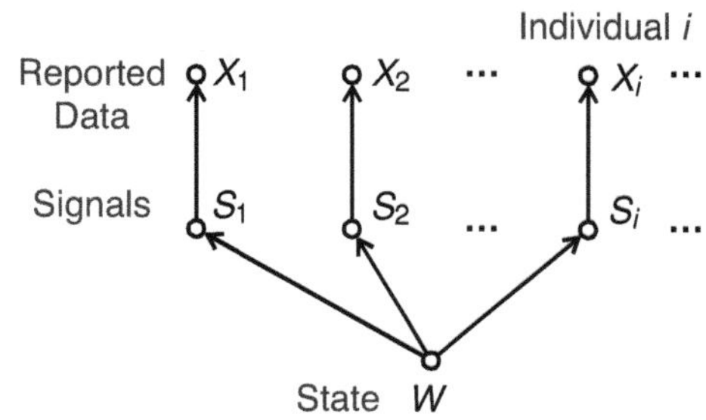

Figure 1: Information structure of the model: The data collector is interested in the state W, which is a binary random variable. Each individual i possesses her private data, which is a binary signal S_i. Conditioned on W, $S_1, S_2, \dots, S_N$ are i.i.d. Individual i's reported data is X_i, which is generated based on S_i using a randomized strategy.

Individuals and Strategies. Consider a population of N individuals and denote the set of individuals by $\mathcal{N} = \{1, 2, \dots, N\}$. Denote all individuals other than some given individual i by "$-i$." Each individual i possesses a binary signal S_i, which is her private data, reflecting her knowledge about the state W. For example, S_i can represent individual i's opinion towards the new technology. Let $\boldsymbol{S} = (S_1, S_2, \cdots, S_N)$. Conditional on the state W, the signals $S_1, S_2, \dots, S_N$ are i.i.d. with the following conditional distributions:

$$\mathbb{P}(S_i = 1 \mid W = 1) = \theta, \quad \mathbb{P}(S_i = 0 \mid W = 1) = 1 - \theta,$$
$$\mathbb{P}(S_i = 0 \mid W = 0) = \theta, \quad \mathbb{P}(S_i = 1 \mid W = 0) = 1 - \theta,$$

where the parameter θ with $0.5 < \theta < 1$ is called *the quality of signals.*

Let X_i denote the data reported by individual i and let $\boldsymbol{X} = (X_1, X_2, \dots, X_N)$. The acceptable values for reported data are 0, 1, and "nonparticipation." So X_i takes values in the set $\mathcal{X} = \{0, 1, \perp\}$, where $\perp$ indicates that individual i declines to participate. A strategy of individual i for data reporting is a mapping $\sigma_i \colon \{0, 1\} \to \mathcal{D}(\mathcal{X})$, where $\mathcal{D}(\mathcal{X})$ is the set of probability distributions on $\mathcal{X}$. Let $\boldsymbol{\sigma} = (\sigma_1, \sigma_2, \dots, \sigma_N)$. The strategy σ_i prescribes a distribution to X_i for each possible value of S_i, which defines the conditional distribution of X_i given S_i. Since we will discuss different strategies of individual i, we let $\mathbb{P}_{\sigma_i}(X_i = x_i \mid S_i = s_i)$ with $x_i \in \mathcal{X}$ and $s_i \in \{0, 1\}$ denote the conditional probabilities defined by strategy σ_i. If a strategy σ_i satisfies that $\mathbb{P}_{\sigma_i}(X_i = 1 \mid S_i = 1) = \mathbb{P}_{\sigma_i}(X_i = 0 \mid S_i = 0)$ and $\mathbb{P}_{\sigma_i}(X_i = \perp \mid S_i = 1) = \mathbb{P}_{\sigma_i}(X_i = \perp \mid S_i = 0) = 0$, we say σ_i is a *symmetric randomized response.* If a strategy σ_i makes X_i and S_i independent, we say σ_i is *non-informative*; otherwise we say σ_i is *informative.*

Mechanism. The data collector uses a payment mechanism $\boldsymbol{R} \colon \mathcal{X}^N \to \mathbb{R}^N$ to determine the amount of payment to each individual, where $R_i(\boldsymbol{x})$ is the payment to individual i when the reported data is $\boldsymbol{X} = \boldsymbol{x}$. We are interested in payment mechanisms in which the payment to each individual is nonnegative, i.e., $R_i(\boldsymbol{x}) \geq 0$ for any individual i and any $\boldsymbol{x} \in \mathcal{X}^N$, which we call *nonnegative mechanisms.*

This constraint is motivated by the fact that in many practical applications such as surveys, the data collector has no means to charge users and can only use payments to incentivize user participation.

Privacy Cost. We quantify the privacy loss incurred when a strategy is in use by the level of (local) differential privacy [8, 7, 19, 9] of the strategy, defined as follows.

DEFINITION 1. *The level of (local) differential privacy, or simply the privacy level, of a strategy σ_i, denoted by $\zeta(\sigma_i)$, is defined to be*

$$\zeta(\sigma_i) = \max\left\{ \ln\left(\frac{\mathbb{P}_{\sigma_i}(X_i \in \mathcal{E} \mid S_i = s_i)}{\mathbb{P}_{\sigma_i}(X_i \in \mathcal{E} \mid S_i = 1 - s_i)} \right) : \mathcal{E} \subseteq \{0, 1, \perp\}, s_i \in \{0, 1\} \right\},$$

where we follow the convention that $0/0 = 1$, and the strategy σ_i is said to be $\zeta(\sigma_i)$-differentially private.

The level of differential privacy quantifies the indistinguishablity between the conditional distributions of the reported data given different values of the signal, therefore measuring how disclosive the strategy is. Note that the amount of privacy leakage quantified by differential privacy is "in addition" to what the adversaries already know. We refer the reader to [8] for more semantic implications of differential privacy.

The privacy loss causes a cost to an individual. We assume that when using strategies with the same privacy level, individuals experience the same cost of privacy. Thus, we model each individual's cost of privacy by a function g of the privacy level. We call g the *cost function* and the cost the *privacy cost.* Our results can be extended to the case where the cost functions are heterogeneous (see the discussion in Section 4.3). We assume that the form of g is publicly known (Ghosh and Roth [15] and subsequent work study the scenario that cost functions are private and design truthful mechanisms to elicit them).

We say the cost function g is *proper* if it satisfies the following three conditions:

$$g(\xi) \geq 0, \quad \forall \xi \geq 0, \tag{1}$$

$$g(0) = 0, \tag{2}$$

$$g \text{ is non-decreasing}, \tag{3}$$

where (1) follows from the fact that a privacy cost is nonnegative, (2) indicates that the privacy cost is 0 when the reported data is independent of the private data, and (3) means that the privacy cost will not decrease when the privacy loss becomes larger. In this paper, we will focus on a proper cost function that is convex, continuously differentiable, and $g(\xi) = 0$ only for $\xi = 0$. With a little abuse of notation, we also use $g(\sigma_i)$ to denote $g(\zeta(\sigma_i))$, which is the privacy cost to individual i when the strategy σ_i is used.

Game Formulation and Nash Equilibrium. In this market model, the data collector first announces a payment mechanism. Then this mechanism induces a strategic form game where the individuals are the players. The utility of each individual is the difference between her payment and her privacy cost. We assume that the individuals are risk neutral, i.e., they are interested in maximizing their expected utility. In this game, the prior distribution P_W, the signal quality parameter θ, the form of the payment mechanism $\boldsymbol{R}$ and the cost function g are common knowledge.

We focus on Nash equilibria of a payment mechanism, where each individual has no incentive to unilaterally change her strategy given other individuals' strategies. Formally, a Nash equilibrium in our model is defined as follows.

DEFINITION 2. *A strategy profile $\boldsymbol{\sigma}$ is a Nash equilibrium in a payment mechanism $\boldsymbol{R}$ if for any individual i and any strategy σ_i',*

$$\mathbb{E}_{\boldsymbol{\sigma}}[R_i(\boldsymbol{X}) - g(\sigma_i)] \geq \mathbb{E}_{(\sigma_i', \boldsymbol{\sigma}_{-i})}[R_i(\boldsymbol{X}) - g(\sigma_i')],$$

where the expectation is over the reported data $\boldsymbol{X}$, and the subscripts $\boldsymbol{\sigma}$ and $(\sigma_i', \boldsymbol{\sigma}_{-i})$ indicate that $\boldsymbol{X}$ is generated by the strategy profile $\boldsymbol{\sigma}$ and $(\sigma_i', \boldsymbol{\sigma}_{-i})$, respectively.

4. THE VALUE OF DATA PRIVACY

We say that the data collector *obtains* ϵ units of privacy from an individual i in a payment mechanism if individual i's best response in a Nash equilibrium of the mechanism is to report data with a privacy level of ϵ. Recall that we are interested in the regime $\epsilon > 0$ since the data collector wants the reported data to be useful for data analysis. Let $\mathcal{R}(i;\epsilon)$ denote the set of nonnegative payment mechanisms in which the data collector obtains ϵ units of privacy from individual i. Then we measure the value of ϵ units of privacy by the minimum payment to individual i of all mechanisms in $\mathcal{R}(i;\epsilon)$. Note that this measure does not depend on the specific identity of i due to the symmetry across individuals. For any mechanism $\boldsymbol{R} \in \mathcal{R}(i;\epsilon)$, let $\boldsymbol{\sigma}^{(\boldsymbol{R};\epsilon)}$ denote the corresponding Nash equilibrium. Then, formally, the value of ϵ units of privacy is measured by

$$V(\epsilon) = \inf_{\boldsymbol{R} \in \mathcal{R}(i;\epsilon)} \mathbb{E}_{\boldsymbol{\sigma}^{(\boldsymbol{R};\epsilon)}}[R_i(\boldsymbol{X})]. \tag{4}$$

In this section, we first derive a lower bound on $V(\epsilon)$ by characterizing the Nash equilibria and replicating mechanisms in $\mathcal{R}(i;\epsilon)$ by genie-aided mechanisms. We then design a payment mechanism in $\mathcal{R}(i;\epsilon)$, and consequently the equilibrium payment to individual i in this mechanism serves as an upper bound of $V(\epsilon)$. The gap between the lower and upper bounds diminishes to zero exponentially fast as the number of individuals becomes large, which indicates that the lower and upper bounds are asymptotically tight.

4.1 Lower Bound

We present a lower bound on $V(\epsilon)$ in Theorem 1 below. For convenience, we define

$$V_{\mathrm{LB}}(\epsilon) = g'(\epsilon) \frac{e^{\epsilon} + 1}{e^{\epsilon}} \left(\frac{\theta}{2\theta - 1}(e^{\epsilon} + 1) - 1 \right), \tag{5}$$

where g' is the derivative of the privacy cost function of an individual and θ is the quality of signals.

THEOREM 1. *The value of ϵ units of privacy measured in (4) for any $\epsilon > 0$ is lower bounded as $V(\epsilon) \geq V_{\mathrm{LB}}(\epsilon)$. Specifically, for any nonnegative payment mechanism $\boldsymbol{R}$, if the strategy of an individual i in a Nash equilibrium has a privacy level of ϵ with $\epsilon > 0$, then the expected payment to individual i at this equilibrium is lower bounded by $V_{\mathrm{LB}}(\epsilon)$.*

We remark that the lower bound in Theorem 1 can be achieved by a hypothetical payment mechanism in which a genie who knows the realization of the underlying state W guides the data collector on how much to pay each individual. Intuitively, the knowledge of the state W provides more information about the system, which helps the data collector to obtain privacy with less payment. While it may sound like a chicken-and-egg problem as the data collector's sole purpose of paying individuals for their private data is to learn the state W, it will become clear that the philosophy carries over and the data collector should utilize the best estimate of W in the payment mechanism to minimize the payment. The insight we gain from this mechanism sheds light on the asymptotically tight upper bound on the value of privacy in Section 4.2.

This genie-aided payment mechanism, denoted by $\widehat{\boldsymbol{R}}^{(\epsilon)}$, determines the payment to each individual i based on her own reported data X_i and the state W as follows:

$$\widehat{R}_i^{(\epsilon)}(X_i, W) = \frac{g'(\epsilon)(e^{\epsilon}+1)^2}{2e^{\epsilon}}\widehat{A}_{X_i,W}, \qquad (6)$$

where

$$\widehat{A}_{1,1} = \frac{1}{(2\theta-1)P_W(1)}, \quad \widehat{A}_{0,0} = \frac{1}{(2\theta-1)P_W(0)},$$
$$\widehat{A}_{0,1} = \widehat{A}_{1,0} = 0.$$

In this mechanism, it can be proved that the best response of individual i is the following symmetric randomized response, denoted by $\sigma_i^{(\epsilon)}$, which is ϵ-differentially private:

$$\mathbb{P}_{\sigma_i^{(\epsilon)}}(X_i = 1 \mid S_i = 1) = \mathbb{P}_{\sigma_i^{(\epsilon)}}(X_i = 0 \mid S_i = 0) = \frac{e^{\epsilon}}{e^{\epsilon}+1},$$
$$\mathbb{P}_{\sigma_i^{(\epsilon)}}(X_i = 1 \mid S_i = 0) = \mathbb{P}_{\sigma_i^{(\epsilon)}}(X_i = 0 \mid S_i = 1) = \frac{1}{e^{\epsilon}+1},$$
$$\mathbb{P}_{\sigma_i^{(\epsilon)}}(X_i = \perp \mid S_i = 1) = \mathbb{P}_{\sigma_i^{(\epsilon)}}(X_i = \perp \mid S_i = 0) = 0.$$

For convenience, we will refer to this strategy as the *ϵ-strategy.* The expected payment to individual i at this strategy equals to the lower bound in Theorem 1.

Next we sketch the proof of Theorem 1. We first give three lemmas that form the basis of the proof, and then present the proof based on that. The proofs of these lemmas can be found in our technical report [31].

4.1.1 Characterization of Nash Equilibria

We first characterize individuals' behavior in a Nash equilibrium. In general, an ϵ-differentially private strategy has uncountably many possible forms. However, provided that the strategy is part of a Nash equilibrium (i.e., a best response of an individual), the following lemma substantially reduces the space of possibilities. We remark that a similar phenomenon for privacy-aware individuals has been observed in [4] in a different setting.

LEMMA 1. *In any nonnegative payment mechanism, an individual's strategy in a Nash equilibrium is either a symmetric randomized response, or a non-informative strategy.*

We remark that Lemma 1 holds for more general probability models of the signals. The proof carries over as long as the support of the joint distribution of the signals is the entire domain $\{0,1\}^N$.

By Lemma 1, if an individual's strategy in a Nash equilibrium has a privacy level of ϵ, where $\epsilon > 0$, this equilibrium strategy is either the ϵ-strategy or the $(-\epsilon)$-strategy. The following lemma says that from the payment perspective, it suffices to further focus on the case that it is the ϵ-strategy.

LEMMA 2. *For any nonnegative payment mechanism $\boldsymbol{R}$ in which the strategy profile $(\sigma_i^{(-\epsilon)}, \boldsymbol{\sigma}_{-i})$ with some $\epsilon > 0$ is a Nash equilibrium, there exists another nonnegative payment mechanism $\boldsymbol{R}'$ in which $(\sigma_i^{(\epsilon)}, \boldsymbol{\sigma}_{-i})$ is a Nash equilibrium, and the expected payment to each individual at these two equilibria of the two mechanisms are the same.*

This lemma is proved by considering the payment mechanism $\boldsymbol{R}'$ that is constructed by applying $\boldsymbol{R}$ on the reported data after modifying X_i to $1 - X_i$.

4.1.2 Genie-Aided Payment Mechanism

A genie-aided payment mechanism $\widehat{\boldsymbol{R}}\colon \mathcal{X}^N \times \{0,1\} \to \mathbb{R}^N$ determines the payment to an individual based on not only the reported data $\boldsymbol{X}$ but also the underlying state W. Compared with a standard payment mechanism, a genie-aided mechanism is hypothetical since the data collector has access to the underlying state, as if she were aided by a genie. We consider nonnegative genie-aided payment mechanisms where $\widehat{R}_i(\boldsymbol{X}, W)$, the payment to individual i, depends on only her own reported data X_i and the underlying state W. We write $\widehat{R}_i(X_i, W)$ to represent $\widehat{R}_i(\boldsymbol{X}, W)$ for conciseness. Therefore, for each individual i, a genie-aided mechanism makes use of the information of W but discards the information in $\boldsymbol{X}_{-i}$. The following lemma shows that the expected payments resulting from any Nash equilibrium of any payment mechanism can be replicated by a genie-aided payment mechanism with the same Nash equilibrium. Thus we can restrict our attention to genie-aided mechanisms to obtain a lower bound on the value of privacy.

LEMMA 3. *For any nonnegative payment mechanism $\boldsymbol{R}$ and any Nash equilibrium $\boldsymbol{\sigma}$ of it, there exists a nonnegative genie-aided mechanism $\widehat{\boldsymbol{R}}$, such that $\boldsymbol{\sigma}$ is also a Nash equilibrium of $\widehat{\boldsymbol{R}}$ and the expected payment to each individual at this equilibrium is the same under $\boldsymbol{R}$ and $\widehat{\boldsymbol{R}}$.*

This lemma is proved by constructing the following genie-aided payment mechanism $\widehat{\boldsymbol{R}}$ according to the desired equilibrium $\boldsymbol{\sigma}$: for any individual i and any $x_i \in \mathcal{X}, w \in \{0,1\}$,

$$\widehat{R}_i(x_i, w) = \overline{R}_i(x_i; w) := \mathbb{E}_{\boldsymbol{\sigma}}[R_i(\boldsymbol{X}) \mid X_i = x_i, W = w].$$

Our intuition is as follows. A genie-aided mechanism can use the state W to generate an incentive to individual i, which "mimics" the incentive provided by the reported data $\boldsymbol{X}_{-i}$ of others. The above genie-aided payment mechanism $\widehat{\boldsymbol{R}}$ is constructed such that no matter what strategy individual i uses, her expected utility is the same under $\boldsymbol{R}$ and $\widehat{\boldsymbol{R}}$. Since an individual calculates her best response according to the expected utility, her equilibrium behavior and expected payment are the same under $\widehat{\boldsymbol{R}}$ and $\boldsymbol{R}$. We remark that the Nash equilibria of a genie-aided mechanism are much easier to analyze since the individuals are decoupled in the payments and thus an individual's strategy does not have an influence on other individuals' utility.

Let $\widehat{\mathcal{R}}(i;\epsilon)$ denote the set of nonnegative genie-aided payment mechanisms in which the ϵ-strategy is an individual i's strategy in a Nash equilibrium, and let $\sigma_i^{(\epsilon)}$ denote the ϵ-strategy. Consider

$$\widehat{V}(\epsilon) = \inf_{\widehat{\boldsymbol{R}} \in \widehat{\mathcal{R}}(i;\epsilon)} \mathbb{E}_{\sigma_i^{(\epsilon)}}\left[\widehat{R}_i(X_i, W)\right],$$

which is a definition similar to the value of ϵ units of privacy, $V(\epsilon)$, measured in (4). Then $\widehat{V}(\epsilon) \leq V(\epsilon)$ for the following reasons. Consider any $\boldsymbol{R} \in \mathcal{R}(i;\epsilon)$, i.e., any nonnegative payment mechanism $\boldsymbol{R}$ in which individual i's strategy in a Nash equilibrium has a privacy level of ϵ. With Lemma 1 and 2, we can assume without loss of generality that this equilibrium strategy is the ϵ-strategy. Then by Lemma 3, we can map $\boldsymbol{R}$ to a $\widehat{\boldsymbol{R}} \in \widehat{\mathcal{R}}(i;\epsilon)$, such that

$$\mathbb{E}_{\boldsymbol{\sigma}(\boldsymbol{R};\epsilon)}[R_i(\boldsymbol{X})] = \mathbb{E}_{\sigma_i^{(\epsilon)}}\left[\widehat{R}_i(X_i, W)\right].$$

Therefore, the infimum over $\widehat{\mathcal{R}}(i;\epsilon)$ is no greater than the infimum over $\mathcal{R}(i;\epsilon)$, i.e., $\widehat{V}(\epsilon) \leq V(\epsilon)$.

4.1.3 Proof of Theorem 1

With Lemma 1, 2 and 3, we can prove the lower bound in Theorem 1 by focusing on the genie-aided mechanisms in $\widehat{\mathcal{R}}(i;\epsilon)$. Then there is no need to consider the strategies of individuals other than individual i since a genie-aided mechanism pays individual i only according to X_i and W. A necessary condition for the ϵ-strategy to be a best response of individual i is that ϵ yields no worse expected payment than other privacy levels. We utilize this necessary condition to obtain a lower bound on the expected payment to individual i, which gives a lower bound on $\widehat{V}(\epsilon)$ and further proves the lower bound in Theorem 1.

Proof of Theorem 1. By Lemma 1, 2 and 3, it suffices to focus on nonnegative genie-aided payment mechanisms in which the ϵ-strategy is an individual i's strategy in a Nash equilibrium, i.e., mechanisms in $\widehat{\mathcal{R}}(i;\epsilon)$. Consider any $\widehat{\boldsymbol{R}} \in \widehat{\mathcal{R}}(i;\epsilon)$ and denote the ϵ-strategy by $\sigma_i^{(\epsilon)}$. Consider the ξ-strategy of individual i with any $\xi \geq 0$ and denote it by $\sigma_i^{(\xi)}$. Then the expected utility of individual i at the strategy $\sigma_i^{(\xi)}$ can be written as

$$\begin{aligned}
&\mathbb{E}_{\sigma_i^{(\xi)}}\left[\widehat{R}_i(X_i, W)\right] - g(\sigma_i^{(\xi)}) \\
&= \sum_{x_i, s_i, w} \mathbb{P}_{\sigma_i^{(\xi)}}(X_i = x_i \mid S_i = s_i)\mathbb{P}(S_i = s_i, W = w)\widehat{R}_i(x_i, w) \\
&\quad - g(\xi), \\
&= \overline{K}_1 \frac{e^{\xi}}{e^{\xi}+1} + \overline{K}_0 \frac{1}{e^{\xi}+1} + \overline{K} - g(\xi),
\end{aligned}$$

where

$$\begin{aligned}
\overline{K}_1 &= \{\widehat{R}_i(1,1)P_W(1)\theta + \widehat{R}_i(1,0)P_W(0)(1-\theta)\} \\
&\quad - \{\widehat{R}_i(0,1)P_W(1)\theta + \widehat{R}_i(0,0)P_W(0)(1-\theta)\}, \\
\overline{K}_0 &= \{\widehat{R}_i(1,1)P_W(1)(1-\theta) + \widehat{R}_i(1,0)P_W(0)\theta\} \\
&\quad - \{\widehat{R}_i(0,1)P_W(1)(1-\theta) + \widehat{R}_i(0,0)P_W(0)\theta\}, \\
\overline{K} &= \widehat{R}_i(0,1)P_W(1) + \widehat{R}_i(0,0)P_W(0).
\end{aligned}$$

It can be seen that $\overline{K}_1$, $\overline{K}_0$ and $\overline{K}$ do not depend on ξ. Let this expected utility define a function f of ξ; i.e.,

$$f(\xi) = \overline{K}_1 \frac{e^{\xi}}{e^{\xi}+1} + \overline{K}_0 \frac{1}{e^{\xi}+1} - g(\xi) + \overline{K}.$$

Then a necessary condition for the ϵ-strategy to be an equilibrium strategy is that ϵ maximizes $f(\xi)$, which implies that $f'(\epsilon) = 0$ since $\epsilon > 0$. Since

$$f'(\xi) = (\overline{K}_1 - \overline{K}_0)\frac{e^{\xi}}{(e^{\xi}+1)^2} - g'(\xi),$$

setting $f'(\epsilon) = 0$ yields that

$$\overline{K}_1 - \overline{K}_0 = g'(\epsilon)\frac{(e^{\epsilon}+1)^2}{e^{\epsilon}}. \tag{7}$$

Now we calculate the expected payment to individual i at the ϵ-strategy:

$$\mathbb{E}_{\sigma_i^{(\epsilon)}}\left[\widehat{R}_i(X_i, W)\right] = -(\overline{K}_1 - \overline{K}_0)\frac{1}{e^{\epsilon}+1} + (\overline{K}_1 + \overline{K}).$$

By definition,

$$\begin{aligned}
\overline{K}_1 + \overline{K} &= \widehat{R}_i(1,1)P_W(1)\theta + \widehat{R}_i(1,0)P_W(0)(1-\theta) \\
&\quad + \widehat{R}_i(0,1)P_W(1)(1-\theta) + \widehat{R}_i(0,0)P_W(0)\theta,
\end{aligned}$$

and

$$\begin{aligned}
\overline{K}_1 - \overline{K}_0 &= \big(\widehat{R}_i(1,1) - \widehat{R}_i(0,1)\big)P_W(1)(2\theta-1) \\
&\quad + \big(\widehat{R}_i(0,0) - \widehat{R}_i(1,0)\big)P_W(0)(2\theta-1).
\end{aligned}$$

Therefore,

$$\begin{aligned}
\overline{K}_1 + \overline{K} &= \frac{\theta}{2\theta-1}(\overline{K}_1 - \overline{K}_0) \\
&\quad + \widehat{R}_i(1,0)P_W(0) + \widehat{R}_i(0,1)P_W(1) \\
&\geq \frac{\theta}{2\theta-1}(\overline{K}_1 - \overline{K}_0) \\
&= g'(\epsilon)\frac{(e^{\epsilon}+1)^2}{e^{\epsilon}}\frac{\theta}{2\theta-1},
\end{aligned}$$

where we have used the nonnegativity of $\widehat{\boldsymbol{R}}$. Then the expected payment to individual i is bounded as follows:

$$\begin{aligned}
&\mathbb{E}_{\sigma_i^{(\epsilon)}}\left[\widehat{R}_i(X_i, W)\right] \\
&= -(\overline{K}_1 - \overline{K}_0)\frac{1}{e^{\epsilon}+1} + (\overline{K}_1 + \overline{K}) \\
&\geq g'(\epsilon)\frac{e^{\epsilon}+1}{e^{\epsilon}}\left(\frac{\theta}{2\theta-1}(e^{\epsilon}+1) - 1\right),
\end{aligned} \tag{8}$$

which proves the lower bound. □

Now beyond the proof, we take a moment to check when this lower bound can be achieved. To achieve the lower bound, we need the equality in (8) to hold and the equation (7) to be satisfied, which is equivalent to the following conditions:

$$\widehat{R}_i(1,0) = 0, \tag{9}$$

$$\widehat{R}_i(0,1) = 0, \tag{10}$$

$$(2\theta-1)\Big(\widehat{R}_i(1,1)P_W(1) + \widehat{R}_i(0,0)P_W(0)\Big) = g'(\epsilon)\frac{(e^{\epsilon}+1)^2}{e^{\epsilon}}. \tag{11}$$

It is easy to check that the genie-aided payment mechanism $\widehat{\boldsymbol{R}}^{(\epsilon)}$ defined in (6) is in $\widehat{\mathcal{R}}(i;\epsilon)$ and satisfies (9)–(11), and therefore achieves the lower bound. Can this lower bound be achieved by a standard nonnegative payment mechanism? Consider any payment mechanism $\boldsymbol{R} \in \mathcal{R}(i;\epsilon)$. Following similar arguments, we can prove that to achieve the lower bound, $\boldsymbol{R}$ needs to satisfy the following conditions:

$$\overline{R}_i(1;0) = 0, \tag{12}$$

$$\overline{R}_i(0;1) = 0, \tag{13}$$

$$(2\theta - 1)\big(\overline{R}_i(1;1)P_W(1) + \overline{R}_i(0;0)P_W(0)\big) = g'(\epsilon)\frac{(e^\epsilon + 1)^2}{e^\epsilon}, \tag{14}$$

where recall that $\overline{R}_i(x_i;w) = \mathbb{E}_{\boldsymbol{\sigma}^{(\boldsymbol{R},\epsilon)}}[R_i(\boldsymbol{X}) \mid X_i = x_i, W = w]$ for $x_i, w \in \{0,1\}$. It can be proved that if $\boldsymbol{R}$ satisfies (12) and (13), then $R_i(\boldsymbol{x}) = 0$ for any $\boldsymbol{x} \in \mathcal{X}^N$, which contradicts (14). Therefore, no standard nonnegative payment mechanism can achieve the lower bound. However, as will be shown in the next section, we can design a class of standard nonnegative payment mechanisms such that the expected payment approaches the lower bound as the number of individuals increases. The design follows the insights indicated by the genie-aided mechanism $\widehat{\boldsymbol{R}}^{(\epsilon)}$: to minimize the payment, the data collector should utilize the best estimate of W in the payment mechanism based on the noisy reports.

4.2 Upper Bound

We present an upper bound on $V(\epsilon)$ in Theorem 2 below. For convenience, we define

$$d = \frac{1}{2}\ln\frac{(e^\epsilon + 1)^2}{4(\theta e^\epsilon + 1 - \theta)((1-\theta)e^\epsilon + \theta)}, \tag{15}$$

where θ is the quality of signal. Note that $d > 0$ for any $\epsilon > 0$. Recall that $V_{\mathrm{LB}}(\epsilon)$ is the lower bound in Theorem 1.

THEOREM 2. *The value of ϵ units of privacy measured in (4) is upper bounded as $V(\epsilon) \le V_{\mathrm{LB}}(\epsilon) + O(e^{-Nd})$, where the $O(\cdot)$ is for $N \to \infty$. Specifically, there exists a nonnegative payment mechanism $\boldsymbol{R}^{(N,\epsilon)}$ in which the strategy profile $\boldsymbol{\sigma}^{(\epsilon)}$ consisting of ϵ-strategies is a Nash equilibrium, and the expected payment to each individual i at this equilibrium is upper bounded by $V_{\mathrm{LB}}(\epsilon) + O(e^{-Nd})$.*

Comparing this upper bound with the lower bound $V_{\mathrm{LB}}(\epsilon)$ in Theorem 1 we can see that the gap between the lower and upper bounds is just the term $O(e^{-Nd})$, which diminishes to zero exponentially fast as N goes to infinity.

We present the payment mechanism $\boldsymbol{R}^{(N,\epsilon)}$ in Section 4.2.1. We will show that under $\boldsymbol{R}^{(N,\epsilon)}$, the strategy profile $\boldsymbol{\sigma}^{(\epsilon)}$ consisting of ϵ-strategies is a Nash equilibrium. Therefore, $\boldsymbol{R}^{(N,\epsilon)}$ is a member of $\mathcal{R}(i;\epsilon)$, and the payment to individual i at $\boldsymbol{\sigma}^{(\epsilon)}$ gives an upper bound on the value of privacy.

The design of $\boldsymbol{R}^{(N,\epsilon)}$ is enlightened by the hypothetical payment mechanism $\widehat{\boldsymbol{R}}^{(\epsilon)}$ defined in (6). But without direct access to the state W, the mechanism $\boldsymbol{R}^{(N,\epsilon)}$ relies on the reported data from an individual i's peers, i.e., individuals other than individual i, to obtain an estimate of W. We borrow the idea of the peer-prediction method [23], which rewards more for the agreement between an individual and her peers to encourage truthful reporting. However, unlike the peer-prediction method, the individuals here have privacy concerns and they will weigh the privacy cost against the payment to choose the best privacy level. We modify the payments in $\widehat{\boldsymbol{R}}^{(\epsilon)}$ to ensure that the ϵ-strategy is still a best response of each individual in $\boldsymbol{R}^{(N,\epsilon)}$, given that other individuals also follow the ϵ-strategy, which yields the desired Nash equilibrium $\boldsymbol{\sigma}^{(\epsilon)}$.

The equilibrium payment to each individual in $\boldsymbol{R}^{(N,\epsilon)}$ converges to the lower bound in Theorem 1 as the number of individuals N goes to infinity. The intuition behind is that as the number of individuals N goes to infinity, the majority of the reported data from other individuals converges to the underlying state W, and thus $\boldsymbol{R}^{(N,\epsilon)}$ works similar as the genie-aided mechanism $\widehat{\boldsymbol{R}}^{(\epsilon)}$, whose equilibrium payment to each individual equals to the lower bound in Theorem 1.

4.2.1 A Payment Mechanism $\boldsymbol{R}^{(N,\epsilon)}$

The payment mechanism $\boldsymbol{R}^{(N,\epsilon)}$ is designed for purchasing private data from N privacy-aware individuals, parameterized by a privacy parameter ϵ, where $N \ge 2$ and $\epsilon > 0$.

1. Each individual reports her data (which can be the decision of not participating).
2. The data collector counts the number of participants, which is denoted by n.
3. For non-participating individuals, the payment is zero.
4. If there is only one participant, pay zero to this participant. Otherwise, for each participating individual i, the data collector computes the variable

$$M_{-i} = \begin{cases} 1 & \text{if } \displaystyle\sum_{j:\, X_j \neq \perp, j \neq i} X_j \ge \left\lfloor \frac{n-1}{2} \right\rfloor + 1, \\ 0 & \text{otherwise,} \end{cases}$$

which is the majority of the other participants' reported data. Then the data collector pays individual i the following amount of payment according to her reported data X_i and M_{-i}:

$$R_i^{(N,\epsilon)}(\boldsymbol{X}) = \frac{g'(\epsilon)(e^\epsilon + 1)^2}{2e^\epsilon} A_{X_i, M_{-i}},$$

where the parameters $A_{1,1}, A_{0,0}, A_{0,1}, A_{1,0}$ are defined in Section 4.2.2.

4.2.2 Payment Parameterization

Let

$$\alpha = \theta\frac{e^\epsilon}{e^\epsilon + 1} + (1-\theta)\frac{1}{e^\epsilon + 1}.$$

The physical meaning of α can be seen by considering the strategy profile $\boldsymbol{\sigma}^{(\epsilon)}$, where given the state W, the reported data $X_1, X_2, \ldots, X_N$ are i.i.d. with

$$\mathbb{P}_{\sigma_i^{(\epsilon)}}(X_i = 1 \mid W = 1) = \mathbb{P}_{\sigma_i^{(\epsilon)}}(X_i = 0 \mid W = 0) = \alpha.$$

Given that the number of participants is n with $n \ge 2$, define the following quantities. Consider a random variable that follows the binomial distribution with parameters $n-1$ and α. Let $\beta^{(n)}$ denote the probability that this random variable is greater than or equal to $\lfloor \frac{n-1}{2} \rfloor + 1$. Let

$$\gamma^{(n)} = \begin{cases} 1 - \dbinom{n-1}{\frac{n-1}{2}} \alpha^{\frac{n-1}{2}} (1-\alpha)^{\frac{n-1}{2}} & \text{if } n-1 \text{ is even,} \\ 1 & \text{if } n-1 \text{ is odd.} \end{cases} \tag{16}$$

To see the physical meaning of $\beta^{(n)}$ and $\gamma^{(n)}$, still consider $\boldsymbol{\sigma}^{(\epsilon)}$, where the number of participants is $n = N$. Then for an individual i,

$$\mathbb{P}_{\boldsymbol{\sigma}^{(\epsilon)}}(M_{-i} = 1 \mid W = 1) = \beta^{(N)},$$

$$\mathbb{P}_{\boldsymbol{\sigma}^{(\epsilon)}}(M_{-i} = 1 \mid W = 0) = \gamma^{(N)} - \beta^{(N)}.$$

With the introduced notation, the parameters $A_{1,1}$, $A_{0,0}$, $A_{0,1}$, $A_{1,0}$ used in the payment mechanism $\boldsymbol{R}^{(N,\epsilon)}$ are defined as follows:

$$A_{1,1} = \frac{P_W(1)(1-\beta^{(n)}) + P_W(0)(1-(\gamma^{(n)}-\beta^{(n)}))}{(2\beta^{(n)}-\gamma^{(n)})(2\theta-1)P_W(1)P_W(0)},$$
$$A_{0,0} = \frac{P_W(1)\beta^{(n)} + P_W(0)(\gamma^{(n)}-\beta^{(n)})}{(2\beta^{(n)}-\gamma^{(n)})(2\theta-1)P_W(1)P_W(0)},$$
$$A_{0,1} = 0,$$
$$A_{1,0} = 0.$$

It is easy to verify that these parameters are nonnegative. Thus $\boldsymbol{R}^{(N,\epsilon)}$ is a nonnegative payment mechanism. The proof of the equilibrium properties of $\boldsymbol{R}^{(N,\epsilon)}$ in Theorem 2 is given below.

4.2.3 *Proof of Theorem 2*

PROOF. It suffices to prove that the strategy profile $\boldsymbol{\sigma}^{(\epsilon)}$ is a Nash equilibrium in $\boldsymbol{R}^{(N,\epsilon)}$ and the expected payment to each individual i at this equilibrium satisfies that $\mathbb{E}_{\boldsymbol{\sigma}^{(\epsilon)}}\left[R_i^{(N,\epsilon)}(\boldsymbol{X})\right] \leq V_{\mathrm{LB}}(\epsilon) + O(e^{-Nd})$, where recall that $V_{\mathrm{LB}}(\epsilon)$ is defined in (5). For conciseness, in the remainder of this proof, we suppress the explicit dependence on N and ϵ, and write $\boldsymbol{R}$ and $\boldsymbol{\sigma}$ to represent $\boldsymbol{R}^{(N,\epsilon)}$ and $\boldsymbol{\sigma}^{(\epsilon)}$, respectively.

We first prove that the strategy profile $\boldsymbol{\sigma}$ is a Nash equilibrium in $\boldsymbol{R}$; i.e., for any individual i, the ϵ-strategy is a best response of individual i when other individuals follow $\boldsymbol{\sigma}_{-i}$. Following the notation in the proof of Lemma 1, for any individual i we consider any strategy σ_i' of individual i and let

$$p_1 = \mathbb{P}_{\sigma_i'}(X_i = 1 \mid S_i = 1), \quad q_1 = \mathbb{P}_{\sigma_i'}(X_i = 0 \mid S_i = 1),$$
$$p_0 = \mathbb{P}_{\sigma_i'}(X_i = 1 \mid S_i = 0), \quad q_0 = \mathbb{P}_{\sigma_i'}(X_i = 0 \mid S_i = 0).$$

Then by the proof of Lemma 1, the best response satisfies either $p_1 = p_0, q_1 = q_0$, or $p_1 = q_0, p_0 = q_1, p_1 + q_1 = 1$, depending on the form of the utility function $U_i(p_1, p_0, q_1, q_0)$, which is the expected utility of individual i at the strategy σ_i' when other individuals follow $\boldsymbol{\sigma}_{-i}$. Thus, we derive the form of $U_i(p_1, p_0, q_1, q_0)$ next. Recall that we let $\overline{R}_i(x_i; w)$ denote $\mathbb{E}_{(\sigma_i', \boldsymbol{\sigma}_{-i})}[R_i(\boldsymbol{X}) \mid X_i = x_i, W = w]$ for $x_i, w \in \{0,1\}$. Then

$$\begin{aligned}
&U_i(p_1, p_0, q_1, q_0)\\
&= \mathbb{E}_{(\sigma_i', \boldsymbol{\sigma}_{-i})}[R_i(\boldsymbol{X}) - g(\zeta(\sigma_i'))]\\
&= K_1 p_1 + K_0 p_0 + L_1 q_1 + L_0 q_0 - g(\zeta(p_1, p_0, q_1, q_0)),
\end{aligned}$$

with

$$K_1 = \{\overline{R}_i(1;1)P_W(1)\theta + \overline{R}_i(1;0)P_W(0)(1-\theta)\},$$
$$K_0 = \{\overline{R}_i(1;1)P_W(1)(1-\theta) + \overline{R}_i(1;0)P_W(0)\theta\},$$
$$L_1 = \{\overline{R}_i(0;1)P_W(1)\theta + \overline{R}_i(0;0)P_W(0)(1-\theta)\},$$
$$L_0 = \{\overline{R}_i(0;1)P_W(1)(1-\theta) + \overline{R}_i(0;0)P_W(0)\theta\}.$$

In the designed mechanism $\boldsymbol{R}$, the payment to individual i only depends on X_i and M_{-i}. Thus we write $R_i(X_i; M_{-i}) = R_i(\boldsymbol{X})$. Then the value of $\overline{R}_i(x_i; w)$ is calculated as follows:

$$\begin{aligned}
\overline{R}_i(1;1) &= \mathbb{E}_{(\sigma_i', \boldsymbol{\sigma}_{-i})}[R_i(\boldsymbol{X}) \mid X_i = 1, W = 1]\\
&= \beta^{(N)} R_i(1;1),\\
\overline{R}_i(1;0) &= \mathbb{E}_{(\sigma_i', \boldsymbol{\sigma}_{-i})}[R_i(\boldsymbol{X}) \mid X_i = 1, W = 0]\\
&= (\gamma^{(N)} - \beta^{(N)}) R_i(1;1),\\
\overline{R}_i(0;1) &= \mathbb{E}_{(\sigma_i', \boldsymbol{\sigma}_{-i})}[R_i(\boldsymbol{X}) \mid X_i = 0, W = 1]\\
&= (1-\beta^{(N)}) R_i(0;0),\\
\overline{R}_i(0;0) &= \mathbb{E}_{(\sigma_i', \boldsymbol{\sigma}_{-i})}[R_i(\boldsymbol{X}) \mid X_i = 0, W = 0]\\
&= (1-(\gamma^{(N)} - \beta^{(N)})) R_i(0;0),
\end{aligned}$$

and it can be verified that K_1, K_0, L_1 and L_0 are all positive. Therefore, by the proof of Lemma 1, the possibility for the best response to be $p_1 = p_0, q_1 = q_0, 0 < p_1 + q_1 < 1$ can be eliminated and the best response strategy must be in one of the following three forms:

$$p_1 = p_0 = q_1 = q_0 = 0, \tag{17}$$
$$p_1 = p_0, \quad q_1 = q_0, \quad p_1 + q_1 = 1, \tag{18}$$
$$p_1 = q_0, \quad p_0 = q_1, \quad p_1 + q_1 = 1. \tag{19}$$

The strategy in (17) is to always not participate, which yields an utility of zero. For strategies in the form of (18) or (19), we can write the expected utility as a function of p_1 and p_0 as follows:

$$\overline{U}_i(p_1, p_0) = \overline{K}_1 p_1 + \overline{K}_0 p_0 + \overline{K} - g(\zeta(p_1, p_0)),$$

where $\overline{K}_1 = K_1 - L_1$, $\overline{K}_0 = K_0 - L_0$, $\overline{K} = L_1 + L_0$, and with a little abuse of notation, $\zeta(p_1, p_0) = \max\left\{\left|\ln \frac{p_1}{p_0}\right|, \left|\ln \frac{1-p_1}{1-p_0}\right|\right\}$. Inserting the value of $R_i(X_i; M_{-i})$ gives

$$\overline{K}_1 = \frac{g'(\epsilon)(e^\epsilon+1)^2}{2e^\epsilon}, \quad \overline{K}_0 = -\frac{g'(\epsilon)(e^\epsilon+1)^2}{2e^\epsilon}.$$

Then a strategy in the form of (18) yields an utility of $\overline{K} > 0$. A strategy in the form of (19) can be written as

$$p_1 = q_0 = \frac{e^\xi}{e^\xi+1}, \quad p_0 = q_1 = \frac{1}{e^\xi+1}.$$

Then the expected utility can be further written as a function f of ξ as follows:

$$f(\xi) = \overline{K}_1 \frac{e^\xi}{e^\xi+1} + \overline{K}_0 \frac{1}{e^\xi+1} - g(|\xi|) + \overline{K}.$$

Therefore, to prove that the ϵ-strategy is a best response of individual i, it suffices to prove that ϵ maximizes $f(\xi)$ and $f(\epsilon) \geq \overline{K}$. For any $\xi < 0$, it is easy to see that

$$\overline{K}_1 \frac{e^\xi}{e^\xi+1} + \overline{K}_0 \frac{1}{e^\xi+1} < 0 < \overline{K}_1 \frac{e^{-\xi}}{e^{-\xi}+1} + \overline{K}_0 \frac{1}{e^{-\xi}+1}.$$

Thus $f(\xi)$ achieves its maximum value at some $\xi \geq 0$. For any $\xi \geq 0$,

$$f'(\xi) = (\overline{K}_1 - \overline{K}_0)\frac{e^\xi}{(e^\xi+1)^2} - g'(\xi),$$
$$f''(\xi) = -(\overline{K}_1 - \overline{K}_0)\frac{e^\xi(e^\xi-1)}{(e^\xi+1)^3} - g''(\xi) \leq 0,$$

where the second inequality is due to the convexity of the cost function g. Therefore, f is concave. Since $f'(\epsilon) = 0$, ϵ maximizes $f(\xi)$. The optimal value is

$$f(\epsilon) = g'(\epsilon)\frac{e^\epsilon - e^{-\epsilon}}{2} - g(\epsilon) + \overline{K}.$$

By the convexity of g, $g(\epsilon) \leq g'(\epsilon)\epsilon \leq g'(\epsilon)\frac{e^\epsilon - e^{-\epsilon}}{2}$. Thus $f(\epsilon) \geq \overline{K}$, which completes the proof for the ϵ-strategy to be a best response of individual i.

Next we calculate the expected payment to individual i at $\boldsymbol{\sigma}$, which can be written as

$$\mathbb{E}_{\boldsymbol{\sigma}}[R_i(\boldsymbol{X})] = -(\overline{K}_1 - \overline{K}_0)\frac{1}{e^{\epsilon}+1} + \overline{K}_1 + \overline{K}.$$

By definitions,

$$\begin{aligned}
&\overline{K}_1 + \overline{K} \\
&= \frac{g'(\epsilon)(e^{\epsilon}+1)^2}{2e^{\epsilon}} \frac{1}{(2\beta^{(N)} - \gamma^{(N)})(2\theta - 1)} \\
&\quad \cdot \Big(2(\beta^{(N)})^2 + (4\theta - 2 - 2\gamma^{(N)})\beta^{(N)} \\
&\quad + 2(1-\theta)\gamma^{(N)} + \beta^{(N)}(1-\beta^{(N)})\frac{P_W(1)}{P_W(0)} \\
&\quad + (\gamma^{(N)} - \beta^{(N)})(1 - (\gamma^{(N)} - \beta^{(N)}))\frac{P_W(0)}{P_W(1)}\Big) \\
&=: \frac{g'(\epsilon)(e^{\epsilon}+1)^2}{2e^{\epsilon}} h(\beta^{(N)}).
\end{aligned}$$

Then

$$\begin{aligned}
\mathbb{E}_{\boldsymbol{\sigma}}[R_i(\boldsymbol{X})] &= \frac{g'(\epsilon)(e^{\epsilon}+1)}{e^{\epsilon}}\left(\frac{1}{2}h(\beta^{(N)})(e^{\epsilon}+1) - 1\right) \\
&= V_{\mathrm{LB}}(\epsilon) + \frac{g'(\epsilon)(e^{\epsilon}+1)^2}{2e^{\epsilon}}\left(h(\beta^{(N)}) - \frac{2\theta}{2\theta-1}\right).
\end{aligned}$$

To derive an upper bound on the expected payment, we first analyze the function h. Rearranging terms gives

$$\begin{aligned}
h(\beta^{(N)}) &= \frac{1}{2\theta-1}\frac{1}{2\beta^{(N)} - \gamma^{(N)}} \\
&\quad \cdot \Bigg((2-t)(\beta^{(N)})^2 + \Big(4\theta - 2 - 2\gamma^{(N)} + \frac{P_W(1)}{P_W(0)} \\
&\quad + (2\gamma^{(N)} - 1)\frac{P_W(0)}{P_W(1)}\Big)\beta^{(N)} \\
&\quad + 2(1-\theta)\gamma^{(N)} + \gamma^{(N)}(1-\gamma^{(N)})\frac{P_W(0)}{P_W(1)}\Bigg),
\end{aligned}$$

where $t = \frac{(P_W(1))^2 + (P_W(0))^2}{P_W(1)P_W(0)} \geq 2$. Taking derivative yields

$$\begin{aligned}
h'(\beta^{(N)}) &= \frac{1}{2\theta-1}\frac{1}{(2\beta^{(N)} - \gamma^{(N)})^2} \\
&\quad \cdot \Bigg(2(2-t)\Big(\beta^{(N)} - \frac{\gamma^{(N)}}{2}\Big)^2 - (\gamma^{(N)})^2 \\
&\quad - \frac{\gamma^{(N)}t}{2}(2 - \gamma^{(N)}) - 2\gamma^{(N)}(1-\gamma^{(N)})\Bigg).
\end{aligned}$$

Therefore, $h'(\beta^{(N)}) \leq 0$ and h is a non-increasing function.

Next we derive a lower bound on $\beta^{(N)}$. Let $Y_1, Y_2, \ldots, Y_{N-1}$ be i.i.d. Bernoulli random variables with parameter α. Then by the definition of $\beta^{(N)}$:

$$\begin{aligned}
\beta^{(N)} &= \mathbb{P}\left(\sum_{l=1}^{N-1} Y_l \geq \left\lfloor \frac{N-1}{2} \right\rfloor + 1\right) \\
&= \gamma^{(N)} - \mathbb{P}\left(\sum_{l=1}^{N-1}(1 - Y_l) \geq N - 1 - \left\lceil \frac{N-1}{2} \right\rceil + 1\right) \\
&\geq \gamma^{(N)} - \mathbb{P}\left(\sum_{l=1}^{N-1}(1-Y_l) \geq \frac{N-1}{2}\right) \\
&\geq \gamma^{(N)} - e^{-(N-1)d},
\end{aligned}$$

where $d = \frac{1}{2}\ln\frac{1}{4\alpha(1-\alpha)} > 0$ is the parameter defined in (15) and the last inequality follow from the Chernoff bound [28].

By the monotonicity of h,

$$\begin{aligned}
&h(\beta^{(N)}) - \frac{2\theta}{2\theta-1} \\
&\leq h\left(\gamma^{(N)} - e^{-(N-1)d}\right) - \frac{2\theta}{2\theta-1} \\
&= \frac{1}{2\theta-1}\frac{1}{\gamma^{(N)} - 2e^{-(N-1)d}} \\
&\quad \cdot \Bigg((2-t)e^{-2(N-1)d} + \Big(2(1-\gamma^{(N)}) + 2\gamma^{(N)}t \\
&\quad - \frac{P_W(1)}{P_W(0)} - (2\gamma^{(N)} - 1)\frac{P_W(0)}{P_W(1)}\Big)e^{-(N-1)d} \\
&\quad + \gamma^{(N)}\frac{P_W(1)}{P_W(0)} + (\gamma^{(N)})^2\frac{P_W(0)}{P_W(1)} - (\gamma^{(N)})^2 t\Bigg) \\
&\leq \frac{1}{2\theta-1}\frac{1}{\gamma^{(N)} - 2e^{-(N-1)d}} \\
&\quad \cdot \Bigg((2-t)e^{-2(N-1)d} + (2(1-\gamma^{(N)}) + t)e^{-(N-1)d} \\
&\quad + \gamma^{(N)}(1-\gamma^{(N)})\frac{P_W(1)}{P_W(0)}\Bigg).
\end{aligned}$$

Recall the definition of $\gamma^{(N)}$ in (16). Then when $N-1$ is odd, $\gamma^{(N)} = 1$, and when $N-1$ is even,

$$\begin{aligned}
1 - \gamma^{(N)} &= \binom{N-1}{\frac{N-1}{2}}\alpha^{\frac{N-1}{2}}(1-\alpha)^{\frac{N-1}{2}} \\
&= e^{-(N-1)d} \cdot \binom{N-1}{\frac{N-1}{2}} 2^{-(N-1)},
\end{aligned}$$

where $\lim_{N\to\infty}\binom{N-1}{\frac{N-1}{2}}2^{-(N-1)} = 0$. Thus $1 - \gamma^{(N)} = O(e^{-Nd})$ as $N \to \infty$.

Therefore,

$$\begin{aligned}
&\mathbb{E}_{\boldsymbol{\sigma}}[R_i(\boldsymbol{X})] \\
&\leq V_{\mathrm{LB}}(\epsilon) + \frac{g'(\epsilon)(e^{\epsilon}+1)^2}{2e^{\epsilon}}\left(h\left(\gamma^{(N)} - e^{-(N-1)d}\right) - \frac{2\theta}{2\theta-1}\right) \\
&\leq V_{\mathrm{LB}}(\epsilon) + \frac{g'(\epsilon)(e^{\epsilon}+1)^2}{2e^{\epsilon}}\frac{1}{2\theta-1}\frac{1}{\gamma^{(N)} - 2e^{-(N-1)d}} \\
&\quad \cdot \left((2-t)e^{-2(N-1)d} + (2(1-\gamma^{(N)}) + t)e^{-(N-1)d} + O(e^{-Nd})\right) \\
&= V_{\mathrm{LB}}(\epsilon) + O(e^{-Nd}),
\end{aligned}$$

as $N \to \infty$, which completes the proof. □

4.3 Extension to Heterogeneous Cost Functions

Our results on the value of privacy are also valid in the scenario where individuals' privacy cost functions are heterogeneous and known. In this case, the value of ϵ units of privacy is still measured by the minimum payment of all nonnegative payment mechanisms under which an individual's best response in a Nash equilibrium is to report the data with a privacy level of ϵ. However, with heterogeneous cost functions, this value differs from individual to individual. Following similar notation, we let $V_i(\epsilon)$ denote the value of ϵ units of privacy to individual i, and let g_i denote the cost function of individual i. Then the following lower and upper bounds, which are almost identical to those in Theorem 1 and 2 except the heterogeneous cost function $g_i(\epsilon)$, hold

$$g_i'(\epsilon)\frac{e^\epsilon+1}{e^\epsilon}\left(\frac{\theta}{2\theta-1}(e^\epsilon+1)-1\right)\leq V_i(\epsilon)$$
$$\leq g_i'(\epsilon)\frac{e^\epsilon+1}{e^\epsilon}\left(\frac{\theta}{2\theta-1}(e^\epsilon+1)-1\right)+O(e^{-Nd}).$$

The lower bound above can be derived directly from the proof of Theorem 1, since the proof does not depend on whether the cost functions are homogeneous or not. The upper bound above is given by a payment mechanism that works similar to $\boldsymbol{R}^{(N,\epsilon)}$, with the g' in $R_i^{(N,\epsilon)}$ replaced by g_i'. In this mechanism, the strategy profile $\boldsymbol{\sigma}^{(\epsilon)}$ is still a Nash equilibrium, and the expected payment to individual i at this equilibrium can still be upper bounded as in Theorem 2 but again with g' replaced by g_i'.

5. PAYMENT VS. ACCURACY

In this section, we apply the fundamental bounds on the value of privacy to the payment–accuracy problem, where the data collector aims to minimize the total payment while achieving an accuracy target in learning the state. The solution of this problem can be used to guide the design of review systems. For example, to evaluate the underlying value of a new product, a review system can utilize the results in this section to design a payment mechanism for eliciting informative feedback from testers.

5.1 Payment–Accuracy Problem

The data collector learns the state W from the reported data $X_1, X_2, \dots, X_N$, which is collected through some payment mechanism, by performing hypothesis testing between the following two hypotheses:

$$H_0\colon W=0,$$
$$H_1\colon W=1.$$

The conditional distributions of the reported data given the hypotheses are specified by the strategy profile in a Nash equilibrium of the payment mechanism. According to Lemma 1, we can write an equilibrium strategy profile in the form of $(\sigma_i^{(\epsilon_i)}) = (\sigma_1^{(\epsilon_1)}, \sigma_2^{(\epsilon_2)}, \dots, \sigma_N^{(\epsilon_N)})$ with $\epsilon_i \in \mathbb{R}\setminus\{0\}\cup\{\perp\!\!\!\perp\}$, where recall that $\sigma_i^{(\epsilon_i)}$ is the ϵ_i-strategy. For ease of notation, a non-informative strategy is also called an ϵ-strategy but with $\epsilon=\perp\!\!\!\perp$. Let $\mathcal{R}(\epsilon_1,\epsilon_2,\dots,\epsilon_N)$ denote the set of nonnegative payment mechanisms in which $(\sigma_i^{(\epsilon_i)})$ is a Nash equilibrium.

We consider an information-theoretic approach based on the Chernoff information [5] to measure the accuracy that can be achieved in hypothesis testing. For each individual i, let $D(\epsilon_i)$ denote the Chernoff information between the conditional distributions of X_i given $W=1$ and $W=0$. The larger $D(\epsilon_i)$ is, the more possible that the two hypotheses can be distinguished. In later discussions we will see that the Chernoff information is closely related to the best achievable probability of error.

The data collector aims to minimize the total payment while achieving an accuracy target. The design choices include the number of individuals N, the parameters $\epsilon_1, \epsilon_2, \dots, \epsilon_N$, and the payment mechanism $\boldsymbol{R}$ in which the strategy profile $(\sigma_i^{(\epsilon_i)})$ is a Nash equilibrium. Then we formulate the mechanism design problem as the following optimization problem, which we call the *payment–accuracy problem*:

$$\min_{\substack{N\in\mathbb{N},\,\epsilon_i\in\mathbb{R}\setminus\{0\}\cup\{\perp\!\!\!\perp\},\forall i\\ \boldsymbol{R}\in\mathcal{R}(\epsilon_1,\epsilon_2,\dots,\epsilon_N)}} \sum_{i=1}^N \mathbb{E}_{(\sigma_i^{(\epsilon_i)})}[R_i(\boldsymbol{X})]$$
$$\text{subject to}\quad e^{-\sum_{i=1}^N D(\epsilon_i)}\leq\tau,$$

where the accuracy target is represented by τ, which is related to the maximum allowable error. We focus on the range $\tau\in(0,1)$ for nontriviality. Let $F(\tau)$ denote the optimal payment in this problem, i.e., the infimum of the total payment while satisfying the accuracy target τ.

5.2 Bounds on the Payment–Accuracy Problem

We present bounds on $F(\tau)$ in Theorem 3 below. For convenience, we define

$$\widetilde{\epsilon}=\inf\left\{\arg\max\left\{\frac{D(\epsilon)}{V_{\rm LB}(\epsilon)}:\epsilon>0\right\}\right\},\quad \widetilde{N}=\left\lceil\frac{\ln(1/\tau)}{D(\widetilde{\epsilon})}\right\rceil, \tag{20}$$

where recall that $V_{\rm LB}(\epsilon)$ is the lower bound in Theorem 1.

THEOREM 3. *The optimal payment $F(\tau)$ in the payment–accuracy problem for a given accuracy target $\tau\in(0,1)$ is bounded as: $(\widetilde{N}-1)V_{\rm LB}(\widetilde{\epsilon})\leq F(\tau)\leq \widetilde{N}V_{\rm LB}(\widetilde{\epsilon})+O(\tau\ln(1/\tau))$, where the $O(\cdot)$ is for $\tau\to 0$.*

The upper bound in Theorem 3 is given by the designed mechanism $\boldsymbol{R}^{(N,\epsilon)}$ with parameters chosen as $\epsilon=\widetilde{\epsilon}$ and $N=\widetilde{N}$. Note that $\widetilde{\epsilon}$ can be proved to have a well-defined finite value independent of τ. By the lower and upper bounds on the value of privacy, the payment to each individual in $\boldsymbol{R}^{(\widetilde{N},\widetilde{\epsilon})}$ is roughly equal to the lower bound $V_{\rm LB}(\widetilde{\epsilon})$. Then Theorem 3 indicates that the total payment of the designed mechanism $\boldsymbol{R}^{(\widetilde{N},\widetilde{\epsilon})}$ is at most one individual's payment away from the minimum, with the diminishing term $O(\tau\ln(1/\tau))$ omitted. Figure 2 shows an illustration of the lower and upper bounds.

Theorem 3 is proved by Lemma 4 and Lemma 5 below, where the lower bound is given by the lower bound on the value of privacy, and the upper bound is given by $\boldsymbol{R}^{(\widetilde{N},\widetilde{\epsilon})}$.

5.2.1 Lower Bound

First, notice that it suffices to limit the choice of each ϵ_i to $(0,+\infty)$ in the payment–accuracy problem, since when $\epsilon_i=\perp\!\!\!\perp$, $D(\epsilon_i)=0$, and when $\epsilon_i<0$, $D(\epsilon_i)=D(|\epsilon_i|)$ and there exists another nonnegative payment mechanism with the same payment property and a Nash equilibrium at $(\sigma_i^{(|\epsilon_i|)})$ by Lemma 2.

Now we use the lower bound on the value of privacy to prove the lower bound on $F(\tau)$. By Theorem 1,

$$\inf_{\boldsymbol{R}\in\mathcal{R}(\epsilon_1,\epsilon_2,\dots,\epsilon_N)}\sum_{i=1}^N\mathbb{E}_{(\sigma_i^{(\epsilon_i)})}[R_i(\boldsymbol{X})]\geq\sum_{i=1}^N V_{\rm LB}(\epsilon_i).$$

Therefore, the optimal payment $F(\tau)$ is lower bounded by the optimal value of the following optimization problem (P1):

$$\min_{N\in\mathbb{N},\,\epsilon_i\in(0,+\infty),\forall i}\sum_{i=1}^N V_{\rm LB}(\epsilon_i)$$
$$\text{subject to}\quad e^{-\sum_{i=1}^N D(\epsilon_i)}\leq\tau. \tag{P1}$$

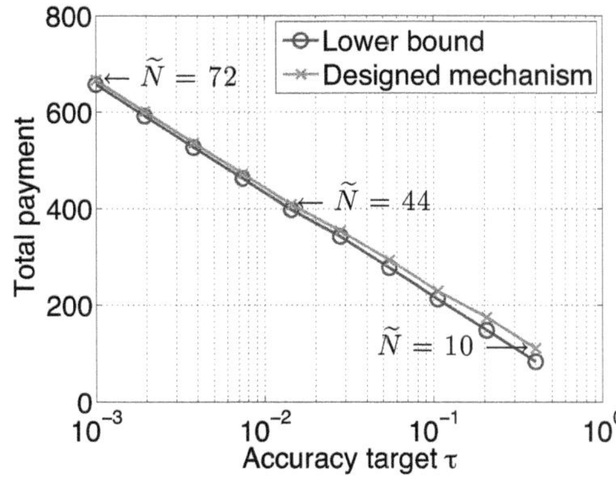

Figure 2: Illustration of the lower and upper bounds in Theorem 3 on the minimum total payment for achieving an accuracy target τ, where the upper bound is given by the designed mechanism $\boldsymbol{R}^{(\widetilde{N},\widetilde{\epsilon})}$. In this example, the prior PMF of the state is $P_W(1) = 0.7$, $P_W(0) = 0.3$. The quality of signals is $\theta = 0.8$. The cost function is $g(\epsilon) = \epsilon$. The range of τ shown in the figure is 0.001–0.4.

LEMMA 4. *Any feasible solution* $(N, \epsilon_1, \epsilon_2, \ldots, \epsilon_N)$ *of* (P1) *satisfies*

$$\sum_{i=1}^{N} V_{\mathrm{LB}}(\epsilon_i) \geq (\widetilde{N} - 1)V_{\mathrm{LB}}(\widetilde{\epsilon}),$$

where $\widetilde{\epsilon}$ *and* $\widetilde{N}$ *are defined in* (20).

Lemma 4 states that the total expected payment of the data collector is at least $(\widetilde{N}-1)V_{\mathrm{LB}}(\widetilde{\epsilon})$. Note that the value given by the genie-aided payment mechanism $\widehat{\boldsymbol{R}}^{(\widetilde{\epsilon})}$ for $\widetilde{N}$ individuals is $\widetilde{N}V_{\mathrm{LB}}(\widetilde{\epsilon})$, which is at most one $V_{\mathrm{LB}}(\widetilde{\epsilon})$ away from the optimal value of (P1). We can think of $V_{\mathrm{LB}}(\epsilon)$ as the price for ϵ units of privacy and $D(\epsilon)$ as the quality that the data collector gets from ϵ units of privacy due to its contribution to the accuracy. Then the intuition for $(\widetilde{N}, \widetilde{\epsilon}, \ldots, \widetilde{\epsilon})$ to be a near-optimal choice is that the privacy level $\widetilde{\epsilon}$ gives the best quality/price ratio and $\widetilde{N}$ is the fewest number of individuals to meet the accuracy target. The proof of Lemma 4 is presented in our technical report [31]. With this lemma, the lower bound on $F(\tau)$ in Theorem 3 is straightforward.

5.2.2 Upper Bound

LEMMA 5. *Choose the parameters in the payment mechanism* $\boldsymbol{R}^{(N,\epsilon)}$ *defined in Section 4.2.1 to be* $\epsilon = \widetilde{\epsilon}$ *and* $N = \widetilde{N}$, *where* $\widetilde{\epsilon}$ *and* $\widetilde{N}$ *are defined in* (20). *Then in the Nash equilibrium* $\boldsymbol{\sigma}^{(\widetilde{\epsilon})}$ *of* $\boldsymbol{R}^{(\widetilde{N},\widetilde{\epsilon})}$, *the accuracy target* τ *can be achieved, and the total expected payment is upper bounded as*

$$\mathbb{E}_{\boldsymbol{\sigma}^{(\widetilde{\epsilon})}}\left[\sum_{i=1}^{\widetilde{N}} R_i^{(\widetilde{N},\widetilde{\epsilon})}(\boldsymbol{X})\right] \leq \widetilde{N}V_{\mathrm{LB}}(\widetilde{\epsilon}) + O(\tau \ln(1/\tau)).$$

This lemma follows from Theorem 2 and we omit the proof here. Since the payment mechanism $\boldsymbol{R}^{(N,\epsilon)}$ together with $\epsilon = \widetilde{\epsilon}$ and $N = \widetilde{N}$ is a feasible solution of the payment–accuracy problem, the upper bound in this lemma gives the upper bound on $F(\tau)$ in Theorem 3.

5.3 Discussions on the Accuracy Metric

When we study the relation between payment and accuracy, the accuracy can also be measured by the best achievable probability of error, defined as

$$p_e = \inf_{\psi} \mathbb{P}_{(\sigma_i^{(\epsilon_i)})}(\psi(\boldsymbol{X}) \neq W),$$

where $\psi(\boldsymbol{x})$ is a decision function, with $\psi(\boldsymbol{x}) = 0$ implying that H_0 is accepted and $\psi(\boldsymbol{x}) = 1$ implying that H_1 is accepted. However, p_e is difficult to deal with analytically since its exact form in terms of $\epsilon_1, \epsilon_2, \ldots, \epsilon_N$ is intractable.

We measure the accuracy based on the Chernoff information, which is an information-theoretic metric closely related to p_e. It can be proved by the Bhattacharyya bound [17] that at the strategy profile $(\sigma_i^{(\epsilon_i)})$,

$$p_e \leq e^{-\sum_{i=1}^{N} D(\epsilon_i)}. \tag{21}$$

Therefore, if we want to guarantee that $p_e \leq p_e^{\max}$ for some maximum allowable probability of error $p_e^{\max}$, we can choose $\tau = p_e^{\max}$ in the payment–accuracy problem. In fact, the metric based on the Chernoff information is very close to the metric p_e, since the upper bound (21) is tight in exponent when all the ϵ_i are the same, i.e., when the reported data is i.i.d. given the hypothesis.

6. CONCLUSIONS

In this paper, we studied "the value of privacy" under a game-theoretic model, where a data collector pays strategic individuals to buy their private data for a learning purpose. The individuals do not consider the data collector to be trustworthy, and thus experience a cost of privacy loss during data reporting. The value of ϵ units of privacy is measured by the minimum payment of all nonnegative payment mechanisms under which an individual's best response in a Nash equilibrium is to report the data with a privacy level of ϵ. We derived asymptotically tight lower and upper bounds on the value of privacy as the number of individuals becomes large, where the upper bound was given by a designed payment mechanism $\boldsymbol{R}^{(N,\epsilon)}$. We further applied these fundamental limits to find the minimum total payment for the data collector to achieve certain learning accuracy target, and derived lower and upper bounds on the minimum payment. The total payment of the designed mechanism $\boldsymbol{R}^{(N,\epsilon)}$ with properly chosen parameters is at most one individual's payment away from the minimum. It would be of great interest to study the value of privacy under (ϵ, δ)-differential privacy, and to extend our results to more general models of private and reported data, e.g., models with larger alphabets for the state, the signals and the reported data.

7. ACKNOWLEDGEMENT

This work was supported in part by the NSF under Grant ECCS-1255425.

8. REFERENCES

[1] ACEMOGLU, D., DAHLEH, M. A., LOBEL, I., AND OZDAGLAR, A. Bayesian learning in social networks. *Review of Econ. Stud. 78*, 4 (Oct. 2011), 1201–1236.

[2] BASSILY, R., AND SMITH, A. Local, private, efficient protocols for succinct histograms. In *Proc. Ann. ACM Symp. Theory of Computing (STOC)* (Portland, OR, 2015), pp. 127–135.

[3] CHEN, Y., CHONG, S., KASH, I. A., MORAN, T., AND VADHAN, S. Truthful mechanisms for agents that value privacy. In *Proc. ACM Conf. Electronic Commerce (EC)* (Philadelphia, PA, 2013), pp. 215–232.

[4] CHEN, Y., SHEFFET, O., AND VADHAN, S. Privacy games. In *Int. Conf. Web and Internet Economics (WINE)* (2014), vol. 8877, pp. 371–385.

[5] COVER, T. M., AND THOMAS, J. A. *Elements of Information Theory*, 2nd ed. John Wiley & Sons, Hoboken, NJ, 2006.

[6] DUCHI, J. C., JORDAN, M. I., AND WAINWRIGHT, M. J. Local privacy and minimax bounds: Sharp rates for probability estimation. In *Advances Neural Information Processing Systems (NIPS)* (Lake Tahoe, NV, Dec. 2013), pp. 1529–1537.

[7] DWORK, C. Differential privacy. In *Proc. Int. Conf. Automata, Languages and Programming (ICALP)* (Venice, Italy, 2006), pp. 1–12.

[8] DWORK, C., MCSHERRY, F., NISSIM, K., AND SMITH, A. Calibrating noise to sensitivity in private data analysis. In *Proc. Conf. Theory of Cryptography (TCC)* (New York, NY, 2006), pp. 265–284.

[9] DWORK, C., AND ROTH, A. The algorithmic foundations of differential privacy. *Found. Trends Theor. Comput. Sci. 9*, 3–4 (Aug. 2014), 211–407.

[10] ERLINGSSON, Ú., PIHUR, V., AND KOROLOVA, A. RAPPOR: Randomized aggregatable privacy-preserving ordinal response. In *Proc. ACM SIGSAC Conf. Computer and Communication Security (CCS)* (Scottsdale, AZ, 2014), pp. 1054–1067.

[11] FANTI, G. C., PIHUR, V., AND ERLINGSSON, Ú. Building a RAPPOR with the unknown: Privacy-preserving learning of associations and data dictionaries. *arXiv:1503.01214 [cs.CR]* (2015).

[12] FLEISCHER, L. K., AND LYU, Y. Approximately optimal auctions for selling privacy when costs are correlated with data. In *Proc. ACM Conf. Electronic Commerce (EC)* (Valencia, Spain, 2012), pp. 568–585.

[13] GHOSH, A., AND LIGETT, K. Privacy and coordination: Computing on databases with endogenous participation. In *Proc. ACM Conf. Electronic Commerce (EC)* (Philadelphia, PA, 2013), pp. 543–560.

[14] GHOSH, A., LIGETT, K., ROTH, A., AND SCHOENEBECK, G. Buying private data without verification. In *Proc. ACM Conf. Economics and Computation (EC)* (Palo Alto, CA, 2014), pp. 931–948.

[15] GHOSH, A., AND ROTH, A. Selling privacy at auction. In *Proc. ACM Conf. Electronic Commerce (EC)* (San Jose, CA, 2011), pp. 199–208.

[16] HSU, J., KHANNA, S., AND ROTH, A. Distributed private heavy hitters. In *Proc. Int. Conf. Automata, Languages and Programming (ICALP)* (Warwick, UK, 2012), pp. 461–472.

[17] KAILATH, T. The divergence and Bhattacharyya distance measures in signal selection. *IEEE Trans. Commun. Technol. 15*, 1 (Feb. 1967), 52–60.

[18] KAIROUZ, P., OH, S., AND VISWANATH, P. Extremal mechanisms for local differential privacy. In *Advances Neural Information Processing Systems (NIPS)* (Montreal, Canada, Dec. 2014), pp. 2879–2887.

[19] KASIVISWANATHAN, S. P., LEE, H. K., NISSIM, K., RASKHODNIKOVA, S., AND SMITH, A. What can we learn privately? *SIAM J. Comput. 40*, 3 (May 2011), 793–826.

[20] KROFT, S. The data brokers: selling your personal information. *CBS News* (Mar. 2014).

[21] LE, T. N., SUBRAMANIAN, V. G., AND BERRY, R. A. The value of noise for informational cascades. In *Proc. IEEE Int. Symp. Information Theory (ISIT)* (Honolulu, HI, 2014), pp. 1101–1105.

[22] LIGETT, K., AND ROTH, A. Take it or leave it: Running a survey when privacy comes at a cost. In *Proc. Int. Workshop Internet and Network Economics (WINE)* (Liverpool, UK, 2012), pp. 378–391.

[23] MILLER, N., RESNICK, P., AND ZECKHAUSER, R. Eliciting informative feedback: The peer-prediction method. In *Computing with Social Trust*, Human–Computer Interaction Series. Springer London, 2009, pp. 185–212.

[24] NISSIM, K., VADHAN, S., AND XIAO, D. Redrawing the boundaries on purchasing data from privacy-sensitive individuals. In *Proc. Conf. Innovations in Theoretical Computer Science (ITCS)* (Princeton, NJ, 2014), pp. 411–422.

[25] PAI, M. M., AND ROTH, A. Privacy and mechanism design. *SIGecom Exch. 12*, 1 (June 2013), 8–29.

[26] ROTH, A., AND SCHOENEBECK, G. Conducting truthful surveys, cheaply. In *Proc. ACM Conf. Electronic Commerce (EC)* (Valencia, Spain, 2012), pp. 826–843.

[27] SHOKRI, R. Privacy games: Optimal user-centric data obfuscation. In *Proc. Privacy Enhancing Technologies (PETS)* (Philadelphia, PA, 2015), pp. 299–315.

[28] SRIKANT, R., AND YING, L. *Communication Networks: An Optimization, Control and Stochastic Networks Perspective.* Cambridge Univ. Press, New York, 2014.

[29] WANG, W., YING, L., AND ZHANG, J. On the relation between identifiability, differential privacy, and mutual-information privacy. In *Proc. Ann. Allerton Conf. Communication, Control and Computing* (Monticello, IL, Sept. 2014), pp. 1086–1092.

[30] WANG, W., YING, L., AND ZHANG, J. A minimax distortion view of differentially private query release. In *Proc. Asilomar Conf. Signals, Systems, and Computers* (Pacific Grove, CA, Nov. 2015).

[31] WANG, W., YING, L., AND ZHANG, J. The value of privacy: Strategic data subjects, incentive mechanisms and fundamental limits. *arXiv:1603.06870 [cs.GT]* (2016).

[32] WARNER, S. L. Randomized response: A survey technique for eliminating evasive answer bias. *J. Amer. Stat. Assoc. 60*, 309 (Mar. 1965), 63–69.

[33] XIAO, D. Is privacy compatible with truthfulness? In *Proc. Conf. Innovations in Theoretical Computer Science (ITCS)* (Berkeley, CA, 2013), pp. 67–86.

Instability in Distributed Mobility Management

Revisiting Configuration Management in 3G/4G Mobile Networks

Yuanjie Li†, Haotian Deng‡, Jiayao Li†, Chunyi Peng‡, Songwu Lu†
†University of California, Los Angeles, *The Ohio State University
yuanjie.li@cs.ucla.edu, deng.264@buckeyemail.osu.edu, likayo@ucla.edu,
chunyi@cse.ohio-state.edu, slu@cs.ucla.edu

ABSTRACT

Mobility support is critical to offering seamless data service to mobile devices in 3G/4G cellular networks. To accommodate policy requests by users and carriers, micro-mobility management scheme among cells (*i.e.*, handoff) is designated to be configurable. Each cell and mobile device can configure or even customize its own handoff procedure. In this paper, we examine the handoff misconfiguration issues in 3G/4G networks. We show that they may incur handoff instability in the form of persistent loops, where the device oscillates between cells even without radio-link and location changes. Such instability is mainly triggered by uncoordinated parameter configurations and inconsistent decision logic in the handoff procedure. It can degrade user data performance, incur excessive signaling overhead, and violate network's expected handoff goals. We derive the instability conditions, and validate them on two major US mobile carrier networks. We further design a software tool for automatic loop detection, and run it over operational networks. We discuss possible fixes to such uncoordinated configurations among devices and cells.

1. INTRODUCTION

The 3G/4G cellular network is the only large-scale infrastructure that offers "anytime, anywhere" mobility support to smartphones and tablets in reality. The key lies in its micro-mobility management scheme, which *determines* the serving cell (also known as base station)[1] and migrates the mobile device from the current cell to the next neighboring one. This procedure is called handoff, the fine-grained mobility scheme in practice.

In this paper, we study how configurations on the management plane affects the handoff behaviors of mobile devices. At first glance, this micro-mobility support scheme seems to warrant no further research; it has been operated for many years and extensive studies have been documented. However, our fresh perspective from the management-plane configurations yields some interesting, yet surprising results.

[1]Each base station may manage multiple cells (antennas), each of which covers a geographical area. In this paper, we use cells and base stations interchangeably, for a slight abuse of notations.

SIGMETRICS '16, June 14-18, 2016, Antibes Juan-Les-Pins, France
 ISBN 978-1-4503-4266-7/16/06. . . $15.00
DOI: http://dx.doi.org/10.1145/2896377.2901457

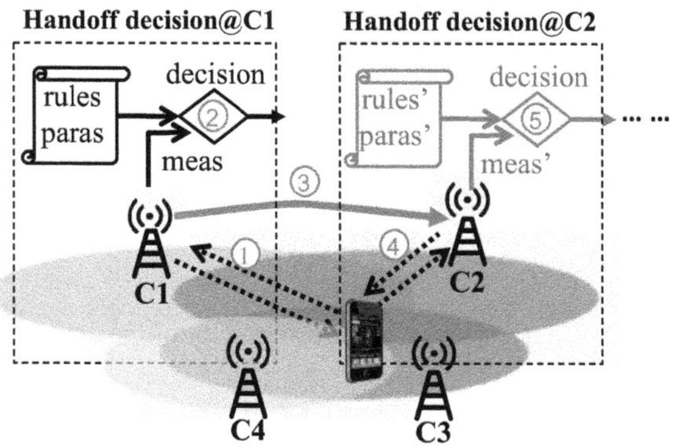

Figure 1: The distributed handoff is configurable.

In a nutshell, the handoff process is distributed in nature, as illustrated in Figure 1. There is no central point which collects all the information and makes decision. Instead, each decision is made locally at a cell or by the mobile device. The target cell is selected by the handoff decision made by the current serving cell or the mobile device. The operation has three components: the local decision logic (rules), tunable parameters and runtime measurements. The decision logic takes both parameters and measurements as inputs (①), and selects the next cell (②). Once the handoff is executed (③), it switches to a new serving cell and starts another handoff decision iteration (④ and ⑤). Note that, both the decision logic and parameters are configurable, in order to meet diverse requirements, such as selecting the best radio quality, letting operators specify their preferences, *etc.*. Moreover, coexistence of heterogeneous technologies (*e.g.*, 3G, 4G LTE, LTE-advanced, small cells) further results in diverse handoff configurations.

In this work, we conduct a systematic study on handoff configurations. We show that, uncoordinated configurations among cells can lead to handoff instability: the mobile device oscillates between a set of cells covering the same area, even when no radio-link or location change is detected. Load balancing is also not the main concern. Instead, uncoordinated parameter settings and loop-prone decision logic among devices and cells are the key drivers to instability. The concrete cases of such instability are covered in five distinctive categories to be reported in §5 and §6.

In each of the five categories, our effort starts from a formal analysis on the handoff (in)stability conditions. While we understand many parameters could be involved, our highlight is not on the qualitative or quantitative impact of each parameter by processing large traces from operational networks. Instead, our focus is on the fundamental understanding from the perspective of structural properties. We thus derive instability conditions that exhibit persistent loops for various forms of handoff misconfigurations. To this end, our modeling setting strives to be as simple as possible, if not overly simplistic in some cases, while still capturing the essence and neglecting secondary details.

We then validate the existence of handoff loops, as well as their impacts, on two US mobile carrier networks. Such empirical assessments are conducted on each problematic category discovered in modeling and analysis. We further design a software tool for automatic loop detection, which applies domain-specific knowledge to check for configuration conflicts in real networks.

Our results show that, handoff instability is not uncommon in reality. We have found 21 instances in the tested scenarios. Instability may occur among homogeneous cells (within 3G or 4G), and among heterogeneous cells (3G/4G/Femtocell). The conflicts can occur not only within existing handoff policies, but also upon configuration updates by carriers. Both configurations and decision logic, from both the network and the user, could result in persistent loops. Certain policy conflicts are even rooted in the problematic network mechanism design (*e.g.*, radio connection control). We notice that persistent loops may be less common than those transient ones (*e.g.*, ping-pong effects), which oscillate between cells due to frequent movement and radio signal strength fluctuations [30, 31]. However, such persistent loops *could* be fully avoided while transient loops cannot due to the nature of the environment dynamics. To this end, we devise loop detection and resolution solutions on both the device and network side, and validate their effectiveness. To our knowledge, this is the first work to report that instability may exhibit due to uncoordinated configurations (among cells and devices) on the management plane of 3G/4G mobile networks.

The rest of the paper is organized as follows. §2 introduces background on handoff configurations and its formulation as a distributed decision process. §3 describes our methodology. §4 gives a brief overview of findings. Using both analysis and empirical study, §5 and §6 describe five categories of instability due to uncoordinated parameters and loop-prone logic, respectively. §7 reports our design of an automatic detection tool and §8 discusses the possible changes on both the carrier and the device to eliminate the loops. §9 compares with the related work and §10 concludes the paper.

2. HANDOFF MANAGEMENT

The 3G/4G network is the largest wireless infrastructure deployed in reality. Its architecture has two main components: radio access network (provisioned by base stations) and core network. The geographic area served by a base station (BS) is called a cell, denoting the coverage of radio access to devices in proximity. At a given location, a device is usually covered by multiple, possibly overlapping cells to ensure seamless service.

In a larger area with many cells, the 3G/4G network offers wide-area mobility support to roaming devices with a two-tier structure. The base stations provide the fine-grained roaming support by handoff, which enables the device to switch its serving cell/base station as it moves. At the coarse granularity, base stations in a geographic area are grouped and managed by a central controller (i.e., mobile switching center (MSC) in 3G, and mobility management entity (MME) in 4G). The controller permits roaming between areas, and further tracks user locations, manages voice/data service contexts and configures forwarding paths.

2.1 Configuration Management for Handoff

Micro-mobility management in current 3G/4G networks is *configurable*. Three components work in concert to make each handoff decision: the *decision logic*, the *tunable parameters* and the *runtime observations (i.e., measurements)*. The decision logic takes both parameters and observations as inputs, and selects the next cell. Tunable parameters specify what kinds of metrics are of interest to the device and the operator. Runtime observations collect latest measurements, thus capturing the dynamic network state.

There are two types of handoffs in 3G/4G networks: (1) *Idle-state handoff*: It is performed by the mobile device, when the device is at the idle state (without ongoing traffic) and has no active connection to the serving cell. This is to prepare the device for network access at any time. (2) *Active-state handoff*: It is initiated by the serving cell, when the device has established the radio connection to the network. We next elaborate on their differences in three components.

∘ **Decision Logics.** This is the algorithm to choose the target cell. The idle-state handoff logic is standardized in 3GPP specifications [5, 10]. Its exact form will be described in §2.2. In contrast, the active-state handoff logic is customizable by the networks.

∘ **Configurable parameters.** They are used by the decision logic. For idle-state handoff, two types of parameters are used: the cell preference, and the radio assessment thresholds. Table 1 summarizes the parameter notations, which are abstracted from actual configurations in operational networks. For active-state handoff, it can further customize its parameter set. Both idle and active state handoffs' parameters are configured by the network, and distributed to the mobile device through broadcast (for idle-state handoff [10]) or dedicated signaling channel (for active-state handoff [6]).

∘ **Runtime observations.** They are usually on the dynamic radio qualities measured by the device, and serve as inputs to the handoff decision logic. The device collects and reports such observations to the handoff decision logic for the decision-making. The idle-state handoff accepts cell radio quality assessments as input, while the active-state can use both the radio quality and customizable observations (*e.g.*, cell load). In practice, to tolerate signal strength oscillations, these observation metrics are typically pre-processed before handoff decision. For example, the received signal strengths used in handoff have been averaged to filter out noises and transients [5, 10]. To stay focused, we assume the observations remain unchanged during each handoff decision process. In reality, we find that this usually holds at the same location, since the handoff decision making is faster than signal strength fluctuations (§7.3).

In summary, handoff configuration specifies key parameters and observation requirements for its decision logic. The parameters span both the user device and the network. Such parameters for the idle-state handoff have been standardized in [10], whereas those for active-state handoff are not standardized and carriers have freedom to customize them. In this work, we do not study abnormal factors, such as inaccurate observations, failure report, etc., but focus on common-case factors. To highlight our findings, we mainly focus on cell preferences and radio quality evaluation thresholds in our analysis and experiments.

2.2 Configurations in Idle-State Handoff

In this section, we use idle-state handoff as an example to present the configurable parameters, decision logic and runtime observations. We denote a handoff execution as $s \xrightarrow{\Omega_s(G_s,O_s)} t$, where s is the serving cell, and t is the target cell selected from candidate cells. Given the serving cell s, Ω_s, G_s and O_s denote the handoff decision logic, tunable parameters and runtime observations, respectively. If the serving cell does not exist (*e.g.*, upon device power-on), we have $s = \emptyset$ and the decision is made by the device.

Figure 2 shows the standardized decision logic for idle-state handoff [3,6]. The decision logic chooses the target cell by comparing the serving cell with each candidate. The runtime observation

Symbol	Description
γ_c	Received signal strength of cell c
$P_{s,c}$	Idle-state preference of cell c at cell s
Θ_s^{serv}	Idle-state threshold of γ_s when s is the serving cell
$\Theta_{s,c}^{low}$	Idle-state threshold of γ_c when s is serving and $P_{s,c} < P_{s,s}$
$\Theta_{s,c}^{eq}$	Idle-state threshold of γ_c when s is serving and $P_{s,s} = P_{s,c}$
$\Theta_{s,c}^{high}$	Idle-state threshold of γ_c when s is serving and $P_{s,c} > P_{s,s}$
$\Theta_{s,c}$	Active-state threshold of γ_c when s is serving with absolute comparison
$\Theta 1_s$	Active-state threshold of γ_s when s is serving with indirect relative comparison
$\Theta 2_{s,c}$	Active-state threshold of γ_c when s is serving with indirect relative comparison
$\Theta_{s,c}$	Active-state threshold of γ_c when s is serving with direct relative comparison

Table 1: Notations.

Idle-state handoff

Input: serving cell s, neighboring cell list C, radio measurements γ for each neighboring cell
Output: target cell t
Step1: initialize candidate cell list $L \leftarrow [\,]$
Step2: pairwise cell comparison
for each cell c **in** C:
  if $P_{s,c} > Ps,s$ **and** $\gamma_c > \Theta_{s,c}^{high}$
    L.append(c)
  elif $P_{s,c} = Ps,s$ **and** $\gamma_c > \gamma_s + \Theta_{s,c}^{eq}$
    L.append(c)
  elif $P_{s,c} < Ps,s$ **and** $\gamma_s < \Theta_s^{serv}$ **and** $\gamma_c > \Theta_{s,c}^{low}$
    L.append(c)
Step3: target cell decision

$$t = \begin{cases} s & \text{if } L \text{ is empty} \\ c & \text{if } c \text{ is the cell in } L \text{ with highest preference } P_{s,c} \end{cases}$$

Figure 2: Idle-state handoff decision logic.

is the received signal strength γ_c from each candidate cell c, measured by the user device. For each candidate cell c, the serving cell s defines two types of configurable parameters: the preference level ($P_{s,c}$) concerning a candidate cell c and a series of signal strength thresholds (Θ_s^{serv}, $\Theta_{s,c}^{low}$, $\Theta_{s,c}^{eq}$, $\Theta_{s,c}^{high}$) that help Ω_s to make a decision. Note that both parameters are needed. Radio signal strength is directly related to wireless transmission performance, as well as the cell type (3G, 4G, macro-cells, or femtocells). The cell preference reflects the precedence of cell types from the perspective of the carrier or the user or both. It supplies a flexible mechanism for the device/network to adjust the priorities.

Specifically, each cell is evaluated with the pre-configured preference and the runtime received signal strength. A target cell is chosen when (1) it is more preferred than the serving cell, and its signal strength is higher than a threshold; or (2) it is equally preferred to the serving cell, and its signal strength is offset higher than the serving cell's, or (3) it is less preferred than the serving cell, but the serving cell's signal strength is lower than a threshold, while the target cell's signal strength is higher than another threshold. If more than one cell outperforms the serving cell, the one with highest preference could be chosen. If a tie exists, the signal strength is used to break the tie.

3. METHODOLOGY

We take a two-step approach to studying the instability of the configured handoff. We first use a modeling framework to derive (in)stability conditions. We then run validation experiments to detect loops, uncover the root causes, and quantify the impact in operational 3G/4G networks.

Modeling and Analysis. Our modeling generally follows a discrete-event style. Each handoff is abstracted as a transition from serving cell s to target cell t. The handoff execution for $s \rightarrow t$ is acted on the serving cell s and the mobile device. So after handoff to a new cell, the execution would change. Consecutive handoffs may occur even with the same observations (*e.g.*, no location/radio condition change). Stability is ensured, if for any invariant observation, a device initially associated with any cell s will always converge to the target t but not move to other cells, *i.e.*

$$\mathbf{s} \rightarrow c_1 \rightarrow c_2 \rightarrow \cdots \rightarrow c_k \rightarrow \mathbf{t}$$

If this property is violated, a *persistent loop* can happen between a set of cells even for some unchanged measurements (or measurements fluctuatiing within a small range, see §5–6). The user would experience data/voice performance degradation. The carrier cannot achieve the designated handoff goal, and may suffer from excessive signaling overhead. The handoff is assumed to always succeed without failures (*e.g.*, we ignore radio-link outage).

Empirical Validation. We next conduct experiments in two metropolitan areas from both west and east coasts over two top-tier U.S. carriers: US-I and US-II. The goal is to (in)validate the existence of each handoff loop and quantify its negative impact. The validation takes two steps. First, we develop a loop detection tool (§7) to check the carriers' handoff policies. The detection algorithm is based on our analytical (in)stability results. It reports the stability violations and its condition for runtime observations. Second, for each stability violation, we conduct validation experiments to test its existence, and quantify its negative impact if it exists.

We run both outdoor and indoor experiments. The outdoor experiments cover 63 different locations over 240 km^2 in the west coast and 260 km^2 in the east coast. Each location is selected by at least 2km apart, in order to obtain different cell coverage. We also collect information on indoor experiments at 50 spots in two 8-floor office buildings and one apartment. In the indoor settings, we mainly collect the radio quality observations at various spots, since most cells, as well as their configurations, are similar across locations. We also deploy four 3G Femtocells in office and at home for indoor tests. We use four Android phone models: Samsung Galaxy S4, S5 and Note 3, and LG Optimus G.

4. OVERVIEW OF FINDINGS

In this work, we classify the instability (IS) cases based on the *causes* of the configuration conflicts. Broadly speaking, there are two classes: *parameter misconfiguration*, and *loop-prone decision logic*. Figure 3 exemplifies more concrete subcategories, and Table 2 summarizes our main findings from operational networks.

uncoordinated parameter configuration (§5). In this category, the instability is observed when cells' tunable parameters are not well coordinated. Such misconfigurations can happen within idle-state handoff and active-state handoff (§5.1 and §5.2). It can also happen between idle and active-state handoffs (§5.3). For idle-state handoff, note that identical decision logic is used among all devices at each location [5, 10]. The uncoordinated parameter configuration is the *only* cause of the persistent loops (proved in §5.2).

loop-prone decision logics (§6). The instability also occurs when different cells apply conflicting decision logics. No matter how well parameters are fine tuned, conflicts always exist between decision logics. The fundamental reason is that, the active-state logic is customizable at each cell and the current standards do not mandate the same decision algorithm. Specifically, the conflicts can happen between active-state logic engines (§6.1), and between active and idle-state decision logics (§6.2). However, no conflicts exist between idle-state engines since they follow identical, standardized algorithms.

5. INSTABILITY BY UNCOORDINATED PARAMETER CONFIGURATION

We have discovered three categories in this class of instability, all of which are caused by uncoordinated parameter configurations.

Category	Loop type	Carrier	Cause of configuration conflicts	Impact
Uncoordinated parameter configurations (§5)	4G-Femtocell-3G	US-I	Conflicting demands between offloading to private Femtocell and high-speed data service to user.	Data drop/delay; excessive signaling overhead; no offloading or high-speed service achieved
	4G-Femtocell-2G-3G	US-I	The mobile device's service-recovery handoff improperly configures high preference to 2G.	No voice service; data drop/delay; excessive signaling overhead; no offloading or high-speed service achieved
	4G-4G	US-I	Partial policy update with incremental 4G infrastructure upgrade.	Failure of user migration to new cells
	Femtocell-3G	US-I	Isolated Femtocell applies aggressive handoff.	Data/voice disruption
Loop-prone decision logic (§6)	4G-4G	US-I	Uncoordinated load balancing between cells.	Load balancing failure
	3G-3G	US-I,US-II	Radio-agnostic connection control by design.	Data delay/drop; offloading failure
	Femtocell-3G	US-I	Radio-agnostic connection control by design.	Data delay/drop; offloading failure

Table 2: Summary of persistent handoff loops.

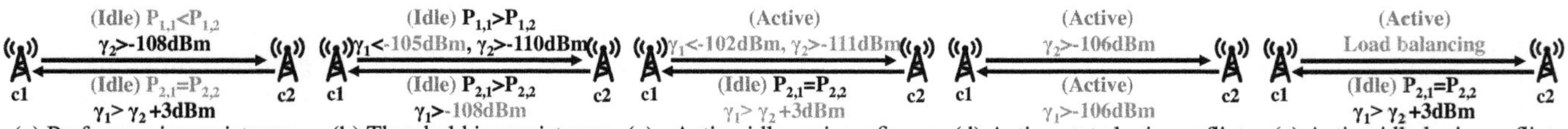

(a) Preference inconsistency (b) Threshold inconsistency (c) Active-idle misconfiguration (d) Active-state logic conflict (e) Active-idle logic conflict

Figure 3: Instability with uncoordinated parameter configuration (a,b,c) and loop-prone decision logic (d,e).

They are illustrated in Figures 3a-3c. We first derive the conditions for parameters and runtime observations that would (not) trigger instability. Our analysis aims to answer two questions: (1) Under which parameter configurations, there *exists* some runtime observations that can trigger instability? (2) Given improper parameter configurations, which runtime observation values will eventually trigger instability? Then we conduct empirical assessments to validate their instances in operational 3G/4G networks.

5.1 Inconsistent Preference Values

In this category, each cell locally configures its preference, but these preferences are not globally coordinated. Figure 3a illustrates a simple two-cell case. In this setting, c_1 configures c_2 to be more preferred to c_1 itself, but c_2 assigns equal preference to both cells. The persistent loop happens if the signal strength satisfies $\gamma_2 > \Theta_{2,1}^{high}(-108\text{dBm})$, and $\gamma_1 > \gamma_2 + \Theta_{2,1}^{high}(3\text{dBm})$. Note that, this loop can occur for *any* threshold settings (in the achievable range).

5.1.1 Deriving Instability Conditions

We first derive the instability conditions for this category. Recall that, in the idle-state handoff (Figure 2), when associated with cell s, the mobile device evaluates each candidate c with the preconfigured preference $P_{s,c}$, and its runtime signal strength γ_c. Each cell c is compared with serving cell s, and would be selected if (1) it is more preferred than the serving cell, and its signal strength is higher than a threshold ($(\gamma_c > \Theta_{s,c}^{high})$); (2) it is equally preferred, and its signal strength is offset higher than the serving cell's ($\gamma_c > \gamma_s + \Theta_{s,c}^{eqn}$), or (3) it is less preferred, but the serving cell's strength is weak ($\gamma_s < \Theta_s^{serv}$), *and* the target cell's signal strength is satisfying ($\gamma_c > \Theta_{s,c}^{low}$). If more than one cell satisfies above condition, the one with highest preference could be chosen.

The following result shows that, persistent loop can be caused by improper configurations of preference values. The good news is that, such persistent loops can be eliminated, when the derived preference conditions are avoided (the proof is in Appendix A):

> **Proposition 1.** *Consider n cells $c_1, c_2, ..., c_n$ that use idle-state handoffs only. A loop $c_1 \to c_2 \to ... \to c_n \to c_1$ can always happen, if and only if their preference settings satisfy: (1) at least one cell c_i sets $P_{i,i} < P_{i,i+1}$, and (2) every cell c_j sets $P_{j,j} \le P_{j,j+1}$, and $P_{n,n} \le P_{n,1}$.* □

Two results follow from Proposition 1. First, some preference settings would *always* trigger persistent loops with some runtime observations. For stability, they should always be avoided. Second, with consistent preference configuration, the idle-state decision logic can always ensure stability for a device. This serves as the foundation for stability analysis on other forms of handoff logic. As we will see in §5.2, there exists *pairwise* coordination methods for loop freedom. Enumerating all possible loops is not needed.

5.1.2 Empirical Validation

In this category, we have been able to identify 17 instances that can cause loops in US-I, using the detection tool to be described in Section 7. These configuration conflicts can happen at the same areas (with different runtime observations), and are reported in all locations. Figure 4 summarizes these loops. The smallest loop involves 3 cells, while the largest one includes 7 cells. Among these loops, 16 out of 17 conflicts would occur with Femtocell deployed, while the remaining one can occur without Femtocell. Our outdoor tests first show that all 2G/3G/4G Macrocells have the problematic configurations, and 61 out of 63 locations (96.8%) have all Macrocells deployed. This implies that a potential loop would exist if a Femtocell were deployed at the spot. We further deploy a Femtocell in a campus building, and conduct indoor experiments in all viable locations. In that floor, 25% of the testing locations satisfy both configuration and signal strength conditions, thus triggering loops. For US-II, we do not observe loops in this category. Based on the causes of the preference conflicts, the loops found in US-I can be further classified in three categories:

∘ **L1: uncoordinated handoff goals.** In this category, 8 variants of loops are reported, all happening between 4G Macrocell, Femtocell and 3G Macrocells. These loops are caused by preference settings for conflicting goals. The 4G Macrocells intend to offload user to his/her private Femtocells, so it assigns Femtocell with highest preference (over 4G/3G Macrocells). The 3G Femtocell has equal preference to all 3G/4G cells. But 3G Macrocells prefers to move the user to high-speed 4G network, so it assigns 3G Femtocell lower preference to 4G. This violates Proposition 1.

We next quantify the negative impacts. We observe that the loop frequently occurs. Figure 5 plots a two-hour log of serving cells in the 40-hour test in one 4G-Femtocell-3G example. Our test further shows that, more than 90% loops happen every <200 seconds. With such high frequency, the carrier can neither offload the users to Femtocell, nor offer high-speed 4G service.

Such frequent handoff loops incur large signaling overhead between the phone and the network. Figure 6a shows that, compared with the 4G case, the current loop increases its signaling to the cell

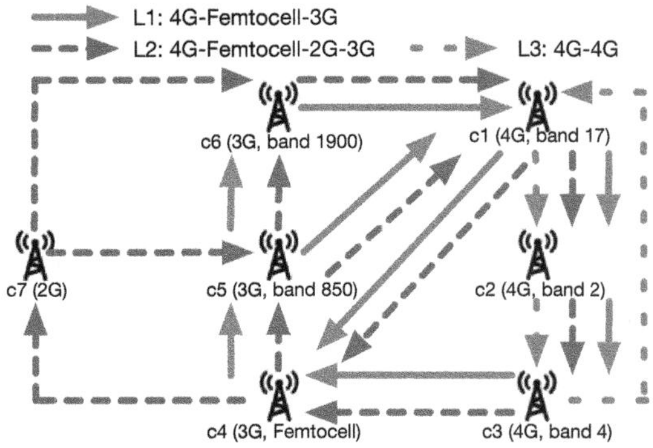

Figure 4: Idle-state persistent loops detected in US-I.

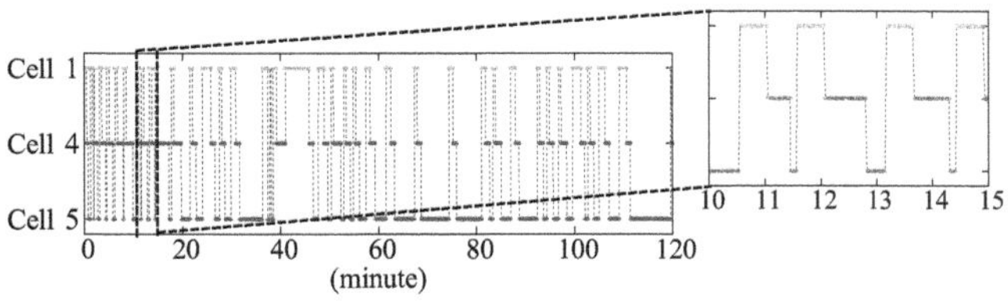

Figure 5: A two-hour log of associated cells at one static phone. The loop is observed despite varying loop cycles.

and to the core network by 7.6x (6329 : 827) and 23.5x (1226 : 58), respectively. These signaling messages are triggered by location update [4], and include messages related to radio resource allocation, data forwarding path reconfigurations and authentications.

These frequent loops can also degrade data performance. To evaluate it, we load a webpage (www.cnn.com) and a music file (about 5MB) every five minutes using Firefox, and record the loading time with/without loop at the same location in Figure 6b and Figure 6c. The loop slows down the webpage downloading by 11x than 4G (33x fold in the worst case). In the worst case, it takes 1.5 minute to download this webpage, whereas it would take 3 seconds using 4G. We observe similar performance slump in the music case with delay increase by 10x (50th) and 14.5x (worst case). The music file can be stably downloaded within 12 seconds using 4G, whereas it takes up to 180 seconds in our test. Such performance degrade is mainly caused by repetitive location update. The location update may trigger data path forwarding reconfiguration and re-authentication, during which the incoming/outgoing traffic would be delayed or dropped. Each 3G and Femtocell location update typically takes 3 to 6 seconds. In the worst case, the Femtocell location update can be further delayed to up to 30s.

Besides data performance, such idle-state persistent loops can also cause call drops. In the same experiment setting, we launch voice calls every five minutes using phone's dialer, and record the failures of voice call setup. We find that the call drop rate is 9.6%. The reason is that, when the call is initiated in presence of loops, the network cannot locate the user to the specific cell, thus unable to establish the voice call session.

∘ **L2: device-side preference misconfiguration.** Our loop detector further reports 8 variants of loops between 4G Macrocells, Femtocell, 2G and 3G Macrocells. Compared with previous category, when leaving the Femtocell, the mobile device handoffs to 2G first, then handoffs to 3G Macrocells. This happens when the Femtocell's signal strength is weak (< -115dBm) but still higher than 4G's high-preference handoff threshold (-116dBm in this scenario). It turns out that, this extra handoff is caused by improper preference configuration on the mobile device. With low signal strength, the device may temporarily lose association to Femtocell. Based on the 3GPP standard, the mobile device resumes the service by scanning all the cells, and associates to the first available one [10]. The order of the scanning is based on a preference list in the phone's SIM card. For some phones, the 2G is listed as highest preference, so the phone moves to 2G instead of 3G Macrocells. Once associated with 2G, the device would immediately handoff to 3G Macrocells, because the 2G cell assigns 3G cells higher preference. This way, the persistent loop continues.

For loops in this category, all negative impacts in 4G-Femtocell-3G loops also retain here. Besides, the device may further lose voice services in 2G cells. The reason is that, some 2G cells cannot support voice and data service *concurrently*. When the device is transmitting data, the voice service would be disabled.

∘ **L3: incremental 4G infrastructure upgrade.** The last variant is a 4G-only loop that appears until recently. We observe that US-I is upgrading its 4G infrastructure, and deploying cells under a new frequency band (c_2 in Figure 4). Before the upgrade, existing 4G cells (c_1 and c_3 in Figure 4) assign equal preferences to each other. US-I intends to migrate users to the new cells, which offers higher bandwidth. To achieve it, some old cells (c_1) assign higher preference to new cells. However, not all cells' preferences are updated timely: equal preference still exists on some cells (c_2). Such partial update cannot migrate user to the new cells: it violates Proposition 1, and incurs loops between cells. This loop has no direct impact on users, because all cells belong to the same location area. But this incurs larger 4G-Femtocell-3G and 4G-Femtocell-2G-3G loops, and indirectly amplifies their negative impacts.

5.2 Inconsistent Thresholds

In this category of instability, handoffs may oscillate among cells with uncoordinated thresholds. This may occur even when the preference values are globally consistent. It can be exemplified in Figure 3b. In the setting, both cells c_1 and c_2 agree that c_1 is preferred, but they apply different rules. Specifically, c_1 uses high-preference rule ($\gamma_2 > \Theta^{high}_{1,2}$ (-108dBm)), and c_2 uses equal-preference rule ($\gamma_1 > \gamma_2 + \Theta^{eq}_{2,1}$ (3dBm)). Therefore, the loop exists as long as the received signal strength meets the above condition. Similar misconfigurations can also occur in active-state handoff.

5.2.1 *Instability Condition*

We next derive the instability condition with respect to the radio threshold. We assume the preference settings are globally consistent, *i.e.* they all see the non-conflicting ordering on cell preference values. The following result shows the necessary and sufficient threshold configurations for any loop-free handoff (the proof is in Appendix B):

Proposition 2. *Consider n cells that use the idle-state handoffs only, and configure consistent preferences. The handoff stability is guaranteed iff. the radio thresholds are coordinated as follows: for every two cells c_i and c_j, (1)$\min_{c_i \to c_k} \Theta^{high}_{i,k} \geq \Theta^{serv}_j$ if $P_i > P_j$[2]; (2) $\min_{c_j \to c_k} \Theta^{high}_{j,k} \geq \Theta^{serv}_i$ if $P_i < P_j$; (3) $\Theta^{eq}_{i,j} + \Theta^{eq}_{j,i} \geq 0$ if $P_i = P_j$.* □

Compared with Proposition 1, Proposition 2 offers a *pairwise* configuration between any two cells. With consistent parameter configurations, two-cell loop avoidance also implies larger loop avoidance.

We further show that instability detection is still polynomial even with inconsistent preference (the proof is in Appendix C):

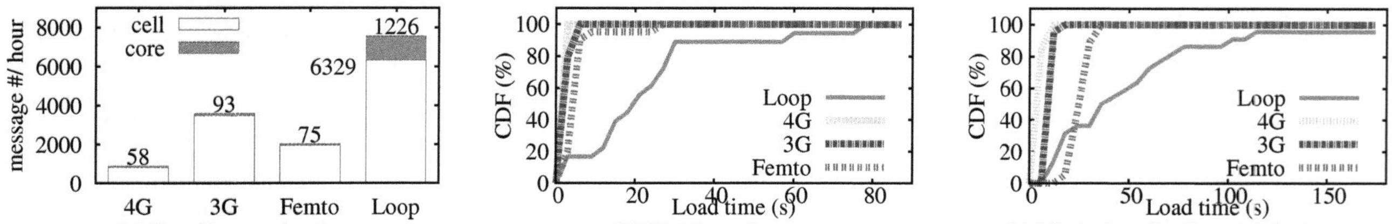

(a) Signaling overhead (b) Web browsing (c) Music downloading and playing

Figure 6: Impacts of loops of L1.

Proposition 3. *Given n cells at a location, the complexity of finding persistent loops is $O(mn)$, where m is the number of idle-state handoff rules from all cells.* □

5.2.2 Empirical Assessment

For this category of idle-state threshold misconfigurations, our experiments report no conflicts in US-I/US-II. The traces show that, both carriers impose stricter conditions over the idle-state thresholds than required (by Proposition 2). The real threshold settings are *fully decoupled* from the preferences: no matter how preferences are configured, the high-preference threshold Θ^{high} (US-I: [-114dBm, -110dBm], US-II: [-114dBm, -111dBm]) is *always* higher than the serving threshold Θ^{serv} (US-I/II: [-120dBm,-116dBm]) between any two cells. This signifies prudent engineering practice, contributing to good operations by both carriers in reality most of the time.

5.3 Active-Idle Misconfiguration

Instability may also be observed when the idle-state handoff is used in some cells but the active-state handoff is adopted in others. For instance, this could occur when the device exchanges highly bursty traffic, e.g., during Web browsing or instant messaging. The device thus stays active with traffic for a while, but then remains idle without traffic. This active/idle state switching is driven by the setup/release of radio connections, and is regulated by the Radio Resource Control (RRC) protocol [6]. For this scenario, uncoordinated configurations between idle and active state handoff may incur instability.

Figure 3c illustrates such an example of two-cell loop. In the setting, c_1's active-state handoff policy evaluates c_1 and c_2's signal strength with two thresholds. But it does not coordinate with c_2's idle-state handoff. So the persistent loops between them can happen when -111dBm$< \gamma_2 < \gamma_1 -$ 3dBm<-105dBm.

5.3.1 Stability Analysis

We next derive the stability conditions when active-state handoff is involved. Different from idle-state handoff, the active-state handoff logic is customizable. It can thus decide whether to access cells' radio qualities in decision. We first assume all cells' active-state handoffs evaluate radio conditions (the remaining cases will be handled by Proposition 6 of next section). Since there can be many ways to define the radio evaluation criteria, we cannot derive the (in)stability conditions in an arbitrary setting. Instead, we analyze a class of criteria, which are widely used in engineering practice [2, 6, 7] and research [24, 27]. To this end, we assume that the active-state handoff adopts the following radio criteria.

Assumption 1. *For any active-state handoff policy $c_i \to c_j$, it evaluates cell radio in the decision logic, and takes one of the following forms: (a)* ***absolute comparison:*** *$\gamma_j > \Theta_{i,j}$ (b)* ***indirect relative comparison:*** *$\gamma_i < \Theta1_i, \gamma_j > \Theta2_{i,j}$; (c)* ***direct relative comparison:*** *$\gamma_j > \gamma_j + \Theta_{i,j}$.*

In §5.3.2, we will validate that this assumption holds in real operational networks. The following configurations ensure stability for active-idle misconfiguration (the proof is in Appendix D):

Proposition 4. *Consider n cells $c_1, c_2, ..., c_n$ that satisfy Assumption 1. The stability is guaranteed, if all cells' active and idle-state handoffs' radio thresholds are coordinated as follows. For every two cells c_i and c_j, consider c_i's idle-state and c_j's active-state parameters: (1)$\min_{c_i \to c_k} \Theta^{high}_{i,k} \geq \Theta1_j$ if $P_i > P_j$ and c_j uses absolute comparison; (2) $\min_{c_j \to c_k} \Theta_{j,k} \geq \Theta^{serv}_i$ if $P_i < P_j$ and c_j uses indirect relative comparison; (3) $\Theta^{eq}_{i,j} + \Theta_{j,i} \geq 0$ if $P_i = P_j$ and c_j uses direct relative comparison.* □

Given Assumption 1, any active-state handoff can be split into two parts: an equivalent "idle-state handoff" and decisions over other observations. Indeed, when only active-state handoffs are used, Proposition 4 is sufficient but not always necessary. Stability can be ensured through other means (*e.g.* coordinating other parameters). The merit of Proposition 4 stems from its support for idle-state handoffs: it ensures stability within active-state handoffs only, *and* between idle and active state handoffs.

5.3.2 Empirical Validation

Validation of Assumption 1. We first exam whether Assumption 1 holds in real mobile networks. Constrained by no access to the operator's internal handoff decision logics, we gauge it from the runtime cellular messages exchanged between the device and the network (the serving cell). This is viable because in 3G/4G active-state handoff decision is device-assisted: the mobile device reports the radio measurement results to the serving cell, and then the serving cell makes the decision. We find that, both US-I and US-II's active-state handoff commands are usually *directly* triggered by 3G/4G RRC radio measurement reports, whose triggering conditions are standardized in [3, 6] and satisfy Assumption 1[3]. So effectively, the serving base station's handoff logic evaluates radio quality that satisfies Assumption 1. To demonstrate this, we calculate (1) the probability that the active-state handoff occurs after the measurement report, and (2) the device-perceived time interval between the delivery of last measurement reports and receipt of the active-state handoff command. Higher occurrence probability and smaller time interval would imply closer relation between active-state handoff and RRC measurement reports.

[3]For example, in 4G RRC, the report criteria A4 and B1 are the absolute comparisons, criteria A5 and B2 are the indirect relative comparisons, and criteria A3 is the direct relative comparison.

		US-I	US-II
#. Active-state handoff		11,050	10,178
Occurrence probability after RRC measurement report	Total	99.7%	97.8%
	Absolute comparison	1.0%	3.2%
	Indirect relative comparison	21.2%	34.2%
	Direct relative comparison	77.5%	60.4%
Interval between handoff command and last RRC measurement report	Min	40.6ms	20.1ms
	Med	79.9ms	60.0ms
	Max	141.4ms	266.5ms

Table 3: Probability and the elapsed time of active-state handoff which is triggered by RRC measurement report [3,6] (satisfying Assumption 1).

Table 3 shows both results. For both US-I and US-II, 99.7% and 97.8% active-state handoff happens after device sends RRC measurement reports, respectively. Among these handoff commands, 77.5% (60.4%) are initiated after RRC measurements triggered by direct relative comparison (*e.g.*, event A3 in 4G RRC). The time interval between the last measurement report (from device) and the handoff commands are short: the medium value is 79.9ms (60.0ms), while the maximum value is 141.4ms (266.5ms) in US-I (US-II). Both imply that, on reception of device's radio measurement reports (satisfying Assumption 1), the serving base station's decision logic immediately determines to trigger active-state handoff. This is coherent with the public literature [2,6,7,24,27].

Validation of active-idle misconfiguration. In this subcategory, our detection tool has found one instance in US-I (L4). We observe threshold incoordination between 3G Macrocell's idle-state handoff and Femtocell's active-state handoff for voice. The scenario is similar to that of Figure 3c. The device oscillates between 3G Macrocell (c_1) and Femtocell (c_2) when $\gamma_1 < -102dBm, \gamma_2 > -111dBm, \gamma_1 > \gamma_2 + 3dBm$. Interestingly, though no threshold misconfiguration is observed at the idle state, it occurs between idle and active-state handoffs.

This threshold incoordination is not shown without reasons. The Femtocell tends to move the active-state user to the Macrocell, even when the Macrocell's signal strength is weaker than the Femtocell's. This is because the Femtocell is deployed by users in an unplanned and isolated fashion. Its radio coverage is smaller than that of the Macrocell's. So the device has a higher chance to leave the Femtocell coverage. To avoid the potential voice call disruption, the Femtocell proactively switches the device to the Macrocell earlier than needed. Unfortunately, this configuration violates Proposition 4, and fails to achieve the expected goal. The device may handoff back to the Femtocell at the idle state under the same observations.

We test this loop at all viable indoor locations. At each spot, we launch a 24-hour test, and periodically load the webpage with Firefox every five minutes. We count the total number of connections, and how many experience the looped transition between two cells. The active-state handoff condition is satisfied with probability 9.4% (see Table 4). However, once satisfied, the loop always occurs in our test. We run the same webpage loading test to assess its impact on user traffic. As shown in Figure 7, this loop incurs extra delay about 40–90 seconds.

6. INSTABILITY BY LOOP-PRONE DECISION LOGIC

In this major class of instability, persistent loops may occur if cells apply conflicting handoff decision logics. Different from uncoordinated parameters, no matter how well parameters are tuned, conflicts always exist between decision engines. The fundamental root cause is that, the active-state handoff logic is customizable at each cell. We further discover two categories of instability in this class, one is between active-state logic (§6.1), and the other between active and idle-state engines (§6.2).

6.1 Active-Active Logic Conflicts

The category of instability may appear due to loop-prone decision logic, despite identical parameters. The root cause is that, active-state handoff may use decision logic different from the common one defined by its idle-state counterpart. Operators may customize the logic.

Figure 3d illustrates a two-cell-loop example. The active-state handoff decision logic at each cell adopts a simple rule: both agree to switch to the other if the signal strength at the neighboring cell is good enough (*e.g.* >-106dBm). However, if both cells satisfy the signal strength condition, the loop would occur. Note that regardless of the radio threshold to be set, the signal strength that satisfies the loop condition always exists.

6.1.1 Analytical Result

We now derive the stability conditions for the active-state decision logic. When all active-state decision engines assess radio quality and satisfy Assumption 1, loop-prone logic can be eliminated as follows (the proof is similar to Appendix D):

Proposition 5. *Consider n cells $c_1, c_2, ..., c_n$ that satisfy Assumption 1. The stability is guaranteed, if all cells' active and idle-state handoffs' radio thresholds are coordinated as follows. For every two cells c_i and c_j, consider c_i's idle-state and c_j's active-state parameters: (1)$\min_{c_i \to c_k} \Theta_{i,k} \geq \Theta 1_j$ if c_i uses indirect relative comparison, and c_j uses absolute comparison; (2) $\min_{c_j \to c_k} \Theta_{j,k} \geq \Theta 1_i$ if c_i uses absolute comparison, and c_j uses indirect relative comparison; (3) $\Theta_{i,j} + \Theta_{j,i} \geq 0$ if c_i and c_j use direct relative comparison.* □

Proposition 5 specifies a sufficient condition for loop-free, active handoffs. It is applicable to *any* handoff decision logic among cells, as long as it assesses radio quality. By coordinating the radio evaluation portion, no observations on the radio quality can lead to a loop. There are two benefits to this approach. First, it does not require coordination of other unknown parameters, thus being flexible and extensible. Second, it is also backward compatible with the idle-state handoff. This helps to prevent persistent loops between active-state handoffs, *and* between active and idle-state handoffs.

6.1.2 Empirical Validation

Our tool also detects one instance (L5) between two 4G cells in US-I at one location (Figure 3d). Both cells try to offload users to each other, when the other's signal strength is higher than certain threshold. However, such load-balancing decisions are not coordinated. A user thus oscillates between these two cells. Fortunately, this loop is not commonly observed. Among all 4G cells we collect, 67% of them use the same policy for the active-state handoff, but its neighboring cells are not observed to use the same rule except at one location. At this location, we conduct 6-hour ping tests and observe 8 loops (every 45 minutes on average) and the minimum one lasts only 43 seconds.

We further discover that, active-state loop-prone handoff engines are less observed due to prudent engineering practice. In US-I/US-II, most Macrocells' active-state decision logic is *more conservative* than their idle-state handoffs' counterpart. The radio quality measurements, which may trigger idle-state handoffs, cannot always trigger active-state handoffs in the same cell. The RRC measurement configuration for active handoffs uses stricter thresholds and report criteria than their idle-state handoff counterpart. The reason is that, active-state handoff is usually activated with data traffic. It tends to be more conservative to ensure the seamless data/voice service. Since the idle-state handoffs' thresholds follow the conservative loop-free setting, it is not surprising to see fewer active-state-only handoff loops.

Another related finding is that, the active-state loop-prone handoff logics are more common in 4G. In both US-I and US-II's 3G Macrocells, we didn't observe loop-prone handoff logics in active state. Our experiments show that, both operators' 3G active-state handoff logics are even more conservative than 4G's active-state counterparts: only handoffs between cells under the same frequency (intra-frequency handoff) are used, whose triggering condition is based on the direct relative comparison between serving and neighboring cells' radio qualities (Assumption 1). The reason is that, different from 4G LTE, 3G UMTS supports *soft handover* between cells under the same frequency. Because of this, intra-frequency handoff offers more seamless data service in mobility, thus more preferred by network operators. This further limits the available candidate cells, thus less prone to loops than 4G.

6.2 Active-Idle Logic Conflicts

This category of instability occurs when some cells apply idle-state handoffs, while others use active-state handoffs. Instability is always triggered if the handoff does not assess radio quality. This can be illustrated by the example of Figure 3e. In this case, c_1's active-state decision never considers the signal strength used by the c_2's idle-state handoff. Instead, c_1 uses load-balancing, regardless of the radio quality. Consequently, the serving cell oscillates between c_1 and c_2 once the switch conditions are satisfied in both handoff iterations. It shows that incoordination between decision logic functions is responsible for this unnecessary loop.

6.2.1 Analytical Result

If the active-state handoff does not assess radio quality, we show that idle-active loops would always occur:

Proposition 6. *Two-cell persistent loop between c_i and c_j always exists, if c_i's active-state logic to c_j does not evaluate radio quality, while c_j applies idle-state decision logic to c_i.* □

The proof can be found in Appendix E. In practice, the idle-state decision logic is available at all devices. Proposition 6 implies that, if a cell c_i's active-state handoff logic does not assess radio quality, the only possibility to avoid loops is that all its neighboring cells do not allow handoffs to c_i. However, this cell would consequently become isolated from others.

6.2.2 Empirical Validation

We have found two instances in this category, one (L6) in US-I and US-II, and the other (L7) in US-I only. L6 happens between two 3G Macrocells, whereas L7 happens between a 3G Macrocell and a Femtocell. The handoff decision logic is shown in Figure 3e, with c_1 = 3G and c_2 = 3G/Femtocell. This setting violates Proposition 4.

Our study shows that, both instances are caused by a design defect in 3G Radio Resource Control (RRC) protocol. The 3G RRC defines an offloading mechanism during connection setup. When a device attempts to setup a radio connection, the cell can reject the device's request, and redirects the device to a nearby cell [3]. However, this redirection *cannot* take cells' radio quality into consideration. Without a connection, the device cannot report the observations to the cell. If the current cell's radio quality is better than neighbors', the offloading cannot succeed, because the device would shift back in idle state.

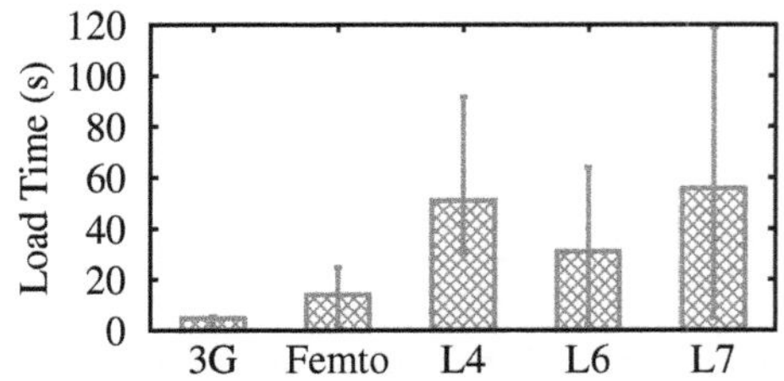

Figure 7: Impacts of loops of active-idle misconfiguration logic conflicts (web page loading).

We quantity both loops' impact under similar experiment settings to those for IS1-C3. We find that L6 and L7 are not commonly observed even when the loop condition is satisfied. L6 and L7 occur at the probability of 2.15% and 0.49% in our observation at one location (Table 4). The serving-cell congestion probability largely decides the loop occurrence. As shown in Figure 7, both loops incur delay about 20–53 seconds (median), up to two minutes. We observe that some phones do not always follow the cell's handoff command. Instead, they seek to reconnect to the serving cell. This is why the user device may still not suffer from it even when the loop condition is met.

7. AUTOMATIC LOOP DETECTION

With above analytical findings, we next design and implement a software tool, which enables automatic detection on handoff instability. Given the parameters and decision logics from cells at a location, our tool reports the conflicting parameters/logics that may incur instability, uncovers their root causes, and identifies the possible runtime observations that will trigger the loop occurrence.

7.1 Design

At first glance, loop detection looks fairly simple. A straightforward straw man solution works as follows. Given handoff configurations from all cells, the tool first enumerates all the looped handoff transitions $c_1 \to c_2 \to ... \to c_n \to c_1$. For each of them, a persistent loop would be reported, if there exist some runtime observations that can satisfy handoff configurations concurrently. To uncover root causes, we search whether there exists a set of configurations for each handoff that can eliminate the loop. If yes, then the loop is incurred by uncoordinated configurations (§5); otherwise, it is due to loop-prone logic (§6).

However, this approach is deemed impractical. Enumerating loops implies state explosions on the number of cells and configurations. Uncovering root causes further incurs exponential search over the configuration space. To address both issues, we apply the domain-specific (in)stability conditions to reduce the complexity. We differentiate loops with/without active-state handoffs, and apply distinctive techniques for loop detection and cause inference.

∘ *Idle-state handoff only.* We adopt a two-step procedure to detect all idle-state handoff loops. First, given all cells at each location, we check if these cells' preference settings are consistent. If so, enumeration can be replaced with pairwise threshold check according to Proposition 2. Otherwise, enumeration with pruning is applied based on Proposition 1. In each round, we seek to find all loops with a cell c_i involved. Starting from c_i, we run a variant DFS algorithm over the graphs of handoff transitions. For each cell c_j to be visited, a variable γ_j is maintained, which denotes the potential radio measurement violating stability. We initialize γ_i, and derive γ_j recursively. When c_j is visited from c_k, (1) if $P_{k,j} > P_{k,k}$, then

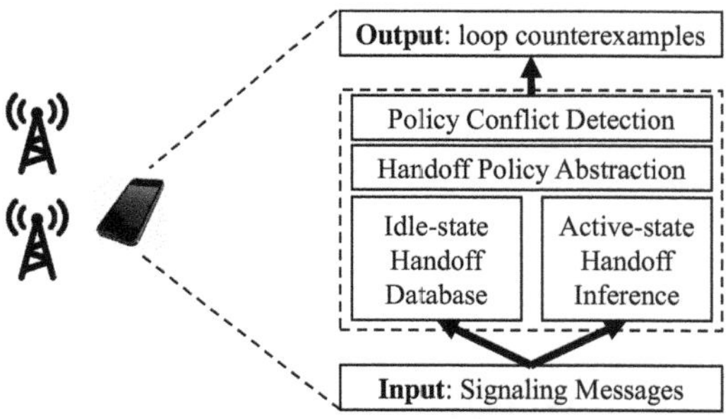

Figure 8: In-device for loop detection.

$\gamma_j \leftarrow \Theta^{high}_{k,j}$; (2) if $P_{k,j} = P_{k,k}$, then $\gamma_j \leftarrow \gamma_k + \Theta^{eq}_{k,j}$; (3) if $P_{k,j} < P_{k,k}$, c_j is pruned if $\gamma_k > \Theta^{serv}_k$; otherwise, $\gamma_j \leftarrow \Theta^{low}_{k,j}$. If c_i is visited again, a loop is reported if γ_i can satisfy the last handoff transition. Once all loops with c_i are found, we remove c_i from the cell list, and detect loops for the remaining cells. The root cause analysis is straightforward, since the loops in this category can only be caused by misconfigurations.

∘ *Active and idle-state handoff.* With active-state handoffs, we apply Propositions 4, 5 and 6 to eliminate unnecessary enumerations. For each cell c, we first check if its active-state handoff execution evaluates radio quality. If not, idle-active handoff loops are reported between c and its neighbors, with the cause "loop-prone logic" (Proposition 6). We further remove c, and replace each handoff transition from c with a new one from c's parents, with the configuration as that for $parent(c) \rightarrow c$. Next, if all cells' handoff executions apply pairwise radio quality evaluation, we check if they satisfy Propositions 4 and 5. If yes, no loops would be reported. This helps to avoid checking other parameters. Otherwise, enumeration would be invoked in the worst case.

7.2 In-phone Implementation

Since we have no access to the cellular network infrastructure, we implement the above design in the mobile device. Figure 8 illustrates our implementation. We first enable in-device cellular configuration collection with *MobileInsight* [1], a system app to collect signaling messages. With these inputs, our tool actively synthesizes the abstract model and applies the loop detection algorithm.

∘ *Handoff configuration collection.* Our implementation proactively switches the phone to every cell at each location (via *e.g.* secret code **#2263#* in Samsung S5), and collects both idle and active-state handoff configurations. The idle-state handoff configurations can be readily derived from the standardized logic and parameters from the *System Information Block (SIB)* messages. The active-state handoff ones are not visible to the device. To infer them, we observe that the serving cells' measurement configurations are available, which are designed for active-state handoffs. These report criteria are standardized in [3, 6] and satisfy Assumption 1. For each cell, our implementation monitors these configurations and handoff commands in *RRCReconfiguration* message, together with the measurements from the device. If a handoff command without measurement is observed, a configuration without radio evaluation is inferred. Otherwise, all measurement reports before the command are treated as potential configurations, and checked in the loop detection.

∘ *Parameter abstraction.* The actual configurations should be mapped to the abstract parameters before detection. Following [3, 6], we perform three parameter conversions before the detection: (1) *threshold set selection*, in which we select the corresponding thresholds based on the usage scenarios (*e.g.* RSRP or RSRQ as the radio metric, normal or VoLTE active-state handoff); (2) *threshold combination*, in which we combine different offsets/hysteresis from real parameters to the thresholds in the model. For example, in the equal-preference, idle-state handoff, the threshold $\Theta^{eq}_{s,c}$ in the model is the sum of the serving cell's hysteresis, the frequency-specific offset, and the cell-specific offset; (3) *threshold scaling*, in which we scale the thresholds based on the speed-scaling factors from SIBs.

∘ *Loop detection.* We implement the detector in Python, which accepts the abstract model as input, and reports the counterexamples. Each report includes the cells in the loop, the conflicting configurations, and the measurements that can trigger the loop. They are used to set up the validation experiments in Sections 5 and 6.

Accuracy analysis. For idle-state handoff only, our tool guarantees that it can find all loops without false positives/negatives. This is because that the phone has full knowledge of the idle-state handoffs, including its decision logics (standardized) and parameters (from the signaling messages). For active-state and active-idle loops, false positive exists. This is because our inference of the decision logics based on Assumption 1 may be incomplete. So the over-detection may exist: active-state and active-idle loops reported by our tool may not always happen in reality. But false negative is still prevented from active-state and active-idle loops: if a loop exists, it would always be detected by our tool.

Limitations. Our current design and implementation have three downsides. First, the loops reported in our design may not always be observed in practice, because the observations triggering the loops may not always appear. To test the loop existence, validation experiments should be conducted. However, they still offer hints for validations, and should be fixed because external measurements cannot always be controlled to avoid loops. Second, the active-state handoff configurations are not accessible to device-side implementation. This causes false positives, and prevents us from uncovering more insights on the active-state handoff. Third, without access to the carrier's handoff configurations, our tool has to be run area-by-area to detect the loops.

7.3 Experiments on Operational Networks

We run the designed tool to validate persistent loops from real carrier configurations, and quantify their negative impacts. Figure 9 summarizes the outdoor and indoor test settings. The cell distribution at different outdoor locations confirms that today's deployment is quite dense and hybrid. At most locations, there are about 8–16 cells. On average, there are about 11 cells in US-I and 10 cells in US-II. The number of unique cells, excluding those observed at multiple locations, are 275 (4G: 120, 3G: 97, 2G: 58) in US-I and 222 (4G: 92, 3G: 66, 2G: 64) in US-II. It confirms that 4G cells have smaller coverage and denser deployment whereas the 2G coverage is much larger. The indoor setting has similar cell density as the outdoor one. Figure 9c plots the median radio signal strength measured at 50 indoor spots in US-I networks. For 2G/3G/4G comparisons, we use normalized percentages obtained from OpenSignal[4], a popular network monitor app, where 0% indicates no coverage and 100% indicates strongest signal strength[5]. It implies that despite higher speed, 4G suffers worse coverage than 3G and 2G in indoor scenarios. The results in US-II are similar and thus omitted here.

We also validate that, the assumption of invariant runtime ob-

[4]http://opensignal.com/android/

[5]4G uses different signal strength metrics from 3G/2G. The minimal strength observed in 3G/2G is -113dBm whereas it is around -125dBm in 4G.

	Avg. cell#/spot		Unique cell#	
	US-I	**US-II**	**US-I**	**US-II**
#4G	2.6	2.1	120	92
#3G	3.4	2.4	97	66
#2G	5.4	5.6	58	64
#All	11.4	10.1	275	222

(a) Statistics of outdoor cell deployment

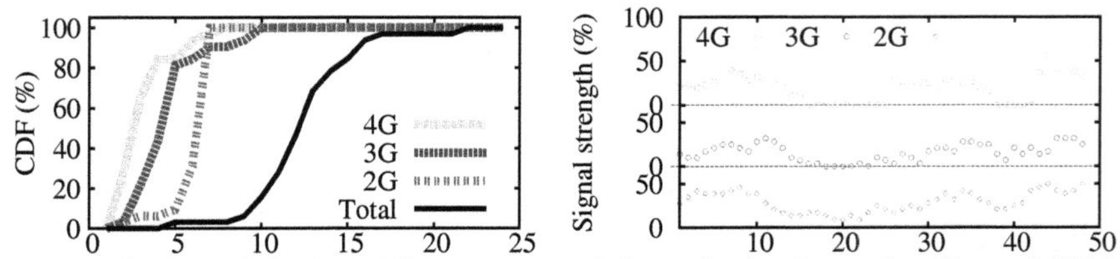

(b) Outdoor cell density in US-I (c) Indoor radio signal strength at 50 spots in US-I

Figure 9: Summary of outdoor and indoor deployment.

	#Scenario instances	Occurrence of Misconfigurations or Loop-prone logic	Loop occurrence (parameter+logic +observation)
L1: 4G-Femto-3G	8	96.8%	25.0%
L2: 4G-Femto-2G-3G	8	96.8%	0.49%
L3: 4G-4G	1	2.2%	2.2%
L4: 3G-Femto	1	96.8%	9.4%
L5: 4G-4G	1	1.6%	1.6%
L6: 3G-3G	1	63.4%	2.15%
L7: 3G-Femto	1	96.8%	0.49%

Table 4: Loop occurrence probability in US-I.

servations in persistent loop is reasonable in practice: in response to runtime radio measurement, both US-I and US-II's handoff decision-makings takes no more than 141.4ms and 266.5ms (§3), respectively. For comparison, for all the tested indoor spots, 95% of cells' signal strength change at same spot takes more than 229.5ms (5.10s) in US-I (US-II), which is much slower than handoff decision making. So during the handoff decision, it is safe to make the invariant runtime observation assumption.

The detailed findings on each category have been described in Sections 5 and 6. With our tool, we have found 21 instances of potential misconfigurations and/or loop-prone logics, which are further classified into 7 categories. For each category, we further run indoor experiments to validate its existence, and estimate its occurrence probability. For each indoor spot, we run a 24-hour test and record the looped handoffs between cells. Table 4 lists the occurrence probability of problematic configurations (left column), and the occurrence probability of loops (right column) observed at one specific location. Other locations have similar results. It shows that, instabilities occur in 2G, 3G and 4G networks, with varying occurrence probabilities. From these instances, we show that, loops with both the uncoordinated configurations and loop-prone decision logic indeed exist. Although carriers have applied at least two prudent rules to mitigate loops, configuration conflicts still exist for various reasons, such as diverse handoff goals, the incremental and/or unplanned cell deployment, the device misconfiguration, and the design defects for the connection control mechanism. Loops incur negative impacts upon both the user and the network. We notice a big distinction between both columns, which reflect the gaps of the root causes and the actual impact. The reason is that, the occurrence of actual loops (right column) is also affected by another runtime observations, which may not always be satisfied. It has two implications. First, misconfigurations or loop-prone logics that may trigger persistent loops are not rare in reality. Most settings are problematic once femtocells are deployed. It indicates that the operator's network infrastructure is not fully upgraded to handle small cells which can be deployed by users. Second, although the misconfigurations occur with high probability, the satisfying signal strength that triggers loops do not always occur. For example, only L1 (25%) is relatively common and other loops like L2, L3, L5, L6 and L7 are rarely observed (below 2%). This is attributed to good practice and satisfactory coverage in radio planning and cell deployment.

8. DISCUSSIONS

We now discuss how to fix the configuration conflicts and their resulting loops. Given that persistent loops hurt both the user performance and the network's operation, we envision that both carriers and users have incentives to remove loops. We next propose solutions to both sides.

8.1 Network-Side Coordination

The carrier should coordinate cells' local configurations to avoid handoff instability. There are two issues to be addressed: (1) How to resolve loops from the existing handoff configurations, and (2) How to avoid new persistent loops from configuration updates?

Fixing existing loops. The carrier can take two steps. First, the operator should check if configuration conflicts exist at each location. This can be done with our loop detection tool (§7).

In the second step, conflicting configurations in loop may be coordinated for stability. It should be noted that, there can be more than one way to fix each loop. Consider the actual loop with the Femtocell involved in Figure 4 (§5.1.2). At least two fixes are available: *(i)* on 4G Macrocell, assign lower preference to Femtocell, or *(ii)* on Femtocell, assign lower preference to 3G Macrocell. The carrier may pick either one based on its demand. For example, applying (i) can provide users with high-speed data service in 4G, while choosing (ii) enables traffic offloading from 4G to 3G.

However, not all schemes are bullet-proof. New loops may appear when fixing old ones. For example, the following scheme can also fix the above loop: *(iii)* on Femtocell, assign higher preference to 3G Macrocell. However, this causes a new loop $Femtocell \rightarrow 3GMacrocell \rightarrow Femtocell$, because it violates Proposition 1. To address this, one could detect the loop again after the fix, and resolve new loops. But this requires enumeration of all configurations. More importantly, there is no guarantee that all loops will be finally fixed.

We propose a general guideline to determine a safe loop fix. Assume a fix requires to modify the configuration for $c_i \rightarrow c_j$. Our guideline imposes a monotonic condition over this fix:

Guideline 1. (Safe configuration update) *For any runtime measurements that cannot trigger $c_i \rightarrow c_j$ before the configuration update, it should not trigger $c_i \rightarrow c_j$ after the update.*

If Guideline 1 is followed, it is straightforward to prove that, for any loop that exists *after* this configuration update, it must have already existed *before* the update. New loops cannot appear thereafter. No extra actions are needed after the old loop fix. So if all fixes obey this rule, all loops will be ultimately fixed.

Handling policy update. The handoff configurations or decision logics can change over time for various reasons, including incremental/unplanned cell deployment, tuning some cells' handoff goals, etc. The carrier may expect to retain stability after the update. We discuss how to achieve this in a single configuration update $c_i \rightarrow c_j$, assuming that stability is guaranteed before the change. Stability with multiple updates can be ensured with each step satisfying the following criteria.

Consider cell c_i adds a new handoff rule to c_j. Two approaches exist to prevent new loops. The first one is to detect loops after the addition, which however implies enumeration of loops (§7). The second is to apply constraints over the new update, without coordinating with others. In §5-6, we have seen two prudent rules from real carriers: (1) for a new idle-state handoff, set threshold Θ^{high} higher than threshold Θ^{serv}, regardless of the preference setting; (2) for a new active-state handoff, set it as at least conservative as the corresponding idle-state handoff. Both rules help to avoid new loops. Propositions 1– 6 also impose such conditions on new updates.

Next consider a configuration deletion: a cell c_i deletes its local handoff toward c_j. The stability is still retained, because no new handoff transitions are introduced.

The last scenario is to modify an existing handoff configuration for $c_i \rightarrow c_j$. This update is equivalent to a two-step procedure: delete the old configuration, and then add the new one. The first step does not cause new loops, while the second step can be safeguarded by above rules for new configurations. Guideline 1 is also applicable here: If the new policy is as conservative as the old one, the overall mobility are still stable after the update.

Runtime mitigation? In addition to configuration coordinations, we are aware that loops can be mitigated at runtime, similar to the transition loops due to radio dynamics. The mobility history can be used to stop the loops by blocking visited cells [9]. Signaling reduction techniques can reduce the impacts [4]. Despite helpful, they do not offer fundamental fixes to loops. Since the configuration-based loops are fixable, the carrier should not rely on runtime mitigations only. Instead, they should fix the configuration conflicts.

Implementation suggestions. To fix existing loops, a centralized controller is needed for configuration coordination. For loops between cells from the same area, loop resolution can be implemented at the location area controller. For other loops, higher-layer controller may be needed. For configuration updates, they can be handled in either centralized or distributed fashions. If loop detection is used, a central controller is still needed. If extra constraints are applied to configuration addition/modification, the resolution can be implemented at each cell. Every cell discovers all neighboring cells' handoff configurations under the self-organizing network (SoN) framework [7, 8], and apply these constraints over its own updates.

8.2 Device-Side Loop Prevention

When loops are not fixed by the carrier, the mobile device has the incentive to prevent itself from suffering from loops. Although the device cannot coordinate configurations among cells, it can configure itself to eliminate loops. At each location, the device can actively collect all cells' configurations, and run the loop detection algorithm (§7). Upon detecting a loop, the device can either statically block some cells, or stop the handoff procedure at runtime. Noted that, this device-side approach cannot replace the network-side configuration coordination. Without the network-side fix, users without this scheme still suffer from persistent loops.

9. RELATED WORK

In recent years, there have been extensive research efforts on 3G/4G mobile networks. They include radio analysis [11,21], TCP over cellular network [18, 29], cross-layer optimization [13, 19], and software-defined cellular networks [17, 20]. On mobility support, extensive optimizations have been proposed for diverse goals, including reducing radio link failure and transient oscillations [14, 24], traffic offloading [12, 16], and supporting heterogeneous network [15, 23]. Instead of optimizing one specific handoff goal, our work focuses on the conflicts between handoff policies (with possibly different goals). Our preliminary work [22] discloses the existence of persistent loops in idle-state handoffs and this work greatly extends it. We conduct a systematic study with both analysis and empirical validation and covers both idle-state handoffs and active-state handoffs.

Misconfigurations and management-plane conflicts have been examined in other Internet systems such as BGP [25], DNS [26], and data center networks [28]. Our work is inspired by such early efforts, but focuses on the management plane for mobility management in 3G/4G mobile networks. We show that policy-driven configurations may lead to instability during handoffs.

10. CONCLUSION

Mobility support is a key utility function offered by 3G/4G cellular networks. As more mobile users are accessing the Internet from their smartphones through the 3G/4G infrastructure, mobility management is likely to become more critical. Like all operational networks, current mobile carriers allow for flexible configurations on their micro-mobility support scheme to address policy concerns. This management-plane aspect on mobility has been largely overlooked by past research efforts. In this work, we seek to conduct a first study toward this general direction.

Our results can be best interpreted from both viewpoints. On one hand, our effort yields some interesting and new findings. The discovered persistent loops, as well as their triggering conditions, have been partially validated in operational networks. Though the incurred damage, in terms of signaling overhead and performance degradation, is not appalling to some users, such problematic issues should be addressed as we seek to build a more dependable, high-performance, mobile network infrastructure. The presented analysis, as well as modeling, despite a little simplistic, also produces some interesting results not reported in the literature. On the other hand, this work is still at the early stage, and the obtained results are likely to be refined over time. Several important issues (e.g., other configuration parameters, and more forms of customized decision logic) have been overlooked so far. Moreover, other structural properties (e.g., whether the handoff process converges to the anticipated cell, and the convergence speed) warrant further efforts. In the broader context, moving beyond current focus on both data and control planes, management plane in 3G/4G mobile networks (hopefully also the upcoming 5G) is still a wide-open research area and deserves more attention. We hope our effort may stimulate more people in the community to work on this important direction.

Acknowledgments: We thank the anonymous reviewers for their constructive comments. We greatly appreciate our shepherd, Dr. Bozidar Radunovic for his valuable feedback. We also thank Jie Zhao for participating in trace collection in this work. This work is supported in part by NSF awards (CNS-1526456, CNS-1526985, CNS-1423576 and CNS-1421440).

11. REFERENCES

[1] Mobileinsight project. http://metro.cs.ucla.edu/mobile_insight.
[2] "ZTE UMTS Handover Description". *http://www.slideshare.net/quyetnguyenhong/zte-umtshandoverdescription.*
[3] 3GPP. TS25.331: Radio Resource Control (RRC), 2006.
[4] 3GPP. TS24.008: Mobile Radio Interface Layer 3, 2012.
[5] 3GPP. TS25.304: User Equipment (UE) Procedures in Idle Mode and Procedures for Cell Reselection in Connected Mode, 2012.
[6] 3GPP. TS36.331: E-UTRA; Radio Resource Control (RRC), 2012.

[7] 3GPP. TS32.522: Self-Organizing Networks (SON) Policy Network Resource Model (NRM) Integration Reference Point (IRP), 2013.
[8] 3GPP. TS32.511: Telecommunication Management; Automatic Neighbor Relation management; Concepts and Requirements, 2014.
[9] 3GPP. TS36.413: S1 Application Protocol (S1AP), 2014.
[10] 3GPP. TS36.304: E-UTRA; User Equipment Procedures in Idle Mode, 2015.
[11] P. K. Athivarapu, R. Bhagwan, S. Guha, V. Navda, and et.al. Radiojockey: mining program execution to optimize cellular radio usage. In *ACM MobiCom*, Aug. 2012.
[12] A. Balasubramanian, R. Mahajan, and A. Venkataramani. Augmenting mobile 3g using wifi. In *ACM MobiSys*, June 2010.
[13] N. Balasubramanian, A. Balasubramanian, and A. Venkataramani. Energy consumption in mobile phones: A measurement study and implications for network applications. In *IMC*, 2009.
[14] C. Brunner, A. Garavaglia, M. Mittal, M. Narang, and J. V. Bautista. Inter-system Handover Parameter Optimization. In *VTC Fall*, 2006.
[15] M. Z. Chowdhury, W. Ryu, E. Rhee, and Y. M. Jang. Handover between Macrocell and Femtocell for UMTS Based Networks. In *IEEE ICACT*, 2009.
[16] W. Dong, S. Rallapalli, R. Jana, L. Qiu, K. Ramakrishnan, L. Razoumov, Y. Zhang, and T. W. Cho. ideal: Incentivized dynamic cellular offloading via auctions. *TON*, 22(4):1271–1284, 2014.
[17] A. Gudipati, D. Perry, L. E. Li, and S. Katti. Softran: Software defined radio access network. In *Proceedings of the second ACM SIGCOMM workshop on Hot topics in software defined networking*, pages 25–30. ACM, 2013.
[18] J. Huang, F. Qian, Y. Guo, Y. Zhou, Q. Xu, Z. M. Mao, S. Sen, and O. Spatscheck. An in-depth study of LTE: Effect of network protocol and application behavior on performance. In *SIGCOMM*, 2013.
[19] U. Javed, D. Han, R. Caceres, J. Pang, S. Seshan, and A. Varshavsky. Predicting handoffs in 3g networks. In *MobiHeld*, 2011.
[20] X. Jin, L. E. Li, L. Vanbever, and J. Rexford. Softcell: scalable and flexible cellular core network architecture. In *CoNEXT*, 2013.
[21] S. Kumar, E. Hamed, D. Katabi, and L. Erran Li. LTE Radio Analytics Made Easy and Accessible. In *ACM SIGCOMM*, 2014.
[22] Y. Li, J. Xu, C. Peng, and S. Lu. A First Look at Unstable Mobility Management in Cellular Networks. In *HotMobile*, Feb 2016.
[23] M. Liu, Z. Li, X. Guo, and E. Dutkiewicz. Performance Analysis and Optimization of Handoff Algorithms in Heterogeneous Wireless Networks. *IEEE Transactions on Mobile Computing*, 7(7):846–857, July 2008.
[24] A. Lobinger, S. Stefanski, T. Jansen, and I. Balan. Coordinating Handover Parameter Optimization and Load Balancing in LTE Self-Optimizing Networks. In *VTC Spring*. IEEE, 2011.
[25] R. Mahajan, D. Wetherall, and T. Anderson. Understanding BGP Misconfiguration. In *ACM SIGCOMM CCR*, 2002.
[26] V. Pappas, Z. Xu, S. Lu, D. Massey, A. Terzis, and L. Zhang. Impact of Configuration Errors on DNS Robustness. In *SIGCOMM*, 2004.
[27] G. P. Pollini. Trends in Handover Design. *IEEE Communications Magazine*, 34(3):82–90, 1996.
[28] P. Sun, R. Mahajan, J. Rexford, L. Yuan, M. Zhang, and A. Arefin. A Network-State Management Service. In *ACM SIGCOMM*, 2014.
[29] F. P. Tso, J. Teng, W. Jia, and D. Xuan. Mobility: A Double-Edged Sword for HSPA Networks: A Large-Scale Test on Hong Kong Mobile HSPA Networks. *IEEE Transactions on Parallel and Distributed Systems*, 23(10):1895–1907, 2012.
[30] Wikipedia. Handover. *http://en.wikipedia.org/wiki/Handover*.
[31] D. Wong and T. J. Lim. Soft handoffs in CDMA Mobile Systems. *IEEE Personal Communications*, 4(6):6–17, 1997.

APPENDIX

A. PROOF FOR PROPOSITION 1

The proof is based on the fact that, the above preference setting is non-decreasing. We can always find a runtime observation that incurs loop as follows: (a) $\gamma_{i+1} > \Theta^{high}_{i,i+1}$, and (b) $\gamma_{j+1} > \Theta^{high}_{j,j+1}$ if $P_{j,j} < P_{j,j+1}$, or $\gamma_{j+1} > \gamma_j + \Theta^{eq}_{j,j+1}$ if $P_{j,j} = P_{j,j+1}$. On the other hand, if above preference setting does not hold, two cases may arise: (1) all cells are of equal preference, then Proposition 2 below will guarantee the loop freedom; (2) at least one cell c_k has $P_{k,k} > P_{k,k+1}$, then the loop can be avoided by setting Θ^{serv}_k equal to the minimum achievable signal strength. □

B. PROOF FOR PROPOSITION 2

The proof starts from the two-cell case. By enumerating all potential looped transitions, we verify that two-cell loops can be eliminated if and only if the above condition holds. This way, the necessity of Proposition 2 is readily guaranteed. The sufficiency of the condition is further proven via contradiction. Assume the above threshold conditions are satisfied, but a larger loop $c_1 \to c_2 ... \to c_n \to c_1$ still exists. There are two possibilities: (a) all cells are of equal preference. By listing their handoff decisions (inequalities) and summing them up, it can be readily shown that (3) is not satisfied; (b) some cells are of different preference. Then it can be shown that there always exists one cell applying high-preference decision, another cell applying low-preference decision, and any cells in between applying equal-preference decision. By listing their handoff decisions (Figure 2) and summing them up, it can be readily shown that (1)–(3) are not satisfied. □

C. PROOF FOR PROPOSITION 3

We prove it by constructing a corresponding algorithm. Given an arbitrary cell c_i, we find all loops with c_i involved. Starting from c_i, we run a variant DFS algorithm by following the idle-state decision rules for transition. In the process, for each cell c_j to be visited, a variable $\gamma_{i,j}$ is maintained, which denotes the potential signal condition violating stability. When c_j is visited by c_k in DFS, (1) if $P_{k,j} > P_{k,k}$, then $\gamma_{i,j} \leftarrow \Theta^{high}_{k,j}$; (2) if $P_{k,j} = P_{k,k}$, then $\gamma_{i,j} \leftarrow \gamma_{i,k} + \Theta^{eq}_{k,j}$; (3) if $P_{k,j} < P_{k,k}$, c_j is pruned in DFS if $\gamma_{i,k} > \Theta^{serv}_k$, otherwise $\gamma_{i,j} \leftarrow \Theta^{low}_{k,j}$. Whenever c_i is visited again, a persistent loop is reported. Once all loops with c_i involved are found, we remove c_i and all the related decision rules from the cell list, and detect loops for the remaining cells. □

D. PROOF FOR PROPOSITION 4

We prove this with a concrete configuration scheme. For every active-state decision logic $c_i \to c_j$, we define an auxiliary "idle-state" handoff logic based on its radio evaluation part. If form (a) in Assumption 1 is used, then the auxiliary logic is defined as $P_{i,j} > P_{i,i}, \Theta^{high}_{i,j} = \Theta_{i,j}$. If (b) is used, it is defined as $P_{i,j} < P_{i,i}, \Theta^{serve}_i = \Theta1_i, \Theta^{low}_{i,j} = \Theta2_{i,j}$. Otherwise, it is defined as $P_{i,j} = P_{i,i}, \Theta^{eq}_{i,j} = \Theta_{i,j}$. This auxiliary logic has the following property: for any runtime observation that can trigger active-state handoff $c_i \to c_j$, it can also trigger this idle-state handoff. Then we replace all active-state handoff policies with auxiliary ones, and apply Propositions 1 on all policies for threshold coordination. Based on the relation between active-state handoff and the auxiliary "idle-state" handoff, this coordination ensures stability among idle and active-sate handoff decisions. □

E. PROOF FOR PROPOSITION 5

It is proven by contradiction. Note that, regardless of the preference and/or threshold setting on c_j, certain cell radio quality γ_i and γ_j can trigger idle-state handoff from c_j to c_i. Without evaluating radio quality, $c_i \to c_j$ can always concurrently happen with $c_j \to c_i$. □

Transiently Secure Network Updates

Arne Ludwig
TU Berlin, Germany
arne@inet.tu-berlin.de

Szymon Dudycz
University of Wroclaw, Poland
szymon.dudycz@gmail.com

Matthias Rost
TU Berlin, Germany
mrost@inet.tu-berlin.de

Stefan Schmid
Aalborg University, Denmark
schmiste@cs.aau.dk

ABSTRACT

Computer networks have become a critical infrastructure. Especially in shared environments such as datacenters it is important that a correct, consistent and secure network operation is guaranteed at any time, even during routing policy updates. In particular, at no point in time should it be possible for packets to bypass security critical waypoints (such as a firewall or IDS) or to be forwarded along loops.

This paper studies the problem of how to change routing policies in a transiently consistent manner. Transiently consistent network updates have been proposed as a fast and resource efficient alternative to per-packet consistent updates. Our main result is a negative one: we show that there are settings where the two basic properties waypoint enforcement and loop-freedom cannot be satisfied simultaneously. Even worse, we rigorously prove that deciding whether a waypoint enforcing, loop-free network update schedule exists is NP-hard. These results hold for both kinds of loop-freedom used in the literature: strong and relaxed loop-freedom. This paper also presents optimized, exact mixed integer programs to compute optimal update schedules. We report on extensive simulation results and initiate the discussion of scenarios where multiple waypoints need to be ensured (also known as service chains).

1. INTRODUCTION

Computer networks are becoming more and more programmable and flexible. In particular, the software-defined networking paradigm enables a logically centralized operation of computer networks: in a Software-Defined Network (SDN), a software controller can install, update and verify "the paths that packets follow", i.e., the (routing) *policies* [5], fast and in a globally consistent manner.

However, today, we do not have a good understanding yet of the opportunities and limitations of a more dynamic network management in general, and the Software-Defined Network (SDN) paradigm in particular. Over the last years, especially the problem of consistent network updates has received much attention [11, 13, 19, 22, 31]. While the logically centralized control introduced by software-defined networking is appealing, an SDN still needs to be regarded as a distributed system, posing non-trivial challenges: in particular, the communication channel between switches and controller exhibits non-negligible and varying delays [6, 13, 18]. The non-atomicity of seemingly atomic data plane updates means that there are periods when the network configuration is incorrect despite looking correct from the control plane perspective [17].

SIGMETRICS '16, June 14–18, 2016, Antibes Juan-Les-Pins, France.

ISBN 978-1-4503-4266-7/16/06...$15.00

DOI: http://dx.doi.org/10.1145/2896377.2901476

In a first line of works, initiated by Reitblatt et al. [31], network updates providing strong consistency guarantees have been studied: even during the transition from an old routing policy π_1 to a new routing policy π_2, the *Per-Packet Consistency* (PPC) property is ensured, i.e., each packet will either be forwarded according to π_1 (exclusively-)or π_2, but not a combination of both. In a second line of works, initiated by Mahajan and Wattenhofer [22], weaker transient consistency properties have been investigated: during a network update, a packet may be forwarded according to the old policy π_1 at some switches and according to the new policy π_2 at other switches; however, the update still provides the most basic transient guarantees, such as *Loop-Freedom* (LF): packets will never be forwarded along a loop. Transiently loop-free updates are an attractive alternative to stronger consistency models such as PPC, as updates take effect earlier, are more resource efficient (no need for extra rules on the switch), and do not require tagging (often problematic given the limited packet header space). Ludwig et al. [19] have observed that besides the canonical *strong* loop-freedom, there exists a *relaxed* notion of loop-freedom which facilitates even faster network updates.

Security critical environments require additional consistency guarantees, beyond loop-freedom. A particularly important one is *Waypoint Enforcement* (WPE): it needs to be ensured that packets traverse specific network functions or middleboxes. In fact, today's computer networks consist of a large number of so-called *middleboxes*, providing a wide spectrum of in-network functionality for security, performance, policy compliance, etc. For example, network policies are often defined in terms of adjacency matrices or big switch abstractions, specifying which traffic is allowed between an ingress network port s and an outgress network port d [14]. In order to enforce such a policy, traffic from s to d needs to traverse a middlebox instance inspecting and classifying the flows. The number of middleboxes in enterprise networks can be of the same order of magnitude as the number of routers [12]. Middleboxes can also be virtualized [1]: such middleboxes can be deployed fast and flexibly on the virtualized network nodes, e.g., running in a virtual machine on a commodity x86 server.

In a nutshell, a transiently consistent waypoint enforcing upate should guarantee that before, during and after the transition from π_1 to π_2, packets traverse a certain middlebox (the waypoint).

1.1 Contributions

This paper studies the problem of how to consistently update a network such that waypoint enforcement and loop-freedom are ensured. In particular, we make the following contributions:

1. **Waypoint enforcement matters:** We show that waypoints may easily be bypassed if no countermeasures are in place. Moreover, we prove that Loop-Freedom (LF) and Waypoint Enforcement (WPE) cannot always be implemented in a wait-free manner, in the sense that the controller must rely on an upper bound estimation for the maximal packet latency in the network.

2. **LF and WPE may conflict:** We show that the transient Waypoint Enforcement WPE property may conflict with Loop-Freedom (LF), in the sense that both properties may not be implementable simultaneously. We also prove that relaxing the notion of loop-freedom, as suggested by Ludwig et al. [19] for performance reasons, does not help to render impossible instances feasible: a given problem instance which cannot be solved under strong loop-freedom, cannot be solved with relaxed loop-freedom either.

3. **NP-hardness:** The main technical result of this paper is a formal proof that the decision problem whether both consistency properties, LF and WPE, can be satisfied simultaneously, is NP-hard. This result holds for both strong and the relaxed loop-freedom.

4. **Multiple waypoints:** We initiate the discussion of how to consistently update routes with more than one waypoint, a.k.a. *service chains.* In particular, we show that flexibilities in the order in which service chain functions are traversed do not help regarding feasibility.

5. **Algorithms:** We present optimized, exact mixed integer algorithms for the different network update variants. While solving mixed integer programs can be resource- and time-consuming in general, we show that in some scenarios, solutions can be computed efficiently, and present a succinct formulation accordingly.

6. **Simulations:** We report on an extensive simulation study. In particular, we find that the scenario size as well as the number of waypoints significantly impacts the runtime. While computing the schedule with a minimum number of rounds is the main objective, we show that for many scenarios the feasibility or the infeasibility can be decided quickly.

1.2 Paper Organization

The remainder of this paper is organized as follows. Section 2 introduces our formal model. Section 3 presents first intuitions and insights. The formal NP-hardness proof is given in Section 4. Section 5 initiates the discussion of multiple waypoints. Section 6 presents different optimized and exact algorithms (mixed integer programs). Simulation results are discussed in Section 7. After reviewing related work in Section 8, we conclude our contribution in Section 9.

2. FORMAL MODEL

We consider a network which is managed by a controller, sending out updates to the different switches across an asynchronous network. As the updates are asynchronous, we require the controller to send out simultaneous updates only to a "safe" subset of nodes. Only after these updates have been confirmed (using acknowledgments), the next subset is updated.

The controller needs to change an old policy resp. *route* π_1 to a new policy resp. route π_2. Both π_1 and π_2 are simple directed paths. Initially, packets are forwarded (using the *old rules*, henceforth also called *old edges*) along π_1, and eventually they should be forwarded according to the new rules of π_2. Packets should never be delayed or dropped at a switch, henceforth also called *node*: whenever a packet arrives at a node, a matching forwarding rule should be present.

Without loss of generality, we assume that π_1 and π_2 lead from a source s to a destination d. Since nodes appearing only in one or none of the two paths are trivially updatable, we focus on the network G induced by the nodes V which are part of *both* policies π_1 *and* π_2, i.e., $V = \{v : v \in \pi_1 \wedge v \in \pi_2\}$. Thus, we can represent the policies as $\pi_1 = (s = v_0, v_1, \ldots, v_{\ell-1} = d)$ and $\pi_2 = (s = v_0, \pi(v_1), \ldots, \pi(v_{\ell-2}), v_{\ell-1} = d)$, for some permutation $\pi : V \setminus \{s,d\} \rightarrow V \setminus \{s,d\}$ and some number ℓ. In fact, we can represent policies in an even more compact way: we are actually only concerned about the nodes $U \subseteq V$ which need to be updated. Let, for each node $v \in V$, $out_1(v)$ (resp. $in_1(v)$) denote the outgoing (resp. incoming) edge according to policy π_1, and $out_2(v)$ (resp. $in_2(v)$) denote the outgoing (resp. incoming) edge according to policy π_2. Moreover, let us extend these definitions for entire node sets S, i.e., $out_i(S) = \bigcup_{v \in S} out_i(v)$, for $i \in \{1,2\}$, and analogously, for in_i. We define s to be the first node (say, on π_1) with $out_1(v) \neq out_2(v)$, and d to be the last node with $in_1(v) \neq in_2(v)$. We are interested in the set of to-be-updated nodes $U = \{v \in V : out_1(v) \neq out_2(v)\}$, and define $n = |U|$. Given this reduction, in the following, we will assume that V only consists of interesting nodes ($U = V$).

Our main objective is to compute update schedules which ensure loop-freedom and waypoint enforcement. We will discuss the two properties in turn.

2.1 Loop-Freedom

We distinguish between *Strong Loop-Freedom* and *Relaxed Loop-Freedom* [19].

2.1.1 Strong Loop-Freedom (SLF)

Our goal is to find an *update schedule* $U_1, U_2, \ldots, U_k$, i.e., a sequence of subsets $U_t \subseteq U$ where the subsets form a partition of U (i.e., $U = U_1 \cup U_2 \cup \ldots \cup U_k$), with the property that for any round t, given that the updates $U_{t'}$ for $t' < t$ have been made, all updates U_t can be performed "asynchronously", that is, in an arbitrary order without violating

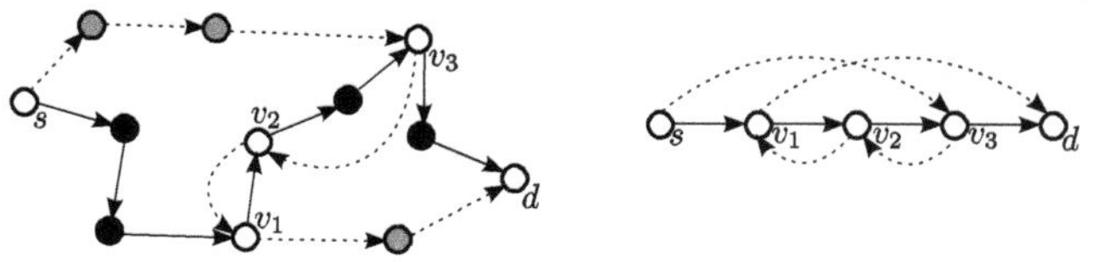

Figure 1: Overview of model and reduction (adopted from [19]). The solid lines show the old policy π_1 and the dashed lines show the new policy π_2. The update problem on the *left* boils down to the update problem for the line representation depicted on the *right* (the old route goes from left to right). Nodes shown in white are the only ones which are part on both paths, and hence relevant for the problem.

loop-freedom. Thus, consistent paths will be maintained for any subset of updated nodes, independently of how long individual updates may take.

More formally, let $U_{<t} = \bigcup_{i=1,\ldots,t-1} U_i$ denote the set of nodes which have already been updated before round t, and let $U_{\leq t}$, $U_{>t}$ etc. be defined analogously. Since updates during round t occur asynchronously, an arbitrary subset of nodes $X \subseteq U_t$ may already have been updated while the nodes $\overline{X} = U_t \setminus X$ still use the old rules, resulting in a temporary forwarding graph $G_t(U, X, E_t)$ over nodes U, where $E_t = out_1(U_{>t} \cup \overline{X}) \cup out_2(U_{<t} \cup X)$. We require that the update schedule $U_1, U_2, \ldots, U_k$ fulfills the property that for all t and for any $X \subseteq U_t$, $G_t(U, X, E_t)$ is loop-free.

Figure 1 illustrates our model [19]: We are given two policies (the old rules of π_1 are *solid*, the new ones of π_2 are *dashed*), see Figure 1 (*left*). We focus on the updateable nodes which are shared by the two policies. Thus, in our example, the update problem can be reduced to the 5-node chain graph in Figure 1 (*right*).

In the following we will call an edge (u, v) of the new policy π_2 *forward*, if v is closer (with respect to π_1) to the destination, resp. *backward*, if u is closer to the destination. It is also convenient to name nodes after their outgoing dashed edges (e.g., *forward* or *backward*); similarly, it is sometimes convenient to say that we *update an edge* when we update the corresponding node.

2.1.2 Relaxed Loop-Freedom (RLF)

Relaxed Loop-Freedom is motivated by the practical observation that transient loops are not very harmful if they do not occur between the source s and the destination d. If relaxed loop-freedom is preserved, only a constant number of packets can loop: we will never push new packets into a loop "at line rate". In other words, even if nodes acknowledge new updates late (or never), new packets will not enter loops. Concretely, and similar to the definition of SLF, we require the update schedule to fulfill the property that for all rounds t and for any subset X, the temporary forwarding graph $G_t(U, X, E'_t)$ is loop-free. The difference is that we only care about the subset E'_t of E_t consisting of edges *reachable from the source s*.

Throughout this paper we refer to Loop-Freedom (LF) whenever the results hold for both SLF and RLF.

2.2 Waypoint Enforcement

In addition to loop-freedom, we want to ensure waypoint-enforcement (WPE). That is, we assume that both the old route π_1 as well as the new route π_2 traverse a special node in the network, henceforth called the *waypoint*. For instance, the waypoint could describe a firewall or intrusion detection system which each packet should traverse: both before, during, as well as after the update.

2.3 Fast Network Updates

We are interested in consistent network updates which are fast: we want to minimize the number of update rounds k in the schedule, where in each round, the controller sends another batch of updates to a subset of nodes, and waits for their completion before starting the next round. This is a natural metric, given the time it takes to update an individual OpenFlow switch today [6, 13, 18].

3. FIRST OBSERVATIONS

To acquaint ourselves with the problem, in this section, we give some examples and also derive first insights.

3.1 Example

Let us consider the example illustrated in Figure 2. The old policy π_1 connects four nodes (switches), from left to right (depicted as a *straight, solid line*, $s \to v_1 \to v_2 \to d$); the new policy π_2 is shown as a *dashed line*. The second node, v_1 (in *black*), represents the waypoint which needs to be enforced.

How can we update the policy π_1 to π_2? A simple solution is to update all nodes *concurrently*. However, as the controller needs to send these commands over the asynchronous network, they may not arrive simultaneously at the nodes, which can result in inconsistent states. For example, if s is updated before v_1 and v_2 are updated, a temporary forwarding path may emerge which violates WPE: packets originating at s will be sent to v_2 and from there to the destination d: the waypoint v_1 is *bypassed*.

One solution to overcome this problem would be to perform the update in *two (communication) rounds*: in the first round, only v_1 and v_2 are updated, and in a second round, once these updates have been performed and acknowledged, the controller also updates s. Note that this 2-round strategy indeed maintains the waypoint at any time during the policy update. However, the resulting solution may still be problematic, as it violates our second desirable transient consistency property, *loop-freedom*: if the update for node v_2 arrives before the update at node v_1, packets may be forwarded in a loop, from nodes v_1 to v_2 and back. Both Waypoint Enforcement WPE as well as Loop-Freedom LF can be ensured (for this specific example) in a *three-round* update: in the first round, only v_1 is updated, in the next round v_2, and finally s.

We, in this paper, are interested in consistent network updates which are *fast*: (parts of) the new paths should be used as soon as possible during the update. Concretely, we want to minimize the *round complexity* of the policy update: the number of communication rounds where in each round, the controller sends another batch of updates to a subset of nodes, and waits for their completion before starting the next round.

3.2 Observation 1: You may have to wait!

It turns out that the transient enforcement of a waypoint is non-trivial. We first show an interesting negative result: it is not possible to implement WPE in a "wait-free manner",

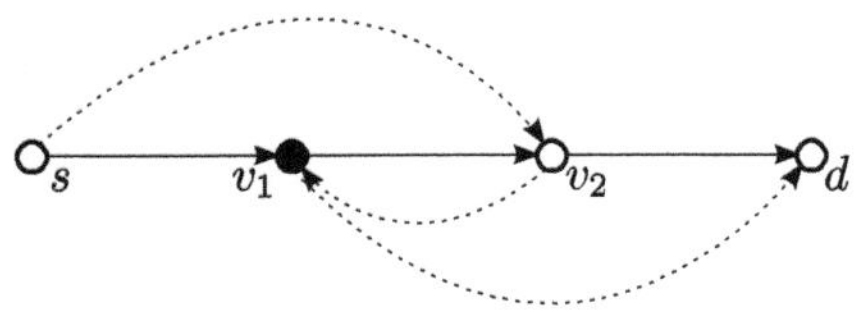

Figure 2: Updating all nodes in one round may violate WPE.

in the following sense: a controller does not only need to wait until the nodes have acknowledged the policy updates of round i before sending out the updates of round $i+1$, but the controller also needs some estimate of the maximal packet latency: if a packet can take an arbitrary amount of time to traverse the network, it is never safe to send out a policy update for certain scenarios. We are not aware of any other transient property for which such a negative result exists. For ease of presentation, we will use the notation $\pi_i^{<wp}$ to refer to the first part of the route given by policy π_i, namely the sub-path from the source to the waypoint, and $\pi_i^{>wp}$ to refer to the second part from the waypoint to the destination.

THEOREM 1. *In an asynchronous environment, a new policy can never be installed without risking the violation of WPE, if a node is part of $\pi_1^{<wp}$ and $\pi_2^{>wp}$.*

PROOF. Consider the example in Figure 2 again, but imagine that the waypoint is at node v_2 instead of node v_1. Assume the following update strategy: in the first round, s and v_2 are updated, and in the second round, v_1. This strategy clearly ensures WPE, *if (but only if)* the updates of Round 2 are sent out after packets forwarded according to the rules before Round 1 have left the system. However, if packets can incur arbitrary delays, then there could always be packets left which are still traversing the old (*solid*) path from s to v_1. These packets have not been routed via the waypoint (v_2) so far but will be sent out to d by v_1 in the new path, violating the WPE property. This problem also exists for any other update strategy. □

Fortunately, in practice, packets do not incur arbitrary delays, and Theorem 1 may only be of theoretical interest: it is often safe to provide an update algorithm with some good upper bound θ on the maximal packet latency. The upper bound θ can be seen as a parameter to tune the safety margin: the higher θ, the higher the probability that any packet is actually waypoint enforced.

3.3 Observation 2: It may be impossible!

We next show a negative result: WPE and LF may conflict, i.e., it is sometimes impossible to simultaneously guarantee both properties.

THEOREM 2. *WPE and LF may conflict.*

PROOF. Consider the example depicted in Figure 3. Clearly, the source s can only be updated once v_3 is updated, otherwise packets will be sent to d directly, which violates WPE. An update of v_3 can only be scheduled after an update of v_2 without risking the violation of LF. However, v_2 needs to wait for v_1 to be updated for the same reasons. This leaves an update of v_1 as the last possibility, which however violates WPE again. Hence there is no update schedule which does not violate either WPE or LF. □

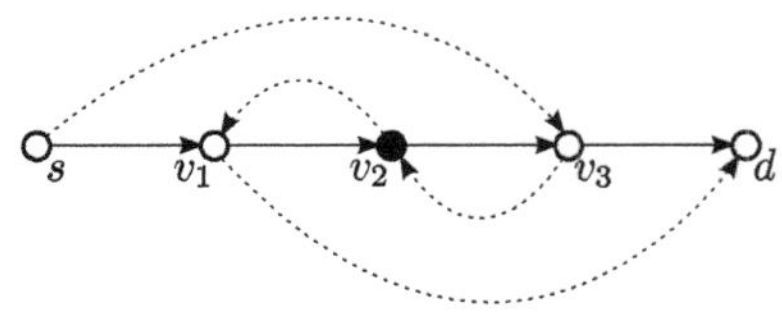

Figure 3: WPE and LF may conflict.

3.4 Observation 3: It does not help to relax!

Given the additional flexibility introduced by relaxed loop-freedom, one could hope that relaxed loop-freedom can also help to overcome the impossibility observed above. However, as we prove in the following, this is never the case.

THEOREM 3. *If there does not exist a strong loop-free solution, there there does also not exist a relaxed solution.*

PROOF. For the sake of contradiction, assume that there exists a scenario which is solvable for RLF but not for SLF. Consider the first round in which the RLF algorithm makes the relevant update which is not possible with SLF. In this configuration, there must exist at least one backward edge and one forward edge which are not updated yet. In a scenario in which all backward edges are already updated, no forward edge can bypass the waypoint if the final policy is consistent. If all forward edges would have already been updated, then the path could easily be completed, updating the backward edges one by one starting with the backward edges connected to the forward edges.

Thus, there exists a forward edge e, which cannot be updated in SLF and by definition must be bypassing the waypoint, as forward edges in SLF cannot create loops. Since this scenario is solvable for RLF, there must exist a backward edge e' that allows the update of e at some point. As e' can only be updated for RLF but not for SLF, it must be an edge which creates a loop which is not on the path between source and destination. However, to enable the update of e, the update of e' must impact the current flow, since an update of e is only possible if the path from the head of e to the destination is leading through the waypoint. Hence, it cannot be the update of e' as it will not change the current flow, which contradicts our assumption. □

4. NP-HARDNESS

Our observation that LF and WPE can conflict may not necessarily be a problem in practice: if these instances can be identified quickly, one could resort to an alternative, possibly more resource-intensive update mechanisms [4, 31]. Unfortunately, however, as we will prove in the following, the underlying decision problem is NP-hard. In particular, we will prove a polynomial-time reduction from 3-SAT: we construct a network update instance according to a 3-SAT formula which is updatable if and only if the 3-SAT formula is satisfiable. We will refer to the 3-SAT formula as $\mathcal{C}$ and to network update instance as $G(\mathcal{C})$.

Notation

In our reduction we will assume that each clause in 3-SAT has exactly 3 literals. We will denote the number of variables as k and the number of clauses as m. The variables will be denoted as $x_1, x_2, \ldots, x_k$ and the clauses as $\mathcal{K}_1, \mathcal{K}_2, \ldots, \mathcal{K}_m$. We will denote the total number of clauses with variable x_i as m_i, number of clauses with literal x_i as p_i and number of clauses with literal $\neg x_i$ as q_i. We will also denote the clauses with literal x_i as $P^i_1, P^i_2, \dots, P^i_{p_i}$ and the clauses with literal $\neg x_i$ as $Q^i_1, Q^i_2, \dots, Q^i_{p_i}$.

General Structure

In the constructed instance there will be a destination d, waypoint wp and auxiliary nodes u_1, u_2, u_3 and δ. For each variable and each clause in 3-SAT we will create a gadget. Additionally for each clause we will add three nodes d^i_1, d^i_2, d^i_3 and for each variable we will add m nodes $r^1_j, \dots, r^m_j$. The source of the path will be the first node in the first clause gadget. The order of gadgets and nodes is presented in Figure 4.

In a gadget for variable x_i there will be a set of nodes connected with clauses containing x_i. Updating one of those edges connecting a clause with the gadget will allow to untangle the corresponding clause (we will define untangling more formally later; generally speaking in order to untangle a clause we need to update one of its edges which corresponds to satisfying it in 3-SAT formula). The variable gadgets will be constructed such that until all clauses are untangled only the edges corresponding to one literal (x_i or $\neg x_i$) can be updated. Therefore the constructed instance will be solvable only if we can untangle all clauses using one literal for each variable, which corresponds to satisfying 3-SAT formula.

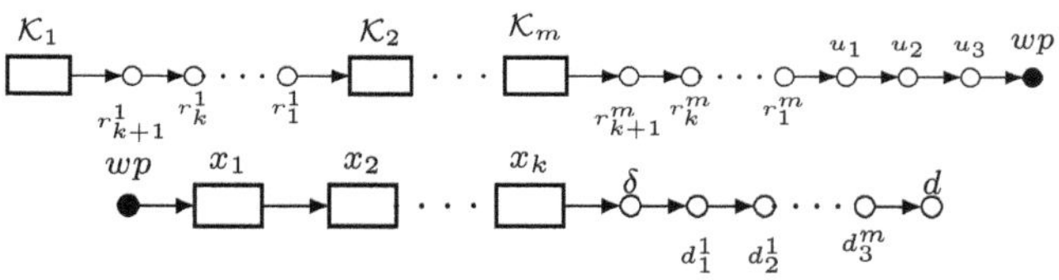

Figure 4: Order of gadgets and nodes. The upper part shows the order from the source to wp. The lower part shows the order from wp to the destination.

Variable Gadgets

For each variable x_j we construct a gadget consisting of four nodes $v^j_1, v^j_2, v^j_3, v^j_4$. These nodes are connected with the edges (v^j_1, v^j_3) and (v^j_2, v^j_4) and there is an edge from v^j_4 to first node of next variable gadget, v^{j+1}_1 (and in case of the last variable gadget there is an edge from v^k_4 to δ). Note that these nodes v^j_4 and v^{j+1}_1 would be combined in our model, but it makes no difference for the problem if we keep both and the proof is easier to follow if we treat them seperately. In the gadget there are also nodes $y^j_1, y^j_2, \dots, y^j_{p_i}$ between v^j_1 and v^j_2 and nodes $z^j_1, z^j_2, \dots, z^j_{q_i}$ between v^j_3 and v^j_4. Clauses $P^j_1, P^j_2, \dots, P^j_{p_i}$ will be connected to $y^j_1, y^j_2, \dots, y^j_{p_i}$, and updating an edge y^j_i will allow clause P^j_i to become untangled. Similarly clauses $Q^j_1, Q^j_2, \dots, Q^j_{q_i}$ will be connected to $z^j_1, z^j_2, \dots, z^j_{q_i}$. In turn nodes $y^j_1, y^j_2, \dots, y^j_{p_i}$ can be updated only if v^j_1 is updated, and $z^j_1, z^j_2, \dots, z^j_{q_i}$ if v^j_2 is updated and v^j_1 is not updated (or all clauses are already untangled). That will allow us to conclude the value of x_j based on whether before all clauses become untangled v^j_1 is updated or not. A construction of the gadget is presented in Figure 5.

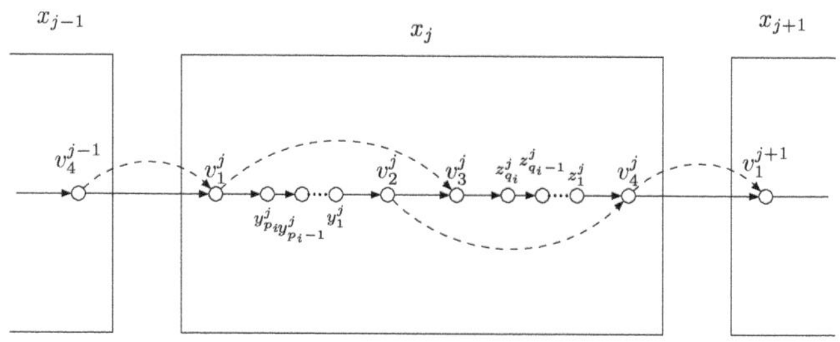

Figure 5: Construction of a variable gadget for x_j.

Clause Gadgets

For each clause $\mathcal{K}_i$ we construct a gadget consisting of nodes $c^i_1, c^i_2, \dots, c^i_6$. Also for each clause we add three nodes (outside of the gadget, close to d, see also Figure 4) d^i_1, d^i_2, d^i_3. For each $j \in \{1,2,3\}$ we add edges (c^i_j, d^i_j) and (d^i_j, c^i_{j+3}). The purpose of nodes d^i_1, d^i_2 and d^i_3 is to delay the update of nodes c^i_1, c^i_2 and c^i_3 until all the clauses are untangled. The construction of a clause gadget is shown in Figure 6.

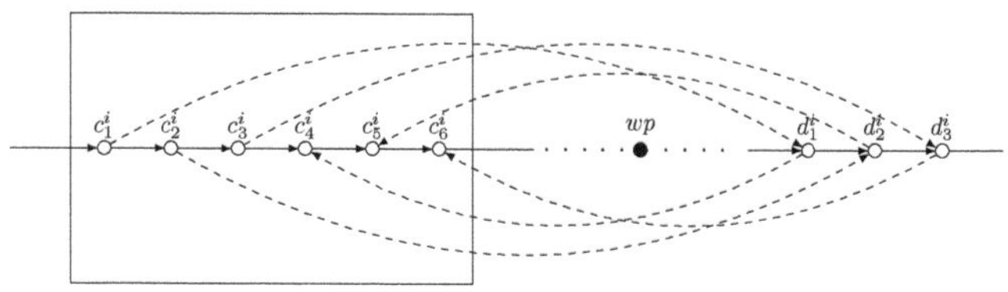

Figure 6: Construction of a clause gadget.

Connecting the Gadgets

Let us consider variable x_i. Let $\mathcal{K}_j = P^i_a$ be any clause containing literal x_i. Then we connect one of the nodes c^j_4, c^j_5, c^j_6 to node y^i_a, and this node to respectively c^{j+1}_1, c^{j+1}_2 or c^{j+1}_3 (if $\mathcal{K}_j$ is the last clause than to u_1, u_2 or u_3 instead). Note, that the nodes $y^i_1, \dots, y^i_{p_i}$ are in reverse order than clauses $P^i_1, \dots, P^i_{p_i}$ (so the earliest clause is connected to the last node). We proceed similarly with clauses $Q^i_1, \dots, Q^i_{q_i}$ and nodes $z^i_1, \dots, z^i_{q_i}$.

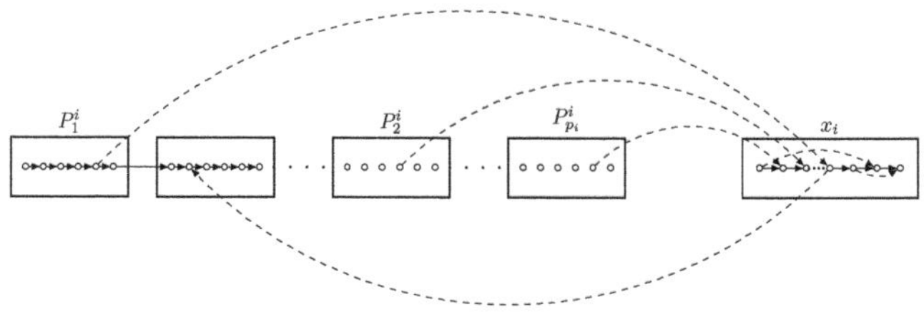

Figure 7: Edges to connect clauses

Connecting the Whole Graph

In addition to the gadgets we need to connect the path to the destination d, the waypoint node wp and the three nodes u_1, u_2, u_3 which will be in the old policy just before the waypoint. We add edges from u_3 to wp, from wp to v^1_1, from u_1 to c^1_2 and from u_2 to c^1_3. After every i-th clause gadget we create $k+1$ nodes $r^i_1, r^i_2, \dots, r^i_{k+1}$ in reverse order, i.e. r^i_{k+1} is the first node after the gadget and r^i_1 is the last.

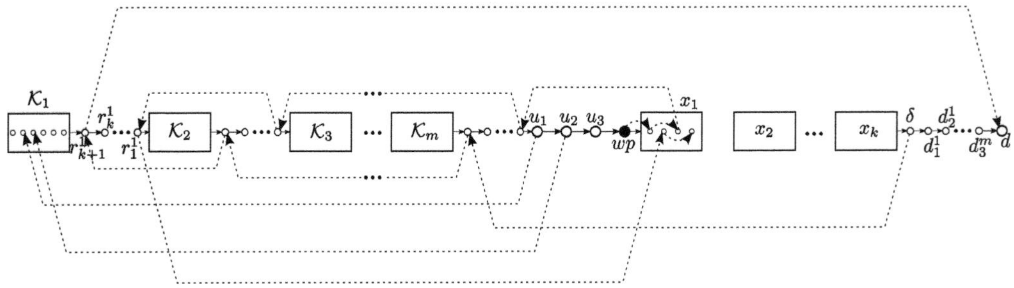

Figure 8: Connecting all paths.

For each variable x_i we create a path starting in v_3^i, then going through nodes $r_i^m, r_i^{m-1}, \ldots, r_i^1$ and ending in v_2^i. We also create a similar path starting in δ, then going through nodes $r_{k+1}^m, r_{k+1}^{m-1}, \ldots, r_{k+1}^1$ and ending in v_d^i. All these edges are shown in Figure 8.

Proof of Correctness

In this section we will prove, that the reduction is correct. We will say that a clause (or clause gadget) is untangled if at least one of the nodes c_4^i, c_5^i or c_6^i is updated. We say that a clause is tangled if it is not untangled.

THEOREM 4. *If $\mathcal{C}$ is satisfiable then there is a schedule for $G(\mathcal{C})$ which satisfies SLF and WPE.*

PROOF. Let σ be an assignment that satisfies $\mathcal{C}$. Then based on σ we will show how to update all nodes in $G(\mathcal{C})$ without violating SLF or WPE. The nodes will be updated according to the following round schedule:

1. For each variable x_i we update v_2^i. Also if $\sigma(x_i) = 1$ we update v_1^i (which makes the update of v_2^i irrelevant as it bypasses v_2^i).
2. For each variable x_i we update either nodes $y_1^i, \ldots, y_{p_i}^i$, if $\sigma(x_i) = 1$, or nodes $z_1^i, \ldots, z_{q_i}^i$ otherwise.
3. Since for each clause $\mathcal{K}_j$ there is at least one literal that satisfies it, we update one of nodes c_4^j, c_5^j, c_6^j which is connected to that literal. The path after these updates is shown on Figure 9.
4. We update nodes r_j^i for all i, j. This can be done, since every clause has at least one outgoing edge and every r_j^i edge has a clause inbetween.
5. We update nodes v_3^i, for all i, and node δ, which connects the path updated in round 4 with the reachable parts behind the waypoint.
6. We update those nodes v_1^i that were not updated earlier, as the path starting at v_3^i is now loop-free.
7. We update those nodes y_j^i and z_j^i that were not updated earlier.
8. We update those nodes c_4^j, c_5^j and c_6^j that were not updated earlier.
9. We update nodes d_1^j, d_2^j, d_3^j, for all j.
10. We update nodes c_1^j, c_2^j, c_3^j, for all j.
11. We update nodes u_1, u_2, u_3 and wp.

None of these updates will violate WPE or SLF. □

THEOREM 5. *If there is a schedule for $G(\mathcal{C})$ which satisfies RLF and WPE then $\mathcal{C}$ is satisfiable.*

We will start by proving the following lemma:

LEMMA 1. *In any correct order of updating edges, as long as some clause gadgets remain tangled, the following conditions hold:*

1. *A node y_j^i can be updated only if node v_1^i is updated. A node z_j^i can be updated only if node v_2^i is updated. Nodes z_j^i and v_1^i cannot be both updated.*
2. *A node r_j^i, for any $i \in \{1, \ldots, m\}$ and $j \in \{1, \ldots, k+1\}$, can be updated only if i-th clause gadget is untangled.*
3. *A node c_j^i, for $j \in \{4, 5, 6\}$ can be updated only if its successor is already updated or if there is $h \in \{4, 5, 6\}$ such that $h < j$ and c_h^i is already updated.*
4. *A node v_3^i, for any i, can be updated if for all $j \in \{0, 1, \ldots, m\}$ r_i^j is updated or if v_2^i is updated, but v_1^i is not. The same applies to node δ.*
5. *Nodes d_1^i and d_2^i and d_3^i, for any i, cannot be updated.*
6. *Node c_3^i cannot be updated. Node c_2^i can be updated only if c_6^{i-1} and its successor are updated, c_5^{i-1} or its successor are not updated and c_4^{i-1} or its successor are not updated. c_1^i can be updated only if c_4^{i-1} or its successor are not updated and either c_6^{i-1} and its successor or c_5^{i-1} and its successor are updated.*

Before proving the lemma, let us make some observations about what these conditions mean in terms of the path traversed by packets. Conditions 1 and 4 guarantee, that if a packet is in v_1^i or v_2^i, for some i, then it will be forwarded to node δ without going through wp. That is because it uses edges from v_1^j and v_2^j to bypass any backward edges. Then Condition 5 guarantees that it travels from δ to d without passing through the waypoint.

Conditions 2, 3 and 6 guarantee that a packet will traverse from the source through all the clauses until it reaches the waypoint. That holds because for each clause, if it is untangled, the packet will be forwarded from some c_j^i to y_l^a, and then, as y_l^a must have been updated before c_j^i, it returns to c_{j-3}^{i+1}. On the other hand, if the clause is tangled, the packet

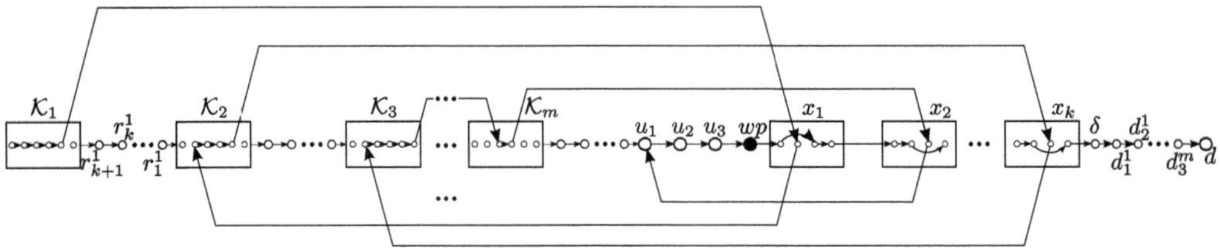

Figure 9: The path after three rounds of updating according to the schedule in proof of Theorem 4.

will go through $r^i_{k+1}, r^i_k, \ldots, r^i_0$ (none of them is updated, since the clause is tangled) to c^{i+1}_1.

Conditions 2 and 4 guarantee that as long as not all clauses are untangled, δ cannot be updated and v^i_3 can be updated only if the path from source to destination does not go through that node.

Let us also notice that if Conditions 5 and 6 hold, then a packet can enter a clause gadget only through nodes c^i_1, c^i_2 and c^i_3, and it is afterwards forwarded to node c^i_4. Therefore it is enough to show that a packet enters a clause gadget twice to prove loop-freedom violation.

PROOF. Let us take any order of updating edges, and consider the first update that violates one of the conditions. If we update any node other than v^i_1 at most one condition is violated. So firstly let's assume that only one condition is violated and consider the cases for which condition it is.

1. Let us assume that y^i_j is updated, but v^i_1 is not. Then the packet goes through all clauses, and then through all previous variable gadgets. Upon entering the gadget for x_i it goes through an edge from y^i_j to $\mathcal{K}_i$ and therefore violates loop-freedom. The case when z^i_j is updated is similar.

2. Let us assume that r^i_j is updated, but the i-th clause is tangled. Then the packet goes through all clause gadgets up to $\mathcal{K}_i$, then it is forwarded to r^i_j. Then there are two possibilities. Firstly it may be forwarded back to r^1_l, for $l \leq j$, and from there to the gadget for x_l. But because Conditions 1, 4 and 5 are satisfied, it would go to the end, without passing through the waypoint. The other case is that it is forwarded back to r^a_l, for some $a < i$ and $l \leq j$, and then re-enters some clause gadget, which would violate loop-freedom.

3. Let us assume that c^i_j is updated but its successor y^l_a and c^i_h, for all $h \in \{4, 5, 6\}$ such that $h < j$, are not. Then the packet traverses through c^i_j without passing through the waypoint, and then it goes to y^l_a. Then it may either be forwarded to v^l_2, which means that it would be forwarded to d without passing through the waypoint, because Conditions 1, 4 and 5 are satisfied, or it travels from some node y^l_g to gadget $\mathcal{K}_f$. But then $f \leq i$, because of the order of nodes $y^l_{p_l}, \ldots, y^l_1$, it would go to a gadget that was already visited, and therefore violate loop-freedom. The case when the successor of c^i_j is z^l_a, for some l, a, is similar.

4. Let us assume that v^i_3 is updated, but there is some r^j_i which is not updated and either v^i_1 is updated or v^i_2 is not. Then the packet, after going through the waypoint, reaches the gadget for x_i. Then, because v^i_1 is updated or v^i_2 is not, it is forwarded to v^i_3. From there it traverses through some backward edges, before it enters some clause gadget (it cannot take backward edges until it goes to r^1_a, and then go forward to some variable gadget, because Condition 2 holds, and not all clauses are untangled). Since all clause gadgets were already visited, it violates loop-freedom.

5. If d^i_j is updated, then the packet traverses through all clause gadgets and variable gadgets until it reaches d^i_j. From there it goes back to c^i_{j+3}. Then there are two possibilities: if it will be forwarded to the next clause gadget, it will violate loop-freedom, because all clauses were already visited. Otherwise, if c^i_{j+3} is updated, the packet is forwarded to some node y^l_a (or z^l_a). From there, it can either be forwarded to some clause gadget, or to x_{l+1}. In both cases, it violates loop-freedom.

6. The condition guarantees that if the packet traverses through c^i_j, for $j \in \{1, 2, 3\}$, then this node cannot be updated. Otherwise, the packet after going to $\mathcal{K}_i$ (without going through the waypoint), would go to d^i_j, and from there to the destination.

Finally let us consider what happens when we update v^i_1 and it violates Conditions 1 and 4. Then the case is similar to violating only Condition 4, that is, the packet traverses through all the clauses to the waypoint, and from there to v^i_1 and next to v^i_3. From there it goes through backward edges and re-enters the clause, which violates loop-freedom. □

Now we are ready to prove Theorem 5.

PROOF. Let us assume that there is a schedule for $G(\mathcal{C})$. Then let us look at the update which untangles the last clause (that is before this update there was an tangled clause, and after this update all clauses are untangled). Then Condition 1 guarantees, that for each variable there is no node corresponding to positive literal (node y^i_a) and a node corresponding to negative literal (node z^i_l) that are both updated. That is because updating node y^i_a requires that v^i_1 is updated, whereas updating node z^i_l requires that v^i_1 is not updated. Therefore in the assignment of variables in $\mathcal{C}$ we set x_i to 1, if at least one of nodes y^i_a, for any a, is updated, or to 0 otherwise. Then because all clauses are untangled, and untangling a clause requires that at least one literal has value 1, this assignment satisfies all formulas in $\mathcal{C}$. □

THEOREM 6. *There is a schedule for $G(C)$ satisfying RLF and WPE iff $\mathcal{C}$ is satisfiable and iff there is a schedule for $G(C)$ satisfying SLF and WPE.*

PROOF. We have shown that the existence of a schedule satisfying RLF and WPE implies that $\mathcal{C}$ is satisfiable. We have also shown that if $\mathcal{C}$ is satisfiable then there is a schedule satisfying SLF and WPE. Because a schedule satisfying SLF and WPE is also a schedule satisfying RLF and WPE, these three statements are equivalent. □

5. EXTENSION TO SERVICE CHAINS

We currently witness a trend towards more complex network services, which concatenate multiple network functions or middleboxes into so-called *service chains* [8, 21, 26, 28, 29]: sequences of network functions which are allocated and stitched together in a flexible manner. For example, a service chain c could define that traffic originating at source s is first steered through an intrusion detection system for security (1st network function), next through a traffic optimizer (2nd network function), and only then is routed towards the destination d. Such advanced network services open an interesting new market for Internet Service Providers, which can become "miniature cloud providers" [30], specialized for in-network processing. Clearly, enforcing multiple waypoints does not render the problem easier.

Interestingly, it is even impossible to compute an update from a route π_1 to a route π_2, if waypoints occur in reverse order in the two policies.

THEOREM 7. *The order, in which two waypoints wp_1 and wp_2 are traversed cannot be changed from π_1 to π_2 without violating either WPE or LF.*

PROOF. Assume that in π_1 packets traverse wp_1 first, followed by wp_2 and vice versa for π_2. By definition, before the start of the update, packets are forwarded according to π_1 and hence, visit wp_1 before wp_2. Due to WPE, both waypoints are on the source-destination path in every round and hence, to change the order of both waypoints, we can identify a single round where this order changes. Otherwise there are either loops or bypassed waypoints. We can assume w.l.o.g. that this round includes an update, which leads to a forwarding of packets to wp_2 before they traversed wp_1 and that this update will be executed as the first update in this round. However, this update immediately bypasses wp_1, since a way back to wp_1 could only exist if this path existed before. Thus, the round before included a loop, as wp_1 was visited before wp_2. □

6. OPTIMAL UPDATE ALGORITHMS

We now present exact algorithms, based on Mixed-Integer Programs (MIPs), for computing update schedules, whenever this is possible. We generalize the Mixed-Integer Program presented in [20] for multiple waypoints and present the following extensions: (1) we model the decision problem by forcing only a single update to take place in each round, (2) present an adaption for realizing the relaxed loop-freedom property, and (3) introduce a *flow extension* that computationally strengthens the formulation. Based on these extensions, we obtain 8 different Mixed-Integer Programming formulations in total. We refer to the formulations by 3 character acronyms of the form -/D | S/R | -/F: the first character indicates whether the decision problem is considered (D) or not (-), the second character indicates whether the strong (S) or the relaxed (R) loop-freedom property is used, and the last indicates whether the flow extension is used (F) or not (-). Hence, DSF will refer to the MIP formulation for the decision variant of the strong loop-freedom property with the flow extension and -R- denotes the basic MIP formulation for the relaxed-loop freedom property without the decision and flow extensions (cf. MIP 1). The models and the extensions are presented in the following.

6.1 Basic Model

According to the line representation presented in Section 3, policies π_1 and π_2 are described as (simple) paths E_{π_1} and E_{π_2} on the common set of nodes V. Both E_{π_1} and E_{π_2} connect the source $s \in V$ to the destination $d \in V$.

The decision of whether switch $v \in V$ shall be updated in any round $r \in \mathcal{R} = \{1, \ldots, |V|-1\}$ is modeled using binary variables $x_v^r \in \{0,1\}$. Constraint 2 of MIP 1 enforces the policy of each node to be changed in exactly one of the rounds. The general objective of the optimization problem is to minimize the number of rounds. This is realized by minimizing the variable $R \geq 0$ which is lower bounded by all the rounds in which an update is performed (see Constraint 1).

Given the assignment of switch updates to rounds, the Constraints 3 and 4 set the variables $y_e^r \in [0,1]$ to indicate whether the edge $e \in E_{\pi_1} \cup E_{\pi_2}$ exists after the (successful) execution of all updates up to and including round r. Note that these variables are actually binary based on their computation as a function of the variables x_v^r. To check that the properties WPE and LF hold, transient states between the rounds $r-1$ and r need to be considered as described below.

Enforcing RLF.

We first outline how to enforce RLF and will then discuss how to adapt the constraints to enforce SLF. To model the RLF property, we need to guarantee the transient states between rounds to be loop-free. Note that the updates for round $r \in \mathcal{R}$ will only be triggered when all updates of nodes in previous rounds were successful. As updates within one round are sent out asynchronously, the updates can be installed in an arbitrary order. To effectively forbid any intermediate cycles it suffices to forbid cycles in the union of edges being installed after the execution of round $r-1$ together with the edges that are enabled in round r. This suffices, as, if there exists a partial update of nodes that forms a transient loop, this loop is also contained in the respective union of the edges.

Specifically, RLF only forbids loops which are reachable from the source node $s \in V$. To this end, we define variables $a_v^r \in \{0,1\}$ to indicate whether a node $v \in V$ may be reachable or *accessible* from the source node s under any order of updates between rounds $r-1$ and r. The variables are set to 1 if, and only if, there exists a (simple) path from s towards v using edges of either the previous round or the current round (see Constraints 5 - 7). Similarly, and based on this reachability information, the variables $y_{u,v}^{r-1 \vee r} \in \{0,1\}$ are set to 1 if the edge $(u,v) \in E$ may be used in the transient state, namely if the edge existed in round $r-1$ or r and u could be reached (see Constraints 8 and 9). Lastly, having reconstructed the information which edges effectively *may* carry flow, we employ the well-known Miller-Tucker-Zemlin constraints (see 10) with corresponding leveling variables $l_v^r \in [0, |V|-1]$ to forbid loops: if traffic may be sent along edge $(u,v) \in E$, i.e., if $y_{u,v}^{r-1 \vee r} = 1$ holds, then $l_v^r \geq l_u^r + 1$ is enforced. Hence, the level variable of the head v of the edge (u,v) is strictly larger than the level variable of its predecessor u. Clearly, an existing cycle does not allow for a feasible assignment of level variables.

We lastly note, that we need to introduce the following constants, modeling the initial state in round 0, for MIP 1 to be well-defined: we set $a_s^0 = 1$, as the source node s is always reachable, and enforce that initially only edges of

Mixed-Integer Program 1: Optimal Rounds (-R-)

$$\min R \quad \text{(Obj)}$$
$$R \geq r \cdot x_v^r \qquad r \in \mathcal{R}, v \in V \quad (1)$$
$$1 = \sum_{r \in \mathcal{R}} x_v^r \qquad v \in V \quad (2)$$
$$y_{u,v}^r = 1 - \sum_{r' \leq r} x_u^{r'} \qquad r \in \mathcal{R},\ (u,v) \in E_{\pi_1} \quad (3)$$
$$y_{u,v}^r = \sum_{r' \leq r} x_u^{r'} \qquad r \in \mathcal{R},\ (u,v) \in E_{\pi_2} \quad (4)$$
$$a_s^r = 1 \qquad r \in \mathcal{R} \quad (5)$$
$$a_v^r \geq a_u^r + y_{u,v}^{r-1} - 1 \qquad r \in \mathcal{R},\ (u,v) \in E \quad (6)$$
$$a_v^r \geq a_u^r + y_{u,v}^{r} - 1 \qquad r \in \mathcal{R},\ (u,v) \in E \quad (7)$$
$$y_{u,v}^{r-1 \vee r} \geq a_u^r + y_{u,v}^{r-1} - 1 \qquad r \in \mathcal{R},\ (u,v) \in E \quad (8)$$
$$y_{u,v}^{r-1 \vee r} \geq a_u^r + y_{u,v}^{r} - 1 \qquad r \in \mathcal{R},\ (u,v) \in E \quad (9)$$
$$y_{u,v}^{r-1 \vee r} \leq \frac{l_v^r - l_u^r - 1}{|V| - 1} + 1 \qquad r \in \mathcal{R},\ (u,v) \in E \quad (10)$$
$$\overline{a}_s^{r,w} = 1 \qquad r \in \mathcal{R}, w \in WP \quad (11)$$
$$\overline{a}_v^{r,w} \geq \overline{a}_u^{r,w} + y_{u,v}^{r-1} - 1 \qquad r \in \mathcal{R}, w \in WP,\ (u,v) \in E_{\overline{\mathsf{WP}}}^{w} \quad (12)$$
$$\overline{a}_v^{r,w} \geq \overline{a}_u^{r,w} + y_{u,v}^{r} - 1 \qquad r \in \mathcal{R}, w \in WP,\ (u,v) \in E_{\overline{\mathsf{WP}}}^{w} \quad (13)$$
$$\overline{a}_d^{r,w} = 0 \qquad r \in \mathcal{R}, w \in WP \quad (14)$$

the old policy E_{π_1} may be used, i.e. we set $y_{u,v}^0 = 1$ for $(u,v) \in E_{\pi_1}$ and $y_{u,v}^0 = 0$ for $(u,v) \in E_{\pi_2}$.

Enforcing WPE.

We denote by $WP \subset V$ the set of waypoints, which may under not be bypassed. For enforcing the WPE property, a reachability construction similar to the one of Constraints 5 - 7 is employed. We define variables $\overline{a}_v^{r,w} \in \{0,1\}$ for each waypoint $w \in WP$, each round $r \in \mathcal{R}$ and each node $v \in V$. Intuitively, $\overline{a}_v^{r,w} = 0$ may only hold, if no path from the source towards the node v exists in the transient state between rounds r and $r-1$, which does not contain waypoint $w \in WP$. To this end, we denote by $E_{\overline{\mathsf{WP}}}^{w} \subset E$ all edges *not* incident to the waypoint w and reachability propagation is only enforced along these edges (cf. Constraints 11 - 13). As Constraint 14 ensures that no packet must arrive at the destination d – using a path in $E_{\overline{\mathsf{WP}}}^{w}$ – no waypoint $w \in WP$ will be bypassed.

6.2 Model Extensions

Based MIP 1, we consider a series of model extensions.

Decision Variant.

First, note that the above presented formulation only considers the *optimization* problem of finding an update schedule using the minimal number of rounds. However, for checking whether a given problem is feasible or not, it will prove useful to consider the respective decision problem. To this end, we may include the following constraint, which only allows one switch to be updated within each round.

$$\sum_{v \in V} x_v^r = 1 \quad r \in \mathcal{R}. \qquad (15)$$

While simple, this constraint can drastically reduce the search space and acts as *symmetry reduction.*

Enforcing SLF.

SLF is strictly stronger than RLF as it forbids cycles under any circumstances, i.e. we forbid cycles even if none of its nodes are (anymore) reachable from the source node. Hence, the reachability variables a_v^r are not needed anymore as all nodes can be considered to be reachable. Therefore, Constraints 5 - 10 can be replaced by the following constraints to enforce the SLF property.

$$y_{u,v}^{r-1 \vee r} \geq y_{u,v}^{r-1} \qquad r \in \mathcal{R},\ (u,v) \in E \quad (16)$$
$$y_{u,v}^{r-1 \vee r} \geq y_{u,v}^{r} \qquad r \in \mathcal{R},\ (u,v) \in E \quad (17)$$
$$y_{u,v}^{r-1 \vee r} \leq \frac{l_v^r - l_u^r - 1}{|V| - 1} + 1 \quad r \in \mathcal{R},\ (u,v) \in E \quad (18)$$

Flow Extension.

A disadvantage of the MIP 1 is the (necessary) use of reachability propagation constraints in the form of binary conjunctions (cf. Constraints 6 - 9): *if* the tail u is reachable *and* the respective edge (u,v) is enabled, *then* the head v is also reachable. These constraints often yield weak linear relaxations [2], which can drastically worsen the solvability in practice. To strengthen the models, we present a multi-commodity flow extension. Concretely, we consider *s*-*d* flows for each round $r \in \mathcal{R}$ to enforce the correctness of the *non-transient* states and introduce flow variables $f_e^r \in [0,1]$ for each round $r \in \mathcal{R}$ and each edge $e \in E_{\pi_1} \cup E_{\pi_2}$. Our extension can be formalized as follows:

$$\sum_{e \in \delta^+(s)} f_e^r = 1 \qquad r \in \mathcal{R} \quad (19)$$
$$\sum_{e \in \delta^+(v)} f_e^r = \sum_{e \in \delta^-(v)} f_e^r \qquad r \in \mathcal{R}, v \in V \setminus \{s,d\} \quad (20)$$
$$f_e^r \leq y_e^r \qquad r \in \mathcal{R}, e \in E_{\pi_1} \cup E_{\pi_2} \quad (21)$$
$$\sum_{e \in \delta^-(w)} f_e^r \geq 1 \qquad r \in \mathcal{R}, w \in WP \quad (22)$$
$$a_v^r \geq f_v^{r-1} \qquad r \in \mathcal{R} \quad (23^*)$$
$$a_v^r \geq f_v^r \qquad r \in \mathcal{R} \quad (24^*)$$

The first two constraints construct *s*-*d* flow, such that the flow starting at the source $s \in V$ must reach the destination $d \in V$. As the flow is upper bounded by the existence of the edges (see Constraint 21), not even fractional cycles may exist after having executed the updates of round $r \in \mathcal{R}$; this is in fact not safe-guarded by MIP 1. Note, that the Constraint 21 is valid both for SLF and RLF, since the flow always emerges at s and all intermediate nodes are therefore reachable.

With respect to the WPE property, the Constraint 22 states that all waypoints must be reached by all of the flow by lower bounding the flow along the the set of incoming edges. Lastly, the Constraints 23* and 24* strenghten the (relaxed) loop detection by bounding the reachability variables a_v^r from below. Note that these constraints are only added, when RLF is considered, as these variables do not exist in the SLF adaption.

7. SIMULATIONS

In our simulations we are specifically interested in the number of scenarios in which LF and WPE conflict and hence are not updateable without violating either one of the two

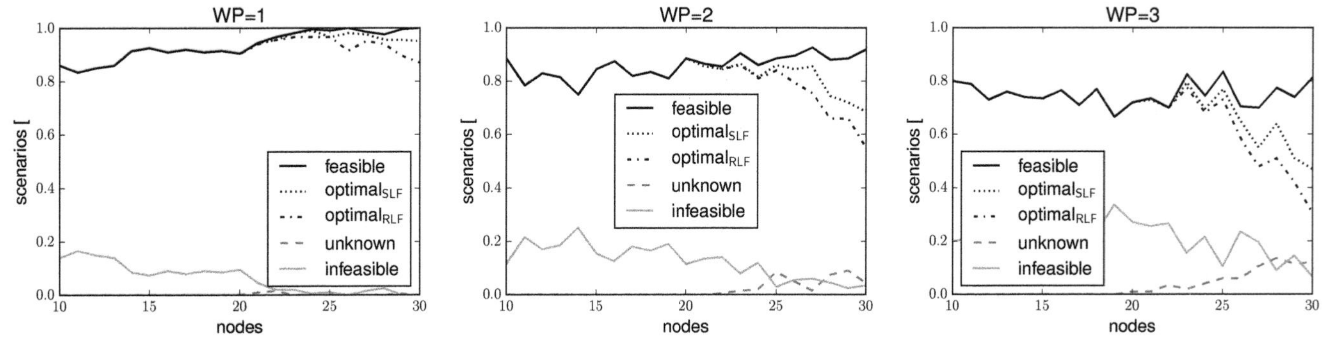

Figure 10: Classification of the generated scenarios according to whether a feasible solution exists, how many optimal solutions can be computed under strong and relaxed loop-freedom, how many scenarios are infeasible and lastly for which percentage of the scenarios neither feasibility nor infeasibility can be proven with any of the algorithms in 10 minutes. As can be seen, the number of waypoints has a distinct impact on the number of feasible scenarios.

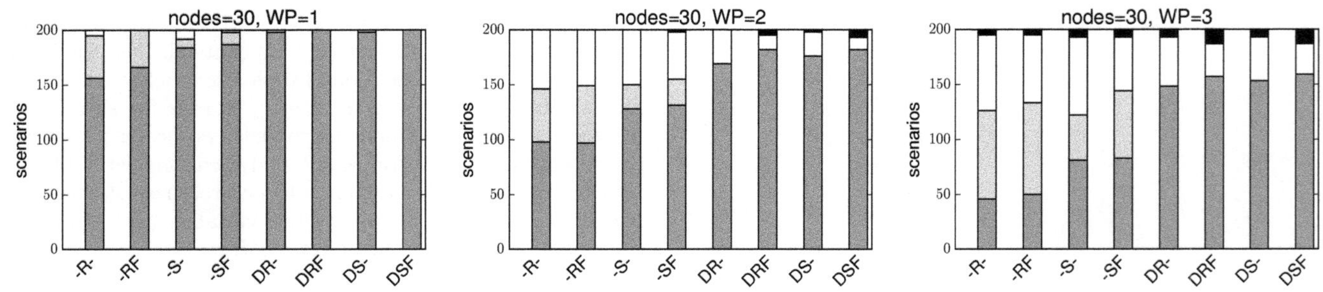

Figure 11: Qualitative evaluation of the algorithm performance for 30 switches and different number of waypoints. The bottom bar (*dark gray*) represents the (*total*) number of scenarios that can be solved optimally, the *light gray* bar represents the number of scenarios for which a feasible solution is found but optimality is not proven, the *white bars* represent the scenarios for which neither feasibility nor infeasibility can be proven in 600 seconds and the *black bars* depict the number of scenarios whose infeasibility is proven successfully.

properties. We generate policy updates randomly and vary the number of nodes as well as the number of waypoints. The generated policies always have a fixed source node $s \in V$ and destination node $d \in V$, and the intermediate nodes' order is shuffled uniformly at random. In cases of multiple adjacent waypoints, we ensure that the order in which the waypoints are traversed by π_1 and π_2 does not differ, as we have already proven in Theorem 7 that these scenarios are unsolvable (and can easily be identified). In addition, we guarantee that no node has the same rule in π_2 as it had in π_1, as those nodes do not need to be considered within our model, since no update and hence, no changes in the forwarding behavior exists. As middleboxes are traversed one by one in the same order, the generated policies can be viewed to model service chains.

We generate updates of lengths $\{10, 11, \ldots, 30\}$, containing one to three waypoints. For each combination of these values, we generate 200 instances (12,600 overall) at random. We use Gurobi 6.5 to solve the respective eight different MIP formulations and terminate experiments, if neither optimality nor infeasibility was shown within 600 seconds.

As to be expected, the feasibility of scenarios is influenced by the number of waypoints within the policy update, see Figure 10. For a single waypoint the percentage of infeasible scenarios is decreasing when increasing the number of nodes. While roughly 15% of the scenarios are infeasible for 10 nodes, for scenarios involving at least 22 nodes only a fraction of at most 3% remain infeasible. These numbers differ when we add more waypoints. With two waypoints the number of infeasible scenarios starts out at 20% and decreases to 5%. Using three waypoints even increases the percentage initially to roughly 30% for smaller instances. More waypoints do not only lead to a higher percentage of infeasible scenarios, but also to more time-intensive computations. While scenarios with one waypoint are solved in nearly all cases within the 600 seconds, the feasibility of roughly 15% of the scenarios cannot be decided with three waypoints at 30 nodes, i.e., within the time limit neither the feasibility nor the infeasibility could be proven using any of the Mixed-Integer Programs. Furthermore, the number of scenarios solved to optimality decreases both with the scenario size and the number of waypoints. Comparing the different notions of Loop-Freedom, we note that for RLF a smaller amount of scenarios could be solved optimally.

The feasibility trends observed in Figure 10 can also be found in Figure 11, which gives an overview of the algorithms' performance for the scenarios containing 30 nodes. Independent of the number of waypoints, it can be observed that the MIP variants, which only allow a single update per round (i.e. the decision variants), find more solutions for the multiple waypoint scenarios than the formulations which aim for a minimization of the number of rounds. Note that when considering the decision variant, any feasible solution is indeed optimal. The flow extension formulations also show a slight benefit compared to its counterparts in terms of the ability to find feasible solutions as well as to detect infeasibilities. However, in scenarios with multiple waypoints, the optimization variants all fail to detect a significant fraction

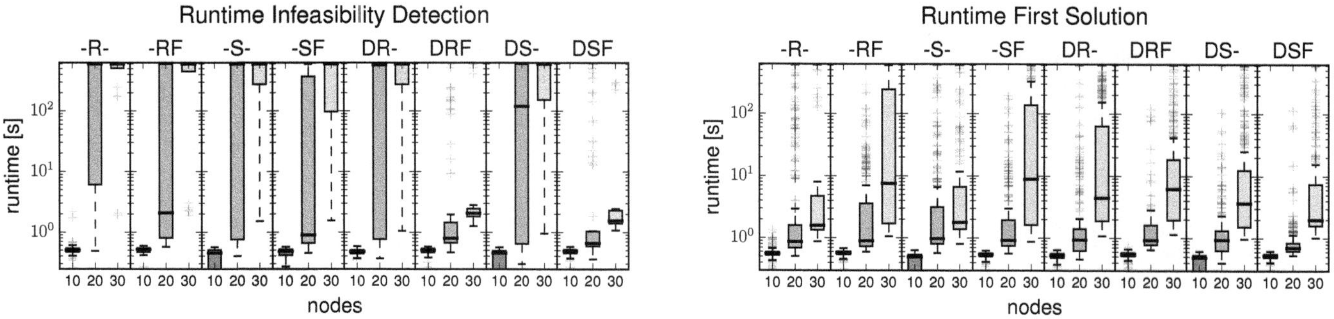

Figure 12: Runtimes for proving the infeasibility of the underlying scenario (*left*) and runtimes for finding the first feasible solution (*right*) aggregated over all number of waypoints and displayed for 10, 20, and 30 nodes as well as for each Mixed-Integer Programming formulation. Note the logarithmic y-axis.

of feasible scenarios as such, i.e. even though solutions exist, none are found within the time limit.

Figure 12 provides a more detailed view on the runtime distributions leading to the increase of undecided scenarios. While there are only very few differences on small scenario sizes, these differences increase with the scenario size. In terms of the infeasibility detection, there is a significant improvement when adding the flow extension to the algorithms, e.g., the median runtime for all algorithms in the 20 node scenario is two orders of magnitude lower with this extension. Especially the decision variants benefit from this extension where the median is also two orders of magnitude lower in the 30 nodes scenarios. Given these results one could possibly use the decision variants as an infeasibility detector while concurrently running an instance of the minimization variant to search for applicable update schedules using the minimal number of rounds. Concretely, in contrast to the benefit for the infeasibility detection, the flow extension prolongs the time until the first solution is found for the minimization algorithms and has roughly no impact in the decision variants. The plots of the runtimes for finding the optimal solution look similar to those for finding the first solution and we hence omit it here.

As the overall goal is to minimize the number of rounds, we lastly present in Figure 13 an ECDF for comparing the minimal number of rounds required to update the different scenarios. We distinguish between RLF and SLF consider scenarios with 10, 20, and 30 nodes. We observe that more than 90% of the scenarios are solvable with at most 10 rounds. Furthermore, the usage of RLF decreases the required number of rounds by roughly one on average.

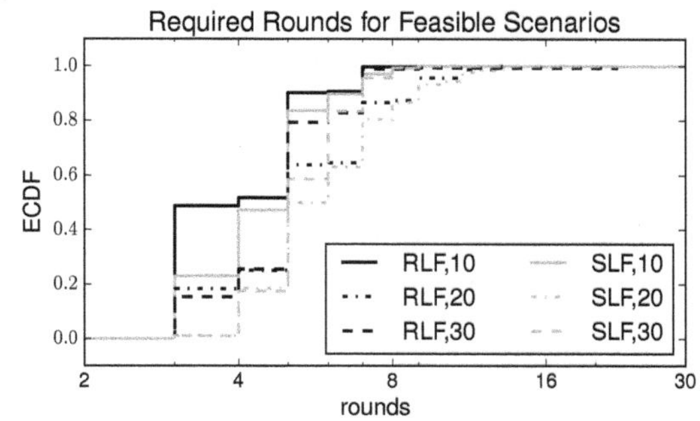

Figure 13: ECDF of the minimal number of required rounds for updating (*feasible*) scenarios with 10 (solid), 20 (dash-dotted), and 30 (dashed) nodes under relaxed (*black*) and strong loop-freedom (*gray*). More than 90% of the scenarios can be solved using 10 or less rounds. Note the logarithmic x-axis.

8. RELATED WORK

Networking routing comes with many policy constraints today, and the impact of these constraints and how to take them into account algorithmically has been studied intensively over the last years, specially in the context of the wide-area Internet [3, 16, 29, 32]. We in this paper are particularly interested in routes maintaining waypoint enforcement guarantees.

The problem of updating [4, 10, 13, 22, 31], synthesizing [24] and checking [15] SDN policies [25] as well as routes [5] has also been studied intensively. In their seminal work, Reitblatt et al. [31] initiated the study of network updates providing strong, per-packet consistency guarantees, and the authors also presented a 2-phase commit protocol. This protocol also forms the basis of the distributed control plane implementation in [4]. Mahajan and Wattenhofer [22] started investigating weaker transient consistency properties—in particular also (strong) loop-freedom—for destination-based routing policies. The measurement studies in [13] and [18] provide empirical evidence for the non-negligible time and high variance of switch updates, further motivating their and our work. In their paper, Mahajan and Wattenhofer proposed an algorithm to "greedily" select a maximum number of edges which can be used early during the policy installation process. Our work builds upon [22], and we consider the scheduling complexity of updating arbitrary routes which are not necessarily destination or shortest-path based. The weak-consistency model introduced in [22] already led to several follow-up papers, for example [19] which also studies round-based models and [7] which studies extensions to jointly optimizing multiple policies. There have recently also been proposals to prioritize shorter policies over longer policies, in order to improve the overall update time [27]. Such a prioritization is meaningful and orthogonal (i.e., could be used in addition) to our approach which optimizes a single policy.

Researchers have also started investigating consistent updates for networks which include (network function virtualized) middleboxes [23]. In their interesting work [9], Ghorbani and Godfrey argue that in the context of network function virtualization, rather stronger consistency properties are required.

A workshop version of this paper appeared at HotNets 2014 [20].

9. CONCLUSION

While software-defined and network function virtualized networks introduce a more flexible and dynamic network operation, this new paradigm also introduces fundamental new challenges. This paper initiated the study of how to update a network in a transiently consistent manner, ensuring two most basic invariants, loop-freedom and waypoint enforcement. We first made several fundamental observations about this problem, and then presented a rigorous proof that it is NP-hard to decide whether a feasible update schedule satisfying both invariants exist. We complemented this negative result with multiple exact algorithms which not only allow to quickly, in practice, identify infeasible instanced (in which case one could resort to update schemes based on tagging), but also to compute optimal transiently consistent update schedules, whenever they exist. We also initiated the discussion of scenarios in which network functions need to be traversed in a certain order, and complemented our formal results with an extensive simulation study. We believe that our paper opens a rich and interesting area of research. Indeed, the required level of consistency often depends on the specific setting, and we will further explore the different notions of consistent updates in the presence of network functionality.

Acknowledgments. This research was supported by the EU project UNIFY FP7-IP-619609 and a German BMBF Software Campus grant (01IS12056).

10. REFERENCES

[1] A. Gember-Jacobson et al. OpenNF: Enabling innovation in network function control. In *Proc. ACM SIGCOMM*, 2014.

[2] D. Bertsimas and R. Weismantel. *Optimization over integers*, volume 13. Dynamic Ideas Belmont, 2005.

[3] M. Caesar and J. Rexford. Bgp routing policies in isp networks. *Netwrk. Mag. of Global Internetwkg.*, 19(6):5–11, Nov. 2005.

[4] M. Canini, P. Kuznetsov, D. Levin, and S. Schmid. A distributed and robust sdn control plane for transactional network updates. In *Proc. IEEE INFOCOM*, 2015.

[5] M. Casado, M. J. Freedman, J. Pettit, J. Luo, N. McKeown, and S. Shenker. Ethane: Taking control of the enterprise. In *Proc. ACM SIGCOMM*, 2007.

[6] A. R. Curtis, J. C. Mogul, J. Tourrilhes, P. Yalagandula, P. Sharma, and S. Banerjee. Devoflow: Scaling flow management for high-performance networks. *SIGCOMM Comput. Commun. Rev.*, 41(4):254–265, 2011.

[7] S. Dudycz, A. Ludwig, and S. Schmid. Can't touch this: Consistent network updates for multiple policies. In *Proc. 46th IEEE/IFIP International Conference on Dependable Systems and Networks (DSN)*, 2016.

[8] ETSI. Network functions virtualisation (nfv); use cases. *http://www.etsi.org/deliver/etsi_gs/NFV/001_099/001/01.01.01_60/gs_NFV001v010101p.pdf*, 2014.

[9] S. Ghorbani and B. Godfrey. Towards correct network virtualization. In *Proceedings of the third workshop on Hot topics in software defined networking*, pages 109–114. ACM, 2014.

[10] H. Harry et al. zUpdate: Updating Data Center Networks with Zero Loss. In *Proc. ACM SIGCOMM*, 2013.

[11] C.-Y. Hong, S. Kandula, R. Mahajan, M. Zhang, V. Gill, M. Nanduri, and R. Wattenhofer. Achieving high utilization with software-driven wan. In *Proc. ACM SIGCOMM*, 2013.

[12] J. Sherry et al. Making middleboxes someone else's problem: Network processing as a cloud service. In *Proc. ACM SIGCOMM*, 2012.

[13] X. Jin, H. Liu, R. Gandhi, S. Kandula, R. Mahajan, J. Rexford, R. Wattenhofer, and M. Zhang. Dionysus: Dynamic scheduling of network updates. In *Proc. ACM SIGCOMM*, 2014.

[14] N. Kang, Z. Liu, J. Rexford, and D. Walker. Optimizing the "one big switch" abstraction in software-defined networks. In *Proc. ACM CoNEXT*, pages 13–24, 2013.

[15] P. Kazemian, M. Chang, H. Zeng, G. Varghese, N. McKeown, and S. Whyte. Real time network policy checking using header space analysis. In *Proc. USENIX NSDI*, 2013.

[16] R. Klöti, V. Kotronis, B. Ager, and X. Dimitropoulos. Policy-compliant path diversity and bisection bandwidth. In *Proc. IEEE INFOCOM*, 2015.

[17] M. Kuzniar, P. Peresini, and D. Kostić. Providing reliable fib update acknowledgments in sdn. In *Proc. ACM CoNEXT*, 2014.

[18] M. Kuźniar, P. Perešíni, and D. Kostić. What you need to know about sdn flow tables. In *Proc. Passive and Active Measurement (PAM)*, pages 347–359. Springer, 2015.

[19] A. Ludwig, J. Marcinkowski, and S. Schmid. Scheduling loop-free network updates: It's good to relax! In *Proc. ACM PODC*, 2015.

[20] A. Ludwig, M. Rost, D. Foucard, and S. Schmid. Good network updates for bad packets: Waypoint enforcement beyond destination-based routing policies. In *Proc. ACM Workshop on Hot Topics in Networks (HotNets)*, 2014.

[21] T. Lukovszki and S. Schmid. Online admission control and embedding of service chains. In *Proc. SIROCCO*, 2015.

[22] R. Mahajan and R. Wattenhofer. On Consistent Updates in Software Defined Networks. In *Proc. ACM HotNets*, 2013.

[23] J. Martins, M. Ahmed, C. Raiciu, and F. Huici. Enabling fast, dynamic network processing with clickos. In *Proc. HotSDN*, pages 67–72, 2013.

[24] J. McClurg, H. Hojjat, P. Cerny, and N. Foster. Efficient synthesis of network updates. In *Proc. ACM SIGPLAN PLDI*, 2015.

[25] C. Monsanto, J. Reich, N. Foster, J. Rexford, and D. Walker. Composing Software Defined Networks. In *Proc. NSDI*, 2013.

[26] P. Skoldstrom et al. Towards unified programmability of cloud and carrier infrastructure. In *Proc. European Workshop on Software Defined Networking (EWSDN)*, 2014.

[27] P. Pereíni, M. Kuzniar, M. Canini, and D. Kostić. Espres: transparent sdn update scheduling. In *Proc. ACM HotSDN*, pages 73–78. ACM, 2014.

[28] R. Hartert et al. Declarative and expressive approach to control forwarding paths in carrier-grade networks. In *Proc. ACM SIGCOMM*, 2015.

[29] R. Soulé et al. Merlin: A language for provisioning network resources. In *Proc. 10th ACM CoNEXT*, 2014.

[30] R. Stoenescu et al. In-net: Enabling in-network processing for the masses. In *Proc. ACM EuroSys*, 2015.

[31] M. Reitblatt, N. Foster, J. Rexford, C. Schlesinger, and D. Walker. Abstractions for network update. In *Proc. ACM SIGCOMM*, pages 323–334, 2012.

[32] L. Sobrinho and T. Quelhas. A theory for the connectivity discovered by routing protocols. In *Proc. IEEE/ACM Trans. Netw.*, 2012.

On the Approximation Error of Mean-Field Models

Lei Ying
School of Electrical, Computer and Energy Engineering
Arizona State University
Tempe, AZ 85287
lei.ying.2@asu.edu

ABSTRACT

Mean-field models have been used to study large-scale and complex stochastic systems, such as large-scale data centers and dense wireless networks, using simple deterministic models (dynamical systems). This paper analyzes the approximation error of mean-field models for continuous-time Markov chains (CTMC), and focuses on mean-field models that are represented as finite-dimensional dynamical systems with a unique equilibrium point. By applying Stein's method and the perturbation theory, the paper shows that under some mild conditions, if the mean-field model is *globally asymptotically stable* and *locally exponentially stable*, the *mean square difference* between the stationary distribution of the stochastic system with size M and the equilibrium point of the corresponding mean-field system is $O(1/M)$. The result of this paper establishes a general theorem for establishing the convergence and the approximation error (i.e., the rate of convergence) of a large class of CTMCs to their mean-field limit by mainly looking into the stability of the mean-field model, which is a deterministic system and is often easier to analyze than the CTMCs. Two applications of mean-field models in data center networks are presented to demonstrate the novelty of our results.

1. INTRODUCTION

The mean-field method is to study large-scale and complex stochastic systems using simple deterministic models. The idea of the mean-field method is to assume the states of nodes in a large-scale system are independently and identically distributed (i.i.d.). Based on this i.i.d. assumption, in a large-scale system, the interaction of a node to the rest of the system can be replaced with an "average" interaction, and the evolution of the system can then be modeled as a deterministic dynamical system, called a *mean-field model.* Then the macroscopic behaviors of the stochastic system can be approximated using the mean-field model, e.g., the stationary distribution of the stochastic system may be approximated using the equilibrium point of the mean-field model.

SIGMETRICS '16, June 14 - 18, 2016, Antibes Juan-Les-Pins, France

ISBN 978-1-4503-4266-7/16/06...$15.00
DOI: http://dx.doi.org/10.1145/2896377.2901463

The mean-field method has important applications in various areas including statistical physics, epidemiology, communication networks, queueing theory, and game theory (e.g., [15, 4, 3, 32, 22, 19, 12, 7, 1, 21, 11]). In particular, over the last few years, it also has emerged as a powerful method for analyzing large-scale cloud computing systems and data center networks. For example, in [22, 32], the mean-field analysis has been used to show that routing each incoming task to the shorter of two randomly sampled servers can significantly reduce queueing delays, a phenomenon called *the power-of-two-choices (Po2)*. The result has been extended to heavy-tailed service-time distributions [9], and to heterogeneous servers [23]. In [31], a mean-field model has been used to quantify the significant benefit of resource pooling. [28] established the asymptotic optimality of the join-idle-queue (JIQ), proposed in [20], using the mean-field model. In [34], a novel randomized load balancing algorithm, named Batch-Filling, has been developed for cloud computing systems with batch arrivals. The algorithm achieves similar delay performance as the power-of-two-choices with a sampling ratio slightly larger than one (i.e., it only samples slightly more than one server on average for each incoming task). In [33], the mean-field analysis has been used for studying the virtual machine placement problem in data center networks. In these applications, the systems under consideration are modeled as CTMCs, and the solutions (equilibrium points) of the corresponding mean-field models are then used to approximate the stationary distributions of the CTMCs.

To justify the mean-field analysis, a critical step is to prove that the stationary distribution of the CTMC indeed converges to the equilibrium point of the mean-field model as the size of the system increases. Consider a family of CTMCs. The Mth CTMC is an M-dimensional continuous-time Markov chain $\mathbf{W}^{(M)} \in \mathcal{U}^M$, where the superscript M is the number of nodes (or called particles) in the system and $\mathcal{U}^M \subseteq \mathbf{R}^M$ is the state space of the CTMC. We assume $\mathcal{U}$ is a finite state space and the CTMC is irreducible. Without loss of generality, let $\mathcal{U} = \{1, \cdots, n\}$. We further define

$$x_i^{(M)}(t) = \frac{1}{M}\sum_{m=1}^{M} \mathbf{1}_{W_m^{(M)}(t)=i}$$

where $\mathbf{1}$ is the indicator function, so $x_i^{(M)}(t)$ is the fraction of nodes in state i at time t. This paper focuses on the case such that $\mathbf{x}^{(M)} = \left\{\mathbf{x}^{(M)}(t), t \geq 0\right\}$ is also an (n-dimensional) CTMC, i.e., the CTMC is a population process

[17, 18]. We remark that many applications of the mean-field method such as those in queueing networks and epidemiology are for population processes.

Now let $\mathbf{x}^{(M)}(\infty)$ denote the stationary distribution of the Mth CTMC. Furthermore, let $\mathbf{x}(t)$ denote the solution of an associated mean-field model and $\mathbf{x}^*$ denote its equilibrium point. Existing approaches for proving the convergence of $\mathbf{x}^{(M)}(\infty)$ to $\mathbf{x}^*$ often involve the following three components.

(1) The first component is to show the convergence of CTMCs to the trajectory of the mean-field model for any finite time interval $[0,t]$, i.e.,

$$\lim_{M\to\infty} \sup_{0\le s\le t} d(\mathbf{x}^{(M)}(s), \mathbf{x}(s)) = 0, \tag{1}$$

where $d(\cdot,\cdot)$ is some measure of distance. This can be proved using different techniques including Kurtz's theorem [17, 18, 22, 34], propagation of chaos [30, 2, 9], or the convergence of the transition semigroup of CTMCs [32, 23].

(2) The second component is to prove the asymptotic stability of the mean-field model, i.e.,

$$\lim_{t\to\infty} \mathbf{x}(t) = \mathbf{x}^*.$$

Lyapunov theorem or LaSalle invariance principle can often be used for proving the stability.

(3) After establishing the previous two results, we obtained

$$\lim_{t\to\infty}\lim_{M\to\infty} \mathbf{x}^{(M)}(t) = \lim_{t\to\infty} \mathbf{x}(t) = \mathbf{x}^*.$$

The convergence of the stationary distributions can then be concluded if we can prove the interchange of the limits, i.e.,

$$\lim_{M\to\infty} \mathbf{x}^{(M)}(\infty) = \lim_{M\to\infty}\lim_{t\to\infty} \mathbf{x}^{(M)}(t)$$
$$=_{(a)} \lim_{t\to\infty}\lim_{M\to\infty} \mathbf{x}^{(M)}(t) = \mathbf{x}^*,$$

where step (a) is called the interchange of the limits.

Since these approaches are all based on the interchange of the limits and use the finite-time convergence (equality (1)) as the stepping stone, they are *indirect* methods of proving

$$\lim_{M\to\infty} \mathbf{x}^{(M)}(\infty) = \mathbf{x}^*.$$

Because of this reason, these approaches can only establish the convergence of mean-field models and the asymptotic behavior of the systems (i.e., for $M=\infty$). The approximation error (or called the rate of convergence) of mean-field models for finite-size systems (e.g., $\|\mathbf{x}^{(M)}(\infty)-\mathbf{x}^*\|$ for a fixed M) is difficult to obtain using these indirect methods.

This paper tackles this fundamental problem and directly studies the approximation error of a large class of mean-field models using Stein's method [26, 27, 6], which is a method to bound the distance of two probability distributions. Our use of Stein's method for the rate of convergence was inspired by the work by Braverman and Dai [10], in which they developed a modular framework with three components for steady-state diffusion approximations and established the rate of convergence to diffusion models for $M/Ph/n+M$ queuing systems. The results in this paper also share similar spirit with the work by Gurvich [14], which establishes the rate of convergence of diffusion models for steady-state approximations for exponentially ergodic Markovian queues. This paper differs from both work in that it considers mean-field models instead of diffusion approximations.

To establish the approximation error, the paper identifies a fundamental connection between the perturbation theory for nonlinear systems and the convergence of mean-field models. The perturbation theory shows that for a stable nonlinear system with exponentially stable equilibrium point, the error of the first-order approximation of the nonlinear system is at the order of $O(\epsilon^2)$, where ϵ is the scaling factor of the perturbation. It turns out the mean-square difference between the stationary distribution of the Mth CTMC and the equilibrium point of the mean-field model is related to the *cumulative* error (integrated over infinite time horizon) of the first-order approximation of the mean-field model. After quantifying the cumulative error, we establish the following results for finite-dimensional mean-field models.

- If the mean-field model is perfect (see definition in Section 2), globally asymptotically stable and locally exponentially stable, then the stationary distributions of the CTMCs converges in the mean-square sense to the equilibrium point of the mean-field model with rate $O(1/M)$ (Theorem 1), specifically, we have the following result on the approximation error

$$E\left[\|\mathbf{x}^{(M)}(\infty)-\mathbf{x}^*\|^2\right] = O(\frac{1}{M}). \tag{2}$$

- If the mean-field model is not perfect, sufficient conditions that guarantee the convergence of the stationary distributions have been obtained in Corollary 1.

We remark that these results are different from the celebrated law of large numbers for Markov chains established by Kurtz [17, 18], where the convergence is established for sample paths of the CTMCs over a finite time interval or for a sequence of t_M which increases M increases [24], not for the stationary distributions of the CTMCs. The contributions of our results are two-fold: First, it provides a *direct* method of studying the convergence of stationary distributions of stochastic systems to their mean-field limits. The method connects the convergence of CTMCs with the stability of the mean-field model. Note that the mean-field model is a deterministic system, so it is often easier to analyze than the CTMCs. Second, the method quantifies the rate of convergence, and provides bounds on the approximation error when using the mean-field limit for approximating the performance of finite-size systems.

We finally comment that the convergence of stationary distributions of one-dimensional discrete-time Markov chains has been studied in [25]. The approximation error of mean-field models for discrete-time Markov chains has been studied in [8], which, however, focuses on numerical methods to compute the error bounds and does not establish a general analytic answer like (2). Furthermore, an approach similar to Stein's method has been used in [29] to prove the tightness of diffusion-scaled stationary distributions for a two-queue system with many servers. The tightness result in [29] establishes an approximation error of the fluid-limit, which is at the same order of the approximation error established in this paper. The key differences are that this paper considers mean-field models for population processes (i.e., with many queues instead of two queues) and establishes sufficient conditions for the convergence and the rate of convergence of a large-class of systems instead of only for a specific system.

2. MEAN-FIELD MODELS

Consider an M-dimensional continuous-time Markov chain $\mathbf{W}^{(M)} \in \mathcal{U}^M$, where the superscript M is the number of nodes (or called particles) in the system and $\mathcal{U}^M \subseteq \mathbf{R}^M$ is the state space of the CTMC. We assume $\mathcal{U}$ is a finite state space and the CTMC is irreducible. Without loss of generality, we assume $\mathcal{U} = \{1, \cdots, n\}$. We further define

$$X_i^{(M)}(t) = \sum_{m=1}^{M} \mathbf{1}_{W_m^{(M)}(t)=i}$$

where $\mathbf{1}$ is the indicator function, so $X_i^{(M)}(t)$ is the number of nodes in state i at time t. We further define

$$\mathbf{x}^{(M)}(t) = \frac{\mathbf{X}^{(M)}(t)}{M},$$

so $x_i^{(M)}(t) \in [0,1]$ represents the *fraction* of nodes in state i at time t. In this paper, we assume $\mathbf{x}^{(M)} = \left\{\mathbf{x}^{(M)}(t), t \geq 0\right\}$ is an (n-dimensional) CTMC. We use $\mathbf{x}^{(M)}(\infty)$ to denote its stationary distribution.

Furthermore, we have a mean-field model described by the following autonomous dynamical system:

$$\dot{\mathbf{x}} \triangleq \frac{d}{dt}x(t) = f(\mathbf{x}(t)) \quad \mathbf{x}(0) = \mathbf{x} \text{ and } \mathbf{x}(t) \in \mathcal{D} \subseteq [0,1]^n, \tag{3}$$

where $\mathcal{D}$ is a compact set. Here, we abuse the notation and use $\mathbf{x}$ to denote the initial condition, which simplifies the notation in the analysis later without causing too much confusion. Assume the system has a unique equilibrium point and let $\mathbf{x}^*$ denote the equilibrium point. The key idea of the mean-field analysis is to use the solution of this deterministic dynamical system to approximate the behavior of the CTMC when M is large; for example, use $\mathbf{x}^*$ to approximate $\mathbf{x}^{(M)}(\infty)$.

Let $Q_{\mathbf{x}^{(M)},\mathbf{y}^{(M)}}$ denote the transition rate of the CTMC from state $\mathbf{x}^M$ to state $\mathbf{y}^M$. A family of CTMCs is called a density-dependent family of CTMCs if the normalized transition rate

$$q_{\mathbf{x}^{(M)},\mathbf{y}^{(M)}} = \frac{1}{M} Q_{\mathbf{x}^{(M)},\mathbf{y}^{(M)}}$$

only depends on $\mathbf{x}^{(M)}$ and $\mathbf{y}^{(M)}$ but is independent of M (see a detailed definition in [22]). For a density-dependent family of CTMCs, the mean-field model can often be obtained by choosing

$$f(\mathbf{x}) = \sum_{\mathbf{y}:\mathbf{y}\neq\mathbf{x}} Q_{\mathbf{x},\mathbf{y}}(\mathbf{y}-\mathbf{x}) = \sum_{\mathbf{y}:\mathbf{y}\neq\mathbf{x}} M q_{\mathbf{x},\mathbf{y}}(\mathbf{y}-\mathbf{x})$$

because $q_{\mathbf{x},\mathbf{y}}$ is the transition rate from $\mathbf{x}$ to $\mathbf{y}$ and $\mathbf{y}-\mathbf{x}$ is the change of system state when such a transition occurs.

We next illustrate the idea using an SIS (susceptible-infected-susceptible) model with an external infection source, which is a variation of the original SIS model.

Example: Let $W_m^{(M)}$ denote the state of an individual such that $W_m^{(M)} = 0$ if the individual is susceptible and $W_m^{(M)} = 1$ if the individual is infected. So $x_0^{(M)}$ is the fraction of susceptible individuals and $x_1^{(M)}$ is the fraction of infected individuals. We assume the recover time of an individual follows an exponential distribution with mean 1. Each infected node randomly selects a node after waiting for a random time that is exponentially distributed with mean $1/\beta$. If the selected node is an susceptible node, it gets infected. Each susceptible node, after it becomes susceptible, gets infected by an external infection source after a random time period that is exponentially distributed with mean $1/\alpha$. Therefore, $\mathbf{W}^{(M)}$, $\mathbf{X}^{(m)}$ and $\mathbf{x}^{(M)}$ are CTMCs. Specifically, $\mathbf{x}^{(M)}$ has the following transition rates, where $x_0^{(M)}$ is the fraction of susceptible individuals and $x_1^{(M)}$ is the fraction of infected individuals:

$$Q_{\mathbf{x}^{(M)},\mathbf{y}^{(M)}} = \begin{cases} M\alpha x_0^{(M)} + M\beta x_0^{(M)} x_1^{(M)}, & \text{if } \mathbf{y}^{(M)} = \mathbf{x}^{(M)} + \frac{1}{M}\begin{pmatrix} -1 \\ 1 \end{pmatrix} \\ M x_1^{(M)}, & \text{if } \mathbf{y}^{(M)} = \mathbf{x}^{(M)} + \frac{1}{M}\begin{pmatrix} 1 \\ -1 \end{pmatrix} \\ -M\alpha x_0^{(M)} - M\beta x_0^{(M)} x_1^{(M)} - M x_1^{(M)}, & \text{if } \mathbf{y}^{(M)} = \mathbf{x}^{(M)} \\ 0 & \text{otherwise.} \end{cases}$$

Note for a given M, computing the stationary distribution of $\mathbf{x}^{(M)}$ is not easy because it has a large state space

$$\left\{\frac{1}{M}, \frac{2}{M}, \cdots, 1\right\}^2$$

and the transition rates are nonlinear functions of the states.

The SIS considered above is a density-dependent CTMC, so we consider the following mean-field model

$$\begin{pmatrix} \dot{x}_0 \\ \dot{x}_1 \end{pmatrix} = f(\mathbf{x}) = \sum_{\mathbf{y}:\mathbf{y}\neq\mathbf{x}} q_{\mathbf{x},\mathbf{y}}(\mathbf{y}-\mathbf{x})$$

$$= (\alpha x_0 + \beta x_0 x_1)\begin{pmatrix} -1 \\ 1 \end{pmatrix} + x_1 \begin{pmatrix} 1 \\ -1 \end{pmatrix}$$

To solve the mean-field model above, we notice that $x_0 + x_1 = 1$ always holds, so we only need to consider

$$\dot{x}_0 = -\alpha x_0 - \beta x_0(1-x_0) + (1-x_0).$$

The equilibrium point can then be obtained by solving

$$0 = -\alpha x_0 - \beta x_0(1-x_0) + (1-x_0).$$

For example, if $\alpha = \beta = 0.5$, then

$$x_0^* = 2 - \sqrt{2} \quad \text{and} \quad x_1^* = \sqrt{2} - 1,$$

which can be used to approximate the fractions of susceptible and infected populations when M is large, i.e., the stationary distribution of $\mathbf{x}^{(M)}$. The simulation results of the fraction of susceptible population with $M = 100$, $1,000$ and $100,000$ are shown in Figure 1, from which the convergence of $x_0^{(M)}$ to $2 - \sqrt{2}$ can be seen clearly. □

3. STEIN'S METHOD FOR QUANTIFYING THE APPROXIMATION ERROR

In this section, we study the convergence and the approximation error (the rate of convergence) of the CTMCs to a mean-field model using Stein's method and the perturbation

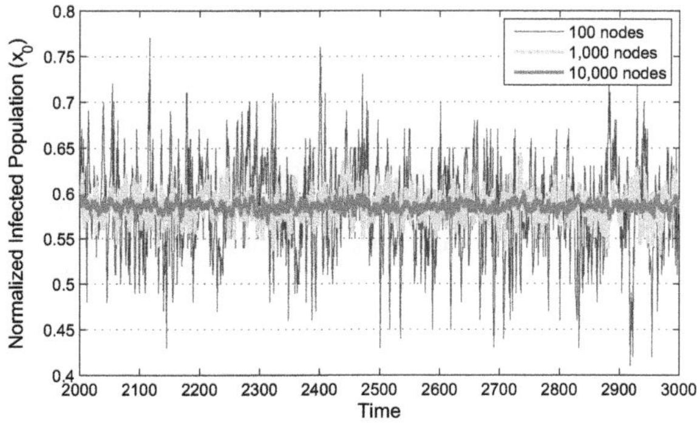

Figure 1: Simulation results of the fraction of susceptible population with $M = 100$, $1,000$, and $100,000$. $\alpha = \beta = 0.5$ in these simulations. The CTMCs were simulated using the uniformization method. The time is the scaled discrete-time used in the uniformization (scaled with M). Specifically, each time slot in the simulation includes M jumps.

theory. Throughout this paper, $\|\cdot\|$ denotes the 2-norm, i.e., $\|\mathbf{x}\| = \sqrt{\sum_i x_i^2}$, and $|\cdot|$ denotes the absolute value. For two vectors $\mathbf{a}, \mathbf{b} \in \mathbf{R}^n$, $\mathbf{a} \cdot \mathbf{b}$ is the dot product. Furthermore, $\nabla g(\mathbf{x})$ denotes the gradient of $g(\mathbf{x})$, and $\nabla x_i(t, \mathbf{x})$ refers to differentiating with respect to the location $\mathbf{x}$, and $\dot{\mathbf{x}}$ is the derivative with respect to time.

Recall the mean-field model defined in equation (3):

$$\dot{\mathbf{x}} = f(\mathbf{x}(t)) \quad \mathbf{x}(0) = \mathbf{x} \text{ and } \mathbf{x}(t) \in \mathcal{D} \subseteq [0,1]^n.$$

The mean-field model is said to be *globally asymptotically stable* if given any initial condition $\mathbf{x}(0) \in \mathcal{D}$ and any $\epsilon > 0$, there exists $t(\mathbf{x}(0), \epsilon)$ such that

$$\|\mathbf{x}(t) - \mathbf{x}^*\| \leq \epsilon \quad \forall t \geq t(\mathbf{x}(0), \epsilon).$$

The mean-field model is said to be *locally exponentially stable* if there exist positive constants ϵ, α and κ such that starting from any initial condition $\|\mathbf{x}(0) - \mathbf{x}^*\| \leq \epsilon$,

$$\|\mathbf{x}(t) - \mathbf{x}^*\| \leq \kappa \|\mathbf{x}(0)\| \exp(-\alpha t).$$

Let $g(\mathbf{x})$ be the solution to the Poisson equation

$$\nabla g(\mathbf{x}) \cdot \dot{\mathbf{x}} = \nabla g(\mathbf{x}) \cdot f(\mathbf{x}) = \sum_{i=1}^{n} (x_i - x_i^*)^2 \qquad (4)$$

Then, the solution has the following form

$$g(\mathbf{x}) = -\int_0^\infty \sum_i (x_i(t, \mathbf{x}) - x_i^*)^2 \, dt$$

when the integral is finite (see [5, 13]), where $\mathbf{x}(t, \mathbf{x})$ is the trajectory of the dynamical system with $\mathbf{x}$ as the initial condition. The integral is finite when the mean-field model is asymptotically stable and locally exponentially stable, which will become clear in Section 5. Note that $-g(\mathbf{x})$ can be viewed as the cumulative square-deviation of the system state from the equilibrium point when the initial condition is $\mathbf{x}$.

Now let $G_{\mathbf{x}^{(M)}}$ denote the generator for the Mth CTMC, then

$$\begin{aligned} G_{\mathbf{x}^{(M)}} g(\mathbf{x}) &= \sum_{\mathbf{y}:\mathbf{y} \neq \mathbf{x}} Q_{\mathbf{x},\mathbf{y}}(\mathbf{x}) (g(\mathbf{y}) - g(\mathbf{x})) \\ &= M \sum_{\mathbf{y}:\mathbf{y} \neq \mathbf{x}} q_{\mathbf{x},\mathbf{y}}(\mathbf{x}) (g(\mathbf{y}) - g(\mathbf{x})). \end{aligned}$$

Since $\mathbf{x}^{(M)}$ is irreducible and has finite state space, $\mathbf{x}^{(M)}$ has a stationary distribution. Initializing $\mathbf{x}^{(M)}(0)$ according to its stationary distribution, and using $E_{\mathbf{x}^{(M)}}[\cdot]$ throughout to the expectation taking over the stationary distribution $\mathbf{x}^{(M)}(\infty)$, we have

$$\begin{aligned} &E_{\mathbf{x}^{(M)}} \left[G_{\mathbf{x}^{(M)}} g(\mathbf{x}) \right] \\ =&E_{\mathbf{x}^{(M)}} \left[M \sum_{\mathbf{y}:\mathbf{y} \neq \mathbf{x}} q_{\mathbf{x},\mathbf{y}}(\mathbf{x}) (g(\mathbf{y}) - g(\mathbf{x})) \right] = 0. \end{aligned} \qquad (5)$$

Then by taking expectation of the Poisson equation (4) over the stationary distribution $\mathbf{x}^{(M)}(\infty)$ and then adding (5) to the equation, we obtain

$$\begin{aligned} &E_{\mathbf{x}^{(M)}} \left[\sum_{i=1}^{n} (x_i - x_i^*)^2 \right] \\ =\ & E_{\mathbf{x}^{(M)}} \left[\nabla g(\mathbf{x}) \cdot f(\mathbf{x}) - M \sum_{\mathbf{y}:\mathbf{y} \neq \mathbf{x}} q_{\mathbf{x},\mathbf{y}} (g(\mathbf{y}) - g(\mathbf{x})) \right] \end{aligned} \qquad (6)$$

Now adding and subtracting $\nabla g(\mathbf{x}) \cdot \sum_{\mathbf{y}:\mathbf{y} \neq \mathbf{x}} q_{\mathbf{x},\mathbf{y}} M(\mathbf{y} - \mathbf{x})$ yields

$$\begin{aligned} &E_{\mathbf{x}^{(M)}} \left[\sum_{i=1}^{n} (x_i - x_i^*)^2 \right] \\ =\ & E_{\mathbf{x}^{(M)}} \Bigg[\nabla g(\mathbf{x}) \cdot f(\mathbf{x}) - \nabla g(\mathbf{x}) \cdot \sum_{\mathbf{y}:\mathbf{y} \neq \mathbf{x}} q_{\mathbf{x},\mathbf{y}} M(\mathbf{y} - \mathbf{x}) \\ & -M \sum_{\mathbf{y}:\mathbf{y} \neq \mathbf{x}} q_{\mathbf{x},\mathbf{y}} (g(\mathbf{y}) - g(\mathbf{x}) - \nabla g(\mathbf{x}) \cdot (\mathbf{y} - \mathbf{x})) \Bigg] \\ =\ & E_{\mathbf{x}^{(M)}} \Bigg[\nabla g(\mathbf{x}) \cdot \left(f(\mathbf{x}) - \sum_{\mathbf{y}:\mathbf{y} \neq \mathbf{x}} q_{\mathbf{x},\mathbf{y}} M(\mathbf{y} - \mathbf{x}) \right) \\ & - \sum_{\mathbf{y}:\mathbf{y} \neq \mathbf{x}} q_{\mathbf{x},\mathbf{y}} M (g(\mathbf{y}) - g(\mathbf{x}) - \nabla g(\mathbf{x}) \cdot (\mathbf{y} - \mathbf{x})) \Bigg]. \end{aligned} \qquad (7)$$

From the equality above, *intuitively*, that

$$E_{\mathbf{x}^{(M)}} \left[\sum_{i=1}^{n} (x_i - x_i^*)^2 \right]$$

converges to zero as $M \to \infty$ can be established if the followings are true:

- Bounded gradient of $g(\mathbf{x})$: $\|\nabla g(\mathbf{x})\|$ is bounded by a constant independent of M.
- Convergence of the generator:

$$\lim_{M \to \infty} E_{\mathbf{x}^{(M)}} \left[\left\| f(\mathbf{x}) - \sum_{\mathbf{y}:\mathbf{y} \neq \mathbf{x}} q_{\mathbf{x},\mathbf{y}} M(\mathbf{y} - \mathbf{x}) \right\| \right] = 0.$$

- Bounded transition-rate of the CTMC: $E_{\mathbf{x}^{(M)}} \left[\sum_{\mathbf{y}:\mathbf{y} \neq \mathbf{x}} q_{\mathbf{x},\mathbf{y}} \right]$ is bounded.

- Diminishing first-order approximation error:

$$\|g(\mathbf{y}) - g(\mathbf{x}) - \nabla g(\mathbf{x}) \cdot (\mathbf{y} - \mathbf{x})\| = O\left(\frac{1}{M^2}\right).$$

  Note that $g(\mathbf{x}) + \nabla g(\mathbf{x}) \cdot (\mathbf{y} - \mathbf{x})$ is the first-order Taylor approximation of $g(\mathbf{y})$.

For many CTMCs and the associated mean-field models, the first three conditions mentioned above can be easily verified. In the following theorem, we will prove that the last condition holds when the mean-field model is globally asymptotically stable and locally exponentially stable (see inequality (11)), and then establish the rate of convergence based on that. The following theorem presents the main result of this paper.

THEOREM 1. *The stationary distributions of the CTMCs* $(\mathbf{x}^{(M)}(\infty))$, *defined in Section 2, converge to the equilibrium point* $(\mathbf{x}^*)$ *of the mean-field model (3) in the mean-square sense with rate* $1/M$, *i.e.,*

$$E_{\mathbf{x}^{(M)}}\left[\sum_{i=1}^{n} (x_i - x_i^*)^2\right] = O\left(\frac{1}{M}\right)$$

when the following conditions hold:

- **Bounded transition-rate condition:** *There exists a constant* $c > 0$ *independent of* M *such that*

$$E_{\mathbf{x}^{(M)}}\left[\sum_{\mathbf{y}:\mathbf{y}\neq\mathbf{x}} q_{\mathbf{x},\mathbf{y}}\right] \leq c.$$

- **Bounded state transition condition:** *There exists a constant* $\tilde{c}$ *independent of* M *such that* $\|\mathbf{x} - \mathbf{y}\| \leq \frac{\tilde{c}}{M}$ *for any* $\mathbf{x}$ *and* $\mathbf{y}$ *such that* $q_{\mathbf{x},\mathbf{y}} \neq 0$.
- **Perfect mean-field model condition:** *The mean-field model (3) is given by*

$$f(\mathbf{x}) = \sum_{\mathbf{y}:\mathbf{y}\neq\mathbf{x}} q_{\mathbf{x},\mathbf{y}} M(\mathbf{y} - \mathbf{x}) \quad \forall\ \mathbf{x}.$$

- **Partial derivative condition:** *The function* $f(\mathbf{x})$ *is twice continuously differentiable.*
- **Stability condition:** *The mean-field model is globally asymptotically stable and is locally exponentially stable.*

REMARK 1. *The first four conditions are easy to verify, so only the stability condition requires nontrivial work. Since a dynamical system has an exponentially stable equilibrium point if and only if the linearized system (at the equilibrium) is exponentially stable (see Theorem 4.15 in [16]), the local exponential stability can be verified by proving the linearized system is exponentially stable (e.g., using Lyapunov method) or numerically verified by calculating the eigenvalues of the state matrix of the mean-field model. The global asymptotical stability in general is studied using the Lyapunov theorem. Two applications of this theorem in data center networks will be presented in Section 4.*

REMARK 2. *It is worth to pointing out that if the mean-field model is unstable but the perfect mean-field model assumption holds. Kurtz's theorem [17, 18] indicates that the sample paths of the CTMCs converge to the trajectory of the mean-field model for any finite time interval, which implies that the CTMCs are "unstable" as well.*

PROOF. We first prove the theorem assuming the mean-field model is globally exponentially stable, and then extend it to the general case. Under the perfect mean-field model assumption, equation (7) becomes

$$\begin{aligned} & E_{\mathbf{x}^{(M)}}\left[\sum_{i=1}^{n} (x_i - x_i^*)^2\right] \\ = \ & E_{\mathbf{x}^{(M)}}\left[-\sum_{\mathbf{y}:\mathbf{y}\neq\mathbf{x}} q_{\mathbf{x},\mathbf{y}} M\left(g(\mathbf{y}) - g(\mathbf{x}) - \nabla g(\mathbf{x}) \cdot (\mathbf{y} - \mathbf{x})\right)\right], \end{aligned}$$

where

$$g(\mathbf{x}) = -\int_0^\infty \sum_i (x_i(t,\mathbf{x}) - x_i^*)^2 \, dt.$$

We next focus on the following term,

$$\begin{aligned} & -\left(g(\mathbf{y}) - g(\mathbf{x}) - \nabla g(\mathbf{x}) \cdot (\mathbf{y} - \mathbf{x})\right) \\ = \ & \int_0^\infty \sum_i \Big((x_i(t,\mathbf{y}) - x_i^*)^2 - (x_i(t,\mathbf{x}) - x_i^*)^2 \\ & -2\left(x_i(t,\mathbf{x}) - x_i^*\right) \nabla x_i(t,\mathbf{x}) \cdot (\mathbf{y} - \mathbf{x}) \Big) \, dt \end{aligned} \quad (8)$$

Note that we exchanged the order of integration and differentiation for the third term. This is can be done because

$$\int_0^\infty 2\left(x_i(t,\mathbf{x}) - x_i^*\right) \nabla x_i(t,\mathbf{x}) \cdot (\mathbf{y} - \mathbf{x}) \, dt$$

is finite, which can be proved using the fact that both $(x_i(t,\mathbf{x}) - x_i^*)$ and $\|\nabla x_i(t,\mathbf{x})\|$ decay exponentially fast to zero as t increases (apply inequalities (20) and (31) with $\mathbf{z} = \mathbf{1}$), and the fact that $\|\mathbf{y} - \mathbf{x}\|$ is bounded due to the bounded state transition condition.

We next define

$$e_i(t) = x_i(t,\mathbf{y}) - x_i(t,\mathbf{x}) - \nabla x_i(t,\mathbf{x}) \cdot (\mathbf{y} - \mathbf{x}),$$

i.e.,

$$x_i(t,\mathbf{y}) = e_i(t) + x_i(t,\mathbf{x}) + \nabla x_i(t,\mathbf{x}) \cdot (\mathbf{y} - \mathbf{x}),$$

so

$$\begin{aligned} & (x_i(t,\mathbf{y}) - x_i^*)^2 - (x_i(t,\mathbf{x}) - x_i^*)^2 \\ & -2\left(x_i(t,\mathbf{x}) - x_i^*\right) \nabla x_i(t,\mathbf{x}) \cdot (\mathbf{y} - \mathbf{x}) \\ = \ & \left(e_i(t) + x_i(t,\mathbf{x}) - x_i^* + \nabla x_i(t,\mathbf{x}) \cdot (\mathbf{y} - \mathbf{x})\right)^2 \\ & - (x_i(t,\mathbf{x}) - x_i^*)^2 - 2\left(x_i(t,\mathbf{x}) - x_i^*\right) \nabla x_i(t,\mathbf{x}) \cdot (\mathbf{y} - \mathbf{x}) \\ = \ & e_i^2(t) + \left(\nabla x_i(t,\mathbf{x}) \cdot (\mathbf{y} - \mathbf{x})\right)^2 + 2e_i(t) \nabla x_i(t,\mathbf{x}) \cdot (\mathbf{y} - \mathbf{x}) \\ & + 2e_i(t)\left(x_i(t,\mathbf{x}) - x_i^*\right) \\ = \ & e_i(t)\left(e_i(t) + 2\nabla x_i(t,\mathbf{x}) \cdot (\mathbf{y} - \mathbf{x}) + 2\left(x_i(t,\mathbf{x}) - x_i^*\right)\right) \\ & + \left(\nabla x_i(t,\mathbf{x}) \cdot (\mathbf{y} - \mathbf{x})\right)^2. \end{aligned}$$

According to the perturbation theory, in particular, inequality (34), when the system is exponentially stable, we have that

$$|e_i(t)| \leq \|\mathbf{e}(t)\| = O\left(\frac{1}{M^2}\right).$$

According to the bounded state transition condition,

$$\|\mathbf{x} - \mathbf{y}\| \leq \frac{\tilde{c}}{M}.$$

Furthermore, both $\nabla x_i(t,\mathbf{x})$ and $x_i(t,\mathbf{x})$ are bounded (see inequalities (20) and (31)) by constants independent of M

and t. Therefore, we can choose a constant b and a sufficiently large $\tilde{M}$ such that for any $M \geq \tilde{M}$,

$$|e_i(t) + 2\nabla x_i(t, \mathbf{x}) \cdot (\mathbf{y} - \mathbf{x}) + 2\left(x_i(t, \mathbf{x}) - x_i^*\right)| \leq b,$$

which implies that

$$\begin{aligned} &|g(\mathbf{y}) - g(\mathbf{x}) - \nabla g(\mathbf{x}) \cdot (\mathbf{y} - \mathbf{x})| \\ \leq & b \int_0^\infty \sum_i |e_i(t)|\, dt + \int_0^\infty \sum_i \left(\nabla x_i(t, \mathbf{x}) \cdot (\mathbf{y} - \mathbf{x})\right)^2 dt, \qquad (9) \\ \leq & b\sqrt{n} \int_0^\infty \|\mathbf{e}(t)\|\, dt + \int_0^\infty \sum_i \left(\nabla x_i(t, \mathbf{x}) \cdot (\mathbf{y} - \mathbf{x})\right)^2 dt, \qquad (10) \end{aligned}$$

where the last inequality is based on the following relation between 1-norm and 2-norm: $\sum_i |e_i(t)| \leq \sqrt{n}\|\mathbf{e}(t)\|$. In Section 5 (in particular, inequality (35)), we will show that under the exponential stability assumption,

$$\int_0^\infty \|\mathbf{e}(t)\|\, dt = O(1/M^2).$$

From the bounded state transition condition, $\|\mathbf{y} - \mathbf{x}\|^2 \leq \frac{\tilde{c}^2}{M^2}$. Therefore,

$$\begin{aligned} &\int_0^\infty \sum_i \left(\nabla x_i(t, \mathbf{x}) \cdot (\mathbf{y} - \mathbf{x})\right)^2 dt \\ \leq & \frac{\tilde{c}^2}{M^2} \int_0^\infty \sum_i \|\nabla x_i(t, \mathbf{x})\|^2\, dt. \end{aligned}$$

Now according to inequality (31), there exist positive constants b_1 and b_2, both independent M, such that

$$\begin{aligned} &\int_0^\infty \sum_i \left(\nabla x_i(t, \mathbf{x}) \cdot (\mathbf{y} - \mathbf{x})\right)^2 dt \\ \leq & \frac{\tilde{c}^2}{M^2} \int_0^\infty b_1 \exp(-b_2 t)\, dt \leq \frac{b_1}{b_2} \frac{1}{M^2}. \end{aligned}$$

Therefore, we can conclude that

$$|g(\mathbf{y}) - g(\mathbf{x}) - \nabla g(\mathbf{x}) \cdot (\mathbf{y} - \mathbf{x})| = O\left(\frac{1}{M^2}\right), \qquad (11)$$

which implies that

$$E_{\mathbf{x}^{(M)}}\left[\sum_{i=1}^n (x_i - x_i^*)^2\right] = O\left(\frac{1}{M}\right) E_{\mathbf{x}^{(M)}}\left[\sum_{\mathbf{y}:\mathbf{y}\neq\mathbf{x}} q_{\mathbf{x},\mathbf{y}}\right]. \qquad (12)$$

Finally, using the bounded transition rate condition, we conclude

$$E_{\mathbf{x}^{(M)}}\left[\sum_{i=1}^n (x_i - x_i^*)^2\right] = O\left(\frac{1}{M}\right). \qquad (13)$$

Now consider the case that the mean-field model is not globally exponentially stable, but is globally asymptotically stable and locally exponentially stable. Recall that $\mathcal{D} \subseteq [0,1]^n$ is compact. According to the definition of global asymptotic stability (Definition 4.4 in [16]), given any $\epsilon > 0$, there exists a finite time t' such that

$$\|\mathbf{x}(t) - \mathbf{x}^*\| \leq \epsilon$$

for any $t \geq t'$. For any finite t, following a similar analysis as in Section 5 (or Section 10.1 in [16]), $\|\mathbf{e}(t, \mathbf{x})\| = O(1/M^2)$ holds.[1] Therefore, we can bound the term (8) by separating the integration into two intervals: from 0 to t', and from t' to ∞, where t' is chosen such that $\mathbf{x}(t)$ converges exponentially to the equilibrium point after t'. Since $\|\mathbf{e}(t', \mathbf{x})\| = O(1/M^2)$, the analysis above applies to the integration over $[t', \infty)$. Hence, the result holds. □

Example: Let us go back to the SIS model introduced in Section 2. A closed-form solution can be obtained for $x_0(t)$. Again assume $\alpha = \beta = 0.5$, then the solution of the ordinary differential equation is

$$x_0(t) = \frac{-e^{-\sqrt{2}t}(2+\sqrt{2})\left(x_0(0) - 2 + \sqrt{2}\right) + (2-\sqrt{2})x_0(0) - 2}{-e^{-\sqrt{2}t}\left(x_0(0) - 2 + \sqrt{2}\right) + x_0(0) - 2 - \sqrt{2}},$$

which converges to $2 - \sqrt{2}$ as $t \to \infty$ independent of $x_0(0)$. Therefore, it is easy to verify that the system is globally, asymptotically stable. Furthermore, the linearized system at the equilibrium is

$$\dot{\epsilon}_0 = -\left(\alpha + \beta(1 - x_0^*) + 1\right)\epsilon_0,$$

where $\epsilon_0 = x_0 - x_0^*$ and x_0^* is the equilibrium value, so the equilibrium point is locally exponentially stable. Furthermore, the mean-field model is perfect in this case and it can be easily verified that all other conditions in Theorem 1 hold. So in the mean square sense, stationary distributions converge to the $x_0 = 2 - \sqrt{2}$ and $x_1 = \sqrt{2} - 1$ with rate $O(1/M)$. Numerical evaluation of $ME_{\mathbf{x}^{(M)}}\left[(x_0 - x_0^*)^2\right]$ versus M is shown in Figure 2, where M varies from 100 to 1,000. We can see that $ME_{\mathbf{x}^{(M)}}\left[\sum_{i=1}^n (x_i - x_i^*)^2\right]$ varies within the interval [0.21, 0.27] while the size of the system increases by 10 times (from 100 to 1,000). The standard deviation (deviation from $2 - \sqrt{2}$) is 0.02177 ($3.72\% \times (2 - \sqrt{2})$) when $M = 100$ and is 0.0068 ($1.16\% \times (2 - \sqrt{2})$) when $M = 1,000$.

From this example, we can see that the mean-field limit is a good approximation of the system when the size of the system is moderate large and the mean-square approximation error of this example is around $\frac{1}{4M}$. □

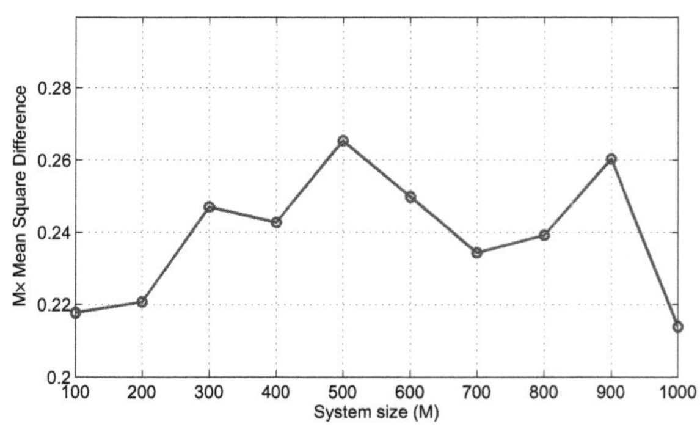

Figure 2: Numerical evaluation of $ME_{\mathbf{x}^{(M)}}\left[(x_0 - x_0^*)^2\right]$ versus M.

Theorem 1 requires a *perfect mean-field model* and *bounded state transitions*. Both conditions can be relaxed, but the rate of convergence will be different.

[1]This holds without exponential stability, but the constant in $O(1/M^2)$ may be a function of t if the system is not exponentially stable.

COROLLARY 1. *Assume partial derivative condition and the stability condition in Theorem 1 hold. The stationary distributions of the CTMCs converge (in the mean square sense) to equilibrium point of the mean-field model, i.e.,*

$$\lim_{M\to\infty} E_{\mathbf{x}^{(M)}}\left[\sum_{i=1}^{n}(x_i - x_i^*)^2\right] = 0$$

when the following conditions also hold:

$$\lim_{M\to\infty} E_{\mathbf{x}^{(M)}}\left[\left\|f(\mathbf{x}) - \sum_{\mathbf{y}:\mathbf{y}\neq\mathbf{x}} q_{\mathbf{x},\mathbf{y}} M(\mathbf{y}-\mathbf{x})\right\|\right] = 0. \quad (14)$$

$$\lim_{M\to\infty} E_{\mathbf{x}^{(M)}}\left[\sum_{\mathbf{y}:\mathbf{y}\neq\mathbf{x}} q_{\mathbf{x},\mathbf{y}} M\|\mathbf{y}-\mathbf{x}\|^2\right] = 0 \quad (15)$$

$$\lim_{M\to\infty} \max_{\mathbf{x},\mathbf{y}:q_{\mathbf{x},\mathbf{y}}>0} \|\mathbf{y}-\mathbf{x}\| = 0 \quad (16)$$

We say that the mean-field model is asymptotically accurate when condition (14) holds, which replaces the perfect mean-field model condition. Conditions (15) and (16) replace the bounded state transition condition.

PROOF. First recall that we have

$$E_{\mathbf{x}^{(M)}}\left[\sum_{i=1}^{n}(x_i - x_i^*)^2\right]$$

$$= E_{\mathbf{x}^{(M)}}\left[\nabla g(\mathbf{x})\cdot\left(f(\mathbf{x}) - \sum_{\mathbf{y}:\mathbf{y}\neq\mathbf{x}} q_{\mathbf{x},\mathbf{y}} M(\mathbf{y}-\mathbf{x})\right)\right.$$

$$\left. - \sum_{\mathbf{y}:\mathbf{y}\neq\mathbf{x}} q_{\mathbf{x},\mathbf{y}} M\left(g(\mathbf{y}) - g(\mathbf{x}) - \nabla g(\mathbf{x})\cdot(\mathbf{y}-\mathbf{x})\right)\right]$$

$$\leq \left(\max_{\mathbf{x}}\|\nabla g(\mathbf{x})\|\right) E_{\mathbf{x}^{(M)}}\left[\left\|f(\mathbf{x}) - \sum_{\mathbf{y}:\mathbf{y}\neq\mathbf{x}} q_{\mathbf{x},\mathbf{y}} M(\mathbf{y}-\mathbf{x})\right\|\right] + \quad (17)$$

$$E_{\mathbf{x}^{(M)}}\left[\sum_{\mathbf{y}:\mathbf{y}\neq\mathbf{x}} q_{\mathbf{x},\mathbf{y}} M\left|g(\mathbf{y}) - g(\mathbf{x}) - \nabla g(\mathbf{x})\cdot(\mathbf{y}-\mathbf{x})\right|\right]. \quad (18)$$

By choosing $\mathbf{z} = \mathbf{1}$ in Section 5, it is easy to verify according to inequality (31) that $(\max_{\mathbf{x}}\|\nabla g(\mathbf{x})\|)$ is upper bounded by a constant independent of M. Therefore, under condition (14), (17) $\to 0$ as $M \to \infty$.

A careful examination of inequality (35) shows that

$$\int_0^\infty \|\mathbf{e}(t)\|\,dt = O\left(\|\mathbf{y}-\mathbf{x}\|^2 \exp\left(\alpha_3'\|\mathbf{y}-\mathbf{x}\|\right)\right).$$

So under condition (16), we have

$$\int_0^\infty \|\mathbf{e}(t)\|\,dt = O\left(\|\mathbf{y}-\mathbf{x}\|^2\right).$$

When condition (16) holds, following the analysis that leads to inequality (10), we can again show that there exists a constant $\tilde{b}$ independent M such that

$$\begin{aligned}&|g(\mathbf{y}) - g(\mathbf{x}) - \nabla g(\mathbf{x})\cdot(\mathbf{y}-\mathbf{x})|\\ \leq\ & \tilde{b}\sqrt{n}\int_0^\infty \|\mathbf{e}(t)\|\,dt + \int_0^\infty \sum_i (\nabla x_i(t,\mathbf{x})\cdot(\mathbf{y}-\mathbf{x}))^2\,dt.\end{aligned}$$

According to inequality (31), we also have

$$\int_0^\infty \sum_i (\nabla x_i(t,\mathbf{x})\cdot(\mathbf{y}-\mathbf{x}))^2\,dt = O\left(\|\mathbf{y}-\mathbf{x}\|^2\right).$$

Therefore, we have

$$(18) = O\left(E_{\mathbf{x}^{(M)}}\left[\sum_{\mathbf{y}:\mathbf{y}\neq\mathbf{x}} q_{\mathbf{x},\mathbf{y}} M\|\mathbf{y}-\mathbf{x}\|^2\right]\right),$$

which converges to zero according to condition (15). Hence, the corollary holds. □

REMARK 3. *When the mean-field model is asymptotically accurate, the convergence rate depends on the convergence rates of (14) and (15).*

4. APPLICATIONS IN DATA CENTER NETWORKS

In this section, we will demonstrate the novelty of Theorem 1 by considering two applications in data center networks: the power-of-two-choices [22, 32] and the virtual machine placement problem [33]. For both problems, mean-field models have been used to analyze the performance of the systems in infinite server regime, but the approximation errors of the mean-field limits for systems with finite number of servers were unknown.

4.1 The power-of-two-choices for servers with f nite buffer

In [22, 32], the authors considered a data center network with M identical servers as shown in Figure 3. Assume tasks arrive at the data center following a Poisson process with rate λM and the processing time of each task is exponentially distributed with mean processing time $\mu = 1$. Each server maintains a queue and $Q_m(t)$ denotes the queue size of server m at time t. For each incoming task, the router (or called scheduler) randomly samples two servers and dispatches the task to the server with a smaller queue size. In this setting, $\mathbf{Q}(t)$ is a CTMC and is a population process.

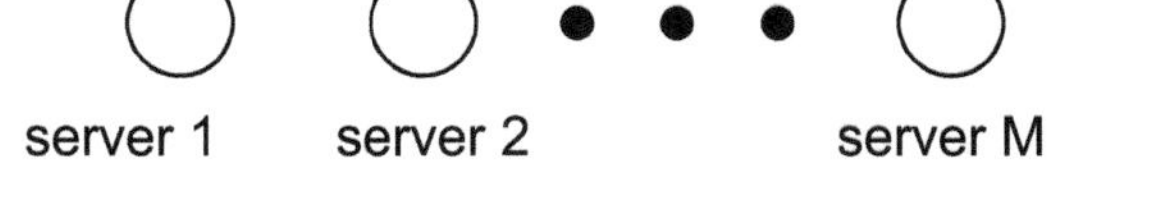

Figure 3: The system has M servers. When a task comes in, the scheduler samples two servers and routes the task to the server with shorter queue. In this example, the scheduler probes server 1 and server M and routes the task to server 1.

Let $s_k^{(M)}(t)$ denote the fraction of servers with queue size *at least* k. Based on the mean-field analysis, it has been shown in [22, 32] that $s_k^{(M)}(\infty)$ weakly converges to s_k^*, where s_k^* is the equilibrium point of the following mean-field system:

$$\dot{s}_k = \begin{cases} \lambda(s_{k-1}^2 - s_k^2) - (s_k - s_{k+1}), & k \geq 1; \\ 1, & k = 0. \end{cases}$$

The mean-field model above is an infinite-dimensional system, so Theorem 1 does not apply. We instead consider finite-buffer servers with buffer size B, for which, the following mean-field model is a perfect mean-field model for the finite-buffer system.

$$\dot{s}_k = \begin{cases} 1, & k = 0; \\ \lambda(s_{k-1}^2 - s_k^2) - (s_k - s_{k+1}), & B-1 \geq k \geq 1; \\ \lambda(s_{k-1}^2 - s_k^2) - s_k, & k = B. \end{cases},$$

and the equilibrium point satisfies the conditions:

$$\begin{aligned} s_0^* &= 1 \\ \lambda({s_{k-1}^*}^2 - {s_k^*}^2) - (s_k^* - s_{k+1}^*) &= 0 \quad B-1 \geq k \geq 1 \\ \lambda({s_{k-1}^*}^2 - {s_k^*}^2) - s_k^* &= 0 \quad k = B. \end{aligned}$$

The existence and uniqueness of the solution has been proved in [22].

Define the Lyapunov function to be

$$V(\mathbf{s}(t)) = \sum_{k=1}^{B} w_k |s_k(t) - s_k^*|$$

for w_k satisfies

$$w_k < w_{k+1} \leq w_k + \frac{w_k(1-\delta) - w_{k-1}}{\lambda(2s_k^* + 1)}$$

for some $\delta > 0$. The existence of such $w_k > 0$ and $\delta > 0$ for the infinite-dimensional mean-field model has been proved in [22]. The same w_k and δ can be used in the finite-dimensional system as well. Following a similar analysis in [22], we obtain

$$\dot{V}(t) \leq -\delta V(t),$$

which implies that

$$\|\mathbf{s}(t) - \mathbf{s}^*\| \leq \frac{1}{w_1} V(t) = \frac{1}{w_1} \sum_{k=1}^{B} w_k |s_k(t) - s_k^*| \leq \frac{V(0)}{w_1} e^{-\delta t}.$$

So the system is globally, exponentially stable. Other conditions in Theorem 1 can be easily verified. So the approximation error in Theorem 1 applies.

4.2 Virtual machine placement in cloud computing systems

In [33], the authors considered a data center network with M identical servers where each server have B units of resources and can host at most B virtual machines (VMs) as shown in Figure 4. Assume VM requests arrive according to a Poisson process with rate λM and the lifetime of each VM is is exponentially distributed with mean lifetime $\mu = 1$. Let $Q_m(t)$ denotes the number of VMs hosted at server m at time t. For each incoming request, the router (or called scheduler) randomly samples two servers and dispatches to the server with a smaller number of VMs. If both servers have already hosted B VMs, the request is blocked. In this setting, $\mathbf{Q}(t)$ again is a CTMC and is a population process.

Let $s_k^{(M)}(t)$ denote the fraction of servers with *at least* k VMs. Based on the mean-field analysis, it has been shown

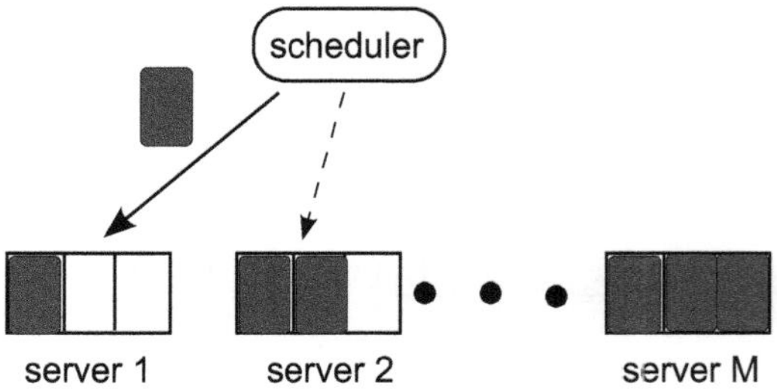

Figure 4: The system has M servers, and each server can host at most three VMs. the scheduler samples two servers and routes the VM request to the server with a smaller number of VMs. In this example, the scheduler routes the VM request to server 1. The request is blocked if both servers are full.

in [33] that $s_k^{(M)}(\infty)$ weakly converges to s_k^*, where s_k^* is the equilibrium point of the following mean-field system:

$$\dot{s}_k = \begin{cases} 1, & k = 0; \\ \lambda(s_{k-1}^2 - s_k^2) - k(s_k - s_{k+1}), & B-1 \geq k \geq 1; \\ \lambda(s_{k-1}^2 - s_k^2) - Bs_k, & k = B. \end{cases}$$

This is a finite-dimensional mean-field model, so Theorem 1 can be applied. The equilibrium point in this case can be recursively solved but the closed-form expression is difficult to obtain. The asymptotic stability of the system has been proved in [33]. We now consider the linearized system at the equilibrium, which is

$$\dot{x}_k = \begin{cases} 0, & k = 0; \\ 2\lambda(s_{k-1}^* x_{k-1} - s_k^* x_k) - k(x_k - x_{k+1}), & B-1 \geq k \geq 1; \\ 2\lambda(s_{k-1}^* x_{k-1} - s_k^* x_k) - Bx_k, & k = B, \end{cases}$$

where $x_k = s_k - s_k^*$.

Define the Lyapunov function to be

$$V(t) = \sum_{k=1}^{B} |x_k|.$$

Note that when $x_k > 0$

$$\begin{aligned} \dot{|x_k|} &= \dot{x}_k \\ &= \begin{cases} 0, & k = 0; \\ 2\lambda(s_{k-1}^* x_{k-1} - s_k^* x_k) - k(x_k - x_{k+1}), & B-1 \geq k \geq 1; \\ 2\lambda(s_{k-1}^* x_{k-1} - s_k^* x_k) - Bx_k, & k = B, \end{cases} \\ &\leq \begin{cases} 0, & k = 0; \\ 2\lambda(s_{k-1}^* |x_{k-1}| - s_k^* |x_k|) - k(|x_k| - |x_{k+1}|), & B-1 \geq k \geq 1; \\ 2\lambda(s_{k-1}^* |x_{k-1}| - s_k^* |x_k|) - B|x_k|, & k = B, \end{cases} \end{aligned}$$

and when $x_k < 0$,

$$\begin{aligned} \dot{|x_k|} &= -\dot{x}_k \\ &= \begin{cases} 0, & k = 0; \\ -2\lambda(s_{k-1}^* x_{k-1} - s_k^* x_k) + k(x_k - x_{k+1}), & B-1 \geq k \geq 1; \\ -2\lambda(s_{k-1}^* x_{k-1} - s_k^* x_k) + Bx_k, & k = B, \end{cases} \\ &\leq \begin{cases} 0, & k = 0; \\ 2\lambda(s_{k-1}^* |x_{k-1}| - s_k^* |x_k|) - k(|x_k| - |x_{k+1}|), & B-1 \geq k \geq 1; \\ 2\lambda(s_{k-1}^* |x_{k-1}| - s_k^* |x_k|) - B|x_k|, & k = B, \end{cases} \end{aligned}$$

It is not difficult to verify that the same inequalities hold when $x_k = 0$. Therefore, we have

$$\dot{V}(t) = \sum_{k=1}^{B} \dot{x}_k = -\sum_{k=1}^{B} |x_k| - 2\lambda s_B^* |x_B| \leq -\sum_{k=1}^{B} |x_k| = -V(t),$$

which implies that

$$\sum_{k=1}^{B} |x_k(t)| = V(t) \leq V(0)e^{-t}.$$

Therefore, the equilibrium point is (locally) exponentially stable. Other conditions in Theorem 1 again can be easily checked, so the approximation bound applies.

For both systems, the convergence of the stationary distributions to the mean-field limits have been proved in the literature based on the interchange of the limits, but the approximation errors (or the rate of convergence) were unknown. The result in this paper not only establishes the approximation errors, but also significantly reduces the additional analysis, in particular, both the convergence in finite time and the interchange of the limits are no longer needed. The purpose of presenting these two applications is to demonstrate the novelty of our result. The mean-field analysis of these two systems has been established in the literature, and is not the focus of this paper. We therefore ignored the details and only presented the key steps. The simulation results that demonstrate the convergence of the finite systems can also be found in the original papers, so were not presented due to page limit.

5. THE PERTURBATION THEORY

In this section, we summarize the results of the perturbation theory for nonlinear systems. These results are special cases of those results presented in [16] because we only need to consider a perturbation to the initial condition. Furthermore, the mean-field model considered in this paper is an autonomous system, which again is a special case of the nonlinear system considered in [16]. For these reasons, the analysis of the perturbation results can be simplified. On the other hand, the perturbation method introduced in [16] only states that the 2-norm of the following error is is at the order of $\|\mathbf{y}-\mathbf{x}\|^2$ independent of t (under certain conditions)

$$\mathbf{e}(t) = \mathbf{x}(t,\mathbf{y}) - \mathbf{x}(t,\mathbf{x}) - \nabla\mathbf{x}(t,\mathbf{x}) \cdot (\mathbf{y}-\mathbf{x})$$

Our result on the rate of convergence, however, requires such an upper bound on the cumulative error, i.e., an upper bound on

$$\int_0^\infty \mathbf{e}(t)\, dt.$$

Therefore, it is necessary to go through the detailed analysis for the system considered in this paper to establish the result for the cumulative error. For the completeness of the paper and the easy reference of the reader, we next introduce the perturbation results in [16] with a more detailed calculation of $\|\mathbf{e}(t)\|$, which shows that not only the approximation error is bounded, but the upper bound decays exponentially to zero as t increases. The analysis closely follows [16].

Consider the system

$$\dot{\mathbf{x}} = f(\mathbf{x}) \tag{19}$$

where $f : \mathcal{D} \subseteq [0,1]^n \to R^n$. *Without the loss of generality, we assume* $\mathbf{x}^* = \mathbf{0}$. We are interested in comparing the solution of this nominal system with the system with a perturbation on the initial condition $\mathbf{x}(0) = \mathbf{x} + \epsilon\mathbf{z}$, where $\mathbf{z} = \frac{1}{\epsilon}(\mathbf{y}-\mathbf{x})$ and is an n-dimensional vector. For the mean-field analysis considered in this paper, $\epsilon = 1/M$. Under the condition of Theorem 1, for any neighboring states $\mathbf{x}$ and $\mathbf{y}$,

$$\|\mathbf{z}\| = \frac{1}{\epsilon}\|(\mathbf{y}-\mathbf{x})\| \leq \tilde{c}.$$

Let $\mathbf{x}(t,\epsilon)$ to denote the solution of the dynamical system with initial perturbation ϵ. Note that the dependence of the solution on $\mathbf{y}-\mathbf{x}$ is omitted to simplify the notation. The analysis holds for any $\mathbf{y}$ and $\mathbf{x}$. We next first repeat the assumptions on the nominal dynamical system.

ASSUMPTION 1. *For any i, the function $f_i(\mathbf{x})$ is twice continuously differentiable. Therefore, the Jacobian matrix of $f(\mathbf{x})$, denoted by $\frac{\partial f}{\partial x}$, is Lipschitz. In other words, there exists a constant $L > 0$ such that*

$$\left\| \frac{\partial f}{\partial x}(\mathbf{x}) - \frac{\partial f}{\partial x}(\mathbf{y}) \right\| \leq L\|\mathbf{x}-\mathbf{y}\|.$$

□

ASSUMPTION 2. *The dynamical system (19) has a unique equilibrium point and is exponentially stable. In other words, there exist positive constants α and κ such that starting from any initial condition $\mathbf{x}(0) \in \mathcal{D}$,*

$$\|\mathbf{x}(t)\| \leq \kappa\|\mathbf{x}(0)\| \exp(-\alpha t). \tag{20}$$

Under this assumption, according to Theorem 4.14 in [16], there exist a Lyapunov function $V(\mathbf{x})$ and positive constants c_u, c_l, c_d, and c_p such that for any $\mathbf{x} \in \mathcal{D}$, the following inequalities hold

$$c_l\|\mathbf{x}\|^2 \leq V(\mathbf{x}) \leq c_u\|\mathbf{x}\|^2$$
$$\dot{V}(\mathbf{x}) \leq -c_d\|\mathbf{x}\|^2$$
$$\|\nabla V(\mathbf{x})\| \leq c_p\|\mathbf{x}\|.$$

□

We first consider the finite Taylor series for $\mathbf{x}(t,\epsilon)$ in terms of ϵ :

$$\mathbf{x}(t,\epsilon) = \mathbf{x}^{(0)}(t) + \epsilon\mathbf{x}^{(1)}(t) + \mathbf{e}(t), \tag{21}$$

and

$$\mathbf{x}(0,\epsilon) = \mathbf{x} + \epsilon\mathbf{z}, \tag{22}$$

where

$$\mathbf{x}^{(0)}(t) = \mathbf{x}(t,0) \text{ and } \mathbf{x}^{(1)}(t) = \left.\frac{d\mathbf{x}}{d\epsilon}(t,\epsilon)\right|_{\epsilon=0}.$$

Substituting (21) into the dynamical system equation, we get

$$\dot{\mathbf{x}}(t,\epsilon) = \dot{\mathbf{x}}^{(0)}(t) + \epsilon\dot{\mathbf{x}}^{(1)}(t) + \dot{\mathbf{e}}(t) = f(\mathbf{x}(t,\epsilon)) \tag{23}$$
$$= h^{(0)}(\mathbf{x}^{(0)}(t)) + h^{(1)}(\mathbf{x}^{(\leq 1)}(t))\epsilon + R_{\mathbf{e}}(t,\epsilon), \tag{24}$$

where $\mathbf{x}^{(\leq 1)} = \left(\mathbf{x}^{(0)}, \mathbf{x}^{(1)}\right)$. The zero-order term $h^{(0)}$ is given by

$$\dot{x}^{(0)}(t) = h^{(0)}\left(\mathbf{x}^{(0)}(t)\right) = f\left(\mathbf{x}^{(0)}(t)\right) \quad \text{with} \quad \mathbf{x}^{(0)}(0) = \mathbf{x},$$

which is the nominal system without the perturbation on the initial condition. The first-order term is given by

$$\begin{aligned} h^{(1)}\left(\mathbf{x}^{(\le 1)}(t)\right) &= \frac{d}{d\epsilon} f(\mathbf{x}(t,\epsilon))\Big|_{\epsilon=0} \\ &= \frac{\partial f}{\partial x}(\mathbf{x}(t,\epsilon))\frac{d\mathbf{x}}{d\epsilon}(t,\epsilon)\Big|_{\epsilon=0} \\ &= \frac{\partial f}{\partial x}(\mathbf{x}^{(0)}(t))\mathbf{x}^{(1)}(t). \end{aligned}$$

Recall that $\frac{\partial f}{\partial x}$ is the Jacobian matrix. Therefore, we have

$$\dot{\mathbf{x}}^{(1)}(t) = \frac{\partial f}{\partial x}(\mathbf{x}^{(0)}(t))\mathbf{x}^{(1)}(t) \quad \text{with} \quad \mathbf{x}^{(1)}(0) = \mathbf{z}. \tag{25}$$

We next study $\mathbf{e}(t) = \mathbf{x}(t,\epsilon) - \mathbf{x}^{(0)}(t) - \epsilon\mathbf{x}^{(1)}(t)$. Combining the results above, we have

$$\begin{aligned} \dot{\mathbf{e}}(t) &= f(\mathbf{x}(t,\epsilon)) - f\left(\mathbf{x}^{(0)}(t)\right) - \epsilon\frac{\partial f}{\partial x}(\mathbf{x}^{(0)}(t))\mathbf{x}^{(1)}(t) \\ \mathbf{e}(0) &= 0. \end{aligned}$$

Now by defining

$$\begin{aligned} &\rho\left(\mathbf{x}^{(\le 1)}(t), \mathbf{e}(t), \epsilon\right) \\ =& f\left(\mathbf{e}(t) + \mathbf{x}^{(0)}(t) + \epsilon\mathbf{x}^{(1)}(t)\right) - f\left(\mathbf{x}^{(0)}(t) + \epsilon\mathbf{x}^{(1)}(t)\right) \\ &- \frac{\partial f}{\partial x}(\mathbf{x}^{(0)}(t))\mathbf{e}(t), \end{aligned}$$

and

$$\begin{aligned} &\gamma\left(\mathbf{x}^{(\le 1)}(t), \epsilon\right) \\ =& f\left(\mathbf{x}^{(0)}(t) + \epsilon\mathbf{x}^{(1)}(t)\right) - f\left(\mathbf{x}^{(0)}(t)\right) - \epsilon\frac{\partial f}{\partial x}(\mathbf{x}^{(0)}(t))\mathbf{x}^{(1)}(t), \end{aligned}$$

we obtain

$$\dot{\mathbf{e}}(t) = \frac{\partial f}{\partial x}(\mathbf{x}^{(0)}(t))\mathbf{e}(t) + \rho\left(\mathbf{x}^{(\le 1)}(t), \mathbf{e}(t), \epsilon\right) + \gamma\left(\mathbf{x}^{(\le 1)}(t), \epsilon\right). \tag{26}$$

Note that both ρ and γ are n-dimensional vectors. It is easy to see that

$$\rho\left(\mathbf{x}^{(\le 1)}(t), 0, \epsilon\right) = \mathbf{0}. \tag{27}$$

According to Taylor's theorem and the mean value theorem, we have

$$\begin{aligned} \gamma_l\left(\mathbf{x}^{(\le 1)}(t), \epsilon\right) &= \epsilon^2 \mathbf{x}^{(1)}(t)^T \mathbf{H}(f_l)(\xi)\mathbf{x}^{(1)}(t) \\ &= \epsilon^2 \sum_{i,j} \frac{\partial^2 f_l}{\partial x_i \partial x_j}(\xi)\left(x_i^{(1)}(t)x_j^{(1)}(t)\right) \end{aligned}$$

for $\xi = \mathbf{x}^{(0)}(t) + \alpha\epsilon\mathbf{x}^{(1)}(t)$ for some $0 \le \alpha \le 1$. $\mathbf{H}(f_l)$ is the Hessian matrix of function $f_l(\mathbf{x})$. Then we have

$$\left|\gamma_l\left(\mathbf{x}^{(\le 1)}(t), \epsilon\right)\right| = \epsilon^2 \left|\sum_{i,j} \frac{\partial^2 f_l}{\partial x_i \partial x_j}(\xi)\left(x_i^{(1)}(t)x_j^{(1)}(t)\right)\right|.$$

Furthermore, we have

$$\begin{aligned} &\frac{\partial \rho_l}{\partial e_i}\left(\mathbf{x}^{(\le 1)}(t), \mathbf{e}(t), \epsilon\right) \\ =& \frac{\partial f_l}{\partial x_i}(\mathbf{e}(t) + \mathbf{x}^{(0)}(t) + \epsilon\mathbf{x}^{(1)}(t)) - \frac{\partial f_l}{\partial x_i}(\mathbf{x}^{(0)}(t)). \end{aligned}$$

According to the mean-value theorem and (27), we have that

$$\begin{aligned} &\rho\left(\mathbf{x}^{(\le 1)}(t), \mathbf{e}(t), \epsilon\right) \\ =& \left(\frac{\partial f}{\partial x}(\tilde{\mathbf{e}}(t) + \mathbf{x}^{(0)}(t) + \epsilon\mathbf{x}^{(1)}(t)) - \frac{\partial f}{\partial x}(\mathbf{x}^{(0)}(t))\right)\mathbf{e}(t), \end{aligned}$$

where $\tilde{\mathbf{e}}(t) = a\mathbf{e}(t)$ for some $0 \le a \le 1$. According to the Lipschitz condition in Assumption (1) and the Cauchy-Schwarz inequality, we have

$$\left\|\rho\left(\mathbf{x}^{(\le 1)}(t), \mathbf{e}(t), \epsilon\right)\right\| \le L\left(\|\mathbf{e}(t)\| + \epsilon\|\mathbf{x}^{(1)}(t)\|\right)\|\mathbf{e}(t)\|.$$

Now we utilize the assumption that the nominal system (19) converges to the equilibrium point exponentially fast from any initial condition in the domain. We use the Lyapunov function in Assumption (2) to bound $\|\mathbf{e}(t)\|$. We start from

$$\begin{aligned} &\dot{V}(\mathbf{e}(t)) \\ =& \nabla V(\mathbf{e}(t)) \cdot \dot{\mathbf{e}}(t) \\ =& \nabla V(\mathbf{e}(t)) \cdot f(\mathbf{e}(t)) + \nabla V(\mathbf{e}(t)) \cdot (\dot{\mathbf{e}}(t) - f(\mathbf{e}(t))) \\ \le_{(a)}& - c_d V(\mathbf{e}(t)) + \nabla V(\mathbf{e}(t)) \cdot (\dot{\mathbf{e}}(t) - f(\mathbf{e}(t))) \\ =& - c_d V(\mathbf{e}(t)) + \nabla V(\mathbf{e}(t)) \cdot \\ &\left(\frac{\partial f}{\partial \mathbf{x}}(\mathbf{x}^{(0)}(t))\mathbf{e}(t) - \frac{\partial f}{\partial \mathbf{x}}(0)\mathbf{e}(t) + \frac{\partial f}{\partial \mathbf{x}}(0)\mathbf{e}(t) - f(\mathbf{e}(t))\right. \\ &\left. + \rho\left(\mathbf{x}^{(\le 1)}(t), \mathbf{e}(t), \epsilon\right) + \gamma\left(\mathbf{x}^{(\le 1)}(t), \epsilon\right)\right) \\ \le& - c_d V(\mathbf{e}(t)) \\ &+ \|\nabla V(\mathbf{e}(t))\| \left(\left\|\frac{\partial f}{\partial \mathbf{x}}(\mathbf{x}^{(0)}(t))\mathbf{e}(t) - \frac{\partial f}{\partial \mathbf{x}}(0)\mathbf{e}(t)\right\|\right. \\ &+ \left\|\frac{\partial f}{\partial \mathbf{x}}(0)\mathbf{e}(t) - f(\mathbf{e}(t))\right\| \\ &\left. + \left\|\rho\left(\mathbf{x}^{(\le 1)}(t), \mathbf{e}(t), \epsilon\right)\right\| + \left\|\gamma\left(\mathbf{x}^{(\le 1)}(t), \epsilon\right)\right\|\right) \end{aligned}$$

where inequality (a) is due to assumption (2) and the last inequality is a result of the Cauchy-Schwarz inequality. Note that based on Assumption (1) and the mean-value theorem, we have

$$\begin{aligned} \left\|\frac{\partial f}{\partial \mathbf{x}}(\mathbf{x}^{(0)}(t))\mathbf{e}(t) - \frac{\partial f}{\partial \mathbf{x}}(0)\mathbf{e}(t)\right\| &\le L\|\mathbf{x}^{(0)}(t)\|\|\mathbf{e}(t)\| \\ \left\|\frac{\partial f}{\partial \mathbf{x}}(0)\mathbf{e}(t) - f(\mathbf{e}(t))\right\| &\le L\|\mathbf{e}(t)\|^2. \end{aligned}$$

We also know that

$$\begin{aligned} \left\|\rho\left(\mathbf{x}^{(\le 1)}(t), \mathbf{e}(t), \epsilon\right)\right\| &\le L\left(\|\mathbf{e}(t)\| + \epsilon\|\mathbf{x}^{(1)}(t)\|\right)\|\mathbf{e}(t)\| \\ \left\|\gamma\left(\mathbf{x}^{(\le 1)}(t), \epsilon\right)\right\| &= \epsilon^2 A(t), \end{aligned}$$

where we define

$$A(t) = \sqrt{\sum_l \left(\sum_{i,j} \frac{\partial^2 f_l}{\partial x_i \partial x_j}(\xi)\left(x_i^{(1)}(t)x_j^{(1)}(t)\right)\right)^2}$$

to simplify the notation.

Summarizing the results above, we get

$$\begin{aligned} &\dot{V}(\mathbf{e}(t)) \\ \le& - c_d V(\mathbf{e}(t)) \\ &+ L\|\nabla V(\mathbf{e}(t))\|\left(\|\mathbf{x}^{(0)}(t)\| + \epsilon\|\mathbf{x}^{(1)}(t)\| + 2\|\mathbf{e}(t)\|\right)\|\mathbf{e}(t)\| \end{aligned}$$

$$
\begin{aligned}
&+ \|\nabla V(\mathbf{e}(t))\| A(t)\epsilon^2 \\
\le &- c_d V(\mathbf{e}(t)) \\
&+ L c_p \left(\|\mathbf{x}^{(0)}(t)\| + \epsilon\|\mathbf{x}^{(1)}(t)\| + 2\|\mathbf{e}(t)\|\right) \|\mathbf{e}(t)\|^2 \\
&+ c_p A(t)\epsilon^2 \|\mathbf{e}(t)\| \\
\le &- c_d V(\mathbf{e}(t)) \\
&+ L\frac{c_p}{c_l}\left(\|\mathbf{x}^{(0)}(t)\| + \epsilon\|\mathbf{x}^{(1)}(t)\| + 2\|\mathbf{e}(t)\|\right) V(\mathbf{e}(t)) \\
&+ \frac{c_p}{\sqrt{c_l}} A(t)\epsilon^2 \sqrt{V(\mathbf{e}(t))}.
\end{aligned}
$$

Define $W(t) = \sqrt{V(t)}$, then we have

$$
\begin{aligned}
&\dot{W}(\mathbf{e}(t)) \\
\le &- \frac{c_d}{2} W(\mathbf{e}(t)) \\
&+ \frac{L}{2}\frac{c_p}{c_l}\left(\|\mathbf{x}^{(0)}(t)\| + \epsilon\|\mathbf{x}^{(1)}(t)\| + 2\|\mathbf{e}(t)\|\right) W(\mathbf{e}(t)) \\
&+ \frac{c_p}{\sqrt{c_1}} A(t)\epsilon^2.
\end{aligned}
$$

By the comparison lemma in [16], we have

$$
W(t) \le \phi(t,0)W(0) + \frac{c_p}{\sqrt{c_1}}\epsilon^2 \int_0^t \phi(t,\tau)A(\tau)\, d\tau \quad (28)
$$

$$
= \frac{c_p}{\sqrt{c_1}}\epsilon^2 \int_0^t \phi(t,\tau)A(\tau)\, d\tau \quad (29)
$$

where the transition function $\phi(t,\tau)$ is

$$
\begin{aligned}
\phi(t,\tau) = \exp\Big(&-\frac{c_d}{2}(t-\tau) \\
&+ \frac{L}{2}\frac{c_p}{c_l}\int_\tau^t \left(\|\mathbf{x}^{(0)}(\gamma)\| + \epsilon\|\mathbf{x}^{(1)}(\gamma)\| + 2\|\mathbf{e}(\gamma)\|\right) d\gamma\Big),
\end{aligned}
$$

and the equality holds because $\mathbf{e}(0) = 0$.

The following lemma proves that the first-order system (25) converges exponentially starting from any initial condition in $\mathcal{D}$.

LEMMA 1. *The first-order system (25) is exponentially stable for any solution $\mathbf{x}^{(0)}(t)$ that starts from $\mathcal{D}$.*

PROOF. That the nominal system is exponentially stable implies that the following linear system

$$
\dot{\mathbf{x}} = \frac{\partial f}{\partial x}(0)\mathbf{x}
$$

is (globally) exponentially stable, and $\frac{\partial f}{\partial x}(0)$ is Hurwitz (Corollary 4.3 in [16]), which further implies that there exists a positive definite symmetric matrix $\mathbf{P}$ such that

$$
V(\mathbf{x}) = \mathbf{x}^T \mathbf{P} \mathbf{x}
$$

is a Lyapunov function for the linear system such that

$$
\dot{V}(\mathbf{x}) \le -\|\mathbf{x}\|^2. \quad (30)
$$

We start from

$$
\begin{aligned}
&\dot{V}(\mathbf{x}^{(1)}(t)) \\
=&\nabla V(\mathbf{x}^{(1)}(t)) \cdot \dot{\mathbf{x}}^{(1)}(t) \\
=&\nabla V(\mathbf{x}^{(1)}(t)) \cdot \frac{\partial f}{\partial x}(0)\mathbf{x}^{(1)}(t) + \nabla V(\mathbf{x}^{(1)}(t)) \cdot \\
&\left(\frac{\partial f}{\partial x}(\mathbf{x}^{(0)}(t))\mathbf{x}^{(1)}(t) - \frac{\partial f}{\partial x}(0)\mathbf{x}^{(1)}(t)\right)
\end{aligned}
$$

$$
\begin{aligned}
\le_{(a)} &- \left\|\mathbf{x}^{(1)}(t)\right\|^2 + 2\lambda_{\max}(\mathbf{P})\, L \left\|\mathbf{x}^{(0)}(t)\right\| \left\|\mathbf{x}^{(1)}(t)\right\|^2 \\
\le &- \frac{1}{\lambda_{\max}(\mathbf{P})} V(\mathbf{x}^{(1)}(t)) + \frac{2\lambda_{\max}(\mathbf{P})}{\lambda_{\min}(\mathbf{P})} L \left\|\mathbf{x}^{(0)}(t)\right\| V\left(\mathbf{x}^{(1)}(t)\right) \\
\le &- \left(\frac{1}{\lambda_{\max}(\mathbf{P})} - \frac{2\lambda_{\max}(\mathbf{P})}{\lambda_{\min}(\mathbf{P})} L \left\|\mathbf{x}^{(0)}(t)\right\|\right) V\left(\mathbf{x}^{(1)}(t)\right)
\end{aligned}
$$

where inequality (a) is based on (30) and the definition of $V(\mathbf{x})$, Assumption (1) and the mean-value theorem, and $\lambda_{\max}(\mathbf{P})$ is the largest eigenvalue of matrix $\mathbf{P}$.

By the comparison lemma, we have

$$
\begin{aligned}
&V(t) \\
\le &\exp\left(-\frac{1}{\lambda_{\max}(\mathbf{P})}t + \frac{2\lambda_{\max}(\mathbf{P})}{\lambda_{\min}(\mathbf{P})} L \int_0^t \left\|\mathbf{x}^{(0)}(\tau)\right\| d\tau\right) V(0) \\
\le &\exp\left(\frac{2\lambda_{\max}(\mathbf{P})\, L\kappa\|\mathbf{x}(0)\|}{\alpha\lambda_{\min}(\mathbf{P})}\right) \exp\left(-\frac{1}{\lambda_{\max}(\mathbf{P})}t\right) V(0),
\end{aligned}
$$

where the last inequality holds because the exponential convergence assumption (2) yields

$$
\int_0^t \left\|\mathbf{x}^{(0)}(\tau)\right\| d\tau \le \int_0^\infty \left\|\mathbf{x}^{(0)}(\tau)\right\| d\tau \le \frac{\kappa\|\mathbf{x}(0)\|}{\alpha}.
$$

Recall that $\mathbf{x}^{(1)}(0) = \mathbf{z}$, so $V(0) = \mathbf{z}^T\mathbf{P}\mathbf{z} = p$ and

$$
\begin{aligned}
&\|\mathbf{x}^{(1)}(t)\|^2 \\
\le &\frac{p}{\lambda_{\min}(\mathbf{P})} \exp\left(\frac{2\lambda_{\max}(\mathbf{P})\, L\kappa\|\mathbf{x}(0)\|}{\alpha\lambda_{\min}(\mathbf{P})}\right) \exp\left(-\frac{1}{\lambda_{\max}(\mathbf{P})}t\right).
\end{aligned} \quad (31)
$$

□

From the lemma above and assumption (1), we have that there exists a constant μ such that

$$
\begin{aligned}
&A(t) \\
\le &\mu\|\mathbf{x}^{(1)}(t)\|^2 \\
\le &\frac{\mu p}{\lambda_{\min}(\mathbf{P})} \exp\left(\frac{2\lambda_{\max}(\mathbf{P})\, L\kappa\|\mathbf{x}(0)\|}{\alpha\lambda_{\min}(\mathbf{P})}\right) \exp\left(-\frac{1}{\lambda_{\max}(\mathbf{P})}t\right).
\end{aligned}
$$

Consider the set such that $\|\mathbf{e}(t)\| \le \frac{c_d c_l}{4 c_p L}$, we have

$$
\begin{aligned}
&\phi(t,\tau) \\
\le &\exp\left(-\frac{c_d}{2}(t-\tau) + \frac{L}{2}\frac{c_p}{c_l}\int_\tau^t \left(\|\mathbf{x}^{(0)}(\gamma)\| + \epsilon\|\mathbf{x}^{(1)}(\gamma)\|\right) d\gamma\right) \\
\le &\exp\Bigg(-\frac{c_d}{4}(t-\tau) + \frac{L}{2}\frac{c_p}{c_l}\Bigg(\frac{\kappa\|\mathbf{x}(0)\|}{\alpha} \\
&+ 2\epsilon\frac{\lambda_{\max}(\mathbf{P})\sqrt{p}}{\sqrt{\lambda_{\min}(\mathbf{P})}} \exp\left(\frac{\lambda_{\max}(\mathbf{P})L\kappa\|\mathbf{x}(0)\|}{\alpha\lambda_{\min}(\mathbf{P})}\right)\Bigg)\Bigg),
\end{aligned}
$$

where last inequality yields from (20) and (31).

Recall we have inequality (29)

$$
W(t) \le \frac{c_p}{\sqrt{c_1}}\epsilon^2 \int_0^t \phi(t,\tau)A(\tau)\, d\tau. \quad (32)
$$

Substituting the bounds on $\phi(t,\tau)$ and $A(\tau)$, we obtain

$$
W(t) \le \epsilon^2 \sqrt{c_1} Z(\|\mathbf{x}(0)\|) \int_0^t \exp\left(-\frac{c_d}{4}(t-\tau) - \frac{1}{\lambda_{\max}(\mathbf{P})}\tau\right) d\tau,
$$

where

$$
Z(\|\mathbf{x}(0)\|)
$$

$$=\frac{c_p}{c_1}\exp\left(\frac{L}{2}\frac{c_p}{c_l}\left(\frac{\kappa\|\mathbf{x}(0)\|}{\alpha}\right.\right.$$
$$\left.\left.\left.+2\epsilon\frac{\lambda_{\max}(\mathbf{P})\sqrt{p}}{\sqrt{\lambda_{\min}(\mathbf{P})}}\exp\left(\frac{\lambda_{\max}(\mathbf{P})L\kappa\|\mathbf{x}(0)\|}{\alpha\lambda_{\min}(\mathbf{P})}\right)\right)\right)\right)\times$$
$$\frac{\mu p}{\lambda_{\min}(\mathbf{P})}\exp\left(\frac{2\lambda_{\max}(\mathbf{P})L\kappa\|\mathbf{x}(0)\|}{\alpha\lambda_{\min}(\mathbf{P})}\right)$$
$$=\frac{c_p\mu p}{c_1\lambda_{\min}(\mathbf{P})}\exp\left(\frac{\kappa L}{\alpha}\left(\frac{c_p}{2c_l}+\frac{2\lambda_{\max}(\mathbf{P})}{\lambda_{\min}(\mathbf{P})}\right)\|\mathbf{x}(0)\|\right.$$
$$\left.+\epsilon\sqrt{p}\frac{c_pL}{c_l}\frac{\lambda_{\max}(\mathbf{P})}{\sqrt{\lambda_{\min}(\mathbf{P})}}\exp\left(\frac{\lambda_{\max}(\mathbf{P})L\kappa\|\mathbf{x}(0)\|}{\alpha\lambda_{\min}(\mathbf{P})}\right)\right).$$

In other words, we have

$$\|\mathbf{e}(t)\|$$
$$\leq\epsilon^2 Z(\|\mathbf{x}(0)\|)\int_0^t \exp\left(-\frac{c_d}{4}(t-\tau)-\frac{1}{\lambda_{\max}(\mathbf{P})}\tau\right)d\tau \quad (33)$$
$$=\begin{cases}\epsilon^2 Z(\|\mathbf{x}(0)\|)\frac{1}{\frac{c_d}{4}-\frac{1}{\lambda_{\max}(\mathbf{P})}}\left(\exp\left(-\frac{1}{\lambda_{\max}(\mathbf{P})}t\right)-\exp\left(-\frac{c_d}{4}t\right)\right), & \text{if } \frac{c_d}{4}\neq\frac{1}{\lambda_{\max}(\mathbf{P})}\\ \epsilon^2 Z(\|\mathbf{x}(0)\|)t\exp\left(-\frac{c_d}{4}t\right), & \text{otherwise.}\end{cases} \quad (34)$$

Then

$$\int_0^\infty \|\mathbf{e}(t)\|\,dt$$
$$\leq \begin{cases}\epsilon^2 Z(\|\mathbf{x}(0)\|)\frac{4\lambda_{\max}(\mathbf{P})}{c_d} & \text{if } \frac{c_d}{4}\neq\frac{1}{\lambda_{\max}(\mathbf{P})}\\ \epsilon^2 Z(\|\mathbf{x}(0)\|)\frac{16}{c_d^2}, & \text{otherwise.}\end{cases}$$
$$=\epsilon^2 Z(\|\mathbf{x}(0)\|)\frac{4\lambda_{\max}(\mathbf{P})}{c_d}.$$

It is easy to see that with properly defined α_1, α_2, α_3 and α_4, we have

$$\int_0^\infty \|\mathbf{e}(t)\|\,dt$$
$$\leq\epsilon^2 p\alpha_1\exp\left(\alpha_2\frac{\|\mathbf{x}(0)\|}{\alpha}+\epsilon\sqrt{p}\alpha_3\exp\left(\alpha_4\frac{\|\mathbf{x}(0)\|}{\alpha}\right)\right). \quad (35)$$

We keep the terms $\|\mathbf{x}(0)\|$ and α to show that the cumulative error depends on the initial condition and the convergence rate of the mean-field model. Furthermore, $p=\mathbf{z}^T\mathbf{P}\mathbf{z}\leq\lambda_{\max}(\mathbf{P})\|\mathbf{z}\|^2$.

6. CONCLUSION

This paper studies the approximation error of a large-class of mean-field models. When the mean-field model is perfect, the mean-square difference (also called the rate of convergence) has been proved to be $O(1/M)$. Based on Stein's method for bounding the distance of probability distributions and the perturbation theory for nonlinear systems, a fundamental connection between the convergence to the mean-field limit and the stability of the mean-field model has been established. Two applications of mean-field models for large-scale data center networks were discussed to demonstrate the novelty of our results.

Acknowledgement

The author is very grateful to Jim Dai and Anton Braverman. Jim's seminar on Stein's method for the steady-state diffusion approximations inspired this work. The discussions with Jim and Anton had continuously stimulated the author during the writing of this paper. This work was supported in part by the NSF under Grant ECCS-1255425.

7. REFERENCES

[1] S. Adlakha and R. Johari. Mean field equilibrium in dynamic games with strategic complementarities. *Operations Research*, 61(4):971–989, 2013.

[2] V. Anantharam and M. Benchekroun. A technique for computing sojourn times in large networks of interacting queues. *Probability in the engineering and informational sciences*, 7(04):441–464, 1993.

[3] F. Baccelli, F. Karpelevich, M. Y. Kelbert, A. Puhalskii, A. Rybko, and Y. M. Suhov. A mean-field limit for a class of queueing networks. *Journal of statistical physics*, 66(3-4):803–825, 1992.

[4] N. T. J. Bailey. *The mathematical theory of infectious diseases and its applications.* Hafner Press, 1975.

[5] A. D. Barbour. Stein's method and Poisson process convergence. *J. Appl. Probab.*, pages 175–184, 1988.

[6] A. D. Barbour and L. H. Chen. *An Introduction to Stein's Method*, volume 4. World Scientific, 2005.

[7] C. Bordenave, D. Mcdonald, and A. Proutiere. A particle system in interaction with a rapidly varying environment: Mean field limits and applications. *Networks and Heterogeneous Media (NHM)*, 2010.

[8] L. Bortolussi and R. A. Hayden. Bounds on the deviation of discrete-time markov chains from their mean-field model. *Performance Evaluation*, 70(10):736–749, 2013.

[9] M. Bramson, Y. Lu, and B. Prabhakar. Asymptotic independence of queues under randomized load balancing. *Queueing Systems*, 71(3):247–292, 2012.

[10] A. Braverman and J. Dai. Stein's method for steady-state diffusion approximations of $m/ph/n+m$ systems. *arXiv preprint arXiv:1503.00774*, 2015.

[11] F. Cecchi, S. C. Borst, and J. S. H. van Leeuwaardena. Mean-field analysis of ultra-dense csma networks. *ACM SIGMETRICS Performance Evaluation Review*, 43(2):13–15, 2015.

[12] A. Chaintreau, J.-Y. Le Boudec, and N. Ristanovic. The age of gossip: spatial mean field regime. In *Proc. Ann. ACM SIGMETRICS Conf.*, pages 109–120, Seattle, Washington, USA, 2009.

[13] F. Gotze. On the rate of convergence in the multivariate clt. *Ann. Probab.*, pages 724–739, 1991.

[14] I. Gurvich et al. Diffusion models and steady-state approximations for exponentially ergodic markovian queues. *Adv. in Appl. Probab.*, 24(6):2527–2559, 2014.

[15] L. P. Kadanoff. More is the same; phase transitions and mean field theories. *Journal of Statistical Physics*, 137(5-6):777–797, 2009.

[16] H. K. Khalil. *Nonlinear systems.* Prentice Hall, 2001.

[17] T. G. Kurtz. Limit theorems for sequences of jump markov processes approximating ordinary differential processes. *J. Appl. Probab.*, 8(2):344–356, 1971.

[18] T. G. Kurtz. *Approximation of population processes*, volume 36. SIAM, 1981.

[19] J.-M. Lasry and P.-L. Lions. Mean field games. *Japanese Journal of Mathematics*, 2(1):229–260, 2007.

[20] Y. Lu, Q. Xie, G. Kliot, A. Geller, J. R. Larus, and A. Greenberg. Join-Idle-Queue: A novel load balancing algorithm for dynamically scalable web services. *Performance Evaluation*, 68(11):1056–1071, 2011.

[21] M. Manjrekar, V. Ramaswamy, and S. Shakkottai. A mean field game approach to scheduling in cellular systems. In *Proc. IEEE Int. Conf. Computer Communications (INFOCOM)*, pages 1554–1562, Toronto, Canada, 2014.

[22] M. Mitzenmacher. *The Power of Two Choices in Randomized Load Balancing.* PhD thesis, University of California at Berkeley, 1996.

[23] A. Mukhopadhyay and R. R. Mazumdar. Analysis of load balancing in large heterogeneous processor sharing systems. *arXiv preprint arXiv:1311.5806*, 2013.

[24] M. F. Norman. A central limit theorem for Markov processes that move by small steps. *Ann. Probab.*, pages 1065–1074, 1974.

[25] M. F. Norman. Limit theorems for stationary distributions. *Ann. Appl. Probab.*, pages 561–575, 1975.

[26] C. Stein. A bound for the error in the normal approximation to the distribution of a sum of dependent random variables. In *Proc. Sixth Berkeley Symp. Math. Stat. Prob.*, pages 583–602, 1972.

[27] C. Stein. Approximate computation of expectations. *Lecture Notes-Monograph Series*, 7:i–164, 1986.

[28] A. L. Stolyar. Pull-based load distribution in large-scale heterogeneous service systems. *arXiv preprint arXiv:1407.6343*, 2014.

[29] A. L. Stolyar. Tightness of stationary distributions of a flexible-server system in the halfin-whitt asymptotic regime. *arXiv preprint arXiv:1403.4896*, 2014.

[30] A.-S. Sznitman. Topics in propagation of chaos. In *Ecole d'été de probabilités de Saint-Flour XIXâĂŤ1989*, pages 165–251. 1991.

[31] J. N. Tsitsiklis and K. Xu. On the power of (even a little) resource pooling. *Stochastic Systems*, 2(1):1–66, 2012.

[32] N. D. Vvedenskaya, R. L. Dobrushin, and F. I. Karpelevich. Queueing system with selection of the shortest of two queues: An asymptotic approach. *Problemy Peredachi Informatsii*, 32(1):20–34, 1996.

[33] Q. Xie, X. Dong, Y. Lu, and R. Srikant. Power of d choices for large-scale bin packing: A loss model. In *Proc. Ann. ACM SIGMETRICS Conf.*, 2015.

[34] L. Ying, R. Srikant, and X. Kang. The power of slightly more than one sample in randomized load balancing. In *Proc. IEEE Int. Conf. Computer Communications (INFOCOM)*, Hong Kong, 2015.

On the Duration and Intensity of Competitions in Nonlinear Pólya Urn Processes with Fitness

Bo Jiang
College of Computer and Information Sciences
University of Massachusetts
Amherst MA, USA
bjiang@cs.umass.edu

Daniel R. Figueiredo
COPPE/PESC
Federal University of Rio de Janeiro (UFRJ)
Rio de Janeiro, Brazil
daniel@land.ufrj.br

Bruno Ribeiro
Department of Computer Science
Purdue University
West Lafayette IN, USA
ribeiro@cs.purdue.edu

Don Towsley
College of Computer and Information Sciences
University of Massachusetts
Amherst MA, USA
towsley@cs.umass.edu

ABSTRACT

Cumulative advantage (CA) refers to the notion that accumulated resources foster the accumulation of further resources in competitions, a phenomenon that has been empirically observed in various contexts. The oldest and arguably simplest mathematical model that embodies this general principle is the Pólya urn process, which finds applications in a myriad of problems. The original model captures the dynamics of competitions between two equally fit agents under linear CA effects, which can be readily generalized to incorporate different fitnesses and nonlinear CA effects. We study two statistics of competitions under the generalized model, namely duration (i.e., time of the last tie) and intensity (i.e., number of ties). We give rigorous mathematical characterizations of the tail distributions of both duration and intensity under the various regimes for fitness and nonlinearity, which reveal very interesting behaviors. For example, fitness superiority induces much shorter competitions in the sublinear regime while much longer competitions in the superlinear regime. Our findings can shed light on the application of Pólya urn processes in more general contexts where fitness and nonlinearity may be present.

Keywords

Competition; Cumulative advantage; Fitness; Nonlinearity; Pólya urn; Duration; Intensity

1. INTRODUCTION

Cumulative advantage (CA) is a ubiquitous phenomenon observed in various systems where agents compete for resources. CA alludes to the capacity that accumulated resources have to foster accumulation of more resources, a principle that appears in the literature under various names such as cumulative advantage [5], preferential attachment [2], "the rich get richer", Matthew effect [6, 17], path-dependent increasing returns [1], and processes with feedback [7, 20].

The oldest and arguably simplest model that embodies CA is the Pólya urn process, which has been widely studied and applied [8, 16, 21]. In particular, one can find applications of Pólya urn model in problems that arise in most areas of science, including biology, physics, economics, and of course, computer science, with a recent example described in Section 2.3. In its simplest form, a Pólya urn has balls with two colors. At each round a ball is chosen uniformly at random from the urn and returned to the urn with another ball of the same color, increasing the number of balls in the urn by one. Note that drawing balls of a given color increases the chance of drawing more balls of the same color, thus embodying the CA phenomenon.

Beyond CA, an observed and recognized characteristics in competitions is *fitness*, which refers to the inherent ability of an agent to accumulate resources that does not depend on the amount of resources already accumulated. A second and more recent consideration, which has also been observed in some contexts, is that the feedback induced by accumulated resources may not be linear as in the simple Pólya urn model. In particular, the propensity to accumulate further resources can be nonlinear in the amount of resources already accumulated. These two generalizations can be easily accommodated in the Pólya urn model by assigning a fixed fitness to each color and by selecting balls not uniformly at random from the urn. Such a model is the object under consideration in this paper (formal definition in Section 2).

Two fundamental characteristics of competitions are their duration and intensity [14]. Duration can be measured as the time required for an agent to take the lead forever, while intensity as the number of times agents tie for the leadership. These two metrics have recently been studied for linear Pólya urn processes with fitness in [14]. The question that we ask here is: What is the impact of introducing nonlinearity in the CA feedback of a Pólya urn process? We address this question by providing a rigorous theoretical understanding of the implications of fitness and nonlinear CA on duration and intensity, along with numerical simulations

SIGMETRICS '16, June 14 - 18, 2016, Antibes Juan-Les-Pins, France

ISBN 978-1-4503-4266-7/16/06... $15.00

DOI: http://dx.doi.org/10.1145/2896377.2901475

to illustrate and support the findings. A summary of our main results is given in Section 2.2.

The rest of this paper is organized as follows. Section 2 formally introduces the nonlinear Pólya urn process with fitness, discusses some related work, and briefly presents a recent application in computer science. Section 3 presents some stochastic ordering results for the metrics investigated. Sections 4 and 5 present the main results on the distributions of duration and intensity, respectively. Section 6 concludes the paper with further discussions.

2. NONLINEAR PÓLYA URN PROCESS

In accordance with the jargon of the Pólya urn model, we will refer to the agents that engage in a competition as *colors*. Consider two colors, labelled 1 and 2. Each color is associated with a positive *fitness* value that reflects its intrinsic competitiveness. Let f_i denote the fitness of color i, $i = 1, 2$, and $r = f_1/f_2$ the fitness ratio. Without loss of generality, we assume that $f_1 \geq f_2$ and hence $r \geq 1$.

The resource that the agents compete for, which is measured in discrete units, will be generically referred to as balls. The competition starts at time $t = 0$ with color i having x_{0i} balls, $i = 1, 2$. We consider a discrete-time process. At each time step, one ball of one of the colors is added to the system. Denote by $X_i(t)$ the number of balls with color i at time t and $\mathbf{X}(t) = (X_1(t), X_2(t))$. The trajectory of the competition $\mathbf{X} = \{\mathbf{X}(t)\}_{t\in\mathbb{N}}$ then forms a discrete-time discrete-space stochastic process. The state space is the first quadrant of the integral lattice $\mathbb{N}^2$. The initial condition is $\mathbf{X}(0) = \mathbf{x}_0 \triangleq (x_{01}, x_{02})$.

In a nonlinear Pólya urn process with fitness, the ball added at time $t+1$ has color i with probability

$$p_i(t) = \frac{f_i X_i(t)^\beta}{f_1 X_1(t)^\beta + f_2 X_2(t)^\beta}.$$

Here $\beta \geq 0$ reflects the strength of the feedback by cumulative advantage. Note that the larger β is, the stronger the feedback. When $\beta = 0$, there is no feedback and the process falls back to a random walk (where the transition probabilities do not depend on $\mathbf{X}(t)$).

More formally, the trajectory $\{\mathbf{X}(t)\}_{t\in\mathbb{N}}$ forms a Markov chain with initial condition $\mathbf{X}(0) = \mathbf{x}_0$ and stationary transition probabilities $\mathbb{P}[\mathbf{X}(t+1) = \mathbf{x}' \mid \mathbf{X}(t) = \mathbf{x}]$ given by

$$Q(\mathbf{x}, \mathbf{x}'; \beta, r) = \begin{cases} \dfrac{r x_1^\beta}{r x_1^\beta + x_2^\beta}, & \text{if } \mathbf{x}' = \mathbf{x} + (1, 0); \\ \dfrac{x_2^\beta}{r x_1^\beta + x_2^\beta}, & \text{if } \mathbf{x}' = \mathbf{x} + (0, 1); \\ 0, & \text{otherwise.} \end{cases} \tag{1}$$

We will call such a process a $(\beta, r, \mathbf{x}_0)$-urn process.

The *duration* and *intensity* of a competition have been defined through events of ties in [14]. We follow the same definitions here. Given a 2D process $\mathbf{X} = \{\mathbf{X}(t)\}_{t\in\mathbb{N}}$, not necessarily an urn process introduced above, we say that a *tie* occurs at time t if $X_1(t) = X_2(t)$. For $n \geq 0$, let $T_n(\mathbf{X})$ be the time of the n-th tie, defined recursively by

$$T_n(\mathbf{X}) = \inf\{t > T_{n-1}(\mathbf{X}) : X_1(t) = X_2(t)\}, \quad n \geq 1,$$

where $T_0(\mathbf{X}) = -1$ by convention. The *duration* $T(\mathbf{X})$ of a competition is defined to be the time of the last tie, i.e.,

$$T(\mathbf{X}) = \sup\{T_n(\mathbf{X}) : n \geq 0, T_n(\mathbf{X}) < +\infty\}.$$

Note that $T(\mathbf{X})$ marks the end of the competition in the sense that there are no more ties after this point in time, hence leaving one of the colors in the lead forever.

Let N_t be the number of ties up to time t, i.e.

$$N_t(\mathbf{X}) = \sum_{j=0}^{t} \mathbf{1}\{X_1(j) = X_2(j)\},$$

where $\mathbf{1}\{A\}$ is the indicator of event A. The *intensity* $N(\mathbf{X})$ of a competition is the total number of ties throughout the competition, i.e.,

$$N(\mathbf{X}) = \lim_{t\to\infty} N_t(\mathbf{X}) = \sum_{t=0}^{\infty} \mathbf{1}\{X_1(t) = X_2(t)\},$$

This measures the intensity of the competition in the sense that it counts the number of potential changes in leadership.

When there is no confusion, we will also write T for $T(\mathbf{X})$, and similarly for T_n, N_t and N. Note that $N = N_T$, $T = T_N$, and that $T < +\infty$ if and only if $N < +\infty$. With an abuse of notation, we will use $T(\beta, r, \mathbf{x}) = T(\beta, r, x_1, x_2)$ to denote $T(\mathbf{X})$ for any $(\beta, r, \mathbf{x})$-urn process $\mathbf{X}$, and similarly for T_n, N_t and N. Throughout the rest of the paper, a boldfaced letter always has two components, e.g. $\mathbf{x} = (x_1, x_2)$ and $\mathbf{Y} = (Y_1, Y_2)$. The notations such as $g(\mathbf{x}) = g(x_1, x_2)$ will be understood without mention.

2.1 Related Work

Given the 90 years since the Pólya urn process was first introduced [8], it is not surprising that many different properties of this process have been characterized through rigorous mathematical treatment as well as simulations. Most work focuses on the so-called *market share*, i.e. the fraction of balls in each color, for which convergence results and limit distributions have been established for different regimes of fitness or feedback strength, but rarely for both [7, 19, 20, 26, 25]. Other properties that have been studied more recently include the probability of ever taking the lead and the onset of monopoly [20, 25]. When the feedback is superlinear ($\beta > 1$), the winning color receives all but a finite number of balls, a phenomenon knowns as *monopoly*, various aspects of which have been studied [19, 20]. The metrics under investigation in this paper, duration and intensity, have been studied in [14] for linear Pólya urn process with fitness.

The *Poissonization* [16] and the exponential embeddding [4] are two major technical tools used in the study of Pólya urn processes. Other methods are surveyed in [21, 26]. We will mainly follow the exponential embedding approach in the present work. We extend existing works by considering the effect of nonlinear CA on duration and intensity. The theoretical findings deepen our understanding of the interaction between fitness and feedback strength in CA competitions, which in turn sheds light on understanding applications that employ such models.

2.2 Overview of Results

Table 1 summarizes our main results on the tail distributions of duration and intensity, which will be detailed in Sections 4 and 5. We have used the standard notations of O, Θ, and Ω in the table. In later sections, we will also use other standard notations such as o and $\sim$ without further mention, where $g(x) \sim h(x)$ means $\lim_x g(x)/h(x) = 1$ in the limiting process under consideration.

	$\mathbb{P}[T(\beta, r, \mathbf{x}_0) \geq t]$		$\mathbb{P}[N(\beta, r, \mathbf{x}_0) \geq n]$	
	$r = 1$	$r > 1$	$r = 1$	$r > 1$
$0 \leq \beta \leq \frac{1}{2}$	1	$e^{-\Omega(t^{1-\beta})}$	1	$O(a^n)$
$\frac{1}{2} < \beta < 1$	$\Theta(t^{\frac{1}{2}-\beta})$	$e^{-\Omega(t^{1-\beta})}$	$\Omega(n^{-\beta})$	$O(a^n)$
$\beta = 1$	$\Theta(t^{-\frac{1}{2}})$	$\Omega(t^{(1-r)x_{01}})$	$\Theta(n^{-1})$	$O(a^n)$
$\beta > 1$	$\Theta(t^{\frac{1}{2}-\beta})$	$\Theta(t^{1-\beta})$	$O(n^{-\beta})$	$O(a^n)$

Table 1: Tail distributions of duration and intensity. Here $a = 2/(r+1)$.

To the best of our knowledge, all results related to nonlinear CA ($\beta \neq 1$) are new, with the exception of the case $\beta \leq 1/2$ and $r = 1$. The linear case ($\beta = 1$) is given in [14], and included here for completeness and comparison.

The results are revealing and worth exploring. In the equal fitness case $r = 1$, we observe a phase transition at $\beta = 1/2$. For $\beta \leq 1/2$, competitions never end [15]. For $\beta > 1/2$, competitions always end, but can be very long and intense, as both duration and intensity have power-law tails.

The picture is dramatically different in the case of different fitnesses. In this case, if $\beta \leq 1$ then the fittest agent is bound to win the competition (i.e., take the lead forever)[1]. If $\beta > 1$, then there is a nonzero probability that the less fit wins (it actually becomes the monopoly) [4]. In the sublinear regime, the fittest color wins relatively quickly with the distribution of duration upper bounded by a Weibull tail. Thus fitness superiority brings a clear advantage in this regime, in sharp contrast to the superlinear regime. Note that not only may the competition duration increase when moving from the linear to superlinear regime depending on r and $\mathbf{x}_0$, but the fittest may even lose the competition! Thus the fittest may have to struggle much more under superlinear CA.

Also observe that moving from equal to non-equal fitness induces longer competitions under superlinear CA. However, there is an advantage in becoming fitter since the chance of winning is greater than under equal fitness (where the chance is 50% if $x_{01} = x_{02}$), but at the expense of engaging in potentially longer competitions. In a nutshell, superlinear CA may exacerbate the strugle of the fittest!

Finally, in the case of different fitnesses, competition intensity is always small, exhibiting an exponential tail. This phenomenon of long (duration) but mild (intensity) competitions has been observed in [14]. We observe here that this phenomenon persists in the presence of nonlinear CA.

2.3 Recent Application to Social Tagging

In this section we briefly describe an example of the applications of Pólya urns in computer science. Such applications could potentially leverage a more general model that incorporates nonlinear CA and fitness. By providing a theoretical understanding of duration and intensity we prepare the ground for the application of more general models.

Social or collaborative tagging refers to the increasingly common process where users *tag* resources within online services [11, 24]. For example, users can bookmark a URL on Delicious[2], annotate pictures on Flickr[1], and use hashtag to mark tweets on Twitter[1]. An important consideration in this context is the dynamics behind tag generation and tag accumulation by the various resources such as URLs, pictures and tweets. In particular, a cumulative advantage effect (i.e., preferential attachment) has been empirically observed in social tagging in the sense that, as resources accumulate more tags, they tend to accumulate even more tags. In order to capture this phenomenon, models that embody cumulative advantage such as Pólya urn and Yule-Simon process have been used to represent how objects accumulate tags [3, 10]. Models that also capture the inherent difference between tags, which can be interpreted as tag fitness [12], and models that leverage tag ranking to assess tag dynamics [24] have also been proposed.

To illustrate such modeling within our framework, consider two URLs competing for bookmarks by users on Delicious, as presented and evaluated in [10]. For $i = 1, 2$, let f_i denote the intrinsic fitness of URL$_i$, and $X_i(t)$ the number of bookmarks that it has received by time t. When the CA feedback has strength $\beta > 0$, how will the two URLs accumulate bookmarks? Will the fittest URL emerge as the unchallenged winner? How many bookmarks will they have accumulated together when this occurs?

An important consideration is the effectiveness of social tagging in describing and assessing online resources [24]. For example, can poor quality URLs be overridden by late coming higher quality URLs in the bookmark competition? The answer to such questions depends fundamentally on the nature of the competition, as defined by the fitnesses $f_{1,2}$ and the feedback strength β. Our work provides a solid theoretical ground for understanding such behaviors. For example, we now know that under superlinear CA much longer competitions can occur (in comparison to linear CA), as well as the fittest losing the competition. Such findings may put into question the effectiveness of social tagging.

3. STOCHASTIC ORDERING RESULTS

In this section, we will show that some of the metrics introduced in Section 2 can be ordered stochastically according to the feedback strength β. We recall the following definition of *stochastic dominance.*

DEFINITION 1 (STOCHASTIC DOMINANCE). *A random variable Z_1* stochastically dominates *a random variable Z_2, if $\mathbb{P}[Z_1 \geq z] \geq \mathbb{P}[Z_2 \geq z]$ for all z. This is denoted by $Z_1 \geq_{\rm st} Z_2$ or $Z_2 \leq_{\rm st} Z_1$.*

3.1 Equal Fitness

The following theorem shows that in the equal fitness case, stronger feedback, i.e. larger β, leads to stochastically shorter and less intense competitions.

THEOREM 1. *Let $\beta \geq \beta' \geq 0$. The following hold,*

(i) $N_t(\beta, 1, \mathbf{x}_0) \leq_{\rm st} N_t(\beta', 1, \mathbf{x}_0)$ for all t;

(ii) $N(\beta, 1, \mathbf{x}_0) \leq_{\rm st} N(\beta', 1, \mathbf{x}_0)$;

(iii) $T_n(\beta, 1, \mathbf{x}_0) \geq_{\rm st} T_n(\beta', 1, \mathbf{x}_0)$ for all n;

(iv) $T(\beta, 1, \mathbf{x}_0) \leq_{\rm st} T(\beta', 1, \mathbf{x}_0)$.

[1]For $\beta = 1$, see [16] for a proof. For $\beta < 1$, see the remark at the end of Section 4.3.3.

[2]delicious.com, www.flickr.com, www.twitter.com

PROOF. Let $\mathbf{X}$ be a $(\beta, 1, \mathbf{x}_0)$-urn process and let $\mathbf{X}'$ be a $(\beta', 1, \mathbf{x}_0)$-urn process. Define a new process $\mathbf{Y}$ by $Y_1(t) = \min\{X_1(t), X_2(t)\}$ and $Y_2(t) = \max\{X_1(t), X_2(t)\}$. Similarly, define $\mathbf{Y}'$ by $Y_1'(t) = \min\{X_1'(t), X_2'(t)\}$ and $Y_2'(t) = \max\{X_1'(t), X_2'(t)\}$.

Let $\{\eta_j\}_{j\in\mathbb{N}}$ be a sequence of independent random variables uniformly distributed on $[0,1]$. Define $\{\mathbf{Z}(t)\}_{t\in\mathbb{N}}$ recursively by $Z_1(0) = \min\{x_{01}, x_{02}\}$, $Z_2(0) = \max\{x_{01}, x_{02}\}$, and

$$Z_1(t+1) = Z_1(t) + \mathbf{1}\left\{Z_1(t) < Z_2(t), \eta_t \le \frac{Z_1(t)^\beta}{Z_1(t)^\beta + Z_2(t)^\beta}\right\},$$
$$Z_2(t+1) = Z_1(t) + Z_2(t) + 1 - Z_1(t+1),$$

Define $\{\mathbf{Z}'(t)\}_{t\in\mathbb{N}}$ by the same equations but with β replaced by β'. Note that $\mathbf{Y} \overset{d}{=} \mathbf{Z}$ and $\mathbf{Y}' \overset{d}{=} \mathbf{Z}'$, where $\overset{d}{=}$ means "equal in distribution". It is also clear that $Z_1(t) \le Z_2(t)$ for all t.

We now show that $Z_1(t) \le Z_1'(t)$ by induction on t. The base case $t = 0$ holds trivially. Assume it holds for t and consider $t+1$. Note that $Z_1(t) + Z_2(t) = Z_1'(t) + Z_2'(t) = x_{01} + x_{02} + t$ and hence $Z_2'(t) \le Z_2(t)$. There are three cases.

- $Z_2'(t) = Z_1'(t) = Z_1(t)$. In this case, $Z_2(t) = Z_1(t)$, and hence $Z_1(t+1) = Z_1(t) \le Z_1'(t) = Z_1'(t+1)$
- $Z_2'(t) = Z_1'(t) \ge Z_1(t) + 1$. In this case, $Z_1(t+1) \le Z_1(t) + 1 \le Z_1'(t) = Z_1'(t+1)$
- $Z_2'(t) > Z_1'(t)$. In this case, $Z_2(t) \ge Z_2'(t) > Z_1'(t) \ge Z_1(t)$. Thus

$$\frac{Z_1(t)^\beta Z_2'(t)^{\beta'}}{Z_2(t)^\beta Z_1'(t)^{\beta'}} = \left(\frac{Z_1(t)}{Z_2(t)}\right)^{\beta-\beta'} \left(\frac{Z_1(t)}{Z_1'(t)} \cdot \frac{Z_2'(t)}{Z_2(t)}\right)^{\beta'} \le 1,$$

and hence

$$\frac{Z_1(t)^\beta}{Z_1(t)^\beta + Z_2(t)^\beta} \le \frac{Z_1'(t)^{\beta'}}{Z_1'(t)^{\beta'} + Z_2'(t)^{\beta'}}.$$

It follows that

$$Z_1(t+1) = Z_1(t) + \mathbf{1}\left\{\eta_t \le \frac{Z_1(t)^\beta}{Z_1(t)^\beta + Z_2(t)^\beta}\right\}$$
$$\le X_1'(t) + \mathbf{1}\left\{\eta_t \le \frac{Z_1'(t)^{\beta'}}{Z_1'(t)^{\beta'} + Z_2'(t)^{\beta'}}\right\} = Z_1'(t+1).$$

In all cases, we have $Z_1(t+1) \le Z_1'(t+1)$, which completes the induction. As a consequence,

$$Z_2(t) - Z_1(t) \ge Z_2'(t) - Z_1'(t) \ge 0, \quad \forall t \ge 0.$$

Thus $\mathbf{Z}$ ties at t only if $\mathbf{Z}'$ also ties at t, which implies $N_t(\mathbf{Z}) \le N_t(\mathbf{Z}')$, $N(\mathbf{Z}) \le N(\mathbf{Z}')$, $T_n(\mathbf{Z}) \ge T_n(\mathbf{Z}')$, and $T(\mathbf{Z}) \le T(\mathbf{Z}')$.

Note that $N_t(\mathbf{X}) = N_t(\mathbf{Y}) \overset{d}{=} N_t(\mathbf{Z})$ and $N_t(\mathbf{X}') = N_t(\mathbf{Y}') \overset{d}{=} N_t(\mathbf{Z}')$, from which *(i)* follows. The same argument also proves *(ii)*, *(iii)* and *(iv)*. Alternatively, *(ii)* follows from *(i)* by letting $t \to \infty$, while *(iii)* follows from *(i)* by the identity $\{T_n \ge t\} = \{N_t \le n\}$. □

3.2 Different Fitnesses

In the case of different fitnesses, there are no such nice ordering results as in Section 3.1, as we will see in Figure 2(b) of Section 4.3. However, we have some partial results, which will be useful later in characterizing the tail distributions of duration and intensity. Note that the results apply to the equal fitness case as well.

The following theorem shows that the time of first tie can be ordered stochastically. The proof uses a coupling argument similar to the one in the proof of Theorem 1 and is found in [13].

THEOREM 2. *Let $\beta \ge \beta' \ge 0$. $T_1(\beta, r, \mathbf{x}_0) \ge_{\text{st}} T_1(\beta', r', \mathbf{x}_0')$, if either of the following conditions holds,*

(i) $r \ge r'$ and $x_{01} \ge x_{01}' \ge x_{02}' \ge x_{02}$;

(ii) $r = r'$ and $x_{01} \le x_{01}' \le x_{02}' \le x_{02}$.

In particular, $T_1(\beta, r, \mathbf{x}_0) \ge_{\text{st}} T_1(\beta', r, \mathbf{x}_0)$.

When competition starts out with a tie, $T_1(\beta, r, x_0, x_0) = T_1(\beta', r, x_0, x_0) = 0$ trivially. What is more interesting in this case is the time of the first return to a tie, which can also be ordered as shown by the next corollary.

COROLLARY 1. *$T_2(\beta, r, x_0, x_0) \ge_{\text{st}} T_2(\beta', r, x_0, x_0)$, if $\beta \ge \beta'$. In particular, the probability of ever tying again satisfies*

$$\mathbb{P}[T_2(\beta, r, x_0, x_0) < \infty] \le \mathbb{P}[T_2(0, r, 0, 0) < \infty] = \frac{2}{r+1}.$$

PROOF. Let $p_r = r/(r+1)$ and $q_r = 1/(r+1)$. By considering the first transition and applying Theorem 2, we obtain

$$\begin{aligned}
&\mathbb{P}[T_2(\beta, r, x_0, x_0) \ge t] \\
&= p_r\mathbb{P}[T_1(\beta, r, x_0+1, x_0) \ge t] + q_r\mathbb{P}[T_1(\beta, r, x_0, x_0+1) \ge t] \\
&\ge p_r\mathbb{P}[T_1(\beta', r, x_0+1, x_0) \ge t] + q_r\mathbb{P}[T_1(\beta', r, x_0, x_0+1) \ge t] \\
&= \mathbb{P}[T_2(\beta', r, x_0, x_0) \ge t].
\end{aligned}$$

which means $T_2(\beta, r, x_0, x_0) \ge_{\text{st}} T_2(\beta', r, x_0, x_0)$. In particular,

$$\begin{aligned}
\mathbb{P}[T_2(\beta, r, x_0, x_0) < \infty] &\le \mathbb{P}[T_2(0, r, x_0, x_0) < \infty] \\
&= \mathbb{P}[T_2(0, r, 0, 0) < \infty] = \frac{2}{r+1},
\end{aligned}$$

where we have used the translation invariance of random walks and the well-known formula for the probability of no return to the origin (see e.g. Section XI.3.c of [9]). □

The next corollary shows that feedback, regardless of its strength β, does not increase competition intensity. In particular, competition always ends if $r > 1$.

COROLLARY 2. *$N(\beta, r, \mathbf{x}_0) \le_{\text{st}} N(0, r, \mathbf{x}_0)$ for any $\beta \ge 0$.*

PROOF. Let $\mathbf{X}$ be a $(\beta, r, \mathbf{x}_0)$-urn process. Let $F_n(z) = \mathbb{P}[X_1(T_n(\mathbf{X})) = z \mid T_n(\mathbf{X}) < \infty]$. Note that $T_n(\mathbf{X})$ is a stopping time of $\mathbf{X}$ for $n \ge 1$. The strong Markov property and Corollary 1 yield

$$\begin{aligned}
&\mathbb{P}[T_{n+1}(\mathbf{X}) < \infty \mid T_n(\mathbf{X}) < \infty] \\
&= \sum_z F_n(z)\mathbb{P}[T_2(\beta, r, z, z) < \infty] \\
&\le \sum_z F_n(z)\mathbb{P}[T_2(0, r, 0, 0) < \infty] = \mathbb{P}[T_2(0, r, 0, 0) < \infty].
\end{aligned}$$

Therefore,

$$\mathbb{P}[N(\beta, r, \mathbf{x}_0) \ge n] = \mathbb{P}[T_n(\mathbf{X}) < \infty]$$

$$= \mathbb{P}[T_1(\mathbf{X}) < \infty] \prod_{j=1}^{n-1} \mathbb{P}[T_{j+1}(\mathbf{X}) < \infty \mid T_j(\mathbf{X}) < \infty]$$
$$\leq \mathbb{P}[T_1(0, r, \mathbf{x}_0) < \infty] \left(\mathbb{P}[T_2(0, r, 0, 0) < \infty]\right)^{n-1}$$
$$= \mathbb{P}[N(0, r, \mathbf{x}_0) \geq n],$$

which means $N(\beta, r, \mathbf{x}_0) \leq_{st} N(0, r, \mathbf{x}_0)$. □

4. TAIL DISTRIBUTION OF DURATION

In this section, we characterize the tail distribution of duration T. The analysis relies on Rubin's exponential embedding that appeared in the appendix of [4]. We first review the exponential embedding in Section 4.1. We then present the tail distribution of T for the case $r = 1$ in Section 4.2 and that for the case $r > 1$ in Section 4.3.

4.1 The Exponential Embedding

Rubin's exponential embedding is a specific representation of an urn process. Let $\{\xi_{kj} : k \in \{1, 2\}, j \in \mathbb{N}\}$ be a set of independent exponential random variables with $\mathbb{E}\xi_{kj} = f_k^{-1} j^{-\beta}$, where f_k is the fitness of color k. Let

$$S_k(x, y) = \sum_{j=x}^{y-1} \xi_{kj},$$

where by convention the sum is zero if $y \leq x$. Given $\mathbf{x}_0$, order $\{S_k(x_{0k}, x_k) : x_k > x_{0k}, k \in \{1, 2\}\}$ in increasing order and let $\tau_1 < \tau_2 < \ldots$ be the resulting sequence. Let

$$X_k(t) = \sup\{x \in \mathbb{N} : S_k(x_{0k}, x) \leq \tau_t\}. \quad (2)$$

Note that $S_k(x_{0k}, x)$ can be considered as the time when color k gets its x-th ball, and $X_k(t)$ is the number of balls with color k when the total number of new balls arriving after time zero is t. The following theorem asserts that the process $\mathbf{X}$ constructed above is a $(\beta, r, \mathbf{x}_0)$-urn process.

THEOREM 3 (RUBIN). *The process $\{\mathbf{X}(t)\}_{t \in \mathbb{N}}$ defined by (2) is a $(\beta, r, \mathbf{x}_0)$-urn process, where $r = f_1/f_2$.*

We will use this representation throughout the rest of Section 4. Without further mention, $\{\xi_{kj}\}$ will always denote the set of independent random variables in this representation and S_k the associated partial sums. We will also use the following notation,

$$\Delta(\mathbf{x}, \mathbf{y}) = \Delta(x_1, x_2, y_1, y_2) = S_1(x_1, y_1) - S_2(x_2, y_2). \quad (3)$$

When $f_k = 1$, the characteristic function of $S_k(x, y)$ is given by

$$\Psi(s; \beta, x, y) = \prod_{j=x}^{y-1} \left(1 - \frac{is}{j^\beta}\right)^{-1}. \quad (4)$$

The quantity $K(\beta, 1, \mathbf{x}_0)$ defined in the following lemma will be used in the statements of the main results of the next two sections. Its proof is found in [13].

LEMMA 1. *If either (i) $\beta > 1$, or (ii) $\beta > 1/2$ and $r = 1$, then*

$$\tilde{\Psi}(s; \beta, r, \mathbf{x}_0) \triangleq \lim_{x \to \infty} \Psi(s; \beta, x_{01}, x) \Psi^*(rs; \beta, x_{02}, x) \quad (5)$$

exists, and

$$K(\beta, r, \mathbf{x}_0) \triangleq \frac{1}{2\pi} \int_{-\infty}^{\infty} \tilde{\Psi}(s; \beta, r, \mathbf{x}_0) ds \quad (6)$$

is a strictly positive real number.

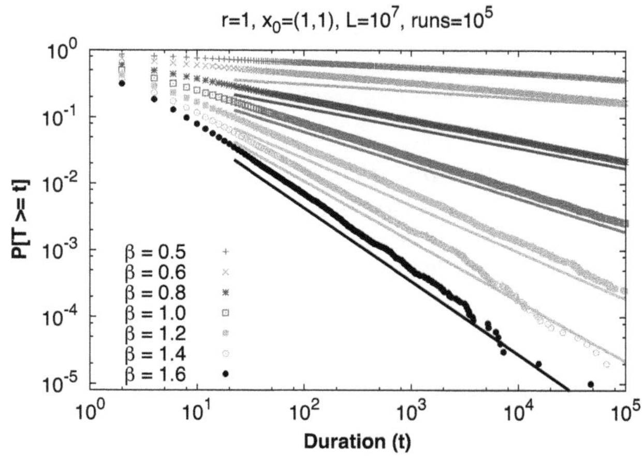

Figure 1: Tail distribution for duration of $r = 1$ and various values of β. Dots (marks) are simulation results. The solid lines have slopes $1/2 - \beta$.

4.2 Equal Fitness

We consider the equal fitness case in this section. Since the transition probability in (1) depends only on r, we assume without loss of generality that $f_1 = f_2 = 1$ throughout this section. The main result is presented in Section 4.2.1. Section 4.2.2 reviews the invariance principle, a key ingredient of the proof, which is given in Section 4.2.3.

4.2.1 Main Result

The following result was proved in [15] (see also Theorem 1 in [19]), from which it follows that $\mathbb{P}[T(\beta, 1, \infty) \geq t] = 1$ for all finite t and $\beta \in [0, 1/2]$.

THEOREM 4 ([15]). *With probability one, $T(\beta, 1, \mathbf{x}_0)$ is finite if and only if $\beta > 1/2$.*

Our focus of this section is thus the regime $\beta > 1/2$. The following theorem shows that $T(\beta, 1, \mathbf{x}_0)$ has a power-law tail with exponent $\beta - 1/2$ in this case, irrespective of the initial condition $\mathbf{x}_0$.

THEOREM 5. *For $\beta > 1/2$,*

$$\mathbb{P}[T(\beta, 1, \mathbf{x}_0) \geq t] \sim \frac{2^{\beta - 1/2}}{\sqrt{(2\beta - 1)\pi}} K(\beta, 1, \mathbf{x}_0) t^{\frac{1}{2} - \beta}. \quad (7)$$

The result is illustrated in Figure 1, which shows the empirical tail distributions of duration from simulations. Each curve is obtained from 10^5 independent runs of $L = 10^7$ time steps each. The same simulation setup is used for all later plots and will not be repeated. Strictly speaking, what are plotted here are the tail distributions of the last tie before the simulation cutoff time L, which are good approximations to the true tail distributions $\mathbb{P}[T(\beta, 1, \mathbf{x}_0) \geq t]$ for $t \ll L$. Similar comments apply to later plots. We observe the stochastic ordering asserted by Theorem 1. Figure 1 also superimposes straight lines with slopes $1/2 - \beta$, which are parallel to the asymptotes of (7). Since we do not have a closed form formula for $K(\beta, 1, \mathbf{x}_0)$, we have arbitrarily chosen the intercepts of these lines to ease comparison of their slopes with those of the simulated curves. Note the good agreement between the corresponding slopes. Note also that for $\beta \le 1/2$, the simulated tail distribution approaches the distribution $\mathbb{P}[T(\beta, 1, \mathbf{x}_0) \ge t] = 1$, and dominates all curves for $\beta > 1/2$. In fact, this stochastic dominance result can be established by the same coupling argument used in the proof of Theorem 1.

4.2.2 The Invariance Principle

In this section, we review a key ingredient of the proof of Theorem 5, i.e. the invariance principle, which asserts that an appropriately scaled random walk converges to a Wiener process in distribution. This has been exploited in the study of nonlinear Pólya urn processes in [19]. We will follow a similar approach, but for our purpose, we will need not only the convergence result but also the rate of convergence, which is provided by the following result of Sakhanenko.

Let $\theta_1, \theta_2, \dots$ be a sequence of independent random variables with $\mathbb{E}\theta_j = 0$ and $\mathbb{E}\theta_j^2 < \infty$ for all j. Define a random process Ξ_θ with piecewise linear continuous sample paths by

$$\Xi_\theta(t) = \sum_{j=1}^{\ell} \theta_j + \frac{t - \sigma_\ell^2}{\mathbb{E}\theta_{\ell+1}^2}\theta_{\ell+1}, \quad \text{for } t \in [\sigma_\ell^2, \sigma_{\ell+1}^2], \ell = 0, 1, \dots,$$

where $\sigma_\ell^2 = \sum_{j=1}^{\ell} \mathbb{E}\theta_j^2$. Note that $\Xi_\theta(\sigma_\ell^2) = \sum_{j=1}^{\ell} \theta_j$.

The following theorem, which is a special case of Theorem 1 of [23], bounds the error incurred by approximating Ξ_θ by a Wiener process.

THEOREM 6 (SAKHANENKO). *Let Ξ_θ be defined as above. For $\alpha \ge 2$, there exists a constant κ and a Wiener process $W = W_\alpha$ such that for any $y > 0$,*

$$\mathbb{P}\left[\sup_{0 \le t < L_\theta^2} |\Xi_\theta(t) - W(t)| \ge 2\kappa\alpha y\right] \le \frac{L_\theta^\alpha}{y^\alpha}, \tag{8}$$

where $L_\theta^\alpha = \sum_{j=1}^{\infty} \mathbb{E}|\theta_j|^\alpha$.

We now apply Theorem 6 to prove the following lemma, which is a key step in the proof of Theorem 5.

LEMMA 2. *Assume $\beta > 1/2$, $c > 0$ and $\epsilon \in (0, c)$. If $x_m \sim m$ and $q_m = \Omega(\sqrt{m})$, then for all large enough m,*

$$\mathbb{P}\left[\sup_{y \ge x_m} \Delta(x_m, x_m, y, y) > \frac{cq_m}{m^\beta}\right] \le 2\bar{\Phi}\left(\frac{c^- q_m}{\sqrt{2m}}\right) + O(m^{-\beta}), \tag{9}$$

and

$$\mathbb{P}\left[\sup_{y \ge x_m} \Delta(x_m, x_m, y, y) > \frac{cq_m}{m^\beta}\right] \ge 2\bar{\Phi}\left(\frac{c^+ q_m}{\sqrt{2m}}\right) - O(m^{-\beta}), \tag{10}$$

where Δ is defined in (3),

$$c^\pm = (c \pm \epsilon)\sqrt{2\beta - 1},$$

and $\bar{\Phi}$ is the CCDF of the standard normal distribution,

$$\bar{\Phi}(z) = \frac{1}{\sqrt{2\pi}} \int_z^\infty e^{-u^2/2} du.$$

PROOF. Let $\theta_j = \xi_{1(j+x_m-1)} - \xi_{2(j+x_m-1)}$ for $j \ge 1$. Define Ξ_θ and L_θ^α as in Theorem 6. Note that

$$\sup_{y \ge x_m} \Delta(x_m, x_m, y, y) = \sup_{\ell \ge 0} \sum_{j=1}^{\ell} \theta_j = \sup_{0 \le t < L_\theta^2} \Xi_\theta(t).$$

Thus

$$E \triangleq \left\{\sup_{y \ge x_m} \Delta(x_m, x_m, y, y) > \frac{cq_m}{m^\beta}\right\} = \left\{\sup_{0 \le t < L_\theta^2} \Xi_\theta(t) > \frac{cq_m}{m^\beta}\right\}.$$

Let W be the Wiener process in Theorem 6, and

$$E_0 = \left\{\sup_{0 \le t < L_\theta^2} |\Xi_\theta(t) - W(t)| > \frac{\epsilon q_m}{2m^\beta}\right\},$$

$$E_\pm = \left\{\sup_{0 \le t < L_\theta^2} W(t) > \left(c \pm \frac{1}{2}\epsilon\right)\frac{q_m}{m^\beta}\right\}.$$

Since $E_+ \subset E \cup E_0$ and $E \subset E_- \cup E_0$, we have

$$\mathbb{P}[E_+] - \mathbb{P}[E_0] \le \mathbb{P}[E] \le \mathbb{P}[E_-] + \mathbb{P}[E_0]. \tag{11}$$

We first show that $\mathbb{P}[E_0] = O(m^{-\beta})$. Theorem 6 yields

$$\mathbb{P}[E_0] \le L_\theta^\alpha \left(\frac{4\alpha\kappa}{\epsilon}\right)^\alpha m^{\alpha\beta} q_m^{-\alpha} \le L_\theta^\alpha \left(\frac{4\alpha\kappa}{\lambda\epsilon}\right)^\alpha m^{\alpha\beta - \alpha/2},$$

where we have used $q_m \ge \lambda\sqrt{m}$ for some $\lambda > 0$ in the last step. Note that

$$|\xi_{1j} - \xi_{2j}|^\alpha \le \max\{\xi_{1j}^\alpha, \xi_{2j}^\alpha\} \le \xi_{1j}^\alpha + \xi_{2j}^\alpha,$$

and $\mathbb{E}\xi_{1j}^\alpha = \mathbb{E}\xi_{2j}^\alpha = \Gamma(\alpha+1)j^{-\alpha\beta}$, where $\Gamma(\cdot)$ is the gamma function. Thus for $\alpha > \beta^{-1}$,

$$L_\theta^\alpha = \sum_{j=1}^{\infty} \mathbb{E}|\theta_j|^\alpha \le 2\sum_{j=x_m}^{\infty} \mathbb{E}\xi_{1j}^\alpha = 2\Gamma(\alpha+1)\sum_{j=x_m}^{\infty} j^{-\alpha\beta}$$

$$\sim 2\Gamma(\alpha+1)\int_m^\infty z^{-\alpha\beta} dz = \frac{2\Gamma(\alpha+1)}{\alpha\beta - 1} m^{1-\alpha\beta}.$$

Set $\alpha = 2 + 2\beta$, which satisfies $\alpha > \beta^{-1}$ for $\beta > 1/2$. It follows that for all large enough m,

$$\mathbb{P}[E_0] = O(m^{-\beta}). \tag{12}$$

Now we compute $\mathbb{P}[E_\pm]$. The well-known formula for the distribution of the maximum of a Wiener process (see (6.5.3) of [22]) yields

$$\mathbb{P}[E_\pm] = 2\bar{\Phi}\left(\frac{(c \pm \epsilon/2)q_m m^{-\beta}}{\sqrt{L_\theta^2}}\right) = 2\bar{\Phi}\left(\frac{c_m^\pm q_m}{\sqrt{2m}}\right), \tag{13}$$

where

$$c_m^\pm = \frac{(c \pm \epsilon/2)\sqrt{2}m^{1/2-\beta}}{\sqrt{L_\theta^2}}.$$

Note that $\mathbb{E}\theta_j^2 = 2\mathrm{Var}[\xi_{1(j+x_m-1)}] = 2(j + x_m - 1)^{-\beta}$. Thus

$$L_\theta^2 = \sum_{j=1}^{\infty} \mathbb{E}\theta_j^2 = 2\sum_{j=x_m}^{\infty} j^{-2\beta} \sim 2\int_m^\infty z^{-2\beta} dz = \frac{2}{2\beta - 1} m^{1-2\beta},$$

from which it follows that

$$c_m^+ \to \left(c + \frac{1}{2}\epsilon\right)\sqrt{2\beta - 1} < c^+,$$

and hence $c_m^+ < c^+$ for large m. Similarly, $c_m^- > c^-$. Therefore, (9) and (10) follow from (11), (12), (13), and the monotonicity of $\bar{\Phi}$. □

Together with some large deviation results, Lemma 2 immediately yields the following bounds on the probability of ever having a tie, which is what will be used directly in the proof of Theorem 5. The proof of Lemma 3 is found in [13].

LEMMA 3. *Suppose $|\rho(\mathbf{x})| = \Omega(1)$, where*

$$\rho(\mathbf{x}) = \frac{x_1 - x_2}{\sqrt{||\mathbf{x}||_1}} = \frac{x_1 - x_2}{\sqrt{x_1 + x_2}}. \tag{14}$$

For $\beta > 1/2$ and $\epsilon > 0$, the following inequalities hold,

$$\mathbb{P}[T_1(\beta,1,\mathbf{x})<\infty] \le 2\bar{\Phi}\left(c_1|\rho(\mathbf{x})|\right) + O(||\mathbf{x}||_1^{-\beta}),$$
$$\mathbb{P}[T_1(\beta,1,\mathbf{x})<\infty] \ge 2\bar{\Phi}\left(c_2|\rho(\mathbf{x})|\right) - O(||\mathbf{x}||_1^{-\beta}),$$

where $c_1 = (1-\epsilon)\sqrt{2\beta-1}$ and $c_2 = \sqrt{2\beta-1}$.

4.2.3 Proof of Theorem 5

Let A_t be the set of states reachable at time t by a $(\beta,1,\mathbf{x}_0)$-urn process, i.e.

$$A_t = \{\mathbf{x}\in\mathbb{N}^2 : ||\mathbf{x}||_1 = ||\mathbf{x}_0||_1 + t,\ x_k \ge x_{0k} \text{ for } k=1,2\}.$$

We will need the following lemma in the proof of Theorem 5.

LEMMA 4. *Let $\mathbf{X}$ be a $(\beta,1,\mathbf{x}_0)$-urn process and $A_t(\delta) = \{\mathbf{x}\in A_t : |\rho(\mathbf{x})| \le \delta\}$, where $\rho(\mathbf{x})$ is defined in (14). For $\beta > 1/2$ and $\gamma < \beta\wedge 1 - 1/2$, where $a\wedge b = \min\{a,b\}$, we have, as $t\to\infty$,*

$$t^{\beta}\mathbb{P}[\mathbf{X}(t)=\mathbf{x}] \to 2^{\beta+1}K(\beta,1,\mathbf{x}_0),$$

uniformly for $\mathbf{x}\in A_t(t^{\gamma})$, where $K(\beta,1,\mathbf{x}_0)$ is given by (6).

PROOF. Note that $\mathbf{X}(t)=\mathbf{x}$ if and only if color 1 gets its x_1-th ball before color 2 gets its (x_2+1)-st ball and at the same time color 2 gets its x_2-th before color 1 gets its (x_1+1)-st ball. Using the exponential embedding, this probability is given by

$$\mathbb{P}[\mathbf{X}(t)=\mathbf{x}] = \mathbb{P}[-\xi_{1x_1} < \Delta(\mathbf{x}_0,\mathbf{x}) < \xi_{2x_2}],$$

where Δ is defined in (3). Let $\psi(s;\mathbf{x})$ denote the characteristic function of $\Delta(\mathbf{x}_0,\mathbf{x})$, i.e.

$$\psi(s;\mathbf{x}) = \Psi(s;\beta,x_{01},x_1)\Psi^*(s;\beta,x_{02},x_2),$$

where Ψ is given by (4). By the inversion formula,

$$\mathbb{P}[-\xi_{1x_1} < \Delta(\mathbf{x}_0,\mathbf{x}) < \xi_{2x_2} \mid \xi_{1x_1},\xi_{2x_2}] = \frac{1}{2\pi}\int_{-\infty}^{\infty}\psi(s;\mathbf{x})\frac{e^{is\xi_{1x_1}} - e^{-is\xi_{2x_2}}}{is}ds.$$

Deconditioning and interchanging the order of integrations by Fubini's theorem, we obtain

$$\begin{aligned}
&\mathbb{P}[-\xi_{1x_1} < \Delta(\mathbf{x}_0,\mathbf{x}) < \xi_{2x_2}]\\
&= \frac{1}{2\pi}\int_{-\infty}^{\infty}\psi(s;\mathbf{x})\frac{\mathbb{E}\left[e^{is\xi_{1x_1}}\right] - \mathbb{E}\left[e^{-is\xi_{1x_2}}\right]}{is}ds\\
&= \frac{1}{2\pi}\int_{-\infty}^{\infty}\psi(s;\mathbf{x})\frac{1}{is}\left[\left(1-\frac{is}{x_1^{\beta}}\right)^{-1} - \left(1+\frac{is}{x_2^{\beta}}\right)^{-1}\right]ds\\
&= \frac{x_1^{-\beta}+x_2^{-\beta}}{2\pi}\int_{-\infty}^{\infty}\psi(s;x_1+1,x_2+1)ds.
\end{aligned}$$

The rest of the proof is found in [13]. We only sketch it here. For $\mathbf{x}\in A_t(t^{\gamma})$, we have $x_1+x_2 = ||\mathbf{x}||_1 = ||\mathbf{x}_0||_1 + t \sim t$, and $x_2 - x_1 = |\rho(\mathbf{x})|\sqrt{||\mathbf{x}||_1} = O(t^{\gamma+1/2}) = o(t^{\beta\wedge 1})$. It follows that as $t\to\infty$,

$$\frac{x_1}{t}\to\frac{1}{2},\ \frac{x_2}{t}\to\frac{1}{2},$$

and

$$\psi(s;x_1+1,x_2+1)\to\tilde{\Psi}(s;\beta,1,\mathbf{x}_0),$$

uniformly for $\mathbf{x}\in A_t(t^{\gamma})$, where $\tilde{\Psi}$ is defined in (5). The proof is then completed by letting $t\to\infty$ and applying the Dominated Convergence Theorem. □

Now we prove Theorem 5.

PROOF OF THEOREM 5. Let $\mathbf{X}$ denote a $(\beta,1,\mathbf{x}_0)$-urn process and A_t the set of reachable states at time t as defined above. Let $\lambda > 0$ and $\gamma\in(0,\beta\wedge 1 - 1/2)$. Let

$$A_t^1 = A_t(\lambda),\quad A_t^2 = A_t\setminus A_t(t^{\gamma}),\quad A_t^3 = A_t(t^{\gamma})\setminus A_t(\lambda),$$

where $A_t(\delta) = \{\mathbf{x}\in A_t : |\rho(\mathbf{x})|\le\delta\}$ as in Lemma 4 and $|A_t(\delta)|\sim\delta t^{1/2}$. Note that $\mathbb{P}[T(\mathbf{X})\ge t] = \sum_{j=1}^{3}P_j$, where

$$P_j = \sum_{\mathbf{x}\in A_t^j}\mathbb{P}[\mathbf{X}(t)=\mathbf{x}]\cdot\mathbb{P}[T_1(\beta,1,\mathbf{x})<\infty].$$

We first bound P_1. Since $|A_t^1|\sim\lambda t^{1/2}$, by Lemma 4,

$$P_1 \le \sum_{\mathbf{x}\in A_t^1}\mathbb{P}[\mathbf{X}(t)=\mathbf{x}] \sim \lambda 2^{\beta+1}K(\beta,1,\mathbf{x}_0)t^{1/2-\beta}.$$

To bound P_2, let $\mathbf{y}_t = \arg\min_{\mathbf{x}\in A_t^2}\rho(\mathbf{x})$. By Theorem 2, $\mathbb{P}[T_1(\beta,1,\mathbf{x})<\infty] \le \mathbb{P}[T_1(\beta,1,\mathbf{y}_t)<\infty]$ for $\mathbf{x}\in A_t^2$. Thus

$$\begin{aligned}
P_2 &\le \mathbb{P}[T_1(\beta,1,\mathbf{y}_t)<\infty]\ \mathbb{P}[\mathbf{X}(t)\in A_t^2] \le \mathbb{P}[T_1(\beta,1,\mathbf{y}_t)<\infty]\\
&\le 2\bar{\Phi}(c_1t^{\gamma}) + O(t^{-\beta}) = o(t^{1/2-\beta}),
\end{aligned}$$

where the last inequality follows from Lemma 3.

Now we bound P_3. By Lemmas 3 and 4,

$$\begin{aligned}
P_3 &= \sum_{\mathbf{x}\in A_t^3}\mathbb{P}[\mathbf{X}(t)=\mathbf{x}]\cdot\mathbb{P}[T_1(\beta,1,\mathbf{x})<\infty]\\
&\sim 2^{\beta}K(\beta,1,\mathbf{x}_0)t^{-\beta}\sum_{\mathbf{x}\in A_t^3}\mathbb{P}[T_1(\beta,1,\mathbf{x})<\infty]\\
&\le 2^{\beta}K(\beta,1,\mathbf{x}_0)t^{-\beta}\sum_{\mathbf{x}\in A_t^3}\bar{\Phi}(c_1|\rho(\mathbf{x})|) + O(t^{\gamma+1/2-2\beta})\\
&\sim 2^{\beta}K(\beta,1,\mathbf{x}_0)t^{1/2-\beta}\int_{\lambda}^{t^{\gamma}}\bar{\Phi}(c_1u)du + o(t^{-\beta})\\
&\le 2^{\beta}K(\beta,1,\mathbf{x}_0)t^{1/2-\beta}\int_{0}^{\infty}\bar{\Phi}(c_1u)du + o(t^{-\beta})\\
&= \frac{2^{\beta-1/2}K(\beta,1,\mathbf{x}_0)}{(1-\epsilon)\sqrt{(2\beta-1)\pi}}t^{1/2-\beta} + o(t^{-\beta}),
\end{aligned}$$

where we have used $\int_0^{\infty}\bar{\Phi}(c_1u)du = c_1^{-1}(2\pi)^{-1/2}$ in the last step. Letting $t\to\infty$, we obtain from the bounds on the P_j's,

$$\limsup_{t\to\infty}\frac{\mathbb{P}[T(\mathbf{X})\ge t]}{t^{1/2-\beta}} \le \lambda 2^{\beta+1}K(\beta,1,\mathbf{x}_0) + \frac{2^{\beta-1/2}K(\beta,1,\mathbf{x}_0)}{(1-\epsilon)\sqrt{(2\beta-1)\pi}}.$$

Letting $\lambda,\epsilon\to 0$,

$$\limsup_{t\to\infty}\frac{\mathbb{P}[T(\mathbf{X})\ge t]}{t^{1/2-\beta}} \le \frac{2^{\beta-1/2}}{\sqrt{(2\beta-1)\pi}}K(\beta,1,\mathbf{x}_0). \tag{15}$$

On the other hand,

$$\begin{aligned}
P_3 &\sim 2^{\beta}K(\beta,1,\mathbf{x}_0)t^{-\beta}\sum_{\mathbf{x}\in A_t^3}\mathbb{P}[T_1(\beta,1,\mathbf{x})<\infty]\\
&\ge 2^{\beta}K(\beta,1,\mathbf{x}_0)t^{-\beta}\sum_{\mathbf{x}\in A_t^3}\bar{\Phi}(c_2|\rho(\mathbf{x})|) - O(t^{\gamma+1/2-2\beta})\\
&\sim 2^{\beta}K(\beta,1,\mathbf{x}_0)t^{1/2-\beta}\int_{\lambda}^{t^{\gamma}}\bar{\Phi}(c_2u)du - o(t^{-\beta}).
\end{aligned}$$

Since $\mathbb{P}[T(\mathbf{X}) \geq t] \geq P_3$, letting $t \to \infty$, we obtain,

$$\liminf_{t\to\infty} \frac{\mathbb{P}[T(\mathbf{X}) \geq t]}{t^{1/2-\beta}} \geq 2^{\beta} K(\beta, 1, \mathbf{x}_0) \int_{\lambda}^{\infty} \bar{\Phi}(c_2 u) du.$$

Letting $\lambda \to 0$ and using $\int_0^\infty \bar{\Phi}(c_2 u)du = c_2^{-1}(2\pi)^{-1/2}$,

$$\liminf_{t\to\infty} \frac{\mathbb{P}[T(\mathbf{X}) \geq t]}{t^{1/2-\beta}} \geq \frac{2^{\beta-1/2}}{\sqrt{(2\beta-1)\pi}} K(\beta, 1, \mathbf{x}_0). \tag{16}$$

Combining (15) and (16) yields (7). □

4.3 Different Fitnesses

We consider in this section the case of different fitnesses. When the feedback is linear ($\beta = 1$), it has been shown in [14] that the duration has a power-law tail with exponent between $(r-1)x_{01}$ and $(r-1)(x_{01} - r^{-1})$. We focus on the superlinear ($\beta > 1$) and sublinear ($\beta < 1$) regimes in this section. The main results are presented in Section 4.3.1. The proof for the superlinear linear regime is given in Section 4.3.2, and that for the sublinear regime is given in Section 4.3.3.

4.3.1 Main Results

The following theorem shows that when the feedback is superlinear, the duration $T(\beta, r, \mathbf{x}_0)$ has a power-law tail with exponent $\beta - 1$. Compared to the duration $T(\beta, 1, \mathbf{x}_0)$ with the same β and $\mathbf{x}_0$ in the equal fitness case, the duration $T(\beta, r, \mathbf{x}_0)$ with $r > 1$ has a significantly heavier tail, which means that in the superlinear regime competitions may become much longer when agents have different fitnesses, similar to the observation in [14] for the linear regime. In contrast to the linear regime, however, the exponent in the superlinear regime does not depend on either the fitness ratio r or the initial condition $\mathbf{x}_0$.

THEOREM 7. *For $r > 1$ and $\beta > 1$,*

$$\mathbb{P}[T(\beta, r, \mathbf{x}_0) \geq t] \sim t^{1-\beta} \frac{(r-1)2^{\beta-1}}{\beta - 1} K(\beta, r, \mathbf{x}_0). \tag{17}$$

If feedback is sublinear, however, $T(\beta, r, \mathbf{x}_0)$ no longer has a power-law tail. As the following theorem shows, the tail distribution of $T(\beta, r, \mathbf{x}_0)$ is upper bounded by a Weibull distribution with shape parameter $1 - \beta$. Thus in the sublinear regime, $T(\beta, r, \mathbf{x}_0)$ with $r > 1$ always has a lighter tail than the corresponding $T(\beta, 1, \mathbf{x}_0)$. In particular, when $\beta = 0$, we recover the known exponential tail of $T(0, r, \mathbf{x}_0)$.

THEOREM 8. *For $r > 1$ and $\beta < 1$,*

$$\limsup_{t\to\infty} \frac{\log \mathbb{P}[T(\beta, r, \mathbf{x}_0) \geq t]}{t^{1-\beta}} \leq \frac{1-r}{1-\beta} 2^{\beta-1} x_{01}^{\beta}. \tag{18}$$

The results are illustrated in Figure 2, which shows the simulated tail distributions of duration for $r = 1.2$ and various β values. Figure 2(a) shows the superlinear regime ($\beta \geq 1$). The power-law exponents from simulations are close to the theoretical values, though the agreement is not as good as in the equal fitness case, as the finite cutoff in simulation time has a greater impact here. Note that the curves for $\beta = 1$ and $\beta = 1.2$ are approximately parallel. This is not a coincidence. For $\beta = 1.2$, Theorem 7 shows that the tail exponent is $\beta - 1 = 0.2$. For $\beta = 1$, [14] shows that the tail exponent is roughly $(r-1)x_{01} = 0.2$. More generally, $T(\beta, r, \mathbf{x}_0)$ with $\beta > 1$ may have a heavier or lighter tail than $T(1, r, \mathbf{x}_0)$, depending on r and $\mathbf{x}_0$.

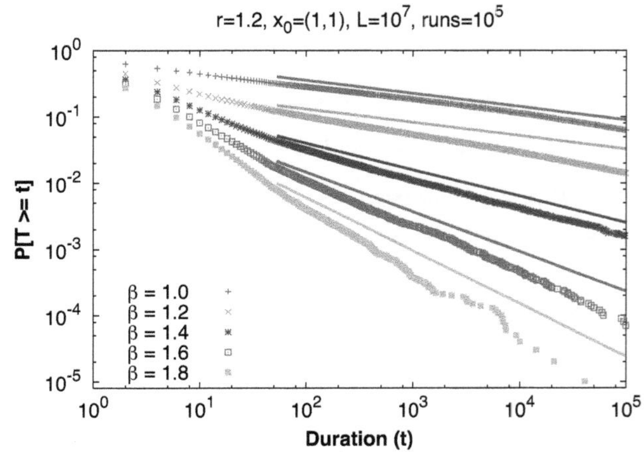

(a) $\beta \geq 1$

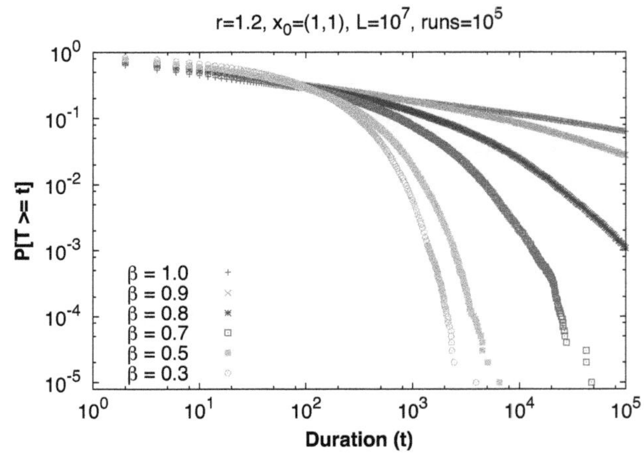

(b) $\beta \leq 1$

Figure 2: Tail distribution of duration for $r = 1.2$ and various values of β. Dots (marks) are simulation results. The solid lines in (a) have slopes $1 - \beta$.

Figure 2(b) shows the sublinear regime ($\beta \leq 1$). As mentioned in Section 3.2, the crossover between the curves indicates that there is no simple stochastic ordering between $T(\beta, r, \mathbf{x}_0)$ of different β. However, the tails are still nicely ordered. Note that a larger β results in a heavier tail, which is opposite to what we observe in the superlinear regime. When β is small, the tail drops very fast. Thus in the sublinear regime having the advantage of a larger fitness clearly manifests itself in shorter competition durations.

4.3.2 Proof of Theorem 7

Before we prove Theorem 7, we first prove the following result on the probability of never tying again when starting from a tie with a large number of balls. As a consequence of this result, for $r > 1$ and large t, the probability of the duration being t has the same order as the probability of having a tie at time t.

LEMMA 5. *For $\beta \geq 0$ and $r \geq 1$, the probability of never tying again satisfies*

$$\lim_{x\to\infty} \mathbb{P}[T_2(\beta, r, x, x) = \infty] = \mathbb{P}[T_2(0, r, 0, 0) = \infty] = \frac{r-1}{r+1}. \tag{19}$$

PROOF. Note that for $\mathbf{x} \sim (x, x)$, the transition probability in (1) satisfies

$$\lim_{x\to\infty} Q(\mathbf{x}, \mathbf{x}+\Delta\mathbf{x}; \beta, r) = Q(0, \Delta\mathbf{x}; 0, r),$$

which is the transition probability of a biased random walk. Thus for fixed $2k$,

$$\lim_{x\to\infty} \mathbb{P}[T_2(\beta, r, x, x) = 2k] = \mathbb{P}[T_2(0, r, 0, 0) = 2k].$$

Since $\mathbb{P}[T_2(\beta, r, x, x) < \infty] = \sum_{k=1}^{\infty} \mathbb{P}[T_2(\beta, r, x, x) = 2k]$, Fatou's Lemma yields

$$\liminf_{x\to\infty} \mathbb{P}[T_2(\beta, r, x, x) < \infty] \geq \sum_{k=1}^{\infty} \lim_{x\to\infty} \mathbb{P}[T_2(\beta, r, x, x) = 2k]$$

$$= \sum_{k=1}^{\infty} \mathbb{P}[T_2(0, r, 0, 0) = 2k] = \mathbb{P}[T_2(0, r, 0, 0) < \infty].$$

Now using Corollary 1, we obtain

$$\lim_{x\to\infty} \mathbb{P}[T_2(\beta, r, x, x) < \infty] = \mathbb{P}[T_2(0, r, 0, 0) < \infty] = \frac{2}{r+1},$$

which immediately implies (19). □

Now we prove Theorem 7.

PROOF OF THEOREM 7. Let $\mathbf{X}$ be a $(\beta, r, \mathbf{x}_0)$-urn process. Note that a tie occurs only at time epochs of the form $t_{2x} = 2x - ||\mathbf{x}_0||_1$ for some integer x. At such a t_{2x}, both colors have x balls. Note that

$$\mathbb{P}[\mathbf{X}(t_{2x}) = (x, x)] = \mathbb{P}[-\xi_{1x} < \Delta(\mathbf{x}_0, x, x) < \xi_{2x}].$$

Repeating the argument in the proof of Lemma 4, we obtain

$$\mathbb{P}[\mathbf{X}(t_{2x}) = (x, x)] \sim (r+1)2^{\beta} K(\beta, r, \mathbf{x}_0) t_{2x}^{-\beta}.$$

Since

$$\mathbb{P}[T(\mathbf{X}) = t_{2x}] = \mathbb{P}[\mathbf{X}(t_{2x}) = (x, x)] \cdot \mathbb{P}[T_2(\beta, r, x, x) = \infty],$$

Lemma 5 then yields

$$\mathbb{P}[T(\beta, r, \mathbf{x}_0) = t_{2x}] \sim (r-1)2^{\beta} K(\beta, r, \mathbf{x}_0) t_{2x}^{-\beta}.$$

Summing over x such that $t_{2x} \geq t$ and using the following Riemann sum approximation,

$$\sum_{x:t_{2x}\geq t} t_{2x}^{-\beta} \sim \int_t^{\infty} \frac{1}{2} z^{-\beta} dz = \frac{1}{2(\beta-1)} t^{1-\beta},$$

we obtain (17). □

4.3.3 *Proof of Theorem 8*

Let $\mathbf{X}$ be a $(\beta, r, \mathbf{x}_0)$-urn process and $t_{2x} = 2x - ||\mathbf{x}_0||_1$ as in the proof of Theorem 7. Note that

$$\mathbb{P}[\mathbf{X}(t_{2x}) = (x, x)] \leq \mathbb{P}[\Delta(\mathbf{x}_0, x+1, x) > 0].$$

Using the standard argument of exponentiation followed by the application of the Markov inequality as in the proof of Chernoff bound, we obtain, for $s < x_{01}^{\beta}$,

$$\mathbb{P}[\mathbf{X}(t_{2x}) = (x, x)] \leq M(s; \beta, x_{01}, x+1) M(-rs; \beta, x_{02}, x),$$

where

$$M(s; \beta, y_1, y_2) = \prod_{j=y_1}^{y_2-1} \left(1 - \frac{s}{j^{\beta}}\right)^{-1}, \quad \text{for } s < y_1^{\beta}, \qquad (20)$$

Note that

$$\log M(s; \beta, x_{01}, x+1) = -\sum_{j=x_{01}}^{x} \log\left(1 - \frac{s}{j^{\beta}}\right) \sim \frac{s x^{1-\beta}}{1-\beta}.$$

and

$$\log M(-rs; \beta, x_{02}, x) = -\sum_{j=x_{02}}^{x-1} \log\left(1 + \frac{rs}{j^{\beta}}\right) \sim -\frac{rs x^{1-\beta}}{1-\beta}.$$

Thus

$$\limsup_{x\to\infty} \frac{\log \mathbb{P}[\mathbf{X}(t_{2x}) = (x, x)]}{x^{1-\beta}} \leq \frac{(1-r)s}{1-\beta}.$$

Letting $s \to x_{01}^{\beta}$, we obtain

$$\limsup_{x\to\infty} \frac{\log \mathbb{P}[\mathbf{X}(t_{2x}) = (x, x)]}{x^{1-\beta}} \leq \frac{1-r}{1-\beta} x_{01}^{\beta}.$$

By Lemma 5,

$$\log \mathbb{P}[T_2(\beta, r, x, x) = \infty] \sim \log \frac{r-1}{r+1} = o(x^{1-\beta}).$$

Since

$$\mathbb{P}[T(\mathbf{X}) = t_{2x}] = \mathbb{P}[\mathbf{X}(t_{2x}) = (x, x)] \cdot \mathbb{P}[T_2(\beta, r, x, x) = \infty],$$

using Lemma 5 and the fact $t_{2x} \sim 2x$, we obtain

$$\limsup_{x\to\infty} \frac{\log \mathbb{P}[T(\beta, r, \mathbf{x}_0) = t_{2x}]}{t_{2x}^{1-\beta}} \leq \frac{1-r}{1-\beta} 2^{\beta-1} x_{01}^{\beta}.$$

Let $0 > C > \frac{1-r}{1-\beta} 2^{\beta-1} x_{01}^{\beta}$. For all large enough x,

$$\mathbb{P}[T(\mathbf{X}) = t_{2x}] \leq e^{C t_{2x}^{1-\beta}}.$$

Summing over x such that $t_{2x} \geq t$, we obtain

$$\mathbb{P}[T(\mathbf{X}) \geq t] = \sum_{x:t_{2x}\geq t} \mathbb{P}[T(\mathbf{X}) = t_{2x}] \leq \frac{1}{2} \int_{t-2}^{\infty} e^{C s^{1-\beta}} ds.$$

By repeated application of l'Hôpital's rule,

$$\limsup_{t\to\infty} \frac{\log \mathbb{P}[T(\mathbf{X}) \geq t]}{t^{1-\beta}} \leq \lim_{t\to\infty} \frac{\log \int_t^{\infty} e^{C s^{1-\beta}} ds}{t^{1-\beta}}$$

$$= \lim_{t\to\infty} \frac{-t^{\beta} e^{C t^{1-\beta}}}{(1-\beta) \int_t^{\infty} e^{C s^{1-\beta}} ds} = C.$$

Letting $C \to \frac{1-r}{1-\beta} 2^{\beta-1} x_{01}^{\beta}$ complets the proof. □

Remark 1. A modification of the above proof shows that color 1 always wins when $\beta < 1$. Indeed, the above proof shows that $\sum_x \mathbb{P}[\Delta(\mathbf{x}_0, x+1, x) > 0] < \infty$. The Borel-Cantelli Lemma then implies that $\Delta(\mathbf{x}_0, x+1, x) \leq 0$ for all large enough x almost surely, from which it follows that $X_1(t) > X_2(t)$ for large enough t.

5. TAIL DISTRIBUTION OF INTENSITY

In this section, we characterize the tail distribution of intensity N. The equal fitness case ($r = 1$) is considered in Section 5.1, and the case of different fitnesses ($r > 1$) is considered in Section 5.2.

5.1 Equal Fitness

We consider the equal fitness case in this section. The main results are presented in Section 5.1.1, and the proofs are given in Section 5.1.2.

5.1.1 *Main Results*

Since T is finite if and only if N is finite, it follows from Theorem 4 that $\mathbb{P}[N(\beta, 1, \infty) \geq n] = 1$ for all finite n, if $\beta \in [0, 1/2]$. Thus, as in Section 4.2, our focus in the present section is the regime $\beta > 1/2$.

The following theorem bounds the tail distribution of intensity. For the sublinear regime $\beta \in (1/2, 1]$, the tail distribution of $N(\beta, 1, \mathbf{x}_O)$ is bounded between two power laws with exponents β and $\beta - 1/2$, respectively. For the superlinear regime $\beta > 1$, we only have an upper bound, but simulations suggest that $N(\beta, 1, \mathbf{x}_O)$ also has a power-law tail in this regime.

THEOREM 9. *(i) For* $\beta \in (1/2, 1]$,

$$\mathbb{P}[N(\beta, 1, \mathbf{x}_O) \geq n] = O(n^{1/2-\beta}), \tag{21}$$

and

$$\mathbb{P}[N(\beta, 1, \mathbf{x}_O) \geq n] = \Omega(n^{-\beta}). \tag{22}$$

(ii) For $\beta \geq 1$,

$$\mathbb{P}[N(\beta, 1, \mathbf{x}_O) \geq n] = O(n^{-\beta}). \tag{23}$$

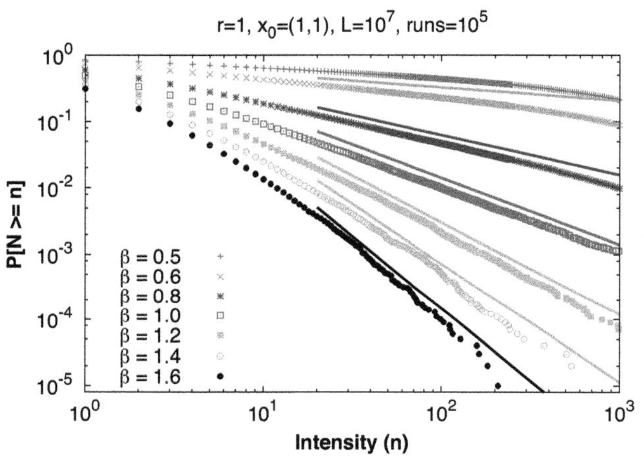

Figure 3: Tail distribution of intensity for $r = 1$ and various values of β. Dots (marks) are simulation results. The solid lines have slopes $1 - 2\beta$.

Figure 3 shows the empirical tail distribution of intensity from simulation. Also superimposed are straight lines with slopes $1 - 2\beta$. Note the good agreement of the simulated slopes with those of the straight lines, which strongly suggests that the intensity $N(\beta, 1, \mathbf{x}_O)$ has a power-law tail with exponent $1 - 2\beta$. We have the following conjecture,

CONJECTURE 1. *For* $\beta > 1/2$, *and some* $C(\beta, \mathbf{x}_O)$,

$$\mathbb{P}[N(\beta, 1, \mathbf{x}_O) \geq n] \sim C(\beta, \mathbf{x}_O) n^{1-2\beta}.$$

5.1.2 *Proof of Theorem 9*

By symmetry, we assume $x_{O1} \geq x_{O2}$ throughout the proof. Note that $N \leq T/2$. Thus for $\beta > 1/2$, Theorem 5 yields,

$$\mathbb{P}[N(\beta, 1, \mathbf{x}_O) \geq n] \leq \mathbb{P}[T(\beta, 1, \mathbf{x}_O) \geq 2n] \sim \frac{K(\beta, 1, \mathbf{x}_O)}{\sqrt{(2\beta - 1)\pi}} n^{\frac{1}{2} - \beta},$$

which implies (21).

Now we prove (22). Since x^β is concave for $\beta \in (1/2, 1]$, by Jensen's inequality, for any $x_1, x_2 > 0$,

$$\frac{x_1^\beta + x_2^\beta}{2} \leq \left(\frac{x_1 + x_2}{2}\right)^\beta,$$

and hence

$$\frac{x_i^\beta}{x_1^\beta + x_2^\beta} \geq \left(\frac{2x_i}{x_1 + x_2}\right)^\beta 2^{-1}.$$

By considering each sample path in the set $\{T_n(\beta, 1, \mathbf{x}_O) = d_O + 2\ell\}$, where $d_O = x_{O1} - x_{O2}$, we obtain

$$\mathbb{P}[T_n(\beta, 1, \mathbf{x}_O) = d_O + 2\ell] \geq \left[\frac{B(x_{O1} + \ell, x_{O1} + \ell)}{B(x_{O1}, x_{O2})} 2^{d_O + 2\ell}\right]^\beta \mathbb{P}[T_n(0, 1, d_O, 0) = d_O + 2\ell], \tag{24}$$

where $B(\cdot, \cdot)$ is the beta function.

Note that

$$\mathbb{P}[N(\beta, 1, \mathbf{x}_O) \geq n] = \mathbb{P}[T_n(\beta, 1, \mathbf{x}_O) < \infty] = \sum_{\ell=n-1}^{\infty} \mathbb{P}[T_n(\beta, 1, \mathbf{x}_O) = d_O + 2\ell].$$

Then (22) follows from (24) and the following lemma.

LEMMA 6. *Let* $\tilde{f}^{(n,d_O)}_{d_O+2\ell} \triangleq \mathbb{P}[T_n(0, 1, d_O, 0) = d_O + 2\ell]$ *be the probability that the* n*-th visit to the origin occurs at time* $d_O + 2\ell$ *in a simple random walk starting from* $d_O \geq 0$. *Then*

$$\sum_{\ell=n-1}^{\infty} \left[\frac{B(x_{O1} + \ell, x_{O1} + \ell)}{B(x_{O1}, x_{O2})} 2^{d_O + 2\ell}\right]^\beta \tilde{f}^{(n,d_O)}_{d_O+2\ell} = \Theta(n^{-\beta}). \tag{25}$$

The proof of (23) follows from the same argument as the proof of (22), except that the directions of all the inequalities get reversed, since x^β is convex for $\beta \geq 1$.

Now we complete the proof of Theorem 9 by proving Lemma 6.

PROOF OF LEMMA 6. Note that for large ℓ,

$$\left[\frac{B(x_{O1} + \ell, x_{O1} + \ell)}{B(x_{O1}, x_{O2})} 2^{d_O + 2\ell}\right]^\beta \sim \frac{C\,\Gamma(2\ell + 2x_{O1} + 1)}{\Gamma(2\ell + 2x_{O1} + 1 + \beta/2)}, \tag{26}$$

where $\Gamma(\cdot)$ is the gamma function, and

$$C = \left[\frac{\sqrt{\pi}}{2^{\|\mathbf{x}_O\|_1 - 3/2} B(x_{O1}, x_{O2})}\right]^\beta.$$

By Eq. (4.4.2) of [18],

$$\frac{\Gamma(2\ell + 2x_{O1} + 1)}{\Gamma(2\ell + 2x_{O1} + 1 + \beta/2)} = {}_0D_1^{-\beta/2}[z^{2x_{O1} + 2\ell}], \tag{27}$$

where ${}_aD_x^{-\alpha}$ is the Riemann-Liouville fractional integral operator defined by

$${}_aD_x^{-\alpha} f = \frac{1}{\Gamma(\alpha)} \int_a^x f(z)(x - z)^{\alpha - 1} dz.$$

Denote the sum in (25) by Λ_n. Combining (26) and (27) yields

$$\Lambda_n \sim C \sum_{\ell=n-1}^{\infty} {}_0D_1^{-\beta/2}[z^{2x_{O1} + 2\ell}] \tilde{f}^{(n,d_O)}_{d_O+2\ell}.$$

By the linearity of Riemann-Liouville integral for power series (see Section 5.2 of [18]),

$$\Lambda_n \sim C\ {}_0D_1^{-\beta/2}\left\{\sum_{\ell=n-1}^{\infty}\tilde{f}_{d_0+2\ell}^{(n,d_0)}z^{2x_{01}+2\ell}\right\}$$
$$= C\ {}_0D_1^{-\beta/2}\left[z^{x_{01}+x_{02}}G_n(z;d_0)\right], \qquad (28)$$

where $G_n(z;d_0)=\sum_{\ell=n-1}^{\infty}\tilde{f}_{d_0+2\ell}^{(n,d_0)}z^{d_0+2\ell}$ is the generating function of $\tilde{f}_{d_0+2\ell}^{(n,d_0)}$, the expression of which is given by the following (see Eq. (A.15) of [14]),

$$G_n(z;d_0)=z^{-d_0}\left(1-\sqrt{1-z^2}\right)^{n+d_0-1}. \qquad (29)$$

Substituting (29) into (28) yields

$$\Lambda_n \sim \frac{C}{\Gamma(\frac{\beta}{2})}\int_0^1 (1-z)^{\frac{\beta}{2}-1}z^{2x_{02}}\left(1-\sqrt{1-z^2}\right)^{n+d_0-1}dz,$$

where we have used $x_{01}+x_{02}-d_0=2x_{02}$. Note that the integrand can be rewritten as

$$(1-z^2)^{\frac{\beta}{2}-1}(1+z)^{1-\frac{\beta}{2}}(1+\sqrt{1-z^2})^{x_{02}}(1-\sqrt{1-z^2})^{n+x_{01}-1},$$

which on $(0,1)$ is bounded between constant multiples of

$$(1-z^2)^{\frac{\beta}{2}-1}(1-\sqrt{1-z^2})^{n+x_{01}-1}.$$

Thus

$$\Lambda_n=\Theta\left(\int_0^1(1-z^2)^{\frac{\beta}{2}-1}\left(1-\sqrt{1-z^2}\right)^{n+x_{01}-1}dz\right).$$

A change of variable $u=\sqrt{1-z^2}$ yields

$$\Lambda_n=\Theta\left(\int_0^1 u^{\beta-1}(1-u)^{n+x_{01}-1}du\right)$$
$$=\Theta(B(\beta,n+x_{01}))=\Theta(n^{-\beta}),$$

which completes the proof. □

5.2 Different Fitnesses

We consider the case of different fitnesses in this section. The following theorem shows that the distribution of the intensity $N(\beta,r,\mathbf{x}_0)$ for $r>1$ always has an exponential tail. Thus competitions are never intense when agents have different fitnesses, irrespective of the feedback strength β and the initial condition $\mathbf{x}_0$.

THEOREM 10. *For $r>1$,*

$$\mathbb{P}[N(\beta,r,\mathbf{x}_0)\ge n]\le r^{-(x_{01}-x_{02})^+}\left(\frac{2}{r+1}\right)^{n-1}, \qquad (30)$$

where $(x)^+=\max\{x,0\}$. In addition,

$$\lim_{n\to\infty}\frac{\log\mathbb{P}[N(\beta,r,\mathbf{x}_0)\ge n]}{n}=\log\left(\frac{2}{r+1}\right). \qquad (31)$$

The result is illustrated in Figure 4, which shows the simulated tail distributions of intensity. Note that the plot uses semi-log scale. The superimposed straight line has the slope $\log\frac{2}{r+1}$ given in (31). Note that the simulated curves all become parallel to the straight line, in good agreement with the theory. Of course, specific β values do affect the leading constants, as reflected by the parallel shifts of the curves.

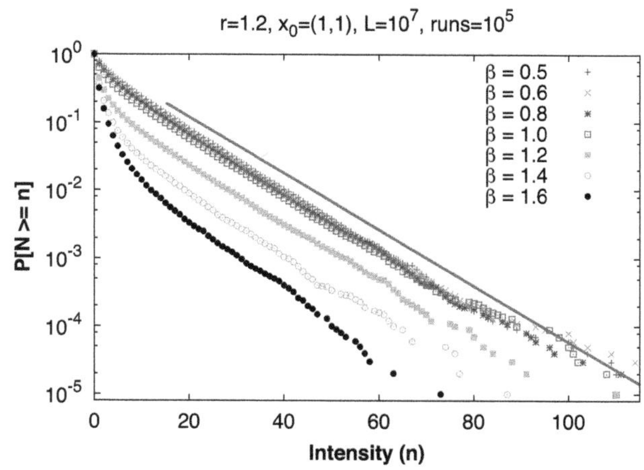

Figure 4: Tail distribution of intensity for $r=1.2$ and various values of β. The dots (marks) are from simulation. The straight line has slope $\log\frac{2}{r+1}$.

PROOF OF THEOREM 10. Eq. (30) follows from Corollary 2 and the well-known formula for $\mathbb{P}[N(0,r,\mathbf{x}_0)\ge n]$ (see e.g. XI.3.d of [9]).

Now we prove (31). Let $\mathbf{X}$ be a $(\beta,r,\mathbf{x}_0)$-urn process and $F_n(z)=\mathbb{P}[X_1(T_n(\mathbf{X}))=z\mid T_n(\mathbf{X})<\infty]$. By the strong Markov property and the fact that $F_n(z)=0$ for $z<n$,

$$\mathbb{P}[T_{n+1}(\mathbf{X})<\infty\mid T_n(\mathbf{X})<\infty]=\sum_{z\ge n}F_n(z)\mathbb{P}[T_2(\beta,r,z,z)].$$

Lemma 5 then implies

$$\lim_{n\to\infty}\mathbb{P}[T_{n+1}(\mathbf{X})<\infty\mid T_n(\mathbf{X})<\infty]=\frac{2}{r+1}. \qquad (32)$$

Since

$$\mathbb{P}[N(\beta,r,\mathbf{x}_0)\ge n]=\prod_{j=0}^{n-1}\mathbb{P}[T_{j+1}(\mathbf{X})<\infty\mid T_j(\mathbf{X})<\infty],$$

(31) follows from (32) and the fact that the Cesàro mean of a convergent sequence converges to the limit of the sequence. □

6. DISCUSSION AND CONCLUSION

Apart from the insights provided by the simulations on our theoretical findings, we illustrate another interesting aspect of the different fitness case. Recall that in the superlinear regime the fittest agent can lose the competition. Does the competition duration depend on the winner? Figure 5 strongly suggests that the answer is yes, which shows the empirical duration distribution conditioned on either 1 or 2 leading the competition at the end of the simulation. For competitions that 1 leads, we observe a power law distribution, consistent with our theoretical findings (the same slopes $1-\beta$ are shown in the plot). However, for competitions that 2 leads, duration seems to be dominated by an exponential tail. Thus, if 2 is to win the competition it has to do so early on: 2 has very little chance of winning if it is trailing behind when a long time has elapsed. However, if 1 is to win, competitions may last very long with 2 putting up a good battle for the lead but losing eventually.

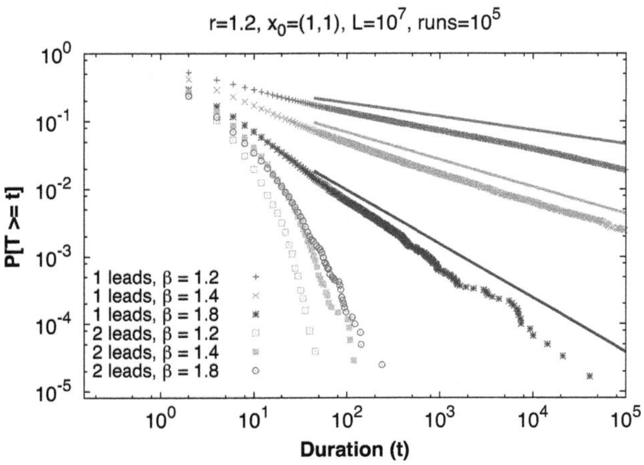

Figure 5: Empirical distribution of duration conditioned on either 1 or 2 leading the competition at the end of simulation time.

This work presented a rigorous mathematical treatment of a nonlinear Pólya urn process which embodies the fitness of agents ($f_{1,2}$) and the feedback strength of CA effect ($\beta > 0$). In particular, we considered sublinear ($\beta < 1$) and superlinear ($\beta > 1$) regimes as well as equal ($f_1 = f_2$) and non-equal ($f_1 \neq f_2$) fitness scenarios and characterized the tail distribution of two important statistics of competitions: duration (i.e., time of the last tie) and intensity (i.e., number of ties). We characterized the complex interactions between fitness superiority and feedback strength, revealing various interesting properties of such competitions, such as the serious struggle of the fittest in the superlinear regime. We believe that our theoretical findings contribute to various applications of the generalized Pólya urn processes that incorporate both fitness and nonlinearity.

7. ACKNOWLEDGEMENTS

This work was supported in part by Army Research Office Contract W911NF-12-1-0385, and ARL Cooperative Agreement W911NF-09-2-0053. D. Figueiredo received financial support through grants from CAPES, FAPERJ and CNPq (Brazil).

8. REFERENCES

[1] W. B. Arthur. *Increasing Returns and Path Dependence in the Economy.* U. Michigan Press, 1994.

[2] A.-L. Barabási and R. Albert. Emergence of scaling in random networks. *Science*, 286(5439):509–512, 1999.

[3] C. Cattuto, V. Loreto, and L. Pietronero. Semiotic dynamics and collaborative tagging. *Proc. National Academy of Sciences*, 104(5):1461–1464, 2007.

[4] B. Davis. Reinforced random walk. *Probability Theory and Related Fields*, 84(2):203–229, 1990.

[5] D. de Solla Price. A general theory of bibliometric and other cumulative advantage processes. *Journal of the American Society for Information Science*, 27(5):292–306, 1976.

[6] T. A. DiPrete and G. M. Eirich. Cumulative advantage as a mechanism for inequality: A review of theoretical and empirical developments. *Annual review of sociology*, pages 271–297, 2006.

[7] E. Drinea, A. Frieze, and M. Mitzenmacher. Balls and bins models with feedback. In *ACM-SIAM Symposium on Discrete Algorithms (SODA)*, pages 308–315, 2002.

[8] F. Eggenberger and G. Pólya. Über die statistik verketteter vorgänge. *Journal of Applied Mathematics and Mechanics/Zeitschrift für Angewandte Mathematik und Mechanik*, 3(4):279–289, 1923.

[9] W. Feller. *An introduction to probability theory and its applications*, volume 1. John Wiley & Sons, 3rd edition, 1968.

[10] S. A. Golder and B. A. Huberman. Usage patterns of collaborative tagging systems. *Journal of information science*, 32(2):198–208, 2006.

[11] M. Gupta, R. Li, Z. Yin, and J. Han. Survey on social tagging techniques. *ACM SIGKDD Explorations Newsletter*, 12(1):58–72, 2010.

[12] H. Halpin, V. Robu, and H. Shepherd. The complex dynamics of collaborative tagging. In *Proceedings of 16th international conference on World Wide Web*, pages 211–220. ACM, 2007.

[13] B. Jiang, D. Figuereido, B. Ribeiro, and D. Towsley. On the duration and intensity of competitions in nonlinear Pólya urn processes with fitness. 2016. Available at `http://arxiv.org/abs/1604.02097`.

[14] B. Jiang, L. Sun, D. Figueiredo, B. Ribeiro, and D. Towsley. On the duration and intensity of cumulative advantage competitions. *Journal of Statistical Mechanics: Theory and Experiment*, 2015(11):P11022, 2015.

[15] K. Khanin and R. Khanin. A probabilistic model for the establishment of neuron polarity. *Journal of Mathematical Biology*, 42(1):26–40, 2001.

[16] H. Mahmoud. *Pólya urn models.* CRC Press, 2008.

[17] R. K. Merton. The matthew effect in science. *Science*, 159:56–63, 1968.

[18] K. B. Oldham and J. Spanier. *The fractional calculus: integrations and differentiations of arbitrary order.* Dover Publications, 2006.

[19] R. I. Oliveira. Balls-in-bins processes with feedback and Brownian Motion. *Combinatorics, Probability and Computing*, 17:87–110, 1 2008.

[20] R. I. Oliveira. The onset of dominance in balls-in-bins processes with feedback. *Random Structures & Algorithms*, 34(4):454–477, 2009.

[21] R. Pemantle. A survey of random processes with reinforcement. *Probability Surveys*, 4(1-79):25, 2007.

[22] S. I. Resnick. *Adventures in stochastic processes.* Birkhäuser, 1992.

[23] A. I. Sakhanenko. Estimates in the invariance principle in terms of truncated power moments. *Siberian Mathematical Journal*, 47(6):1113–1127, 2006.

[24] C. Wagner, P. Singer, M. Strohmaier, and B. A. Huberman. Semantic stability in social tagging streams. In *Proceedings of 23rd international conference on World Wide Web*, pages 735–746, 2014.

[25] T. Wallstrom. The equalization probability of the Pólya urn. *The American Mathematical Monthly*, 119(6):516–518, 2012.

[26] T. Zhu. *Nonlinear Pólya urn models and self-organizing processes.* PhD thesis, University of Pennsylvania, 2009.

Asymptotics of Insensitive Load Balancing and Blocking Phases

Matthieu Jonckheere
Universidad de Buenos Aires and Conicet,
Buenos Aires, Argentina
mjonckhe@dm.uba.ar

Balakrishna J. Prabhu
LAAS-CNRS
Université de Toulouse, CNRS
Toulouse, France
balakrishna.prabhu@laas.fr

ABSTRACT

Load balancing with various types of load information has become a key component of modern communication and information systems. In many systems, characterizing precisely the blocking probability allows to establish a performance trade-off between delay and losses. We address here the problem of giving robust performance bounds based on the study of the asymptotic behavior of the insensitive load balancing schemes when the number of servers and the load scales jointly. These schemes have the desirable property that the stationary distribution of the resulting stochastic network depends on the distribution of job sizes only through its mean. It was shown that they give good estimates of performance indicators for systems with finite buffers, generalizing henceforth Erlang's formula whereas optimal policies are already theoretically and computationally out of reach for networks of moderate size.

We study a single class of traffic acting on a symmetric set of processor sharing queues with finite buffers and we consider the case where the load scales with the number of servers. We characterize the response of symmetric systems under those schemes at different scales and show that three amplitudes of deviations can be identified according to whether $\rho < 1$, $\rho = 1$, and $\rho > 1$. A central limit scaling takes place for a sub-critical load; for $\rho = 1$, the number of free servers scales like $n^{\frac{\theta}{\theta+1}}$ (θ being the buffer depth and n being the number of servers) and is of order 1 for super-critical loads. This further implies the existence of different phases for the blocking probability. Before a (refined) critical load $\rho_c(n) = 1 - an^{-\frac{\theta}{\theta+1}}$, the blocking is exponentially small and becomes of order $n^{-\frac{\theta}{\theta+1}}$ at $\rho_c(n)$. This generalizes the well-known Quality and Efficiency Driven (QED) regime or Halfin-Whitt regime for a one-dimensional queue, and leads to a generalized staffing rule for a given target blocking probability.

Keywords: Insensitive load balancing, blocking phases, mean-field scalings, QED-Jagerman-Halfin-Whitt regime.

SIGMETRICS '16, June 14-18, 2016, Antibes Juan-Les-Pins, France
© 2016 ACM. ISBN 978-1-4503-4266-7/16/06...$15.00
DOI: http://dx.doi.org/10.1145/2896377.2901454

1. INTRODUCTION

Load balancing is a critical component in multi-servers systems such as call centers, server farms, as well as in distributed systems with many applications running on different servers (see, for example, a load balancing simulation case study for the ATLAS Experiment's data acquisition network at CERN [5]). Despite its intensive use, there are few efficient rules of thumb for dynamic load balancing schemes i.e. when the decision of the dispatcher depends on the instantaneous load (e.g. number of jobs) at each server, for which performance evaluation is within reach using currently known techniques. This fact becomes even more evident for large systems with asymmetric server speeds and blocking, where both the precise structure of optimal policies (for specific traffic descriptions) and their performance elude current knowledge and techniques.

Two types of ideas were largely employed to overcome this difficulty: considering large scale networks and obtain asymptotic results using propagation of chaos on the one hand; restricting the load balancing schemes to obtain more tractable reversible processes on the other hand. We aim here at combining both techniques and show that it may lead to very precise results which are typically out of reach with other techniques. In turn, these results allow to give universal (i.e. valid for all job-size distributions) lower bound of performance. In particular, different asymptotic scalings for the blocking probability can be identified: an exponentially small blocking probability for sub-critical loads; a polynomial order in the critical regime; and a constant level for super-critical loads. Before describing our contribution more precisely, let us recall the vast effort of research in the two mentioned directions.

A first way of overcoming the computing difficulty of load balancing problems for processor sharing systems (and more generally symmetric queues) with generic job-size distribution is by restricting the routing policies so that the stationary regime of the system becomes invariant to the job-size distribution (except for its mean), leading to the insensitive load balancing (see [4] for more details). To understand the underlying principles, it is useful to come back to the very properties of the Erlang formula which was clearly a revolution for performance evaluation of telephone networks and arguably the true start of queuing theory. The Erlang formula, which gives the probability of loss for a set of telephone lines, bases its lasting success on simplicity and robustness:

1. the only assumptions which are required to apply the formula are Poisson arrivals and independent calls durations;

2. the formula is insensitive to the call duration distribution and depends on a unique parameter: the traffic intensity; and

3. it can efficiently be computed using a recursive formula.

At the mathematical level, the key property is the reversibility of the birth-and-death processes modeling the system under Markovian assumptions which implies the insensitivity property: the stationary measure of the system does not depend on the whole call distribution but only on its mean.

Those same principles were translated to performance models of best effort and voice traffic in [4, 3] for models with balanced allocations and in [4, 2] for models with dynamic insensitive load balancing. For multi-class networks with insensitive load balancing, Markov Decision Programming techniques were employed in [18], structural results were provided in [13] while extensive simulations were proposed in [24]. All this research dealt with networks of fixed size and allowed to draw the following conclusions. For networks with a unique class of traffic, the insensitive load balancing compares very accurately to optimal policies for a given job-size distribution, while delay estimation are a bit less accurate [4, 2]. The penalization imposed by reversibility is greater for multi-class networks while the sensitivity (of optimal sensitive policies) also deteriorates [18, 13]. Hence a small to moderate price has to be paid for robustness and simplicity. It is perhaps counter-intuitive to notice that for models with infinite buffers, this price becomes very high. It was indeed proved that if the state space is infinite and in the absence of blocking, the optimal insensitive load balancing (for any reasonable criterion) is static (i.e., does not depend on the queue-lengths) and is hence much less efficient than a state-dependent sensitive load balancing [12]. For sensitive schemes like join-the-shortest-queue, there is no characterization of the stationary measures in a general setting (see, for example, the approximations in [16]).

On the other side of the spectrum, a specific attention has been given in the last decades to mean-field type results for different type of networks with load balancing applications. In particular, a great deal of research, which started with the seminal works of [20, 26], has been dedicated to prove mean-fields limits for schemes like join-the-shortest-of-d (JSQ(d)) among n queues where n is large. For example, transient functional law of large numbers and propagation of chaos were obtained in [8] for FIFO scheduling, [25] obtains mean-field limit for the join-the-idle queue (JIQ) while [21] computes the diffusive limit in the Halfin-Whitt regime for a class of policies of which JIQ and JSQ(d) policies are a special case. For general service time distributions, propagation of chaos properties and asymptotic behaviour of the number of occupied servers were obtained for the JSQ policy in [6]. All these results concern systems without blocking and are sensitive to the job-size distribution. For systems with blocking, the recent work of [22] computes the mean-field limit for the JSQ(d) scheme and exponentially distributed job sizes.

It is hence natural and complementary to look at insensitive networks with a very large number of servers and given buffer depth in order to see if the results obtained for finite networks scale appropriately. As detailed below, this leads to very precise results which are qualitatively different from the case without blocking and are out of reach for sensitive policies with blocking. This in turn provides simple dimensioning rules.

Contributions

We study the asymptotics of a set of n processor sharing servers, each with buffer size θ, fed by a Poisson process of intensity ρn when n gets large, under the family of insensitive load balancing schemes shown to be optimal (in the class of insensitive load balancing) in [2]. A more detailed description of the model is given in the next section.

Building on closed-form expressions for the stationary measure, we characterize precisely the asymptotics of the stationary measure and the blocking probability for various scalings of the load. Consequently, we provide universal benchmarks for achievable performance which have no known counterpart for sensitive policies.

We first obtain the stationary measure of the number of occupied servers and give its transient mean-field limit. Considering the symmetric version of the model, we show that the functional law of large numbers also holds for the stationary version of the system (limits in n and t commute). The existence and uniqueness of the limiting stationary probabilities are proved through a monotonicity argument involving the Erlang formula, while the stationary point is characterized through the Erlang formula. This implies simple conclusions on the asymptotic behavior of the blocking probability: the blocking is asymptotically vanishing for the sub-critical ($\rho < 1$) case and is equal to $1 - \rho^{-1}$ for the super-critical case $\rho > 1$. In both cases, this blocking probability corresponds to the optimal blocking probability achievable by any non anticipating policy. Of course this is far from being sufficiently informative and we are led to focus on a more detailed study of the stationary distribution for large n, establishing both large deviations principles for sub- and super-critical cases and moderate deviations results. We show that, when $\rho < 1$ is fixed, the blocking probability is exponentially small, and we characterize the most probable deviations from the mean-field limit. The large deviation cost is shown to be a sum of two terms: the "distance" to the stationary point from distributions with a given mean plus the cost of having a different mean from the true stationary mean. We also show that a central limit theorem is valid for the occupation numbers around the stationary point of the mean-field in the sub-critical regime. For the critical case $\rho = 1$, the right scaling is not anymore of order $\sqrt{n}$. Using local limit theorems and exploiting the characterization of deviations from the mean-field limits, we show that the number of free servers scales like $n^{\frac{\theta}{\theta+1}}$, the limiting distribution depending on θ and coinciding with the normal distribution only for $\theta = 1$. In a third step, we study the critical case at a finer scale and show that a qualitative phase transitions occurs at the critical load $\rho_c(n) = 1 - an^{-\frac{\theta}{\theta+1}}$ where θ is the buffer depth. The blocking probability is exponentially small until $\rho_c(n)$ and of order $n^{-\frac{\theta}{\theta+1}}$ at this critical load. This generalizes the Halfin-Whitt regime established for the $M/M/n/n$ system, (in that case, the correct scaling for the moderate deviations stayed of order $\sqrt{n}$), and show that the popular staffing rule established for the $M/M/n/n$ system does actually change with the value of θ when load balancing is employed. The super-critical regime is simpler to characterize, the deviations being of order 1. We illustrate these findings on simple numerical experiments. Finally, we comment on how these results can be used for performance planning, for instance in trading delay for blocking, while controlling the level of blocking fixing the number of servers and how the level of information needed for a possible implementation can be reduced. We also give insights on possible future work.

2. REVIEW OF THE OPTIMAL INSENSITIVE LOAD BALANCING POLICY

Notation. We use the following notations common to all sections. For any vector space (the exact one under consideration will be clear from the context), let e_i be the point defined by $(e_i)_i = 1,\ (e_i)_j = 0, j \neq i$. We denote:

$$|x| = \sum_{i=1}^{k} x_i \quad \text{and} \quad \binom{|x|}{x} = \frac{|x|!}{x_1! \dots x_k!}.$$

We denote by $\mathbf{1}_S$ the indicator function of S, that is the map taking value 1 inside S and 0 outside and denote respectively by $\mathbb{R}_+$ and $\mathbb{R}_+^*$ the set of non-negative and positive reals.

This section is a review of the relevant definitions, merits and results known for the insensitive load-balancing policy investigated in this paper. The narrative here is for a more general model than the one we shall analyze. Nonetheless, it gives a flavour of the possible generalizations, some of which are elaborated upon in Section 6.

Consider a dispatcher and a set of n processor sharing servers with speed μ_i for $i = 1\dots,n$. Jobs with i.i.d. sizes sampled from a generic distribution of mean 1 arrive to the dispatcher according to a Poisson process of intensity λ. The dispatcher routes an incoming job to one of the servers according to the following insensitive load balancing rule. Let $\theta = (\theta_1, \dots, \theta_n)$ a vector of natural numbers and $\mathcal{X} \subset \mathbb{N}^n$ a finite coordinate convex set describing the constraints on the number of jobs in each server (for instance $\mathcal{X} = \{x : x_i \leq \theta_i, \forall i = 1 \dots n\}$). Then, the incoming job is routed to server i with probability

$$a_i^\theta(x) = \frac{\theta_i - x_i}{\sum_{j=1}^{N}(\theta_j - x_j)} 1_{x+e_i \in \mathcal{X}}. \qquad (1)$$

Note that with this rule, the number of jobs in server i is smaller than θ_i for all $i = 1 \dots n$. One can view θ_i as the buffer size of server i but it could be a smaller number chosen to guarantee a certain rate of service. Also note that this rule depends on the speeds μ_i only through the vector θ. Nevertheless this load balancing rule was proved to be optimal[1] in the set of insensitive load balancing (for a unique class of traffic) in [2], i.e., given the speeds μ_i there exists an optimal vector θ such that this rule is optimal among all insensitive load balancing.

Let X be the stochastic process valued in $\mathcal{X}$ describing the number of on going jobs in each server. Under Poisson arrivals and exponentially distributed job sizes, X is a continuous-time jump Markov process, on the state space $\mathcal{X}$, with infinitesimal generator $Q = (q(x,y))_{x,y\in\mathcal{X}}$ given by

[1]Optimal in the sense that it minimizes the blocking probability or any convex criterion.

$\forall x \in \mathcal{X}$,

$$\begin{cases} q(x, x - e_i) &= \mu_i & \text{if } x - e_i \in \mathcal{X} \\ q(x, x + e_i) &= \lambda a_i(x) & \text{if } x + e_i \in \mathcal{X} \\ q(x, y) &= 0 & \text{if } y \in \mathcal{X},\ y \neq x - e_i, x + e_i\,. \end{cases} \qquad (2)$$

We recall that the family of insensitive load balancing corresponds to the routing rates $\lambda_i() = \lambda a(\cdot)$ such that there exists a balance function $\Lambda : \mathcal{X} \to \mathbb{R}_+^*$,

$$\forall i,\ \forall x \in \mathcal{X}, x + e_i \in \mathcal{X}, \quad \lambda_i(x) = \Lambda(x + e_i)/\Lambda(x), \qquad (3)$$

which is equivalent to the detailed balance criterion. The relationship between this criterion and insensitivity was first formulated in [28]. Under condition (3), the process X is reversible and the stationary distribution is given by

$$\pi(x) = \frac{\Lambda(x)\Phi(x)}{\sum_{y\in\mathcal{X}} \Phi(y)\Lambda(y)}, \qquad (4)$$

with

$$\Phi(x) = \prod_{i=1}^{n} \mu_i^{-x_i}.$$

For the optimal insensitive load balancing corresponding to the mentioned rates $\lambda a_i(\cdot)$, the routing balance function Λ takes the form

$$\Lambda(x) = \Lambda_\theta(x) = \binom{|\theta - x|}{\theta - x} \lambda^{|x|}, \qquad (5)$$

where $\binom{|\theta-x|}{\theta-x} = \frac{|\theta-x|!}{\prod_{i=1}^{n}(\theta_i - x_i)!}$ are the multinomial coefficients.

The blocking probability, B_θ, of an arriving job can be determined using the PASTA property to be $\pi(\theta)$.

3. MODEL AND PRELIMINARY RESULTS

In the rest of the paper, we shall assume that the servers are homogeneous, that is, they have the same speed and the same buffer size. (We shall comment later on the possibility of extending those results). Without loss of generality, let the common speed be 1. The common buffer size will be taken to be θ. (From now on, θ is a natural number and not a vector as in the previous section). For the asymptotic analysis we have in mind, it turns out to be more convenient to define the state as the number of servers processing a certain number of jobs instead of the number of jobs being processed in every server. Let $\mathcal{S} = \{s \in \{0, 1, \dots, n\}^{\theta+1} : \sum_{i=0}^{\theta} s_i = n\}$ be the set of states where s_i corresponds to the number of servers with i jobs. In state $s \in \mathcal{S}$, the insensitive load balancing rule described in Section 2 will route an incoming job to a server with i jobs at rate

$$\lambda_i(s) = \lambda \frac{(\theta - i)s_i}{n\theta - \bar{s}}, \qquad (6)$$

where $\bar{s} = \sum_{i=0}^{\theta} i s_i$.

Let $\{S^{(n)}(t) \in \mathcal{S}\}_{t\geq 0}$ be a stochatic process denoting, at time t, the number of servers with i jobs, $i = 0, \dots, \theta$. Under Poisson arrivals and exponentially distributed job sizes, $S^{(n)}(t)$ is a continuous-time jump Markov process on the state space $\mathcal{S}$ with the following transition rates

$$S^{(n)}(t) \to \begin{cases} S^{(n)}(t) + e_i - e_{i-1} & \text{at rate } \lambda_{i-1}(s), i \geq 1; \\ S^{(n)}(t) + e_i - e_{i+1} & \text{at rate } s_{i+1}, \end{cases} \tag{7}$$

assuming that the transitions take the process to a state within $\mathcal{S}$.

The reversibility property of X is preserved by S. More precisely,

Theorem 1. *If the job-size distribution is exponential, the process $S^{(n)}(t)$ is a reversible Markov process and its stationary distribution is given by*

$$\pi^{(n)}(s) = \pi_0^{(n)} \frac{(n\theta - \bar{s})!}{(n\theta)!} \binom{n}{s} \prod_{k=0}^{\theta} \left(\frac{\theta!}{(\theta - k)!} (n\rho)^k \right)^{s_k}, \tag{8}$$

where is the total number of jobs in the system, and $\rho = \lambda/n$ is the load per server, and $\pi_0^{(n)}$ corresponds to the probability of the state with all servers empty, that is, $\bar{s} = 0$ and $s = (n, 0, \dots, 0)$.

Proof. A sufficient condition for a probability measure to be the stationary measure of a Markov chain is that it satisfy the local balance equations. Consider two states s and $s + e_i - e_{i-1}$, both within $\mathcal{S}$. From (8),

$$\frac{\pi^{(n)}(s + e_i - e_{i-1})}{\pi^{(n)}(s)} = \frac{\lambda(\theta - (i-1))s_{i-1}}{n\theta - \bar{s}} \frac{1}{(s_i + 1)\mu}, \tag{9}$$

$$= \frac{\lambda_{i-1}(s)}{(s_i + 1)}, \tag{10}$$

which are in the same proportion as the local transition rates between these two states as computed from (7). □

Corollary 1. *Using the PASTA property, the blocking probability is given by*

$$B_\theta^{(n)} = \pi_0^{(n)} \frac{(n\rho)^{n\theta}(\theta!)^n}{(n\theta)!}. \tag{11}$$

Instead of using $\pi_0^{(n)}$ as the normalizing constant, we can resort to $B^{(n)}$ for this purpose, and rewrite (8) as

$$\pi^{(n)}(s) = B_\theta^{(n)}(n\theta - \bar{s})! \binom{n}{s} \prod_{k=0}^{\theta} \left(\frac{1}{(\theta - k)!} (n\rho)^{k-\theta} \right)^{s_k}, \tag{12}$$

A special case that will reappear throughout this paper is the one with $\theta = 1$, which corresponds to the classical $M/M/n/n$ queue or the Erlang loss system. Upon setting $\theta = 1$ in (8), we obtain:

$$\pi^{(n)}(s_0) = \frac{(n\rho)^{(n-s_0)}}{(n - s_0)!} \pi(0), \tag{13}$$

$$\text{where } \pi_0^{(n)} = \sum_{k \leq n} \frac{(n\rho)^{n-k}}{(n-k)!}. \tag{14}$$

where s_0 is the number of empty servers. We hence retrieve the formula corresponding to the $M/M/n/n$ queue, as expected.

We remind the reader that for the JSQ policy, the stationary measure is quite intricate to compute even for the case of two servers [16], making it difficult to predict the performance of this policy.

Once the stationary measure is determined, the stationary performance measures such as the mean soujourn time and the blocking probability can be numerically computed for any given set of parameters such as n, θ, or ρ. However, for large n or ρ close to 1, the relationship between the performance measures and the parameters can be obtained in a more palatable (and exploitable) form using asymptotic analysis. The following sections will follow this path leading to a mean-field limit as well as the characterization of the large and moderate deviations.

4. A MEAN-FIELD DETERMINISTIC LIMIT

In this section, we give the limiting transient and stationary behaviour in case of exponentially distributed job-sizes when n diverges. This limit called the mean-field limit has become a classical asymptotic regime for the analysis of large queuing systems and particle systems with a large number of servers or particles [17, 1, 15, 22]. In load-balancing applications, this type of analysis has been used for several policies whose stationary measure is either unknown or known for relatively small values of the number of servers (for example, shorter of d choices [20], joining the shortest queue [22]). Indeed, for data-centers that can have hundreds to thousands of servers, the mean-field limit can give a first-order approximation to the system behaviour both in the transient and in the stationary phase.

In the mean-field limit, dynamics for the fraction of servers containing a certain number of jobs are as follows.

Theorem 2. *Fix a ρ and a $\theta \geq 1$. For exponentially distributed job-sizes, for all fixed time, $S^{(n)}(t)/n \xrightarrow{\mathcal{L}^2} y(t)$, which is the solution of the following set of differential equations:*

$$\frac{dy_j(t)}{dt} = \rho \frac{\theta - (j-1)}{\theta - \sum_k k y_k(t)} y_{j-1}(t) + y_{j+1}(t) - \rho \frac{\theta - j}{\theta - \sum_k k y_k(t)} y_j(t) - y_j(t), \; 0 < j < \theta, \tag{15}$$

$$\frac{dy_\theta(t)}{dt} = \rho \frac{1}{\theta - \sum_k k y_k(t)} y_{\theta-1}(t) - y_\theta(t), \tag{16}$$

$$\frac{dy_0(t)}{dt} = y_1(t) - \rho \frac{\theta}{\theta - \sum_k k y_k(t)} y_0(t). \tag{17}$$

with $y(0) = \lim_{n\to\infty} \frac{S^{(n)}(0)}{n}$.

Proof. For Poisson arrivals and exponentially distributed job-sizes, the technical difficulty is much less compared to that for generic job-size distribution. We hence do not give the details of the proof but only sketch the argument. Fix a time interval $[0, t]$. The process is trivially tight and assuming exponential job-size makes it Markov. Dynkin's formula allows to write this Markov process as a drift part plus a martingale and calculating the increasing process of the martingale, one proves that the martingale part goes to 0. As a consequence, the process converges along subsequences to a deterministic process in $\mathcal{L}^2$. It remains to prove that the limit is unique which is easy in this case since using the regularity of the rates of the process, the limit is a differential equation with a Lipschitz drift. □

Remark 1. *We expect the results to hold under generic job-sizes distribution but the proof becomes much more technical as one has to work with measure-valued processes and falls* *out of the scope of this paper. Results like asymptotic independence for randomized load balancing schemes such as join the shortest of d queues with generic job-sizes have been proved in [6].*

Theorem 3. *For $0 < \rho \leq 1$, the unique steady-state solution of the system of equations (15)–(17) is given by*

$$\hat{p}_j = \left(\frac{\theta - \hat{c}}{\rho}\right)^{\theta - j} \frac{1}{(\theta - j)!} \hat{p}_\theta, \tag{18}$$

$$\text{with } \hat{p}_\theta = \frac{1}{\sum_{k=0}^{\theta} \left(\frac{\theta - \hat{c}}{\rho}\right)^k \frac{1}{k!}}. \tag{19}$$

where

$$\hat{c} = \theta - \rho Erl_\theta^{-1}(1 - \rho), \tag{20}$$

with Erl_θ^{-1} as the inverse function of the Erlang blocking viewed as a function of the traffic intensity for a fixed buffer depth θ.

If $\rho > 1$, the unique solution is $\hat{c} = \theta$, $\hat{p}_j = 0$, for $j \leq \theta - 1$ and $\hat{p}_\theta = 1$.

Proof. Suppose first $\rho < 1$. It can be easily verified that, with

$$\hat{c} = \sum_{k=0}^{\theta} k \hat{p}_k, \tag{21}$$

(18) and (19) is the steady-state solution of (15)–(17). We now show that $\hat{c}$ as defined in (21) verfies (20).

After some simple algebraic manipulations, it can be verified that the fixed point equation (21) is equivalent to the equation

$$(1 - \rho) \sum_{k=0}^{\theta} \left(\frac{\theta - x}{\rho}\right)^k \frac{1}{k!} = \left(\frac{\theta - x}{\rho}\right)^\theta \frac{1}{\theta!} \tag{22}$$

in the set $[0, \theta]$. Thus solving (21) boils down to finding a traffic intensity $a := \frac{\theta - x}{\rho}$ such that the Erlang blocking formula with intensity a gives $1 - \rho$, i.e.:

$$Erl_\theta(a) = \frac{a^\theta \frac{1}{\theta!}}{\sum_{k=0}^{\theta} a^k \frac{1}{k!}} = (1 - \rho).$$

By a simple sample path argument, the Erlang formula is an increasing function of a that is 0 in 0 and 1 in $+\infty$. Hence, it is invertible and there is a unique $a > 0$ such that $Erl_\theta(a) = 1 - \rho$. Now observe that by a conservation argument (the traffic entering vs traffic outgoing) we have that for all a:

$$a(1 - Erl_\theta(a)) \leq \theta,$$

which boils down (given the definition of a) to

$$a \leq \frac{\theta}{\rho}.$$

which in turns gives a unique solution to

$$\frac{\theta - x}{\rho} = a.$$

Now consider $\rho > 1$. It is straightforward to verify that $\hat{c} = \theta$, $\hat{p}_j = 0$, for $j \leq \theta - 1$ and $\hat{p}_\theta = 1$ is a solution. If $\hat{c} < \theta$, then the drift of the differential equation (19) cannot be 0 which implies that the solution given is unique. □

Using the generic method developed in [17] to inverse limits in n and t under the assumption of reversibility of the Markov process under study (which is indeed verified here), we can state that

Proposition 1. *For $\rho < 1$, $\pi^{(n)}$ converges point wise to p when n and t converge to infinity.*

Proof. [17] allows to state that if there is convergence for fixed time intervals, if the process is reversible for fixed n, and if there exists a unique stationary limiting point, (which we have verified) in the previous Proposition, then the conclusion of the Proposition hold. □

Remark 2. *By insensitivity, taking limit in time first define a sequence of limiting distribution $\pi^{(n)}$ which do not depend on the specific job-size distribution and which converges towards p.*

4.1 Performance consequences

Let B_θ denote the stationary blocking probability in the mean-field limit, that is, when $n \to \infty$ and $t \to \infty$. Using the PASTA property for fixed n, the blocking probability of a job is the probability that it finds all the servers in their blocking state *i.e.*, that upon arrival all the servers have θ tasks.

Before deriving B_θ, we first give a lower bound on the blocking probability that could be achieved by any non-anticipating and size-unaware load balancing policy.

Proposition 2. *For $\theta > 0$, the blocking probability of any non-anticipating and size-unaware load balancing policy is greater than* $\max(0, 1 - \rho^{-1})$.

Proof. We give the argument for $\rho > 1$. The argument for $\rho \leq 1$ is similar. Consider the system in which the resources are pooled, that is, there is one server of service rate of $n\mu$ and buffer size $n\theta$. By a path-wise argument for Markovian versions of the systems (implying by insensitivity the result for all service times in stationary regime), the blocking probability of this system will be less than any system with a set of disjoints servers. In the pooled system, the scaled number of tasks in the system $\frac{X(t)}{n}$ will follow the differential equation:

$$\dot{x}(t) = \rho - 1, \; 0 < x(t) < \theta, \tag{23}$$

$$\rho(1 - \hat{B}_\theta) = 1, \; x(t) = \theta. \tag{24}$$

When $x(t)$ is in the interior of the state space, all tasks will be accepted. On the boundary $x(t) = \theta$, the tasks which cause overflow will be blocked. Hence, the blocking probability will be

$$\underline{B}_\theta = 1 - \rho^{-1}.$$

□

We now be shown that the insensitive load-balancing policy achieves this lower bound which is independent of θ.

Proposition 3. *The limiting blocking probability of the insensitive load balancing policy is given by*

$$B_\theta = \begin{cases} 0 & \text{if } \rho < 1; \\ 1 - \rho^{-1} & \text{otherwise.} \end{cases} \tag{25}$$

Proof. For $\rho < 1$, it can be seen that $\hat{p}_\theta < 1$, and therefore, $B_\theta = 0$.

For $\rho \geq 1$, we shall prove first this result for $\theta = 1$. For $\theta = 1$, from (21),

$$c = p_1,$$

and from (18),

$$p_1 = \frac{\rho(1-B_1)}{1-p_1}(1-p_1) = \rho(1-B_1).$$

Since $p_1 \leq 1$, B_1 is such that $\rho(1-B_1) = 1$. That is, $B_1 = 1 - \rho^{-1}$.

Using Proposition 3 in [2], $B_\theta \leq B_1$ for all $\theta \geq 1$. Now, using the lower bound in proposition 2, this implies that $B_\theta = B_1$. □

The stationary blocking probability of the insensitive policy is thus minimal in the considered class of policies, and it is independent of θ. Hence, even a buffer of size 1 is sufficient to get the optimal stationary behavior. We would like to point out that the optimality is only valid in the limit $n \to \infty$. In order to compute the blocking probability (or other performance measures) for values of n that are large but finite, one has to look at finer scales, which will be the objective of Section 5.

5. FINER SCALES AND ESTIMATES

While the results of the previous section are interesting for some performance metrics like the mean number of customers (which gives the mean waiting time via Little's formula), they are too rough to be really informative in terms of blocking probabilities. Indeed, any reasonable dynamic load balancing may achieve the given bounds. To get useful and discriminative estimates, we hence need to investigate the process $S^{(n)}$ at finer scales. In particular, we aim at determining when blocking can be considered a large deviation event (with a probability exponentially small in n) and when it will be in the scale of the central limit theorem.

Some of the proofs and intermediate results used in this section are given in the research report [14].

5.1 Large deviations

Let $\mathcal{P} = \{p \in \mathbb{R}_+^\theta : \sum_{i=0}^{\theta} p_i = 1\}$. For $c > 0$, denote $\mathcal{S}_c^{(n)} = \{s \in \mathcal{S} : \bar{s} = nc\}$, and $\mathcal{P}_c^{(n)} = \{q \in \mathcal{P} : nq \in \mathcal{S}_c^{(n)}\}$. Since $\bar{s} = \sum_k k s_k$, we have $\sum_k q_k = c$, $\forall q \in \mathcal{S}_c^{(n)}$. Thus, $\mathcal{P}_c^{(n)}$ is the set of discrete probability distributions taking values on a lattice of unit size $1/n$ and having a first moment of c.

Define $p \in \mathcal{P}_c^{(n)}$ by

$$p_k(c) := \frac{1}{(\theta-k)!}\left(\frac{\theta-c}{\rho}\right)^{\theta-k}\frac{1}{\psi(c)}. \tag{26}$$

where

$$\psi(c) = \sum_{k=0}^{\theta}\frac{1}{k!}\left(\frac{\theta-c}{\rho}\right)^k, \tag{27}$$

is a normalizing constant which ensures that p is a probability vector. There need not be a vector in $\mathcal{P}_c^{(n)}$ satisfying (26), in which case we define p to be the vector[2] in $\mathcal{P}_c^{(n)}$ which is closest (say in norm l^1) to satisfying (26). To simplify the notation, let $\pi^{(n)}(q;c) = \pi^{(n)}(nq)\mathbb{1}_{\{q\in\mathcal{P}_c\}}$ be the stationary probability of observing $q \in \mathcal{P}_c^{(n)}$.

Let

$$\bar{c} = \arg\max_{c\in[0,\theta]} e^c\psi(c). \tag{28}$$

We first characterize $\bar{c}$. As a consequence of the definition of ψ, simple algebraic computations show that $\bar{c}$ coincides (as it intuitively should) with the asymptotic mean value $\hat{c}$ found in Theorem 3, i.e.,

Proposition 4. $\bar{c} = \hat{c} = \theta - \rho Erl_\theta^{-1}(1-\rho)$.

The proof of the proposition is similar to the one for $\hat{c}$ in Theorem 3.

Let $\hat{p} = p(\hat{c})$. The large deviation cost is shown to be a sum of two terms: the "distance" to the stationary point from distributions with equal means plus the cost of having a different mean from the stationary mean. More precisely, we have the following large deviation estimates for $S^{(n)}$:

Theorem 4. *For $\rho < 1$,*

$$\lim_{n\to\infty}\frac{1}{n}\log\left(\frac{\pi^{(n)}(q;c)}{\pi^{(n)}(\hat{p};\hat{c})}\right) = (c-\hat{c}) + \log\left(\frac{\psi(c)}{\psi(\hat{c})}\right) - D_{KL}(q(c)\|p(c)). \tag{29}$$

Proof. Applying Stirling's approximation in the term containing $n\theta$ in (12) and noting that $\sum_k kq_k = c$, we get

$$\pi^{(n)}(q;c) \sim B_\theta^{(n)}(2\pi(n\theta-nc))^{1/2}e^{-n\theta+nc} \cdot \binom{n}{nq}\prod_{k=0}^{\theta}\left(\frac{1}{(\theta-k)!}\left(\frac{n\theta-nc}{n\rho}\right)^{\theta-k}\right)^{nq_k} \tag{30}$$

$$= B_\theta^{(n)}(2\pi(n\theta-nc))^{1/2}e^{-n\theta+nc}\psi^n \cdot \binom{n}{nq}\prod_{k=0}^{\theta}p_k^{nq_k}, \tag{31}$$

Thus, $\pi^{(n)}(q;c)$ is proportional to the multinomial distribution with p_k as the probability of success of the kth class. Using Stirling's approximation in (31), we get

$$\pi^{(n)}(q;c) \sim B_\theta^{(n)}(2\pi(n\theta-nc))^{1/2}e^{-n\theta+nc}\psi^n(2\pi n)^{-\theta/2} \cdot \prod_{k=0}^{\theta}\left(\frac{p_k}{q_k}\right)^{nq_k}\frac{1}{q_k^{1/2}}, \tag{32}$$

from which the desired result can be deduced. □

Corollary 2. *For $\rho < 1$,*

$$\lim_{n\to\infty} -\frac{1}{n}\log\left(\frac{\pi^{(n)}(q;c)}{\pi^{(n)}(p;c)}\right) = D_{KL}(q\|p). \tag{33}$$

Corollary 2 says that, conditioned on observing nc jobs in the system, the probability of observing a certain distribution of jobs over the servers concentrates around p. The probability of observing any other $q \in \mathcal{P}_c^{(n)}$ decreases exponentially with rate $nD_{KL}(q\|p)$, that is the Kullback-Liebler distance serves as the large-deviations rate function. This result is akin to Sanov's theorem in information theory [7].

[2] When the value of c is clear from the context, we will use the notation p instead of $p(c)$.

Corollary 3. *For $\rho < 1$,*

$$\lim_{n\to\infty} \frac{1}{n} \log\left(\frac{\pi^{(n)}(p;c)}{\pi^{(n)}(p;\hat{c})}\right) = (c-\hat{c}) + \log\left(\frac{\psi(c)}{\psi(\hat{c})}\right). \quad (34)$$

Corollary 3 states that the scaled number of tasks in the system concentrates around $\hat{c}$ exponentially with rate$(c - \hat{c}) + \log(\psi(c)/\psi(\hat{c}))$.

5.2 Asymptotics for the blocking probability

In this section, we shall look at the asymptotics for the blocking probability which is the main performance measure of interest for our system. Two different asymptotic regimes will be considered: *(i)* the number of servers, n scales, linearly with the arrival rate, $n\rho$; and *(ii)* the Halfin-Whitt regime [9] which has a linear term as in *(i)* along with a sub-linear term that represents the safety margin.

The starting point for both these asymptotic regimes will be an integral characterization of B_θ which is derived from the generating function of the stationary measure (see Theorem 13 in the research report).

Theorem 5. *For $\rho \in (0,1)$, the blocking B_θ has the asymptotic form:*

$$\lim_{n\to\infty} B_\theta^{(n)} \exp(nR(\gamma_{\theta,\rho})) \left(\frac{2\pi n}{\alpha_{\theta,\rho}}\right)^{1/2} = 1. \quad (35)$$

where

$$R(t) = \log\left(\sum_{k=0}^{\theta} \frac{t^k}{k!}\right) - \rho t, \quad (36)$$

$$\gamma_{\theta,\rho} = \arg\max_{t\in(0,\infty)} R(t) = \frac{\theta - \hat{c}}{\rho}, \quad (37)$$

and

$$\alpha_{\theta,\rho} = \frac{(1-\rho)}{\rho}\left(\frac{\theta}{\rho\gamma_{\theta,\rho}} - 1\right). \quad (38)$$

Corollary 4. *For $\theta = 1$, $\gamma_{\theta,\rho} = \frac{1-\rho^{-1}}{\rho}$ and $\alpha_{\theta,\rho} = 1$. Thus,*

$$B_1^{(n)} \sim e^{n(1-\rho)}\rho^n(2\pi n)^{-1/2}. \quad (39)$$

For the proof of Theorem 5, we shall need the following result whose proof follows along the same lines as that of Theorem 3.

Lemma 1. *Let $\gamma_{\theta,\rho} = \arg\max_{t\in(0,\infty)} R(t)$. Then, $\gamma_{\theta,\rho}$ is the unique solution of the equation*

$$(1-\rho)\sum_{k=0}^{\theta} \frac{x^k}{k!} = \frac{x^\theta}{\theta!}, \quad (40)$$

is $x = Erl_\theta^{-1}(1-\rho)$.

Proof of Theorem 5. Using calculations on the generating functions for the stationary probability (see Appendix *A*.4 of the research report), we obtain that

$$\lim_{n\to\infty} B_\theta^{(n)} n\rho \int_0^\infty \left(\sum_{k=0}^{\theta} \frac{1}{k!}t^k\right)^n e^{-tn\rho} dt = 1. \quad (41)$$

The asymptotic form of the integral can be determined using Laplace's method, which says that

$$\int_0^\infty e^{nf(t)}dt \approx e^{nf(t_0)}\left(\frac{2\pi}{n(-f''(t_0))}\right)^{1/2}, \quad (42)$$

where t_0 is the unique maximizer of f in $(0,\infty)$.

Define:

$$R(t) = \log\left(\sum_{k=0}^{\theta} \frac{t^k}{k!}\right) - \rho t. \quad (43)$$

Then

$$\lim_{n\to\infty} B_\theta^{(n)} e^{nR(t_0)}\left(\frac{2\pi n\rho^2}{-R''(t_0)}\right)^{1/2} = 1. \quad (44)$$

where t_0 maximizes R and is characterized in Lemma 1. For Laplace's method to be applicable, one needs $R''(t_0) < 0$. This is shown in Lemma 2 which appears in Appendix *A*.3 of the research report. We shall now compute $\alpha_{\theta,\rho} = -\rho^{-2}R''(\gamma_{\theta,\rho})$, and the main result then follows from (44).

Let $g_\theta(t) = \sum_{k=0}^{\theta} \frac{t^k}{k!}$. Since $\gamma_{\theta,\rho}$ is the maximizer of $R(t)$, we have $R'(\gamma_{\theta,\rho}) = 0$, which upon rearrangement gives

$$\frac{g_{\theta-1}(\gamma_{\theta,\rho})}{g_\theta(\gamma_{\theta,\rho})} = \rho. \quad (45)$$

From the definition of g_θ and Lemma 1, we have $g_\theta(\gamma_{\theta,\rho}) = \frac{1}{1-\rho}\frac{\gamma_{\theta,\rho}^\theta}{\theta!}$, and

$$g_{\theta-2}(\gamma_{\theta,\rho}) = g_{\theta-1}(\gamma_{\theta,\rho}) - \frac{\gamma_{\theta,\rho}^{\theta-1}}{(\theta-1)!} \quad (46)$$

$$= \frac{\gamma_{\theta,\rho}^\theta}{\theta!}\left(\frac{\rho}{1-\rho} - \frac{\theta}{\gamma_{\theta,\rho}}\right) \quad (47)$$

Thus,

$$R''(\gamma_{\theta,\rho}) = \frac{g_{\theta-2}(\gamma_{\theta,\rho})}{g_\theta(\gamma_{\theta,\rho})} - \left(\frac{g_{\theta-1}(\gamma_{\theta,\rho})}{g_\theta(\gamma_{\theta,\rho})}\right)^2 \quad (48)$$

$$= \rho - \frac{(1-\rho)\theta}{\gamma_{\theta,\rho}} - \rho^2 \quad (49)$$

from which the expression for $\alpha_{\theta,\rho}$ follows. □

For $\rho > 1$, we cannot use the directly use the technique that was used for $\rho < 1$ because the maximum of $R(t)$ in the interval $[0,\infty)$ occurs at $t = 0$, which is not an interior point of the support of R. So, we shall resort to a theorem due to Erdelyi that treats this case.

Theorem 6. *Let $\rho > 1$ and $n(\rho - 1)$ be bounded away from 0. As $n \to \infty$,*

$$B_\theta^{(n)} \sim 1 - \rho^{-1} + \frac{1}{(\rho-1)^\theta n^\theta} + o(n^{-\theta}). \quad (50)$$

Proof. We shall apply the Erdelyi theorem (see Theorem 1.1 in the arXiv preprint of [23] for a precise statement with the notation relevant for our proof) with $f(t) = -R(t)$ and $[a,b) = [0,\infty)$. Let us verify that the four conditions of this theorem are satisfied by $-R(t)$.

For $\rho \geq 1$, the function $-R(t)$ is increasing in the interval $[0,\infty)$ with minimum at $t = 0$. To see this,

$$-R'(t) = \rho - \frac{\sum_{k=0}^{\theta-1}\frac{t^k}{k!}}{\sum_{k=0}^{\theta}\frac{t^k}{k!}} \geq 1 - \frac{\sum_{k=0}^{\theta-1}\frac{t^k}{k!}}{\sum_{k=0}^{\theta}\frac{t^k}{k!}} \geq 0.$$

From Lemma 4 in the Appendix B of the research report, in a neighborhood of 0, $-R(t)$ is analytic with expansion

$$-R(t) = (\rho-1)t + \frac{t^{\theta+1}}{(\theta+1)!} + o(t^{\theta+1}), \quad (51)$$

and $-R(t)$ is continuously differentiable with an analytic derivative. Finally, to show the absolute convergence of the integral, note that

$$\int_0^{\infty} e^{-n(-R(t))}dt \leq \int_0^{\infty} e^{-n(\rho-1)t}dt = \frac{1}{n(\rho-1)} < \infty, \quad (52)$$

as long as $n(\rho-1)$ is bounded away from 0. Thus, all the necessary conditions required by Erdelyi theorem are satisfied.

The various parameters in the asymptotic expansion (1.5) in [23] are: $R(0)=0$, $\alpha=1$, $a_0=\rho-1$, $a_1=\ldots=a_{\theta-1}=0$, $a_\theta=\frac{1}{(\theta+1)!}$, which gives $\beta_0=(\rho-1)^{-1}$, $\beta_1=\ldots\beta_{\theta-1}=0$ and $\beta_\theta=-\frac{(\rho-1)^{-(\theta+2)}}{\theta!}$, so that

$$\int_0^{\infty} e^{nR(t)}dt \sim \frac{1}{(\rho-1)n} - \frac{1}{(\rho-1)^{\theta+2}n^{\theta+1}} + o(n^{-(\theta+1)}) \quad (53)$$

Substituting the above asymptotic expansion in (41), we get the claimed result. □

Since $R(0)=0$, there is no exponential decay of the blocking probability when $\rho>1$.

Corollary 5. *Setting $\theta=1$ in the above theorem, we get the corresponding result for $\theta=1$ obtained in [10] (see Theorem 13 in there).*

The previous theorems give the asymptotics of the blocking probability for a fixed load per server for large number of servers. For $\rho<1$, the blocking probability goes to 0 exponentially quickly in n while for $\rho>1$ it goes to $1-\rho^{-1}$, a strictly positive quantity. The next theorem looks at the scaling law that results in a polynomial blocking probability. For the Erlang C model, that is, a system without blocking, this regime has the following interpretation: if the cost of servers is high, Halfin and Whitt [9] observed that it could be beneficial to reduce the number of servers in such a way such that the probability of waiting is no longer exponentially small but decays as $n^{-1/2}$. This increase in the waiting probability has the benefit of requiring $\lambda+O(\lambda^{1/2})$ instead of $b\lambda$, $b>1$, servers. Thus, one gains in the cost and the utilization of servers at the expense of the waiting probability. In order to evoke this trade-off between these two quantities, this scaling regime is also called the Quality and Efficiency Driven (QED) regime. We note that this asymptotic regime was already studied for the Erlang B system in Jagerman [10] (see Theorem 14) but the interpretation in terms of a trade-off is due to Halfin and Whitt [9] for systems without blocking and Whitt [27] for systems with blocking.

The following theorem gives the QED scaling for the balanced load-balancing policy and can be viewed as a generalization of the QED result for the Erlang loss model.

Theorem 7. *For $a \in (\infty,\infty)$, let*

$$n\rho = n + an^{1/(\theta+1)}. \quad (54)$$

Then,

$$\lim_{n\to\infty} B_\theta^{(n)} n^{\theta/(\theta+1)} \int_0^{\infty} \exp\left(au - \frac{u^{(\theta+1)}}{(\theta+1)!}\right) du = 1. \quad (55)$$

Proof. The proof follows a similar reasoning as in the proof of Theorem 14 in [10]. From (41) and using Lemma 4 in the Appendix B of the research report, we get

$$1 = \lim_{n\to\infty} B_\theta^{(n)} n\rho \int_0^{\infty} \left(\sum_{k=0}^{\theta} \frac{1}{k!}t^k\right)^n e^{-tn\rho}dt \quad (56)$$

$$\sim \lim_{n\to\infty} B_\theta^{(n)} n\rho \int_0^{\infty} \exp\left(nt - n\frac{t^{(\theta+1)}}{(\theta+1)!} - tn\rho\right) dt \quad (57)$$

$$\sim \lim_{n\to\infty} B_\theta^{(n)} n\rho \int_0^{\infty} \exp\left(an^{1/(\theta+1)}t - \frac{nt^{(6+1)}}{(\theta+1)!}\right) dt \quad (58)$$

Setting $u = tn^{1/(\theta+1)}$ in the above integral gives the stated result. □

Note that a can be positive or negative, which means that even with a total charge larger than the number of servers, the blocking probability can decay to 0 provided that (54) is satisfied asymptotically. When $a=0$ and using simple computations, the above theorem leads to the following corollary:

Corollary 6. *If $\rho=1$:*

$$B_\theta^{(n)} \sim \frac{(\theta+1)!^{\frac{1}{\theta+1}}}{\theta+1}\Gamma\Big(\frac{1}{\theta+1}\Big)n^{-\theta/(\theta+1)}, \quad (59)$$

where Γ is the Gamma function.

Note that for $\theta=1$, we retrieve that:

$$B_1^{(n)} \sim (0.5\pi n)^{-1/2}. \quad (60)$$

5.3 Moderate deviations

Using the previous estimates on the blocking probability (i.e. on the normalizing constant of the stationary distribution) we can now characterize the deviations around $\hat{p}$ of size smaller than $O(n)$ for a fixed value of ρ. Three amplitudes of deviations will be identified according to whether $\rho<1$, $\rho=1$, and $\rho>1$. The proof for the three results in this subsection appear in the appendix of the research report.

The first result is for $\rho<1$ and is a central-limit-theorem-type scaling when the deviations around the mean are of the order of $\sqrt{n}$.

Theorem 8. *For $\rho<1$,*

$$\frac{1}{\sqrt{n}}\left(\left(S^{(n)}(\infty)\right)_{0\le i<\theta} - n(\hat{p})_{0\le i<\theta}\right) \xrightarrow[n\to\infty]{d} \mathcal{N}(0,\Sigma), \quad (61)$$

where

$$\Sigma^{-1} = \psi(1,1,\ldots,1)\cdot(1,1,\ldots,1)^\top - \left(\frac{1}{\theta-\hat{c}}\right)(\theta,\theta-1,\ldots,1)\cdot(\theta,\theta-1,\ldots,1)^\top + \begin{pmatrix} 1/\hat{p}_0 & 0 & \ldots & 0 \\ 0 & 1/\hat{p}_1 & \ldots & 0 \\ \vdots & \ldots & \ddots & \vdots \\ 0 & 0 & \ldots & 1/\hat{p}_{\theta-1} \end{pmatrix} \quad (62)$$

Corollary 7. *For $\rho < 1$, $\theta = 1$, we have $\hat{c} = \rho$, $\hat{p}_0 = 1 - \rho$ and $\psi = \rho^{-1}$ leading to $\Sigma^{-1} = \rho^{-1}$ and:*

$$\frac{S_0^{(n)}(\infty) - n(1-\rho)}{\sqrt{n\rho}} \xrightarrow[n\to\infty]{d} \mathcal{N}(0,1). \qquad (63)$$

The next case corresponds to $\rho = 1$. For $a, z \in \mathbb{R}$ and $\theta \geq 1$, define

$$\widehat{\Phi}_\theta(z;a) = \int_z^\infty \exp\left(au - \frac{u^{(\theta+1)}}{(\theta+1)!}\right) du. \qquad (64)$$

For $\theta = 1$ and $a = 0$, $(2\pi)^{-1/2}\widehat{\Phi}_\theta$ reduces to the complementary cumulative distribution function of the standard normal distribution.

Theorem 9. *For $\rho = 1$ and $z \in \mathbb{R}_+$,*

$$\lim_{n\to\infty} \mathbb{P}\left(\frac{S_{\theta-1}^{(n)}(\infty)}{n^{\theta/(\theta+1)}} > z\right) = \frac{\widehat{\Phi}_\theta(z;0)}{\widehat{\Phi}_\theta(0;0)}, \qquad (65)$$

Corollary 8. *For $\rho = 1$, $\theta = 1$, and $z > 0$,*

$$\lim_{n\to\infty} \mathbb{P}\left(\frac{S^{(n)}(\infty)}{\sqrt{n}} > z\right) = 2(1 - \Phi(z)), \qquad (66)$$

where Φ is the distribution function of the standard normal distribution.

Unlike in the $\rho < 1$ case, the deviations are now no longer of $O(\sqrt{n})$ but are of higher order. On the other hand, the fluctuations take $S^{(n)}$ with high probability only to states with either $\theta - 1$ or θ jobs. All other configurations are on a scale lower than $n^{\theta/(\theta+1)}$. This is in contrast with the behavior for $\rho < 1$ where the fluctuations can take the process to states with number of jobs ranging from 0 to θ. Thus, for $\rho = 1$, conditioned on being accepted, a customer has a high probability of being routed to a server $\theta - 1$ jobs. This property has a direct consequence on the state information the dispatcher needs to take routing decisions. We shall elaborate upon this in Section 6.

Finally, for $\rho > 1$, the following result shows that the deviations around $n\theta$ are of $O(1)$ and are geometrically distributed. Moreover, the excursions take $S^{(n)}$ only to states with $S_{\theta-1}^{(n)} > 0$ and $S_i^{(n)} = 0$ for $i < \theta - 1$. That is, at a random time, there will be a geometrically distributed number of servers with $\theta - 1$ clients and there will be no servers with less than $\theta - 1$ clients. We give more precise on the blocking probability later on.

Theorem 10.
For $\rho > 1$,

$$S_{\theta-1}^{(n)}(\infty) \xrightarrow[n\to\infty]{d} Geo(\rho^{-1}), \qquad (67)$$

and the blocking probability is

$$B_\theta^{(n)} \sim 1 - \rho^{-1}. \qquad (68)$$

The previous theorems give a more precise characterization of the system state as well as its performance for a fixed value of ρ (not depending on n) both in terms of blocking and waiting time. In particular, for $\rho < 1$, the blocking is exponentially small in n while the mean sojourn time is

$$\frac{1}{\rho}\sum_i \frac{\theta - i}{\theta - \hat{c}} i\hat{p}_i,$$

with a deviation of order $\frac{1}{\sqrt{n}}$.

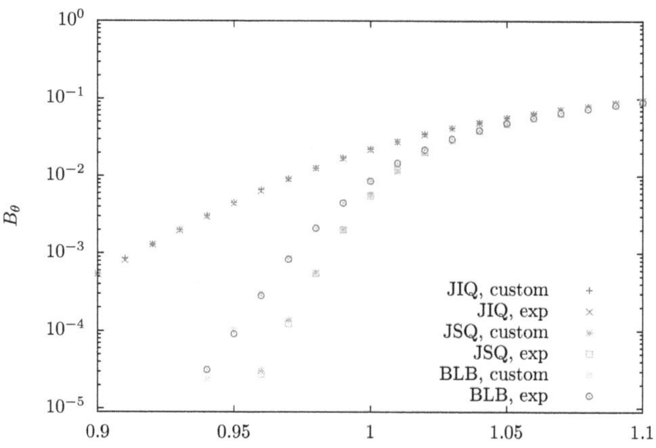

Figure 1: Comparison of the blocking probability for different policies. Number of servers is 20. Buffer size is 10.

5.4 Numerical experiments

We first provide a comparison in Figure 1, of the blocking probability obtained by the insensitive policy analysed in this paper (which is denoted by BLB in the figure) with that of two other policies, namely JSQ and JIQ. The results were obtained through simulations. There are 20 servers each with a buffer size of 10. Two different job-size distributions were used: *(i)* exponential; and *(ii)* a discrete distribution, which we call custom, with point masses at 0.1 and 10. The probability of job-size being 0.1 (resp. 10) was 9/9.9 (resp. 0.9/9.9).

The JSQ policy is known to be optimal for exponential job-size distributions and homogeneous server speeds, and thus gives a natural benchmark for comparison. The JIQ policy is an interesting policy from the practical point of view as it requires little state information compared to JSQ and the insensitive policy while at the same time it is optimal in the mean-field limit, that is its blocking probability goes to 0 when the number of servers goes to ∞. We have not included the JSQ(d) policy in our comparison as this policy is not optimal in the mean-field limit. We observed in the simulations that in the symmetric case and for high loads, the performance of JSQ and JIQ changes very little when changing the job-size distribution.

While JIQ requires less state information, it can be see that even for a load of 0.9, a few orders of magnitude of gains can be obtained by using the state information. The drawback of JIQ comes from the fact that at high loads, it behaves more and more like Bernoulli routing since there are fewer empty servers available. Thus, while JIQ is optimal in the mean-field limit, the number of servers required to get close this limit will be much higher than that of JSQ or the insensitive policy, motivating the asymptotics expressions for fixed n that we provided. For systems with a smaller number of servers in which state information can be obtained relatively cheaply, JSQ or balanced policies can give a considerable performance advantage over JIQ.

As mentioned in the Introduction, in the case of symmetric server speeds, our motivation for studying the insensitive policy comes mainly from the fact that precise asymptotic estimates can be obtained which is obviously not the case with JSQ and JIQ. For asymmetric server speeds, insensitive policies might actually present performance gains over

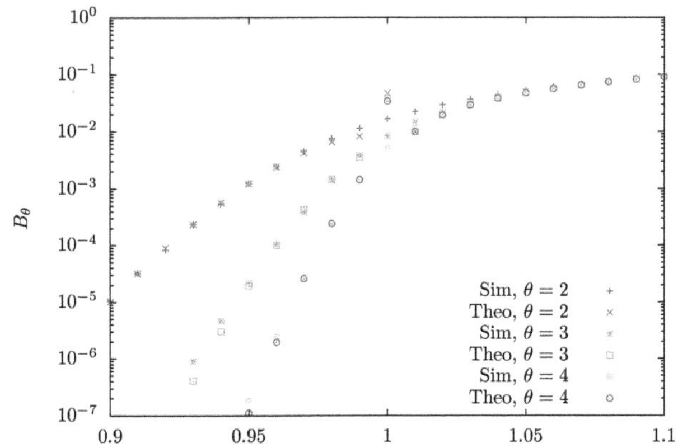

Figure 2: Comparison of the blocking probability computed from Theorems 5 and 10 with that obtained from simulations. Number of servers is 200.

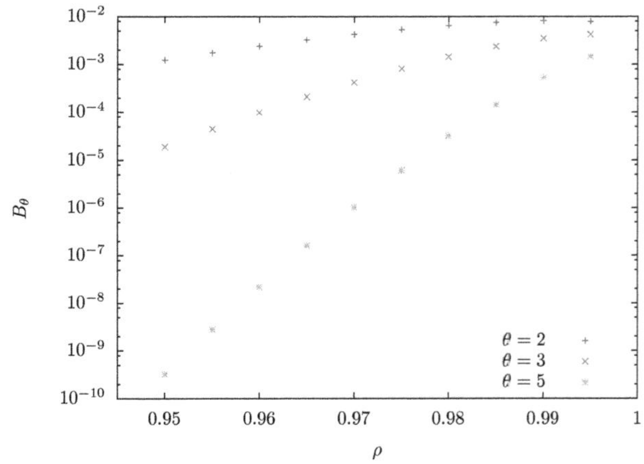

Figure 3: Decay of the blocking probability as predicted by Theorem 5. Number of servers is 100.

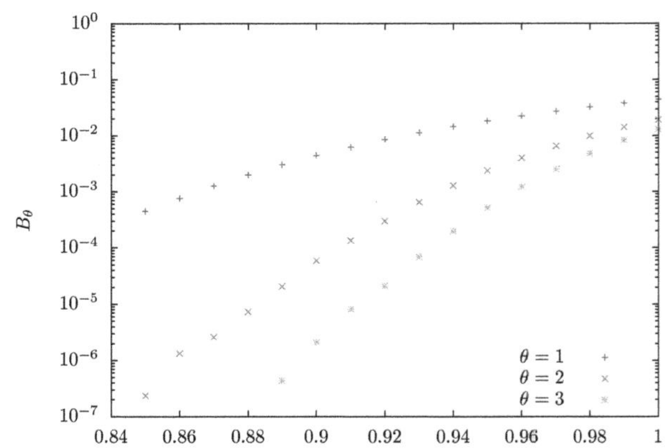

Figure 4: Benefits of resource pooling in terms of the blocking probability. Number of servers in the baseline system is 300.

JSQ. However, a detailed analysis of the asymmetric case falls outside the scope of this paper. Nevertheless, we give the stationary distribution for this case (see Theorem 11 in Section 6) from which asymptotic results similar to the ones in this paper can be derived.

We now illustrate the relationship between the blocking probability and the various parameter such as θ, n and λ for the insensitive policy. First, we evaluate the predictive abilities of some of the results obtained in this section by comparing them with the blocking probability obtained from simulating the Markov chain $S^{(n)}$. In Figure 2, we plot the blocking probability for $n = 200$ servers and for different values of ρ and θ. The theoretical values were calculated using Theorem 5 for $\rho < 1$, Theorem 9 for $\rho = 1$, and Theorem 10 for $\rho > 1$.

We observe that even for $n = 200$ the prediction is already reasonably accurate for $\theta = 2$ and $\theta = 3$, except for loads very close to 1 where the accuracy is less (this comes from a singularity in the expression of the blocking probability at 1).

Theorem 7 says that the decay of the blocking probability goes from polynomial to exponential when the load per server ρ is below $1 + an^{-1/\theta}$. As θ increases the frontier between the exponential and polynomial decay goes closer to $\rho = 1$. In other words, for a given n as θ increases, the blocking probability starts to decay exponentially from a value to ρ which is closer to 1. This phenomenon is shown in figure 3, in which the blocking probability was computed using Theorem 5.

In the final experiment, we illustrate the benefits of resource pooling. We compare three different systems, which we index by θ, each corresponding to $\theta = 1, 2, 3$. In system θ, there are n/θ servers each of service rate θ and buffer size of θ. That is, the three systems have the same total service rate and the total buffer size but differ in the number of servers as well as in the service rate and buffer size of individual servers. For the $\theta = 1$ system there are 300 servers so that the $\theta = 2$ (resp., $\theta = 3$) system has 150 (resp., 100) each of service rate 2 (resp., 3). Figure 4 illustrates the blocking probability as a function of ρ for the three systems. The data for this plot was obtained through simulations. For example, for a load of 0.9 the blocking probability for $\theta = 1$ system is 4.4×10^{-3} while for the system with $\theta = 2$ the corresponding value is 6×10^{-5} which represents a considerable reduction in the blocking probability.

6. ENGINEERING INSIGHTS AND FUTURE WORK

Performance planning

The asymptotic analysis of insensitive load balancing allows to give a conservative planning for managing the performance relationship engaged between delay guarantees depending on θ, blocking guarantees depending both on n, θ and ρ, and given levels of loads. Indeed, in many applications, a given level of quality of service in terms of delay has to be reached and this can be done by fixing θ. For a given buffer depth θ the mean delay of a job entering the system will be less than θ (the server speed and the mean job-size are fixed to 1). On the other hand, for a given θ and n, we have precisely characterized the asymptotics of the blocking probability, unveiling the critical load $\rho_c(n)$ as the frontier of the acceptable blocking probability for most applications. Hence, one can adapt the number of servers n to cope with a target blocking probability given the load or adapt the load given the number of servers. Note that this planning is completely out of reach for specific sensitive policies.

Another way of looking at it is by considering the staffing rule which is the number of servers necessary to obtain a vanishing blocking probability in the limit when the total charge is large. In [10] and [27], the staffing rule for $\theta = 1$ was shown to be $\lambda + O(\lambda^{1/2})$, that is, at least these many servers are required to get a vanishing blocking probability when λ is large.

Theorem 7 generalizes the known results for $\theta = 1$ to larger values of θ leading to the following staffing rule:

Proposition 5. *For a fixed target blocking probability, the number of servers has to scale as $\lambda + a\lambda^{1/(\theta+1)}$, where a is determined by the target blocking probability and can computed using (55).*

Practical schemes under the critical load

One of the major criticisms of state-dependent policies such as JSQ or the policy under study in this paper is that the dispatcher needs to know the state of every server in order to route an incoming job. The process of collecting state information can add significant delays and lead to lost revenue [19]. Practical policies such as JSQ(d) [20] or JIQ [19] play on the trade-off between information and optimality, and aim to perform much better than state-independent policies while at the same time needing much less information than the whole set of servers. For example, JSQ(d), with the knowledge of the state of only d (which can be fixed number independent of n) servers, has a considerable gain at least in the case of exponentially distributed job-sizes and in the absence of blocking when $d = 2$ compared to $d = 1$.

While at first glance, the insensitive load balancing policy seems to require full state information, Theorem 9 lends a helping hand in alleviating this need. Recall that this theorem has the following implication: for $\rho = 1$ and n large, most of the servers will have either θ or $\theta - 1$ jobs. One possible scheme to exploit this property is based on the idea first proposed for JIQ, which was motivated by the observation that collecting state information at arrival instants should be avoided in order to reduce delays for jobs. In JIQ, the servers inform the dispatcher (or leave information on a bulletin board) when they become idle. The dispatcher[3] then knows which servers are idle, and it routes an incoming packet to one of these servers, if there is one, otherwise it routes based on no information. Thus, upon arrival a job can be routed immediately based on state information collected previously.

For the insensitive policy one can conceive a scheme in which servers inform the dispatcher whether they have $\theta - 1$ or fewer than $\theta - 1$ jobs (this scheme automatically implies that the dispatcher also knows which servers have θ jobs). When a job arrives, the dispatcher will need to determine the state of only those servers with less than $\theta - 1$ jobs. Since this number is expected to be on a smaller scale than $n^{\theta/(\theta+1)}$ (thanks to Theorem 9), one can expect to reduce the information flow between the servers and dispatchers at arrival instants. One of our future works will be to characterize precisely the variations in the number of servers with fewer than $\theta - 1$ jobs. A back of the envelope calculation based upon the proof of Theorem 9 leads one to believe that there will $O(n^{(k+1)/(\theta+1)})$ servers with k jobs and hence $O(n^{(\theta-1)/(\theta+1)})$ servers with less that $\theta - 1$ jobs but this remains to be rigorously investigated.

Of course this reasoning is valid for a given blocking probability of order $n^{-\frac{\theta}{\theta+1}}$ and this could be significantly reduced for other blocking targets (and hence other loads).

Multi-speed servers

This planning is of course simplified by the fact that we considered a symmetric system depending only on three possibly inter-dependent parameters (n, ρ, θ). In a future work, we aim at generalizing the analysis to servers with different speeds or even to servers with state dependent speed. Though this generalization falls out of the scope of this paper, let us underline the possibility of this analysis by giving its first step, the expression of the stationary measure for the occupation of a multi-speed server farm.

Consider a server farm with n servers that are classified according to their speed into J different types. A server of type j has speed c_j, buffer size of θ_j, and there are n_j servers of type j.

As for the symmetric system, it is convenient here to study the number of servers processing jobs instead of the number of jobs being processed. Let $\mathcal{S}_j = \{s \in \{0, 1, \ldots, n_j\}^{\theta_j} : \sum_{i=0}^{\theta_j - 1} s_i \le n_j\}$, and let $\mathcal{S}^{(n)} = \prod_{j=1}^{J} \mathcal{S}_j$. Further, let $\{S^{(n)}(t) \in \mathcal{S}\}_{t\ge 0}$, where $n = \sum_{i=1}^{J} n_j$. Let $S^{(n)}(t)$ be a random process defined on $\mathcal{S}^{(n)}(t)$, where the component (i, j) of $\mathcal{S}^{(n)}(t)$ denotes the number of servers of type j with i customers at time t.

We shall use a boldface font to denote an element of $\mathcal{S}_j$, and use calligraphic font to denote an element of $\mathcal{S}^{(n)}$. So, $\mathbf{s}_j$ would be an vector in $\mathcal{S}_j$, and an element $\mathsf{s} \in \mathcal{S}^{(n)}$ can be written as $\mathsf{s} = (\mathbf{s}_1, \mathbf{s}_2, \ldots, \mathbf{s}_J)$.

In state s, the arrival rate to servers of type j and i tasks is given by

$$\lambda_{i,j}(\mathsf{s}) = \frac{(\theta_j - i)s_{i,j}}{\sum_j (n_j\theta_j - \bar{s}_j)} n\rho, \quad (69)$$

where $\bar{s}_j = \sum_i i s_{i,j}$ is the total number of tasks in severs of type j.

Theorem 11. *If the job-size distribution is exponential, the process $\mathcal{S}(t)$ is a reversible Markov process and its stationary distribution of $\mathcal{S}^{(n)}(t)$ is given by*

$$\pi(\mathsf{s}) = \pi(0)\frac{(n\theta - \bar{\mathsf{s}})!}{(n\theta)!}\prod_{j=1}^{J}\binom{n_j}{\mathbf{s}_j}\prod_{k=0}^{\theta}\left(\frac{\theta_j!(n\rho_j)^k}{(\theta_j - k)!}\right)^{s_{k,j}}, \quad (70)$$

where $\bar{\mathsf{s}} = \sum_j \bar{s}_j$ is the total number of tasks in the system, and $\rho_j = \rho c_j^{-1}$.

Given this first result established, all the steps presented in the presented analysis might (and should) be considered. This would in particular allow to characterize the optimal trunk reservation parameters (θ_i) for various trade-off of loads, delays and blocking.

Future research directions

Other than the directions described in the previous subsection, several open questions deserve attention. A natural related model would be the generalization of the Erlang C model, that is, the model in studied in this work but with a common waiting room where arrivals wait when all the

[3]We are assuming a single dispatcher.

servers are in the blocking phase. More fundamental questions that merit investigation are:

- Can similar results be established for sensitive policies (like join the shortest of d queues among n)? Are the meaningful scalings similar?
- Can we quantify the optimality gaps for specific families of job-size distributions?
- Can we obtain even finer estimates for the blocking probabilities in the QED regime, in the spirit of the body of work establishing precise asymptotics for Erlang's formula [11]?

7. ACKNOWLEDGEMENTS

This work was partially supported by the Basque Center for Applied Mathematics, the Bizkaia Talent and European Commission through COFUND programme (reference AYD-000-273), and by the STIC-AmSud project N° 14STIC03.

8. REFERENCES

[1] BENAÏM, M. *Dynamics of stochastic approximation algorithms.* Séminaire de Probabilités XXXIII, Lecture Notes in Math. Springer, Berlin, 1999.

[2] BONALD, T., JONCKHEERE, M., AND PROUTIÈRE, A. Insensitive load balancing. *SIGMETRICS Perform. Eval. Rev. 32*, 1 (2004), 367–377.

[3] BONALD, T., MASSOULIÉ, L., PROUTIÈRE, A., AND VIRTAMO, J. A queueing analysis of max-min fairness, proportional fairness and balanced fairness. *Queueing Syst. Theory Appl. 53*, 1-2 (2006), 65–84.

[4] BONALD, T., AND PROUTIÈRE, A. Insensitive bandwidth sharing in data networks. *Queueing Syst. Theory Appl. 44*, 1 (2003), 69–100.

[5] BONAVENTURA, M., FOGUELMAN, D., AND CASTRO, R. Discrete event modeling and simulation-driven engineering for the atlas data acquisition network. *Computing in Science & Engineering 18*, 3 (2016). To appear.

[6] BRAMSON, M., LU, Y., AND PRABAKHAR, B. Asymptotic independence of queues under randomized load balancing. *Queueing Syst 71* (2012), 247–292.

[7] COVER, T. M., AND THOMAS, J. A. *Elements of Information Theory.* Hoboken. Hoboken, New Jersey: Wiley Interscience., 2006.

[8] GRAHAM, C. Chaoticity on path space for a queueing network with selection of the shortest queue among several. *J. Appl. Probab. 37*, 1 (2000), 198–211.

[9] HALFIN, S., AND WHITT, W. Heavy-traffic limits for queues with many exponential servers. *Operations Research 29*, 3 (1981), 567–588.

[10] JAGERMAN, D. L. Some properties of the Erlang loss function. *Bell System Technical Journal 53*, 3 (1974), 525–551.

[11] JANSSEN, A. J. E. M., VAN LEEUWAARDEN, J. S. H., AND ZWART, A. P. Corrected asymptotics for a multi-server queue in the Halfin-Whitt regime. *Queueing Systems: Theory and Applications 58*, 4 (2008), 261–301.

[12] JONCKHEERE, M. Insensitive versus efficient dynamic load balancing in networks without blocking. *Queueing Syst. 54*, 3 (2006), 193–202.

[13] JONCKHEERE, M., AND MAIRESSE, J. Towards an Erlang formula for multiclass networks. *Queueing Systems 66*, 1 (2010), 53–78.

[14] JONCKHEERE, M., AND PRABHU, B. J. Asymptotics of Insensitive Load Balancing and Blocking Phases. HAL preprint. Available at https://hal.archives-ouvertes.fr/hal-01299605, 2016.

[15] KIPNIS, C., AND LANDIM, C. *Scaling Limits of Interacting Particle Systems.* Grundlehren der mathematischen Wissenschaften. Springer Berlin Heidelberg, 2013.

[16] KNESSL, C., AND YAO, H. On the finite capacity shortest queue problem. *Progress in Applied Mathematics 2*, 1 (2011), 1–34.

[17] LE BOUDEC, J. The stationary behaviour of fluid limits of reversible processes is concnetrated on stationary points. *Networks and hetegnereous media 8*, 2 (2013), 1529–540.

[18] LEINO, J., AND VIRTAMO, J. Insensitive load balancing in data networks. *Comput. Netw. 50*, 8 (2006), 1059–1068.

[19] LU, Y., XIE, Q., KLIOT, G., GELLER, A., LARUS, J. R., AND GREENBERG, A. Join-idle-queue: A novel load balancing algorithm for dynamically scalable web services. *Perform. Eval. 68*, 11 (Nov. 2011), 1056–1071.

[20] MITZENMACHER, M. The power of two choices in randomized load balancing. *Ph.D. Thesis* (1996).

[21] MUKHERJEE, D., BORST, S. C., VAN LEEUWAARDEN, J. S. H., AND WHITING, P. A. Universality of Load Balancing Schemes on Diffusion Scale. *ArXiv e-prints* (Oct. 2015).

[22] MUKHOPADHYAY, A., KARTHIK, A., MAZUMDAR, R. R., AND GUILLEMIN, F. Mean field and propagation of chaos in multi-class heterogeneous loss models. *Performance Evaluation 91* (2015), 117 – 131. Special Issue: Performance 2015.

[23] NEMES, G. An explicit formula for the coefficients in Laplace's method. *Constructive Approximation 38*, 3 (2013), 471–487. Preprint on arXiv:1207.5222.

[24] PLA, V., VIRTAMO, J., AND MARTINEZ-BAUSET, J. Optimal robust policies for bandwidth allocation and admission control in wireless networks. *Computer Networks 52*, 17 (2008), 3258 – 3272.

[25] STOLYAR, A. Pull-based load distribution among heterogeneous parallel servers: the case of multiple routers. *ArXiv e-prints* (2015).

[26] VVEDENSKAYA, N. D., DOBRUSHIN, R. L., AND KARPELEVICH, F. I. Queueing system with selection of the shortest of two queues: An assymptotic approach. *Problems of Information Transmission 32*, 1 (1996), 15–27.

[27] WHITT, W. Heavy traffic approximations for service systems with blocking. *Bell System Technical Journal 63*, 4 (1984), 689–708.

[28] WHITTLE, P. Partial balance and insensitivity. *Journal of Applied Probability 22*, 1 (1985), 168–176.

Understanding Latency Variation in Modern DRAM Chips: Experimental Characterization, Analysis, and Optimization

Kevin K. Chang[1] Abhijith Kashyap[1] Hasan Hassan[1,2]
Saugata Ghose[1] Kevin Hsieh[1] Donghyuk Lee[1] Tianshi Li[1,3]
Gennady Pekhimenko[1] Samira Khan[4] Onur Mutlu[5,1]
[1]Carnegie Mellon University [2]TOBB ETÜ [3]Peking University [4]University of Virginia [5]ETH Zürich

ABSTRACT

Long DRAM latency is a critical performance bottleneck in current systems. DRAM access latency is defined by three fundamental operations that take place within the DRAM cell array: *(i) activation* of a memory row, which opens the row to perform accesses; *(ii) precharge*, which prepares the cell array for the next memory access; and *(iii) restoration* of the row, which restores the values of cells in the row that were destroyed due to activation. There is significant latency variation for each of these operations across the cells of a single DRAM chip due to irregularity in the manufacturing process. As a result, some cells are *inherently* faster to access, while others are inherently slower. Unfortunately, existing systems do not exploit this variation.

The goal of this work is to *(i)* experimentally characterize and understand the latency variation across cells within a DRAM chip for these three fundamental DRAM operations, and *(ii)* develop new mechanisms that exploit our understanding of the latency variation to reliably improve performance. To this end, we comprehensively characterize 240 DRAM chips from three major vendors, and make several new observations about latency variation within DRAM. We find that *(i)* there is large latency variation across the cells for each of the three operations; *(ii)* variation characteristics exhibit significant spatial locality: slower cells are clustered in certain regions of a DRAM chip; and *(iii)* the three fundamental operations exhibit different reliability characteristics when the latency of each operation is reduced.

Based on our observations, we propose Flexible-LatencY DRAM (FLY-DRAM), a mechanism that exploits latency variation across DRAM cells within a DRAM chip to improve system performance. The key idea of FLY-DRAM is to exploit the spatial locality of slower cells within DRAM, and access the faster DRAM regions with reduced latencies for the fundamental operations. Our evaluations show that FLY-DRAM improves the performance of a wide range of applications by 13.3%, 17.6%, and 19.5%, on average, for each of the three different vendors' real DRAM chips, in a simulated 8-core system. We conclude that the experimental characterization and analysis of latency variation within modern DRAM, provided by this work, can lead to new techniques that improve DRAM and system performance.

SIGMETRICS '16, June 14–18, 2016, Antibes Juan-Les-Pins, France.

DOI: http://dx.doi.org/10.1145/2896377.2901453

1. INTRODUCTION

Over the past few decades, the long latency of memory has been a critical bottleneck in system performance. Increasing core counts, emergence of more data-intensive and latency-critical applications, and increasingly limited bandwidth in the memory system are together leading to higher memory latency. Thus, low-latency memory operation is now even more important to improving overall system performance [9, 11, 16, 27, 36, 37, 38, 45, 49, 53, 54, 56, 66, 68, 70, 79].

The latency of a memory request is predominantly defined by the timings of two fundamental operations: *activation* and *precharge*. These operations take place on the two-dimensional arrays of memory *cells* that store data. Activation is the process of "opening" a row of cells, in order to allow data within that row to be accessed. Once a row is *activated*, the memory controller can read from or write to it one cache line at a time. Precharge is the process of "closing" the activated row, and preparing the cell array for the next memory access. Once the array is *precharged*, another row can be activated. Specifically for DRAM, we also need to consider the latency of a third operation, known as *restoration*. A DRAM cell uses a capacitor, whose charge level represents the stored data value. The activation process of a row affects the charge level in the capacitor, which can destroy the data value stored within the cell. To prevent data loss, DRAM must *restore* the charge level of each DRAM cell in the row to reflect the cell's data value before activation, which takes time.

The latencies of these three DRAM operations, as defined by vendor specifications, have *not* improved significantly in the past decade, as depicted in Figure 1. This is especially true when we compare latency improvements to the capacity ($64\times=\frac{8Gb}{128Mb}$) and bandwidth improvements ($16\times\approx\frac{2133MT/s}{133MT/s}$) [21, 23, 37, 38, 70] commodity DRAM chips experienced in the past decade. In fact, the activation and precharge latencies *increased* from 2013 to 2015, when DDR DRAM transitioned from the third generation (12.5ns for DDR3-1600J [21]) to the fourth generation (14.06ns for DDR4-2133P [23]). As the latencies specified by vendors have not reduced over time, the system performance bottleneck caused by raw main memory latency remains largely unaddressed in modern systems.

In this work, we observe that the three fundamental DRAM operations can *actually* complete with a much lower

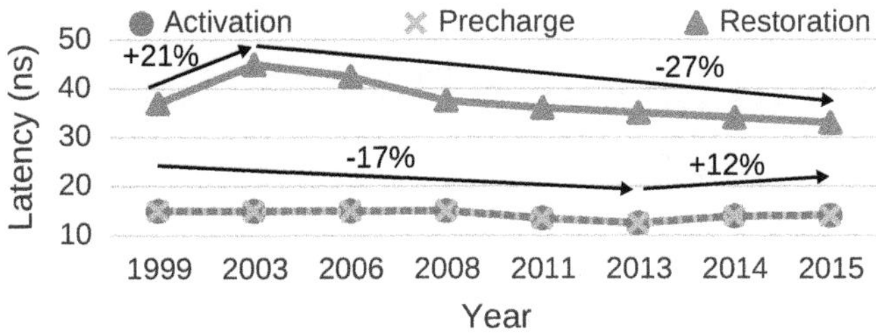

Figure 1: DRAM latency trends over time [20, 21, 23, 51].

latency for many DRAM cells than the specification, because *there is inherent latency variation present across the DRAM cells within a DRAM chip.* This is a result of manufacturing process variation, which causes the *sizes* and *strengths* of cells to be different, thus making some cells faster and other cells slower to be accessed reliably [15, 31, 41]. The speed gap between the fastest and slowest DRAM cells is getting worse [5, 57], as the technology node continues to scale down to sub-20nm feature sizes. Unfortunately, instead of optimizing the latency specifications for the common case, DRAM vendors use a single set of standard access latencies, which provide reliable operation guarantees for the *worst case* (i.e., slowest cells), to maximize manufacturing yield.

We find that the (widening) speed gap among DRAM cells presents an opportunity to reduce DRAM access latency. If we can understand and characterize the inherent variation in cell latencies, we can use the resulting understanding to reduce the access latency for those rows that contain faster cells. **The goal of this work** is to *(i)* experimentally characterize and understand the impact of latency variation in the three fundamental DRAM operations for cell access (activation, precharge, and restoration), and *(ii)* develop new mechanisms that take advantage of this variation to improve system performance.

To this end, we build an FPGA-based DRAM testing infrastructure and characterize 240 DRAM chips from three major vendors. We analyze the variations in the latency of the three fundamental DRAM operations by operating DRAM at multiple reduced latencies. Faster cells do not get affected by the reduced timings, and can be accessed reliably without changing their stored value; however, slower cells *cannot* be reliably read with reduced latencies for the three operations, leading to bit flips. In this work, we define a *timing error* as a bit flip in a cell that occurs due to a reduced-latency access, and characterize timing errors incurred by the three DRAM operations. Our experimental characterization yields six new **key observations**.

First, we find that significant variation is present in modern DRAM chips for the latencies of all three fundamental DRAM operations. For example, we observe that 68%, 100%, and 36% of cache lines can be read reliably when activation/restoration/precharge latencies are reduced by 43%/36%/43%, respectively, across all 240 of our tested DRAM chips. We conclude that exploiting latency variation in DRAM cells has the potential to greatly reduce the access latency.

Second, we find that when we reduce the latency for different DRAM operations, there is spatial locality in inherently slower cells: such cells are clustered in certain *regions* of a DRAM chip, as opposed to being randomly distributed. We conclude that such spatial locality can be exploited to develop low-cost mechanisms to reduce latency, where fast regions are accessed with lower latency, and slow regions are accessed with the standard high latency.

Third, when we reduce the three latencies, we observe that each latency exhibits a different level of impact on the inherently-slower cells. Lowering the activation latency affects *only* the cells read in the first accessed cache line. In contrast, lowering the restoration or precharge latencies affects *all* cells in the row. We explain in detail why this is the case. We also find that the number of timing errors introduced is very sensitive to reductions in activation and precharge latencies, but not that sensitive to reduction in restoration latency. We conclude that different levels of mitigation are required to address the timing errors that result from lowering each of the different DRAM operation latencies, and that reducing restoration latency does not introduce timing errors in our experiments.

Fourth, we analyze the number of timing errors that occur when DRAM access latencies are reduced, and experimentally demonstrate that most of the erroneous cache lines have a single-bit error, with only a small fraction of cache lines experiencing more than one bit flip. We conclude, therefore, that using simple error-correcting codes (ECC) can correct most of these errors, thereby enabling lower latency for many inherently slower cells.

Fifth, we find no clear correlation between temperature and variation in cell access latency. We believe that it is not essential for latency reduction techniques that exploit such variation to be aware of the operating temperature.

Sixth, we find that the stored data pattern in cells affects access latency variation. Certain patterns lead to more timing errors than others. For example, the bit value `1` can be read significantly more reliably at a reduced access latency than the bit value `0`. We conclude that it is promising to investigate asymmetric data encoding or error correction mechanisms that favor `1`s over `0`s.

Based on these major conclusions from our comprehensive analysis and characterization of 240 DRAM chips from three major DRAM manufacturers, we propose and evaluate a new mechanism, called FLY-DRAM (Flexible-LatencY DRAM). FLY-DRAM's key idea is to *(i)* categorize the DRAM cells into fast and slow regions, *(ii)* expose this information to the memory controller, and *(iii)* reduce overall DRAM latency by accessing the fast regions with a lower latency. Our simulation-based analysis shows that FLY-DRAM improves the performance of a wide range of applications in an 8-core system. Based on our experimental observations, we also discuss a page allocator design that exploits the latency variation in DRAM to improve system performance.

We hope that our extensive analysis leads to other new mechanisms to improve DRAM performance and reliability. To facilitate this, we will make our characterization results for all tested DRAM chips and the FLY-DRAM simulator publicly available [10].

To our knowledge, this is the first work to make the following major contributions:

- It experimentally demonstrates and characterizes the significant variation in latency of three fundamental DRAM operations (activation, restoration, and precharge) across different cells within a DRAM chip.
- It experimentally demonstrates that reducing the latency of each of these three fundamental DRAM operations has a different effect on slower cells. It shows that *(i)* while the

memory controller can introduce timing errors in slower cells by reducing the activation and precharge latencies, it can reduce the restoration latency without impacting these cells, thus providing greater opportunities to improve performance without causing timing errors; and *(ii)* errors due to reducing the activation latency appear only in the first cache line accessed in a row, limiting the scope of impact.

- It experimentally demonstrates that access latency variation exhibits spatial locality within DRAM, and that the error rate with reduced latencies is correlated with the stored data pattern in cells, but not with temperature.
- It proposes a new mechanism, FLY-DRAM, which exploits the lower latencies of DRAM regions with faster cells by introducing heterogeneous timing parameters into the memory controller. We find that FLY-DRAM improves performance in an 8-core system by 13.3%, 17.6%, and 19.5%, on average, for each of the three different vendors' real DRAM chips, across a wide range of applications.

2. BACKGROUND & MOTIVATION

In this section, we first provide necessary background on DRAM organization and operation to enable a better understanding of the major DRAM timing parameters we will characterize. Then, we discuss how we can exploit DRAM variation to reduce the DRAM access latency.

2.1 High-Level DRAM System Organization

A modern DRAM system consists of a hierarchy of channels, modules, ranks, and chips, as shown in Figure 2a. Each *memory channel* drives DRAM commands, addresses, and data between a memory controller in the processor and one or more DRAM modules. Each *module* contains multiple DRAM chips that are divided into one or more ranks. A *rank* refers to a group of chips that operate in lock step to provide a wide data bus (usually 64 bits), as a single DRAM chip is designed to have a narrow data bus width (usually 8 bits) to minimize chip cost. Each of the eight chips in the rank shown in Figure 2a transfers 8 bits simultaneously to supply 64 bits of data.

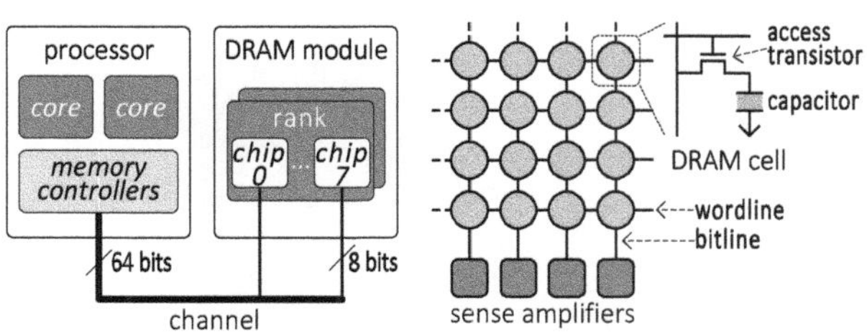

(a) DRAM System (b) DRAM Bank

Figure 2: DRAM system organization.

2.2 Internal DRAM Organization

Within a DRAM chip, there are multiple banks (e.g., eight in a typical DRAM chip [21]) that can process DRAM commands independently from each other to increase parallelism. A *bank* consists of a 2D-array of DRAM cells that are organized into rows and columns, as shown in Figure 2b. A row typically consists of 8K cells. The number of rows varies depending on the chip density. Each DRAM cell has *(i)* a *capacitor* that stores binary data in the form of electrical charge (i.e., fully charged and discharged states represent 1 and 0, respectively), and *(ii)* an *access transistor* that serves as a switch to connect the capacitor to the *bitline*. Each column of cells share a bitline, which connects them to a *sense amplifier*. The sense amplifier senses the charge stored in a cell, converts the charge to digital binary data, and buffers it. Each row of cells share a wire called the *wordline*, which controls the cells' access transistors. When a row's wordline is enabled, the entire row of cells gets connected to the row of sense amplifiers through the bitlines, enabling the sense amplifiers to sense and latch that row's data. The row of sense amplifiers is also called the *row buffer*.

2.3 Accessing DRAM

Accessing (i.e., reading from or writing to) a bank consists of three steps: *(i)* **Row Activation & Sense Amplification**: opening a row to transfer its data to the row buffer, *(ii)* **Read/Write**: accessing the target column in the row buffer, and *(iii)* **Precharge**: closing the row and the row buffer. We use Figure 3 to explain these three steps in detail. The top part of the figure shows the phase of the cells within the row that is being accessed. The bottom part shows both the DRAM command and data bus timelines, and demonstrates the associated timing parameters.

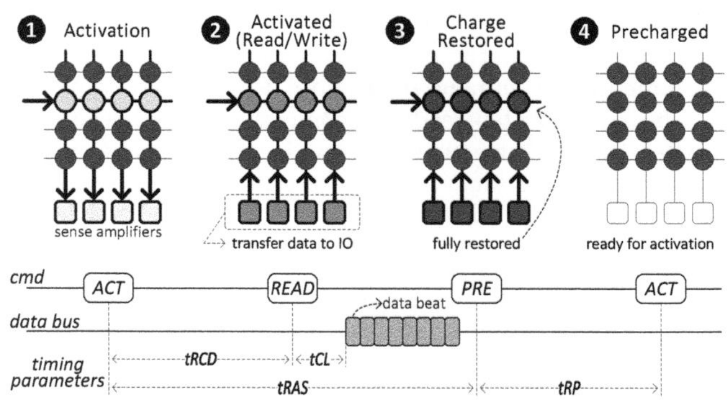

Figure 3: Internal DRAM phases, DRAM command/data timelines, and timing parameters to read a cache line.

Initial State. Initially, the bank remains in the *precharged* state (❹ in Figure 3), where all of the components are ready for activation. All cells are fully charged, represented with the dark grey color (a darker cell color indicates more charge). Second, the bitlines are charged to $V_{DD}/2$, represented as a thin line (a thin bitline indicates the initial voltage state of $V_{DD}/2$; a thick bitline means the bitline is being driven). Third, the wordline is disabled with 0V (a thin wordline indicates 0V; a thick wordline indicates V_{DD}). Fourth, the sense amplifier is *off* without any data latched in it (indicated by lighter color in the sense amplifier).

Row Activation & Sense Amplification Phases. To open a row, the memory controller sends an ACTIVATE command to raise the wordline of the corresponding row, which connects the row to the bitlines (❶). This triggers an *activation*, where charge starts to flow from the cell to the bitline (or the other way around, depending on the initial charge level in the cell) via a process called *charge sharing*. This process perturbs the voltage level on the corresponding bitline by a small amount. If the cell is initially charged (which we assume for the rest of this explanation, without loss of generality), the bitline voltage is perturbed upwards. Note that this causes the cell itself to discharge, losing its data temporarily (hence the lighter color of the accessed row), but this charge will be restored as we will describe below. After the activation phase, the sense amplifier *senses* the voltage perturbation on the bitline, and turns *on* to further *amplify* the voltage level on the bitline by injecting more charge into the bitline and the cell (making the activated row darker in ❷). When the bitline is amplified to a certain voltage level (e.g., $0.8V_{DD}$), the sense amplifier latches in the cell's data, which transforms it into binary data (❷). At this point in time, the data can be read from the sense amplifier. The latency of these two phases (activation and sense amplification) is called the *activation latency*, and is defined as **tRCD** in the standard DDR interface [21, 23]. This activation latency specifies the latency from the time an ACTIVATE command is issued to the time the data is ready to be accessed in the sense amplifier.

Read/Write & Restoration Phases. Once the sense amplifier (row buffer) latches in the data, the memory controller can send a READ or WRITE command to access the corresponding column of data within the row buffer (called a *column access*). The column access time to read the cache line data is called **tCL** (**tCWL** for writes). These parameters define the time between the column command and the appearance of the *first beat of data* on the data bus, shown at the bottom of Figure 3. A *data beat* is a 64-bit data transfer from the DRAM to the processor. In a typical DRAM [21], a column READ command reads out 8 data beats (also called an 8-beat burst), thus reading a complete 64-byte cache line.

After the bank becomes activated and the sense amplifier latches in the binary data of a cell, it starts to *restore* the connected cell's charge back to its original fully-charged state (❸). This phase is known as *restoration*, and can happen in parallel with column accesses. The restoration latency (from issuing an ACTIVATE command to fully restoring a row of cells) is defined as **tRAS**, as shown in Figure 3.

Precharge Phase. In order to access data from a different row, the bank needs to be re-initialized back to the precharged state (❹). To achieve this, the memory controller sends a PRECHARGE command, which *(i)* disables the wordline of the corresponding row, disconnecting the row from the sense amplifiers, and *(ii)* resets the voltage level on the bitline back to the initialized state, $V_{DD}/2$, so that the sense amplifier can sense the charge from the newly opened row. The latency of a precharge operation is defined as **tRP**, which is the latency between a PRECHARGE and a subsequent ACTIVATE within the same bank.

Summary. As shown at the bottom of Figure 3, the latency of back-to-back accesses to different rows in DRAM is decided by tRAS + tRP (restoration latency + precharge latency). The latency of accessing data from a row is decided by tRCD (activation latency), and is then followed by tCL and the data transfer latency (both of which are independent of the activation/restoration/precharge operations). In this work, we focus on the three critical timing parameters: tRCD, tRP, and tRAS.

2.4 Opportunities for Reducing Latency

DRAM standards define fixed values that are used for each of the timing parameters that we have described (e.g., DDR3 DRAM [21, 24]). Unfortunately, these latencies do *not* reflect the *actual* time the DRAM operations take for each cell. This is because the true access latency varies for each cell, as every cell is different in size and strength due to manufacturing process variation effects. For simplicity, and to ensure that DRAM yield remains high, DRAM manufacturers define a single set of latencies that guarantees reliable operation, based on the *slowest* cell in *any* DRAM chip across *all* DRAM vendors. As a result, there is a significant opportunity to reduce DRAM latency if, instead of always using worst-case latencies, we employ the true latency for each cell that enables the three operations reliably.

Our goal in this work is to *(i)* understand the impact of cell variation in the three fundamental DRAM operations for cell access (activation, precharge, and restoration); *(ii)* experimentally characterize the latency variation in these operations; and *(iii)* develop new mechanisms that take advantage of this variation to reduce the latency of these three operations.

To achieve this goal, we discuss the impact of reducing activation (Section 4), precharge (Section 5), and restoration (Section 6) latencies on DRAM cells by experimentally analyzing and characterizing the latency variation in cells in 240 real DRAM chips.

3. EXPERIMENTAL METHODOLOGY

To study the effect of using different timing parameters on modern DDR3 DRAM chips, we developed a DRAM testing platform that allows us to precisely control the value of timing parameters and the tested DRAM location (i.e., banks, rows, and columns) within a module. The testing platform, shown in Figure 4, consists of Xilinx FPGA boards [80] and host PCs. We use the RIFFA [19] framework to communicate data over the PCIe bus from our customized *testing software* running on the host PC to our customized *test engine* on the FPGA. Each DRAM module is tested on an FPGA board, and is located inside a heat chamber that is connected to a temperature controller. Unless otherwise specified, we test modules at an ambient temperature of 20±1°C. We examine various temperatures in Section 4.5.

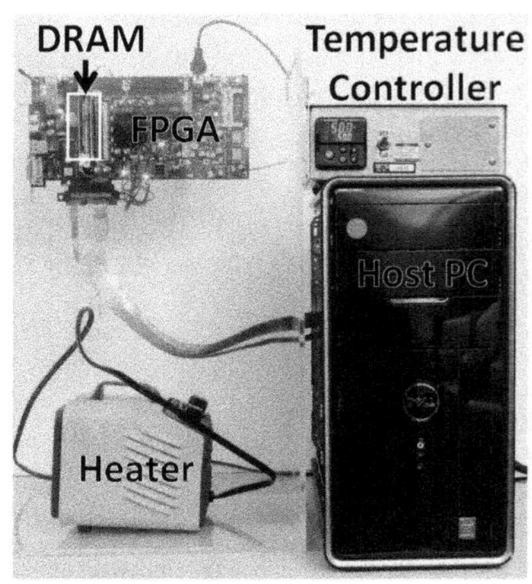

Figure 4: FPGA-based DRAM testing infrastructure.

3.1 DRAM Test

To achieve the goal of controlling timing parameters, our FPGA test engine supports a list of DRAM commands that get processed directly by the memory controller on the FPGA. Then, on the host PC, we can write a *test* that specifies a sequence of DRAM commands along with the delay between the commands (i.e., timing parameters). The test sends the commands and delays from the host PC to the FPGA test engine.

Test 1 shows the pseudocode of a test that reads a cache line from a particular bank, row, and column with timing parameters that can be specified by the user. The test first sends an ACTIVATE to the target row (line 2). After a tRCD delay that we specify (line 3), it sends a READ (line 4) to the target cache line. Our test engine enables us to specify the exact delay between two DRAM commands, thus allowing us to tune certain timing parameters. The read delay (tCL) and data transfer latency (BL) are two DRAM internal timings that cannot be changed using our infrastructure. After our test waits for the data to be fully transferred (line 5), we precharge the bank (line 6) with our specified tRP (line 7). We describe the details of the tests that we created to characterize latency variation of tRCD, tRP, and tRAS in the next few sections.

```
1 ReadOneCacheLine(my_tRCD, my_tRP, bank, row, col)
2   ACT(bank, row)
3   cmdDelay(my_tRCD)        ▷ Set activation latency (tRCD)
4   READ(bank, row, col)
5   cmdDelay(tCL +BL)             ▷ Wait for read to finish
6   PRE(bank)
7   cmdDelay(my_tRP)         ▷ Set precharge latency (tRP)
8   readData()      ▷ Send the read data from FPGA to PC
```

Test 1: Read a cache line with specified timing parameters.

3.2 Characterized DRAM Modules

We characterize latency variation on a total of 30 DDR3 DRAM modules, comprising 240 DRAM chips, from the three major DRAM vendors that hold more than 90% of the market share [2]. Table 1 lists the relevant information about the tested DRAM modules. All of these modules are *dual in-line* (i.e., 64-bit data bus) with a single rank of DRAM chips. Therefore, we use the terms *DIMM* (dual in-line memory module) and module interchangeably. In the rest of the paper, we refer to a specific DIMM using the label D_v^n, where n and v stand for the DIMM number and vendor, respectively. In the table, we group the DIMMs based on their model number, which provides certain information on the process technology and array design used in the chips.

Vendor	DIMM Name	Model	Timing (ns) (tRCD/tRP/tRAS)	Assembly Year
A Total of 8 DIMMs	D_A^{0-1}	M0	13.125/13.125/35	2013
	D_A^{2-3}	M1	13.125/13.125/36	2012
	D_A^{4-5}	M2	13.125/13.125/35	2013
	D_A^{6-7}	M3	13.125/13.125/35	2013
B Total of 9 DIMMs	D_B^{0-5}	M0	13.125/13.125/35	2011-12
	D_B^{6-8}	M1	13.125/13.125/35	2012
C Total of 13 DIMMs	D_C^{0-5}	M0	13.125/13.125/34	2012
	D_C^{6-12}	M1	13.125/13.125/36	2011

Table 1: Properties of tested DIMMs.

4. ACTIVATION LATENCY ANALYSIS

In this section, we present our methodology and results on varying the activation latency, which is expressed by the tRCD timing parameter. We first describe the nature of errors caused by tRCD reduction in Section 4.1. Then, we describe the FPGA test we conducted on the DRAM modules to characterize tRCD variation in Section 4.2. The remaining sections describe different major observations we make based on our results.

4.1 Behavior of Activation Errors

As we discuss in Section 2.3, tRCD is defined as the minimum amount of time between the ACTIVATE and the first column command (READ/WRITE). Essentially, tRCD represents the time it takes for a row of sense amplifiers (i.e., the row buffer) to sense and latch a row of data. By employing a lower tRCD value, a column READ command may potentially read data from sense amplifiers that are still in the *sensing and amplification* phase, during which the data has not been fully latched into the sense amplifiers. As a result, reading data with a lowered tRCD can induce timing errors (i.e., flipped bits) in the data.

To further understand the nature of activation errors, we perform experiments to answer two fundamental questions: *(i)* Does lowering tRCD incur errors on *all* cache lines read from a sequence of READ commands on an opened row? *(ii)* Do the errors propagate back to the DRAM cells, causing *permanent* errors for all future accesses?

4.1.1 Errors Localized to First Column Command

To answer the first question, we conduct Test 2 that first activates a row with a specific tRCD value, and then reads every cache line in the entire row. By conducting the test on every row in a number of DIMMs from all three vendors, we make the following observation.

```
ReadOneRow(my_tRCD, bank, row)
  ACT(bank, row)
  cmdDelay(my_tRCD)                 ▷ Set activation latency
  for c ← 1 to Col_MAX
    READ(bank, row, c)                ▷ Read one cache line
    findErrors()              ▷ Count errors in a cache line
  cmdDelay(tCL + BL)
  PRE(bank)
  cmdDelay(tRP)
```

Test 2: Read one row with a specified tRCD value.

Observation 1: *Activation errors are isolated to the cache line from the first* READ *command, and do not appear in subsequently-read cache lines from the same row.*

There are two reasons why errors do *not* occur in the subsequent cache line reads. First, a READ accesses only its corresponding sense amplifiers, without accessing the other columns. Hence, a READ's effect is isolated to its target cache line. Second, by the time the second READ is issued, a sufficient amount of time has passed for the sense amplifiers to properly latch the data. Note that this observation is independent of DIMMs and vendors as the fundamental DRAM structure is similar across different DIMMs. We discuss the number of activation errors due to different tRCD values for each DIMM in Section 4.3.1.

4.1.2 Activation Errors Propagate into DRAM Cells

To answer our second question, we run two iterations of Test 2 (i.e., reading a row that is activated with a specified tRCD value) on the same row. The first iteration reads a row that is activated with a lower tRCD value, then closes the row. The second iteration re-opens the row using the standard tRCD value, and reads the data to confirm if the errors remain in the cells. Our experiments show that if the first iteration observes activation errors within a cache line, the second iteration observes the same errors. This demonstrates that activation errors not only happen at the sense amplifiers but also propagate back into the cells.

We hypothesize this is because reading a cache line early causes the sense amplifiers to latch the data based on the *current* bitline voltage. If the bitline voltage has not yet fully developed into V_{DD} or 0V, the sense amplifier latches in unknown data and amplifies this data to the bitline, which is then restored back into the cell during restoration phase.

Observation 2: *Activation errors occur at the sense amplifiers and propagate back into the cells. The errors persist until the data is overwritten.*

After observing that reducing activation latency results in timing errors, we now consider two new questions. First, after how much activation latency reduction do DIMMs start observing timing errors? Second, how many cells experience activation errors at each latency reduction step?

4.2 FPGA Test for Activation Latency

To characterize activation errors across every cell in DIMMs, we need to perform an ACTIVATE and a READ on one cache line at a time since activation errors only occur in one cache line per activation. To achieve this, we use Test 3, whose pseudocode is below, for every cache line within a row.

```
1 tRCDColOrderTest(my_tRCD, data)
2   for b ← 1 to Bank_MAX
3     for c ← 1 to Col_MAX                        ▷ Column first
4       for r ← 1 to Row_MAX
5         WriteOneCacheLine(b, r, c, data)
6         ReadOneCacheLine(tRCD, tRP, b, r, c)
7         assert findErrors() == 0                 ▷ Verify data
8         ReadOneCacheLine(my_tRCD, tRP, b, r, c)
9         findErrors()          ▷ Count errors in a cache line
```

Test 3: Read each cache line with a specified tRCD value.

The test iterates through each cache line (lines 2-4) and performs the following steps to test the cache line's reliability under a reduced tRCD value. First, it opens the row that contains the target cache line, writes a specified data pattern into the cache line, and then precharges the bank (line 5). Second, the test re-opens the row to read the cache line with the standard tRCD (line 6), and verifies if the value was written properly (line 7). Then it precharges the bank again to prepare for the next ACTIVATE. Third, it re-activates the row using the reduced tRCD value (*my_tRCD* in Test 3) to read the target cache line (line 8). It records the number of timing errors (i.e., bit flips) out of the 64-byte (512-bit) cache line (line 9).

In total, we have conducted more than 7500 rounds of tests on the DIMMs shown in Table 1, accounting for at least 2500 testing hours. For each round of tests, we conducted Test 3 with a different tRCD value and data pattern. We tested five different tRCD values: 12.5ns, 10ns, 7.5ns, 5ns, and 2.5ns. Due to the slow clock frequency of the FPGA, we can only adjust timings at a 2.5ns granularity. We used a set of four different data patterns: `0x00`, `0xaa`, `0xcc`, and `0xff`. Each data pattern represents the value that was written into each byte of the entire cache line.

4.3 Activation Error Distribution

In this section, we first present the distribution of activation errors collected from all of the tests conducted on every DIMM. Then, we categorize the results by DIMM model to investigate variation across models from different vendors.

4.3.1 Total Bit Error Rates

Figure 5 shows the box plots of the *bit error rate* (BER) observed on every DIMM as tRCD varies. The BER is defined as the fraction of activation error bits in the total population of tested bits. For each box, the bottom, middle, and top lines indicate the 25th, 50th, and 75th percentile of the population. The ends of the whiskers indicate the minimum and maximum BER of all DIMMs for a given tRCD value. Note that the y-axis is in log scale to show low BER values. As a result, the bottom whisker at tRCD=7.5ns cannot be seen due to a minimum value of 0. In addition, we show *all* observation points for each specific tRCD value by overlaying them on top of their corresponding box. Each point shows a BER collected from one round of Test 3 on one DIMM with a specific data pattern and a tRCD value. Based on these results, we make several observations.

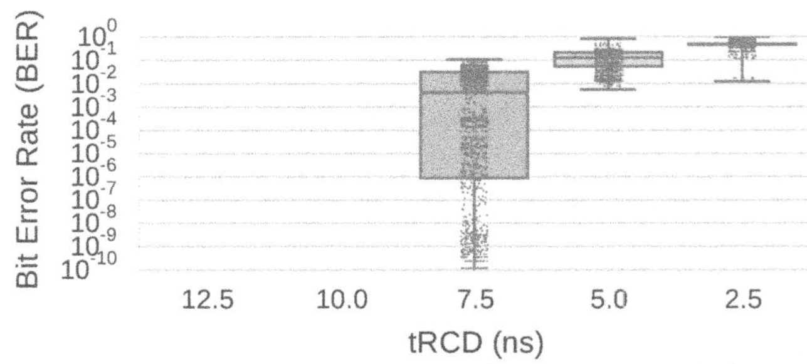

Figure 5: Bit error rate of all DIMMs with reduced tRCD.

First, we observe that BER exponentially increases as tRCD decreases. With a lower tRCD, fewer sense amplifiers are expected to have enough strength to properly sense the bitline's voltage value and latch the correct data. Second, at tRCD values of 12.5ns and 10ns, we observe no activation errors on any DIMM. This shows that the tRCD latency of the slowest cells in our tested DIMMs likely falls between 7.5 and 10ns, which are lower than the standard value (13.125ns). The manufacturers use the extra latency as a *guardband* to provide additional protection against process variation.

Third, the BER variation among DIMMs becomes smaller as tRCD value decreases. The reliability of DIMMs operating at tRCD=7.5ns varies significantly depending on the DRAM models and vendors, as we demonstrate in the Section 4.3.2. In fact, some DIMMs have no errors at tRCD=7.5ns, which cannot be seen in the plot due to the log scale. When tRCD reaches 2.5ns, most DIMMs become rife with errors, with a median BER of 0.48, similar to the probability of a coin toss.

4.3.2 Bit Error Rates by DIMM Model

Since the performance of a DIMM can vary across different models, vendors, and fabrication processes, we provide a detailed analysis by breaking down the BER results by DIMM model (listed in Table 1). Figure 6 presents the distribution of every DIMM's BER grouped by each vendor and model combination. Each box shows the quartiles and median, along with the whiskers indicating the minimum and maximum BERs. Since all of the DIMMs work reliably at 10ns and above, we show the BERs for tRCD=7.5ns and tRCD=5ns.

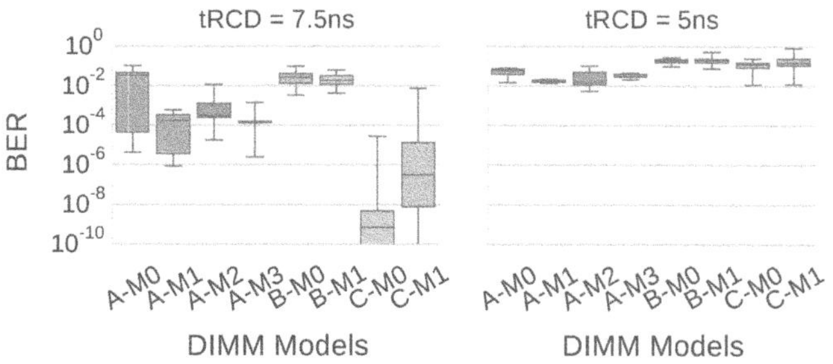

Figure 6: BERs of DIMMs grouped by model, when tested with different tRCD values.

By comparing the BERs across models and vendors, we observe that BER variation exists not only across DIMMs from different vendors, but also on DIMMs manufactured from the same vendor. For example, for DIMMs manufactured by vendor C, *Model 0* DIMMs have fewer errors than *Model 1* DIMMs. This result suggests that different DRAM models have different circuit architectures or process technologies, causing latency variation between them.

Similar to the observation we made across different DIMM models, we observe variation across DIMMs that have the same model. Due to space constraints, we omit figures to demonstrate this variation, but all of our results are available online [10]. The variation across DIMMs with the same model can be attributed to process variation due to the imperfect manufacturing process [5, 41, 55, 57].

4.4 Impact of Data Pattern

In this section, we investigate the impact of reading different data patterns under different tRCD values. Figure 7 shows the average BER of test rounds for three representative DIMMs, one from each vendor, with four data patterns. We do not show the BERs at tRCD=2.5ns, as rows cannot be reliably activated at that latency. We observe that pattern `0x00` is susceptible to more errors than pattern `0xff`, while the BERs for patterns `0xaa` and `0xcc` lie in between.[1] This can be clearly seen on D_C^0, where we observe that `0xff` incurs 4 orders of magnitude fewer errors than `0x00` on average at tRCD=7.5ns. We make a similar observation for the rest of the 12 DIMMs from vendor C.

With patterns `0xaa` and `0xcc`, we observe that bit `0` is more likely to be misread than bit `1`. In particular, we examined the flipped bits on three DIMMs that share the same model as D_C^0, and observed that *all of the flipped bits* are due to bit `0` flipping to `1`. From this observation, we can infer that there is a bias towards bit `1`, which can be more reliably read under a shorter activation latency than bit `0`.

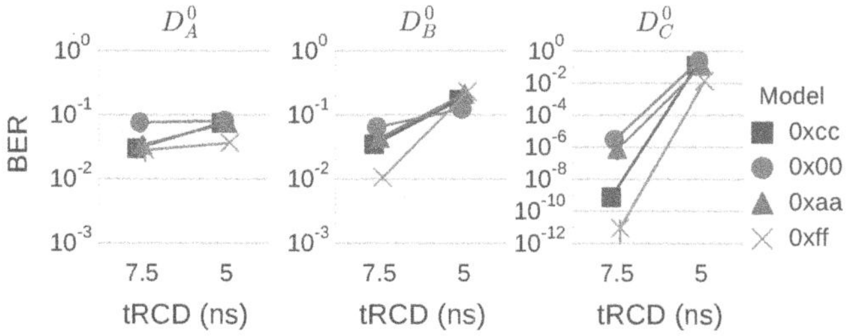

Figure 7: BERs due to four different data patterns on three different DIMMs as tRCD varies.

[1] In a cache line, we write the 8-bit pattern to every byte.

We believe this bias is due to the sense amplifier design. One major DRAM vendor presents a circuit design for a contemporary sense amplifier, and observes that it senses the V_{DD} value on the bitline faster than 0V [42]. Hence, the sense amplifier is able to sense and latch bit `1` faster than `0`. Due to this pattern dependence, we believe that it is promising to investigate asymmetric data encoding or error correction mechanisms that favor `1`s over `0`s.

Observation 3: *Errors caused by reduced activation latency are dependent on the stored data pattern. Reading bit 1 is significantly more reliable than bit 0 at reduced activation latencies.*

4.5 Effect of Temperature

Temperature is an important external factor that may affect the reliability of DIMMs [12, 29, 43, 63]. In particular, Schroeder et al. [63] and El-Sayed et al. [12] do not observe clear evidence for increasing DRAM error rates with increased temperature in data centers. Other works find that data retention time strongly depends on temperature [29, 43, 59]. However, none of these works have studied the effect of temperature on DIMMs when they are operating with a lower activation latency.

To investigate the impact of temperature on DIMMs operating with an activation latency lower than the standard value, we perform experiments that adjust the *ambient temperature* using a closed-loop temperature controller (shown in Figure 4). Figure 8 shows the average BER of three example DIMMs under three temperatures: 20°C, 50°C, and 70°C for tRCD=7.5/5ns. We include error bars, which are computed using 95% confidence intervals.

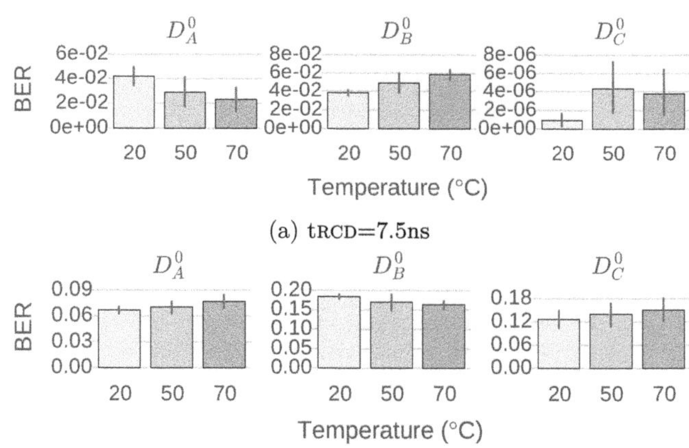

(a) tRCD=7.5ns

(b) tRCD=5ns

Figure 8: BERs of three example DIMMs operating under different temperatures.

We make two observations. First, at tRCD=7.5ns (Figure 8a), every DIMM shows a different BER trend as temperature increases. By calculating the *p-value* between the BERs of different temperatures, we find that the change in BERs is not statistically significant from one temperature to another for two out of the three tested DIMMs, meaning that we cannot conclude that BER increases at higher temperatures. For instance, the p-values between the BERs at 20°C and 50°C for D_A^0, D_B^0, and D_C^0 are 0.084, 0.087, and 0.006, respectively. Two of the three DIMMs have p-values greater than an α of 0.05, meaning that the BER change is statistically insignificant. Second, at lower tRCD values (5ns), the difference between the BERs due to temperature becomes even smaller.

Observation 4: *Our study does not show enough evidence to conclude that activation errors increase with higher temperatures.*

4.6 Spatial Locality of Activation Errors

To understand the locations of activation errors within a DIMM, we show the probability of experiencing at least one bit error in each cache line over a large number of experimental runs. Due to limited space, we present the results of two representative DIMMs from our experiments.

Figure 9 shows the locations of activation errors in the first bank of two DIMMs using tRCD=7.5ns. Additional results showing the error locations in every bank for some DIMMs are available online [10]. The x-axis and y-axis indicate the cache line number and row number (in thousands), respectively. In our tested DIMMs, a row size is 8KB, comprising 128 cache lines (64 bytes). Results are gathered from 40 and 52 iterations of tests for D_C^0 and D_A^3, respectively.

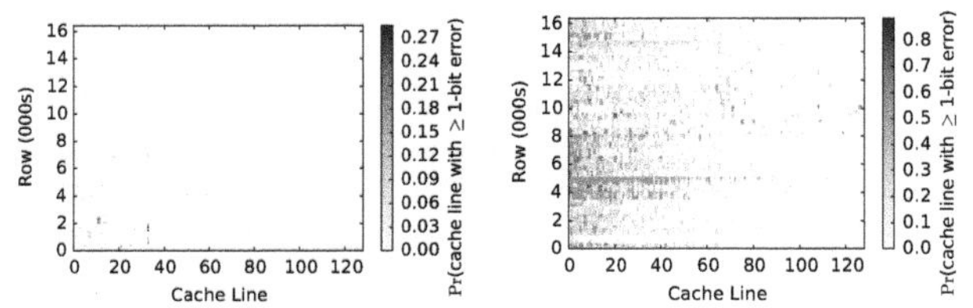

(a) Bank 0 of D_C^0 (b) Bank 0 of D_A^3

Figure 9: Probability of observing activation errors.

The main observation on D_C^0 (Figure 9a) is that errors tend to cluster at certain *columns of cache lines*. For the majority of the remaining cache lines in the bank, we observe no errors throughout the experiments. We observe similar characteristics in other DIMMs from the same model. In addition, we observe clusters of errors at certain regions. For example, D_A^3 (Figure 9b) shows that the activation errors repeatedly occur within the first half of the majority of rows.

We hypothesize that the cause of such spatial locality of errors is due to the locality of variation in the fabrication process during manufacturing: certain cache line locations can end up with less robust components, such as weaker sense amplifiers, weaker cells, or higher resistance bitlines.

Observation 5: *Activation errors do not occur uniformly within DRAM. They instead exhibit strong spatial concentration at certain regions.*

4.7 Density of Activation Errors

In this section, we investigate how errors are distributed within the erroneous cache lines. We present the distribution of error bits at the granularity of *data beats*, as conventional error-correcting codes (ECC) work at the same granularity. We discuss the effectiveness of employing ECC in Section 4.8. Recall from Section 2.3 that a cache line transfer consists of eight 64-bit data beats.

Figure 10 shows the distribution of error bits observed in each data beat of all erroneous cache lines when using tRCD=7.5ns. We show experiments from 9 DIMMs, categorized into three DIMM models (one per vendor). We select the model that observes the lowest average BER from each vendor, and show the frequency of observing 1, 2, 3, and $\geq$4 error bits in each data beat. The results are aggregated from all DIMMs of the selected models. We make two observations.

First, most data beats experience only fewer than 3 error bits at tRCD=7.5ns. We observe that more than 84%, 53%, and 91% of all the recorded activation errors are just 1-bit errors for DIMMs in A-M1, B-M1, and C-M0, respectively. Across all of the cache lines that contain at least one error bit, 82%, 41%, and 85% of the data beats that make up each cache line have no errors for A-M1, B-M1, and C-M0, respectively. Second, when tRCD is reduced to 5ns, the number of errors increases. The distribution of activation errors in data beats when using tRCD=5ns is available online [10], and it shows that 68% and 49% of data beats in A-M1 and C-M0 still have no more than one error bit.

Observation 6: *For cache lines that experience activation errors, the majority of their constituent data beats contain either no errors or just a 1-bit error.*

4.8 Effect of Error Correction Codes

As shown in the previous section, a majority of data beats in erroneous cache lines contain only a few error bits. In contemporary DRAM, ECC is used to detect and correct errors at the granularity of data beats. Therefore, this creates an opportunity for applying error correction codes (ECC) to correct activation errors. To study of the effect of ECC, we perform an analysis that uses various strengths of ECC to correct activation errors.

Figure 11 shows the percentage of cache lines that do *not* observe any activation errors when using tRCD=7.5ns at various ECC strengths, ranging from single to triple error bit correction. These results are gathered from the same 9 DIMMs used in Section 4.7. The first bar of each group is the percentage of cache lines that do not exhibit any activation errors in our experiments. The following data bars show the fraction of error-free cache lines after applying single, double, and triple error correction codes.

We make two observations. First, without any ECC support, a large fraction of cache lines can be read reliably without any errors in many of the DIMMs we study. Overall, 92% and 99% of cache lines can be read without any activation errors from A-M1 and C-M0 DIMMs, respectively. On the other hand, B-M1 DIMMs are more susceptible to reduced activation latency: only 12% of their cache lines can be read without any activation errors.

Observation 7: *A majority of cache lines can be read without any activation errors in most of our tested DIMMs. However, some DIMMs are very susceptible to activation errors, resulting in a small fraction of error-free cache lines.*

Second, ECC is very effective in correcting the activation errors. For example, with a single error correction code (1EC), which is widely deployed in many server systems, the fraction of reliable cache lines improves from 92% to 99% for A-M1 DIMMs. Even for B-M1 DIMMs, which exhibit activation errors in a large fraction of cache lines, the triple error correcting code is able to improve the percentage of error-free cache lines from 12% to 62%.

Observation 8: *ECC is an effective mechanism to correct activation errors, even in modules with a large fraction of erroneous cache lines.*

5. PRECHARGE LATENCY ANALYSIS

In this section, we present the methodology and results on varying the precharge latency, represented by the tRP

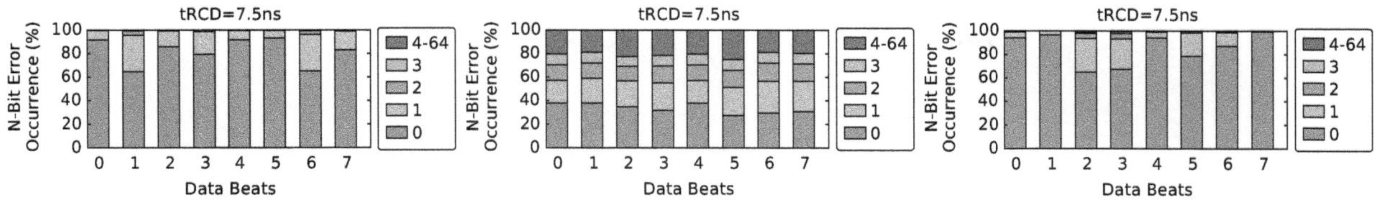

(a) A-M1 (b) B-M1 (c) C-M0

Figure 10: Breakdown of the number of error bits observed in each data beat of erroneous cache lines at tRCD=7.5ns.

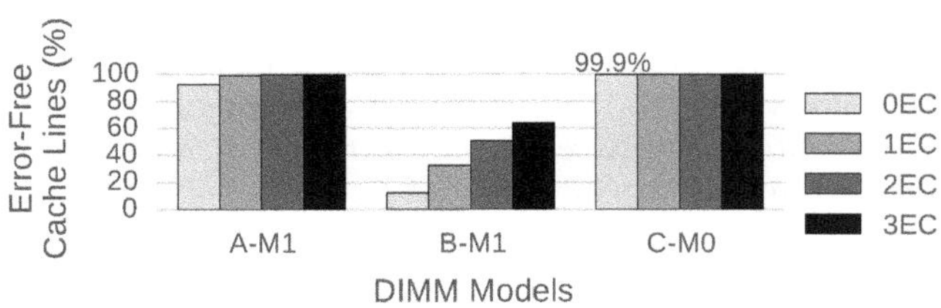

Figure 11: Percentage of error-free cache lines with various strengths of error correction (EC), with tRCD=7.5ns.

timing parameter. We first describe the nature of timing errors caused by reducing the precharge latency in Section 5.1. Then, we describe the FPGA test we conducted to characterize tRP variation in Section 5.2. In the remaining sections, we describe four major observations from our result analysis.

5.1 Behavior of Precharge Errors

In order to access a new DRAM row, a memory controller issues a PRECHARGE command, which performs the following two functions in sequence: *(i)* it closes the currently-activated row in the array (i.e., it disables the activated row's wordline); and *(ii)* it reinitializes the voltage value of every bitline inside the array back to $V_{DD}/2$, to prepare for a new activation.

Reducing the precharge latency by a small amount affects only the reinitialization process of the bitlines without interrupting the process of closing the row. The latency of this process is determined by the *precharge unit* that is placed by each bitline, next to the sense amplifier. By using a tRP value lower than the standard specification, the precharge unit may not have sufficient time to reset the bitline voltage from either V_{DD} (`bit 1`) or 0V (`bit 0`) to $V_{DD}/2$, thereby causing the bitline to float at some other intermediate voltage value. As a result, in the *subsequent* activation, the sense amplifier can incorrectly sense the wrong value from the DRAM cell due to the extra charge left on the bitline. We define precharge errors to be timing errors due to reduced precharge latency.

To further understand the nature of precharge errors, we use a test similar to the one for reduced activation latency in Section 4.1. The test reduces only the precharge latency, while keeping the activation latency at the standard value, to isolate the effects that occur due to a reduced precharge latency. We attempt to answer two fundamental questions: *(i)* Does lowering the precharge latency incur errors on multiple cache lines in the row activated *after* the precharge? *(ii)* Do these errors propagate back to the DRAM cells, causing permanent errors for all future accesses?

5.1.1 Precharge Errors Are Spread Across a Row

Throughout repeated test runs on DIMMs from all three vendors, we observe that reducing the precharge latency induces errors that are spread across multiple cache lines in the row activated after the precharge. This is because reducing the tRP value affects the latency between two *row-level* DRAM commands, PRECHARGE and ACTIVATE. As a result, having an insufficient amount of precharge time for the array's bitlines affects the entire row.

Observation 9: *Timing errors occur in multiple cache lines in the row activated after a precharge with reduced latency.*

Furthermore, these precharge errors are due to the sense amplifiers sensing the wrong voltage on the bitlines, causing them to latch incorrect data. Therefore, as the restoration operation reuses the data latched in the sense amplifiers, the wrong data is written back into the cells.

5.2 FPGA Test for Precharge Latency

In contrast to activation errors, precharge errors are spread across an *entire* row. As a result, we use a test that varies tRP at the row level. The pseudocode of the test, Test 4, is shown below.

```
TRPRowOrderTest(my_tRP, data)
  for b ← 1 to Bank_MAX
    for r ← 1 to Row_MAX                          ▷ Row order
      WriteOneRow(b, r, data)
      ReadOneRow(tRCD, tRP, b, r)
      WriteOneRow(b, r + 1, data_bar)             ▷ Inverted data
      ReadOneRow(tRCD, tRP, b, r + 1)
      assert findErrors() == 0   ▷ Verify data, data_bar
      ReadOneRow(tRCD, my_tRP, b, r)
      findErrors()                    ▷ Count errors in row r
```

Test 4: Read each row with a specified tRP value.

In total, we have conducted more than 4000 rounds of tests on the DIMMs shown in Table 1, which accounts for at least 1300 testing hours. We use three groups of different data patterns: (`0x00`, `0xff`), (`0xaa`, `0x33`), and (`0xcc`, `0x55`). Each group specifies two different data patterns, which are the inverse of each other, placed in consecutive rows in the same array. This ensures that as we iterate through the rows in order, the partially-precharged state of the bitlines will not favor the data pattern in the adjacent row to be activated.

5.3 Precharge Error Distribution

In this section, we first show the distribution of precharge errors collected from all of the tests conducted on every DIMM. Then, we categorize the results by DIMM model to investigate variation across models from different vendors.

5.3.1 Total Bit Error Rates

Figure 12 shows the box plots of the BER observed for every DIMM as tRP is varied from 12.5ns down to 2.5ns. Based on these results, we make several observations. First, similar to the observation made for activation latency, we do not observe errors when the precharge latency is reduced to 12.5

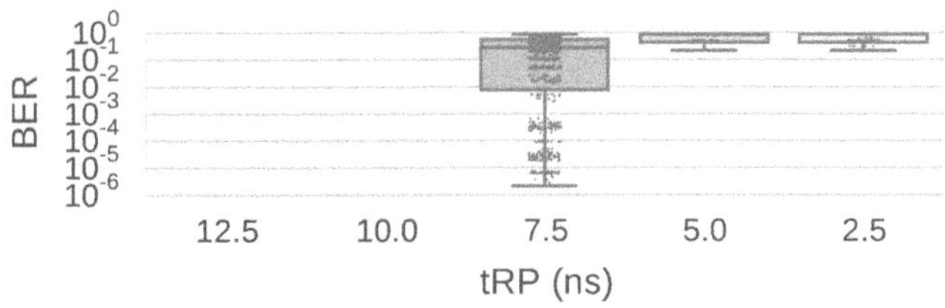

Figure 12: Bit error rate of all DIMMs with reduced tRP.

and 10ns, as the reduced latencies are still within the guardband provided. Second, the precharge BER is significantly higher than the activation BER when errors start appearing at 7.5ns – the median of the precharge BER is 587x higher than that of the activation BER (shown in Figure 5). This is partially due to the fact that reducing the precharge latency causes the errors to span across multiple cache lines in an *entire row*, whereas reducing the activation latency affects *only the first cache line* read from the row. Third, once tRP is set to 5ns, the BER exceeds the tolerable range, resulting in a median BER of 0.43. In contrast, the activation BER does not reach this high an error rate until the activation latency is lowered down to 2.5ns.

Observation 10: *With the same amount of latency reduction, the number of precharge errors is significantly higher than the number of activation errors.*

5.3.2 Bit Error Rates by DIMM Model

To examine the precharge error trend for individual DIMM models, we show the BER distribution of every DIMM categorized by DRAM model in Figure 13. Similar to the observation we made for activation errors in Section 4.1, variation exists across different DIMM models. These results provide further support for the existence and prevalence of latency variation in modern DRAM chips.

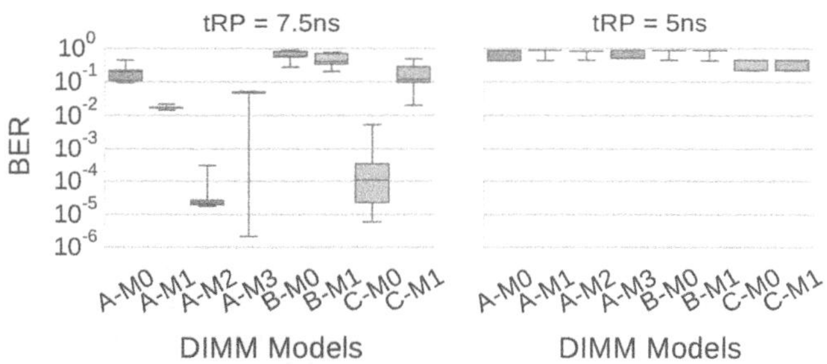

Figure 13: BERs of DIMMs grouped by model, when tested with different tRP values.

5.4 Spatial Locality of Precharge Errors

In this section, we investigate the location and distribution of precharge errors. Due to the large amount of available data, we show representative results from a single DIMM, $\mathtt{D}_C^0$ (model C-M0). All of our results for all DIMMs will be made available publicly [10]. Figure 14 shows the probability of each cache line seeing at least a one-bit precharge error in Bank 0 and Bank 7 of $\mathtt{D}_C^0$ when we set tRP to 7.5ns. The x-axis indicates the cache line number, and the y-axis indicates the row number (in thousands). The results are gathered from 12 iterations of tests. We make several observations based on our results.

First, some banks do not have any precharge errors throughout the experiments, such as Bank 0 (Figure 14a, hence the plot is all white). Similar to the activation errors, precharge errors are *not* distributed uniformly across locations within DIMMs. Second, Figure 14b shows that the errors concentrate on a certain region of rows, while the other regions experience much fewer or no errors. This demonstrates that certain sense amplifiers, or cells at certain locations are more robust than others, allowing them to work reliably under a reduced precharge latency.

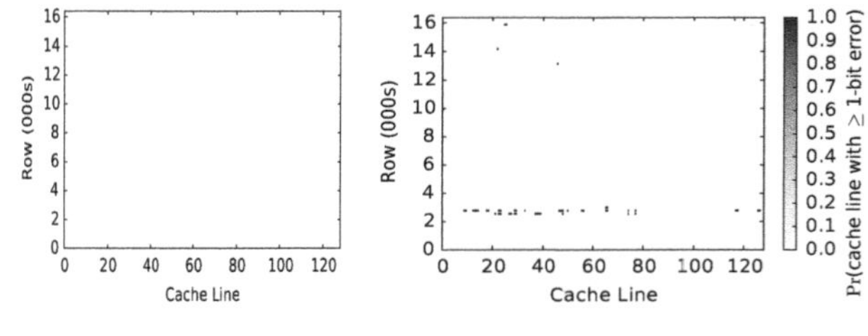

(a) Bank 0 of $\mathtt{D}_C^0$ (b) Bank 7 of $\mathtt{D}_C^0$

Figure 14: Probability of observing precharge errors.

Observation 11: *Precharge errors do not occur uniformly within DIMMs, but exhibit strong spatial concentration at certain regions.*

Overall, we observe that 71.1%, 13.6%, and 84.7% of cache lines contain no precharge errors when they are read from A-M1, B-M1, and C-M0 model DIMMs, respectively, with tRP=7.5ns. Similar to the trend discussed in Section 4.8, C-M0 DIMMs have the highest fraction of reliable cache lines among the DIMMs tested, while B-M1 DIMMs experience the largest amount of errors. Even though the number of error-free cache lines at tRP=7.5ns is lower than that at tRCD=7.5ns, the portion is still significant enough to show the prevalence of precharge latency variation in modern DIMMs.

Observation 12: *When precharge latency is reduced, a majority of cache lines can be read without any timing errors in some of our tested DIMMs. However, other DIMMs are largely susceptible to precharge errors, resulting in a small fraction of error-free cache lines.*

6. RESTORATION LATENCY ANALYSIS

In this section, we present a methodology and findings on varying the restoration latency, defined by the tRAS timing parameter. First, we elaborate on the impact of reducing tRAS on performance and reliability in Section 6.1. Then, we explain our FPGA test conducted to characterize tRAS variation, and present our observations.

6.1 Impact of Reduced tRAS

As mentioned in Section 2.3, tRAS specifies the minimum amount of time between issuing an ACTIVATE and a PRECHARGE command to a bank. By reducing tRAS, we can complete an access to one row faster, and quickly switch to access the next row. From the perspective of *reliability*, reducing the restoration latency may potentially induce errors in the cells due to having insufficient time to restore the lost charge back to the cells. When a row of cells is activated, the cells temporarily lose their charge to the bitlines, so that the sense amplifiers can sense the charge. During the restoration phase, the sense amplifiers restore charge back into the cells, bringing them back to the fully-charged state. By reducing the restoration latency, the amount of restored charge reduces, and the cells may not reach the fully-charged state. As a result, a subsequent access to the same row may not able to sense the correct value, thereby leading to errors.

6.2 Test Methodology and Results

To characterize the variation in restoration latency (tRAS), we consider another important factor that affects the amount of charge stored in DRAM cells, which is *leakage*. DRAM cells lose charge over time, thus requiring a periodic *refresh* operation to restore the charge. Reducing the restored charge in the cells can cause them to lose too much charge before the next refresh, generating an error.

To perform a conservative characterization, we integrate this leakage factor into our test methodology. We access each row by issuing a pair of commands, ACTIVATE and PRECHARGE, with a specific tRAS value between these two commands. Then, we wait for a full refresh period (defined as 64ms in the DRAM standard [21, 23]) before we access the row again to verify the correctness of its data. We test this sequence on a representative set of DIMMs from all three DRAM vendors and we use four data patterns: `0x00`, `0xff`, `0xaa`, and `0xcc`.

In our previously described tests on activation and precharge variation, we test every time step from the default timing value to a minimum value of 2.5ns, with a reduction of 2.5ns per step. Instead of reducing tRAS all the way down to 2.5ns from its standard value of 35ns, we lower it until $t\text{RAS}_{min} = t\text{RCD}+t\text{CL}+\text{BL}$, which is the latency of activating a row and reading a cache line from it. In a typical situation where the memory controller reads or writes a piece of data after opening a row, lowering tRAS below $t\text{RAS}_{min}$ means that the memory controller can issue a PRECHARGE while the data is still being read or written. Doing so risks terminating READ or WRITE operations prematurely, causing unknown behavior.

In order to test tRAS with a reasonable range of values, we iterate tRAS from 35ns to $t\text{RAS}_{min}$. Our $t\text{RAS}_{min}$ is calculated by using the standard tCL=13.125ns and BL=5ns along with a fast tRCD=5ns. $t\text{RAS}_{min}$ is rounded up to the nearest multiple of 2.5ns, which is *22.5ns*.

We do not observe errors across the range of tRAS values we tested in any of our experiments. This implies that charge restoration in modern DRAMs completes within the duration of an activation and a read. Therefore, tRAS can be reduced aggressively without affecting data integrity.

Observation 13: *Modern DIMMs have sufficient timing margin to complete charge restoration within the period of an* ACTIVATE *and a* READ. *Hence,* tRAS *can be reduced without introducing any errors.*

7. EXPLOITING LATENCY VARIATION

Based on our extensive experimental characterization, we propose two new mechanisms to reduce DRAM latency for better system performance. Our mechanisms exploit the key observation that different DIMMs have different amounts of tolerance for lower DRAM latency, and there is a strong correlation between the location of the cells and the lowest latency that the cells can tolerate. The first mechanism (Section 7.1) is a pure hardware approach to reducing DRAM latency. The second mechanism (Section 7.2) leverages OS support to maximize the benefits of the first mechanism.

7.1 Flexible-Latency DRAM

As we discussed in Sections 4.6 and 5.4, the timing errors caused by reducing the latency of the activation/precharge operations are concentrated on certain DRAM regions, which implies that the latency heterogeneity among DRAM cells exhibits strong locality. Based on this observation, we propose *Flexible-LatencY DRAM (FLY-DRAM)*, a software-transparent design that exploits this heterogeneity in cells to reduce the overall DRAM latency. The key idea of FLY-DRAM is to determine the shortest reliable access latency of each DRAM region, and to use the memory controller to apply that latency to the corresponding DRAM region at runtime. There are two key design challenges of FLY-DRAM, as we discuss below.

The first challenge is determining the shortest access latency. This can be done using a *latency profiling* procedure, which *(i)* runs Test 3 (Section 4.2) with different timing values and data patterns, and *(ii)* records the smallest latency that enables reliable access to each region. This procedure can be performed at one of two times. First, the system can run the procedure the very first time the DRAM is initialized, and store the profiling results to non-volatile memory (e.g., disk or flash memory) for future reference. Second, DRAM vendors can run the procedure at manufacturing time, and embed the results in the Serial Presence Detect (SPD) circuitry (a ROM present in each DIMM) [22]. The memory controller can read the profiling results from the SPD circuitry during DRAM initialization, and apply the correct latency for each DRAM region. While the second approach involves a slight modification to the DIMM, it can provide better latency information, as DRAM vendors have detailed knowledge on DRAM cell variation, and can use this information to run more thorough tests to determine a lower bound on the latency of each DRAM region.

The second design challenge is limiting the storage overhead of the latency profiling results. Recording the shortest latency for each cache line can incur a large storage overhead. For example, supporting four different tRCD and tRP timings requires 4 bits per 512-bit cache line, which is almost 0.8% of the entire DRAM storage. Fortunately, the storage overhead can be reduced based on a new observation of ours. As shown in Figures 9a and 9b, timing errors typically concentrate on certain DRAM *columns*. Therefore, FLY-DRAM records the shortest latency *at the granularity of DRAM columns*. Assuming we still need 4 bits per DRAM cache line, we need only 512 bits per DRAM bank, or an insignificant 0.00019% storage overhead for the DIMMs we evaluated. One can imagine using more sophisticated structures, such as Bloom Filters [4], to provide finer-grained latency information within a reasonable storage overhead, as shown in prior work on variable DRAM refresh time [44, 59]. We leave this for future work.

The FLY-DRAM memory controller *(i)* loads the latency profiling results into on-chip SRAMs at system boot time, *(ii)* looks up the profiled latency for each memory request based on its memory address, and *(iii)* applies the corresponding latency to the request. By reducing the latency values of tRCD, tRAS, and tRP for some memory requests, FLY-DRAM improves overall system performance, which we quantitatively demonstrate in the next two sections.

7.1.1 Evaluation Methodology

We evaluate the performance of FLY-DRAM on an eight-core system using Ramulator [32, 33], an open-source cycle-level DRAM simulator, driven by CPU traces generated from Pin [46]. We will make our source code publicly available [10]. Table 2 summarizes the configuration of our evaluated system. We use the standard DDR3-1333H timing parameters [21] as our baseline.

Processor	8 cores, 3.3 GHz, OoO 128-entry window
LLC	8 MB shared, 8-way set associative
DRAM	DDR3-1333H [21], open-row policy [61], 2 channels, 1 rank per channel, 8 banks per rank, Baseline: tRCD/tCL/tRP = 13.125ns, tRAS = 36ns

Table 2: Evaluated system configuration.

FLY-DRAM Configuration. To conservatively evaluate FLY-DRAM, we use a randomizing page allocator that maps each virtual page to a randomly-located physical page in memory. This allocator essentially distributes memory accesses from an application to different latency regions at random, and is thus unaware of FLY-DRAM regions.

Because each DIMM has a different fraction of fast cache lines, we evaluate FLY-DRAM on three different yet representative real DIMMs that we characterized. We select one DIMM from each vendor. Table 3 lists the distribution of cache lines that can be read reliably under different tRCD and tRP values, based on our characterization. For each DIMM, we use its distribution as listed in the table to model the percentage of cache lines with different tRCD and tRP values. For example, for D_A^2, we set 93% of its cache lines to use a tRCD of 7.5ns, and the remaining 7% of cache lines to use a tRCD of 10ns. Although these DIMMs have a small fraction of cache lines (<10%) that can be read using tRCD=5ns, we conservatively set tRCD=7.5ns for them to ensure high reliability. FLY-DRAM dynamically sets tRCD and tRP to either 7.5ns or 10ns for each memory request, based on which cache line the request is to. For the tRAS timing parameter, FLY-DRAM uses 27ns ($\lceil$tRCD+tCL$\rceil$) for all cache lines in these three tested DIMMs, as we observe no errors in any of the tested DIMMs due to lowering tRAS (see Section 6.2).

DIMM Name	Vendor	Model	tRCD Dist. (%)		tRP Dist. (%)	
			7.5ns	10ns	7.5ns	10ns
D_A^2	A	M1	93	7	74	26
D_B^7	B	M1	12	88	13	87
D_C^2	C	M0	99	1	99	1

Table 3: Distribution of cache lines under various tRCD and tRP values for three characterized DIMMs.

FLY-DRAM Upper-Bound Evaluation. We also evaluate the upper-bound performance of FLY-DRAM by assuming that *every* DRAM cell is fast (i.e., 100% of cache lines can be accessed using tRCD/tRP=7.5ns).

Applications and Workloads. To demonstrate the benefits of FLY-DRAM in an 8-core system, we generate 40 8-core multi-programmed workloads by assigning one application to each core. For each 8-core workload, we randomly select 8 applications from the following benchmark suites: SPEC CPU2006 [73], TPC-C/H [75], and STREAM [48]. We use PinPoints [58] to obtain the representative phases of each application. Our simulation executes at least 200 million instructions on each core [9, 16, 35, 38].

Performance Metric. We measure system performance with the *weighted speedup (WS)* metric [69], which is a measure of job throughput on a multi-core system [13]. Specifically, $WS = \sum_{i=1}^{N} \frac{IPC_i^{shared}}{IPC_i^{alone}}$. N is the number of cores in the system. IPC_i^{shared} is the IPC of an application that runs on $core_i$ while other applications are running on the other cores. IPC_i^{alone} is the IPC of an application when it runs alone in the system without any other applications. Essentially, WS is the sum of every application's slowdown compared to when it runs alone on the same system.

7.1.2 Multi-Core System Results

Figure 15 illustrates the system performance improvement of FLY-DRAM over the baseline for 40 workloads. The x-axis indicates the evaluated DRAM configurations, as shown in Table 3. The percentage value on top of each box is the average performance improvement over the baseline.

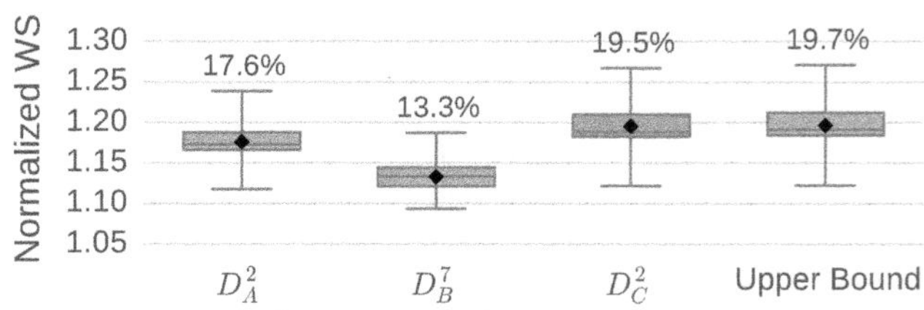

Figure 15: System performance improvement of FLY-DRAM for various DIMMs (listed in Table 3).

We make the following observations. First, FLY-DRAM improves system performance significantly, by 17.6%, 13.3%, and 19.5% on average across all 40 workloads for the three real DIMMs that we characterize. This is because FLY-DRAM reduces the latency of tRCD, tRP, and tRAS by 42.8%, 42.8%, and 25%, respectively, for many cache lines. In particular, DIMM D_C^2, whose great majority of cells are reliable at low tRCD and tRP, performs within 1% of the upper-bound performance (19.7% on average). Second, although DIMM D_B^7 has only a small fraction of cells that can operate at 7.5ns, FLY-DRAM still attains significant system performance benefits by using low tRCD and tRP latencies (10ns), which are 23.8% lower than the baseline, for the majority of cache lines. We conclude that FLY-DRAM is an effective mechanism to improve system performance by exploiting the widespread latency variation present across DRAM cells.

7.2 Discussion: DRAM-Aware Page Allocator

While FLY-DRAM significantly improves system performance in a software-transparent manner, we can take better advantage of it if we expose the different latency regions of FLY-DRAM to the software stack. We propose the idea of a DRAM-aware page allocator in the OS, whose goal is to better take advantage of FLY-DRAM by intelligently mapping application pages to different-latency DRAM regions in order to improve performance.

Within an application, there is heterogeneity in the access frequency of different pages, where some pages are accessed much more frequently than other pages [3, 60, 70, 74, 77, 83]. Our DRAM-aware page allocator places more frequently-accessed pages into lower-latency regions in DRAM. This *access frequency aware placement* allows a greater number of DRAM accesses to experience a reduced latency than a page allocator that is oblivious to DRAM latency variation, thereby likely increasing system performance.

For our page allocator to work effectively, it must know which pages are expected to be accessed frequently. In order to do this, we extend the OS system calls for memory allocation to take in a Boolean value, which states whether the memory being allocated is expected to be accessed frequently. This information either can be annotated by the programmer, or can be estimated by various dynamic profiling techniques [1, 6, 26, 47, 60, 74, 77, 83]. The page allocator uses this information to find a free physical page in DRAM that suits the expected access frequency of the application page that is being allocated.

We expect that by using our proposed page allocator, FLY-DRAM can perform close to the upper-bound performance reported in Section 7.1.2, even for DIMMs that have a smaller fraction of fast regions.

8. RELATED WORK

To our knowledge, this is the first work to *(i)* provide a detailed experimental characterization and analysis of latency variation for three major DRAM operations (tRCD, tRP, and tRAS) *across different cells within a DRAM chip*, *(ii)* demonstrate that a reduction in latency for each of these fundamental operations has a different impact on slower cells, *(iii)* show that access latency variation exhibits spatial locality, *(iv)* demonstrate that the error rate due to reduced latencies is correlated with the stored data pattern but not conclusively correlated with temperature, and *(v)* propose mechanisms that take advantage of variation *within a DRAM chip* to improve system performance.

DRAM Latency Variation. Adaptive-Latency DRAM (AL-DRAM) also characterizes and exploits DRAM latency variation, but does so at a much coarser granularity [37]. This work experimentally characterizes latency variation across different DRAM chips under different operating temperatures. AL-DRAM sets a uniform operation latency for the *entire* DIMM. In contrast, our work characterizes latency variation *within each chip*, at the granularity of individual DRAM cells. Our mechanism, FLY-DRAM, can be combined with AL-DRAM to further improve performance.

Chandrasekar et al. study the potential of reducing some DRAM timing parameters [7]. Similar to AL-DRAM, this work observes and characterizes latency variation *across* DIMMs, whereas our work studies variation across cells *within a DRAM chip*.

DRAM Error Studies. There are several studies that characterize various errors in DRAM. Many of these works observe how specific factors affect DRAM errors, analyzing the impact of temperature [12, 37] and hard errors [18]. Other works have conducted studies of DRAM error rates in the field, studying failures across a large sample size [40, 50, 63, 71, 72]. There are also works that have studied errors through controlled experiments, investigating errors due to retention [28, 29, 43, 59], disturbance from neighboring DRAM cells [34], and latency variation *across DRAM chips* [7, 37]. None of these works study errors due to latency variation across the cells within a DRAM chip, which we extensively characterize in our work.

DRAM Latency Reduction. Several types of commodity DRAM (Micron's RLDRAM [52] and Fujitsu's FCRAM [62]) provide low latency at the cost of high area overhead [35, 38]. Many prior works (e.g., [8, 9, 17, 35, 38, 45, 56, 65, 66, 70, 84]) propose various architectural changes *within* DRAM chips to reduce latency. In contrast, FLY-DRAM does not require any changes to a DRAM chip. Other works [16, 36, 64, 67, 68] reduce DRAM latency by changing the memory controller, and FLY-DRAM is complementary to them.

ECC DRAM. Many memory systems incorporate ECC DIMMs, which store information used to correct data during a read operation. Prior work (e.g., [14, 25, 29, 30, 39, 76, 78, 81, 82]) proposes more flexible or more powerful ECC schemes for DRAM. While these ECC mechanisms are designed to protect against faults using standard DRAM timings, we show that they also have the potential to correct timing errors that occur due to reduced DRAM latencies.

9. CONCLUSION

This paper provides the first experimental study that comprehensively characterizes and analyzes the latency variation within modern DRAM chips for three fundamental DRAM operations (activation, precharge, and restoration). We find that significant latency variation is present across DRAM cells in all 240 of our tested DRAM chips, and that a large fraction of cache lines can be read reliably even if the activation/restoration/precharge latencies are reduced significantly. Consequently, exploiting the latency variation in DRAM cells can greatly reduce the DRAM access latency. Based on the findings from our experimental characterization, we propose and evaluate a new mechanism, FLY-DRAM (Flexible-LatencY DRAM), which reduces DRAM latency by exploiting the inherent latency variation in DRAM cells. FLY-DRAM reduces DRAM latency by categorizing the DRAM cells into fast and slow regions, and accessing the fast regions with a reduced latency. We demonstrate that FLY-DRAM can greatly reduce DRAM latency, leading to significant system performance improvements on a variety of workloads.

We conclude that it is promising to understand and exploit the inherent latency variation within modern DRAM chips. We hope that the experimental characterization, analysis, and optimization techniques presented in this paper will enable the development of other new mechanisms that exploit the latency variation within DRAM to improve system performance and perhaps reliability.

ACKNOWLEDGMENTS

We thank our shepherd Christopher Stewart, anonymous reviewers, and SAFARI group members for feedback. We acknowledge the support of Google, Intel, Nvidia, and Samsung. This research was supported in part by the ISTC-CC, SRC, and NSF (grants 1212962 and 1320531). Kevin Chang is supported in part by the SRCEA/Intel Fellowship.

References

[1] N. Agarwal *et al.*, "Page Placement Strategies for GPUs Within Heterogeneous Memory Systems," in *ASPLOS*, 2015.

[2] H. Bauer *et al.*, "Memory: Are Challenges ahead?" March 2016. Available: http://www.mckinsey.com/industries/semiconductors/our-insights/memory-are-challenges-ahead

[3] A. Bhattacharjee and M. Martonosi, "Thread Criticality Predictors for Dynamic Performance, Power, and Resource Management in Chip Multiprocessors," in *ISCA*, 2009.

[4] B. H. Bloom, "Space/Time Tradeoffs in Hash Coding with Allowable Errors," *CACM*, July 1970.

[5] K. Chakraborty and P. Mazumder, *Fault-Tolerance and Reliability Techniques for High-Density Random-Access Memories*. Prentice Hall, 2002.

[6] R. Chandra *et al.*, "Scheduling and Page Migration for Multiprocessor Compute Servers," in *ASPLOS*, 1994.

[7] K. Chandrasekar *et al.*, "Exploiting Expendable Process-Margins in DRAMs for Run-Time Performance Optimization," in *DATE*, 2014.

[8] K. K.-W. Chang *et al.*, "Improving DRAM Performance by Parallelizing Refreshes with Accesses," in *HPCA*, 2014.
[9] K. K. Chang *et al.*, "Low-Cost Inter-Linked Subarrays (LISA): Enabling Fast Inter-Subarray Data Movement in DRAM," in *HPCA*, 2016.
[10] CMU SAFARI Research Group Source Code Repository, https://github.com/CMU-SAFARI.
[11] J. Dean and L. A. Barroso, "The Tail at Scale," *CACM*, 2013.
[12] N. El-Sayed *et al.*, "Temperature Management in Data Centers: Why Some (Might) Like It Hot," in *SIGMETRICS*, 2012.
[13] S. Eyerman and L. Eeckhout, "System-Level Performance Metrics for Multiprogram Workloads," *IEEE Micro*, 2008.
[14] S.-L. Gong *et al.*, "CLEAN-ECC: High Reliability ECC for Adaptive Granularity Memory System," in *MICRO*, 2015.
[15] T. Hamamoto *et al.*, "On the Retention Time Distribution of Dynamic Random Access Memory (DRAM)," in *IEEE TED*, 1998.
[16] H. Hassan *et al.*, "ChargeCache: Reducing DRAM Latency by Exploiting Row Access Locality," in *HPCA*, 2016.
[17] H. Hidaka *et al.*, "The Cache DRAM Architecture," *IEEE Micro*, 1990.
[18] A. A. Hwang *et al.*, "Cosmic Rays Don't Strike Twice: Understanding the Nature of DRAM Errors and the Implications for System Design," in *ASPLOS*, 2012.
[19] M. Jacobsen *et al.*, "RIFFA 2.1: A Reusable Integration Framework for FPGA Accelerators," *RTS*, 2015.
[20] JEDEC, "DDR2 SDRAM Standard," 2009.
[21] JEDEC, "DDR3 SDRAM Standard," 2010.
[22] JEDEC, "Standard No. 21-C. Annex K: Serial Presence Detect (SPD) for DDR3 SDRAM Modules," 2011.
[23] JEDEC, "DDR4 SDRAM Standard," 2012.
[24] JEDEC, "Low Power Double Data Rate 3 (LPDDR3)," 2012.
[25] X. Jian *et al.*, "Low-Power, Low-Storage-Overhead Chipkill Correct via Multi-Line Error Correction," in *SC*, 2013.
[26] X. Jiang *et al.*, "CHOP: Adaptive Filter-Based DRAM Caching for CMP Server Platforms," in *HPCA*, 2010.
[27] S. Kanev *et al.*, "Profiling a Warehouse-Scale Computer," in *ISCA*, 2015.
[28] S. Khan *et al.*, "PARBOR: An Efficient System-Level Technique to Detect Data Dependent Failures in DRAM," in *DSN*, 2016.
[29] S. Khan *et al.*, "The Efficacy of Error Mitigation Techniques for DRAM Retention Failures: A Comparative Experimental Study," in *SIGMETRICS*, 2014.
[30] J. Kim *et al.*, "Bamboo ECC: Strong, Safe, and Flexible Codes for Reliable Computer Memory," in *HPCA*, 2015.
[31] K. Kim and J. Lee, "A New Investigation of Data Retention Time in Truly Nanoscaled DRAMs," in *EDL*, 2009.
[32] Y. Kim *et al.*, "Ramulator," https://github.com/CMU-SAFARI/ramulator.
[33] Y. Kim *et al.*, "Ramulator: A Fast and Extensible DRAM Simulator," *IEEE CAL*, 2015.
[34] Y. Kim *et al.*, "Flipping Bits in Memory Without Accessing Them: An Experimental Study of DRAM Disturbance Errors," in *ISCA*, 2014.
[35] Y. Kim *et al.*, "A Case for Exploiting Subarray-Level Parallelism (SALP) in DRAM," in *ISCA*, 2012.
[36] C. J. Lee *et al.*, "DRAM-Aware Last-Level Cache Writeback: Reducing Write-Caused Interference in Memory Systems," in *HPS Technical Report*, 2010.
[37] D. Lee *et al.*, "Adaptive-Latency DRAM: Optimizing DRAM Timing for the Common-Case," in *HPCA*, 2015.
[38] D. Lee *et al.*, "Tiered-Latency DRAM: A Low Latency and Low Cost DRAM Architecture," in *HPCA*, 2013.
[39] S. Li *et al.*, "MAGE: Adaptive Granularity and ECC for Resilient and Power Efficient Memory Systems," in *SC*, 2012.
[40] X. Li *et al.*, "A Realistic Evaluation of Memory Hardware Errors and Software System Susceptibility," in *USENIX ATC*, 2010.
[41] Y. Li *et al.*, "DRAM Yield Analysis and Optimization by a Statistical Design Approach," in *IEEE TCSI*, 2011.
[42] K.-N. Lim *et al.*, "A 1.2V 23nm 6F2 4Gb DDR3 SDRAM With Local-Bitline Sense Amplifier, Hybrid LIO Sense Amplifier and Dummy-Less Array Architecture," in *ISSCC*, 2012.
[43] J. Liu *et al.*, "An Experimental Study of Data Retention Behavior in Modern DRAM Devices: Implications for Retention Time Profiling Mechanisms," in *ISCA*, 2013.
[44] J. Liu *et al.*, "RAIDR: Retention-Aware Intelligent DRAM Refresh," in *ISCA*, 2012.
[45] S.-L. Lu *et al.*, "Improving DRAM Latency with Dynamic Asymmetric Subarray," in *MICRO*, 2015.
[46] C.-K. Luk *et al.*, "Pin: Building Customized Program Analysis Tools with Dynamic Instrumentation," in *PLDI*, 2005.
[47] J. Marathe and F. Mueller, "Hardware Profile-Guided Automatic Page Placement for ccNUMA Systems," in *PPoPP*, 2006.
[48] J. D. McCalpin, "STREAM Benchmark."
[49] S. A. McKee, "Reflections on the Memory Wall," in *CF*, 2004.
[50] J. Meza *et al.*, "Revisiting Memory Errors in Large-Scale Production Data Centers: Analysis and Modeling of New Trends from the Field," in *DSN*, 2015.
[51] Micron Technology, Inc., "128Mb: x4, x8, x16 Automotive SDRAM," 1999.
[52] Micron Technology, Inc., "576Mb: x18, x36 RLDRAM3," 2011.
[53] O. Mutlu, "Memory Scaling: A Systems Architecture Perspective," *IMW*, 2013.
[54] O. Mutlu and L. Subramanian, "Research Problems and Opportunities in Memory Systems," *SUPERFRI*, 2015.
[55] S. Nassif, "Delay Variability: Sources, Impacts and Trends," in *ISSCC*, 2000.
[56] S. O *et al.*, "Row-Buffer Decoupling: A Case for Low-Latency DRAM Microarchitecture," in *ISCA*, 2014.
[57] M. Onabajo and J. Silva-Martinez, *Analog Circuit Design for Process Variation-Resilient Systems-on-a-Chip.* Springer, 2012.
[58] H. Patil *et al.*, "Pinpointing Representative Portions of Large Intel Itanium Programs with Dynamic Instrumentation," in *MICRO*, 2004.
[59] M. K. Qureshi *et al.*, "AVATAR: A Variable-Retention-Time (VRT) Aware Refresh for DRAM Systems," in *DSN*, 2015.
[60] L. E. Ramos *et al.*, "Page Placement in Hybrid Memory Systems," in *ICS*, 2011.
[61] S. Rixner *et al.*, "Memory Access Scheduling," in *ISCA*, 2000.
[62] Y. Sato *et al.*, "Fast Cycle RAM (FCRAM): A 20-ns Random Row Access, Pipe-Lined Operating DRAM," in *VLSIC*, 1998.
[63] B. Schroeder *et al.*, "DRAM Errors in the Wild: A Large-Scale Field Study," in *SIGMETRICS*, 2009.
[64] V. Seshadri *et al.*, "The Dirty-Block Index," in *ISCA*, 2014.
[65] V. Seshadri *et al.*, "Fast Bulk Bitwise AND and OR in DRAM," *IEEE CAL*, 2015.
[66] V. Seshadri *et al.*, "RowClone: Fast and Energy-Efficient In-DRAM Bulk Data Copy and Initialization," in *MICRO*, 2013.
[67] V. Seshadri *et al.*, "Gather-Scatter DRAM: In-DRAM Address Translation to Improve the Spatial Locality of Non-Unit Strided Accesses," in *MICRO*, 2015.
[68] W. Shin *et al.*, "NUAT: A Non-Uniform Access Time Memory Controller," in *HPCA*, 2014.
[69] A. Snavely and D. Tullsen, "Symbiotic Jobscheduling for a Simultaneous Multithreading Processor," in *ASPLOS*, 2000.
[70] Y. H. Son *et al.*, "Reducing Memory Access Latency with Asymmetric DRAM Bank Organizations," in *ISCA*, 2013.
[71] V. Sridharan *et al.*, "Memory Errors in Modern Systems: The Good, the Bad, and the Ugly," in *ASPLOS*, 2015.
[72] V. Sridharan and D. Liberty, "A Study of DRAM Failures in the Field," in *SC*, 2012.
[73] Standard Performance Evaluation Corp., "SPEC CPU2006," http://www.spec.org/cpu2006.
[74] K. Sudan *et al.*, "Micro-Pages: Increasing DRAM Efficiency with Locality-Aware Data Placement," in *ASPLOS*, 2010.
[75] Transaction Performance Processing Council, "TPC Benchmarks," http://www.tpc.org/.
[76] A. N. Udipi *et al.*, "LOT-ECC: Localized and Tiered Reliability Mechanisms for Commodity Memory Systems," in *ISCA*, 2012.
[77] B. Verghese *et al.*, "Operating System Support for Improving Data Locality on CC-NUMA Compute Servers," in *ASPLOS*, 1996.
[78] C. Wilkerson *et al.*, "Reducing Cache Power with Low-cost, Multi-bit Error-correcting Codes," in *ISCA*, 2010.
[79] M. V. Wilkes, "The Memory Gap and the Future of High Performance Memories," *SIGARCH CAN*, 2001.
[80] Xilinx, "ML605 Hardware User Guide," Oct. 2012.
[81] D. H. Yoon *et al.*, "BOOM: Enabling Mobile Memory Based Low-Power Server DIMMs," in *ISCA*, 2012.
[82] D. H. Yoon and M. Erez, "Virtualized ECC: Flexible Reliability in Main Memory," in *ASPLOS*, 2010.
[83] H. Yoon *et al.*, "Row Buffer Locality Aware Caching Policies for Hybrid Memories," in *ICCD*, 2012.
[84] T. Zhang *et al.*, "Half-DRAM: A High-Bandwidth and Low-Power DRAM Architecture from the Rethinking of Fine-Grained Activation," in *ISCA*, 2014.

Hash, Don't Cache (the Page Table)

Idan Yaniv
Technion – Israel Institute of Technology
idanyani@cs.technion.ac.il

Dan Tsafrir
Technion – Israel Institute of Technology
dan@cs.technion.ac.il

ABSTRACT

Radix page tables as implemented in the x86-64 architecture incur a penalty of four memory references for address translation upon each TLB miss. These 4 references become 24 in virtualized setups, accounting for 5%–90% of the runtime and thus motivating chip vendors to incorporate page walk caches (PWCs). Counterintuitively, an ISCA 2010 paper found that radix page tables with PWCs are superior to hashed page tables, yielding up to 5x fewer DRAM accesses per page walk. We challenge this finding and show that it is the result of comparing against a suboptimal hashed implementation—that of the Itanium architecture. We show that, when carefully optimized, hashed page tables in fact outperform existing PWC-aided x86-64 hardware, shortening benchmark runtimes by 1%–27% and 6%–32% in bare-metal and virtualized setups, without resorting to PWCs. We further show that hashed page tables are inherently more scalable than radix designs and are better suited to accommodate the ever increasing memory size; their downside is that they make it more challenging to support such features as superpages.

> *"In all affairs it's a healthy thing now and then to hang a question mark on the things you have long taken for granted." (B. Russell)*

> *"The backbone of the scientific method involves independent validation of existing work. Validation is not a sign of mistrust—it is simply how science is done." (D. Feitelson)*

1. INTRODUCTION

Computer systems typically utilize translation lookaside buffers (TLBs) to accelerate the conversion of virtual addresses to physical addresses. The TLB is consulted upon each memory reference, and if it misses, the hardware retrieves the absent translation using the corresponding page tables and places it in the TLB. In the x86-64 architecture, the page tables are hierarchical, organizing the translations in a 4-level radix tree. Finding a missing translation in this hierarchy—a.k.a. "walking" the page tables—thus incurs an overhead of four memory references. Although the TLB often avoids this overhead (when it hits), TLB misses might still degrade performance substantially and might account for up to 50% of the application runtime [9, 10, 14, 34, 38].

Attempting to mitigate the cost of TLB misses, hardware vendors introduced special page walk caches (PWCs) to accelerate the page table walks [5, 27]. PWCs store partial translations—of prefixes of virtual addresses—thus allowing the hardware to quickly skip over upper levels in the radix tree hierarchy instead of traversing them. In the best-case scenario, when the table walker always hits the PWC, a walk requires only one memory access instead of four. SPEC CPU2006 benchmarks, for example, require 1.13 memory references per walk, on average [9].

Utilizing PWCs to shorten table walks is specifically tailored for the radix tree structure of x86 page tables. Shortening table walks can, in principle, be achieved without resorting to PWCs by replacing the radix page tables with *hashed* page tables, which yield short page walks by design [22, 29, 39]. Assuming no hash collisions, a hashed page table walk consists of only one memory reference rather than four, similarly to the best-case scenario of radix page tables with PWCs.

Arguably, as hashed page tables obviate the need for PWCs, they may constitute an appealing alternative to the commonly used radix page tables design. Counterintuitively, however, an ISCA 2010 study by Barr et al. [9] proclaimed that radix page tables are more efficient than hashed page tables:

> *"... this paper contributes to the age-old discourse concerning the relative effectiveness of different page table organizations. Generally speaking, earlier studies concluded that organizations based on hashing [...] outperformed organizations based upon radix trees for supporting large virtual address spaces [29, 39]. However, these studies did not take into account the possibility of [PWCs] caching page table entries from the higher levels of the radix tree. This paper shows that [PWC-aided] radix tables cause up to 20% fewer total memory accesses and up to 400% [=5x] fewer DRAM accesses than hash-based tables".*

Barr et al. explained that this poor performance is the result of: (1) hashed page tables being "unable to take advantage of the great locality seen in virtual address space usage" since hashing scatters the page table entries (PTEs) associated with virtually-adjacent pages, as opposed to radix tables, which tightly pack such PTEs within the same cache lines; (2) radix page tables having "a smaller page table entry size,

SIGMETRICS '16, June 14 - 18, 2016, Antibes Juan-Les-Pins, France

ISBN 978-1-4503-4266-7/16/06...$15.00

DOI: http://dx.doi.org/10.1145/2896377.2901456

because [hashed page tables] must include a tag in the page table entry", making hashed PTEs consume significantly more cache lines; and (3) the presence of hash collisions, inevitably increasing the number of memory accesses required per walk to "more than one reference to follow a collision chain."

In this study, we find that, in fact, hashed page tables *can* be more performant than radix page tables. We contend that the above findings by Barr et al. do not apply to hashed page tables in general; rather, they are specific to the hashed page table implementation that the authors used for their evaluation—the Itanium architecture [19,25]. We present three optimizations that correspondingly tackle the aforementioned three flaws in this hashed page table design: (1) utilizing a hashing scheme that maps groups of PTEs of virtually-adjacent pages into the same cache line [39]; (2) leveraging properties of hashed paging (inapplicable to radix page tables) that allow us to pack PTEs more densely and thereby fit more of them per cache line; and, consequently, (3) substantially reducing the load factor of the hash table, thus decreasing the number of collisions and lowering the page walk latency.

Our **first contribution**, therefore, is to show that the ISCA 2010 findings are not applicable to hashed page tables in general. We do so by experimentally demonstrating (1) why the Itanium design is suboptimal and (2) how to optimize it to be more performant than the radix design. Our proposed hashed page table reduces benchmark runtimes by 1%–27% compared to the 4-level radix page tables baseline with PWCs as implemented in current x86-64 hardware.

The ISCA 2010 work pertains to bare-metal (non-virtual) setups only. Here we also consider virtualized setups, because they substantially increase the page walk length and amplify the overhead caused by TLB misses. Hardware-assisted virtualization utilizes two layers of page tables, one for the host system and one for the guest virtual machine. The translation process of simultaneously walking these page tables is done in a "two-dimensional" (2D) manner, requiring 24 instead of 4 memory references [5,6,26]. Such 2D page walks make up 5%–90% of the total runtime when TLB miss rates are high, prompting hardware vendors to extend PWC support to virtualized setups [4,28]. Previous work showed a 15%–38% improvement in guest performance by extending the PWCs to store entries from both the guest and the host page tables [11].

Our **second contribution** is the design, optimization, and experimental evaluation of a 2D hashed page table hierarchy suitable for virtualized setups. Our insight is that the number of memory accesses required to satisfy one TLB miss when using a d-dimensional page table is $2^d - 1$ for hashed page tables and $5^d - 1$ for (4-level) radix page tables, making hashed page tables exponentially more efficient. Thus, for a 2D paging system suitable for current virtualized setups ($d = 2$), our hashed page table allows for walks consisting of only 3 (rather than 24) memory references, assuming no hash collisions.

Interestingly, to achieve optimal performance, we find that the hashed page tables of the host and guest should be configured to impose different locality granularities on the PTEs that they house. The host should group PTEs of virtually-adjacent pages at the granularity of cache lines, whereas the guest should group such PTEs at the granularity of pages. With such granularities, a host PTE that maps (part of) the guest's hashed page table can be utilized to access a page-worth of guest PTEs associated with virtually-adjacent guest pages. This design is thus compatible with the locality of reference often observed in real workloads.

Our newly proposed 2D hashed page table design reduces benchmark runtimes by 6%–32% as compared to the 2D radix page table design of existing x86-64 hardware (which employs PWCs that support 2D table walks).

Our **third contribution** is a qualitative assessment of the scalability of the two competing page table designs. Radix page tables rely on PWCs, whose size is physically limited—equivalently to other level-one caches whose speed must be on par with that of the processor (L1, TLB-L1). As emerging workloads access larger memory regions with lower locality, their radix page tables grow larger and harder to cache. We demonstrate the performance consequences of the PWC size limit by simulating unrealistically perfect PWCs (infinite, always hit) and showing that the resulting performance improvement can approach 19% and 35% in bare-metal and virtualized setups, for some workloads. Hashed page tables, in contrast, are insensitive to the application's memory footprint or access pattern, approaching their optimal performance whenever their load factor is low enough to curb hash collisions. They are also practical and viable, whereas optimal, unlimited-size PWCs are not. Although hashed page tables are not without their drawbacks—these will be enumerated and discussed—we nonetheless conclude that the hashed page table design is more scalable than the radix page table design.

2. RADIX PAGE TABLES

2.1 Bare-Metal Address Translation

Modern computer systems typically utilize virtual memory to make application programming easier. Each process exists in its own contiguous virtual address space, so applications do not need to be aware of each other. Other benefits of virtual memory include improved security due to memory isolation, and the ability to use more memory than physically available by swapping data to/from secondary storage. Virtual memory is supported by both software and hardware. The operating system (OS) is responsible for assigning physical memory to virtual memory, and the memory management unit (MMU) carries out the address translation upon each memory access. The commonly used page size in x86 and other architectures is (2^{12} =) 4KB. Therefore, the 12 least significant bits of each address (virtual or physical) serve as the offset within the page, and the remaining bits serve as the page number. The virtual memory subsystem maps virtual page numbers (VPNs) to physical page numbers (PPNs). Per-process VPN to PPN mappings are stored in the page table of the process and are cached by the TLB.

The x86 architecture uses radix page tables, which are also called multilevel, hierarchical, and forward-mapped. As their name suggests, radix page tables store VPN to PPN mappings in a radix tree data structure. On current 64-bit architectures, the tree consists of a four-level hierarchy when standard 4KB pages are used [5,26]. Accordingly, walking the page table in order to perform a VPN to PPN translation requires four memory references. Page sizes larger than 4KB are also supported so as to increase the memory coverage of the TLB [36]. When larger pages are used, the table walk is shortened to three or two steps, depending on the page size.

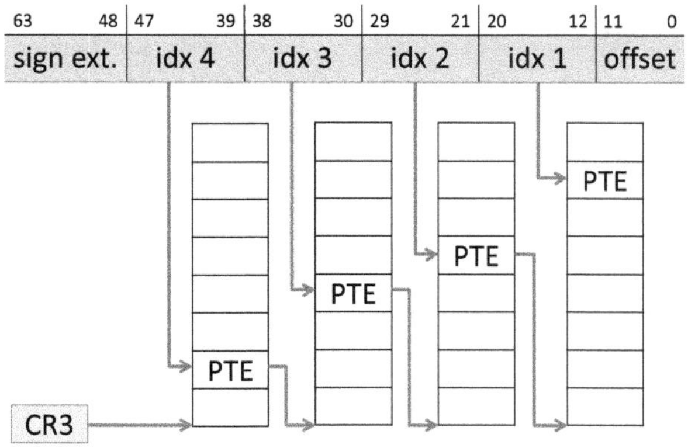

Figure 1: Bare-metal radix page table walk.

63 52	51 12	11 0
0's padding	PPN	attributes

Table 1: Radix PTE structure.

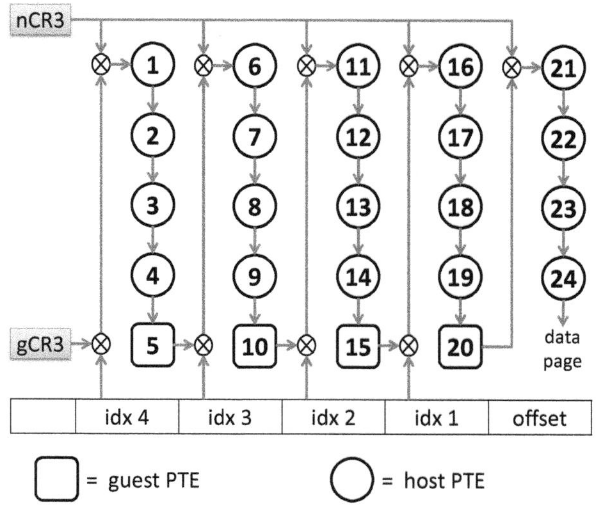

Figure 2: 2D radix page table walk.

Figure 1 depicts the radix page table structure and page walk process. Current x86-64 processors utilize 48-bit virtual addresses and no more than 52 bits for the physical addresses. With 4KB pages, the 48-bit virtual address decomposes into a 36-bit VPN and a 12-bit page offset. The 36-bit VPN further decomposes into four 9-bit indexes, such that each index selects a PTE from its corresponding level in the tree. Each PTE contains the physical address of a table in the next level. The topmost, root level table is pointed to by the CR3 register. PTEs in the lowest level contain the PPNs of the actual program pages. Since the page indexes consist of 9 bits, there are $2^9 = 512$ PTEs in each tree node, and since the tree nodes reside in 4KB pages ($= 2^{12}$ bytes), each PTE consists of $2^{12}/2^9 = 8$ bytes. PTEs encode more information than just the next PPN, in the format shown in Table 1.

Notably, PTEs are stored in the regular L1, L2 and L3 caches to accelerate the page walks [7]. In modern x86-64 processors, these caches consist of 64-byte cache lines. Radix page tables arrange the PTEs contiguously, one after the other, so each cache line encapsulates exactly eight PTEs. Lowest level PTEs that are co-located within a cache line correspond to eight consecutive pages that are contiguous in the virtual memory space. Thus, whenever the MMU accesses a PTE, its seven same-line neighboring PTEs are implicitly prefetched to the data cache hierarchy, and there is a non-negligible chance that these seven will be accessed soon due to spatial locality.

2.2 Two-Dimensional Address Translation

Machine virtualization technology allows multiple guest OSes to run on the same physical host system encapsulated within virtual machines (VMs). Guests do not control the physical host resources, and what they consider to be physical memory addresses are in fact guest physical addresses. The host creates this abstraction by introducing another dimension of address translation, called the nested dimension. In the past, this abstraction was created using "shadow page tables," a software-only technique that involves write-protecting the memory pages that the guest is using as page tables [2]. Each update of these pages triggers an exit to the host, which is thus made aware of the guest's view of its memory. The host in fact maintains another set of pages—the shadow pages—that serve as the real page table hierarchy of the guest.

Shadow page tables are difficult to implement and induce substantial overheads caused by the repeated guest-host switches upon modifications of write-protected pages [12, 13]. These drawbacks motivated chip vendors to provide hardware constructs that directly support the host in its efforts to efficiently maintain the illusion that guest OSes control the physical memory. Both AMD and Intel have implemented *nested paging* [4, 28], which supports two levels of address translation. The guest maintains a set of page tables that map between guest virtual addresses (GVAs) to guest physical addresses (GPAs). The host maintains a different set of page tables that map GPAs to host physical addresses (HPAs). The hardware is responsible for seamlessly "concatenating" the two layers of translation, by performing a *two-dimensional page walk* (as opposed to the one-dimensional page walk in bare-metal setups). Nested paging lets the guest manage its own page tables and eliminates the need for host intervention. The downside is that nested paging squares the number of memory references required to obtain a translation.

Figure 2 outlines a 2D page walk in the x86-64 architecture. The MMU references the memory hierarchy 24 times in the order given by the numbered shapes. The squares (numbered 5, 10, 15, and 20) denote the guest PTEs, and the circles (numbered 1–4, 6–9, 11–14, 16–19, and 21–24) denote the host PTEs. The four references to guest PTEs are analogous to the four references in the 1D page walk. Bare-metal page walks access PTEs by their physical addresses, whereas guests access PTEs by their GPAs. Each of these four GPAs is translated with a nested page walk to produce the HPA of the corresponding PTE. The guest page walk outcome is a fifth GPA that points to the requested data page. It requires an additional nested page walk before the page walk process is complete (numbered 21–24). Note that 2D page walks make use of two separate CR3 registers for the guest and the nested dimensions. The guest CR3 register and the virtual page number combine to start the guest page table walk. The nested CR3 register is used five times to initialize each of the five nested page table walks.

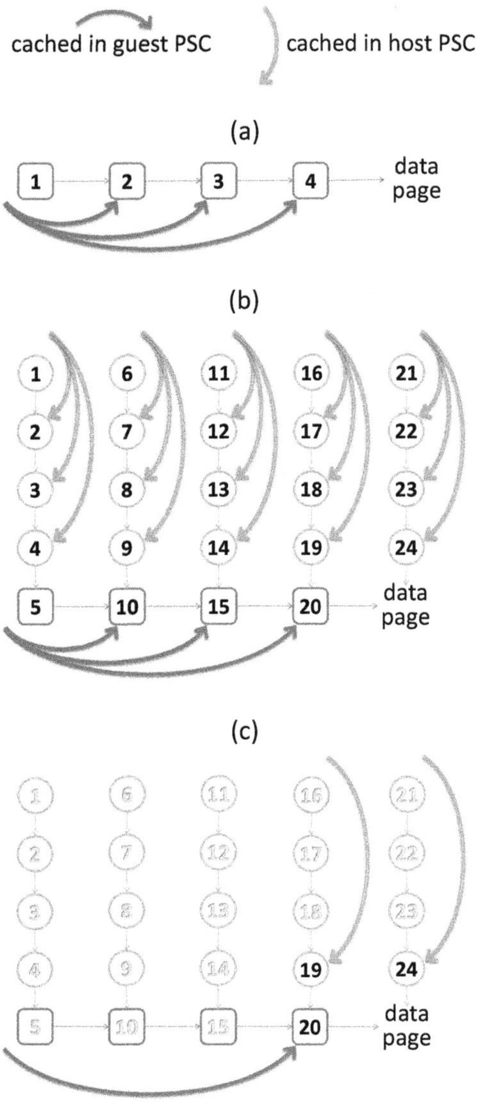

Figure 3: Page walk caches.

3. PAGE WALK CACHES

Radix page table walks require expensive memory references, and 2D page walks all the more. This motivated hardware vendors to present MMU caches, which accelerate address translation by caching parts of the page walk process. However, as with every cache, their performance degrades when the working set of partial translations is too large. In this section, we survey the existing implementations of MMU caches in bare-metal and virtualized hardware. To the best of our knowledge, Intel has not published detailed information on the x86-64 hardware that speeds up 2D page walks. We therefore introduce a simple yet not previously reported MMU cache design, which we set as the Intel baseline design for our evaluation in section 5.

3.1 Caching One-Dimensional Page Walks

MMU caches accelerate bare-metal page walks [9] by storing PTEs from the higher levels of the radix tree in small low-latency caches. Higher level PTEs are good cache candidates because they map large regions of virtual memory, so many workloads use only a small set of them with considerable reuse. PTEs from the lowest level are harder to cache; indeed, TLBs utilize hundreds of entries to effectively cache the lowest level PTEs, whereas MMU caches typically contain dozens of entries.

AMD and Intel provide different implementations of MMU caches. AMD's *page walk caches* (PWCs) tag the PTEs with their physical addresses in memory, so the PWC serves as a dedicated "L1D cache" for page walks.[1] When the MMU finds a PTE in the page walk cache, it immediately reads it and saves a reference to the memory hierarchy. Intel's *paging-structure caches* (PSCs) tag the PTEs with prefixes of the virtual page number corresponding to their location in the radix tree. That is, PTEs from the topmost level are tagged by the uppermost 9-bit index from the VPN, PTEs from the next level are tagged by two 9-bit indexes, and PTEs from the third level are tagged by three 9-bit indexes. If the MMU finds a PTE in the paging-structure cache, the page walk process can begin from that PTE. Therefore, the MMU searches for an entry with the longest matching tag, to shorten the page walk as much as possible. Figure 3(a) illustrates a radix page walk process that utilizes a paging structure cache. In the best-case scenario, when a third level PTE is found in the MMU cache, the page walk process skips over three levels in the tree and directly accesses the lowest level PTE.

3.2 Caching Two-Dimensional Page Walks

As stated earlier, 2D radix page tables lengthen the page walk to 24 memory references. Thus, extending MMU caches to speed up 2D page walks is crucial. AMD's page walk caches are physically tagged, so they can be extended to hold guest and host PTEs in the same cache according to their host physical addresses. Indeed, AMD researchers showed that caching PTEs from the guest and host dimension in the PWC brings a 15%–38% improvement in guest performance [11].

Our performance measurements on an Intel platform indicate that Intel's microarchitectures also implement hardware that accelerates 2D page walks. Alas, we do not know the exact implementation details of that hardware. We therefore offer a new, readily-implementable extension of Intel's PSCs, which boosts 2D page walks. Because Intel's paging structure caches tag PTEs with their guest virtual addresses, they can only keep guest PTEs. We propose to add another, separate PSC that stores host PTEs tagged by their host virtual addresses. Figure 3(b) depicts a 2D page walk process in a processor that utilizes two PSCs for the guest and host. The two PSCs operate in the guest and host dimensions independently and decrease the overall page walk latency. In the best-case scenario, depicted in Figure 3(c), we hit both PSCs, and the 2D page walk shortens to only three memory references. Since our proposed design is a straightforward generalization of Intel's microarchitecture, we will further assume it is the nominal Intel design.

Previous works [9, 14] explored the different types of MMU caches and showed that they achieve similar performance gains. Our simulation results corroborate this finding; thus we examine only PSCs in our experiments and assume the same analysis can be applied to other kinds of MMU caches. For simplicity, we will use the terms "MMU caches," "page walk caches," and "paging structure caches" interchangeably.

[1] We remark that AMD microarchitectures caches PTEs in the L2 and L3 caches only [11].

4. HASHED PAGE TABLES

Hashed page tables [22], as their name suggests, store mappings from virtual to physical pages in a hash table. When assuming no hash collisions, only one memory access is required for address translation, regardless of the workload's memory consumption or access pattern. As radix page walks involve four memory references, hashed page tables should perform better than radix page tables, without requiring PWCs. But recent results by Barr et al. [9] surprisingly found that PWC-aided radix page tables are superior to hashed page tables, "increas[ing] the number of DRAM accesses per walk by over 400%."[2] The authors identified three drawbacks of hashed page tables underlying this poor performance: (1) hashing scatters the mappings of consecutive pages in different cache lines, so hashed page tables are unable to leverage the spatial locality seen in many workloads; (2) hashed PTEs are bigger than radix PTEs, leading to higher memory usage; and (3) hash collisions occur frequently, resulting in more memory references per page walk.

We contend that these drawbacks are specific to the Itanium design that Barr et al. used for their evaluation [19, 25]. We demonstrate that these drawbacks do not apply to hashed paging in general, and that hashed page tables can be optimized through a series of improvements that make them better performing than PWC-aided radix page tables. In this section, we first describe the basic Itanium design assessed by Barr et al. [9] (§4.1). We then point out the problems in this design (§4.2) and propose optimizations that address them (§4.3). Last, we describe how hashed page tables can be applied in virtual systems, and how they can shrink the 2D page walk cost (§4.4).

4.1 The Basic Design

The Itanium architecture utilizes a hashed page table when its virtual hash page table (VHPT) is configured to use "long format" PTEs [19, 25]. The VHPT resides in the virtual memory space, which the OS pins to the physical memory. The long format PTEs consist of 32 bytes that house full translation information, including protection keys, page sizes, and reserved bits for software use. The latter may store any value, notably an address that points to a collision chain. The Itanium architecture explicitly requires the OS's involvement on hash collisions. The hardware page walker hashes into a single table slot, raising a TLB miss fault that invokes an OS handler upon a hash collision. The OS can then resolve the collision as it pleases, e.g., by searching for the translation somewhere else in the hash table, or by using some auxiliary OS-defined data structure.

Barr et al. chose the latter alternative. They utilized "chain tables", which hold PTEs whose hash slots were already taken, resolving hash collisions with the *closed addressing* method [15]. With this design, entries that hash to the same table slot form a collision chain, which is a simple linked list where each entry points to the next. The chain's head is stored directly in the table, and the other nodes are stored in the aforementioned chain table data structure. Both the hash table and the chain table are allocated upon startup. To avoid dynamic resizing, the maximal number of PTEs should be known. When assuming no sharing of physical pages between processes, this number is bounded by the number of physical pages [29]. Thus, if the chain table size is set to this maximal number of PTEs, no dynamic resizing is needed.

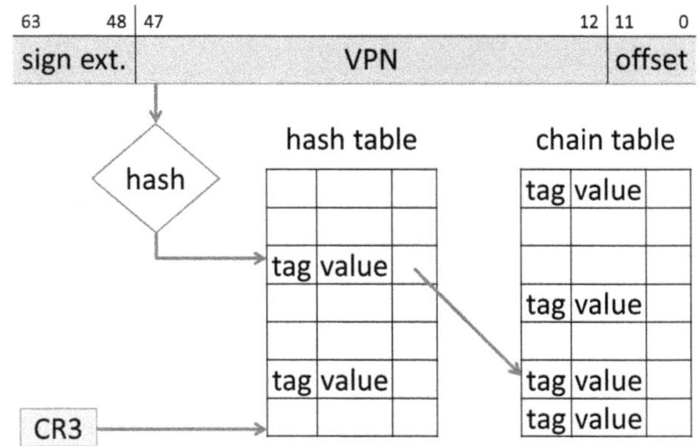

Figure 4: Hashed page table utilizing closed addressing.

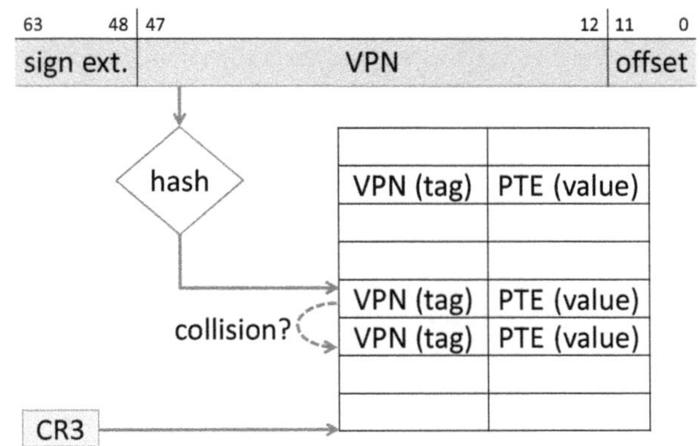

Figure 5: Hashed page table utilizing open addressing.

Figure 4 depicts the Itanium hashed page table variant that was used by Barr et al. Unlike the per-process radix page tables, there is a single, big hashed page table shared among all processes, pointed to by the CR3 register. Each slot in the hash table consists of three fields: tag (VPN), value (PTE), and a pointer to the next node in the collision chain. When translating an address, the 36-bit VPN hashes to some slot, and it is then compared to the tag stored in that slot to detect if a hash collision has occurred. If the tag mismatches, the next node in the collision chain is examined. The search continues until a match is found or the chain ends, indicating that the element is not in the table. Our simulation of the basic Itanium design reproduces the methodology of Barr et al., which does not account for the additional overheads incurred due to chain table lookups being handled by software. (Subsequent simulated versions implement the search entirely in hardware, as will be later explained.)

4.2 Flaws of the Basic Design

The basic hashed design as implemented in the Itanium architecture has several weaknesses. First, the hashed page table does not cache the PTEs effectively since it scatters the PTEs of virtually adjacent pages to non-adjacent table slots that reside in distinct cache lines. Radix page tables, on the other hand, keep the mappings of virtually adjacent pages contiguously in the physical memory, tightly packing

[2]The primary focus of the paper by Barr et al. was, in fact, on optimizing PWCs.

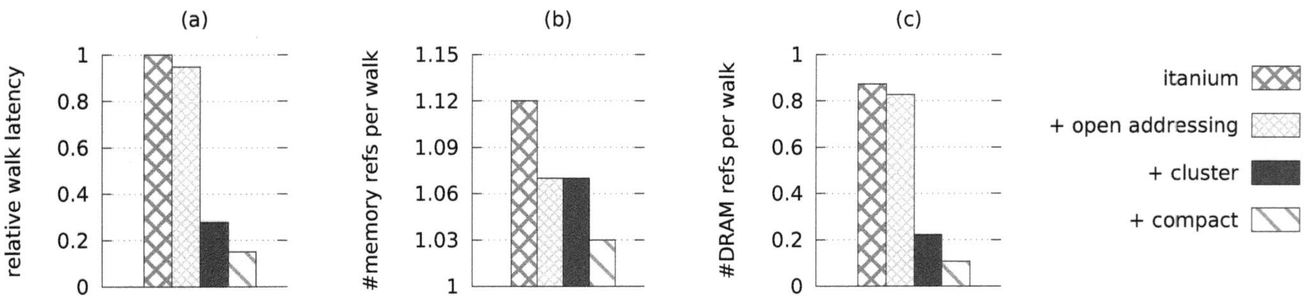

Figure 6: Optimizing the hashed page table gradually cuts down the walk latency and the number of references to the memory and DRAM. (Showing results for the 433.milc benchmark in bare-metal setup.)

their PTEs in cache lines. When one page is referenced, it is often the case that its virtually neighboring pages will soon be accessed as well, because many workloads exhibit locality of reference. Correspondingly, when one PTE is referenced, there is a greater chance that the PTEs of virtually adjacent pages will be referenced soon. Consequently, when the page walker references a radix PTE and inserts it into the cache, it also inserts the PTEs of neighboring pages, which reside in the same cache line, thereby eliminating cache misses in future page walks. Hashed designs, on the other hand, are less likely to prefetch PTEs of neighboring pages into the cache. They thus increase the number of costly DRAM references due to cache misses.

Hashed page tables also require additional memory since they must keep the tags and chain pointers to resolve potential hash collisions. In the Itanium design, the 32-bytes long PTE houses the "short" 8-byte PTE version along with its matching 36-bit VPN and an 8-byte chain pointer. A 64-byte cache line thus contains exactly two long PTE slots, in contrast to the radix page table design whereby each cache line contains eight PTEs. Hashed performance therefore degrades because the caches can hold four times fewer hashed PTEs than radix PTEs. Hashed page tables reference a larger working set of cache lines than do radix designs, so they may cause more cache misses during page walks.

The rate of hash table collisions is mainly determined by the ratio of occupied slots to the total number of slots, also called the *load factor* [15]. The hash table performance degrades as the load factor grows, since more occupied slots increase the likelihood that different elements will hash to the same slot. Importantly, for a fixed load factor, the rate of hash collisions is not affected by the workload memory footprint or access pattern, if uniform hashing is assumed [15]. The basic design sets the maximum load factor to 1/2 by allocating a hash table with twice the number of slots required to map the resident physical pages. That is, two 32-byte slots are allocated for each 4KB page in the physical memory. The hash table thus consumes 1.6% of the physical memory.

Another drawback of the Itanium hashed page table is that it requires an additional data structure—the chain table. Ideally, without hash collisions, the chain table is unnecessary since the hash table has enough space to contain all the PTEs. But hash collisions cannot be completely eliminated, so some memory must be allocated to the chain table. Radix designs are thus more space efficient, because they do not require additional data structures.

4.3 Optimizations

We now describe three optimizations aimed at remedying the flaws of the basic Itanium design. Figure 6 shows that the improvements reduce the page walk latency, as well as the number of references to the memory and the DRAM, for a specific SPEC CPU2006 benchmark (433.milc). We present the results for a single benchmark since the other benchmarks exhibit the same qualitative behavior.

Open Addressing

Our first proposal is to get rid of the wasteful chain table by switching to the *open addressing* method [15], which stores all PTEs in the hash table slots. Figure 5 illustrates the hashed page table structure and hashed page walk process in the open addressing scheme. Each slot in the hash table consists of three fields: tag (VPN), value (PTE), and an "empty" bit to mark a free slot. The chain pointers are no longer used to resolve hash collisions; when a tag mismatch occurs, the next slot in the hash table is examined. The search ends when a match is found or an empty slot is reached, indicating that the element is not found in the table.

Besides saving the memory required by the chain table, the open addressing scheme has another, more important advantage: it discards the chain pointers that lie inside PTEs. We can therefore shrink the table slots of the open addressing design to 16 bytes, as each slot contains only a 36-bit VPN and its matching 8-byte PTE. Consequently, the hashed page table size is cut by half. We can turn this space we saved to good use by lowering the load factor and shortening the hash table lookup. The open addressing design in Figure 6 sets the load factor to 1/4, without using additional memory over the basic Itanium design. Decreasing the load factor indeed lowers the average number of memory references per walk, as can be seen in Figure 6(b).

PTE Clustering

Our second proposal is to utilize *clustered page tables*—a hashed page tables variant that pack the mappings of consecutive pages in the same hash table slot [39], thereby making the page table easier to cache for workloads with a high degree of locality. The number of PTEs that occupy the same slot is called the *clustering factor*. It is normally chosen to be the largest possible such that each table slot fits into a single cache line. If the table slots are smaller than a cache line, the clustered page table does not exploit the spatial locality to its maximum. And if the table slots are bigger than a

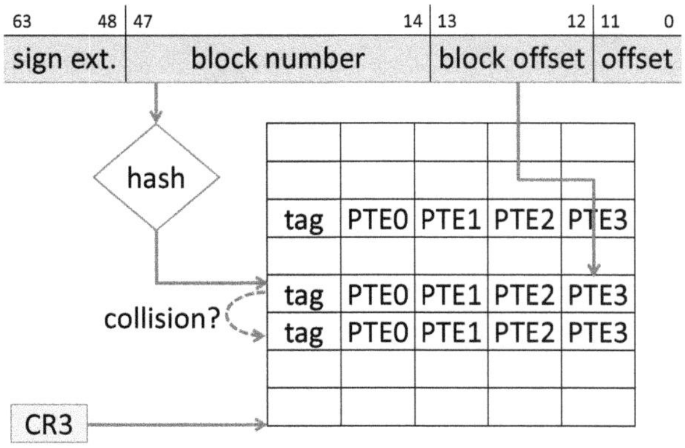

Figure 7: Clustered page table walk.

cache line, the tag (block number) and the value (PTE) may reside in different lines, so probing a single slot may require two memory references. Because hashed PTEs are 16 bytes long, and since x86-64 processors use 64-byte cache lines, the optimal clustering factor is four; radix designs still pack twice more, that is, eight PTEs per cache line.

Figure 7 depicts the clustered page table structure and the clustered page walk process. The hash table lookup follows that of hashed page tables with minor changes. The 36-bit VPN decomposes to a page block number (bits 14:47) and page block offset (bits 12:13). The block number hashes to a table slot, and the block offset indexes into the array of PTEs stored in the slot. When a mismatch occurs between the block number and the tag in the slot, the next slot in the table is examined. Each hash table slot is 64 bytes long, to hold a single tag (34-bit block number) and four values (four PTEs, 8 bytes each).

Figure 6(c) provides the average number of DRAM references per walk. We see that clustering the PTEs as was just described takes advantage of the locality seen in this workload and generates fewer DRAM references than the basic design.

PTE Compaction

We propose a new technique that further improves hashed page tables by compacting eight adjacent PTEs in a single 64-byte cache line, resulting in the spatial locality of hashed page tables similar to that of the x86-64 radix page tables. The clustered page tables, as were previously defined, cannot pack eight PTEs and a tag in a single cache line, since PTEs are 8 bytes long. But we can exploit the unused topmost bits of each PTE and store the tag in this unused space. Specifically, the x86-64 architecture reserves bits 52:63 of the PTE as available for use by the system software in long addressing mode [5]. If we group all the available bits from the eight PTEs, we have more than enough space to store the 33-bit page block number, which serves as the tag. Table 2 shows the possible layout of a hash table slot containing eight PTEs. We use 8 bytes for the tag and 7 bytes for each of the eight PTEs. This layout is valid even for architectures with 56-bit physical addresses, i.e., 64 petabytes of physical memory, which is more than enough for the foreseeable future. Note that the compaction technique can only be applied in tandem with clustered page tables, since they amortize the space overhead of the tag over many PTEs.

8 B	7 B	7 B		7 B	7 B
tag	PTE0	PTE1	...	PTE6	PTE7

Table 2: Compact cluster of PTEs.

Compacting the PTEs cuts the number of hash table slots by half, as each slot now holds eight PTEs instead of four. If we fix the load factor, compaction thus saves half the memory used by the hashed page table. Alternatively, we can decrease the load factor and reduce the hash table lookup complexity. The compact design in Figure 6 implements the compaction of eight PTEs in a cache line and sets the load factor to 1/8, bringing the average page walk cost close to a single memory reference per walk, without using additional memory over the previous designs. We see that it also exploits the spatial locality and further reduces the number of DRAM references.

Note that radix paging hardware cannot easily implement a compaction scheme that derives benefit from the unused bits in the PTEs. Current radix hardware packs eight PTEs in a cache line, and it can pack two additional PTEs if the unused bits were utilized. That is, the radix hardware can pack a maximum of 10 PTEs in a cache line and hence no more than 640 PTEs in a 4KB page. But trying to pack 640 PTEs in a page will demand a more complex calculation of the radix tree indexes, via a sequence of three divide and modulo operations, which cannot be parallelized. Current radix paging hardware exploits the fact that each page contains a power-of-two number of PTEs to immediately extract the indexes to the radix tables without having to calculate them. Specifically, each 4KB page contains exactly 512 PTEs, and the 36-bit virtual page number directly decomposes to the four 9-bit radix tree indexes, as explained in section 2.

> TO SUMMARIZE: Itanium hashed page tables can be improved via three optimizations. First, utilizing an open, rather than closed addressing scheme shrinks the table slots and reduces the load factor. Second, clustering adjacent PTEs leverages the spatial locality seen in many workloads. Third, compacting the PTEs makes it possible to pack eight PTEs per cache line, similarly to the x86-64 radix design, thereby (i) equalizing the number of cache lines occupied by the two virtual memory implementations, as well as (ii) further decreasing the load factor and eliminating almost all hash collisions.

In section 5, we show that our optimized hashed page tables indeed reduce benchmark runtimes by 1%–27% compared to x86-64 PWC-aided radix page tables.

4.4 Two-Dimensional Hashed Page Tables

Hashed page tables reduce the page walk cost in bare-metal setups, so they may be able to shorten 2D page walks in virtualized setups as well. We now design and optimize 2D hashed page tables, which implement the guest and the host page tables with hashed schemes. Figure 8 outlines a 2D hashed page walk, which references the memory hierarchy three times per TLB miss, assuming no hash collisions. The 36-bit VPN hashes to a slot in the guest page table. This index combines with the guest CR3 register to generate the GPA of the guest PTE. We perform a nested page walk (step 1 in the figure) to translate the GPA to a HPA. Only then can we access the guest PTE (step 2 in the figure) and discover

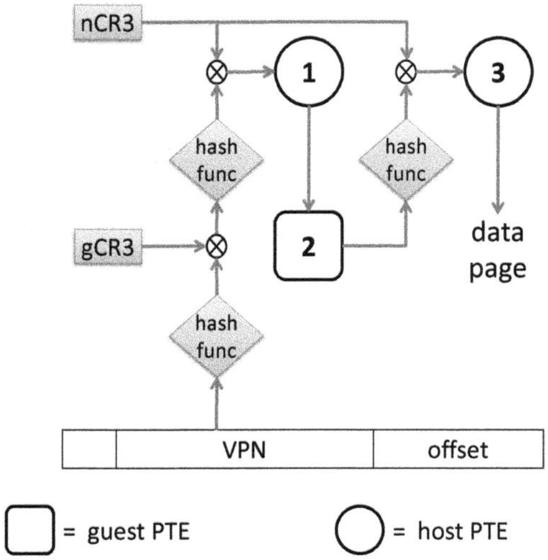

Figure 8: 2D hashed page table walk.

the GPA of the data page. We finish the page walk process with a second nested page walk (step 3 in the figure), which finds the HPA of the data page. The nested CR3 register is used two times during the page walk to initialize each of the two nested page table walks.

A 2D hashed page table is no more than two separate 1D hashed page tables for the guest and the host. We applied the three optimizations that we proposed for 1D hashed paging to both the guest and the host page tables. We initially believed that these two page tables should be tuned the same, i.e., adopting the open addressing scheme, clustering and compacting eight PTEs in a cache line, and thereby reducing the load factor to 1/8. To validate our belief, we scanned the design space of 2D hashed page tables. Surprisingly, we discovered that the guest and host page tables should be configured differently to realize the full potential of 2D hashed page tables.

Our analysis helped us to spot a subtle difference between the guest and the host page tables: the former maps the application pages, whereas the latter also maps the pages assigned to the guest page table. The host page table is able to leverage the locality of reference to the guest page table in the same way it benefits from locality in the application data. When the guest page table is scattered over many pages (in the host address space), the host page table keeps that many translations to map these pages. To minimize the number of required host translations, we should attempt to minimize the number of pages used by the guest page table. Therefore, we increase the clustering factor of the guest page table from 8 to 512, such that the mappings of each group of 512 consecutive pages will condense into a single page instead of lying in multiple pages. Figure 9 indicates that increasing the clustering factor of the guest page table from 8 to 512 reduces the page walk latency (for a specific benchmark).

Furthermore, when the host page table clusters contiguous translations in the same cache line, it can leverage locality at granularity of several pages. Assuming the host page table uses a clustering factor of 8, when the guest page table is spread over many blocks of 8 pages, the host translations consume more cache lines. To minimize the working set of cache lines that hold host page table mappings, we should attempt to minimize the number of 8-page blocks used by the guest page table. Therefore, we increase the clustering factor of the guest page table even further, from 512 to 4096. Figure 9 shows that increasing the guest clustering factor even further to 4096 reduces the page walk latency.

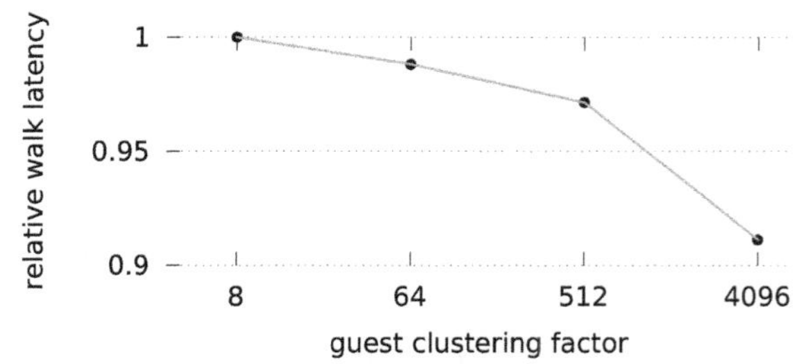

Figure 9: The walk latency of 2D hashed page table decreases as the guest clustering increases.

To SUMMARIZE: In virtualized setups, the hashed paging scheme is more efficient than radix paging, because it incurs a TLB miss penalty of only 3 (rather than 24) memory references, assuming no hash collisions. To further improve their performance, we find that 2D hashed page tables should also cluster guest PTEs in granularity of several pages.

In section 5, we show that our newly proposed 2D hashed page tables reduce benchmark runtimes by 6%–32% as compared to the current x86-64 hardware (which employs PWCs that support 2D table walks).

5. HASHED VERSUS RADIX PAGING

In this section, we first describe the methodology we use to evaluate page table designs. Next, we measure the performance gap between present x86-64 hardware and perfect, unrealistic PWCs. We then compare hashed paging to radix paging; our results show that hashed page tables can bring notable performance benefits in bare-metal and virtualized setups. Finally, we enumerate the practical drawbacks and problems of hashed paging.

5.1 Methodology

Our goal is to estimate the performance of nonexistent hardware, such as the proposed hashed page tables or radix paging with perfect PWCs. To this end, we apply the de facto methodology of recent microarchitectural research concerning virtual memory [10, 14, 18]. First, we develop an approximate performance model, which assumes, for simplicity, that the application runtime (measured in cycles) is a linear function of the *walk cycles*, i.e., the cycles spent during page walks:

$$runtime = A * walk\_cycles + B.$$

The model parameters A, B are benchmark specific, and we find them by measuring a real system running each benchmark separately. Second, we calculate the walk cycles of new page table designs from our memory simulator, which we implemented and thoroughly tested. Last, we plug the simulation results into the linear performance model to predict the runtime of the benchmarks on these new designs.

The performance model is gauged for each benchmark individually with experiments conducted on a Linux server equipped with an Intel processor, as outlined in Table 3. Our Intel processor provides monitoring hardware that is able to measure the cycles spent during page walks (events 0x0408, x0449 in the Sandy Bridge microarchitecture [27]). The connection between the walk cycles and the application runtime is not immediate, as the walk cycles overlap with other processor activities in modern, pipelined, out-of-order CPUs. But the walk cycles certainly hint at the application performance; thus our assumption that the relationship is linear. Finding the model parameters A, B is simple given two points on the line. We obtain the first point from measurement with the default 4KB pages used, and the second point after configuring the system to use 2MB pages via the Transparent Huge Pages feature [1].

Having the performance curve, we can now apply it to evaluate several hardware designs. We develop a trace-based simulator, and generate traces dynamically with Intel's Pin binary instrumentation tool [31, 32, 34]. For each memory reference in the trace, the simulator initially consults the TLB for address translation, walks the page table hierarchy upon a TLB miss, and then performs the memory access. The simulator outputs the number of references to all the relevant hardware structures (L1/L2 TLB, L1 data cache, L2/L3 caches, DRAM, and PWCs when available). The walk cycles are then calculated via summing the access latencies to each hardware component, weighted by the access frequency. The microarchitecture parameters were taken from the closely related studies by Bhattacharjee et al. [14] and Gandhi et al. [18] as outlined in Table 3.

We note that memory simulators are able to produce accurate estimations of the walk cycles, because the page walk process is sequential, where each reference to the memory hierarchy depends on the previous one. We sample a small, representative subset of the full memory address trace following the statistical sampling technique by Wunderlich et al. [40]; we verified that our sampling simulator is accurate, yielding cycle estimates within $\pm 5\%$ of the full run outcome with 95% confidence. The trace-based approach, together with sampling, enables us to evaluate new architecture designs relatively quickly. Average programs run 5x–50x slower under the simulator, so we can inspect realistic workloads with big memory footprints. As Pin is limited to instrumentation in user mode only, we measured the TLB misses and the walk cycles invoked by the kernel via performance counters and verified that they are negligible.

bare-metal system		
processor	dual-socket Intel Xeon E5-2420 (SandyBridge), 6 cores/socket, 2 threads/core, 1.90 GHz	
memory hierarchy	component	latency [cycles]
	64 KB L1 data cache (per thread)	4
	64 KB L1 inst. cache (per thread)	not simulated
	512 KB L2 cache (per core)	12
	15 MB L3 cache (per chip)	30
	96 GB DDR2 SDRAM	100
TLB	64 entries L1 data TLB 128 entries L1 instruction TLB (not simulated) 512 entries L2 TLB all TLBs are 4-way associative	
PSC	2 entries PML4 cache, 4 entries PDP cache 32 entries PDE cache, 4-way associative all caches have 2 cycles access latency	
operating system	Ubuntu 14.04.2 LTS, kernel version 3.13.0-55	
fully virtualized system		
host	QEMU emulator version 2.0.0 with KVM support	
PSCs	separate PSCs for the guest and the host, each of the same size as the bare-metal PSC	
operating system	Ubuntu 14.04.2 LTS, kernel version 3.13.0-55 for both the guest and the host	

Table 3: Details of the experimental platform; the microarchitectural parameters were also used in the simulator.

5.2 Radix Paging with PWCs Does Not Scale

Perfect PWCs, which theoretically eliminate all misses, cut down bare-metal and virtualized page walks considerably, to one and three memory references per walk, respectively. But realistic PWCs have finite sizes that limit their performance. Our analysis shows that the gap between the performance of actual (x86-64) and ideal (infinite and always hit) PWCs can be significant in memory intensive workloads, as depicted in Figure 10 for three benchmark suites. The first suite is the canonical **SPEC CPU2006** [20], whose benchmarks typically exhibit negligible TLB miss rates and hence are largely unaffected by PWCs. We therefore limit our analysis to only those benchmarks that are sensitive to PWC misses, enjoying a performance improvement of at least 1% when PWCs are perfect—these are mcf, cactusADM, and xalancbmk. The performance of the remaining 28 SPEC CPU2006 benchmarks neither improves nor degrades when employing perfect PWCs (or our optimized hashed design). The second benchmark suite is **Graph500** [8, 35], which ships with several implementations and a scalable input generator; we use the shared memory (OpenMP) version with eight threads, and we test three different input sizes: 4GB, 8GB, and 16GB. The third suite is **GUPS** [30, 33], which likely approximates an upper bound on the performance improvement that perfect PWCs offer, randomly accessing a large in-memory table; we use three table sizes: 2GB, 8GB, and 32GB.

Figure 10 shows that PWC misses degrade the performance by up to 19% and 35% in bare-metal and virtualized setups. When focusing on Graph500 and GUPS, we see that the effectiveness of the PWCs monotonically drops due to (1) bigger memory footprints (compare benchmarks in the same suite) and (2) lower locality of reference (compare GUPS benchmarks to Graph500 benchmarks with similar/smaller size).

Figure 10 further demonstrates that the gap between real and ideal PWCs is larger in the virtualized case, because 2D radix page walks are longer and harder to cache. We generalize this observation and qualitatively show that radix paging scales poorly as more layers of virtualization are added. Specifically, we prove that the *page walk length* (number of memory references required to obtain a translation) grows exponentially with the number of virtualization layers. For a nested setup with d virtualization layers and a page walk length of L in each layer, we show that the *overall* page walk length is $(L+1)^d - 1$. Consequently, the overall page walk length in a d-dimensional page table is $5^d - 1$ for radix paging, whereas it is $2^d - 1$ for hashed paging, assuming no hash collisions. Thus, 2D radix page walks are exponentially longer, and the effectiveness of the PWC drops as it struggles to cache these longer walks.

The formula for the d-dimensional overall page walk length is proved by induction. The base case ($d = 1$) is trivial. The inductive step assumes (1) a d-dimensional nested virtualiza-

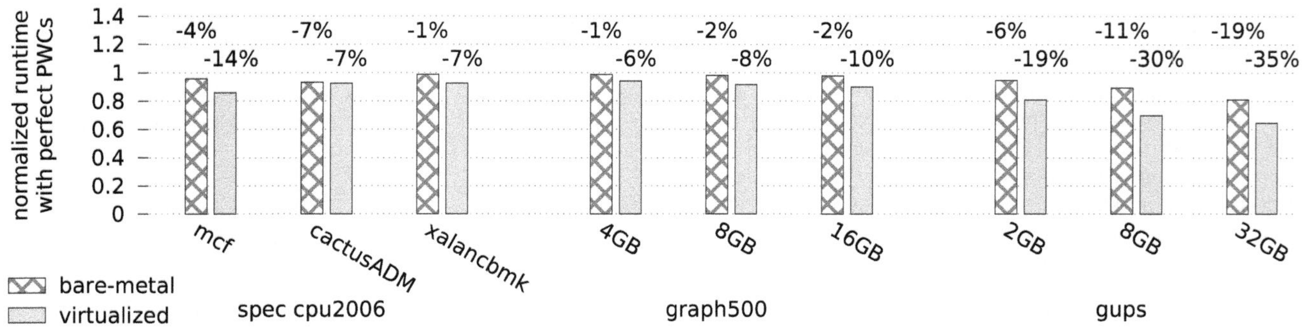

Figure 10: Simulating perfect PWCs (infinite and always hit) as compared to actual PWCs. Clearly, memory intensive workloads could achieve notable improvement gains if all PWC misses were eliminated.

tion hierarchy, denoted g, with an overall page walk length of $L_g = (L+1)^d - 1$, and (2) a host h with page walk length of $L_h = L$. With this notation, our formula trivially stems from the following lemma.

LEMMA 1. *If we host g on top of h, then the overall page walk length will become $(L_g + 1) \cdot (L_h + 1) - 1$.*

PROOF. Before hosting g on top of h, our induction hypothesis implies that a virtual memory reference by g induces $L_g + 1$ physical memory references: L_g for the table walk, plus one for the application data pointed to by the PTE at the end of the walk. Likewise, a virtual memory reference by h induces $L_h + 1$ physical memory references. When hosting g's nested hierarchy on top of h, each of the $L_g + 1$ guest physical references must now be translated to host physical addresses, so we end up with $(L_g + 1) \cdot (L_h + 1)$ references to the physical memory, which includes the access to the application data at the end of the table walk. We thus subtract one memory reference from this result. □

5.3 Hashed Paging Performs Better

Our two competing designs are hashed paging and radix paging with PWCs. The comparison between them is not "fair," since the latter employs additional cache structures—the PWCs—skewing the odds in its favor. Still, we find that hashed page tables perform better than radix tables for the workloads tested. (Recall that we focus on workloads that stress the TLB and PWCs; for workloads that experience few TLB and PWC misses, as do most SPEC CPU2006 benchmarks, hashed paging and radix paging perform similarly.) Figure 11 depicts the runtime improvement achieved by using hashed paging rather than radix paging with PWCs. The Graph500 and GUPS benchmarks show larger improvement gains as the memory footprint grows, because the PWC efficiency degrades, while hashed page tables require the same number of memory references per walk. The figure also confirms that the improvement opportunity from using hashed page tables is greater in the virtualized case, since hashed paging is exponentially more efficient, as was discussed above.

We now provide an in-depth analysis of hashed paging performance by comparing Figure 11 to Figure 10—the differences are summarized in Table 4. We see that, for the Graph500 and GUPS benchmarks, perfect PWCs reduce the runtime more than hashed page tables. The reason for this performance gap is the difference in the page walk length. Radix paging with perfect PWCs require 1 and 3 memory references per walk in bare-metal and virtualized setups, while hashed page tables exhibit hash collisions and thus require a few more, that is, 1.08 and 3.33 references on average. Our results confirm that reducing the hash table load factor and, hence, decreasing the hash collision rate closes the gap between the two designs.

Interestingly, Table 4 shows that hashed paging outperforms perfect PWCs for the three SPEC CPU2006 benchmarks that we examined. Radix paging with PWCs incurs additional cycles to search the PWCs, whereas hashed paging does not. Our analysis indicates that this PWC overhead, albeit small, is noticeable in the mcf and xalancbmk benchmarks. Table 4 also reveals that hashed paging cuts the cactusADM bare-metal runtime by 27%, whereas the perfect PWCs design reduces it by 7%. This significant performance gap merits further discussion, as it cannot be attributed to the PWC latency alone.

CactusADM solves a set of partial differential equations. The main loop references, on each iteration, multiple array elements whose virtual addresses are separated by a constant stride [21]. Since radix page tables map virtual addresses contiguously, the PTEs matching these virtual addresses also reside in physical addresses separated by a constant stride. And so, if the PTEs map to the same set in the data caches on the first iteration, they will conflict again on each subsequent iteration. Our analysis indicates that the lowest level PTEs, which are left out of the PWCs, indeed conflict in the L1 data cache due to this access pattern. We experimentally substantiated this finding by verifying that an (impractical) fully associative L1 data cache almost completely eliminates the L1 misses during page walks. Hashed page tables, on the other hand, are less sensitive to such cache pathologies because they randomly scatter the PTEs in the physical memory allocated to the hash table, lowering the probability for successive misses due to cache conflicts. The hashed paging randomization reduces the likelihood of encountering a worst-case input, similarly to the memory layout randomization that is used in STABILIZER to get predictable performance [16].

TO SUMMARIZE: The performance of radix page tables depends on PWCs, so their effectiveness degrades when workloads access larger and larger memory regions with lower locality. In contrast, our optimized hashed page tables cut the page walk overhead without resorting to PWCs, as their performance is unaffected by the memory footprint or the access pattern of the application.

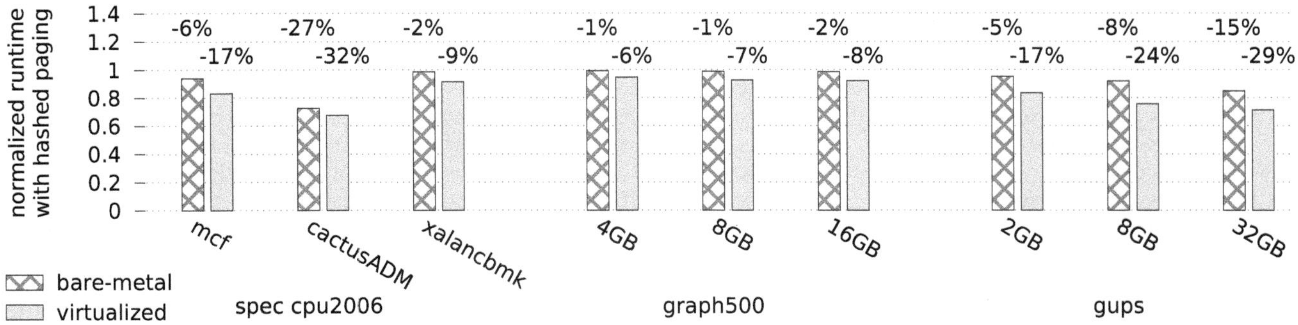

Figure 11: Normalized benchmark runtimes of hashed paging relative to radix paging with (real) PWCs.

benchmark	*bare-metal*		*virtualized*	
	perfect PWCs	*hashed paging*	*perfect PWCs*	*hashed paging*
SPEC mcf	-4%	-6%	-14%	-17%
SPEC cactusADM	-7%	-27%	-7%	-32%
SPEC xalancbmk	-1%	-2%	-7%	-9%
graph500 4GB	-1%	-1%	-6%	-6%
graph500 8GB	-2%	-1%	-8%	-7%
graph500 16GB	-2%	-2%	-10%	-8%
GUPS 2GB	-6%	-5%	-19%	-17%
GUPS 8GB	-11%	-8%	-30%	-24%
GUPS 32GB	-19%	-15%	-35%	-29%

Table 4: The runtime improvement achieved when utilizing (1) ideal PWCs and (2) hashed paging, as compared to radix paging with real PWCs. The improvement provided by hashed paging is comparable to that of ideal PWCs. The exception is cactusADM, for which hashed paging offers a much greater improvement due to radix caching pathologies.

5.4 Drawbacks of Hashed Paging

Practical implementation of hashed page tables is hindered by several obstacles [17]. First, hashed page tables are designed to avoid dynamic resizing, so they are allocated once and spread over a large memory area. This necessitates sharing the page table between all processes, contrary to the per-process page table employed with radix paging. Using a single page table for all processes has some advantages, e.g., saving the overhead of allocating and deallocating page tables as processes are created and terminated. One of the drawbacks is that killing a process requires a linear scan of the hash table to find and delete the associated PTEs, though this can be carried out lazily. Deleting a slot from an open addressed hash table is another challenge. Just marking the deleted slot as "empty" might truncate search chains that probed this slot, found it occupied and moved on to the next probe. Therefore, deleted slots should be distinguished with a special "deleted" value. But marking deleted slots has the undesirable side effect of a longer hash table lookup, because it no longer depends solely on the load factor.

Page tables should also support several features besides mapping virtual to physical addresses. Such features include sharing memory between processes and multiple page sizes. A feasible solution for both requirements is to add another level of translation, as implemented in the Power architecture [23, 37]. The Power architecture defines three types of addresses: effective, virtual, and physical. Each process owns a separate effective memory space, but the virtual address space is shared by all processes. This way, applications can share data by translating different effective segments to the same virtual segment. The effective and virtual address spaces are divided to 256MB segments, whereas the virtual and physical address spaces are divided to 4KB pages by default. Recent versions of Power allow different segments to be configured with different virtual memory page sizes: 4KB, 64KB, 16MB, or 16GB [24]. Multiple page sizes may boost performance with fewer virtual to physical translations, at the cost of potential waste of memory that was allocated but never used.

The Power architecture requires a two-level translation procedure for each memory reference: the first stage translates effective to virtual addresses, and the second stage translates virtual to physical addresses via hashed page tables. The Power architecture employs a closed addressing scheme, where each hash table slot contains a group of 8 PTEs, which form a constant size list. The hardware page walker uses two different hash functions to obtain two such groups of PTEs. If the VPN is not found in one of the 16 PTEs, the hardware triggers a page-fault interrupt that the OS must resolve.

This study investigates page table design with respect to their performance. In real environments that employ hashed page tables, we acknowledge that the aforementioned difficulties are likely to have an adverse affect on performance. Quantifying the precise implications is a nontrivial task; we leave this study for future work.

6. RELATED WORK

6.1 Optimizing MMU Caches

Several studies proposed optimizations to make MMU caches more efficient. Barr et al. [9] offered three new designs that, along with the existing designs by Intel and AMD, encompass the whole design space of MMU caches. They found that the optimal design is the "unified translation cache" with a modified insertion policy. This design caches entries from the different levels of the radix tree in the same structure, as AMD's page walk cache does. This makes it a flexible design, unlike Intel's Paging Structure Cache, which allocates a fixed portion of the cache to each tree level. But unified caches are not able to adapt well to workloads of varying sizes, because lower-levels PTEs, which have low reuse, may evict higher-levels PTEs, which show greater reuse. Therefore, the authors proposed the novel "variable insertion-point LRU replacement policy," and showed that it performs better than the LRU algorithm. Their scheme favors higher-level PTEs by inserting entries from the second level into a recency position below the most recently used position. Employing this scheme raises the hit rates for the third and fourth level PTEs, but the hit rates for the second level remain very low, so page walks require two memory references on average. In other words, the proposed design still suffers from misses caused by the limited capacity of PWCs and is not able to close the performance gap to obtain the results of perfect PWCs or hashed page tables.

Bhattacharjee et al. [14] suggested two techniques to improve the performance and coverage of MMU caches. The first modifies the operating system to allocate pages for the radix page table in a way that encourages coalescing, i.e., in a way that is likely to place the page table pages in consecutive physical addresses. Coalescing can save valuable PWC entries with modest hardware changes, by detecting coalescing pages and unifying the corresponding PTEs into a single PWC entry. The authors focused on coalescing page table data from the lowest level in the radix tree, and they showed that on average dozens of pages can be coalesced.

The second technique proposed by Bhattacharjee et al. replaces the per-core PWCs with a single PWC with the same total capacity, which is shared between the cores. The shared PWC has higher access latency because it is a large structure that resides outside the core. But the authors proved that it yields higher hit rates that compensate for the longer access time and boost the performance of parallel and multiprogrammed workloads. The two techniques are orthogonal and, when applied together, achieve performance close to perfect PWCs. However, the study examined small to medium-sized applications, with memory footprints smaller than 8GB, so future studies will have to check that these results hold for big memory workloads as well. Assessing the performance of the proposed methods for virtualized systems with 2D page walks was not included in the study and certainly deserves examination.

6.2 Speculative Inverted Shadow Page Tables

Ahn et al. [3] studied the hardware support for 2D page walks in x86 architectures. First, they suggested shrinking the nested page walk by using a linear page table in the nested dimension. This design cuts the 2D page walk from 24 to 9 memory references, but is impractical for guests with 64-bit virtual address space, since linear page tables allocate a PTE for each page in the guest virtual space. Virtual machines with a 64-bit must use a hashed page table instead, because they can efficiently map addresses from a wide range to values in a fixed small range.

The authors also introduced the "speculative inverted shadow page table" (SISPT) to reduce the cost of 2D page walks. SISPT is a variant of shadow page tables and hashed page tables, which acts as a third-level TLB that resides in the physical memory. When the hardware finds the translation in the SISPT, it obtains it with a single memory reference; otherwise, it invokes a page fault to be handled by the operating system. Not all translations are stored in the SISPT, so the guest and nested page tables are maintained to provide a complete memory mapping. Given the large size of the SISPT, it is shared between all virtual machines and the processes inside them. Synchronization between the SISPT and the full page table requires hypervisor intervention at context switches and other page table updates. This is the primary overhead associated with shadow paging (and with every software managed TLB). To eliminate the overhead of hypervisor interventions, the SISPT does not try to remain consistent with guest page table updates. On a TLB miss, the processor speculatively executes with the mapping found at the SISPT while simultaneously performing a full 2D walk. If the processor finds the speculated translation to be incorrect, the processor pipeline is flushed and the SISPT is updated. The SISPT mechanism presents a trade-off between decreased page walk latency and increased complexity of hardware (the added page walker and the speculative execution engine).

Choosing which guest and nested page tables are used to keep the full mapping is independent of the SISPT design choice. The different alternatives have little effect on the overall performance, because the speculative walks hide most of the non-speculative walk latencies. But quick 2D page walks are still essential; without them, the core will be stalled waiting for the correct translation. Thus, our 2D hashed page tables may be used as the backing page tables to shorten the non-speculative page walks.

6.3 Direct Segments

Basu et al. [10] analyzed big-memory server workloads such as databases, in-memory caches, and graph analytics. They found that these workloads pay a high price for page-based virtual memory but often do not need the benefits that virtual memory offers: they rarely use swapping, allocate most of their memory on startup, and grant read-write permissions to nearly all their memory. The authors therefore suggested that such applications may benefit from using paging only in a small portion of their address space, while translating the rest of the address space via segmentation. Their idea, "direct segments," requires modest hardware and software changes. Each core is equipped with three registers, `base`, `limit` and `offset`, which map a large, contiguous portion of the process's virtual address space. The hardware translates the virtual addresses lying in the range [`base`,`limit`) to physical addresses by simply adding the constant `offset`, without resorting to the TLB. The OS is responsible for allocating the required physical memory and setting these registers accordingly. While direct segments eliminate the majority of the TLB misses in big-memory workloads, they are less suitable for compute workloads with unpredictable memory usage and for environments where many processes execute for short periods.

The authors also extended direct segments to reduce the address translation overhead in virtualized setups [18]. They offered three modes of operation: direct segments in the guest dimension (guest direct), in the host dimension (VMM direct), or in both (dual direct). The modes present different trade-offs between performance and restrictions on other virtual memory features. The guest and the VMM modes achieve near bare-metal performance with modifications confined to the guest and the hypervisor, respectively, whereas the third mode achieves almost zero translation overhead. However, the dual direct mode requires changes in the guest and the hypervisor, and it provides limited support for memory overcommitment and sharing pages between virtual machines. The VMM mode allows swapping in the guest, whereas the guest mode supports page sharing and live migration of virtual machines. Fragmentation can prevent the creation of direct segments and can be removed via compaction.

7. CONCLUSIONS

Virtual memory offers many advantages and plays a vital role in computer systems, but it comes at the price of performance degradation. The commonly used x86-64 radix page tables require 4 and 24 memory references per walk in bare-metal and virtualized systems. Current radix designs attempt to hide these expensive accesses to the memory hierarchy with PWCs. But this approach is suboptimal, as emerging big-data workloads reference vast amounts of memory with low locality. In contrast, the number of required memory references along a hashed page walk does not depend on the application memory footprint or access locality. We show that carefully designing hashed page tables shrinks bare-metal and virtualized page walks to just above one and three memory reference per walk, respectively, without resorting to PWCs. The disadvantage of hashed page tables is that they make it more challenging to efficiently provide such functionalities as superpages and page sharing.

8. ACKNOWLEDGMENTS

We thank Thomas Barr, Alan Cox, and Scott Rixner for providing valuable feedback and sharing with us their memory simulator, which allowed us to reproduce and compare against their results [9]. We thank the anonymous reviewers and our shepherd, Alex Liu, for their feedback. This project has received funding from the European Union's Horizon 2020 research and innovation programme under grant agreement No. 688386 (OPERA).

9. REFERENCES

[1] Transparent hugepage support. https://www.kernel.org/doc/Documentation/vm/transhuge.txt, 2016. Linux documentation page (Accessed: Apr 2016).

[2] Keith Adams and Ole Agesen. A comparison of software and hardware techniques for x86 virtualization. In *ACM Architectural Support for Programming Languages and Operating Systems (ASPLOS)*, pages 2–13, 2006. http://dx.doi.org/10.1145/1168857.1168860.

[3] Jeongseob Ahn, Seongwook Jin, and Jaehyuk Huh. Revisiting hardware-assisted page walks for virtualized systems. In *ACM/IEEE International Symposium on Computer Architecture (ISCA)*, pages 476–487, 2012. http://dx.doi.org/10.1145/2366231.2337214.

[4] AMD, Inc. *AMD-V Nested Paging*, 2008. White Paper available at: http://developer.amd.com/wordpress/media/2012/10/NPT-WP-11-final-TM.pdf. (Accessed: Apr 2016).

[5] AMD, Inc. *AMD64 Architecture Programmer's Manual, Volume 2*, 2013. http://amd-dev.wpengine.netdna-cdn.com/wordpress/media/2012/10/24593_APM_v21.pdf. (Accessed: Apr 2016).

[6] ARM Holdings. *ARM Cortex-A53 MPCore Processor, Technical Reference Manual*, 2014. http://infocenter.arm.com/help/topic/com.arm.doc.ddi0500d/DDI0500D_cortex_a53_r0p2_trm.pdf. (Accessed: Apr 2016).

[7] Vlastimil Babka and Petr Tůma. Investigating cache parameters of x86 family processors. In *SPEC Benchmark Workshop on Comput. Performance Evaluation and Benchmarking*, pages 77–96, 2009. http://dx.doi.org/10.1007/978-3-540-93799-9_5.

[8] David A. Bader, Jonathan Berry, Simon Kahan, Richard Murphy, E. Jason Riedy, and Jeremiah Willcock. Graph 500 benchmark. http://www.graph500.org/specifications, 2011. Version 1.2 (Accessed: Apr 2016).

[9] Thomas W. Barr, Alan L. Cox, and Scott Rixner. Translation caching: Skip don't walk (the page table). In *ACM/IEEE International Symposium on Computer Architecture (ISCA)*, pages 48–59, 2010. http://dx.doi.org/10.1145/1815961.1815970.

[10] Arkaprava Basu, Jayneel Gandhi, Jichuan Chang, Mark D. Hill, and Michael M. Swift. Efficient virtual memory for big memory servers. In *ACM/IEEE International Symposium on Computer Architecture (ISCA)*, pages 237–248, 2013. http://dx.doi.org/10.1145/2485922.2485943.

[11] Ravi Bhargava, Benjamin Serebrin, Francesco Spadini, and Srilatha Manne. Accelerating two-dimensional page walks for virtualized systems. In *ACM Architectural Support for Programming Languages and Operating Systems (ASPLOS)*, pages 26–35, 2008. http://dx.doi.org/10.1145/1346281.1346286.

[12] Nikhil Bhatia. Performance evaluation of AMD RVI hardware assist. Technical report, VMware, Inc., 2009. http://www.cse.iitd.ernet.in/~sbansal/csl862-virt/2010/readings/RVI_performance.pdf. (Accessed: Apr 2016).

[13] Nikhil Bhatia. Performance evaluation of Intel EPT hardware assist. Technical report, VMware, Inc., 2009. http://www.vmware.com/pdf/Perf_ESX_Intel-EPT-eval.pdf. (Accessed: Apr 2016).

[14] Abhishek Bhattacharjee. Large-reach memory management unit caches. In *IEEE/ACM International Symposium on Microarchitecture (MICRO)*, pages 383–394, 2013. http://dx.doi.org/10.1145/2540708.2540741.

[15] Thomas H. Cormen, Charles E. Leiserson, Ronald L. Rivest, and Clifford Stein. *Introduction to Algorithms*. The MIT Press, 3rd edition, 2009.

[16] Charlie Curtsinger and Emery D Berger. STABILIZER: Statistically sound performance evaluation. In *ACM Architectural Support for Programming Languages and Operating Systems (ASPLOS)*, pages 219–228, 2013. http://dx.doi.org/10.1145/2451116.2451141.

[17] Cort Dougan, Paul Mackerras, and Victor Yodaiken. Optimizing the idle task and other MMU tricks. In *USENIX Symposium on Operating Systems Design and Implementation (OSDI)*, pages 229–237, 1999. http://citeseerx.ist.psu.edu/viewdoc/summary?doi=10.1.1.68.1609.

[18] Jayneel Gandhi, Arkaprava Basu, Mark D. Hill, and Michael M. Swift. Efficient memory virtualization: Reducing dimensionality of nested page walks. In *IEEE/ACM International Symposium on Microarchitecture (MICRO)*, pages 178–189, 2014. http://dx.doi.org/10.1109/MICRO.2014.37.

[19] Charles Gray, Matthew Chapman, Peter Chubb, David Mosberger-Tang, and Gernot Heiser. Itanium: A system implementor's tale. In *USENIX Annual Technical Conference (ATC)*, pages 264–278, 2005.

http://citeseerx.ist.psu.edu/viewdoc/summary?doi=10.1.1.104.3059.

[20] John L. Henning. SPEC CPU2006 benchmark descriptions. *ACM SIGARCH Computer Architecture News (CAN)*, 34(4):1–17, sep 2006. http://dx.doi.org/10.1145/1186736.1186737.

[21] John L. Henning. SPEC CPU2006 memory footprint. *ACM SIGARCH Computer Architecture News (CAN)*, 35(1):84–89, mar 2007. http://doi.acm.org/10.1145/1241601.1241618.

[22] Jerry Huck and Jim Hays. Architectural support for translation table management in large address space machines. In *ACM/IEEE International Symposium on Computer Architecture (ISCA)*, pages 39–50, 1993. http://dx.doi.org/10.1145/165123.165128.

[23] IBM Corporation. *PowerPC Microprocessor Family: The Programming Environments Manual for 32 and 64-bit Microprocessors*, 2005. https://wiki.alcf.anl.gov/images/f/fb/PowerPC_-_Assembly_-_IBM_Programming_Environment_2.3.pdf. (Accessed: Apr 2016).

[24] IBM Corporation. *AIX Version 6.1 Performance Management*, first edition, 2007. http://ps-2.kev009.com/basil.holloway/ALLPDF/sc23525300.pdf. (Accessed: Apr 2016).

[25] Intel Corporation. *Intel Itanium Architecture Software Developer's Manual, Volume 2*, 2010. http://tinyurl.com/itanium2. (Accessed: Apr 2016).

[26] Intel Corporation. *Intel 64 and IA-32 Architectures Software Developer's Manual, Volume 3A*, 2015. http://tinyurl.com/intel-x86-3a. (Accessed: Apr 2016).

[27] Intel Corporation. *Intel 64 and IA-32 Architectures Software Developer's Manual, Volume 3B*, 2015. http://tinyurl.com/intel-x86-3b. (Accessed: Apr 2016).

[28] Intel Corporation. *Intel 64 and IA-32 Architectures Software Developer's Manual, Volume 3C*, 2015. http://tinyurl.com/intel-x86-3c. (Accessed: Apr 2016).

[29] Bruce L. Jacob and Trevor N. Mudge. A look at several memory management units, TLB-refill mechanisms, and page table organizations. In *ACM Architectural Support for Programming Languages and Operating Systems (ASPLOS)*, pages 295–306, 1998. http://dx.doi.org/10.1145/291069.291065.

[30] David Koester and Bob Lucas. RandomAccess – GUPS (Giga updates per second). http://icl.cs.utk.edu/projectsfiles/hpcc/RandomAccess/. (Accessed: Apr 2016).

[31] Jun Min Lin, Yu Chen, Wenlong Li, Zhao Tang, and Aamer Jaleel. Memory characterization of SPEC CPU2006 benchmark suite. In *Workshop for Computer Architecture Evaluation using Commercial Workloads (CAECW)*, 2008. http://www.jaleels.org/ajaleel/publications/SPECanalysis.pdf. (Accessed: Apr 2016).

[32] Chi-Keung Luk, Robert Cohn, Robert Muth, Harish Patil, Artur Klauser, Geoff Lowney, Steven Wallace, Vijay Janapa Reddi, and Kim Hazelwood. Pin: Building customized program analysis tools with dynamic instrumentation. In *ACM International Conference on Programming Languages Design and Implementation (PLDI)*, pages 190–200, 2005. http://dx.doi.org/10.1145/1065010.1065034.

[33] Piotr R Luszczek, David H Bailey, Jack J Dongarra, Jeremy Kepner, Robert F Lucas, Rolf Rabenseifner, and Daisuke Takahashi. The HPC challenge (HPCC) benchmark suite. In *ACM/IEEE International Conference on High Performance Computing, Networking, Storage and Analysis (SC)*, 2006. http://dx.doi.org/10.1145/1188455.1188677. An SC tutorial, available via http://icl.cs.utk.edu/projectsfiles/hpcc/pubs/sc06_hpcc.pdf. (Accessed: Apr 2016).

[34] Collin McCurdy, Alan L. Cox, and Jeffrey Vetter. Investigating the TLB behavior of high-end scientific applications on commodity microprocessors. In *IEEE International Symposium on Performance Analysis of Systems and Software (ISPASS)*, pages 95–104, 2008. http://dx.doi.org/10.1109/ISPASS.2008.4510742.

[35] Richard C. Murphy, Kyle B. Wheeler, and Brian W. Barrett. Introducing the Graph 500. In *Cray User Group Conference (CUG)*, 2010. https://cug.org/5-publications/proceedings_attendee_lists/CUG10CD/pages/1-program/final_program/CUG10_Proceedings/pages/authors/11-15Wednesday/14C-Murphy-paper.pdf. (Accessed: Apr 2016).

[36] Juan Navarro, Sitaram Iyer, Peter Druschel, and Alan Cox. Practical, transparent operating system support for superpages. In *USENIX Symposium on Operating Systems Design and Implementation (OSDI)*, pages 89–104, 2002. http://dx.doi.org/10.1145/844128.844138.

[37] C. Ray Peng, Thomas A. Petersen, and Ron Clark. The PowerPC architecture: 64-bit Power with 32-bit compatibility. In *IEEE Computer Society International Computer Conference (COMPCON)*, pages 300–307, 1995. http://dx.doi.org/10.1109/CMPCON.1995.512400.

[38] Cristan Szmajda and Gernot Heiser. Variable radix page table: A page table for modern architectures. In *Advances in Computer Systems Architecture, Asia-Pacific Conference (ACSAC)*, pages 290–304, 2003. http://dx.doi.org/10.1007/978-3-540-39864-6_24.

[39] M. Talluri, M. D. Hill, and Y. A. Khalidi. A new page table for 64-bit address spaces. In *ACM Symposium on Operating Systems Principles (SOSP)*, pages 184–200, 1995. http://dx.doi.org/10.1145/224056.224071.

[40] Roland E. Wunderlich, Thomas F. Wenisch, Babak Falsafi, and James C. Hoe. SMARTS: Accelerating microarchitecture simulation via rigorous statistical sampling. In *ACM/IEEE International Symposium on Computer Architecture (ISCA)*, pages 84–97, 2003. http://dx.doi.org/10.1145/859618.859629.

Exploiting Core Criticality for Enhanced GPU Performance

Adwait Jog[1] Onur Kayiran[2] Ashutosh Pattnaik[3] Mahmut T. Kandemir[3]
Onur Mutlu[4,5] Ravishankar Iyer[6] Chita R. Das[3]

[1]College of William and Mary [2]Advanced Micro Devices, Inc.
[3]Pennsylvania State University [4]ETH Zürich [5]Carnegie Mellon University [6]Intel

ABSTRACT

Modern memory access schedulers employed in GPUs typically optimize for memory throughput. They implicitly assume that *all* requests from different cores are equally important. However, we show that during the execution of a subset of CUDA applications, different cores can have different amounts of tolerance to latency. In particular, cores with a larger fraction of warps waiting for data to come back from DRAM are less likely to tolerate the latency of an outstanding memory request. Requests from such cores are more critical than requests from others. Based on this observation, this paper introduces a new memory scheduler, called *(C)ritica(L)ity (A)ware (M)emory (S)cheduler* (CLAMS), which takes into account the latency-tolerance of the cores that generate memory requests. The key idea is to use the fraction of critical requests in the memory request buffer to switch between scheduling policies optimized for criticality and locality. If this fraction is below a threshold, CLAMS prioritizes critical requests to ensure cores that cannot tolerate latency are serviced faster. Otherwise, CLAMS optimizes for locality, anticipating that there are too many critical requests and prioritizing one over another would not significantly benefit performance.

We first present a core-criticality estimation mechanism for determining critical cores and requests, and then discuss issues related to finding a balance between criticality and locality in the memory scheduler. We progressively devise three variants of CLAMS, and show that the *Dynamic CLAMS* provides significantly higher performance, across a variety of workloads, than the commonly-employed GPU memory schedulers optimized solely for locality. The results indicate that a GPU memory system that considers both core criticality and DRAM access locality can provide significant improvement in performance.

1. INTRODUCTION

Graphics Processing Units (GPUs) are becoming increasingly popular for general purpose computing due to their capability in providing large improvements in performance and energy efficiency compared to CPUs [1–3,11,24,49,55–57,59, 69,77,80,90]. GPUs achieve significant speedups by exploiting high thread-level parallelism (TLP). They launch thousands of threads across multiple cores to mask the performance bottlenecks of a single thread. Threads are typically grouped into fixed-sized batches known as *warps* or *wavefronts*. To serve the high memory-demands of thousands of concurrently executing threads, many modern GPUs use GDDR5 memory, which typically has 3-4 times the peak-bandwidth of the high-end DDR4 memories used in chip multiprocessors.

Although high-bandwidth memory systems have increased GPU performance substantially, memory bandwidth is still precious and a critical performance determinant [27,31,39, 41,43,68,72,88]. In fact, it will be more so as compute resources on GPUs continue to increase [28,38,41,43]. To address this, a large body of work has focused on improving bandwidth utilization (e.g., [4,7,40,41,68,88]), and caching efficiency in GPUs (e.g., [5,35,41,58,75]). However, past works primarily focus on improving application performance by treating all threads and memory requests with *equal* importance. This phenomenon stems from the fact that GPUs typically focus on improving the collective performance of multiple concurrently executing threads, by overlapping their execution. In the same vein, the commonly-used memory request scheduling policy, First-ready First-Come First-Served (FR-FCFS) [73, 74, 93], implicitly assumes that all memory requests are *equally critical* for overall performance, and hence, it aims to maximize memory data throughput rather than minimize latency of specific requests or cores.

We observe that, in a subset of CUDA applications, due to the contention of memory requests from different cores in the memory system (along with interconnects and shared caches), and the inability of the FR-FCFS memory scheduler to distinguish between the memory requests originating from different cores, GPU cores experience significant variation in average memory access latencies. Due to such variation, the number of stalling warps that belong to the cores that suffer from higher memory access latencies is typically higher than that of other cores, making the former type of cores less latency tolerant, i.e., more *critical* for overall performance. Thus, because different cores have varying degrees of tolerance to latency during execution, their corresponding memory requests have varying degrees of criticality.

In contrast to the purely locality-focused memory schedulers, **our goal** in this work is to design a memory scheduler that is cognizant of the latency tolerance of cores. One simple idea based on our observation is to detect and *always prioritize* critical requests over non-critical requests.

SIGMETRICS '16, June 14-18, 2016, Antibes Juan-Les-Pins, France

DOI: http://dx.doi.org/10.1145/2896377.2901468

As the cores that lack enough warps to hide the long memory latencies are more likely to quickly stall for the data to come back, prioritizing requests from such cores in the memory controller provides a way of pro-actively avoiding them from getting stalled. However, we find that such a memory scheduler that is focused *purely* on core criticality degrades DRAM access locality significantly. This motivates us to explore more intelligent memory scheduling schemes that consider *both criticality and locality*. To this end, we introduce the *(C)ritica(L)ity (A)ware (M)emory (S)cheduler* (CLAMS) for GPUs, which achieves a fine balance between core criticality and DRAM access locality.

The CLAMS design comprises four steps. First, it periodically calculates the current level of latency tolerance of a GPU core. It does so by periodically calculating the fraction of short-latency warps on the core.[1] A core is expected to be more latency tolerant if most of the launched warps are short-latency warps that execute compute instructions or that find their required data in privates caches. Second, CLAMS periodically ranks the cores based on their current level of latency tolerance, and tags the memory requests with the core's rank. The ranking is done in such a way that the cores that have lower latency tolerance are ranked lower. Third, based on the value of the rank, CLAMS determines whether or not a request should be considered critical. To do so, it uses a criticality-rank threshold (Th_{CR}), which specifies *up to which rank* a request should be considered as *critical*. Fourth, CLAMS decides whether or not a critical request should be prioritized in the memory scheduler, by also taking into account DRAM access (row-buffer) locality. It does so by periodically calculating the percentage of requests that are considered as critical in the memory request buffer, and comparing it to a value called the scheduling-mode threshold (Th_{SM}). If the percentage of critical requests is below Th_{SM}, CLAMS goes into criticality mode, where it prioritizes critical requests to ensure cores that cannot tolerate latency are serviced faster. Otherwise, CLAMS operates in locality mode, where it optimizes for locality (like existing schedulers), anticipating that there are too many critical requests to prioritize one over another.

To our knowledge, this is the first work that observes latency tolerance differences between GPU cores and exploits such differences to improve GPU resource management, focusing on memory request scheduling. This paper makes the following **contributions:**

• We introduce the concept of core-criticality in GPUs. We show that all GPU cores do *not* possess the same latency tolerance at all times, and this variation in latency tolerance across cores is one of the key reasons for different levels of criticality among memory requests, which is not exploited by current GPU memory request schedulers.

• We introduce the first GPU memory scheduler, CLAMS, which takes into account core-criticality and achieves a fine balance between criticality and locality via our new dynamic criticality estimation mechanism. We propose three different designs for CLAMS: static, semi-dynamic (Semi-Dyn) and dynamic (Dyn) based on how required thresholds (Th_{CR} and Th_{SM}) are computed, and find that Dyn-CLAMS is the best performer due to its ability to compute these thresholds at runtime and thereby adapt dynamically to varying application demands.

[1]Section 3 describes our exact mechanism to measure the latency tolerance of a core.

• We present a comprehensive experimental evaluation of three CLAMS designs as compared to commonly used FR-FCFS [73,74,93] and FR-FCFS-Cap [62] memory schedulers using a variety of CUDA applications. Our results show that Dyn-CLAMS reduces the latency of critical memory requests by 35%, resulting in an average 9% IPC improvement (maximum 15%) over the FR-FCFS scheduler, and is within 1% of an idealized CLAMS design that uses best threshold values profiled separately for *each* application. Furthermore, the performance of none of the evaluated applications degrades with our mechanism.

2. BACKGROUND AND MOTIVATION

A typical GPU consists of multiple simple cores, also called streaming-multiprocessors[2] [67] in NVIDIA terminology. Each core is associated with private L1 data, texture and constant caches, along with software-managed scratchpad memory. The cores are connected to memory channels (partitions) via an interconnection network. Each memory partition is associated with a shared L2 cache, and its associated memory requests are handled by a GDDR5 memory controller. When an application kernel is launched on a GPU, the memory requests originating from different cores interfere at various levels of the GPU memory hierarchy, such as the interconnect, last-level caches, and main-memory. At each of these levels, the underlying shared resource management policies do *not* consider the source core-ids of the requests while making decisions, and therefore might allocate shared resources across different cores in an *uneven* fashion. Our detailed analysis shows that such uneven allocation can lead to significant variation in average memory latencies across different GPU cores.

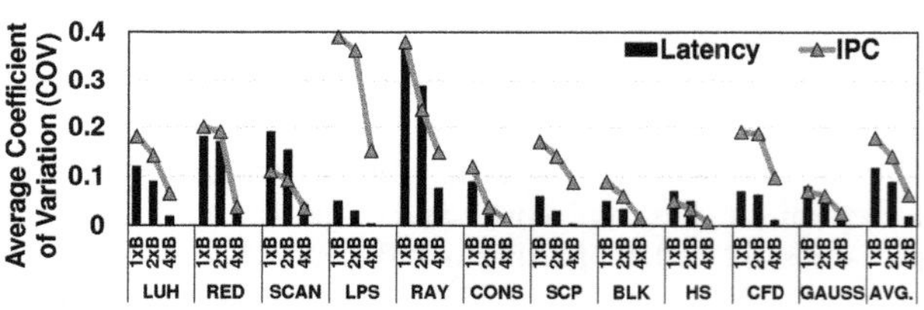

Figure 1: Average Coefficient of Variation (COV) in memory access latencies and in IPCs across different GPU cores.

To understand this variation, we calculate the *coefficient of variation (COV)* in memory access latencies, which is defined as the ratio of standard deviation over arithmetic mean of the average memory access latencies experienced by different cores. Figure 1 shows the COV in memory access latencies as well as COV in IPCs across different cores for 11 different CUDA applications, averaged across fixed epochs[3], for three different scenarios: applications when executed on a GPU that has 1) equal to (1xB), 2) double (2xB), and 3) quadruple (4xB) the peak memory bandwidth of our baseline GPU architecture. In the baseline scenario (1xB), we observe significant COV in latencies across cores for applications like `LUH` (13%), `RAY` (33%), `SCAN` (19%), and `RED` (18%). Because of such variation, many GPU cores experience higher memory access latencies than others. Therefore, such cores have a high number of stalling warps on memory,

[2]In this paper, we use the term *core* for a streaming-multiprocessor (SM).

[3]Epoch length is 10K cycles.

making them *less latency tolerant* than other cores. This might also result in higher stall times for these cores, leading to significant COV in IPCs across different cores, as shown in Figure 1.

We observe significant COV in both latencies and IPCs for **RAY**, **LUH**, and **RED**, stressing the fact that variation in latencies can lead to significant variation in IPCs across cores. In addition to this observation, we notice two contrasting cases. First, in **SCAN**, variation in latencies across cores is higher than variation in IPCs. This is because **SCAN** is able to tolerate higher latencies up to a certain level, which reduces the variation in IPCs. Second, in **LPS** and **CFD**, much lower variation in latencies across cores is present compared to variation in IPCs. This is because CTA and instruction-mix load imbalance [6,43,54,89] across cores also causes IPC variation during application execution. Finally, we observe that increasing the peak memory bandwidth leads to a significant decrease in COV in latencies as well as in IPCs, implying that memory bandwidth contention of different cores in the memory system is a major cause of COV in latencies as well as in IPCs.

Our goal is to develop a mechanism that prioritizes the cores that suffer from lower latency tolerance. Improving the performance of these cores would improve overall system performance by enabling these cores to make progress (Section 3.1). We expect such a mechanism to specifically benefit those applications that have significant COV in both latencies and IPCs (e.g., **RAY**, **LUH**, and **RED**), and not so for those applications that have small COV (e.g., **BLK**, **HS**). Such a mechanism can be employed at various levels. For example, a warp scheduler can be employed to control the progress of each core separately. However, since the cores contend for the memory system resources, especially main memory bandwidth, a memory scheduling mechanism can be more effective to expedite the requests of cores with lower latency tolerance, and is therefore the focus of this paper. Thus, in this work, we design a new GPU memory scheduler that is aware of the latency tolerance of individual cores.

3. CORE CRITICALITY: BASIC IDEAS AND METRICS

In this section, we describe and analyze the metrics to gauge the latency tolerance of a core and its variance across cores.

3.1 Latency Tolerance as a Measure of Core Criticality

A GPU core achieves high latency tolerance by hosting a large number of warps. If some warps get blocked because of pending DRAM accesses, the remaining warps can continue their execution and potentially mask the long latency penalties of the blocked warps. In order to quantify the level of latency tolerance on a GPU core, we employ a two-step strategy. The first step is to classify the warps as *short-latency* and *long-latency* warps. The short-latency warps are the issued warps that do not have any pending memory request(s). In other words, they are currently executing either compute instructions or instructions whose required data is already present in the private caches. Therefore, these short-latency warps are expected to provide latency tolerance to the core in the presence of the remaining long-latency warps whose execution might be blocked for hundreds of cycles due to pending memory request(s). After classifying the warps into short-latency vs. long-latency, the second step is to periodically[4] calculate *the ratio of short-latency warps over total issued warps.* Note that the sum of short-latency and long-latency warps is equal to the total issued warps, and thus this ratio can take a value between 0 and 1. *We use this ratio as a metric to gauge the latency tolerance of a core.* We call it the *short-latency ratio.* A high value of this ratio indicates that the core has a high percentage of short-latency warps, suggesting that the core has high latency tolerance.

We observe in our experiments that, relative change in IPC and relative change in our latency tolerance metric has an average correlation of 74% across our application suite (described in Section 6). This means that improving the latency tolerance of a core might improve its IPC. We also observe that a mechanism that prioritizes the memory requests of cores that have lower latency tolerance can have higher impact on overall performance. For example, it is more advantageous to make one more additional warp ready to execute in a core with zero short-latency warps (i.e., a core with no latency tolerance) compared to doing so in a core with a large number of short-latency warps (i.e., a core with enough latency tolerance).

To analyze the criticality of cores, we quantize our latency tolerance metric, short-latency ratio, into eight equal parts.[5] Based on this value, we assign a criticality *rank* to a core. Essentially, each equal part of the short-latency ratio corresponds to a rank. For example, if this ratio is less than or equal to $\frac{1}{8}$, the core is considered to be the most critical and is in *rank-1* state. Similarly, if a core's short-latency ratio is greater than $\frac{7}{8}$, that core is considered to be the least critical, and is in *rank-8* state.

Formally, we consider a core to be *critical* if the current *rank* of the core is less than or equal to a *Criticality-Rank-Threshold* (Th_{CR}). In other words, the value of Th_{CR} specifies ***up to which rank*** the core should be considered as *critical.* For example, a Th_{CR} value of 4 implies that the core is considered critical only if its current rank is less than or equal to rank 4.

3.2 Understanding Variation of Criticality Across Cores

Not only the latency tolerance of a core can change during execution, but we also observe that there is a *wide variation in latency tolerance across GPU cores.* To measure this variation, we introduce a metric, called *percentage of critical cores (PCC)*, which is defined as the percentage of GPU cores that are in the critical state. Since a core is treated as critical based on the chosen value of Criticality-Rank-Threshold (Th_{CR}), PCC needs to be defined for a particular value of Th_{CR}. Hence, we define PCC(Th_{CR}) as the percentage of critical cores (PCC) for a particular Th_{CR}, where Th_{CR} can take any integer from 1 to 8. If PCC(Th_{CR}) is 100%, it means that all cores are critical, and have similar latency tolerance. If PCC(Th_{CR}) is 0%, it means that all cores are non-critical. In both

[4]In our experiments, we calculate this ratio over an epoch of 128 cycles (a threshold that is determined empirically).

[5]We could divide this ratio into more than eight parts to get a finer granularity picture of the current latency tolerance of a core, but our detailed studies show that eight parts provide sufficient granularity to understand and distinguish between the latency tolerance of different cores.

cases, the variation in criticality across cores is insignificant. On the other hand, if the value of PCC(Th_{CR}) is in mid-range, then some cores are critical and the remaining cores are not. Therefore, the value of PCC(Th_{CR}) gives a notion of the variation in criticality across cores. For a better understanding of the PCC metric, consider Figure 2, which shows the rank of three cores of a GPU. We notice that if Th_{CR} is chosen as 1, PCC is 0%, as all cores have higher rank than 1 and no core is considered critical. With Th_{CR} equal to 4, the value of PCC is 33%, as the rank of core-3 is less than the chosen value of Th_{CR}, making it the only critical core in the system. With Th_{CR} equal to 7, the value of PCC is 100%, as all cores are considered critical because the rank of every core is less than Th_{CR}.

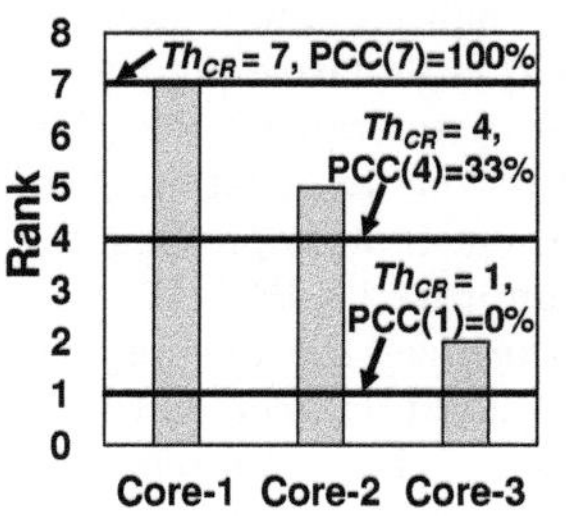

Figure 2: Example demonstrating the PCC metric.

We observe that as Th_{CR} increases, the number of critical cores also increases (or remains the same). Therefore, PCC(Th_{CR}) also increases (or remains the same) as Th_{CR} increases from 1 to 8. Formally, $[PCC(a) \geq PCC(b)]$, if $(a > b)$.

3.2.1 *Analysis of the PCC metric.*

Figure 3 shows PCC(Th_{CR}) over time (sampled every 1K cycles) for four applications, for three different values of Th_{CR} ($Th_{CR} = \{1, 4, 7\}$), over time. We make three main observations from this figure.

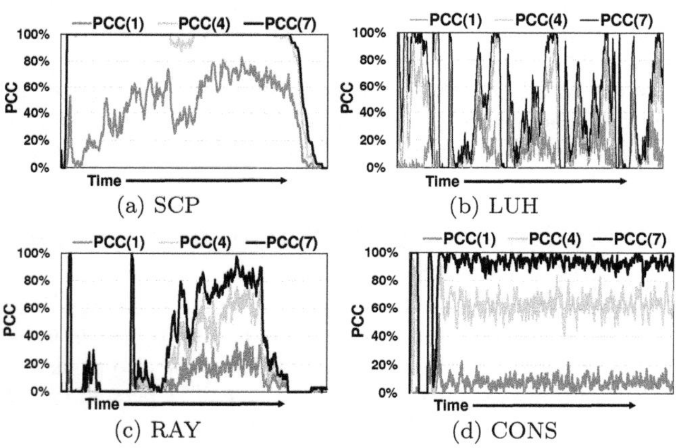

(a) SCP (b) LUH

(c) RAY (d) CONS

Figure 3: PCC metric over time with different criticality-rank thresholds.

Observation I: PCC is dependent on the chosen criticality-rank threshold. During application execution, the instantaneous PCC(Th_{CR}) is a function of the chosen Th_{CR} value. For example, in **SCP**, values of PCC(Th_{CR} = 1) and PCC(Th_{CR} = 7) at a given time are very different. This follows from our previous discussion: as Th_{CR} increases, the number of critical cores increases, leading to high PCC values. The other three applications (**LUH**, **RAY**, **CONS**) also exhibit this trend.

Observation II: PCC varies within an application over time. Even for a fixed value of Th_{CR}, PCC(Th_{CR}) may not be constant throughout execution. For example, as observed prominently in **LUH** and **RAY**, PCC(Th_{CR} = 4) can be different over time, implying that the number of critical cores for the same value of Th_{CR} is not constant over time. In **CONS**, the change in PCC(Th_{CR}) over time is not very prominent, and PCC(Th_{CR} = 4) is in the mid-range (40-60%), implying that roughly half the cores are critical.

Observation III: PCC varies across applications. Across applications, even for the same value of Th_{CR}, PCC(Th_{CR}) can be very different. For example, at Th_{CR} = 4, **RAY** and **SCP** have very different PCC(Th_{CR} = 4) values (**SCP**'s is fairly higher than **RAY**'s). This indicates that, with Th_{CR} = 4, the number of critical cores for **SCP** is higher than that of **RAY**.

We also analyze the effect of memory bandwidth on the PCC metric. Figure 4 plots PCC[6] for varying amounts of main memory bandwidth (as described in Figure 1). We make one major observation:

Observation IV: PCC reduces significantly as main memory bandwidth increases. This trend is consistent with our discussions from Section 2 that the variation average memory latency observed by different cores (i.e., variation in criticality across different cores) reduces with higher memory bandwidth.

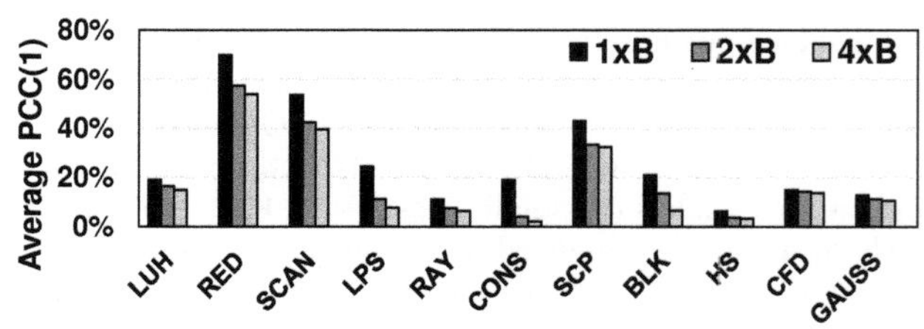

Figure 4: Effect of main memory bandwidth on PCC.

4. ANALYZING CRITICALITY IN THE MEMORY SYSTEM

Cores with low latency tolerance are less likely to tolerate the latency of an outstanding memory request, making their requests more critical. Thus, our goal is to design a *criticality-aware* memory-scheduler that takes advantage of differences in criticality among requests and prioritizes the latency-critical requests to improve system performance. One of the important steps in designing such a memory scheduler is to gauge the variation in criticality across GPU cores. As discussed in Section 3.2, the PCC(Th_{CR}) metric is one of the key indicators of existence of different levels of criticality among cores, and in turn their corresponding memory requests. If the PCC(Th_{CR}) metric indicates that the latency tolerance variance across cores exists for a particular value of Th_{CR}, the memory scheduler can potentially prioritize requests from cores that have lower ranks. This is because such cores are more likely to have a large number of stalled warps that are waiting for memory requests to be serviced. We can prioritize requests from such cores to *proactively* avoid causing these cores to stall. However, note that as PCC(Th_{CR}) is dependent on Th_{CR}, we need to carefully examine the PCC(Th_{CR}) values for all possible

[6]We choose to show results for PCC with Th_{CR} = 1 because the critical cores at this Th_{CR} have the least latency tolerance, and reducing PCC(1) by prioritizing the memory requests of such cores is advantageous for improving overall performance (Section 3.1).

values of Th_{CR}, to understand at what level of Th_{CR} does substantial latency criticality variation across cores exist (if at all). If the PCC(Th_{CR}) metric does not indicate significant variance at any Th_{CR} level, the memory requests from different cores will have similar latency criticality. If this is the case, the memory scheduler can focus on preserving locality (like an existing GPU memory scheduler) since giving some requests higher priority than others is less likely to improve system performance.

The calculation of PCC(Th_{CR}) requires global information exchange across cores, and the hardware overhead of calculating this information and then communicating it directly to the memory controllers (MCs) periodically can be expensive. Instead, we propose to capture the variations in latency tolerance across cores directly at the MCs. To do so, we relay the current latency tolerance level of a core to the GPU memory scheduler by tagging the memory requests originating from that core with the core's current rank, and then calculating, at the MC, a metric called percentage of critical requests (PCR), which is defined as percentage of critical memory requests present in the MC memory request buffer. Again, because the decision of defining requests (or cores as we discussed before in Section 3.2) as critical is dependent on the value of Th_{CR}, we define PCR(Th_{CR}), which is the percentage of critical requests (*the requests that are tagged with rank values less than or equal to* Th_{CR}) in the MC request buffer. *Note that the observations discussed for PCC(Th_{CR}) in Section 3.2 hold true for PCR(Th_{CR}) as well. This is because the only difference of PCR(Th_{CR}) from PCC(Th_{CR}) is that PCR(Th_{CR}) considers criticality of requests instead of their corresponding cores.*

In Figure 5, we plot PCR(Th_{CR}) over time for the same four applications shown in Figure 3, for the same values of $Th_{CR} = \{1, 4, 7\}$. We observe that in both Figure 3 and Figure 5, applications have very similar patterns: PCR(Th_{CR} plots over time, shown in Figure 5, are highly correlated with the PCC(Th_{CR}) curves shown in Figure 3) Thus, a criticality-aware memory scheduler could make scheduling decisions based on PCR(k) $\forall k \in \{1...8\}$ information calculated locally at the MC, instead of using the global PCC(k), $\forall k \in \{1...8\}$ information.

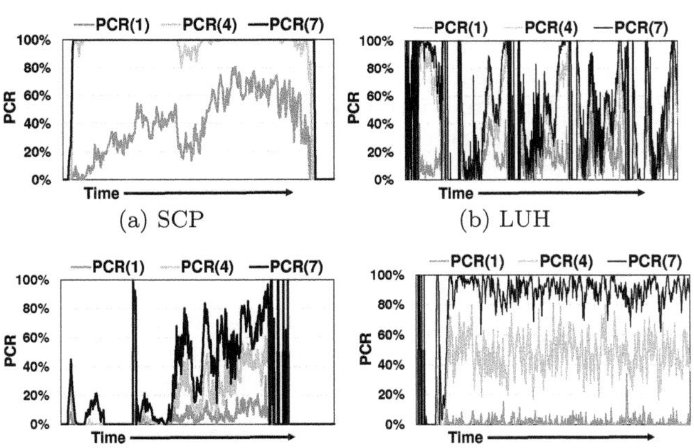

(a) SCP (b) LUH (c) RAY (d) CONS

Figure 5: PCR metric over time with different criticality-rank thresholds.

Relaying each core's rank information to the MC, and then periodically calculating PCR(Th_{CR}) at the MC has two primary benefits: (1) this percentage can be calculated locally at the MC without requiring communication across MCs, as we just discussed, (2) the calculations to find the appropriate Th_{CR} value (discussed in Section 5) and other optimizations can also be done locally at the MCs.

Scope of Criticality Aware Scheduling. To understand the scope (i.e., potential opportunity) of criticality-aware memory scheduling in GPU workloads, we investigate the existence of memory requests with different criticality-ranks at the MCs at the same time. Figure 6 depicts the distribution of criticality-rank differences across DRAM requests, where criticality-rank difference is defined as the difference between the highest and the lowest criticality-rank of the memory requests present in the MC at the same time. This data is for one of the MCs (we observe similar distributions in other MCs), when more than one request is present in the MC buffer. In Figure 6, `diff-0` denotes the percentage of DRAM cycles during which *all* the memory requests in the buffer have the same criticality-rank. Similarly, `diff-1` denotes the percentage of DRAM cycles during which the difference between the highest and the lowest rank of the memory requests in the MC at the same instant is 1. Note that as the maximum possible rank is 8, the difference of the highest and the lowest rank can range from 0 to 7.

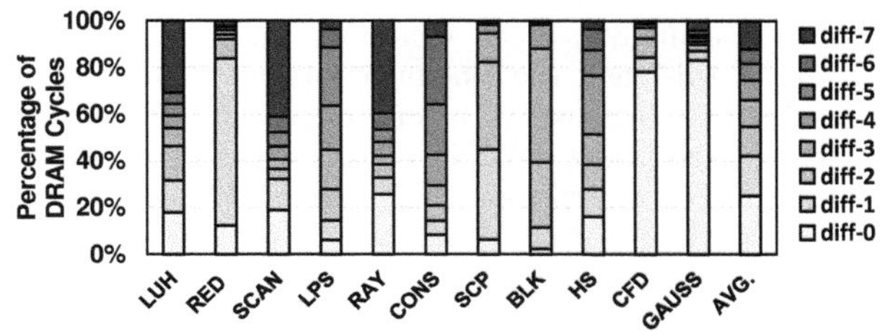

Figure 6: Distribution of criticality-rank differences across requests in the memory controller.

As we observe from Figure 6, the rank range present in the MC significantly varies across applications. In applications such as `LUH` and `RAY`, the difference in ranks is significant during most of the execution, while in other applications such as `GAUSS` and `CFD`, the difference is 0 most of the time. Therefore, in these applications, the scope of criticality-aware memory scheduling is likely to be lower. We observe that many applications (e.g., `RAY`, `LUH`, `CONS`, `RED`) have enough scope for criticality-based prioritization.

We conclude from these results that a memory scheduler that exploits the criticality differences across different cores' memory requests has promising scope to improve overall system performance.

5. DESIGN AND IMPLEMENTATION

5.1 Design Challenges of CLAMS

We identify two major challenges in designing CLAMS:

(I) Co-existence of critical and non-critical requests. In order to allow criticality-based prioritization, one of the important challenges is to find Th_{CR} such that both critical and non-critical requests coexist in the MC buffer. From our prior discussions, we observe that a high value of Th_{CR} might lead to *too* many cores and their corresponding requests to be considered as critical. On the other hand, a low value of Th_{CR} might lead to a *very* small number of cores and their corresponding requests to be considered as critical. In both scenarios, the MC buffer contains either only critical requests or only non-critical requests. This prevents the scheduler to take advantage of the differences between the ranks of the requests in the MC buffer. Therefore, *to increase the opportunities for criticality-based prioritization by distinguishing critical requests from others, it is imperative to find an appropriate Th_{CR} value that can enable substantial coexistence of both critical and non-critical requests in the system.*

(II) Balancing DRAM access locality and criticality. Even though choosing an appropriate Th_{CR} enables the co-existence of both critical and non-critical requests in the system, it might not achieve a good balance between exploiting locality (using the baseline scheduling policy that aims to maximize row buffer hit rate) and exploiting criticality (using our new policy that prioritizes critical requests). To address this trade-off, we periodically calculate PCR(Th_{CR}) to switch between scheduling policies optimized for criticality or locality. Over execution, if PCR(Th_{CR}) is *below* a threshold, which we call the *Scheduling-Mode-Threshold* (Th_{SM}), the scheduler prioritizes critical requests to ensure that the cores that cannot tolerate latency are serviced faster. However, if PCR(Th_{CR}) exceeds Th_{SM}, this implies that the differences in latency criticality have become insignificant and there are too many critical requests to prioritize one over another. In this case, the scheduler returns to the baseline mode of prioritizing row buffer hit requests. It is challenging to find an appropriate value for Th_{SM}, because a too high value for Th_{SM} would push the scheduler to serve critical requests for a longer time, potentially hampering locality. A too low value for Th_{SM} would not provide enough opportunities for criticality based prioritization. Therefore, it is important to find an appropriate Th_{SM} value to achieve a balance between exploiting locality and exploiting criticality.

Table 1 summarizes all metrics and thresholds we consider to design the CLAMS scheduler. We will make use of these in our descriptions in the rest of Section 5.

Table 1: List of CLAMS related metrics and thresholds.

Acronym	Description
PCC	Percentage of GPU cores in the critical state
PCR	Percentage of critical memory requests present in the MC request buffer
PCR_b	Ratio between the number of critical requests and the total number of requests, destined to b^{th} bank.
Th_{CR}	Specifies the rank up to which the core should be considered critical.
Th_{SM}	Specifies the threshold below which the scheduler prioritizes critical requests.

5.2 Design Overview of CLAMS

We propose three different schemes for calculating Th_{CR} and Th_{SM}. The first scheme is called as *Static-CLAMS* because it uses a *single and fixed* set of values for Th_{CR} and Th_{SM} for all applications. However, we find that these fixed and independent choices of Th_{CR} and Th_{SM} make it difficult to simultaneously address the two design challenges (Section 5.1). Therefore, our second scheme, called *Semi-Dyn-CLAMS*, dynamically calculates Th_{CR} based on: 1) a fixed value of Th_{SM}, and 2) PCR(k), $\forall k \in \{1...8\}$ information, calculated within an MC (Section 4). This scheme dynamically finds Th_{CR} but still uses a static value for Th_{SM}. Our third scheme is called *Dyn-CLAMS* because it dynamically calculates both Th_{CR} and Th_{SM}. It uses the same method as Semi-Dyn-CLAMS to calculate Th_{CR} and then dynamically updates Th_{SM} based on the calculated Th_{CR}. The thresholds calculated by these schemes are used to determine the *working mode* of CLAMS. The two working modes in which CLAMS scheduler can issue requests to the banks are *locality mode* and *criticality mode.*

Locality mode. This is the default scheduling mode in which CLAMS is locality-focused. It prioritizes: 1) row-hit requests over all other requests, 2) critical requests over other requests, 3) older requests over younger ones. Hence, if there are no critical requests present, this mode follows the baseline FR-FCFS scheduling policy [74, 93], which prioritizes: 1) row-hit requests over all other requests, 2) older requests over younger ones.

Criticality mode. In this mode, CLAMS is criticality-focused, and optimizes mainly for criticality. It prioritizes: 1) critical requests over all other requests, 2) row hit requests over other requests, 3) older requests over younger ones. Hence, if there are no critical requests present, this mode falls back to the baseline FR-FCFS policy.

Mode Selection. The decision to be in criticality or locality mode is based on the value of PCR calculated on a per bank basis, using the per-bank value $PCR_b(Th_{CR})$, which is defined as the ratio between the number of critical requests destined to b^{th} bank and the total number of requests destined to b^{th} bank. The particular mode is decided based on Eq.1.

$$PCR_b(Th_{CR}) \begin{cases} \leq Th_{SM} & \textit{criticality mode} \\ > Th_{SM} & \textit{locality mode} \\ = 0 & \textit{criticality} = \textit{locality mode.} \end{cases} \quad (1)$$

In the special case, when there are no critical requests destined to b^{th} bank ($PCR_b(Th_{CR}) = 0$), criticality and locality mode follow exactly the same request service order.

Inter-Core vs. Intra-Core Criticality. The goal of switching to the criticality mode is to prioritize critical memory requests over other requests belonging to *different* cores. However, because of the procedure we follow to tag criticality rank with a memory request, it might happen that both critical and non-critical requests from the **same** core might co-exist in an MC. As our schemes (explained next) do not explicitly consider core-ids while serving requests, it might happen that our prioritization mechanism might prefer a critical request over another; both belonging to the *same* core. This procedure has limited benefit, because requests from the same core have similar utility unless they have different *intra-core* criticality typically caused due to memory divergence [5, 11]. In our work, we are more interested in *inter-core* criticality, which is due to the fact that different cores have different levels of latency tolerance. Our detailed analysis shows that our schemes benefit more from *inter-core* criticality. On average, in criticality mode, 76% of the decisions to prioritize critical requests over non-critical ones are made for requests from different cores.

5.3 Design of the Static-CLAMS Memory Scheduler

This is the simplest of our proposed schemes. It uses fixed values for both the thresholds to identify the working mode. However, such fixed and independent choices for threshold values make the two design challenges of CLAMS harder to solve effectively (Section 5.1). To understand this, consider Figure 7, where we show the distribution of memory requests for one of the MCs (distribution for other MCs are similar) across different criticality-ranks when executed on our baseline architecture that employs FR-FCFS.

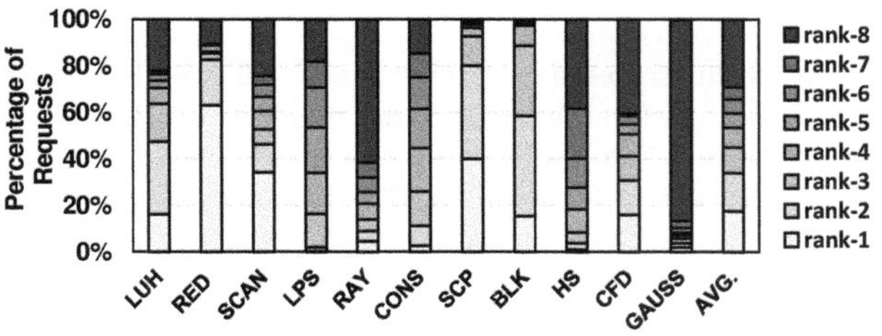

Figure 7: Distribution of requests in different criticality-rank states.

We observe, from the AVG. bar, that Th_{CR}=4 leads to co-existence of both critical and non-critical requests in the MC buffer. However, this value of Th_{CR} does not provide substantial coexistence in *every* application. For example in, SCP, with Th_{CR}=4, a majority of the requests are critical. Therefore, with this value of Th_{CR} along with Th_{SM}=20%, the scheduler will be in locality mode *most of the time*[7], as it will detect that there are too many critical requests in the MC. On the other hand, with Th_{SM}=80%, the scheduler will be mostly in criticality mode. This can degrade DRAM row buffer locality, leading to significant loss in performance. From this discussion, we conclude that: *(1) there is a need for adapting the Th_{CR} to the executing application, and (2) Th_{CR} and Th_{SM} should not be determined independently of each other.*

5.4 Design of the Semi-Dyn-CLAMS Memory Scheduler

The primary goal of Semi-Dyn-CLAMS is to calculate Th_{CR} with the help of a fixed Th_{SM} value and PCR(k) information, $\forall k \in \{1...8\}$[8]. This procedure achieves two additional sub-goals. First, Semi-Dyn-CLAMS makes Th_{CR} dependent on Th_{SM}, as it calculates Th_{CR} dynamically based on the fixed Th_{SM} value. Therefore, Semi-Dyn-CLAMS does *not* determine Th_{CR} and Th_{SM} independently, which is desirable based on the discussion in Section 5.3. Second, it makes Th_{CR} and Th_{SM} cognizant of *all* the requests in the MC request buffer, i.e., the PCR(k), $\forall k$ information. This is important because as PCR(k) and PCC(k) values are correlated (Section 4), making Th_{CR} and Th_{SM} aware of PCR(k), in turn, makes them aware of the current state of variation in criticality across cores.

To increase the opportunities of driving the memory scheduler in criticality mode, we dynamically find Th_{CR} such that the percentage of requests that are critical, denoted by PCR(Th_{CR}), is less than or equal to a fixed Th_{SM} value, but also as close as possible to Th_{SM}. In other words, we need to find the highest Th_{CR} such that PCR(Th_{CR}) is less than or equal to a fixed Th_{SM} value. After obtaining Th_{CR}, the scheduler will mostly be in criticality mode because we have ensured that over a window, PCR(Th_{CR}) is less than or equal to Th_{SM}. However, after being in criticality mode, if PCR (even with Th_{CR} = 1) exceeds the fixed value of Th_{SM}, the scheduler switches to locality mode, because our scheme detects that there are *too* many critical requests to prioritize and thus the latency tolerance variation across cores is not significant. Therefore, in such scenarios, we set Th_{CR}=8, which makes all requests to be considered critical. Such a value of Th_{CR} value will always drive the scheduler to locality mode, because PCR(8) is always equal to 1 and greater than Th_{SM}. We empirically find that Th_{SM} prefers to be in a mid-range (40% provided the best average performance results, Section 7). This is expected because, mid-range percentage of critical requests allows the coexistence of both critical and non-critical requests in MC.

Figure 8 illustrates the operation of Semi-Dyn-CLAMS over time, where we choose Th_{SM}=40% (❶). Assume only three values of Th_{CR} = {1,4,7} are possible for illustration purposes (in our final evaluation, we consider the full range from 1 to 8). We observe from Figure 8a that, in CONS, Th_{CR} is chosen as 4 most of the time because this value of Th_{CR} is the highest possible value of Th_{CR} such that PCR(Th_{CR}) is less than or equal to Th_{SM}=40%. Therefore, in CONS, the scheduler will mostly be in criticality mode. In SCP (Figure 8b), the situation is different. By choosing the same value of Th_{SM}=40% in the first half of the execution, the scheduler will be in criticality mode most of the time, as PCR(1) is lower than Th_{SM}=40%. However, during the second half of the execution, SCP prefers locality mode (❷), where PCR(1) line is above the horizontal line of Th_{SM}=40% (❶). During this time, there is no Th_{CR} such that PCR(Th_{CR}) is less than Th_{SM}=40%, and hence our scheme detects that there are too many critical requests (even with Th_{CR}=1). We set the scheduler to go in locality mode by setting Th_{CR}=8.

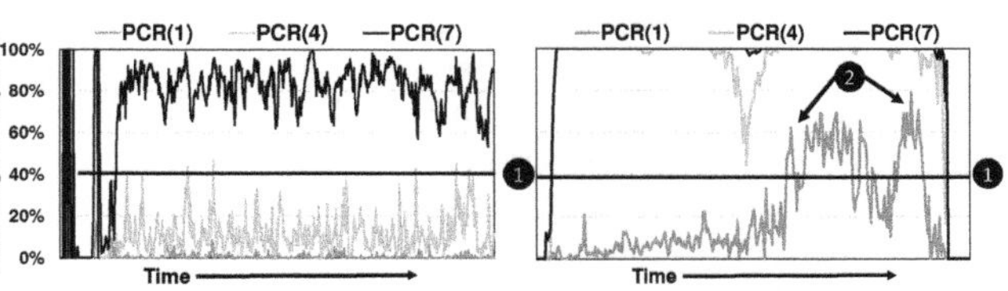

(a) CONS (b) SCP

Figure 8: Execution of CONS and SCP to illustrate the working of Semi-Dyn-CLAMS. Th_{CR} values are calculated dynamically.

Discussion. Recall that the actual mode selection is based on Eq.1, which compares the value of $PCR_b(Th_{CR})$ (and not PCR(Th_{CR})) with the value of Th_{SM}. Therefore, even though Semi-Dyn-CLAMS selects a value of Th_{CR} such that PCR(Th_{CR}) is lower than (or equal to) Th_{SM}, it is not necessary that $PCR_b(Th_{CR})$ will also be lower than (or equal to) to Th_{SM}. Therefore, even though Semi-Dyn-CLAMS overall strives to keep the scheduler in the criticality mode, while ensuring that both critical and non-critical requests have substantial presence in MC, during actual issue of requests to the memory banks, the scheduler can be in any of the modes – locality or criticality. However, if, $\forall k \in \{1..8\}$, PCR(k) is greater than the Th_{SM} value, the scheduler switches to the locality mode by setting the Th_{CR}

---

[7]Note that the actual working mode selection is based on Eq. 1, where $PCR_b(Th_{CR})$ (and not PCR(Th_{CR})) is used. Thus, the actual decision of being in criticality mode or locality mode is made on a per-bank basis. Section 5.4 provides more details.

[8]This information is updated every 512 cycles. We also used three other sampling size windows (256, 1024, 2048) cycles. The difference in overall average performance is less than 1%, implying that sampling window size does not have a significant impact on our design.

value to 8. This value of 8 will always switch the scheduler to the locality mode, because, by definition, both PCR(8) and $PCR_b(8)$ are always equal to 1, and therefore, it will be always greater than Th_{SM}. We use this analysis as a foundation for our next scheme.

Importance of $PCR_b(Th_{CR})$ and PCR(k)$\forall k$. For calculating the appropriate Th_{CR}, Semi-Dyn-CLAMS consults PCR(k), $\forall k$ information, but the scheduler makes actual decisions on the working modes based on the current set of requests to be issued to the bank, i.e., by examining $PCR_b(Th_{CR})$. This has two advantages. First, the actual mode decision is aware of the current state of the requests destined to each bank. Second, this decision is also aware of the status of all the requests in the MC, which, in turn, is also aware of PCC information.

5.5 Design of Dyn-CLAMS Memory Scheduler

We find Semi-Dyn-CLAMS to be an aggressive design in taking advantage of criticality because of two reasons. First, Semi-Dyn-CLAMS always strives to find opportunities to work in criticality mode. Second, Semi-Dyn-CLAMS goes into locality mode only when there are too many critical requests at Th_{CR}=1 (PCR(1) > Th_{SM}) in the MC buffer. Due to these two reasons, we observe significant loss in locality and performance in some applications (e.g., SCP and RAY) where locality is very important.

Even though Semi-Dyn-CLAMS calculates a Th_{CR} value that facilitates the scheduler to be in criticality mode, when it actually issues requests to the bank, the scheduler might actually pick locality mode based on the $PCR_b(Th_{CR})$ value for each bank (Section 5.4). The goal of Dyn-CLAMS is to improve locality by increasing such opportunities.

To do so, we eliminate one of the important limitations of Semi-Dyn-CLAMS: that it still uses a fixed value of Th_{SM}. In other words, in Semi-Dyn-CLAMS, Th_{CR}-Th_{SM} dependence is only *one way*, and Th_{SM} is *not* updated based on the calculated Th_{CR} value. Therefore, the *key idea* of Dyn-CLAMS is to first gauge the negative effect of the loss in row-locality on the latency tolerance (i.e., performance) of the cores by dynamically examining Th_{CR}, and then restoring the loss by lowering the value of Th_{SM} as much as possible while maintaining the same value of Th_{CR} calculated using Semi-Dyn-CLAMS. This is because, with a lower value of Th_{SM}, the scheduler is more likely to work in locality mode (see Eq. 1).

Dyn-CLAMS uses exactly the same procedure as adopted by Semi-Dyn-CLAMS to calculate Th_{CR}, but in addition, also lowers Th_{SM}. At the beginning of every window, we start with a fixed Th_{SM} value (Th_{SMinit}) to determine Th_{CR} using Semi-Dyn-CLAMS. The value of Th_{SMinit} is equal to 40%, which we calculated based on extensive experimental evaluation. After calculating Th_{CR}, we update (lower) the value of Th_{SM} to PCR(Th_{CR}). By doing so, Th_{CR} remains the same as per Semi-Dyn-CLAMS scheme, but Th_{SM} is reduced. Thus, both Th_{CR} and Th_{SM} values are updated dynamically.

Figure 9 illustrates this scheme. For CONS, we observed in Semi-Dyn-CLAMS (Figure 8) that Th_{CR} is usually 4, but in Dyn-CLAMS, while maintaining the same Th_{CR}, the value of Th_{SM} is lowered (pointed by ❶ → ❸) such that it closely resembles the PCR(4) curve. Similarly, in SCP, the value of Th_{SM} is lowered to match closely with PCR(1). However, in cases when SCP prefers locality mode (❷), Semi-Dyn-CLAMS sets Th_{CR} to 8, and Dyn-CLAMS sets Th_{SM} to 0, making the scheduler work in locality mode. Table 2 formally describes the procedures adopted by our schemes.

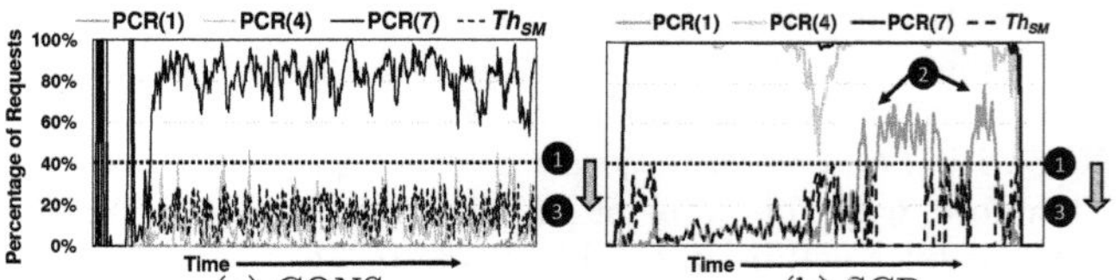

(a) CONS (b) SCP

Figure 9: Execution of CONS and SCP to illustrate the working of Dyn-CLAMS. Th_{SM} is dynamically updated based on Th_{CR}.

5.6 Hardware Overheads

We describe the hardware overheads of the three flavors of CLAMS. All three flavors requires logic to tag a memory request with the criticality of the core that generates it.

Tagging memory requests with core criticality. Each core is assigned with a rank depending on its current state of latency tolerance. As the maximum possible number of warps on a core is 48, we need two 13-bit counters to store the windowed-average of short-latency and issued warps over 128 cycles. We calculate the rank using one 13-bit divider and eight comparators. This rank is stored in a 3-bit register. At the time when a memory request is issued, we tag the memory request with the corresponding core's rank.

(I) Static-CLAMS. Two 8-bit up-down counters per-bank (max. MC buffer size is 256) are required to track the number of critical and pending memory requests. For mode selection, we compare the value of $PCR_b(Th_{CR})$ to a fixed value of Th_{SM} with the help of comparator. Th_{CR} (3 bits) and Th_{SM} (7 bits) values are stored as fixed thresholds in registers at the MC.

(II) Semi-Dyn-CLAMS. We calculate PCR(k) $\forall k$ per MC over a window of 512 cycles by keeping track of the critical requests and the number of total requests at the MC. We need one 9-bit counter per rank and one 9-bit counter

Table 2: Pseudo code for our proposed schemes

Semi-Dyn-CLAMS (Section 5.4)	Dyn-CLAMS (Section 5.5)

$Th_{CR} = 8$.
for $k \in \{1...7\}$ **do**
if (0 < PCR(k) $\leq Th_{SM}$ < PCR(k+1)) **then**
Th_{CR} = k.
end if; end for
return Th_{CR}.
	$Th_{SM} = Th_{SMinit}$; $Th_{CR} = 8$.
	for $k \in \{1...7\}$ **do**
	if (0 < PCR(k) $\leq Th_{SM}$ < PCR(k+1)) **then**
	Th_{CR} = k; Th_{SM} = PCR(Th_{CR}).
	end if; end for
	if Th_{CR} = 8 **then** Th_{SM} = 0%. **end if**
	return (Th_{CR}, Th_{SM}).

Table 3: Key configuration parameters of the simulated GPU configuration.

Core Features	1400MHz core clock, 32 cores (streaming multi-processors), SIMT width = 32 (16 × 2), Greedy-then-oldest first (GTO) dual warp scheduler [67], Thread-blocks are scheduled on SMs in a load-balanced fashion
Resources / Core	48KB shared memory, 32KB register file, Max. 1536 threads (48 warps, 32 threads/warp)
Private Caches / Core	16KB 4-way L1 data cache, 12KB 24-way texture cache, 8KB 2-way constant cache, 2KB 4-way I-cache, 128B cache block size
Shared L2 Cache	16-way 128 KB/memory channel (768KB in total), 128B cache block size
Features	Memory coalescing and inter-warp merging enabled, immediate post dominator based branch divergence handling
Memory Model	6 GDDR5 Memory Controllers (MC), FR-FCFS scheduling, 256 max. common request buffer for all 8 banks per MC, 924 MHz memory clock Global address space is interleaved among partitions in chunks of 256 bytes Hynix GDDR5 Timing, t_{CL} = 12, t_{RP} = 12, t_{RC} = 40, t_{RAS} = 28, t_{CCD} = 2, t_{RCD} = 12, t_{RRD} = 6, t_{CDLR} = 5, t_{WR} = 12
Interconnect	1 crossbar/direction (32 cores, 6 MCs), 1400MHz interconnect clock, islip VC and switch allocators

to keep track of the pending memory requests. We take a snapshot of these counters in extra storage, and then flush the counters. We then calculate PCR(k) $\forall k$ based on the snapshot values, and store them in 8 PCR(k) registers. To calculate Th_{CR}, we compare the fixed Th_{SM} value with 8 PCR(k) registers.

(III) Dyn-CLAMS. This scheme updates Th_{SM} with the value of PCR(Th_{CR}), Thus, it does not require extra overhead over Semi-Dyn-CLAMS. The information for all schemes is computed locally at the MCs. The total storage required for one of the MCs is 43B.

6. EVALUATION METHODOLOGY

We simulate the baseline architecture described in Table 3 using GPGPU-Sim v3.2.1 [6], a cycle-accurate GPU simulator. We studied 11 applications (Table 4) from various suites such as SDK [66], Rodinia [12], LLNL [42], and SHOC [13]. We classify these applications into two classes. Class-A applications show high-to-moderate scope for criticality-aware scheduling because of the presence of variation in criticality across cores (see Figure 1). The other applications are classified as Class-B because of low scope for criticality-aware scheduling (see Figure 6 and Figure 1). All the applications are executed until completion, except for LUH, CONS, and CFD, where we execute 500 million instructions.

Table 4: Evaluated applications. Table also shows: 1) Average occupancy (occ) of a GPU core in terms of warps, 2) Average Th_{CR} and Th_{SM} calculated using Semi-Dyn-CLAMS and Dyn-CLAMS, respectively, and 3) % of critical requests served in criticality-mode with Dyn-CLAMS (%-cri).

Application	Abbr.	Class	occ	Th_{CR}	Th_{SM}	%-cri
Lulesh [42]	LUH	A	18	4	13%	46
Reduction [13]	RED	A	15	1	16%	38
Scan [13]	SCAN	A	14	4	16%	42
Laplace 3D [66]	LPS	A	11	4	23%	32
Ray Tracing [66]	RAY	A	16	6	11%	40
Convolution [66]	CONS	A	15	5	21%	45
Scalar Product [66]	SCP	B	30	1	10%	66
BlackScholes [66]	BLK	B	32	2	8%	70
Hotspot [12]	HS	B	23	6	17%	17
CFD Solver [12]	CFD	B	45	2	4%	10
Gaussian [12]	GAUSS	B	8	6	6%	2

7. EXPERIMENTAL RESULTS

In this section, we analyze the performance of three CLAMS designs, along with two more memory schedulers: FR-FCFS-Cap-Best and Static-CLAMS-Best. FR-FCFS-Cap (streak control) scheduler [62] enforces a *cap* on the younger row-hit requests that can be serviced before an older row request to the same bank. When the cap is reached, FCFS policy is applied. While such a cap alleviates the starvation problem for waiting requests, it is not aware of the criticality of requests it is servicing. We show the results of FR-FCFS-Cap-Best that picks the best performing *cap* threshold, profiled separately for *each* application. Evaluated choices for *cap* values are 2, 4, 6, 8, 12 and 16. Static-Best-CLAMS is the Static-CLAMS scheduler that uses the best performing combination of Th_{CR} and Th_{SM}, profiled separately for *each* application. In contrast to Static-Best-CLAMS, Static-CLAMS uses a *single* set of thresholds (Th_{CR}=4 and Th_{SM}=20%) that provides the best *average* performance across *all* applications. The values of these thresholds are chosen from a pool of 42 (7 × 6) different combinations formed using fixed values of Th_{CR} (1 through 7) and Th_{SM} (0% through 100% in steps of 20%). Note that both FR-FCFS-Cap-Best and Static-Best-CLAMS are hard to implement as they require an exhaustive search across many threshold combinations on a per application basis. We observe that the FR-FCFS-Cap results are very sensitive to thresholds and a single threshold does not work well for all the applications. Dynamic adaptation of such thresholds is non-trivial and that is why we propose CLAMS.

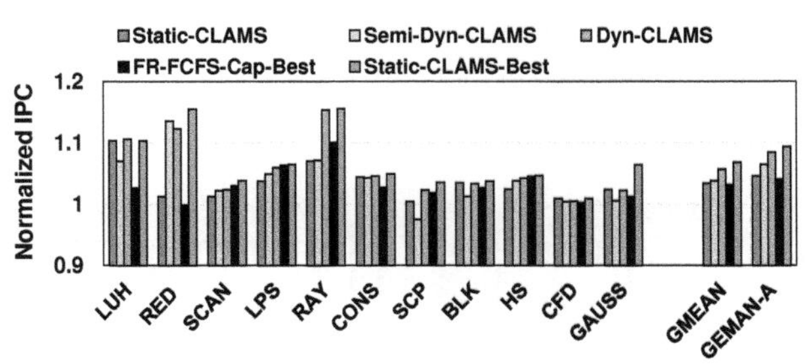

Figure 10: Performance results normalized to FR-FCFS.

Figure 10 shows the IPC improvement over FR-FCFS of proposed memory schedulers. We provide two averages, GMEAN for all applications, and GMEAN-A for only Class-A applications. We also present auxiliary metrics related to DRAM and GPU cores in Figure 11. Figure 11a shows the Row Buffer Hit Rate (RBHR) to measure DRAM locality. Figure 11b depicts the latency of critical memory requests (with respective values of Th_{CR}), and Figure 11c shows the core stall cycles during which GPU cores are not able to issue any warps. Reductions in critical request latencies and

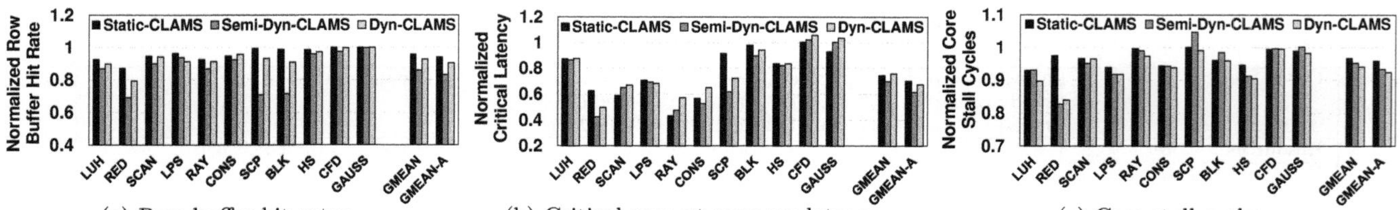

(a) Row buffer hit rates (b) Critical request memory latency (c) Core stall cycles

Figure 11: (a) DRAM row buffer hit rate, (b) memory latency of critical requests, (c) core stall cycles. Results are normalized to FR-FCFS.

core stall cycles are attributed to our prioritization schemes which favor critical requests. All results are normalized to the baseline FR-FCFS scheduler.

Analysis of Static-CLAMS. Using a single set of thresholds (Th_{CR}=4 and Th_{SM}=20%) for all applications does not lead to significant improvements over FR-FCFS in SCP and RED. This is expected because with Th_{CR}=4, a high percentage of requests are treated as critical, and using Th_{SM}=20% along with it pushes the scheduler to work mostly in locality mode. However, for LUH, we observe 10% IPC improvement, because static thresholds address both the design challenges reasonably (Section 5.1). On average, Static-CLAMS provides 3% IPC improvement for all 11 applications. Although none of the applications experience performance degradation, this scheme is still far from the upper-bound performance achievable with Static-Best-CLAMS.

Analysis of Semi-Dyn-CLAMS. We first analyze the dynamic changes in Th_{CR} calculated by the Semi-Dyn-CLAMS scheme for two applications – SCP and CONS. Figure 12 shows these results for two fixed values (40%, 80%) of Th_{SM}. We first start when Th_{SM}=40%. In SCP, Semi-Dyn-CLAMS chooses Th_{CR}=1 in the first half of the execution (Ⓐ) (as expected from our discussion in Section 5). In the second half of the execution (Ⓑ), we observe many switches to Th_{CR}=8 as Semi-Dyn-CLAMS detects that there are too many critical requests and hence switches to locality mode. In CONS, our scheme chooses Th_{CR} between 4 and 5 and mostly remains in criticality mode. However, when Th_{SM} is set to 80%, we observe an increase in Th_{CR} values for SCP in the first half of the execution (Ⓐ), and Semi-Dyn-CLAMS switches to locality mode less often (because fewer instances are observed where Th_{CR}=8). This is expected because with a higher Th_{SM} value, the scheduler will switch to criticality mode more often.

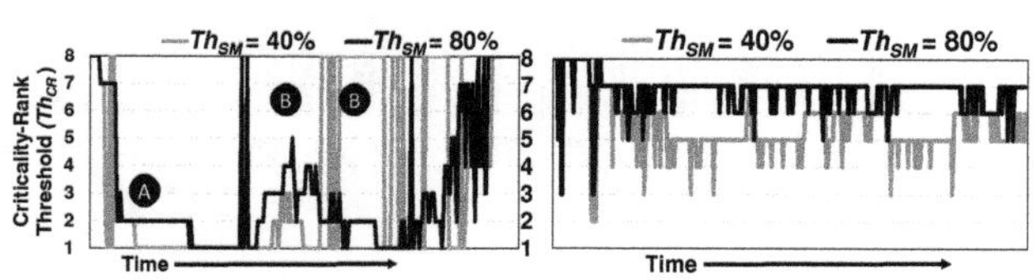

(a) SCP (b) CONS

Figure 12: Changes in Th_{CR} observed with Semi-Dyn-CLAMS. When Th_{CR}=8, the scheduler is in locality mode.

On average, Semi-Dyn-CLAMS provides 5% IPC improvement over FR-FCFS. RED, RAY, and LPS experience 13%, 7%, and 5% improvement, respectively. As desired, this scheme attempts to push the scheduler mostly to criticality mode, which helps to reduce the latency of critical requests further by 6% (at the cost of 10% reduction in RBHR) compared to Static-CLAMS. This in turn reduces the core stall cycles further by 2% compared to Static-CLAMS (Figure 11c). In SCP, row buffer hit rate is hampered the most, by 30% (Figure 11a), leading to 5% performance degradation compared to FR-FCFS. On the other hand, in RED, even though RBHR is reduced by 20%, performance improves significantly (by 12%) due to the reduction in critical request latency and core stall cycles. Our detailed analysis shows that, in RED, the impact of locality on performance is much lower than that of criticality, and vice versa in SCP. Our next scheme, Dyn-CLAMS is expected to recover the loss in locality and performance by reducing the Th_{SM} value dynamically.

Analysis of Dyn-CLAMS. We first analyze the dynamic changes in Th_{SM} calculated by the Dyn-CLAMS scheme for two applications – SCP and CONS. Figure 13 shows these changes when Th_{SMinit} = 40% and 80%. We start with analyzing the Th_{SM} curves when Th_{SMinit}=40%. In SCP and CONS, we find that the value of Th_{SM} is less than or equal to 40%. This helps the scheduler to switch to locality mode more frequently, as discussed in Section 5.5. During the phases when Th_{CR}=8 (as pointed in Figure 12 by Ⓑ), Th_{SM} value is 0% (Ⓑ), pushing the scheduler to always be in locality mode. For Th_{SMinit} = 80% curves, we observe that the value of Th_{SM} is much higher due to the increase in Th_{CR} values.

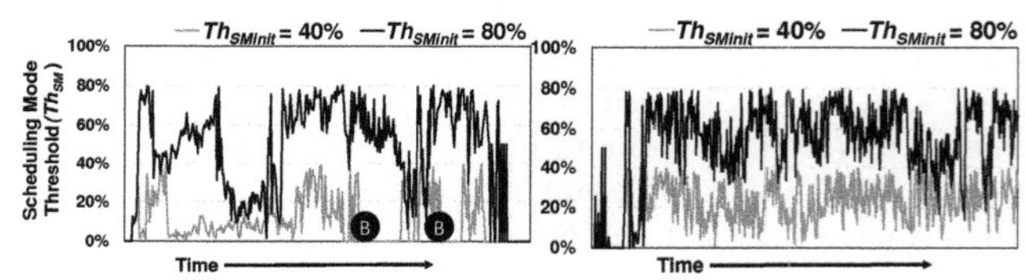

(a) SCP (b) CONS

Figure 13: Changes in Th_{SM} observed with Dyn-CLAMS.

On average, Dyn-CLAMS performs better than all three memory scheduling schemes except the upper bound Static-Best-CLAMS. RED, RAY, and LUH are the best performers with 15%, 15%, and 10% improvement over FR-FCFS, respectively. This scheme is especially useful for applications where exploiting locality is at least as important as exploiting criticality. For example, in SCP and RAY, RBHR is improved by 5% and 7%, respectively (Figure 11a), leading to additional benefits over Semi-Dyn-CLAMS. We also observe reduction in PCC(1) for these applications (22%, 25%, and 6%, respectively), as expected from our discussion in Section 3.2.

We further observe from Figure 10 that the gap between Dyn-CLAMS and Static-CLAMS-Best is not significant for many applications, suggesting that Dyn-CLAMS is able to dynamically calculate the best static combinations of thresholds for each application, as shown in Table 4, without the need for any offline application profiling. We also report the percentage of critical requests that are served in criticality mode (%-cri) in Table 4. For SCP and BLK, even though %-cri is very high, Dyn-CLAMS does not show benefit because the *number* of critical requests is small. For Class-A applications, %-cri is significant, which shows that Dyn-CLAMS is able to improve performance by prioritizing critical requests. In summary, Dyn-CLAMS achieves 9% IPC improvement over FR-FCFS, 5% over FR-FCFS-Cap-Best, and also is within 1% of the Static-CLAMS-Best for Class-A applications. The performance of none of the Class-B applications degrades with our third, most dynamic scheme.

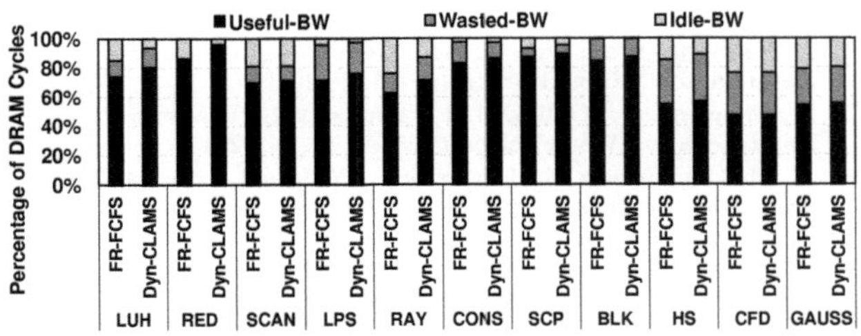

Figure 14: Useful, wasted, and idle DRAM bandwidth distribution with baseline FR-FCFS ad Dyn-CLAMS.

To get a deeper understanding into these performance results, Figure 14 shows the break down of the memory bandwidth for FR-FCFS and Dyn-CLAMS schemes into the following components: (A) *Useful-BW:* the percentage of DRAM cycles during which the application moves data (reads and writes) over the DRAM interface, (B) *Wasted-BW:* the percentage of DRAM cycles during which no data is transferred over the DRAM interface due to DRAM timing constraints [9], but there are pending memory requests in the MC buffer, and (C) *Idle-BW:* the percentage of DRAM cycles during which there are no requests pending in the MC buffer, and hence DRAM is idle. We observe that IPC and Useful-BW are highly correlated, which is consistent with the findings shown by Guz et al. [31, 32]. We further observe that Wasted-BW increases in LUH and RAY with Dyn-CLAMS because of the loss in RBHR. This is expected as the loss in locality causes more row conflicts. However, in SCAN, in spite of the reduction in RBHR, we observe negligible reduction in Wasted-BW. This is because Dyn-CLAMS enables more cores to be active at a time, allowing requests from more cores to take advantage of BLP. This increase in BLP helps to mask the negative effects of the loss in locality.

Brief Summary of Sensitivity Studies. For Semi-Dyn-CLAMS, increasing the Th_{SM} value from 20% to 40% improves the performance of applications (e.g., CONS, RED) that prefer the criticality mode. However, beyond Th_{SM}=40%, performance of most applications (except RED) saturates. Performance starts declining after Th_{SM}=60% due to the steep decrease in RBHR. We observe similar trends for Th_{SMinit} in Dyn-CLAMS. On average, a value of 40% for both Th_{SM} and Th_{SMinit} leads to the best average performance results across all our applications.

8. RELATED WORK

To our knowledge, this is the first paper that develops (1) the notion of *core criticality* in GPU systems, (2) mechanisms to dynamically estimate core criticality for different GPU cores, and (3) techniques that use such criticality estimation mechanisms to improve GPU performance via sophisticated memory request scheduling. As such, this paper is related to past works on criticality estimation in CPUs, memory scheduling (for both GPUs and CPUs), and in general other scheduling mechanisms in GPUs. We briefly summarize the prior work related to this paper in these broad categories.

Criticality Related Studies in CPUs. There have been several works that identified critical instructions [10, 21–23, 78, 79, 81], critical threads [8, 9, 17, 20, 36, 37, 86], critical applications [14, 18, 47, 48, 63], critical memory requests [4, 26, 33, 34, 45, 51, 70, 87], and critical network packets [15, 16, 29, 30], within the context of a CPU system, and developed mechanisms to analyze and/or prioritize them. None of these works identify or exploit the notion of *core criticality* we describe and analyze in this paper, which is specific to GPU systems. Srinivasan et al. [78] contrasts criticality and locality by performing a limit study that gives the maximum potential of exploiting critical memory requests. A follow-up work [79] gives a practical algorithm for identifying critical memory requests within the context of CPUs that employ out-of-order execution and explores caching mechanisms for exploiting both criticality and locality. Other works, mentioned above, take advantage of criticality information of various entities, including instructions, threads, applications, memory requests, and network packets, by developing different notions of criticality. In comparison, the criticality notion we introduce and exploit in this paper is based on the latency tolerance of a GPU core, which is very different from that of prior works.

Memory Scheduling in CPUs. Several works exploited various notions of criticality for memory request scheduling in CPU systems. Ebrahimi et al. [20] propose parallel application memory scheduling, where the memory scheduler prioritizes critical threads in multi-threaded CPU programs, where critical threads are estimated to be those that are likely on the critical path of execution. Ghose et al. [26] use load criticality information for effective memory scheduling in CPU systems. In contrast to their static memory controller policy that always favors critical requests, we develop memory scheduling mechanisms that can *dynamically* switch between criticality and locality modes. Ausavarungnirun et al. [4] propose a memory scheduler to maintain row-buffer locality in CPU-GPU fused architectures while providing high CPU performance. Our insights can be combined with the insights of this work: if we want to use our techniques for GPUs present in the CPU-GPU fused architectures [4, 44], we should also consider latency tolerance of CPU cores and include that information in the prioritization mechanisms at the memory controller.

There are numerous other memory scheduling techniques [19, 33, 46–48, 52, 53, 60–63, 65, 71, 76, 82–85, 87, 92] designed for various goals in multi-core and multi-threaded systems. None of these works are designed for GPUs and, hence, their notion of request criticality, when it exists, is very different from our notion of core criticality.

Memory Scheduling in GPUs. Lakshminarayana et al. [50] explored a DRAM scheduling policy that chooses between two policies: Shortest Job First (SJF) and FR-FCFS. Their scheme uses a statically determined parameter that needs to be uniquely calculated for each application. As this scheduler does not adapt to dynamic needs of criticality and locality in the application, it can potentially degrade per-

[9]Note that, improving RBHR and bank-level parallelism (BLP) can reduce this Wasted-BW.

formance compared to FR-FCFS [50]. On the other hand, CLAMS *dynamically* detects the preferred mode (locality or criticality) for applications at runtime and switches between two modes: Criticality and Locality. Due to its heavily dynamic nature in adapting thresholds used to workload characteristics, we find that our mechanism does not degrade any workload's performance. Yuan et al. [91] propose an arbitration mechanism in the interconnection network to restore the lost row buffer locality caused by the interleaving of requests. They showed that performance of in-order DRAM is competitive to FR-FCFS. In this paper, we show qualitatively and quantitatively that CLAMS outperforms FR-FCFS. Ausavarungnirun et al. [5] develop a technique that can prioritize some warps over others based on the latency tolerance characteristics of the warps. Our core-level criticality based mechanisms can be combined with such warp-level criticality based mechanisms for higher performance improvements.

Warp Scheduling in GPUs. Narasiman et al. [64] and Gebhart et al. [25] proposed two-level warp schedulers to improve latency tolerance and energy consumption in GPUs, respectively. Rogers et al. [75] and Jog et al. [41] proposed warp schedulers to reduce contention in caches. Lee et al. [54] proposed a criticality-aware warp scheduler that prefers critical warps over others for better latency tolerance. None of these works specifically coordinate with the underlying memory schedulers for orchestrated warp and memory scheduling decisions. CLAMS provides a substrate to foster such research, as it incorporates the core-criticality information while making memory scheduling decisions.

9. CONCLUSIONS

We introduce the notion of core criticality in GPUs, a measure of latency tolerance of a GPU core, and a new GPU memory scheduler, called CLAMS, which exploits this new measure to improve GPU performance. Our scheduler takes into account the latency tolerance of GPU cores and prioritizes memory requests from such cores, when doing so would be beneficial. CLAMS dynamically determines the importance of exploiting core criticality versus exploiting DRAM locality by monitoring the fraction of critical requests in the memory request buffers. As such, it can adapt well to changing workload demands by swiftly switching between two scheduling policies optimized for criticality and locality. Our evaluations show that CLAMS provides significant performance benefits for the class of applications that exhibit high variance in criticality across cores, without hurting the performance of other applications. We conclude that considering core criticality is a promising way to improve GPU performance and hope future works can take advantage of the notion of core criticality for other system optimizations. In particular, we believe a promising area of research is to explore this notion within the context of heterogeneous CPU-GPU memory systems.

ACKNOWLEDGMENTS

We thank the anonymous reviewers for their feedback. This research is supported in part by NSF grants #1205618, #1213052, #1212962, #1302225, #1302557, #1317560, #1320478, #1320531, #1409095, #1409723, #1439021, #1439057, and #1526750. Adwait Jog also acknowledges the start-up grant from College of William and Mary.

REFERENCES

[1] M. Abdel-Majeed and M. Annavaram, "Warped Register File: A Power Efficient Register File for GPGPUs," in *HPCA*, 2013.

[2] M. Abdel-Majeed *et al.*, "Warped Gates: Gating Aware Scheduling and Power Gating for GPGPUs," in *MICRO*, 2013.

[3] M. Arora *et al.*, "Redefining the Role of the CPU in the Era of CPU-GPU Integration," *IEEE Micro*, 2012.

[4] R. Ausavarungnirun *et al.*, "Staged Memory Scheduling: Achieving High Prformance and Scalability in Heterogeneous Systems," in *ISCA*, 2012.

[5] R. Ausavarungnirun *et al.*, "Exploiting Inter-Warp Heterogeneity to Improve GPGPU Performance," in *PACT*, 2015.

[6] A. Bakhoda *et al.*, "Analyzing CUDA Workloads Using a Detailed GPU Simulator," in *ISPASS*, 2009.

[7] M. Bauer *et al.*, "CudaDMA: Optimizing GPU Memory Bandwidth via Warp Specialization," in *SC*, 2011.

[8] A. Bhattacharjee and M. Martonosi, "Thread criticality predictors for dynamic performance, power, and resource management in chip multiprocessors," in *ISCA*, 2009.

[9] Q. Cai *et al.*, "Meeting Points: Using Thread Criticality to Adapt Multicore Hardware to Parallel Regions," in *PACT*, 2008.

[10] J. Casmira and D. Grunwald, "Dynamic Instruction Scheduling Slack," in *Kool Chips Workshop in conjunction with MICRO*, 2000.

[11] N. Chatterjee *et al.*, "Managing DRAM Latency Divergence in Irregular GPGPU Applications," in *SC*, 2014.

[12] S. Che *et al.*, "Rodinia: A Benchmark Suite for Heterogeneous Computing," in *IISWC*, 2009.

[13] A. Danalis *et al.*, "The Scalable Heterogeneous Computing (SHOC) benchmark suite," in *GPGPU*, 2010.

[14] R. Das *et al.*, "Application-to-Core Mapping Policies to Reduce Memory System Interference in Multi-Core Systems," in *HPCA*, 2013.

[15] R. Das *et al.*, "Application-aware prioritization mechanisms for on-chip networks," in *MICRO*, 2009.

[16] R. Das *et al.*, "Aérgia: exploiting packet latency slack in on-chip networks," in *ISCA*, 2010.

[17] K. Du Bois *et al.*, "Criticality stacks: Identifying critical threads in parallel programs using synchronization behavior," in *Proceedings of the 40th Annual International Symposium on Computer Architecture*, ser. ISCA '13. New York, NY, USA: ACM.

[18] E. Ebrahimi *et al.*, "Fairness via Source Throttling: A Configurable and High-Performance Fairness Substrate for Multi-Core Memory Systems," in *ASPLOS*, 2010.

[19] E. Ebrahimi *et al.*, "Prefetch-Aware Shared Resource Management for Multi-Core Systems," in *ISCA*, 2011.

[20] E. Ebrahimi *et al.*, "Parallel application memory scheduling," in *MICRO*, 2011.

[21] B. Fields *et al.*, "Slack: maximizing performance under technological constraints," in *ISCA*, 2002.

[22] B. Fields *et al.*, "Focusing processor policies via critical-path prediction," in *ISCA*, 2001.

[23] B. A. Fields *et al.*, "Interaction cost and shotgun profiling," 2004.

[24] J. Gai *et al.*, "More IMPATIENT: A Gridding-accelerated Toeplitz-based Strategy for non-Cartesian High-resolution 3D MRI on GPUs," *JPDC*, 2013.

[25] M. Gebhart *et al.*, "Energy-efficient Mechanisms for Managing Thread Context in Throughput Processors," in *ISCA*, 2011.

[26] S. Ghose *et al.*, "Improving Memory Scheduling via Processor-Side Load Criticality Information," in *ISCA*, 2013.

[27] N. Goswami *et al.*, "Power-performance Co-optimization of Throughput Core Architecture using Resistive Memory," in *HPCA*, 2013.

[28] N. Goswami *et al.*, "Exploring GPGPU Workloads: Characterization Methodology, Analysis and Microarchitecture Evaluation Implications," in *IISWC*, 2010.

[29] B. Grot *et al.*, "Kilo-NOC: A Heterogeneous Network-on-Chip Architecture for Scalability and Service Guarantees," in *ISCA*, 2011.

[30] B. Grot *et al.*, "Preemptive Virtual Clock: A Flexible, Efficient, and Cost-effective QOS Scheme for Networks-on-Chip," in *MICRO*, 2009.

[31] Z. Guz *et al.*, "Many-Core vs. Many-Thread Machines: Stay Away From the Valley," *IEEE CAL*, 2009.

[32] Z. Guz *et al.*, "Threads vs. Caches: Modeling the Behavior of Parallel Workloads," in *ICCD*, 2010.

[33] E. Ipek *et al.*, "Self-Optimizing Memory Controllers: A Reinforcement Learning Approach," in *ISCA*, 2008.

[34] M. K. Jeong *et al.*, "A QoS-aware memory controller for dynamically balancing GPU and CPU bandwidth use in an MPSoC," in *DAC*, 2012.

[35] W. Jia *et al.*, "Characterizing and Improving the Use of Demand-fetched Caches in GPUs," in *ICS*, 2012.

[36] J. A. Joao *et al.*, "Bottleneck Identification and Scheduling in Multithreaded Applications," in *ASPLOS*, 2012.

[37] J. A. Joao *et al.*, "Utility-based Acceleration of Multithreaded Applications on Asymmetric CMPs," in *ISCA*, 2013.

[38] A. Jog *et al.*, "Application-aware Memory System for Fair and Efficient Execution of Concurrent GPGPU Applications," in *GPGPU*, 2014.

[39] A. Jog *et al.*, "Anatomy of GPU Memory System for Multi-Application Execution," in *MEMSYS*, 2015.

[40] A. Jog *et al.*, "Orchestrated Scheduling and Prefetching for GPGPUs," in *ISCA*, 2013.

[41] A. Jog *et al.*, "OWL: Cooperative Thread Array Aware Scheduling Techniques for Improving GPGPU Performance," in *ASPLOS*, 2013.

[42] I. Karlin *et al.*, "Exploring Traditional and Emerging Parallel Programming Models using a Proxy Application," in *IPDPS*, 2013.

[43] O. Kayiran *et al.*, "Neither More Nor Less: Optimizing Thread-level Parallelism for GPGPUs," in *PACT*, 2013.

[44] O. Kayiran *et al.*, "Managing GPU Concurrency in Heterogeneous Architectures," in *MICRO*, 2014.

[45] S. Khan *et al.*, "Improving Cache Performance by Exploiting Read-Write Disparity," in *HPCA*, 2014.

[46] H. Kim *et al.*, "Bounding memory interference delay in COTS-based multi-core systems," in *RTAS*, 2014.

[47] Y. Kim *et al.*, "ATLAS: A Scalable and High-performance Scheduling Algorithm for Multiple Memory Controllers," in *HPCA*, 2010.

[48] Y. Kim *et al.*, "Thread Cluster Memory Scheduling: Exploiting Differences in Memory Access Behavior," in *MICRO*, 2010.

[49] D. Kirk and W. W. Hwu, *Programming Massively Parallel Processors.* Morgan Kaufmann, 2010.

[50] N. B. Lakshminarayana *et al.*, "DRAM Scheduling Policy for GPGPU Architectures Based on a Potential Function," *IEEE CAL*, 2012.

[51] C. J. Lee *et al.*, "Improving Memory Bank-Level Parallelism in the Presence of Prefetching," in *MICRO*, 2009.

[52] C. J. Lee *et al.*, "Prefetch-Aware DRAM Controllers," in *MICRO*, 2008.

[53] C. J. Lee *et al.*, "DRAM-Aware Last-Level Cache Writeback: Reducing Write-Caused Interference in Memory Systems," in *HPS Technical Report.* University of Texas at Austin, 2010.

[54] S.-Y. Lee and C.-J. Wu, "CAWS: Criticality-aware Warp Scheduling for GPGPU Workloads," in *PACT*, 2014.

[55] S.-Y. Lee and C.-J. Wu, "Characterizing GPU Latency Hiding Ability," in *ISPASS*, 2014.

[56] V. W. Lee *et al.*, "Debunking the 100X GPU vs. CPU Myth: An Evaluation of Throughput Computing on CPU and GPU," in *ISCA*, 2010.

[57] J. Leng *et al.*, "GPUWattch: Enabling Energy Optimizations in GPGPUs," in *ISCA*, 2013.

[58] D. Li *et al.*, "Priority-Based Cache Allocation in Throughput Processors," in *HPCA*, 2015.

[59] E. Lindholm *et al.*, "NVIDIA Tesla: A Unified Graphics and Computing Architecture," *IEEE Micro*, 2008.

[60] T. Moscibroda and O. Mutlu, "Memory Performance Attacks: Denial of Memory Service in Multi-Core Systems," in *USENIX Security*, 2007.

[61] S. P. Muralidhara *et al.*, "Reducing Memory Interference in Multicore Systems via Application-Aware Memory Channel Partitioning," in *MICRO*, 2011.

[62] O. Mutlu and T. Moscibroda, "Stall-Time Fair Memory Access Scheduling for Chip Multiprocessors," in *MICRO*, 2007.

[63] O. Mutlu and T. Moscibroda, "Parallelism-Aware Batch Scheduling: Enhancing Both Performance and Fairness of Shared DRAM Systems," in *ISCA*, 2008.

[64] V. Narasiman *et al.*, "Improving GPU Performance via Large Warps and Two-level Warp Scheduling," in *MICRO*, 2011.

[65] K. J. Nesbit *et al.*, "Fair Queuing Memory Systems," in *MICRO*, 2006.

[66] NVIDIA, "CUDA C/C++ SDK Code Samples," 2011. http://developer.nvidia.com/cuda-cc-sdk-code-samples

[67] NVIDIA, "Fermi: NVIDIA's Next Generation CUDA Compute Architecture," 2011.

[68] G. Pekhimenko *et al.*, "A Case for Toggle-Aware Compression for GPU Systems," in *HPCA*, 2016.

[69] B. Pichai *et al.*, "Architectural Support for Address Translation on GPUs: Designing Memory Management Units for CPU/GPUs with Unified Address Spaces," in *ASPLOS*, 2014.

[70] M. K. Qureshi *et al.*, "A Case for MLP-Aware Cache Replacement," ser. ISCA, 2006.

[71] N. Rafique *et al.*, "Effective Management of DRAM Bandwidth in Multicore Processors," in *PACT*, 2007.

[72] M. Rhu *et al.*, "A Locality-Aware Memory Hierarchy for Energy-Efficient GPU Architectures," in *MICRO*, 2013.

[73] S. Rixner, "Memory Controller Optimizations for Web Servers," in *MICRO*, 2004.

[74] S. Rixner *et al.*, "Memory Access Scheduling," in *ISCA*, 2000.

[75] T. G. Rogers *et al.*, "Cache-Conscious Wavefront Scheduling," in *MICRO*, 2012.

[76] V. Seshadri *et al.*, "The dirty-block index," in *ISCA*, 2014.

[77] A. Sethia *et al.*, "APOGEE: Adaptive Prefetching on GPUs for Energy Efficiency," in *PACT*, 2013.

[78] S. T. Srinivasan and A. R. Lebeck, "Load latency tolerance in dynamically scheduled processors," in *MICRO*, 1998.

[79] S. Srinivasan *et al.*, "Locality vs. Criticality," in *ISCA*, 2001.

[80] S. S. Stone *et al.*, "Accelerating advanced MRI reconstructions on GPUs," *J. Parallel Distrib. Comput.*, 2008.

[81] S. Subramaniam *et al.*, "Criticality-Based Optimizations for Efficient Load Processing," in *HPCA*, 2009.

[82] L. Subramanian *et al.*, "The Blacklisting Memory Scheduler: Achieving High Performance and Fairness at Low Cost," in *ICCD*, 2014.

[83] L. Subramanian *et al.*, "BLISS: Balancing Performance, Fairness and Complexity in Memory Access Scheduling," *IEEE TPDS*, 2016.

[84] L. Subramanian *et al.*, "The Application Slowdown Model: Quantifying and Controlling the Impact of Inter-application Interference at Shared Caches and Main Memory," in *MICRO*, 2015.

[85] L. Subramanian *et al.*, "MISE: Providing performance predictability and improving fairness in shared main memory systems," in *HPCA*, 2013.

[86] M. A. Suleman *et al.*, "Accelerating Critical Section Execution with Asymmetric Multi-core Architectures," in *ASPLOS*, 2009.

[87] H. Usui *et al.*, "DASH: Deadline-Aware High-Performance Memory Scheduler for Heterogeneous Systems with Hardware Accelerators," in *ACM TACO*, 2016.

[88] N. Vijaykumar *et al.*, "Enabling Efficient Data Compression in GPUs," in *ISCA*, 2015.

[89] J. Wang and Y. Sudhakar, "Characterization and Analysis of Dynamic Parallelism in Unstructured GPU Applications," in *IISWC*, 2014.

[90] X. L. Wu *et al.*, "Impatient MRI: Illinois Massively Parallel Acceleration Toolkit for image reconstruction with enhanced throughput in MRI," in *ISBI*, 2011.

[91] G. Yuan *et al.*, "Complexity Effective Memory Access Scheduling for Many-core Accelerator Architectures," in *MICRO*, 2009.

[92] J. Zhao *et al.*, "FIRM: Fair and high-performance memory control for persistent memory systems," in *MICRO*, 2014.

[93] W. K. Zuravleff and T. Robinson, "Controller for a Synchronous DRAM that Maximizes Throughput by Allowing Memory Requests and Commands to be Issued Out of Order, US Patent," 1997.

A Service System with Randomly Behaving On-demand Agents

Lam M. Nguyen
ISE Department
Lehigh University
Bethlehem, PA 18015
lmn214@lehigh.edu

Alexander L. Stolyar
ISE Department
Lehigh University
Bethlehem, PA 18015
stolyar@lehigh.edu

ABSTRACT

We consider a service system where agents (or, servers) are invited on-demand. Customers arrive as a Poisson process and join a customer queue. Customer service times are i.i.d. exponential. Agents' behavior is random in two respects. First, they can be invited into the system exogenously, and join the agent queue after a random time. Second, with some probability they rejoin the agent queue after a service completion, and otherwise leave the system. The objective is to design a real-time adaptive agent invitation scheme that keeps both customer and agent queues/waiting-times small. We study an adaptive scheme, which controls the number of pending agent invitations, based on queue-state feedback.

We study the system process fluid limits, in the asymptotic regime where the customer arrival rate goes to infinity. We use the machinery of switched linear systems and common quadratic Lyapunov functions to derive sufficient conditions for the local stability of fluid limits at the desired equilibrium point (with zero queues). We conjecture that, for our model, local stability is in fact sufficient for global stability of fluid limits; the validity of this conjecture is supported by numerical and simulation experiments. When the local stability conditions do hold, simulations show good overall performance of the scheme.

1. INTRODUCTION

This model is a generalization of that in [9, 7]. It was originally motivated (see [9]) by applications to call/contact centers [1], where what we call agents are "special agents", or "knowledge workers," whose time is expensive, so that it is inefficient to have them working fixed shifts, with inevitable periods of idle time due to random fluctuations in customer demand. It is much more reasonable to invite them on-demand in real time; however, designing an efficient agent invitation strategy is non-trivial due to randomness in agent behavior. Besides efficiency (in terms of minimizing customer and agent waiting times), another highly desirable feature of the invitation scheme is simplicity and robustness.

SIGMETRICS '16 June 14-18, 2016, Antibes Juan-Les-Pins, France

ACM ISBN 978-1-4503-4266-7/16/06.

DOI: http://dx.doi.org/10.1145/2896377.2901484

The model we consider is generic and has other applications, or potential applications. One example is telemedicine [2], in which case "agents" are doctors, invited on-demand to serve patients remotely. Another example is crowdsourcing-based customer service [3]. Also note that the model has relation to classical assemble-to-order models, where customers are orders and "invited agents" are products, which cannot be produced/assembled instantly. The model is also related to "double-ended queues" [5] and matching systems [4]; although in such models arrivals of all types into the system are typically exogenous, as opposed to being controlled.

We study a feedback-based adaptive scheme of [9, 7]. We consider the system in the asymptotic regime where the customer arrival rate becomes large while the distributions of an agent response times and a service time are fixed. We show convergence of the fluid-scaled process to the fluid limit (Theorem 1). The fluid limit trajectories have very complicated behavior – there are two domains where they follow different ODEs, and a "reflecting" boundary. This poses big challenges for proving *global stability* of the fluid limits, understood as the convergence of their trajectories to the equilibrium point, at which the queues are zero. Given that, the focus of this paper and our main results concern the system *local stability* at the equilibrium point, understood as the stability of the dynamic system which describes fluid limit trajectories away from the boundary. We use the machinery of switched linear systems and common quadratic Lyapunov functions [8] to obtain our **main results** (Theorem 2), providing sufficient local stability conditions. The details of our model, results, proofs, conjectures and numerical/simulation experiments are in [6].

2. MODEL AND ALGORITHM

Customers arrive according to a Poisson process, and join the customer queue waiting for an available agent and are served in the order of their arrival. There is an infinite pool of potential agents, which can be invited to serve customers. Once being invited, an agent joins the agent queue after a random, exponentially distributed, time with mean $1/\beta$. The customer and agent queues cannot be positive simultaneously: the head-of-the-line customer and agents are immediately matched, leave their queues, and together go to service. Each service time is an exponentially distributed random variable with mean $1/\mu$; after the service completion, the customer leaves the system, while the agent rejoins the agent queue with probability $\alpha \in [0, 1)$. Let $X(t)$ be the number of pending agents that have been invited but have not decided to accept or decline the invitations at time t. We define $Y(t) = Q_a(t) - Q_c(t)$ as the difference of the number of customers in the agent queue and in the customer queue at time t. Let $Z(t)$ be the number of customers (or agents) in service at time t. The system state can be described by three variables X, Y, Z.

The feedback scheme in [9] maintains a "target" $X_{target}(t)$ for the number of invited agents $X(t)$. $X_{target}(t)$ is changed by $\Delta X_{target}(t) = [-\gamma\Delta Y(t) - \epsilon Y(t)\Delta t]$ at each time t when $Y(t)$ changes by $\Delta Y(t)$ (+1 or −1), where $\gamma > 0$ and $\epsilon > 0$ are the algorithm parameters and Δt is the time duration from the previous change of Y. New agents are invited if and only if $X(t) < X_{target}(t)$, where $X(t)$ is the actual number of invited (pending) agents; therefore, $X(t) \geq X_{target}(t)$ holds at all times. In addition, $X_{target}(t) \geq 0$; i.e. if an update of $X_{target}(t)$ makes it negative, its value is immediately reset to zero. To simplify our theoretical analysis, we consider a "stylized" version, which has the same basic dynamics, but keeps $X_{target}(t)$ integer and assumes that $X(t) = X_{target}(t)$ at all times; the latter is equivalent to assuming that not only agent invitations can be issued instantly, but they can also be withdrawn at any time. Formally, the stylized scheme is defined as follows. There are four types of mutually independent, and independent of the past, events that affect the dynamics of $X(t)$, $Y(t)$ and $Z(t)$ in a small time interval $[t, t+dt]$: (i) a customer arrival, (ii) an agent acceptance, (iii) an additional event, and (iv) a service completion with probabilities Λdt, $\beta X(t)dt$, $\epsilon|Y(t)|dt$, and $\mu Z(t)dt$, respectively. The changes at these event times are described as follows: (i) Upon a customer arrival, if $Y(t) > 0$, $Z(t)$ changes by $\Delta Z(t) = 1$; and if $Y(t) \leq 0$, $\Delta Z(t) = 0$. $\Delta Y(t) = -1$ and $\Delta X(t) = \gamma$. (ii) Upon the acceptance of an invitation, if $Y(t) < 0$, $\Delta Z(t) = 1$; and if $Y(t) \geq 0$, $\Delta Z(t) = 0$. $\Delta Y(t) = 1$ and $\Delta X(t) = -(\gamma \wedge X(t))$. (iii) Upon the third type of event, if $X(t) \geq 1$, $\Delta X(t) = -\text{sgn}(Y(t))$; and if $X(t) = 0$, $\Delta X(t) = 1$ if $Y(t) < 0$ and $\Delta X(t) = 0$ if $Y(t) \geq 0$. (iv) Upon the service completion, (a) with probability α, if $Y(t) < 0$, $\Delta Z(t) = 0$; and if $Y(t) \geq 0$, $\Delta Z(t) = -1$; $\Delta Y(t) = 1$ and $\Delta X(t) = -(\gamma \wedge X(t))$. (b) With probability $(1-\alpha)$, $\Delta Z(t) = -1$.

3. MAIN RESULTS

We consider a sequence of systems, indexed by a scaling parameter $r \to \infty$. In the system with index r, the arrival rate is λr, while the parameters α, β, μ, ϵ, γ are constant. The corresponding process is (X^r, Y^r, Z^r), where $X^r = (X^r(t), t \geq 0)$, $Y^r = (Y^r(t), t \geq 0)$ and $Z^r = (Z^r(t), t \geq 0)$. Let $W = |Y| + 2Z$ be the total number of customers and agents in the system. We are using a new process (X, Y, W), which is more convenient for the analysis. We define new fluid-scaled processes with centering $(\bar{X}^r, \bar{Y}^r, \bar{W}^r) = r^{-1}(X^r - \lambda r(1-\alpha)/\beta, Y^r, W^r - 2\lambda r/\mu)$.

THEOREM 1. *Consider a sequence of processes* $(\bar{X}^r, \bar{Y}^r, \bar{W}^r)$, $r \to \infty$, *with deterministic initial states such that* $(\bar{X}^r(0), \bar{Y}^r(0), \bar{W}^r(0)) \to (x(0), y(0), w(0))$ *for some fixed* $(x(0), y(0), w(0)) \in \mathbb{R}^3$, $x(0) \geq -\lambda(1-\alpha)/\beta$. *Then, these processes can be constructed on a common probability space, so that the following holds. W.p.1, from any subsequence of r, there exists a further subsequence such that*

$$(\bar{X}^r, \bar{Y}^r, \bar{W}^r) \to (x, y, w) \quad u.o.c. \quad as \quad r \to \infty \tag{1}$$

where $(x, y, w) = [(x(t),\ t \geq 0), (y(t),\ t \geq 0), (w(t),\ t \geq 0)]$ *is a locally Lipschitz trajectory such that at any regular point* $t \geq 0$

$$\begin{cases} x' = \begin{cases} -\gamma y' - \epsilon y, & if\ x > -\frac{\lambda(1-\alpha)}{\beta} \\ [-\gamma y' - \epsilon y] \vee 0, & if\ x = -\frac{\lambda(1-\alpha)}{\beta} \end{cases} \\ y' = \beta x + \frac{1}{2}\alpha\mu(w - |y|) \\ w' = \beta x + \frac{1}{2}(\alpha - 2)\mu(w - |y|). \end{cases} \tag{2}$$

Consider a dynamic system

$$\begin{cases} x' = -\gamma y'(t) - \epsilon y \\ y' = \beta x + \frac{1}{2}\alpha\mu(w - |y|) \\ w' = \beta x + \frac{1}{2}(\alpha - 2)\mu(w - |y|), \end{cases} \tag{3}$$

which is (2) "away from boundary," i.e. when $x > -\frac{\lambda(1-\alpha)}{\beta}$.

THEOREM 2. *For any set of positive* β, μ, *and* $\alpha \in (0, 1)$, *there exist values of* $\gamma > 0$ *and* $\epsilon > 0$ *satisfying either*

$$\begin{cases} \frac{\beta\gamma^2}{4} < \epsilon < \frac{\beta\gamma^2}{2} \\ \epsilon > \frac{\beta\gamma^2}{2} - \left(\frac{\alpha\gamma\mu}{2} - \frac{(1-\alpha)\mu^2}{2\beta}\right) \\ \gamma > \frac{(1-\alpha)\mu}{\alpha\beta} \end{cases} \quad or \quad \begin{cases} \epsilon < \frac{\beta\gamma^2}{2} - \frac{\alpha\gamma\mu}{2} \\ \gamma > \frac{\alpha\mu}{\beta}. \end{cases} \tag{4}$$

For the parameters, satisfying either the left or right condition of (4), common quadratic Lyapunov function of the system (3) exists, and the system (3) is exponentially stable.

Note that the right condition of (4) is more robust and is easier to achieve in practice. Indeed, for any given $\epsilon > 0$, it holds for all sufficiently large γ.

4. REFERENCES

[1] Z. Aksin, M. Armony, and V. Mehrotra. The modern call center: a multi-disciplinary perspective on operations management research. *Production and Operations Management*, 16(6):665–688, 2007.

[2] American Telemedicine Association. *Core Operational Guidelines for Telehealth Services Involving Provider-Patient Interactions*, 2014.

[3] P. Formisano. Flexibility for changing business needs: Improve customer service and drive more revenue with a virtual crowdsourcing solution. *White paper*, 2014.

[4] I. Gurvich and A. Ward. On the dynamic control of matching queues. *Stochastic Systems*, 4(2):479–523, 2014.

[5] B. R. K. Kashyap. The double-ended queue with bulk service and limited waiting space. *Operations Research*, 14(5):822–834, 1966.

[6] L. Nguyen and A. Stolyar. A service system with randomly behaving on-demand agents, 2016. http://arxiv.org/pdf/1603.03413v1.pdf.

[7] G. Pang and A. Stolyar. A service system with on-demand agent invitations. *Queueing Systems*, 2015. http://arxiv.org/pdf/1409.7380v2.pdf.

[8] R. Shorten, F. Wirth, O. Mason, K. Wulff, and C. King. Stability criteria for switched and hybrid systems. *SIAM Review*, 49(4):545–592, 2007.

[9] A. Stolyar, M. Reiman, N. Korolev, V. Mezhibovsky, and H. Ristock. Pacing in knowledge worker engagement, 2010. *United States Patent Application 20100266116-A1.*

An Analysis of Load Imbalance in Scale-out Data Serving

Stanko Novakovic
EPFL
stanko.novakovic@epfl.ch

Alexandros Daglis
EPFL
alexandros.daglis@epfl.ch

Edouard Bugnion
EPFL
edouard.bugnion@epfl.ch

Babak Falsafi
EPFL
babak.falsafi@epfl.ch

Boris Grot
University of Edinburgh
boris.grot@ed.ac.uk

ABSTRACT

Despite the natural parallelism across lookups, performance of distributed key-value stores is often limited due to load imbalance induced by heavy skew in the popularity distribution of the dataset. To avoid violating service level objectives expressed in terms of tail latency, systems tend to keep server utilization low and organize the data in micro-shards, which in turn provides units of migration and replication for the purpose of load balancing. These techniques reduce the skew, but incur additional monitoring, data replication and consistency maintenance overheads. This work shows that the trend towards extreme scale-out will further exacerbate the skew-induced load imbalance, and hence the overhead of migration and replication.

CCS Concepts

•**Computer systems organization** → *Distributed architectures;*

Keywords

Load imbalance; Replication

1. INTRODUCTION

A significant portion of contemporary web-scale applications is latency-sensitive. However, designing a datacenter-scale system that guarantees low latency for the majority of user requests is notoriously challenging. Such latency-critical systems are often powered by in-memory distributed key-value stores (KVS), which span hundreds of servers and provide the means for locating and retrieving data fast by using consistent hashing. The flexibility and scalability of using KVS in a scale-out environment has led to its broad use as a state-of-the-art approach for low-latency data serving applications. However, a substantial pain point of the approach is that it leads to severe inter-server load imbalance whenever the data popularity distribution is skewed.

SIGMETRICS '16 June 14-18, 2016, Antibes Juan-Les-Pins, France

ACM ISBN 978-1-4503-4266-7/16/06.

DOI: http://dx.doi.org/10.1145/2896377.2901501

To ensure good quality of service under skewed workloads, providers set strict service-level objectives (SLO), requiring the service deployment to respond to user requests within a short and bounded delay. What makes the challenge even harder is that designing for the average latency is not enough; a good service guarantees that the vast majority of the requests will meet the SLO, and thus targets a 99th or even 99.9th percentile latency of just a few milliseconds [3]. To satisfy such strict latency requirements and at the same time sufficiently utilize the available resources and deliver high throughput, providers rely on various migration and replication schemes.

In this work we first characterize the skew in data serving workloads and show that the trend towards extreme scale-out [4] will further exacerbate the load imbalance problem. We then argue that such increase in load imbalance will raise the frequency of migration and replication operations to keep the system at the desired level of utilization [6].

2. SCALE-OUT-INDUCED IMBALANCE

KVS typically handle very large collections of data items and millions or billions of user requests per second. In such a setting, skewed distributions emerge naturally, as the popularity of the data items varies greatly. Previous work has shown that popularity distributions in real-world KVS workloads follow a power-law distribution, resulting in an access frequency imbalance, commonly referred to as *skew* [1]. This skewed distribution is often modeled by the power-law Zipfian distribution [2]. A classic example of such skewed popularity distribution is a social network, where a very small subset of users is extremely popular as compared to the average user. These two distinct user categories (popular versus the rest) result in a popularity distribution with a skyrocketing peak and a long tail.

Dataset distribution across the deployment's collection of servers is typically done by grouping data items into "micro-shards", each server being responsible for hosting and serving hundreds or thousands of them from its local memory [3]. This data distribution is done by applying a hash function on the *key* of the data items, which maps each of them to a micro-shard and each micro-shard to a server. In practice, a collection of micro-shards mapping to a single server represents a single data *shard* that is served by its corresponding server. Thus, even after grouping data items together into shards, the presence of the original popularity skew is still observable as a popularity skew across shards.

We define the *shard skew* as the access ratio between the hottest server and the average. Shard skew arises in a data-

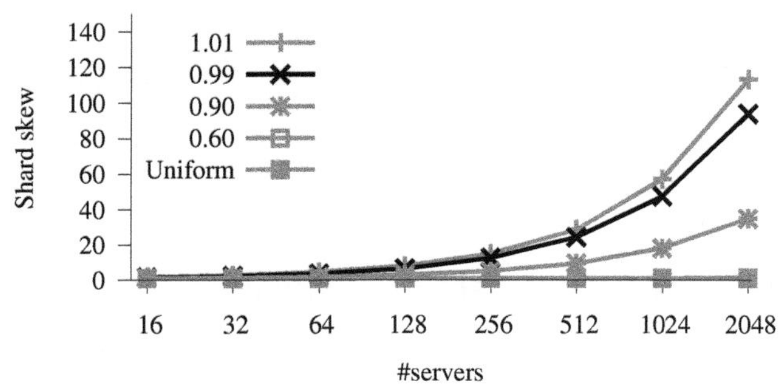

Figure 1: Shard-skew sensitivity as a function of Zipfian exponent and the number of servers.

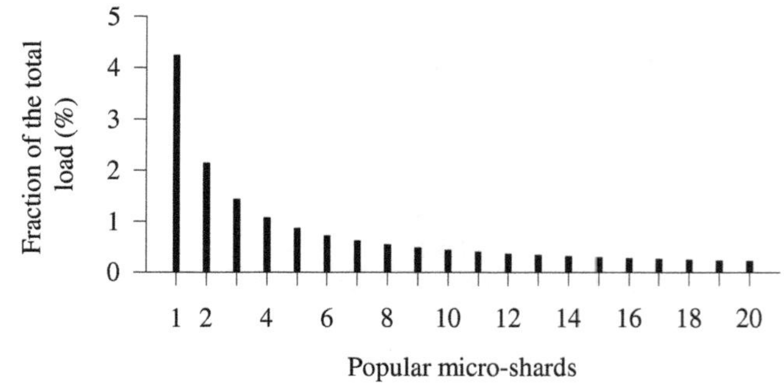

Figure 2: The 20 most popular micro-shards out of 512000 micro-shards (sorted), $\alpha = 0.99$

center deployment as a function of the exponent α of the dataset's power-law distribution. The exponent α is determined by the dataset it models. $\alpha = 0.99$ is the typical data popularity distribution used in KVS research. Some studies show that the popularity distribution skew in real-world datasets can be lower than that, but also even higher (e.g., up to $\alpha = 1.01$ [5]).

Fig. 1 shows that the shard skew becomes more dramatic as the number of servers grows. The number of servers is proportional to the dataset size and inversely proportional to the per-server DRAM capacity. For $\alpha = 0.6$, the shard skew only grows to 1.4× from 1 to 2048 servers, meaning that such a distribution would result in only 1.4× lower efficiency than a perfectly balanced distribution. At the same time, both $\alpha = 0.99$ and $\alpha = 1.01$ show unambiguously that the shard skew dramatically limits performance. For example, doubling the number of servers from 1024 to 2048 with $\alpha = 0.99$ leads to shard skew increasing near-linearly by 1.97×. Although capacity would double, the throughput would remain nearly identical.

3. DYNAMIC REPLICATION

Service providers are well aware of the problems arising from skew-induced load imbalance [3, 6]: servers that hold the most popular micro-shards can quickly become overwhelmed with user requests, degrading the whole system's performance and service quality. Data replication is a widely-used technique for dealing with such load imbalance in the datacenter. We focus on dynamic replication, where the system takes replication decisions based on the current load. Dynamic replication is never free, it requires: (i) close load monitoring; (ii) the actual replication of micro-shards and keeping the metadata up to date; (iii) maintaining consistency of a large number of micro-shard replicas.

To evaluate the impact of the trend towards extreme scale-out on the overhead of dynamic replication, we designed a model of a distributed key-value store. The model is configured with 1 billion keys, with Zipfian $\alpha = 0.99$ key popularity, hashed into 512×1000 micro-shards on the cluster. Using the information about the load associated with each of the micro-shards, we can compute the upper bound on how many replicas are required for each one of them. A suitable metric for computing this bound is the ratio between the micro-shard's load (λ_i) and the average server load ($\lambda_{avg} = \frac{1}{N}$, where N is the number of servers in the cluster).

Fig. 2 shows the 20 most popular micro-shards in our dataset. The hottest micro-shard alone accounts for 4.2% of the total traffic, which is 20× the average load of an entire server in a 512-node cluster, and 85× in a 2048-node cluster of the same aggregate capacity. For a read-only workload, one solution is to combine aggressive replication across the cluster with caching at the application tier [5, 6]. Unfortunately, neither replication nor caching is free for read-write workloads, as each copy needs to be updated on each write, regardless of the consistency model. The cost of keeping the replicas consistent increases with the size of the cluster, as more replicas are required to achieve better balance.

We conclude that the problem of serving large datasets will increase with the trend towards extreme scale-out [4], i.e., the dynamic replication of micro-shards scales unfavorably with the increase in server count. Emerging low-latency rack-scale fabrics [7] may provide a way to efficiently aggregate memory to reduce the pressure on dynamic replication.

Acknowledgments. This work has been partially funded by the *Workloads and Server Architectures for Green Datacenters* project of the Swiss National Science Foundation, the Nano-Tera *YINS* project, and the *Scale-Out NUMA* project of the Microsoft-EPFL Joint Research Center.

4. REFERENCES

[1] B. Atikoglu, Y. Xu, E. Frachtenberg, S. Jiang, and M. Paleczny. Workload analysis of a large-scale key-value store. In *SIGMETRICS '12*, 2012.

[2] L. Breslau, P. Cao, L. Fan, G. Phillips, and S. Shenker. Web Caching and Zipf-like Distributions: Evidence and Implications. In *INFOCOM '99*, 1999.

[3] J. Dean and L. A. Barroso. The tail at scale. *Commun. ACM*, 56(2):74–80, 2013.

[4] Facebook. Introducing "Yosemite": the first open source modular chassis for high-powered microservers, 2015.

[5] B. Fan, H. Lim, D. G. Andersen, and M. Kaminsky. Small cache, big effect: provable load balancing for randomly partitioned cluster services. In *SOCC '11*, 2011.

[6] Q. Huang, H. Gudmundsdottir, Y. Vigfusson, D. A. Freedman, K. Birman, and R. van Renesse. Characterizing Load Imbalance in Real-World Networked Caches. In *HOTNETS-XIII*, 2014.

[7] S. Novakovic, A. Daglis, E. Bugnion, B. Falsafi, and B. Grot. Scale-out NUMA. In *ASPLOS-XIX*, 2014.

Analyzing the Power Consumption of the Mobile Page Load

Yi Cao Javad Nejati Pavan Maguluri Aruna Balasubramanian Anshul Gandhi
Stony Brook University
{yicao1, jnejati, smaguluri, arunab, anshul} @cs.stonybrook.edu

1. INTRODUCTION

A large portion of today's Web traffic comes from mobiles devices. User experience of mobile Web pages has become an important factor that content providers and service providers want to improve. One metric for evaluating user experience is the mobile Web performance, specifically the page load time (PLT). While improving mobile Web performance has drawn increasing attention [2], most optimizations tend to overlook an important metric, *energy*. PLT and energy are distinct metrics; we observe in our experiments that these metrics may not always be correlated. Given the importance of battery life for mobile users, we argue that Web page optimizations should also be evaluated for their impact on energy consumption.

However, examining the energy effects of a Web optimization is challenging, even if one has access to power monitors, for several reasons. First, Web page loads experience high variance due to network conditions and device scheduling. Our own experiments show that the energy consumption of a Web page can vary by about 30% under the same experimental setup. Second, Web pages can be highly complex since they are composed of distinct *components*, which are individual page load activities such as loading objects, parsing the page, or evaluating Javascript. There are also many levels of dependencies among those components during the page load process. Without detailed application-level semantics, it is hard to tease out the energy contribution of each component. Third, the page load process is short-lived, ranging from several milliseconds to a few seconds. Although different power models [3, 5] for mobile devices have been proposed, they do not work well for such short-lived applications. This is because such models require fine-grained *resource monitoring*, which incurs substantial overhead and impacts model accuracy.

2. RECON

We present RECON(REsource- and COmpoNent-based modeling), a model that addresses all of the challenges outlined above to accurately predict the energy consumption of any mobile Web page load. The design of RECON is motivated by the fact that resource monitoring incurs significant overheads at fine-grained time scales, and does not provide insights into the page load process. Instead, RECON collects resource-level data at *coarse* granularity, and then exploits low-level *page load semantics*. RECON extracts page load semantics using WProf-M [4], a tool that decomposes the page load process into various components. In effect, RECON augments coarse-grained resource monitoring with component-level information, resulting in high prediction accuracy and providing benefits over individual resource-only or component-only models.

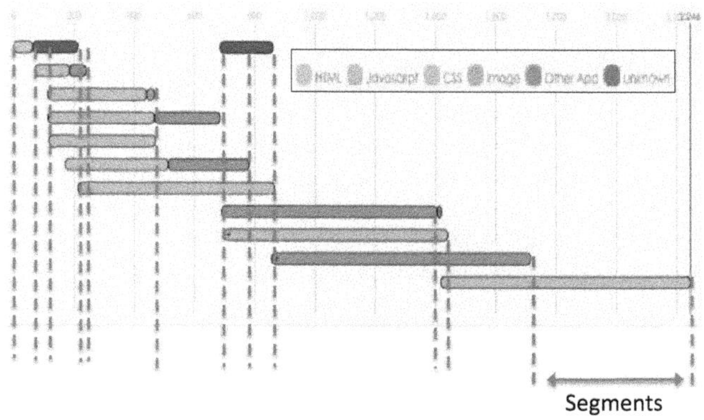

Figure 1: Using WProf-M to decompose the components when loading the *instagram.com* Web page.

Our modeling approach breaks down the page load process into "segments", where a segment is defined as an interval of page load activity during which the components of the Web page do not change. By definition, a segment is composed of at least one component. Further, the entire page load process can be partitioned into discrete (non-overlapping) segments. Figure 1 shows how we partition a page load into segments using WProf-M's component-level decomposition. We then model the power consumption of a segment, s, as:

$$\hat{P}_s = w_0 + \sum_{i \in Resources} w_i R_i + \sum_{j \in s} w_j, \qquad (1)$$

where i represents the various resources we monitor, including CPU utilization and frequency, bytes and packets transmitted through the WiFi interface; R_i represents the average value for that resource during s; j represents a component, and thus $j \in s$ is the set of all components that make up segment s; finally, w_i and w_j are coefficients (independent of s) representing the power contribution of the resources

SIGMETRICS '16 June 14-18, 2016, Antibes Juan-Les-Pins, France

ACM ISBN 978-1-4503-4266-7/16/06.
DOI: http://dx.doi.org/10.1145/2896377.2901491

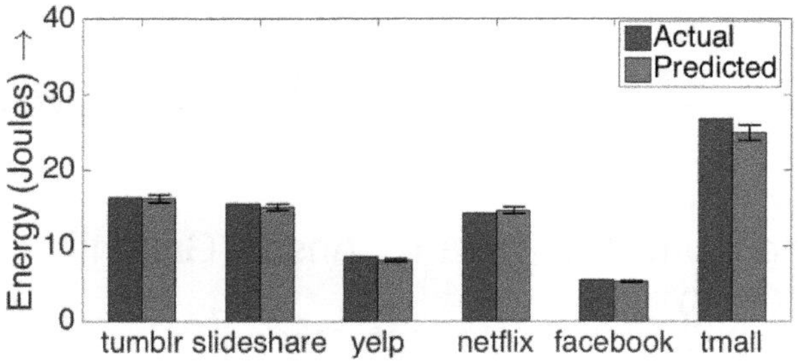

Figure 2: Actual vs. predicted energy consumption for 6 popular Web pages.

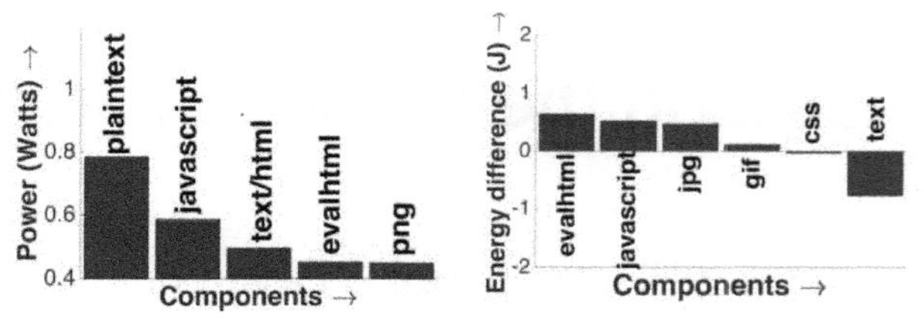

Figure 3: Left: predicted per-component power consumption for *alexa.com*; Right: changes in per-component energy consumption for *fico.com* due to compression.

and components. w_0 is also a coefficient, and represents the baseline power consumption of the phone which could be attributed to background activities, screen brightness, etc. Our next task is to determine the values of these coefficients.

We use multiple linear regression to derive the weights vector, $\vec{w}$, that is indicative of the power contribution of each component and resource, and the baseline power. Once we derive the weights, we can compute the energy consumption of the segment by multiplying the predicted power with the segment length (obtained via WProf-M); summing over all segments gives us the Web page energy consumption.

In the training period, we monitor the ground-truth power consumption by using the Monsoon Power Monitor [1]. We train our regression model on nine instantiations of a given Web page and test on the tenth instantiation. Our error results are based on a 10-fold cross validation.

3. RESULTS

We validate RECON on the Samsung Galaxy S4 and S5 devices using 50 popular Web pages chosen from *alexa.com*. Our results show that RECON's average prediction error for energy consumption across these Web pages is 4.48%, and the average segment-level energy consumption prediction error is less than 8.88%. Figure 2 shows the actual and predicted mean energy consumption for 6 popular Web pages, and the confidence intervals around the predicted mean.

4. APPLICATIONS: OPTIMIZATION

An important application of RECON is studying the energy effects of Web optimizations. To that end, we consider four popular optimizations: *Compression, Minification, Inlining* and *Ad-block*. Our mean prediction error for Web page energy consumption under these optimizations is a low 5.45%. In addition to accurately predicting the energy effects of an optimization, RECON also provides Web developers with several useful applications in optimization:

4.1 Breaking down total power consumption

RECON decomposes the total energy consumption of a Web page into component-level energy consumption, so that we know each component's contribution to the total energy consumption. For example, Figure 3 (left) shows the predicted per-component energy usage for *alexa.com*. Further, RECON allows Web developers to visualize how an optimization affects component-level energy consumption. Figure 3 (right) shows the change in predicted per-component energy usage under compression for *fico.com*. We see that, after compression, the energy consumption of evalhtml and Javascript increases, indicating that compression is not useful for these components. On the other hand, the energy consumption for text decreases, suggesting that text compression is useful.

4.2 Analyzing why energy consumption changes

With the help of RECON, we can explore not only *how* but also *why* energy consumption changes due to an optimization. For example, the inlining optimization embeds all the external Javascripts and CSS in the root HTML file. Inlining avoids small downloads, so the energy consumption due to downloading decreases. However, inlining lengthens the HTML evaluation, which, according to RECON, is a power-hungry component. In our experiments with *netflix.com*, we found the total energy consumption increases on inlining although the PLT decreases.

5. CONCLUSION

RECON provides Web developers with quick and accurate power predictions of the mobile page load. Moreover, RECON helps users explore how and why energy consumption changes due to an optimization. Our end-goal in this research is to enable and promote simultaneous energy- and performance-analysis of Web pages; RECON is an important step in this direction.

Acknowledgements

We gratefully acknowledge the anonymous reviewers for their feedback. This work was supported by the National Science Foundation through the grant CNS-1551909 and a Google Research Grant R2-2015-839.

6. REFERENCES

[1] Monsoon Power Monitor. http://msoon.github.io/powermonitor/.

[2] M. Butkiewicz, D. Wang, Z. Wu, H. V. Madhyastha, and V. Sekar. Klotski: Reprioritizing Web Content to Improve User Experience on Mobile Devices. In *NSDI 2015*, pages 439–453.

[3] X. Chen, N. Ding, A. Jindal, Y. C. Hu, M. Gupta, and R. Vannithamby. Smartphone energy drain in the wild: Analysis and implications. In *SIGMETRICS 2015*, pages 151–164.

[4] X. S. Wang, A. Balasubramanian, A. Krishnamurthy, and D. Wetherall. Demystifying Page Load Performance with WProf. In *NSDI 2013*, pages 473–485.

[5] L. Zhang, B. Tiwana, Z. Qian, Z. Wang, R. P. Dick, Z. M. Mao, and L. Yang. Accurate online power estimation and automatic battery behavior based power model generation for smartphones. In *CODES+ISSS 2010*, pages 105–114.

Automated Test Location Selection for Cellular Network Upgrades

Mubashir Adnan Qureshi*, Ajay Mahimkar+, Lili Qiu*
Zihui Ge+, Sarat Puthenpura+, Nabeel Mir+, Sanjeev Ahuja+
UT Austin* AT&T+

ABSTRACT

Cellular networks are constantly evolving due to frequent changes in radio access and end user equipment technologies, applications, and traffic. Network upgrades should be performed with extreme caution since millions of users heavily depend on the cellular networks. Before upgrading the entire network, it is important to conduct field evaluation of upgrades.The choice and number of field test locations have significant impact on the time-to-market and confidence in how well various network upgrades will work out in the rest of the network. We propose a novel approach – *Reflection* to automatically determine where to conduct the upgrade field tests to accurately identify important features that affect the upgrade and predict for the performance of untested locations. We demonstrate its effectiveness using real traces collected from a major US cellular network as well as synthetic traces.

Motivation: Cellular networks play a significant role in today's communication. To many users, it is often the only means of getting connectivity. The cellular networks are extremely complex and constantly evolving at a rapid pace. Changes are introduced to either support new service features (*e.g.*, Voice over LTE), technologies (*e.g.*, LTE-advanced, small cells), fix software bugs, or expand network coverage. Deploying changes in a cellular network should be done with extreme caution in order to avoid any unexpected performance degradation or failures. Extensive testing is typically conducted in large-scale laboratory settings, but it is virtually impossible to replicate the large-scale, diverse variations and extreme complexity of real operational networks. Thus, the changes are tested on a smaller scale in the field. This small scale testing in the field is referred to as the *First Field Application (FFA)*.

The goal of FFA testing is to identify and infer the performance impacts of the change and make a recommendation for a go/no-go decision for a network-wide roll-out. If the desirable service performance impacts (*e.g.*, improvements or at times no change in performance) are observed after the FFA, the decision is to go-ahead with the roll-out. However, if performance degradations are observed, the changes need to be rolled back at the FFA locations and further analysis needs to be conducted in lab settings. Once the field test finishes, the network-wide roll-out begins at a rapid pace. Any unexpected issues discovered in the network-wide roll-out would slow down the process. Thus, careful planning of field tests is important to ensure smooth network-wide deployment.

SIGMETRICS '16 June 14-18, 2016, Antibes Juan-Les-Pins, France

ACM ISBN 978-1-4503-4266-7/16/06.
DOI: http://dx.doi.org/10.1145/2896377.2901505

Challenge: A major challenge faced by the network operations and engineering teams in the planning and design of fields tests is *what selection criteria to employ for selecting the network elements to be used for the field tests?* This is an important and unique challenge arising from the tremendous diversity in cellular networks. Such diversity introduces the following issues: (i) *Extremely large search space:* There are tens of thousands of cellular base stations (referred to as eNodeBs in LTE) to choose from, each with hundreds of features. Which features to consider and which nodes to test have significant impact on the accuracy and predictability of the tests. (ii) *Interactions between features:* It is often impossible to know in advance which features will interact negatively with a new network change. Ideally we should automatically discover this undesirable interaction based on the limited FFA tests, and resolve the issue before the network-wide roll-out. (iii) *Very low sampling for FFA locations:* Since one of the FFA goals is to minimize the risk of negative impact on network locations, the network operation teams have a very low sampling budget (*e.g.*, 1%).

The current practice used by the operation team is to test the change using high traffic with the assumption that negative impacts are more likely to occur under high traffic. The current practice assumes that if the network change performs well at high traffic locations, then it will perform well at low or moderate traffic locations. Moreover, the service performance indicators are also stable at locations with high traffic, which enables accurate before/after analysis of upgrade impacts. However, it is common that contrasting performance impacts can happen due to features unrelated to traffic. For example, the change may not work well with some particular software version installed on some nodes thus resulting in performance degradation. Thus, it is important to select FFA locations that capture a diverse set of features.

Overview of our approach: We propose a new approach *Reflection* that systematically utilizes a diverse set of features (*e.g.*, software/hardware configuration, radio parameters, user population, mobility patterns, network topology) and automatically identifies the FFA test locations that would improve the predictability between the performance impacts during FFA and network-wide deployment. Having predictable performance behaviors with FFA ensures a smooth and rapid wide-scale roll-out. Through automated and effective analysis of a wide variety of features, *Reflection* "reflects" the impacts observed during FFA and predicts the performance of the post-FFA wide-scale deployment.

Reflection first extracts the features to be used for test planning and performance analysis, and post processes the raw input. Then it performs the first phase test planning, applies upgrades to the testing locations, assesses performance impact diagnoses test performance to identify important features, uses the diagnosis results to guide subsequent test planning, and iterates until the maximum number of phases is reached. In the end, it outputs the final diagnosis results for the important features and predicts performance at untested eNodeBs using the same diagnosis algorithm. In the interest of space, below we focus on first phase test planning, diagnosis, and subsequent test planning, since they are most challenging.

One way to design test cases is to diversify all features (*e.g.*, for each feature, select test case that involves different values of that feature). However, the number of test cases grows exponentially with the number of features, which can be prohibitively expensive. In practice, only a small number of features are important to the performance, and these important features may not be known in advance. Therefore, we develop a *multi-phase test planning*. The intuition behind our multi-phase test planning approach is that if we know the performance at different eNodeBs with different feature values, we can more effectively design the tests. Thus, instead of designing complete tests in advance and conducting all tests in one shot, we use the performance outcome from previous tests to guide the subsequent test design. This multi-phase test planning is practical since major cellular service providers schedule FFA in a staggered manner.

First phase: During the first phase, we pick nodes that offer the best coverage over all features so that we can assess the impact of each of these features to narrow down to a smaller subset of candidate features that are likely to be important. We develop a greedy algorithm that selects feature values that maximize the minimum hamming distance among them. Minimum hamming distance is used as the optimization metric because it captures the number of features whose impacts can be assessed (*e.g.*, if we select two feature values: 000 vs. 111, we can assess the impact of three features by comparing the performance when each feature takes a value 0 versus 1). Specifically, we first randomly select a feature value combination to test. In the next iteration, we add a feature value combination that has the largest hamming distance from the one selected earlier. This is because it allows us to estimate impact of two features by computing the difference between when one feature takes a value 0 versus takes a value 1. Note that this comes with a caveat, which assumes that the impact of the interaction between the two features is likely to be smaller than the impact of an individual feature, which is likely to hold in practice. In the third iteration, we pick a feature combination that maximizes the minimum hamming distance from the two we picked so far: $max\ min_i\ hamming(n_i, n')$, where n_i are the set of feature combinations already selected and n' denotes the new feature combination to add. We iterate until we select enough eNodeBs to test.

Diagnosis: Given the performance from the nodes tested during the first phase, we develop an iterative algorithm to identify the features that explain the contrasting performance impact. If there is no contrasting impact then we can go ahead with network wide roll-out. For each unique feature value combination, we compute the degradation probability using the traces. Our approach iteratively adds one feature at a time to optimize a metric. To start with, it computes a metric for each feature and selects the one that optimizes this metric. Then it fixes this feature, and iteratively adds one feature at a time so that the new feature in conjunction with the previously selected features optimizes the metric. It iterates until adding a feature does not significantly improve the metric.

We develop a new diagnosis metric based on *z statistics:*

$$\frac{\sum_i \sum_{j \neq i} |z_{ij}|}{\|\#regions\| \times (\|\#regions\| - 1)},$$

where $z_{ij} = \frac{p_i - p_j}{\sqrt{p_{ij}(1-p_{ij})(1/n_i+1/n_j)}}$ and $p_{ij} = \frac{x_i+x_j}{n_i+n_j}$, i and j denote one of the feature combinations defined by the currently selected features (*e.g.*, 00, 01, 10, 11 for two binary features), $\|\#regions\|$ is the total number of regions defined by the selected features (*e.g.*, two binary features define 4 regions: 00, 01, 10, 11), x_i and x_j are the number of degraded eNodeBs for the i-th and j-th feature combinations, and n_i and n_j are the corresponding total number of eNodeBs.

The metric tries to capture the average difference between the z scores across all regions defined by the selected features. The intuition is that important features yield larger difference in the degradation probabilities across different regions defined by the selected features. But instead of directly using probability difference, we weigh the probability difference based on the number of samples in the cluster since a large difference under a small sample size does not mean much but the same difference under a large sample size means more. A major *advantage* of our metric is that it captures statistical significance of the derived probabilities.

Subsequent phase: During the subsequent testing phase, we focus on testing only these candidate features by selecting nodes that offer the best coverage over the candidate features so that we can further narrow down to the final set of features that we consider as important. In this way, we can significantly reduce the number of test cases. It is similar to the first phase: it also employs a similar greedy algorithm that maximizes the minimum hamming distance between selected nodes. There are two main difference between the first and subsequent phases. First, since the first phase already narrows down to a subset of candidate features, the second phase only diversifies over these candidate features. Second, the second phase should add new nodes to test that complement the nodes already tested during the first phase. This can be achieved by selecting a new feature value that maximizes the minimum hamming distance from all the selected nodes so far, including those selected in the first phase and the previous iterations of the second phase.

After testing on these eNodeBs selected during the second phase, we run the diagnosis algorithm. Note that by now we see the performance outcomes from all nodes selected in all test phases, so we use the performance information from all tests as the input to identify the important features that contribute to the performance difference.

Once we know which features are important, we can derive a degradation probability for each combination of important features (*e.g.*, for K important features that take binary values, we derive degradation probabilities for 2^K important feature combinations: from 00...0 to 11...1). Then we can predict the degradation probability of an untested location by classifying it into one of 2^K important feature combinations and apply the previously derived degradation probability to make a prediction. This method easily supports non-binary features, as well.

Summary of evaluation results: We evaluate *Reflection* using one-year data collected from a major cellular service provider in US. Our results show that *Reflection* only requires testing 2% nodes to identify the features that affect degradation and accurately predicts the performance outcome of the remaining 98% untested nodes. For the operational case studies provided by the cellular provider, we were able to accurately identify the set of features responsible for contrasting performance impact using our diagnosis approach. Furthermore using synthetic traces, we show that our planning algorithm consistently outperforms random selection based planning method and our diagnosis algorithm can accurately identify the features responsible for contrasting performance impact while minimizing the number of false positives and false negatives.

CAR: A Compression-Aware Refresh Approach to Improve Memory Performance and Energy Efficiency

Wenjie Liu¶, Ping Huang§, Kun Tang§, Ke Zhou¶* and Xubin He§
¶ Wuhan National Laboratory for Optoelectronics, Huazhong University of Science and Technology
§ Department of Electrical and Computer Engineering, Virginia Commonwealth University

ABSTRACT

DRAM memory is suffering increasingly aggravating refresh penalty, which no longer causes trivial performance degradation and power consumption. As memory capacity increases, refresh penalty has become increasingly worse as more rows have to be refreshed. In this work, we propose a simple, practical, and effective refresh approach called *CAR (Compression-Aware Refresh)* to efficiently mitigate refresh overheads. We apply data compression technique to store data in compressed format so that data blocks which are originally distributed across all the constituent chips of a rank only need to be stored in a subset of those chips, leaving banks in the remaining chips not fully occupied. As a result, the memory controller can safely skip refreshing memory rows which contain no useful data without compromising data integrity. Such a compression-aware refresh scheme can result in significant refresh savings and thus improve overall memory performance and energy efficiency. Moreover, to further take advantage of data compression, we adopt the rank subsetting technique to enable accesses to only those occupied chips for memory requests accessing compressed data blocks. Evaluations using benchmarks from SPEC CPU 2006 and the *PARSEC 3.0* on the recent DDR4 memory systems have shown that CAR can achieve up to 1.66 $\times$ performance improvement (11.7% on average).

1. INTRODUCTION

Memory performance is crucial to the overall system performance as it provides an intermediate stage to bridge the huge gap between the performance anticipated by processors and the stagnant operations of disk system or flash storage. As data-intensive workloads and big-data applications become more and more prevalent, the requirement for high performance and large capacity from the memory system has steadily increased. Furthermore, memory subsystem contributes a significant percentage of the overall system energy consumption.

Modern DRAM memory technology is primarily built with capacitive cells, each of which contains one capacitor and one transistor. Information in a cell is represented by the charges trapped in the capacitor. Since trapped charges leak over time by its very nature, DRAM cells must be *refreshed* periodically to guarantee data integrity [1]. The basic requirement is that every memory cell must be refreshed at least once within its so-called *retention time* window [2] even when the whole memory system is in idle state, otherwise data loss might occur. However, refresh operation brings about significant performance and energy overheads, causing "*Refresh Wall*" problem [1]. Even worse, as memory density increases, the refresh overheads grow substantially since there are more rows that need to be refreshed and the device unavailable time increases commensurately. It is projected that in future 64Gb devices, refresh operations would account for 50% of energy consumption and degrade 50% memory throughput at the same time [1]. High refresh overheads have become a critically detrimental factor to memory performance and energy efficiency and it is extremely beneficial to mitigate refresh overheads.

In this paper, we propose a low-complexity, practical, and straightforward approach to mitigate refresh overheads in respects of both performance and energy. Many previous works [3] have revealed that most cache lines are reasonably compressible, implying there exist a good opportunity to achieve refresh savings via data compression. We employ the well-known low-complexity, low-latency base-delta-immediate (BDI) [3] compression algorithm as our compression engine to minimize introduced overheads. With compression, a 64-byte data block only requires a portion of the original space, resulting in *sparse* banks which are eligible for not being refreshed. In order to take advantage of the compressed data, *Rank Subsetting* [4] is ultilized to partially access a rank (i.e., access the chips containing post-compression content) and obtain reduced memory traffic and access energy.

2. COMPRESSION-AWARE REFRESH

2.1 Overall Architecture

Figure 1 shows a simplified schematic view of our proposed CAR architecture. As shown in the figure, we add a compression engine in the memory controller. The compression engine performs compression and decompression for cache lines. Cache lines required by the processor are first brought into the memory controller for decompression and then returned to the processor. New cache lines coming from the processor are compressed and then stored in the memory banks. The number of banks (in different chips) that a cache line actually occupies depends on the compressed size. Depending on the compression ratio, cache lines might be compressed into variable sizes. In the figure, we assume a memory system comprising 8 chips, each of which is responsible for 8 bytes of a 64-byte cache line. Due to compression, banks in some of those chips may contain much less data than when cache lines are stored in uncompressed format. Those banks are called *sparse* banks. Memory rows in sparse banks may not need to be refreshed, as they contain invalidate data, reducing the amount of rows that need to be

*Corresponding author.

SIGMETRICS '16 June 14-18, 2016, Antibes Juan-Les-Pins, France

ACM ISBN 978-1-4503-4266-7/16/06.
DOI: http://dx.doi.org/10.1145/2896377.2901498

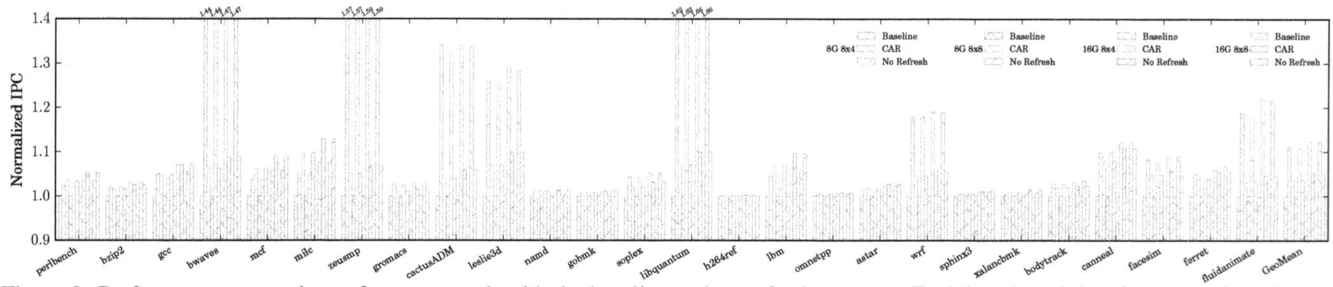

Figure 3: Performance comparison of our approach with the baseline and no refresh systems. Each benchmark has four sets of results and the middle legend in each set represents CAR and labels the memory configuration for the set. CAR can improve performance as much as 1.66× for *libquantum*, with an average of 11.7% (It should be noted that the maximum and average refresh performance penalty is 12.8% and 4.4%, respectively).

refreshed. We also make necessary changes to the refresh mechanism to skip refreshing memory rows containing invalidate data.

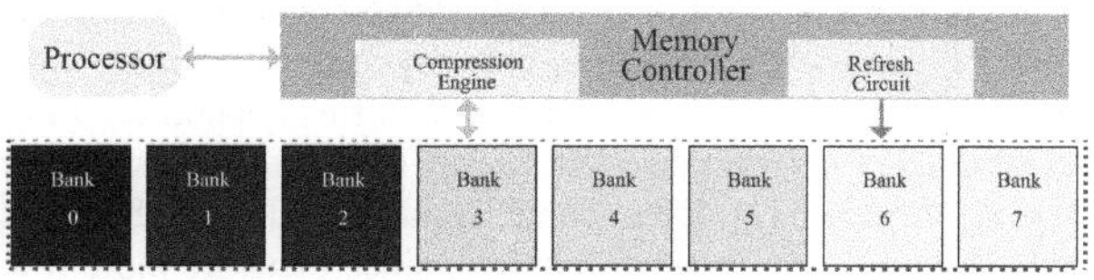

Figure 1: A simplified schematic overview of CAR architecture. Cache line compression results in *sparse* banks in which memory rows may not need refresh. The different colors represent different degrees of sparseness of the bank.

2.2 Refresh Reduction

In order to safely skip refreshing invalid cache lines in a *sparse* bank, we need to track which rows in the bank are valid. To fulfill this purpose, we devise a two-level vector data structure. As it is shown in Figure 2, the first-level is called *refresh indicator vector*, an n-bit vector. Each bit of this vector corresponds to a row in the bank and when the bit is set, the corresponding row is indicated as valid and needs refresh. The second-level is called *utilization vector*, an $(n*m)$-bit vector. Every m-bit acts as a counter to remember the number of valid cache lines the corresponding row currently contains. Whenever a compressed cache line takes space from a bank, the corresponding row counter of the bank is incremented by one. On the other hand, whenever a cache line becomes short (due to overwriting) and needs less space, then the counter corresponding to the released row is decremented by one. When a counter decreases to zero, meaning the corresponding row contains no valid cache lines, the corresponding row bit in the first-level vector is reset to 0, indicating to the memory controller to skip refreshing the corresponding row. The changes in compressed size cause counter values to be changed. Row granularity refresh controlling is possible as retention time based refresh approaches rely on similar row granularity refresh [2, 5]. When a bank receives a refresh command to refresh a set of rows, it checks the first-level vector to see which rows do not need to be refreshed. For those rows, it simply increments the refresh counter and does not perform refresh, as what a "dummy refresh" [5] does.

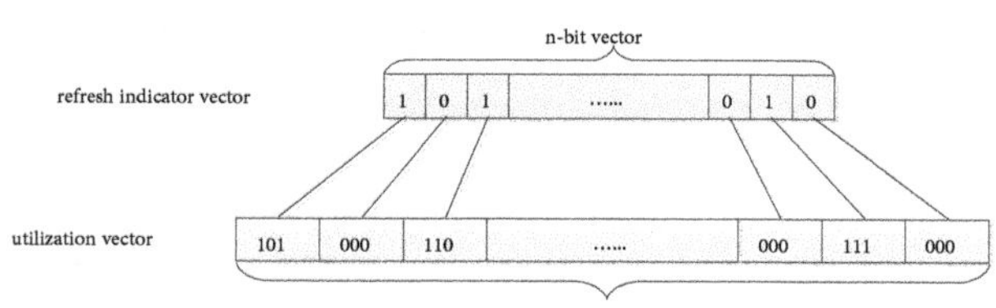

Figure 2: A two-level data structure used to efficiently track rows that do not need refresh. The first-level vector indicates which rows need refresh. The second-level vector tracks the row utilizations.

Assume an 8×8 memory system and the row size is 4KB. Then a 64-byte cache line is evenly distributed among eight banks in the eight different chips. Each bank takes 8 bytes of the cache line. Therefore, a 4KB row in a bank contains data from $\frac{4KB}{8B} = 512$ cache lines, resulting in each row counter in the *utilization vector* requiring $\log_2 512 = 9$ bits (i.e., $m = 9$). Besides, it requires one more bit for each bank row in the *refresh indicator vector*. In total, this two-level vector data structure incurs 10 bits overhead for each 4KB bank row.

3. PRELIMINARY RESULTS

We compare our approach with a no-compression, no rank subsetting, auto refresh (1x FGR mode) baseline memory system and a no-compression, no rank subsetting, no-refresh ideal memory system. Instruction Per Cycle (IPC) metric is employed to compare the performance of our approach *CAR* with the baseline and no refresh systems. Figure 3 demonstrates the normalized IPC comparison results. As it is shown in the figure, CAR is able to improve performance as much as 1.66× for *libquantum*, with an average of 11.7%. Our approach can efficiently alleviate refresh performance penalty. Generally speaking, non-intensive applications suffer from refresh penalty less than intensive applications, as fewer requests are blocked. More compressible and intensive applications benefit more from CAR.

4. ACKNOWLEDGMENTS

The research is supported in part by the National Natural Science Foundation of China (NSFC) under grant No.61232004, 61502189, and 61572012, the Education Ministry of Hubei Province of China under No. B2015054 and U.S. NSF under grants CNS1218960 and CCF1547804.

5. REFERENCES

[1] M. K. Qureshi, D. H. Kim, S. Khan, P. Nair, and O. Mutlu, "AVATAR: A Variable-Retention-Time (VRT) Aware Refresh for DRAM Systems," in *DSN*, 2015.

[2] J. Liu, B. Jaiyen, R. Veras, and O. Mutlu, "RAIDR: Retention-Aware Intelligent DRAM Refresh," in *ISCA*, 2012.

[3] G. Pekhimenko, V. Seshadri, O. Mutlu, P. B. Gibbons, M. A. Kozuch, and T. C. Mowry, "Base-Delta-Immediate Compression: Practical Data Compression for On-Chip Caches," in *PACT*, 2012.

[4] H. Zheng, J. Lin, Z. Zhang, E. Gorbatov, H. David, and Z. Zhu, "Mini-Rank: Adaptive DRAM Architecture for Improving Memory Power Efficiency," in *MICRO*, 2008.

[5] I. Bhati, Z. Chishti, S.-L. Lu, and B. Jacob, "Flexible Auto-Refresh: Enabling Scalable and Energy-Efficient DRAM Refresh Reductions," in *ISCA*, 2015.

Contrasting Effects of Replication in Parallel Systems: From Overload to Underload and Back

Felix Poloczek
University of Warwick / TU Berlin

Florin Ciucu
University of Warwick

ABSTRACT

Task replication has recently been advocated as a practical solution to reduce latencies in parallel systems. In addition to several convincing empirical studies, analytical results have been provided, yet under some strong assumptions such as independent service times of the replicas, which may lend themselves to some contrasting and perhaps contriving behavior. For instance, under the independence assumption, an overloaded system can be stabilized by a replication factor, but can be sent back in overload through further replication. Motivated by the need to dispense with such common and restricting assumptions, which may cause unexpected behavior, we develop a unified and general theoretical framework to compute tight bounds on the distribution of response times in general replication systems. These results immediately lend themselves to the optimal number of replicas minimizing response time quantiles, depending on the parameters of the system (e.g., the degree of correlation amongst replicas).

1. INTRODUCTION

Given the late abundance of computing resources, a natural and yet very simple way to improve latencies is *replication*. In the context of a multi-server (parallel) system, the idea is merely to replicate a task into multiple copies/replicas, and to execute each replica on a different server. By leveraging the statistical variability of the servers themselves, as execution platforms, it is expected that some replicas would finish much faster than others. The key gain of executing multiple replicas is not to reduce the average latency, but rather the latency tail which is recognized as critically important for ensuring a consistently fluid/natural responsiveness of systems.

While the idea of using redundant requests is not new, as it has been used to demonstrate significant speedups in parallel programs [3], it has become very attractive with its implementation in the MapReduce framework through the so-called 'backup-tasks' [1]. Thereafter there has been a surge of high-quality empirical work which has convincingly demonstrated the benefits of using redundancy for significant latency improvement.

Such empirical work has been complemented by several excellent analytical studies, which have provided fundamental insight into the benefits of replication. Constrained by analytical tractability, most of these works make several strong assumptions: not only the arrivals are Poisson and the service times are exponentially distributed, but the service times of the replicas plus the corresponding original tasks are statistically independent [2]. By challenging these assumptions, we first provide some elementary analytical arguments, that the benefits of replication are highly dependent on both the distributional and correlation structures of the service times. Second, we develop a general analytical framework to compute stochastic bounds on the response time distributions in replication systems. In particular, our framework covers scenarios with Markovian arrivals, general service time distributions, and a correlation model amongst the original and replicated tasks.

SIGMETRICS '16 June 14-18, 2016, Antibes Juan-Les-Pins, France

ACM ISBN 978-1-4503-4266-7/16/06.

DOI: http://dx.doi.org/10.1145/2896377.2901499

2. ELEMENTARY INSIGHTS

We consider a parallel system with K homogeneous servers with identical speeds. A stream of tasks arrives at a dispatcher according to some stationary and ergodic point process; the interarrival times are denoted by t_i with mean $E[t_1] = \frac{1}{\lambda}$.

Upon its arrival, job i is replicated to $k \leq K$ servers where they are processed with service times $x_{i,1}, \ldots, x_{i,k}$, respectively. We first assume the family of service times $\{x_{i,j} \mid i \geq 1,\ 1 \leq j \leq k\}$ are i.i.d. and drawn from some general distribution subject to a finite moment generating function; the average is set to $E[x_1] = \frac{1}{\mu}$.

A necessary and sufficient condition for stability in a scenario with replication factor $0 \leq k \leq K$ is

$$\mathbb{E}[\min\{x_1, \ldots, x_k\}] < \frac{K}{k}\mathbb{E}[t_1] \ . \tag{1}$$

Denoting the CCDF of x_i by $f(x) := \mathbb{P}(x_1 \geq x)$, we observe from the previous stability conditions that the 'best' replication-factor k is

$$\operatorname*{argmin}_k k \int f^k(x)dx \ . \tag{2}$$

Depending on the distribution of the x_i, each of the replication strategies 1) No-Replication (i.e., $k = 1$), 2) Full-Replication (i.e., $k = K$), and 3) Partial-Replication (i.e., $1 < k < K$) can be the 'best':

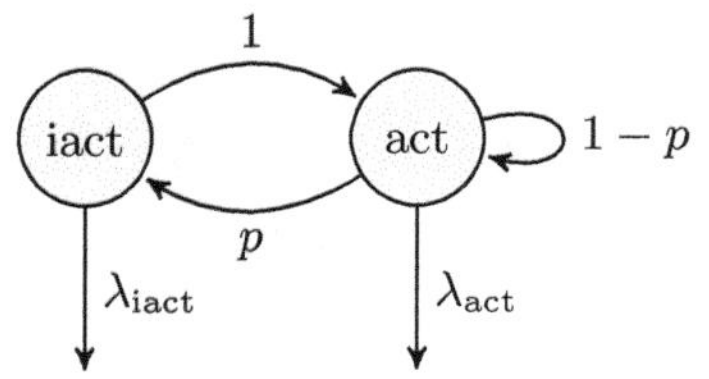

Figure 1: Two-state Markov chain $Z(n)$

No-Replication: Uniform: Assuming uniformly distributed service times, i.e., $x_i \sim \mathcal{U}_{[0,1]}$, replication is detrimental:

$$k\mathbb{E}\left[\min\{x_1,\dots,x_k\}\right] = \int_0^1 kx^k dx = \frac{k}{k+1} \;.$$

Full-Replication: Weibull: Assume Weibull distributed service times, i.e., $f(x) = e^{-(x/\lambda)^\alpha}$. For $\alpha < 1$, a higher degree of replication is 'better':

$$k\mathbb{E}\left[\min\{x_1,\dots,x_k\}\right] = k\frac{\lambda}{k^{1/\alpha}}\Gamma(1+1/\alpha) \;.$$

Partial Replication: Pareto: Assume Pareto distributed service times, i.e., $f(x) = x^{-\alpha}$ for $x \geq 1$. For suffiently small $\alpha > 1$, Partial-Replication is 'best':

$$k\mathbb{E}\left[\min\{x_1,\dots,x_k\}\right] = k + \frac{k}{k\alpha - 1} \;.$$

This last example highlights that the performance of replication strategies heavily depends on the replication factor k, the service time distribution, and other underlying assumptions. In particular, performance is not monotonic in k, and thus an optimization framework is desirable.

3. THEORY

For simplicity, we assume that K is an integral multiple of k. Further, the jobs are assigned to the $\frac{K}{k}$ batches in a round robin scheme, i.e. the interarrival times for one batch can be described as:

$$\tilde{t_i} := \sum_{j=0}^{K/k-1} t_{(i-1)\frac{K}{k}+j} \;.$$

The *steady-state* response time r has a representation:

$$r =_{\mathcal{D}} \max_{n\geq 1}\left\{\sum_{i=1}^{n+1}\min_{j\leq k}\{x_{i,j}\} - \sum_{i=1}^{n}\tilde{t}_i\right\} \;. \tag{3}$$

We consider the following correlation model for the replicas (from [4]):

$$x_{i,j} = \delta y_i + (1-\delta)\, y_{i,j} \;,$$

where the random variables y_i and $y_{i,j}$ are i.i.d. Here, the parameter $\delta \in [0,1]$ describes the degree of correlation amongst the replicas; $\delta = 0$ corresponds to the i.i.d. case.

For the interarrival times, we consider two scenarios. In the first scenario the $\{t_i\}$ are i.i.d., in the second scenario they have a Markovian structure as in Figure 1: the Markov chain $Z(n)$ alternates between *active* and *inactive* periods; while active, exponentially distributed interarrival times are generated (parameter λ_{act}). While inactive, *one* interarrival time (exponentially distributed, parameter $\lambda_{\text{inact}} < \lambda_{\text{act}}$) is generated, and the chain jumps back to the active state.

For $0 \leq \theta < \lambda_{\text{iact}}$, let T_θ denote the following matrix:

$$T_\theta := \begin{pmatrix} 0 & \frac{\lambda_{\text{act}}}{\lambda_{\text{act}}+\theta} \\ p\frac{\lambda_{\text{iact}}}{\lambda_{\text{iact}}+\theta} & (1-p)\frac{\lambda_{\text{act}}}{\lambda_{\text{act}}+\theta} \end{pmatrix} \;.$$

Further, let $\xi(\theta)$ denote the spectral radius of T_θ, and $h = (h_{\text{act}}, h_{\text{iact}})$ be a corresponding eigenvector.

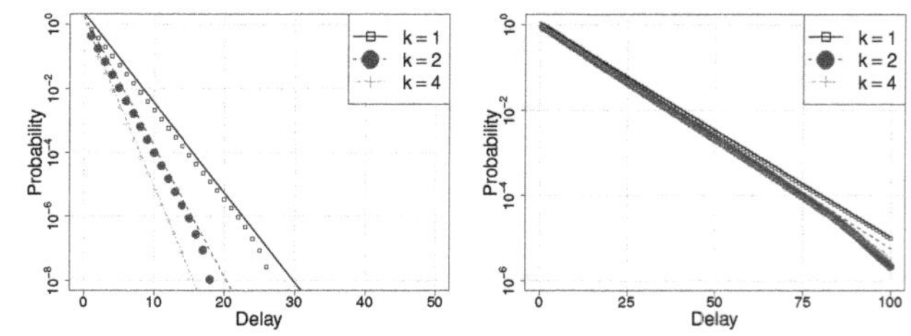

(a) i.i.d. scenario (b) Markovian scenario

Figure 2: Stochastic bounds vs. simulation results accounting for 10^9 packets ($K = 4$, $\rho = .75$, $\mu = 1$, $\delta = .5$)

THEOREM 1. *For the two scenarios above, let*

$$\theta_{iid} := \sup\left\{\theta \geq 0 \;\middle|\; \mathbb{E}\left[e^{\theta\delta y_i}\right]\mathbb{E}\left[e^{\theta(1-\delta)\min_{j\leq k}\{y_{i,j}\}}\right] \mathbb{E}\left[e^{-\theta t_i}\right]^{\frac{K}{k}} \leq 1\right\}$$

$$\theta_{mkv} := \sup\left\{\theta \geq 0 \;\middle|\; \mathbb{E}\left[e^{\theta\delta y_i}\right]\mathbb{E}\left[e^{\theta(1-\delta)\min_{j\leq k}\{y_{i,j}\}}\right] \xi^{\frac{K}{l}}(\theta) \leq 1\right\}$$

Then for the response time holds for all $\sigma \geq 0$:

$$\mathbb{P}(r_{iid} \geq \sigma) \leq \mathbb{E}\left[e^{\theta_{iid}\min_{j\leq k}\{x_{1,j}\}}\right] e^{-\theta_{iid}\sigma}$$

$$\mathbb{P}(r_{mkv} \geq \sigma) \leq \mathbb{E}\left[e^{\delta\theta_{mkv}y_i}\right]\mathbb{E}\left[e^{(1-\delta)\theta_{mkv}\min_{j\leq k}\{y_{i,j}\}}\right] e^{-\theta_{mkv}\sigma}$$

To numerically compare our stochastic bounds to simulation results we refer to Figure 2; we remark that in both considered scenarios, the bounds are remarkably accurate.

This work was partially funded by the DFG grant Ci 195/1-1.

4. REFERENCES

[1] J. Dean and S. Ghemawat. Mapreduce: Simplified data processing on large clusters. *Communications of the ACM*, 51(1):107–113, Jan. 2008.

[2] K. Gardner, S. Zbarsky, S. Doroudi, M. Harchol-Balter, and E. Hyytiä. Reducing latency via redundant requests: Exact analysis. In *ACM Sigmetrics*, pages 347–360, 2015.

[3] G. D. Ghare and S. T. Leutenegger. Improving speedup and response times by replicating parallel programs on a snow. In *10th International Conference on Job Scheduling Strategies for Parallel Processing (JSSPP)*, pages 264–287, 2004.

[4] G. Joshi, Y. Liu, and E. Soljanin. On the delay-storage trade-off in content download from coded distributed storage systems. *IEEE Journal on Selected Areas in Communications (JSAC)*, 32(5):989–997, May 2014.

Explicit Back-off Rates for Achieving Target Throughputs in CSMA/CA Networks

Benny Van Houdt
Dept. Mathematics and Computer Science
University of Antwerp, Belgium
benny.vanhoudt@uantwerpen.be

ABSTRACT

CSMA/CA networks have often been analyzed using a stylized model that is fully characterized by a vector of back-off rates and a conflict graph. We present an explicit formula for the unique vector of back-off rates $\vec{\nu}(\vec{\theta})$ needed to achieve any achievable throughput vector $\vec{\theta}$ provided that the network has a *chordal* conflict graph. These back-off rates are such that the back-off rate of a node only depends on its own target throughput and the target throughput of its neighbors and can be determined in a *distributed* manner. We also introduce a distributed chordal approximation algorithm for general conflict graphs which is shown (using numerical examples) to be more accurate than the Bethe approximation.

1. INTRODUCTION

An often studied model for CSMA/CA networks is the so-called *ideal* model [2, 4, 5, 6, 8, 9, 11, 12]. The ideal CSMA/CA model considers a network with a fixed set of n nodes and is fully characterized by a fixed conflict graph G and a fixed vector of back-off rates $\vec{\nu} = (\nu_1, \ldots, \nu_n)$. The conflict graph G identifies the pairs of nodes that interfere with each other, while the vector $(\nu_1, \ldots, \nu_n)$ determines the mean time that the nodes have to sense the channel idle before they are allowed to start a transmission.

One of the key assumptions of the ideal CSMA/CA model is that sensing is instantaneous, which implies that collisions cannot occur (as the probability that two nodes start transmitting at exactly the same time is zero). Another important assumption is that each of the n nodes always has packets ready for transmission, that is, the network is assumed to be saturated. Further perfect sensing and packet transmission is assumed.

While the product form solution for the steady state probabilities of the ideal CSMA/CA model has been established long ago [2] and the set Γ of achievable throughput vectors $\vec{\theta} = (\theta_1, \ldots, \theta_n)$ has been identified in [6], very few explicit results are available on how to set the back-off rates $\vec{\nu}$ to achieve a given vector $\vec{\theta} \in \Gamma$ (where Γ clearly depends on the conflict graph G). In [9] an explicit formula was presented to achieve fairness in a line network where each node interferes with its β left and right nodes. More recently, by relying on some existing results in statistical physics, explicit formulas for the back-off vector needed to achieve a given throughput vector were presented in case the conflict graph is a tree [12]. The existence of a unique vector of back-off rates for each achievable throughput vector was proven in [8].

In this paper[1] we identify a set of conflict graphs G for which simple explicit expressions can be obtained for the vector of back-off rates $\vec{\nu}$ that achieves a given throughput vector $\vec{\theta} \in \Gamma$. We show that an explicit expression can be obtained for any *chordal* conflict graph, thereby generalizing existing results for line networks and networks that have a tree as a conflict graph. These explicit expressions are such that the back-off rate ν_i of node i only depends on its own target throughput θ_i and the target throughput of its neighbors in the conflict graph G. Further we present a distributed chordal approximation for general conflict graphs that is more accurate than the Bethe approximation [12].

2. MODEL DESCRIPTION

Consider a network consisting of n nodes that is fully characterized by a vector of back-off rates $(\nu_1, \ldots, \nu_n)$ and an *undirected* conflict graph $G = (V(G), E(G))$, with $V(G) = \{1, \ldots, n\}$. A node is either active or inactive at any point in time. The conflict graph G specifies which pairs of nodes cannot be simultaneously active, that is, nodes i and j cannot be active simultaneously if and only if $(i,j) \in E(G)$. When a node becomes active, it remains active for some time before becoming inactive again. An inactive node can only become active if none of its neighbors in G are active. When a node becomes inactive it starts a back-off period. As soon as one of the neighbors of an inactive node in G becomes active, the back-off period of the inactive node is frozen and resumes when all of its neighbors are inactive again. A node becomes active when its back-off period ends.

If the duration of the active period is exponential (with mean 1) and the back-off period is exponentially distributed with mean $1/\nu_i$ for node i, it is well-known [2] that this network evolves as a reversible Markov chain on the state space

$$\Omega = \{(z_1, \ldots, z_n) \in \{0,1\}^n | z_i z_j = 0 \text{ if } (i,j) \in E(G)\},$$

where node i is active in state $(z_1, \ldots, z_n)$ if and only if $z_i = 1$. The steady state probabilities $\pi(\vec{z})$, with $\vec{z} = (z_1, \ldots, z_n)$

[1]A full version of this paper is available at [10].

SIGMETRICS '16 June 14-18, 2016, Antibes Juan-Les-Pins, France

ACM ISBN 978-1-4503-4266-7/16/06.
DOI: http://dx.doi.org/10.1145/2896377.2901482

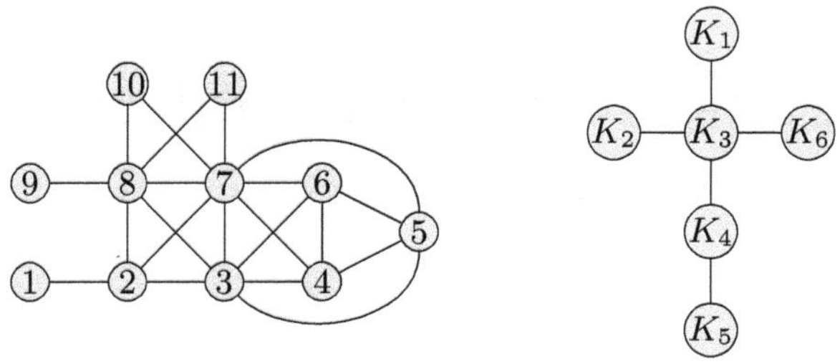

Figure 1: Example of a chordal graph G with $n = 11$ nodes (left) and one of its clique trees (right). This graph contains 6 maximal cliques $K_1 = \{1, 2\}, K_2 = \{3, 4, 5, 6, 7\}, K_3 = \{2, 3, 7, 8\}, K_4 = \{7, 8, 10\}, K_5 = \{8, 9\}$ and $K_6 = \{7, 8, 11\}$.

of this Markov chain are given by

$$\pi(\vec{z}) = \frac{1}{Z_n} \prod_{i=1}^{n} \nu_i^{z_i},$$

where $Z_n = \sum_{\vec{z} \in \Omega} \prod_{i=1}^{n} \nu_i^{z_i}$ is the normalizing constant. The throughput θ_i of node i equals $\theta_i = \sum_{\vec{z} \in \Omega, z_i = 1} \pi(\vec{z})$, for $i = 1, \ldots, n$. In [6] the set Γ of achievable throughput vectors $\vec{\theta} = (\theta_1, \ldots, \theta_n)$ was shown to equal the interior of the convex hull of Ω and for each achievable vector $\vec{\theta} \in \Gamma$ there exists a unique vector $\vec{\nu} = (\nu_1, \ldots, \nu_n)$ of back-off rates that achieves $\vec{\theta}$ [8].

3. MAIN RESULT

In this section we present an explicit formula for the back-off rates needed to achieve any achievable target throughput vector when the conflict graph G is chordal. A chordal graph $G = (V(G), E(G))$ is one in which all cycles consisting of more than 3 nodes have a *chord*. A chord of a cycle is an edge joining two nonconsecutive nodes of the cycle. A graph is chordal if and only if it has a perfect elimination ordering [1], which is an ordering of the nodes of the graph such that, for each $v \in V(G)$, v and the neighbors of v that occur after v in the order form a clique.

Let $\mathcal{K}_G = \{K_1, \ldots, K_m\}$ be the set of maximal cliques of G. A clique tree $T = (\mathcal{K}_G, \mathcal{E})$ is a tree in which the nodes correspond to the maximal cliques and the edges are such that the subgraph of T induced by the maximal cliques that contain the node v is a subtree of T for any $v \in V$. An example of a chordal graph G and possible clique tree T is given in Figure 1. One can show that a graph G is chordal if and only if it has at least one clique tree (see Theorem 3.1 in [1]). A clique tree T of a chordal graph can be constructed in linear time and contains at most $V(G)$ nodes.

THEOREM 1. *Consider a network with a chordal conflict graph G. Let $\vec{\theta} = (\theta_1, \ldots, \theta_n)$ be a positive vector with $T = \max_{j \in \mathcal{K}_G} \sum_{s \in K_j} \theta_s < 1$. The throughput of node i, for $i = 1, \ldots, n$, in a network with conflict graph G matches θ_i if and only if the back-off rates are set as*

$$\nu_i(\vec{\theta}) = \theta_i \frac{\prod_{(K,K') \in \mathcal{E}, i \in K \cap K'} \left(1 - \sum_{s \in K \cap K'} \theta_s\right)}{\prod_{K \in \mathcal{K}_G, i \in K} \left(1 - \sum_{s \in K} \theta_s\right)}, \qquad (1)$$

for $i = 1, \ldots, n$, where $T = (\mathcal{K}_G, \mathcal{E})$ is any clique tree of G.

Input: A chordal conflict graph G
Output: Back-off rates $\nu_1(\vec{\theta}), \ldots, \nu_n(\vec{\theta})$
Determine a perfect elimination ordering of G
for $i = 1$ *to* n **do**
  Let $\alpha(i)$ be the node in position i in this order;
end
for $i = 1$ *to* n **do**
  Let $\mathcal{M}_{\alpha(i)} = \mathcal{N}_{\alpha(i)} \cap \{\alpha(i+1), \ldots, \alpha(n)\}$;
end
$\nu_{\alpha(n)}(\vec{\theta}) = \theta_{\alpha(n)} / (1 - \theta_{\alpha(n)})$;
for $i = n - 1$ **down to** 1 **do**
  $\nu_{\alpha(i)}(\vec{\theta}) = \theta_{\alpha(i)} / (1 - \theta_{\alpha(i)} - \sum_{s \in \mathcal{M}_{\alpha(i)}} \theta_s)$;
  for $j \in \mathcal{M}_{\alpha(i)}$ **do**
    $\nu_j(\vec{\theta}) = \nu_j(\vec{\theta}) \frac{1 - \sum_{s \in \mathcal{M}_{\alpha(i)}} \theta_s}{1 - \theta_{\alpha(i)} - \sum_{s \in \mathcal{M}_{\alpha(i)}} \theta_s}$;
  end
end

Algorithm 1: Algorithm to determine the unique back-off rates for any $\vec{\theta} \in \Gamma$ in a network with a chordal conflict graph G.

The next property shows that the back-off rates as specified by (1) can be computed using Algorithm 1. The first step of this algorithm exists in determining a perfect elimination ordering of G, which can be achieved in $O(|V(G)| + |E(G)|)$ time using the maximum cardinality search (MCS) algorithm [7]. The MCS algorithm determines the perfect elimination ordering by picking $\alpha(n)$ at random and subsequently determines $\alpha(i)$ by selecting the node with the most neighbors in $\{\alpha(i+1), \ldots, \alpha(n)\}$, breaking ties arbitrarily.

PROPOSITION 1. *The back-off rates $\nu_i(\vec{\theta})$ as computed by Algorithm 1 are equal to* (1) *irrespective of the perfect elimination ordering used.*

The back-off rates $\nu_i(\vec{\theta})$ can also be determined in a fully distributed manner with limited message passing. More specifically, it suffices for node i to discover its set of neighbors $\mathcal{N}_i$ in the conflict graph G, their target throughputs $\{\theta_j | j \in \mathcal{N}_i\}$ as well as the set of neighbors $\mathcal{N}_j$ for each $j \in \mathcal{N}_i$. With this information node i can construct the subgraph $G[\mathcal{N}_i^+]$ of the conflict graph G induced by i and its neighbors. To obtain its back-off rate $\nu_i(\vec{\theta})$ node i executes Algorithm 1 on the graph $G[\mathcal{N}_i^+]$ and sets its own back-off rate accordingly.

PROPOSITION 2. *The back-off rate for node $i \in V$ given by executing Algorithm 1 on the conflict graph G is identical to the rate obtained for node i when executing Algorithm 1 on the subgraph $G[\mathcal{N}_i^+]$ of G induced by the nodes in $\mathcal{N}_i \cup i$.*

4. CHORDAL APPROXIMATION

In this section we present a *chordal* approximation for the rates $\nu_i(\vec{\theta})$ for a general conflict graph G that is exact when the conflict graph is chordal. To study the accuracy of the proposed approximation we considered a class of conflict graphs obtained by placing a set of n nodes in a random manner in the unit square and assumed that node i and j are in conflict when the Euclidean distance between node i and j was below some threshold (see Figure 2).

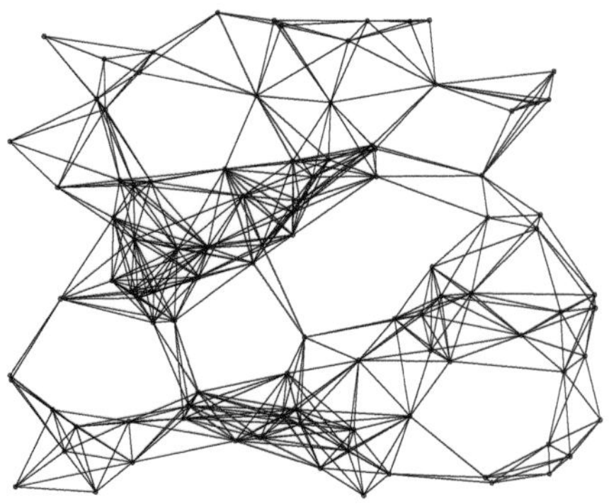

Figure 2: Non-chordal conflict graph with $n = 100$ nodes and 485 edges.

Input: A general conflict graph $G = (V, E)$
Output: A maximal chordal subgraph $\tilde{G} = (V, \tilde{E})$ and peo α

```
1  for v ∈ V do
2  |  C(v) = ∅;
3  end
4  k = |V|; Ẽ = ∅;
5  Select any v0 ∈ V; set S_k = {v0}; α(k) = v0;
6  for u ∈ V \ S_k with (u, v0) ∈ E do
7  |  if C(u) ⊆ C(v0) then
8  |  |  C(u) = C(u) ∪ {v0}; Ẽ = Ẽ ∪ (u, v0);
9  |  end
10 end
11 Let v0 ∈ V \ S_k with |C(v0)| ≥ |C(v)| for v ∈ V \ S_k;
12 Set α(k − 1) = v0; S_{k−1} = S_k ∪ {v0}; k = k − 1;
13 if k > 1 then
14 |  Go to line 6;
15 end
```

Algorithm 2: MAXCHORD algorithm of [3].

The idea behind the proposed distributed chordal approximation exists in letting node i determine its back-off rate by computing a maximal chordal subgraph G_i of $G[\mathcal{N}_i^+]$ and computing its back-off rate using Algorithm 1 on G_i. To determine the subgraph G_i node i runs the MAXCHORD algorithm of [3] on $G[\mathcal{N}_i^+]$ with $v_0 = i$ in line 5 (see Algorithm 2). We refer to this approximation as the *local* chordal subgraph approximation. When the graph G is chordal this distributed algorithm corresponds to the distributed algorithm of Section 3 and is therefore exact.

Note the Bethe approximation of [12] corresponds to using the subtree consisting of the edges (i, j) with $j \in \mathcal{N}_i$, instead of the maximal chordal subgraph G_i and applying Algorithm 1 on this subtree. As such the local chordal subgraph approximation takes more conflicts into account when determining the back-off rates and it is expected to be more accurate than the Bethe approximation. This was confirmed using numerical experiments, with Figure 3 showing one particular example when using both approximations on the conflict graph of Figure 2 and setting the target throughput of each node equal to 0.04.

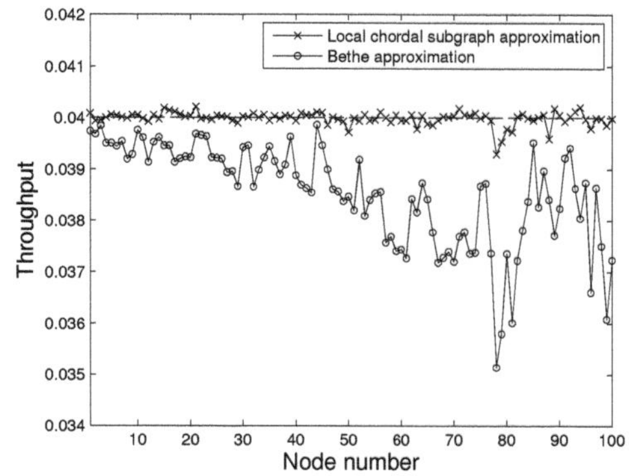

Figure 3: Throughputs of *local* chordal subgraph and Bethe approximation for the conflict graph in Figure 2 (by simulation) when the target throughput $\theta_i = 0.04$ for all i.

5. REFERENCES

[1] J. Blair and B. W. Peyton. An introduction to chordal graphs and clique trees. In *Graph Theory and Sparse Matrix Computation*, volume 56 of *The IMA Volumes in Mathematics and its Applications*, pages 1–29. Springer New York, 1993.

[2] R. Boorstyn, A. Kershenbaum, B. Maglaris, and V. Sahin. Throughput analysis in multihop CSMA packet radio networks. *IEEE Transactions on Communications*, 35(3):267–274, 1987.

[3] P. Dearing, D. Shier, and D. Warner. Maximal chordal subgraphs. *Discrete Applied Mathematics*, 20(3):181 – 190, 1988.

[4] M. Durvy, O. Dousse, and P. Thiran. On the fairness of large CSMA networks. *IEEE Journal on Selected Areas in Communications*, 27(7):1093–1104, 2009.

[5] L. Jiang, D. Shah, J. Shin, and J. Walrand. Distributed random access algorithm: scheduling and congestion control. *IEEE Trans. Inform. Theory*, 56(12):6182–6207, 2010.

[6] L. Jiang and J. Walrand. A distributed CSMA algorithm for throughput and utility maximization in wireless networks. *IEEE/ACM Transactions on Networking*, 18(3):960–972, June 2010.

[7] R. Tarjan. Maximum cardinality search and chordal graphs. Unpublished Lecture Notes CS 259, 1976.

[8] P. M. van de Ven, A. J. E. M. Janssen, J. S. H. van Leeuwaarden, and S. C. Borst. Achieving target throughputs in random-access networks. *Perform. Eval.*, 68(11):1103–1117, Nov. 2011.

[9] P. M. van de Ven, J. S. H. van Leeuwaarden, D. Denteneer, and A. J. E. M. Janssen. Spatial fairness in linear random-access networks. *Perform. Eval.*, 69(3-4):121–134, Mar. 2012.

[10] B. Van Houdt. Explicit back-off rates for achieving target throughputs in CSMA/CA networks. *CoRR*, abs/1602.08290, 2016.

[11] X. Wang and K. Kar. Throughput modeling and fairness issues in CSMA/CA based ad-hoc networks. In *Proc. of IEEE INFOCOM*, 2005.

[12] S. Yun, J. Shin, and Y. Yi. CSMA using the Bethe approximation: scheduling and utility maximization. *IEEE Transactions on Information Theory*, 61(9):4776–4787, 2015.

Freestyle Dancing: Randomized Algorithms for Dynamic Storage Load-Balancing

Liang Liu[†], Yating Wang[†], Lance Fortnow[†], Jin Li[‡], Jun Xu[†]
[†]Georgia Institute of Technology [‡]Microsoft Research Technologies
{lliu315, fortnow}@gatech.edu, Jinl@microsoft.com

ABSTRACT

In this work, we study a challenging research problem that arises in minimizing the cost of storing customer data online for reliable accesses in a cloud. It is how to near-perfectly balance the remaining capacities of all disks across the cloud system while adding new file blocks so that the inevitable event of capacity expansion can be postponed as much as possible. The challenges of solving this problem are twofold. First, new file blocks are added to the cloud concurrently by many dispatchers (computing servers) that have no communication or coordination among themselves. Though each dispatcher is updated with information on disk occupancies, the update is infrequent and not synchronized. Second, for fault-tolerance purposes, a combinatorial constraint has to be satisfied in distributing the blocks of each new file across the cloud system. We propose a randomized algorithm, in which each dispatcher independently samples a blocks-to-disks assignment according to a probability distribution on a set of assignments conforming to the aforementioned combinatorial requirement. We show that this algorithm allows a cloud system to near-perfectly balance the remaining disk capacities as rapidly as theoretically possible, when starting from any unbalanced state that is correctable mathematically.

Categories and Subject Descriptors

C.1.2 [Multiple Data Stream Architectures]
E.2 [Data Storage Representations]

Keywords

Load Balance, Capacity Distribution, Load Distribution, Birkhoff Decomposition

1. INTRODUCTION

A cloud service provider needs to provide its customers with reliable accesses to their own data, despite service disruptions of its disks, computers, and networks, caused possibly by power failures, hardware malfunctions, scheduled maintenances/upgrades, operator errors, etc. This disruption tolerance capability is achieved typically through a combination of two risk control measures. One is erasure coding [4], that is, to divide a customer file into b blocks, and then encode them into $b+b' = k$ blocks (by adding b' blocks of redundancies) so that missing one or two such blocks due to aforementioned disruptions will not prevent the file from being decoded and delivered to the customer. The other is "geographic" diversity, that is, to strategically distribute these (coded) blocks across the cloud system so that a typical service disruption event may affect the access to at most one or two such (coded) blocks.

In this work, we study a research problem concerning how to near-perfectly balance the remaining capacities of all disks across the cloud system while adding new file blocks so that the inevitable event of capacity expansion can be postponed as much as possible. This problem is challenging due to two constraints the proposed load-balancing solution has to work under. The first constraint is the aforementioned "geographic" diversity requirement. At the cloud service provider we are working with, the disk servers of the entire cloud system is logically divided into mn equal-capacity partitions – called cells – organized as an $m \times n$ matrix. This partitioning is done in such a way that, with high probability, at most one row and/or one column (of storage servers) of will be impacted at any time by an aforementioned service disruption event [6]. Hence the diversity requirement translates into that, when a new customer file, consisting of k coded blocks, is added to the cloud system, no cell can take in more than one such block, and no two cells that take in a block can be on the same row or on the same column of the matrix.

The second constraint is "distributed independent dispatching". In a cloud environment, new files are added to the system by a large number of front-end computing servers that interact with customers, which we call dispatchers. "Distributed independent dispatching" means that no communication or coordination is allowed among dispatchers when they add new files to the disks, because such communication or coordination is prohibitively expensive in a large cloud environment with a large number of dispatchers geographically distributed across the world. In addition, to minimize reporting overheads, dispatchers obtain accurate reporting of the loads (occupancy ratios) of all disks (cells) in a cloud system quite infrequently (say once a day). It can be shown this second constraint rules out naive solutions such as a (deterministic) greedy approach, in which we try to place k blocks in a diverse set of k cells that collectively have the smallest overall occupancy ratios.

2. THE LOAD-BALANCING PROBLEM AND OUR SOLUTION

In this work, we propose a randomized load-balancing algorithm that works as follows. Each dispatcher, upon receiving a disk occupancy report, precomputes a probability distribution over a set of possible blocks-to-cells assignments conforming to the afore-

SIGMETRICS '16 June 14-18, 2016, Antibes Juan-Les-Pins, France

ACM ISBN 978-1-4503-4266-7/16/06.
DOI: http://dx.doi.org/10.1145/2896377.2901481

mentioned diversity requirement. Note that every such assignment corresponds to a k-matching when the rows and the columns of the matrix are viewed as the two independent vertex sets in a bipartite graph. Later on, when a dispatcher has to add (the k blocks of) a new file to the cloud system, it randomly samples a blocks-to-cells assignment according to the computed distribution, and dispatches the blocks accordingly. Note it is important to do this in two steps, since the first step – computing the desired distribution – which is done offline, could take a long time (typically minutes). The second step – making random assignments based on the precomputed probability distribution – on the other hand, must be finished in milliseconds in order not to "freeze" the cloud service.

Our main research problem is therefore to identify (mathematically) and compute a suitable probability distribution, that, after a large number of random blocks-to-cells assignments are made – independently by many dispatchers – according to the distribution, the residual spaces of all disks in the cloud system will be made very close to one another, even when they are far apart to start with. A major contribution of this work is to identify and efficiently compute such a distribution. Armed with this distribution, our randomized load-balancing algorithm can balance the disk loads across different cells almost as perfectly as the idealized scheme (centralized control with perfect and timely knowledge of the loads of all cells), under the diversity constraint.

Computing this probability distribution above has indeed been studied in the mathematics literature [2, 1, 5]. Here we describe this computation in this context of cloud storage load-balancing. Let $L = \{l_{ij}\}$ be the load matrix of the cloud system in the sense l_{ij} is the total storage load of the cell on the i_{th} row and j_{th} column of the cloud matrix. The computation consists of two steps. The first step is to derive the minimum target load level $\hat{l}$ that can be reached by all cells simultaneously by the aforementioned idealized scheme [5]. Let L_T be an $m \times n$ matrix every element of which has value $\hat{l}$. The second step is to decompose the difference matrix $L_T - L$ into a linear combination of k-matchings [2, 1]. By normalizing the coefficients in the linear combination, we arrive at the probability distribution. This decomposition problem can be converted to the Birkhoff-Von Neumann (BVN) decomposition of an $(m+n-k) \times (m+n-k)$ doubly stochastic matrix. By using the most efficient algorithm discovered so far for BVN decomposition [3], the complexity of computing this probability distribution is $O\big((m+n-k)^3 \log(m+n-k)\big)$. One of our contributions is to propose a deterministic algorithm that can reduce this complexity to $O\big((m+n)\log(m+n) + (3k)^3 \log(3k)\big)$. For small k values that are typical for storage erasure codes, the latter complexity can be several orders of magnitude smaller than the former, for very large cloud size ($m \times n$). We omit this algorithm here due to lack of space.

After a certain number of assignments are made according to the this probability distribution, the loads across cells should become quite balanced. At that point, the load-balancing operation in the cloud system enters a cruising stage. In the cruising stage, a dispatcher adds statistically the same number of blocks to each cell so as not to change the status quo. We achieve it by using a "plane sweep" algorithm at every dispatcher. This algorithm limits the maximum such variation caused by a single dispatcher to at most two blocks. In addition, the algorithm instances at different dispatchers are independently randomly parameterized to keep the actions of different dispatchers, and hence the cells where such maximum variations occur, statistically independent of one another. The basic idea of the algorithm is for a dispatcher to make successive assignments using the same $k \times k$ k-matching matrix π that is shifted in a "sweeping pattern" over time.

3. EVALUATION

We perform a simulation study to evaluate two properties of our load-balance scheme. One is how balanced our scheme can achieve and maintain in the cloud. The other one is how fast our scheme can restore the balanced state after some typical breakdown scenarios. The parameters we use in the simulation are as follows: $m = 60$, $n = 20$, $k = 18$. In addition, each cell can hold 1.5×10^7 blocks and the total number of new blocks to be added to the cloud system per day is about 0.1% of the cloud storage capacity. In the simulation, we use metric $D = \max l_{ij} - \bar{l}$, the difference between the load ratio of the most heavily loaded cell and the average load ratio to measure how well loads are balanced across the cells, and call this D the *positive load ratio deviation*. D reflects the evenness of load distribution.

According to our simulation results (1200 simulation runs, each of which simulates 800 days that gradually fills up the cloud storage from 0% to 80% loaded), with our load balancing scheme, D could be maintained at smaller than 0.03% of each cell's maximum capacity with overwhelming probability. That means with overwhelming probability, the utilization ratio of the cloud could reach 79.97% without any cell's load exceeding 80%.

We also evaluate how fast and effectively our load-balancing scheme can "fix" load-imbalance caused by a hardware failure scenario. We assume that the hardware failure makes one row of cells unaccessible for as long as a week (7 days). We made 100 simulation runs for this scenario. Our results show that during the hardware failure period, the deviation D increases to about 0.003% of a cell's capacity. After the row impacted by the hardware failure comes back into service, our weighted randomized assignment algorithm restores the balance within four days, or after new blocks, in the amount no more than $0.1\% \times 4 = 0.4\%$ of the total storage of the cloud system, are assigned.

Acknowledgment

This work is supported in part by US NSF through grants CNS-1248117 and CNS-1423182.

4. REFERENCES

[1] BIRKHOFF, D. Tres observaciones sobre el algebra lineal. *Universidad Nacional de Tucuman Revista , Serie A 5* (1946), 147–151.

[2] CHANG, C.-S., CHEN, W.-J., AND HUANG, H.-Y. Birkhoff-von neumann input buffered crossbar switches. In *INFOCOM 2000. Nineteenth Annual Joint Conference of the IEEE Computer and Communications Societies. Proceedings. IEEE* (Mar 2000), vol. 3, pp. 1614–1623 vol.3.

[3] GOEL, A., KAPRALOV, M., AND KHANNA, S. Perfect matchings in $O(n \log n)$ time in regular bipartite graphs. *CoRR abs/0909.3346* (2009).

[4] HUANG, C., SIMITCI, H., XU, Y., OGUS, A., CALDER, B., GOPALAN, P., LI, J., AND YEKHANIN, S. Erasure coding in windows azure storage. In *Presented as part of the 2012 USENIX Annual Technical Conference (USENIX ATC 12)* (Boston, MA, 2012), USENIX, pp. 15–26.

[5] MENDELSOHN, N. S., AND DULMAGE, A. L. The convex hull of sub-permutation matrices. *Proceedings of the American Mathematical Society 9* (1958), 253–254.

[6] MICROSOFT AZURE STORAGE TEAM. Introducing zone redundant storage. bit.ly/1LFsA44, 2014.

Joint Data Purchasing and Data Placement in a Geo-Distributed Data Market

Xiaoqi Ren, Palma London, Juba Ziani, Adam Wierman*
California Institute of Technology
{xren, plondon, jziani, adamw}@caltech.edu

ABSTRACT

This paper studies design challenges faced by a geo-distributed cloud data market: which data to purchase (data purchasing) and where to place/replicate the data (data placement). We show that the joint problem of data purchasing and data placement within a cloud data market is NP-hard in general. However, we give a provably optimal algorithm for the case of a data market made up of a single data center, and then generalize the structure from the single data center setting and propose Datum, a near-optimal, polynomial-time algorithm for a geo-distributed data market.

1. INTRODUCTION

Ten years ago computing infrastructure was a *commodity*. Now, computing power and memory are *services* that can be cheaply subscribed to and scaled as needed via cloud providers like Amazon EC2, Microsoft Azure, etc.

We are beginning the same transition with respect to *data*. Data is broadly being gathered, bought, and sold in various marketplaces. However, it is still a commodity, often obtained through offline negotiations between providers and companies. Acquiring data is now one of the key bottlenecks for new tech startups.

This is beginning to change with the emergence of *cloud data markets*, which offer a single, logically centralized point for buying and selling data. Multiple data markets have recently emerged in the cloud, e.g., Microsoft Azure DataMarket [1], Factual [2], InfoChimps [3], Xignite [4], IUPHAR [5], etc. A rich literature has studied on cloud data market pricing. **This paper focuses on the engineering side of the design of a data market**, which has been ignored to this point. Supposing that prices are given, there are two important challenges that remain for the operation of a data market: 1) *data purchasing:* given prices and contracts offered by data providers, which providers should a data market purchase from to satisfy a set of client queries with minimal cost? 2) *data placement:* How should purchased data be stored and replicated throughout a geo-distributed data market in order to minimize bandwidth and latency costs? And which clients should be served from which replicas given the locations and data requirements of the clients?

In this paper, we present Datum, which jointly optimizes data purchasing and data placement costs for a geo-distributed data market. Datum first optimizes data purchasing as if the data market was made up of a single data center (given carefully designed "transformed" costs) and then, given the data purchasing decisions, optimizes data placement/replication. The "transformed" costs are designed to allow an architectural decomposition of the joint problem into subproblems that manage data purchasing (external operations of the data market) and data placement (internal operations of the data market). This decomposition is of crucial operational importance because it means that internal placement and routing decisions can proceed without factoring in data purchasing costs, mimicking operational structures of geo-distributed analytics systems today.

We have evaluated Datum using a case study, which shows that Datum is near-optimal (within 1.6%) in practical settings. Further, the performance of Datum improves upon approaches that neglect data purchasing decisions by > 45%. Details are reported in the full version of this paper [6].

2. MODELING THE DATA CLOUD

We consider a setting where there are P data providers selling different data to C clients. Each data provider offers a set of quality levels $\mathcal{L}$. We use $q(l,p)$ to denote the data quality level l, offered by data provider p and use $f(l,p)$ to denote the fee charged by provider p for data of quality level l. Each client c sends a *query* to the data center, requesting particular data from multiple data providers. Denote the set of data providers required by the request from client query c by $G(c)$. The client query also specifies a minimum desired quality level, $w_c(p)$, for each data provider p it requests.

The data cloud in this marketplace is an aggregator and intermediary. We model the data cloud as a geographically distributed cloud consisting of D data centers. Each data center aggregates data from geographically separate local data providers, and data from data providers may be (and often is) replicated across multiple data centers within the data cloud. Denote the cost to transfer data of quality $q(l,p)$, originating from data provider p, from data center d to client c by $\alpha_{d,c}(l,p)$. And denote the cost to transfer data of quality $q(l,p)$ from data provider p to data center d by $\beta_{p,d}(l)$. Define binary variable $x_{d,c}(l,p)$ such that

*This work is partially supported by NSF grants CNS-1254169, CNS-1319820, NETS-1518941, and BSF grant 2012348.

SIGMETRICS '16 June 14-18, 2016, Antibes Juan-Les-Pins, France

ACM ISBN 978-1-4503-4266-7/16/06.
DOI: http://dx.doi.org/10.1145/2896377.2901486

$x_{d,c}(l,p) = 1$ if and only if data of quality $q(l,p)$, originating from data provider p, is transferred from data center d to client c. Define binary variable $y_{p,d}(l)$ such that $y_{p,d}(l) = 1$ if and only if data of quality $q(l,p)$ is transferred from data provider p to data center d.

Our goal is to provide a design that minimizes the operational costs of a data cloud. These costs include:

1) The *operation cost* due to transferring data of all quality levels from data providers to data centers.

$$\text{OperCost} = \sum_{p=1}^{P} \sum_{l=1}^{L_p} \sum_{d=1}^{D} \beta_{p,d}(l) y_{p,d}(l).$$

2) The *execution cost* due to transferring data of all quality levels from data centers to clients.

$$\text{ExecCost} = \sum_{c=1}^{C} \sum_{p \in G(c)} \sum_{l=1}^{L_p} \sum_{d=1}^{D} \alpha_{d,c}(l,p) x_{d,c}(l,p).$$

3) The *purchasing cost* (PurchCost) due to buying data from the data provider. Due to space limit, we only discuss the widely adopted per-query data contracting model here.

$$\text{PurchCost} = \sum_{c=1}^{C} \sum_{p \in G(c)} \sum_{l=1}^{L_p} \sum_{d=1}^{D} f(l,p) x_{d,c}(l,p).$$

Given the cost models described above, we can now represent the goal of the data cloud via the following integer linear program (ILP).

$$\min_{x,y} \quad \text{OperCost} + \text{ExecCost} + \text{PurchCost} \tag{1}$$

$$\text{subject to} \quad x_{d,c}(l,p) \le y_{p,d}(l) \ \forall c,p,l,d \tag{1a}$$

$$\sum_{l=1}^{L_p} \sum_{d=1}^{D} x_{d,c}(l,p) = 1, \ \forall c, p \in G(c) \tag{1b}$$

$$\sum_{l=1}^{L_p} \sum_{d=1}^{D} x_{d,c}(l,p) q(l,p) \ge w_c(p), \ \forall c, p \in G(c) \tag{1c}$$

$$x_{d,c}(l,p) \ge 0, \forall c,p,l,d \tag{1d}$$

$$y_{p,d}(l) \ge 0, \ \forall p,l,d \tag{1e}$$

$$x_{d,c}(l,p), y_{p,d}(l) \in \{0,1\}, \forall c,p,l,d \tag{1f}$$

3. Datum

Our first result, stated below, highlights that cost minimization for a data cloud is NP-hard.

THEOREM 1. *The cost minimization problem for a geo-distributed data cloud given in* (1) *is NP-hard.*

More specifically, the reduction leading to Theorem 1 highlights that the data cloud optimization problem is equivalent to the *non-metric* uncapacitated facility location problem Nevertheless, even though our problem can, in general, be viewed as the non-metric uncapacitated facility location, it does have a structure in real-world situations that we can exploit to develop practical algorithms.

In particular, in the case of a data cloud made up of a single data center, though the problem is still an uncapacitated facility location problem, there is a structure that allows us to design an algorithm with polynomial running time that gives an exact optimal solution. The details of the algorithm and corresponding proof can be found in [6].

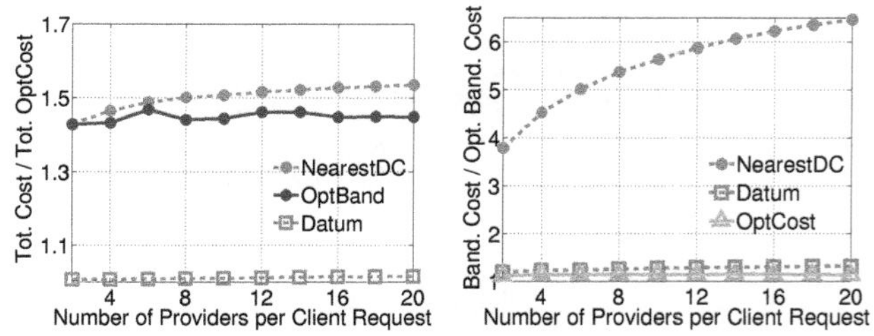

(a) Total Cost (b) Bandwidth Cost

Figure 1: Datum **is near optimal.**

Unlike the data cloud cost minimization problem for a single data center, the general data cloud cost minimization is NP-hard. However, the exact solution for single data center case inspires our design, Datum, for cost minimization in a geo-distributed data cloud.

The idea underlying Datum is to, first, optimize data purchasing decisions as if the data market was made up of a single data center (given carefully designed "transformed" costs). Then, second, given the data purchasing decisions, Datum optimizes data placement/replication decisions .

The sketch of Datum is as following. A detailed description of each steps of the algorithm can be found in [6].

Step 1: Define V as the set of all possible subsets of data centers. Reformulate the problem and for data centers, replace subscription d with v to add two new constraints to (1). Those two new constraints guarantee the decoupling of data purchasing and data placement.

Step 2: Aggregate variables x and y with respect to subscription v, and treat the geo-distributed data cloud as a single data center with proper parameter approximation. This leaves the "single data center" problem and thus can be solved optimally in polynomial time.

Step 3: The results of Step 2 determines which quality levels should be purchased and which quality levels should be delivered to each client. Then the remaining problem to determine data placement and data replication an be solved optimally in polynomial time.

4. CASE STUDY

We illustrate the performance of Datum using a case study of a geo-distributed data cloud running in North America. A detailed description of the settings can be found in [6]. Figure 1(a) illustrates the costs savings Datum provides. It highlights that Datum provides near-optimal performance (within 1.6% of optimal) in realistic settings via a polynomial-time algorithm that is provably optimal in the case of a data cloud running on a single data center. Additionally, Datum provides > 45% improvement over current design proposals for geo-distributed data analytics systems.

References

[1] Microsoft Azure. https://azure.microsoft.com/en-us/, 2015.
[2] Factual. https://www.factual.com/, 2015.
[3] Infochimps. http://www.infochimps.com/, 2015.
[4] Xignite. http://www.xignite.com/, 2015.
[5] The IUPHAR/BPS Guide to Pharmacology. http://www.guidetopharmacology.org/, 2015.
[6] X.Ren, P. London, J. Ziani, and A. Wierman. Joint Data Purchasing and Data Placement in a Geo-Distributed Data Market. http://arxiv.org/abs/1604.02533.

Majority Rule Based Opinion Dynamics with Biased and Stubborn Agents

Arpan Mukhopadhyay
University of Waterloo
Waterloo, Canada
a3mukhop@uwaterloo.ca

Ravi R. Mazumdar
University of Waterloo
Waterloo, Canada
mazum@uwaterloo.ca

Rahul Roy
Indian Statistical Institute, Delhi
rahul@isid.ac.in

ABSTRACT

In this paper, we investigate the impact of majority-rule based random interactions among agents in a large social network on the diffusion of opinions in the network. Opinion of each agent is assumed to be a binary variable taking values in the set $\{0, 1\}$. Interactions among agents are modeled using the majority rule, where each agent updates its opinion at random instants by adopting the '*majority*' opinion among a group of randomly sampled agents. We investigate two scenarios that respectively incorporate 'bias' of the agents towards a specific opinion and stubbornness of some of the agents in the majority rule dynamics. For the first scenario, where all the agents are assumed to be '*biased*' towards one of the opinions, it is shown that the agents reach a *consensus* on the preferred opinion (with high probability) only if the initial fraction of agents having the preferred opinion is above a certain threshold. Furthermore, the mean time taken to reach the consensus is shown to be logarithmic in the network size. In the second scenario, where the presence of '*stubborn*' agents, who never update their opinions, is assumed, we characterize the equilibrium distribution of opinions of the non-stubborn agents using mean field techniques. The mean field limit is shown to have multiple *stable* equilibrium points which leads to a phenomenon known as *metastability*.

Keywords

Opinion dynamics, majority rule, mean field, metastability

1. INTRODUCTION

With the widespread use of online social networking opinions of individuals are constantly being shaped by social interactions. In many cases, the individuals face only two choices concerning a specific issue (e.g. Windows/Linux, pro-/anti-government, etc.). In such cases, the opinions can be treated as binary variables taking values in the set $\{0, 1\}$. The interactions among agents are generally modeled using simple rules that capture the essential features of individuals in a society such as their tendency to mimic their neighbors or to conform with the majority. The celebrated *voter model* [1, 2, 3], where an agent simply copies the opinion of another randomly sampled neighbor, captures the tendency of an individual to mimic other individuals in the society. In this paper, we focus on a more realistic model of social interaction, given by the *majority rule* model [4, 5, 6], where an updating agent samples multiple individuals at an update instant and adopts the opinion of the majority of the sampled neighbors.

More formally, we consider a network of N agents, where each agent can communicate with any other agent.[1] Opinion of each agent is assumed to be a binary variable taking values in the set $\{0, 1\}$. Initially, α fraction of agents is assumed to have opinion $\{1\}$. The agents consider updating their opinions at points of independent unit rate Poisson processes associated with themselves. At a point of the Poisson process associated with itself, an agent either retains or updates its opinion. If an agent decides to update its opinion, then it interacts with two[2] agents chosen uniformly at random (with replacement) and adopts the majority opinion among the three agents which include the two sampled agents and the updating agent itself.

In all previous works on majority rule models, it is assumed that an agent updates its opinion at each point of the Poisson process associated with itself. However, the decision of an agent to update or retain its past opinion depends on factors such as the preference of the agent to current opinion and the propensity of the agent to change opinions. We incorporate the effects of these factors separately in the scenarios described below.

2. MAJORITY RULE WITH 'BIASED' AGENTS

We first consider the case where the agents are biased towards one of the two opinions. In particular, we assume, without loss of generality, that opinion $\{1\}$ is preferred to opinion $\{0\}$ by all the agents in the network. This is modeled as follows: Each agent with opinion $i \in \{0, 1\}$ updates its opinion at a point the unit rate Poisson point process associated with itself with probability q_i and retains its opinion with probability with probability $p_i = 1 - q_i$. In case,

[1]Note that results of this paper hold even when the agents have fixed neighborhoods whose sizes grow as $O(N)$.

[2]The analysis can be generalized to the case where an agent samples $2K$ agents at an update instant.

SIGMETRICS '16 June 14-18, 2016, Antibes Juan-Les-Pins, France

ACM ISBN 978-1-4503-4266-7/16/06.

DOI: http://dx.doi.org/10.1145/2896377.2901488

the agent decides to update its opinion, the update occurs following the majority rule discussed above. We assume $q_0 > q_1$ ($p_0 < p_1$) to imply that the agents having opinion $\{0\}$ update their opinions more frequently than the agents having opinion $\{1\}$. In this sense, the agents are biased towards opinion $\{1\}$.

Clearly, in this case, the network gets absorbed (in a finite time) in a state where all agents adopt the same opinion. This is referred to as the *consensus* state. Our interest is to find out the probability with which consensus is achieved on the preferred opinion $\{1\}$. We also intend to characterize the mean time to reach the consensus state.

The probability $E_N(n)$ with which the network reaches consensus on opinion $\{1\}$ starting from $n \in \{1, 2, \ldots, N\}$ agents having opinion $\{1\}$ can be shown to be given by

$$E_N(n) = \frac{1}{(1+r)^{N-1}} \sum_{k=0}^{n-1} \binom{N-1}{k} r^k, \tag{1}$$

where $r = q_1/q_0 < 1$ and $E_N(0) = 0$. Now let $x^{(N)}(t)$ denote the fraction (among N total agents) of agents having opinion $\{1\}$ at time $t \geq 0$. We show that if $x^{(N)}(0) \Rightarrow \alpha \in [0,1]$ as $N \to \infty$, where '$\Rightarrow$' denotes weak convergence, then $x^{(N)}(\cdot) \Rightarrow x(\cdot)$ as $N \to \infty$, where $x(\cdot)$ is the unique process satisfying

$$\dot{x}(t) = (q_0 + q_1)x(t)(1 - x(t))\,(x(t) - \kappa_q)\,, \tag{2}$$

with $x(0) = \alpha$ and $\kappa_q = q_1/(q_0 + q_1)$. The process $x(\cdot)$ is known as the mean field limit of the network and the properties of the network for large N can be studied via this process. From (2) it follows that for $x(0) = \alpha > \kappa_q$, $x(t) \to 1$ as $t \to \infty$. Therefore, the mean consensus time, for large N, can be approximated as the time taken by the process $x(\cdot)$ to reach the state $1 - 1/N$ from state α. We denote the approximate mean consensus time by $\bar{T}_N(\alpha)$. Now, solving (2) with the above limits we obtain

$$\begin{aligned}\bar{T}_N(\kappa_q + \epsilon) \approx \frac{1}{q_0 + q_1}\Bigg[&\frac{1}{\kappa_q(1-\kappa_q)} \ln(N(1-\kappa_q) - 1) \\ &- \frac{1}{\kappa_q}\ln(N-1) - \frac{1}{\kappa_q(1-\kappa_q)}\ln\epsilon \\ &+ \frac{1}{\kappa_q}\ln(\kappa_q + \epsilon) + \frac{1}{1-\kappa_q}\ln(1 - \kappa_q - \epsilon)\Bigg]\end{aligned} \tag{3}$$

Similar expression hold for $x(0) = \alpha < \kappa_q$. It is clear from (3) that the mean consensus time grows as $O(\ln N)$. It is also clear that the network will reach consensus on opinion $\{1\}$ with high probability only when the fraction $x^{(N)}(0) > \kappa_q$.

3. MAJORITY RULE WITH 'STUBBORN' AGENTS

We next consider the case where γ_i fraction of agents in the network always have opinion $i \in \{0, 1\}$. We call these agents as the *stubborn* agents. The other $(1 - \gamma_0 - \gamma_1)$ fraction of agents, referred to as the *non-stubborn* agents, update their opinions at each point of the Poisson processes associated with themselves. Clearly, the presence of stubborn agents prevents the network from reaching a consensus state. It can be shown that the evolution of the fraction of non-stubborn agents having opinion $\{1\}$ converges as $N \to \infty$ to the mean field process $x(\cdot)$ given by

$$\dot{x}(t) = (1-x)[(1-\gamma_0-\gamma_1)x+\gamma_1]^2 - x[(1-\gamma_0-\gamma_1)(1-x)+\gamma_0]^2. \tag{4}$$

The right hand side of (4) is a cubic polynomial in $x(t)$. Hence, there can be at most three equilibrium points of the process $x(\cdot)$. It can be shown that depending on the values of γ_0 and γ_1, the mean field has either exactly one or exactly two stable equilibrium points.

If there exist multiple equilibrium points of the process $x(\cdot)$ then the mean field convergence implies that the equilibrium fraction of non-stubborn agents having opinion $\{1\}$ fluctuates between the regions corresponding to the stable equilibrium points of the mean field, spending long intervals in each configuration. This phenomenon as formally known as metastability. In Figure 1, we show the sample path of the process $x^{(N)}(\cdot)$ which denotes the fraction of non-stubborn agents having opinion $\{1\}$. We see that even at steady state the process switches back and forth between regions corresponding to the stable equilibrium points of $x(\cdot)$. This provides numerical evidence of the metastable behavior of the network.

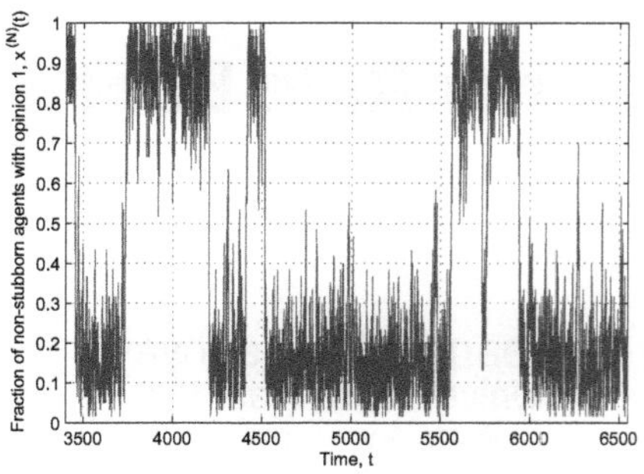

Figure 1: Majority rule with stubborn agents: Sample path of the process $x^{(N)}(\cdot)$ with $N = 100$, $\gamma_0 = \gamma_1 = 0.2$.

4. REFERENCES

[1] R. A. Holley and T. M. Liggett. Ergodic theorems for weakly interacting infinite systems and the voter model. *Annals of Applied Probability*, 3(4), 1975.

[2] P. Clifford and A. Sudbury. A model for spatial conflict. *Biometrika*, 60(3):581–588, 1973.

[3] J. T. Cox. Coalescing random walks and voter model consensus times on the torus in $\mathbb{Z}^d$. *Annals of Probability*, 17(4), 1989.

[4] P. L. Krapivsky and S. Redner. Dynamics of majority rule in two-state interacting spin systems. *Physical Review Letters*, 90(23):238701, 2003.

[5] P. Chen and S. Redner. Consensus formation in multi-state majority and plurality models. *Journal of Physics A: Mathematical and General*, 38(33):7239, 2005.

[6] P. Chen and S. Redner. Majority rule dynamics in finite dimensions. *Physical Review E*, 71(3):036101, 2005.

Mean Field Equilibria of Pricing Games in Internet Marketplaces

Vamseedhar Reddyvari Raja
Texas A&M University

Vinod Ramaswamy
University of Colorado, Boulder

Srinivas Shakkottai
Texas A&M University

Vijay Subramanian
University of Michigan

ABSTRACT

We model an Internet marketplace using a set of servers that choose prices for performing jobs. Each server has a queue of unfinished jobs, and is penalized for delay by the market maker via a holding cost. A server completes jobs with a low or high "quality", and jobs truthfully report the quality with which they were completed. The best estimate of quality based on these reports is the "reputation" of the server. A server bases its pricing decision on the distribution of its competitors offered prices and reputations. An entering job is given a random sample of servers, and chooses the best one based on a linear combination of price and reputation. We seek to understand how prices would be determined in such a marketplace using the theory of Mean Field Games. We show the existence of a Mean Field Equilibrium and show how reputation plays a role in allowing servers to declare larger prices than their competitors. We illustrate our results by a numerical study of the system via simulation with parameters chosen from data gathered from existing Internet marketplaces.

1. INTRODUCTION

The world has recently seen an explosion in the growth of Internet marketplaces. Marketplaces that enable small scale goods sellers to reach their target audience range from broad ones such as Amazon and Ebay, or more specialized ones such as Swappa [2] and Hacker's List [1]. The heterogeneous mix of agents who have different lifetimes and differing abilities to complete jobs has meant that establishing credentials in a marketplace is usually by means of a reputation scheme, wherein users that have interacted with these agents leave feedback based on their experience. It has been empirically observed that having a higher reputation carries a sale price premium to the tune of about $5-10\%$ [3]. We too observed the same phenomenon in data that we gathered from Swappa. It is also observed in [3] that delays in processing jobs are considered quite unfavorably. How then should an agent with a certain reputation and a certain number of pending jobs to be completed, price his good or service against competing offers?

Our objective in this work is to study the dynamics of competition across agents providing a nominally identical service or good in an Internet marketplace. Here, the agents offering service have an inherent competence or quality of service that is unknown to potential customers. Customers are only aware of the posted reputation, and take a decision on which agent to choose for service based on a combination of the offered price and reputation. The marketplace is intersted in ensuring high throughput and low delays, and hence imposes a holding cost on each agent based on its number of pending jobs. The agent providing service has a random lifetime, after which he leaves the system. Such behavior is typical of small scale service providers and retailers. The challenge faced by an agent is to tradeoff the need to set a low price to incentivize customers to explore its service (and potentially enhance its reputation), while at the same time trying to maximize its payoff at the current reputation by setting higher prices. While doing so, the agent needs to model the likely prices set by the competing providers.

Modeling the actions of each individual competitor in a marketplace where the number of agents is very large is prohibitively complex for any particular agent. Indeed, given that a potential customer only views the offered prices and reputations of a finite subset of agents, a particular agent is unlikely to have gone head-to-head with any of the competitors it faces for some particular job if the agent lifetimes are all randomly drawn. Thus, it might in fact be unnecessary for any agent to compute the behavior of each potential competitor in order to determine the optimal price. This setting of infinite agents, each with ephemeral lifetimes and with random finite subsets interacting with each other at each step is the typical setting of a mean field game.

The Mean Field Game (MFG) is the limiting case of a Bayesian game under which the number of agents becomes large, and the interactions between any finite subset of agents becomes infrequent. When these conditions are met, it is an

Research was funded in part by NSF grants CNS-1149458, AST 1443891, EFRI-1440969, IIS-1538827, AST-1343381 and AST-1516075. Any opinions, findings, and conclusions or recommendations expressed in this material are those of the authors and do not necessarily reflect the views of the funding agencies

SIGMETRICS '16 June 14-18, 2016, Antibes Juan-Les-Pins, France

ACM ISBN 978-1-4503-4266-7/16/06.
DOI: http://dx.doi.org/10.1145/2896377.2901495

accurate approximation to assume that the states and hence the actions of any finite subset of competitors are independent of each other, which is the so-called chaos hypothesis. This hypothesis provides the basis for the MFG under which we consider the system from the viewpoint of a single agent that has a belief that his opponents actions would be drawn independently of each other from some candidate probability distribution, and takes a best response action based on his current state and this belief. The system is said to be at a Mean Field Equilibrium (MFE) if this action is itself a sample consistent with the candidate distribution. The MFG approach has recently been used in several different problems on games with a large number of agents, each subset of which meet infrequently [4–7].

2. MEAN FIELD MODEL

We consider a system with NM agents that are randomly permuted and divided into N clusters with M agents in each cluster. At each discrete time instant $k = 1, 2, 3, \cdots, M$ jobs arrive into the system, and each job is assigned to a different cluster. Each agent in a cluster specifies a price (that we refer to as a bid) for completion of the job, and if its bid is accepted by the job, the agent is awarded the payment stated in its bid. We study the system in the mean field regime in which $N \to \infty$.

State Space of Agent: The state of this agent consists of the queue length, the service quality and its reputation. We denote the residual work load in the queue just before time instant k by $q_k \in [0, \infty]$. An agent can complete each job with either a "high" quality w.p. η or "low" quality w.p. $1-\eta$. The marketplace tries to estimate the agents's quality via a reputation scheme in which customers provide feedback on whether they received high or low quality service. The reputation of an agent is estimated via a $\beta-$distribution $\beta(\alpha_k, \beta_k)$.

State Transitions: The state of the system could change due to departures, arrivals or regenrations. At each time slot, the server completes $d_k \sim \Phi$ units of work and the queue state changes from q_k to $(q_k - d_k)^+$.

We assume a new job of unit size arrives in the cluster of the selected agent at each time slot. Let $x_k \in [0, \infty]$ be the bid submitted by the server in slot k (the equivalent random variable is denoted X_k). If the server wins the auction, the queue state q_k changes to $q_k + 1$. As indicated above, with each arrival, the reputation changes to $(\alpha_k + 1, \xi_k + 1)$ with probability η and $(\alpha_k, \xi_k + 1)$ with probability $1 - \eta$.

Each server has a geometrically distributed lifetime and can quit in any time slot w.p. $1 - \delta$. When regeneration occurs the agent's initial state is $(R_q, R_\alpha, R_\xi, R_\eta)$ drawn from the distribution Ψ.

Bid, Payment and Cost: The marketplace charges a holding cost $C(q_k)$ to the sever at each time slot k. Also, at each time slot if the server's bid is accepted, it obtains a payment equal to its bid y_k (random variable Y_k). The net payoff for the agent in time slot k is $y_k w_k - C(q_k)$.

Effective Bid and Customer Choice: Customers (jobs) choose the agents (servers) based on both the bid amount as well as reputation. We model the *effective bid* of the server as the linear combination $x_k \triangleq y_k - z g(\alpha_k, \xi_k)$, where $g(\alpha, \xi) = \alpha/\xi$ and z is a parameter that trades off bid and reputation. X_k is used to denote the random variable corresponding to effective bid. Then the assumption is that customers choose the agent that has the lowest effective bid.

DEFINITION 1 (MEAN FIELD EQUILIBRIUM). *Let ρ be a candidate effective bid distribution and θ_ρ be a stationary policy for an agent. Then, we say that (ρ, θ_ρ) constitutes a mean field equilibrium if*

1. *θ_ρ is an optimal policy for the decision problem in* (1), *given effective bid distribution ρ; and*

$$V_{\rho,\eta} = \sup_{\theta \in \Theta} \mathbb{E}_\theta \left[\sum_{t=k}^{\infty} \delta^t \left(-C(Q_t) + r_\rho(X_t, A_t, \Xi_t) \right) \right] \quad (1)$$

2. *$\rho(x) = \gamma(x) \triangleq \Pi_\rho\Big(\big\{(q, \alpha, \xi, \eta) : (q, \alpha, \xi, \eta) \in \theta_\rho^{-1}([-z, x])\big\}\Big), \forall x \in \mathbb{R}^+$, where $\Pi_\rho(q, \alpha, \xi, \eta)$ is the steady state distribution.*

The main result we proved in this paper is that there exists an MFE (ρ, θ_ρ) such that $\rho(x) = \gamma(x)$. We establishied continuity and compactness of mapping from ρ to γ and make use of Schauder fixed point theorem to prove this result.

3. CONCLUSION

In this paper we considered the problem of determining the optimal price (bid) selection policy in a competitive marketplace that has many service providers that are relatively short lived. We setup a model in which jobs come at a steady rate into the marketplace and use both reputation and price jointly as a means of selecting a service provider. We showed that our marketplace can be thought of a version of a first price reverse auction, and characterized the best response bidding policy under the mean field assumption. We also showed that the assumption is valid by proving the existence of a MFE. We gathered data to find an accurate parameter to represent the tradeoff between reputation and offered price, and then numerically studied the system to understand the interplay between the diffrent state variables of an agent. On methodological side, we belive that there might be a more general result in our work regarding the understanding of the role of the "type" in a mechanism design setting, which we will explore in the future. We also are continuing our data collection efforts in order to study many different service marketplaces to understand pricing behavior.

4. REFERENCES

[1] Hacker's List. https://hackerslist.com.

[2] Swappa. https://swappa.com/.

[3] A. Ghose, P. G. Ipeirotis, and A. Sundararajan. Opinion mining using econometrics: A case study on reputation systems. In *Annual Meeting-Association for Computational Linguistics*, volume 45, page 416, 2007.

[4] K. Iyer, R. Johari, and M. Sundararajan. Mean field equilibria of dynamic auctions with learning. *Management Science*, 60(12):2949–2970, 2014.

[5] J. Li, R. Bhattacharyya, S. Paul, S. Shakkottai, and V. Subramanian. Incentivizing sharing in realtime D2D streaming networks: A mean field game perspective. In *Proceedings of IEEE Infocom*, Hong Kong, 2015.

[6] M. Manjrekar, V. Ramaswamy, and S. Shakkottai. A mean field game approach to scheduling in cellular systems. In *Proceedings of IEEE Infocom*, Toronto, Canada, 2014.

[7] J. Xu and B. Hajek. The supermarket game. In *ISIT*, 2012.

Modeling SMR Drive Performance

Mansour Shafaei
shafaei@ece.neu.edu

Mohammad Hossein Hajkazemi
hajkazemi@ece.neu.edu

Peter Desnoyers
pjd@ccs.neu.edu

Abutalib Aghayev
agayev@cs.cmu.edu

1. INTRODUCTION

Shingled Magnetic Recording (SMR) provides higher track density by overlapping adjacent tracks, resulting in data loss on a "downstream" track if the upstream track is overwritten. To prevent such loss, disk surfaces are typically divided into *bands* separated by guard regions wider than the head width; these bands may then be sequentially written and re-written without cross-band interference. Drive-managed SMR devices handle the resulting write constraints by incorporating an internal translation layer, much like SSDs, presenting a standard re-writeable block interface to the host. Generally-available SMR drives seen to date utilize a variant of the set-associative translation layer [2]: a static LBA-to-physical location mapping is used, writes are staged into a log or *persistent cache*, and are then de-staged to their "home" location via a band-at-a-time cleaning process.

In this work, we present a model based on detailed evaluation of the Seagate ST5000AS0011, a 5 TB device-managed SMR drive, which predicts mean latency and throughput within less than 3% in most cases. It predicts tail latency, measured as RMS latency error, within 25%—only modestly higher than the 10% variation seen between nominally identical drives.

2. TRANSLATION LAYER BEHAVIOR

To model the behavior of the drive, in addition to well-known disk behavior we need to understand the following performance issues: **Writes**: what is the latency and throughput of writes to the staging area? **Reads**: again, how do reads to data which is in the staging area perform? **Cleaning**: when does cleaning begin? How much time will it take e.g. after a specific workload? **Interference**: how are host reads and writes scheduled when the device is cleaning?

For this poster we focus on cleaning and interference, and present the following characteristics without discussion: (a) rotation time is ≈10 ms (5900 RPM), (b) every 240th write is delayed about 350 ms, (c) bands are 20 tracks, or ≃37 MiB at the outer and ≃17 MiB at inner diameter.

SIGMETRICS '16 June 14-18, 2016, Antibes Juan-Les-Pins, France

ACM ISBN 978-1-4503-4266-7/16/06.

DOI: http://dx.doi.org/10.1145/2896377.2901496

2.1 Cleaning

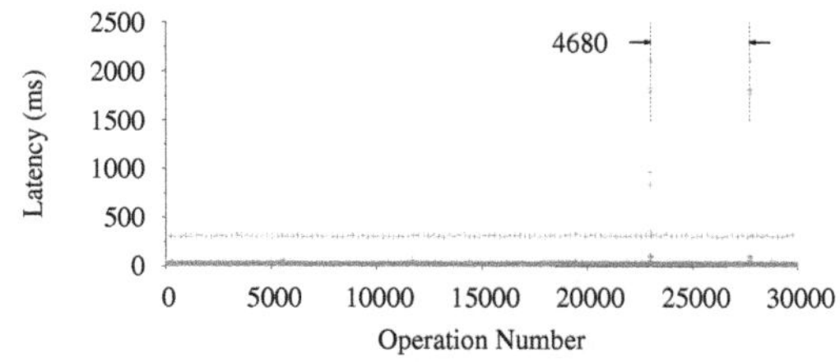

Figure 1: Sequential write latencies, 16 KB blocks, at outer diameter

Figure 1 shows latency for synchronous, sequential 16 KiB writes; two episodes of cleaning may be seen, marked by several > 1 s latency writes. We note that (a) cleaning is first triggered after 22,987 writes, (b) multiple writes complete with different latencies during each cleaning episode, and (c) the cleaning episodes occur every 4680 writes, or 74 MiB (2 bands):

- Foreground cleaning is triggered when the on-disk cache of ≃23,000 "slots" is filled, where a slot holds one synchronous write. (or multiple writes when writing with queue depth > 1)
- Writes are interleaved with cleaning, as more than one write completes during each cleaning episode.
- Two bands are cleaned during each cleaning episodes. (verified at different points on disk)

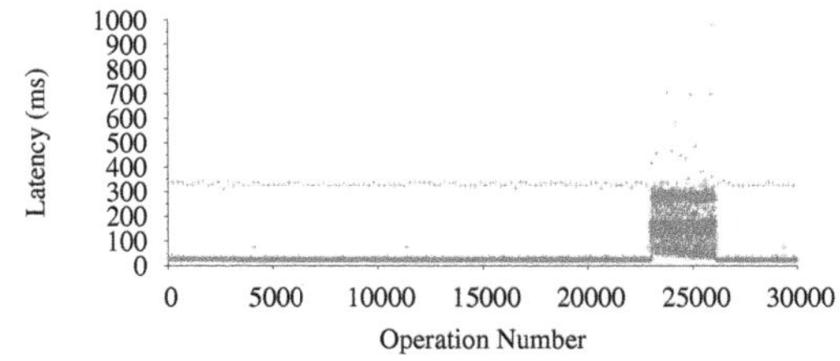

Figure 2: Random write latency (10 GiB range), 32 KB blocks

In Figure 2 we see write latency for random writes across a 10 GiB LBA range (277 bands): again cleaning begins after 22,987 writes, but now a long period of cleaning is seen, followed by another cleaning-free interval of nearly 23,000 writes. Previous work [1] has found that cleaning is performed in FIFO order, with the write at the tail of the persistent cache (and all others from the same band) being merged and de-staged. In the experiment in Figure 2 each band cleaned opens up about 23,000/277 or 83 cache

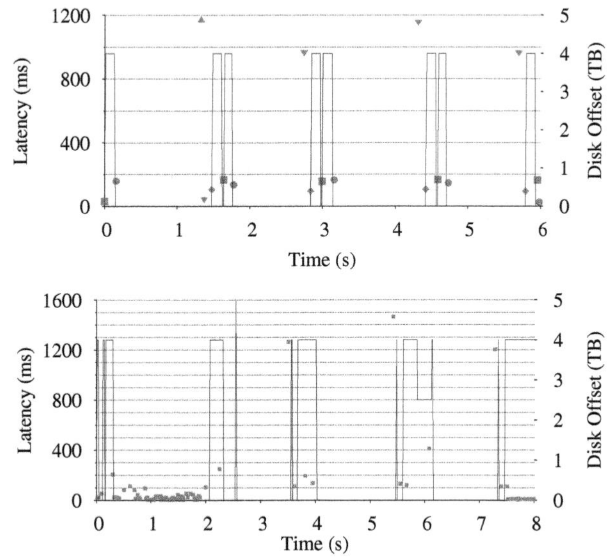

Figure 3: Head position and write (top)/read (bottom) latencies, 4 TB

slots on average, but (usually) only one at the tail of the log; eventually the last few bands with data scattered through the cache are cleaned, and writes are able to proceed against a virtually empty cache. In the case of the drive examined, there are two separate limits which force cleaning: a maximum map size (no more than 23,000 active slots in the cache) and a maximum log size (head-tail no more than 1.5·23,000 slots, active or inactive).

2.2 Interference

We note that write latency during cleaning is much higher in the sequential case, over 2 seconds, vs. 300-400 ms for random writes. This may be explained by Figure 3, showing read and write latencies as well as disk head position during a single cleaning episode, as well as Algorithm 1, the inferred cleaning algorithm.

Algorithm 1 Inferred cleaning algorithm

```
for band i in 1, 2 do
    while data left do
        read up to 15MB from data band
        collect band i writes from persistent cache
        write merged data to persistent cache
        write back to band i
    end while
end for
```

In each graph in Figure 3 we see two bands being cleaned, each being cleaned in two stages; each state (a) reads a portion of the original band data from its home location (head at 4 TB), (b) reads all persistent cache slots containing data from that portion of the band (head at 0 TB), (c) writes a copy of the merged band in or near the persistent cache (head still at 0 TB), and (d) overwrites the corresponding data band portion. A single high-latency interruption is seen due to step (b), while additional shorter delays are due to steps (a), (c), and (d). (note that the reads completing during the first collection phase in the bottom graph are to the exact band being cleaned; all other reads would be blocked.)

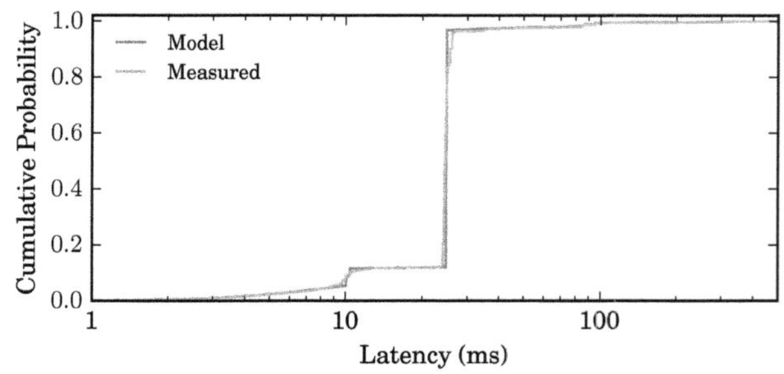

Figure 4: Latency CDF: Model vs. drive (mds_0)

The difference in cleaning duration may be seen to be due to the organization of the cache, and in particular that cache slots are aligned on roughly 0.2 rotation boundaries. The collection phase thus (typically) takes 2 ms per cache slot to be read; in the random/10 GiB case this is about 100 slots, while in the sequential case it is $\frac{1}{2}band/16KiB$ or about 1000.

Note on sequential write performance: When writing sequential data with write cache disabled, performance suffers two-fold. First, there is a five-fold operation amplification when writing: if byte B' replaces byte B, then (1) B' is written to cache, (2) B is read during cleaning, (3) B' is read from cache, (4) B' is written back to cache, and (5) B' is written to the data band. Secondly, for every cache slot (i.e. N writes, where N is the queue depth when writing) there is an additional 2 ms rotational overhead during cleaning.

3. MODEL EVALUATION

We evaluate a model based on these measured characteristics on selected MSR Cambridge traces and others; in Figure 4 we see real-drive and model latency CDFs for one such trace. To quantify the difference between modeled and measured behavior we use two metrics: (a) relative error of mean latency (or throughput), and (b) Ruemmler and Wilkes' demerit parameter [3], the RMS horizontal distance between measured cumulative distribution functions, which is far more sensitive to errors in tail latency:

$$\sqrt{\int_0^1 \left(CDF_1^{-1}(p) - CDF_2^{-1}(p)\right)^2 dp}$$

Perfect alignment between model and drive is not really possible: measuring nominally identical drives on the same traces, we found mean latency matched within about 0.5%, but RMS error ranged from 5% to 13%. Comparing the model with real drive performance on the same traces we found (in almost all cases) mean latency errors less than 10%, and RMS errors of less than 25%.

This work was supported in part by NSF award CNS-1149232.

4. REFERENCES

[1] A. Aghayev and P. Desnoyers. Skylight-a window on shingled disk operation. In *FAST*, pages 135–149, 2015.
[2] Y. Cassuto, M. A. Sanvido, C. Guyot, D. R. Hall, and Z. Z. Bandic. Indirection systems for shingled-recording disk drives. In *MSST*, pages 1–14. IEEE, 2010.
[3] C. Ruemmler and J. Wilkes. An introduction to disk drive modeling. *Computer*, 27(3):17–28, 1994.

Multipath Streaming: Fundamental Limits and Efficient Algorithms

Richard Combes
Centrale-Supelec / L2S
richard.combes@supelec.fr

Habib Sidi
INRIA
habisd1@gmail.com

Salah Elayoubi
Orange Labs / SystemX
salaheddine.elayoubi
@orange.com

ABSTRACT

We investigate streaming over multiple links. We provide lower bounds on the starvation probability of any policy and simple, order-optimal policies with matching and tractable upper bounds ([1],[2]).

1. THE MODEL

We consider a file divided in N chunks of unit size, indexed by $n \in \{1,\dots,N\}$. There are $K \geq 1$ links, on which any chunk can be requested. When a requested chunk is received on a link, it is placed in a buffer. After a prebuffering time denoted by $B > 0$ the file is read at unit speed. Namely, at time $n + B$, if chunk n is present in the buffer then it is read, and otherwise starvation occurs. The goal is to design request policies that minimize the starvation probability. We denote by π the request policy where $\pi_n = k$ if chunk n is requested on link k. We assume that if two chunks $n < n'$ are requested on the same link then n is requested before n'. We define $d_k(n) = \sum_{n'=1}^{n} \mathbf{1}\{\pi_{n'} = k\}$, the number of chunks comprised between 1 and n requested on link k. We denote by $X_k(\ell)$ the delay of the ℓ-th chunk requested on link k. Namely, if $\pi_n = k$, chunk n arrives at time $\sum_{\ell=1}^{d_k(n)} X_k(\ell)$. The starvation probability P^N is the probability that there exists a chunk that does not arrive in time. We consider "static" policies where π does not depend on $(X_k(\ell))_{\ell,k}$ and "oracle" policies where π is an arbitrary function of $(X_k(\ell))_{\ell,k}$.

Assumption 1 (i.i.d. delays). *For all k, $(X_k(\ell))_{\ell\geq 0}$ is an i.i.d sequence with expectation μ_k, variance σ_k^2 and cumulant generating function $G_k(a) = \log(\mathbb{E}[e^{aX_k(\ell)}])$. Further, $G_k(a) < +\infty$ on an open neighbourhood of 0.*

[1]An extended version of this work is available at: http://arxiv.org/abs/1602.07112

[2]This work has been performed in the framework of the IDEFIX project, funded by the ANR under contract number ANR-13-INFR-0006

SIGMETRICS '16 June 14-18, 2016, Antibes Juan-Les-Pins, France

ACM ISBN 978-1-4503-4266-7/16/06.

DOI: http://dx.doi.org/10.1145/2896377.2901485

Assumption 2 (Markovian delays). *For all k there exists a continuous time, stationary ergodic Markov chain on a discrete space $\mathcal{S}$ denoted by $(S_k(t))_{t\in\mathbb{R}}$ with stationary distribution m_k and transition rate matrix $Q^k = (q^k(i,j))_{i,j\in\mathcal{S}}$. There exists a function $r : \mathcal{S} \to \mathbb{R}^+$ such that for all ℓ, k:*

$$\tau_k(\ell) = \min\left\{t \geq 0 : \int_0^t r(S_k(u))du \geq \ell\right\},$$

with $X_k(\ell) = \tau_k(\ell) - \tau_k(\ell-1)$ and $\mu_k = \mathbb{E}[X_k(\ell)]$.

We define $r_k = 1/\mu_k$, the average data rate of link k, and $R = \sum_{k=1}^{K} r_k$ the sum of data rates. We distinguish three regimes: underload ($R > 1$), critical ($R = 1$) and overload ($R < 1$). We define the frequency vector $f = (f_1, ..., f_K)$, with $f_k = r_k/R$. We denote by $P^N(\pi, B)$ the starvation probability for N chunks, prebuffering time B and policy π.

2. PERFORMANCE LIMITS

Theorem 1 is a lower bound on the starvation probability that holds for all oracle policies. For large files ($N \to \infty$), there are sharp transitions between regimes: to ensure that $P \not\to 1$ we require $B = \mathcal{O}(1)$ (underload), $B = \mathcal{O}(\sqrt{N})$ (critical) and $B = \mathcal{O}(N)$ (overload).

Theorem 1. *The following holds for all oracle policies π. (i) For all $B \geq 0$ and $N \geq 1$ we have:*

$$P^N(\pi, B) \geq \mathbb{P}\left[\exists n \in \{1, ..., N\} : \sum_{k=1}^{K} D_k(n, B) < n\right]$$

$$D_k(n, B) = \max\{d \geq 0 : \sum_{\ell=1}^{d} X_k(\ell) \leq B + n\}.$$

(ii) Consider i.i.d. delays. If $R \leq 1$, for all $b \geq 0$ we have:

$$\liminf_{N\to\infty} P^N(\pi, (R^{-1} - 1)N + b\sqrt{N}) \geq \prod_{k=1}^{K} \Psi\left(\frac{b}{\sigma_k\sqrt{f_k}}\right),$$

with $\Psi(x) = \frac{1}{\sqrt{2\pi}}\int_x^{+\infty} e^{-\frac{z^2}{2}}dz$.

3. EFFICIENT ALGORITHM

To obtain an efficient policy, chunks should be requested on link k at frequency f_k, so that $d_k(n) \approx nf_k, \forall k, n$. Policy π is f-upper balanced if $d_k^\pi(n) \leq (n + K - 1)f_k \;\forall k, n$.

Proposition 1. *Consider π such that for all $n \geq 0$:*

$$\pi_n \in \arg\min_k \frac{d_k^\pi(n-1) + 1}{f_k}$$

with ties broken arbitrarily. Then π is f-upper balanced.

4. PERFORMANCE: I.I.D. DELAYS

Consider i.i.d. delays and define $F_k(a) = G_k(a) - a/f_k$. Define $a_k^\star = +\infty$ if $X_k(\ell) < 1/f_k$ a.s. and $a_k^\star = \max\{a \geq 0 : F_k(a) = 0\}$ otherwise. We calculate $a_k^\star$ below for exponential delays and sub-Gaussian delays, which includes bounded and Gaussian delays. We say that $X_k(\ell)$ is v_k^2-sub-Gaussian if $G_k(a) \leq a\mu_k + a^2 v_k^2/2, \forall a \geq 0$.

PROPOSITION 2. *Consider $R > 1$.*
(i) If $X_k(\ell) \sim Exp(r_k)$, then $a_k^\star = r_k(1 + W(-Re^{-R})/R)$ with W the Lambert function.
(ii) If $X_k(\ell)$ is v_k^2-sub-Gaussian then $a_k^\star \geq 2\mu_k(R-1)/v_k^2$.

Theorem 2 gives upper bounds on the starvation probability of upper balanced policies, and shows that they are order optimal: the pre-buffering times have the same scaling as the lower bound of Theorem 1.

THEOREM 2. *Let π be f-upper balanced. Define $N_k = f_k N$ and $\mathcal{G}_k = \{a : F_k(a) \geq 0\}$.*
(i) For all $b \geq 0$ and $N \geq 1$ we have:

$$P^N(\pi, b + K - 1) \leq 1 - \prod_{k=1}^{K} \left[1 - \min_{a_k \in \mathcal{G}_k} e^{N_k F_k(a_k) - a_k b}\right].$$

(ii) If $R > 1$, we have $a_k^\star > 0$ and for all $N \geq 1$ and $b \geq 0$:

$$P^N(\pi, b + K - 1) \leq 1 - \prod_{k=1}^{K} \left[1 - e^{-a_k^\star b}\right].$$

(iii) If $R \leq 1$, and $X_k(\ell)$ is v_k^2-sub-Gaussian for all k, then for all $b \geq 0$ and $N \geq 1$:

$$P^N(\pi, (R^{-1} - 1)N + b + K - 1) \leq 1 - \prod_{k=1}^{K} \left[1 - e^{-\frac{b^2}{2v_k^2}}\right].$$

5. PERFORMANCE: MARKOV DELAYS

For Markovian delays, the problem is mostly intractable, and we consider a regime where $S_k(t)$ evolves on a "faster time scale" than the streaming flow of interest. This regime makes sense since typical streaming flows are long while link variability is caused by short phenomena such as fading, medium access protocols and short-lived elastic flows. We replace $(S_k(t))_t$ by the accelerated process $(S_k(\phi t))_t$ with speed $\phi > 0$. We use Lemma 1, which shows that the amount of data received on a link can be approximated by a Wiener process. We identify $r(.)$ with $(r(i))_{i \in \mathcal{S}}$.

LEMMA 1 (BHATTACHARYA, 82). *Define $G^\phi(t) = \sqrt{\phi} \int_0^t (r(S_k(\phi u)) - r_k) du$. Consider $g^k = (g^k(i))_{i \in \mathcal{S}}$ a solution to the Poisson equation: $Q^k g^k = r(.) - r_k$. Define the asymptotic variance $\overline{\sigma}_k^2 = -2\sum_{i \in \mathcal{S}} r(i) g^k(i) m_k(i)$. Then $G^\phi(.)$ converges to a Wiener process with drift 0 and variance $\overline{\sigma}_k^2$, when $\phi \to \infty$.*

Theorem 3 gives upper bounds on the starvation probability of upper balanced policies. Statement (i) shows that for $R > 1$ fixed and $\phi \to \infty$ we have $P \to 0$ i.e. the link variability disappears due to the ergodic theorem. Statement (ii) deals with the case where R depends on ϕ and approaches 1 as $\phi \to \infty$. In cases of interest $\overline{\sigma}_k^2$ can be calculated explicitly making our performance bounds tractable as shown below.

THEOREM 3. *Let π be f-upper balanced.*
(i) Consider $R > 1$ and $b > 0$ fixed. Then for all $N \geq 1$:

$$P^{N,\phi}(\pi, b + K - 1) \underset{\phi \to \infty}{\to} 0.$$

(ii) Consider $C_1, C_2 \geq 0$, define $b^\phi = C_2/\sqrt{\phi}$ and assume that $R = R^\phi \equiv 1/(1 - C_1/\sqrt{\phi})$. Then for all $N \geq 1$:

$$\limsup_{\phi \to \infty} P^{N,\phi}(\pi, b^\phi + K - 1)$$

$$\leq 1 - \prod_{k=1}^{K} \left(1 - \mathbb{P}\left[\max_{t \in \{K, \ldots, N+K-1\}} \overline{\sigma}_k W(t) - r_k C_1 t \geq f_k C_2\right]\right).$$

with $(W(t))_t$ a standard Wiener process.
(iii)(a) If $C_1 = 0$, $R^\phi = 1$ and for all $N \geq 1$:

$$\limsup_{\phi \to \infty} P^{N,\phi}(\pi, b^\phi + K - 1)$$

$$\leq 1 - \prod_{k=1}^{K} \left(1 - 2\Psi\left(\frac{f_k C_2}{\overline{\sigma}_k \sqrt{N + K - 1}}\right)\right)$$

(iii)(b) If $C_1 > 0$, for all $N \geq 1$:

$$\limsup_{\phi \to \infty} P^{N,\phi}(\pi, b^\phi + K - 1) \leq 1 - \prod_{k=1}^{K} \left(1 - e^{-2\frac{r_k^2 C_1 C_2}{\overline{\sigma}_k^2}}\right).$$

6. SOME RELEVANT LINK MODELS

6.1 Wireless links with random access

We consider Bianchi's model with one back-off stage, window size W and collision probability p (calculated through a fixed point equation). If a transmission is successful one transmits a frame, otherwise one waits for a duration uniformly distributed in $[0, W]$. A chunk is composed of n_f frames. The cumulant generating function of delays is:

$$G(a) = n_f \left(a + \log\left(\frac{p}{1 - (1-p)h(aW)}\right)\right)$$

with $h(a) = (e^a - 1)/a$ and a such that $(1-p)h(aW) < 1$.

6.2 Wireless ON-OFF channels

A link is shared between a secondary user and a primary user whose activity follows a two-states Markov process independent from the secondary user activity. The secondary user transmits at rate 1 when the primary user is not active. The transition rate matrix is $Q = \begin{pmatrix} -\beta & \beta \\ \alpha & -\alpha \end{pmatrix}$. The stationary distribution is $m = (\frac{\alpha}{\alpha+\beta}, \frac{\beta}{\alpha+\beta})$, the expected data rate is $r = \frac{\beta}{\alpha+\beta}$. The Poisson equation yields: $\overline{\sigma}^2 = \frac{2\beta\alpha}{(\alpha+\beta)^3}$.

6.3 Links with short lived flows

A link is shared between the streaming flow and $S(t)$ short flows following an M/M/1 process with load $\rho < 1$. When there are n small flows, the streaming flow transmits at rate $r(n)$ (e.g. $r(n) = 1/(1+n)$ for fair rate sharing). The stationary distribution is $m(n) = \rho^n(1-\rho)$. The expected data rate is $\overline{r} = \sum_{n \geq 0} r(n)\rho^n(1-\rho)$. Define $\overline{R}(n) = r(n) - \overline{r}$. Solving the Poisson equation we get:

$$\overline{\sigma}^2 = 2\rho \sum_{n \geq 0} \sum_{i=0}^{n-1} \overline{R}(n)\overline{R}(i)(\rho^n - \rho^i).$$

Network Calculus Analysis of a Feedback System with Random Service

Alireza Shekaramiz*, Jörg Liebeherr*, Almut Burchard**
* Department of ECE, University of Toronto, Canada.
** Department of Mathematics, University of Toronto, Canada.
E-mail: {ashekaramiz, jorg}@ece.utoronto.ca; almut@math.toronto.edu.

ABSTRACT

Feedback mechanisms are integral components of network protocols and traffic control algorithms. Their performance evaluation is hard due to intricate time correlations introduced by feedback. Network calculus has been successfully applied for the analysis of feedback mechanisms in deterministic systems. However, an extension to random systems has remained an open problem for more than a decade. We present a stochastic network calculus analysis of a random system with feedback, specifically, a window flow control system with random service and fixed feedback delay. We quantify the service impediment due to the feedback mechanism by deriving statistical lower bounds on the available service, and obtain complementary upper bounds. We also discover special cases where an exact description of the service is feasible.

1. INTRODUCTION

The network calculus offers a system theoretical approach for the analysis of networks that can express complex arrival and service processes [3]. Network calculus can be used for the analysis of deterministic systems as well as stochastic ones. Whereas, over the last ten years, many key results of the deterministic network calculus have been shown to also hold under probabilistic assumptions, there has not been a successful treatment of stochastic feedback systems. Here we present progress on the analysis of stochastic feedback systems with methods of the stochastic network calculus. Following the literature on the deterministic analysis of feedback systems [2, 3], we study a window flow control system, which enforces that only a limited number of w bits, referred to as *window size*, can be in transit at any time. The delay of the feedback is assumed to be d time units. The feedback signal opens or closes a throttle that prevents traffic from entering the network. A recent paper [5] addresses the same problem as us, but only derives time-dependent (delay) bounds. Our work resolves key difficulties that can be used to complete their analysis. The details of our results and proofs are provided in [1].

SIGMETRICS '16 June 14-18, 2016, Antibes Juan-Les-Pins, France

ACM ISBN 978-1-4503-4266-7/16/06.

DOI: http://dx.doi.org/10.1145/2896377.2901487

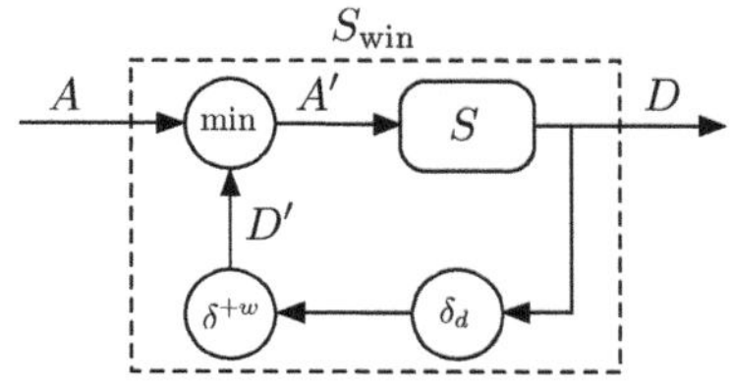

Figure 1: Model with window size $w > 0$ and feedback delay $d \geq 0$.

2. BIVARIATE NETWORK CALCULUS

We perform our analyzes within the $(\wedge, \otimes)$-dioid algebra of bivariate functions. We indicate $\mathcal{F}$ as the family of bivariate functions which are non-negative and non-decreasing in the second argument, and $\mathcal{F}_o$ as the subfamily with $f(t,t) = 0$ for $f \in \mathcal{F}_o$. For $f, g \in \mathcal{F}$ the minimum $(\wedge)$ is defined as $f \wedge g\,(s,t) = \min\{f(s,t), g(s,t)\}$, and the convolution $(\otimes)$ is defined as $f \otimes g\,(s,t) = \min_{s \le \tau \le t}\{f(s,\tau) + g(\tau,t)\}$ with the neutral element δ, i.e., $f \otimes \delta = \delta \otimes f = f$. These two operations form dioid algebras on the sets $\mathcal{F}$ and $\mathcal{F}_o$ [3]. The convolution operation in these dioids is associative, but not commutative. A process $f \in \mathcal{F}_o$ is called subadditive if $f(s,t) \le f(s,\tau) + f(\tau,t)$ holds for $s \le \tau \le t$. We define the subadditive closure of $f \in \mathcal{F}$ by $f^* = \bigwedge_{n=0}^{\infty} f^{(n)}$, where $f^{(0)} = \delta$, $f^{(1)} = f$, $f^{(n+1)} = f^{(n)} \otimes f \quad (n \ge 1)$. The available service at a network element is described by a process $S(s,t) \in \mathcal{F}_o$ that satisfies the input-output relationship $D(0,t) \ge A \otimes S(0,t)$ for any arrival process $A(0,t)$ and corresponding departure process $D(0,t)$ at that element. The service offered by a sequence of network elements with service processes $S_1, S_2, \ldots, S_N$ is given by their convolution $S_1 \otimes S_2 \otimes \ldots \otimes S_N$.

3. PROBLEM DESCRIPTION

We analyze the network with window flow control in Fig. 1. Traffic with arrival process $A(s,t)$ is serviced by a network element with service process $S(s,t)$, subject to the additional constraint that the total backlog in the element at any time may not exceed $w > 0$. (The excess traffic is held in a FIFO buffer at the network entrance). The feedback information consists of the value of the departure function delayed by $d \ge 0$ time slots, i.e., $D(s, t-d)$. The delay of $d \ge 0$ is given by a service process δ_d, defined as $\delta_d = \delta(s, t-d)$ such that $f(s,t-d) = f \otimes \delta_d(s,t)$ for every $f \in \mathcal{F}$. The network service is given by a service process S, i.e., $D(0,t) \ge A' \otimes S(0,t)$. For $w > 0$ we define a function δ^{+w} where $\delta^{+w}(s,t) = w$ for $s \ge t$ and $\delta^{+w}(s,t) = \infty$ for $s < t$, which allows us to write $f(s,t) + w = f \otimes \delta^{+w}(s,t)$.

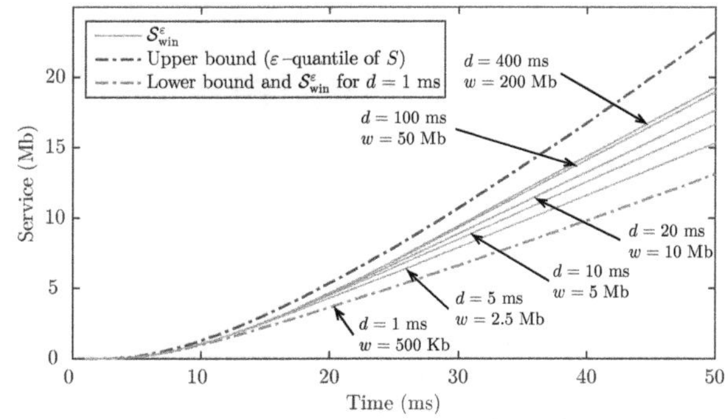

Figure 2: $\mathcal{S}^{\varepsilon}_{\mathrm{win}}(0,t)$ **(**$\varepsilon = 10^{-6}$**,** $w/d = 500$ **Mbps).**

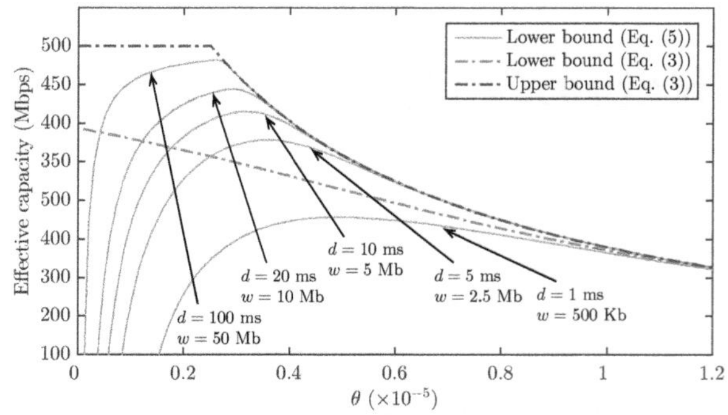

Figure 3: $\gamma_{\mathrm{win}}(-\theta)$ **(**$w/d = 500$ **Mbps).**

Using the derivations in [2, 3], the flow control system can be represented by an equivalent service process S_{win} given by

$$S_{\mathrm{win}} = (S \otimes \delta_d \otimes \delta^{+w})^* \otimes S = \bigwedge_{n=0}^{\infty} (S \otimes \delta_d \otimes \delta^{+w})^{(n)} \otimes S\,.$$

The analysis of such a system with random service process $S \in \mathcal{F}_o$ requires the computation of a subadditive closure as well as distribution of minima involving a bivariate random service process S. We assume a nonzero feedback delay since for a system with no feedback delay ($d = 0$), a subadditive $S \in \mathcal{F}_o$ yields the trivial result of $S_{\mathrm{win}} = S$, i.e., the feedback has no impact on the overall service. We use the moment-generating functions (MGF) network calculus [4] for our analysis ($M_X(\theta) = E[e^{\theta X}]$ denotes the MGF of a random variable X for any $\theta \in \mathbb{R}$). For a network system with service element S, a statistical service bound $\mathcal{S}^{\varepsilon}$ of a bivariate service process S for a given $\varepsilon > 0$ [4] is defined as $\mathrm{P}\big(S(s,t) \le \mathcal{S}^{\varepsilon}(s,t)\big) \le \varepsilon$. A statistical service bound can be computed from M_S as

$$\mathcal{S}^{\varepsilon}(s,t) = \sup_{\theta>0} \frac{1}{\theta}\big\{\log\varepsilon - \log M_S(-\theta,s,t)\big\}\,. \qquad (1)$$

An alternative measure, which is useful when reasoning about long-term traffic rates and scaling properties, is the effective capacity $\gamma_S(-\theta)$, defined for $\theta > 0$ by

$$\gamma_S(-\theta) = \lim_{t\to\infty} -\frac{1}{\theta t}\log M_S(-\theta,0,t)\,. \qquad (2)$$

4. EQUIVALENT SERVICE PROCESSES

Our first result provides an exact characterization of S_{win} for the special case $d = 1$.

LEMMA 1. *Consider a feedback system as in Fig. 1 with an additive service process* $S(s,t) = \sum_{k=s}^{t-1} c_k$*, where* $(c_k)_{k\ge1}$ *is an arbitrary sequence of non-negative random variables. For* $d = 1$ *and* $w > 0$*, the equivalent service process is given by* $S_{\mathrm{win}}(s,t) = \sum_{k=s}^{t-1} \min\{c_k, w\}$*.*

The following theorem shows that the exact result from Lemma 1 provides a lower bound on S_{win} for $d > 1$ in terms of the ratio w/d.

THEOREM 1. *Given a (not necessarily additive) service process* $S \in \mathcal{F}_o$*. Let* S_{win} *be the equivalent service process for a feedback system with parameters* $d > 0$ *and* $w > 0$*. Then*

$$S'(s,t) \;\le\; S_{\mathrm{win}}(s,t) \;\le\; \min\big\{S(s,t), \lceil \tfrac{t-s}{d} \rceil\, w\big\}\,, \qquad (3)$$

where S' *is the equivalent service process with* $d' = 1$ *and* $w' = w/d$*.*

Theorem 1 holds for general service processes and the bounds on the average rates depend only on ratio w/d.

5. VARIABLE BIT RATE SERVICE

We apply our results to a work-conserving FIFO buffer with a random time-variable service rate, which we refer to as variable bit rate (VBR) server. The VBR server offers the service process $S(s,t) = \sum_{k=s}^{t-1} c_k$, as in Lemma 1. We assume that the c_k's are i.i.d. random variables, with MGF $M_c(\theta) = E[e^{\theta c_k}]$. The MGF of S is $M_S(\theta,s,t) = (M_c(\theta))^{t-s}$, and the effective capacity has the simple expression $\gamma_S(-\theta) = -\frac{1}{\theta}\log M_c(-\theta)$. In Theorem 2 we present bounds on the MGF of the equivalent service process S_{win} of a VBR server in the feedback system of Fig. 1. The bounds are expressed in terms of a statistical service bound for a chosen violation probability $\varepsilon > 0$ (using Eq. (1)) and in terms of the effective capacity (from Eq. (2)), both of which require bounds on the MGF of S_{win}, denoted by $M_{S_{\mathrm{win}}}$.

THEOREM 2. *Let* $S(s,t)$ *be a VBR server with feedback as described above. Then, for every* $\theta > 0$*,*

$$M_{S_{\mathrm{win}}}(-\theta,s,t) \le \Big(\big(M_c(-\theta)\big)^d + de^{-\theta w}\Big)^{\lfloor \frac{t-s}{d} \rfloor}\,. \qquad (4)$$

A lower bound on the effective capacity of $S_{\mathrm{win}}(s,t)$ *is given for* $\theta > 0$ *by*

$$\gamma_{\mathrm{win}}(-\theta) \ge \gamma_S(-\theta) - \frac{1}{d\theta}\log\Big(1 + de^{\theta(d\gamma_S(-\theta)-w)}\Big)\,. \qquad (5)$$

For a numerical evaluation we consider a VBR server with an exponential distribution with an average service rate of 1 Gbps. For a fixed ratio w/d, Fig. 3 depicts statistical service bounds $\mathcal{S}^{\varepsilon}_{\mathrm{win}}(0,t)$ as functions of time (using Eq. (1), Eq. (3), and Eq. (4)), and Fig. 4 evaluates the lower bounds of the effective capacity γ_{win} from Eq. (5).

6. REFERENCES

[1] A. Shekaramiz, J. Liebeherr, A. Burchard. Window flow control systems with random service. *arXiv:1507.04631*, July 2015.

[2] R. Agrawal, R. L. Cruz, C. Okino, and R. Rajan. Performance bounds for flow control protocols. *IEEE/ACM Trans. Netw.*, 7(3):310–323, June 1999.

[3] C.-S. Chang. *Performance Guarantees in Communication Networks*. Springer Verlag, 2000.

[4] M. Fidler. An end-to-end probabilistic network calculus with moment generating functions. In *IEEE IWQoS*, pages 261–270, June 2006.

[5] M. A. Beck, J. B. Schmitt. Window flow control in stochastic network calculus - The general service case In *Proc. ACM VALUETOOLS*, January 2016.

QoE Analysis of a Large-Scale Live Video Streaming Event

Adnan Ahmed
The University of Iowa

Zubair Shafiq
The University of Iowa

Amir Khakpour
Verizon Digital Media Services

ABSTRACT

Streaming video has received a lot of attention from industry and academia. In this work, we study the characteristics and challenges associated with large-scale *live* video delivery. Using logs from a commercial Content Delivery Network (CDN), we study live video delivery for a major entertainment event that was streamed by hundreds of thousands of viewers in North America. We analyze Quality-of-Experience (QoE) for the event and note that a significant number of users suffer QoE impairments. As a consequence of QoE impairments, these users exhibit lower engagement metrics.

Keywords

Content Delivery; Live Video; Quality of Experience

1. INTRODUCTION

An increasingly large number of content publishers now broadcast their video content live over the Internet. This growth is a consequence of low costs of content delivery and the adoption of advertisement/subscription based revenue models. Content publishers typically contract third-party Content Delivery Networks (CDNs) to provide high quality over-the-top video streaming services.

According to Cisco [1], more than 64% of the global Internet traffic was video in 2014. The stakeholders in the Internet video ecosystem, such as content providers, CDNs, and ISPs need to frequently upgrade their infrastructure to meet the increasing demands of Internet video and user expectations for high quality. As a result, researchers in academia and industry are actively studying various aspects of over-the-top streaming video delivery.

Prior literature includes studies on analyzing the impact of Quality-of-Service (QoS) metrics, such as bandwidth, packet loss and received signal strength, on the performance of specific applications, including streaming video [11, 6]. More recently, researchers have introduced video-specific Quality-of-Experience (QoE) metrics, such as *rate of buffering* and *average bitrate*, in the pursuit to understand and quantify user experience. However, prior studies have been limited mainly to on-demand streaming video. In the recent years, live video streaming has been gaining popularity for various events like sports (MLB World Series, NCAA Basketball Finals etc.[5]) and eSports (Twitch, Azubu etc.[4]). This paradigm, therefore, presents interesting opportunities for video delivery and QoE optimizations due to the unique traffic dynamics and access patterns. Towards this end, we study a large-scale live video streaming event. We focus on a popular entertainment awards event in 2015 that was streamed live by a commercial CDN. We quantify user perceived video quality in terms of QoE metrics such as rate of buffering, average bitrate, rate of fluctuation, etc. We then analyze the statistics of these QoE metrics and observe that a significant number of users suffer from QoE impairments.

SIGMETRICS '16 June 14-18, 2016, Antibes Juan-Les-Pins, France

ACM ISBN 978-1-4503-4266-7/16/06.

DOI: http://dx.doi.org/10.1145/2896377.2901504

2. DATA

Video is by far the biggest source of traffic on the Internet. Video can be classified into three categories: bandwidth-sensitive *streaming stored video* (Netflix, YouTube, Hulu, etc.), bandwidth- and delay-sensitive *streaming live video* (Twitch, NFL Live, CNNgo, etc.), and delay-sensitive *interactive live video* (Skype, Facetime, Google Hangouts, etc.). We focus our attention on *streaming live video* for which while the network must provide the steady-state throughput that is more than the video bitrate, excessive delays can still be an issue due to the live nature of the event. QoE for streaming video is determined by a wide range of factors such as encoding bitrate, buffering rate, etc. Understanding the relationship between QoE and user engagement is an active area of research [3, 9, 2, 10].

Adaptive bitrate controllers are used to dynamically adapt video quality based on various factors such as network bandwidth estimation and player buffer occupancy [7, 12]. The video is encoded at multiple discrete bitrates (quality levels A to G) and divided in segments of 2-10 seconds. The client-side video player estimates the available network bandwidth and requests the video segments at a suitable bitrate. Our data set is composed of server-side HTTP logs from a commercial CDN network which was responsible for online streaming of the live event. The information is collected at multiple Points of Presence (PoPs) across the USA. The HTTP logs contain client information and the requested video chunks. We measure QoE metrics using the timestamps and bitrates of the requested chunks. Overall, our data set contains 625,626 users and more than 21 million minutes worth of video view time. The live event lasted for approximately five hours.

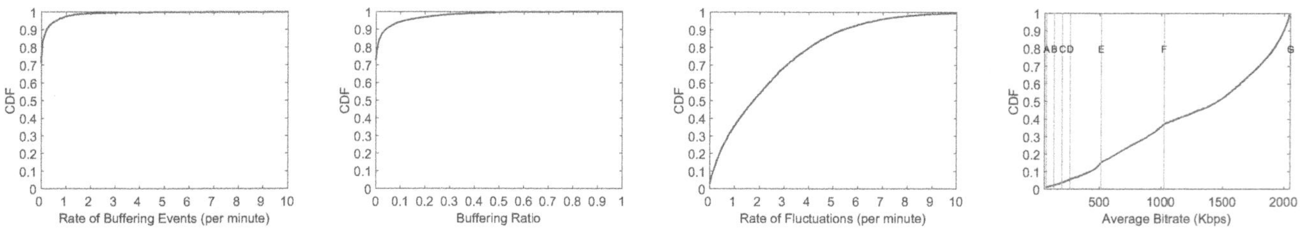

(a) Rate of buffering (b) Buffering ratio (c) Rate of fluctuation (d) Average bitrate

Figure 1: Distributions of QoE metrics. Overall, most users experience few buffering events at high average bitrate. We do observe a tail of users experiencing higher buffering, more fluctuations, and lower bitrate than other users.

3. QOE MEASUREMENT

In this section, we conduct a systematic measurement of video QoE and study its impact on user engagement. Commonly used QoS metrics like end-to-end delay, loss and bandwidth, do not directly tie-in to the end-user experience. For example, even if the user is getting low delays at the network level, he/she could be experiencing serious problems at the application level which may arise due to unexpected cross-layer interactions or application layer issues. Therefore, it is important to quantify metrics that directly capture end-user experience. We first define a set of video-specific metrics that are used to quantify QoE [3, 2].

Average Bitrate. Since the video player at the client can request video segments at different bitrates, we use the average bitrate to quantify the overall video quality experienced by the user.

Rate of Fluctuation. We calculate the rate of fluctuation (per minute) as a video QoE metric. Frequent changes in video bitrate may degrade user experience.

Rate of Buffering. We calculate the rate of buffering as the number of buffering events per minute over the duration of the video session. As reported in prior literature [3, 9, 8], buffering events can have a significant negative impact on user engagement.

Buffering Ratio. We calculate buffering ratio as the fraction of time spent in buffering events over the duration of the video session.

Figure 1 plots the cumulative distribution functions (CDFs) of the QoE metrics. In Figure 1(a), we note that a vast majority of users experience relatively low rate of buffering. For instance, almost 95% of users experience less than 0.5 buffering events per minute on average. Similarly, in Figure 1(b), we note low buffering ratios for most users. More specifically, more than 90% of users have buffering ratio lower than 0.05. In Figure 1(c), we observe that users do experience relatively more video quality fluctuations than buffering events. For example, about 50% of users experience more than 2 fluctuations per minute on average. In Figure 1(d), we note that a majority of users watch the video stream at a high bitrate. In particular, more than 60% of users watch the video stream at a bitrate of at least 1 Mbps (i.e., quality level F) on average. Overall, we observe that a small number of users in the tail of QoE distributions suffer from frequent buffering events, frequent video quality fluctuations, and low average bitrate. Our further analysis shows that these "tail" users have lower engagement than other users.

4. CONCLUSION

In this paper, we analyzed QoE metrics for a large-scale live video streaming event. We analyze server side logs to extract video QoE metrics for more than 600K users across USA for a large-scale live video streaming event. We note that a significant number of tail users suffer QoE impairments. As reported in prior literature, we observe that these tail users have lower engagement compared to other users.

Acknowledgement

This material is based in part upon work supported by the National Science Foundation under Grant Number CNS-1464110.

5. REFERENCES

[1] Cisco Visual Networking Index: Forecast and Methodology, 2014-2019.

[2] A. Balachandran, V. Sekar, A. Akella, S. Seshan, I. Stoica, and H. Zhang. Developing a Predictive Model of Quality of Experience for Internet Video. In *ACM SIGCOMM*, 2013.

[3] F. Dobrian, A. Awan, D. Joseph, A. Ganjam, J. Zhan, V. Sekar, I. Stoica, and H. Zhang. Understanding the Impact of Video Quality on User Engagement. In *ACM SIGCOMM*, 2011.

[4] L. Eadicicco. 10 Facts About Twitch. http://www.businessinsider.com/statistics-about-twitch-2014-8, August 2014.

[5] M. Fisher. The Next Chapter in Live Streaming. http://qwilt.com/the-next-chapter-in-live-streaming-in-which-certai, April 2014.

[6] P. Gill, M. Arlitt, Z. Li, and A. Mahanti. YouTube Traffic Characterization: A View From the Edge. In *ACM Internet Measurement Conference (IMC)*, 2007.

[7] T.-Y. Huang, R. Johari, N. McKeown, M. Trunnell, and M. Watson. A Buffer-Based Approach to Rate Adaptation: Evidence from a Large Video Streaming Service. In *ACM SIGCOMM*, 2014.

[8] J. Jiang, V. Sekar, I. Stoica, and H. Zhang. Shedding Light on the Structure of Internet Video Quality Problems in the Wild. In *ACM Conference on Emerging Networking EXperiments and Technologies (CoNEXT)*, 2013.

[9] S. S. Krishnan and R. K. Sitaraman. Video Stream Quality Impact Viewer Behavior: Inferring Causality Using Quasi-Experimental Designs. In *ACM Internet Measurement Conference (IMC)*, 2012.

[10] M. Z. Shafiq, J. Erman, L. Ji, A. X. Liu, J. Pang, and J. Wang. Understanding the Impact of Network Dynamics on Mobile Video User Engagement. In *ACM SIGMETRICS*, 2014.

[11] M. Z. Shafiq, L. Ji, A. X. Liu, J. Pang, S. Venkataraman, and J. Wang. A First Look at Cellular Network Performance during Crowded Events. In *ACM SIGMETRICS*, 2013.

[12] X. Yin, A. Jindal, V. Sekar, and B. Sinopoli. A Control-Theoretic Approach for Dynamic Adaptive Video Streaming over HTTP. In *ACM SIGCOMM*, 2015.

Safe Randomized Load-Balanced Switching by Diffusing Extra Loads

Sen Yang
Georgia Institute of Technology
sen.yang@gatech.edu

Bill Lin
University of California, San Diego
billlin@ece.ucsd.edu

Jun (Jim) Xu
Georgia Institute of Technology
jx@cc.gatech.edu

ABSTRACT

Load-balanced switch architectures are known to be scalable in both size and speed, which is of interest due to the continued exponential growth in Internet traffic. However, the main drawback of load-balanced switches is that packets can depart out of order from the switch. Randomized load-balancing of application flows by means of hashing on the packet header is a well-known simple solution to this packet reordering problem in which all packets belonging to the same application flow are routed through the same intermediate port and hence the same path through the switch. Unfortunately, this method of load-balancing can lead to instability, depending on the mix of flow sizes and durations in the group of flows that gets randomly assigned to route through the same intermediate port. In this paper, we show that the randomized load-balancing of application flows can be enhanced to provably guarantee both stability and packet ordering by extending the approach with *safety* mechanisms that can *uniformly diffuse* packets across the switch whenever there is a build-up of packets waiting to route through the some intermediate port. Although simple and intuitive, our experimental results show that our extended randomized load-balancing approach significantly outperforms existing load-balanced switch architectures.

Categories and Subject Descriptors

C.2.1 [**Computer-Communication Networks**]: Network Architecture and Design—*Packet-switching networks*; C.2.6 [**Computer-Communication Networks**]: Internetworking—*Routers*

Keywords

Load-balanced switches; throughput guarantees

1. INTRODUCTION

To keep up with the relentless growth of the Internet traffic, network operators need high-performance switch architectures that can scale well in both size and speed, provide throughput guarantees, achieve low latency, and maintain packet ordering. However, conventional switch architectures like centrally-scheduled input-queued crossbar switches are not scalable.

Alternatively, a promising scalable class of switch architecture is the load-balanced switch (LBS), which was first introduced by Chang et al. [1, 2], and later further developed by others. These architectures rely on two switching stages for routing packets. The first switching stage connects the first stage of input ports to the center stage of intermediate ports, and the second switching stage connects the center stage of intermediate ports to the final stage of output ports. Both switching stages execute a deterministic connection pattern such that each input is connected to each output of a switching stage at $1/N$th of the time.

Although the basic load-balanced switch originally proposed in [1] is capable of achieving throughput guarantees, it has the critical problem that packet departures can be badly out of order. This is detrimental to Internet traffic since TCP falsely regards out-of-order packets as indications of congestion and packet loss. One simple approach for ensuring correct packet order in an application flow, which is all that matters, is randomized load-balancing. This approach, also known as "TCP hashing," force all packets that belong to the same application flow to go through the same intermediate port, by determining the intermediate port each packet should be headed to via hashing (on its header). Although simple and intuitive, the main drawback of the randomized approach is that stability cannot be guaranteed.

Alternatively, most existing approaches that can guarantee both stability and packet ordering are based on some form of complete or partial aggregation of packets into frames or stripes. Uniform Frame Spreading (UFS) [5], Full-Order Frames First (FOFF) [5], Padded Frames (PF) [4], and Sprinklers [3] are representative examples of such approaches. However, these methods pay a significant price for ensuring packet ordering in that they perform significantly worse than the originally proposed basic load-balanced switch [1].

2. OUR APPROACH

To remedy the problems that lead to instability in the randomized load-balancing approach, we extend it with two *safety* mechanisms. First, let λ_{ij} be the arrival rate for VOQ_{ij}, the Virtual Output Queue (VOQ) of packets arriving at input port i with output destination j. Depending on the hash values of their flow identifiers, the set of TCP/UDP flows within VOQ_{ij} can be partitioned into N subsets called

SIGMETRICS '16 June 14-18, 2016, Antibes Juan-Les-Pins, France

ACM ISBN 978-1-4503-4266-7/16/06.
DOI: http://dx.doi.org/10.1145/2896377.2901480

bins, numbered $1, 2, \cdots, N$. Each bin m, $m = 1, 2, \cdots, N$, corresponds to the set of flows that are hashed (and hence need to be switched) to intermediate port m. Using a simple credit scheme, without any knowledge of the value of λ_{ij}, we can limit the rate at which packets in each bin are served (switched) to at most λ_{ij}/N. In fact, this credit scheme guarantees something even stronger: The actual long-term service rates of these bins, after the rate-limiting, are identical. The first safety mechanism, when enforced on every VOQ, clearly ensures no overloading at any input port *by the "normal" (i.e., rate-limited) traffic.*

However, by limiting the service rate of each such bin at an input port to λ_{ij}/N, those bins with traffic arrival rates exceeding that limit (e.g., bins that contain elephant flows) can grow in size. To ensure that these bins don't grow infinitely, thus leading to instability, we implement a second safety mechanism in which once a build-up of packets at a bin exceeds some threshold $W \geq N$ in size, we "evacuate" the excess load by *uniformly diffusing* the build-up of packets across all intermediate ports (i.e., a full-frame of N packets are uniformly spread one-to-one to the N intermediate ports). We introduce an easy-to-implement technique to ensure packet ordering when this evacuation mechanism kicks in, which involves requiring a "to-be-evacuated" bin to wait till it is safe (from packet reordering) to do so. Due to this waiting, careful scheduling is needed to coordinate an "orderly evacuation" of all bins being evacuated at any input port to ensure switch stability under 100% traffic load.

We prove that our Safe Randomization Switch (SRS) scheme can achieve 100% throughput (i.e., rate-stable), while guaranteeing packet order, under any admissible[1] arrival traffic that is allowed to change rapidly dynamically over time. In arriving at this proof, we have invented a general methodology for proving the stability of queues. Our proof is based on the following extremal argument in spirit (but not exactly in this form). Suppose SRS is not stable so that the total length $Q(t)$ of a subset of queues in SRS, as a function of time t, does not satisfy the stability condition $\lim_{t\to\infty} \frac{Q(t)}{t} = 0$. Then we define $\gamma \equiv \limsup_{t\to\infty} \frac{Q(t)}{t} > 0$. Let t_i, $i = 1, 2, \ldots$, be a sequence of time such that $\lim_{i\to\infty} t_i = \infty$ and $\lim_{i\to\infty} \frac{Q(t_i)}{t_i} = \gamma$. Starting with this time sequence t_i, by the properties of the aforementioned credit scheme (for rate-limiting "TCP hashed" traffic into each intermediate port) and the aforementioned scheduler for the orderly evacuation, and through standard busy period arguments, we can construct another sequence of time t'_i, $i = 1, 2, \cdots$, such that $\lim_{i\to\infty} t'_i = \infty$ and $\limsup_{i\to\infty} \frac{Q(t'_i)}{t'_i} > \gamma$, which contradicts the definition of γ. Given how general this methodology is, we believe it can be applied to some other queueing theory problems, especially where circumstances make it hard to use the standard fluid analysis.

3. EVALUATION

In this section, we compare the performance of our proposed SRS approach with other existing load-balanced switching algorithms, including the basic load-balancing scheme [1], UFS [5], FOFF [5], PF [4], and the recently proposed Sprinklers scheme [3]. The basic load-balancing scheme (labeled "Basic") does not guarantee packet ordering, but it provides the lower bound of the average delay that a load-balanced switch can achieve.

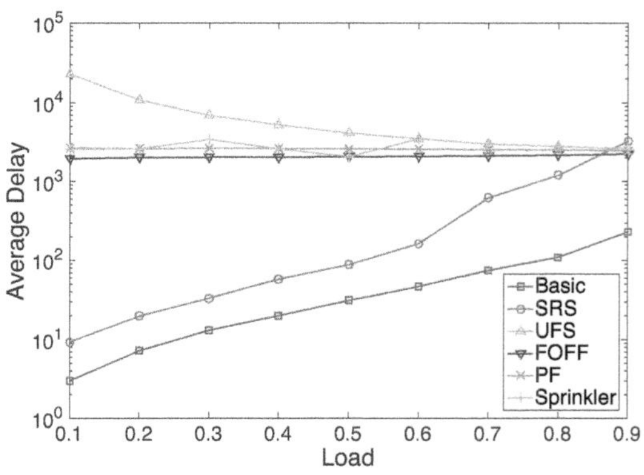

Figure 1: Average delay under uniform traffic.

In the experiments we assume uniform distribution[2] of the destination ports for the arrival flows – i.e. a new flow goes to output j with probability $\frac{1}{N}$. The results are shown in Fig. 1. Several observations can be made from the above experiments. First, the average delay of SRS is significantly better than the existing methods of UFS, FOFF, PF, and Sprinklers for all traffic loads up to about $\lambda < 0.9$ and the average delay is only slightly more for $\lambda \geq 0.9$. Furthermore, in comparison to the basic load-balanced switch approach that does not guarantee packet order, the performance of SRS follows roughly the same trend as the basic LBS approach. In summary, perhaps surprisingly, the SRS solution is able to achieve significantly better results than existing methods, especially under low-to-moderate loads, based on the simple mechanism of hashing.

Acknowledgement: This work has been supported in part by NSF projects CNS 1248117, CNS 1218092, CNS 1423182, CNS 1422286.

4. REFERENCES

[1] Chang, C.-S., Lee, D.-S., and Jou, Y.-S. Load balanced birkhoff–von neumann switches, part i: one-stage buffering. *Computer Communications 25*, 6 (2002), 611–622.

[2] Chang, C.-S., Lee, D.-S., and Lien, C.-M. Load balanced birkhoff–von neumann switches, part ii: multi-stage buffering. *Computer Communications 25*, 6 (2002), 623–634.

[3] Ding, W., Xu, J., Dai, J. G., Song, Y., and Lin, B. Sprinklers: A randomized variable-size striping approach to reordering-free load-balanced switching. In *ACM CoNext, the 10th International Conference on Emerging Networking EXperiments and Technologies* (2014), ACM.

[4] Jaramillo, J. J., Milan, F., and Srikant, R. Padded frames: a novel algorithm for stable scheduling in load-balanced switches. *Networking, IEEE/ACM Transactions on Networking 16*, 5 (2008), 1212–1225.

[5] Keslassy, I. *The load-balanced router.* PhD thesis, Stanford University, 2004.

[1]Here "admissible" means the long-run-average total rate of all traffic destined for any output port must exist and is no more than 1 (i.e., 100% loaded).

[2]We also conducted experiments for quasi-diagonal traffic and the conclusion is roughly the same.

Searching For A Single Community in a Graph

Avik Ray
ECE, UT Austin
avik@utexas.edu

Sujay Sanghavi
ECE, UT Austin
sanghavi@mail.utexas.edu

Sanjay Shakkottai
ECE, UT Austin
shakkott@austin.utexas.edu

ABSTRACT

In standard graph clustering/community detection, one is interested in partitioning the graph into more densely connected subsets of nodes. In contrast, the *search* problem of this paper aims to only find the nodes in a *single* such community, the target, out of the many communities that may exist. To do so , we are given suitable side information about the target; for example, a very small number of nodes from the target are labeled as such.

We consider a general yet simple notion of side information: all nodes are assumed to have random weights, with nodes in the target having higher weights on average. Given these weights and the graph, we develop a variant of the method of moments that identifies nodes in the target more reliably, and with lower computation, than generic community detection methods that do not use side information and partition the entire graph.

Keywords

community detection, stochastic block model, side-information

1. INTRODUCTION

Community detection, or graph clustering, is the classic problem of finding subsets of nodes such that each subset has higher connectivity within itself, as compared to the average connectivity of the graph as a whole. Typically, when graphs represent similarity or affinity relationships between nodes, these subsets represent communities of similar nodes. Also typically, this problem has primarily been considered in the unsupervised setting, where the only input is the graph itself and the objective is to partition all or most of the nodes.

In this paper we look at a different, but related, community detection task, which we will refer to as the *search problem*. Our objective is to use the graph to find a single community of nodes – which we will call the *target community* – for which we have been given some relevant but quite noisy side information. We would like to do so more reliably, and with lower computation, than existing methods that do not use side information.

Our motivations are two-fold: *(i)* it is often the case that the network analyst is looking for nodes with a-priori specified characteristics e.g. in military/intelligence settings, and *(ii)* it is rare that we are faced with a "pure" graph analysis problem; typically there is extra non-graphical side information that, if used properly, could make the inference task easier.

Our contributions are as follows.

(i) We develop a simple yet generic framework for how side-information is to be specified: each node is given a (possibly random) weight, with nodes in the target community having higher weight on average than nodes not in the target – we call these *biased weights*.

(ii) Given such biased weights, we develop a variant of the 2nd order method of moments – to find the nodes in the target community. We call this *Community Search* algorithm.

(iii) Our main results characterize the effectiveness of this algorithm in finding the target community; we study this in the standard stochastic block model setting with many communities. Analytically, we show that it matches (potentially upto log factors) the analytical guarantees of the state of the art unsupervised community detection methods; empirically, we show that the method outperforms these methods even with very noisy side information (e.g. very small number of labeled nodes), and has significantly lower computational complexity.

2. SETTINGS AND ALGORITHM

Consider a graph $G = (V, E)$ with n nodes and k communities that partition the vertex set as $V = \cup_{i=1}^{k} V_i$. Let $\alpha_i = |V_i|/n$ be the fraction of nodes in the i-th community. The edge set E is generated according to the standard stochastic block model [2] with edge probabilities p, q, $0 < q < p < 1$.

In the search problem we are interested in the recovery of *one* target community, say V_1. The side-information is in the form of *biased node weights.* Each node $j \in V$ is assigned a weight $w_j > 0$ by a random process; these weights satisfy the condition $E[w_j | j \in V_1] > E[w_j | j \in V_i]$ for all $i \neq 1$. These biased weights may be computed using a set of *labeled nodes* from the target community $\mathcal{L} \subset V_1$.

The main goal is to solve this search problem faster than the time required to recover all k communities, and without any loss in estimation accuracy.

Algorithm: We now describe our main algorithm called **Community Search**. X be the adjacency matrix of the

SIGMETRICS '16 June 14-18, 2016, Antibes Juan-Les-Pins, France

ACM ISBN 978-1-4503-4266-7/16/06.

DOI: http://dx.doi.org/10.1145/2896377.2901494

graph G. Also define community membership vectors $\mu_1, \ldots, \mu_k$ where $\mu_i \in \mathbb{R}^n$, as follows. Let $\mu_{j,i}$ be the $j-$th coordinate of vector μ_i. Then $\mu_{j,i} = p$ if $j \in V_i$, $\mu_{j,i} = q$ otherwise. Note that these μ_i-s are linearly independent and the community memberships of the nodes can be obtained from these membership vectors via thresholding. The aim of our algorithm is to estimate the membership vector of the first community μ_1 (which can then be used to recover nodes in V_1). For any two subsets $P, Q \subset [n]$ let $X_{P,Q}$ denote the submatrix of X corresponding to the rows and columns in set P and Q respectively. The input parameters to Algorithm 1 are the adjacency matrix X, number of communities k, the set of biased node weights $(w_1, \ldots, w_n)$, and a threshold τ. The output is the community estimate $\hat{V}_1$.

Algorithm 1 Community Search

Input: Adjacency matrix X, k, biased weights $(w_1, \ldots, w_n)$, threshold τ
Output: $\hat{V}_1$

1: Partition nodes into four sets P_1, P_2, P_3, P_4 at random. Let $n_i = |P_i|$
2: Compute matrices $\hat{A}_1 = \frac{1}{\sqrt{n_3}} X_{P_1,P_3}$, $\hat{A}_2 = \frac{1}{\sqrt{n_3}} X_{P_2,P_3}$
3: Compute vector $\hat{m}_1 = \frac{1}{n_1} \sum_{j \in P_1} X_{P_1,j}$
4: Compute matrix $\hat{B} = \frac{1}{n_4} \sum_{j \in P_4} w_j X_{P_1,j} X^T_{P_2,j}$
5: $\hat{\mu}_{P_1}, \hat{\alpha}_1 \leftarrow$ SearchSubroutine$(\hat{A}_1, \hat{A}_2, \hat{B}, \hat{m}_1, k)$
6: Compute $V_{P_1} = \{j \in P_1 : \hat{\mu}_{P_1,j} > \tau\}$
7: Repeat steps 2-5 with P_i's rotated in order to estimate $\hat{\mu}_{P_2}, \hat{\mu}_{P_3}, \hat{\mu}_{P_4}$. Use them to compute $V_{P_2}, V_{P_3}, V_{P_4}$. Return community $\hat{V}_1 = V_{P_1} \cup V_{P_2} \cup V_{P_3} \cup V_{P_4}$

Algorithm 2 SearchSubroutine

Input: $\hat{A}_1, \hat{A}_2, \hat{B}, \hat{m}_1, k$
Output: $\hat{\mu}_1, \hat{\alpha}_1$

1: Compute rank k-svd of matrices $\hat{A}_1, \hat{A}_2 : \hat{A}_1 = U_1 D_1 V_1^T$, $\hat{A}_2 = U_2 D_2 V_2^T$
2: Compute matrices $W_1 = U_1 D_1^{-1}$, $W_2 = U_2 D_2^{-1}$
3: Let u_1 be the largest left singular vector of $W_1^T \hat{B} W_2$
4: Compute $z = U_1 D_1 u_1$
5: Compute $a = u_1^T W_1^T \hat{m}_1$
6: Return $\hat{\mu}_1 \leftarrow z/a$ and $\hat{\alpha}_1 \leftarrow a^2$

3. RESULTS

In this section we present our main results. When side information is available in the form of biased weights w_j for each node $j \in V$, these weights need to be *informative* about the target community V_1 so that it could be recovered. We quantify this in the following set of assumptions.

(A1) Average weight bias: Under this condition the expected weight of a node in community V_1 is greater than the expected weight of a node in any other community V_i. Precisely the weights satisfy: $E[w_j|j \in V_1] > E[w_j|j \in V_i]$, $\forall i \neq 1$

(A2) Weight concentration: Let $\alpha_{max} = \max_{i \in [k]} \alpha_i$ and $\alpha_{min} = \min_{i \in [k]} \alpha_i$. Define $\sigma_1(R) := E[w_j|j \in V_1]$, $\gamma_2 := \max_{i \in [k], j \in V} |w_j - E[w_j|j \in V_i]|$, and $\xi(n) = o(\sqrt{\log n})$ be any slowly growing function. Then with high probability the maximum deviation of the weights are bounded as follows.

$$\frac{\gamma_2}{\sigma_1(R)} = O\left(\min\left\{\frac{\alpha^4_{min}(p-q)^4}{\alpha^4_{max} p^4 \xi(n)}, \frac{\alpha^5_{min}\sqrt{n}(p-q)^5}{\alpha^4_{max} p^{4.5} \xi(n)} - 1\right\}\right)$$

(A3) p, q separation: Let p, q, n satisfy $\frac{(p-q)^3}{p^2} = \tilde{\Omega}\left(\frac{\alpha_{max}}{\alpha^3_{min} n}\right)$ This condition fundamentally determines when communities are identifiable in a stochastic block model and similar conditions are required for other community detection algorithms [2, 1].

Theorem 1 shows that under the above assumptions on the biased weights Algorithm 1 can reconstruct community V_1 with high accuracy.

THEOREM 1. *Consider a (n, k, p, q) stochastic block model satisfying condition (A3). Given biased weights $(w_1, \ldots, w_n)$ satisfying conditions (A1), (A2), then Algorithm 1 recovers community V_1 with fraction of error nodes $o(1)$ with high probability.*

Biased weights, as required in Theorem 1, can be obtained from a small set of labeled nodes $\mathcal{L}$ as follows. Weight w_i is simply the number of nodes in $\mathcal{L}$ that are at distance of $r + 1$ hops from node i.

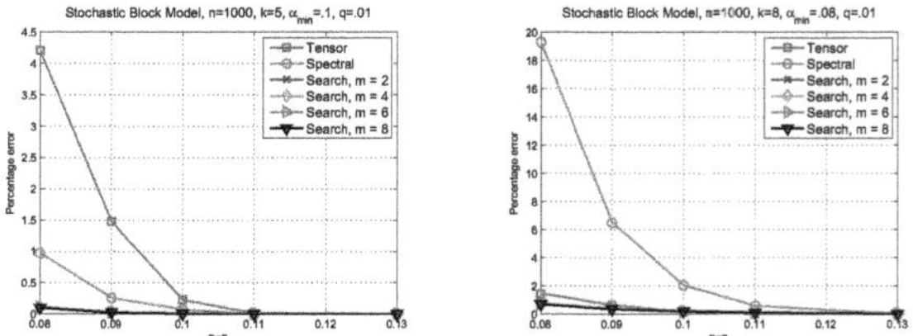

(a) $n = 1000$, $k = 5$ (b) $n = 1000$, $k = 8$

Figure 1: Figure comparing the average error performance of Community Search algorithm with Spectral clustering [3] and Tensor decomposition [1] algorithms in two stochastic block models with $n = 1000$, $k \in \{5, 8\}$. We use m labeled node from target cluster as side information and compute biased weights. The Community Search algorithm outperforms both Spectral clustering and Tensor decomposition.

Experiments: In synthetic graphs generated using stochastic block model we observe that the Community Search algorithm exhibits greater accuracy (Figure 1) and more than 3X speedup over Spectral clustering [3] and Tensor decomposition [1] algorithms.

4. ACKNOWLEDGMENTS

We would like to acknowledge support from NSF grants CNS-1320175, 0954059; ARO grants W911NF-15-1-0227, W911NF-14-1-0387; and the US DoT supported D- STOP Tier 1 University Transportation Center.

5. REFERENCES

[1] A. Anandkumar, R. Ge, D. Hsu, and S. M. Kakade. A tensor spectral approach to learning mixed membership community models, 2013. http://arxiv.org/abs/1302.2684.

[2] A. Condon and R. M. Karp. Algorithms for graph partitioning on the planted partition model. *Random Structures and Algorithms*, 18(2):116–140, 2001.

[3] A. Y. Ng, M. I. Jordan, and Y. Weiss. On spectral clustering: Analysis and an algorithm. *Advances in neural information processing systems*, 2:849–856, 2002.

Shoot for the Moon and You Will Never Miss: Characterizing and Detecting Aimbots in Online Games

Daiping Liu*, Xing Gao*†, Mingwei Zhang‡, Haining Wang*

*University of Delaware {dpliu,hnw}@udel.edu
†College of William and Mary xgao01@email.wm.edu
‡Intel Labs mingwei.zhang@intel.com

1. INTRODUCTION

The online game market is one of the fastest growing entertainment industries in the world. By 2016, the size of global game market is forecasted to reach $86.1 billion. Among the many genres of online games, first person shooter (FPS) is the second most popular. Due to the popularity and economic importance of FPS games, it is imperative to shield them from cheating for the benefit of both game operators and players, especially considering that the competitive nature of FPS games provides strong incentives to cheat. With regard to FPS games, the most common cheat is the use of automated tools to aim and shoot more accurately, also known as *aimbots*. While people have proposed different approaches for detecting fully automated bots, none of them can detect aimbots. Aimbot detection is notoriously difficult because aimbots are completely passive (i.e., no tampering with game data or code) and interact with human players intensively (i.e., semi-automatic).

In this work, we propose an accurate and robust server-side aimbot detector, called AimDetect. We define eight novel features to model the differences between aimbots and honest players from two aspects: (1) the anomalous behaviors stemming from the automation of aimbots and (2) the blatant nature of cheaters. All these features can be precisely measured on the server-side and also be universally extracted across most modern FPS games. These features are then fed into a novel two-layer classification framework, which accurately determines if a player is using aimbot. In the first step, a machine-learning algorithm is invoked every time a kill event occurs. The learned model classifies each kill as from aimbots or honest players. We currently utilize Support Vector Machine (SVM) for this step. AimDetect considers every kill event as an independent observation. To further reduce false alarms, in the second step, a sequential hypothesis testing algorithm is used to compute a comprehensive anomaly score over a sequence of observations. Evaluation results show that our two-layer classifier significantly outperforms traditional single-layer approach.

To demonstrate the efficacy of AimDetect, we implement a prototype and evaluate its performance using the traces collected on a public game server. One challenge here is to collect ground truth data from our field deployment. To this end, we devise a novel and generic technique called *bait-target* that can effectively identify modern aimbots. We set up a public game server hosting CS-1.6 and we ran our field measurement for one month. The evaluation results show that AimDetect is able to capture almost all aimbots with only 0.7% false positive rate.

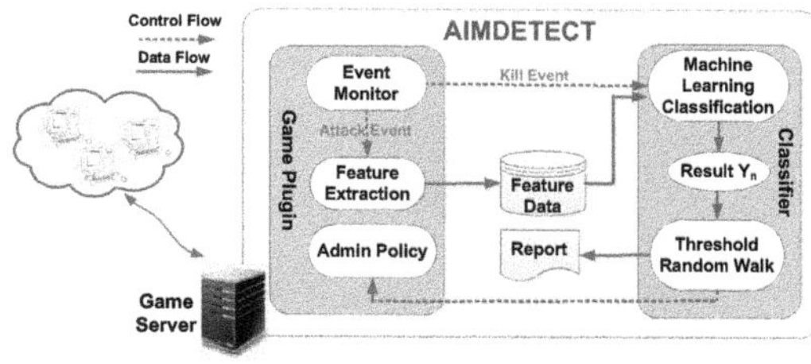

Figure 1: Overview of AIMDETECT

2. AIMDETECT DESIGN

At a high level, AimDetect is motivated by our measurement results that aimbots usually manifest themselves through a series of suspicious behavioral patterns. Figure 1 illustrates the architecture of AimDetect, which completely resides on game servers and consists of an in-game plugin and a stand-alone classifier. The in-game plugin has three modules: event monitor, feature extraction, and administration policy. The first module monitors in-game events like aiming at an enemy, death and hit. These events drive the feature extraction module, which collects predefined in-game features as listed in Table 1. Administrators can set policies that are executed when aimbots are detected. The stand-alone classifier will be invoked once a kill event is captured in the event monitor. Our classifier comprises two steps. First, the collected features are fed into a machine learning classification system, which determines whether the killer uses aimbot. Each kill could be considered as an independent observation. Then, to reduce false positives, which are less tolerable than false negatives in production games, we compute a comprehensive anomaly score over a sequence of observations, instead of deciding on one single observation. A sequential hypothesis testing algorithm, specifically Threshold Random Walk (TRW), is utilized in the second step. When an aimbot is detected, the classifier will notify the in-game plugin to execute preset policies.

3. AIMDETECT EVALUATION

Server Deployment. We host CS-1.6 on our public server. CS-1.6 represents one of the most popular modern FPS games. Our CS-1.6 server is published on www.game

SIGMETRICS '16 June 14-18, 2016, Antibes Juan-Les-Pins, France

ACM ISBN 978-1-4503-4266-7/16/06.
DOI: http://dx.doi.org/10.1145/2896377.2901503

Feature	Description
F_1	Num of attack attempts before a kill
F_2	Num of deaths before a kill
F_3	Time to kill
F_4	Cursor acceleration
F_5	Ratio of hits when the attackers are crouching
F_6	State-aware hits
F_7	State-aware hit ratio
F_8	Suspiciousness of headshots

Table 1: Feature set defined in AimDetect.

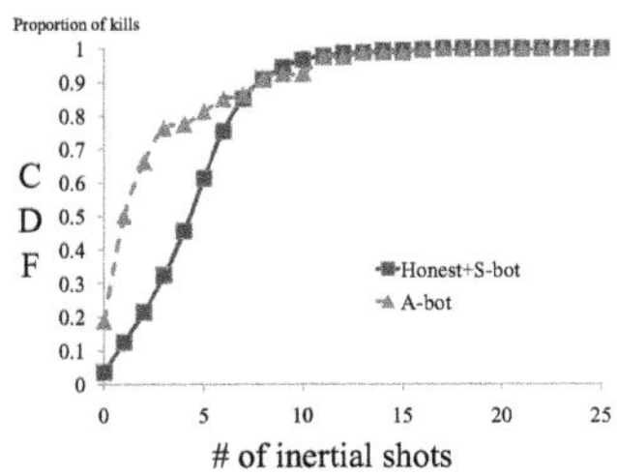

Figure 2: Statistics of inertial shots.

tracker.com/games/cs. We allocate 32 slots, the maximum number a server could host.

Bait-Target Design. To collect ground truth data on our field deployment, we devise bait-targets. The basic idea is to simulate an opponent using a human-invisible bot, which is referred to as a bait-target, as a trap to catch aimbots. We design bait-target by leveraging our key observation: when a player kills an opponent, he will highly likely shoot one or more bullets, which we call *inertial shots.* Figure 2 presents the statistics of inertial shots for aimbots and honest players. We find that only 3.6% of kills come with no inertial shots and for each player, most of their kills have at least one inertial shot. Thus, our observation would hold in most cases.

The position where a bait-target is placed can also affect the detection accuracy. If a bait-target is placed very close to a player's crosshair or it is placed near a real opponent, many false alarms could be raised. However, if a bait-target is placed far away from a player's crosshair, we may miss most aimbots. We decide to place a bait-target *exactly above the victim* upon a kill event. When a player just kills an opponent, its crosshair should be close to the victim and thus an honest player's inertial shots are usually gathered around the victim. However, aimbots can *immediately* catch a next valid target, causing their inertial shots to hit the bait-target. Figure 3 illustrates the placement of a bait-target.

Dataset. Our dataset contains one-month traces. During our deployment, 294 non-empty connections from 131 distinct IP addresses play in our server. These IP addresses are mapped to 31 countries. In total, using bait-targets, we can identify 38 aimbots.

Evaluation Results. We first evaluate if SVM is able to correctly classify those kills from honest players and aimbots. The accuracy of the classifier is affected by the size of its training set. Thus, we evaluate the performance of SVM by varying the training set size from 300 to 1,100 kills. For each size, we test 10 times with kills from randomly selected honest and cheating players. The averaged results are shown in Figure 4. We can see that the accuracy increases as the training set grows. However, after the training set reaches 900, the accuracy will stabilize at around 92%. So, our further evaluation is based on a training set of size 900. And we randomly generate five pairs of training and testing sets. In this setting, our SVM classifier achieves true positive rate (TPR_s) of 83.6% and false positive rate (FPR_s) of 5.8%.

Figure 3: An example of bait-target. The bait-target is rendered as visible for illustration purpose.

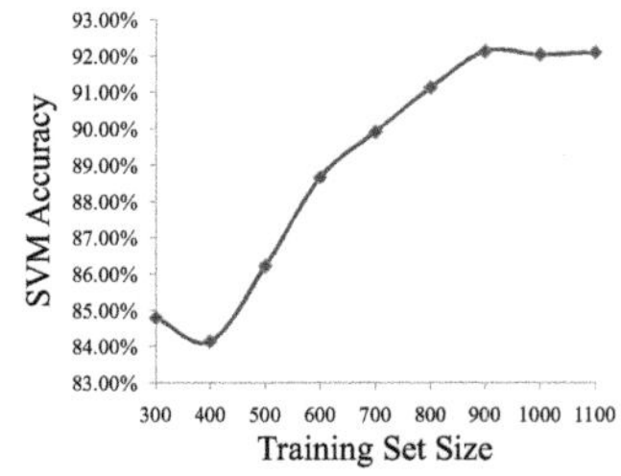

Figure 4: Training set size *v.s.* SVM accuracy.

Although our SVM classifier only achieves acceptable performance, SVM + TRW can significantly improve the detection accuracy of AimDetect. TRW has four parameters, θ_0, θ_1, α, and β. Based on the results of the SVM classifier, θ_1 can be set to 83.6% and θ_0 to 5.8%; α and β are user-chosen false positive and false negative rates for TRW. Table 2 lists the final accuracy of AimDetect with different settings of α and β. The results are averaged on the five pairs of training and testing sets.

AimDetect is able to achieve a quite promising TPR_{s+t} in all settings. For specific training sets, when α and β decrease, some false negatives occur because more observations are needed. The FPR_{s+t} in all settings are acceptable, and when α and β are set quite low (i.e., 0.001), the FPR_{s+t} even drops to 0.7%.

α	β	TPR_{s+t}	FPR_{s+t}
0.05	0.05	100%	7.5%
0.01	0.01	99%	4%
0.005	0.005	98.5%	1.9%
0.001	0.001	97.6%	0.7%

Table 2: Detection performance of SVM + TRW.

4. CONCLUSION

We have designed and implemented an accurate and robust server-side aimbot detector, AimDetect. AimDetect utilizes a set of novel features to model the behavioral patterns of aimbots and honest players, which stem from both the automation of aimbots and the blatant nature of cheaters. These features are then fed into a two-step classifier, which first classifies each kill event as from either honest players or aimbots using SVM and then employs TRW to compute a comprehensive anomaly score. Our evaluation results show that AimDetect is able to capture almost all of the aimbots with quite low false positive rate.

Spatial *Multi-LRU* Caching for Wireless Networks with Coverage Overlaps

Anastasios Giovanidis
CNRS & Télécom ParisTech - LTCI
23, Avenue d'Italie, 75013, Paris, France
giovanid@enst.fr

Apostolos Avranas
Télécom ParisTech - LTCI, Paris, France
& AUTh, Thessaloniki, Greece
eavranasa@gmail.com

ABSTRACT

This article introduces a novel family of decentralised caching policies for wireless networks, referred to as spatial *multi-LRU*. Based on these, cache inventories are updated in a way that provides content diversity to users that are covered by, and thus have access to, more than one station. Two variations are proposed, the *multi-LRU-One* and *-All*, which differ in the number of replicas inserted in the involved edge caches. Che-like approximations are proposed to accurately predict their hit probability under the Independent Reference Model (IRM). For IRM traffic multi-LRU-One outperforms multi-LRU-All, whereas when the traffic exhibits temporal locality the -All variation can perform better.

Keywords

Caching; LRU; Multi-coverage areas; Point Processes; Che

1. INTRODUCTION

We consider the wireless edge of a content centric network, which consists of a set of transmitting nodes (base stations (BSs), pico-, nano- stations, or WIFI hotspots) taking fixed positions on a planar area, and a set of users dynamically arriving at this area and asking for service. A user can be covered by multiple of these nodes (say m), but she/he will *choose only one* to be served from. All nodes are equipped with memory of size K objects, which offers the possibility to cache a fraction of the existing data. When the user's request is found in the cache of some covering station, then the user is served directly by this one. Otherwise, the request is retrieved from the core network.

The *hit probability*, is defined as the probability that a user will find her/his demand cached in the memory of one of the covering cells. So how does one optimally manage the available cache inventories? There is a trade-off. Popular objects should be made widely available, while less popular content should also be included for diversity. Cache management policies can be grouped into two categories:

SIGMETRICS '16 June 14-18, 2016, Antibes Juan-Les-Pins, France

ACM ISBN 978-1-4503-4266-7/16/06.
DOI: http://dx.doi.org/10.1145/2896377.2901483

(i) *Policies with per-reQuest updates* (POQ), where updates of the cache content are done locally and are triggered by the users on a per-request basis. For these, file popularity information is not available. The Least-Recently-Used (LRU and q-LRU) policies fall in this category.

(ii) *Policies with Popularity updates* (POP), where exact information over content popularities is available, and is used to infrequently update cache inventories. This category covers the Least-Frequently-Used (LFU), as well as policies that result from solutions of optimisation problems with a-priori knowledge of additional system information, e.g. the *Greedy Full Information (GFI)* [3], and the *Probabilistic Block Placement (PBP)* [1]. POP should have higher hit-probability than POQ due to the extra information.

2. SPATIAL MULTI-LRU

This work introduces a novel family of distributed cache management POQ policies that profit from multi-coverage. These are the *spatial multi-LRU* policies and are based on the (single-)LRU. The main idea is that, since a user can check all the caches of covering BSs for the demanded object, and download it from any one that has it in its inventory, cache updates and object insertions can be done in a more efficient way than just applying single-LRU independently to all caches. The fact that the user triggers a cache's update/insertion action, allows each cache to be indirectly informed about the inventory content of its neighbours. Variations of the multi-LRU family differ in the number of inserted contents in the network, after a missed content demand. Differences can also appear in the update phase.

- **multi-LRU-One:** Action is taken only in *one* cache out of the covering m. (a. Update) If the content is found in a non-empty subset of the m caches, only one cache from the subset is used for download and, for this, the content is moved to the most-recently-used position. (b. Insertion) If the object is not found in *any* cache, it is inserted only in one while its least-recently-used object is evicted. This one cache can be chosen as the closest to the user, a random one, or from some other criterion. (Here, we choose the *closest* node).
- **multi-LRU-All:** Insertion action is taken in *all* m caches. (a. Update) If the content is found in a non-empty subset of the m caches, all caches from this subset are updated. (b. Insertion) If the object is not found in *any* cache it is inserted in all m. A variation based on q-LRU can be proposed, where the object is inserted in each cache with probability $q > 0$.

The motivation behind the different versions of the multi-LRU policies is the following. When a user has more than one opportunity to be served due to multi-coverage, she/he can benefit from a larger cache memory (the sum of memory sizes from covering nodes.). In this setting, the optimal insertion of new content and update actions are not yet clear. If multi-LRU-One is applied, a single replica of the missed content is left down in one of the $m > 1$ caches, thus favouring diversity among neighbouring caches. If multi-LRU-All is used, m replicas are left down, one in each cache, thus spreading the new content over a larger geographic area (the union of m covering cells), at the cost of diversity. q-multi-LRU-All is in-between the two, leaving down a smaller than m number of replicas. A-priori, it is unclear which one will perform better with respect to hit probability.

The performance largely depends on the type of incoming traffic. For fixed object catalogue and stationary traffic, diversity in the cache inventories can be beneficial, whereas for time-dependent traffic with varying catalogue, performance can be improved when many replicas of the same object are available, before its popularity perishes.

3. NETWORK MODEL

Wireless Multi-Coverage: For the analysis, the positions of transmitters coincide with the atoms from the realisation of a 2-dimensional *stationary* point process, $\Phi_b = \{x_i\}$ with intensity $\lambda_b > 0$ in $[m^{-2}]$. The type is left general, e.g. a homogeneous *Poisson Point Process* (PPP), or a *square lattice.*

There are two different planar areas (*cells*) associated with each atom x_i. The first is the *Voronoi cell* $\mathcal{V}(x_i) \subset \mathbb{R}^2$, which is the geometric locus of all planar points closer to x_i than to any other station. The second one is the *Coverage cell* $\mathcal{C}_i$, which is a (possibly random) area $\mathcal{C}_i$ of wireless coverage associated with x_i. When users arrive inside the coverage cell of x_i they can be served from it by downlink transmission. In general $\mathcal{C}_i$ is different from $\mathcal{V}(x_i)$. Coverage cells can overlap. Voronoi cells do not overlap, per definition.

Suppose that a user arrives at some random position and time (say the Cartesian origin $o := (0,0)$ at $t_o = 0$). This is the *typical user.* The *coverage number* $\mathcal{N}$ (as in [1]) is the random variable (r.v.) for the number of coverage cells that cover o. It depends on the PP Φ_b and the downlink transmission scheme. It has mass function $p_m := \mathbb{P}[\mathcal{N} = m]$, $m = 0, \ldots, M$, with $\sum_{m=1}^{M} p_m = 1$ and $N_{BS} := \mathbb{E}[\mathcal{N}]$. The values of the probabilities depend on the coverage model. Special cases include: the SINR *Model*, and the SNR/*Boolean Model.* In both, $\mathcal{C}_i$ is the set of planar points for which the received signal quality from x_i exceeds some threshold T.

Spatial Traffic Model: Each user is assumed to arrive at some planar location with a request for a specific data object, stay there during service and then leave. We model the users by a marked PPP in $\mathbb{R}^2 \times \mathbb{R} \times \mathbb{N}$, $\Phi_u = \{(\psi_i, t_i, v_i)\}$ with intensity $\lambda_u > 0$ in $[m^{-2}sec^{-1}]$. The variables refer to position, time and object index. All objects have the same size, normalised to 1. Two types of traffic are considered:

(A) Spatial Independent Reference Model (IRM). (i) The Φ_u is a homogeneous PPP in both space and time. (ii) There is an object catalogue $\mathcal{F}$ with finite size F. (iii) Each object $c_j \in \mathcal{F}$ has a constant and known probability a_j to be requested (i.e. object *popularity*). Objects are ordered by popularity $a_1 \geq a_2 \geq \ldots \geq a_F$. It holds, $\sum_{j=1}^{F} a_j = 1$. An example is Zipf distribution, with exponent $0 < \gamma < 2$.

(B) Temporal Locality Model. (i) Given a time instant, users on the plane form a homogeneous PPP. (ii) The object catalogue is not fixed over time. New objects appear with rate λ_{obj} in $[sec^{-1}]$. (iii) Each object has a finite lifespan τ_j $[sec]$ drawn from a distribution with finite expected value. After the lifespan expires, the object ceases to interest users. (iv) During its lifespan, the object popularity may vary based on some function that controls shape (rectangle, exponentially decreasing, etc.). Models of this type have been proposed in [4]. The average spatial popularity per object is equal to λ_u/λ_{obj} $[m^{-2}]$.

Storage: A storage space of size $K \geq 1$ objects is installed and available on each transmitter node x_i of Φ_b. The cache inventory of each node is a (varying over time) subset of objects, with number of elements not greater than K.

4. CHE-LIKE APPROXIMATIONS

The main difficulty, when trying to work analytically with spatial multi-LRU, is that the hit probability of some cache depends on the hit probability of its neighbours and the neighbours of its neighbours. This is because the coverage area of each node has many sub-areas of multi-coverage by different node subsets, which makes analysis neither easy, nor exact. For spatial IRM traffic, we can use the approach of Che for one cache and single-LRU [2], to derive similar approximations for the multi-LRU cache management policies. Che assumes that, the maximum uninterrupted period of an object within the cache, from its last request to eviction, can be approximated by the same constant *characteristic time* T_C for all objects.

Similarly, in all multi-LRU variations, we assume that any object in each cache has the same characteristic time T_C. Additional case-tailored approximations are made to obtain very accurate analytical formulas for the hit-performance.

4.1 multi-LRU-One (Che with CIA)

By definition of this policy variation, the cache influenced by a user is her/his geographically closest. Consequently, only the users within the *Voronoi cell* of a node, also covered by this node, can trigger an action of update or insertion at its cache. Because Voronoi cells do not overlap, the influence of the neighbouring stations' traffic on the inventory of x_i should be small. So, we use a *Cache Independence Approximation* (CIA), based on which, each cache performs single-LRU for the users that arrive within its Voronoi cell. Then with IRM traffic, for a typical user covered by m stations, with average Voronoi surface $|\mathcal{V}| < |\mathcal{C}|$, the expression for the hit-probability per object j in cache x_i is

$$P_{hit,i}(j) \overset{IRM}{=} 1 - e^{-a_j \lambda_u |\mathcal{V}| T_C}, \; i \in \{1, \ldots, m\}. \quad (1)$$

The characteristic time is found by solving the equation

$$\sum_{j=1}^{F} (1 - e^{-a_j \lambda_u |\mathcal{V}| T_C}) = K. \quad (2)$$

Furthermore, the independence due to the CIA, has the result that, when the user is covered by m stations, her/his hit probability is simply the product of hit probabilities of all these stations. Consequently, the total hit probability is

$$P_{hit} \overset{(1)}{=} \sum_{j=1}^{F} a_j \sum_{m=0}^{M} p_m \left(1 - e^{-a_j \lambda_u m |\mathcal{V}| T_C}\right). \quad (3)$$

For both the PPP and square lattice model of node positions, the average size of a Voronoi cell is equal to $|\mathcal{V}| = \lambda_b^{-1}$.

4.2 multi-LRU-All (Che with CSA)

By definition of this variation, users falling on any point within the *Coverage cell* of a node x_i can trigger an action of update or insertion at its cache inventory.

In this case, we use a different approximation, the *Cache Similarity Approximation* (CSA), which states that inventories of neighbouring caches have the same content. This is motivated by the fact that new content is simultaneously installed in all caches of nodes covering a user, when the user triggers insertion.For IRM traffic, the probability for a typical user (covered by m stations), requesting for object j to find it in cache x_i is

$$P_{hit,i}(j) \overset{IRM}{=} 1 - e^{-a_j \lambda_u |\mathcal{C}| T_C}. \quad (4)$$

For the characteristic time, we solve the equation

$$\sum_{j=1}^{F} (1 - e^{-a_j \lambda_u |\mathcal{C}| T_C}) = K. \quad (5)$$

Since neighbouring caches have the same content, the total miss probability when a set of m stations cover a typical user is equal to the probability that no other user with the same demand arrives within the total area of coverage during the characteristic time T_C (otherwise the content is definitely in all caches, either because of update or insertion. Then, the total hit probability is

$$P_{hit} = \sum_{j=1}^{F} a_j \sum_{m=0}^{M} p_m \left(1 - e^{-a_j \lambda_u |\mathcal{A}_m| T_C}\right), \quad (6)$$

where we denote by $\mathcal{A}_m$ the total area of coverage from the m stations, having surface

$$|\mathcal{A}_m| = \left| \bigcup_{\ell=1}^{m} \mathcal{C}_i \right|, \quad m = 0, \ldots, M. \quad (7)$$

It holds $|\mathcal{A}_0| = 0$, for $m = 0$. In the Boolean model $|\mathcal{A}_1| = |\mathcal{C}_1| = \pi R_b^2$, while the surface of $\mathcal{A}_m$ is a superposition of m overlapping discs with equal radius R_b. The main difficulty in calculating the approximate hit probability for multi-LRU-All with the above formulas, is to obtain exact values for the total surface $|\mathcal{A}_m|$.

5. REFERENCES

[1] B. Blaszczyszyn and A. Giovanidis. Optimal geographic caching in cellular networks. *IEEE Intl. Conf. on Commun. (ICC)*, 2015.

[2] H. Che, Y. Tung, and Z. Wang. Hierarchical web caching systems: Modeling, design and experimental results. *IEEE JSAC*, 20(7):1305–1314, Sept. 2002.

[3] N. Golrezaei, K. Shanmugam, A. Dimakis, A. Molisch, and G. Caire. FemtoCaching: Wireless video content delivery through distributed caching helpers. *Proc. IEEE INFOCOM*, 2012.

[4] S. Traverso, M. Ahmed, M. Garetto, P. Giaccone, E. Leonardi, and S. Niccolini. Unravelling the impact of temporal and geographical locality in content caching systems. *IEEE Trans. Multimedia*, 17(10):1839–1854, 2015.

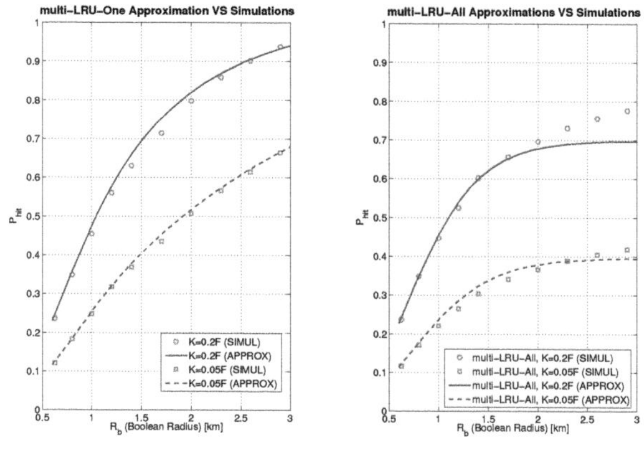

(a) multi-LRU-One (b) multi-LRU-All

Figure 1: Verification of Che-Like approximations for multi-LRU-One, and -All. Poisson/Boolean, IRM. $\lambda_b = 0.5$ [km^{-2}], $\lambda_u = 80$ [$m^{-2}hour^{-1}$], $F = 10000$, $\gamma = 0.78$. Two curves: $K = 0.2F$ or $K = 0.05F$.

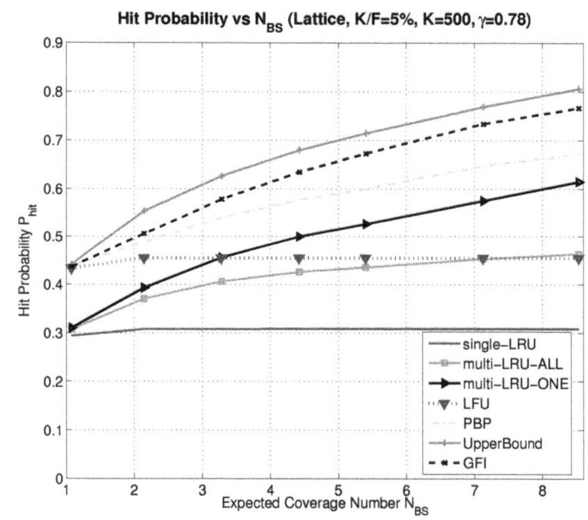

Figure 2: Performance evaluation for Hit Performance of caching policies. Lattice/Boolean, IRM.

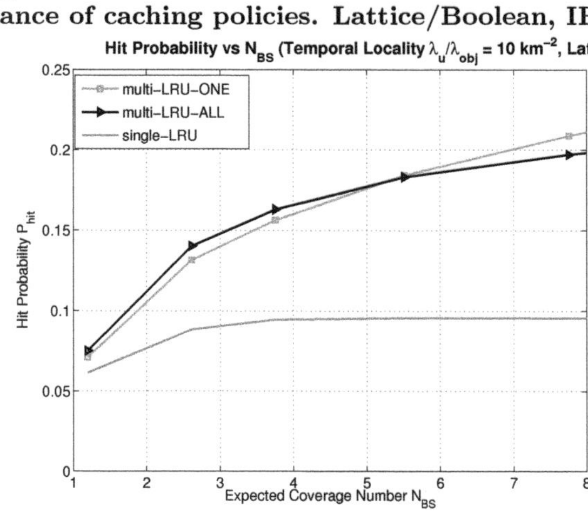

Figure 3: Performance evaluation for Hit Performance. Lattice/Boolean, Temporal locality.

SSD Failures in Datacenters: What, When and Why?

Iyswarya Narayanan*, Di Wang†, Myeongjae Jeon†, Bikash Sharma†, Laura Caulfield†, Anand Sivasubramaniam*, Ben Cutler†, Jie Liu†, Badriddine Khessib†, Kushagra Vaid†
*The Pennsylvania State University, †Microsoft Corporation
*{iun106,anand}@cse.psu.edu
†{wangdi,myeoje,bsharma,laura.caulfield,bcutler,jie.liu,bkhessib,kvaid}@microsoft.com

ABSTRACT

Despite the growing popularity of Solid State Disks (SSDs) in the datacenter, little is known about their reliability characteristics in the field. The little knowledge is mainly vendor supplied, which cannot really help understand how SSD failures can manifest and impact production systems, in order to take appropriate actions. Besides failure data, a detailed characterization requires wide spectrum of data about factors influencing SSD failures, right from provisioning (what models? where and when deployed? etc.) to the operational ones (workloads, read-write intensities, write amplification, etc.). We analyze over half a million SSDs that span multiple generations spread across several datacenters which host a wide range of workloads over nearly 3 years. By studying the diverse set of factors on SSD failures, and their symptoms, our work provides the first look at the *what, when and why* characteristics of SSD failures in production datacenters.

Keywords

solid state drives; reliability; datacenters;

1. INTRODUCTION

With several attractive performance properties, energy efficiencies, growing densities, non-mechanical components, and continually dropping cost per gigabyte, NAND-flash based Solid State Drives (SSDs) are gaining rapid adoption in datacenters [1]. However, with SSDs being relatively in their infancy compared to their HDD counterparts (past 5-8 years compared to several decades), little is understood about their failure properties in production environments.

Understanding SSD failure characteristics can be extremely valuable in several ways in designing, provisioning and operating them in datacenters. However, the current knowledge about SSD failure rates is primarily based on accelerated lab testing (e.g. [2]). Over and beyond the parameters and the ranges that they are tested for, numerous other factors in a production environment (e.g., diverse workloads, environment conditions, etc.) may not have been considered. A datacenter operator may need to understand the what, when and why characteristics for appropriate provisioning and operational decisions, that may not easily be captured using a single (failure rate) metric [3], or by analyzing various influencing factors independently [4]. By jointly evaluating diverse set of factors on SSD failures, and their symptoms, we provide the first glimpse of SSD failure characteristics in production environment.

SIGMETRICS '16 June 14-18, 2016, Antibes Juan-Les-Pins, France

ACM ISBN 978-1-4503-4266-7/16/06.
DOI: http://dx.doi.org/10.1145/2896377.2901489

2. DATA COLLECTION

We analyze data from over half a million SSDs of different generations (those just deployed to those nearing end of life) from two different vendors that span five very large datacenters and several edge datacenters, over a span of nearly 3 years. These SSDs serve data for a wide spectrum of workloads including Big Data Analytics, Content Distribution Caches, Web Search Engines, and Management software, that exhibit diverse read-write characteristics. Table 1 summarizes the salient characteristics of these SSDs.

Model	Size	Avg. Age	Reads/disk	Writes/disk
1-A	160GB	3.17 yrs.	NA	42.8 TB
1-B	160GB	3.31 yrs.	138.7 TB	25.1 TB
1-C	160GB	2.69 yrs.	99.9 TB	11.7 TB
1-D	480GB	1.92 yrs.	145.2 TB	40.3 TB
2-A	480GB	1.8 yrs.	NA	NA

Table 1: SSDs under study. Reads/disk and Writes/disk mean the average amount of data read and written, respectively, per disk since its deployment. NA indicates unavailable data.

3. SSD RELIABILITY

DEFINITION 1. *Fail-stopped/Failed Device - We identify an SSD to fail-stop, if the result of some underlying SSD events/failures propagates to the corresponding server, causing it to be shutdown for external investigation[1]. The device will be replaced/ repaired subsequently[2]. We refer to devices that fail-stops anytime during our observation window, as a "Failed", and all the other devices as "Healthy" ones.*

In this work, we focus on such fail-stop failure as they are significant in our dataset, and their consequent downtime implies: (i) lower QoS and availability to hosted applications and/or (ii) higher expenses in provisioning extra capacities to guarantee a promised availability to these applications.

[1]We investigated failure tickets and identified SSDs as the failure source.

[2]Yet, we conservatively term it as failed in this study, since the downtime is itself a significant concern/cost. Over 80% of the fail-stopped SSDs were replaced in our observed datacenters during the observation window.

Figure 1 shows Annualized Failure Rate (AFR) of the SSD models. Model 2-A, an enterprise class SSD, has much lower AFR compared to the other consumer class models. For the latter, SSD specifications report AFRs between 0.61% - 0.73%. However, except model 1-A which is in the specified range, both model 1-B and 1-C exceed the published AFR, while model 1-D is well below. *This indicates that a production datacenter environment running real workloads can affect a SSD's failure characteristics very differently from the operating conditions imposed by their corresponding manufacturer's test environments.*

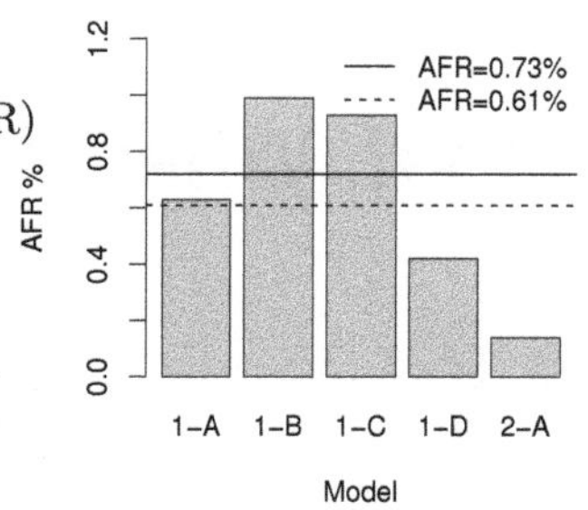

Figure 1: AFR for SSD models. Horizontal lines are reported by vendors.

3.1 SSD Failure Symptoms

Even before the onset of a fail-stop failure, SSDs can exhibit the following symptoms – Reallocated Sector Count, Program/Erase Fail Count, Data Errors (CRC and Uncorrectable Errors), and SATA Downshift Count – captured using SMART attributes. Some of these symptoms can by themselves be debilitating enough to be viewed as a "failure" in certain situations [3], even if they do not immediately result in a fail-stop. However, we still treat these as symptoms, and consider only the fail-stop events to be failures.

Figure 2 shows AFR for two groups of devices, those exhibiting symptoms and those not. The presence of any of these symptoms increases AFR by as much as 3X to 20X, with data errors being more significant. Further analysis suggests that, there is a higher likelihood of the symptoms preceding SSD failures, with an intense manifestation preventing their survivability beyond a few months. However, these symptoms alone are not a sufficient indicator for diagnosing failures, motivating the need to analyze the effect of other factors on SSD failure characteristics.

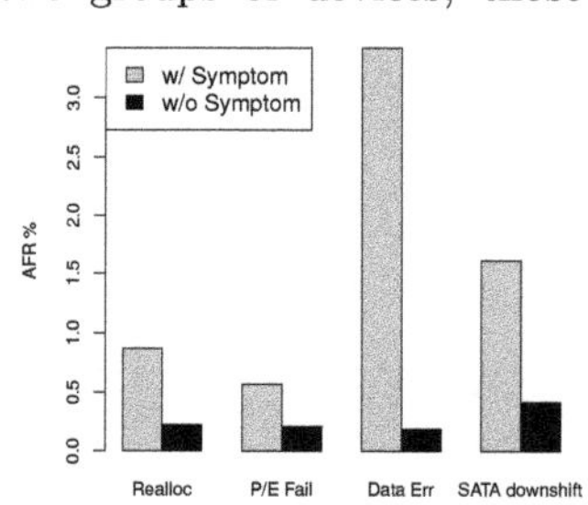

Figure 2: AFR in the presence and absence of symptoms.

3.2 SSD Failure Factors

We study factors from various levels in the datacenter hierarchy that can affect SSD reliability. This includes:

i) ***Device level factors*** of Host Writes, Reads, NAND Writes, Read-Write Ratio, and Write Amplification Factors.
ii) ***Server level factors*** of SSD Space Utilization, HDD Space Utilization, Processor and Memory utilization.
iii) ***Datacenter level factors*** of Rack SKU and Datacenter facility which is a proxy for various design decisions such as availability, cooling, and packaging.

We observe that provisioning (what model? SKU? facility?) and operational parameters (read/write rates, write amplification, SSD and HDD space utilization, etc.) all show some correlation with SSD failures. This motivates the need for understanding their order of importance (to be useful to a datacenter operator), and a systematic multi-factor analysis to better answer the what, when and why of SSD failures.

3.3 Characterization of failed devices

What? We characterize the SSDs based on their *signature*, which comprise of symptoms and factors. Using machine learning based approach, we evaluate the signature and classify them into "failed" or "healthy". It uses Random Forest for classification and obtains the relative order of important features using Permutation Feature Ranking.

Our result based on 5-fold cross validation shows that: (i) Failed devices can be differentiated from healthy ones with high precision (87%) and recall (71%) using failure signatures from tens of important factors and their threshold values; (ii) Failure symptoms including data errors and reallocated sectors, device and server level workload related factors such as total NAND writes, total reads and writes, memory utilization, etc. rank higher in identifying failures;

When? To understand when a device fails, we leverage the high frequency and lower error rate *rules* identified by the Random Forest to classify the devices' signatures. We represent the time at which a device's signature matches the classification rules as t_m and the actual time of failure as t_f, $t_f >= t_m$. We study the relation between the time to fail (t_f-t_m) and the rules themselves.

We observe that devices are more likely to fail in less than a month, if the matched failure signatures include failure symptoms. But, they tend to survive longer if the matched failure signatures are entirely based on workload factors.

Why? To understand the possible causes of SSD failures, we study the causal relationship between correlating factors, symptoms and failures. Typically, randomized controlled experimens are used to find such relationships. However, they are often impractical or even infeasible due to their time and cost constraints. Hence, we resort to finding causal relationships from the observational data using causal graphical models and Pearl's do-calculus.

The results suggest that i) symptoms (data errors and reallocations) as well as the device model have direct impact on failures; ii) other design/provisioning factors and operational/workload factors impact failures via media wearout; iii) the factors with strong causal impact match well with the ones identified using Permutation Feature Ranking.

4. ACKNOWLEDGMENTS

This work was supported by National Science Foundation under grants 1302225 and 1302557.

5. REFERENCES

[1] D. G. Andersen and S. Swanson. Rethinking Flash in the Data Center. *IEEE Micro*, 2010.

[2] L. M. Grupp, A. M. Caulfield, J. Coburn, S. Swanson, E. Yaakobi, P. H. Siegel, and J. K. Wolf. Characterizing Flash Memory: Anomalies, Observations, and Applications. In *MICRO*, 2009.

[3] J. Meza, Q. Wu, S. Kumar, and O. Mutlu. A Large-Scale Study of Flash Memory Failures in the Field. In *ACM SIGMETRICS*, 2015.

[4] B. Schroeder, R. Lagisetty, and A. Merchant. Flash reliability in production: The expected and the unexpected. In *USENIX FAST*, 2016.

The Power of d Choices for Redundancy

Kristen Gardner
Carnegie Mellon University
Pittsburgh, PA
ksgardne@cs.cmu.edu

Samuel Zbarsky
Carnegie Mellon University
Pittsburgh, PA
szbarsky@andrew.cmu.edu

Mor Harchol-Balter
Carnegie Mellon University
Pittsburgh, PA
harchol@cs.cmu.edu *

Alan Scheller-Wolf
Carnegie Mellon University
Pittsburgh, PA
awolf@andrew.cmu.edu

ABSTRACT

An increasingly prevalent technique for improving response time in queueing systems is the use of redundancy. In a system with redundant requests, each job that arrives to the system is copied and dispatched to multiple servers. As soon as the first copy completes service, the job is considered complete, and all remaining copies are deleted. A great deal of empirical work has demonstrated that redundancy can significantly reduce response time in systems ranging from Google's BigTable service to kidney transplant waitlists.

We propose a theoretical model of redundancy, the Redundancy-d system, in which each job sends redundant copies to d servers chosen uniformly at random. We derive the first exact expressions for mean response time in Redundancy-d systems with any finite number of servers. We also find asymptotically exact expressions for the distribution of response time as the number of servers approaches infinity.

1. INTRODUCTION

Redundancy – the idea of dispatching multiple copies of the same job and waiting for the first copy to complete service – is an important strategy for reducing response times in applications ranging from Google's BigTable service to kidney transplant waitlists.

Redundancy provides significant response time improvements because it exploits two sources of variability. First, queueing times across servers can be highly variable due to load from different applications. Redundant requests wait in the queue at multiple servers, so they experience the *minimum queueing time* across these servers. Second, the *same* job might see highly variable service times at different servers. For example, in computer systems applications such as web queries, external factors such as network interference, disk seek time, and background tasks can cause a query to be slowed down unpredictably. This slowdown dominates the computation time required for the query, which is inherently quite small. This causes the query's actual service time to be very long relative to its inherent size. For example, a web query can be slowed down by up to a factor of 27 due to unpredictable background load [4]. Sending redundant requests enables a job to receive the *minimum service time* across servers.

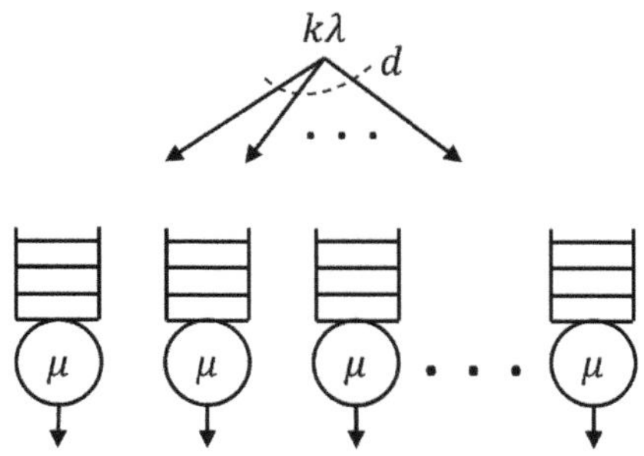

Figure 1: The Redundancy-d system consists of k servers, each providing independent exponential service times with rate μ. Jobs arrive to the system as a Poisson process with rate $k\lambda$. Each job sends copies to d servers chosen uniformly at random. A job is complete when its first copy completes service.

While it is clear that redundancy can lead to a significant reduction in response time, it is often difficult to determine how much redundancy is needed to obtain such improvements. Is sending only two copies enough to achieve most of the potential benefit? What is the additional benefit of increasing the number of copies?

We study these questions in a theoretical model called the Redundancy-d system (see Figure 1). The Redundancy-d system consists of k servers; each arriving job makes d copies of itself and dispatches these copies to d different servers chosen uniformly at random. The job is considered complete as soon as the first copy completes service.

Our *primary contribution* is providing the first exact analysis of response time in the Redundancy-d system. First, we derive exact closed-form expressions for mean response time as a function of the number of servers k and the number of

*This work was supported by NSF awards CMMI-1538204, CMMI-1334194, and CSR-1116282; by the Intel Science and Technology Center for Cloud Computing; and by a Google Faculty Research Award 2015/16.

SIGMETRICS '16 June 14-18, 2016, Antibes Juan-Les-Pins, France

ACM ISBN 978-1-4503-4266-7/16/06.
DOI: http://dx.doi.org/10.1145/2896377.2901497

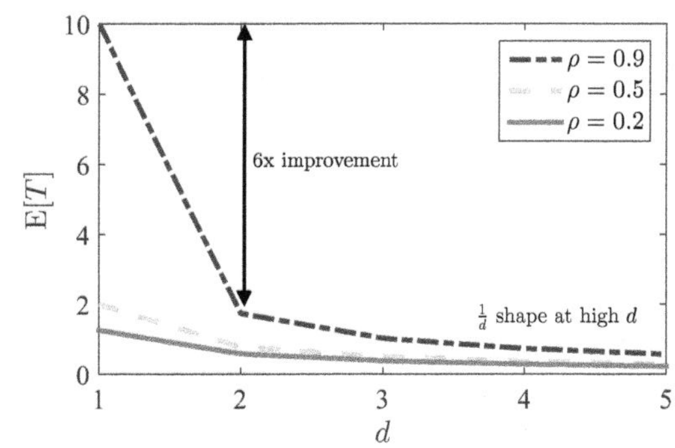

Figure 2: Mean response time $\mathrm{E}[T]$ as a function of d under low ($\rho = 0.2$, solid red line), medium ($\rho = 0.5$, dashed green line), and high ($\rho = 0.9$, dot-dashed blue line) load.

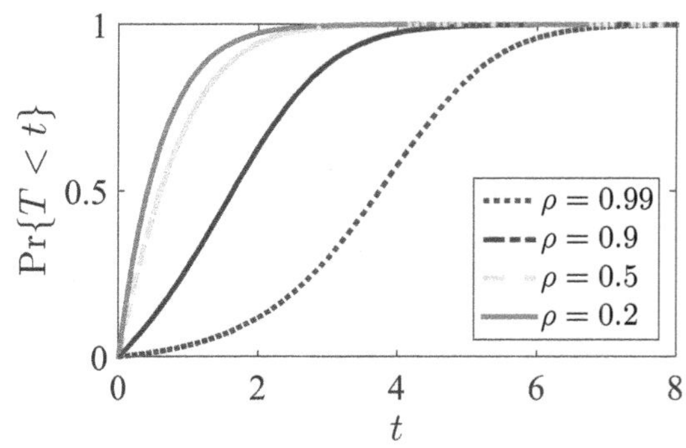

Figure 3: Probability that response time $T < t$ when $d = 2$ under low ($\rho = 0.2$, solid red line), medium ($\rho = 0.5$, dashed green line), high ($\rho = 0.9$, dot-dashed blue line), and very high ($\rho = 0.99$, dotted purple line) load.

copies per job, d, by modeling the system as a Markov chain. Second, we consider the system in the limit as the number of servers k approaches infinity. Under a standard asymptotic independence assumption, we derive an asymptotically exact expression for the distribution of response time. Our exact analysis allows us to quantify the magnitude of the benefit from increasing d.

2. MAIN RESULTS

Let $\rho = \frac{\lambda}{\mu}$ denote the system load. This is the total arrival rate to the system ($k\lambda$) divided by the maximum service rate of the system ($k\mu$). The system is stable as long as $\rho < 1$.

THEOREM 1. *The mean response time in the Redundancy-d system with k servers is*

$$\mathrm{E}[T] = \sum_{i=d}^{k} \frac{1}{k\mu \frac{\binom{k-1}{d-1}}{\binom{i-1}{d-1}} - k\lambda}. \tag{1}$$

We derive the result in Theorem 1 by modeling the system as a Markov chain. Following [1], our system state is a list of all jobs in the system in the order in which they arrived, where we track the d specific servers to which each job sent its copies. The general form of the limiting distribution of the state space is an immediate consequence of Theorem 1 in [1]. Unfortunately, knowing the limiting distribution's form does not tell us the normalizing constant, nor does it immediately yield results for mean number in system and mean response time. To find mean response time, we must first find $\Pr\{m \text{ jobs in system}\}$ by summing over all $\binom{k}{d}$ possible choices of servers for each queue position. We develop a novel state aggregation approach that uses recurrence relations to obtain the result given in Theorem 1 (see [2]).

THEOREM 2. *Assuming queues are d-wise asymptotically independent as $k \to \infty$, the response time in the Redundancy-d system with $d > 1$ has c.c.d.f.*

$$\Pr\{T > t\} = \left(\frac{1}{\rho + (1-\rho)e^{t\mu(d-1)}}\right)^{\frac{d}{d-1}}. \tag{2}$$

Theorem 2 relies on the assumption that queues are asymptotically independent as $k \to \infty$ (see [2] for definition); this is a standard assumption that has been shown to hold in several related systems (e.g., [3]). Our proof of Theorem 2 involves considering a tagged arrival to the Redundancy-d system, and asking why that arrival would have not yet departed by time t. There are two possibilities: either the job has a large size, or the job experiences a long queueing time. In the latter case, the long queueing time can again be attributed to the preceding arrival having a large size or a long queueing time. This recursive formulation leads to a system of differential equations, which we solve to obtain the result in Theorem 2.

Our exact analysis allows us to quantify the response time benefit obtained from increasing d. Figure 2 shows mean response time, $\mathrm{E}[T]$, in the Redundancy-d system as a function of d for low, medium, and high load. At all loads, $\mathrm{E}[T]$ decreases as d increases. The most significant improvement occurs between $d = 1$ and $d = 2$: $\mathrm{E}[T]$ decreases by up to a factor of 6. Figure 3 shows that this improvement is even bigger at the tail of response time; the 95th percentile of response time decreases by up to a factor of 8 when $\rho = 0.9$. From Theorem 2, we see that as d becomes large, mean response time scales in proportion to $\frac{1}{d}$, indicating that there is decreasing marginal benefit from further increasing d.

3. REFERENCES

[1] K. Gardner, S. Zbarsky, S. Doroudi, M. Harchol-Balter, E. Hyytiä, and A. Scheller-Wolf. Reducing latency via redundant requests: Exact analysis. In *SIGMETRICS*, June 2015.

[2] K. Gardner, S. Zbarsky, M. Harchol-Balter, and A. Scheller-Wolf. Analyzing response time in the Redundancy-d system. Technical report, CMU-CS-15-141R, 2016.

[3] N. Vvedenskaya, R. Dobrushin, and F. Karpelevich. Queueing system with selection of the shortest of two queues: An asymptotic approach. *Probl. Peredachi Inf.*, 32(1):20–34, 1996.

[4] Y. Xu, M. Bailey, B. Noble, and F. Jahanian. Small is better: Avoiding latency traps in virtualized data centers. In *Proceedings of the 4th annual Symposium on Cloud Computing*, page 7. ACM, 2013.

Time-Based Bandwidth Allocation for Heterogeneous Storage

Hui Wang
Rice University, ECE Department
6100 Main St. Houston, TX, USA
hw5@rice.edu

Peter Varman
Rice University, ECE Department
6100 Main St. Houston, TX, USA
pjv@rice.edu

ABSTRACT

Providing fairness and system efficiency are important, often conflicting, requirements when allocating shared resources. In a hybrid storage system the problem is complicated by the high variability in request service times, caused by speed differences between heterogeneous devices and workload-specific variations in access time within a device.

This paper describes a model for fair *time-based* resource allocation in a hybrid storage system that has better fairness and efficiency than traditional IOPS-based schemes. An analytical model is developed and an optimal algorithm for fairly allocating device times to applications while maximizing the system throughput or utilization is presented. The results are validated using Linux implementations.

1. INTRODUCTION

In this paper we propose a model called Time-Based Bandwidth Allocation (TBBA) for storage systems made up of two types of devices: hard disks (HDs) and solid state drives (SSDs). The maximum throughput of these devices can vary significantly depending on the mix of reads and writes, and random and sequential IOs in the workload. When request service times are variable, the capacity of the device is not fixed but itself varies with the actual mix of requests served. This make it difficult to apply resource-allocation techniques which implicitly assume that the resource capacities are independent of the allocations.

We generalize the Bottleneck Aware Allocation (BAA) model for multiple resources that we proposed in [7] to handle the case when requests may have variable service times. The BAA model maximizes system utilization while preserving the fairness properties of policies like Dominant Resource Fairness [1] (DRF). The DRF policy allocates multiple resources among clients to equalize their dominant shares and is shown to have excellent fairness properties like *envy-freedom* and *sharing incentive*. In contrast, BAA partitions clients into bottleneck sets and only requires equalizing dominant shares within a set. By relaxing the constraint between clients in different bottleneck sets, BAA maximizes system utilization while maintaining all the fairness properties of DRF, thus achieving both fairness and high efficiency.

TBBA decides how much time on each device to allocate to the clients to maximize system utilization and maintain fairness. TBBA generalizes policies for time allocation on a single device like the HD or SSD in isolation *e.g.* PARDA [2], Argon [5], Fahrrad [4], and FIOS [3] to handle multiple resource types.

2. MODEL

The system consists of n clients that access a hybrid storage array. Clients' IO requests are directed to either the SSD or the HD. The fraction of requests of client i to the SSD (HD) is its *hit ratio* (respectively *miss ratio*) and is denoted by h_i (respectively m_i). The service times of client i for HD and SSD requests are denoted by t_i^d and t_i^s respectively.

A client is *bottlenecked* on either the HD or the SSD depending on its balance factor. The *balance factor* δ_i of a continuously backlogged client i, is the ratio of the time spent servicing its SSD requests to the time spent on its HD requests; *i.e.* $\delta_i = (h_i \times t_i^s)/(m_i \times t_i^d)$. If $\delta_i > 1$ then i is bottlenecked on the SSD, while $\delta_i < 1$ indicates it is bottlenecked on the HD. The clients are partitioned into two sets S and D consisting of the clients that are bottlenecked on the SSD ($\delta_i \geq 1$) and HD ($\delta_j < 1$) respectively.

Define the *entitlement* E_i of client i as its throughput when it is allocated $1/n$ sec of time on the system every second. $E_i = 1/(n \times m_i \times t_i^d)$ for $i \in D$, and $E_j = 1/(n \times h_j \times t_j^s)$ for $j \in S$. The actual *throughput* of client i is denoted by A_i. Define the *amplification factor* of client i as the ratio A_i/E_i, the ratio of its actual throughput to its entitlement.

We now describe fairness requirements for the allocation. **Local Fairness** [7]: For clients i and j in the same bottleneck set, local fairness requires that their throughputs are in proportion to their entitlements *i.e.* $A_i/A_j = E_i/E_j$. Rearranging, $A_i/E_i = A_j/E_j$ *i.e.* the amplification factor of all clients in a bottleneck set is the same. Denote the amplification factor for clients in D by ρ_d and in S by ρ_s. Hence, the throughput of client $i \in D$ and $j \in S$ can be written as: $A_i = \rho_d E_i$ and $A_j = \rho_s E_j$ respectively.
Sharing Incentive [1, 7]: SI requires that each client gets a throughput that is at least equal to its entitlement. That is for all clients i, $E_i \geq A_i$. Hence, $\rho_d \geq 1$ and $\rho_s \geq 1$.
Envy-Freedom (EF) [1, 7]: An allocation is EF if no client can increase its throughput by swapping its allocation with another client. This means that no client should get more time than any other client on *both* devices. Clients in the

SIGMETRICS '16 June 14-18, 2016, Antibes Juan-Les-Pins, France

ACM ISBN 978-1-4503-4266-7/16/06.
DOI: http://dx.doi.org/10.1145/2896377.2901492

same bottleneck set are automatically envy free. Let $i \in D$ and $j \in S$. Let T_i^d and T_i^s denote the time allocated to client i on the HD and SSD respectively. EF between i and j requires that: $T_i^d \geq T_j^d$ and $T_j^s \geq T_i^s$.

The mathematical formulation of EF constraints follow. Now $T_k^d = A_k \times m_k \times t_k^d$ and $T_k^s = A_k \times h_k \times t_k^s$ for any client k, $A_i = \rho_d E_i$ and $A_j = \rho_s E_j$. Substituting in the time inequalities in the previous paragraph and recalling the definition of the balance factor δ_i, we get the condition for EF: $\forall i \in D, j \in S$, $\rho_s/\rho_d \leq min_j\{\delta_j : j \in S\}$ and $\rho_s/\rho_d \geq max_i\{\delta_i : i \in D\}$. Define $\mu = max_{i \in D}\ \{\delta_i\}$ and $\nu = min_{j \in S}\ \{\delta_j\}$. From the above discussion, we can formulate the fairness criteria of TBBA in terms of three simple constraints on ρ_s and ρ_d. Specifically:

$$\rho_d \geq 1 \qquad \rho_s \geq 1 \qquad \nu \geq \frac{\rho_s}{\rho_d} \geq \mu \tag{1}$$

Resource Constraints: The resource constraints require that the total time allocated on the devices be constrained by the real time available. The time allocated per second on the HD and the SSD must both be no more than 1, leading to the capacity constraints:

$$\rho_d|D| \ + \ \rho_s \sum_{j \in S} 1/\delta_j \leq n \qquad \rho_d \sum_{i \in D} \delta_i + \rho_s|S| \leq n \tag{2}$$

Objective Functions: The goal is to maximize either the system throughput Γ (IOPS) (sum of client throughputs) or the system utilization Υ (sum of device busy times). These can be written as:

$$\Gamma = \rho_d \sum_{i \in D} E_i + \rho_s \sum_{j \in S} E_j \quad \Upsilon = \frac{\rho_d}{n} \sum_{i \in D}(1+\delta_i) + \frac{\rho_s}{n} \sum_{j \in S}(1+\frac{1}{\delta_j})$$

The above formulation of the problem as a linear programming optimization can be solved for ρ_s and ρ_d using standard LP solvers. We next present a direct way to calculate the optimal solutions that is more efficient.

3. ALLOCATION ALGORITHMS

We first describe the algorithm for maximizing system utilization subject to fairness requirements. We refer to the optimal solution as the *fairopt* operating point. The algorithm determines the fairopt values, ρ_s^* and ρ_d^*; the optimal allocation A_i is found by scaling the entitlement E_i by either ρ_s^* ($i \in S$) or ρ_d^* ($i \in D$). The fairopt operating point must satisfy: (i) at least one of the devices must be fully utilized (Pareto optimality) (ii) ρ_s^*/ρ_d^* must lie in the interval $[\mu, \nu]$ (EF, equation 1) (iii) $\rho_s^*, \rho_d^* \geq 1$ (SI, equation 1).

The allocation algorithm is shown in Algorithm 1. We first find $\omega = \rho_s/\rho_d$ at which *both* the HD and the SSD are fully utilized, by equating the left-hand sides of the resource constraint equations (2). Simplifying, we get:

$$\omega = \rho_s/\rho_d \ = \ \sum_{i \in D}(1-\delta_i) / \sum_{j \in S}(1-1/\delta_j) \tag{3}$$

If ω lies between μ and ν, then the resulting allocation can be shown to satisfy EF and SI [6]. This is the *fairopt* operating point for case 1 of Algorithm 1. If ω lies outside the EF interval $[\mu.\nu]$ then ρ_s/ρ_d must be changed, decreasing the utilization of one of the devices. Case 2 considers the case where $\omega < \mu$. In order to increase ρ_s/ρ_d the utilization of the HD must be reduced. At the *fairopt* point we must have $\rho_s/\rho_d = \mu$ and the SSD must be fully utilized. Similarly, in case 3 we need to decrease ρ_s/ρ_d by decreasing the SSD utilization while keeping the HD at 100% utilization. At the *fairopt* point we must have $\rho_s/\rho_d = \nu$ and the HD fully utilized. The complete proofs of the claims are available in the full paper and in [6].

Algorithm 1: Find_Max_Fair_Utilization
Step 1 Compute $\omega = \sum_{i \in D}(1-\delta_i)/\sum_{j \in S}(1-1/\delta_j)$
Step 2 Calculate ω^*: fairopt value of ρ_s/ρ_d
$\omega \in [\mu, \nu]$: $\omega^* = \omega$; $\rho_d^* = n/\sum_{i \in D}(\delta_i + \omega|S|)$; $\rho_s^* = \rho_d^* \times \omega$;
$\omega < \mu$: $\omega^* = \mu$; $\rho_d^* = n/\sum_{i \in D}(\delta_i + \mu|S|)$; $\rho_s^* = \rho_d^* \times \mu$;
$\omega > \nu$: $\omega^* = \nu$; $\rho_d^* = n/(|D| + \nu \sum_{j \in S} 1/\delta_j)$; $\rho_s^* = \rho_d^* \times \nu$;
Step 3 Calculate client allocations
$\forall\ i$: if $i \in D$ $A_i = \rho_d E_i$; else if $i \in S$ $A_i = \rho_s E_i$

We now describe the modifications necessary to find the *fairopt* operating point when the goal is to maximize the total throughput rather than the utilization. The two goals can sometimes be in conflict with each other: that is, the throughput can increase while the utilization decreases or vice versa [6].

We identify the limiting values of ρ_s/ρ_d for which SI is satisfied while one device in fully utilized. Specifically, define $\nu' = \rho_s/\rho_d$ where $\rho_d = 1$ and the SSD is 100% utilized; the unique solution is $\nu' = (n - \sum_{i \in D} \delta_i)/|S|$. Similarly, $\mu' = |D|/(n - \sum_{j \in S} 1/\delta_j)$ is the unique value of ρ_s/ρ_d when $\rho_s = 1$ and the HD is 100% utilized.

In Algorithm 2 below, $\mathrm{T}(x)$ computes the total system throughput for its argument $x = \rho_s/\rho_d$. In the case when utilization and throughput increase or decrease in tandem, the points of maximum throughput and maximum utilization are the same (operating point ω), and the fairopt point is the same as in Algorithm 1. Otherwise, the maximum fair throughput is attained at the point when the utilization is minimum subject to Pareto optimality (at least one device fully utilized) and fairness (satisfies SI and EF); these are exactly the points μ' and ν'.

Algorithm 2: Find_Max_Fair_Throughput
Step 1 Compute ω, μ', and ν'.
Step 2 Compute ν^* and μ^*:
$\nu^* = min\{\nu, \nu'\} = min\{\nu,\ (n - \sum_{i \in D} \delta_i)/|S|\}$
$\mu^* = max\{\mu, \mu'\} = max\{\mu,\ |D|/(n - \sum_{j \in S} 1/\delta_j)$
Step 3 Calculate optimal fair throughput T^*
$\mu \leq \omega \leq \nu$: $T^* = \max(T(\omega), T(\mu^*), T(\nu^*))$
$\omega < \mu$: $T^* = \max(T(\mu), T(\nu^*))$
$\omega > \nu$: $T^* = \max(T(\mu^*), T(\nu))$

4. PERFORMANCE EVALUATION

We implemented a prototype in the Linux system by interposing the TBBA scheduler in the IO path. Raw IO is performed to eliminate the influence of OS buffer caching. The storage server includes a 1 TB SCSI Western Digital hard disk (7200 RPM 64MB Cache SATA 6.0 Gb/s) and 120 GB SAMSUNG 840 Pro Series SSD. Since we needed to emulate different proportions of HD and SSD requests, we randomly partitioned the blocks between the two devices to meet the assumed hit ratio of the workload. We compare the TBBA performance with Linux CFQ, Time-Based DRF [1] scheduler, and IO-Based Weighted Fair Queuing (WFQ) scheduler with equal weights. More experimental results are available in [6].

Table 1: Allocations (IOPS) in Linux system

	TBBA	CFQ	DRF	WFQ
C_1	280	308	341	355
C_2	280	308	341	355
C_3	212	252	260	355
C_4	4256	2959	2328	355
Total	5028	3827	3270	1420

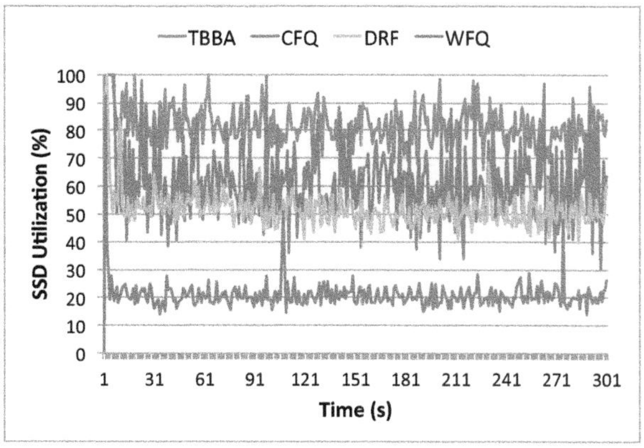

Figure 1: SSD device utilization. HD utilization is 100% for all schedulers.

In this experiment, there are four clients with hit ratios 0.8, 0.8, 0.8, 0.99 and read ratios 0.5, 0.5, 1.0 and 1.0. We estimate the service times for each device by system profiling. The average HD (SSD) service times for reads and writes are 6 ms and 3 ms (0.17 ms and 0.09 ms) respectively. The average HD times t_i^d for the clients are 4.5 ms, 4.5 ms, 6.0 ms and 6.0 ms respectively, and the average SSD times t_j^s are 0.13 ms, 0.13 ms, 0.17 ms and 0.17 ms respectively. Computing, $\delta_1 = 0.12$, $\delta_2 = 0.12$, $\delta_3 = 0.11$ and $\delta_4 = 2.8$, so $C1$, C_2 and $C_3 \in D$ and $C_4 \in S$.

The system throughput and allocation for each client are shown in Table 1. TBBA gets significantly higher throughput than all the other schedulers. WFQ gets the lowest throughput because it tries to equalize the IOPS for each client without considering the system bottleneck and the difference of service times for each client. The SSD utilizations of the four schedulers are shown in Figure 1. TBBA has the highest SSD utilization. It is not fully utilized because TBBA will not sacrifice fairness to maximize the system throughput. In TBBA's allocation, $C1$, C_2 and C_3 get around 250 ms per second on the HD, and C_4 gets 716 ms on the SSD. Each client gets at least it's fair share (1/4s on their bottleneck devices every second), so Sharing Incentive is satisfied. No one gets higher allocation on both devices so Envy-freedom also holds.

Synchronous IO In the second part of this experiment, we also evaluated the performance for synchronous read/writes using the four schedulers. In this case the average HD read and writes times are 7.5 ms and 8.5 ms respectively, and the SSD times are 0.17 ms and 1.0 ms respectively.

The system throughputs of TBBA, CFQ, DRF and IO-Based WFQ were measured as 3667 IOPS, 3230 IOPS, 2135 IOPS and 800 IOPS respectively, following the trend of the asynchronous reads and writes. The SSD utilization of the four schedulers are shown in Figure 2. We verifed that TBBA satisfies all the fairness properties as well.

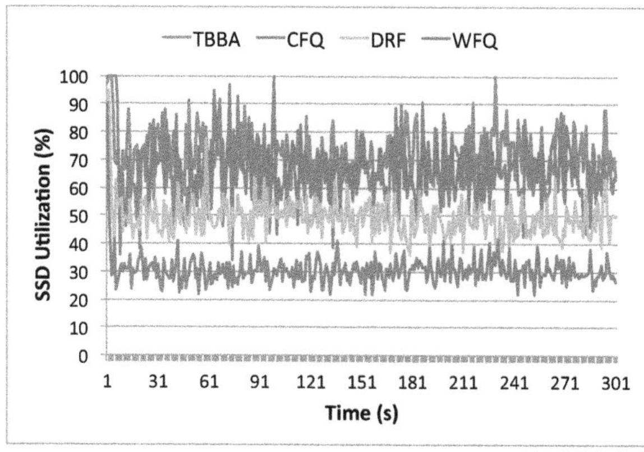

Figure 2: SSD device utilization (Synchronous IOs): HD utilization 100% for all schedulers.

5. CONCLUSIONS

In this paper, we proposed a model, Time-Based Bandwidth Allocation (TBBA), for allocating multiple resources based on a generalized version of time slicing. We used the TBBA model to fairly time-multiplex a hybrid storage system while maximizing system throughput or utilization. A computationally-efficient algorithm for computing the allocation is presented and empirical results of a Linux-based implementation are described.

6. ACKNOWLEDGMENTS

Supported in part by NSF grant CCF-1421434. Hui Wang is currently at LinkedIn, Mountain View, CA.

7. REFERENCES

[1] A. Ghodsi, M. Zaharia, B. Hindman, A. Konwinski, S. Shenker, and I. Stoica. Dominant resource fairness: fair allocation of multiple resource types. In *USENIX NSDI*, pages 24–24, 2011.

[2] A. Gulati, I. Ahmad, and C. Waldspurger. PARDA: Proportional Allocation of Resources in Distributed Storage Access. In *USENIX FAST*, pages 85–98, 2009.

[3] S. Park and K. Shen. Fios: A fair, efficient flash i/o scheduler. In *USENIX FAST*, pages 203–211, 2012.

[4] A. Povzner, T. Kaldewey, S. Brandt, R. Golding, T. M. Wong, and C. Maltzahn. Efficient guaranteed disk request scheduling with Fahrrad. *ACM SIGOPS Oper. Syst. Rev.*, 42(4):13–25, 2008.

[5] M. Wachs, M. Abd-El-Malek, E. Thereska, and G. R. Ganger. Argon: performance insulation for shared storage servers. In *USENIX FAST*, pages 5–5, 2007.

[6] H. Wang. *Resource Allocation Models for Multi-Tiered Storage: Balancing System Efficiency and QoS*. PhD thesis, Rice University, Houston, TX, USA, 2015.

[7] H. Wang and P. Varman. Balancing fairness and efficiency in tiered storage systems with bottleneck-aware allocation. In *USENIX FAST*, pages 229–242, 2014.

Towards Multi-Resource Fair Allocation with Placement Constraints

Wei Wang[†], Baochun Li[‡], Ben Liang[‡], Jun Li[‡]
[†]Hong Kong University of Science and Technology, [‡]University of Toronto
weiwa@cse.ust.hk, {bli, liang, junli}@ece.utoronto.ca

ABSTRACT

Multi-resource fair schedulers have been widely implemented in compute clusters to provide service isolation guarantees. Existing multi-resource sharing policies, notably *dominant resource fairness* (DRF) and its variants, are designed for unconstrained jobs that can run on all machines in a cluster. However, an increasing number of datacenter jobs specify *placement constraints* and can only run on a particular class of machines meeting specific hardware/software requirements (*e.g.*, GPUs or a particular kernel version). We show that directly extending existing policies to constrained jobs either compromises isolation guarantees or allows users to gain more resources by deceiving the scheduler. It remains unclear how multi-resource fair sharing is defined and achieved in the presence of placement constraints. We address this open problem by a new sharing policy, called *task share fairness* (TSF), that provides provable isolation guarantees and is strategy-proof against gaming the allocation policy. TSF is shown to be envy-free and Pareto optimal as well.

1. INTRODUCTION

Datacenter jobs are characterized by a high degree of demand diversity across *multiple resource types*. For example, business analytics jobs are usually CPU-intensive; machine learning jobs are often memory- or I/O-bound. Multi-resource fair allocation is therefore needed to provide *predictable service isolation*, where a job is guaranteed to receive a fair share of datacenter resources, regardless of the other jobs' behaviors.

Dominant resource fairness (DRF) [2] is the *de facto* sharing policy for multi-resource allocation. With DRF, jobs receive the same share of *dominant resource*—defined for each job as the one whose percentage share is the maximum across all resources. DRF is proved to possess a number of highly desirable sharing properties—notably *sharing incentive* and *strategy-proofness*—and is widely implemented as a resource scheduler in systems like Hadoop YARN and Apache Mesos.

SIGMETRICS '16 June 14-18, 2016, Antibes Juan-Les-Pins, France

ACM ISBN 978-1-4503-4266-7/16/06.
DOI: http://dx.doi.org/10.1145/2896377.2901493

We note that the successful application of DRF is limited to *unconstrained jobs* that can run on all machines in a datacenter, provided that the machine has sufficient resources to accommodate a job. However, incompatibilities between machine configurations and prerequisites of job execution are frequently encountered in datacenters. As a result, an increasing number of jobs specify *placement constraints*, restricting them to run on a particular class of machines meeting specific hardware/software requirements [4]. For example, a CUDA job must run on machines with GPUs; a DNS service requires machines with public IP addresses. It is reported in [4] that approximately 50% of Google's cluster jobs have simple, yet restrictive, placement constraints. We show that directly applying DRF and its variants to these jobs compromises fairness guarantees. It remains unclear how multi-resource fair allocation should be defined and achieved for jobs with placement constraints.

In this paper, we answer this open question with a new sharing policy, called *task share fairness* (TSF). We show that TSF satisfies a number of desirable sharing properties that are widely recognized to be most important for cluster resource management [2, 3]. In particular, with TSF, jobs are better off sharing the datacenter dynamically (*sharing incentive*); no job can receive more resources by lying about its demands and/or constraints (*strategy-proofness*); no job would envy the allocation of another (*envy-freeness*); no job can increase its allocation without decreasing that of another (*Pareto optimality*). To our knowledge, TSF is the first multi-resource allocation policy meeting all these important properties in the presence of placement constraints.

2. DESIRABLE SHARING PROPERTIES

In this paper, we focus on *hard, non-combinatorial* placement constraints (*i.e.*, a job's constraint is independ of the other jobs' placements). In particular, we model constraints as a bipartite graph consisting of job vertices and machine vertices. An edge is connected between a job vertex and a machine vertex if the job can run on the machine. We model a datacenter as a shared cluster consisting of a number of machines with multiple resources, *e.g.*, CPU, memory, *etc.* Each job runs many parallel tasks. A task is characterized by a *demand vector*, which specifies the amount of resources needed during the task's runtime.

As observed by DRF [2], there are four properties that *any* datacenter scheduler should satisfy: sharing incentive, strategy-proofness, envy-freeness, and Pareto optimality.

Sharing incentive. Consider some *arbitrary* original allocation of resources where each job is given a dedicated

Table 1: Properties of DRF variants and TSF in the presence of constraints: sharing incentive (SI), strategy-proofness (SP), envy-freeness (EF), and Pareto optimality (PO).

Property	Per-Machine DRF	DRFH	CDRF	TSF
SI			✓	✓
SP	✓	✓		✓
EF	✓	✓		✓
PO		✓	✓	✓

resource pool to run their tasks. Suppose now the jobs share their resources with others. A new allocation of the shared resources is said to provide *sharing incentive*, if it allows each job to run no fewer tasks than the job would have run in its original dedicated resource pool.

Strategy-proofness. No job can run more tasks by lying about its resource demands and/or constraints.

Envy-freeness. Assume job i can run n_i tasks with its own allocation and can run $n_{i\leftrightarrow j}$ tasks after exchanging its allocation with another job j. We have $n_i \geq \frac{w_i}{w_j} n_{i\leftrightarrow j}$ for all i and j, where w_i and w_j are the *weights* of two jobs. The weight of a job can be computed from its original dedicated resource pool as defined in the sharing incentive property.

Pareto optimality. Any attempt to launch more tasks for a job results in fewer tasks for another.

It is worth mentioning that our requirement of sharing incentive generalizes that of existing work as the dedicated resource pools given to jobs can be *arbitrary*, while existing work only considers *equal partitioning* [1, 2, 5] (each of N jobs is given $1/N$ of the total resources). In addition, jobs now have *two-dimensional* strategies, one for demand and another for constraints. Existing work, however, can only handle one-dimensional strategies, where jobs either game the demands [1, 2, 5] or the constraints [3], but not both.

Can the four properties be satisfied using existing sharing policies? To answer this question, we start with CMMF allocation [3] that generalizes max-min fairness to constrained jobs for single-resource sharing. However, because CMMF is a *market-based* allocation [3], it is not strategy-proof in the multi-resource environment [2]. We next turn to three DRF variants that generalize DRF to a compute cluster consisting of multiple heterogeneous machines: Per-Machine DRF [1, 5], DRFH [5], and CDRF [1]. Table 1 summarizes their properties. We see that none of them retains all the required properties in the presence of placement constraints.

3. TASK SHARE FAIRNESS

We propose a new multi-resource sharing policy, called *task share fairness* (TSF), that retains all the properties described in §2 for constrained jobs (see Table 1). TSF computes the *task share* for each job, defined as the ratio between the number of tasks allocated and the maximum number of tasks the job can run if *we remove its constraints and allocate it the entire datacenter.* One can interpret task share as the *job slowdown* due to resource sharing and placement constraints. TSF simply applies *max-min fair allocation with respect to the jobs' task share.*

A toy example of TSF. We consider a 3-node cluster shown in Fig. 1, where machines m_1 and m_3 have the same configuration of ⟨9 CPUs, 12 GB RAM⟩, while m_2 has ⟨3 CPUs, 4 GB RAM⟩. There are three jobs. The task of j_1 demands ⟨1 CPU, 2 GB⟩ and can be executed on all machines but m_3; the task of j_2 demands ⟨3 CPUs, 1 GB⟩ and can run on m_2 only; the task of j_3 demands ⟨1 CPU, 4 GB⟩ and can run on all machines. Suppose that we have allocated 6 tasks to j_1 on m_1, 1 to j_2 on m_2, and 3 to j_3 on m_3. We compute the task shares of these three jobs as follows.

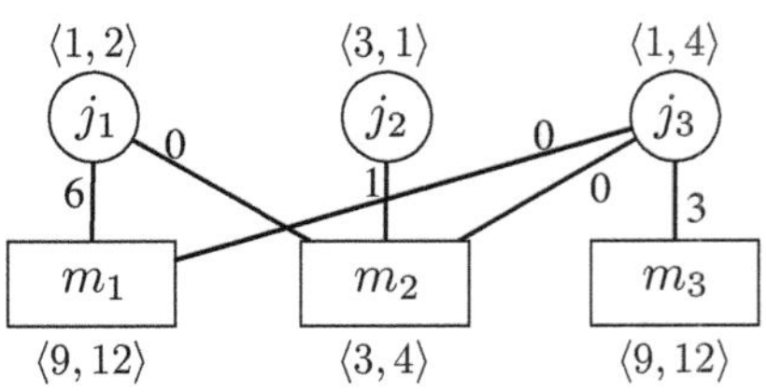

Figure 1: An example of a TSF allocation.

- For j_1, we remove its constraints and let it monopolize the entire cluster. In this hypothetical scenario, j_1 can run 14 tasks: 6 on m_1, 2 on m_2, and 6 on m_3. Therefore, the task share of j_1 is $\frac{6}{14} = \frac{3}{7}$.
- For j_2, we remove its constraints and let it monopolize the cluster. This allows j_2 to run 7 tasks: 3 on m_1, 1 on m_2, and 3 on m_3. The task share of j_2 is $\frac{1}{7}$.
- For j_3, its tasks can be executed on all machines. If monopolizing the cluster, j_3 can run 7 tasks: 3 on m_1, 1 on m_2, and 3 on m_3. The task share of j_3 is $\frac{3}{7}$.

To see that the allocation above realizes TSF, we first show that the minimum task share (*i.e.*, $\frac{1}{7}$ for j_2) is maximized. This is because j_2 is allocated the entire m_2—the only machine j_2 can run tasks on—so that its task share cannot be further increased. We next see that the second lowest task share is also maximized, because both j_1 and j_3 receive the same share $\frac{3}{7}$, and no more task can be allocated.

We may generalize TSF to weighted jobs. In particular, an allocation is said to achieve *weighted TSF* if any attempt to allocate more tasks to a user would result in fewer tasks allocated to another with an equal or lower *weighted task share*, defined for each job as the task share normalized by its weight. The following theorem states that weighted TSF retains all the required properties described in §2.

Theorem 1. *Assume originally each job i is given a dedicated resource pool and can run k_i tasks in it. If jobs instead share their resources and re-allocate them using TSF with weight $w_i = k_i/h_i$ for job i, the allocation is strategy-proof, envy-free, Pareto optimal, and provides sharing incentive.*

4. REFERENCES

[1] E. Friedman, A. Ghodsi, and C.-A. Psomas. Strategyproof allocation of discrete jobs on multiple machines. In *ACM EC*, 2014.

[2] A. Ghodsi, M. Zaharia, B. Hindman, A. Konwinski, S. Shenker, and I. Stoica. Dominant resource fairness: Fair allocation of multiple resource types. In *USENIX NSDI*, 2011.

[3] A. Ghodsi, M. Zaharia, S. Shenker, and I. Stoica. Choosy: Max-min fair sharing for datacenter jobs with constraints. In *ACM EuroSys*, 2013.

[4] B. Sharma, V. Chudnovsky, J. L. Hellerstein, R. Rifaat, and C. R. Das. Modeling and synthesizing task placement constraints in google compute clusters. In *ACM SoCC*, 2011.

[5] W. Wang, B. Liang, and B. Li. Multi-resource fair allocation in heterogeneous cloud computing systems. *IEEE Trans. Parallel Distrib. Syst.*, 26(10):2822–2835, 2015.

Trading Discount for Reputation? – On the Design and Analysis of E-Commerce Discount Mechanisms

Hong Xie, Richard T.B. Ma
School of Computing
National University of Singapore
{xieh,tbma}@comp.nus.edu.sg

John C.S. Lui
Department of Computer Science & Engineering
The Chinese University of Hong Kong
cslui@cse.cuhk.edu.hk

ABSTRACT

We develop an optimization framework to trade short-term profits for reputation (i.e., reducing *ramp-up time*). We apply the stochastic bandits framework to design an online discounting mechanism which infers the optimal discount from a seller's historical transaction data. We conduct experiments on an eBay's dataset and show that our online discounting mechanism can trade 60% of the short-term profits for reducing the ramp-up time by 40%.

Categories and Subject Descriptors

H.4 [**World Wide Web**]: Web applications – Electronic commerce

Keywords

Reputation; Discount; E-commerce

1. INTRODUCTION

Reputation system has become an indispensable component of modern E-commerce systems (e.g., Alibaba, Amazon, eBay, etc), as it helps buyers make informed decisions in choosing trustworthy sellers [3]. Because it is quite common for a buyer to purchase products from a seller whom he has never transacted with before in an E-commerce system, it is critical for buyers to know whether a seller is trustworthy or not [3]. One inefficiency of the reputation system is that new sellers may need to spend substantial amount of time to attain a trustworthy reputation [4], and we call this the "*ramp-up time*". It was found out in [4] that sellers in eBay need to spend around eight hundred days to get ramped up. Reducing the ramp-up time is highly desirable for sellers in real world E-commerce systems. To reduce the ramp-up time, more than 11,000 sellers in Taobao have been identified to accelerate the reputation accumulating process even via illegitimate methods, i.e., fake transactions [5]. Another evidence is the emergence of professional fake-transaction services [5]. Typical companies providing such services include Lantian [1] with 6,700,000 fake-transactions (estimated) per year [5].

In this work, we propose a legitimate way to accelerate the reputation accumulating process through price discounts. The idea is that by providing some price discounts, a new seller can attract more buyers even when the seller has a low reputation score. The challenge is to determine the appropriate price discount. The larger the discounts, the more buyers a new seller can attract. However, it also reduces his profits, which is critical to a new seller to survive in a competitive E-commerce system. So, the first challenge we need to address is to *quantify the tradeoffs in selecting the appropriate price discounts.* Secondly, sellers usually have no prior knowledge on buyers' preferences over price discounts, i.e., for some buyers, a small discount is sufficient to attract them to purchase a product, while other buyers may need to have a higher price discount to lure them for a transaction. The second challenge we want to address is *to learn (or infer) the buyers' preferences and set the appropriate price discounts simultaneously.*

SIGMETRICS '16 June 14-18, 2016, Antibes Juan-Les-Pins, France

ACM ISBN 978-1-4503-4266-7/16/06.
DOI: http://dx.doi.org/10.1145/2896377.2901500

2. SYSTEM MODEL

A buyer pays the seller $p \in [0,1]$ to purchase a product. We consider a normalized manufacturing cost $c \in [0,1]$. After selling a product, the E-commerce system charges a transaction fee $\tau \in [0,1)$ from the seller. Let u be the unit profit of a seller after selling one product, we have $u = p - c - \tau$.

• **Reputation System Model:** We consider an eBay-like reputation system. After receiving a product, a buyer provides a rating to indicate the quality of the transaction, such as the product quality, the shopping experience, etc. The feedback rating can be one of three levels, i.e., $\{1\,(\text{positive}), 0\,(\text{neutral}), -1\,(\text{negative})\}$. We use a probabilistic model to capture human factors such as personal preferences, biases in ratings. Denote P^+, P^0, P^- as the probability that a seller receives a positive, neutral and negative rating respectively. Note that $P^+ + P^0 + P^- = 1$. One can vary the values of P^+, P^0, P^- to reflect different levels of personal biases. A seller's reputation is quantified by the total sum of all his feedback ratings. Denote $r \in \mathbb{Z}$ be the reputation score of a seller. A new seller who just joins an E-commerce system is initialized with $r = 0$. We use a continuous time system to characterize the reputation update dynamics. Let $r(t)$ denote a seller's reputation score at time $t \in [0, \infty)$. When a seller joins an E-commerce system (at time $t = 0$), his reputation is initialized as $r(0) = 0$.

E-commerce systems usually classify sellers into different types based on their reputation scores. For example in eBay, sellers are classified into thirteen types, i.e., {no star, 1 star, 2 stars, ..., 12 stars}. Formally, our model classifies sellers into $S+1$ types, i.e., {0 star, 1 star, ..., S stars}. Denote $\mathcal{S} : \mathbb{Z} \to \{0, 1, \ldots, S\}$ as a map which prescribes a number of stars for each reputation score, $\mathcal{S}(r) = 0$, if $r < n_1$ and $\mathcal{S}(r) = S$ if $r \geq n_S$. For $i = 1, \ldots, S-1$, $\mathcal{S}(r) = i$ if $n_i \leq r < n_{i+1}$. We use a Poisson process to characterize the buyers' arrival process. One can vary the arrival rate of the Poisson process to differentiate sellers in terms of the reputation. More concretely, the larger the number of stars, the higher is the arrival rate. Denote λ_s, where $s \in \{0, 1, \ldots, S\}$, be the buyers' arrival rate when a seller has a number of s stars. We have $\lambda_i \leq \lambda_j$ for $0 \leq i \leq j \leq S$.

• **The Price Discount Model:** A seller can set one of $M + 1$ potential price discount levels $\{0, 1, \ldots, M\}$, where $M \in \mathbb{N}$. Here, level 0 corresponds to the case that a seller does *not* provide any discount. The higher the discount level, the larger the discount on the price. Denote $P_m, m = 0, 1, \ldots, M$, as the probability that a buyer who clicks into an online store will purchase a product if the seller sets a level m price discount. We require $P_0 < P_1 < \ldots < P_M$ to signify that the larger the price discount, the higher the probability that a buyer will purchase a product. The values of P_m, where $m = 0, 1, \ldots, M$ are unknown to sellers. Note that the transaction's arrival process is still a Poisson counting process (via Poisson thinning argument). Denote $\lambda(t, m)$ as the transaction's rate at time t when a seller sets a level m discount. we have $\lambda(t, m) = \lambda_s P_m$, if $\mathcal{S}(r(t)) = s$

• **Ramp-Up Time:** Recall that new sellers are initialized with 0 star, with which it is quite diff cult to attract buyers. Hence, one critical metric for sellers is the minimum time it takes to earn enough credits. Let $T(s) \triangleq \arg\min_t\{\mathcal{S}(r(t)) \geq s\}$ denote the minimum time to earn a number of $s \in \{0, 1, \ldots, S\}$ stars. Note that sellers can set a target on the number of stars to be earned.

3. DESIGN OBJECTIVE

• **Metrics:** Denote $\mathcal{M}$ as a mechanism which prescribes a price discount level for each product sold in the ramp-up process. The ramp up process is def ned as the process for a new seller to earn s stars. One benef t of the mechanism $\mathcal{M}$ is in reducing the ramp-up time since setting a price discount can attract more buyers.

Def nition 3.1. *Denote $T(s, \mathcal{M})$ as the ramp-up time corresponds to the mechanism $\mathcal{M}$. Def ne $\mathcal{R}(s, \mathcal{M}) \triangleq \frac{E[T(s)] - E[T(s, \mathcal{M})]}{E[T(s)]}$, as the ramp-up time reduction achieved by the mechanism $\mathcal{M}$.*

Notice that the mechanism $\mathcal{M}$ achieves the ramp-up time reduction at the expense of losing some short-term prof ts. Denote $G(s)$ and $G(s, \mathcal{M})$ as the short-term prof ts, which are earned in the ramp-up process when a seller sets no discount at all and uses the discount mechanism $\mathcal{M}$ respectively.

Def nition 3.2. *Def ne $\mathcal{L}(s, \mathcal{M}) \triangleq \frac{E[G(s)] - E[G(s, \mathcal{M})]}{E[G(s)]}$ as the short-term prof t loss due to the mechanism $\mathcal{M}$.*

• **Design Tradeoffs:** Our objective is to design a mechanism $\mathcal{M}$ which trades price discounts for reputation subject to different tradeoffs between the *ramp-up time* and the *short-term prof t loss*:

$$\max_{\mathcal{M}} \quad z(s, \mathcal{M}) \triangleq \alpha \mathcal{R}(s, \mathcal{M}) - (1 - \alpha)\mathcal{L}(s, \mathcal{M}) \tag{1}$$

$s.t. \mathcal{M}$ sets discounts for products sold in the ramp-up process,

where $\alpha \in [0, 1]$ denotes a balance factor which can be controlled by a seller. The value of α ref ects the aggressiveness of a seller in reducing the ramp-up time.

4. DISCOUNT MECHANISM

Mechanism: We apply the UCB algorithm [2] to set the appropriate discount. We outline the mechanism in Algorithm 1, where w_i denotes the waiting time of i-th transaction. In Algorithm 1, step one to step six correspond to initialization, where the seller tries each discount once. Step eight is the key step, which sets the appropriate discount based on historical transaction data.

Algorithm 1 : Online Discounting Mechanism

1: **for** $i = 1$ to $M + 1$ **do**
2: Set level $i - 1$ discount for i-th transaction, i.e., $m_i \leftarrow i - 1$.
3: Observe the waiting time w_i of i-th transaction
4: $R_{m_i} \leftarrow -\alpha \lambda_{\mathcal{S}(r_i)} P_0 w_i - (1 - \alpha)\frac{d_{m_i} p}{u}$, $N_{m_i} \leftarrow 1$
5: update reputation score r
6: **end for**
7: **while** $r < n_s$ **do**
8: $m_i \leftarrow \arg\max_m \left\{ \frac{R_m}{N_m} + \max\left\{ \frac{4\ln(i-1)}{N_m}, \sqrt{\frac{4\ln(i-1)}{N_m}} \right\} \right\}$
9: Observe the waiting time w_i of the i-th transaction
10: $R_{m_i} \leftarrow R_{m_i} - \alpha \lambda_{\mathcal{S}(r_i)} P_0 w_i - (1 - \alpha)\frac{d_{m_i} p}{u}$, $N_{m_i} \leftarrow N_{m_i} + 1$
11: update reputation score r
12: **end while**

Experiments on eBay Data: We crawled a dataset from eBay in April 2013. It contains of 18,533,913 historical ratings which are received by 4,362 sellers from the f rst day that a seller joins the eBay till April 2013. We consider six levels of discounts and $d_m = m \times 5\%$. We synthesize $P_0, P_1, \ldots, P_5$ to ref ect the real-world scenario as accurate as possible. We consider four representative types of buyers' preference to discounts: (1) **Sigmoid:** $P_m = 0.5/(1 + e^{-(m-3)})$; (2) **Concave:** $P_m = 0.0237(m + 1)^{0.5}$; (3) **Linear:** $P_m = 0.0237(m + 1)$; (4) **Convex:** $P_m = 0.0237(m + 1)^{1.5}$, where $m = 0, 1, \ldots, 5$ and the parameters 0.0237 and 0.5 are carefully selected to guarantee that the value of P_0 is the same for these four preference models. Without loss of generality, sellers aim to earn f ve stars in our experiments. Figure 1(a) shows that as the α increases, the ramp-up time reduction increases. However, as shown in Figure 1(b) that this is achieved at a price of losing more short-term prof ts. If a seller has a moderate investing budget (i.e., $\alpha = 0.6$) our mechanism can reduce the ramp-up time by at least 40% by trading 60% of the short-term prof ts.

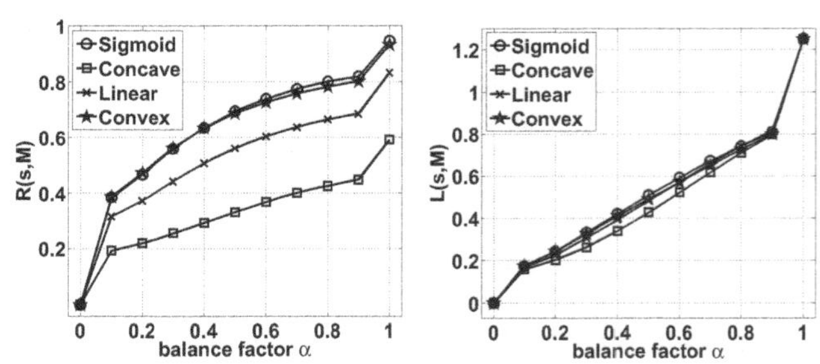

(a) Ramp-up time reduction (b) Short-term prof ts loss

Figure 1: Ramp-up time and short-term prof ts.

5. REFERENCES

[1] http://www.88sxy.com/.
[2] P. Auer, N. Cesa-Bianchi, and P. Fischer. Finite-time analysis of the multiarmed bandit problem. *Machine learning*, 47(2-3):235–256, 2002.
[3] P. Resnick, K. Kuwabara, R. Zeckhauser, and E. Friedman. Reputation systems. *Commun. ACM*, 43(12):45–48, Dec. 2000.
[4] H. Xie and J. C. Lui. Modeling ebay-like reputation systems: Analysis, characterization and insurance mechanism design. *Performance Evaluation*, 91:132–149, 2015.
[5] H. Xu, D. Liu, H. Wang, and A. Stavrou. E-commerce reputation manipulation: The emergence of reputation-escalation-as-a-service. In *Proc. of WWW*, 2015.

Author Index

Aghayev, Abutalib 389
Ahmed, Adnan 395
Ahuja, Sanjeev 371
Alizadeh, Mohammad 75
Avrachenkov, Konstantin 165
Avranas, Apostolos 403
Balasubramanian, Aruna 369
Bojja Venkatakrishnan,
Shaileshh 75
Bresler, Guy 207
Brinton, Christopher G. 235
Buchnik, Eliav 51
Bugnion, Edouard 367
Burchard, Almut 393
Burle, Sai Kiran 13
Cao, Yi 369
Caulfield, Laura 407
Chaintreau, Augustin 25, 179
Chandrasekaran, Balakrishnan 89
Chang, Kevin K. 323
Chen, Niangjun 193
Chiang, Mung 235
Ciucu, Florin 375
Cohen, Edith 51
Combes, Richard 391
Comden, Joshua 193
Cullina, Daniel 63
Cutler, Ben 407
Daglis, Alexandros 367
Dai, Haipeng 139
Das, Chita R. 351
Deng, Haotian 261
Desnoyers, Peter 389
Dudyzc, Szymon 273
Elayoubi, Salah 391
Falsafi, Babak 367
Fanti, Giulia 153
Ferragut, Andrés 101
Figueiredo, Daniel R. 299
Fortnow, Lance 381
Gabielkov, Maksym 179
Gamarnik, David 1
Gandhi, Anshul 193, 369
Gao, Xing 401
Gardner, Kristen 409
Garetto, Michele 37
Ge, Zihui 371
Ghose, Saugata 323
Giovanidis, Anastasios 403
Grot, Boris 367
Ha, Sangtae 235
Hajkazemi,
Mohammad Hossein 389
Harchol-Balter, Mor 73, 409
Hassan, Hasan 323
He, Xubin 373
Hsieh, Kevin 323
Huang, Ping 373
Ioannidis, Stratis 113
Iyer, Ravishankar 351
Jacquet, Philippe 125
Jeon, Myeongjae 407
Jiang, Bo 299
Joe-Wong, Carlee 235
Jog, Adwait 351
Jonckheere, Matthieu 311
Kairouz, Peter 153
Kandemir, Mahmut T. 351
Kashyap, Abhijith 323
Kayiran, Onur 351
Khakpour, Amir 395
Khan, Samira 323
Khessib, Badriddine 407
Kiyavash, Negar 63
Lee, Donghyuk 323
Legout, Arnaud 179
Leonardi, Emilio 37
Li, Baochun 415
Li, Jiayao 261
Li, Jin 381
Li, Jun 415
Li, Meng 139
Li, Tianshi 323
Li, Yuanjie 261
Liang, Ben 415
Liebeherr, Jorg 393
Lin, Bill 397
Liu, Alex X. 139
Liu, Daiping 401
Liu, Jia 221
Liu, Jie 407
Liu, Liang 381
Liu, Wenjie 373
Liu, Zhenhua 193
Loguinov, Dmitri 127
London, Palma 383
Lu, Songwu 261
Ludwig, Arne 273
Lui, John C. S. 417
Ma, Richard T. B. 417
Maggs, Bruce 89
Maguluri, Pavan 369
Maguluri, Siva Theja 13
Mahimkar, Ajay 371
Mazumdar, Ravi R. 385
Mir, Nabeel 371
Mukhopadhyay, Arpan 385
Mutlu, Onur 323, 351
Nam, Yun Seong 89
Narayanan, Iyswarya 407
Nejati, Javad 369
Nguyen, Lam M. 365
Novakovic, Stanko 367
Oh, Sewoong 153
Paganini, Fernando 101
Pattnaik, Ashutosh 351
Pekhimenko, Gennady 323
Peng, Chunyi 261
Poloczek, Felix 375
Prabhu, Balakrishna J. 311
Puthenpura, Sarat 371
Puzhavakath Narayanan,
Shankaranarayanan 89
Qiu, Lili 371
Qureshi, Mubashir Adnan 371
Ramachandran, Arthi 179
Ramaswamy, Vinod 387
Ramchandran, Kannan 153
Rao, Sanjay 89
Ray, Avik 399
Reddyvari Raja, Vamseedhar 387
Ren, Xiaoqi 383
Ribeiro, Bruno 165, 299
Rodríguez, Ismael 101
Rost, Matthias 273
Roy, Rahul 385
Sanghavi, Sujay 399
Scheller-Wolf, Alan 409

Schmid, Stefan 273
Shafaei, Mansour 389
Shafiq, Zubair 395
Shah, Devavrat 207
Shakkottai, Sanjay 399
Shakkottai, Srinivas 387
Shamsi, Zain 127
Sharma, Bikash 407
Shekaramiz, Alireza 393
Sidi, Habib 391
Sivakumar, Ashiwan 89
Sivasubramaniam, Anand 407
Sreedharan, Jithin K. 165
Srikant, R 13
Stolyar, Alexander L. 365
Subramanian, Vijay 387
Tan, Chee Wei 235
Tang, Kun 373
Torrisi, Giovanni-Luca 37
Towsley, Don 25, 299
Tsafrir, Dan 337
Tsitsiklis, John N. 1
Vaid, Kushagra 407
Van Houdt, Benny 377
Varman, Peter 411
Viswanath, Pramod 75, 153
Voloch, Luis Filipe 207
Wang, Di 407
Wang, Haining 401
Wang, Hui 411
Wang, Wei 139, 415
Wang, Weina 249
Wang, Yating 381
Wierman, Adam 193, 383
Xia, Cathy H. 25
Xie, Hong 417
Xu, Jun (Jim) 381, 397
Yang, Sen 397
Yaniv, Idan 337
Yeh, Edmund 113
Ying, Lei 249, 285
Zbarsky, Samuel 409
Zeng, Yun 25
Zhang, Junshan 249
Zhang, Mingwei 401
Zheng, Liang 235
Zhong, Yuankun 139
Zhou, Ke 373
Ziani, Juba 383
Zubeldia, Martin 1

www.ingramcontent.com/pod-product-compliance
Ingram Content Group UK Ltd.
Pitfield, Milton Keynes, MK11 3LW, UK
UKHW051511290926
15471UKWH00008B/1555

9 781450 346009